MAUDSLEY AND BURN'S TRUSTS AND TRUSTEES: CASES AND MATERIALS

MAUDSLEY AND BURN'S
TRUSTS AND TRUSTEES

CASES AND MATERIALS

Seventh Edition

G J VIRGO BCL, MA

Barrister of Lincoln's Inn

Professor of English Private Law, University of Cambridge

Fellow of Downing College, Cambridge

E H BURN BCL, MA

Barrister and Honorary Bencher of Lincoln's Inn

Emeritus Student of Christ Church, Oxford

Formerly Professor of Law in the City University

OXFORD
UNIVERSITY PRESS

OXFORD

UNIVERSITY PRESS

Great Clarendon Street, Oxford OX2 6DP

Oxford University Press is a department of the University of Oxford.
It furthers the University's objective of excellence in research, scholarship,
and education by publishing worldwide in

Oxford New York

Auckland Cape Town Dar es Salaam Hong Kong Karachi
Kuala Lumpur Madrid Melbourne Mexico City Nairobi
New Delhi Shanghai Taipei Toronto

With offices in

Argentina Austria Brazil Chile Czech Republic France Greece
Guatemala Hungary Italy Japan Poland Portugal Singapore
South Korea Switzerland Thailand Turkey Ukraine Vietnam

Oxford is a registered trade mark of Oxford University Press
in the UK and in certain other countries

Published in the United States
by Oxford University Press Inc., New York

© Oxford University Press, 2008

British Library Cataloguing in Publication Data

Data available

Library of Congress Cataloging in Publication Data

Data available

Typeset by Newgen Imaging Systems (P) Ltd., Chennai, India
Printed in Great Britain
on acid-free paper by
Ashford Colour Press Ltd, Gosport, Hampshire

ISBN 978-0-19-921904-9

1 3 5 7 9 10 8 6 4 2

PREFACE

In preparing this new edition we have made a number of significant changes, but the heart of the book remains the same: a casebook concerning the law of trusts and trustees. This is a body of law which is traditionally considered to be difficult to understand. This is partly because it is sometimes, unfairly, considered to be a subject which is old-fashioned and not relevant today. It is true that much of the law does derive from old cases, but its significance today cannot be doubted, especially in the corporate and commercial world. We have sought to reflect this in the extracts from cases and materials which we have used.

Structurally the book has changed significantly since the last edition, partly to ensure that it better reflects the syllabus of law schools, but also to ensure that the disparate parts of the subject fit together more coherently in the light of new trends and developments. Previous editions had a substantial part covering Trusts and Taxes. Much of this has been removed, not because it is unimportant, but because it tends not to be covered in law schools as part of a trusts course. It remains true, however, that studying the trust without tax is like Hamlet without the prince. So we have sought to give an idea in Chapter 1 of the underlying significance of taxation to trust law.

The book is now divided into seven parts. The first provides an introduction to the trust and to equity; the second focuses on the express trust, specifically types of express trust, the requirements of the trust, its creation and the position of beneficiaries; the third part relates to implied and imputed trusts, namely resulting trust, constructive trusts and a new chapter on the common-intention constructive trusts; the fourth part relates to purpose trusts, both non-charitable and charitable; the fifth part to trustees, their powers, duties and fiduciary obligations; the sixth part to the liability of trustees for breach of trust. Finally, to reflect the syllabus of law schools, a new part is concerned with other equitable orders, such as the injunction, specific performance and search orders. Sometimes these equitable orders may be of relevance to claims relating to trustees, but this part is more significant in illustrating the role of equity in civil litigation generally.

Another significant development in this edition is the inclusion of a wider range of extracts from academic commentaries and also more text to explain some of the more difficult aspects of the law. We have retained and expanded the practice of previous editions to include questions which encourage the reader to think about the implications of the material which has been read, and also further reading which can be undertaken to broaden the reader's understanding of the subject.

Since the publication of the sixth edition there have been a number of significant statutory and judicial developments in the law. The key statutory provisions are the Pensions Act 2004, the Mental Capacity Act 2005 and, most significant of all, the Charities Act 2006, which includes for the first time a statutory definition of charity.

We have also included a variety of materials from the Charity Commission, including its guidance on the interpretation of public benefit.

There has been widespread judicial activity since the publication of the last edition. The House of Lords has considered the nature of the common-intention constructive trust; the meaning of trustee *de son tort*; the award of compound interest and the nature of liability for unconscionable receipt of property in breach of trust or fiduciary duty.

The Privy Council has examined the nature of trust powers; disclosure of documents to beneficiaries and the meaning of dishonesty in the action for dishonestly assisting a breach of trust or fiduciary duty.

Important decisions of the Court of Appeal have concerned the role of the constructive trust to save a failed gift; the common-intention constructive trust; estoppel; fiduciary duties; remedies for breach of fiduciary duty; the action of dishonest assistance and the operation of the Civil Liability (Contribution) Act 1978.

Significant decisions at first instance include those which have considered sham trusts; the remedial constructive trust; property holding by unincorporated associations; the effect of trustee mistakes; the recognition that profits arising from breach of fiduciary duty can be held on constructive trust, and tracing.

We have also included some important decisions from the Commonwealth which have considered the test of certainty of subject matter; the award of exemplary damages for breach of fiduciary duty and the nature of liability for knowing receipt of property which has been transferred in breach of trust or fiduciary duty.

Finally the Law Commission has continued to be active in this area, publishing significant reports on the property interests of cohabitants; on capital and income in trusts and on trustee exemption clauses.

We would both like to thank Marilyn Kennedy-McGregor, Barrister of Gray's Inn and of Lincoln's Inn, and John Cartwright, Student of Christ Church, Oxford, for their help and support in the preparation of this edition. We would also like to thank the publishers, who have been responsible for the compilation of the Table of Cases, Statutes and Statutory Instruments and the Index. Graham Virgo would like to thank Amy Goymour, Hopkins Parry Fellow at Downing College, Cambridge, and his students for their advice in preparing this edition, and Cally, Elizabeth and Jonathan for their support and encouragement.

This edition purports to state the law as it was on 31 January 2008, but it has been possible to incorporate more recent developments where space has permitted.

G.J.V   E.H.B.
Downing College   Christ Church
Cambridge   Oxford

CONTENTS

PART III IMPLIED AND IMPUTED TRUSTS

PART IV   PURPOSE TRUSTS

11 CHARITABLE TRUSTS: FAILURE OF PURPOSES 544

12 CHARITABLE TRUSTS: REGULATION AND MANAGEMENT 579

PART V TRUSTEES

13 GENERAL PRINCIPLES RELATING TO TRUSTEES

ACKNOWLEDGEMENTS

Grateful acknowledgement is made to all the authors and publishers of copyright material that appears in this book, and in particular to the following for permission to reprint material from the sources indicated:

Parliamentary copyright material is reproduced with the permission of the Controller of Her Majesty's Stationery Office on behalf of Parliament. Other Crown copyright material is reproduced under Class Licence Number XXXXXXXX with the permission of the Controller of HMSO and the Queen's Printer.

Bailli

Daraydan Holdings Ltd and others v Solland International Ltd and others [2004] EWHC 622 (Ch) [2005] Ch 119

Oxley v Hiscock [2004] EWCA Civ 546 [2005] Fam 211. Paragon Finance v DB Thakerar and Co [1999] 1 All ER 400

Cambridge University Press
Maitland: Lectures on Equity 2nd edn

Fontana Press
Hackney Understanding Equity and Trusts

ICLR

Agip (Africa) Ltd v Jackson [1990] Ch 265
Air Jamaica Ltd v Charlton [1999] 1 WLR 1399
Alsop Wilkinson v Neary [1996] 1 WLR 1220
American Cyanamid Co v Ethicon Ltd [1975] AC 396
Armitage v Nurse [1998] Ch 241
Ashburn Anstalt v Arnold [1989] Ch 1
Re Astor's Settlement Trust [1952] Ch 534
Attenborough v Solomon [1913] AC 76
Re Ball's Settlement Trusts [1968] 1 WLR 899
Banner Homes Group plc v Luff Developments Ltd [2000] Ch 372
Barclays Bank v Quistclose Investments Ltd [1970] AC 567
Barlow Clowes International Ltd v Eurotrusts International Ltd [2005] UKPC 37, [2006] 1 WLR
Re Barlow's Will Trusts [1979] 1 WLR 278
Bartlett v Barclays Bank Trusts Co Ltd (No. 1) [1980] Ch 515
Beswick v Beswick [1968] AC 58
Biscoe v Jackson (1887) 35 Ch D 460

Re Gray [1925] Ch 362
Re Grove-Grady [1929] 1 Ch 557
Guild v Inland Revenue Commissioners [1992] 12 AC 310
Guinness plc v Saunders [1990] 2 AC 663
Re Gulbenkian's Settlements [1970] AC 508
Re Hagger [1930] 2 Ch 190
Re Hallett's Estate (1880) 13 Ch D 696
Harries v Church Commissioners for England [1992] 1 WLR 1241
Re Harwood [1936] Ch 285
Re Hetherington [1990] Ch 1
Holder v Holder [1968] Ch 353
Re Holt's Settlement [1969] 1 Ch 100
Re Hooper [1932] 1 Ch 38
Re Hopkins' Will Trust [1965] Ch 669
Hunter v Moss [1994] 1 WLR 452
IRC v Baddeley [1995] AC 572
IRC v Educational Grants Association Ltd [1967] Ch 123
IRC v McMulleh [1981] AC 1
Incorporated Council of Law Reporting for England and Wales v Attorney General
    [1972] Ch 73
Re JW Laing Trust [1984] Ch 143
Jaggard v Sawyer [1995] 1 WLR
Johnson v Agnew [1980] AC 367
Joseph Rowntree Memorial Trusts Housing Association Ltd v Attorney-General
    [1983] Ch 159
Re Kay's Settlement [1939] Ch 329
Re Keeler's Settlement Trusts [1981] Ch 156
Re Keen [1937] Ch 236
Klug v Klug [1918] 2 Ch 67
Knocker v Youle [1986] 1 WLR 934
Re Koeppler Will Trusts [1986] Ch 423
Re Lepton's Charity [1972] Ch 276
Letterstedt v Broers (1884) 9 App Cas 371
Re Lipinski's Will Trusts [1976] Ch 235
Leahy v Attorney-General for New South Wales [1959] AC 457
Lloyds Bank plc v Rosset [1991] AC 107
Re Londonerry's Settlement [1965] Ch 918
Re Macadam [1946] Ch 73
MacNiven v Westmoreland Investments Ltd [2001] UKHL 6 [2003] 1 AC 311
Re McGeorge [1963] Ch 544
McGovern v Attorney-General [1982] Ch 321
Mettoy Pension Trustees Ltd v Evans [1990] 1 WLR 1587
National Anti-Vivisection Society v IRC [1948] AC 318

Twinsectra Ltd v Yardley [2002] UKHL 12, [2002] 2 AC 164
Vandervell v Inland Revenue Commissioners [1967] 2 AC 291
Re Vandervell's Trusts (no. 2) [1974] Ch 269
Varsani v Jessani [1999] Ch 219
Re West Sussex Constabulary's Widows, Children and Benevolent (1930) Fund
    Trusts [1971] Ch 1
Westdeutsche Landesbank Girzocentrale v Islington LBC [1996] AC 669
Re Weston's Settlement [1969] 1 Ch 223
Williams-Ashman v Price and Williams [1942] Ch 219
Williams's Trustees v Inland Revenue Commissioners [1947] AC 447
Re Wright [1954] Ch 347
Re Wrightson [1908] 1 Ch 789
Yaxley v Gotts [2000] Ch 162

LexisNexis (All ER)

Abou-Rahmah v Abacha [2006] EWCA Civ 1492 [2007] 1 All ER (Comm 827)
Artistic Upholstery Ltd v Art Forma (Furniture) Ltd [1999] 4 All ER 277
Buttle v Saunders [1950] 2 All ER 193
Conservative and Unionist Central Office v Burrell [1980] [1982] 3 All ER 42, [1982]
    2 All ER 1
Re Evans [1999] 2 All ER 777
Foster v Spencer [1996] 2 All ER 672
Goulding v James [1997] 2 All ER 239
Lloyds Bank plc v Carrick [1996] 4 All ER 630
Mason v Farbrother [1983] 2 All ER 1078
Paragon Finance v DB Thakerar and Co [1999] 1 All ER 400
Re Polly Peck International (no. 2) [1998] 3 All ER 812
Warren v Gurney [1944] 2 All ER 472

Lexis Nexis AU

Williams v Commissioner of Inland Revenue [1965] NZLR 395

Lloyds Rep Bank
Box v Barclays Bank Trusts Co Ltd (No. 1) [1980], Marveva Compania Naviera SA v
    International Bulkcarriers SA [1975]

MLR

Modern Law Review
MLR (1951) 14 MLR 136, 139–140 (JDB Mitchell)
MLR (1973) 36 MLR 210,212–214 (SM Bandali)

NSWC (via www.lawlink.nsw.gov.au)
White v Shortall [2006] NSWC 1379

NZLR
Williams v Commissioner of Inland Revenue [1965] NZLR 395

Restitution Law Review
Restitution Law Review: [1998] 57–58 (G. Virgo)

Sweet & Maxwell
Goff & Jones: The Law of Restitution 7th edn 2007, Hanbury & Martin: Modern
  Equity 17th edn 2005, Lewin on Trusts 18th edn 2008, Parker & Mellows: Modern
  Law of Trusts 8th edn 2003.
Law Quarterly Review: (1965) 81 LQR 196–198 (REM), (1970) 86 LQR 20 (PVB),
  (1994) LQR 335,336–339 (D. Hayton), (2001) 117 LQR 575,584,587–588 (Lord
  Templeman), (2005) 121 LQR 452, 453 (M. Conaglen)

SCLR
M'Caig v University of Glasgow (1907) SC 231
M'Caig's Trustees v Kirk-Session of United Free Church of Lismore (1915) SC 426
Reproduced with permission of The Scottish Council of Law Reporting

The Legal Intelligencer (via www.law.com)
Richard v The Hon AB Mackay (March 14,1987) (1997)

Tottel Publishing
Whitehouse and Hassall: Trusts of Land, Trustee Delegation and the Trustee Act
2000 2nd edn 2001

Thomson
Proprietary Restitution in Equity in Commercial Law (2005) by S Degeling and J
Edelman. Reproduced with permission by the © Lawbook Co, part of Thomson Legal
& Regulatory Limited, http://www.thomson.co.au

Wiley-Blackwell
Modern Law Review
(1951) 14 MLR 136, 139–140 (JDB Mitchell)
(1973) 36 MLR 210, 212–214 (SM Bandali). Reproduced with permission of Wiley-
Blackwell Publishing Limited

CROSS-REFERENCES

The following books have been cross-referenced, and abbreviated as follows:

H&M	Hanbury and Martin, *Modern Equity* (17th edn 2005)
Lewin	*Lewin on Trusts* (18th edn 2008)
P&M	Parker and Mellows: *The Modern Law of Trusts* (8th edn 2003)
P&S	Pearce and Stevens, *The Law of Trusts and Equitable Obligations* (4th edn, 2006)
Pettit	*Equity and the Law of Trusts* (10th edn 2005)
Snell	*Snell's Equity* (31st edn 2005)
T&H	Thomas and Hudson, *The Law of Trusts* (2004)
U&H	Underhill and Hayton: *Law Relating to Trusts and Trustees* (17th edn 2006)

CROSS-REFERENCES

The following books have been cross-referenced and abbreviated as follows:

H&M	Hanbury and Martin, *Modern Equity* (17th edn 2005)
Lewin	*Lewin on Trusts* (18th edn 2008)
P&M	Parker and Mellows: *The Modern Law of Trusts* (8th edn 2003)
P&S	Pearce and Stevens: *The Law of Trusts and Equitable Obligations* (4th edn 2006)
Pettit	*Equity and the Law of Trusts* (10th edn 2005)
Snell	*Snell's Equity* (31st edn 2005)
T&H	Thomas and Hudson: *The Law of Trusts* (2004)
U&H	Underhill and Hayton: *Law Relating to Trusts and Trustees* (17th edn 2006)

TABLE OF STATUTES

This Table is sorted as follows: UK legislation, foreign legislation, European legislation and international instruments

FOREIGN LEGISLATION

AUSTRALIA

BERMUDA

BRITISH VIRGIN ISLANDS

CANADA

CAYMAN ISLANDS

CYPRUS

TABLE OF STATUTORY INSTRUMENTS

TABLE OF CASES

Page references in **bold** type indicate where a case is set out in part or full

PART I

INTRODUCTION TO TRUSTS

1

THE NATURE OF A TRUST

I EQUITY AND TRUSTS[1]

A EQUITY[2]

Charles Dickens' *Bleak House*, first published in 1853, contains this description of equity as practised in the courts of the time:

On such an afternoon, some score of members of the High Court of Chancery bar ought to be—as here they are—mistily engaged in one of the ten thousand stages of an endless cause, tripping one another up on slippery precedents, groping knee-deep in technicalities, running their goat-hair and horse-hair warded heads against walls of words, and making a pretence of equity with serious faces, as players might.

Everyone is yawning 'for no crumb of amusement ever falls from Jarndyce and Jarndyce (the cause in hand), which was squeezed dry years upon years ago'.

---

[1] H&M, pp. 3–73; Lewin, pp. 3–15; P&M, pp. 1–12; P&S pp. 3–31; Pettit pp. 1–23; Snell pp. 3–25; T&H pp. 13–23, 47–52; U&H, pp. 2–6, 49–65.

[2] Worthington, *Equity* (2nd ed., 2006), pp. 3–21; *What About Law?* (ed. Barnard, O'Sullivan and Virgo, 2007), Ch. 6.

That case involved a disputed inheritance and, as Dickens says: 'this scarecrow of a suit has, in course of time, become so complicated, that no man alive knows what it means'. By the end of the novel, judgment is given but the legal costs which have been incurred are so great that they devour most of the estate which was disputed in the first place.

This is the equity of the nineteenth century, which was concerned with death and succession, taxes and debts. This is dry and technical law. But equity today is very different. Although the modern subject is built on the old cases, the principles which underpin those cases have been refined over the years and are of real significance today, often in contexts very different from inheritance disputes. For example, much modern commercial law, especially company law, has been dramatically influenced by equity.

(i) What is equity?[3]

English case law can be divided into the common law and equity. The common law has been developed by the judges in the courts over hundreds of years. But there is another stream of judge-made law known as equity. To understand why we have two different streams of judge-made law we need to go back in time to the medieval ages. This was the period when judge-made law started to develop rapidly. Legal principles, some of which are still relevant today, started to emerge. However, the general attitude of the judges was strict and inflexible. Although there was room for judicial creativity, the judges tended to interpret the law rigidly and developed it through the elaboration of ever more complicated rules. In particular, claims brought by individual litigants had to fall within clearly established categories and, if they did not, they would fail. If no remedy was awarded or was even available, it was possible to petition the King to seek justice. The King delegated this function to his principal minister, the Chancellor, who exercised his judgment according to his conscience. Equity in this period was discretionary and vague, as was famously described by John Selden, a legal author in the seventeenth century:

Equity is a roguish thing: for law we have a measure, know what to trust to; equity is according to the conscience of him that is chancellor, and as that is larger or narrower, so is equity. [It is] as if they should make the standard for the measure we call a foot a chancellor's foot; what an uncertain measure would this be! One chancellor has a long foot, another a short foot, a third an indifferent foot. 'Tis the same in the chancellor's conscience.[4]

Eventually a separate court was established, known as the Court of Chancery, to deal with the petitions to the Chancellor and it was the law that was developed and applied in this court which became known as equity. The purpose of this body of law was

---

[3] Baker, *Introduction to Legal History* (4th edn., 2002), pp. 97–116. See also M. Macnair, 'Equity and Conscience' (2007) OJLS 659.

[4] *Table Talk of John Selden* (F. Pollock ed.) (1927), p. 43.

to temper the rigidity in the application of the law by common law judges.[5] From the seventeenth century onwards this body of law became more systematic. By the Judicature Acts 1873 and 1875 the common law and equitable jurisdictions were fused. But this was simply a fusion of the administration of the legal systems. It followed that a court could apply rules of both the common law and equity. But the Acts did not involve a fusion of equity and common law as bodies of law. Indeed, section 25 of the Judicature Act 1873 recognised that where there was a conflict between the rules of equity and the rules of the common law the former prevailed.

Equity is still sometimes described as operating to modify the rigidity of the common law. But, to the extent that this indicates that equity is vague and unprincipled, it is untrue. For much of equity today is rule-based and certain; precedent is followed. But it does not follow that, as it is sometimes quaintly put, equity is 'past the age of child-bearing'. Equity can still be used to create new doctrines and to develop existing ones to provide solutions to problems which are ignored by the common law.

Although the common law and equity are distinct, there have been calls for assimilation of the two systems, otherwise known as fusion.[6] Where there is no need for separate rules at law and in equity, such as the rules on tracing,[7] assimilation is appropriate. But there is a danger that rapid assimilation of rules which have existed for a long time will mean that the subtleties and nuances of the law will be lost.[8]

Lord Millett, 'Proprietary Restitution' in *Equity in Commercial Law* (ed. Degeling and Edelman)(2005), p. 309

Those who favour the fusion of law and equity might perhaps reflect that the three greatest systems of jurisprudence in the Western world have all been dual systems. Jewish law had its written and oral law; Roman law its civil and praetorian or bonitary law; English law common law and equity. In each case the duality served a similar function. One system provided certainty; the other the necessary flexibility and adaptability to enable justice to be done. But the common law and equity are not two separate and parallel systems of law. The common law is a complete system of law which could stand alone, but which if not tempered by equity would often be productive of injustice; while equity is not a complete and independent system of law and could not stand alone.

(ii) The contribution of equity

Equity has made a profound contribution to many areas of the law, especially as regards the identification of rights and the development of important remedies, such as the order of specific performance[9] to make the defendant perform his obligations

---

[5] See *Earl of Oxford's Case* (1615) 1 Ch Rep 1.

[6] See, especially, Burrows: *Hochelga Lectures: Fusing Common Law and Equity: Remedies, Restitution and Reform* (2002); (2002) 22 OJLS 1.   [7] See p. 896, below.

[8] See Virgo in *Rationalizing Property, Equity and Trusts: Essays in Honour of Edward Burn* (ed. Getzler) (2003), p. 106. See also [1994] Conv 13 (J. Martin).   [9] See p. 1031, below.

under a contract, or injunctions[10] to stop the defendant from committing a wrong. Equity has been influential in many other ways. For example, equity can be used to regulate exploitative transactions, such as where one party unduly influences another to enter into a disadvantageous contract or to make a gift. Equity is also responsible for the recognition and regulation of certain types of relationship known as fiduciary relationships.[11] A fiduciary is somebody who is in a relationship of trust and confidence with somebody else, known as the principal. The fiduciary is expected to be loyal to the principal and to maintain the highest standards of behaviour in looking after the principal's interests. Typical fiduciary relationships are those of company directors with their company, and solicitors with their clients.

B TRUSTS

The most important contribution of equity to English law is undoubtedly the trust. The crucial feature of the trust is that property is held by one person for the benefit of another. This is recognised through the division of property rights. One person holds the legal title to the property but does not have absolute ownership. This is the trustee. As far as the common law is concerned that person is the legal owner. But equity can see that the legal owner holds the property not for himself but for the benefit of somebody else, known as the beneficiary. In equity the beneficiaries under a trust are the owners of the beneficial interests given to them. Trustees' ownership is wholly burdensome. The trusteeship obligates them to manage the property in the exclusive interest of the beneficiaries, and imposes onerous duties and liabilities upon them. All the advantage is with the beneficiaries.

There is a variety of reasons why someone would wish to create a trust. There may be a particular advantage in having trustees managing and administering the property. This might be because the beneficiaries are too young to do so or cannot be trusted with the property. Or the trust might be a convenient way of holding the property for the mutual benefit of a group of people. This is one of the main reasons why the trust is used in the commercial world. For example, it is used as a mechanism for managing pension funds,[12] where the pension fund is held by trustees for the benefit of employees; or as a mechanism for a group of people investing their funds by means of a unit or investment trust, where trustees hold investments in a large range of stock exchange securities in trust for members of the public who have purchased units or shares in the trust fund.[13]

Another purpose of the trust is that it can provide a means for avoiding tax, by transferring property to somebody whose tax liability might be smaller because they

---

[10] See p. 1012, below.   [11] See p. 778, below.   [12] See p. 69, below.

[13] Financial Services and Markets Act 2000, Part XVII, Ch. III (unit trusts authorised by the Financial Services Authority).

pay a lower rate of tax on their income. The trust is also increasingly important in the commercial context as a tax-saving device, especially if the trust is located overseas in a tax haven. But there is a danger that the trust might be open to abuse and there is complex law to ensure that the trust is not used as an illegitimate method of tax evasion.

In the family context, the trust may be used to avoid having the whole of a family's capital being owned by one person. In some circumstances it will be preferable to provide for successive enjoyment of the property; in others for the enjoyment to be shared; or to provide protection against creditors; or to provide for interests to arise in the future. When property is held in a way other than the *absolute* ownership of one person, it is usually held under some form of trust. In the case of land, for example, this has been achieved by the use of a trust of land.[14]

Maitland: *Selected Essays,* p. 129

If we were asked what is the greatest and most distinctive achievement performed by Englishmen in the field of jurisprudence I cannot think that we should have any better answer to give than this, namely, the development from century to century of the trust idea.[15]

II DEFINITION AND CLASSIFICATION OF TRUSTS[16]

A DEFINITION OF THE TRUST

Maitland: *Lectures on Equity* (2nd edn), p. 44

Where judges and text-writers fear to tread professors of law have to rush in. I should define a trust in some such way as the following—when a person has rights which he is bound to exercise upon behalf of another or for the accomplishment of some particular purpose he is said to have those rights in trust for that other or for that purpose and he is called a trustee.

It is a wide, vague definition, but the best that I can make. I shall comment on it by distinguishing cases of trust from some other cases.

---

[14] Under the Trusts of Land and Appointment of Trustees Act 1996, s. 1.

[15] Of Maitland Scrutton LJ said in *Holmes–Laski Letters* (1913), vol 2, at p. 1142: 'Most historians throw light on dark places; he threw a searchlight into the unknown.' And MacNaghten J said, at p. 1412: 'Maitland was not a lawyer at all, but a poet.' Both are cited by Sir Robert Megarry in *Inns Ancient and Modern* (Selden Society 1977), p. 3. See also (2001) 60 CLJ 265 (S.F.C. Milsom).

[16] H&M, pp. 47–73; Lewin, pp. 3–23; P&M, pp. 12–22; P&S pp. 111–120; Pettit pp. 27–28; Snell pp. 463–472; T&H pp. 13–31; U&H, pp. 6–10.

Underhill and Hayton: *Law of Trusts and Trustees* (17th edn), p. 2

A trust is an equitable obligation, binding a person (called a trustee) to deal with property (called trust property) owned by him as a separate fund, distinct from his own private property, for the benefit of persons (called beneficiaries or, in old cases, *cestuis que trust*), of whom he may himself be one, and any one of whom may enforce the obligation.[17]

Scott and Ascher on Trusts (5th edn, 2006), §2.1.3

Even if it were possible to frame an exact definition of a legal concept, the definition would be of little practical value. One cannot use a definition as a major premise, from which to deduce rules governing conduct. Our law has not developed that way. The definition must derive from the rules, and not vice versa. For the most part, all one can do is to attempt to describe a legal concept in such a way that others will know, at least in a general way, what one is talking about.

Notwithstanding these limitations, each of the Restatements of Trusts has attempted to define, or at least to describe, an express trust. According to the Third Restatement, an express trust is 'a fiduciary relationship with respect to property, arising from a manifestation of intention to create that relationship and subjecting the person who holds title to the property to duties to deal with it for the benefit of charity or for one or more persons, at least one of whom is not the sole trustee.'[18] In this definition, or description, the following characteristics stand out: (1) a trust is a relationship; (2) it is a relationship of a fiduciary character; (3) it is a relationship with respect to property, not one involving merely personal duties; (4) it subjects the person who holds title to the property to duties to deal with it for the benefit of charity or one or more persons, at least one of whom is not the sole trustee; and (5) it arises as a result of a manifestation of an intention to create the relationship. It is the combination of these characteristics that well describes the notion of the trust as it has developed in Anglo-American law.

Parkinson, 'Reconceptualising the Express Trust' (2002) 61 CLJ 657, 683

I would want to define the private express trust, including the charitable trust, in the following terms:

> An express trust is an equitable obligation[19] binding a person ('the trustee') to deal with identifiable property to which he or she has legal title[20] for the benefit of others to whom he or she is in some

---

[17] Approved by Cohen J in *Re Marshall's Will Trusts* [1945] Ch 217 at 219; and by Romer LJ in *Green v Russell* [1959] 2 QB 226 at 241. *Cestuis que trust* is the correct plural: (1910) 26 LQR 196 (C. Sweet).

[18] Restatement (Third) of Trusts § 2 (2003). This definition varies little from that of the Second Restatement. See Restatement (Second) of Trusts § 2 (1959).

[19] It is this which distinguishes the trust from other forms of obligation, for the obligation is equitable in nature and consequently enforceable by means of the full range of equitable remedies appropriate to the situation.

[20] On this definition it is sufficient that the trustee has legal title to identifiable property. That property may be held within a larger mass as long as it is capable of identification within that mass. This definition also covers the situation where a trustee is required to provide for another person out of an estate, for the subject matter of the trust is identified, and for the purposes of satisfying the trust obligation the definition does not require precise quantification of the amount to be sued for.

way accountable. Such obligations may either be for the benefit of persons who have proprietary rights in equity, of whom he or she may be one, or for the furtherance of a sufficiently certain purpose[21] which can be enforced by someone intended to have a right of enforcement under the terms of the trust[22] or by operation of law.[23,24]

T. Honoré, 'Trusts: The Inessentials' in *Rationalizing Property, Equity and Trusts: Essays in Honour of Edward Burn* (ed. J. Getzler), p. 8

[Trust law] is a branch of the law designed to allow people to set aside assets to be administered for purposes of private or public benefit in the confidence that the state, through its courts or other agencies, will, if called upon, see to it that the assets are applied for those purposes.

B CLASSIFICATION OF TRUSTS[25]

It is possible to classify trusts in a number of ways. Traditionally, trusts are characterised in terms of identifiable legal categories. Alternatively, trusts can be characterised by reference to particular events by reference to which trusts arise, such as agreement, wrongdoing and, possibly, unjust enrichment.[26]

(i) Express trusts

The main form of trust is the express trust,[27] which is created intentionally by the settlor (if the trust is created by somebody whilst he is alive who 'settles' property on trust) or the testator (if the trust is created by somebody in a will). An express trust may be created by the settlor declaring that he holds property on trust for another or by the transfer of the legal title to the property to vest in another person who holds for the beneficiaries.

---

[21] This requirement deals with one of the objections to the trust in *Re Astor's Settlement Trusts* [1952] Ch 534 (that it was too vague). See p. 359, below.

[22] On this definition, it is not necessary that the enforcer be provided for expressly in the terms of the trust. It is sufficient that the court will recognise that it was the intention of the settlor that certain persons should have a right of enforcement. In *Re Denley* [1969] 1 Ch 373, p. 375, below, Goff J took the view that the employees of the company for whose benefit the sports ground was to be established would have such an enforcement right....

[23] This part of the definition is necessary in order to bring the charitable trust within the definition. Charitable trusts are enforceable by the Attorney-General as a matter of law, not because this is so provided in the trust instrument.

[24] See also (2001) 117 LQR 96 (D. Hayton); (1995) 105 Yale LJ 625 (J. Langbein).

[25] [1999] LMCLQ 111, 115–117 (C. Rickett and R. Grantham).

[26] See Chambers, *Resulting Trusts* (1997), p. 5. See also (1999) 28 *Univ. of Western Australia Law Review* 13 (P. Birks) and N. McBride in *Restitution and Equity, Volume 1: Resulting Trusts and Equitable Compensation* (2000) (ed. P. Birks and F. Rose), pp. 23–38.   [27] See (2002) 61 CLJ 657 (P. Parkinson).

(ii) Fixed and Discretionary trusts

The express trust can either be fixed or discretionary. In a fixed trust the interest or share of the beneficiaries is laid down in the trust instrument. For example, a father may put in his will that, if he dies before his three children attain the age of 18, his property should be transferred to trustees for the benefit of the children in equal shares. If the father dies before the children become 18 the trustees would have legal title to the property, but they would not be able to benefit from it since they would have to manage the property for the children until they attained 18. Each child would have a fixed equitable interest in one-third of the property until they became 18, when the legal interest in their share of the property would be transferred to them.

Alternatively, in an express discretionary trust[28] the trustees own the property at law but no beneficiary has an existing equitable interest in the property. Rather, the trustees have a discretion to distribute the property as they wish to people from a particular class of potential beneficiaries. So, for example, the trust may give to the trustees a discretion to use the trust property to pay for the education of children of employees from a particular business. The trustees would be free to decide how they could allocate trust funds to such children in such amounts as they considered to be appropriate, but the trustee is obliged to distribute the property.[29]

(iii) Inter vivos and testamentary trusts

Trusts may be created *inter vivos* or by will. On death, the owner of property has to do something with it. He cannot take it with him. He may give it to a devisee or legatee absolutely, or may create successive interests; for example, a husband may leave property to his wife for her life and after her death to their children. Within limits, a testator can do as he wishes with his property and will usually decide after consulting his family, his friends, and his solicitor; in any event he should make a will as soon as he has property, even an insurance policy, to leave.

(iv) Bare and special trusts

A bare trust[30] arises where property is vested in the trustee for the benefit of another without the settlor requiring how the property should be used.[31] So, for example, if the settlor transfers property to trustees to hold on trust for the beneficiary absolutely, this will be a bare trust. The trustee of a bare trust must permit the beneficiary to enjoy the property and must follow the beneficiary's instructions as to the disposal of it.

A special trust is one where special duties are imposed on the trustee to manage the property and to distribute it to the beneficiaries.

---

[28] See p. 44, below.

[29] Compare with a fiduciary power (see p. 43, below) where the trustee is not obliged to exercise the power.

[30] See *Re Cunningham and Frayling* [1891] 2 Ch 567 at 572; *Tomlinson v Glyns Executor and Trustee Co* [1970] Ch 112 at 125, 126.

[31] For a statutory definition of 'bare trust' see the Trusts of Land and Appointment of Trustees Act 1996, s. 19 (3).

(v) Public and Private trusts

Trusts may be created for public (i.e. charitable) purposes as well as for individuals or a class of people. The latter are private trusts, since they are not created for the benefit of the public; the former are public trusts because there is a public benefit, as is required by the Charities Act 2006. Public or charitable trusts form a large and important area of the law of trusts. They are specially favoured by the law, being in effect free from liability to tax, and being permitted to continue in perpetuity. Many English charities are ancient. The total number of charities registered with the Charity Commission in 2007 was over 190,000.[32]

(vi) Implied trusts

In some circumstances a trust results in favour of the settlor, and this is usually, but not necessarily, consistent with the settlor's intention, albeit implied rather than express.[33] So, for example, the settlor may be presumed to intend a trust for himself where he creates an express trust which fails, so that the trustee will hold on trust for the settlor. Similarly, a presumed intent will be implied where a purchaser pays for property which is received by another person. That other person will be presumed to hold on trust for the purchaser.

(vii) Imputed trusts

Another type of trust is known as the constructive trust.[34] This arises through the application of legal rules rather than being expressly created by a settlor or testator. These trusts arise in a wide variety of circumstances, such as the prevention of fraud.

III DISTINGUISHING TRUSTS FROM OTHER CONCEPTS[35]

A BAILMENT[36]

Maitland: *Lectures on Equity* (2nd edn), p. 45

We must distinguish the trust from the bailment. This is not very easy to do, for in some of our classical text-books perplexing language is used about this matter. For example, Blackstone

---

[32] Charity Commission website: <http://www.charity-commission.gov.uk>.
[33] See Chapter 6.
[34] See Chapter 7. This term is, however, sometimes used to describe trusts which are properly classified as implied rather than imputed. See p. 323, below.
[35] H&M, pp. 47–67; Lewin, pp. 12–15; P&M, pp. 22–36; Pettit, pp. 28–41; Snell pp. 472–479; T&H, pp. 42–47; U&H, pp. 10–40.
[36] H&M, pp. 48–49; Lewin, p. 14; Pettit, p. 28; Snell, pp. 472–473; T&H, pp. 45–46; U&H, pp. 24–25; A. Bell in *Interests in Goods* (ed. N. Palmer and E. McKendrick) (2nd edn, 1998), Chap. 19; Bridge, *Personal*

defines a bailment thus: 'Bailment, from the French *bailler,* is a delivery of goods in trust, upon a contract expressed or implied, that the trust shall be faithfully executed on the part of the bailee' (*Comm*. II, 451).

Here a bailment seems to be made a kind of trust. Now of course in one way it is easy enough to distinguish a bailment from those trusts enforced by equity, and only by equity, of which we are speaking. We say that the rights of a bailor against his bailee are legal, are common law rights, while those of a *cestui que trust* against his trustee are never common law rights. But then this seems to be a putting of the cart before the horse; we do not explain why certain rights are enforced at law while other rights are left to equity.

Let us look at the matter a little more closely. On the one hand we will have a bailment— A lends B a quantity of books—A lets to B a quantity of books in return for a periodical payment—A deposits a lot of books with B for safe custody. In each of these cases B receives rights from A, and in each of these cases B is under an obligation to A; he is bound with more or less rigour to keep the books safely and to return them to A. Still we do not I think conceive that B is bound to use on A's behalf the rights that he, B, has in the books. Such rights as B has in them he has on his own behalf, and those rights he may enjoy as seems best to him. On the other hand, S is making a marriage settlement and the property that he is settling includes a library of books; he vests the whole ownership of these books in T and T' who are to permit S to enjoy them during his life and then to permit his firstborn son to enjoy them and so forth. Not unfrequently valuable chattels are thus settled so that whoever dwells in a certain mansion during the continuance of the settlement shall have the use of the pictures, books, plate, and so forth. Now here T and T' are full owners of the chattels. S and the other *cestui que trusts* have no rights in the chattels, but T and T' are bound to use their rights according to the words of the settlement, words which compel them to allow S and the other *cestui que trusts* to enjoy those things.

You may say the distinction is a fine one, almost a metaphysical one—and very likely I am not stating it well—but there are two tests which will bring out the distinction. The one is afforded by the law of sale, ...

A is the bailor, B is the bailee of goods; B sells the goods to X, the sale not being authorised by the terms of the bailment and not being made in market overt or within the Factors' Acts.[37] X, though he purchases in good faith, and though he has no notice of A's rights, does not get a good title to the goods. A can recover them from him; if he converts them to his use he wrongs A. Why? Because he bought them from one who was not owner of them. Turn to the other case. T is holding goods as trustee of S's marriage settlement. In breach of trust he sells them to X; X buys in good faith and has no notice of the trust. X gets a good title to the goods. T was the owner of the goods; he passed his rights to X; X became the owner of the goods and S has no right against X—for it is an elementary rule, to which I must often refer hereafter, that trust rights can not be enforced against one who has acquired legal (i.e. common law) ownership bona fide,

Property Law (3rd edn, 2002), pp. 33–43; Crossley Vaines, *Personal Property* (5th edn, 1973), chap. 6; Gleeson, *Personal Property Law* (1997), pp. 34–44; Palmer, *Bailment* (2nd edn, 1991); Worthington, *Personal Property Law: Text and* Materials (2000), p. 81; *Aluminium Industrie Vaassen BV v Romalpa Aluminium Ltd* [1976] 1 WLR 676; *Re Goldcorp Exchange* [1995] 1 AC 74 at 97.

37 See Factors Act 1889, ss. 2, 8, 9; Sale of Goods Act 1979, ss. 21–26; Consumer Credit Act 1974, Sch. 4, para. 22. The rule of market overt was abolished by the Sale of Goods (Amendment) Act 1994, s. 1.

for value, and without notice of the existence of those trust rights. Here you see one difference between the bailee and the trustee...[38]

Cases can be conceived where it would be difficult to say whether there was a bailment by deposit or a trust. For instance, I go abroad in a hurry and do not know whether I shall return. I send a piano to a friend, and I say to him, 'Take care of my piano and if I don't return give it to my daughter'. This may be construed both ways, as a bailment or as a trust. Perhaps the age of my daughter—a thing strictly irrelevant—would decide which way it would go.

B AGENCY[39]

The relationship between trustee and beneficiary, and that between principal and agent, is *fiduciary*. For that reason there are many similarities between them. The crucial distinction is that the agency relationship is *personal*; the trust relationship *proprietary*.

Hanbury & Martin: *Modern Equity* (17th edn), pp. 49–50

The relationship of principal and agent, which is normally contractual, is governed by rules of common law and equity, while the relationship of trustee and beneficiary, which is rarely contractual, is exclusively equitable. The function of an agent is to represent the principal in dealings with third parties, while a trustee does not bring the beneficiaries into any relationship with third parties. There are, however, many similarities.[40] The relationship of trustee and beneficiary is fiduciary; that of principal and agent is normally fiduciary, but not inevitably so. Both trustees and agents must act personally and not delegate their duties; neither may make unauthorised profits from their office.

A significant distinction arises from the fact that the relationship of principal and agent is primarily debtor/creditor, while a trust is proprietary: the trust property vests in the trustee and the beneficiaries are the equitable owners. The crucial point here is that a proprietary right (so long as the property or its proceeds can be identified) is not affected by the defendant's insolvency, whereas a personal claim will abate with the claims of other creditors if the defendant cannot pay in full.

An agent does not necessarily hold any property for the principal. Even if he does, he may merely have possession rather than title. The principal will have proprietary rights against the agent only if the agent has acquired title to property for the benefit of the principal. That proposition is clear enough in the abstract, but it is often extremely difficult to gauge, especially where the subject matter is money... (i) whether the agent has acquired title or mere possession, and (ii) if he has acquired title, whether there is an intention to create a trust or to allow the agent to take an absolute title subject to a merely personal monetary obligation.

---

[38] This paragraph was cited with approval by Mummery LJ in *MCC Proceeds Inc v Lehman Bros International (Europe)* [1998] 4 All ER 675 at 688.

[39] H&M, pp. 49–50; Lewin, pp. 13–14; P&M, p. 32; Pettit, pp. 29–30; Snell, p. 473; T&H, p. 46; U&H, pp. 10–12; (1892) 8 LQR 220 (C. Sweet); Hanbury, *Principles of Agency* (2nd edn, 1952) pp. 3–10; *Bowstead and Reynolds on Agency* (18th edn, 2006), pp. 23–24.

[40] See *Fridman's Law of Agency* (7th edn, 1996), pp. 23–27.

C CONTRACT[41]

Trust and contract are very different concepts. Contract is a common law concept based upon agreement, requiring either a deed or consideration, and creates a personal right against the other party. The trust is an equitable concept, dependent typically upon the intention of the settlor, and creating a proprietary interest in the beneficiary. Nevertheless, there are situations in which the dividing line is not clear.

(i) Debt[42]

A debt is often contractual, although does not necessarily have to be, and sometimes there are real difficulties in distinguishing trust and debt. Essentially, however, a debt is a personal obligation, whereas a trust is proprietary.

Morley v Morley
(1678) 2 Cas in Ch 2 (Lord Nottingham LC)

The Defendant was Trustee for the Plaintiff an Infant, and received for him 40*l.* in Gold; a Servant of the Defendant living in the House with him robbed his Master of 200*l.* and the 40*l.* out of his House. The Robbery, *viz.* That the Defendant was robbed of Money, was proved; the Sum of 40*l.* was proved by only the Defendant's Oath.

LORD CHANCELLOR: He was to keep it but as his own, and allowed it on Account; so in Case of a Factor; so in Case of a Person robbed, for he cannot possibly have other Proof.

In **Duggan v Governor of Full Sutton Prison** [2004] 1 WLR 1010 the Court of Appeal held that the rule in the Prison Rules, that any prisoner who had cash in prison was required to pay it into an account under the governor's control, created a relationship of debtor and creditor and did not impose a trust. It followed that the governor was not obliged to invest the money in an interest-bearing account. There was nothing in the circumstances to lead equity to impose a trust, and in particular there was nothing in the Prison Rules which indicated that a trust was intended.

A line of cases suggests that, where a lender is sufficiently well-advised to make his loan in specific legal language, if the borrower becomes insolvent he may convert what on the face of it is a debt into a trust, thereby avoiding the consequence of being an unsecured creditor. This trust has become known as the *Quistclose* trust, after the name

---

[41] H&M, pp. 50–55; Lewin, pp. 12–13; P&M, pp. 22–29; Pettit, pp. 28–29; Snell, pp. 473–475; T&H, pp. 43–45; U&H, pp. 12–21.

[42] See generally *Space Investments Ltd v Canadian Imperial Bank of Commerce Trust Co (Bahamas) Ltd* [1986] 1 WLR 1072; (1987) 103 LQR 433 (R. M. Goode); *Ross v Lord Advocate* [1986] 1 WLR 1077; (1987) 50 MLR 231 (M. Percival). For an example of a debt which is the subject matter of a trust, see *Barclays Bank plc v Willowbrook International Ltd* [1987] 1 FTLR 386 (when A charges to B a debt owed to A by C, any money paid by C to A is held by A as constructive trustee for B).

of the case in which the House of Lords first recognised it.[43] Although the existence of this trust is now well established, the ambit of this trust device remains unclear and the proper method for analysing the trust has proved to be highly controversial, even as to whether it is always a trust, although the preferable view is that this is simply a matter of contractual construction.[44]

(ii) Settlements and Covenants to Settle

It is important also to distinguish between the creation of a trust or settlement, and a covenant or contract to create one. Once a settlement is created, in equity the beneficiaries become owners of their share of the settled property. But if the settlor has covenanted to create a settlement or to add property to an existing settlement, the rights of the intended beneficiaries depend on whether or not they can compel the settlor to complete the settlement. Traditionally, they cannot do so if they are volunteers; for equity does not assist a volunteer.[45] But the effect of this principle has now been modified following the enactment of the Contracts (Rights of Third Parties) Act 1999.[46]

(iii) Unincorporated Associations

An unincorporated association is not a 'legal person', and questions arise as to the means by which the property of such an association is held. Is it owned by the members jointly? Or held by the committee members or club officials on trust for the members? Or for the purposes of the association? Or held by them subject to contractual rights in favour of the members?

The answers to these questions can determine the validity of a gift to an unincorporated association, and are also relevant to the solution of problems concerning the disposal of assets on a dissolution.[47]

(iv) Contractual Licences

In the context of the rights of a contractual licence to occupy land, there is some authority for imposing a constructive trust where justice and good conscience require it.[48] This is so where land subject to a contractual licence is sold to a third party, and the courts have sought to avoid the result that the purchaser, not being bound by the contract, can evict the licensee, by imposing a constructive trust upon him or her.[49]

---

[43] *Barclays Bank plc v Quistclose Investments Ltd* [1970] AC 567, see p. 239, below.
[44] See p. 255, below.   [45] See p. 161, below.   [46] See p. 169, below.
[47] See p. 235, below.   [48] See *Ashburn Anstalt v Arnold* [1989] Ch 1, p. 310, below.
[49] See p. 310, below.

D   GIFTS[50]

Thomas and Hudson, *The Law of Trusts* (2004), pp. 46–47

A gift involves the outright transfer of property rights in an item of property from an absolute owner of those rights to a volunteer (that is, someone who has given no consideration for the transfer). The recipient (or donee) becomes absolute owner of that property as a result of the transfer. In some senses the recipient of a gift appears to occupy a similar position to the beneficiary under a trust. The settlor transfers absolute title in property by dividing between the legal title vested in the trustee and the equitable title vested in the beneficiary. The beneficiary is not required (by the general law of trusts) to have given consideration for that transfer. In that sense the beneficiary is a volunteer. One of the core equitable principles... is that equity will not assist a volunteer.[51] However, the significant difference between a gift and a trust is that legal title has been assigned to the trustee on the basis that the trustee is required to deal with the property for the benefit of the beneficiary. In short, equity is acting on the conscience of the trustee in her treatment of the trust fund, rather than seeking to benefit a beneficiary. It is a by-product of the control of the trustee's conscience that the beneficiary takes equitable title in the property.

E   CONDITIONS AND CHARGES[52]

In **Attorney-General v The Cordwainers' Company** (1833) 3 My & K 534,[53] the testator, by his will dated 31 March, 1547, devised the Falcon Inn and adjoining premises in Fleet Street to the Cordwainers' Company 'for the only interest, use and performation of this my last will and testament...' The will required the Cordwainers' Company to pay £6 a year to the testator's brother David and after David's death to his widow; to make certain payments to charity and to the officers of the company for attending certain masses; a gift over to David in fee, on failure by the Company to carry out the terms of the will, the company then 'to be clearly expelled, discharged, and put out of the premises'.

The rents of the premises were £12 6s. 8d. in 1547. They had risen to £358 in 1833. The question was whether the Company, having carried out the terms of the will, was entitled to the surplus, or whether they held the premises as trustees, and were obligated to hold the surplus on charitable trusts. The Master of the Rolls (Sir John Leach) held that they held the premises subject to a condition, and, upon due performance of the condition, were entitled to keep the surplus beneficially. He said (at 542):

The first question is whether this testator intended the corporation to take as mere trustees, or whether he intended to give them any beneficial interest. The next consideration is whether, if the corporation were to take as trustees, they were to be trustees for mere charitable purposes.

---

[50] T&H pp. 46–47.   [51] See p. 161, below.

[52] H&M, pp. 55–56; Lewin, pp. 87–88; P&M, pp. 32–33; U&H, pp. 47–49; (1952) 11 CLJ 240 (T.C. Thomas).

[53] See also *Re Oliver* (1890) 62 LT 533 (devise of real estate to nephew, 'he also paying thereout' certain legacies. Held to create a charge and not a trust. The nephew not obligated to account for surplus).

It does not appear to me that the words of this devise do constitute this corporation mere trustees. The estate is absolutely given to them; not upon trust, but for the use, interest, and performance of the testator's will. It is rather a gift upon condition, than a gift upon trust. They are to take the estate so devised to them, upon condition that they perform the duties which by the terms of the will are imposed upon them. Those duties are not for mere charitable purposes. Half the property that this testator disposes of is disposed of to his brother; an annuity of £6 is given to his brother for his life; and after his brother's death there is no disposition of this annuity, except that £2 a year are given to his widow if she survived him. These are not charitable purposes. It is plain that a beneficial estate was intended to be given to the Cordwainers' Company, because the testator expressly declares that, if the condition upon which this estate is devised to the corporation be not performed, the brother shall enter and defeat the estate given to the Cordwainers' Company. Defeat what estate? An estate given to them in mere trust, from which they were to derive no benefit? Is it to be supposed that this was considered by the testator in the nature of a penalty? The imposition of a penalty for non-performance of the condition implies a benefit, if the condition be performed, and is inconsistent with any other intention, than that the testator meant to give a beneficial interest to the company upon the terms of complying with the directions contained in his will. There is, therefore, no trust, either express or implied, for charitable purposes further than to the extent of the special charge imposed; and, upon all the principles applied in this Court to such a case, this information must be dismissed.

In **Re Frame** [1939] Ch 700[54] a testator bequeathed property to Mrs. Ada Taylor, his housekeeper 'on condition that she adopts my daughter Alma Edwards and also gives to my daughters Jessie Edwards and May Alice Edwards the sum of 5*l.* each, and a like sum of 5*l.* to my son Alexander Edwards'. SIMONDS J construed this gift as a trust for the maintenance of Alma, and held that Mrs. Taylor was bound to provide maintenance for Alma even if, as happened, she was unsuccessful in an application to adopt her. In considering the effect of the words quoted above, he said at 703:

The question is what those words mean. I have listened to an able and interesting argument on these questions: whether the condition is a condition subsequent or a condition precedent; whether, if it be a condition precedent, the condition has become impossible of performance, and whether, if so, the gift fails; whether, if it be a condition subsequent, the donee has failed, through no fault of her own, to comply with the condition, and whether, in that event, the gift has failed. As I listened to that argument it impressed itself more and more on me that, after all, this was not a condition at all, for, in my view, on the true construction of this clause, the word 'condition' is not used in its strict legal sense. It is a gift to Mrs. Taylor on condition, in the sense of on the terms or on the trust that she does certain things, and that, I think, becomes clearer when it is realized that the condition relates not only to the adoption of one daughter, but to the payment of certain sums to other daughters. A devise, or bequest, on condition that the devisee or legatee makes certain payments does not import a condition in the strict sense of the word, but a trust, so that, though the devisee or legatee dies before the testator and the gift does not take effect, yet the payments must be made; for it is a trust, and no trust fails for want of trustees. When I come to look at the condition, it seems clear that what the testator intended was that Mrs. Taylor should receive certain moneys

---

[54] Cf. *Re Brace* [1954] 1 WLR 955 ('on condition that she will always provide a house for my daughter Doris at...').

on the term that she performed certain acts. Much argument has been directed to what is involved in the condition that 'she adopts my daughter'. It seems clear that whether or not an adoption under the authority of an order made under the Adoption of Children Act 1926 is necessary, what is intended is not any single formal act, but a series of acts to establish as between Mrs. Taylor and the testator's daughter the relationship of parent and child—in a word, Mrs. Taylor was to treat the child as if she were her daughter, because that is what adoption means. Is that a trust which the Court can enforce? It includes not only the parental duties of care, advice, and affection, but also the duty of maintenance. This Court cannot compel, so far as adoption involves the giving of care, advice and affection that such things be given. But, seeing that it involves the duty of maintenance, that is a trust which the Court can enforce, directing, if necessary, an inquiry in that regard. It will not allow the whole trust to fail because in part it cannot be enforced.

Therefore, I come to the conclusion that the gift to Mrs. Taylor of all the money and insurance policies—what that means will have to be considered—on condition 'that she adopts my daughter' involves that she receives those things, whatever they may be, on trust to make proper provision for the maintenance of the child as her adopted daughter. That is a trust which can be enforced, and, if necessary, an inquiry can be directed in regard to it.

F INTERESTS UNDER A WILL OR INTESTACY[55]

(i) The Distinction between a Personal Representative and a Trustee

Attenborough v Solomon
[1913] AC 76 (HL, **Viscount Haldane, Lords Atkinson** and **Shaw of Dunfermline**)

The testator, who died in 1878, devised and bequeathed his residuary estate to his two sons, A.A. Solomon ('A.A.') and J.D. Solomon upon trust to sell, and to divide the proceeds of sale among his children equally. Within a year, the debts and legacies had been paid, and the residuary account passed, but the estate had not been finally distributed.

In 1892, A.A. pledged some silver plate, part of the residuary estate, with George Attenborough and Sons, pawnbrokers, the appellants, to secure a personal loan. The appellants had no reason to believe that A.A. was not the absolute owner. The matter came to light when A.A. died in 1907.

The question was whether the appellants obtained any rights over the plate, as pawnbrokers. They would do so if A.A. had acted as an executor, since the power of

[55] H&M, pp. 56–62; Lewin, pp. 10–12, 471–472; P&M, pp. 29–32; Pettit, pp. 37–40; Snell, pp. 477–479; U&H, pp. 23–28; (1955) 19 Conv (NS) 199 (B.S. Ker); [1984] Conv 423 (C. Stebbings); [1990] Conv 257 (C. Stebbings); (1991) 11 OJLS 609 (C. Stebbings).

disposal of personalty by executors is *several*; but not if A.A. were a trustee, because the trustee's power of disposal is *joint*.[56]

Held. The appellants obtained no title because A.A. was a trustee.

Viscount Haldane LC: The general principles of law which govern this case are not doubtful. The position of an executor is a peculiar one. He is appointed by the will, but then, by virtue of his office, by the operation of law and not under the bequest in the will, he takes a title to the personal property of the testator, which vests him with the *plenum dominium* over the testator's chattels. He takes that, I say, by virtue of his office. The will becomes operative so far as its dispositions of personalty are concerned only if and when the executor assents to those dispositions. It is true that by virtue of his office he has a general power to sell or pledge for the purpose of paying debts and getting in the money value of the estate. He is executor and he remains executor for an indefinite time. Authorities were cited to us by [counsel for the appellants] to the effect that an executor can sell at a period long after the death of the testator, and that where it is a question of conveyancing, as for instance in the case of the sale of leaseholds by the executor, the purchaser is not entitled to make requisitions as to whether debts remain unpaid, because the executor's office remains intact and he may exercise his functions at any time. That is true as a general principle, and I have no comment to make upon it except that it is qualified by another principle, which is this: the office of executor remains, with its powers attached, but the property which he had originally in the chattels that devolved upon him, and over which these powers extended, does not necessarily remain. So soon as he has assented, and this he may do informally and the assent may be inferred from his conduct, the dispositions of the will become operative, and then the beneficiaries have vested in them the property in those chattels. The transfer is made not by the mere force of the assent of the executor, but by virtue of the dispositions of the will which have become operative because of this assent.

Now, my Lords, in view of the residuary account passed as it was and in the form it was, in view of the evidence of Mr. J.D. Solomon, and in view of the fourteen years which had passed since the testator died before the time when Mr. A.A. Solomon made the pledge to the appellants in 1892, I am of opinion that the true inference to be drawn from the facts is that the executors considered that they had done all that was due from them as executors by 1879, and were content when the residuary account was passed that the dispositions of the will should take effect. That is the inference I draw from the form of the residuary account; and the inference is strengthened when I consider the lapse of time since then, and that in the interval nothing was done by them purporting to be an exercise of power as executors. My Lords, if this be so, this appeal must be disposed of on the footing that in point of fact the executors assented at a very early date to the dispositions of the will taking effect. It follows that under these dispositions the residuary estate, including the chattels in question, become vested in the trustees as trustees. That they were the same persons as the executors does not affect the point, or in my opinion present the least obstacle to the inference. But if that was so, then the title to the silver plate of A.A. Solomon as executor had ceased to exist before he made the pledge of 1892. What then was the position of the appellants? By the law of England the property in a chattel must always

---

[56] Law Reform Committee 23rd Report (*The Powers and Duties of Trustees*) 1982, Cmnd 8733, para. 7.12 recommends that 'personal representatives should be placed under a duty to act unanimously (subject to any contrary provision in the will) when disposing of property from the deceased's estate'. See also Law Commission Report: *Title on Death* 1989 (Law Com. No. 184), paras. 2.10–2.19 and Law of Property (Miscellaneous Provisions) Act 1994, s. 16.

be in one person or body of persons. When the person who owns the chattel makes a pledge of it to a pawnbroker he is not purporting to part with the full property or giving any thing which is in the nature of a title to that property to the pawnee, excepting to a limited extent. The expression has been used that the pawnee in such a case has got a special property in the chattel. My Lords, that is true in this sense, that the pawnbroker is entitled to hold the chattel upon the terms that when the possession has been lawfully given to him it is not to be taken away from him, and that if default is made in the redemption of the pledge, or it may be in the payment of interest, he may go further and by virtue of his contract, assuming it to be valid, sell the chattel. But the contract of pawn is simply an illustration of that contract of bailment of which Holt CJ gave the famous exposition in the great case of *Coggs v Bernard* (1703) 2 Ld Raym 909; and it rests upon this foundation, that the property remains in the bailor, and that the bailee, whether it be a bailment by way of pawn or in any other form, simply takes at the outside a right to the possession dependent on the validity of the title of the bailor with the other rights possibly superadded to which I have referred. If that be true, upon no hypothesis did the appellants get a legal title to the property in the plate. When A.A. Solomon handed over these articles of silver to Messrs. Attenborough he had no property to pass as executor; and they got no contractual rights which could prevail against the trustees. The latter were the true owners and they are now in a position to maintain an action, which under the old forms would have been an action of trover or detinue, to recover possession of the chattels free from the restrictions on the right to reclaim possession which were sought to be imposed by the contract between A.A. Solomon and the appellants. My Lords, the property, if I am right in the inference which I draw from the circumstances of the case, was vested not in A.A. Solomon, but in A.A. Solomon and his co-trustee jointly in 1892, when the attempted pledge was made; and I see no answer to the case made for the respondents that the present trustees, in whom that property is now vested, are entitled to recover it.

In **Re King's Will Trusts** [1964] Ch 542, PENNYCUICK J held that personal representatives could not exercise the statutory powers of appointing new trustees nor could they rely upon the provisions of Trustee Act 1925, section 40,[57] to vest realty in newly appointed trustees, unless they had assented in writing in accordance with the Administration of Estates Act 1925, section 36(4), to the vesting of the realty in themselves as trustees.

The testatrix, by her will dated 12 June, 1939, appointed X, Y and Z to be her executors, and X and Y her trustees. The estate contained land. As a result of various deaths and purported appointments of new trustees, Mr. Assheton, the plaintiff, claimed that he was the sole surviving trustee, and that the legal estate was vested in him. The defendant was the sole surviving personal representative (by representation). The question was whether the various appointments of trustees by X and Y and their successors were valid appointments; and whether, if they were valid, the legal estate was now vested, by virtue of Trustee Act 1925, section 40, in the plaintiff.

PENNYCUICK J held that the legal estate was in the defendant. Before personal representatives could become trustees of land, it was necessary that they should formally assent in writing in their own favour under section 36(4), just as they would in favour

---

[57] See p. 632, below.

of other persons. The deed of appointment of new trustees did not operate as such assent.

With personalty an assent can be implied. With realty, it must be in writing. *Re King's Will Trusts* is contrary to the earlier practice of many conveyancers,[58] but in the absence of evidence of widespread problems resulting from this decision, the Law Commission recommended that no change be made.[59]

(ii) The Nature of the Interest of a Legatee or Devisee

Commissioner of Stamp Duties (Queensland) v Livingston[60]
[1965] AC 694 (PC, **Viscount Radcliffe, Lords Reid, Evershed, Pearce** and **Upjohn**)

A testator, H.D. Livingston, died domiciled in New South Wales, leaving to his widow absolutely an estate which consisted of real and personal property in Queensland and in New South Wales.

While the estate was still in the course of administration, the widow (Mrs. Coulson) died intestate, also domiciled in New South Wales.

One question was whether succession duty was payable on the widow's death in respect of the Queensland property left to her in the will. Under the relevant Queensland statute succession duty was payable in respect of 'every devolution by law of any beneficial interest in property…upon the death of any person…'.

Held. No duty was payable in Queensland. The widow did not hold a beneficial interest in the property, but merely a chose in action which was situated in New South Wales.

Viscount Radcliffe: When Mrs. Coulson died she had the interest of a residuary legatee in the testator's unadministered estate. The nature of that interest has been conclusively defined by decisions of long-established authority, and its definition no doubt depends upon the peculiar status which the law accorded to an executor for the purposes of carrying out his duties of administration. There were special rules which long prevailed about the devolution of freehold land and its liability for the debts of a deceased, but subject to the working of these rules whatever property came to the executor *virtute officii* came to him in full ownership, without distinction between legal and equitable interests. The whole property was his. He held it for the purpose of carrying out the functions and duties of administration, not for his own benefit; and these duties would be enforced upon him by the Court of Chancery, if application had to be made for that purpose by a creditor or beneficiary interested in the estate. Certainly, therefore, he was in a fiduciary position with regard to the assets that came to him in the right of his office,

---

[58] (1964) 28 Conv (NS) 298 (J.F. Garner). The equitable beneficial interest may still pass under an implied assent by a personal representative: *Re Edwards' Will Trusts* [1982] Ch 30; [1981] Conv 450 (G. Shindler); [1982] Conv 4 (P.W. Smith).

[59] Law Commission Report: *Title on Death* 1989 (Law Com. No. 184); para. 1.5–1.6.

[60] (1965) CLJ 44 (S.J. Bailey); *Crowden v Aldridge* [1993] 1 WLR 433; [1994] Conv 446 (J.G. Ross Martyn). See also *Official Receiver in Bankruptcy v Schultz* (1990) 170 CLR 306; [1992] Conv 92 (J.K. Maxton).

and for certain purposes and in some aspects he was treated by the court as a trustee. 'An executor,' said Kay J in *Re Marsden* (1884) 26 Ch D 783 at 789, 'is personally liable in equity for all breaches of the ordinary trusts which in Courts of Equity are considered to arise from his office.' He is a trustee 'in this sense'.

It may not be possible to state exhaustively what those trusts are at any one moment. Essentially, they are trusts to preserve the assets, to deal properly with them, and to apply them in a due course of administration for the benefit of those interested according to that course, creditors, the death duty authorities, legatees of various sorts, and the residuary beneficiaries. They might just as well have been termed 'duties in respect of the assets' as trusts. What equity did not do was to recognise or create for residuary legatees a beneficial interest in the assets in the executor's hands during the course of administration. Conceivably, this could have been done, in the sense that the assets, whatever they might be from time to time, could have been treated as a present, though fluctuating, trust fund held for the benefit of all those interested in the estate according to the measure of their respective interests. But it never was done. It would have been a clumsy and unsatisfactory device from a practical point of view; and, indeed, it would have been in plain conflict with the basic conception of equity that to impose the fetters of a trust upon property, with the resulting creation of equitable interests in that property, there had to be specific subjects identifiable as the trust fund. An unadministered estate was incapable of satisfying this requirement. The assets as a whole were in the hands of the executor, his property; and until administration was complete no one was in a position to say what items of property would need to be realised for the purposes of that administration or of what the residue, when ascertained, would consist or what its value would be. Even in modern economies, when the ready marketability of many forms of property can almost be assumed, valuation and realisation are very far from being interchangeable terms.

At the date of Mrs. Coulson's death, therefore, there was no trust fund consisting of Mr. Livingston's residuary estate in which she could be said to have any beneficial interest, because no trust had as yet come into existence to affect the assets of his estate. The relation of her estate to his was exactly the same as that of Mrs. Tollemache's estate to that of her deceased husband's, as analysed in the well-known decision of *Lord Sudeley v A-G* [1897] AC 11. Just as Mr. Tollemache's rights in the mortgages of New Zealand land were the property of his executors for the purposes of the administration of his estate, and no one else had any property interest in them, so Mr. Livingston's property in Queensland, real or personal, was vested in his executors in full right, and no beneficial property interest in any item of it belonged to Mrs. Coulson at the date of her death. In their Lordships' opinion the decision of the *Sudeley* case is conclusive on this issue. It is sufficient to quote the words of Lord Herschell, which do no more than reflect the reasoning and views of all the members of the House who took part in the decision. 'I do not think,' he said at 18, speaking of Mrs. Tollemache's executors, 'that they have any estate, right, or interest, legal or equitable, in these New Zealand mortgages so as to make them an asset of her estate.'

It is evident that there would not have been the divisions of opinion in the Australian courts that have arisen in this case, if the proposition laid down by the *Sudeley* decision had always been regarded as being as final and comprehensive as, in their Lordships' opinion, it was intended to be. There has been a reluctance to accept Lord Herschell's words at their face value and, it would seem, a feeling that they ought to be treated as subject to some limitation that does justice to the 'interest' that a residuary legatee possesses in his testator's estate. The judgment of Jordan CJ in *McCaughey v Stamp Duties Comr* (1945) 46 NSWR 192 contains a reasoned statement of some of these misgivings, which were again referred to in the High Court of Australia in *Smith v Layh* (1953) 90 CLR 102 at 108–109; and cases in England such as *Re*

Cunliffe-Owen [1953] Ch 545 indicate a certain unease at relating *Sudeley* to other English decisions. Basically, these criticisms appear to arise from an incomplete assessment of the legal position of assets which belong to an executor for the purposes of his administration and from a use of the word 'interest' that is not sufficiently precise to meet the requirements of a taxing Act to which questions of locality and valuation are all important. But since these criticisms have been made, it is desirable that this opinion should notice and comment upon them...

... their Lordships regard it as clearly established that Mrs. Coulson was not entitled to any beneficial interest in any property in Queensland at the date of her death. What she was entitled to in respect of her rights under her deceased husband's will was a chose in action, capable of being invoked for any purpose connected with the proper administration of his estate; and the local situation of this asset, as much under Queensland law as any other law, was in New South Wales, where the testator had been domiciled and his executors resided and which constituted the proper forum of administration of his estate.

In **Lall v Lall** [1965] 1 WLR 1249, the question was whether the right of a widow under the Intestates' Estates Act 1952 to require the matrimonial home to be appropriated towards the satisfaction of her share of an intestate's estate gave the widow standing to defend an action for possession of the house. No grant of administration had been made. BUCKLEY J held, following *Commissioner of Stamp Duties (Queensland) v Livingston*, that it did not.

In **Eastbourne Mutual Building Society v Hastings Corpn** [1965] 1 WLR 861, PLOWMAN J quoted VISCOUNT RADCLIFFE to summarise the principle of the *Livingston* case as follows:

Therefore, while it may well be said in a general way that a residuary legatee has an interest in the totality of the assets... it is in their Lordships' opinion inadmissible to proceed from that to the statement that such a person has an equitable interest in any particular one of those assets, for such a statement is in conflict with the authority of both *Sudeley* [1897] AC 11 and *Barnardo* [1921] 2 AC 1 and is excluded by the very premise on which those decisions were based.

(1970) 86 LQR 20 (P.V.B.)

In **Re Leigh's Will Trusts** [1970] Ch 277, a testatrix specifically bequeathed 'all shares which I hold and any other interest or assets which I may have' in a named company. The testatrix never had any shares or interest of her own in the company, but both at the time she made her will and at her death she was the sole administratrix and beneficiary of her intestate husband's unadministered estate. That estate included some shares in and a debt due from the company. The question for Buckley J was whether those shares and debt passed under the bequest. The testatrix could not have bequeathed them in her capacity of administratrix, but what of her position as sole beneficiary?

The position of a person entitled to the residue or upon an intestacy while the administration is continuing was reviewed by Viscount Radcliffe in *Stamp Duties Comr (Queensland) v Livingston* [1965] AC 694 and, as Buckley J observed, may be summarised in four propositions:

(1) The entire ownership of the assets of the estate remains during the course of administration in the personal representative;

(2) No person entitled to residue or upon an intestacy has any proprietary interest in any particular asset in the estate;

(3) Each such person has a right to require the deceased's estate to be duly administered;[61]

(4) That right is a chose in action which is transmissible.

It follows that the only disposable interest which the testatrix had was the chose in action which could be transmitted to one or more beneficiaries. Buckley J held that the testatrix had 'an interest in the company both in respect of the shares and of the debt sufficient to answer the description in the specific bequest to the [specific legatee], which was accordingly effective to entitle [him] to receive such of the shares and so much of the debt as in the due administration of [the husband's] estate should eventually fall into the possession of the executors of the testatrix' (p. 283).[62]

This decision is understandable on the facts of the case but may be difficult to apply in other circumstances. Suppose that the testatrix already had some shares in the company. Would the gift in the will have carried the additional shares comprised in the unadministered estate? Then again, suppose that the shares had been sold to pay the husband's debts. Could the specific legatee have recourse to the doctrine of marshalling and require to be compensated out of other assets of the husband's estate? And if they had not been sold, how far do the executors have to go to procure them? Buckley J said: 'What she could transmit was her own right to require the administrator of her husband's estate, whoever he might be, to administer his estate in any manner she or her personal representative might require consistent with the rights of any other persons having rights against the estate. This right she could transmit to her executor, coupled with a duty to exercise it in a particular manner. By her will she has, in my judgment, clearly indicated that her executor should so exercise this right as to procure the 51 shares, and the company's indebtedness should to the largest possible extent become available to satisfy the specific bequest' (p. 284). Is the executor bound, if necessary to save the shares, to use the testatrix's own estate to pay off the husband's debts? Alternatively, does the doctrine of ademption apply to any extent if the shares are sold (a) before the testatrix makes her will, or (b) before she dies, or (c) after her death? It may be some time before the implications of this decision are fully worked out.'[63]

In **Wu Koon Tai v Wu Yau Loi** [1997] AC 179 LORD BROWNE-WILKINSON said, on behalf of the Privy Council, at 188:

In principle, there is no reason why a devisee of land comprised in an unadministered estate cannot enter into a binding contract to sell that land. True, until completion of the administration and the vesting of the property in the devisee, the devisee cannot convey the land in specie.

---

[61] See *Passant v Jackson* [1986] STC 164 at 167, *per* SLADE LJ.

[62] See also *Earnshaw v Hartley* [2000] Ch 155 (beneficial interest in an unadministered estate held to be sufficient for purposes of Limitation Act 1980, Sch. 1, para. 9).

[63] Cf. *Re K* [1986] Ch 180, p. 305, below, where residuary beneficiaries under an unadministered estate had not acquired 'an interest in property' under the Forfeiture Act 1982, s. 2 (7).

But their Lordships were referred to no authority to suggest that such devisee cannot validly contract to sell the land at a time when his interest is a mere chose in action or expectancy. Their Lordships can see no distinction in principle between such a contract and a contract for value to assign a future chose in action. As and from the date when the chose in action comes into existence, the contract becomes specifically enforceable.

(iii) Executor's Duty is to the Estate as a Whole

In **Re Hayes' Will Trusts** [1971] 1 WLR 758,[64] the testator appointed four persons to be executors and trustees of his will, of whom the testator's son was one. The will gave to the executors a power to sell certain land, expressly authorising sale to his son 'despite his being a trustee, and in his case at the value placed upon the same for purposes of estate duty'.

The executors agreed to sell the land to the son at the agreed estate duty valuation. The other beneficiaries objected that the sale price was too low.

Ungoed-Thomas J held that the executors were under no duty to agree an estate duty valuation which held an even balance between the beneficiaries, as trustees would have to do. Their duty was to the estate as a whole, and the estate duty valuation should be agreed in the ordinary way. He said at 764:

It is of course rightly common ground that 'my trustees' in agreeing the estate duty valuation were acting as executors under statutory powers conferred by section 15(f) of the Trustee Act 1925. They were not acting under any powers conferred by the will, including in particular clause 5(iii). I am completely satisfied that in fixing and agreeing the amount of the estate duty valuation Mr. Cooper, who was acting for the executors, was completely unaffected by the existence of the power to sell to the son. So this power to agree the estate duty valuation is to be considered as a purely personal representative administration power. It is well established that the estate being administered by a personal representative is the personal representative's property. Of course he has fiduciary duties with regard to it and their performance will be secured by the court; and he may be made liable for breaches of his fiduciary duties. But no legatee, devisee or next-of-kin has any beneficial interests in the assets being administered. His position is quite different from that of a trustee, who holds property for beneficiaries and has a duty to hold the balance evenly between the beneficiaries to whom the property belongs and for whom the trustee holds it. It does not necessarily follow that the duty of an executor in the course of administering the estate is subject to the trustee's duty of holding the balance evenly between the beneficiaries. Whether he has such a duty has to be independently considered in the light of his own different fiduciary functions and obligations: see *Stamp Duties Comr (Queensland) v Livingston* [1965] AC 694 at 707, 708 [p. 21, above]. Those functions are to get in the testator's estate, preserve its properties, discharge its liabilities and distribute the resulting net assets. The legal personal representatives would in due course be concerned to obtain a proper discharge for the net assets and thus to ascertain who were entitled to them and to ensure that the assets were distributed to those entitled. But even then they would not be concerned in the course of acting as legal personal representatives with any conflicting interests of beneficiaries under testamentary trusts but only with the trustees of that trust; and not the less so even if they themselves happen to be such trustees. In our case there is not even

---

[64] (1971) 36 Conv (NS) 136 (J.F. Mummery).

the possibility of argument that the farms were in the personal representatives' hands freed of administration and merely held for distribution; and therefore held by the legal personal representative on trust for the beneficiaries. Such an argument would be plainly contrary to the established facts. So the legal personal representative functions, so far at any rate as they arise in our case, are functions which relate to the process of ascertaining the net assets available for distribution and not at all functions in the distribution itself.

Much the most important authority on this part of this case is *Re Charteris* [1917] 2 Ch 379. It appears from the recital of facts in the report supplemented by Swinfen Eady LJ's references in the course of his judgment, that a testatrix gave her residue to her executors and trustees upon trust for sale and to raise a legacy to be held by them on trust for A for life and over. She gave them power to appropriate in satisfaction of the legacy and to postpone sale: and she provided that interest on the amount of the legacy in so far as there was no appropriation should be at 3½ per cent and in so far as there was appropriation the interest would be the income of the appropriated investments. The balance of residue she gave to residuary legatees. It seems that the powers of the executors and trustees to postpone the sale of residue out of whose proceeds the legacy was to be paid and to appropriate it to the legacy were powers given to them in their capacity as executors: but even if they were given to them as trustees then *a fortiori* the observations made in the judgment would be applicable to them as executors, because, as already indicated, the fiduciary nexus between trustees and beneficiaries fastens directly on the trust property and is in that respect stronger than the fiduciary nexus between executor and beneficiary.

The executors decided to postpone sale and thus not to appropriate investments to the legacy. As the life tenant's interest on appropriated investments would be higher than the 3½ per cent interest on the amount of the legacy, the life tenant objected to this course. The postponement in itself operated, as was fully realised by the executors when they made their decision, wholly in the interests of the residuary legatee and contrary to the interests of the pecuniary legatee. The bona fides of the executors was not questioned. The objection failed...

The most likely price, in the absence of consultation between the valuers representing conflicting interests, would presumably be the mean price. The habitual well-recognised process of arriving at that price is for executors to put in the lowest price within the range and then to confer with the district valuer who acts to safeguard the revenue. Such has been the accepted process of arriving at the price which the 'property would fetch if sold in the open market' and it seems to me to be as likely as any to arrive at that price within the margin which is the price most likely to be the market price. That was what was done in our case: and Mr. Cooper's evidence, which I accept, is that the price agreed was the fair and proper price and was in fact in this case the mean price within the marginal limits ranging from 10 per cent above to 10 per cent below it.

G   TRUSTS IN PUBLIC LAW[65]

In considering the use of the term 'trust' in relation to the Crown, LORD SELBORNE LC said in **Kinloch v Secretary of State for India** (1882) 7 App Cas 619 at 625:

Now the words 'in trust for' are quite consistent with, and indeed are the proper manner of expressing, every species of trust—a trust not only as regards those matters which are the proper subjects for an equitable jurisdiction to administer, but as respects higher matters, such

---

[65]   H&M, pp. 72–73; Lewin, pp. 30–31; P&M, pp. 18–20; Snell p. 479; U&H, p. 10.

as might take place between the Crown and public officers discharging, under the directions of the Crown, duties or functions belonging to the prerogative and to the authority of the Crown. In the lower sense they are matters within the jurisdiction of, and to be administered by, the ordinary courts of equity; in the higher sense they are not. What their sense is here, is the question to be determined, looking at the whole instrument and its nature and effect.

And LORD DIPLOCK in **Town Investments Ltd v Department of the Environment** [1978] AC 359 at 382:

My Lords, I would not exclude the possibility that an officer of state, even though acting in his official capacity, may in some circumstances hold property subject to a trust in private law for the benefit of a subject; but clear words would be required to do this and, even where the person to be benefited is a subject, the use of the expression 'in trust' to describe the capacity in which the property is granted to an officer of state is not conclusive that a trust in private law was intended; for 'trust' is not a term of art in public law and when used in relation to matters which lie within the field of public law the words 'in trust' may do no more than indicate the existence of a duty owed to the Crown by the officer of state, as servant of the Crown, to deal with the property for the benefit of the subject for whom it is expressed to be held in trust, each duty being enforceable administratively by disciplinary sanctions and not otherwise: *Kinloch v Secretary of State for India* (1882) 7 App Cas 619, per Lord Selborne LC, at 625–626. But even if the legal relationship of trustee and *cestui qui trust* under a trust in private law is capable of existing between an officer of state in his official capacity and a subject, the concept of such relationship being capable of existing between him as trustee and the Crown as *cestui qui trust* is in my view wholly irreconcilable with the legal nature in public law of the relationship between the Crown and its servants or, in more modern parlance, the government and the ministers who form part of it.[66]

In **Lonrho Exports Ltd v Export Credits Guarantee Department** [1999] Ch 158, 178, LIGHTMAN J recognised that the Crown might act as trustee for nationals or corporations.

IV RECOGNITION OF TRUSTS BY NON-TRUST STATES[67]

The concept of a trust originated in England and followed the flag to all common law jurisdictions. Civil law states have never adopted trusts,[68] but the 1984 Hague Convention on the Law Applicable to Trusts and their Recognition seeks to bring

---

[66] See also *Tito v Waddell (No 2)* [1977] Ch 106 at 210–226, per Megarry V-C.

[67] H&M, pp.45–46; Lewin, pp. 400–418; P&M, pp. 841–847; Pettit, pp. 25–26; T&H, pp. 1315–1375; U&H, pp. 1235–1306; Dicey, Morris and Collins *Conflict of Laws* (14th edn, 2006), pp. 1302–1331; Cheshire and North, *Private International Law* (13th edn, 2001), pp. 1030–1044; Harris, *The Hague Trusts Convention* (2002); (1987) 36 ICLQ 260 (D.J. Hayton); (1987) 35 AJCL 307 (E. Gaillard and D. Trautman); (1987) 131 SJ 827 (T. Prime); (1987) 36 ICLQ 454 (A. Wallace); (1989) BTR 41, 65 (J.F. Avery Jones *et al*).

[68] On the proposed new law of trusts in France, see [1992] Conv 407 (H. Dyson); Bérando, *Les Trusts Anglo-Saxon et le Droit Français* (1992). On Roman Law, see Johnston, *The Roman Law of Trusts* (1988).

about international recognition of the concept. It does so by establishing uniform conflict of laws rules (reflecting those of England and Wales), which are to be applied by all signatories. Accordingly, the trust concept is not introduced into the domestic law of non-trust states.

The Recognition of Trusts Act 1987 enabled the United Kingdom to ratify the Convention.

RECOGNITION OF TRUSTS ACT 1987[69]

1. Applicable law and recognition of trusts

(1) The provisions of the Convention set out in the Schedule to this Act shall have the force of law in the United Kingdom.

(2) Those provisions shall, so far as applicable, have effect not only in relation to the trusts described in Articles 2 and 3 of the Convention but also in relation to any other trusts of property arising under the law of any part of the United Kingdom or by virtue of a judicial decision whether in the United Kingdom or elsewhere.

SCHEDULE

Section 1

CONVENTION ON THE LAW APPLICABLE TO TRUSTS AND
ON THEIR RECOGNITION

CHAPTER I—SCOPE

Article 1

This Convention specifies the law applicable to trusts and governs their recognition.

Article 2

For the purposes of this Convention, the term 'trust' refers to the legal relationship created—inter vivos or on death—by a person, the settlor, when assets have been placed under the control of a trustee for the benefit of a beneficiary or for a specified purpose.

A trust has the following characteristics—

(a) the assets constitute a separate fund and are not a part of the trustee's own estate;

(b) title to the trust assets stands in the name of the trustee or in the name of another person on behalf of the trustee;

(c) the trustee has the power and the duty, in respect of which he is accountable, to manage, employ or dispose of the assets in accordance with the terms of the trust and the special duties imposed upon him by law.

---

[69] Recognition of Trusts Act 1987 (Overseas Territories) Order 1989 (S.I. 1989 No. 673).

The reservation by the settlor of certain rights and powers, and the fact that the trustee may himself have rights as beneficiary, are not necessarily inconsistent with the existence of a trust.

Article 3

The Convention applies only to trusts created voluntarily and evidenced in writing.

CHAPTER II—APPLICABLE LAW

Article 6

A trust shall be governed by the law chosen by the settlor. The choice must be express or be implied in the terms of the instrument creating or the writing evidencing the trust, interpreted, if necessary, in the light of the circumstances of the case.

Where the law chosen under the previous paragraph does not provide for trusts or the category of trust involved, the choice shall not be effective and the law specified in Article 7 shall apply.

Article 7

Where no applicable law has been chosen, a trust shall be governed by the law with which it is most closely connected.

In ascertaining the law with which a trust is most closely connected reference shall be made in particular to—

  (a) the place of administration of the trust designated by the settlor;
  (b) the situs of the assets of the trust;
  (c) the place of residence or business of the trustee;
  (d) the objects of the trust and the places where they are to be fulfilled.

Article 8

The law specified by Article 6 or 7 shall govern the validity of the trust, its construction, its effects and the administration of the trust.

In particular that law shall govern—

  (a) the appointment, resignation and removal of trustees, the capacity to act as a trustee, and the devolution of the office of trustee;

  (b) the rights and duties of trustees among themselves;

  (c) the right of trustees to delegate in whole or in part the discharge of their duties or the exercise of their powers;

  (d) the power of trustees to administer or to dispose of trust assets, to create security interests in the trust assets, or to acquire new assets;

  (e) the powers of investment of trustees;

  (f) restrictions upon the duration of the trust, and upon the power to accumulate the income of the trust;

(g) the relationships between the trustees and the beneficiaries including the personal liability of the trustees to the beneficiaries;

(h) the variation or termination of the trust;

(i) the distribution of the trust assets;

(j) the duty of trustees to account for their administration.

CHAPTER III—RECOGNITION

Article 11

A trust created in accordance with the law specified by the preceding Chapter shall be recognised as a trust.

Such recognition shall imply, as a minimum, that the trust property constitutes a separate fund, that the trustee may sue and be sued in his capacity as trustee, and that he may appear or act in this capacity before a notary or any person acting in an official capacity.

In so far as the law applicable to the trust requires or provides, such recognition shall imply in particular—

(a) that personal creditors of the trustee shall have no recourse against the trust assets;

(b) that the trust assets shall not form part of the trustee's estate upon his insolvency or bankruptcy;

(c) that the trust assets shall not form part of the matrimonial property of the trustee or his spouse nor part of the trustee's estate upon his death;

(d) that the trust assets may be recovered when the trustee, in breach of trust, has mingled trust assets with his own property or has alienated trust assets. However, the rights and obligations of any third party holder of the assets shall remain subject to the law determined by the choice of law rules of the forum.

Article 14

The Convention shall not prevent the application of rules of law more favourable to the recognition of trusts.

CHAPTER IV—GENERAL CLAUSES

Article 17

In the Convention the word 'law' means the rules of law in force in a State other than its rules of conflict of laws.[70]

---

[70] Thus excluding the doctrine of *renvoi*.

Article 18

The provisions of the Convention may be disregarded when their application would be manifestly incompatible with public policy.

V TAXATION OF TRUSTS[71]

A GENERAL

Taxation is often a prominent consideration in the decision to create a trust. It is consequently important both to be aware of the application of the tax regime where trusts are involved, and, more significantly, to understand why trusts might be created to avoid or minimise a tax liability.

Three taxes in particular are relevant to trusts, namely Income Tax, Capital Gains Tax, and Inheritance Tax. Other taxes may also affect trusts—for instance Stamp Duty and Value Added Tax—but these are of comparatively subordinate importance. Inheritance Tax is the tax which usually concerns the trust lawyer most. At first sight, this might seem odd. The great bulk of the government's tax revenue is derived from the taxation of income, not capital; and, despite some stringent anti-avoidance provisions, settlements can be used to minimise Income Tax. In reality, however, taxation is concerned not just with raising revenue but also with the redistribution of wealth within society. Such redistribution can only be achieved, it is said, by preventing aggregations of capital from passing unbroken from generation to generation.

Although a knowledge of the law of taxation is important to understand why the device of the trust might be used to avoid or reduce tax liability, this work will not examine this complex body of law in any detail.

Thomas and Hudson, *The Law of Trusts*, p. 50

The core, technical advantage of the trust [to reduce tax liability] is the possibility that more than one person owns the trust property at one and the same time such that the question as to which of them is to bear the liability to pay tax on any income or capital gain of the trust is a complex one. While UK revenue law has developed sophisticated rules governing the allocation of liability to tax and the rate at which tax will be paid by means of statute, and frequently ever more sophisticated rules preventing the avoidance of tax through the use of trusts by means of statute and of case law, trusts nevertheless offer great possibilities for the minimization of the settlor's personal liability to tax due to the division in the ownership of property between trustee and beneficiary on the creation of a trust, coupled with the opportunities for structuring the ownership of property and selecting the people who should own it, which the trust device presents.

[71] H&M, pp. 217-238; P&M, pp. 624–652; P&S, pp. 144–150; Pettit pp. 24–25; T&H pp. 50–52; Thomas, *Taxation and Trusts* (1981); Tiley, *Revenue Law* (5th edn, 2005).

B MITIGATION, AVOIDANCE AND EVASION[72]

Taxpayers have resorted increasingly to tax evasion, tax avoidance, and tax mitiga-tion[73] and the trust can be used as a device to do any of these. Tax evasion is the crim-inal breach of the tax laws. The distinction between tax mitigation and tax avoidance was recognised by LORD NOLAN in **Inland Revenue Commissioners v Willoughby** [1997] 1 WLR 1071 at 1079:

The hallmark of tax avoidance is that the taxpayer reduces his liability to tax without incurring the economic consequences that Parliament intended to be suffered by any taxpayer qualifying for such reduction in his tax liability. The hallmark of tax mitigation, on the other hand, is that the taxpayer takes advantage of a fiscally attractive option afforded to him by the tax legisla-tion, and genuinely suffers the economic consequences that Parliament intended to be suffered by those taking advantage of the option.[74]

Thomas and Hudson, *The Law of Trusts,* p. 51

The settlor may name persons other than himself to be the beneficiaries of the trust and there-fore claim to have no rights to the [property]. Those beneficiaries might be the settlor's own infant children (who would probably have no other taxable income) or a company controlled by the settlor. Other common tax avoidance schemes using trusts involve trustees resident in other tax jurisdictions where little or no tax is payable (such as the Cayman Islands or the British Virgin Islands) to raise an argument that the trust ought not to be liable to UK taxation in any event but rather to tax at the lower rate applicable in that other jurisdiction.

The general response to tax avoidance remains in the hands of the judiciary. The most controversial matter for the courts concerns determining where the line should be drawn between legitimate tax mitigation and unacceptable tax avoidance.

LORD TOMLIN said in **Inland Revenue Commissioners v Duke of Westminster** [1936] AC 1 at 19:[75]

Every man is entitled if he can to arrange his affairs so that the tax attaching under the appro-priate Acts is less than it otherwise would be. If he succeeds in ordering them so as to secure that result, then, however unappreciative the Commissioners of Inland Revenue or his fellow taxpayers may be of his ingenuity, he cannot be compelled to pay an increased tax.[76]

[72] See B. McFarlane and E. Simpson, 'Tackling Avoidance' in *Rationalizing Property, Equity and Trusts* (ed. J. Getzler) pp. 135–186.
[73] See (2001) 117 LQR 575 (Lord Templeman).
[74] The usefulness of the distinction between avoidance and mitigation was doubted by LORD HOFFMANN in *MacNiven v Westmoreland Investments Ltd* [2003] 1 AC 311 at 355.
[75] The Duke, instead of paying his gardener £3 a week in wages, covenanted to pay him £1.18s a week for seven years and the gardener was expected not to take the balance of £1.2s. It was held that the Duke was entitled to deduct the payment in computing his total income for surtax, the gardener being an annuitant under Schedule D and not an employee under Schedule E. Most covenants between individuals made after 14 March, 1988 were rendered ineffective for the purposes by Finance Act 1988, s. 36, inserting s. 347A into Income and Corporation Taxes Act 1988.
[76] See also *Ayrshire Pullman Motor Services and D M Ritchie v IRC* (1929) 14 TC 754 at 763, where Lord Clyde said: 'No man in this country is under the smallest obligation, moral or other, so as to arrange

The ambit of the *Westminster* principle has been restricted by subsequent decisions. In a series of cases beginning with *Ramsay v IRC* [1982] AC 300 and reaching a high-water mark with *Furniss v Dawson* [1984] AC 474, the House of Lords, though paying lip service to the *Westminster* principle, held that where there is a pre-ordained series of transactions, or a single composite scheme, into which steps are inserted solely for the purpose of avoiding tax and which otherwise have no commercial or business purpose, the court may disregard those steps and, instead of taxing the transactions or scheme as found, may tax what it identifies as the 'relevant transaction'. In other words, the *Ramsay/Furniss* principle is that the tax liability of a person involved in a scheme may be determined on the basis of a constructive transaction as opposed to the actual transaction to which he was a party.

The classic statement of the new principle was put forward by LORD BRIGHTMAN in **Furniss v Dawson** [1984] AC 474 at 526:

My Lords, in my opinion the rationale of the new approach is this. In a pre-planned tax-saving scheme, no distinction is to be drawn for fiscal purposes, because none exists in reality, between (i) a series of steps which are followed through by virtue of an arrangement which falls short of a binding contract, and (ii) a like series of steps which are followed through because the participants are contractually bound to take each step *seriatim*. In a contractual case the fiscal consequences will naturally fall to be assessed in the light of the contractually agreed results. For example, equitable interests may pass when the contract for sale is signed. In many cases equity will regard that as done which is contracted to be done. *Ramsay* says that the fiscal result is to be no different if the several steps are pre-ordained rather than pre-contracted....

   The formulation by Lord Diplock in *IRC v Burmah Oil Co Ltd* [1982] STC 30 at 33 expresses the limitations of the *Ramsay* principle. First, there must be a pre-ordained series of transactions; or, if one likes, one single composite transaction. This composite transaction may or may not include the achievement of a legitimate commercial (i.e. business) end... Secondly, there must be steps inserted which have no commercial (business) *purpose* apart from the avoidance of a liability to tax—not 'no business *effect*'. If those two ingredients exist, the inserted steps are to be disregarded for fiscal purposes. The court must then look at the end result. Precisely how the end result will be taxed will depend on the terms of the taxing statute sought to be applied....

   The formulation, therefore, involves two findings of fact, first, whether there was a pre-ordained series of transactions, i.e. a single composite transaction, secondly, whether that transaction contained steps which were inserted without any commercial or business purpose apart from a tax advantage, Those are facts to be found by the commissioners. They may be primary facts or, more probably, inferences to be drawn from the primary facts. If they are inferences, they are nevertheless facts to be found by the commissioners.

This far-reaching principle was severely restricted by the decision of the House of Lords in **Craven v White** and associated appeals [1989] AC 398. LORD OLIVER OF AYLMERTON (with whom LORDS KEITH OF KINKEL and JAUNCEY OF TULLICHETTLE expressly

his legal relations to his business or to his property as to enable the Inland Revenue to put the largest possible shovel into his stores.'

concurred) reviewed *Ramsay v IRC* and *Furniss v Dawson*, and identified the limits of the doctrine established in them. LORD OLIVER OF AYLMERTON said at 514:

As the law currently stands, the essentials emerging from *Furniss v Dawson* [1984] AC 474 appear to me to be four in number: (1) that the series of transactions was, at the time when the intermediate transaction was entered into, pre-ordained in order to produce a given result; (2) that that transaction had no other purpose than tax mitigation; (3) that there was at that time no practical likelihood that the pre-planned events would not take place in the order ordained, so that the intermediate transaction was not even contemplated practically as having an independent life; and (4) that the pre-ordained events did in fact take place. In these circumstances the court can be justified in linking the beginning with the end so as to make a single composite whole to which the fiscal results of the single composite whole are to be applied.

I do not, for my part, think that *Furniss v Dawson* goes further than that. The intellectual basis for the decision was *Ramsay* and the criteria for the application of the *Ramsay* doctrine were those enunciated by Lord Brightman. On those criteria, I see no escape from the conclusion reached in all the three appeals in the High Court and in the Court of Appeal that the appellants must fail. Nor do I readily see that the criteria are logically capable of expansion so as to apply to any similar case except one in which, when the intermediate transaction or transactions take place, the end result which in fact occurs is so certain of fulfilment that it is intellectually and practically possible to conclude that there has indeed taken place one single and indivisible process. To permit this it seems to me essential that the intermediate transaction bears the stamp of interdependence at the time when it takes place. A transaction does not change its nature because of an event, then uncertain, which subsequently occurs and *Ramsay* is concerned not with re-forming transactions but with ascertaining their reality. There is a real and not merely a metaphysical distinction between something that is done as a preparatory step towards a possible but uncertain contemplated future action and something which is done as an integral and interdependent part of a transaction already agreed and, effectively, pre-destined to take place. In the latter case, to link the end to the beginning involves no more than recognising the reality of what is effectively a single operation *ab initio*. In the former it involves quite a different process, *viz.* that of imputing to the parties, ex post facto, an obligation (either contractual or quasi-contractual) which did not exist at the material time but which is to be attributed from the occurrence or juxtaposition of events which subsequently took place. That cannot be extracted from *Furniss v Dawson* as it stands nor can it be justified by any rational extension of the *Ramsay* approach. It involves the invocation of a different principle altogether, that is to say, the reconstruction of events into something that they were not, either in fact or in intention, not because they in fact constituted a single composite whole but because, and only because, one or more of them was motivated by a desire to avoid or minimise tax. That may be a very beneficial objective but it has to be recognised that the rational basis of *Ramsay* and *Furniss v Dawson* then becomes irrelevant and is replaced by a principle of nullifying a tax advantage derived from any 'associated operation'. The legislature has not gone this far and the question is should or can your Lordships?

My Lords, I do not think so. I am at one with those of your Lordships who find the complicated and stylised antics of the tax avoidance industry both unedifying and unattractive but I entirely dissent from the proposition that because there is present in each of the three appeals before this House the element of a desire to mitigate or postpone the respondents' tax burdens, this fact alone demands from your Lordships a predisposition to expand the scope of the doctrine of

Ramsay and of *Furniss v Dawson* beyond its rational basis in order to strike down a transaction which would not otherwise realistically fall within it.

Nor do I consider that the *Ramsay* approach, which is no doubt applicable to a much wider variety of transactions than those embraced in the instant appeals, requires further exposition or clarification. Its basis is manifest and has been clearly explained by Lord Wilberforce. What the appellants urge upon your Lordships is a restatement of the approach in a formula based, as it seems to me, not upon a much wider, but at the moment undefined, general principle of judicial disapprobation of the lawful rearrangement of the subject's affairs designed to produce a result which is fiscally advantageous to him in relation to a transaction into which he anticipates entering. That is essentially a legislative exercise and one upon which, in my opinion, your Lordships should hesitate long before embarking.

The House of Lords has continued to emphasise that the principle is as much one of statutory construction as it is of transaction reconstruction. In **IRC v McGuckian** [1997] 1 WLR 991, LORD STEYN said at 999:

During the last 30 years there has been a shift away from literalist to purposive methods of construction. Where there is no obvious meaning of a statutory provision the modern emphasis is on a contextual approach designed to identify the purpose of a statute and to give effect to it. But, under the influence of the narrow *Duke of Westminster* doctrine [1936] AC 1 at 19, tax law remained remarkably resistant to the new non-formalist methods of interpretation. It was said that the taxpayer was entitled to stand on a literal construction of the words used regardless of the purpose of the statute: *Pryce v Monmouthshire Canal and Railway Cos* (1879) 4 App Cas 197 at 202-203; *Cape Brandy Syndicate v IRC* [1921] 1 KB 64 at 71; *IRC v Plummer* [1980] AC 896. Tax law was by and large left behind as some island of literal interpretation...

...the intellectual breakthrough came in 1981 in the Ramsay case, and notably in Lord Wilberforce's seminal speech which carried the agreement of Lord Russell of Killowen, Lord Roskill and Lord Bridge of Harwich. Lord Wilberforce restated the principle of statutory construction that a subject is only to be taxed upon clear words [1982] AC 300 at 323.... To the question 'What are clear words?' he gave the answer that the court is not confined to a literal interpretation. He added 'There may, indeed should, be considered the context and scheme of the relevant Act as a whole, and its purpose may, indeed should, be regarded.' This sentence was critical. It marked the rejection by the House of pure literalism in the interpretation of tax statutes....

The new *Ramsay* principle [1982] AC 300 was not invented on a juristic basis independent of statute. That would have been indefensible since a court has no power to amend a tax statute. The principle was developed as a matter of statutory construction. That was made clear by Lord Wilberforce in the *Ramsay* case and is also made clear in subsequent decisions in this line of authority: see the review in the dissenting speech of Lord Goff of Chieveley in *Craven v White* [1989] AC 398 at 520–521. The new development was not based on a linguistic analysis of the meaning of particular words in a statute. It was founded on a broad purposive interpretation, giving effect to the intention of Parliament. The principle enunciated in the *Ramsay* case was therefore based on an orthodox form of statutory interpretation. And in asserting the power to examine the substance of a composite transaction the House of Lords was simply rejecting formalism in fiscal matters and choosing a more realistic legal analysis.

A more recent decision of the House of Lords on tax avoidance is **MacNiven v Westmoreland Investments Ltd** [2001] UKHL 6, [2003] 1 AC 311.[77] LORD HOFFMANN said at 327:

My Lords, it seems to me that what Lord Wilberforce was doing in *Ramsay* was no more (but certainly no less) than to treat the statutory words 'loss' and 'disposal' as referring to commercial concepts to which a juristic analysis of the transaction, treating each step as autonomous and independent, might not be determinative. What was fresh and new about *Ramsay* was the realisation that such an approach need not be confined to well recognised accounting concepts such as profit and loss but could be the appropriate construction of other taxation concepts as well.

His Lordship considered American authorities and continued:

The speeches in *Ramsay* and subsequent cases contain numerous references to the 'real' nature of the transaction and to what happens in 'the real world'. These expressions are illuminating in their context, but you have to be careful about the sense in which they are being used. Otherwise you land in all kinds of unnecessary philosophical difficulties about the nature of reality and, in particular, about how a transaction can be said not to be a 'sham' and yet be 'disregarded' for the purpose of deciding what happened in 'the real world'. The point to hold onto is that something may be real for one purpose but not for another. When people speak of something being a 'real' something, they mean that it falls within some concept which they have in mind, by contrast with something else which might have been thought to do so, but does not. When an economist says that real incomes have fallen, he is not intending to contrast real incomes with imaginary incomes. The contrast is specifically between incomes which have been adjusted for inflation and those which have not. In order to know what he means by 'real', one must first identify the concept (inflation adjustment) by reference to which he is using the word.

Thus in saying that the transactions in *Ramsay* were not sham transactions, one is accepting the juristic categorisation of the transactions as individual and discrete and saying that each of them involved no pretence. They were intended to do precisely what they purported to do. They had a legal reality. But in saying that they did not constitute a 'real' disposal giving rise to a 'real' loss, one is rejecting the juristic categorisation as not being necessarily determinative for the purposes of the statutory concepts of 'disposal' and 'loss' as properly interpreted. The contrast here is with a commercial meaning of these concepts. And in saying that the income tax legislation was intended to operate 'in the real world', one is again referring to the commercial context which should influence the construction of the concepts used by Parliament....

The point I wish to emphasise is that Lord Brightman's formulation in *Furniss v Dawson,* like Lord Diplock's formulation in *IRC v Burmah Oil Co Ltd* [see p. 33, above] is not a principle of construction. It is a statement of the consequences of giving a commercial construction to a fiscal concept. Before one can apply Lord Brightman's words, it is first necessary to construe the statutory language and decide that it refers to a concept which Parliament intended to be given a commercial meaning capable of transcending the juristic individuality of its component parts. But there are many terms in tax legislation which cannot be construed in this way.

---

[77] (2001) 117 LQR 575 (Lord Templeman), (2001) 60 CLJ 259 (G. Virgo). See also *Barclays Mercantile Business Finance v Mawson* [2004] UKHL 51, [2005] STC I, *IRC v Scottish Provident* (2004) UKHL 52, [2005] STC 15, *Macdonald (Inspector of Taxes) v Dextra Accessories Ltd* [2005] UKHL 47, [2005] STC III; *West (Inspector of Taxes) v Trennery* [2005] UKHL 5, [2005] STC 214.

They refer to purely legal concepts which have no broader commercial meaning. In such cases, the *Ramsay* principle can have no application.

In *Barclays Mercantile Business Finance Ltd v Mawson* [2004] UKHL 51, [2005] STC 1 the distinction between commercial and legal concepts was rejected and the House of Lords emphasised the significance of statutory construction when considering tax avoidance.

MacNiven shows the need to focus carefully upon the particular statutory provision and to identify its requirements before one can decide whether circular payments or elements inserted for the purpose of tax avoidance should be disregarded or treated as irrelevant for the purposes of the statute. In the speech of Lord Hoffmann in *MacNiven* it was said that if a statute laid down requirements by reference to some commercial concept such as gain or loss, it would usually follow that elements inserted into a composite transaction without any commercial purpose could be disregarded, whereas if the requirements of the statute were purely by reference to its legal nature (in *MacNiven*, the discharge of a debt) then an act having that legal effect would suffice, whatever its commercial purpose may have been. This is not an unreasonable generalisation, indeed perhaps something of a truism, but we do not think that it was intended to provide a substitute for a close analysis of what the statute means. It certainly does not justify the assumption that an answer can be obtained by classifying all concepts *a priori* as either 'commercial' or 'legal'. That would be the very negation of purposive construction.

(2001) 117 LQR 575, 584, 587–588 (Lord Templeman)[78]

There is no principle which either requires or permits a court to divide tax avoidance into two categories, namely one category where the courts have regard to the entire transaction and look to see if any steps within it should be disregarded as having no commercial purpose except for the avoidance of tax otherwise payable, and another category where the courts look at steps which form part of a transaction but without regard to the entire transaction. The argument of Lord Hoffmann, which attempts to create such categories, and then asserts that the Westmoreland scheme falls into the second category, reflects ingenuity but not principle....

The formulation by Lord Brightman in *Furniss,* which defeats a tax avoidance scheme based on artificial steps, is founded on fairness. A taxpayer who avoids tax by artificial means frustrates the intention of Parliament that a taxable event shall be taxed. The scheme reduces the yield of tax to the Treasury and thus to the public. After the decision of the House of Lords in *Ramsay,* the Chancellor of the Exchequer announced that the decision had saved the Revenue £300 million a year. Tax avoidance schemes are also unfair to taxpayers who accept the fiscal consequences of taxable events, or who do not know or cannot afford or are not in a position to indulge in such schemes.

No one has ever advanced a convincing reason for allowing tax avoidance schemes based on artificial steps to distort the operation of taxing statutes and frustrate the intentions of Parliament.

[78] See also Lord Templeman, 'Form and Substance' in *Rationalizing Property, Equity and Trusts* (ed. J. Getzler) pp. 130–134.

The *Westmoreland* case fails to apply the principles and precedents established by *Ramsay, Burmah* and *Furniss*. The future is uncertain because of the attempt by Lord Hoffmann to distinguish that which cannot logically be distinguished. It is sometimes alleged that the trio of cases which introduced the judicial approach to tax avoidance schemes in 1982 and 1984 led to uncertainty. It is true that corporations and their advisers were deterred from inventing fresh artificial steps for fear of their being unsuccessful. But there never was any difficulty in identifying steps which had no business purpose save for the avoidance of tax which would otherwise be payable, until the *Westmoreland* case muddied the waters. Reliance can no longer be placed on the judiciary to deter corporations, and other wealthy taxpayers, from avoiding the taxation consequences of taxable events by means of artificial steps which have no purpose or effect save avoidance. Parliament has recently taken up the battle against fraud on the Revenue. The tax evader commits a criminal offence punishable with prison, penalties and fines. The tax avoider commits no offence and only risks failure to avoid the tax. Parliament could by legislation restore the certainty that steps with no business purpose except the avoidance of tax shall be ignored in the computation of the tax sought to be avoided thus restoring the principles which were established in the past and the precedents which have been discarded. Now that Parliament is concerned to draft tax legislation in a language which is intelligible, the definition of tax avoidance and the consequences of tax avoidance formulated by Lord Brightman in *Furniss* form a solid foundation for restoring logic and certainty to the law.

C   INCOME TAX

Where income arises from a trust, its taxation takes place at two different stages. The trustees are chargeable because they receive the income, and the beneficiaries are assessable on any income received from the trust, but their assessment will take account of any Income Tax already paid by the trustees. However, where the trust is a bare trust the beneficiary is taxed as though he were the absolute owner of the property.[79]

Income arising from trust assets (which is usually investment income) is treated as the income of the trustees: it is not deemed to be the settlor's income; nor are the trustees agents for the beneficiaries. Trustees are chargeable to Income Tax simply because they are in receipt of the income.[80] It makes no difference that the beneficiaries may be entitled to it, not even if there is only one beneficiary and he is *sui juris*.[81] Moreover, the taxation of trustees differs considerably from that of individuals. In general, the whole of the income of a trust is taxable. It makes no difference whether the income is absorbed by the expenses of administration, or paid to beneficiaries, or accumulated.

---

[79] *Baker v Archer-Shee* [1927] AC 844.
[80] *Williams v Singer* [1921] 1 AC 65.
[81] *IRC v Hamilton-Russell's Executors* [1943] 1 All ER 474.

D   CAPITAL GAINS TAX

Capital Gains Tax is a tax chargeable on capital gains accruing to a person in a year of assessment during any part of which he is resident in the United Kingdom or during which he is ordinarily resident in the United Kingdom, i.e. it is a tax on the difference in the value of a chargeable asset between the date of its acquisition and the date of its disposal.

The particular relevance of Capital Gains Tax to the decision to establish a trust is that a settlor who settles property on trust will not be liable for any subsequent capital gain unless he retains an interest in the settlement. The trustees will be chargeable to Capital Gains Tax on any gains made in disposing of assets in the course of administering the trust. Generally a disposal by a beneficiary of his interest under a settlement does not result in a Capital Gains Tax liability.

E   INHERITANCE TAX

Inheritance Tax was introduced in 1986 as a replacement for Capital Transfer Tax which had been introduced in 1975. It is governed by the Inheritance Tax Act 1984 and the Finance Act 1986. It is a direct tax on the transfer (or the deemed transfer) of capital. It falls primarily on the estate passing on death, but it is also a tax on certain lifetime gifts. There are certain exempt transfers, notably between spouses: Section 18, Inheritance Tax Act, 1984.

PART II

EXPRESS PRIVATE TRUSTS

2

THE NATURE AND TYPES OF TRUSTS AND POWERS

I DISTINGUISHING BETWEEN TRUSTS AND POWERS[1]

A trust is imperative; a power discretionary. A trustee must perform the duties connected with his trust. A power, whether held in a fiduciary capacity or otherwise, may be exercised or not at the discretion of the donee of the power.

Express private trusts primarily fall into two main categories: the fixed trust and the discretionary trust. A fixed trust arises where the interest or share of the beneficiary is laid down in the trust instrument; for example, 'on trust for my children in equal shares'. A discretionary trust is a trust in which the share of each member of the class of beneficiaries is determined by the discretion of the trustees; but there is still an obligation upon the trustees to make the division; for example: 'on trust for such of my children as my trustees shall select'. The discretion of a discretionary trustee can be characterised as a power, in the sense that the trustee can choose who is to benefit. However, this power must be exercised and so it is sometimes called a trust power.

Trustees may also have other powers which they are not obliged to exercise. These are called fiduciary powers. Since a trustee is a fiduciary he or she must consider the exercise of the power but is not required to exercise it. Examples of powers include: 'with power to appoint in favour of such of my children and in such proportions as my trustees shall think fit'; or, to give a more sophisticated example: 'with power to appoint to such of my children, grandchildren and their spouses and the employees

---

[1] See H&M, pp. 62–67; Lewin, pp. 981–992; P&M, pp. 203–212; Pettit, pp. 30–37; P&S, pp. 120–121; Snell, pp. 235–251, 475–477; U&H, pp. 35–40.

and ex-employees and their dependants of X company and in such proportions ... etc'. Powers may also be given to people who are not trustees.[2] These are called mere powers and the donee of the power is not even required to consider the exercise of it.

The distinction between trust and power becomes blurred in the case of discretionary trusts,[3] especially in the case of 'non-exhaustive' discretionary trusts—those in which the trustees may decide not to distribute any income at all, but rather to accumulate it. With an 'exhaustive' discretionary trust, it is the duty of the trustees to exercise their discretion in favour of one or more members of the class of beneficiaries. If they fail to do so, the court will make an order for equal division among the beneficiaries, or in such proportions as is appropriate in the circumstances.[4] Further, the class of beneficiaries, if they are of full age and under no disability, and if between them they are entitled to the whole of the beneficial interest, may terminate the trust.[5]

Most of the cases upon the distinction between trusts and powers have arisen in connection with the question whether a disposition is void for uncertainty. These cases[6] are no longer of practical significance, because it was decided in *McPhail v Doulton*[7] that, in the case of discretionary trusts, the test of certainty of objects should be the same as that established for powers in *Re Gulbenkian's Settlements*.[8] However, the distinction remains important in the trust context as regards the determination of the trustee's obligations. It is therefore important to determine whether the trust is fixed or discretionary and whether a trustee's power is a trust power or a fiduciary power. Whether a particular disposition creates a power or a trust is a question of the intention of the settlor as ascertained from a construction of the language of the instrument.

A   TRUST POWERS AND FIDUCIARY POWERS

In **McPhail v Doulton**[9] the House of Lords had to consider whether a clause in a deed created a trust or a fiduciary power. The clause stated that trustees should apply

[2] For the distinction between a fiduciary power and a mere power, see H&M, p. 172; *Re Gulbenkian's Settlements* [1970] AC 508 at 518 *per* Lord Reid; *Re Hay's Settlement Trusts* [1982] 1 WLR 202 at 209 [p. 51, below] *per* Megarry V-C; *Turner v Turner* [1983] 2 All ER 745 [p. 54, below]; *Breadner v Granville-Grossman* [2001] Ch 523 at 540 (Park J) [p. 46, below].

[3] See (1970) *Annual Survey of Commonwealth Law* 187 (J.D. Davies); (1974) 37 MLR 643 (Y. Grbich). On discretionary trusts generally, see H&M, pp. 201–216; Lewin, pp. 21–22; P&M, pp. 41, 179–182; P&S, pp. 446–461; Pettit, pp. 76–79; Snell, pp. 507–508; T&H, pp. 28–30; U&H, pp. 84–87.

[4] *McPhail v Doulton* [1971] AC 424 below; *Re Locker's Settlement Trusts* [1977] 1 WLR 1323 [p. 97, n. 53, below].   [5] *Re Smith* [1928] Ch 915 [p. 193, below].

[6] *IRC v Broadway Cottages Trust* [1955] Ch 20; *Re Hooper's Settlement* (1955) 34 ATC 3; *Re Sayer Trust* [1957] Ch 423; *Re Eden* [1957] 1 WLR 788; *Re Saxone Shoe Co Ltd's Trust Deed* [1962] 1 WLR 943; *Re Leek* [1969] 1 Ch 563.

[7] [1971] AC 424 [p. 91, below]. See also *Twinsectra Ltd v Yardley* [2002] UKHL 12, [2002] 2 AC 164, para. 16 (Lord Hoffmann).   [8] [1970] AC 508 [p. 90, below].

[9] See p. 91, below as regards the relevance of the case to the appropriate test for certainty of objects.

the net income of a fund for officers and employees and their relatives or dependents in 'such amounts at such times and on such conditions (if any) as [the trustees] think fit...' The trustees were under no obligation to exhaust the income in any one year. They could realise capital for the purpose of making such grants if the income was insufficient. It was also provided (clause 10) that 'no person shall have any right title or interest in the fund otherwise than pursuant to the exercise of such discretion'. The House of Lords held that the deed created a trust power rather than a fiduciary power.

LORD WILBERFORCE, at p. 448, identified the crucial distinction between trusts and powers.

It is striking how narrow and in a sense artificial is the distinction, in cases such as the present, between trusts or as the particular type of trust is called, trust powers, and powers. It is only necessary to read the learned judgments in the Court of Appeal to see that what to one mind may appear as a power of distribution coupled with a trust to dispose of the undistributed surplus, by accumulation or otherwise, may to another appear as a trust for distribution coupled with a power to withhold a portion and accumulate or otherwise dispose of it. A layman and, I suspect, also a logician would find it hard to understand what difference there is.

It does not seem satisfactory that the entire validity of a disposition should depend on such delicate shading. And if one considers how in practice reasonable and competent trustees would act, and ought to act, in the two cases, surely a matter very relevant to the question of validity, the distinction appears even less significant. To say that there is no obligation to exercise a mere power and that no court will intervene to compel it, whereas a trust is mandatory and its execution may be compelled, may be legally correct enough but the proposition does not contain an exhaustive comparison of the duties of persons who are trustees in the two cases. A trustee of an employees' benefit fund, whether given a power or a trust power, is still a trustee and he would surely consider in either case that he has a fiduciary duty: he is most likely to have been selected as a suitable person to administer it from his knowledge and experience, and would consider he has a responsibility to do so according to its purpose. It would be a complete misdescription of his position to say that, if what he has is a power unaccompanied by an imperative trust to distribute, he cannot be controlled by the court unless he exercised it capriciously, or outside the field permitted by the trust (cf. *Farwell on Powers*, 3rd edn, p. 524). Any trustee would surely make it his duty to know what is the permissible area of selection and then consider responsibly, in individual cases, whether a contemplated beneficiary was within the power and whether, in relation to other possible claimants, a particular grant was appropriate.

Correspondingly a trustee with a duty to distribute, particularly among a potentially very large class, would surely never require the preparation of a complete list of names, which anyhow would tell him little that he needs to know. He would examine the field, by class and category; might indeed make diligent and careful inquiries, depending on how much money he had to give away and the means at his disposal, as to the composition and needs of particular categories and of individuals within them; decide upon certain priorities or proportions, and then select individuals according to their needs or qualifications. If he acts in this manner, can it really be said that he is not carrying out the trust?

Differences there certainly are between trust (trust powers) and powers, but as regards validity, should they be so great as that in one case complete, or practically complete, ascertainment is needed, but not in the other? Such distinction as there is would seem to lie in the extent of the survey which the trustee is required to carry out: if he has to distribute the whole of a fund's income, he must necessarily make a wider and more systematic survey than if his duty is expressed in terms of a power to make grants. But just as, in the case of a power, it is possible to underestimate the fiduciary obligation of the trustee to whom it is given, so, in the case of a trust (trust power), the danger lies in overstating what the trustee requires to know or to inquire into before he can properly execute his trust. The difference may be one of degree rather than of principle: in the well-known words of Sir George Farwell, *Farwell on Powers,* (3rd edn, 1916), p. 10, trusts and powers are often blended, and the mixture may vary in its ingredients.

With this background I now consider whether the provisions of clause 9(a) constitute a trust or a power. I do so briefly because this is not a matter on which I or, I understand, any of your Lordships have any doubt. Indeed, a reading of the judgments of Goff J and of the majority in the Court of Appeal leave the strong impression that, if it had not been for their leaning in favour of possible validity and the state of the authorities, these learned judges would have found in favour of a trust. Naturally read, the intention of the deed seems to me clear: clause 9(a), whose language is mandatory ('shall'), creates, together with a power of selection, a trust for distribution of the income, the strictness of which is qualified by clause 9(b), which allows the income of any one year to be held up and (under clause 6(a)) either placed, for the time, with a bank, or, if thought fit, invested. Whether there is, in any technical sense, an accumulation seems to me in the present context a jejune[10] inquiry: what is relevant is that clause 9(c) marks the difference between 'accumulations' of income and the capital of the fund: the former can be distributed by a majority of the trustees, the latter cannot. As to clause 10, I do not find in it any decisive indication. If anything, it seems to point in favour of a trust, but both this and other points of detail are insignificant in the face of the clearly expressed scheme of clause 9. I therefore agree with Russell LJ and would to that extent allow the appeal, declare that the provisions of clause 9(a) constitute a trust and remit the case to the Chancery Division for determination whether on this basis clause 9 is (subject to the effects of section 164 of the Law of Property Act, 1925) valid or void for uncertainty.

In **Breadner v Granville-Grossman** [2001] Ch 523, Park J said at 540:

50.   It is trite law that there is a distinction between two kinds of dispositive discretions which may be vested in trustees. There are discretions which the trustees have a duty to exercise (sometimes called 'trust powers'), and discretions which the trustee may exercise but have no duty to exercise (sometimes called 'mere powers'). The distinction is most familiar in the context of discretions to distribute income. In cases of trust powers the trustees are bound to distribute the income, but have a discretion as to how it should be divided between the beneficiaries. In cases of mere powers the trustees have two discretions—first a discretion whether to distribute the income or not, and second, if they decide that they will exercise

---

[10] Meaning 'without interest or significance'.

the first discretion, a further discretion as to how to divide the income between the bene-ficiaries. In the latter kind of case there will usually be a default trust which deals with the income if the trustees do not exercise their discretion to distribute it. Typically the default trust will provide for the undistributed income to be accumulated or to be paid as of right to a beneficiary whose interest in it is vested but defeasible by the trustees exercising their discretion to distribute.

51.   The distinction is explained by Lord Upjohn in *Re Gulbenkian's Settlement Trusts* [1970] AC 508 at 525, and illustrated by *Re Locker's Settlement Trusts* [1977] 1 WLR 1323, (a trust power case), and *Re Allen-Meyrick's Will Trusts* [1966] 1 WLR 499, (a mere power case).

52.   Sometimes the distinction does not matter, but there is an important difference between the two kinds of case if the trustees do not exercise the discretion to distribute income within the normal time for exercising it. That time is usually 'a reasonable time'. If there is a trust power and, although the trustees are required to exercise it within a reasonable time, they do not do so, the discretion still exists. If the trustees are willing to exercise it, albeit later than they should have done, the court will probably permit them to do so. That is what happened in *Re Locker's Settlement Trusts*. Alternatively the court will exercise the discretion itself. But if the discretion to distribute income is a mere power, and the trustees do not exercise it within a reasonable time of the receipt of an item of income, the discretion no longer exists as respects that income. The default trusts take effect indefeasibly. That is what happened in *Re Allen-Meyrick's Will Trusts*.

53.   The distinction between trust powers and mere powers is, as I have said, most com-monly encountered in connection with powers to distribute income. But the distinction also exists in connection with other kinds of dispositive powers, including powers of appointment.

In **Schmidt v Rosewood Trust Ltd** [2003] UKPC 26, [2003] 2 AC 709, see p. 743 below, the Privy Council commended Park J's analysis as follows:

40.   This passage gives a very clear and eminently realistic account of both the points of difference and the similarities between a discretionary trust and a fiduciary dispositive power. The outstanding point of difference is of course that under a discretionary trust of income distribution of income (within a reasonable time) is mandatory, the trustees' discretion being limited to the choice of the recipients and the shares in which they are to take. If there is a small, closed class of discretionary objects who are all *sui juris*, their collective entitlement gives them a limited power of disposition over the income subject to the discretionary trust, as is illustrated by *Re Smith* [1928] Ch 915 and *Re Nelson* (1918) reported as a note to *Re Smith*, at p. 920. But the possibility of such a collective disposition will be rare, and on his own the object of a discretionary trust has no more of an assignable or transmissible interest than the object of a mere power.

41.   Apart from the test for certainty being the same and the fact that an individual's inter-est or right is non-assignable, there are other practical similarities between the positions of the two types of object. Either has the negative power to block a family arrangement or similar transaction proposed to be effected under the rule in *Saunders v Vautier* (1841) 4 Beav 115 [see p. 191, below] (unless in the case of a power the trustees are specially authorised to release, that is to say extinguish, it). Both have a right to have their claims properly considered by the

trustees. But if the discretion is exercisable in favour of a very wide class the trustees need not survey mankind from China to Peru (as Harman J, echoing Dr Johnson, said in *Re Gestetner Settlement* [1953] Ch 672, 688–689) if it is clear who are the prime candidates for the exercise of the trustees' discretion.

In **Burrough v Philcox** (1840) 5 My & Cr 72, John Walton, the testator, gave life interests in a trust fund to his two children with remainders to their issue, but if each of the children should die without leaving lawful issue (as happened), then the survivor of the children should have power to dispose, by will, 'amongst my nephews and nieces, or their children, either all to one of them or to as many of them as my surviving child shall think proper'. There was no gift over in default.

The question was whether this language created a trust in favour of the nephews and nieces, or whether it was a power.

LORD COTTENHAM held that it was a trust. The living nephews and nieces took in equal shares. He said at 89:

The question is, whether these nephews and nieces and their children, take any interest in the property, independently of the power; that is, whether the power given to the survivor of the son and daughter is a mere power, and the interests of the nephews and nieces and their children were, therefore, to depend upon the exercise of it, or whether there was a gift to them, subject only to the power of selection given to the survivor of the son and daughter.

[His Lordship referred to *Duke of Marlborough v Lord Godolphin* (1750) 2 Ves Sen 61; *Brown v Higgs* (1800) 5 Ves 495 at 506; *Harding v Glyn* (1739) 1 Atk 469, and *Witts v Boddington* (1790) 3 Bro CC 95, and continued:] These and other cases shew that when there appears a general intention in favour of a class, and a particular intention in favour of individuals of a class to be selected by another person, and the particular intention fails, from that selection not being made, the Court will carry into effect the general intention in favour of the class. When such an intention appears, the case arises, as stated by Lord Eldon in *Brown v Higgs* (1803) 8 Ves 561 at 574, of the power being so given as to make it the duty of the donee to execute it; and, in such case, the Court will not permit the objects of the power to suffer by the negligence or conduct of the donee, but fastens upon the property a trust for their benefit.

In **Re Weekes' Settlement** [1897] 1 Ch 289, Mrs. Slade, by her will, gave a life interest in certain property to her husband 'and I give to him power to dispose of all such property by will amongst our children ...' The will contained no gift in default of appointment. The husband failed to make any appointment. The question was whether the children were entitled in equal shares or whether the property passed to the heir at law of Mrs. Slade.

ROMER J held that the heir at law was entitled. He said at 292:

Now, apart from the authorities, I should gather from the terms of the will that it was a mere power that was conferred on the husband, and not one coupled with a trust that he was bound to exercise. I see no words in the will to justify me in holding that the testatrix intended that the children should take if her husband did not execute the power.

This is not a case of a gift to the children with power to the husband to select, or to such of the children as the husband should select by exercising the power.

If in this case the testatrix really intended to give a life interest to her husband and a mere power to appoint if he chose, and intended if he did not think fit to appoint that the property should go as in default of appointment according to the settlement, why should she be bound to say more than she has said in this will?

I come to the conclusion on the words of this will that the testatrix only intended to give a life interest and a power to her husband—certainly she has not said more than that.

Am I then bound by the authorities to hold otherwise? I think I am not. The authorities do not shew, in my opinion, that there is a hard and fast rule that a gift to A for life with power to A to appoint among a class and nothing more must, if there is no gift over in the will, be held a gift by implication to the class in default of the power being exercised. In my opinion the cases shew (though there may be found here and there certain remarks of a few learned judges which, if not interpreted by the facts of the particular case before them, might seem to have a more extended operation) that you must find in the will an indication that the testatrix did intend the class or some of the class to take—intended in fact that the power should be regarded in the nature of a trust—only a power of selection being given, as, for example, a gift to A for life with a gift over to such of a class as A shall appoint.

B POWERS[11]

(i) Ambit and Exercise of Powers

It has been a matter of some controversy as to whether the rules relating to the certainty with which objects of a power can be identified are the same as for the identification of beneficiaries of a trust. This is considered below.[12] A further important issue concerns how trustees should exercise their powers.

In **Re Hay's Settlement Trusts** [1982] 1 WLR 202,[13] under clause 4 of a settlement made in 1958, trustees held the trust fund 'for such persons or purposes as the trustees shall by deed...executed within 21 years from the date hereof appoint'. The trustees were prohibited from appointing the settlor, her husband, or any past or present trustee. During the first five years any undisposed income was to be accumulated and capitalised. Thereafter the income was to be held on a discretionary trust, until the power was exercised or exhausted (whichever was the first to occur).

In 1969 the trustees purported to exercise their power under clause 4 by a deed of appointment. Clause 1 of the deed of appointment gave to the trustees power to hold

[11] H&M, pp. 62–67, 171–189; Lewin, pp. 981–1114; P&M, pp. 32–34; P&S, pp. 418–445; Pettit, pp. 30–37; Snell, pp. 235–251; T&H, pp. 28–29; U&H, pp. 35–40; *Farwell on Powers* (3rd edn, 1916); Thomas, *Powers* (1998); (1957) 35 *Canadian Bar Review* 1060 (O.R. Marshall); (1953) 69 LQR 334 (D.M. Gordon); (1949) 13 Conv (NS) 20 (J.G. Fleming); (1954) 18 Conv (NS) 565 (F.R. Crane); (1971) CLJ 68 (J.A. Hopkins); (1971) 87 LQR 31 (J.W. Harris); (1976) 54 Can BR 229 (M.C. Cullity); (1977) 3 *Monash University Law Review* 210 (Y. Grbich); (1982) 98 LQR 551 (C.T. Emery). [12] See p. 90, below.
[13] [1982] Conv 432 (A. Grubb).

the fund 'for such...persons and such purposes as shall be appointed', and clause 2 divided the undisposed income to be held on an intermediate discretionary trust, similar to the power in clause 4 of the settlement, 'for the benefit of any...persons whatsoever (the settlor, her husband or any past or present trustee excepted) as the trustees shall appoint'.

SIR ROBERT MEGARRY V-C held that the intermediate power to appoint under clause 4 of the 1958 settlement was valid, but that the discretionary trust of income created under clause 2 of the 1969 deed of appointment was void. He said at 207:

The starting point must be to consider whether the power created by the first limb of clause 4 of the settlement is valid. The essential point is whether a power for trustees to appoint to anyone in the world except a handful of specified persons is valid. Such a power will be perfectly valid if given to a person who is not in a fiduciary position: the difficulty arises when it is given to trustees, for they are under certain fiduciary duties in relation to the power, and to a limited degree they are subject to the control of the courts. At the centre of the dispute there are *Re Manisty's Settlement* [1974] Ch 17 (in which Templeman J differed from part of what was said in the Court of Appeal in *Blausten v IRC* [1972] Ch 256); *McPhail v Doulton* [1971] AC 424 ... and *Re Baden's Deed Trusts (No 2)* [1973] Ch 9 ... [14] Mr. Child, I may say, strongly contended that *Re Manisty's Settlement* was wrongly decided.

In *Re Manisty's Settlement* [1974] Ch 17,[15] a settlement gave trustees a discretionary power to apply the trust fund for the benefit of a small class of the settlor's near relations, save that any member of a smaller 'excepted class' was to be excluded from the class of beneficiaries. The trustees were also given power at their absolute discretion to declare that any person, corporation or charity (except a member of the excepted class or a trustee) should be included in the class of beneficiaries. Templeman J held that this power to extend the class of beneficiaries was valid.

In *Blausten v IRC* [1972] Ch 256, which had been decided some 18 months earlier, the settlement created a discretionary trust of income for members of a 'specified class' and a power to pay or apply capital to be held on trust for them. The settlement also gave the trustees power 'with the previous consent in writing of the settlor' (at 272) to appoint any other person or persons (except the settlor) to be included in the 'specified class'. The Court of Appeal decided the case on a point of construction; but Buckley LJ, at 271, also considered a contention that the trustees' power to add to the 'specified class' was so wide that it was bad for uncertainty, since the power would enable anyone in the world save the settlor to be included. He rejected this contention on the ground that the settlor's prior written consent was requisite to any addition to the 'specified class'; but for this, it seems plain that he would have held the power void for uncertainty. Orr LJ, at 274, simply concurred, but Salmon LJ, at 274, expressly confined himself to the point of construction, and said nothing about the power to add to the 'specified class'. In *Re Manisty's Settlement* [1974] Ch 17 at 29, Templeman J rejected the view of Buckley LJ on this point on the ground that *Re Gestetner Settlement* [1953] Ch 672; *Re Gulbenkian's Settlements* [1970] AC 508 and the two *Baden* cases did not appear to have been fully explored in the *Blausten* case, and the case did not involve any final pronouncement on the point. In general I respectfully agree with Templeman J.

[14] For *McPhail v Doulton* and *Re Baden (No 2)*, see pp. 91–101, below.
[15] (1973) 37 Conv NS 355 (F.R. Crane); (1974) CLJ 66 (J.A. Hopkins).

I propose to approach the matter by stages. First, it is plain that if a power of appointment is given to a person who is not in a fiduciary position, there is nothing in the width of the power which invalidates it *per se*. The power may be a special power with a large class of persons as objects; the power may be what is called a 'hybrid' power, or an 'intermediate' power, authorising appointment to anyone save a specified number or class of persons; or the power may be a general power. Whichever it is, there is nothing in the number of persons to whom an appointment may be made which will invalidate it. The difficulty comes when the power is given to trustees as such, in that the number of objects may interact with the fiduciary duties of the trustees and their control by the court. Mr. Child's argument carried him to the extent of asserting that no valid intermediate or general power could be vested in trustees.

That brings me to the second point, namely, the extent of the fiduciary obligations of trustees who have a mere power vested in them, and how far the court exercises control over them in relation to that power. In the case of a trust, of course, the trustee is bound to execute it, and if he does not, the court will see to its execution. A mere power is very different. Normally the trustee is not bound to exercise it, and the court will not compel him to do so. That, however, does not mean that he can simply fold his hands and ignore it, for normally he must from time to time consider whether or not to exercise the power, and the court may direct him to do this. When he does exercise the power, he must, of course (as in the case of all trusts and powers) confine himself to what is authorised, and not go beyond it. But that is not the only restriction. Whereas a person who is not in a fiduciary position is free to exercise the power in any way that he wishes, unhampered by any fiduciary duties, a trustee to whom, as such, a power is given is bound by the duties of his office in exercising that power to do so in a responsible manner according to its purpose. It is not enough for him to refrain from acting capriciously; he must do more. He must 'make such a survey of the range of objects or possible beneficiaries...' as will enable him to carry out his fiduciary duty. He must find out 'the permissible area of selection and then consider responsibly, in individual cases, whether a contemplated beneficiary was within the power and whether, in relation to other possible claimants, a particular grant was appropriate': *Re Baden (No 1)* [1971] AC 424 at 449, 457, *per* Lord Wilberforce...[16]

That brings me to the third point. How is the duty of making a responsible survey and selection to be carried out in the absence of any complete list of objects? This question was considered by the Court of Appeal in *Re Baden (No 2)* [1973] Ch 9. That case was concerned with what, after some divergencies of judicial opinion, was held to be a discretionary trust and not a mere power, but plainly the requirements for a mere power cannot be more stringent than those for a discretionary trust. The duty, I think, may be expressed along the following lines: I venture a modest degree of amplification and exegesis of what was said on pp. 20, 27. The trustee must not simply proceed to exercise the power in favour of such of the objects as happen to be at hand or claim his attention. He must first consider what persons or classes of persons are objects of the power within the definition in the settlement or will. In doing this, there is no need to compile a complete list of the objects, or even to make an accurate assessment of the number of them: what is needed is an appreciation of the width of the field, and thus whether a selection is to be made merely from a dozen or, instead, from thousands or millions... Only when the trustee has applied his mind to 'the size of the problem' should he then consider in individual cases

---

[16] See also *Vestey v IRC (No 2)* [1979] Ch 198 at 205–206, *per* Walton J; *Turner v Turner* [1984] Ch 100 [p. 54, below].

whether in relation to other possible claimants, a particular grant is appropriate. In doing this, no doubt he should not prefer the undeserving to the deserving; but he is not required to make an exact calculation whether, as between deserving claimants, A is more deserving than B: see *Re Gestetner Settlement* [1953] Ch 672, 688, approved in *Re Baden (No 1)* [1971] AC 424, 453.

If I am right in these views, the duties of a trustee which are specific to a mere power seem to be threefold. Apart from the obvious duty of obeying the trust instrument, and in particular of making no appointment that is not authorised by it, the trustee must, first, consider periodically whether or not he should exercise the power; second, consider the range of objects of the power; and third, consider the appropriateness of individual appointments. I do not assert that this list is exhaustive; but as the authorities stand it seems to me to include the essentials, so far as relevant to the case before me....

On this footing, the question is thus whether there is something in the nature of an inter-mediate power which conflicts with these duties in such a way as to invalidate the power if it is vested in a trustee. The case that there is rests in the main on *Blausten v IRC* [1972] Ch 256, which I have already summarised. The power there was plainly a mere power, and it authorised the trustees, with the settlor's previous consent in writing, to add any other person or persons (except the settlor) to the specified class.

In that case Buckley LJ referred to the power as being one the exercise of which the trustees were under a duty to consider from time to time, and said, at 272:

> 'If the class of persons to whose possible claims they would have to give consideration were so wide that it really did not amount to a class in any true sense at all no doubt that would be a duty which it would be impossible for them to perform and the power could be said to be invalid on that ground. But here, although they may introduce to the specified class any other person or persons except the settlor, the power is one which can only be exercised with the previous consent in writing of the settlor... Therefore on analysis the power is not a power to introduce anyone in the world to the specified class, but only anyone proposed by the trustees and approved by the settlor. This is not a case in which it could be said that the settlor in this respect has not set any metes and bounds to the beneficial interests which he intended to create or permit to be created under this settlement.'

After referring to *Re Park* [1932] 1 Ch 580, 583, Buckley LJ went on, at 273:

> '...this is not a power which suffers from the sort of uncertainty which results from the trustees being given a power of so wide an extent that it would be impossible for the court to say whether or not they were properly exercising it and so wide that it would be impossible for the trustees to consider in any sensible manner how they should exercise it, if at all, from time to time. The trustees would, no doubt, take into consideration the possible claims of anyone having any claim upon the beneficence of the settlor. That is not a class of persons so wide or so indefinite that the trustees would not be able rationally to exercise their duty to consider from time to time whether or not they should exercise the power.'

It seems quite plain that Buckley LJ considered that the power was saved from invalidity only by the requirement for the consent of the settlor. The reason for saying that in the absence of such a requirement the power would have been invalid seems to be twofold. First, the class of persons to whose possible claims the trustees would be duty-bound to give consideration was so wide as not to form a trust class, and this would make it impossible for the trustees to perform their duty of considering from time to time whether to exercise the power.

I feel considerable difficulty in accepting this view. First, I do not see how mere numbers can inhibit the trustees from considering whether or not to exercise the power, as distinct from deciding in whose favour to exercise it. Second, I cannot see how the requirement of the settlor's consent will result in any 'class' being narrowed from one that is too wide to one that is small enough. Such a requirement makes no difference whatever to the number of persons potentially included: the only exclusion is still the settlor. Thirdly, in any case I cannot see how the requirement of the settlor's consent could make it possible to treat 'anyone in the world save X' as constituting any real sort of a 'class', as that term is usually understood.

The second ground of invalidity if there is no requirement for the settlor's consent seems to be that the power is so wide that it would be impossible for the trustees to consider in any sensible manner how to exercise it, and also impossible for the court to say whether or not they were properly exercising it. With respect, I do not see how that follows. If I have correctly stated the extent of the duties of trustees in whom a mere power is vested, I do not see what there is to prevent the trustees from performing these duties. It must be remembered that Buckley LJ, though speaking after *Re Gulbenkian's Settlements* [1970] AC 508 and *Re Baden (No 1)* [1971] AC 424 had been decided, lacked the advantage of considering *Re Baden (No 2)* [1973] Ch 9, which was not decided until some five months later. He thus did not have before him the explanation in that case of how the trustees should make a survey and consider individual appointments in cases where no complete list of objects could be compiled. I also have in mind that the settlor in the present case is still alive, though I do not rest my decision on that.

From what I have said it will be seen that I cannot see any ground upon which the power in question can be said to be void. Certainly it is not void for linguistic or semantic uncertainty; there is no room for doubt in the definition of those who are or are not objects of the power. Nor can I see that the power is administratively unworkable. The words of Lord Wilberforce in *Re Baden (No 1)* at 457, are directed to discretionary trusts, not powers. Nor do I think that the power is void as being capricious. In *Re Manisty's Settlement* [1974] Ch 17, 27, Templeman J appears to be suggesting that a power to benefit 'residents of Greater London' is void as being capricious 'because the terms of the power negative any sensible intention on the part of the settlor'. In saying that, I do not think that the judge had in mind a case in which the settlor was, for instance, a former chairman of the Greater London Council, as subsequent words of his on that page indicate. In any case, as he pointed out earlier in the page, this consideration does not apply to intermediate powers, where no class which could be regarded as capricious has been laid down. Nor do I see how the power in the present case could be invalidated as being too vague, a possible ground of invalidity considered in *Re Manisty's Settlement,* at 24. Of course, if there is some real vice in a power, and there are real problems of administration or execution, the court may have to hold the power invalid: but I think that the court should be slow to do this.

Dispositions ought if possible to be upheld, and the court ought not to be astute to find grounds upon which a power can be invalidated. Naturally, if it is shown that a power offends against some rule of law or equity, then it will be held to be void: but a power should not be held void upon a peradventure. In my judgment, the power conferred by clause 4 of the settlement is valid.

With that, I turn to the discretionary trust of income under clause 2 of the deed of appointment.

His Lordship held that this discretionary trust of income was void as an excessive execution of the power since trustees could not delegate their powers unless authorised,[17] and continued:

That, I think, suffices to dispose of the case. I have not dealt with the submission which Mr. Child put in the forefront of his argument. This was that even if the power had been wide enough to authorise the creation of the discretionary trust, that trust was nevertheless bad as being a trust in favour of 'so hopelessly wide' a definition of beneficiaries 'as not to form "anything like a class" so that the trust is administratively unworkable': see *Re Baden (No 1)* at 457, *per* Lord Wilberforce. I do not propose to go into the authorities on this point. I consider that the duties of trustees under a discretionary trust are more stringent that those of trustees under a power of appointment (see, for example, *Re Baden (No 1)* at 457), and as at present advised I think that I would, if necessary, hold that an intermediate trust such as that in the present case is void as being administratively unworkable. In my view there is a difference between a power and a trust in this respect. The essence of that difference, I think, is that beneficiaries under a trust have rights of enforcement which mere objects of a power lack. But in this difficult branch of the law I consider that I should refrain from exploring without good reason any matters which do not have to be decided.

In **Turner v Turner** [1984] Ch 100, three appointments made by family trustees under a fiduciary power were held void. MERVYN DAVIES J said at 106:

The question is whether or not the trustees so far failed to direct their minds to the matter of their discretionary powers of appointment that the deeds of appointment ought not to be regarded as an exercise of the powers of appointment. To see such a question asked is at first sight surprising but the evidence given in this case shows good reason for it . . . It is quite clear from the correspondence that the trustees were no more than ciphers.

His Lordship quoted from MEGARRY V-C in *Re Hay's Settlement Trusts* [1982] 1 WLR 202 at 209, [p. 49, above] and continued:

Accordingly the trustees exercising a power come under a duty to consider. It is plain on the evidence that here the trustees did not in any way 'consider' in the course of signing the three deeds in question. They did not know they had any discretion during the settlor's lifetime, they did not read or understand the effect of the documents they were signing and what they were doing was not preceded by any decision. They merely signed when requested. The trustees therefore made the appointments in breach of their duty, in that it was their duty to 'consider' before appointing, and this they did not do. . . .

His Lordship referred to *Pilkington v IRC* [1964] AC 612 [p. 770, below] and *Re Abrahams' Will Trusts* [1969] 1 Ch 463, and continued:

The authorities I have mentioned, including *Re Hastings-Bass* [1975] Ch 25 [p. 660, below] permit the inference that, in a clear case on the facts, the court can put aside the purported exercise of a fiduciary power, if satisfied that the trustees never applied their minds at all to the exercise of the discretion entrusted to them. If appointors fail altogether to exercise the duties of consideration referred to by Sir Robert Megarry V-C then there is no exercise of the power and the purported appointment is a nullity. Applying those principles to this case I am satisfied on the evidence that all three purported appointments ought to be set aside.

---

[17] See now Trustee Act 2000, s 26 (b): p. 702, below.

(ii) Intervention of the Court

Mettoy Pension Trustees Ltd v Evans[18]
[1990] 1 WLR 1587 (Ch D, **Warner J**)

Mettoy Company plc, whose main business was the manufacture of 'Corgi' toys at Swansea, set up a pension fund for its employees. Under rule 13(5) the company had a power of appointment in favour of the pensioners, with a gift over to itself in default of appointment. A separate trustee company was trustee of the fund. The company went into liquidation with a substantial surplus in the fund. The main question was whether the liquidator could release the power and thus secure the surplus for the general creditors.

Held. The liquidator could not. (i) The power was fiduciary; (ii) It could not be released by the liquidator because he would be in a position where his duty and interest conflicted; and (iii) The court could intervene to protect the pensioners.

Warner J: Mr. Walker suggested a classification, which I accept, of fiduciary discretions into four categories. In this classification, category 1 comprises any power given to a person to determine the destination of trust property without that person being under any obligation to exercise the power or to preserve it. Typical of powers in this category is a special power of appointment given to an individual where there is a trust in default of appointment. In such a case the donee of the power owes a duty to the beneficiaries under that trust not to misuse the power, but he owes no duty to the objects of the power. He may therefore release the power but he may not enter into any transaction that would amount to a fraud on the power, a fraud on the power being a wrong committed against the beneficiaries under the trust in default of appointment: see *Re Mills* [1930] 1 Ch 654 and *Re Greaves* [1954] Ch 434. It seems to me to follow that, where the donee of the power is the only person entitled under the trust in default of appointment, the power is not a fiduciary power at all, because then the donee owes no duty to anyone. That was the position in *Re Mills* [1930] 1 Ch 654 and will be the position here if the discretion in the last paragraph of rule 13(5) of the 1983 rules is in category 1. Category 2 comprises any power conferred on the trustees of the property or on any other person as a trustee of the power itself: *per* Romer LJ, at p. 669. I will, as Chitty J did in *Re Somes* [1896] 1 Ch 250, 255, call a power in this category 'a fiduciary power in the full sense'. Mr. Walker suggested as an example of such powers vested in persons other than the trustees of the property the powers of the managers of a unit trust. A power in this category cannot be released: the donee of it owes a duty to the objects of the power to consider, as and when may be appropriate, whether and if so how he ought to exercise it: and he is to some extent subject to the control of the courts in relation to its exercise: see, for instance, *Re Abrahams' Will Trusts* [1969] 1 Ch 463, 474, *per* Cross J; *Re Manisty's Settlement* [1974] Ch 17, 24 [p. 50, above] *per* Templeman J; and *Re Hay's Settlement Trusts* [1982] 1 WLR 202, 210 [p. 49, above] *per* Sir Robert Megarry V-C. Category 3 comprises any discretion which is really a duty to form a judgment as to the existence or otherwise of particular circumstances giving rise to particular consequences. Into this category fall the discretions that were in question in such cases as *Weller v Kerr* (1866)

[18] [1991] Conv 364 (J.E. Martin); [1991] All ER Rev 203 (P.J. Clarke); (1991) 106 LQR 214 (S. Gardner); (1990) 53 MLR 377 (R. Nobles). See also *Re Hastings-Bass* [1975] Ch 25 [p. 660, below] and *Breadner v Granville-Grossman* [2001] Ch 523, 542 (Park J) [p. 46, above].

LR 1 Sc & Div 11; *Dundee General Hospitals Board of Management v Walker* [1952] 1 All ER 896 and the two cases reported by Lexis that I have already mentioned, namely *Kerr v British Leyland (Staff) Trustees Ltd* [1986] CA Transcript 286 and *Mihlenstedt v Barclays Bank International Ltd* [1989] IRLR 522. Category 4 comprises discretionary trusts, that is to say cases where someone, usually but not necessarily the trustees, is under a duty to select from among a class of beneficiaries those who are to receive, and the proportions in which they are to receive, income or capital of the trust property. Mr. Walker urged me to eschew the phrases 'trust power,' 'power coupled with a duty,' 'power coupled with a trust' and 'power in the nature of a trust', which, as he demonstrated by means of an impressive survey of reported cases, have been variously used to describe discretions in categories 2, 3 and 4.

In the present case the question is whether the discretion given to the employer by the last paragraph of rule 13(5) of the 1983 rules is in category 1 or category 2.

I have come to the conclusion that the discretion conferred on the employer by the last paragraph of rule 13(5) of the 1983 rules is a fiduciary power in the full sense. The considerations that have led me to that conclusion are these. If that discretion is not such a fiduciary power it is, from the point of view of the beneficiaries under the scheme, illusory. As I have pointed out, the words conferring the power mean no more, on that construction of them, than that the employer is free to make gifts to those beneficiaries out of property of which it is the absolute beneficial owner, so that at best those words amount to what Hutchison J in *El Awadi v Bank of Credit and Commerce International SA Ltd* [1990] 1 QB 606, 617 called 'a true but pointless assertion'. The *Courage Group* case [1987] 1 WLR 495 illustrates one possible consequence of the discretion being of that nature. If the employer were acquired by a take-over raider (to use Millet J's expression in that case) there would be nothing whatever to prevent that raider from rendering itself entitled to the entire surplus. On the simple cesser of the employer's business at a time when the employer was solvent, the position would be governed (in 1983) by the principle of *Parke v Daily News Ltd* [1962] Ch 927 as modified by section 74 of the Companies Act 1980. The exercise of the discretion would accordingly in general require the approval of a resolution of the shareholders, and it is doubtful if such a resolution could approve its exercise in favour of beneficiaries other than employees or former employees, for instance their widows. If, as has happened in this case, the employer should become insolvent, the discretion would inevitably not be exercised, because it would become exercisable on behalf of the employer by someone, be he receiver or liquidator, whose duties to creditors required him to refrain from exercising it....

The question then arises, if the discretion is a fiduciary power which cannot be exercised either by the receivers or by the liquidator, who is to exercise it? I heard submissions on that point. The discretion cannot be exercised by the directors of the company, because on the appointment of the liquidator all the powers of the directors ceased. I was referred to a number of authorities on the circumstances in which the court may interfere with or give directions as to the exercise of discretions vested in trustees, namely *Gisborne v Gisborne* (1877) 2 App Cas 300; *Re Hodges* (1878) 7 Ch D 754; *Tabor v Brooks* (1878) 10 Ch D 273; *Klug v Klug* [1918] 2 Ch 67 [p. 656, below]; *Re Allen-Meyrick's Will Trusts* [1966] 1 WLR 499; *McPhail v Doulton* [1971] AC 424 [p. 91, below]; *Re Manisty's Settlement* [1974] Ch 17, 25–26; and *Re Locker's Settlement* [1977] 1 WLR 1323 [p. 97, n. 53, below]. None of those cases deals directly with a situation in which a fiduciary power is left with no one to exercise it. They point however to the conclusion that in that situation the court must step in. Mr. Inglis-Jones and Mr. Walker urged me to say that in this case the court should step in by giving directions to the trustees as to the distribution of the surplus in the pension fund. They relied in particular on the passage in *McPhail v Doulton,* where Lord Wilberforce said, at 456, 457:

> 'As to powers, I agree with my noble and learned friend Lord Upjohn in *Re Gulbenkian's Settlements* [1970] AC 508 [p. 90, below] that although the trustees may, and normally will, be under a fiduciary duty to consider whether or in what way they should exercise their power, the court will not normally compel its exercise. It will intervene if the trustees exceed their powers, and possibly if they are proved to have exercised it capriciously. But in the case of a trust power, if the trustees do not exercise it, the court will: I respectfully adopt as to this the statement in Lord Upjohn's opinion (at 525). I would venture to amplify this by saying that the court, if called upon to execute the trust power, will do so in the manner best calculated to give effect to the settlor's or testator's intentions. It may do so by appointing new trustees, or by authorising or directing representative persons of the classes of beneficiaries to prepare a scheme of distribution, or even, should the proper basis for distribution appear by itself directing the trustees so to distribute. The books give many instances where this has been done, and I see no reason in principle why they should not do so in the modern field of discretionary trusts.'

Clearly, in the first two sentences of that passage Lord Wilberforce was referring to a discretion in category 2 and in the following part of it to a discretion in category 4. In that latter part he was indicating how the court might give effect to a discretionary trust when called on to execute it. It seems to me however that the methods he indicated could be equally appropriate in a case where the court was called on to intervene in the exercise of a discretion in category 2. In saying that, I do not overlook that, in *Re Manisty's Settlement* [1974] Ch 17 at 25, Templeman J expressed the view that the only right and the only remedy of an object of the power who was aggrieved by the trustees' conduct would be to apply to the court to remove the trustees and appoint others in their place. However, the earlier authorities to which I was referred, such as *Re Hodges* (1878) 7 Ch D 754 and *Klug v Klug* [1918] 2 Ch 67, had not been cited to Templeman J. I conclude that, in a situation such as this, it is open to the court to adopt whichever of the methods indicated by Lord Wilberforce appears most appropriate in the circumstances.

That brings me back to the question what should be done about its exercise, a question which I dealt with in part earlier, when I concluded that the court could adopt any of the methods indicated by Lord Wilberforce in *McPhail v Doulton* [1971] AC 424 at 457. No one suggests that I should, in this case, appoint new trustees. So the question is what directions I should give under paragraph (3) of the originating summons. That is a question on which, as I mentioned earlier, I have heard some evidence, particularly evidence from the actuaries, but on which further evidence will be necessary, and on which I have heard no submissions. When counsel have had an opportunity of considering my judgment, I will hear them as to the form of the order I should make at this stage.

[1991] Conv 364, at 365–366 (J.E. Martin)

Previous authorities have suggested that the only way the court can intervene in the case of a power is by the appointment of new trustees.[19] This, for some reason, has not been requested

---

[19] See *Re Manisty's Settlement* [1974] Ch 17.

in the present case.[20] In upholding the possibility of a more positive intervention, Warner J relied on *Klug v Klug*,[21] where the court in effect directed the exercise of the power of advancement.

In **Breadner v Granville-Grossman** [2001] Ch 523[22] [p. 46, above] trustees had exercised a mere power of appointment one day late. They sought a determination from the court that the exercise of the power was valid. PARK J relied on *Re Hastings-Bass* [1975] Ch 25 [p. 660, below] and *Mettoy Pension Trustees Ltd v Evans* [1990] 1 WLR 1587 [p. 55, above] to draw a distinction between cases where the trustees have acted and cases where they have failed to act. In the former cases the courts may be prepared to declare the act to be ineffective, because, for example, the trustees have taken into account irrelevant considerations. Where, however, the trustees have failed to act, the court will not intervene. It followed that, since the trustees had failed to exercise the power in time, the power had expired and it was not open to the court to assume that the power had been exercised in time.

Counsel for the trustees further argued that an alternative method for treating the exercise of the power as valid was by reference to the doctrine of awarding 'equitable relief against the defective execution of a power'. The effect of this equitable doctrine would be to act on the consciences of those who would otherwise benefit from the failure to exercise the power in time 'and compel them to perfect the intention of the trustees to exercise the power'.[23] PARK J recognised the existence of this principle but concluded that it was inapplicable in this case primarily because the parties who would benefit from the failure to exercise the power had not acted unconscionably, and also because the doctrine did not apply where a power had not been exercised.

(iii) Fraud on a Power[24]
Hanbury and Martin: *Modern Equity* (17th edn, 2005), p. 182

An appointor, in the typical case of a special power of appointment with a gift over in default, is under no duty to exercise the power; but if he chooses to exercise the power, he must exercise it honestly.[25] Unless he is a fiduciary,[26] he need not weigh the merits of the possible beneficiaries; he may appoint all the available assets to any one beneficiary, who may indeed be himself.[27] But he must exercise it within the limits imposed by the donor or testator who created it.[28] If,

---

[20] See (1991) 107 LQR 214 (S. Gardner), suggesting that the trustee company was the obvious substitute, and that this would have been the most appropriate means of intervention. Gardner also suggests that one result of the assimilation of remedies might be that 'administrative unworkability' now applies to fiduciary powers as well as to discretionary trusts: see p. 102, below. There would have been no problem in *Mettoy* itself because the class of pensioners would not give rise to difficulty under this principle.

[21] [1918] 2 Ch 67 [see p. 656, below] not cited in *Re Manisty's Settlement*, note 19 above. But see Gardner, ibid, where it is considered that the older cases relied on, such as *Klug*, do not give great support to the judicial exercise of fiduciary discretions.   [22] [2000] All ER Rev 248 (P.J. Clarke).

[23] [2001] Ch 523 at 545.

[24] See H&M, pp. 182–186; Lewin, pp. 1083–1095; P&M, pp. 220–224; P&S, pp. 429–432; Snell, pp. 243–248; T&H, pp. 579–611; Thomas, *Powers*, pp. 453–494.   [25] *Cloutte v Storey* [1911] 1 Ch 18.

[26] In which case, see *Re Hay's Settlement Trust* [1982] 1 WLR 202 [p. 49, above].

[27] *Re Penrose* [1933] Ch 793.

[28] (1977) 3 *Monash University Law Review* 210 (Y. Grbich), describing the doctrine of fraud on a power as an '*ultra vires* appointments' doctrine.

of course, he expressly exceeds those limits the exercise of the power will be void unless it can be cut down by severing the invalid excess.[29] But the doctrine of fraudulent exercise of a power goes further than this, for it extends to the intent with which a power is exercised. The theory is that, in the case of a special power, the property is vested in those entitled in default of its exercise subject to its being divested by a proper exercise of the power,[30] and that an exercise of the power for any 'sinister object' is not proper, is a fraud on those entitled in default, and void.[31] It should be appreciated that the term 'fraud' is used here in a special sense: 'the equitable doctrine of "fraud on a power" has little, if anything, to do with fraud'.[32] It signifies 'in more modern parlance an improper use of the power for a collateral purpose'.[33]

(iv) Power of Testamentary Disposition

The courts have said that the power of testamentary disposition is a personal one which cannot be delegated to another; and, that, with the exception of charitable gifts and general and special powers of appointment,[34] a testator cannot leave it to someone else to make a will for him. This supposed anti-delegation rule does not apply to trusts created *inter vivos*, and was rejected in *Re Beatty*[35] by HOFFMANN J in the case of a testamentary disposition to trustees to allocate to or among such person or persons as they think fit. 'The common law rule...is a chimera, a shadow cast by the rule of certainty, having no independent existence.'[36]

QUESTIONS

1. Tabulate the duties of trustees/donees of powers for the following:
   (a) fixed trusts
   (b) trusts with a power of selection: e.g. *Burrough v Philcox* (1840) 5 My & Cr 72 [p. 48, above]
   (c) trust powers/discretionary trusts
      (i) exhaustive
      (ii) non-exhaustive

---

[29] *Churchill v Churchill* (1867) LR 5 Eq 44; *Re Oliphant* (1917) 86 LJ Ch 452.

[30] *Re Brooks' Settlement Trusts* [1939] Ch 993.

[31] *Vatcher v Paull* [1915] AC 372. *Cf Re Greaves* [1954] Ch 434 at 446.

[32] *Medforth v Blake* [2000] Ch 86 at 103.

[33] *Hillsdown Holdings plc v Pensions Ombudsman* [1997] 1 All ER 862 at 883.

[34] *Re Park* [1932] 1 Ch 580; *Re Abrahams' Will Trusts* [1969] 1 Ch 463; *Re Gulbenkian's Settlements* [1970] AC 508; *Re Manisty's Settlement* [1974] Ch 17; *Re Hay's Settlement Trusts* [1982] 1 WLR 202.

[35] [1990] 1 WLR 1503, explaining *Chichester Diocesan Fund and Board of Finance Inc v Simpson* [1944] AC 341 [p. 537, below]; (1991) 107 LQR 211 (J.D. Davies).

[36] At 1509. The power was an intermediary or hybrid power: it was not a general power because of its fiduciary nature; nor a special power because there was no class: [1991] Conv 138 (J. Martin).

(d) fiduciary powers

(e) non-fiduciary/mere powers.

See H&M, pp. 62–67, 211–216. How do you account for the differences?

2. To what extent does the trustee of a discretionary trust run the risk of personal liability if he disposes of the fund without considering a beneficiary of whom he was unaware? How should he protect himself? (1970) 34 Conv (NS) 287 (F.R. Crane); Trustee Act 1925, s. 61; p. 871, below.

3. Does administrative unworkability invalidate:

(a) powers, or

(b) fixed trusts

as well as discretionary trusts? See p. 102, below; H&M, pp. 110–112; P&M, pp. 71–75; (1991) 107 LQR 214 (S. Gardner). Consider in this context *Re Beatty* [1990] 1 WLR 1503 [p. 104, below]; *Mettoy Pension Trustees Ltd v Evans* [1990] 1 WLR 1587 [p. 55, above].

II PARTICULAR TYPES OF EXPRESS TRUST

A PROTECTIVE TRUSTS[37]

A protective trust is a useful way of protecting a beneficiary against the effects of misfortune or his or her own extravagance. It represents a compromise between two forces: the desire on the one hand to make a person's property available for his creditors; and on the other to enable family property to be available for the support of the family in the event of the insolvency of the head of the family. A protective trust shows the furthest extent to which English law will permit property to be denied to creditors. Most American jurisdictions allow beneficial interests under trusts to be inalienable, and this has allowed the development of what are called 'spendthrift trusts'.[38]

---

[37] H&M, pp. 191–200; Lewin, pp. 186–189; P&M, pp. 264–270; P&S, pp. 138–140; Pettit, pp. 79–81; Snell, pp. 508–510; T&H, pp. 253–264; U&H, pp. 267, 911; (1957) 21 Conv (NS) 110, 323 (L.A. Sheridan); (1967) 31 Conv (NS) 117 (A.J. Hawkins).

[38] Scott, *Law of Trusts* (1987) § 151; Griswold, *Spendthrift Trusts* (2nd edn, 1947); Keeton, *Modern Developments in the Law of* Trusts (1971), chap. 15. In England from the early nineteenth century until 1935 it was possible to create a trust for the separate use of a married woman and to impose a restraint upon anticipation or alienation. See Law Reform (Married Women and Tortfeasors) Act 1935 and Married Women (Restraint upon Anticipation) Act 1949.

The basis of a protective trust is a determinable life interest,[39] determined upon a stated event, which is usually any situation in which the income or any part of it becomes payable to anyone other than the beneficiary. A settlor cannot create in himself an interest which is determinable upon his own bankruptcy.[40] He may make the interest determinable upon any event *other than* bankruptcy,[41] or may create an interest in *another* person which is determinable upon that other's bankruptcy.

When the determining event occurs, the life interest is forfeited. That is not necessarily a disaster; forfeiture means that the life tenant is no longer entitled; therefore, his creditors (or the trustee in bankruptcy) cannot claim. But on the forfeiture of the life interest, other trusts then arise; which, in the case of the protective trust provisions contained in Trustee Act 1925, section 33, will be discretionary trusts, with the original life tenant a member of the class of beneficiaries.

As will be seen, a settlor may spell out the terms of a protective trust. But, since 1925, he may take advantage of Trustee Act 1925, section 33, and declare that property is held 'on protective trusts'.[42]

(i) Trustee Act 1925, s. 33

TRUSTEE ACT 1925

33. Protective Trusts

(1) Where any income, including an annuity or other periodical income payment, is directed to be held on protective trusts for the benefit of any person (in this section called 'the principal beneficiary') for the period of his life or for any less period, then, during that period (in this section called the 'trust period') the said income shall, without prejudice to any prior interest, be held on the following trusts, namely:

(i) Upon trust for the principal beneficiary during the trust period or until he, whether before or after the termination of any prior interest, does or attempts to do or suffers any act or thing, or until any event happens, other than an advance under any statutory or express power, whereby, if the said income were payable during the trust period to the principal beneficiary absolutely during that period, he would be deprived of the right to receive the same or any part thereof,[43] in any of which cases, as well as on the termination of the trust period, whichever first happens, this trust of the said income shall fail or determine.

---

[39] Which must be distinguished from a gift subject to a condition subsequent: *Brandon v Robinson* (1811) 18 Ves 429; *Rochford v Hackman* (1852) 9 Hare 475; *Re Scientific Investment Pension Plan Trusts* [1999] Ch 53 [p. 64, below].

[40] *Re Burroughs-Fowler* [1916] 2 Ch 251; Trustee Act 1925, s. 33 (3) [p. 62, below].

[41] *Re Detmold* (1889) 40 Ch D 585 [p. 62, below].

[42] Or words making clear that this was intended: *Re Wittke* [1944] Ch 166 ('upon protective trusts for the benefit of my sister'); *Re Platt* [1950] CLY 4386 ('for protective life interest').

[43] *Re Smith's Will Trusts* (1981) 131 NLJ 292 [p. 63, below].

(ii) If the trust aforesaid fails or determines during the subsistence of the trust period, then, during the residue of that period, the said income shall be held upon trust for the application thereof for the maintenance or support, or otherwise for the benefit, of all or any one or more exclusively of the other or others of the following persons[44] (that is to say)—

(a) the principal beneficiary and his or her spouse or civil partner,[45] if any, and his or her children or more remote issue, if any; or

(b) if there is no spouse or civil partner or issue of the principal beneficiary in existence, the principal beneficiary and the persons who would, if he were actually dead, be entitled to the trust property or the income thereof or to the annuity fund, if any, or arrears of the annuity, as the case may be;

as the trustees in their absolute discretion, without being liable to account for the exercise of such discretion, think fit.

(2) This section does not apply to trusts coming into operation before the commencement of this Act, and has effect subject to any variation of the implied trusts aforesaid contained in the instrument creating the trust.

(3) Nothing in this section operates to validate any trust which would, if contained in the instrument creating the trust, be liable to be set aside.

(ii) Forfeiture

The courts have often had to determine whether or not a particular event has effected a forfeiture. When the question arises upon an express trust, the result depends upon a construction of the language of the forfeiture provisions, which may or may not differ materially from the Trustee Act 1925, section 33. It will be seen that in some of the cases it is to the advantage of the life tenant to establish that there was a forfeiture; sometimes not.

(a) Effective forfeiture

In **Re Detmold** (1889) 40 Ch D 585, under a marriage settlement of the settlor's own property, the income was payable to himself 'during his life, or till he shall become bankrupt, or shall...suffer something whereby [the income], or some part thereof, would...by operation or process of law, if belonging absolutely to him, become vested in or payable to some other person', and after the determination of the trust in favour of the settlor, upon trust to pay the income to his wife. In July 1888 an order was made appointing a judgment creditor of the settlor to be receiver of the income; and in September 1888 the settlor was adjudicated bankrupt.

---

[44] See Family Law Reform Act 1987, s. 1, Sch. 2, para 2. Relationships are to be construed without regard to illegitimacy.   [45] As amended by the Civil Partnership Act 2004.

NORTH J, in holding that the wife was entitled to the income, said at 588:

The limitation of the life interest to the settlor was validly determined by the fact that, in consequence of the order appointing the receiver, he ceased to be entitled to receive the income. This took place before the bankruptcy, and, therefore, the forfeiture is valid against the trustee in bankruptcy.

In **Re Balfour's Settlement** [1938] Ch 928, the income of a settled fund was payable to Mr. Balfour for life or until he should 'do or suffer something whereby the same or some part thereof would through his act or default or by operation or process of law or otherwise if belonging absolutely to him become vested in or payable to some other person', with a discretionary trust over. During 1933 to 1936 the sole trustee advanced to him part of the capital at his request and in breach of trust. Balfour was then adjudicated bankrupt. FARWELL J held that his interest had determined, because the trustees had asserted their right to impound the income prior to the date of the bankruptcy; and therefore nothing passed to the trustee in bankruptcy.[46]

In **Re Baring's Settlement Trusts** [1940] Ch 737, under a family settlement a wife had a protected life interest with the income payable to her 'until some event should happen whereby the income...would become...payable to...some other person', with a discretionary trust over. Her husband obtained a sequestration order against her property on her failure to obey a court order to return her infant children to the jurisdiction of the court. When she eventually returned with the children, the question arose whether the life interest was forfeited. MORTON J held that it was, although the sequestration order was only temporary. He said, at 753, that the settlor 'intended that there should be a continuous benefit to the beneficiaries so that either the tenant for life should be in a position to have the income or the discretionary trust should arise'.

In **Re Dennis's Settlement Trusts** [1942] Ch 283,[47] under a family settlement of 1923 the settlor's son, then an infant, was given a protected life interest 'until any act or event should happen whereby the income would...become vested in...some other person'. On his attaining twenty-one in 1935, a supplemental deed was executed providing that for the next six years the trustees should pay to him only part of the income and accumulate the balance for him. FARWELL J held that this rearrangement caused a forfeiture.

In **Re Smith's Will Trusts** (1981) 131 NLJ 292, a trustee bank held the residue of a testator's estate on trusts, *inter alia*, (a) to pay to the testator's daughter 'for her own absolute use and benefit' up to £10,000, if she so requested, and (b) to hold the income of the residue and of the balance, after any payments to her under (a), on protective trusts for her life. In 1976 she requested and received £10,000 for the purchase of a house. MEGARRY V-C held that the life interest of the daughter determined under Trustee Act 1925, section 33(1)(i). When the payment was made, she was 'deprived

---

[46] Cf. *Re Brewer's Settlement* [1896] 2 Ch 503, where the bankruptcy took place before the trustees exercised their right. [47] (1942) 58 LQR 312 (R.E.M.).

of the right to receive part of the income' from the residue 'directed to be held on protective trusts'.

In **Gibbon v Mitchell** [1990] 1 WLR 1304, Mr. Gibbon purported to surrender his protected life interest in favour of his two children, with a view to reducing the effect of inheritance tax. He was not advised that the effect of the deed would be to forfeit his life interest and to bring into operation the discretionary trusts under section 33, unless an order of the court was first obtained under the Variation of Trusts Act 1958 [p. 832, below], which would remove the protection annexed to the life interest. MILLETT J ordered that the deed should be set aside for mistake.

In **Re Scientific Investment Pension Plan Trusts** [1999] Ch 53, clause 24 in the trust deed of a pension scheme prohibited the assignment by any member of any benefit arising under the scheme and stated that, if anything happened whereby any benefit was vested in somebody else, then the member would forfeit all rights to the benefit and the trustees of the scheme would hold the benefit on trust for the scheme's general purposes, but with a discretionary power to apply it for the benefit of the member's dependants in cases of hardship. Renton was a member of the scheme. His employment ceased in 1991. He was made bankrupt in 1992.

Held. Since his rights under the scheme were determinable on a particular event, the effect of the bankruptcy order was to forfeit his interest under the scheme.

RATTEE J said at 59:

Mr. Renton's trustee in bankruptcy submits that clause 24 of the trust deed is void and of no effect. This argument is based on the well established principle that a forfeiture provision in a will or other trust instrument purporting to forfeit, in the event of voluntary or involuntary alienation, an absolute or life interest given by the relevant instrument is void as repugnant to the essential alienability of the interest given. The court has for long recognised a distinction between the grant of a determinable interest, granted on terms that it is determinable, for example, in the event of alienation or bankruptcy, which is effective according to its terms, and the purported grant of an absolute or limited interest not expressed to be so determinable, coupled with a provision purporting to forfeit the interest on alienation or bankruptcy. The latter provision is held to be void as repugnant to the essential nature of the interest given. In *Brandon v Robinson* (1811) 18 Ves 429, 433–434 Lord Eldon LC explained the distinction thus:

'There is no doubt, that property may be given to a man, until he shall become bankrupt. It is equally clear, generally speaking, that if property is given to a man for his life, the donor cannot take away the incidents to a life estate; and, as I have observed, a disposition to a man, until he shall become bankrupt, and after his bankruptcy over, is quite different from an attempt to give to him for his life, with a proviso that he shall not sell or alien it.'

The statutory protective trusts provided by section 33 of the Trustee Act 1925 are, of course, an example of the former type of limitation, namely an interest until purported alienation with a gift over. The distinction is not a particularly attractive one, being based on form rather than substance. The effect intended to be achieved by both forms of limitation would appear to be the same. However, the distinction is, for good or ill, firmly embedded in the law. On the other hand, it is clear that which form of limitation the donor intended is to be gathered from the whole of the words used in the relevant trust instrument. No particular form of words is necessary for one or the other.

His Lordship referred to *Rochford v Hackman* (1852) 9 Hare 475 and continued:

Thus the position appears from the authorities to which I have referred to be as follows.

(a) A forfeiture clause purporting to forfeit an absolute interest in possession in the event of alienation will be void.

(b) So will be such a clause which purports similarly to forfeit a life or other limited interest in possession which is not, on the true construction of the instrument creating it, made determinable in the same events as those in which the forfeiture is expressed to operate.

(c) On the other hand, there is nothing objectionable about such a forfeiture clause which purports to defeat a future interest in the event of purported alienation before it falls into possession or to create a gift over in the event in which an income interest in possession is, on the true construction of the trust instrument, expressed to be determinable.

If a forfeiture clause purports to apply both to interests in possession within (a) or (b) above and to future or determinable interests within (c) above, it will be wholly void, even as to interests within (c) above, as to which it would have been valid if limited to interests within that class: *Re Smith* [1916] 1 Ch 369.

His Lordship construed clause 24 and concluded that it made the benefits determinable in specified events and so the clause was effective to forfeit the benefits.[48]

(b) Ineffective forfeiture

In **Re Tancred's Settlement** [1903] 1 Ch 715 at 723, Sir Seymer Tancred was entitled under a deed of 1891 to income for life or 'until he should dispose or attempt to dispose of the…income…or do something whereby the income…would become payable to or vested in some other person'. In 1896 he assigned his life interest to the trustees of his marriage settlement, of which he was tenant for life and solely entitled to the income, and appointed them his attorneys to receive the income; and authorised them to charge their expenses to the fund. BUCKLEY J held that there was no forfeiture.

In **Re Westby's Settlement** [1950] Ch 296, the Court of Appeal held that there was no forfeiture where the tenant for life under a protective trust was of unsound mind, and fees became payable out of the estate to the Supreme Court Funds under section 148 (3) of the Lunacy Act 1890.[49]

---

[48] Section 14(3) of the Welfare Reform and Pensions Act 1999 prevents the forfeiture of rights under pension schemes when a member of the scheme has been declared bankrupt.

[49] See now Mental Health Act 1983, s. 106 (6).

In **Re Oppenheim's Will Trusts** [1950] Ch 633, HARMAN J, in holding that, where a tenant for life under a protective trust was certified as a person of unsound mind, the appointment of a receiver did not effect a forfeiture, said at 636:

I think that a man who has a statutory agent, as this man has, can give by his agent a personal discharge no less than ... if he were on the top of Mount Everest, his banker could give a personal discharge on his behalf. It seems to me also that the forfeiture was not intended to operate in a case of this kind where no one else will be entitled to the benefit of the income in the event which has happened. It was intended to prevent the income from getting into other hands. That does not occur in the present case.

In **Re Longman** [1955] 1 WLR 197, a son was entitled to the income from a trust fund subject to a forfeiture 'if he should commit any act whereby any part of the income ... became vested in or payable to any other person'. In 1953 he authorised his trustees to pay money to his creditors 'from the dividend due to me in July next from [a certain company]'. The company, however, did not declare a dividend. DANCKWERTS J held that this prevented a forfeiture and said at 199:

It seems to me that the authorities given by the son were completely nugatory, and that there was nothing on which they could operate and they never did operate on anything.

In **Re Mair** [1935] Ch 562, FARWELL J held that an order made under section 57 of the Trustee Act 1925,[50] authorising the trustees to raise money to enable a tenant for life under a protective trust to 'pay certain pressing liabilities' did not effect a forfeiture. He said, at 565:

If and when the Court sanctions an arrangement or transaction under section 57, it must be taken to have done it as though the power which is being put into operation had been inserted in the trust instrument as an overriding power ... The forfeiture clause remains attached to the income which is payable to the tenant for life from time to time ...

It must, however, be remembered that if a scheme sanctioned by the court involves, as in *Re Salting* [1932] 2 Ch 57, an agreement or covenant by the tenant for life to pay premiums on policies or other like payments with a proviso that if they are not duly paid the trustees are to pay them out of income, the failure to pay by the tenant for life will create a forfeiture, since it will be that act or omission of the tenant for life that creates the forfeiture and not the exercise by the Court of its overriding power.

Hanbury & Martin: *Modern Equity* (17th edn), pp. 198–199

It is not clear whether a forfeiture is effected when a court order is made which alters a protected life interest under a marriage settlement.[51] In *Re Richardson's Will Trusts*,[52] the court ordered that the principal beneficiary should charge his interest with an annual payment of £50

---

[50] See p. 749, below.

[51] Which the court has power to do under the Matrimonial Causes Act 1973, s. 24 (1).

[52] [1958] Ch 504, illustrating the advantage of establishing a series of protective trusts, 'one set until the beneficiary is twenty-five, another from twenty-five to thirty-five, a third from thirty-five to forty-five, and another for the rest of his life'. A forfeiture of, or a charge upon, the principal beneficiary's interest in one of the trusts would not affect his interest in subsequent trusts. He would get a fresh start. (1958) 74 LQR 182 (R.E.M.) [p. 67, below].

in favour of his divorced wife. The charge was held to create a forfeiture. On the other hand, in *General Accident Fire and Life Assurance Corpn Ltd v IRC*[53] an order diverting part of the income from the life tenant in favour of a former wife was held not to effect a forfeiture.

These cases are distinguishable on a narrow ground of construction of section 33.[54] But the broader ground of the decision, that this situation has no relevance to the real purpose of protective trusts, would seem to apply to the charge in *Re Richardson's Will Trusts*[55] as much as to the diversion of part of the income in the *General Accident* case.[56] It is submitted that the principle of the *General Accident* case is sound. As Donovan LJ said,[57] '...the section is intended as a protection to spendthrift or improvident or weak life tenants. But it can give...no protection against the effect of a court order such as was made here. Furthermore, if such order involves a forfeiture much injustice could be done.' Perhaps the problem can be rationalised with the cases on section 57 by saying with Russell LJ, who made clear, however, that he did not rest his decision on this approach: 'the settlement throughout was potentially subject in all its trusts to such an order as was made'.[58] *Re Richardson's Will Trusts*[59] was not mentioned; but an earlier case on the Matrimonial Causes Act 1859 in favour of forfeiture, *Re Carew,*[60] was overruled. It is tempting to say that *Re Richardson's Will Trusts* is wrong; but it should be noted that in that case, as in *Re Carew*, the decision in favour of forfeiture forwarded the broad policy of section 33; for the forfeiture in those cases allowed the discretionary trusts to operate when otherwise the trustee in bankruptcy would have claimed the interest.

(1958) 74 LQR 182, 184 (R.E.M.)

This sequence of events points a moral for draftsmen. Hitherto the normal course of drafting has been to give a life interest simply 'on protective trusts', with or without variations. The result is that a single mistaken act by the beneficiary may deprive him of his determinable life interest and reduce him for the rest of his life to the status of merely one of the beneficiaries of a discretionary trust. *Re Richardson* suggests that there may be advantages in setting up a series of protective trusts, e.g., one set until the beneficiary is twenty-five, another from twenty-five to thirty-five, a third from thirty-five to forty-five, and another for the rest of his life. The result would be that a youthful indiscretion at say, twenty-two, would not irretrievably condemn the beneficiary to the mere hopes of a beneficiary under a discretionary trust, dependent upon the exercise of the trustees' discretion, but would give him a fresh start when he was twenty-five. Again, a bankruptcy at the age of thirty would not *per se* mean that when he was twice that age he would still have not an income as of right, but a mere hope of a well-exercised discretion. Indeed, instead of relating the stages to the age of the beneficiary, they might be related to a period of time (e.g. five years) after the occurrence of any event which had made the initial trust pass from Stage 1 to Stage 2. England lacks the device of the spendthrift trust in the American sense, but it is far from clear that the fullest possible use is being made of the existing machinery of protective and discretionary trusts.

53 [1963] 1 WLR 1207.
54 Ibid, see Donovan LJ at 1217 and Russell LJ at 1221; (1963) 27 Conv (NS) 517 (F.R. Crane).
55 [1958] Ch 504. 56 [1963] 1 WLR 1207. 57 Ibid., *per* Donovan LJ at 1218.
58 Ibid at 1222. 59 [1958] Ch 504. 60 (1910) 103 LT 658.

(iii) The Effect of Forfeiture

In **Re Gourju's Will Trusts** [1943] Ch 24, Mrs. Gourju was a protected life tenant under her husband's will. She resided at Nice. That part of France was occupied by the Germans in June, 1940. By the Trading with the Enemy Act 1939 and Orders made thereunder,[61] she became disentitled to receive the income of the fund, and her protected life interest was forfeited. The Custodian of Enemy Property could not claim the income, for he had no better claim than Mrs. Gourju. The discretionary trusts came into effect. The trustees wished to accumulate the income and pay it at the end of the war to Mrs. Gourju. SIMONDS J held that they could not do so. Their duty was to pay to one or more of the members of the discretionary class.

Underhill and Hayton: *Law of Trusts and Trustees* (17th edn), pp. 265–266

Another point that not infrequently arises is whether, under a discretionary trust... *where the settlor is a third party,* and the defeasible life interest has been forfeited either by bankruptcy or alienation (voluntary or involuntary), the trustees can, *under the discretion* vested in them, continue to pay the income to the person whose life interest has determined. Obviously the object of such trusts is to enable this to be done if it can be. The authorities are, however, against the right of the trustees to do this,[62] on the ground apparently that the life tenant, being bound to hand over to his creditor or assignee whatever his interest in the income may be, is none the less bound with regard to such part of the income as may be paid to him by the trustees in the exercise of their discretion; and that they, having notice of this equity, are equally bound not to pay him. This may seem to be a *reductio ad absurdum*, since the trustees could not under any circumstances pay any part of the income to the creditor or assignee,[63] so that it is difficult to see how the latter could suffer by the payment being made to the life tenant himself, or what claim he could have upon the trustees. Nevertheless, trustees under such circumstances have been made liable to the creditor or assignee,[64] although, curiously enough, it is well settled that they are at liberty to *expend* the income for his benefit.[65] In one case it was held that the trustees might apply such part as they thought fit of the income for the benefit of the person whose life interest had determined without reference to any debt which such person might owe to the trust estate.[66] This case is distinct from that which has been more frequently before the courts where the contest is between the tenant of a protected life interest and his own assignee. The law is,

---

[61] Trading With the Enemy (Custodian) Order 1939. Later Orders contained a proviso that vesting in the Custodian of Enemy Property should not take place if it would cause a forfeiture.

[62] *Re Coleman* (1888) 39 Ch D 443; *Re Neil* (1890) 62 LT 649, explained by Stirling LJ in *Re Fitzgerald* [1904] 1 Ch 573 at 593.

[63] *Re Bullock* (1891) 64 LT 736; *Train v Clapperton* [1908] AC 342; *Re Laye* [1913] 1 Ch 298; *Re Hamilton* (1921) 124 LT 737. But cf. *Lord v Bunn* (1843) 2 Y & C Ch Cas 98, which seems *contra* at first sight, but really turned on a question of construction.

[64] *Re Coleman*, note 62 above; *Re Neil*, note 62 above, explained by Stirling LJ in *Re Fitzgerald*, note 62 above.

[65] *Re Bullock*, note 63 above and cf. *Re Coleman*, ibid; and *Re Neil*, ibid. But see *Re Ashby* [1892] 1 QB 872, where Vaughan Williams J thought that the bankrupt might be liable to account for sums paid to him, though, perhaps, just for the surplus above that needed for his mere support. See also *Re Allen-Meyrick's Will Trusts* [1966] 1 WLR 499 at 503.   [66] *Re Eiser's Will Trusts* [1937] 1 All ER 244.

therefore, in an anomalous and unsatisfactory state; and it is not considered that it has been in any way altered by the introduction by section 33 of the Trustee Act 1925[67] of the statutory 'protective trusts'...

It needs scarcely be said that, until they have notice of an act amounting to forfeiture, the trustees are justified in paying the income to the first beneficiary.[68]

B OCCUPATIONAL PENSION FUND TRUSTS[69]

Trusts of pension funds, otherwise known as occupational pension schemes, are trusts which are subject to the same basic principles as apply to any express trust. Indeed, some of the leading cases on the modern law of trusts are pension trust cases.[70] However, sometimes these basic principles have been modified, most importantly by the Pensions Act 1995,[71] meaning that it is appropriate to treat the occupational pension fund trust as a distinct form of express trust.

(i) The Nature of Occupational Pension Fund Trusts

In **Air Jamaica Ltd v Charlton** [1999] 1 WLR 1399 [p. 205, below] LORD MILLETT, delivering the opinion of the Privy Council, said at 1407:

A pension scheme can, in theory at least, be established by contract between the employer and each employee and without using the machinery of a trust. Such a scheme would have to be very simple. It would look very like a self-employed pension policy. There would be no trust fund and no trustees. The employer would simply contract with each of his employees that, if the employee made weekly payments to the employer, the employer would pay the employee a pension on retirement or a lump sum on death. The employer would not make any contributions itself, since there would be no one to receive them. But the benefits would be calculated at a higher level than would be justified by the employee's contributions alone.

The company's pension scheme was, however, of a very different kind. A trust fund was established with its own trustees. Contributions, whether by members or by the company, were paid into the trust fund, and the trustees were given powers of investment over the fund. The

---

[67] See p. 61, above.   [68] *Re Long* [1901] WN 166.

[69] H&M, pp. 477–499; P&M, pp. 503–542; P&S, pp. 638–653; Pettit, pp. 426–427; T&H, pp. 1415–1502; U&H, pp. 61–65. See generally Ellison, *Pensions: Law and Practice* (1988); (1992) 6 *Trust Law International* 119 (Lord Browne-Wilkinson); (1993) 56 MLR 471 (G. Moffatt); (1994) 14 LS 345 (R. Nobles); (1996) 59 MLR 241 (R. Nobles); [1997] Conv 89 (M. Milner); (2000) 14 *Trust Law International* 201 (S.E.K. Hulme); (2000) 14 *Trust Law International* 66 (Lord Millett); [2005] Conv 229 (D. Hayton).

[70] *Wilson v Law Debenture Trust Corpn plc* [1995] 2 All ER 337 (principle that trustees not bound to give reasons to the beneficiaries for the exercise of their discretions applied to pension fund trustees); *Air Jamaica Ltd v Charlton* [1999] 1 WLR 1399 [p. 205, below] (resulting trust); *Cowan v Scargill* [1985] Ch 270 [p. 705, below] (ethical considerations in making investment decisions); *Mettoy Pension Trustees Ltd v Evans* [1990] 1 WLR 1587 [p. 55, above] (release of fiduciary power); *Edge v Pensions Ombudsman* [2000] Ch 602 (duty to exercise discretion for proper purpose).

[71] See p. 71, below. For example, the general rule that trustees must act unanimously is modified for trustees of occupational pension funds who can act by majority decision: Pensions Act 1995, s. 32.

benefits were funded in part by contributions and in part by the income of the investments held in the fund. The interposition of a trust fund between the company and the members meant that payment of benefits to members was the responsibility of the trustees, not the company. The machinery employed was that of a trust, not a contract.[72]

This is not to say that the trust is like a traditional family trust under which a settlor voluntarily settles property for the benefit of the object of his bounty. The employee members of an occupational pension scheme are not voluntary settlors. As has been repeatedly observed, their rights are derived from their contracts of employment as well as from the trust instrument. Their pensions are earned by their services under their contracts of employment as well as by their contributions. They are often not inappropriately described as deferred pay. This does not mean, however, that they have contractual rights to their pensions. It means only that, in construing the trust instrument, regard must be had to the nature of an occupational pension and the employment relationship that forms its genesis.

In the present case prospective employees were informed that the company maintained a pension scheme for its staff and that membership was compulsory for those under 55 years of age. They were told the amount of the employee's contribution, and that the company paid 'an amount not less than the employee's contribution, plus any amount necessary to support the financial viability of the scheme'. Even if these can be regarded as imposing contractual obligations on the company, the only obligation which was undertaken by the company, and one which it has fully performed, was to make contributions to the fund. The obligation to make pension payments was not a contractual obligation undertaken by the company, but a trust obligation imposed on the trustees. Their Lordships agree with the observation of Carey JA, who was dissenting in the Court of Appeal, that each employee becomes a member of the pension scheme by virtue of his employment, but that his entitlement to a pension arises under the trusts of the scheme.

Their Lordships should add for completeness that, while the members' entitlements arise under the trusts of the pension plan, the company's obligation to deduct contributions from members and to pay them to the trustees together with its own matching contributions, is contractual. The company undertook this obligation by its covenant with the trustees in the trust deed. The obligation was, however, subject to the power of the company unilaterally to discontinue the plan under section 13.2 of the plan.

It is well established that, absent statutory intervention, such pensions schemes are subject to the rule against perpetuities:[73] see, for example, *Lucas v Telegraph Construction and Maintenance Co Ltd* [1925] LN 211; *Re Flavel's Will Trusts* [1969] 1 WLR 444; *Re Thomas Meadows & Co Ltd and Subsidiary Companies (1960) Staff Pension Scheme Rules* [1971] Ch 278. Following the decision of Russell J in the *Telegraph* case [1925] LN 211 the Superannuation and other Trust Funds (Validation) Act 1927 was hurriedly introduced in England with retrospective effect to exempt pension schemes from the rule against perpetuities provided that certain criteria were satisfied. That Act has since been repealed and replaced by the Social Security Act 1973[74] which makes special provision for all qualifying occupational pension schemes to be exempt from the rule. Similar legislation has been introduced in most other common law jurisdictions both in the Commonwealth and in the United States. Unhappily no such legislation has been enacted in Jamaica, where no steps have been taken to modernise

---

[72] See p. 72, below.   [73] See p. 110, below.
[74] See now the Pension Schemes Act 1993, s. 163.

the rule as was done in England by the Perpetuities and Accumulations Act 1964. The company's pension scheme is thus subject to the common law rule against perpetuities unaffected by any legislative amendment.

(ii) The Pensions Acts 1995 and 2004

The enactment of the Pensions Act 1995 followed a review of pensions law by the Pension Law Review Committee, chaired by Professor Roy Goode.[75] The subsequent enactment of the Pensions Act 2004 has resulted in the creation of a Pensions Regulator and a Pension Protection Fund.

Goode Report: *Pensions Law Reform* 1993 (Cm. 2342), paras. 4.1.5, 4.1.8–4.1.14 and 4.2.3

The framework and policies of occupational pensions law

4.1.5   The root of the problem is that there is no comprehensive legal framework governing occupational pensions.... Pensions law is an amalgam of equity and trust law, contract and labour law, heavily overlaid with complex legislation governing the occupational pensions aspects of social security, taxation and financial services. One can search in vain for a code in which the essential rights and obligations flowing from the establishment of pension schemes are clearly laid out. Much of the law is to be found only in reports of court decisions about the interpretation of scheme documents and the duties of trustees and employers at common law. Legislation is at present spread over more than thirty statutes and well over a hundred statutory instruments. The planned consolidation Act for occupational pensions will certainly improve matters. But it will do nothing to resolve the much greater problem of complex subordinate legislation, not to mention the profusion of memoranda, guidance notes, practice notes and other documents produced by the various government departments and professional bodies. Nor will it deal with the fundamental weakness of the present system, the lack of a properly structured framework of rights and obligations.

The role and adequacy of trust law

4.1.8   The weaknesses to which we have drawn attention have led to suggestions that trust law should be abandoned for occupational pensions, and that pension rights should be defined by contract and/or legislation. Following on the Maxwell affair [76] some commentators have derided trust law as medieval and archaic and as having failed its purpose in the pensions field.

4.1.9   Trust law is indeed of considerable antiquity, but it has shown a remarkable ability to adapt itself to modern commercial requirements. Indeed, the full range and power of the modern trust are to be found not in the family trust, with which the pension trust is customarily contrasted, but with the trust used in commerce and finance. The trust is not only a means of segregating assets for the protection of the beneficiaries, thus insulating them from the consequences of the settlor's bankruptcy; its equally important function is to provide a mechanism

---

[75] See (1993) 7 *Trust Law International* 91 (D. Chatterton); [1993] Conv 283 (D. Hayton).

[76] About £450 million had been misappropriated from the pension funds of employees of Mirror Group Newspapers and the Maxwell Communications Company by Robert Maxwell.

for the collective representation and protection of members of a group of people linked by a common interest. Good examples of such a mechanism are the unit trust and the bond or debenture trust deed. Under these, the individual interests of substantial numbers of holders of units, bonds and debenture stock are channelled into the trust and held and protected by the trustees for the benefit of all holders, so providing the collective mechanism without which efficient administration would be impossible. This mechanism is valuable even where there is no trust property in the normal sense, merely an aggregation of personal rights.[77]

4.1.10   In our consultation document we directly posed the question whether the use of the trust should be abandoned. Whilst there were those who continued to advocate the movement from trust to contract, there was a widespread recognition of the need to retain trust law as the basis of pension scheme regulation. It was felt that trust law embodies highly developed concepts of fiduciary responsibility which it is important to preserve...

4.1.11   Though contract law has a role to play in the field of pensions it is not in itself adequate to take over the functions performed by the trust. Individual employment contracts on their own provide neither the security resulting from a segregation of assets nor the collective mechanism that is so important for the administration of pension schemes. If the employer operating an unfunded scheme becomes insolvent the scheme members are merely unsecured creditors. Moreover, under English law contract rights cannot in general be enforced by or against those who are strangers to the contract, so that a contract between employer and employee would not of itself be enough to give the employee a right to take proceedings against third parties (for example, fund managers) for failing in their duty.[78]

4.1.12   The dissatisfaction expressed with the trust as an institution, understandable though this may be in the light of pension fund losses resulting from improper conduct, is largely misplaced, for it demands more of trust law than this can reasonably be expected to perform. The deliberate misappropriation of trust funds is both a civil wrong and a criminal offence. Trust law cannot in itself prevent breaches of trust any more than criminal law can prevent the commission of crimes.

4.1.13   The rules of trust law are not, for the most part, statutory. They have been developed by the courts over a long period and are based on the assumption that every settlor is free to write his or her own trust rules. That approach is inevitable, for to override the provisions of a lawful trust would be tantamount to legislation, and it is the function of Parliament, not the courts, to legislate. Trust law plays little part in the normal employer–employee contract, though the flexibility of trust law has enabled the courts to distinguish the pension trust from the family trust and to emphasise the significance of the contract of employment for the exercise of powers conferred by the scheme documents. Trust law itself cannot prescribe rules to secure the solvency of schemes, or the monitoring of pension funds. That too is the function of Parliament.

4.1.14   We therefore endorse the view expressed in the great weight of evidence submitted to us that trust law in itself is broadly satisfactory and should continue to provide the foundation for interests, rights and duties arising in relation to pension schemes. But some of the principles of trust law require modification in their application to pensions. In particular, some curbs need

[77] For example, where unsecured bonds are issued, so that there are no assets securing repayment, there will still be a trust deed providing for the appointment of trustees for the bondholders and conferring powers on the trustees to take action for the protection of all bondholders if, for example, the issuer of the bond defaults in payment.

[78] See now Contracts (Rights of Third Parties) Act 1999 [p. 169, below].

to be placed on the permissible content of scheme rules, especially in relation to certain of the powers that can be reserved to the employer and the trustees and the scope of exemptions given to trustees from liability for breach of duty. Trust law also requires statutory reinforcement in other ways. This is reflected in the growing volume of legislation enacted in recent times to strengthen the rights of scheme members and the duties of employers, trustees, auditors and actuaries. The question is whether this legislation is adequate or has always moved in the right direction. We have already made clear our view that what is now needed is comprehensive legislation to regulate occupational pension schemes.

The family trust and the pension trust

4.2.3   In the early days of occupational pension schemes there was a much closer affinity than at present between the pension trust and the traditional family trust. Pensions were in many cases seen as acts of bounty, tangible expressions of gratitude by the employer for long and faithful service. In those cases, as with the family trust it was for the settlor, the employer, to decide upon what terms his or her bounty were to be provided. The employees were not seen as having any interest in the constitution or administration of the scheme; it was not for them to look a gift horse in the mouth. That approach has long since changed. Pension benefits are now seen as an integral part of a total remuneration package earned by service and contributed to by the employee....

The Goode Committee recommended that the rights of pension beneficiaries should be enhanced and safeguarded by the enactment of special rules which go beyond the protection given to beneficiaries under general trust law. The Pensions Act 1995 implemented most of these recommendations, some in modified form.[79] In particular, the Act introduced reforms relating to the appointment, removal and disqualification of trustees (sections 16–31); wide investment powers (sections 33–36); a requirement to appoint professional advisers (sections 47–48); a minimum funding requirement to prevent a shortfall of funds in the case of funded schemes (sections 56–61); and restrictions on employers' rights to surplus funds (sections 37, 73–77).[80] The Pensions Ombudsman also was given jurisdiction to investigate and determine complaints relating especially to the maladministration of pension fund trusts.[81]

The Pensions Act 2004 replaces the Occupational Pensions Regulatory Authority, which was established by the 1995 Act, with the Pensions Regulator. The 2004 Act also establishes a Pension Protection Fund to compensate members of occupational pension schemes who suffer as a result of fraud, or from their company going into insolvency, and the pension fund not having sufficient assets to meet its liabilities to its members.

---

[79] (1996) 59 MLR 241 (R. Nobles).   [80] See *National Grid Co plc v Mayes* [2001] 1 WLR 864.
[81] Pension Schemes Act 1993, ss. 146–151, as amended by Pensions Act 1995, s. 157. See *Law Debenture Trust Corpn plc v Pensions Ombudsman* [1998] 1 WLR 1329; *Hillsdown Holdings plc v Pensions Ombudsman* [1997] 1 All ER 862; *Edge v Pensions Ombudsman* [2000] Ch 602; (2000) 14 *Trust Law International* 146 (J. Farrand).

QUESTIONS

1. Is it appropriate for pension funds to be subject primarily to trust law rather than to contract law? See *Air Jamaica v Charlton* [1999] 1 WLR 1399, [p. 69, above]; The Goode Report, [p. 71, above].

2. What should happen to the surplus of a pension fund? Should it be paid to the employer (or creditors of the employer if it is insolvent); the employees; or pass to the State as *bona vacantia*? See Pensions Act 1995, s. 37, as amended by Pensions Act 2004, s. 250; *National Grid Co plc v Mayes* [2001] 1 WLR 864; H&M, pp. 492–494; (2000) 14 TLI 66 (Lord Millett); (2001) 15 TLI 130 (N. Davies); (2003) 17 TLI 2 (D. Pollard).

3. Should the law relating to pension trusts be developed differently from that relating to conventional private trusts? See [2005] Conv 229 (D. Hayton).

3

THE REQUIREMENTS
OF A TRUST

The key requirement of an express trust is that the settlor or testator intended to create a trust. It follows that the settlor must have capacity to create a trust.[1] Consequently a settlement made by a child is voidable by the child before or reasonably soon after he attains the age of 18,[2] and a settlement made by a mentally incapacitated person is void.[3]

In addition to the necessary intention to create a trust, there are various other requirements which must be satisfied before a trust can be validly created. These include:

(i)   certainties of subject matter and beneficiaries;

(ii) the existence of beneficiaries who are able to enforce the trust;

(iii) compliance with the perpetuity rules.

Formalities for the creation of a trust are considered in chapter 4.

---

[1] See H&M, pp. 77–79; Lewin, pp. 83–103; P&M, pp. 95–96; Pettit, pp. 42–44; U&H, pp. 329–335.

[2] *Edwards v Carter* [1893] AC 360.

[3] *Re Beaney* [1978] 1 WLR 770. But note the Mental Capacity Act 2005 by virtue of which the court may make a settlement of property or execute a will on behalf of a person who lacks mental capacity: s. 18(1)(h),(i).

I CERTAINTY[4]

A trust cannot be created unless there is certainty in respect of: the intention to create a trust; the property which is the subject matter of the trust; and (charitable trusts apart) the beneficiaries. These are the 'three certainties'.[5] Various principles are identified in the case law to assist in determining whether the three certainties are satisfied; but ultimately this will depend upon careful construction of the language of the instrument under consideration. It is important to be aware at the outset that the problems of uncertainty can easily be avoided by careful drafting of the trust instrument or by providing mechanisms for the resolution of uncertainty, such as giving the trustees the power to resolve any uncertainty. Sometimes, however, it is necessary to determine whether the trust is invalid for uncertainty, and this is where the principles in this part come into operation.

The three aspects of the 'certainty' problem are treated separately here. In many cases, however, they overlap. So, for example, it has been recognised that 'uncertainty in the subject of the gift has a reflex action upon the previous words, and throws doubt upon the intention of the testator, and seems to shew that he could not possibly have intended his words of confidence, hope, or whatever they may be—his appeal to the conscience of the first taker—to be imperative words'.[6] Similarly, a division of property among various beneficiaries may create uncertainty as to both the property and the beneficiaries.[7]

There is sometimes confusion between these rules of certainty and some related rules. First, the certainty rules apply quite differently to charitable trusts.[8] There, the requirement is that the trust must be exclusively charitable, but there is no need to specify which particular charity is to benefit. Second, the rule that the objects of a trust (the beneficiaries) must be certain leaves open the question, discussed below,[9] whether there can be a non-charitable purpose trust, without human beneficiaries. In so far as this is possible, the purposes must be sufficiently certain.[10] Third, it is important to appreciate the relationship between these rules and discretionary trusts.[11] It is possible to leave uncertain which members of a group of beneficiaries will benefit and which share any one will receive, provided that the property available for distribution is certain, the class of beneficiaries is sufficiently certain, and the discretionary power of selection is vested in some person or persons. If no provision is made for the exercise of the discretion, the disposition is void for uncertainty.[12] Fourth, problems of uncer-

---

[4] H&M, pp. 94–116; Lewin, pp. 83–102; P&M, pp. 46–74; P&S pp. 160–168; Pettit pp. 44–56; Snell pp. 486–492; T&H pp. 55–123; U&H, pp. 97–139.

[5] *Knight v Knight* (1840) 3 Beav 148 at 173, *per* Lord Langdale MR.

[6] *Mussoorie Bank v Raynor* (1882) 7 App Cas 321 at 331, *per* Sir Arthur Hobhouse; *Re Adams and the Kensington Vestry* (1884) 27 Ch D 394. See p. 78, below.

[7] *Boyce v Boyce* (1849) 16 Sim 476.   [8] See p. 536, below.   [9] See p. 357, below.

[10] *Re Astor's Settlement Trusts* [1952] Ch 534 [see p. 359, below].   [11] See p. 91, below.

[12] *Sprange v Barnard* (1789) 2 Bro CC 585.

tainty also arise where the gift is to ascertainable beneficiaries, but their qualification is subject to a condition.[13] However, the court will adopt a common-sense approach to the construction of documents, and will seek to resolve any ambiguity in favour of upholding the trust if possible.

The rules on certainty continue to be practically necessary because, if there is uncertainty relating to the trust, it will not be possible for the court to administer it if the trustee fails to do so.

A CERTAINTY OF INTENTION

(i) General principles

In **Gold v Hill** [1999] 1 FLR 54 [p. 124, below] the deceased had said to his solicitor 'if anything happens to me you will have to sort things out. You know what to do. Look after Carol [his mistress] and the kids'. CARNWATH J, in considering whether this was sufficiently certain to create a trust, said at 64:

As to the precise terms of the trust, there is potential ambiguity in the words used, but the general intention is clear, that is to provide help for Carol to look after herself and her children. In legal terms it would be possible to interpret that in various ways . . . : a gift to the three of them jointly; a gift to Carol in the expectation (not legally enforceable) that she would use it for her and the children; or, as proposed by the amended pleading, a gift to her on trust for her and the two children. It would be unfortunate if the difficulty of distinguishing precisely between these possibilities, which are probably of little practical difference, should have the effect of defeating the gift altogether and producing a result directly contrary to Mr. Gilbert's intention.

I remind myself of what was said by Lord Upjohn in *Re Gulbenkian's Settlements* [1970] AC 508, 522 as to the task of the court in construing such documents, applying the usual canons of construction. He said:

'. . . very frequently, whether it be in wills, settlements or commercial agreements, the application of such fundamental canons leads nowhere, the draftsman has used words wrongly, his sentences border on the illiterate and his grammar may be appalling. It is then the duty of the court by the exercise of its judicial knowledge and experience in the relevant matter, innate common sense and desire to make sense of the settlor's or party's expressed intentions, however obscure and ambiguous the language that may have been used, to give a reasonable meaning to that language if it can do so without doing violence to it. The fact that the court has to see whether the clause is "certain" for a particular purpose does not disentitle the court from doing otherwise than, in the first place, trying to make sense of it.'

---

[13] *Re Allen* [1953] Ch 810; *Re Tuck's Settlement Trusts* [1978] Ch 49[p. 668, below]; *Re Barlow's Will Trusts* [1979] 1 WLR 278 [p. 104, below]. For problems of uncertainty in connection with conditions subsequent, see *Clayton v Ramsden* [1943] AC 320; *Blathwayt v Baron Cawley* [1976] AC 397; *Re Jones* [1953] Ch 125 [p. 667, below]. See generally H&M, pp. 348–354; Cheshire and Burn, *Modern Law of Real Property* (17th edn, 2006), pp. 566–581.

Applying that approach, it seems to me that the most likely interpretation of Mr. Gilbert's intentions, as expressed in the 'enrolment card' and elaborated by his conversation with Mr. Gold, was, as pleaded in the amended statement of claim, namely that he should hold them as trustee for her to apply those moneys for the use and benefit of herself and her children.

As MEGARRY J said in **Re Kayford Ltd** [1975] 1 WLR 279 at 28:

It is well settled that a trust can be created without using the word 'trust' or 'confidence' or the like: the question is whether in substance a sufficient intention to create a trust has been manifested.

This requirement is strictly applied.[14] A testator may say that he 'hopes' or 'expects' or 'has full confidence' that a legatee will apply property for the benefit of others. Somehow a line has to be drawn between requests and obligations. The approach of the courts has varied on this question. In the early nineteenth century, an intention to create a trust would readily be found.[15] Later a stricter construction was applied, the turning point usually being said to be the Court of Appeal decision in *Lambe v Eames* in 1871.[16]

Re Adams and the Kensington Vestry
(1884) 27 Ch D 394 (CA, **Baggallay, Cotton** and **Lindley LJJ**)

George Smith, the testator, provided in his will as follows: 'I give, devise, and bequeath all my real and personal estate and effects whatsoever and wheresoever unto and to the absolute use of my wife, Harriet Smith, her executors, administrators and assigns, in full confidence that she will do what is right as to the disposal thereof between my children, either in her lifetime or by will after her decease.'

The question was whether this was an absolute gift, or whether the property was subject to a trust in favour of the children.

Held. The widow took absolutely.

14 *Jones v Lock* (1865) 1 Ch App 25 [p. 151, below]; *Swiss Bank Corpn v Lloyds Bank Ltd* [1982] AC 584; *Re Multi Guarantee Co Ltd* [1987] BCLC 257. For a less strict approach, see *Paul v Constance* [1977] 1 WLR 527 [p. 153, below].   15 H&M, p. 95.

16 (1871) 6 Ch App 597. For other cases where it was held that no trust was created, see *Mussoorie Bank Ltd v Raynor* (1882) 7 App Cas 321 ('feeling confident that she will act justly to our children in dividing the same when no longer required by her'); *Re Diggles* (1888) 39 Ch D 253 ('it is my desire that she allows A.G. an annuity of £25 during her life'); *Re Hamilton* [1895] 2 Ch 370 ('I wish them to bequeath the same equally between the families of O and P'); *Re Williams* [1897] 2 Ch 12 ('in the fullest trust and confidence that she will carry out my wishes in the following particulars'); *Re Johnson* [1939] 2 All ER 458 ('I request that C on her death leave her property to my four sisters'); *Swain v Law Society* [1983] 1 AC 598 ('on behalf of all solicitors'); *Re Challoner Club Ltd* (1997) The Times, 4 November (club members' contribution to be placed in a separate bank account and not to be touched until the club's future had been resolved). See also, in the context of secret trusts, *Re Snowden* [1979] Ch 528 [p. 136, below]. Contrast *Comiskey v Bowring-Hanbury* [1905] AC 84 (testator gave to his wife 'the whole of my real and personal estate ... in full confidence that she will make such use of it as I should have made myself and that at her death she will devise it to such one or more of my nieces as she may think fit and in default of any disposition by her thereof by her will ... I hereby direct that all my estate and property acquired by her under this my will shall at her death be equally divided among the surviving said nieces'). H.L. held by a majority that there was an intention to make a gift to the wife, with an executory gift over of the whole property at her death to such of her nieces as should survive her, shared according to the wife's will, and otherwise equally. Lord Lindley (dissenting) construed the limitation as showing an intention to make an absolute gift to the wife.

Cotton LJ: The question before us is whether, upon the true construction of the will of *George Smith,* he imposed upon his wife *Harriet* a trust. Now just let us look at it, in the first instance, alone, and see what we can spell out of it, and what was expressed by the will. Reading that will, and I will not repeat it, because it has been already read, it seems to me perfectly clear what the testator intended. He leaves his wife his property absolutely, but what was in his mind was this: 'I am the head of the family, and it is laid upon me to provide properly for the members of my family—my children: my widow will succeed me when I die, and I wish to put her in the position I occupied as the person who is to provide for my children.' Not that he entails upon her any trust so as to bind her, but he simply says, in giving her this, I express to her, and call to her attention, the moral obligation which I myself had and which I feel that she is going to discharge. The motive of the gift is, in my opinion, not a trust imposed upon her by the gift in the will. He leaves the property to her; he knows that she will do what is right, and carry out the moral obligation which he thought lay on him, and on her if she survived him, to provide for the children. But it is said that the testator would be very much astonished if he found that he had given his wife power to leave the property away. That is a proposition which I should express in a different way. He would be much surprised if the wife to whom he had left his property absolutely should so act as not to provide for the children, that is to say, not to do what is right. That is a very different thing. He would have said: 'I expected that she would do what was right, and therefore I left it to her absolutely. I find she has not done what I think is right, but I cannot help it, I am very sorry that she has done so.' That would be the surprise, I think, that he would express, and feel, if he could do either, if the wife did what was unreasonable as regards the children.

But, then, it is said there is authority against that, and I am in no way disposed, if there be any definite canon or rule of construction established, to depart from that, because that must introduce great uncertainty. But undoubtedly, to my mind, in the later cases, especially *Lambe v Eames* (1871) 6 Ch App 597 and *Re Hutchinson and Tenant* (1878) 8 Ch D 540, both the Court of Appeal and the late Master of the Rolls shewed a desire really to find out what, upon the true construction, was the meaning of the testator, rather than to lay hold of certain words which in other wills had been held to create a trust, although on the will before them they were satisfied that that was not the intention. I have no hesitation in saying myself, that I think some of the older authorities went a great deal too far in holding that some particular words appearing in a will were sufficient to create a trust. Undoubtedly confidence, if the rest of the context shews that a trust is intended, may make a trust, but what we have to look at is the whole of the will which we have to construe, and if the confidence is that she will do what is right as regards the disposal of the property, I cannot say that that is, on the true construction of the will, a trust imposed upon her. Having regard to the later decisions, we must not extend the old cases in any way, or rely upon the mere use of any particular words, but, considering all the words which are used, we have to see what is their true effect, and what was the intention of the testator as expressed in his will. In my opinion, here he has expressed his will in such a way as not to shew an intention of imposing a trust on the wife, but on the contrary, in my opinion, he has shewn an intention to leave the property, as he says he does, to her absolutely.

In **Re Steele's Will Trusts**[17] [1948] Ch 603, the testatrix, who died in 1929, provided by clause 2 of her will as follows: 'I give my diamond necklace to my son to go and be held as an heirloom by him and by his eldest son on his decease and to go and descend to the

---

[17] (1968) 32 Conv (NS) 361 (P.St.J. Langan); Pettit, p. 47.

eldest son of such eldest son and so on to the eldest son of his descendants as far as the rules of law and equity will permit (and I request my said son to do all in his power by his will or otherwise to give effect to this my wish).' This provision was basically the same as that which had been held in *Shelley v Shelley* (1868) LR 6 Eq 540 to create a trust.

WYNN-PARRY J, while noting the extent to which the construction placed upon precatory expressions had changed since 1868, upheld it as creating a trust. He said at 609:

> The case of *Shelley v Shelley* has stood for eighty years and I have before me a will which, as I have already observed, is, as regards the relevant passage, couched in exactly the same language *mutatis mutandis* as that which was considered by Wood V-C in *Shelley v Shelley*. That appears to me to afford the strongest indication that the testatrix in this case, by her will, which appears clearly upon the face of it to have been a will prepared with professional aid, indicated that the diamond necklace in question should devolve in the same manner as the jewellery was directed to devolve by the order in *Shelley v Shelley*. Having regard to that strong indication of intention, and having regard to the fact that I cannot see any good reason why, notwithstanding the admitted trend of modern decisions, I should treat *Shelley v Shelley* as wrongly decided and therefore a case which I ought not to follow, I come to the conclusion that I must declare that upon the true construction of the will of the testatrix the diamond necklace should have been held upon trust for Charles Steele for his life and after his death for the second plaintiff Charles Ronald Steele for his life and after his death for David Steele, the third plaintiff, for his life and after the death of the survivor of them upon trust for the eldest son or grandson of the third plaintiff David Steele and otherwise in the manner decided in *Shelley v Shelley* including the ultimate trust in default of any male issue of David Steele (who takes an absolutely vested interest) in favour of Charles Steele absolutely and that the order in this case will follow *mutatis mutandis* the minutes which appear in the case of *Shelley v Shelley*.

(ii) Sham Trusts

When considering whether there was an intention to create a trust it is important to determine whether the intention is to create a genuine trust or a trust which is a sham or a pretence.[18]

In **Midland Bank plc v Wyatt** [1997] 1 BCLC 242, the plaintiffs obtained a charging order over the Wyatts' interest in the matrimonial home. Wyatt alleged that he had previously made a declaration of trust in respect of his interest in the home for the benefit of his wife and daughters. The plaintiff alleged that this was a sham transaction and void. DAVID YOUNG QC said at 252:

> I do not believe Mr. Wyatt had any intention, when he executed the trust deed, of endowing his children with his interest in Honer House, which at the time was his only real asset. I consider

---

[18] See *Shalson v Russo* [2005] Ch 281 [p. 81, below]; *A v A (St George Trustees Ltd) Intervening* [2007] EWHC 99 (Fam) [p. 81, below]. Note also *WT Ramsay Ltd v IRC* [1982] AC 300 where the House of Lords considered sham transactions for the purpose of tax avoidance schemes: see p. 33, above. Lord Wilberforce, at 323, said that a sham transaction professes to be one thing but is in fact something different. See also *Snook v London and West Riding Investments Ltd* [1967] 2 QB 786, 902 (Diplock LJ); *Hitch v Stone (Inspector of Taxes)* [2001] EWCA Civ 63, [2001] STC 214. See generally (2008) CLJ 176 (M. Conaglen).

the trust deed was executed by him, not to be acted upon but to be put in the safe for a rainy day. As Mr. Wyatt states in his affidavit, it was to be used as a safeguard to protect his family from long-term commercial risk, should he set up his own company. As such, I consider the declaration of trust was not what it purported to be but a pretence, or as it is sometimes referred to, a 'sham'. The fact that Mr. Wyatt executed the deed with the benefit of legal advice from Mr. Ellis does not, in my view, affect the status of the transaction. It follows that even if the deed was entered into without any dishonest or fraudulent motive, but was entered into on the basis of mistaken advice, in my judgment such a transaction will still be void and therefore an unenforceable transaction if it was not intended to be acted upon but was entered into for some different or ulterior motive. Accordingly I find that the declaration of trust sought to be relied upon by Mr. Wyatt is void and unenforceable.

In **Shalson v Russo** [2003] EWHC 1637 (Ch), [2005] Ch 281 RIMER J recognised that both the settlor and the trustee must intend the trust to be a sham. If the settlor lacks the intention to create a trust but the trustee does not, the trust can still be valid.[19]

In **A v A (St George Trustees Ltd) intervening** [2007] EWHC 99 (Fam), MUNBY J said:

41   In the present case there have been, from time to time, a number of different trustees of the trusts. The question therefore arises as to which of the trustees' intentions are relevant for this purpose. Put somewhat differently, the question arises as to whether a trust which is not a sham can subsequently become a sham and, conversely, whether a trust which is a sham can subsequently lose that character....

42   It seems to me that as a matter of principle a trust which is not initially a sham cannot subsequently become a sham...Once a trust has been properly constituted, typically by the vesting of the trust property in the trustee(s) and by the execution of the deed setting out the trusts upon which the trust property is to be held by the trustee(s), the property cannot lose its character as trust property save in accordance with the terms of the trust itself, for example, by being paid to or applied for the benefit of a beneficiary in accordance with the terms of the trust deed. Any other application of the trust property is simply and necessarily a breach of trust; nothing less and nothing more.

43   A trustee who has bona fide accepted office as such cannot divest himself of his fiduciary obligations by his own improper acts. If therefore, a trustee who has entered into his responsibilities, and without having any intention of being party to a sham, subsequently purports, perhaps in agreement with the settlor, to treat the trust as a sham, the effect is not to create a sham where previously there was a valid trust. The only effect, even if the agreement is actually carried into execution, is to expose the trustee to a claim for breach of trust and, it may well be, to expose the settlor to a claim for knowing assistance[20] in that breach of trust. Nor can it make any difference, where the trust has already been properly constituted, that a trustee may have entered into office—may indeed have been appointed a trustee in place of an honest trustee— for the very purpose and with the intention of treating the trust for the future as a sham. If, having been appointed trustee, he has the trust property under his control, he cannot be heard to dispute either the fact that it is trust property or the existence of his own fiduciary duty....

45   I turn to consider the converse case. Can a trust which is initially a sham subsequently lose that character? I see no reason in principle why that should not be possible. The situation

---

[19] See also *Chase Manhattan Equities Ltd v Goodman* [1991] BCLC 897; *Grupo Torras SA v Al Sabah* [2004] WTLR 1 (Deputy Bailiff of the Royal Court of Jersey).   [20] See p. 982, below.

is best explained by an example. S has purportedly vested property in T1 as trustee of a trust which is in fact, consistently with their common intention, a sham from the outset. T1 now wishes to retire as 'trustee'. S, executing all the appropriate documents, purports to appoint T2 as T1's successor and to transfer the 'trust property' into T2's name. Now if T2 knows that the 'trust' is a sham and accepts appointment as 'trustee' intending to perpetuate the sham, then nothing has changed. The 'trust' was a sham whilst T1 was the 'trustee' and remains a sham even though T1 has been replaced by T2. But what if T2 does not know that the 'trust' was a sham, and accepts appointment believing the ' trust' to be entirely genuine and intending to perform his fiduciary duties conscientiously and strictly in accordance with what he believes to be a genuine trust deed? I cannot see any reason why, in that situation, what was previously a sham should not become, even if only for the future, a genuine trust.

46   On the contrary, principle argues compellingly that in such circumstances there is indeed, for the future, a valid and enforceable trust. After all, in the circumstances I have postulated, the trust property has been vested in someone who accepts that he holds the property as trustee on the trusts of a document which he believes to be a genuine instrument. He has no intention that the arrangement should be a sham....

49   The corollary of all this can be stated very simply. Whatever the settlor or anyone else may have intended, and whatever may have happened since it was first created, a trust will not be a sham—in my judgment cannot as a matter of law be a sham—if *either* i) the original trustee(s), or ii) the current trustee(s), were not, because they lacked the relevant knowledge and intention, party to the sham at the time of their appointment. In the first case, the trust will never have been a sham. In the second case, the trust, even if it was previously a sham, will have become a genuine—a valid and enforceable—trust as from the date of appointment of the current trustee(s).

50   There has been some debate in the authorities as to what is required to establish the requisite common *intention*. In *Midland Bank plc v Wyatt* [1995] 1 FLR 696 [p. 80, above] the Deputy Judge, Mr David Young QC, said at page 699 that:

> ' a sham transaction will still remain a sham transaction even if one of the parties to it merely went along with the "shammer" not either knowing or caring about what he or she was signing. Such a person would still be a party to the sham and could not rely on any principle of estoppel such as was the case in *Snook*'...

What is required is a common *intention,* but reckless indifference will be taken to constitute the necessary intention.

A declaration of trust may also be set aside where it is made to defraud creditors.[21] Section 423 of the Insolvency Act 1986[22] provides that a transaction, including a gift, which was at an undervalue[23] and which was intended to put assets beyond the

---

[21] H&M, pp. 358–364; Lewin, pp. 191–197; P&M, pp. 255–262; Pettit, pp. 232–234; Snell, pp. 500–506; T&H, pp. 265–281; U&H, pp. 359–363. Note also the law on voidable preferences: Insolvency Act 1986, ss. 238, 239; *Farepak Foods and Gifts Ltd v Revenue and Customs* [2006] EWHC 3272 (Ch).

[22] See also Insolvency Act 1986, s. 339: transactions at an undervalue where the transferor is declared bankrupt within five years of the transaction, but there is no need to prove an intent to defraud creditors. See, for example, *Hill v Haines* [2007] EWCA Civ 1284, [2007] 50 EG 109 (CS). *Singla v Brown* [2007] EWHC 405 (Ch), [2008] 2 WLR 283.

[23] See *Re MC Bacon Ltd* [1990] BCLC 324; *Agricultural Mortgage Corpn plc v Woodward* [1995] 1 EGLR 1 (creation of tenancy for wife set aside, even though it was at full value, since wife achieved benefits greater than those conferred by the tenancy itself).

reach of creditors[24] or to prejudice their interests in a claim against the transferor,[25] may be set aside and the court may order any property transferred under the transaction to be returned. So, for example, if a settlor creates a settlement not for value in order to defraud creditors, this trust can be set aside and the settled property be restored to the settlor.

This is illustrated by **IRC v Hashmi** [2002] EWCA Civ 981, [2002] WTLR 1027 where a tenant had acquired the freehold and purported to declare a trust of this for his son. The tenant had been under-declaring his profits and so potentially was liable to the Inland Revenue. In concluding that he had intended to put the property beyond the reach of his creditors, ARDEN LJ said, at p. 1035:

It is sufficient if the statutory purpose can properly be described as a purpose and not merely as a consequence . . . it will often be the case that the motive to defeat creditors and the motive to secure family protection will co-exist in such a way that even the transferor himself may be unable to say what was uppermost in his mind. . . . for something to be a purpose it must be a real substantial purpose . . .

> QUESTION
>
> What is the effect of a decision that a trust is a sham? See *Hitch v Stone* [2001] EWCA Civ 63, [2001] STC 214, para.87 (Arden LJ): *A v A* [2007] EWHC 99 (Fam), paras. 56–57 (Munby J).

B   CERTAINTY OF SUBJECT MATTER

It is possible to declare a trust over all kinds of property.

In **Swift v Dairywise Farms Ltd** [2000] 1 WLR 1177[26] it was held that milk quotas (which give the holder an exemption from a levy which would otherwise be payable) could form the subject matter of a trust. In justifying this decision JACOBS J referred to the wide definition of property in section 436 of the Insolvency Act 1986:

'property' includes money, goods, things in action, land and every description of property wherever situated and also obligations and every description of interest, whether present or future or vested or contingent, arising out of, or incidental to property.[27]

---

[24] *IRC v Hashmi* [2002] EWCA Civ 981, [2002] WTLR 1027.

[25] *Hill v Spread Trustee Co Ltd* [2006] EWCA Civ 542, [2007] 1 WLR 2404 (purpose in making a settlement to induce the Revenue to make an incorrect assessment of Capital Gains Tax: within s. 423).

[26] [2000] All ER Rev 247 (P.J. Clarke).

[27] In *Don King Productions Inc. v Warren* [2000] Ch 291 the Court of Appeal accepted that personal and unassignable rights could be held on trust. Criticised [1999] LMCLQ 353 (A. Tettenborn).

However, the declaration of trust will only be valid if the subject matter of the trust can be identified with sufficient certainty.

In **Palmer v Simmonds** (1854) 2 Drew 221, the testatrix, by her will, gave her residuary estate to Thomas Harrison 'for his own use and benefit, as I have full confidence in him, that if he should die without lawful issue he will ... leave the bulk of my said residuary estate unto' certain named persons.

The expression of confidence was sufficient, according to the practice at that time, to manifest an intention to create a trust. The question was whether the subject matter of the trust was sufficiently certain. KINDERSLEY V-C held that it was not. He said at 227:

What is the meaning then of bulk? The appropriate meaning, according to its derivation, is something which bulges out, &c. [His Honour referred to *Todd's Johnson and Richardson's Dictionary* for the different meanings and etymology of the word.] Its popular meaning we all know. When a person is said to have given the bulk of his property, what is meant is not the whole but the greater part, and that is in fact consistent with its classical meaning. When, therefore, the testatrix uses that term, can I say she has used a term expressing a definite, clear, certain part of her estate, or the whole of her estate? I am bound to say she has not designated the subject as to which she expresses her confidence; and I am therefore of opinion that there is no trust created; that *Harrison* took absolutely, and those claiming under him now take.[28]

Re Golays' Will Trusts[29]
[1965] 1 WLR 969 (ChD, **Ungoed-Thomas J**)

By his will, the testator directed his executors 'to let Tossy—[whom he named]—to enjoy one of my flats during her lifetime and to receive a reasonable income from my other properties. ...' The question was whether the gift of the income was void for uncertainty.

Held. The gift was valid.

Ungoed-Thomas J: Another question that arises is whether this gift of reasonable income fails for uncertainty.

There are two classes of case with which I am concerned in interpreting this particular provision in the will: the first is where a discretion is given to specified persons to quantify the amount; the other class of case is where no such discretion is expressly conferred upon any specified person.

The question therefore comes to this: Whether the testator by the words 'reasonable income' has given a sufficient indication of his intention to provide an effective determinant of what he intends so that the court in applying that determinant can give effect to the testator's intention.

---

[28] For other testamentary gifts which failed, see *Sprange v Barnard* (1789) 2 Bro CC 585 ('the remaining part of what is left'); *Boyce v Boyce* (1849) 16 Sim 476 ('all my other houses'); *Re Jones* [1898] 1 Ch 438 ('such parts of my ... estate as she shall not have sold'); *Re Last* [1958] P 137 ('anything that is left'); *Anthony v Donges* [1998] 2 FLR 775 ('such minimal part of my estate [to which my wife is] entitled for maintenance purposes'). Cf. *T Choithram International SA v Pagarani* [2001] 1 WLR 1 (PC) left open whether a gift of 'all my wealth' was void for uncertainty.   [29] (1965) 81 LQR 481 (R.E.M.).

Whether the yardstick of 'reasonable income' were applied by trustees under a discretion given to them by a testator or applied by a court in course of interpreting and applying the words 'reasonable income' in a will, the yardstick sought to be applied by the trustees in the one case and the court in the other case would be identical. The trustees might be other than the original trustees named by the testator and the trustees could even surrender their discretion to the court. It would seem to me to be drawing too fine a distinction to conclude that an objective yardstick which different persons sought to apply would be too uncertain, not because of uncertainty in the yardstick but as between those who seek to apply it.

In this case, however, the yardstick indicated by the testator is not what he or some other specified person subjectively considers to be reasonable but what he identifies objectively as 'reasonable income'. The court is constantly involved in making such objective assessments of what is reasonable and it is not to be deterred from doing so because subjective influences can never be wholly excluded. In my view the testator intended by 'reasonable income' the yardstick which the court could and would apply in quantifying the amount so that the direction in the will is not in my view defeated by uncertainty.

Another aspect of the certainty of subject matter requirement is whether the property which is subject to the trust is itself identifiable.[30] If the trust property cannot be ascertained then the trust will be void for uncertainty.[31]

In **Hunter v Moss** [1994] 1 WLR 452,[32] the defendant was the registered owner of 950 shares in a company (MEL) with an issued share capital of 1,000 shares. He made an oral declaration of trust in favour of the plaintiff relating to 5 per cent of the company's issued share capital (i.e. 50 shares). The Court of Appeal held that the trust was not void for uncertainty.

DILLON LJ said at 457:

I pass then to the second point of uncertainty. It is well established that for the creation of a trust there must be the three certainties referred to by Lord Langdale in *Knight v Knight* (1840) 3 Beav 148. One of those is, of course, that there must be certainty of subject matter. All these shares were identical in one class: 5 per cent was 50 shares and the defendant held personally more than 50 shares.... Again, it would not be good enough for a settlor to say 'I declare that I hold 50 of my shares on trust for B', without indicating the company he had in mind of the various companies in which he held shares. There would be no sufficient certainty as to the subject matter of the trust. But here the discussion is solely about the shares of one class in the one company.

It is plain that a bequest by the defendant to the plaintiff of 50 of his ordinary shares in MEL would be a valid bequest on the defendant's death which his executors or administrators would be bound to carry into effect. Mr. Hartman sought to dispute that and to say that if, for instance, a shareholder had 200 ordinary shares in ICI and wanted to give them to A, B, C and D equally he could do it by giving 200 shares to A, B, C and D as tenants in common,

---

[30] *Westdeutsche Landesbank Girozentrale v Islington London Borough Council* [1996] AC 669 at 705 (Lord Browne-Wilkinson).

[31] *Re Stapylton Fletcher Ltd* [1994] 1 WLR 1181 and *Re Goldcorp Exchange Ltd* [1995] 1 AC 74 (PC); (1994) CLJ 443 (L.S. Sealy); [1994] All ER Rev 250 (P.J. Clarke); (1995) 9 *Trust Law International* 43, 45 (P. Birks).

[32] (1994) 110 LQR 335 (D. Hayton); (1995) 48 CLP 113 (A. Clarke); [1994] All ER Rev 249 (P.J. Clarke); (1994) CLJ 448 (M. Ockleton); [1996] Conv 223 (J. Martin).

but he could not validly do it by giving 50 shares to A, 50 shares to B, 50 shares to C and 50 shares to D, because he has not indicated which of the identical shares A is to have and which B is to have. I do not accept that. That such a testamentary bequest is valid, appears sufficiently from *Re Clifford* [1912] 1 Ch 29 and *Re Cheadle* [1900] 2 Ch 620....

Mr. Hartman, however, relied on two authorities in particular. One is a decision of Oliver J in *Re London Wine Co (Shippers) Ltd* [1986] PCC 121 which was decided in 1975. That was a case in which the business of the company was that of dealers in wine and over a period it had acquired stocks of wine which were deposited in various warehouses in England. Quantities were then sold to customers by the company, but in many instances the wine remained at the warehouse. There was no appropriation—on the ground, as it were—from bulk, of any wine, to answer particular contracts. But the customer received from the company a certificate of title for wine for which he had paid which described him as the sole and beneficial owner of such-and-such wine of such-and-such a vintage. The customer was charged for storage and insurance, but specific cases were not segregated or identified.

Subsequently, at a stage when large stocks of wine were held in various warehouses to the order of the company and its customers, a receiver was appointed by a debenture holder. The question that arose was whether the customers who had received these certificates of title had a good title to the quantity of wine referred to in the certificate as against the receiver appointed under a floating charge. The judge held that it could not be said that the legal title to the wine had passed to individual customers and the description of the wine did not adequately link it with any given consignment or warehouse. And, furthermore, it appeared that there was a lack of comparison at the time the certificates were issued in that, in some cases, the certificates were issued before the wine which had been ordered by the company had actually been received by the company. It seems to me that that case is a long way from the present. It is concerned with the appropriation of chattels and when the property in chattels passes. We are concerned with a declaration of trust, accepting that the legal title remained in the defendant and was not intended, at the time the trust was declared, to pass immediately to the plaintiff. The defendant was to retain the shares as trustee for the plaintiff.[33]

Mr. Hartman also referred to *MacJordan Construction Ltd v Brookmount Erostin Ltd* (1991) 56 BLR 1, a decision of this court. The position there was that MacJordan were sub-contractors for Brookmount as main contractors. There was retention money kept back by Brookmount which, on the documents, was to be held on a trust for the sub-contractors, but it had not been set aside as a separate fund when a receiver was appointed by the main contractor, Brookmount's bank. It was, consequently, held that MacJordan were not entitled to payment in full of the retention moneys in priority to the receiver and the secured creditor. It was common ground in that case that, prior to the appointment of the receivers, there were no identifiable assets of Brookmount impressed with the trust applicable to the retention fund. At best, there was merely a general bank account.

In reliance on that case Mr. Hartman submitted that no fiduciary relationship can attach to an unappropriated portion of a mixed fund. The only remedy is that of a floating charge.[34] He referred to a passage in the judgment of Lord Greene MR in *Re Diplock* [1948] Ch 465 at 519–520 where he said:

> 'The narrowness of the limits within which the common law operated may be linked with the limited nature of the remedies available to it... In particular, the device of a declaration of charge

---

[33] See now the Sale of Goods (Amendment) Act 1995, by virtue of which purchasers of an unascertained part of a bulk of goods take an undivided share of the bulk.   [34] See p. 945, below.

was unknown to the common law and it was the availability of that device which enabled equity to give effect to its wider conception of equitable rights.'

So Mr. Hartman submitted that the most that the plaintiff could claim is to have an equitable charge on a blended fund....

As I see it, however, we are not concerned in this case with a mere equitable charge over a mixed fund. Just as a person can give, by will, a specified number of his shares of a certain class in a certain company, so equally, in my judgment, he can declare himself trustee of 50 of his ordinary shares in MEL or whatever the company may be and that is effective to give a beneficial proprietary interest to the beneficiary under the trust. No question of a blended fund thereafter arises and we are not in the field of equitable charge.

In **Re Harvard Securities Ltd** [1997] 2 BCLC 369[35] a company purchased shares on behalf of clients and retained legal title in the shares as nominee for each client. The company went into liquidation. The question for the court was whether the clients of the company had a beneficial interest in the shares even though the shares had not been allocated to them. NEUBERGER J held that he was bound by *Hunter v Moss* and consequently it was possible to create a trust of some shares from a class of shares. He distinguished, at 384, *Hunter v Moss* from other cases which had held that trusts of unascertained goods would not be recognised[36] 'on the ground that *Hunter* was concerned with shares as opposed to chattels'.

(1994) LQR 335, 336–339 (D. Hayton)

Fortunately, there is clear authority for the case where A contracts to sell 50 of his 950 bottles of Chateau Lafite 1961 to B, who pays A the price, or purports to declare himself trustee of 50 of those 950 bottles for B. Oliver J (as he then was) in *Re London Wine Co (Shippers) Ltd* [1986] PCC 121, following the Court of Appeal in *Re Wait* [1927] 1 Ch 606, held that until 50 bottles are specifically appropriated to meet the contract, uncertainty of the specific subject matter thereof means that no proprietary interest passes to B. At some length, after full argument, he also pointed out that such a conclusion could not be avoided by any alleged constructive or express trust of 50 bottles because the subject matter of the trust would be uncertain until 50 specific bottles were set aside for B. One would therefore have thought it obvious that the intended trust of 50 shares for Hunter would have failed for want of certainty, especially when he was not a purchaser but a donee and 'equity will not assist a volunteer'; 'equity will not perfect an imperfect gift'. Indeed, 'equity follows the law', so surely one needs a specific appropriation at law and in equity where concerned with assets forming an unidentified part of a fungible bulk.

Surprisingly, Dillon LJ simply said of *Re London Wine*, 'That case is a long way from the present. It is concerned with the appropriation of chattels and when property in chattels passes. We are concerned with a declaration of trust.' A possible, old-fashioned, but surely specious, distinction (made at first instance by Colin Rimer, QC as deputy High Court judge in

---

[35] (1998–9) 9 *King's College Law Journal* 112 (T. Villiers). See also *Re CA Pacific Finance Ltd* [2000] 1 BCLC 494 (Court of First Instance, Hong Kong Special Administrative Region).

[36] Especially *Re Stapylton Fletcher Ltd* [1994] 1 WLR 1181 and *Re Goldcorp Exchange Ltd* [1995] 1 AC 74 (PC). He also referred to *Re Wait* [1927] 1 Ch 606.

Hunter v Moss [1993] 1 WLR 934 at 946) might be that one could distinguish tangibles from intangibles, but Dillon LJ did not make this distinction and, indeed, Professor Goode in (1987) 103 LQR 438 at 459 accepts *Re London Wine* as requiring separate appropriation equally for tangibles and intangibles. *Prima facie*, it seems that while all shares of a particular class must be absolutely identical, the odd bottle or two in a batch of 950 might be defective. However, such an odd distinction does not seem sufficient to justify equity going out of its way to assist a volunteer by perfecting an imperfect gift of intangibles, even if one might also argue that sections 16–19 of the Sale of Goods Act 1979 contain a comprehensive code on passing of legal and equitable title to goods so excluding liberal development of the equitable rules that is not similarly excluded for intangibles. Furthermore, will all shares in a consolidated holding of 950 shares really be identical if an incorporated parcel of 50 happens to represent a forged gratuitous transfer?

Dillon LJ then dealt with *MacJordan Construction Ltd v Brookmount Erostin Ltd* (1991) 56 BLR 1 but did not get to the heart of it. On Brookmount making interim payments to MacJordan for construction work pursuant to an architect's certificate, it was entitled to retain a percentage which it was contractually obliged to set aside in a separate trust account. It never set up such an account before going into receivership, when there was about £157,000 in its bank account and when £109,000 ought to have been set aside. Although 'equity considers as done that which ought to have been done', the Court of Appeal could not ascertain precisely which of Brookmount's money should have been set aside on trust for MacJordan so that MacJordan could not be treated as having an equitable interest in any specific part of the £157,000....

He cited *Re Clifford* [1912] 1 Ch 29 and *Re Cheadle* [1900] 2 Ch 620 for such a testamentary bequest being valid, which is indisputable. However he ignored the fact that there is a crucial difference between such a testamentary bequest, where undoubtedly the testator has effectively divested himself of his legal and beneficial ownership, and an *inter vivos* declaration of oneself as trustee for another, where the disputed question is whether or not the settlor has effectively divested himself of this beneficial ownership in specific property.

It is elementary that a bequest is a perfect gift that is completed by the testator's death. Thereupon, certain property, namely the testator's whole estate, passes to the executor, who has full ownership without distinction between legal and equitable interests therein, subject to fiduciary obligations to administer it by paying debts, expenses, taxes, etc., and then implementing the executory trusts of the testator to the extent that there is sufficient property left to satisfy such trusts. The intended beneficiaries only have an equitable chose in action until the executor has completed the administration of the estate: *Comr of Stamp Duties v Livingston* [1965] AC 694 [p. 21, above].

It follows that the only *inter vivos* situation analogous to the testamentary situation instanced by Dillon LJ is that where the settlor makes a perfect gift of specific property to a trustee so as to divest himself of legal and beneficial ownership thereof, e.g. by transferring 950 shares to a trustee and imposing equitable obligations upon the trustee to distribute 50 to X and 900 to Y.

The position is very different where the settlor, S, retains the legal title and intends to declare a trust so as to make a perfect gift to X of the equitable interest in specific property. S can intend either that X is to be equitably entitled to one-nineteenth of each of S's 950 shares, so that S and X are equitable tenants in common, or, as in *Hunter v Moss*, that X is to be exclusively entitled in equity to 50 of S's 950 shares. In the former case, X has a certain equitable interest in one-nineteenth of every share; but in the latter case S has not yet divested himself of any beneficial interest in any specific shares because he has not set aside a specific 50 shares for X, so surely the equitable gift is imperfect and X has no equitable rights in any shares. If S then changes his mind, it follows that equity will not compel him to perfect his imperfect gift by treating the latter type of intention as the former: [compare] *Milroy v Lord* (1862) 4 De G F & J 264 [p. 157, below]. In contrast, if S had declared himself trustee of 50 for X and 900 for Y, then he would have divested himself of all beneficial interest in his 950 shares. Thus, under the rule in *Saunders v Vautier* (1841) 4 Beav 115 [p. 191, below] if X and Y agreed, being between them absolutely entitled to the whole equitable interest in the 950, they could jointly call for the shares.

In **White v Shortall** [2006] NSWC 1379 although CAMPBELL J, sitting in the New South Wales Court of Appeal, did not consider the reasoning in *Hunter v Moss* to be persuasive, he did conclude that the purported declaration of a trust of 222,000 shares out of 1.5 million was valid. He said, at para. 210:

The declaration of trust left him free to deal with the parcel of 1.5 million shares as he pleased, provided that it was not reduced below 222,000, provided that any encumbrances on the shareholding were such that at least 222,000 were left unencumbered, and provided that the plaintiff was entitled to call for the transfer of 222,000 shares at any time... If there were to be any declaration of dividend or return of capital prior to the time that the plaintiff had the 222,000 shares transferred to her, the plaintiff would be entitled to receive an appropriate proportionate part of the dividend or return of capital.... A trust of this kind is not analogous to a simple trust, where a single and discrete item is held on a bare trust for a single beneficiary. Rather, it is a trust of the fund (the entire shareholding of 1.5 million shares) for two different beneficiaries... It is because the trust is construed as being of the entire shareholding that it is not necessary for the plaintiff to be able to point to some particular share and be able to say 'That share is mine.'... In the present case, one can identify the property that is subject to the trust (the entire shareholding), one can identify the trustee (the defendant), and one can identify the beneficiaries (the plaintiff as to 222,000 shares, the defendant as the to the rest). That is all that is needed for a valid trust.[37]

C CERTAINTY OF OBJECTS

Prior to *McPhail v Doulton* [1971] AC 424 [p. 91, below] the requirement for certainty of objects was expressed by one rule for trusts and another for powers. As explained above,[38] powers and trusts are different concepts. It is not inevitable that the test for validity on the grounds of certainty should be the same for each. The rule for powers was settled in *Re Gulbenkian's Settlements* [1970] AC 508 [p. 90, below] which laid down that the requirement for certainty was met if it was possible to determine with certainty whether any given individual was or was not a member of the class.[39]

[37] See p. 910, below, for an analogous analysis of equitable proprietary interests in a mixed fund.
[38] See p. 43, above.
[39] Following the formulation of the rule in *Re Gestetner Settlement* [1953] Ch 672 at 688, *per* Harman J: 'whether any given postulant is a member of the specified class'.

The rule for trusts, before *McPhail v Doulton,* was stricter. It had been laid down in *IRC v Broadway Cottages Trust*[40] that a trust was void for uncertainty unless it was possible, at the time when the trust came into operation, to make a list of all the beneficiaries, the so-called 'complete list test'. This rule was thought to be necessary in order to make a distribution possible if the trustees, in breach of their duty, failed to make a selection. The method of distribution, it was said, would be by equal division among the members of the class of beneficiaries on the principle that Equality is Equity; and equal division was only possible if it was known how many shares there would be.[41] As will be seen, *McPhail v Doulton* applied, as the test for certainty of beneficiaries under a *discretionary* trust,[42] the test which had been applied to powers in *Re Gulbenkian's Settlements.* The problem of determining the division if the trustees failed to select was not insuperable where the trustees have a discretion as to which beneficiaries will be selected: the court would find a way. The problem was artificial, in that it had never arisen in the form of trustees refusing to select beneficiaries. Rather the issue had only arisen when the trustees had asked the court whether a selection would be valid. Reluctant trustees could in any case be replaced. Further, in modern trusts with the employees of a business tycoon as beneficiaries, and not merely members of the family as was usually the case with older trusts, equal division would be absurd. The older, stricter, complete list rule, however, still applies to fixed trusts, where the interest or share of a beneficiary is laid down in the trust instrument.[43] This is because, where the trust property is to be divided among the beneficiaries in equal shares, it could, as a practical matter, only be shared equally among the members of the group of beneficiaries if it was possible to make an exact and precise list of the members. In the case of a fixed trust, therefore, the rule of *Broadway Cottages* must apply.

Finally, a word of warning about terminology. The language of the cases dealing with the requirement for certainty in trusts and powers must be read with some care. The dividing line between trusts and powers is not always made clear; the use of phrases such as 'trust powers' and 'powers in the nature of a trust',[44] shows this. Such phrases refer to trusts in which the trustees have a power of selection; as in a discretionary trust.[45] Trustees are required to exercise a trust power. This should be contrasted with a mere power, which need not be exercised.[46]

(i) Powers

In **Re Gulbenkian's Settlements** [1970] AC 508, a settlement contained a power to appoint in favour of Mr. Gulbenkian 'any wife and his children or remoter issue...and any person...in whose house or apartments or in whose company or under whose care or control or by or with whom [he] may from time to time be employed or residing'. The question was whether the power was void for uncertainty. It was unanimously upheld

[40] [1955] Ch 20.   [41] *Burrough v Philcox* (1840) 5 My & Cr 72 [p.48, above].
[42] See p. 44, above; p. 91, below.   [43] See p. 10, above.
[44] See *Breadner v Granville-Grossman* [2001] Ch 523 at 540, (Park J), p. 46, above.
[45] See [1984] Conv 227 (R. Bartlett and C. Stebbings).   [46] See p. 44, above.

by the House of Lords. A power is valid if it could be said with certainty whether any given individual was or was not a member of the class. LORD UPJOHN said at 523:

In my opinion, this clause is not void for uncertainty, and the Court of Appeal were quite right to overrule the decision of Harman J in *Re Gresham's Settlement* [1956] 1 WLR 573, where he held a similar clause was void on that ground.

My Lords, that is sufficient to dispose of the appeal, but, as I have mentioned earlier, the reasons of two members of the Court of Appeal went further and have been supported by counsel for the respondents with much force and so must be examined.

Lord Denning MR [1968] Ch 126 at 134E, propounded a test in the case of powers collateral, namely, that if you can say of one particular person meaning thereby, apparently, any one person only that he is clearly within the category the whole power is good though it may be difficult to say in other cases whether a person is or is not within the category, and he supported that view by reference to authority. Winn LJ at 138E said that where there was not a complete failure by reason of ambiguity and uncertainty the court would give effect to the power as valid rather than hold it defeated since it will have wholly failed, which put—though more broadly—the view expressed by the Master of the Rolls. Counsel for the respondents in his second line of argument relied upon these observations as a matter of principle but he candidly admitted that he could not rely upon any authority. Moreover, the Master of the Rolls at 133B, expressed the view that the different doctrine with regard to trust powers should be brought into line with the rule with regard to conditions precedent and powers collateral...

But with respect to mere powers, while the court cannot compel the trustees to exercise their powers, yet those entitled to the fund in default must clearly be entitled to restrain the trustees from exercising it save among those within the power. So the trustees or the court must be able to say with certainty who is within and who is without the power. It is for this reason that I find myself unable to accept the broader proposition advanced by Lord Denning MR and Winn LJ mentioned earlier, and agree with the proposition as enunciated in *Re Gestetner Settlement* [1953] Ch 672 and the later cases.

(ii) Discretionary Trust

(a) The Is or Is Not Test

McPhail v Doulton[47]
[1971] AC 424 (HL, Lords Reid, Hodson, Viscount Dilhorne, Lords Guest and Wilberforce)

A deed, executed on 17 July, 1941, by the settlor, Mr. Baden, provided that a fund was to be held upon certain trusts in favour of the staff of Matthew Hall and Co Ltd and their relatives and dependants.

---

[47] This case is also known as *Re Baden (No. 1)* (1970) 34 Conv (NS) 287 (F. Crane); (1971) CLJ 68 (J.A. Hopkins); (1971) CLP 133 (H. Cohen); (1971) 87 LQR 31 (J.W. Harris); (1973) 5 *New Zealand Universities Law Review* 348; (1974) 37 MLR 643 (Y.F.R. Grbich); (1973) 7 *Victoria University of Wellington Law Review* 258 (L. McKay); (1975) 4 *Anglo-American Law Review* 442 (S. Fradley); (1982) 98 LQR 551 (C.T. Emery); [1984] Conv 22 (P. Matthews), 304 (J. Martin), 307 (D. Hayton). Law Commission 8th Annual Report 1972–1973 (Law Com 1973 No. 58), para 68.

The deed provided (clause 9(a)) that the trustees should apply the net income in making grants at their absolute discretion 'to or for the benefit of any of the officers and employees or ex-officers or ex-employees of the company or to any relatives or dependants of any such persons in such amounts at such times and on such conditions (if any) as they think fit. . . .'

Two main questions arose: whether the deed created a power or a trust; and whether it was void for uncertainty. At first instance,[48] Goff J held that it was a power and not a trust and that it was valid: applying as the test of certainty that applied by the Court of Appeal in *Re Gulbenkian's Settlements:*[49] namely, that a power was valid if it was sufficiently certain to enable any one claimant to show that he comes within the description. The Court of Appeal[50] agreed (Harman and Karminski LJJ, Russell LJ dissenting) that it was a power and not a trust; but remitted the case to the Chancery Division to determine the validity upon the application of the test for certainty of powers which had been laid down by the House of Lords in *Re Gulbenkian's Settlements.*[51] The decision of the Court of Appeal was appealed to the House of Lords.

Held. The deed created a trust and not a power (Lords Hodson and Guest dissenting). The test for certainty for discretionary trusts was the same as that for powers, i.e. whether it could be said with certainty that any given individual was or was not a member of the class. The case was remitted to the Chancery Division for the determination of validity upon this basis. Brightman J upheld its validity and this was affirmed by the Court of Appeal in *Re Baden's Deed Trusts (No. 2).*[52]

Lord Wilberforce: In this House, the appellants contend, and this is the first question for consideration, that the provisions of clause 9(a) constitute a trust and not a power. If that is held to be the correct result, both sides agree that the case must return to the Chancery Division for consideration, on this footing, whether this trust is valid. But here comes a complication. In the present state of authority, the decision as to validity would turn on the question whether a complete list (or on another view a list complete for practical purposes) can be drawn up of all possible beneficiaries. This follows from the Court of Appeal's decision in *IRC v Broadway Cottages* [1955] Ch 20, as applied in later cases by which, unless this House decides otherwise, the Court of Chancery would be bound. The respondents invite your Lordships to review this decision and challenge its correctness. So the second issue which arises, if clause 9(a) amounts to a trust, is whether the existing test for its validity is right in law and, if not, what the test ought to be.

Having concluded that clause 9(a) constituted a trust [see p. 44, above] his Lordship continued:

This makes it necessary to consider whether, [in remitting the case to the Chancery Division to determine whether clause 9(a) was void for uncertainty], the court should proceed on the basis

48 [1967] 1 WLR 1457.
49 [1968] Ch 126, following *Re Allen* [1953] Ch 810; *Re Leek* [1967] Ch 1061; affd [1969] 1 Ch 563; *Re Gibbard's Will Trusts* [1967] 1 WLR 42.   50 [1969] 2 Ch 388.
51 [1970] AC 508 [p. 90, above].   52 [1973] Ch 9 [p. 97, below].

that the relevant test is that laid down in *IRC v Broadway Cottages Trust* [1955] Ch 20 or some other test.

That decision gave the authority of the Court of Appeal to the distinction between cases where trustees are given a *power* of selection and those where they are bound by a *trust* for selection. In the former case the position, as decided by this House, is that the power is valid if it can be said with certainty whether any given individual is or is not a member of the class and does not fail simply because it is impossible to ascertain every member of the class: *Re Gulbenkian's Settlements* [1970] AC 508. But in the latter case it is said to be necessary, for the trust to be valid, that the whole range of objects (I use the language of the Court of Appeal) should be ascertained or capable of ascertainment.

The respondents invited your Lordships to assimilate the validity test for trusts to that which applies to powers. Alternatively they contended that in any event the test laid down in the *Broadway Cottages* case was too rigid, and that a trust should be upheld if there is sufficient practical certainty in its definition for it to be carried out, if necessary with the administrative assistance of the court, according to the expressed intention of the settlor. I would agree with this, but this does not dispense from examination of the wider argument. The basis for the *Broadway Cottages* principle is stated to be that a trust cannot be valid unless, if need be, it can be executed by the court, and (though it is not quite clear from the judgment where argument ends and decision begins) that the court can only execute it by ordering an equal distribution in which every beneficiary shares. So it is necessary to examine the authority and reason for this supposed rule as to the execution of trusts by the court.

Assuming, as I am prepared to do for present purposes, that the test of validity is whether the trust can be executed by the court, it does not follow that execution is impossible unless there can be equal division.

As a matter of reason, to hold that a principle of equal division applies to trusts such as the present is certainly paradoxical. Equal division is surely the last thing the settlor ever intended: equal division among all may, probably would, produce a result beneficial to none. Why suppose that the court would lend itself to a whimsical execution? And as regards authority, I do not find that the nature of the trust, and of the court's powers over trusts, calls for any such rigid rule. Equal division may be sensible and has been decreed, in cases of family trusts, for a limited class; here there is life in the maxim 'equality is equity', but the cases provide numerous examples where this has not been so, and a different type of execution has been ordered, appropriate to the circumstances.

Moseley v Moseley (1673) Cas temp Finch 53 is an early example, from the time of equity's architect, where the court assumed power (if the executors did not act) to nominate from the sons of a named person as it should think fit and most worthy and hopeful, the testator's intention being that the estate should not be divided. In *Clarke v Turner* (1694) Freem Ch 198, on a discretionary trust for relations, the court decreed conveyance to the heir-at-law judging it 'most reputable for the family that the heir-at-law should have it'. In *Warburton v Warburton* (1702) 4 Bro Parl Cas 1, on a discretionary trust to distribute between a number of the testator's children, the House of Lords affirmed a decree of Lord Keeper Wright that the eldest son and heir, regarded as necessitous, should have a double share, the court exercising its own discretionary judgment against equal division.

These are examples of family trusts but in *Richardson v Chapman* (1760) 7 Bro Parl Cas 318 the same principle is shown working in a different field. There was a discretionary trust of the testator's 'options' (namely, rights of presentation to benefices or dignities in the Church) between a number of named or specified persons, including present and former chaplains and other domestics; also 'my worthy friends and acquaintance, particularly the Reverend Dr. Richardson of Cambridge'. The House of Lords (reversing Lord Keeper Henley) set aside a 'corrupt' presentation and ordered the trustees to present Dr. Richardson as the most suitable person. The grounds of decision in this House, in accordance with the prevailing practice, were not reported, but it may be supposed that the reported argument was accepted that where the court sets aside the act of the trustee, it can at the same time decree the proper act to be done, not by referring the matter to the trustee's discretion, but by directing him to perform as a mere instrument the thing decreed (ibid., 326, 327). This shows that the court can in a suitable case execute a discretionary trust according to the perceived intention of the trustee. It is interesting also to see that it does not seem to have been contended that the trust was void because of the uncertainty of the words 'my worthy friends and acquaintance'. There was no doubt that Dr. Richardson came within the designation.

In the time of Lord Eldon, the Court of Chancery adopted a less flexible practice: in *Kemp v Kemp* (1795) 5 Ves 849 Sir Richard Arden MR, commenting on *Warburton v Warburton* (1702) 4 Bro Parl Cas 1 ('a very extraordinary' case), said that the court now disclaims the right to execute a power (i.e. a trust power) and gives the fund equally. But I do not think that this change of attitude, or practice, affects the principle that a discretionary trust *can*, in a suitable case, be executed according to its merits and otherwise than by equal division. I prefer not to suppose that the great masters of equity, if faced with the modern trust for employees, would have failed to adapt their creation to its practical and commercial character. Lord Eldon himself, in *Morice v Bishop of Durham* (1805) 10 Ves 522, laid down clearly enough that a trust fails if the object is insufficiently described or if it cannot be carried out, but these principles may be fully applied to trust powers without requiring a complete ascertainment of all possible objects. His earlier judgment in the leading, and much litigated, case of *Brown v Higgs* (1803) 8 Ves 561 shows that he was far from fastening any rigid test of validity upon trust powers. After stating the distinction, which has ever since been followed, between powers, which the court will not require the donee to execute, and powers in the nature of a trust, or trust powers, he says of the latter that if the trustee does not discharge it, the court will, *to a certain extent,* discharge the duty in his room and place. To support this, he cites *Harding v Glyn* (1739) 1 Atk 469, an early case where the court executed a discretionary trust for 'relations' by distributing to the next-of-kin.

I dwell for a moment upon this point because, not only was *Harding v Glyn* described by Lord Eldon 8 Ves 561 at 570 as having been treated as a clear authority in his experience for a long period, but the principle of it was adopted in several nineteenth-century authorities. When the *Broadway Cottages Trust* case came to be decided in 1955, these cases were put aside as anomalous (see [1955] Ch 20 at 33, 35), but I think they illustrate the flexible manner in which the court, if called on, executes trust powers for a class. At least they seem to prove that the supposed rule as to equal division does not rest on any principle inherent in the nature of a trust. They prompt me to ask why a practice, or rule, which has been long followed and found useful in 'relations' cases should not also serve in regard to 'employees', or 'employees and their relatives', and whether a decision which says the contrary is acceptable.

I now consider the modern English authorities, particularly those relied on to show that complete ascertainment of the class must be possible before it can be said that a discretionary trust is valid.

Re Ogden [1933] Ch 678 is not a case which I find of great assistance. The argument seems to have turned mainly on the question whether the trust was a purpose trust or a trust for ascertained objects. The latter was held to be the case and the court then held that all the objects of the discretionary gift could be ascertained. It is weak authority for the requirement of complete ascertainment.

The modern shape of the rule derives from *Re Gestetner Settlement* [1953] Ch 672, where the judgment of Harman J, to his later regret, established the distinction between discretionary powers and discretionary trusts. The focus of this case was upon powers. The judgment first establishes a distinction between, on the one hand, a power collateral, or appurtenant, or other powers 'which do not impose a trust on the conscience of the donee' (at 684), and on the other hand a trust imposing a duty to distribute. As to the first, the learned judge said: 'I do not think it can be the law that it is necessary to know of all the objects in order to appoint to one of them'. As to the latter he uses these words, at 685: 'it seems to me there is much to be said for the view that he must be able to review the whole field in order to exercise his judgment properly'. He then considers authority on the validity of powers, the main stumbling-block in the way of his own view being some words used by Fry J in *Blight v Hartnoll* (1881) 19 Ch D 294 at 301, which had been adversely commented on in *Farwell on Powers* (3rd edn, at pp. 168, 169), and I think it worth while quoting the words of his conclusion. He says [1953] Ch 672 at 688, 689:

> 'The settlor had good reason, I have no doubt, to trust the persons whom he appointed trustees; but I cannot see here that there is such a duty as makes it essential for these trustees, before parting with any income or capital, to survey the whole field, and to consider whether A is more deserving of bounty than B. That is a task which was and which must have been known to the settlor to be impossible, having regard to the ramifications of the persons who might become members of this class.
>
> If, therefore, there be no duty to distribute, but only a duty to consider, it does not seem to me that there is any authority binding on me to say that this whole trust is bad. In fact, there is no difficulty, as has been admitted, in ascertaining whether any given postulant is a member of the specified class. Of course, if that could not be ascertained the matter would be quite different, but of John Doe or Richard Roe it can be postulated easily enough whether he is or is not eligible to receive the settlor's bounty. There being no uncertainty in that sense, I am reluctant to introduce a notion of uncertainty in the other sense, by saying that the trustees must worry their heads to survey the world from China to Peru, when there are perfectly good objects of the class in England.'

Subject to one point which was cleared up in this House in *Re Gulbenkian's Settlements* [1970] AC 508, all of this, if I may say so, seems impeccably good sense, and I do not understand the learned judge to have later repented of it. If the judgment was in any way the cause of future difficulties, it was in the indication given—not by way of decision, for the point did not arise—that there was a distinction between the kind of certainty required for powers and that required for trusts. There is a difference perhaps but the difference is a narrow one, and if one is looking to reality one could hardly find better words than those I have just quoted to describe what trustees, in either case, ought to know. A second look at this case, while fully justifying the decision, suggests to me that it does not discourage the application of a similar test for the validity of trusts.

So I come to *IRC v Broadway Cottages Trust* [1955] Ch 20. This was certainly a case of trust, and it proceeded on the basis of an admission, in the words of the judgment, 'that the class of "beneficiaries" is incapable of ascertainment'. In addition to the discretionary trust of income, there was a trust of capital for all the beneficiaries living or existing at the terminal date. This necessarily involved equal division and it seems to have been accepted that it was void for uncertainty since there cannot be equal division among a class unless all the members of the class are known. The Court of Appeal applied this proposition to the discretionary trust of income, on the basis that execution by the court was only possible on the same basis of equal division. They rejected the argument that the trust could be executed by changing the trusteeship, and found the relations cases of no assistance as being in a class by themselves. The court could not create an arbitrarily restricted trust to take effect in default of distribution by the trustees. Finally they rejected the submission that the trust could take effect as a power: a valid power could not be spelt out of an invalid trust.

My Lords, it will have become apparent that there is much in this which I find out of line with principle and authority but before I come to a conclusion on it, I must examine the decision of this House in *Re Gulbenkian's Settlements* on which the appellants placed much reliance as amounting to an endorsement of the *Broadway Cottages* case. But is this really so?

[His Lordship examined the case and continued:] What this does say, and I respectfully agree, is that, in the case of a trust, the trustees must select from the class. What it does not say, as I read it, or imply, is that in order to carry out their duty of selection they must have before them, or be able to get, a complete list of all possible objects.

So I think that we are free to review the *Broadway Cottages* case. The conclusion which I would reach, implicit in the previous discussion, is that the wide distinction between the valid-ity test for powers and that for trust powers is unfortunate and wrong, that the rule recently fastened upon the courts by *IRC v Broadway Cottages Trust* ought to be discarded, and that the test for the validity of trust powers ought to be similar to that accepted by this House in *Re Gulbenkian's Settlements* for powers, namely, that the trust is valid if it can be said with certainty that any given individual is or is not a member of the class.

I am interested, and encouraged, to find that the conclusion I had reached by the end of the argument is supported by distinguished American authority. Professor Scott in his well-known book on trusts (*Scott on Trusts* (1939)) discusses the suggested distinction as regards validity between trusts and powers and expresses the opinion that this would be 'highly technical' (s. 122, p. 613). Later in the second *Restatement of Trusts* (1959), s. 122 (which *Restatement* aims at stating the better modern view and which annotates the *Broadway Cottages* case), a common test of invalidity is taken, whether trustees are 'authorised' or 'directed': this is that the class must not be so indefinite that it cannot be ascertained whether any person falls within it. The reporter is Professor Austin Scott. In his abridgement, published in 1960 (*Scott's Abridgment of The Law of Trusts,* s. 122, p. 239), Professor Scott maintains the same position:

> 'It would seem that if a power of appointment among the members of an indefinite class is valid, the mere fact that the testator intended not merely to confer a power but to impose a duty to make such an appointment should not preclude the making of such an appointment. It would seem to be the height of technicality that if a testator *authorises* a legatee to divide the property among such of the testator's friends as he might select, he can properly do so, but that if he *directs* him to make such a selection, he will not be permitted to do so.'

Assimilation of the validity test does not involve the complete assimilation of trust pow-ers with powers. As to powers, I agree with my noble and learned friend Lord Upjohn in *Re Gulbenkian's Settlements* that although the trustees may, and normally will, be under a fiduciary duty to consider whether or in what way they should exercise their power, the court will not normally compel its exercise. It will intervene if the trustees exceed their powers, and possibly if they are proved to have exercised it capriciously. But in the case of a trust power, if the trustees do not exercise it, the court will: I respectfully adopt as to this the statement in Lord Upjohn's opinion at 525. I would venture to amplify this by saying that the court, if called upon to execute the trust power, will do so in the manner best calculated to give effect to the settlor's or testator's intentions. It may do so by appointing new trustees, or by authorising or directing representative persons of the classes of beneficiaries to prepare a scheme of distribution, or even, should the proper basis for distribution appear by itself directing the trustees so to distribute.[53] The books give many instances where this has been done, and I see no reason in principle why they should not do so in the modern field of discretionary trusts (see *Brunsden v Woolredge* (1765) Amb 507; *Supple v Lowson* (1773) Amb 729; *Liley v Hey* (1842) 1 Hare 580 and *Lewin on Trusts* (16th edn, 1964) p. 630). Then, as to the trustees' duty of inquiry or ascertainment, in each case the trustees ought to make such a survey of the range of objects or possible beneficiaries as will enable them to carry out their fiduciary duty (cf. *Liley v Hey*). A wider and more comprehensive range of inquiry is called for in the case of trust powers than in the case of powers.

Two final points: first, as to the question of certainty. I desire to emphasise the distinction clearly made and explained by Lord Upjohn at 524, between linguistic or semantic uncertainty which, if unresolved by the court, renders the gift void, and the difficulty of ascertaining the existence or whereabouts of members of the class, a matter with which the court can appropriately deal on an application for directions. There may be a third case where the meaning of the words used is clear but the definition of beneficiaries is so hopelessly wide as not to form 'anything like a class' so that the trust is administratively unworkable or in Lord Eldon's words one that cannot be executed: *Morice v Bishop of Durham* (1805) 10 Ves 522 at 527. I hesitate to give examples for they may prejudice future cases, but perhaps 'all the residents of Greater London' will serve. I do not think that a discretionary trust for 'relatives' even of a living person falls within this category.[54]

I would allow the appeal. . . .

On remittance to the Chancery Division, BRIGHTMAN J and the Court of Appeal (SACHS, MEGAW and STAMP LJJ) in **Re Baden's Deed Trusts (No 2)** [1973] Ch 9[55] found that the test for certainty was satisfied. The wide differences in their application of the test demonstrates how difficult it may prove to be in practice.

Sachs LJ: The next point as regards [this] approach that requires consideration is the contention, strongly pressed by Mr. Vinelott, that the court must always be able to say whether any

---

[53] In *Re Locker's Settlement* [1977] 1 WLR 1323 the existing trustees of an exhaustive discretionary trust, who had failed to make annual distribution of income, were nevertheless allowed to apply their discretion in the distribution of the income, but 'only in favour of such objects or some or one of them as would have been objects of the said discretion had it been exercised within a reasonable time after receipt of the income' (*per* Goulding J at 1327); [1978] Conv 166 (F.R. Crane); (1978) 94 LQR 177. The court has similar powers of intervention in the case of a fiduciary power: *Mettoy Pension Trustees Ltd v Evans* [1990] 1 WLR 1587 [p. 55, above].

[54] See *Blausten v IRC* [1972] Ch 256 at 271–273, where some of these points are further discussed; *Re Manisty's Settlement* [1974] Ch 17 at 27–29, where Templeman J, discussing this point in the context of intermediate powers (i.e. a power to appoint to anybody except certain people or groups of people), said, at 27: 'a power to benefit residents of Greater London is capricious because the terms of the power negative any sensible intention on the part of the settlor'; (1974) 38 Conv (NS) 269 (L. McKay); *Re Hay's Settlement Trusts* [1982] 1 WLR 202 [p. 49, above] (where Megarry V-C 'thought that he would, if necessary, hold' that an intermediate discretionary trust would be void for administrative unworkability); [1982] Conv 432 (A. Grubb); *R v District Auditor, ex p West Yorkshire Metropolitan County Council* [1986] RVR 24 [p. 102 below].

[55] (1973) 36 Conv (NS) 351 (D.J. Hayton); (1973) CLJ 36 (J.A. Hopkins); *Re Bethel* (1971) 17 DLR (3d) 652; (1971) *Annual Survey of Commonwealth Law* 377; (1981) 9 *Sydney Law Review* 58 (R.P. Austin).

given postulant is *not* within the relevant class as well as being able to say whether he is within it. In construing the words already cited from the speech of Lord Wilberforce in the *Baden* case (as well as those of Lord Reid and Lord Upjohn in the *Gulbenkian* case), it is essential to bear in mind the difference between conceptual uncertainty and evidential difficulties...[56]

As Mr. Vinelott himself rightly observed, 'the court is never defeated by evidential uncertainty', and it is in my judgment clear that it is conceptual certainty to which reference was made when the 'is or is not a member of the class' test was enunciated. (Conceptual uncertainty was in the course of argument conveniently exemplified, rightly or wrongly matters not, by the phrase 'someone under a moral obligation' and contrasted with the certainty of the words 'first cousins'.) Once the class of person to be benefited is conceptually certain it then becomes a question of fact to be determined on evidence whether any postulant has on inquiry been proved to be within it: if he is not so proved, then he is not in it. That position remains the same whether the class to be benefited happens to be small (such as 'first cousins') or large (such as 'members of the X Trade Union' or 'those who have served in the Royal Navy'). The suggestion that such trusts could be invalid because it might be impossible to prove of a given individual that he was *not* in the relevant class is wholly fallacious—and only Mr. Vinelott's persuasiveness has prevented me from saying that the contention is almost unarguable...

In agreement with the practical approach of Brightman J [1972] Ch 607 at 625, I consider that the trustees, or if necessary the court, are quite capable of coming to a conclusion in any given case as to whether or not a particular candidate could properly be described as a dependant—a word that, as the judge said, 'conjures up a sufficiently distinct picture'. I agree, too, that any one wholly or partly dependent on the means of another is a 'dependant'. There is thus no conceptual uncertainty inherent in that word and the executors' contentions as to the effect of its use fail.

As regards 'relatives' Brightman J, after stating, at 625, 'it is not in dispute that a person is a relative of an...employee..., if both trace legal descent from a common ancestor': a little later said: 'in practice, the use of the expression "relatives" cannot cause the slightest difficulty'. With that view I agree for the reasons he gave when he correctly set out the evidential position.

Megaw LJ: The main argument of Mr. Vinelott was founded upon a strict and literal interpretation of the words in which the decision of the House of Lords in *Re Gulbenkian's Settlements* [1970] AC 508 was expressed. That decision laid down the test for the validity of powers of selection. It is relevant for the present case, because in the previous excursion of this case to the House of Lords [1971] AC 424 it was held that there is no relevant difference in the test of validity, whether the trustees are given a power of selection or, as was held by their Lordships to be the case in this trust deed, a trust for selection. The test in either case is what may be called the *Gulbenkian* test. The *Gulbenkian* test, as expressed by Lord Wilberforce at 450, and again in almost identical words at 454, is this:

> '...the power is valid if it can be said with certainty whether any given individual is or is not a member of the class and does not fail simply because it is impossible to ascertain every member of the class.'

---

[56] In *Re Tuck's Settlement Trusts* [1978] Ch 49 at 60, Lord Denning MR described this distinction as a 'deplorable dichotomy', serving only to defeat the settlor's intention. But the distinction was acknowledged by HL in *Blathwayt v Baron Cawley* [1976] AC 397 at 425.

The executors' argument concentrates on the words 'or is not' in the first of the two limbs of the sentence quoted above: 'if it can be said with certainty whether any given individual is *or is not* a member of the class'. It is said that those words have been used deliberately, and have only one possible meaning; and that, however startling or drastic or unsatisfactory the result may be—and Mr. Vinelott does not shrink from saying that the consequence is drastic—this court is bound to give effect to the words used in the House of Lords' definition of the test. It would be quite impracticable for the trustees to ascertain in many cases whether a particular person was *not* a relative of an employee. The most that could be said is: 'there is no proof that he is a relative'. But there would still be no 'certainty' that such a person was not a relative. Hence, so it is said, the test laid down by the House of Lords is not satisfied, and the trust is void. For it cannot be said with certainty, in relation to any individual, that he is not a relative.

I do not think it was contemplated that the words 'or is not' would produce that result. It would, as I see it, involve an inconsistency with the latter part of the same sentence: 'does not fail simply because it is impossible to ascertain every member of the class'. The executors' contention, in substance and reality, is that it *does* fail 'simply because it is impossible to ascertain every member of the class'.

The same verbal difficulty, as I see it, emerges also when one considers the words of the suggested test which the House of Lords expressly rejected. That is set out by Lord Wilberforce in a passage immediately following the sentence which I have already quoted. The rejected test was in these terms [1971] AC 424 at 450: '... it is said to be necessary ... that the whole range of objects ... should be ascertained or capable of ascertainment'. Since that test was rejected, the resulting affirmative proposition, which by implication must have been accepted by their Lordships, is this: a trust for selection will not fail simply because the whole range of objects cannot be ascertained. In the present case, the trustees could ascertain, by investigation and evidence, many of the objects: as to many other theoretically possible claimants, they could not be certain. Is it to be said that the trust fails because it cannot be said with certainty that such persons are not members of the class? If so, is that not the application of the rejected test: the trust failing because 'the whole range of objects cannot be ascertained'?

In my judgment, much too great emphasis is placed in the executor's argument on the words 'or is not'. To my mind, the test is satisfied if, as regards at least a substantial number of objects, it can be said with certainty that they fall within the trust; even though, as regards a substantial number of other persons, if they ever for some fanciful reason fell to be considered, the answer would have to be, not 'they are outside the trust', but 'it is not proven whether they are in or out'. What is a 'substantial number' may well be a question of common sense and of degree in relation to the particular trust: particularly where, as here, it would be fantasy, to use a mild word, to suggest that any practical difficulty would arise in the fair, proper and sensible administration of this trust in respect of relatives and dependants.

I do not think that this involves, as Mr. Vinelott suggested, a return by this court to its former view which was rejected by the House of Lords in the *Gulbenkian* case. If I did so think, I should, however reluctantly, accept Mr. Vinelott's argument and its consequences. But as I read it, the criticism in the House of Lords of the decision of this court in that case related to this court's acceptance of the view that it would be sufficient if it could be shown that *one single person* fell within the scope of the power or trust. The essence of the decision of the House of Lords in the *Gulbenkian* case, as I see it, is *not* that it must be possible to show with certainty that any given person *is* or *is not* within the trust; but that it is not, or may not be, sufficient to be able to show that one individual person is within it. If it does not mean that, I do not know where the line is supposed to be drawn, having regard to the clarity and emphasis with which the House of Lords has laid down that the trust does not fail because the whole range of objects cannot be ascertained.

I would dismiss the appeal.

Stamp LJ: Mr. Vinelott, fastening on those words, 'if it can be said with certainty that any given individual is or is not a member of the class', submitted in this court that a trust for distribution among officers and employees or ex-officers or ex-employees or any of their relatives or dependants does not satisfy the test. You may say with certainty that any given individual is or is not an officer, employee, ex-officer or ex-employee. You may say with certainty that a very large number of given individuals are relatives of one of them; but, so the argument runs, you will never be able to say with certainty of many given individuals that they are not. I am bound to say that I had thought at one stage of Mr. Vinelott's able argument that this was no more an exercise in semantics and that the phrase on which he relies indicated no more than that the trust was valid if there was such certainty in the definition of membership of the class that you could say with certainty that some individuals were members of it: that it was sufficient that you should be satisfied that a given individual presenting himself has or has not passed the test and that it matters not that having failed to establish his membership—here his relationship—you may, perhaps wrongly, reject him. There are, however, in my judgment serious difficulties in the way of a rejection of Mr. Vinelott's submission.

The first difficulty, as I see it, is that the rejection of Mr. Vinelott's submission involves holding that the trust is good if there are individuals—or even one—of whom you can say with certainty that he is a member of the class. That was the test adopted by and the decision of the Court of Appeal in the *Gulbenkian* case where what was under consideration was a power of distribution among a class conferred upon trustees as distinct from a trust for distribution: but when the *Gulbenkian* case came before the House of Lords that test was decisively rejected and the more stringent test upon which Mr. Vinelott insists was adopted. Clearly Lord Wilberforce in expressing the view that the test of validity of a discretionary trust ought to be similar to that accepted by the House of Lords in the *Gulbenkian* case did not take the view that it was sufficient that you could find individuals who were clearly members of the class; for he himself remarked, towards the end of his speech as to the trustees' duty of inquiring or ascertaining, that in each case the trustees ought to make such a survey of the range of objects or possible beneficiaries as will enable them to carry out their fiduciary duty. It is not enough that trustees should do nothing but distribute the fund among those objects of the trust who happen to be at hand or present themselves. Lord Wilberforce, after citing that passage which I have already quoted from the speech of Lord Upjohn in the *Gulbenkian* case, put it more succinctly by remarking that what this did say (and he agreed) was that the trustees must select from the class, but that passage did not mean (as had been contended) that they must be able to get a complete list of all possible objects. I have already called attention to Lord Wilberforce's opinion that the trustees ought to make such a survey of the range of objects or possible beneficiaries as will enable them to carry out their fiduciary duty, and I ought perhaps to add that he indicated that a wider and more comprehensive range of inquiry is called for in the case of what I have called discretionary trusts than in the case of fiduciary powers. But, as I understand it, having made the appropriate survey, it matters not that it is not complete or fails to yield a result enabling you to lay out a list or particulars of every single beneficiary. Having done the best they can, the trustees may proceed upon the basis similar to that adopted by the court where all the beneficiaries cannot be ascertained and distribute upon the footing that they have been: see, for example, *Re Benjamin* [1902] 1 Ch 723. What was referred to as 'the complete ascertainment test' laid down by this court in the *Broadway Cottages* case is rejected. So also is the test laid down by this court in the *Gulbenkian* case. Validity or invalidity is to depend upon whether you can say of any individual — and the accent must be upon that word 'any', for it is not simply the individual whose claim you are considering who is spoken of—'is or is not a member of the class', for only thus can you make a survey of the range of objects or possible beneficiaries.

If the matter rested there, it would in my judgment follow that, treating the word 'relatives' as meaning descendants from a common ancestor, a trust for distribution such as is here in question would not be valid. Any 'survey of the range of the objects or possible beneficiaries' would certainly be incomplete, and I am able to discern no principle upon which such a survey could be conducted or where it should start or finish. The most you could do, so far as regards relatives, would be to find individuals who are clearly members of the class—the test which was accepted in the Court of Appeal, but rejected in the House of Lords, in the *Gulbenkian* case.

The matter does not, however, rest there . . . *Harding v Glyn* (1739) 1 Atk 469 . . . was an early case where the court executed a discretionary trust for 'relations'—and it is a discretionary trust for relations that I am considering—by distributing to the next of kin in equal shares[57] . . .

Harding v Glyn accordingly cannot be regarded simply as a case where in default of appointment a gift to the next-of-kin is to be implied as a matter of construction, but as authority endorsed by the decision of the House of Lords [1971] AC 424, that a discretionary trust for 'relations' was a valid trust to be executed by the court by distribution to the next-of-kin. The class of beneficiaries thus becomes a clearly defined class and there is no difficulty in determining whether a given individual is within it or without it.

Does it then make any difference that here the discretionary trust for relations was a reference not to the relations of a deceased person but of one who was living? I think not. The next-of-kin of a living person are as readily ascertainable at any given time as the next-of-kin of one who is dead.

Hackney: *Understanding Equity and Trusts* (1987), pp. 58–59

Since courts are prepared to strike down dispositions in favour of classes of objects on the grounds that the objects are too uncertain, they have signalled that the settlor's views, or those of the trustees, are not conclusive on the question of validity. Here, as in the matter of intention and subject matter, a number of interests are at stake, some of them conflicting. Settlors have their own conflicting interests. In general terms they want a relaxed test, as that will result in a greater chance of their dispositions being held valid. But they do not want too relaxed a test, as they do not want trustees to be able to play fast and loose with their intentions. Objects or potential objects (those within range of the settlor's benevolent intentions) have a similar dilemma: wide tests will increase their chances of qualifying, but once qualified they will not want a test so wide that they cannot easily calculate their chances of success if they wish to challenge a particular appointment by a trustee on the grounds that the appointee was a non-object. The trustee's selfish interest is in a tightly drawn test. He must administer the trust properly, according to its terms. A conscientious trustee will want a test that allows him to do that with a minimum of doubt, and of course he faces the unique difficulty that if he pays to the wrong objects either on a valid or invalid trust or power, he will have to make good the deficit, and though courts have power to excuse him, they do not always do so. A trustee in sympathy with the aims of the settlor will be likely to want a test which is less strict, and so he too will settle for

---

[57] Cf *Re Barlow's Will Trusts* [1979] 1 WLR 278 [p. 104, below], where 'relations' was held to mean everyone related by blood to the testatrix.

a compromise. The public interest is in having a test which does not result in continuous litiga-tion. Litigation is a particular evil in this part of the law, which is overwhelmingly dominated by planning considerations. The ideal is that the law should be capable of formulation in such a way that legal advisers can produce instruments that are free of legal defect and which can operate entirely outside the court. Until court lists are much reduced, courts have better things to do than involve themselves in the luxury of avoidable disputes about certainty of objects, which both hold up other business and cost money to beneficiaries. It is an abuse of judicial power for a judge to say he is happy to have a relaxed test in the interests of enhancing settlors' wishes, and that if anyone has any problem with operating it, all they have to do is go along to see him. The public also presumably has some input in the kind of freedom of disposition which they are happy for settlors to have, and this may differ from the freedom they might themselves wish, were they not considering the public interest.

(b) Administrative Unworkability. Capricious

In **R v District Auditor, ex p West Yorkshire Metropolitan County Council** [1986] RVR 24,[58] a local authority resolved to create a trust under which the trustees were 'to apply and expend the Trust Fund for the benefit of any or all or some of the inhabitants of the County of West Yorkshire' in four specified ways. It was conceded that this was not a charitable trust, because one of its objects, the dissemination of information about the proposed abolition of the metropolitan county councils, was not charitable.[59] In holding that the trust could not take effect as an express private trust, LLOYD LJ said at 26:

Counsel for the county council did not seek to argue that the trust is valid as a charitable trust, though he did not concede the point in case he should have second thoughts in a higher court. His case was that the trust could take effect as an express private trust. For the creation of an express private trust three things are required. First, there must be a clear intention to create the trust. Secondly there must be certainty as to the subject matter of the trust; and thirdly there must be certainty as to the persons intended to benefit. Two of the three certainties, as they are familiarly called, were present here. Was the third? He argued that the beneficiaries of the trust were all or some of the inhabitants of the county of West Yorkshire. The class might be on the large side, containing as it does some 2½ million potential beneficiaries. But the defini-tion, it was said, is straightforward and clear-cut. There is no uncertainty as to the concept. If anyone were to come forward and claim to be a beneficiary, it could be said of him at once whether he was within the class or not.

I cannot accept counsel for the county council's argument. I am prepared to assume in favour of the council, without deciding, that the class is defined with sufficient clarity. I do not decide the point because it might, as it seems to me, be open to argument what is meant by 'an inhabit-ant' of the county of West Yorkshire. But I put that difficulty on one side. For there is to my mind a more fundamental difficulty. A trust with as many as 2½ million potential beneficiaries is, in my judgment, quite simply unworkable. The class is far too large. In *Re Gulbenkian's Settlements* [1970] AC 508 Lord Reid said at 518:

'It may be that there is a class of case where, although the description of a class of beneficiaries is clear enough, any attempt to apply it to the facts would lead to such administrative difficulties that it would for that reason be held to be invalid.'

[58] (1986) CLJ 391 (C. Harpum).   [59] See p. 536, below.

His Lordship quoted Lord Wilberforce's final paragraph in *McPhail v Doulton* [1971] AC 424 at 457 [p. 97, above] and continued:

It seems to me that the present trust comes within the third case to which Lord Wilberforce refers. I hope I am not guilty of being prejudiced by the example which he gave. But it could hardly be more apt, or fit the facts of the present case more precisely.

I mention the subsequent decisions in *Re Baden's Deed Trusts (No 2)* [1972] Ch 607, and on appeal [1973] Ch 9 [p. 97, above] and *Re Manisty's Settlement* [1974] Ch 17 [p. 50] with misgiving, since they were not cited in argument. The latter was a case of an intermediate power, that is to say, a power exercisable by trustees in favour of all the world, other than members of an excepted class. After referring to *Gulbenkian* and the two *Baden* cases, Templeman J (as he then was) said:

'I conclude...that a power cannot be uncertain merely because it is wide in ambit.'

A power to benefit, for example, the residents of Greater London might, he thought, be bad, not on the ground of its width but on the ground of capriciousness, since the settlor could have no sensible intention to benefit 'an accidental conglomeration of persons' who had 'no discernible link with the settlor'. But that objection could not apply here. The council had every reason for wishing to benefit the inhabitants of West Yorkshire.

Lord Wilberforce's dictum has also been the subject of a good deal of academic comment and criticism, noticeably by L. McKay (1974) 38 Conv 269 and C.T. Emery (1982) 98 LQR 551. I should have welcomed further argument on these matters, but through no fault of counsel for the county council this was not possible. So I have to do the best I can.

My conclusion is that the dictum of Lord Wilberforce remains of high persuasive authority, despite *Re Manisty*. *Manisty's* case was concerned with a power, where the function of the court is more restricted. In the case of a trust, the court may have to execute the trust. Not so in the case of a power. That there may still be a distinction between trusts and powers in this connection was recognised by Templeman J himself in the sentence immediately following his quotation of Lord Wilberforce's dictum, when he said:

'In these guarded terms Lord Wilberforce appears to refer to trusts which may have to be executed and administered by the court and not to powers where the court has a very much more limited function.'

There can be no doubt that the declaration of trust in the present case created a trust and not a power. Following Lord Wilberforce's dictum, I would hold that the definition of the beneficiaries of the trust is 'so hopelessly wide' as to be incapable of forming 'anything like a class'. I would therefore reject counsel for the county council's argument that the declaration of trust can take effect as an express private trust.

Since, as I have already said, it was not argued that the trust can take effect as a valid charitable trust, it follows that the declaration of trust is ineffective. What we have here, in a nutshell, is a non-charitable purpose trust. It is clear law that, subject to certain exceptions, such trusts are void: see *Lewin on Trusts*, 16th edn, pp. 17–19.[60] The present case does not come within any of the established exceptions. Nor can it be brought within the scope of such recent decisions as *Re Denley's Trust Deed* [1969] 1 Ch 373 [p. 375, below] and *Re Lipinski's*

---

[60] See Chapter 9, below.

Will Trusts [1976] Ch 235 [p. 372, below] since there are, for the reasons I have given, no ascertained or ascertainable beneficiaries.[61]

(c) Many Certain Categories; One Uncertain

Hanbury & Martin: *Modern Equity* (17th edn, 2005), p. 114

Further difficulties could arise with a definition of a class of beneficiaries which contained a long series of categories which complied with the *McPhail v Doulton* test, but to which there was added one category which did not. What, for example, would the court say to a trust in the same language as that in *McPhail v Doulton* but to which there was added 'any person to whom I may be under a moral obligation and any of my old friends'? ... which is, let it be assumed, conceptually uncertain. The same problem could arise in a case of power.

In this situation, the class as the whole does not satisfy the test. It would however be unfortunate to declare the whole trust void because of the final addition. After all, the trust is workable as it is. Such a trust, however, may be held void unless it is possible to excise the offending phrase by severance; this suggestion has sometimes been made,[62] but the severance principle has yet to be established. Thus in *Re Wright's Will Trusts*,[63] where the class consisted of identifiable named charities and other bodies which could not be identified, the Court of Appeal refused to give effect to the gift in favour of the named charities only.

(iii) Gift Subject to a Condition Precedent

In **Re Barlow's Will Trusts** [1979] 1 WLR 278,[64] the testatrix died in 1975, owning a large collection of valuable pictures. By her will she gave some of them to her executor upon trust for sale, and added a direction to him 'to allow any member of my family and any friends of mine who may wish to do so to purchase any of such pictures' at a valuation made in 1970 or at probate value whichever should be the lower.

In holding that the direction was valid, Browne-Wilkinson J said at 280:

The main questions which arise for my decision are (a) whether the direction to allow members of the family and friends to purchase the pictures is void for uncertainty since the meaning of the word 'friends' is too vague to be given legal effect; and (b) what persons are to be treated as being members of the testatrix's family. I will deal first with the question of uncertainty.

Those arguing against the validity of the gift in favour of the friends contend that, in the absence of any guidance from the testatrix, the question 'Who were her friends?' is incapable of being answered. The word is said to be 'conceptually uncertain' since there are so

---

[61] See *Re Beatty* [1990] 1 WLR 1503 (fiduciary power given to trustees in favour of 'such person or persons as they think fit' held valid without consideration of administrative unworkability); [1991] Conv 138 (J. Martin). Note *Gibbs v Harding* [2007] EWHC 3(Ch); [2008] 2 WLR 361, para. 15 (Lewison J) (that for the black community of four London boroughs unworkable as a private trust but valid as a charitable trust).

[62] *Per* Sachs LJ in *Re Leek* [1969] 1 Ch 563 at 586 (assuming, however, that legislation would be required); and in the case of a power Winn LJ in *Re Gulbenkian's Settlements* [1968] Ch 126 at 138 (CA); cf. decisions on trusts which are not exclusively charitable [p. 536, below].

[63] (1999) 13 *Trust Law International* 48 (decided 1982).

[64] [1980] Conv 263 (L. McKay); (1982) 126 SJ 518 (N.D.M. Parry); (1982) 98 LQR 551, 562–567 (C.T. Emery).

many different degrees of friendship and it is impossible to say which degree the testatrix had in mind. In support of this argument they rely on Lord Upjohn's remarks in *Re Gulbenkian's Settlements* [1970] AC 508, and the decision of the House of Lords in [*McPhail v Doulton*] [1971] AC 424, to the effect that it must be possible to say who is within and who without the class of friends. They say that since the testatrix intended all her friends to have the opportunity to acquire a picture, it is necessary to be able to ascertain with certainty all the members of that class.

Mr. Shillingford, who argued in favour of the validity of the gift, contended that the test laid down in the *Gulbenkian* and *Baden* cases was not applicable to this case; the test, he says, is that laid down by the Court of Appeal in *Re Allen* [1953] Ch 810, as appropriate in cases where the validity of a condition precedent or description is in issue, namely, that the gift is valid if it is possible to say of one or more persons that he or they undoubtedly qualify even though it may be difficult to say of others whether or not they qualify.

The distinction between the *Gulbenkian* test and the *Re Allen* test is, in my judgment, well exemplified by the word 'friends'. The word has a great range of meanings; indeed, its exact meaning probably varies slightly from person to person. Some would include only those with whom they had been on intimate terms over a long period; others would include acquaintances whom they liked. Some would include people with whom their relationship was primarily one of business; others would not. Indeed, many people, if asked to draw up a complete list of their friends, would probably have some difficulty in deciding whether certain of the people they knew were really 'friends' as opposed to 'acquaintances'. Therefore, if the nature of the gift was such that it was legally necessary to draw up a complete list of 'friends' of the testatrix, or to be able to say of any person that 'he is not a friend', the whole gift would probably fail even as to those who, by any conceivable test, were friends.

But in the case of a gift of a kind which does not require one to establish all the members of the class (e.g. 'a gift of £10 to each of my friends'), it may be possible to say of some people that on any test, they qualify. Thus in *Re Allen* at 817, Sir Raymond Evershed MR took the example of a gift to X 'if he is a tall man'; a man 6 ft. 6 ins. tall could be said on any reasonable basis to satisfy the test, although it might be impossible to say whether a man, say, 5ft. 10ins. high satisfied the requirement.

So in this case, in my judgment, there are acquaintances of a kind so close that, on any reasonable basis, anyone would treat them as being 'friends'. Therefore, by allowing the disposition to take effect in their favour, one would certainly be giving effect to part of the testatrix's intention even though as to others it is impossible to say whether or not they satisfy the test.

In my judgment, it is clear that Lord Upjohn in *Re Gulbenkian's Settlements* [1970] AC 508 was considering only cases where it was necessary to establish all the members of the class. He makes it clear, at 524, that the reason for the rule is that in a gift which requires one to establish all the members of the class (e.g. 'a gift to my friends in equal shares') you cannot hold the gift good in part, since the quantum of each friend's share depends on how many friends there are. So all persons intended to benefit by the donor must be ascertained if any effect is to be given to the gift. In my judgment, the adoption of Lord Upjohn's test by the House of Lords in the *Baden* case is based on the same reasoning, even though in that case the House of Lords held that it was only necessary to be able to survey the class of objects of a power of appointment and not to establish who all the members are.

But such reasoning has no application to a case where there is a condition or description attached to one or more individual gifts; in such cases, uncertainty as to some other persons who may have been intended to take does not in any way affect the quantum of the gift to persons who undoubtedly possess the qualification. Hence, in my judgment, the different test laid down in *Re Allen* [1953] Ch 810.

The recent decision of the Court of Appeal in *Re Tuck's Settlement Trusts* [1978] Ch 49 [p. 668, below] establishes that the test in *Re Allen* is still the appropriate test in considering such gifts, notwithstanding the *Gulbenkian* and *Baden* decisions: see *per* Lord Russell of Killowen at 65.

Accordingly, in my judgment, the proper result in this case depends on whether the disposition in clause 5(a) is properly to be regarded as a series of individual gifts to persons answering the description 'friend' (in which case it will be valid), or a gift which requires the whole class of friends to be established (in which case it will probably fail).

The effect of clause 5(a) is to confer on friends of the testatrix a series of options to purchase. Although it is obviously desirable as a practical matter that steps should be taken to inform those entitled to the options of their rights, it is common ground that there is no legal necessity to do so. Therefore, each person coming forward to exercise the option has to prove that he is a friend; it is not legally necessary, in my judgment, to discover who all the friends are. In order to decide whether an individual is entitled to purchase, all that is required is that the executors should be able to say of that individual whether he has proved that he is a friend. The word 'friend', therefore, is a description or qualification of the option holder.

It was suggested that by allowing undoubted friends to take I would be altering the testatrix's intentions. It is said that she intended all her friends to have a chance to buy any given picture, and since some people she might have regarded as friends will not be able to apply, the number of competitors for that picture will be reduced. This may be so; but I cannot regard this factor as making it legally necessary to establish the whole class of friends. The testatrix's intention was that a friend should acquire a picture. My decision gives effect to that intention.

I therefore hold that the disposition does not fail for uncertainty, but that anyone who can prove that by any reasonable test he or she must have been a friend of the testatrix is entitled to exercise the option. Without seeking to lay down any exhaustive definition of such test, it may be helpful if I indicate certain minimum requirements:

(a) The relationship must have been a longstanding one.

(b) The relationship must have been a social relationship as opposed to a business or professional relationship.

(c) Although there may have been long periods when circumstances prevented the testatrix and the applicant from meeting, when circumstances did permit they must have met frequently.

If in any case the executors entertain any real doubt whether an applicant qualifies, they can apply to the court to decide the issue.

Finally on this aspect of the case I should notice two further cases to which I was referred. The first is *Re Gibbard's Will Trusts* [1967] 1 WLR 42 in which Plowman J upheld the validity of a power to appoint to 'any of my old friends'. It is not necessary for me to decide whether that decision is still good law, in that it applied the *Re Allen* test to powers of appointment. But it does show that, if the *Re Allen* test is the correct test, the word 'friends' is not too uncertain to be given effect.

Secondly, in *Re Lloyd's Trust Instruments* (24 June, 1970, unreported) but extracts from which are to be found in *Brown v Gould* [1972] Ch 53, 56–57, Megarry J stated, at 57:

'If there is a trust for "my old friends", all concerned are faced with uncertainty as to the concept or idea enshrined in those words. It may not be difficult to resolve that "old" means not "aged" but "of long standing"; but then there is the question of how long is "long". Friendship, too, is a concept with almost infinite shades of meaning. Where the concept is uncertain, the gift is void. Where the concept is certain, then mere difficulty in tracing and discovering those who are entitled normally does not invalidate the gift.'

The extract that I have read itself shows that Megarry J was considering a trust for 'my old friends' (which required the whole class to be ascertained) and not such a case as I have to deal with. In my judgment, that dictum was not intended to apply to such a case as I have before me.

I turn now to the question who are to be treated as 'members of my family'. It is not suggested that this class is too uncertain. The contest is between those who say that only the next-of-kin of the testatrix are entitled, and those who say that everyone related by blood to the testatrix are included.

His Lordship then held that everyone related by blood to the testatrix was included.

D ABSENCE OF CERTAINTIES

Snell, *Snell's Equity* (31st edn, 2005), p. 492

The effect of the absence of any of the certainties may be summarised as follows. The paramount certainty is that of subject-matter, in the first sense; if there is no certainty as to the property to be held upon trust, the entire transaction is nugatory. Next, if that certainty is present but there is no certainty of words, the person entitled to the trust property holds free from any trust. Finally, if both these certainties are present but there is uncertainty of objects, there is a resulting trust for the settlor, for 'once establish that a trust [of definite property] was intended, and the legatee cannot take beneficially';[65] the same applies where there is uncertainty of the subject-matter as regards the beneficial interest, unless one of the beneficiaries can establish a claim to the whole.

It will be noticed that the order in which these points should be considered is the natural order of any limitation in trust, e.g. where trustees hold 'Blackacre in trust for A and B equally'.

QUESTIONS

1. Why do different rules concerning certainty of subject matter apply to testamentary bequests and to *inter vivos* settlements?

2. If A declared that he held 100 of his 1,000 shares in B Ltd on trust for C, and then sold 200 of his shares, whose shares has he sold? If A used the proceeds of sale to buy lottery tickets and one of them won the jackpot (say, £10 million), who can claim the jackpot?

---

[65] *Briggs v Penny* (1851) 3 Mac & G 546 at 557, *per* Lord Truro LC.

3. What are the tests for certainty of objects, in each of the following categories:

   (a) fixed trusts

   (b) discretionary trusts

      (i) exhaustive

      (ii) non-exhaustive

   (c) fiduciary powers

   (d) non-fiduciary/mere powers

   (e) gifts subject to a condition?

   See p. 43, above and H&M, pp. 62–67, 94–116, 211–216.
   How do you account for the differences?

4. Do you think that the test for certainty laid down in *Re Gulbenkian's Settlements* and *McPhail v Doulton* is sound? How would you formulate the test after reading *Re Baden's Deed Trusts (No 2)* [1973] Ch 9? See H&M, pp. 66–67, 103–115.

5. Is there a workable distinction between conceptual and evidential certainty?

6. How far can questions of uncertainty be resolved by a third party whom the settlor or testator has made an arbiter of the matter? *Re Tuck's Settlement Trusts* [1978] Ch 49 [p. 668, below]; *Re Leek* [1969] 1 Ch 563; *Re Coates* [1955] Ch 495 (forgotten friends); *Re Wright's Will Trusts* [1981] LS Gaz R 841, where JUDGE BLACKETT-ORD V-C opined that a residuary gift to trustees 'to use the same at their absolute discretion for such people and institutions as they think may have helped me or my late husband' would be void for being conceptually uncertain or impracticable; *Re Tepper's Will Trusts* [1987] Ch 358 [p. 668, n. 87, below]; (1983) 133 NLJ 915 (P. Matthews).

7. Do you think that *Re Barlow's Will Trusts* [1979] 1 WLR 278 [p. 104, above] was rightly decided on the basis of (a) authority and (b) policy? [1980] Conv 263 (L. McKay); (1982) 126 SJ 518 (N.D.M. Parry); (1982) 98 LQR 551, 562–567 (C.T. Emery); U&H, pp. 131–132.

8. If you were advising a client who wishes to set up a trust for the benefit of their friends, what would you advise them to do? See *Schmidt v Rosewood Trust Ltd* [2003] UKPC 26, [2003] 2 AC 709, at para. 35.

II THE BENEFICIARY PRINCIPLE[66]

The orthodox view is that a private trust can only exist if the trustees hold the trust property on trust for ascertainable individuals—or for such as will be ascertained during the period of perpetuity.[67] Various reasons are given. The beneficial interest must

---

[66] H&M, pp. 371–372; Lewin, pp. 102–103; P&M, pp. 74–78; P&S pp. 378–380; Pettit pp. 56–57; T&H pp. 154–155; U&H, pp. 145–147.   [67] *Re Flavel's Will Trusts* [1969] 1 WLR 444, especially at 446–447.

be vested in somebody within the period of perpetuity.[68] The court must be able to enforce a trust, and there must therefore be ascertainable persons in whose favour the court can decree performance. A trust is obligatory; and there cannot be an obligation unless there is a corresponding right. Finally, a purpose must be sufficiently certain; 'benevolent' or 'patriotic' or 'public' purposes are too vague. None of these reasons applies to charitable trusts. Charitable trusts are a special type of purpose trust,[69] one which is of special importance to society, and one which is therefore given special privileges in terms of perpetuity, taxation and enforcement.[70] The Attorney-General is charged with the duty of enforcement of charitable trusts.

Some cases at first instance have upheld non-charitable purpose trusts.[71] The modern trend however is to declare them void; and the court will not extend the confines of existing decisions. Even those have been described by HARMAN LJ as 'troublesome, anomalous and aberrant'.[72] We will consider in Chapter 9 the ways in which it is possible to achieve a non-charitable purpose without setting up a trust.

It has been argued that the orthodox view that English law does not recognise purpose trusts is incorrect.[73] Although this may be correct when the old authorities are examined, it is clear from the more recent authorities that the settled view is that non-charitable purpose trusts are not generally considered to be valid in English law. This view is now so entrenched that it is unlikely to be overturned save by legislation.

In **Morice v Bishop of Durham** (1804) 9 Ves 399; on appeal (1805) 10 Ves 522, there was a bequest to the Bishop upon trust for 'such objects of benevolence and liberality as the Bishop of Durham in his own discretion shall most approve of'. This was held not to be a charitable trust. As there were no ascertainable beneficiaries the trust failed. SIR WILLIAM GRANT MR said at 404:

The only question is whether the Trust, upon which the residue of the personal Estate is bequeathed, be a trust for charitable purposes. That it is upon some trust, and not for the personal benefit of the Bishop is clear from the words of the Will; and is admitted by his Lordship; who expressly disclaims any beneficial interest. That it is a Trust, unless it be of a charitable nature, too indefinite to be executed by this Court, has not been, and cannot be denied. There can be no Trust over the exercise of which this Court will not assume a control; for an uncontrollable power of disposition would be Ownership, and not Trust. If there be a clear Trust, but for uncertain objects, the property, that is the subject of the trust, is undisposed of, and the benefit of such Trust must result to those, to whom the Law gives Ownership in default of disposition by the former owner. But this doctrine does not hold good with regard to Trusts for Charity. Every other Trust must have a definite object. There must be somebody, in whose favour the Court can decree performance.

---

[68] See p. 110, below.   [69] See p. 410, below.   [70] See p. 410, below.

[71] See p. 366, below. Further, article 2 of the Hague Convention on the Law Applicable to Trusts and on their Recognition (1984), incorporated into English law by the Recognition of Trusts Act 1987, defines a trust to include one 'for a specified purpose'.

[72] *Re Endacott* [1960] Ch 232 at 251; *Re Wood* [1949] Ch 498.

[73] Baxendale-Walker, *Purpose Trusts* (1999).

III PERPETUITY RULES[74]

For a trust to be valid it must comply with a variety of rules known as the perpetuity rules. Failure to comply with these rules will render the trust void.[75]

A THE RULE AGAINST REMOTENESS OF VESTING

A trust must vest within the perpetuity period otherwise it will be void. The perpetuity period is traditionally assessed by reference to a relevant life in being plus 21 years, but it is possible to specify that it will be a period not more than 80 years long.[76] At common law this was determined when the trust was declared. Now, by the Perpetuities and Accumulations Act 1964, section 3, the trust will only be void once it is clear that it will vest outside the perpetuity period. The Law Commission has recommended that this rule against perpetuity should be replaced by a statutory perpetuity period of 125 years and the principle of 'wait and see' should apply.[77]

B THE RULE AGAINST INALIENABILITY

The rule against perpetuities may also affect the duration of a trust, since a trust will be void[78] if, by its terms, the capital is required to be tied up for a time in excess of the perpetuity period.[79] This is known as the rule against excessive duration or the 'Rule against Inalienability'.[80] It is not applicable to trusts for charitable purposes; the community interest is that charitable trusts should last for ever,[81] but it does apply to non-charitable purpose trusts.[82]

---

[74] H&M, pp. 373–374; Lewin, pp. 136–165; P&M, pp. 238–255; P&S pp. 404–405; Pettit pp. 217–218, 247–248; T&H pp. 204–252; U&H, pp. 280–285. See generally Cheshire and Burn, *Modern Law of Real Property* (17th edn, 2006), pp. 509ff; Megarry & Wade, *Law of Real Property* (6th edn, 2000), pp. 291ff; Morris & Leach, *Rule against Perpetuities* (2nd edn, 1962 and Supplement); Maudsley, *The Modern Law of Perpetuities* (5th edn, 1984).

[75] But see [1996] Conv 24, 27–28 (J. Jaconelli) arguing that such trusts are voidable i.e. they stand until they are terminated.

[76] Perpetuities and Accumulations Act 1964, s. 1.

[77] Law Com No. 251, 1998: para 1.15.   [78] See H&M, p. 387.

[79] See *Re Lipinski's Will Trusts* [1976] Ch 235 [p. 372, below]. The rule is not affected by the Perpetuities and Accumulations Act 1964: s. 15(4).

[80] (2006) 26 LS 414 (I. Dawson).

[81] See p. 411, below.   [82] See p. 366, below.

4

CREATION OF EXPRESS TRUSTS

In Chapter 3 we considered the requirements for an express trust to be valid. In this chapter we are concerned with the formalities relating to the creation of trusts, and related matters. In order to create an express trust two distinct formality issues need to be considered. The first relates to the formalities for the declaration of trusts and, once a trust has been declared, for the disposition of equitable interests. The second concerns the formalities for the constitution of trusts, by which property is vested in trustees.

I FORMALITIES FOR THE DECLARATION OF TRUSTS AND DISPOSITION OF PROPERTY[1]

A *INTER VIVOS*

(i) *Declaration of Trusts*

Writing is not required for trusts of pure personalty.[2] Trusts of land or interests in land must, however, be evidenced by writing.

---

[1] H&M, pp. 79–94; Lewin, pp. 39–47; P&M, pp. 96–114; P&S pp. 195–210; Pettit pp. 85–97; Snell pp. 484–486; T&H pp. 126–133; U&H, pp. 287–305, 314–316.

[2] *Re Kayford Ltd* [1975] 1 WLR 279; *Paul v Constance* [1977] 1 WLR 527.

LAW OF PROPERTY ACT 1925

53. Instruments required to be in writing

(1) Subject to the provisions hereinafter contained with respect to the creation of interests in land by parol—

    (b) a declaration of trust respecting any land or any interest therein must be manifested and proved by some writing signed by some person who is able to declare such trust or by his will.[3]

(2) This section does not affect the creation or operation of resulting, implied or constructive trusts.[4]

Where land is conveyed *inter vivos* to a donee on an oral trust for a third party, so failing to comply with the requirements of section 53(1)(b), a constructive trust will be enforced where this is necessary to prevent fraud, by virtue of the maxim that equity will not permit a statute to be used as an instrument for fraud.[5]

(ii) Disposition of equitable interests

LAW OF PROPERTY ACT 1925

53. Instruments required to be in writing

(1) Subject to the provisions hereinafter contained with respect to the creation of interests in land by parol—

    (c) a disposition of an equitable interest or trust subsisting at the time of the disposition, must be in writing[6] signed by the person disposing of the same.[7] or by his agent thereunto lawfully authorised in writing or by will.[8]

---

[3] Failure to comply with this provision renders the trust unenforceable: *Gardner v Rowe* (1828) 5 Russ 258. This provision does not apply to trusts of land arising from joint ownership: *Roy v Roy* [1996] 1 FLR 541.

[4] *Bannister v Bannister* [1948] 2 All ER 133; *Oughtred v IRC* [1960] AC 206 [p. 118, below]; *Hodgson v Marks* [1971] Ch 892; (1971) 35 Conv (NS) 255, at 260–266 (I. Leeming); *Binions v Evans* [1972] Ch 359; *Ottaway v Norman* [1972] Ch 698 [p. 132, below].

[5] *Taylor v Salmon* (1838) 4 My & Cr 134; *Davies v Otty (No 2)* (1865) 35 Beav 208; *Rochefoucauld v Boustead* [1897] 1 Ch 196; *Bannister v Bannister* [1948] 2 All ER 133; *Re Nichols* [1974] 1 WLR 296 at 301; (1984) CLJ 306 (T.E. Youdan); [1986] 36 *Northern Ireland Legal Quarterly* 358 (M.P. Thompson); [1987] Conv 246 (J.D. Feltham); [1988] Conv 267 (T.G. Youdan); *Du Boulay v Raggett* (1988) 58 P & CR 138. See H&M, pp. 80–82; N. Hopkins, 'Conscience, discretion and the creation of property rights' (2006) 4 LS 475 (use of constructive trust triggered by unconscionability).

[6] The writing need not contain details of the trust where the assignee is to hold in a fiduciary capacity: *Re Tyler* [1967] 1 WLR 1269 [p. 122, below].

[7] This may be satisfied by joinder of documents: *Re Danish Bacon Co Ltd Staff Pension Fund Trusts* [1971] 1 WLR 248 [p. 113, below].

[8] Failure to comply with this provision renders the disposition void: H&M, p. 82. See *Halloran v Minister Administering National Parks and Wildlife Act 1974* [2006] HCA 3, (2006) 80 *Australian Law Journal Reports* 519; [2006] Conv 390 (P.G. Turner).

For section 53(1)(c) to be at least potentially applicable the crucial requirement is that there must be an equitable interest or trust which is subsisting at the time of the disposition.[9] Consequently, the provision will not apply to a declaration of trust which creates an equitable interest. It will be seen that the application of section 53(1)(c) in different types of situation has been inconsistent.[10] Different types of disposition will be examined but, in each case, determining whether writing is required will depend on whether the interest which is being disposed of was subsisting at the time. If writing is required then it is also necessary to examine what will constitute writing for these purposes.

(a) Assignment of Equitable Interest

In **Re Danish Bacon Co Ltd Staff Pension Fund Trusts** [1971] 1 WLR 248, an employee had the right to nominate a person to receive benefits due under the company's pension fund in the case of death before qualifying for a pension. An employee had nominated his wife in the approved form which was duly signed and witnessed. He then changed the nomination by letter to the company. The question was whether, on the assumption that section 53(1)(c) applied.[11] the documents together could supply the necessary writing. MEGARRY J said at 254:

I have been referred to no authority on the point relating to the words in section 53(1)(c) which run 'a disposition...must be in writing...'; indeed, despite the riches of authority on this point under section 40,[12] section 53(1)(c) appears to be wholly barren. However, if a statutory requirement that a 'memorandum' shall be 'in writing' may be satisfied by two or more documents, I do not see why two or more documents should not satisfy the requirement that a 'disposition' shall be 'in writing'. True, section 40(1) is merely directed to providing written evidence of a transaction, whereas under section 53(1)(c) (unlike section 53(1)(b)) the matter is one not merely of evidence but of the disposition itself. Yet two documents are used in constituting a strict settlement of land or establishing a trust for sale of land, and there are well-established rules for the incorporation of documents in a will; and if two or more documents, when read together, dispose of an equitable interest, I do not see why the court should insist on separating them and subjecting each separately to the test of section 53(1)(c).[13]

(b) Direction to Trustees to Hold on Trust for Another

In **Grey v Inland Revenue Commissioners** [1960] AC 1[14] the question was whether an instruction by a beneficiary to the trustees to hold upon different trusts was a disposition of a subsisting equitable interest within the Law of Property Act 1925,

[9] *Kinane v Mackie-Conteh* [2005] EWCA Civ 45; [2005] Conv 501 (B. McFarlane).

[10] See generally [1979] Conv 17; (1975) 7 *Ottawa Law Review* 483 (G. Battersby); (1984) 47 MLR 385 (B. Green).

[11] Which it presumably did because the employee had an existing equitable interest as regards payment of the pension.

[12] See Law of Property (Miscellaneous Provisions) Act 1989 s. 2, which repeals and replaces LPA 1925, s. 40 by a requirement that a contract for the sale or other disposition of land can *only* be made *in* writing; Cheshire and Burn's *Modern Law of Real Property* (17th edn, 2006), p. 91.

[13] See *Crowden v Aldridge* [1993] 1 WLR 433.   [14] (1960) CLJ 31 (J.W.A. Thornley).

s. 53(1)(c). As it was put in argument by Pennycuick QC at 4, 'If X holds property in trust for A as absolute equitable owner and A then directs X to hold the property on the settlement of trusts for the benefit of B, C and D, and X accepts the trust, is that direction a "disposition" of a subsisting equitable interest within the meaning of section 53?'

The settlor, Mr. Hunter, had made six settlements of nominal sums in favour of his grandchildren. Subsequently he transferred substantial blocks of shares to the trustees, which they held on trust for him. Then he orally instructed the trustees to hold the shares upon the trusts of the six settlements. Finally, documents were executed in confirmation of the oral declaration, and these were executed by Mr. Hunter. The question was whether the trusts of the shares had been created by the oral declaration or by the later documents.

This mattered because it affected liability to pay Stamp Duty. Stamp Duty was payable *ad valorem*[15] upon a 'conveyance on sale', which includes 'every instrument...whereby any property, or any estate or interest in any property, upon the sale thereof is transferred to or vested in a purchaser, or any other person on his behalf or by his direction'.[16] Thus 'the thing which is made liable to the duty is an "instrument". If a contract of purchase and sale, or conveyance by way of purchase and sale, can be, or is carried out without an instrument, the case is not within the section, and no tax is imposed. It is not the transaction of purchase and sale which is struck at; it is the instrument whereby the purchase and sale are effected which is struck at'.[17]

Whether the trusts of the shares in *Grey v IRC* were created by the oral direction or by the later documents depended on whether the oral declaration was valid. It would be valid as an oral *declaration* of a trust of personalty; but not if it was a *disposition* of a subsisting equitable interest.

The House of Lords decided that it was a disposition. The equitable interest was to pass from Mr. Hunter to the beneficiaries. That 'amounted in any ordinary sense of the words to a "disposition of an equitable interest or trust subsisting at the time of the disposition",' *per* LORD RADCLIFFE at 15. There was no necessity to construe the word 'disposition' in the light of the language of the Statute of Frauds (1677), which dealt with 'grants and assignments'. The passing of the interest could only be effected by an instrument in writing. It was thus effected by the later document, and that document was liable to *ad valorem* Stamp Duty.[18]

(c) Conveyance of Legal Estate by Nominee

In **Vandervell v Inland Revenue Commissioners** [1967] 2 AC 291.[19] Vandervell decided to give to the Royal College of Surgeons sufficient money to endow a Chair of

---

[15] Meaning a tax assessed by the value of the land.

[16] Stamp Act 1891, s. 54, now repealed by Finance Act (FA)1999, s. 139, Sch. 20, Pt. V (2).

[17] *Per* LORD ESHER in *IRC v Angus* (1889) 23 QBD 579 at 589.

[18] Followed by PC in *Baird v Baird* [1990] 2 AC 548; [1990] Conv 458 (G. Kodilinye).

[19] (1966) 24 CLJ 19 (G.H. Jones); (1967) 31 Conv (NS) 175 (S.M. Spencer); (1967) 30 MLR 461 (N. Strauss); *IRC v Hood Barrs (No 2)* (1963) 41 TC 339; (2002) CLJ 169 (R.C. Nolan).

Pharmacology. This was to be done by transferring a holding of shares in Vandervell Products Ltd., which were vested in the National Provincial Bank Ltd. on trust for Vandervell, to the Royal College, and then declaring dividends on the shares, for which the Royal College would be free of liability to tax because it is a charity. An option to repurchase the shares for £5,000 was given to Vandervell Trustees Ltd., a company which acted as trustee for the Vandervell family trusts. The bank transferred the shares, and the dividends were declared.

The Revenue assessed Vandervell to Surtax on the dividends on the ground that he had not divested himself absolutely of all interest in the shares.[20] This was upheld by the House of Lords. Vandervell Trustees Ltd. held the option on a resulting trust for Vandervell. One argument for the Revenue was that the bank had conveyed only the legal estate in the shares to the Royal College of Surgeons; the equitable interest remained in Vandervell because he had failed to effect its disposition in writing as required by section 53(1)(c). In rejecting this argument, LORD UPJOHN said at 311:

[Section 53(1)(c) was] applied in *Grey* [1960] AC 1 [p. 113, above], and *Oughtred* [1960] AC 206 [p. 118, below], to cases where the legal estate remained outstanding in a trustee and the beneficial owner was dealing and dealing only with the equitable estate. That is understandable; the object of the section, as was the object of the old Statute of Frauds, is to prevent hidden oral transactions in equitable interests in fraud of those truly entitled, and making it difficult, if not impossible, for the trustees to ascertain who are in truth his beneficiaries. But when the beneficial owner owns the whole beneficial estate and is in a position to give directions to his bare trustee with regard to the legal as well as the equitable estate there can be no possible ground for invoking the section where the beneficial owner wants to deal with the legal estate as well as the equitable estate . . .

Counsel for the Crown admitted that where the legal and beneficial estate was vested in the legal owner and he desired to transfer the whole legal and beneficial estate to another he did not have to do more than transfer the legal estate and he did not have to comply with section 53(1)(c); and I can see no relevant difference between that case and this.

R. Nolan, Vandervell v IRC: *A Case of Overreaching* (2002) 61 CLJ 169, 188

The doctrine of overreaching can be used to explain and justify their Lordships' decision in *Vandervell* that the Royal College of Surgeons got good legal title to 100,000 'A' shares in Vandervell Products Ltd., free of Vandervell's prior equitable interest in them, even though Vandervell had not transferred that interest to the Royal College in accordance with section 53(1)(c) of the Law of Property Act 1925. Vandervell, without any need for formality, instructed National Provincial Bank Ltd. to give away its legal title to the shares, free of his equitable interest in them. The shares were transferred to the Royal College, and re-registered in its name, so it acquired good legal title to them. The gift of the shares also overreached Vandervell's equitable interest in them. Consequently, the Royal College acquired the shares

[20] See Income Tax Act 1952, s. 415; this became Income & Corporation Taxes Act 1988, ss. 684, 685 and was repealed by FA 1995, Sch. 29, Pt. VIII (8).

free of that interest. No aspect of these transactions amounted to the disposition of a subsisting equitable interest, within section 53(1)(c).

This explanation of their Lordships' decision relies on a well understood and well accepted doctrine, overreaching, which is very commonly encountered in the administration of trusts: it does not relegate a case so practically important as *Vandervell* to the status of a useful 'anomaly' or 'exception'. Understanding their Lordships' decision in terms of such a familiar, well known, doctrine has another major benefit. The substantial body of law relating to over-reaching can be used to establish the limits within which *Vandervell* should properly be applied: it can be used to establish the consequences which may follow in a variety of circumstances when a nominee, acting on instructions from his beneficiary, deals with an asset he holds for that beneficiary. Finally, this explanation of their Lordships' decision helps to reconcile *Vandervell* with other cases on section 53(l)(c), cases which those who teach the law of trusts must explain as best they can.

(d) Constitution of Trust following Resulting Trust

In 1961 Vandervell Trustees Ltd. exercised the option, taking £5,000 from the Vandervell children's settlement for the purpose. The Royal College of Surgeons transferred the shares to Vandervell Trustees Ltd. The Revenue made a further claim on the ground that Vandervell Trustees Ltd. had held the shares on trust for Vandervell. In 1965 Vandervell executed a deed, formally transferring to the children's settlement any right or interest which he might still have in the shares.

Vandervell having died, his estate sued Vandervell Trustees Ltd. for the return of the dividends paid on the shares since 1961. They succeeded before Megarry J, but failed in the Court of Appeal in **Re Vandervell's Trusts (No 2)** [1974] Ch 269.[21] On the question of the way in which the equitable interest, previously enjoyed in the option, had left Vandervell, Lord Denning said at 320:

Mr. Balcombe for the executors admitted that the intention of Mr. Vandervell and the trustee company was that the shares should be held on trust for the children's settlement. But he said that this intention was of no avail. He said that during the first period, Mr. Vandervell had an equitable interest in the property, namely, a resulting trust; that he never disposed of this equitable interest (because he never knew he had it): and that in any case it was the disposition of an equitable interest which, under section 53 of the Law of Property Act 1925, had to be in writing, signed by him or his agent, lawfully authorised by him in writing (and there was no such writing produced). He cited *Grey v IRC* [1960] AC 1 and *Oughtred v IRC* [1960] AC 206.

There is a complete fallacy in that argument. A resulting trust for the settlor is born and dies without any writing at all. It comes into existence whenever there is a gap in the beneficial ownership. It ceases to exist whenever that gap is filled by someone becoming beneficially entitled. As soon as the gap is filled by the creation or declaration of a valid trust, the resulting trust comes to an end. In this case, before the option was exercised, there was a gap in the beneficial ownership. So there was a resulting trust for Mr. Vandervell. But, as soon as the option was exercised and the shares registered in the trustees' name, there was created a valid trust of

---

[21] (1974) 38 Conv 405 (P.J. Clarke); (1975) 38 MLR 557 (J.W. Harris).

the shares in favour of the children's settlement. Not being a trust of land, it could be created without any writing. A trust of personalty can be created without writing. Both Mr. Vandervell and the trustee company had done everything which needed to be done to make the settlement of these shares binding on them. So, there was a valid trust: see *Milroy v Lord* (1862) 4 De GF & J 264 at 274, *per* Turner LJ.[22]

But STEPHENSON LJ had doubts. He said at 322:

To expound my doubts would serve no useful purpose; to state them shortly may do no harm. The cause of all the trouble is what the judge called [1974] Ch 269 at 298, 'this ill-fated option' and its incorporation in a deed which was 'too short and simple' to rid Mr. Vandervell of the beneficial interest in the disputed shares, as a bare majority of the House of Lords held, not without fluctuation of mind on the part of one of them (Lord Upjohn), in *Vandervell v IRC* [1967] 2 AC 291 at 314–317. The operation of law or equity kept for Mr. Vandervell or gave him back an equitable interest which he did not want and would have thought he had disposed of if he had ever known it existed. It is therefore difficult to infer that he intended to dispose or ever did dispose of something he did not know he had until the judgment of Plowman J in *Vandervell v IRC* [1966] Ch 261 at 273, which led to the deed of 1965, enlightened him, or to find a disposition of it in the exercise by the trustee company in 1961 of its option to purchase the shares. And even if he had disposed of his interest, he did not dispose of it by any writing sufficient to comply with section 53(1)(c) of the Law of Property Act 1925.

(e) Declaration by Equitable Owner of Himself as Trustee

(1958) 74 LQR 180 at 182 (P.V.B.)

Does a declaration of trust [by an equitable owner] operate to transfer the equitable interest from donor to donee? It is suggested that when the donor declares himself a trustee of his equitable interest, he retains his equitable interest but a subsidiary equitable interest becomes vested in the donee. He might well have active duties, if, for example, he had declared a discretionary trust. Trusts of equitable interests do not seem to have received much attention in this country but are well recognised on the other side of the Atlantic and referred to in *Scott on Trusts* (2nd edn, 1956), p. 645 as subtrusts. Thus the *Restatement of the Law of Trusts,* Vol. 1, s. 83 declares that 'an equitable interest, if transferable, can be held in trust' and gives the following illustration: 'A, the owner of a bond, declares himself a trustee of it for B. B declares himself a trustee for C of his interest in the bond. B is trustee for C of his equitable interest in the bond. On the other hand, when the donor directs the trustees to hold property on trust for the donee, the donor does indeed disappear from the picture. Whether he says to the trustees, "I assign my equitable interest to you to hold upon the trusts of the settlements", so that it merges in the legal interest, or says more simply, "I direct you to hold the property" upon such trusts, he has, it would seem, purported to assign or dispose of his equitable interest in the property, which he cannot do orally.[23]

---

[22] See p. 157, below.
[23] See *Grainge v Wilberforce* (1889) 5 TLR 436; *DHN Food Distributors Ltd v Tower Hamlets London Borough Council* [1976] 1 WLR 852; (1977) 93 LQR 171 (D. Sugarman and F. Webb).

(f) Oral Contract for the Sale of Shares

Oughtred v Inland Revenue Commissioners[24]
[1960] AC 206 (HL, Viscount Radcliffe, Lords Cohen, Keith of Avonholm, Denning and Jenkins)

100,000 preference shares and 100,000 ordinary shares in William Jackson and Son Ltd were held upon trust for Mrs. Oughtred for life and after her death on trust for her son Peter absolutely. Mrs Oughtred also held 72,700 shares absolutely.

On Mrs. Oughtred's death, Estate Duty would be payable at the rate applicable to the aggregated value of the settled property and her own free estate. In order to reduce the liability to Estate Duty,[25] Mrs. Oughtred and her son Peter orally agreed that she would transfer to him her 72,700 shares, and Peter would release to his mother his remainder interest in the 200,000 preference and ordinary shares. Subsequently, documents covering these transfers were executed. The Revenue claimed Stamp Duty upon the transfer of Peter's interest in the 200,000 shares. The key issue for the court was whether the oral contract had been effective to transfer the property in the shares. If it had been effective then Stamp Duty was not payable.

Held (Viscount Radcliffe and Lord Cohen dissenting). Stamp Duty was payable.

Lord Jenkins: It is said further that in the present case the disputed transfer transferred nothing beyond a bare legal estate, because, in accordance with the well-settled principle applicable to contracts of sale, between contract and completion the appellant became under the oral agreement beneficially entitled in equity to the settled shares, subject to the due satisfaction by her of the purchase consideration, and accordingly the entire beneficial interest in the settled shares had already passed to her at the time of the execution of the disputed transfer, and there was nothing left upon which the disputed transfer could operate except the bare legal estate.

The Commissioners of Inland Revenue seek to meet this argument by reference to section 53(1)(c) of the Law of Property Act, 1925. They contend that as the agreement of 18 June, 1956, was an oral agreement it could not, in view of section 53(1)(c), effect a disposition of a subsisting equitable interest or trust, and accordingly that Peter's subsisting equitable interest under the trusts of the settlement, in the shape of his reversionary interest, remained vested in him until the execution of the disputed transfer, which in these circumstances operated as a transfer on sale to the appellant of Peter's reversionary interest and additionally as a transfer not on sale to the appellant of the legal interest in the settled shares. It was by this process of reasoning that the Commissioners arrived at the opinion expressed in the case stated that the disputed transfer attracted both the *ad valorem* duty exigible on a transfer on sale of the reversionary interest and also the fixed duty of 10s.

This argument is attacked on the appellant's side by reference to subsection (2) of section 53 of the Act of 1925, which excludes the creation or operation of resulting, implied or constructive trusts from the provisions of subsection (1). It is said that inasmuch as the oral agreement was an agreement of sale and purchase it gave rise, on the principle to which I have already adverted, to a constructive trust of the reversionary interest in favour of the appellant

[24] Followed in *Parinv (Hatfield) Ltd v Inland Revenue Commissioners* [1998] STC 305.
[25] Estate Duty has been replaced by Inheritance Tax. See p. 39, above.

subject to performance by her of her obligation to transfer to Peter the free shares forming the consideration for the sale. It is said that this trust, being constructive, was untouched by section 53(1)(c) in view of the exemption afforded by section 53(2), and that the appellant's primary argument still holds good.

I find it unnecessary to decide whether section 53(2) has the effect of excluding the present transaction from the operation of section 53(1)(c), for, assuming in the appellant's favour that the oral contract did have the effect in equity of raising a constructive trust of the settled shares for her untouched by section 53(1)(c), I am unable to accept the conclusion that the disputed transfer was prevented from being a transfer of the shares to the appellant on sale because the entire beneficial interest in the settled shares was already vested in the appellant under the constructive trust, and there was accordingly nothing left for the disputed transfer to pass to the appellant except the bare legal estate. The constructive trust in favour of a purchaser which arises on the conclusion of a contract for sale is founded upon the purchaser's right to enforce the contract in proceedings for specific performance. In other words, he is treated in equity as entitled by virtue of the contract to the property which the vendor is bound under the contract to convey to him. This interest under the contract is no doubt a proprietary interest of a sort, which arises, so to speak, in anticipation of the execution of the transfer for which the purchaser is entitled to call. But its existence has never (so far as I know) been held to prevent a subsequent transfer, in performance of the contract, of the property contracted to be sold from constituting for Stamp Duty purposes a transfer on sale of the property in question. Take the simple case of a contract for the sale of land. In such a case a constructive trust in favour of the purchaser arises on the conclusion of the contract for sale, but (so far as I know) it has never been held on this account that a conveyance subsequently executed in performance of the contract is not stampable *ad valorem* as a transfer on sale. Similarly, in a case like the present one, but uncomplicated by the existence of successive interests, a transfer to a purchaser of the investments comprised in a trust fund could not, in my judgment, be prevented from constituting a transfer on sale for the purposes of Stamp Duty by reason of the fact that the actual transfer had been preceded by an oral agreement for sale.

In truth, the title secured by a purchaser by means of an actual transfer is different in kind from, and may well be far superior to, the special form of proprietary interest which equity confers on a purchaser in anticipation of such transfer.

This difference is of particular importance in the case of property such as shares in a limited company. Under the contract the purchaser is no doubt entitled in equity as between himself and the vendor to the beneficial interest in the shares, and (subject to due payment of the purchase consideration) to call for a transfer of them from the vendor as trustee for him. But it is only on the execution of the actual transfer that he becomes entitled to be registered as a member, to attend and vote at meetings, to effect transfers on the register, or to receive dividends otherwise than through the vendor as his trustee.

Viscount Radcliffe (dissenting): The reason of the whole matter, as I see it, is as follows: On 18 June, 1956, the son owned an equitable reversionary interest in the settled shares: by his oral agreement of that date he created in his mother an equitable interest in his reversion, since the subject matter of the agreement was property of which specific performance would normally be decreed by the court. He thus became a trustee for her of that interest *sub modo*:[26] having regard to subsection (2) of section 53 of the Law of Property Act, 1925, subsection (1) of

----

26 Meaning 'within limits'.

that section did not operate to prevent that trusteeship arising by operation of law. On 26 June Mrs. Oughtred transferred to her son the shares which were the consideration for her acquisition of his equitable interest: upon this transfer he became in a full sense and without more the trustee of his interest for her. She was the effective owner of all outstanding equitable interests. It was thus correct to recite in the deed of release to the trustees of the settlement, which was to wind up their trust, that the trust fund was by then held upon trust for her absolutely. There was, in fact, no equity to the shares that could be asserted against her, and it was open to her, if she so wished, to let the matter rest without calling for a written assignment from her son. Given that the trustees were apprised of the making of the oral agreement and of Mrs. Oughtred's satisfaction of the consideration to be given by her, the trustees had no more to do than to transfer their legal title to her or as she might direct. This and no more is what they did.

It follows that, in my view, this transfer cannot be treated as a conveyance of the son's equitable reversion at all. The trustees had not got it: he never transferred or released it to them: how then could they convey it? With all respect to those who think otherwise, it is incorrect to say that the trustees' transfer was made either with his authority or at his discretion. If the recital as to Mrs. Oughtred's rights was correct, as I think that it was, he had no remaining authority to give or direction to issue. A release is, after all, the normal instrument for winding up a trust when all the equitable rights are vested and the legal estate is called for from the trustees who hold it. What the release gave the trustees from him was acquittance for the trust administration and accounts to date, and the fact that he gave it in consideration of the legal interest in the shares being vested in his mother adds nothing on this point. Nor does it, with respect, advance the matter to say, correctly, that at the end of the day Mrs. Oughtred was the absolute owner of the shares, legal and equitable. I think that she was: but that is description, not analysis. The question that is relevant for the purpose of this appeal is how she came to occupy that position; a position which, under English law, could be reached by more than one road.

In **Neville v Wilson** [1997] Ch 144[27] shareholders of a company ('J.E.N.') had entered into an oral agreement with one another in 1969 for the informal liquidation of the company. Part of this agreement was to the effect that the company's equitable interest in the shares of another company should be divided amongst the shareholders according to their existing shareholdings. The issue for the court was whether this agreement was effective to dispose of the company's interest in its shares.

Held: The effect of the agreement was to constitute each shareholder a constructive trustee of the shares so that section 53(2) LPA 1925 applied.

Nourse LJ said at 155:

'The effect of the agreement, more closely analysed, was that each shareholder agreed to assign his interest in the other shares of J.E.N.'s equitable interest in exchange for the assignment by the other shareholders of their interests in his own *aliquot* share.[28] Each individual agreement having been a disposition of a subsisting equitable interest not made in writing, there then arises the question whether it was rendered ineffectual by section 53 of the Law of Property Act 1925.

---

[27] (1997) 113 LQR 213 (P. Milne), [1996] Conv 368 (M. Thompson), (1996) 55 CLJ 436 (R. Nolan). See also *Slater v Simm* [2007] EWHC 951 (Ch), [2007] WTLR 1043.

[28] Meaning a part of a larger holding.

[His Lordship quoted section 53(1) and continued:] The simple view of the present case is that the effect of each individual agreement was to constitute the shareholder an implied or constructive trustee for the other shareholders, so that the requirement for writing contained in subsection (1)(c) of section 53 was dispensed with by subsection (2). That was the view taken by Upjohn J [1958] Ch 383 at first instance and by Lord Radcliffe in the House of Lords in *Oughtred v Inland Revenue Commissioners*. In order to see whether it is open to us to adopt it in this court, we must give careful consideration to those views and to the other speeches in the House of Lords.

[His Lordship referred to various dicta from *Oughtred* and continued:] The views of their Lordships as to the effect of section 53 can be summarised as follows. Lord Radcliffe, agreeing with Upjohn J, thought that subsection (2) applied. He gave reasons for that view. Lord Cohen and Lord Denning thought that it did not. Although neither of them gave reasons, they may be taken to have accepted the submissions of Mr. Wilberforce at 220–222. Lord Keith and Lord Jenkins expressed no view either way. We should add that when the case was in this court Lord Evershed MR, in delivering the judgment of himself, Morris and Ormerod LJJ said [1958] Ch 678 at 687:

'In this court the case for the Crown has, we think, been somewhat differently presented, and in the end of all, the question under section 53 of the Law of Property Act 1925, does not, in our judgment, strictly call for a decision. We are not, however, with all respect to the judge, prepared to accept, as we understand it, his conclusions upon the effect of section 53 of the Law of Property Act 1925.'

The basis of this court's decision was the same as that adopted by the majority of the House of Lords.

We do not think that there is anything in the speeches in the House of Lords which prevents us from holding that the effect of each individual agreement was to constitute the shareholder an implied or constructive trustee for the other shareholders. In this respect we are of the opinion that the analysis of Lord Radcliffe, based on the proposition that a specifically enforceable agreement to assign an interest in property creates an equitable interest in the assignee, was unquestionably correct; cf. *London and South Western Railway Co v Gomm* (1882) 20 Ch D 562, 581, *per* Sir George Jessel MR. A greater difficulty is caused by Lord Denning's outright rejection of the application of section 53(2), with which Lord Cohen appears to have agreed.

So far as it is material to the present case, what subsection (2) says is that subsection (1)(c) does not affect the creation or operation of implied or constructive trusts. Just as in *Oughtred v Inland Revenue Commissioners* the son's oral agreement created a constructive trust in favour of the mother, so here each shareholder's oral or implied agreement created an implied or constructive trust in favour of the other shareholders. Why then should subsection (2) not apply? No convincing reason was suggested in argument and none has occurred to us since. Moreover, to deny its application in this case would be to restrict the effect of general words when no restriction is called for, and to lay the ground for fine distinctions in the future. With all the respect which is due to those who have thought to the contrary, we hold that subsection (2) applies to an agreement such as we have in this case.

For these reasons we have come to the conclusion that the agreement entered into by the shareholders of J.E.N. in about April 1969 was not rendered ineffectual by section 53 of the Act of 1925.

However, in **United Bank of Kuwait plc v Sahib** [1997] Ch 107 CHADWICK J said at 129:

I should, perhaps, add (without seeking to decide the point) that I am far from persuaded that section 53(2) of the Law of Property Act 1925 can have any application in a case where it is sought to avoid the effect of section 53(1)(c) by relying on an oral contract to make the disposition which section 53(1)(c) requires to be in writing. The point arose in *Oughtred v Inland Revenue Commissioners* [1960] AC 206. It was put, succinctly, by counsel for the Inland Revenue (Mr. Wilberforce QC) in argument, at 221: 'it cannot be right that an oral contract can transfer property when an oral disposition cannot.' Lord Denning, at 233 accepted the point. So also, I think, did Lord Cohen, at 230. Lord Radcliffe did not accept it, at 227. Lord Jenkins, with whose judgment Lord Keith of Avonholm agreed, found it unnecessary to decide the point, at 239. I am happy to be able to take the same course. It is unnecessary to decide that point in the present case.[29]

(1996) CLJ 436, 438 (R. Nolan)

[*Neville v Wilson*] illustrates the extreme technicality and artificiality of the case law which has grown up around the Law of Property Act 1925 section 53(1)(c). If a person directs his trustees that the assets they hold for him are now to be held for someone else, then this amounts to a disposition of that person's *subsisting* equitable interest, within section 53(1)(c) (*Grey v IRC* [1960] AC 1 [p. 113, above]). Yet according to *Neville v Wilson,* if a person does not unilaterally tell his trustees what to do, but instead contracts for value to dispose of his beneficial interest, that is not a disposition of a *subsisting* equitable interest within section 53(1)(c), because technically what is involved is the creation of a *new* equitable interest in the purchaser, coupled with destruction of the 'old' equitable interest in the hands of the vendor; and this is so, even though that 'new' interest is logically identical to the 'old' (cp. *Grey v IRC* [1958] Ch 375 at 382, *per* Uphohn J; [1958] Ch 690 at 715, *per* Lord Evershed MR).

(g) Disposition to Fiduciary

In **Re Tyler** [1967] 1 WLR 1269, Miss Tyler, by her will, appointed Mr. King and Mrs. Green her executors. Shortly after its execution, she placed £1,500 in the hands of Mr. King, and on 9 May, 1951 she wrote a letter instructing him to use as much of the money (income or capital) as was needed to provide reasonable care and comfort for Mrs. Green; and to dispose of the surplus at Mrs. Green's death as the testatrix had previously indicated to Mr. King. The testatrix died, then Mr. King, and finally Mrs. Green.

The instructions for disposal of the surplus on Mrs. Green's death were that £500 should be paid to Mr. King's executors if (as happened) he should die before Mrs. Green, and the rest divided among a number of charitable institutions.

This summons was brought to determine on what trusts the fund was held on Mrs. Green's death.

---

29 This aspect of the case was not considered on appeal to the Court of Appeal: [1997] Ch 107.

PENNYCUICK J held that the evidence to support the executors' claim to £500 was insufficient, and that this sum was held on a resulting trust for Miss Tyler's estate. The balance of the fund went to charity. On the question of the observance of the necessary formalities, he said at 1274:

We do not know whether there was an interval of time between the payment by Miss Tyler to Mr. King of the £1,500 and the statement by her to him of her wishes with regard to it. On that footing there would have been an interval of time during which Mr. King held the £1,500 on a resulting trust for Miss Tyler. The first question which has been argued is whether a trust was validly constituted as regards formalities, having regard, in particular, to section 53 of the Law of Property Act, 1925, which contains the following provision: ...

It is now well established that the requirement applies to equitable interest in personalty as well as in land. It seems to me that, even on the view of the facts most unfavourable to the creation of a valid trust for this purpose, that is that there was a payment to Mr. King before any trusts were declared, there has been in this case sufficient compliance with the requirements of section 53. The letter of 9 May constitutes, it seems to me, a valid assignment in writing of an equitable interest by Miss Tyler to Mr. King, assuming that such an equitable interest existed. There is nothing in section 53 which requires that, where the assignee is to hold in a fiduciary capacity, the writing shall comprise the particulars of the trust. I conclude, then, that in May, 1951, a trust was validly created so far as formality is concerned.

(h) Under the Variation of Trusts Act 1958

The question of the operation of section 53(1)(c) in relation to the equitable interests of consenting adults when a variation of a trust is effected under the Variation of Trusts Act 1958 was discussed in *Re Holt's Settlement* [1969] 1 Ch 100. This is dealt with in Chapter 17, below.

(i) Nomination of Benefits

In **Re Danish Bacon Co Ltd Staff Pension Fund Trusts** [1971] 1 WLR 248 [p. 113, above], although it was not necessary to decide whether the interest was one to which section 53(1)(c) applied, MEGARRY J said at 255:

Whether section 53(1)(c) does apply is a matter upon which I am by no means clear; and in view of what I have already decided on the section, I do not have to resolve that point. However, it has been extensively argued, and I think I should give some indication of my views. What I am concerned with is a transaction whereby the deceased dealt with something which *ex hypothesi* could never be his. He was not disposing of his pension, nor of his right to the contributions and interest if he left the company's service. He was dealing merely with a state of affairs that would arise if he died while in the company's pensionable service, or after he had left it without becoming entitled to a pension. If he did this, then the contributions and interest would, by force of the rules, go either to his nominee, if he had made a valid nomination, or to his personal representatives, if he had not. If he made a nomination, it was revocable at any time before his death.

The question is thus whether an instrument with this selective, contingent and defeasible quality, which takes effect only on the death of the person signing it, can fairly be said to be 'a disposition of an equitable interest or trust subsisting at the time of the disposition'.

Mr. Ferris put much emphasis on the word 'subsisting': however wide the word 'disposition' might be in its meaning, there was no disposition of a subsisting equity, he said. I should hesitate to describe an instrument which has a mere possibility of becoming a 'disposition' as being in itself a disposition *ab initio*; and I agree that the word 'subsisting' also seems to point against the nomination falling within section 53(1)(c)...I very much doubt whether the nomination falls within section 53(1)(c); but as I have indicated, I do not have to decide that point, and I do not do so.

In **Gold v Hill** [1999] 1 FLR 54 the deceased had nominated a solicitor as the beneficiary of a life insurance policy. During an informal conversation the deceased had informed the solicitor of the nomination and of his desire that the solicitor should use the proceeds of the policy for the benefit of the woman with whom the deceased was living. One question which CARNWATH J considered was whether this nomination in the form of a trust was valid since it had not been made in writing. His Lordship referred to *Re Danish Bacon Co Ltd Staff Pension Fund Trusts* [1971] 1 WLR 248 and held that the nomination did not have to be made in writing because it did not involve the disposition of an equitable interest and it was irrelevant that the nomination was made in the form of a trust. He said at 65:

The true view is that the trust did not crystallise until the sum became payable upon death. Until then, there is no subsisting equitable interest capable of being disposed of within the meaning of section 53.

(j) Disclaimer of Beneficial Interest

In **Re Paradise Motor Co Ltd** [1968] 1 WLR 1125, the question arose whether the disclaimer of a beneficial interest in shares was required to be evidenced in writing under section 53(1)(c). In holding that it did not, DANCKWERTS LJ said at 1143:

The...argument was that there could here be no disclaimer of the beneficial interest in the shares because a disclaimer would, by re-transfer, be a disposition of an equitable interest in property, and neither of the suggested disclaimers was in writing signed by [the disclaimant]: see the Law of Property Act, 1925, section 53(2). We think that the short answer to this is that a disclaimer operates by way of avoidance and not by way of disposition. For the general aspects of disclaimer we refer briefly to the discussion in *Re Stratton's Disclaimer* [1958] Ch 42.[30]

In **Newlon Housing Trust v Alsulaimen** [1999] 1 AC 313, in determining the meaning of 'disposition' for the purposes of section 24 of the Matrimonial Causes Act 1973 (property adjustment orders), LORD HOFFMANN said at 316:

The question is therefore whether the termination of a tenancy can be a disposition of property. 'Disposition' is a familiar enough word in the law of property and ordinarily means an act by which someone ceases to be the owner of that property in law or in equity: see the formulation

---

[30] A disclaimer is not treated as a disposition for the purposes of inheritance tax: Inheritance Tax Act (IHTA) 1984, s. 17.

by Mr. R.O. Wilberforce QC in *Grey v Inland Revenue Commissioners* [1960] AC 1, 18. In some contexts it may include the case in which the property ceases to exist.... But, be that all as it may, I think it is essential to the notion of a disposition of property in this context that there is property of which the disponor disposes, whether to someone else or not. It is this property which the court can restore to his estate by setting aside the disposition.

(iii) Reform

Law Commission, Seventh Programme of Reform (No. 259, 1999), pp. 14–15

Formalities
At present there are certain statutory formal requirements for the creation of trusts and interests in land and for the disposition of equitable interests.[31] These date back to 1677. These provisions are now a cause of some difficulty. First, the requirement that a trust of land is unenforceable unless evidenced in writing[32] has led to the judicial development of so-called 'common intention' constructive trusts, as a means of giving effect to informal agreements between the parties. The resulting body of law is widely regarded as uncertain and unsatisfactory. In relation to other forms of property, where there are no equivalent formal requirements, very similar informal arrangements have been found to create express trusts,[33] and the difficulties associated with common intention constructive trusts have not arisen. Secondly, the requirement that a disposition of a subsisting equitable interest must be made in writing[34] is not only inherently unsatisfactory as it has been interpreted[35] but it is perceived to be a problem in relation to certain forms of electronic trading in securities.[36] Thirdly, developments in electronic commerce mean that formal requirements need to be reviewed to ensure that they can accommodate widely used forms of electronic communication.[37]

Law Commission, 2000 Annual Report (Law Com. No. 268, 2001), p. 36

We are currently reviewing the project to see whether it may be possible to address the most pressing problems quickly by use (for example) of an Order made under section 8 of the Electronic Communications Act 2000.

---

[31] See LPA 1925, s. 53.
[32] LPA 1925, s. 53(1)(b). See p. 112, above.
[33] See *Paul v Constance* [1977] 1 WLR 527.
[34] LPA 1925, s. 53(1)(c). See p. 112, above.
[35] It appears to have no clear rationale: see *Neville v Wilson* [1997] Ch 144 [p. 120, above], holding that a specifically enforceable contract to assign an equitable interest was effective to transfer that interest without the need for writing. It is not easy to see why the specific enforceability or otherwise of an agreement should determine whether formal requirements of writing apply.
[36] The legal issues are complex. The problem typically arises where a custodian holds the securities in intangible electronic form for the benefit of investors, and then trades in them.
[37] See, in particular, the UNCITRAL Model Law on Electronic Commerce, Article 6, which may be incorporated into English law in the near future.

QUESTIONS

1. How would you have decided:

    (a) *Re Vandervell's Trusts (No 2)* [1974] Ch 269 [p. 116, above]; [1979] Conv 17, at pp. 31–37 (G. Battersby); (1974) Conv (NS) 405 (P.J. Clarke); (1975) 38 MLR 557 (J.W. Harris)?

    (b) *Oughtred v IRC* [1960] AC 206 [p. 118, above]; [1979] Conv 17, at pp. 26–31 (G. Battersby)?

    (c) *Neville v Wilson* [1997] Ch 144 [p. 120, above]?

2. Is it possible to reconcile the approach of the House of Lords in *Oughtred v IRC* with that of the Court of Appeal in *Neville v Wilson?* Is it significant that *Oughtred* was a Stamp Duty case? See [1996] Conv 368, 370–371 (M.P. Thompson), (1996) CLJ 436, 438 (R. Nolan), H&M, pp. 91–92.

3. Is it useful to explain the analysis in *Vandervell v Inland Revenue Commissioners* [1967] 2 AC 291 [p. 114, above], as being founded on the over-reaching doctrine? See (2002) CLJ 169 (R.C. Nolan).

B   BY WILL[38]

(i) Formalities for Testamentary Dispositions

WILLS ACT 1837

9. Signing and attestation of wills

No will shall be valid unless—

   (a) it is in writing, and signed by the testator, or by some other person in his presence and by his direction; and

   (b) it appears that the testator intended by his signature to give effect to the will; and

   (c) the signature is made or acknowledged by the testator in the presence of two or more witnesses present at the same time; and

   (d) each witness either—

       (i)   attests and signs the will; or

---

[38] H&M, p. 94; Lewin, pp. 74–82; P&M, p. 97 ; P&S pp. 198–199; Pettit pp. 96–97; Snell p. 485; T&H pp. 127–128; U&H, p. 305. For detailed commentary on this section, see *Theobald on Wills* (16th edn, 2001), chap. 4; *Williams on Wills* (9th edn, 2008), chaps. 10–16. For testamentary formalities in the conflict of laws, see Wills Act 1963.

      (ii)   acknowledges his signature, in the presence of the testator (but not necessarily in the presence of any other witness),

but no form of attestation shall be necessary.[39]

Section 9 prescribes the formalities which are necessary for the validity of a testamentary disposition. It is important that strict formalities should attend a will. If a problem should arise, the testator is no longer with us and cannot be consulted. The imposition of certain formalities reduces the chance of mistake, or of ill-considered and hasty dispositions.

(ii) Testamentary Dispositions which Fail to Comply with the Wills Act 1837 [40]

What should be done if the testator's intention is obvious, but a formality is lacking? Perhaps there was only one witness; or perhaps two witnesses attested the will, but not in the presence of the testator. In this situation, the well-intentioned formalities become a burden, unnecessarily invalidating the will. Further, what should the court do if a beneficiary fraudulently obtains a benefit for himself?—as by promising orally that he would hold certain property, left to him in the will, on trust for another?[41] Equity strives, where possible, to prevent a statute being used as a cloak for fraud. The secret trust doctrines grew up in this context.[42] and reasonably clear rules were laid down to meet the situation where, by the terms of the will, the gift was made to a legatee absolutely (a 'fully secret' trust); for there was in that situation a possibility of fraud. The problem is more difficult where the gift is to a legatee 'on such trusts as I have declared (or shall declare)' (a 'half-secret' trust). The legatee here takes in a fiduciary capacity, and cannot fraudulently claim for himself. It would be strange if the mention of the trust *prevented* its being enforced as a secret trust; but, there being no possibility of fraud, its enforcement must be based upon some doctrine other than that of fraud.

    Secret trusts however are only one of various methods of effecting testamentary dispositions without spelling out the disposition in the will, which will be considered in this section.

---

[39] As substituted by Administration of Justice Act 1982, s. 17. See Law Reform Committee 22nd Report (Cmnd 7902), Part II.

[40] H&M, p. 149–169; Lewin, pp. 74–75; P&M, p. 114–134; P&S pp. 211–233; Pettit pp. 127–135; Snell pp. 551–560; T&H pp. 895–904; U&H, pp. 316–328; (1915) 28 *Harvard Law Review* 236, 366 (G.P. Costigan); (1937) 53 LQR 501 (W.S. Holdsworth); (1947) 12 Conv (NS) 28 (J.G. Flemming); (1951) 67 LQR 314 (L.A. Sheridan); (1963) 27 Conv (NS) 92 (J.A. Andrews); (1972) 36 Conv (NS) 113 (R. Burgess); (1972) 23 *Northern Ireland Law Quarterly* 263 (R. Burgess); [1979] Conv 360 (P. Matthews); [1980] Conv 341 (D.R. Hodge); [1981] Conv 335 (T.G. Watkin); [1985] Conv 248 (B. Perrins); [1995]; Conv 366 (D. Wilde); [1996] Conv 302 (C.E.F. Rickett); (1999) 115 LQR 631 (P. Critchley); [2000] Conv 420 (D. Kincaid); Oakley, *Constructive Trusts* (3rd edn, 1997), chap. 5; Miller, *Machinery of Succession,* (2nd edn, 1996) pp. 223–230; *Theobald on Wills* (note 38 above), chaps. 6, 11; *Williams on Wills* (note 38 above), chap. 36.

[41] A similar problem arises where land is conveyed *inter vivos* to a donee on an oral trust for a third party; thus failing to comply with LPA 1925, s. 53(1)(b) [p. 112, above].

[42] *McCormick v Grogan* (1869) LR 4 HL 82 at 88, 89, 97 [p. 133, below]. See also *Thynn v Thynn* (1684) 1 Vern 296; *Crook v Brooking* (1688) 2 Vern 50 *per* Lord Jeffreys LC; *Drakeford v Wilks* (1747) 3 Atk 539. See now *Re Snowden* [1979] Ch 528 [p. 136, below], *per* Megarry V-C.

(a) Incorporation by Reference

In the Goods of Smart [43]
[1902] P 238 (PD, **Gorell Barnes J**)

By a will made in 1895, the testatrix directed that, after a life interest, her trustees should give to such of her friends as she might designate certain articles to be specified in a book or memorandum to be found with her will. Such a book or memorandum was prepared in 1898 or 1899. Subsequently (27 July, 1900) a codicil was executed which confirmed the will, but did not refer to the book.

Held. The 'book or memorandum' was referred to as a future document and could not be admitted to probate.

Gorell Barnes J: Before referring very briefly to the cases, it seems to me desirable to state how the principle upon which this matter ought to be decided appears to my mind. It seems to me that it has been established that if a testator, in a testamentary paper duly executed, refers to an existing unattested testamentary paper, the instrument so referred to becomes part of his will; in other words, it is incorporated into it; but it is clear that, in order that the informal document should be incorporated in the validly executed document, the latter must refer to the former as a written instrument then existing—that is, at the time of execution—in such terms that it may be ascertained. A leading case upon this subject is *Allen v Maddock* (1858) 11 Moo PCC 427, and it is desirable also to refer to *In the Goods of Mary Sunderland* (1866) LR 1 P & D 198. It will be seen from a statement of the principle in the form I have just given, that the document which it is sought to incorporate must be existing at the time of the execution of the document into which it is to be incorporated, and there must be a reference in the properly executed document to the informal document as an existing one, and not as a future document. If the document is not existing at the time of the will, but comes into existence afterwards, and then, after that again, there is a codicil confirming the will, the question arises, as it has done in a number of these cases, whether that document is incorporated. It appears to me that, following out the principle which I have already referred to, the will may be treated, by the confirmation given by the codicil, as executed again, and as speaking from the date of the codicil, and if the informal document is existing then, and is referred to in the will as existing, so as to identify it, there will be incorporation; but if the will, treated as being re-executed at the date of the codicil, still speaks in terms which shew that it is referring to a future document, then it appears to me there is no incorporation.

(b) Facts of Independent Legal Significance

Jarman on Wills (8th edn, 1951), p. 153

In *Stubbs v Sargon*[44] it was contended that, on the same principle, a devise of realty to 'the persons who shall be in co-partnership with me at the time of my decease, or to whom I shall

---

[43] *Allen v Maddock* (1858) 11 Moo PCC 427; *Re Jones' Will Trusts* [1942] Ch 328; *Re Edwards' Will Trusts* [1948] Ch 440 [p. 130, below]; *Re Schintz's Will Trusts* [1951] Ch 870; *Re Tyler* [1967] 1 WLR 1269; *Re Berger* [1990] Ch 118; cf *In the Goods of Lady Truro* (1866) LR 1 P & D 201; *Theobald on Wills* (note 38 above), pp. 59–61.   [44] (1837) 2 Keen 255; on appeal (1838) 3 My & Cr 507.

have disposed of my business' was void, as leaving it for the testator by some further act, not authorised by the Statute of Frauds, to select the devise. But Lord Langdale, and on appeal Lord Cottenham, held the devise good. Lord Cottenham compared the case to that of a father having two sons, and devising his property to such one of them as should not become entitled to an estate from a third person; here the act of a third person determines who shall take the father's estate. But the act is not testamentary; if it were, one man would be making another man's will. And if not testamentary when done by a third person, it cannot be so when done by the testator himself; otherwise a testator could not devise to such person as, at his death, should be his wife or servant. And Lord Langdale said, if the description was such as to distinguish the devisee from every other person, it was sufficient without entering into the question whether the description was acquired by the devisee after the date of the will, or by the testator's own act in the ordinary course of his affairs, or in the management of his property.

The question is, therefore: is the supplementary act testamentary? If it is, the devise is void; if it is not, then, although it is the sole act of the testator, the devise is good.

The point frequently arises where a testator by his will directs part of his property to be disposed of in such way as he shall by letter, memorandum, etc., or the like, direct; it is clear that no such document can have any testamentary operation, unless executed as a will, or incorporated by a subsequent will or codicil.[45]

Scott: *Trusts* (4th edn, 1989), § 54.2

Where disposition is determined by facts of independent significance. There is another doctrine of the law of wills which is sometimes confused with the doctrine of incorporation by reference. Even though a disposition cannot be fully ascertained from the terms of the will, it is not invalid if it can be ascertained from facts which have significance apart from their effect upon the disposition in the will. Indeed it is frequently necessary to resort to extrinsic evidence to identify the persons who are to take or the subject matter of a disposition. Thus a bequest to the children or the heirs or next of kin of a named person requires a resort to extrinsic evidence to establish their identity, but it is of course valid. So also a disposition in favor of persons who are in the employ of the testator at the time of his death, or a disposition in favor of such person or institution as may care for the testator during his old age or last illness, is valid. So too the property given may be ascertained by extrinsic facts; thus a bequest of money in banks, securities in a safe-deposit box, or furniture in a designated room or house, is valid. On the other hand, the disposition is invalid where the facts from which it is to be ascertained have no independent significance; thus a disposition in favor of such persons as may be named in an unattested memorandum, or such property as may be designated in such a memorandum, is invalid unless it can be upheld on the doctrine of incorporation by reference, since the designation in the memorandum has no significance apart from the disposition of the property by the will...this doctrine, like that of incorporation by reference, is a general doctrine of the law of wills...

(c) Gifts to Trustees of an Existing Settlement

A testamentary gift may be made as an addition to an existing settlement by 'incorporating' the settlement into the will by reference in accordance with the principles of incorporation by reference. But difficulties will obviously arise where the settlement

---

[45] See *Re Jones' Will Trusts* [1942] Ch 328 [p. 130, below].

is amended; for the amended settlement will be a new document. If the rules of the doctrine of incorporation by reference are strictly observed, it seems that the only alternative solutions are either to hold that the settlement is void, or to enforce it in its *un*amended form. Neither solution is satisfactory.

In **Re Edwards' Will Trusts** [1948] Ch 440.[46] a settlor, in 1935, made a 'pilot' settlement of £100, the fund to be held upon trust, as to income and capital, for such persons as the settlor should by a memorandum direct, and subject thereto, upon trust for his wife and children. By his will, made on the same date but afterwards, the settlor directed that his residuary estate should be held upon the trusts of the settlement 'so far as such trusts and provisions are subsisting and capable of taking effect'. By a subsequent memorandum dated November 1937, he laid down certain trusts upon which part of the fund was to be held. Seven years later, he died. The question was whether the residuary estate was held upon the trusts of the settlement; and, if so, whether these were the original trusts, or those laid down in the memorandum of 1937. The Court of Appeal held that the will incorporated the settlement in its original unamended form. LORD GREENE MR said at 446:

The settlement here is a document which can be perfectly well identified, and there is no rule of law to the contrary. It can accordingly be incorporated as a piece of writing into the testamentary disposition. Indeed, if the settlement, instead of being a thing having value and force in itself, had been merely a memorandum previously executed to which, in his will, he referred, it could perfectly well have been admitted to probate as a testamentary instrument. The question then would have arisen, what provisions in this instrument are valid and what are invalid? I start then with the proposition that the incorporation of this document into the will is a permissible and easy matter. When I say incorporation, I am referring to what I may perhaps call the mechanical act of incorporation by reading the language of it into the will itself. We have now got therefore to a stage where there is a will, part of the directions of which cannot operate any more than they could operate if they had been contained, as in the case of *Re Jones* [1942] Ch 328, in the will itself. The presence of that invalid provision in the case of *Re Jones* did not involve its being struck out of the probate and treated as not being part of the will, nor do I see any reason why the invalidity of a provision contained in this settlement should be any reason for excluding it from the testamentary directions of the deceased. The result of his having in that identifiable document included something which the law does not allow to have effect, is a matter to be considered after probate when the question of the validity of his testamentary dispositions arises. The result therefore is that there is here a composite will consisting of a combination of the actual will itself plus the provisions of the settlement...

It seems to me that the directions for incorporation are directions to read into the will the entirety of a document which the testator no doubt thought would be effective. But if, on writing them into the will, it turns out that part of them is invalid from some rule of law, as in the present case, I cannot read the testator's directions as meaning that, therefore, the whole process of incorporation must be abandoned. I think that the effect of it is that so much of the settlement as can validly have operation as part of a testamentary disposition is left to take effect according to its true construction.

---

[46] *Re Jones*, ibid; *Re Schintz's Will Trusts* [1951] Ch 870; *Re Cooper* [1939] Ch 811 [p. 144, below].

(d) Secret Trusts[47]

1. Fully Secret Trusts

A testator sometimes makes a gift by will which is absolute on its face, but which is intended to be held by the legatee (or devisee) upon trust. This may be, as was commonly the situation in the older cases, a method of giving property to a mistress or to an illegitimate child, without the fact being made public by inclusion in the will. The testator could give the legacy to a trusted friend, absolutely, relying on the friend to hand over the legacy as required. The situation has also arisen where an aged testatrix is unable to make up her mind as to her wishes, usually in relation to trinkets; she leaves the property to a solicitor, who will see to its disposal according to later verbal instructions.[48]

The difficulty is that such intended trusts do not comply with the necessary formalities of the Wills Act 1837. If they are not to be enforced in favour of the intended beneficiaries, what should happen? It is inequitable for the legatee to keep it for himself. Equity will not allow a statute to be used as an instrument of fraud. Fraud would be prevented if the legatee was required to hold upon a resulting trust for the estate. But this is a denial of the testator's intention. Provided that the intended trusts are communicated to the legatee *prior to* the testator's death, such trusts are enforced in favour of the intended beneficiary.[49]

Thynn v Thynn
(1684) 1 Vern 296 (Ch, **Earl of Guildford, Lord Keeper**)

The Case was, that Mr. *Thynn,* of *Eagham,* Deceased, having made a Will, and thereby made his Wife sole Executrix; the Defendant Mr. *Thynn* the Son, hearing of this Will, came to his Mother in the Life-time of his Father, and perswaded her, that there being many Debts, the Executorship would be troublesome to her; and desired that he might be nam'd Executor;[50]—for that he by reason of his Privilege of Parliament could struggle the better with the Creditors, and perswaded his Mother to move his Father in it; declaring that he would be only an Executor in Trust for her: And the Mother accordingly prevails on the Father that it might be so: And thereupon Mr. *Thynn* the Son gets a new Will drawn, whereby a Legacy of 50l. only is given to his Mother, and therein he makes himself sole Executor; and cancels the former Will, tho' the Father opposed the doing thereof; and the last Will was read over so low, that the Testator could not hear it; and when he called to have it read louder, the Scrivenor cried, he was afraid of disturbing his Worship. The Defendant having thus made himself sole Executor, and procured

---

[47] H&M, p. 153–169; Lewin, pp. 75–82; P&M, p. 114–134; P&S pp. 211–233; Pettit pp. 127–135; Snell pp. 555–560; T&H pp. 895–904; U&H, pp. 317–328; Oakley, *Constructive Trusts* (3rd edn), pp. 243–263; [2004] Conv 388 (M. Pawlowski and J. Brown); [2005] Conv 492 (E. Challinor); [2006] Conv 203 (R. Meager). See also articles referred to at p. 127, note 40 above.

[48] See e.g. *Re Snowden* [1979] Ch 528 [p. 136, below].

[49] The same principle applies where an existing legacy is not revoked: *Chamberlaine v Chamberlaine* (1678) Freem Ch 34; *Moss v Cooper* (1861) 1 John & H 352; and where an intestate, in reliance upon the undertaking of next of kin, fails to make a will: *Stickland v Aldridge* (1804) 9 Ves 516, and where a legatee undertakes to dispose of property on death in a particular manner: *Ottaway v Norman* [1972] Ch 698 [p. 132, below].

[50] Before the Executors Act 1830, an executor was permitted to retain beneficially property not otherwise disposed of by the will.

this Will to be executed, where only a Legacy of 50l. was given to his Mother, set up for himself, and denied the Trust for his Mother: And in his two first Answers he denied the Will was drawn by his Directions, and that the 50l. therein given to his Mother was without the Testator's Privity; but in his third Answer he confessed it.

Upon the whole Matter, it appeared to be, as well as a Fraud, as also a Trust, the Lord *Keeper*, notwithstanding the Statute of *Frauds* and *Perjuries*, tho' no Trust was declar'd in Writing, decreed it for the Plaintiff, and Order'd that the Defendant should be examined on Interrogatories for discovery of the Estate.

In **Kasperbauer v Griffith** (2000) 1 WTLR 333 PETER GIBSON LJ identified the essential features of a fully secret trust.[51]

...the authorities make plain that what is needed is (i) an intention by the testator to create a trust, satisfying the traditional requirement of three certainties (that is to say certain language in imperative form, certain subject matter and certain objects or beneficiaries); (ii) the communication of the trust to the legatees, and (iii) acceptance of the trust by the legatee, which acceptance can take the form of silent acquiescence. The crucial question in the present case is whether there was that intention and, as Brightman J said in *Ottaway v Norman* [1972] Ch 698, 711 [p. 133, below], it is an essential element that the testator must intend to subject the legatee to an obligation in favour of the intended beneficiary. That will be evidenced by appropriately imperative, as distinct from precatory language.

Informal Disclosure of Existence and Terms of Trust

Ottaway v Norman
[1972] Ch 698[52] (ChD, **Brightman J**)

By his will, dated 8 March, 1960, Mr. Ottaway devised his freehold bungalow, called 'Ashcroft', and its contents to Miss Hodges, his housekeeper; with one-half of his residuary estate to her, and the other half to his son, William. During his lifetime Ottaway orally communicated his intention to Miss Hodges that she should leave the bungalow and its contents, and it was alleged, so much of her residuary estate as should remain undisposed of at her death, to the plaintiffs, William and William's wife Dorothy.

A few months after Ottaway's death in 1963, Miss Hodges made a will which accorded with this arrangement. But in 1967 she made a new will in which she devised the bungalow to the defendant and his wife. The plaintiff alleged that Miss Hodges had agreed to leave the bungalow, its contents, and her residuary estate to them, and brought an action for a declaration that the defendant, who was Miss Hodges's executor, held the property on a constructive trust for them. In the evidence, the

[51] This was approved by Nourse LJ in *Margulies v Margulies* (1999–2000) 2 ITELR 641. See also *Brown v Pouran* [1995] 1 NZLR 352; [1996] Conv 302 (C.E.F. Rickett).
[52] (1972) 36 Conv (NS) 113 (R. Burgess), 129 (D.J. Hayton); (1973) 36 MLR 210 (S.M. Bandali) p. 291, below, post; [1971] *Annual Survey of Commonwealth Law* 384 (J. Hackney).

undertaking in respect of the bungalow was established, but not that in respect of the residuary estate.

Held. The defendant held the bungalow on a constructive trust for the plaintiffs.

Brightman J: It will be convenient to call the person upon whom such a trust is imposed the 'primary donee' and the beneficiary under that trust the 'secondary donee'. The essential elements which must be proved to exist are:

(i)   the intention of the testator to subject the primary donee to an obligation in favour of the secondary donee;

(ii)   communication of that intention to the primary donee; and

(iii) the acceptance of that obligation by the primary donee either expressly or by acquiescence.

It is immaterial whether these elements precede or succeed the will of the donor. I am informed that there is no recent reported case where the obligation imposed on the primary donee is an obligation to make a will in favour of the secondary donee as distinct from some form of *inter vivos* transfer. But it does not seem to me that there can really be any distinction which can validly be taken on behalf of the defendant in the present case. The basis of the doctrine of a secret trust is the obligation imposed on the conscience of the primary donee and it does not seem to me that there is any materiality in the machinery by which the donor intends that that obligation shall be carried out.

Mr. Buckle, for Mr. Norman, relied strongly on *McCormick v Grogan* (1869) LR 4 HL 82. In that case a testator in 1851 had left all his property by a three-line will to his friend Mr. Grogan. In 1854 the testator was struck down by cholera. With only a few hours to live he sent for Mr. Grogan. He told Mr. Grogan in effect that his will and a letter would be found in his desk. The letter named various intended beneficiaries and the intended gifts to them. The letter concluded with the words:

'I do not wish you to act strictly on the foregoing instructions, but leave it entirely to your own good judgment to do as you think I would, if living, and as the parties are deserving.'

An intended beneficiary whom Mr. Grogan thought it right to exclude sued. I will read an extract from the speech of Lord Westbury, at 97, because Mr. Buckle relied much upon it.

'...the jurisdiction which is invoked here by the appellant is founded altogether on personal fraud. It is a jurisdiction by which a Court of Equity, proceeding on the ground of fraud, converts the party who has committed it into a trustee for the party who is injured by that fraud. Now, being a jurisdiction founded on personal fraud, it is incumbent on the court to see that a fraud, a *malus animus*, is proved by the clearest and most indisputable evidence.'

Lord Westbury continued, at 97:

'You are obliged, therefore, to shew most clearly and distinctly that the person you wish to convert into a trustee acted *malo animo*. You must shew distinctly that he knew that the testator or the intestate was beguiled and deceived by his conduct. If you are not in a condition to affirm that without any misgiving, or possibility of mistake, you are not warranted in affixing on the individual the *delictum* of fraud, which you must do before you convert him into a trustee. Now are there any indicia of fraud in this case?'

Lord Westbury then examined the facts with which that case was concerned.

Founding himself on Lord Westbury Mr. Buckle sought at one stage to deploy an argument that a person could never succeed in establishing a secret trust unless he could show that the primary donee was guilty of deliberate and conscious wrongdoing of which he said there was no evidence in the case before me. That proposition, if correct, would lead to the surprising result that if the primary donee faithfully observed the obligation imposed on him there would not ever have been a trust at any time in existence. The argument was discarded, and I think rightly. Mr. Buckle then fastened on the words 'clearest and most indisputable evidence' and he submitted that an exceptionally high standard of proof was needed to establish a secret trust. I do not think that Lord Westbury's words mean more than this: that if a will contains a gift which is in terms absolute, clear evidence is needed before the court will assume that the testator did not mean what he said. It is perhaps analogous to the standard of proof which this court requires before it will rectify a written instrument, for there again a party is saying that neither meant what they have written...[53]

Having heard the evidence I have no doubt in my mind that I have received an accurate account of all essential facts from William and Mrs. Dorothy Ottaway (the plaintiffs). I find as a fact that Mr. Harry Ottaway intended that Miss Hodges should be obliged to dispose of the bungalow in favour of the plaintiffs at her death; that Mr. Harry Ottaway communicated that intention to Miss Hodges; and that Miss Hodges accepted the obligation. I find the same facts in relation to the furniture, fixtures and fittings which passed to Miss Hodges under clause 4 of Mr. Harry Ottaway's will. I am not satisfied that any similar obligation was imposed and accepted as regards any contents of the bungalow which had not devolved on Miss Hodges under clause 4 of Mr. Harry Ottaway's will.

I turn to the question of money. In cross-examination William said the trust extended to the house, furniture and money:

> 'Everything my father left to Miss Hodges was to be in the trust. The trust comprised the lot. She could use the money as she liked. She had to leave my wife and me whatever money was left.'

In cross-examination Mrs. Dorothy Ottaway said that her understanding was that Miss Hodges was bound to make a will giving her and her husband the bungalow, contents and any money she had left. 'She could please herself about the money. She did not have to save it for us. She was free to spend it.' It seems to me that two questions arise. First, as a matter of fact, what did the parties intend should be comprised in Miss Hodges's obligation? All money which Miss Hodges had at her death including both money which she had acquired before Mr. Harry Ottaway's death and money she acquired after his death from all sources? Or only money acquired under Mr. Harry Ottaway's will? Secondly, as a matter of law, if such an obligation existed would it create a valid trust? On the second question I am content to assume for present purposes but without so deciding that if property is given to the primary donee on the understanding that the primary donee will dispose by his will of such assets, if any, as he may have at his command at his death in favour of the secondary donee, a valid trust is created in favour of the secondary donee which is in suspense during the lifetime of the primary donee, but attaches to the estate of the primary donee at the moment of the latter's death. There would seem to be at least

---

[53] Not followed in *Re Snowden* [1979] Ch 528 at 534–537 [p. 136, below], where Megarry V-C applied the ordinary civil standard of proof on a balance of probabilities, unless fraud was alleged against the alleged trustee.

some support for this proposition in an Australian case to which I was referred: *Birmingham v Renfrew* (1937) 57 CLR 666.[54] I accept that the parties mentioned money on at least some occasions when they talked about Mr. Harry Ottaway's intentions for the future disposition of Ashcroft. I do not, however, find sufficient evidence that it was the intention of Mr. Harry Ottaway that Miss Hodges should be compelled to leave all her money, from whatever source derived, to the plaintiffs. This would seem to preclude her giving even a small pecuniary legacy to any friend or relative. I do not think it is clear that Mr. Harry Ottaway intended to extract any such far-reaching undertaking from Miss Hodges or that she intended to accept such a wide obligation herself. Therefore the obligation, if any, is in my view, to be confined to money derived under Mr. Harry Ottaway's will. If the obligation is confined to money derived under Mr. Harry Ottaway's will, the obligation is meaningless and unworkable unless it includes the requirement that she shall keep such money separate and distinct from her own money. I am certain that no such requirement was ever discussed or intended. If she had the right to mingle her own money with that derived from Mr. Harry Ottaway, there would be no ascertainable property upon which the trust could bite at her death. This aspect distinguishes this case from *Re Gardner* [1920] 2 Ch 523.

There is another difficulty. Does money in this context include only cash or cash and investments, or all movable property of any description? The evidence is quite inconclusive. In my judgment the plaintiff's claim succeeds in relation to the bungalow and in relation to the furniture, fixtures and fittings which devolved under paragraph 4 of Mr. Harry Ottaway's will subject, of course, to normal wastage, fair wear and tear, but not to any other assets.

In **Re Boyes** (1884) 26 Ch D 531, a legacy was given to the testator's solicitor, who was told that it was to be held upon trust, but he was not informed, until after the testator's death, what the trusts were. Among the testator's papers, a letter was found which said that the residuary estate was to be held on trust for a lady to whom the testator was not married. The solicitor desired to carry out the testator's wishes.

KAY J held that he took as trustee, holding on a resulting trust for the testator's next-of-kin, and said at 536:

The essence of all those decisions is that the devisee or legatee accepts a particular trust which thereupon becomes binding upon him, and which it would be a fraud in him not to carry into effect... The defendant is a trustee of this property for the next-of-kin of the testator. I can only hope that they will consider the claim which this lady has upon their generosity.

The delivery of a sealed letter during the testator's lifetime is a sufficient communication provided that it is known to contain the terms of a trust and is accepted as such. For 'a ship which sails under sealed orders, is sailing under orders though the exact terms are not ascertained by the captain till later'.[55]

---

54 See also *Re Cleaver* [1981] 1 WLR 939 [p. 292, below], where Nourse J relied on *Birmingham v Renfrew* in the context of mutual wills and cited extracts from the judgment of Dixon J.

55 *Re Keen* [1937] Ch 236 at 242, *per* Lord Wright MR; *Re Boyes* (1884) 26 Ch D 531 at 536.

Standard of Proof

In **Re Snowden** [1979] Ch 528[56] the testatrix aged 86 made her will six days before she died; she left her residuary estate to her brother Bert absolutely. Bert died six days after the testatrix, leaving all his property to his son. Evidence was given by members of the firm of solicitors who had prepared and witnessed the will that the testatrix 'wished to be fair to everyone', and that she wanted Bert to 'look after the division for her'.

SIR ROBERT MEGARRY V-C held there was no secret trust but only a moral obligation on Bert, and therefore his son was absolutely entitled to the residue.[57] He said at 534:

One question that arises is whether the standard of proof required to establish a secret trust is merely the ordinary civil standard of proof, or whether it is a higher and more cogent standard. If it is the latter, I feel no doubt that the claim that there is a secret trust must fail. On this question, *Ottaway v Norman* [1972] Ch 698 [p. 132, above] was cited; it was, indeed, the only authority that was put before me. According to the headnote, the standard of proof 'was not an exceptionally high one but was analogous to that required before the court would rectify a written instrument'. When one turns to the judgment, one finds that what Brightman J said at 712, was that Lord Westbury's words in *McCormick v Grogan* (1869) LR 4 HL 82 at 97, a case on secret trusts, did not mean that an exceptionally high standard of proof was needed, but meant no more than that:

'if a will contains a gift which is in terms absolute, clear evidence is needed before the court will assume that the testator did not mean what he said. It is perhaps analogous to the standard of proof which this court requires before it will rectify a written instrument, for there again a party is saying that neither meant what they have written.'

[His Lordship referred to *Ottaway v Norman* and continued:]

I feel some doubt about how far rectification is a fair analogy to secret trusts in this respect. Many cases of rectification do of course involve a party in saying that neither meant what they have written, and requiring that what they have written should be altered. On the other hand, the whole basis of secret trusts, as I understand it, is that they operate outside the will, changing nothing that is written in it, and allowing it to operate according to its tenor, but then fastening a trust on to the property in the hands of the recipient. It is at least possible that very different standards of proof may be appropriate for cases where the words of a formal document have to be altered and for cases where there is no such alteration but merely a question whether, when the document has been given effect to, there will be some trust of the property with which it dealt.... I am not sure that it is right to assume that there is a single, uniform standard of proof for all secret trusts. The proposition of Lord Westbury in *McCormick v Grogan* with which Brightman J was pressed in *Ottaway v Norman* was that the jurisdiction in cases of secret trust was

'founded altogether on personal fraud. It is a jurisdiction by which a Court of Equity, proceeding on the ground of fraud, converts the party who has committed it into a trustee for the party

[56] [1979] Conv 448 (F.R. Crane); (1979) 38 CLJ 26 (C.E.F. Rickett); (1991) 107 LQR 194 (B. Robertson). See also *Re Cleaver* [1981] 1 WLR 939 at 947–948 [p. 292, below], where Nourse J held that mutual wills need only be proved on the balance of probabilities.

[57] See also *Kasperbauer v Griffith* (2000) 1 WTLR 333 and *Margulies v Margulies* (1999–2000) 2 ITELR 641.

who is injured by that fraud. Now, being a jurisdiction founded on personal fraud, it is incumbent on the court to see that a fraud, a *malus animus*, is proved by the clearest and most indisputable evidence.'

Of that, it is right to say that the law on the subject has not stood still since 1869, and that it is now clear that secret trusts may be established in cases where there is no possibility of fraud. *McCormick v Grogan* has to be read in the light both of earlier cases that were not cited, and also of subsequent cases, in particular *Blackwell v Blackwell* [1929] AC 318 [p. 139, below]. It seems to me that fraud comes into the matter in two ways. First, it provides an historical explanation of the doctrine of secret trusts; the doctrine was evolved as a means of preventing fraud. That, however, does not mean that fraud is an essential ingredient for the application of the doctrine; the reason for the rule is not part of the rule itself. Second, there are some cases within the doctrine where fraud is indeed involved. There are cases where for the legatee to assert that he is a beneficial owner, free from any trust, would be a fraud on his part.

It is to this latter aspect of fraud that it seems to me that Lord Westbury's words are applicable. If a secret trust can be held to exist in a particular case only by holding the legatee guilty of fraud, then no secret trust should be found unless the standard of proof suffices for fraud. On the other hand, if there is no question of fraud, why should so high a standard apply? In such a case, I find it difficult to see why the mere fact that the historical origin of the doctrine lay in the prevention of fraud should impose the high standard of proof for fraud in a case in which no issue of fraud arises. In accordance with the general rule of evidence, the standard of proof should vary with the nature of the issue and its gravity: see *Hornal v Neuberger Products Ltd* [1957] 1 QB 247.

Now in the present case there is no question of fraud. The will directed the residue to be held in trust for the brother absolutely, and the only question is whether or not the beneficial interest thus given to him has been subjected to a trust, and if so, what that trust is. The trust, if it is one, is plainly one which required the brother to carry it out: it was he who was to distribute the money and see that everything was dealt with properly, and not the trustees of the will. There was thus no attempt to cancel the testamentary trust of residue for the brother and require the trustees of the will to hold the residue on the secret trust instead. Accordingly I cannot see that rectification provides any real analogy. The question is simply that of the ordinary standard of evidence required to establish a trust.

I therefore hold that in order to establish a secret trust where no question of fraud arises, the standard of proof is the ordinary civil standard of proof that is required to establish an ordinary trust. I am conscious that this does not accord with what was said in *Ottaway v Norman* [1972] Ch 698; but I think the point was taken somewhat shortly there, and the judge does not seem to have had the advantage of having cited to him the authorities that I have considered. For those reasons I have overcome my hesitation in differing from him. I cannot therefore dispose of the case summarily on the footing that a high standard of proof has plainly not been achieved, but I must consider the evidence in some detail to see whether the ordinary standard of proof has been satisfied. The initial question, of course, is whether the brother was bound by a secret trust, or whether he was subject to no more than a moral obligation.

[His Lordship considered the evidence and continued:] The general picture which seems to me to emerge from the evidence is of a testatrix who for long had been worrying about how to divide her residue and who was still undecided. She had a brother whom she trusted implicitly and who knew her general views about her relations and her property. She therefore left her residue to him in the faith that he would, in due time and in accordance with her general wishes, make in her stead the detailed decisions about the distribution of her residue which had for so long troubled her and on which she was still undecided. He was her trusted brother, more wealthy than she, and a little older. There was thus no need to bind him by any legally enforceable trust; and I cannot see any real indication that she had any thought of doing this. Instead, she simply left him, as a matter of family confidence and probity, to do what he thought she would have done if she had ever finally made up her mind. In short, to revert to the language of Christian LJ in *McCormick v Grogan* (1867) IR 1 Eq 313 at 328, I cannot see any real evidence that she intended the sanction to be the authority of a court of justice and not merely the conscience of her brother. I therefore hold that her brother took the residue free from any trust.

2. Half-Secret Trusts

The gift may be to a legatee, not absolutely, but in a fiduciary capacity. Different questions then arise. If the legacy is 'to X upon such trusts as I have orally declared (or shall orally declare) to him', it is clear that X can never claim beneficially. The property is given to him as trustee. We saw that the reason which the judges have given for enforcing fully secret trusts was the prevention of fraud. If, in a half-secret trust, there is no possibility of fraud, how can the court justify the imposition of a trust on that ground?

One possible solution is to refuse to enforce half-secret trusts and to hold that the beneficial interest returns to the testator's estate by way of resulting trust. It would however be a strange rule of law which says that a gift to X absolutely (on a fully secret trust) makes X hold upon trust for Y; yet a gift to X *upon trust* (on a half-secret trust) will be held on a resulting trust. That would mean that the mention of the intended trust in the will would prevent its taking effect. It seems therefore that (a) half-secret trusts should be no less readily enforced than fully secret trusts; (b) fraud is not an adequate basis for the enforcement of half-secret trusts: (c) some other and better rationale is required. The cases will show that some courts have used the analogy of the doctrine of incorporation by reference[58] to meet this problem; with the result that half-secret trusts communicated before or at the time of the will may be enforced; but not those communicated between the date of the will and the death of the testator.[59] Clearly this is inadequate. An attempt is made at the end of this chapter to suggest a theory which is capable of providing a rational basis for the enforcement of secret trusts.[60]

But the problem is wider than this. The question is not merely: on what basis can we enforce these trusts? The question should be: bearing in mind the sound policy in favour of formalities in wills, and the express terms of the Wills Act 1837, section 9, are the reasons for the enforcement of informal dispositions so compelling that it is

[58] See p. 128, above.

[59] But see *Gold v Hill* [1999] 1 FLR 54 [p.144, below].

[60] See [1979] Conv 360 (P. Matthews) where it is argued that the incorporation by reference doctrine is the true basis of half-secret trusts; [1980] Conv 341 (D.R. Hodge) where it is argued that the fraud theory is the true basis of *all* secret trusts: 'the essence of the fraud being found, not in the element of personal gain in the secret trustee, but in the facts that the deceased's confidence is being betrayed and the secret beneficiaries being deprived of benefits which, but for the trustee's action, would have been secured to them by other means' (p. 348). See also [1995] Conv 364 (D. Wilde) and (1999) 115 LQR 631 (P. Critchley).

necessary to enforce them, or some of them? Having answered that question, the earlier one becomes relevant.

Blackwell v Blackwell
[1929] AC 318 (HL, **Lord Hailsham LC, Viscount Sumner, Lords Buckmaster, Carson** and **Warrington**)

The testator, Mr. Blackwell, by a codicil to his will, gave to five persons the sum of £12,000, the income to be applied 'for the purposes indicated by me to them', with power to apply £8,000 of the capital 'to such person or persons indicated by me to them', as they thought fit. The objects of the trust were communicated orally to the trustees, and accepted by them prior to the execution of the codicil. These were in favour of a lady and her illegitimate son. The widow challenged the validity of the trust and claimed the £12,000 as part of the residue.

Held. The trust was valid, and oral evidence was admissible to prove it.

Viscount Sumner: In itself the doctrine of equity, by which parol evidence is admissible to prove what is called 'fraud' in connection with secret trusts, and effect is given to such trusts when established, would not seem to conflict with any of the Acts under which from time to time the Legislature has regulated the right of testamentary disposition. A Court of conscience finds a man in the position of an absolute legal owner of a sum of money, which has been bequeathed to him under a valid will, and it declares that, on proof of certain facts relating to the motives and actions of the testator, it will not allow the legal owner to exercise his legal right to do what he will with his own. This seems to be a perfectly normal exercise of general equitable jurisdiction. The facts commonly but not necessarily involve some immoral and selfish conduct on the part of the legal owner. The necessary elements, on which the question turns, are intention, communication, and acquiescence. The testator intends his absolute gift to be employed as he and not as the donee desires; he tells the proposed donee of this intention and, either by express promise or by the tacit promise, which is signified by acquiescence, the proposed donee encourages him to bequeath the money in the faith that his intentions will be carried out. The special circumstance, that the gift is by bequest only makes this rule a special case of the exercise of a general jurisdiction, but in its application to a bequest the doctrine must in principle rest on the assumption that the will has first operated according to its terms. It is because there is no one to whom the law can give relief in the premises, that relief, if any, must be sought in equity. So far, and in the bare case of a legacy absolute on the face of it, I do not see how the statute-law relating to the form of a valid will is concerned at all, and the expressions, in which the doctrine has been habitually described, seem to bear this out. For the prevention of fraud equity fastens on the conscience of the legatee a trust, a trust, that is, which otherwise would be inoperative; in other words it makes him do what the will in itself has nothing to do with; it lets him take what the will gives him and then makes him apply it, as the Court of conscience directs, and it does so in order to give effect to wishes of the testator, which would not otherwise be effectual.

To this two circumstances must be added to bring the present case to the test of the general doctrine, first, that the will states on its face that the legacy is given on trust but does not state what the trusts are, and further contains a residuary bequest, and, second, that the legatees are acting with perfect honesty, seek no advantage to themselves, and only desire, if the Court will permit them, to do what in other circumstances the Court would have fastened it on their conscience to perform.

Since the current of decisions down to *Re Fleetwood* (1880) 15 Ch D 594 and *Re Huxtable* [1902] 2 Ch 793 has established that the principles of equity apply equally when these circumstances are present as in cases where they are not, the material question is whether and how the Wills Act affects this case. It seems to me that, apart from legislation, the application of the principle of equity, which was made in *Fleetwood's* and *Huxtable's* cases, was logical, and was justified by the same considerations as in the cases of fraud and absolute gifts. Why should equity forbid an honest trustee to give effect to his promise, made to a deceased testator, and compel him to pay another legatee, about whom it is quite certain that the testator did not mean to make him the object of this bounty? In both cases the testator's wishes are incompletely expressed in his will. Why should equity, over a mere matter of words, give effect to them in one case and frustrate them in the other? No doubt the words 'in trust' prevent the legatee from taking beneficially, whether they have simply been declared in conversation or written in the will, but the fraud, when the trustee, so called in the will, is also the residuary legatee, is the same as when he is only declared a trustee by word of mouth accepted by him. I recoil from interfering with decisions of long standing, which reject this anomaly, unless constrained by statute.

The answer is put in the phrase, 'this is making the testator's will for him', instead, that is, of limiting him to the will made in statutory form. What then of the legislation? Great authorities seem to have expressed an opinion, that this equitable principle, as a whole, conflicts with section 9 of the Wills Act. Lord Cairns in 1868 says that when a devisee seeks to apply what has been devised to him otherwise than in accordance with the testator's intentions, communicated by him and accepted, 'it is in effect a case of trust, and in such case the Court will not allow the devisee to set up the Statute of Frauds, or, rather, the Statute of Wills.... But in this the Court does not violate the spirit of the statutes; but for the ... prevention of fraud, it engrafts the trusts on the devise by admitting evidence which the statute would in terms exclude, in order to prevent a devisee from applying property to a purpose foreign to that for which he undertook to hold it': *Jones v Badley* (1868) 3 Ch App 362 at 364 ...

His Lordship discussed the relationship between the equitable principle and the Wills Act 1837, section 9, and continued:

Accordingly, I think the conclusion is confirmed, which the frame of section 9 of the Wills Act seems to me to carry on its face, that the legislation did not purport to interfere with the exercise of a general equitable jurisdiction, even in connection with secret dispositions of a testator, except in so far as reinforcement of the formalities required for a valid will might indirectly limit it. The effect, therefore, of a bequest being made in terms on trust, without any statement in the will to show what the trust is, remains to be decided by the law as laid down by the Courts before and since the Act and does not depend on the Act itself.

The limits, beyond which the rules as to unspecified trusts must not be carried, have often been discussed. A testator cannot reserve to himself a power of making future unwitnessed dispositions by merely naming a trustee and leaving the purposes of the trust to be supplied afterwards, nor can a legatee give testamentary validity to an unexecuted codicil by accepting an indefinite trust, never communicated to him in the testator's lifetime: *Johnson v Ball* (1851) 5 De G & Sm 85; *Re Boyes* (1884) 26 Ch D 531; *Riordan v Banon* (1876) IR 10 Eq 469; *Re Hetley* [1902] 2 Ch 866. To hold otherwise would indeed be to enable the testator to 'give the go-by' to the requirements of the Wills Act, because he did not choose to comply with them. It is communication of the purpose to the legatee, coupled with acquiescence or promise on his part, that removes the matter from the provision of the Wills Act and brings it within the law of trusts, as applied in this instance to trustees, who happen also to be legatees. If I am right in thinking that there is no contradiction of the Wills Act in applying the same rule, whether the trustee is or is not so described in the will, and the whole topic is detached from the enforcement of the Wills Act itself, then, whether the decisions in equity are or are not open to doubt in themselves, I think that, in view of the subject-matter of these decisions and the length of time during which they have been acquiesced in, your Lordships may well in accordance with precedent refuse to overrule them lest titles should be rendered insecure and settlements, entered into in reliance on their authority, should now be disturbed. It is to be remembered that the rule as to trusts not expressed in a will is not limited to relations such as the testator in this case was concerned to provide for, but may have been applied in many other connections. I pretend to no means of knowledge of my own, but it seems to me probable that effect has been given to these cases to a substantial extent and therefore that, to avoid possible injustice, your Lordships should refuse to interfere with them now. Accordingly in my opinion the appeal fails on all grounds.

Time of Communication and Acceptance

Re Keen
[1937] Ch 236 (CA, **Lord Wright MR**, **Greene** and **Romer LJJ**)

A testator, Mr. Keen, by clause 5 of his will, gave £10,000 to trustees 'to be held upon trust and disposed of by them among such person, persons or charities as may be notified by me to them … during my lifetime'. Prior to the execution of the will, he handed to one of the trustees a sealed envelope, containing the name of a lady who was to be the beneficiary. The trustee did not open the envelope until after the testator's death, but he was aware of the fact that it contained the beneficiary's name.

Held. The reservation of a power to make future unattested dispositions is contrary to the Wills Act 1837. Furthermore, the communication, being prior to the execution of the will, was inconsistent with the terms of the will. The legacy therefore fell into residue.

Lord Wright MR: The summons came before Farwell J, who decided adversely to the claims of the lady on the short ground that she could not prove that she was a person notified to the trustees by the testator during his lifetime within the words of clause 5. His opinion seems to be that the clause required the name and identity of the lady to be expressly disclosed to the trustees during the testator's lifetime so that it was not sufficient to place these particulars in the physical possession of the trustees or one of them in the form of a memorandum which they were not to read till the testator's death.

I am unable to accept this conclusion, which appears to me to put too narrow a construction on the word 'notified' as used in clause 5 in all the circumstances of the case. To take a parallel, a ship which sails under sealed orders, is sailing under orders though the exact terms are not ascertained by the captain till later. I note that the case of a trust put into writing which is placed in the trustees' hands in a sealed envelope, was hypothetically treated by Kay J as possibly constituting a communication in a case of this nature: *Re Boyes* (1884) 26 Ch D 531 at 536. This, so far as it goes, seems to support my conclusion. The trustees had the means of knowledge available whenever it became necessary and proper to open the envelope. I think Mr. Evershed was right in understanding that the giving of the sealed envelope was a notification within clause 5.

This makes it necessary to examine the matter on a wider basis, and to consider the principles of law which were argued both before Farwell J and this Court, but which the judge found it merely necessary to mention. There are two main questions: first, how far parol evidence is admissible to define the trust under such a clause as this, and, secondly and in particular, how far such evidence if admissible at all would be excluded on the ground that it would be inconsistent with the true meaning of clause 5.

It is first necessary to state what, in my opinion, is the true construction of the words of the clause.

These words, in my opinion, can only be considered as referring to a definition of trusts which have not yet at the date of the will been established and which between that date and the testator's death may or may not be established. Mr. Roxburgh has strenuously argued, basing himself in particular on the word 'may', that the clause even though it covers future dispositions, also includes a disposition antecedent to or contemporaneous with the execution of the will. I do not think that even so wide a construction of the word 'may' would enable Mr. Roxburgh's contention to succeed, but in any case I do not feel able to accept it. The words of the clause seem to me to refer only to something future and hypothetical, to something as to which the testator is reserving an option whether to do or not to do it. . . .

The principles of law or equity relevant in a question of this nature have now been authoritatively settled or discussed by the House of Lords in *Blackwell v Blackwell* [1929] AC 318 [p. 139, above]. In 1869 in *McCormick v Grogan* (1869) LR 4 HL 82 the House of Lords had held that a secret trust, that is a trust created by an expression of the testator's wishes communicated to and accepted by the legatee, bound the conscience of the legatee, though in the terms of the will the bequest was absolute. Such a trust was held to be altogether outside the will; the will took effect according to its terms and the property passed absolutely to the legatee: but the Court, it was held, would compel the legatee to apply that property according to the undertaking he had assumed to carry out the wishes of the testator. It would be a fraud or breach of faith not to fulfil the undertaking which the legatee had given to carry out the purposes for which the bequest to him was made.

No complication was involved in such a case by reason of section 9 of the Wills Act, 1837. The testamentary disposition, which had been duly attested, received full effect. But a different question had to be considered when in the will itself the property was left to the legatee in trust, but neither the nature of the trust nor its beneficiaries were defined in the will. That was the case decided in *Blackwell v Blackwell*. . . .

As in my judgment clause 5 should be considered as contemplating future dispositions and as reserving to the testator the power of making such dispositions without a duly attested codicil simply by notifying them during his lifetime, the principles laid down by Lord Sumner must be fatal to the appellant's claim. Indeed they would be equally fatal even on the construction for which Mr. Roxburgh contended, that the clause covered both anterior or contemporaneous notifications as well as future notifications. The clause would be equally invalid, but, as already explained, I cannot accept that construction. In *Blackwell v Blackwell* [1929] AC 318; *Re Fleetwood* (1880) 15 Ch D 594 and *Re Huxtable* [1902] 2 Ch 793 the trusts had been specifically declared to some or all of the trustees at or before the execution of the will and the language of the will was consistent with that fact. There was in these cases no reservation of a future power to change the trusts, in whole or in part. Such a power would involve a power to change a testamentary disposition by an unexecuted codicil and would violate section 9 of the Wills Act. This was so held in *Re Hetley* [1902] 2 Ch 866. *Johnson v Ball* (1851) 5 De G & Sm 85 is again a somewhat different example of the rule against dispositions made subsequently to the date of the will in cases where the will in terms leaves the property on trust, and shows that the position may be different from the position where the will in terms leaves the gift absolutely. The trusts referred to but undefined in the will must be described in the will as established prior to or at least contemporaneously with its execution.

But there is still a further objection which in the present case renders the appellant's claim unenforceable; the trusts which it is sought to establish by parol evidence would be inconsistent with the express terms of the will. That such an objection is fatal appears from the cases already cited, such as *Re Huxtable*. In that case an undefined trust of money for charitable purposes was declared in the will as in respect of the whole corpus, and accordingly evidence was held inadmissible that the charitable trust was limited to the legatee's life so that he was free to dispose of the corpus after his death. Similarly in *Johnson v Ball* the testator by the will left the property to trustees upon the uses contained in a letter signed 'by them and myself': it was held that evidence was not admissible to show that though no such letter was in existence at the date of the will, the testator had made a subsequent declaration of trust; the Court held that these trusts could not be enforced. Lord Buckmaster in *Blackwell's* case [1929] AC 318 at 331 described *Johnson v Ball* as an authority pointing to 'a case where the actual trusts were left over after the date of the will to be subsequently determined by the testator'. That in his opinion would be a contravention of the Wills Act. I know of no authority which would justify such a contravention. Lord Buckmaster also quotes at 330 the grounds on which Parker V-C based his decision as being both 'that the letter referred to in the will had no existence at the time when the will was made and that supposing it referred to a letter afterwards signed it is impossible to give effect to it as a declaration of the trusts, since it would admit the document as part of the will and it was unattested'.

In the present case, while clause 5 refers solely to a future definition or to future definitions of the trust subsequent to the date of the will, the sealed letter relied on as notifying the trust was communicated (as I find the facts) before the date of the will. That it was communicated to one trustee only and not to both would not, I think, be an objection (see Lord Warrington's observation in the *Blackwell* case at 341). But the objection remains that the notification sought to be put in evidence was anterior to the will and hence not within the language of clause 5, and inadmissible simply on that ground as being inconsistent with what the will prescribes.

It is always with reluctance that a Court refuses to give effect to the proved intention of the testator. In the present case it may be said that the objection is merely a matter of drafting and that the decision in *Blackwell v Blackwell* would have been applicable if only clause 5 had been worded as applying to trusts previously indicated by the testator. The sealed letter would then have been admissible, subject to proof of the communication and acceptance of the trust. This may be true, but the Court must deal with the matter as in fact it is. It would be impossible to give effect to the appellant's contention without not merely extending the rule laid down in *Blackwell v Blackwell*, but actually contravening the limitations which have been placed on that rule as necessarily arising from the Wills Act and, in addition, from the fact that the conditions prescribed by the will cannot be contradicted.

The appeal must be dismissed and the decision of Farwell J affirmed.

In **Re Bateman's Will Trusts** [1970] 1 WLR 1463, a testator directed his trustee to set aside £24,000 and pay the income 'to such persons and in such proportions as shall be stated by me in a sealed letter in my own handwriting addressed to my trustees'. There was no evidence as to whether a sealed letter had been written and addressed to the trustees by the testator at the date of the will. PENNYCUICK V-C held that the direction was invalid, and said at 1468:

These words clearly, I think, import that the testator may, in the future, after the date of the will, give a sealed letter to his trustees. It is impossible to confine the words to a sealed letter already so given. If that is the true construction of the wording, it is not in dispute that the direction is invalid.

   I was referred to one or two cases on the point, in particular, *Re Keen's Estate* [1937] Ch 236, in the Court of Appeal, and *Re Jones* [1942] Ch 328, *per* Simonds J. I do not think it necessary to go further into those cases because it is really clear and not in dispute that once one must construe the direction as admitting of a future letter then the direction is invalid, as an attempt to dispose of the estate by a non-testamentary instrument.[61]

In **Gold v Hill** [1999] 1 FLR 54, the testator, after he had made his will, nominated his solicitor as a beneficiary of a life insurance policy. The testator orally informed the solicitor that he wanted him to use the proceeds of the money to look after the testator's cohabitant and children. It was held, by analogy with secret trusts, that the solicitor held the money as a constructive trustee for the cohabitant and children. CARNWATH J said at 163:

The nomination, like a testamentary disposition, does not transfer or create any interest until death. It is consistent with the principle of *Blackwell v Blackwell* [p. 139, above], that the nominee should take under the rules of the policy, but then be required to 'apply it as the court of conscience directs' and so 'to give effect to the wishes of the testator'. Such doubts as there may be, in the case of testamentary dispositions, as to the effectiveness of an intention communicated *after* the execution of the will, appear to be derived from the particular rules applying to wills. There is no reason why they should create similar difficulties in the case of nominations. Since the nomination has no effect until the time of death, it should be sufficient that the nature of the trust is sufficiently communicated prior to that time.

Alterations to the Trust Property

In **Re Cooper** [1939] Ch 811 a testator left £5,000 to two trustees, to whom he communicated the terms of the trust before he had executed his will in February 1938. The trustees acquiesced. By a later will in March, the testator purported to cancel the earlier will except for certain bequests, and then added: 'the sum of £5,000 bequeathed to my trustees in the will now cancelled is to be increased to £10,000, they knowing my wishes regarding that sum'. This increase was never communicated by the testator

---

[61] *Riordan v Banon* (1876) IR 10 Eq 469; cf. *Balfe v Halpenny* [1904] 1 IR 486; *Re Browne* [1944] IR 90; (1951) 67 LQR 413 (L.A. Sheridan); [1992] Conv 202 (J. Mee) and (1991) 5 *Trust Law International* 69 (P. Couglan); *Re Prendiville* (5 December 1990, unreported).

to the trustees. The Court of Appeal held that the first £5,000 was subject to a secret trust, but that the additional £5,000 went on a resulting trust. Sir Wilfrid Greene MR said at 817:

The substance of the matter is that, having imposed on the conscience of these two trustees the trust in relation to the legacy of 5000l. and having written that legacy into his will of February, 1938, by this will he in effect is giving another legacy of the same amount to be held upon the same trusts. It seems to me that upon the facts of this case it is impossible to say that the acceptance by the trustees of the onus of trusteeship in relation to the first and earlier legacy is something which must be treated as having been repeated in reference to the second legacy or the increased legacy, whichever way one chooses to describe it. In order that a secret trust might be made effective with regard to that added sum in my opinion precisely the same factors were necessary as were required to validate the original trusts, namely, communication, acceptance or acquiescence, and the making of the will on the faith of such acceptance or acquiescence. None of these elements, as I have said, were present. It is not possible, in my opinion, to treat the figure of 5000l. in relation to which the consent of the trustees was originally obtained as something of no essential importance. I cannot myself see that the arrangement between the testator and the trustees can be construed as though it had meant '5000l. or whatever sum I may hereafter choose to bequeath'. That is not what was said and it was not with regard to any sum other than the 5000l. that the consciences of the trustees (to use a technical phrase) were burdened. It must not be thought from what I have been saying that some trifling excess of the sum actually bequeathed over the figure mentioned in the first bequest to the trustees would necessarily not be caught. Such an addition might come within the rule of de minimis if the facts justified it. Similarly it must not be thought that, if a testator, having declared to his trustees trusts in relation to a specified sum, afterwards in his will inserts a lesser sum, that lesser sum would not be caught by the trusts. In such a case the greater would I apprehend be held to include the less.

Surplus After Performing the Trust

In **Re Rees** [1950] Ch 204 a testator, the Reverend Rees, appointed his solicitor and Mr. Hopkins as executors and trustees of his will, and in clause 3 left the whole of his property 'unto my trustees absolutely they well knowing my wishes concerning the same'. At the execution of the will the testator told his trustees that he left his estate to them on their assurance that they would make certain payments out of it 'and on the understanding that any surplus was to be retained by them for their own use'.

On the death of the testator in 1944, the payments were made, leaving a substantial surplus in the hands of the trustees. The Court of Appeal, affirming Vaisey J [1949] Ch 541, held that the surplus did not vest in the trustees absolutely and beneficially, but went on a resulting trust for the testator's next-of-kin. Evershed MR said at 207:

There are two distinct points. The first is one of the construction of the will. On its true interpretation, does clause 3 confer on the persons named as trustees an interest in the property on trust only, or does it give the property to those two persons conditionally on their discharging the wishes communicated to them? The second point which arises, if the first is decided adversely to the plaintiff, is this: although the form of the will on its proper reading, creates only a trust estate in the trustees, can they, nevertheless, by oral evidence, prove that they held it on trust, having discharged the several payments to which I have already alluded, for the two trustees beneficially or the survivor of them? I will deal with the two questions in that order.

His Lordship construed the clause as conferring upon the trustees an interest in trust only, and continued:

That makes it necessary to consider the second question. As I have already indicated, I agree with the judge that to admit evidence to the effect that the testator informed one of the executors—or, I will assume in Mr. Milner Holland's favour, both of the executors—that he intended them to take beneficial interests and that his wishes included that intention, would be to conflict with the terms of the will as I have construed them; for the inevitable result of admitting that evidence and giving effect to it would be that the will would be regarded not as conferring a trust estate only upon the two trustees, but as giving them a conditional gift which on construction is the thing which, if I am right, it does not do.[62]

3. Tenants in Common and Joint Tenants

In **Re Stead** [1900] 1 Ch 237, FARWELL J had to consider a gift by will to two persons as joint tenants which had been made upon the faith of an antecedent promise by one of them to hold upon secret trusts. He said at 241:

If A induces B either to make, or to leave unrevoked, a will leaving property to A and C as tenants in common, by expressly promising, or tacitly consenting, that he and C will carry out the testator's wishes, and C knows nothing of the matter until after A's death, A is bound, but C is not bound: *Tee v Ferris* (1856) 2 K & J 357; the reason stated at 368 being, that to hold otherwise would enable one beneficiary to deprive the rest of their benefits by setting up a secret trust. If, however, the gift were to A and C as joint tenants, the authorities have established a distinction between those cases in which the will is made on the faith of the antecedent promise by A and those in which the will is left unrevoked on the faith of a subsequent promise. In the former case, the trust binds both A and C: *Russell v Jackson* (1852) 10 Hare 204; *Jones v Badley* (1868) 3 Ch App 362, the reason stated being that no person can claim an interest under a fraud committed by another; in the latter case A and not C is bound: *Burney v Macdonald* (1845) 15 Sim 6 and *Moss v Cooper* (1861) 1 John & H 352, the reason stated at 367 being that the gift is not tainted with any fraud in procuring the execution of the will. Personally I am unable to see any difference between a gift made on the faith of an antecedent promise and a gift left unrevoked on the faith of a subsequent promise to carry out the testator's wishes; but apparently a distinction has been made by the various judges who have had to consider the question. I am bound, therefore, to decide in accordance with these authorities....

(1972) 88 LQR at 228 (B. Perrins)

The 'reasons stated' by Farwell J in *Re Stead* are at first sight contradictory. One consideration is that a person must not be allowed, by falsely setting up a secret trust, to deprive

---

[62] See *Re Tyler* [1967] 1 WLR 1269 at 1277, where Pennycuick J said 'I will make no pretence of finding that reasoning easy'.

another of his benefits under the will. Apparently this is decisive if the parties are tenants in common but not if they are joint tenants. On the other hand one person must not profit by the fraud of another. Apparently this is decisive only if the parties are joint tenants and not if they are tenants in common. Yet again it is apparently only fraud in procuring the execution of a will that is relevant, and not fraud in inducing a testator not to revoke a will already made. All very confusing, but add *Huguenin v Baseley* (1807) 14 Ves 273 and the whole picture springs into focus and the confusion disappears. Returning to A and C, whether they are tenants in common or joint tenants, C is not bound *if his gift was not induced by the promise of A* because to hold otherwise would be to enable A to deprive C of his benefit by setting up a secret trust; but C is bound *if his gift was induced by the promise of A* because he cannot profit by the fraud of another; and if the trust was communicated to A after the will was made, then C takes free *if his gift was not induced by the promise of A* because if there is no inducement there is no fraud affecting C.

This, it is submitted, is what was decided by the cases cited in Farwell J's judgment.

4. Theoretical Basis of Secret Trusts[63]

In **Re Young** [1951] Ch 344 a testator made a bequest to his wife, and imposed a condition that she should, *inter alia*, make certain bequests which he had communicated to her. One of them was a gift of £2,000 in favour of Mr. Cobb, the testator's chauffeur. Cobb attested the will. An attesting witness cannot receive a legacy under the will.[64] DANCKWERTS J held that Cobb was entitled to the £2,000. This was a gift to him under an oral trust declared by the testator and not a bequest under the will. He said at 350:

There is one other point, which is rather interesting, concerning the validity of one of these legacies. The widow has testified that the testator's intention, as communicated to her, was that the man who had been employed by the testator for many years as chauffeur and general factotum should receive a legacy of £2,000. The chauffeur was one of the two attesting witnesses to the will, and if he takes the legacy under the terms of the will the result of section 15 of the Wills Act, 1837, is to make his legacy ineffective. The question is whether he takes the legacy under the will. Mr. Christie, on behalf of the next-of-kin, referred to *Re Fleetwood* (1880) 15 Ch D 594, a case of a secret trust, decided by Hall V-C, where it was held that, as a woman intended to be a beneficiary was one of the attesting witnesses to the fourth codicil, the trust for her failed as to her beneficial interest, as it would have done, Hall V-C said, had it been declared in the codicil. It appears that the point was not argued in that particular case, which was concerned with a number of other points; and it seems to me that that particular decision is contrary to principle. The whole theory of the formation of a secret trust is that the Wills Act has nothing to do with the matter because the forms required by the Wills Act are entirely disregarded, since the persons do not take by virtue of the gift in the will, but by virtue of the secret trusts imposed upon the beneficiary, who does in fact take under the will.

In the Irish case of *O'Brien v Condon* [1905] 1 IR 51 Sir Andrew Porter MR had to consider the matter with the decision of *Re Fleetwood* before him. He pointed out in a judgment which

---

[63] See articles referred to at p. 127, n. 40, above.

[64] Wills Act 1837, s. 15, modified by Wills Act 1968 which allows the attesting witness-legatee to take if the will was duly executed without his attestation.

seems to me to be entirely in accordance with principle and common sense that *Re Fleetwood* was inconsistent with the principle of the matter, and inconsistent with certain other cases, one of which was a decision of the House of Lords on an Irish appeal, namely *Cullen v A-G for Ireland* (1866) LR 1 HL 190. Sir Andrew Porter MR pointed out in *O'Brien v Condon* at 59 that the point was not argued before Hall V-C in *Re Fleetwood,* and accordingly he decided to differ from the decision in *Re Fleetwood* and to apply what seems to me to be the proper statement of the principle. I agree with the decision in *O'Brien v Condon* and I think it right to follow it in the circumstances of this case, because the particular point was not argued before Hall V-C and I think that his judgment on it was given *per incuriam.*

It seems to me that according to *Cullen v A-G for Ireland,* and the later decision of *Re Gardner* [1923] 2 Ch 230, every consideration connected with this principle requires me to reach the conclusion that a beneficiary under a secret trust does not take under the will, and that he is not, therefore, affected by section 15 of the Wills Act, 1837.

Hanbury & Martin: *Modern Equity* (17th edn., 2005), pp. 165–168

It is one thing to say that the trust operates outside the will, but it is another to say just how and when the trust takes effect. . . . the most natural way for this to occur is to treat the communication to the trustee as the declaration of trust, and the vesting of the property in the trustee by the will as the constitution of the trust. If this is so, it is a lifetime declaration, and the Wills Act has no effect upon it; the only statutory formalities that are relevant are Law of Property Act 1925, section 53(1)(b).[65] which requires that declarations of trusts of land should be evidenced in writing; but this would not affect the rule requiring a fraudulent trustee in a fully secret trust of land to hold on a constructive trust.[66] There would be no awkward distinction between declarations prior to and subsequent to the will in half-secret trusts;[67] the sole question would be whether or not a trust was declared of the property before the death, and whether that trust became properly constituted by the vesting of the property in the trustee.

We have seen that the usual rule in the case of property coming to a person who had previously declared himself trustee of it was that the trust did not become constituted without a further manifestation of intention.[68] It was submitted that where a third person accepted an instruction to hold the property on certain trusts and the settlor subsequently transferred the property to him without further declaration, the trust would be constituted. It should make no difference whether the property passed to the trustee by a conveyance or by a will.[69] It will probably fail however if the trustee predeceases the testator, at any rate in the case of a fully

---

[65] See p. 112, above; *Re Baillie* (1886) 2 TLR 660 at 661; but there was no writing in *Ottaway v Norman* [1972] Ch 698 [p.000, above].   [66] LPA 1925, s. 53(2).

[67] *Re Keen* [1937] Ch 236 [p.132, above].

[68] See p. 141, below.

[69] As with the property received by Miss Towry Law from her sister and conveyed to the trustees; *Re Ellenborough* [1903] 1 Ch 697 [p.182, below]; *Re Adlard* [1954] Ch 29; *Re Ralli's Will Trusts* [1964] Ch 288 [p.159, below].

secret trust.[70] Assuming its terms were known, it may be that a half-secret trust could be saved by the maxim 'a trust does not fail for want of a trustee'.[71] ...

Until the property has so vested, there is no completely constituted trust; the declaration can have no effect and cannot create property rights. The will can be revoked or altered, or the property may be disposed of during the testator's lifetime. The testator can revoke his instructions to the secret trustee at any time,[72] and if he acts as if he had forgotten the declaration or assumed it to be no longer existent, no doubt it will be treated as having expired. No rational theory, it is suggested, can be found which will justify the remarkable decision in *Re Gardner (No 2)*.[73] We have seen that a wife left her estate to her husband for life,[74] and that after his death, it was to be held on secret trust for five named beneficiaries. One of the beneficiaries predeceased the wife. The representatives of the deceased beneficiary successfully claimed the share.

A gift by will normally lapses if the donee predeceases the testator,[75] and the estate of the donee can only claim if the donee acquired some interest in the property before he died. No such interest could exist in this case; and the theory which suggests that a secret trust can be treated as a lifetime declaration of trust does not suggest that any interest is obtained by any beneficiary prior to the constitution of the trust by vesting of the legal estate in the trustee.

QUESTIONS

1. Should secret trusts be classified as express, implied, or constructive trusts? Why? Is this a matter of practical significance? p. 301, below; H&M, pp. 168–169; Lewin pp. 77–78; P&M, pp. 132–134; P&S 232–233; Pettit, pp. 129–130; Snell, pp. 558–560; T&H, pp. 903–904; (1951) 67 LQR 314 at 323ff (L.A. Sheridan); [1979] Conv 341 at 348 (D.R. Hodge); Oakley, *Constructive Trusts* (3rd edn), pp. 260–263; *Ottaway v Norman* [1972] Ch 698 [p. 132, above]; *Re Baillie* (1886) 2 TLR 660 at 661; *Gold v Hill* [1999] 1 FLR 54 [p. 144, above]. See also *Brown v Pourau* [1995] 1 NZLR 352; [1996] Conv 302 (C.E.F. Rickett).

2. Is it advisable, as a matter of policy to enforce (a) fully secret trusts, (b) half-secret trusts? H&M, p. 169; (1951) 67 LQR 314 at 328 (L.A. Sheridan); [1981] Conv 335 (T.G. Watkin); Scott, *Trusts* (3rd edn, 1997), §55.9.

[70] *Re Maddock* [1902] 2 Ch 220 at 251; Oakley, *Constructive Trusts* (3rd edn), p. 250; cf. [2000] Conv 420, 439 (D. Kincaid).

[71] Unless the particular trustee is regarded as essential to the trust. For the view that a half-secret trust would also fail, see [1995] Conv 366, 373 (D. Wilde); cf. Oakley, ibid, p. 250.

[72] But any substituted instructions given after the will is executed will be invalid in the case of a half-secret trust. See also [2004] Conv 388 (M. Pawlowski and J. Brown).

[73] [1923] 2 Ch 230. See Oakley, *Constructive* Trusts (3rd ed.), p. 251, suggesting that there is no clear rule against a non-testamentary trust for a dead person. This is doubtful, as such a beneficiary has no legal personality, unless it is clear that his estate is intended to take.

[74] *Re Gardner (No. 1)* [1920] 2 Ch 523.

[75] A special exception is made in the case of children of the testator who predecease him, leaving issue: Wills Act 1837, s. 33. Such a gift takes effect in favour of the issue.

3. 'The fraud theory is, consistently with the authorities, available to justify the enforcement of all secret trusts.' (D.R. Hodge in [1980] Conv 341 at 348) 'The ghost of fraudulent behaviour in the area of secret trusts still lingers. It should be exorcised once and for all.' (C.E.F. Rickett in (1979) 38 CLJ 260 at 264).

  What is meant by fraud? Does the ghost still linger, and, if so, should it be exorcised? See (1999) 115 LQR 631 (P. Critchley).

4. Why is the rule in half-secret trusts for the time of communication and acceptance different from that in fully secret trusts? Should it be?

5. To what extent does the doctrine of secret trusts apply to *inter vivos* dispositions? See (1951) 67 LQR 314 at 323; *Re Tyler* [1967] 1 WLR 1269 at 1275.

  V sells and conveys two cottages to P. By a separate oral agreement P allows V to occupy one of the cottages rent free for so long as he desires. Consider how V can be protected if P claims possession. By a constructive trust (*Bannister v Bannister* [1948] 2 All ER 133)? By an estoppel licence? If both methods are applicable, which is to be preferred?

II CONSTITUTION OF TRUSTS[76]

An express trust only exists if the trust is constituted by title to the trust property being vested in the trustee. A trust can be constituted in two ways: by declaration of oneself as a trustee or by transfer of property to trustees.

A DECLARATION OF ONESELF AS TRUSTEE[77]

If the settlor declares himself trustee, there is no problem of constitution of the trust since the property is already vested in the settlor. The problem in this context relates to whether there has been a declaration of trust. 'Men often mean to give things to their kinsfolk, they do not often mean to constitute themselves trustees.'[78] It is necessary to show that the settlor manifested an intention to declare himself trustee. Nothing else will do. An intention to give will not be construed as an intention to declare himself trustee. 'An imperfect gift is no declaration of trust.'[79]

---

[76] H&M, pp. 117–147; Lewin, pp. 47–67; P&M, pp.135–176; P&S pp. 168–195; Pettit pp. 98–126; Snell pp. 494–499; T&H pp.125–152; U&H, pp. 187–231.

[77] H&M, pp. 126–130; Lewin, pp. 39–41; P&M, pp. 139–141; P&S, pp. 169–173; Pettit, pp. 102–103; Snell, p. 498; T&H, pp. 140–145; U&H, pp. 188–194.

[78] Maitland, *Equity* (2nd edn, 1929) p. 72. See *Pappadakis v Pappadakis* (2000) The Times, 19 January (a failed assignment could not take effect as a trust since the purported assignor had not intended the assignment to be a declaration of trust).   [79] Maitland, *Equity* (2nd edn) p. 72.

Jones v Lock
(1865) 1 Ch App 25 (CA in Ch, **Lord Cranworth LC**)

On returning from a business visit to Birmingham, Mr. Jones was reproved by his family for not bringing a present for his baby son. He produced a cheque for £900 payable to himself, and said: 'Look you here, I give this to baby; it is for himself, and I am going to put it away for him, and will give him a great deal more along with it.' He placed the cheque in the baby's hand. His wife feared that the baby might tear it, and Jones added: 'Never mind if he does; it is his own, and he may do what he likes with it.' He took the cheque back and locked it in the safe. Six days later he died. The question was whether the baby was entitled to the cheque.

Held. There had been no gift to the baby;[80] and no declaration of trust in his favour.

Lord Cranworth LC: This is a special case, in which I regret to say that I cannot bring myself to think that, either on principle or on authority, there has been any gift or any valid declaration of trust. No doubt a gift may be made by any person *sui juris* and *compos mentis,* by conveyance of a real estate or by delivery of a chattel; and there is no doubt also that, by some decisions, unfortunate I must think them, a parol[81] declaration of trust of personalty may be perfectly valid even when voluntary. If I give any chattel that, of course, passes by delivery, and if I say, expressly or impliedly, that I constitute myself a trustee of personalty, that is a trust executed, and capable of being enforced without consideration. I do not think it necessary to go into any of the authorities cited before me; they all turn upon the question, whether what has been said was a declaration of trust or an imperfect gift. In the latter case the parties would receive no aid from a Court of equity if they claimed as volunteers.[82] But when there has been a declaration of trust, then it will be enforced, whether there has been consideration or not. Therefore the question in each case is one of fact; has there been a gift or not, or has there been a declaration of trust or not? I should have every inclination to sustain this gift, but unfortunately I am unable to do so; the case turns on the very short question whether *Jones* intended to make a declaration that he held the property in trust for the child; and I cannot come to any other conclusion than that he did not. I think it would be of very dangerous example if loose conversations of this sort, in important transactions of this kind, should have the effect of declarations of trust.

His Lordship then commented on the evidence, and said that no doubt it was a fair representation of what had actually taken place, that the father had really had an intention of settling something on the child, and that his giving the note to the child was symbolic of what he meant to do. However, it was not his meaning to enable the child, by his next friend, to bring an action of trover for the cheque or file a bill for the £900. Jones had merely meant to say that now he could make a provision for the boy; and what he had said to the solicitor was quite consistent with this.

It was all quite natural, but the testator would have been very much surprised if he had been told that he had parted with the £900, and could no longer dispose of it. It all turns upon the facts,

---

[80] Because the gift of a non-bearer cheque requires endorsement. Under Cheques Act 1957, s. 2, endorsements in blank of cheques payable to order are not necessary as far as the rights of a collecting bank are concerned; and under Bills of Exchange Act 1882, s. 81A (as inserted by Cheques Act 1992), a cheque is not transferable if it is crossed and bears the words 'account payee' across its face.

[81] Meaning 'without writing'.   [82] See p. 161, below.

which do not lead me to the conclusion that the testator meant to deprive himself of all property in the note, or to declare himself a trustee of the money for the child. I extremely regret this result, because it is obvious that, by the act of God, this unfortunate child has been deprived of a provision which his father meant to make for him.

Richards v Delbridge
(1874) LR 18 Eq 11 (Ch, Sir George Jessel MR)

Mr. Delbridge was tenant of premises where he carried on business as a bone-manure merchant. He was assisted by Mr. Richards, his infant grandson. Shortly before Delbridge's death, he indorsed on the lease, and signed the following memorandum: 'This deed and all thereto belonging I give to *Edward Bennetto Richards* from this time forth, with all the stock-in-trade.' He delivered the document to Richards' mother to hold for him, and then died, making no mention of this property in his will. The question was whether, on Delbridge's death, the lease and business passed to Richards, or whether it passed under the will.

Held. It passed under the will. There was no conveyance to, or declaration of trust in favour of, Richards.

Sir George Jessel MR: The principle is a very simple one. A man may transfer his property, without valuable consideration, in one of two ways: he may either do such acts as amount in law to a conveyance or assignment of the property, and thus completely divest himself of the legal ownership, in which case the person who by those acts acquires the property takes it beneficially, or on trust, as the case may be; or the legal owner of the property may, by one or other of the modes recognised as amounting to a valid declaration of trust, constitute himself a trustee, and, without an actual transfer of the legal title, may so deal with the property as to deprive himself of its beneficial ownership, and declare that he will hold it from that time forward on trust for the other person. It is true he need not use the words, 'I declare myself a trustee', but he must do something which is equivalent to it, and use expressions which have that meaning; for, however anxious the Court may be to carry out a man's intention, it is not at liberty to construe words otherwise than according to their proper meaning....

The true distinction appears to me to be plain, and beyond dispute: for a man to make himself a trustee there must be an expression of intention to become a trustee, whereas words of present gift shew an intention to give over property to another, and not retain it in the donor's own hands for any purpose, fiduciary or otherwise.

In *Milroy v Lord* (1862) 4 De GF & J 264 at 274 [p. 157, below], Lord Justice Turner, after referring to the two modes of making a voluntary settlement valid and effectual, adds these words: 'The cases, I think, go further, to this extent, that if the settlement is intended to be effectuated by one of the modes to which I have referred, the Court will not give effect to it by applying another of those modes. If it is intended to take effect by transfer, the Court will not hold the intended transfer to operate as a declaration of trust, for then every imperfect instrument would be made effectual by being converted into a perfect trust.'

In **Middleton v Pollock** (1876) 2 Ch D 104.[83] Mr. Pollock, a solicitor, received money for investment from various clients. The money was so intermingled that it was

---

[83] *Gee v Liddell* (1866) 35 Beav 621.

impossible to trace that invested by each client. Pollock died heavily insolvent. Before his death, he made declarations of trust in favour of selected clients, mostly relatives and friends. The one selected for trial as a representative case was that of a relative, Miss Elliott.

Miss Elliott's money had never been invested. Before he died, Pollock indorsed a bill of exchange in her favour, and signed a declaration that he held certain leaseholds on trust for her to secure the repayment to her of the money owed, plus interest. Miss Elliott knew nothing of this. The question was whether Miss Elliott (and the others similarly placed) was entitled to the property in preference to the general creditors. SIR GEORGE JESSEL MR held that she was, as there had been a valid declaration of trust in favour of Miss Elliott. The trust could not be avoided as a fraudulent preference under 13 Eliz. c. 5 [p. 82, above], as it was made bona fide and for valuable consideration.

In **Paul v Constance** [1977] 1 WLR 527.[84] Mr. Constance was separated from his wife and lived with the plaintiff. He received £950 as damages resulting from an injury at work, and he and the plaintiff decided to put it into a deposit account at Lloyds Bank.

Because of the embarrassment which would be caused by having an account in two different names, the account was opened in Mr. Constance's name only. He indicated on various occasions that he wished it to be the plaintiff's as much as his. On his death, Mrs. Constance claimed the deposit as part of her husband's estate. The plaintiff sought a declaration that the deposit was held on trust for her.

In finding for the plaintiff. SCARMAN LJ, after referring to *Jones v Lock* (1865) 1 Ch App 25 [p. 151, above], and *Richards v Delbridge* (1874) LR 18 Eq 11 [p. 152, above], said at 531:

There is no suggestion of a gift by transfer in the present case. The facts of the two cases do not, therefore, very much help the submission of Mr. Blythe but he was able to extract from them this principle: that there must be a clear declaration of trust and that means there must be clear evidence from what is said or done of an intention to create a trust—or, as Mr. Blythe put it, 'an intention to dispose of a property or a fund so that somebody else to the exclusion of the disponent acquires the beneficial interest in it'. He submitted that there was no such evidence. When one looks at the detailed evidence to see whether it goes as far as that—and I think that the evidence does have to go as far as that—one finds that from the time that the deceased received his damages right up to his death he was saying, on occasions, that the money was as much the plaintiff's as his. When they discussed the damages, how to invest them or what to do with them and when they discussed the bank account, he would say to her: 'the money is as much yours as mine'.

The judge, rightly treating the basic problem in the case as a question of fact, reached this conclusion. He said: 'I have read through my notes and I am quite satisfied that it was the intention of Mrs. Paul and Mr. Constance to create a trust in which both of them were interested.' In this court the issue becomes: was there sufficient evidence to justify the judge in reaching that conclusion of fact? In submitting that there was, Mr. Wilson draws attention first and foremost to the words used. When one bears in mind the unsophisticated character of the deceased and his relationship with the plaintiff during the last few years of his life, Mr. Wilson submits that the

---

[84] Criticised in Heydon and Loughlan, *Cases and Materials on Equity and Trusts* (6th edn, 2002), pp. 132–134. See also *Harrison v Gibson* [2006] 1 WLR 1212; *Gibbs v Harding* [2007] EWHC 3 (Ch); [2008] 2 WLR 361.

words that he did use on more than one occasion, 'this money is as much yours as mine', convey clearly a present declaration that the existing fund was as much the plaintiff's as his own. The judge accepted that conclusion. I think that he was well justified in doing so and, indeed, I think that he was right to do so.

It might, however, be thought that this was a borderline case, since it is not easy to pinpoint a specific moment of declaration, and one must exclude from one's mind any case built upon the existence of an implied or constructive trust, for this case was put forward at the trial and is now argued by the plaintiff as one of express declaration of trust. It was so pleaded and it is only as such that it may be considered in this court. The question, therefore, is whether, in all the circumstances, the use of those words on numerous occasions as between the deceased and the plaintiff constituted an express declaration of trust. The judge found that they did. For myself, I think that he was right so to find. I therefore would dismiss the appeal.[85]

In **Rowe v Prance** [1999] 2 FLR 787, the defendant had conducted an extra-marital relationship with the plaintiff for 14 years. The defendant had told the plaintiff that he would divorce his wife, sell the matrimonial home and use the proceeds to purchase a yacht, which would be their home whilst they sailed round the world. The defendant did not divorce his wife or sell the matrimonial home but did purchase the yacht, which was registered in his sole name because, the plaintiff said, the defendant had told her that she did not have an Ocean Master's Certificate. Neither did the defendant. The defendant described the yacht frequently as 'our boat'. After the relationship had ended, the plaintiff claimed that the defendant had expressly constituted himself as trustee of the boat. NICHOLAS WARREN QC found for the plaintiff. He emphasised that, since the subject matter of the trust was personalty, writing was not needed.[86] He concluded that the description of the boat as 'ours' meant that the shares of the plaintiff and the defendant should be equal.

In **Re B (Child: Property Transfer)** [1999] 2 FLR 418 a financial provision order had been made under the Guardianship of Minors Act 1971 following the termination of the relationship of an unmarried father and mother. Part of this order stated that the mother should obtain the legal interest in the family home for the 'benefit of the said child of this family'. The child argued that this created an express trust. Her argument was rejected. ROBERT WALKER LJ said at 424:

A line of authority shows that the expression 'for the benefit of' is not, despite its obvious family resemblance to words such as 'beneficial' and 'beneficiary', a particularly apt or reliable indicator of an intention to create a trust.

T Choithram International SA v Pagarani
[2001] 1 WLR 1 (PC, **Lords Browne-Wilkinson, Jauncey of Tullichettle, Clyde, Hobhouse of Woodborough and Millett.)**[87]

The donor (TCP), who was seriously ill, executed a trust deed to establish a philanthropic foundation. Having appointed himself one of the trustees, he stated orally that he gave

[85] See *Re Vandervell's Trusts (No 2)* [1974] Ch 269 [p. 211, below], where the declaration was made by the trustees with the consent of the beneficial owner. [86] See p. 111, above.
[87] (2001) 60 CLJ 483 (J. Hopkins); [2001] Conv 515 (C. Rickett); [2001] All ER Rev 265 (P.J. Clarke).

all of his estate to the foundation. TCP died before deposit balances and shares had been transferred to the foundation. The plaintiffs claimed that they were entitled to TCP's estate on an intestacy because he had not made a valid gift to the foundation. The trial judge and the Court of Appeal of the British Virgin Islands found for the plaintiffs.

Held: TCP had intended to make an immediate irrevocable gift to the foundation. Since TCP was one of the trustees of the foundation he was bound by the trust and so the gift to the foundation was properly vested in all the trustees.

Lord Browne-Wilkinson: Their Lordships then turn to the central and most important question: on the basis that TCP intended to make an immediate absolute gift 'to the foundation' but had not vested the gifted property in all the trustees of the foundation, are the trusts of the foundation trust deed enforceable against the deposits and the shares or is this (as the judge and the Court of Appeal held) a case where there has been an imperfect gift which cannot be enforced against TCP's estate whatever TCP's intentions[?]

The judge and the Court of Appeal understandably took the view that a perfect gift could only be made in one of two ways, *viz* (a) by a transfer of the gifted asset to the donee, accompanied by an intention in the donor to make a gift; or (b) by the donor declaring himself to be a trustee of the gifted property for the donee. In case (a), the donor has to have done everything necessary to be done which is within his own power to do in order to transfer the gifted asset to the donee. If the donor has not done so, the gift is incomplete since the donee has no equity to perfect an imperfect gift: *Milroy v Lord* (1862) 4 De GF & J 264 [p. 157, below]; *Richards v Delbridge* (1874) LR 18 Eq 11 [p. 152, above]; *Re Rose* [1949] Ch 78 [p. 162, below]; *Re Rose* [1952] Ch 499 [p. 161, below]. Moreover, the court will not give a benevolent construction so as to treat ineffective words of outright gift as taking effect as if the donor had declared himself a trustee for the donee: *Milroy v Lord*. So, it is said, in this case TCP used words of gift to the foundation (not words declaring himself a trustee): unless he transferred the shares and deposits so as to vest title in all the trustees, he had not done all that he could in order to effect the gift. It therefore fails. Further it is said that it is not possible to treat TCP's words of gift as a declaration of trust because they make no reference to trusts. Therefore the case does not fall within either of the possible methods by which a complete gift can be made and the gift fails. Though it is understandable that the courts below should have reached this conclusion since the case does not fall squarely within either of the methods normally stated as being the only possible ways of making a gift, their Lordships do not agree with that conclusion. The facts of this case are novel and raise a new point. It is necessary to make an analysis of the rules of equity as to complete gifts. Although equity will not aid a volunteer, it will not strive officiously to defeat a gift. This case falls between the two common-form situations mentioned above. Although the words used by TCP are those normally appropriate to an outright gift—'I give to X'—in the present context there is no breach of the principle in *Milroy v Lord* if the words of TCP's gift (i.e. to the foundation) are given their only possible meaning in this context. The foundation has no legal existence apart from the trust declared by the foundation trust deed. Therefore the words 'I give to the foundation' can only mean 'I give to the trustees of the foundation trust deed to be held by them on the trusts of foundation trust deed'. Although the words are apparently words of outright gift they are essentially words of gift on trust.

But, it is said, TCP vested the properties not in *all* the trustees of the foundation but only in one, i.e. TCP. Since equity will not aid a volunteer, how can a court order be obtained vesting the gifted property in the whole body of trustees on the trusts of the foundation[?] Again, this represents an over-simplified view of the rules of equity. Until comparatively recently the great majority of trusts were voluntary settlements under which beneficiaries were volunteers having given no value. Yet beneficiaries under a trust, although volunteers, can enforce the trust against the trustees. Once a trust relationship is established between trustee and beneficiary, the fact that a beneficiary has given no value is irrelevant. It is for this reason that the type of perfected gift referred to in class (b) above is effective since the donor has constituted himself a trustee for the donee who can as a matter of trust law enforce that trust.

What then is the position here where the trust property is vested in one of the body of trustees, viz. TCP? In their Lordships' view there should be no question. TCP has, in the most solemn circumstances, declared that he is giving (and later that he has given) property to a trust which he himself has established and of which he has appointed himself to be a trustee. All this occurs at one composite transaction taking place on 17 February. There can in principle be no distinction between the case where the donor declares himself to be sole trustee for a donee or a purpose and the case where he declares himself to be one of the trustees for that donee or purpose. In both cases his conscience is affected and it would be unconscionable and contrary to the principles of equity to allow such a donor to resile from his gift. Say, in the present case, that TCP had survived and tried to change his mind by denying the gift. In their Lordships' view it is impossible to believe that he could validly deny that he was a trustee for the purposes of the foundation in the light of all the steps that he had taken to assert that position and to assert his trusteeship. In their Lordships' judgment in the absence of special factors where one out of a larger body of trustees has the trust property vested in him he is bound by the trust and must give effect to it by transferring the trust property into the name of all the trustees.

The plaintiffs relied on the decision of Sir John Romilly MR in *Bridge v Bridge* (1852) 16 Beav 315 as showing that the vesting of the trust property in one trustee, the donor, out of many is not sufficient to constitute the trust: see at 324. Their Lordships have some doubt whether that case was correctly decided on this point, the judge giving no reasons for his view. But in any event it is plainly distinguishable from the present case since the judge considered that the trust could not be fully constituted unless the legal estate in the gifted property was vested in the trustees and in that case the legal estate was vested neither in the donor nor in any of the other trustees.

Therefore in their Lordships' view the assets, if any, validly included in TCP's gift to the foundation are properly vested in the trustees and are held on the trusts of the foundation trust deed.

B   TRANSFER OF THE TRUST PROPERTY TO TRUSTEES[88]

The other method of constituting a trust is for the settlor to transfer the property to the trustees. The method of transfer varies with the property in question. A legal estate in unregistered land must be transferred by deed,[89] in registered land by registration;[90] stocks and shares by an appropriate form of transfer;[91] equitable interests[92]

[88] H&M, pp.120–123; Lewin, pp. 47–67; P&M, pp.136–139; P&S pp. 173–174; Pettit pp. 99–102; Snell pp. 496–498; T&H pp.120–126; U&H, pp. 194–199.   [89] LPA 1925, s. 52(1).
[90] Land Registration Act 2002.
[91] See Companies Act 2006 ss. 544, 770–774; Stock Transfer Act 1963, s. 1.
[92] LPA 1925, s. 53 (1)(c) [p. 112, above].

and copyright by writing;[93] chattels by deed of gift[94] or by an intention to give coupled with a delivery of possession;[95] a bill of exchange by indorsement;[96] and various other types of property by their own special procedure. The vesting of the trust property in the trustee *constitutes* the trust. In a completely constituted trust, there is no need for consideration; and the question of whether a beneficiary is a volunteer is immaterial.

(i) Legal Interests

Milroy v Lord[97]
(1862) 4 De GF & J 264 (CA in Ch, **Knight Bruce** and **Turner LJJ**)

The settlor executed a voluntary deed, purporting to transfer fifty shares in the Bank of Louisiana to Mr. Lord to be held on trust for the plaintiffs, and later handed to him the share certificates. At the time, Lord held a general power of attorney, which would have entitled him to transfer the settlor's shares. However the shares could only be transferred by registration of the transferee in the books of the bank, and this was never done. The question was whether a trust of the shares had been created in favour of the plaintiffs.

Held (reversing STUART V-C). No trust existed.

Turner LJ: Under the circumstances of this case, it would be difficult not to feel a strong disposition to give effect to this settlement to the fullest extent, and certainly I spared no pains to find the means of doing so, consistently with what I apprehend to be the law of the Court; but, after full and anxious consideration, I find myself unable to do so. I take the law of this Court to be well settled, that, in order to render a voluntary settlement valid and effectual, the settlor must have done everything which, according to the nature of the property comprised in the settlement, was necessary to be done in order to transfer the property and render the settlement binding upon him. He may of course do this by actually transferring the property to the persons for whom he intends to provide, and the provision will then be effectual, and it will be equally effectual if he transfers the property to a trustee for the purposes of the settlement, or declares that he himself holds it in trust for those purposes; and if the property be personal, the trust may, as I apprehend, be declared either in writing or by parol; but, in order to render the settlement binding, one or other of these modes must, as I understand the law of this Court, be resorted to, for there is no equity in this Court to perfect an imperfect gift. The cases I think

---

93 Copyright, Designs and Patents Act 1988, s. 90 (3).

94 *Jaffa v Taylor Gallery Ltd* (1990) The Times, 21 March: trust of painting validly constituted without physical delivery to the trustees (one of whom was in Ireland) on the ground that the formal declaration of trust contained in the deed transferred the property in the painting to the trustees, each of whom had a copy of the document and agreed to act. See also *T Choithram International SA v Pagarani* [2001] 1 WLR 1, p.154, above.

95 *Ryall v Rowles* (1750) 1 Ves Sen 348; *Irons v Smallpiece* (1819) 2 B & Ald 551; *Cochrane v Moore* (1890) 25 QBD 57; *Lock v Heath* (1892) 8 TLR 295; *Kilpin v Ratley* [1892] 1 QB 582; *Re Cole* [1964] Ch 175; *Thomas v Times Book Co Ltd* [1966] 1 WLR 911 (the original manuscript of *Under Milk Wood*). See (1964) 27 MLR 357 (A.C. Diamond); (1953) CLJ 355 (J.W.A. Thornely).

96 Bills of Exchange Act 1882, s. 31; *Whistler v Forster* (1863) 14 CBNS 248; see, however, Cheques Act 1957, ss. 1, 2.   97 See also *Macedo v Stroud* [1922] 2 AC 330.

go further to this extent, that if the settlement is intended to be effectuated by one of the modes to which I have referred, the Court will not give effect to it by applying another of those modes. If it is intended to take effect by transfer, the Court will not hold the intended transfer to operate as a declaration of trust, for then every imperfect instrument would be made effectual by being converted into a perfect trust. These are the principles by which, as I conceive, this case must be tried.

Applying, then, these principles to the case, there is not here any transfer either of the one class of shares or of the other to the objects of the settlement, and the question therefore must be, whether a valid and effectual trust in favour of those objects was created in the defendant *Samuel Lord* or in the settlor himself as to all or any of these shares. Now it is plain that it was not the purpose of this settlement, or the intention of the settlor, to constitute himself a trustee of the bank shares. The intention was that the trust should be vested in the defendant *Samuel Lord,* and I think therefore that we should not be justified in holding that by the settlement, or by any parol declaration made by the settlor, he himself became a trustee of these shares for the purposes of the settlement. By doing so we should be converting the settlement or the parol declaration to a purpose wholly different from that which was intended to be effected by it, and, as I have said, creating a perfect trust out of an imperfect transaction....

The more difficult question is, whether the Defendant *Samuel Lord* did not become a trustee of these shares? Upon this question I have felt considerable doubt; but in the result, I have come to the conclusion that no perfect trust was ever created in him. The shares, it is clear, were never legally vested in him; and the only ground on which he can be held to have become a trustee of them is, that he held a power of attorney under which he might have transferred them into his own name; but he held that power of attorney as the agent of the settlor; and if he had been sued by the Plaintiffs as trustee of the settlement for an account under the trust, and to compel him to transfer the shares into his own name as trustee, I think he might well have said—These shares are not vested in me; I have no power over them except as the agent of the settlor, and without his express directions I cannot be justified in making the proposed transfer, in converting an intended into an actual settlement. A Court of Equity could not, I think, decree the agent of the settlor to make the transfer, unless it could decree the settlor himself to do so, and it is plain that no such decree could have been made against the settlor. In my opinion, therefore, this decree cannot be maintained as to the fifty *Louisiana Bank* shares.

In **Paul v Paul** (1882) 20 Ch D 742.[98] property was settled, in a marriage settlement, upon the spouses successively for life, with remainder to the children of the marriage. If there were no children of the marriage, the wife took absolutely on surviving the husband; and, if she died in his lifetime, she was given a power to appoint by will, and in default of appointment, the property passed to the wife's next-of-kin excluding the husband.

There were no children of the marriage. The spouses asked that the capital of the fund should be paid to them because the only persons who had any interest therein were the next-of-kin who were volunteers, and whose interest the wife could defeat by exercising her power of appointment, or by surviving her husband.

The Court of Appeal refused the application. The funds were settled. The trust in favour of the next-of-kin was constituted. It was immaterial that they were volunteers.

[98] See also *Jefferys v Jefferys* (1841) Cr & Ph 138; *Re Bowden* [1936] Ch 71; and *T Choithram International SA v Pagarani* [2001] 1 WLR 1 [p.154, above].

Re Ralli's Will Trusts
[1964] Ch 288 (ChD, **Buckley J**)

A testator, who died in 1899, left his residuary estate on trust for his wife for life, and then for his two daughters, Helen and Irene absolutely. Helen, by her marriage settlement, covenanted to settle after-acquired property in favour, in the events which happened, of the children of Irene. On the death of Helen and of the testator's widow, the plaintiff, who was Irene's husband, was sole surviving trustee, both of the testator's will and of the marriage settlement; and Helen's share of the residuary estate was thus vested in him. The question was whether the plaintiff held it on trust for those interested under Helen's will, or on the trusts of Helen's marriage settlement.

Held. The plaintiff held Helen's share upon the trusts of the marriage settlement. The property was vested in the trustee of the marriage settlement, and it made no difference that it came to him in his capacity as trustee of the will trusts.

Buckley J: The investments representing the share of residue in question, which I shall call 'the fund', stand in the name of the plaintiff. This is because he is now the sole surviving trustee of the testator's will. Therefore, say the defendants, he holds the fund primarily on the trusts of the will, that is to say, in trust for them as part of Helen's estate. The plaintiff is, however, also the sole surviving covenantee under clause 7 of the settlement as well as the sole surviving trustee of that settlement. This, however, affords him no answer, say the defendants, to their claim under the will unless the plaintiff, having transferred the fund to them in pursuance of the trusts of the will, could compel them to return it in pursuance of their obligation under the covenant, and this, they say, he could not do. In support of this last contention they rely on *Re Plumptre's Marriage Settlement* [1910] 1 Ch 609; *Re Pryce* [1917] 1 Ch 234 and *Re Kay's Settlement* [1939] Ch 329 [p. 173, below].

The plaintiff, on the other hand, contends that, as he already holds the fund, no question of his having to enforce the covenant arises. The fund, having come without impropriety into his hands, is now, he says, impressed in his hands with the trusts upon which he ought to hold it under the settlement; and because of the covenant it does not lie in the mouth of the defendants to say that he should hold the fund in trust for Helen's estate. He relies on *Re Bowden* [1936] Ch 71 ... The plaintiff also relies on *Re Adlard* [1954] Ch 29, where Vaisey J followed *Re Bowden*, and on the observations of Upjohn J in *Re Burton's Settlements* [1955] Ch 82 at 104.

Mr. Goff for the defendants says that *Re Bowden* and *Re Adlard* are distinguishable from the present case because in each of those cases the fund had reached the hands of the trustees of the relevant settlement and was held by them in that capacity, whereas in the present case the fund is, as he maintains, in the hands of the plaintiff in the capacity of trustee of the will and not in the capacity of trustee of the settlement. He says that *Re Burton's Settlements,* the complicated facts of which I forbear to set out here, should be distinguished on the ground that, when the settlement there in question was made, the trustee of that settlement and the trustee of the settlement under which the settlor had expectations was the same, so that the settlor by her settlement gave directions to the trustee of the settlement under which she had expectations, who then already held the relevant fund.

Sir Milner Holland, for the plaintiff, says that the capacity in which the trustee has become possessed of the fund is irrelevant. Thus in *Strong v Bird* (1874) LR 18 Eq 315 an imperfect gift was held to be completed by the donee obtaining probate of the donor's will of which he was executor, notwithstanding that the donor died intestate as to her residue and that the donee was not a person entitled as on her intestacy. Similarly in *Re James* [1935] Ch 449 a grant of administration to two administrators was held to perfect an imperfect gift by the intestate to one of them, who had no beneficial interest in the intestate's estate.

In my judgment the circumstance that the plaintiff holds the fund because he was appointed a trustee of the will is irrelevant. He is at law the owner of the fund, and the means by which he became so have no effect upon the quality of his legal ownership. The question is: for whom, if anyone, does he hold the fund in equity? In other words, who can successfully assert an equity against him disentitling him to stand upon his legal right? It seems to me to be indisputable that Helen, if she were alive, could not do so, for she has solemnly covenanted under seal to assign the fund to the plaintiff, and the defendants can stand in no better position. It is, of course, true that the object of the covenant was not that the plaintiff should retain the property for his own benefit, but that he should hold it on the trusts of the settlement. It is also true that, if it were necessary to enforce performance of the covenant, equity would not assist the beneficiaries under the settlement, because they are mere volunteers;[99] and that for the same reason the plaintiff, as trustee of the settlement, would not be bound to enforce the covenant and would not be constrained by the court to do so, and indeed, it seems, might be constrained by the court not to do so. As matters stand, however, there is no occasion to invoke the assistance of equity to enforce the performance of the covenant. It is for the defendants to invoke the assistance of equity to make good their claim to the fund. To do so successfully they must show that the plaintiff cannot conscientiously withhold it from them. When they seek to do this, he can point to the covenant which, in my judgment, relieves him from any fiduciary obligation he would otherwise owe to the defendants as Helen's representatives. In so doing the plaintiff is not seeking to enforce an equitable remedy against the defendants on behalf of persons who could not enforce such a remedy themselves: he is relying upon the combined effect of his legal ownership of the fund and his rights under the covenant. That an action on the covenant might be statute-barred is irrelevant, for there is no occasion for such an action.[100]

BUCKLEY J also held that a clause in the settlement providing that 'all the property comprised within the terms of [the covenant] shall become subject in equity to the settlement hereby covenanted to be made thereof' had the effect of imposing a trust independently of the vesting of the property in the trustee. It is difficult, however, to see that the provision could be more than a future declaration of a trust of unascertained property, and therefore void. See *Re Anstis* (1886) 31 Ch D 596.

(ii) Equitable Interests

A trust of an equitable interest may be constituted by an assignment of that interest to trustees; being a disposition of an equitable interest, it must be in writing under section 53(1)(c) of the Law of Property Act 1925 [p. 112, above].

---

[99] Now see Contracts (Rights of Third Parties) Act 1999 [p.169, below].
[100] Cf. *Re Brooks' Settlement Trusts* [1939] Ch 993 [p.183, below].

In **Kekewich v Manning** (1851) 1 De GM & G 176.[101] trustees held shares on trust for A for life remainder to B absolutely. B assigned his equitable interest to C to hold on trust for D. This was held to create a trust of B's equitable interest in remainder.

C INCOMPLETELY CONSTITUTED TRUSTS; FAILED GIFTS

It was seen in *Milroy v Lord*[102] that it is a fundamental principle that 'equity will not assist a volunteer'. This means that if a settlor fails to transfer property to a trustee then equity will not intervene to save the trust by treating the settlor as a trustee who holds the property on trust. Similarly, if a donor purports to transfer legal title to property to a donee but fails to do so effectively, then equity will not intervene to save the gift.

However, it is not true to say that equity will never assist volunteers. There are a number of cases where equity has done so.

(i) Settlor or Donor has done all Necessary to Transfer Title

Re Rose[103]
[1952] Ch 499 (CA, **Evershed MR, Jenkins** and **Morris LJJ**)

On 30 March, 1943 the settlor made two transfers of shares in an unlimited company in the form required by its Articles of Association. Under the Articles, the directors of the company could refuse, at their discretion, to register a transfer. The transfers were registered on 30 June, 1943. The settlor died at a time when Estate Duty would have been payable on the shares if the effective date of the transfer was 30 June, but not if it was 30 March. The Crown claimed the duty.[104]

Held (affirming ROXBURGH J). No duty payable. The settlor had done everything in his power to effect the transfer.

Evershed MR: The burden of the case presented by the Crown may be briefly put as it was formulated in reply by Mr. Pennycuick. This document, he said, on the face of it, was intended to operate and operated, if it operated at all, as a transfer. If for any reason it was at its date incapable of so operating, it is not legitimate, either by reference to the expressed intention in the document or on well-established principles of law, to extract from it a wholly different

---

[101] *Gilbert v Overton* (1864) 2 Hem & M 110 (assignment of agreement for lease).

[102] (1862) 4 De GF & J 264 [p. 157, above].

[103] (1976) 40 Conv (NS) 139 (L. McKay), where the reasoning of the decision is criticised. See also (1998) CLJ 46, 48–53 (S. Lowrie and P. Todd) and Oakley, *Constructive Trusts* (3rd edn), chap. 8. *Re Rose* was described in *Rowlandson v National Westminster Bank Ltd* [1978] 1 WLR 798 at 802, as 'a gloss' on the principle of perfect gifts. See *Re Fry* [1946] Ch 312; *Re Paradise Motor Co Ltd* [1968] 1 WLR 1125; *Vandervell v IRC* [1967] 2 AC 291 at 330; *Tett v Phoenix Property and Investment Co Ltd* [1984] BCLC 599; *Mascall v Mascall* (1984) 50 P & CR 119 [p. 164, below]; *Trustee of the Property of Pehrsson v von Greyerz* (unreported) 16 June 1999 (PC); *Brown & Root Technology Ltd v Sun Alliance and London Assurance Co Ltd* [2001] Ch 733.

[104] Estate Duty was replaced by Capital Transfer Tax, itself replaced by Inheritance Tax in IHTA 1984 [p. 39, above].

transaction—that is, to make it take effect not as a transfer but as a declaration of trust. Now I agree that on the face of the document it was obviously intended (if you take the words used) to operate and operate immediately as a transfer—'I do hereby transfer to the transferee' these shares 'to hold unto the said transferee, subject to the several conditions on which I held the same at the time of the execution hereof'. It plainly was intended to operate immediately as a transfer of rights. To some extent at least, it is said, it could not possibly do so. To revert to the illustration which has throughout been taken, if the company had declared a dividend during this interregnum, it is not open to question that the company must have paid that dividend to the deceased. So that *vis-à-vis* the company, this document did not, and could not, operate to transfer to Mrs. Rose the right against the company to claim and receive that dividend. Shares, Mr. Pennycuick says, are property of a peculiar character consisting, as it is sometimes put, of a bundle of rights—that is, rights against or in the company. It has followed from his argument that if such a dividend had been paid, the deceased could, consistently with the document to which he has set his hand and seal, have retained that dividend, and, if he had handed it over to his wife, it would have been an independent gift. I think myself that such a conclusion is startling. Indeed, I venture to doubt whether to anybody but a lawyer such a conclusion would even be comprehensible—at least without a considerable amount of explanation. That again is not conclusive; but I confess that I approach a matter of this kind with a pre-conceived notion that a conclusion that offends common sense, so much as this would *prima facie* do, ought not to be the right conclusion.

His Lordship examined *Milroy v Lord* in detail, and referred to the dictum of Turner LJ which is reprinted above at p. 157.

Those last few sentences form the gist of the Crown's argument and on it is founded the broad, general proposition that if a document is expressed as, and on the face of it intended to operate as, a transfer, it cannot in any respect take effect by way of trust—so far I understand the argument to go. In my judgment, that statement is too broad and involves too great a simplification of the problem; and is not warranted by authority. I agree that if a man purporting to transfer property executes documents which are not apt to effect that purpose, the court cannot then extract from those documents some quite different transaction and say that they were intended merely to operate as a declaration of trust, which *ex facie* they were not: but if a document is apt and proper to transfer the property—is in truth the appropriate way in which the property must be transferred—then it does not seem to me to follow from the statement of Turner LJ that, as a result, either during some limited period or otherwise, a trust may not arise, for the purpose of giving effect to the transfer. The simplest case will, perhaps, provide an illustration. If a man executes a document transferring all his equitable interest, say, in shares, that document, operating, and intended to operate, as a transfer, will give rise to and take effect as a trust; for the assignor will then be a trustee of the legal estate in the shares for the person in whose favour he has made an assignment of his beneficial interest. And, for my part, I do not think that the case of *Milroy v Lord* (1862) 4 De GF & J 264 is an authority which compels this court to hold that in this case—where, in the terms of Turner LJ's judgment, the settlor did everything which, according to the nature of the property comprised in the settlement, was necessary to be done by him in order to transfer the property—the result necessarily negatives the conclusion that, pending registration, the settlor was a trustee of the legal interest for the transferee.

The view of the limitations of *Milroy v Lord,* which I have tried to express, was much better expressed by Jenkins J in the recent case which also bears the same name of *Re Rose* [1949] Ch 78 (though that is a coincidence). It is true that the main point, the essential question to be determined, was whether there had been a transfer *eo nomine*[105] of certain shares within the meaning of a will. The testator in that case, Rose, by his will had given a number of shares to one Hook but the gift was subject to this qualification, 'if such shares have not been transferred to him previously to my death'. The question was, had the shares been transferred to him in these circumstances? He had executed (as had this Mr. Rose) a transfer in appropriate form and handed the transfer and the certificate to Hook; but, at the time of his death, the transfer had not been registered. It was said, therefore, that there had been no transfer; and (following Mr. Pennycuick's argument) there had been no passing to Hook of any interest, legal or benefi-cial, whatever, by the time the testator died. If that view were right then, of course, Hook would be entitled to the shares under the will. But my brother went a little more closely into the matter, because it was obvious that on one view of it, if it were held that there was a 'transfer' within the terms of the will, though the transfer was inoperative in the eye of the law and not capable of being completed after the death, then Mr. Hook suffered the misfortune of getting the shares neither by gift *inter vivos* nor by testamentary benefaction. Therefore, my brother considered the case of *Milroy v Lord*, and in regard to it he used this language [1949] Ch 78 at 89:

> 'I was referred on that to the well known case of *Milroy v Lord*, and also to the recent case of *Re Fry* [1946] Ch 312. Those cases, as I understand them, turn on the fact that the deceased donor had not done all in his power, according to the nature of the property given, to vest the legal interest in the property in the donee. In such circumstances it is, of course, well settled that there is no equity to complete the imperfect gift. If any act remained to be done by the donor to complete the gift at the date of the donor's death the court will not compel his personal representatives to do that act and the gift remains incomplete and fails. In *Milroy v Lord* the imperfection was due to the fact that the wrong form of transfer was used for the purpose of transferring certain bank shares. The document was not the appropriate document to pass any interest in the property at all.'

Then he refers to *Re Fry*, which is another illustration.[106]

> 'In this case, as I understand it, the testator had done everything in his power to divest himself of the shares in question to Mr. Hook. He had executed a transfer. It is not suggested that the transfer was not in accordance with the company's regulations. He had handed that transfer together with the certificate to Mr. Hook. There was nothing else the testator could do.'

I venture respectfully to adopt the whole of the passage I have read which, in my judgment, is a correct statement of the law. If that be so, then it seems to me that it cannot be asserted on the authority of *Milroy v Lord*, and I venture to think it also cannot be asserted as a matter of logic and good sense or principle, that because, by the regulations of the company, there had to be a gap before Mrs. Rose could, as between herself and the company, claim the rights which the shares gave her *vis-à-vis* the company, the deceased was not in the meantime a trustee for her of all his rights and benefits under the shares. That he intended to pass all those rights, as I have said, seems to be too plain for argument. I think the matter might be put perhaps in a somewhat different fashion, though it reaches the same end. Whatever might be the position during the period between the execution of this document and the registration of the shares, the transfers were on 30 June, 1943, registered. After registration, the title of Mrs. Rose was beyond doubt complete in every respect; and if the deceased had received a dividend between execution and registration and Mrs. Rose had claimed to have that dividend handed to her, what would have been the deceased's answer? It could no longer be that the purported gift was imperfect; it had been made perfect. I am not suggesting that the perfection was retroactive. But what else could

---

[105] Meaning 'by that name'.　　[106] See also *Re Transatlantic Life Assurance Co Ltd* [1980] 1 WLR 79.

he say? How could he, in the face of his own statement under seal, deny the proposition that he had, on 30 March, 1943, transferred the shares to his wife?—and by the phrase 'transfer the shares' surely must be meant transfer to her 'the shares and all my right title and interest thereunder'. Nothing else could sensibly have been meant. Nor can he, I think, make much of the fact that this was a voluntary settlement on his part. Being a case of an unlimited company, as I have said, Mrs. Rose had herself to undertake by covenant to accept the shares subject to their burdens—in other words, to relieve the deceased of his liability as a corporator. I find it unnecessary to pursue the question of consideration, but it is, I think, another feature which would make exceedingly difficult and, sensibly impossible, the assertion on the deceased's part of any right to retain any such dividend.[107]

In **Mascall v Mascall** (1984) 50 P & CR 119[108] the plaintiff executed a transfer of a house with registered title in favour of his son, and also handed the land certificate to him. Before the documents were sent to the Land Registry for the registration of the son as proprietor, the plaintiff and his son had a serious row. The plaintiff then sought a declaration that the transfer was void. In holding that there had been an effective gift to the son, LAWTON LJ referred to *Milroy v Lord* and *Re Rose* and said at 125:

In my judgment, that is the situation here. The plaintiff had done everything in his power to transfer the house to the defendant. He had intended to do it. He had handed over the land certificate. He had executed the transfer and all that remained was for the defendant, in the ordinary way of conveyancing, to submit the transfer for stamping and then to ask the Land Registry to register his title. Mr. Pearson sought to say that, in relation to registered land, if not to unregistered land, the plaintiff could have done more because he himself, pursuant to section 18 of the Land Registration Act 1925, could have asked the Land Registry to register the transfer and he had not done so; therefore he had not done everything within his power. In my judgment, that is a fallacious argument. He had done everything in his power in the ordinary way of the transfer of registered property and, in the ordinary way, it was for the defendant to get the Land Registry to register him as the proprietor of the property. In those circumstances, it seems to me that the deputy judge's judgment was correct and I would dismiss the appeal.[109]

(ii) Unconscionability[110]

Pennington v Waine[111]
[2002] EWCA Civ 227, [2002] 1 WLR 2075 (**Arden, Clarke, Schiemann LJJ**)

Mrs. Ada Crampton told her nephew, Harold Crampton, that she wanted to give him 400 shares in a company and for him to become a director of the company, for which

---

[107] See *Mallott v Wilson* [1903] 2 Ch 494, where Byrne J held that, where an intended trustee disclaimed an interest transferred on trust as soon as he knew of it, the transfer constituted the trust until disclaimer, whereupon the legal estate, now clothed with the trusts, revested in the settlor. For criticism, see [1981] Conv 141 (P. Matthews).   [108] (1985) 82 LS Gaz 1629 (H. Wilkinson).

[109] In *Brown & Root Technology Ltd v Sun Alliance and London Assurance Co Ltd* [2001] Ch 733 it was held, in the context of a dispute about the assignment of a lease which had not been registered, that the *Re Rose* principle did not apply as regards legal, rather than equitable, rights. See (1999) 50 *Northern Ireland Law Quarterly* 90 (A. Dowling).   [110] Snell, pp. 548–551.

[111] (2003) CLJ 263 (A. Doggett); [2003] Conv 364 (J. Garton); [2002] LMCLQ 296 (H. Tijo and T.M. Yeo); [2002] All ER Rev 229 (P.J. Clarke); [2006] Conv 192 (M. Halliwell); [2006] Conv 411 (H.T. Chee).

he needed to own at least one share. They both signed the share transfer form which was delivered to the company's auditor, Mr. Pennington, but was not delivered to the company before she died. The trial judge held that the transfer of shares was effective when the donor had signed the form and so the shares did not form part of her residuary estate.

Held. Since the nephew had been informed of the gift and had been made a director it would have been be unconscionable for the donor to revoke the gift which was effective in equity.

Arden LJ:

52 This appeal raises the question of what is necessary for the purposes of a valid equitable assignment of shares by way of gift. If the transaction had been for value, a contract to assign the share would have been sufficient: neither the execution nor the delivery of an instrument of transfer would have been required. However, where the transaction was purely voluntary, the principle that equity will not assist a volunteer must be applied and respected. [Her Ladyship referred to *Milroy v Lord* (1862) 4 De GF & J 264 [p. 157, above], *Jones v Lock* (1865) 1 Ch App 25 [p. 151, above], *Warriner v Rogers* (1873) LR 16 Eq 340 and *Richards v Delbridge* (1874) LR 18 Eq 11 [p. 152, above], and continued:] Accordingly the gift must be perfected, or 'completely constituted'.

53 The principle that equity will not assist a volunteer has been lucidly explained in Maitland, *Lectures on Equity* (1909), p 73:

'I have a son called Thomas. I write a letter to him saying "I give you my Blackacre estate, my leasehold house in the High Street, the sum of £1,000 Consols standing in my name, the wine in my cellar". This is ineffectual—I have given nothing—a letter will not convey freehold or leasehold land, it will not transfer Government stock, it will not pass the ownership in goods. Even if, instead of writing a letter, I had executed a deed of covenant—saying not I do convey Blackacre, I do assign the leasehold house and the wine, but I covenant to convey and assign—even this would not have been a perfect gift. It would be an imperfect gift, and being an imperfect gift the court will not regard it as a declaration of trust. I have made quite clear that I do not intend to make myself a trustee, I meant to give. The two intentions are very different—the giver means to get rid of his rights, the man who is intending to make himself a trustee intends to retain his rights but to come under an onerous obligation. The latter intention is far rarer than the former. Men often mean to give things to their kinsfolk, they do not often mean to constitute themselves trustees. An imperfect gift is no declaration of trust. This is well illustrated by the cases of *Richards v Delbridge* (1874) LR 18 Eq 11 and *Heartley v Nicholson* (1875) LR 19 Eq 233.'

54 Thus explained, the principle that equity will not assist a volunteer at first sight looks like a hard-edged rule of law not permitting much argument or exception. Historically the emergence of the principle may have been due to the need for equity to follow the law rather than an intuitive development of equity. The principle against imperfectly constituted gifts led to harsh and seemingly paradoxical results. Before long, equity had tempered the wind to the shorn lamb (i.e. the donee). It did so on more than one occasion and in more than one way.

55 First it was held that an incompletely constituted gift could be upheld if the gift had been completed to such an extent that the donee could enforce his right to the shares as against third parties without forcing the donor to take any further step. Accordingly, if a share transfer has been executed by the donor and duly presented to the company for registration, the donee would be entitled, if necessary, to apply to the court for an order for rectification of the share register under section 359 of the Companies Act 1985. Such an order would not, of course, be granted

if for example the directors had a discretion to refuse to register the transfer and had timeously passed a valid resolution to decline to register the transfer: see *Buckley on the Companies Acts* (looseleaf ed), para 359.277.

56   That exception was extended in *Rose v Inland Revenue Comrs* [1952] Ch 499 and other cases by holding that for this exception to apply it was not necessary that the donor should have done all that it was necessary to be done to complete the gift, short of registration of the transfer. On the contrary it was sufficient if the donor had done all that it was necessary for him or her to do.

57   There is a logical difficulty with this particular exception because it assumes that there is a clear answer to the question, when does an equitable assignment of a share take place? In fact the question is circular. For if by handing the form of transfer to Mr. Pennington in this case, Ada completed the transaction of gift and the equitable assignment of the 400 shares, Harold can bring an action against Mr. Pennington to recover the shares as his property, and the principle that equity will not assist a volunteer is not infringed. If on the other hand, by handing the share transfer to Mr. Pennington, Ada did not complete the transaction of gift or the equitable assignment of the shares, Harold cannot recover the shares because to do so would mean compelling the donor or the donor's agent to take some further step. The equitable assignment clearly occurs at some stage before the shares are registered. But does it occur when the share transfer is executed, or when the share transfer is delivered to the transferee, or when the transfer is lodged for registration, or when the pre-emption procedure in article 8 is satisfied or the directors resolve that the transfer should be registered? I return to this point below.

58   According to counsel's researches, the situation in the present case has not arisen in any reported cases before. I note that in her recent work, *Personal Property Law, Text, Cases and Materials* (2000), p 241 Professor Sarah Worthington takes it as at axiomatic that

'notwithstanding any demonstrable intention to make a gift, there will be no effective gift in equity if the donor simply places matters (such as completed transfer forms accompanied by the relevant share certificates) in the hands of the donor's agents. In those circumstances the donor remains at liberty to recall the gift simply by revoking the instructions previously given to the agent. The donor has not done all that is necessary, and the donee is not in a position to control completion of the transfer. It follows that the intended gift will not be regarded as complete either at law or in equity.'

59   Secondly equity has tempered the wind (of the principle that equity will not assist a volunteer) to the shorn lamb (the donee) by utilising the constructive trust. This does not constitute a declaration of trust and thus does not fall foul of the principle (see *Milroy v Lord* (1862) 4 De GF & J 264 and *Jones v Lock* (1865) LR 1 Ch App 25) that an imperfectly constituted gift is not saved by being treated as a declaration of trust. Thus, for example, in *T Choithram International SA v Pagarani* [2001] 1 WLR 1 [p. 154, above], the Privy Council held that the assets which the donor gave to the foundation of which he was one of the trustees were held upon trust to vest the same in all the trustees of the foundation on the terms of the trusts of the foundation. This particular trust obligation was not a term of the express trust constituting the foundation but a constructive trust adjunct to it. So, too, in *Rose v Inland Revenue Comrs* [1952] Ch 499, the Court of Appeal held that the beneficial interest in the shares passed when the share transfers were delivered to the transferee, and that consequently the transferor was a trustee of the legal estate in the shares from that date. At one stage in his judgment Sir Raymond Evershed MR went further and held that an equitable interest passed when the document declaring a gift was executed. [Her Ladyship quoted from Evershed MR's judgment [see p. 161, above] and continued:]

60   Thirdly equity has tempered the wind to the shorn lamb by applying a benevolent construction to words of gift. As explained above an imperfect gift is not saved by being treated as a declaration of trust. But where a court of equity is satisfied that the donor had an intention to make an immediate gift, the court will construe the words which the donor used as words effecting a gift or declaring a trust if they can fairly bear that meaning and otherwise the gift will fail. This point can also be illustrated by reference to *T Choithram International SA v Pagarani* [2001] 1 WLR 1. [Arden LJ referred to the case, and continued:]

61   Accordingly the principle that, where a gift is imperfectly constituted, the court will not hold it to operate as a declaration of trust, does not prevent the court from construing it to be a trust if that interpretation is permissible as a matter of construction, which may be a benevolent construction. The same must apply to words of gift. An equity to perfect a gift would not be invoked by giving a benevolent construction to words of gift or, it follows, words which the donor used to communicate or give effect to his gift.

62   The cases to which counsel have referred us do not reveal any, or any consistent single policy consideration behind the rule that the court will not perfect an imperfect gift. The objectives of the rule obviously include ensuring that donors do not by acting voluntarily act unwisely in a way that they may subsequently regret. This objective is furthered by permitting donors to change their minds at any time before it becomes completely constituted. This is a paternalistic objective, which can outweigh the respect to be given to the donor's original intention as gifts are often held by the courts to be incompletely constituted despite the clearest intention of the donor to make the gift. Another valid objective would be to safeguard the position of the donor: suppose, for instance, that (contrary to the fact) it had been discovered after Ada's death that her estate was insolvent, the court would be concerned to ensure that the gift did not defeat the rights of creditors. But, while this may well be a relevant consideration, for my own part I do not consider that this need concern the court to the exclusion of other considerations as in the event of insolvency there are other potent remedies available to creditors where insolvents have made gifts to defeat their claims: see for example sections 339 and 423 of the Insolvency Act 1986. There must also be, in the interests of legal certainty, a clearly ascertainable point in time at which it can be said that the gift was completed, and this point in time must be arrived at on a principled basis.

63   There are countervailing policy considerations which would militate in favour of holding a gift to be completely constituted. These would include effectuating, rather than frustrating, the clear and continuing intention of the donor, and preventing the donor from acting in a manner which is unconscionable. As Mr. McGhee pointed out, both these policy considerations are evident in *T Choithram International SA v Pagarani* [2001] 1 WLR 1. It does not seem to me that this consideration is inconsistent with what Jenkins LJ said in *Re McArdle* [1951] Ch 669. His point was that there is nothing unconscionable in simply (without more) changing your mind. That is also the point which Professor Worthington makes in the passage I have cited.

64   If one proceeds on the basis that a principle which animates the answer to the question whether an apparently incomplete gift is to be treated as completely constituted is that a donor will not be permitted to change his or her mind if it would be unconscionable, in the eyes of equity, *vis-à-vis* the donee to do so, what is the position here? There can be no comprehensive list of factors which makes it unconscionable for the donor to change his or her mind: it must depend on the court's evaluation of all the relevant considerations. What then are the relevant facts here? Ada made the gift of her own free will: there is no finding that she was not competent to do this. She not only told Harold about the gift and signed a form of transfer which she delivered to Mr. Pennington for him to secure registration: her agent also told Harold that he need take

no action. In addition Harold agreed to become a director of the company without limit of time, which he could not do without shares being transferred to him. If Ada had changed her mind on (say) 10 November 1998, in my judgment the court could properly have concluded that it was too late for her to do this as by that date Harold signed the form 288A, the last of the events identified above, to occur.

65   There is next the pure question of law: was it necessary for Ada deliver the form of transfer to Harold? . . . . . .

66   Even if I am correct in my view that the Court of Appeal took the view in *Rose v Inland Revenue Comrs* that delivery of the share transfers was there required, it does not follow that delivery cannot in some circumstances be dispensed with. Here, there was a clear finding that Ada intended to make an immediate gift. Harold was informed of it. Moreover, I have already expressed the view that a stage was reached when it would have been unconscionable for Ada to recall the gift. It follows that it would also have been unconscionable for her personal representatives to refuse to hand over the share transfer to Harold after her death. In those circumstances, in my judgment, delivery of the share transfer before her death was unnecessary so far as perfection of the gift was concerned.

CLARKE LJ agreed that the appeal should be dismissed, although his analysis was rather different:

104   It appears to me that the logic of those passages from the judgment of Sir Raymond Evershed MR [in *Rose v IRC*] supports the proposition that where the document used to transfer the property is, as he put it, 'apt and proper to transfer the property' and 'is in truth the appropriate way in which the property must be transferred', the court will give effect to the transfer on the basis that the transferor has done everything in his power to effect the transfer. In this context, since the transfer form evidences a present transfer, the property being transferred is the equitable interest in the shares. It cannot be the legal interest in them because the legal interest can only be transferred on registration. In these circumstances Sir Raymond Evershed MR thought that the equitable interest was transferred as at the date of execution, whereafter the transferor held the legal interest as trustee for the transferee. . . .

115   Finally, [*T Choithram International SA v Pagarani* [2001] 1 WLR 1] seems to me to give some assistance to the analysis set out above. As Arden LJ has observed, Lord Browne-Wilkinson, at p11, highlighted the contrast between the maxim that equity will not aid a volunteer and the maxim that it will not strive officiously to defeat a gift. It seems to me that if equity refuses to aid Harold on the facts of this case, it will prefer the former maxim to the latter, whereas all the circumstances of the case lead to the conclusion that it should give effect to the gift which Ada intended.

116   *T Choithram International SA v Pagarani* . . . seems to me to be an example of a case in which the court held that enough had been done to enable equity to assist the donee. I would accept Mr. McGhee's submission that equity will intervene only where the donor has done everything in his power to perfect the gift cannot be absolutely true since there is always something more that the donor could have done. Thus, even if Ada had delivered the transfer form to Harold, she could have done more by making a specific request to the company to register the shares in Harold's name. In my opinion Ada executed a valid equitable assignment in favour of Harold by signing the form in circumstances in which she had no intention of revoking it in the future. This is not, therefore a case of an imperfect gift (or assignment) of her equitable interest. As I see it, she thereafter held the legal interest in the shares in trust for Harold, who, as between him and her, would thereafter have been beneficially entitled to any dividend declared on the shares.

D COVENANTS TO SETTLE

It is important to distinguish between the creation of a trust or settlement and a covenant or contract to create one. Once a settlement is created, the beneficiaries become owners in equity of their share of the settled property. But if the settlor has covenanted to create a settlement or to add property to an existing settlement, the rights of the intended beneficiaries depend on whether or not they can compel the settlor to complete the settlement. Traditionally, they could not do so if they were volunteers; for equity does not assist a volunteer. If, however, a person had provided consideration, including marriage consideration, they could enforce the covenant. This doctrine has now been qualified by the Contracts (Rights of Third Parties) Act 1999, the effect of which is that in certain circumstances a third party who has not provided consideration will nevertheless be able to enforce the covenant in his own right. Although this statutory reform reduces the importance of the doctrine that volunteers cannot enforce a covenant to settle, it does not render that doctrine irrelevant. This is because the 1999 Act only applies to those covenants which were entered into after 11 May, 2000.[112] It follows that it remains necessary to consider the old cases which recognise that volunteers cannot enforce a covenant and those which identify methods for avoiding this principle.

(i) Contracts (Rights of Third Parties) Act 1999[113]

CONTRACTS (RIGHTS OF THIRD PARTIES) ACT 1999

1. Rights of third party to enforce contractual term

(1) Subject to the provisions of this Act, a person who is not a party to a contract (a 'third party') may in his own right enforce a term of the contract if—

    (a) the contract expressly provides that he may, or

    (b) subject to subsection (2), the term purports to confer a benefit on him.

(2) Subsection (1)(b) does not apply if on a proper construction of the contract it appears that the parties did not intend the term to be enforceable by the third party.

(3) The third party must be expressly identified in the contract by name, as a member of a class or as answering a particular description but need not be in existence when the contract is entered into.

---

[112] Contracts (Rights of Third Parties) Act 1999, s. 10(2). Alternatively, the Act will apply to covenants entered into after 11 November, 1999 if the contract expressly provides that the Act shall apply: ibid, s. 10(3).

[113] H&M, pp. 130–131; Lewin, pp. 88–89; P&M, p. 171; P&S p. 191; Pettit pp. 108–109; Snell pp. 474–475; T&H pp. 147–149; U&H, pp. 217–220; Cheshire, Fifoot and Furmston, *Law of Contract* (15th edn, 2007) (2007), pp. 588–593; Treitel, *The Law of Contract* (12th edn, 2007), pp. 691–698; (2001) 60 CLJ 353 (N. Andrews). The Contracts (Rights of Third Parties) Act 1999 implements Law Commission Report No. 242 (1996) *Privity of Contract: Contract for the Benefit of Third Parties*.

(4) This section does not confer a right on a third party to enforce a term of a contract otherwise than subject to and in accordance with any other relevant terms of the contract.

(5) For the purpose of exercising his right to enforce a term of the contract, there shall be available to the third party any remedy that would have been available to him in an action for breach of contract if he had been a party to the contract (and the rules relating to damages, injunctions, specific performance[114] and other relief shall apply accordingly).

(6) Where a term of a contract excludes or limits liability in relation to any matter references in this Act to the third party enforcing the term shall be construed as references to his availing himself of the exclusion or limitation.

(7) In this Act, in relation to a term of a contract which is enforceable by a third party—

'the promisor' means the party to the contract against whom the term is enforceable by the third party, and 'the promisee' means the party to the contract by whom the term is enforceable against the promisor.

2. Variation and rescission of contract

(1) Subject to the provisions of this section, where a third party has a right under section 1 to enforce a term of the contract, the parties to the contract may not, by agreement, rescind the contract, or vary it in such a way as to extinguish or alter his entitlement under that right, without his consent if—

(a) the third party has communicated his assent to the term to the promisor,

(b) the promisor is aware that the third party has relied on the term, or

(c) the promisor can reasonably be expected to have foreseen that the third party would rely on the term and the third party has in fact relied on it.

(2) The assent referred to in subsection (1)(a)—

(a) may be by words or conduct, and

(b) if sent to the promisor by post or other means, shall not be regarded as communicated to the promisor until received by him.

(3) Subsection (1) is subject to any express term of the contract under which—

(a) the parties to the contract may by agreement rescind or vary the contract without the consent of the third party, or

(b) the consent of the third party is required in circumstances specified in the contract instead of those set out in subsection (1)(a) to (c).

---

[114] At common law a volunteer beneficiary who was party to a deed could sue on it for damages but could not obtain specific performance of the deed: *Cannon v Hartley* [1949] Ch 213. The better view is that the same rule should apply under the 1999 Act. See H&M, p. 131.

(4) Where the consent of a third party is required under subsection (1) or (3), the court or arbitral tribunal may, on the application of the parties to the contract, dispense with his consent if satisfied—

   (a) that his consent cannot be obtained because his whereabouts cannot reasonably be ascertained, or

   (b) that he is mentally incapable of giving his consent.

(5) The court or arbitral tribunal may, on the application of the parties to a contract, dispense with any consent that may be required under subsection (1)(c) if satisfied that it cannot reasonably be ascertained whether or not the third party has in fact relied on the term.

(6) If the court or arbitral tribunal dispenses with a third party's consent, it may impose such conditions as it thinks fit, including a condition requiring the payment of compensation to the third party.

(ii) Covenants to Settle Before 11 May, 2000[115]

(a) Is the person who wishes to enforce the covenant a volunteer?

As regards covenants made before 11 May, 2000 the general rule that equity will not assist a volunteer applies. This is most likely to be relevant in connection with family settlements; either where the covenantor has failed to comply with a covenant to establish a settlement, or where a spouse, being a beneficiary under a marriage settlement, covenants to settle after-acquired property and fails to do so. At the outset it is important to determine whether or not the person who wishes to enforce the covenant is a volunteer.

Pullan v Koe[116]
[1913] 1 Ch 9 (ChD, **Swinfen Eady J**)

A marriage settlement dated May 1859, which settled property on trusts for a husband and wife and prospective children, contained a provision that the wife should settle after-acquired property of the value of £100 or upwards. In 1879, she received a present of £285 from her mother. The money was paid into her husband's bank account, on which she had power to draw. Part was then invested in bearer bonds or debentures;

---

[115] H&M, pp. 131–139; Lewin, pp. 89–92; P&M, pp. 170–176; P&S pp. 191–195; Pettit pp. 105–117; Snell pp. 130–131; T&H pp. 149–151; U&H, pp. 220–231. See also (1960) 76 LQR 100 (D.W. Elliott); (1962) 78 LQR 228 (J.A. Hornby); (1965) 23 CLJ 46 (G.H. Jones); (1966) 29 MLR 397 (D. Matheson); (1966) 8 *Malaya Law Review* 153 (M. Scott); [1967] *Annual Survey of Commonwealth Law* 387 (J.D. Davies); (1969) 85 LQR 213 (W.A. Lee); (1975) 91 LQR 236 (J.L. Barton); (1976) 92 LQR 427 (R.P. Meagher and J.R.F. Lehane); (1979) 32 CLP 1 (C.E.F. Rickett); (1981) 34 CLP 189 (C.E.F. Rickett); [1982] Conv 280 (M.W. Friends); 352 (S. Smith); (1982) 98 LQR 17 (J.D. Feltham); (1986) 60 *Australian Law Journal* 387 (S. Lindsay and P. Ziegler); *Perspectives of Law* (ed. R. Pound) (1964), p. 240 (R.H. Maudsley); Gardner, *An Introduction to the Law of Trusts* (2nd edn., 2002), chap. 4.

[116] *Re D'Angibau* (1879) 15 Ch D 228; *Re Plumptre's Marriage Settlement* [1910] 1 Ch 609; *Re Cook's Settlement Trusts* [1965] Ch 902 [p. 175, below]; cf. *Paul v Paul* (1882) 20 Ch D 742.

and the interest paid to the account. The bonds remained at the bank. In 1909, the husband died. The trustees of the settlement, acting on behalf of the wife and children, claimed the bonds from the husband's executor. The defendants relied on the Statutes of Limitation.

Held. The trustees succeeded. The £285 was subject to a trust in favour of those within the marriage consideration, and was now represented by the bonds.

Swinfen Eady J: It was contended that the bonds never in fact became trust property, as both the wife and husband were only liable in damages for breach of covenant, and that the case was different from cases where property which has once admittedly become subject to the trusts of an instrument has been improperly dealt with, and is sought to be recovered. In my opinion as soon as the 285l. was paid to the wife it became in equity bound by and subject to the trusts of the settlement. The trustees could have claimed that particular sum, could have obtained at once the appointment of a receiver of it, if they could have shewn a case of jeopardy, and, if it had been invested and the investment could be traced, could have followed the money and claimed the investment.

This point was dealt with by Jessel MR in *Smith v Lucas* (1881) 18 Ch D 531 at 543, where he said:

'What is the effect of such a covenant in equity? It has been said that the effect in equity of the covenant of the wife, as far as she is concerned, is that it does not affect her personally, but that it binds the property: that is to say, it binds the property under the doctrine of equity that that is to be considered as done which ought to be done. That is in the nature of specific performance of the contract no doubt. If, therefore, this is a covenant to settle the future-acquired property of the wife, and nothing more is done by her, the covenant will bind the property.'

Again in *Collyer v Isaacs* (1881) 19 Ch D 342 at 351, Jessel MR said:

'A man can contract to assign property which is to come into existence in the future, and when it has come into existence, equity, treating as done that which ought to be done, fastens upon that property, and the contract to assign thus becomes a complete assignment. If a person contracts for value, e.g., in his marriage settlement, to settle all such real estate as his father shall leave him by will, or purports actually to convey by the deed all such real estate, the effect is the same. It is a contract for value which will bind the property if the father leaves any property to his son.'

The property being thus bound, these bonds became trust property, and can be followed by the trustees and claimed from a volunteer.

Again the trustees are entitled to come into a Court of Equity to enforce a contract to create a trust, contained in a marriage settlement, for the benefit of the wife and the issue of the marriage, all of whom are within the marriage consideration. The husband covenanted that he and his heirs, executors, and administrators should, as soon as circumstances would admit, convey, assign, and surrender to the trustees the real or personal property to which his wife should become beneficially entitled. The trustees are entitled to have that covenant specifically enforced by a Court of Equity. In *Re D'Angibau* (1879) 15 Ch D 228 at 242 and in *Re Plumptre's Marriage Settlement* [1910] 1 Ch 609 at 616 it was held that the Court would not interfere in favour of volunteers, not within the marriage consideration, but here the plaintiffs are the contracting parties and the object of the proceeding is to benefit the wife and issue of the marriage.

Re Kay's Settlement
[1939] Ch 329 (Ch D, **Simonds J**)[117]

In 1907 Miss Kay, a spinster, executed a voluntary conveyance in favour of herself for life and after her death for her issue, containing a covenant to settle after-acquired property. She married and had three children and became entitled to other property. She refused a request by the trustees of the settlement to bring in the property on the ground that, as the settlement was purely voluntary, they ought not to take steps to enforce the covenant or to recover damages.

Held. Trustees directed not to take any such steps.

Simonds J: The trustees have issued this summons, making as parties to it, first, the settlor herself and, secondly, her infant children, who are beneficiaries under the settlement. But, be it observed, though beneficiaries, her children are, for the purpose of this settlement, to be regarded as volunteers, there being no marriage consideration, which would have entitled them to sue, though they are parties to this application. The trustees ask whether, in the event which has happened of the settlor having become entitled to certain property, they should take proceedings against her to compel performance of the covenant or to recover damages on her failure to implement it.... The settlor has appeared by Mr. Evershed and has contended, as she was entitled to contend, that the only question before the Court was whether the trustees ought to be directed to take such proceedings; that is to say, she contended that the only question before the Court was precisely that question which Eve J had to deal with in *Re Pryce* [1917] 1 Ch 234. She has said that the question before me is not primarily whether, if she were sued, such an action would succeed (as to which she might have a defence, I know not what), but whether, in the circumstances as they are stated to the Court, the trustees ought to be directed to take proceedings against her.

As to that, the argument before me has been, on behalf of the children of the marriage, beneficiaries under the settlement, that, although it is conceded that the trustees could not successfully take proceedings for specific performance of the agreements contained in the settlement, yet they could successfully, and ought to be directed to, take proceedings at law to recover damages for the non-observance of the agreements contained in the settlement.... In the circumstances I must say that I felt considerable sympathy for the argument which was put before me by Mr. Winterbotham on behalf of the children, that there was, at any rate, on the evidence before the Court to-day, no reason why the trustees should not be directed to take proceedings to recover what damages might be recoverable at law for breach of the agreements entered into by the settlor in her settlement. But on a consideration of *Re Pryce* it seemed to me that so far as this Court was concerned the matter was concluded and that I ought not to give any directions to the trustees to take the suggested proceedings.

In *Re Pryce* the circumstances appear to me to have been in no wise different from those which obtain in the case which I have to consider. In that case there was a marriage settlement made in 1887. It contained a covenant to settle the wife's after-acquired property....

[His Lordship set out the after-acquired property and continued:] The husband died in 1907, and there was no issue of the marriage. Subject to his widow's life interest in both funds, the ultimate residue of the wife's fund was held in trust for her statutory next-of-kin, and the husband's fund was held in trust for him absolutely. The widow was also tenant for life under

[117] See also *Cannon v Hartley* [1949] Ch 213.

her husband's will. The trustees of the marriage settlement in that case took out a summons 'to have it determined whether these interests and funds were caught by the provisions of the settlement, and, if so, whether they should take proceedings to enforce them'....

Eve J, in a considered judgment, held that although the interests to which I have referred were caught by the covenant of the wife and the agreement by the husband respectively, yet the trustees ought not to take any steps to recover any of them. In the case of the wife's fund he said that her next-of-kin were volunteers, who could neither maintain an action to enforce the covenant nor for damages for breach of it, and that the Court would not give them by indirect means what they could not obtain by direct procedure; therefore he declined to direct the trustees to take proceedings either to have the covenant specifically enforced or to recover damages at law. The learned judge, as I have said, took time to consider his judgment. Many of the cases which have been cited to me, though not all of them apparently, were cited to him, and after deciding that no steps should be taken to enforce specific performance of the covenant he used these words [1917] 1 Ch 234 at 241:

'The position of the wife's fund is somewhat different, in that her next-of-kin would be entitled to it on her death; but they are volunteers, and although the Court would probably compel fulfilment of the contract to settle at the instance of any persons within the marriage consideration—see *per* Cotton LJ in *Re D'Angibau* (1879) 15 Ch D 228 at 242—and in their favour will treat the outstanding property as subjected to an enforceable trust—*Pullan v Koe* [1913] 1 Ch 9 [p. 171, above]—"volunteers have no right whatever to obtain specific performance of a mere covenant which has remained as a covenant and has never been performed"; see *per* James LJ in *Re D'Angibau* at 246. Nor could damages be awarded either in this Court, or, I apprehend, at law, where, since the Supreme Court of Judicature Act, 1873,[118] the same defences would be available to the defendant as would be raised in an action brought in this Court for specific performance or damages.'

That is the exact point which has been urged on me with great insistence by Mr. Winterbotham. Whatever sympathy I might feel for his argument, I am not justified in departing in any way from this decision, which is now twenty-one years old. The learned judge went on:

'In these circumstances, seeing that the next-of-kin could neither maintain an action to enforce the covenant nor for damages for breach of it, and that the settlement is not a declaration of trust constituting the relationship of trustee and *cestui que trust* between the defendant and the next-of-kin, in which case effect could be given to the trusts even in favour of volunteers, but is a mere voluntary contract to create a trust, ought the Court now for the sole benefit of these volunteers to direct the trustees to take proceedings to enforce the defendant's covenant? I think it ought not; to do so would be to give the next-of-kin by indirect means relief they cannot obtain by any direct procedure, and would in effect be enforcing the settlement as against the defendant's legal right to payment and transfer from the trustees of the parents' marriage settlement.'

It is true that in those last words the learned judge does not specifically refer to an action for damages, but it is clear that he has in his mind directions both with regard to an action for specific performance and an action to recover damages at law—or, now, in this Court.

In those circumstances it appears to me that I must follow the learned judge's decision and I must direct the trustees not to take any steps either to compel performance of the covenant or to recover damages through her failure to implement it.

[118] Now Supreme Court Act 1981, s. 49.

Re Cook's Settlement Trusts
[1965] Ch 902 (Ch D, **Buckley J**)

In 1934, by an agreement and subsequent settlement of family property, made between Sir Herbert Cook, Bart., Sir Francis Cook (his son), and the trustees of the settlement, certain pictures became the absolute property of Sir Francis Cook. In the settlement, Sir Francis covenanted (clause 6) for valuable consideration that if any of those pictures should be sold during his lifetime, the net proceeds of sale should be paid to the trustees of the settlement to be held upon the trusts of the settlement.

In 1962, Sir Francis gave a Rembrandt (a picture of Titus) to his wife. She desired to sell it. The question was whether, on the sale of the Rembrandt, the trustees were obligated to take steps to enforce the performance of the covenant.

Held. As the beneficiaries had given no consideration for the covenant, they could not require the trustees to take steps to enforce it. Nor were they beneficiaries of a trust of the promise.[119]

Buckley J: Mr. Goff, appearing for Sir Francis, has submitted first that, as a matter of law, the covenant contained in clause 6 of the settlement is not enforceable against him by the trustees of the settlement...[He] submits that the covenant was a voluntary and executory contract to make a settlement in a future event and was not a settlement of a covenant to pay a sum of money to the trustees. He further submits that as regards the covenant all the beneficiaries under the settlement are volunteers, with the consequence that not only should the court not direct the trustees to take proceedings on the covenant but it should positively direct them not to take proceedings. He relies upon *Re Pryce* [1917] 1 Ch 234 and *Re Kay's Settlement* [1939] Ch 329.

Counsel for the second and third defendants have contended that on the true view of the facts there was an immediate settlement of the obligation created by the covenant, and not merely a covenant to settle something in the future. It was said, as Mr. Monckton put it, that by the agreement Sir Herbert bought the rights arising under the covenant for the benefit of the *cestuis que trustent* under the settlement and that, the covenant being made in favour of the trustees, these rights became assets of the trust. He relied on *Fletcher v Fletcher* (1844) 4 Hare 67; *Williamson v Codrington* (1750) 1 Ves Sen 511 and *Re Cavendish Browne's Settlement Trusts* [1916] WN 341. I am not able to accept this argument. The covenant with which I am concerned did not, in my opinion, create a debt enforceable at law, that is to say, a property right, which, although to bear fruit only in the future and upon a contingency, was capable of being made the subject of an immediate trust, as was held to be the case in *Fletcher v Fletcher*. Nor is this covenant associated with property which was the subject of an immediate trust as in *Williamson v Codrington*. Nor did the covenant relate to property which then belonged to the covenantor, as in *Re Cavendish Browne's Settlement Trusts*. In contrast to all these cases, this covenant upon its true construction is, in my opinion, an executory contract to settle a particular fund or particular funds of money which at the date of the covenant did not exist and which might never come into existence. It is analogous to a covenant to settle an expectation or

---

[119] Appeal compromised. The picture was later sold at Christies for 760,000 guineas. See The Times, 7 November, 1964, p. 5 and 20 March, 1965, p. 10.

to settle after-acquired property. The case, in my judgment, involves the law of contract, not the law of trusts.

As an alternative argument, Mr. Brightman formulated this proposition, which he admitted not to be directly supported by any authority, but he claimed to conflict with none: that where a covenantor has for consideration moving from a third party covenanted with trustees to make a settlement of property, the court will assist an intended beneficiary who is a volunteer to enforce the covenant if he is specially an object of the intended trust or (which Mr. Brightman says is the same thing) is within the consideration of the deed. In formulating this proposition Mr. Brightman bases himself on language used by Cotton LJ in *Re D'Angibau* (1879) 15 Ch D 228 at 242 and by Romer J in *Cannon v Hartley* [1949] Ch 213 at 223. As an example of a case to which the proposition would apply, Mr. Brightman supposes a father having two sons who enters into an agreement with his elder son and with trustees whereby the father agrees to convey an estate to his elder son absolutely in consideration of the son covenanting with his father and the trustees, or with the trustees alone, to settle an expectation on trusts for the benefit of the younger son. The younger son is a stranger to the transaction, but he is also the primary (and special) beneficiary of the intended settlement. A court of equity should, and would, Mr. Brightman contends, assist the younger son to enforce his brother's covenant and should not permit the elder son to frustrate the purposes of the agreement by refusing to implement his covenant although he has secured the valuable consideration given for it. The submission is not without attraction, for it is not to be denied that, generally speaking, the conduct of a man who, having pledged his word for valuable consideration, takes the benefits he has so obtained and then fails to do his part, commands no admiration. I have, therefore, given careful consideration to this part of the argument to see whether the state of the law is such as might justify me (subject to the construction point) in dealing with the case on some such grounds.

There was no consideration for Sir Francis's covenant moving from the trustees; nor, of course, was there any consideration moving from Sir Francis's children. [His Lordship referred to *A-G v Jacobs-Smith* [1895] 2 QB 341 at 353; *Hill v Gomme* (1839) 5 My & Cr 250 at 254; *Harvey v Ashley* (1748) 3 Atk 607 at 610; *Re D'Angibau* (1879) 15 Ch D 228; *Green v Paterson* (1886) 32 Ch D 95, and continued:]

These authorities show that there is an equitable exception to the general rule of law which I have mentioned where the contract is made in consideration of marriage and the intended beneficiary who seeks to have the contract enforced is within the marriage consideration. They do not support the existence of any wider exception save perhaps in the case of a beneficiary who is not within the marriage consideration but whose interests under the intended trusts are closely interwoven with interests of others who are within that consideration. They do not support the view that any such exception exists in favour of a person who was not a party to the contract and is not to be treated as though he had been and who has given no consideration and is not to be treated as if he had given consideration. Where the obligation to settle property has been assumed voluntarily it is clear that no object of the intended trusts can enforce the obligation. Thus in *Re Kay's Settlement* [1939] Ch 329, a spinster made a voluntary settlement in favour of herself and her issue which contained a covenant to settle after-acquired property. She later married and had children who, as volunteers, were held to have no right to enforce the covenant. Mr. Brightman distinguishes that case from the present on the ground that in *Re Kay's Settlement* the settlement and covenant were entirely voluntary, whereas Sir Francis received consideration from Sir Herbert; but Sir Francis received no consideration from his own children. Why, it may be asked, should they be accorded an indulgence in a court of equity which they would not have been accorded had Sir Herbert given no consideration? As regards them the covenant must, in my judgment, be regarded as having been given voluntarily. A plaintiff is not entitled to claim equitable relief against another merely because the latter's conduct is unmeritorious. Conduct by A which is unconscientious in relation to B so as to entitle B to equitable relief may not be unconscientious in relation to C so that C will have no standing to claim relief notwithstanding that the conduct in question may affect C. The father in Mr. Brightman's fictitious illustration could after performing his part of the contract release his elder son from the latter's covenant with him to make a settlement on the younger son, and the younger son could, I think, not complain. Only the covenant with the trustees would then remain, but this covenant would be a voluntary one, the trustees having given no consideration. I can see no reason why in these circumstances the court should assist the younger son to enforce the covenant with the trustees. But the right of the younger son to require the trustees to enforce their covenant, could not, I think, depend on whether the father had or had not released his covenant. Therefore, as it seems to me, on principle the younger son would not in any event have an equitable right to require the trustees to enforce their covenant. In other words, the arrangement between the father and his elder son would not have conferred any equitable right or interest upon his younger son.

I reach the conclusion that Mr. Brightman's proposition is not well-founded. There is no authority to support it and *Green v Paterson* (1886) 32 Ch D 95 is, I think, authority the other way. Accordingly, the second and third defendants are not, in my judgment, entitled to require the trustees to take proceedings to enforce the covenant even if it is capable of being construed in a manner favourable to them.

His Lordship then held that the words 'in case any of such pictures shall be sold' in clause 6 of the settlement following the covenant that Sir Francis would not during his lifetime sell without previous notice in writing to the trustees, only referred to a sale by Sir Francis and did not contain any embargo on a disposition of the works of art in any other way, e.g. by gift.

(b) Can a volunteer ever enforce a covenant?

1. Action for Damages by Trustees

Pettit: *Equity and the Law of Trusts* (10th edn, 2006), pp. 103–104

ii Beneficiary a volunteer—the equitable rules

If the trust is completely constituted the fact that a beneficiary is a volunteer is irrelevant: he is just as much entitled to enforce the trust as a *cestui que trust* who has provided consideration. If, however, the trust is not completely constituted, a volunteer beneficiary will gain no assistance from a court of equity. This can be illustrated by *Re Plumptre's Marriage Settlement*.[120] There, under a marriage settlement made in 1878, certain funds coming from the wife's father were settled upon the usual trusts of a wife's fund, with an ultimate remainder, in the events which happened, for the wife's statutory next-of-kin. The settlement contained an

[120] [1910] 1 Ch 609; *Jefferys v Jefferys* (1841) Cr & Ph 138; *Re D'Angibau* (1879) 15 Ch D 228, CA.

after-acquired property clause, which was held to cover a sum of stock given by the husband to the wife, which she subsequently sold and reinvested and which remained registered in her name on her death in 1909. The facts of this case, it will have been observed, are very similar to those in *Pullan v Koe*[121] and it was likewise held that any action at law would be barred by the Statute of Limitation. By contrast with *Pullan v Koe,* however, the beneficiaries under the settlement who were seeking to enforce the covenant, that is the next-of-kin, were not within the marriage consideration but were mere volunteers. It was accordingly held that they could not enforce the covenant against the husband, as administrator of his wife's estate.

As appears from the above cases, the fact that the obligation is contained in a deed makes no difference in equity which has no special regard to form.[122] It may well be asked, however, whether the trustees with whom the covenant is made can, or should, bring an action at law for damages since the common law regards consideration and the formality of a deed as alternative requirements. On this question it has been held that volunteers cannot compel trustees to take proceedings for damages, and further, that if the trustees ask the court for directions as to what they should do, they will be directed not to take any steps either to compel performance of the covenant or to recover damages through the failure to implement it. Thus in the leading case of *Re Pryce,*[123] there was a marriage settlement under which the wife covenanted to settle after-acquired property. The beneficial limitations of funds brought into the settlement by the wife (including any after-acquired property) were successive life interests to the wife and the husband, remainder to the children of the marriage (of whom there were never in fact any), and an ultimate remainder to the wife's next-of-kin, who were of course volunteers. The husband was dead and the wife did not wish the covenant to be enforced. The court held that the trustees *ought* not to take any steps to compel the transfer or payment to them of the after-acquired property. Notwithstanding powerful academic criticism,[124] *Re Pryce*[125] and *Re Kay's Settlement*[126] were followed in *Re Cook's Settlement Trusts.*[127]

iii Beneficiary a covenantee

Even where a *cestui que trust* is a volunteer, there is a clear decision at first instance,[128] that if the covenant is made with him, there is no answer to an action by him at common law on the covenant, and substantial damages for breach thereof will be awarded. But, as a volunteer, he will not be able to obtain the equitable remedy of specific performance.

iv Performance of unenforceable covenant

It is clear that if the settlor has in fact transferred property to trustees in compliance with an unenforceable covenant to settle the same in favour of volunteers, he thereby completely constitutes the trust, and cannot thereafter claim to recover the property, which must be held by the trustees on the declared trusts.[129]

---

[121] [1913] 1 Ch 9.

[122] See eg *Jefferys v Jefferys*, note 120 above; *Kekewich v Manning* (1851) 1 De GM & G 176.

[123] [1917] 1 Ch 234; *Re Kay's Settlement* [1939] Ch 329, [1939] 1 All ER 245. See 'Incompletely Constituted Trusts' by R.H. Maudsley in *Perspectives of Law* (ed. R. Pound), p. 240.

[124] (1960) 76 LQR 100 (D.W. Elliott); (1962) 76 LQR 228 (J.A. Hornby). As to the position if trustees do not ask the court for directions, but choose to bring an action see D.W. Elliott, ibid; [1988] Conv 19 (D. Goddard); R.H. Maudsley, note 123 above, p. 244; [1967] *Annual Survey of Commonwealth Law* 392 (J.D. Davies).

[125] Note 123 above.   [126] Note 123 above.   [127] [1965] Ch 902.

[128] *Cannon v Hartley* [1949] Ch 213.

[129] *Paul v Paul* (1882) 20 Ch D 742; *Re Adlard* [1954] Ch 29; *Re Ralli's Will Trusts* [1964] Ch 288.

In **Re Cavendish Browne's Settlement Trusts** [1916] WN 341, Catherine Cavendish Browne made a voluntary settlement containing a covenant 'to convey and transfer to the trustees all the property, both real and personal, to which she was absolutely entitled by virtue of the joint operation of the wills of' J.H. and A. Cavendish Browne. When Catherine died, she had not yet assured to the trustees a share of unconverted real estate in Canada, to which she had become entitled under the two wills. The question was whether the value of the share or any part of it ought to be paid to the trustees by way of damages for breach of covenant. YOUNGER J 'without delivering a final judgment, held on the authority of *Williamson v Codrington* (1750) 1 Ves Sen 511; *Cox v Barnard* (1850) 8 Hare 310; *Fletcher v Fletcher* (1844) 4 Hare 67; *Re Parkin* [1892] 3 Ch 510; *Ward v Audland* (1847) 16 M & W 862; *Lloyd's v Harper* (1880) 16 Ch D 290; *Davenport v Bishopp* (1843) 2 Y & C Ch Cas 451; *Clough v Lambert* (1839) 10 Sim 174; *Synge v Synge* [1894] 1 QB 466; *Spickernell v Hotham* (1854) Kay 669; *Re Plumptre's Marriage Settlement* [1910] 1 Ch 609 that the trustees were entitled to recover [from Catherine's administrators] substantial damages for breach of the covenant to assure, and that the measure of damages was the value of the property which would have come to the hands of the trustees if the covenant had been duly performed.'

2. Trust of the Promise

If there was a trust of the promise, there would be a constituted trust of a chose in action, and such a trust could be enforced by the trustee for the benefit of the beneficiary,[130] or by the beneficiary for his own benefit, joining the trustee as co-claimant or as defendant.[131]

Fletcher v Fletcher

(1844) 4 Hare 67 (Ch, **Wigram V-C**)

By a voluntary deed, Mr. Fletcher covenanted with trustees to pay to them £60,000, which the trustees were to hold upon trust for, in the events which happened, Ellis's illegitimate son. The trustees were unaware of the deed, which was found among Fletcher's papers after his death. The trustees did not wish to establish the trust except under an order of the court. The question was whether the son could enforce the covenant against the father's executor.

Held. The son was entitled to enforce the covenant, although it was voluntary.

Wigram V-C: It is not denied that, if the plaintiff in this case had brought an action in the name of the trustees, he might have recovered the money; and it is not suggested, that if the trustees had simply allowed their name to be used in the action, their conduct could have been impeached. There are two classes of cases, one of which is in favour of, and the other, if applicable, against, the plaintiff's claim. The question is, to which of the two classes it belongs.

---

[130] *Lloyd's v Harper* (1880) 16 Ch D 290. See also *Barclays Bank plc v Willowbrook International Ltd* [1987] 1 FTLR 386; *Harrison v Tew* [1989] QB 307.

[131] *Affréteurs Réunis SA v Leopold Walford (London) Ltd* [1919] AC 801.

In trying the equitable question I shall assume the validity of the instrument at law. If there was any doubt of that it would be reasonable to allow the Plaintiff to try the right by suing in the name of the surviving trustee. The first proposition relied upon against the claim in equity was, that equity will not interfere in favour of a volunteer. That proposition, though true in many cases, has been too largely stated. A court of equity, for example, will not, in favour of a volunteer, enforce the performance of a contract in specie. That it will, however, sometimes act in favour of a volunteer is proved by the common case of a volunteer on a bond who may prove his bond against the assets. Again, where the relation of trustee and *cestui que trust* is constituted, as where property is transferred from the author of the trust into the name of a trustee, so that he has lost all power of disposition over it, and the transaction is complete as regards him, the trustee, having accepted the trust, cannot say he holds it, except for the purposes of the trust; and the Court will enforce the trust at the suit of a volunteer. According to the authorities, I cannot, I admit, do anything to perfect the liability of the author of the trust, if it is not already perfect. This covenant, however, is already perfect. The covenantor is liable at law, and the Court is not called upon to do any act to perfect it. One question made in argument has been, whether there can be a trust of a covenant the benefit of which shall belong to a third party; but I cannot think there is any difficulty in that. Suppose, in the case of a personal covenant to pay a certain annual sum for the benefit of a third person, the trustee were to bring an action against the covenantor; would he be afterwards allowed to say he was not a trustee? If he cannot do so after once acknowledging the trust, then there is a case in which there is a trust of a covenant for another. In the case of *Clough v Lambert* (1839) 10 Sim 174 the question arose; the point does not appear to have been taken during the argument, but the Vice-Chancellor of England was of opinion that the covenant bound the party; that the *cestui que trust* was entitled to the benefit of it; and that the mere intervention of a trustee made no difference. The proposition, therefore, that in no case can there be a trust of a covenant is clearly too large, and the real question is whether the relation of trustee and *cestui que trust* is established in the present case.

Maudsley: *Perspectives of Law* (ed. R. Pound), p. 248

There was, then, a trust of the promise, and the plaintiff as beneficiary of this trust, could enforce it. But it seems to me that there are one or two difficulties in holding that a trust of a chose in action was created on the facts of this particular case.[132] In the first place, positive evidence of intention is lacking. Ellis Fletcher, the covenantor, covenanted that he would pay the £60,000 to trustees 'to be held on the following trusts'. There is clearly a trust which will affect the money once it is received by the trustee, but no manifestation of an intention by either party to create a trust of a chose in action. Secondly . . . it seems to me that a trust of this nature should be created, if at all, by the obligee and not by the obligor; and there was evidence of the fact that the trustee did not enter into the arrangement intending to be a trustee of a promise, for he did not know about it, and wished to decline the trust as soon as he did hear about it.

---

[132] For difficulties in deciding whether in any particular case there is a manifestation of the intention to create a trust, see *Re Engelbach's Estate* [1924] 2 Ch 348; *Vandepitte v Preferred Accident Insurance Corpn of New York* [1933] AC 70; *Re Schebsman* [1944] Ch 83; *Green v Russell* [1959] 2 QB 226; *Scruttons Ltd v Midland Silicones Ltd* [1962] AC 446; *Beswick v Beswick* [1968] AC 58; *Woodar Investment Development Ltd v Wimpey Construction (UK) Ltd* [1980] 1 WLR 277; *Forster v Silvermere Golf and Equestrian Centre Ltd* (1981) 42 P & CR 255. See also (1982) 98 LQR 17 (J.D. Feltham).

A trust of tangible property is declared by the owner of the property, whether he keeps the property himself or transfers it to another on trust; a trust of a debt is declared by the creditor. A covenantor should not claim, at one swoop, to burden himself with the promise of the payment of money to a promisee, and impose trusts upon the promisee behind his back. It is not as if he were assigning the benefit of a promise, or transferring the money; in such cases he could of course impose trusts on the promise or on the money. The logic of the matter seems to me to be that if A covenants to pay money to B which B is to hold on trust for C, the trusts on which money will be held, when paid over, can be declared by A; but a trust of A's promise should be declared by the person who has the benefit of the promise, namely B; and this will usually be proved by showing that B contracted as trustee for the persons nominated by the covenantor. Both these difficulties are overcome by the rules of the Restatement that the inference in these cases is that the promisee becomes trustee of his rights under the promise, and that, in the case of a voluntary covenant to settle, the settlor is the promisor.[133]

E TRUSTS OF FUTURE PROPERTY[134]

In **Norman v Federal Commissioner of Taxation** (1963) 109 CLR 9. WINDEYER J said, at 24:

As to attempted assignments of things not yet in existence:

As it is impossible for anyone to own something that does not exist, it is impossible for anyone to make a present gift of such a thing to another person, however sure he may be that it will come into existence and will then be his to give. He can, of course, promise that when the thing is his he will make it over to the intended donee. But in the meantime he may change his mind and when the time comes refuse to carry out his promise, even though it were by deed. A court of law could not compel him to perform it. A court of equity would not. Courts of equity never had the objections to all agreements about future interests that, until the seventeenth century, were deeply rooted in the common law. Equity did not share the view that such agreements were void on the ground of maintenance. But things not yet in existence could only be the subject of agreement, not of present disposition. And, in relation to promises and agreements, equity has been faithful to its maxim that it does not come to the aid of volunteers. For equity a deed does not make good a want of consideration.

If we turn from attempted gifts of future property to purported dispositions of it for value, the picture changes completely. The common law objection remains. But in equity a would-be present assignment of something to be acquired in the future is, when made for value, construed as an agreement to assign the thing when it is acquired. A court of equity will ensure that the would-be assignor performs this agreement, his conscience being bound by the consideration. The purported assignee thus gets an equitable interest in the property immediately the legal ownership of it is acquired by the assignor, assuming it to have been sufficiently described to be then identifiable. The prospective interest of the assignee is in the meantime protected by equity. These principles, which now govern assignments for value of property to be acquired in

---

[133] §26, Comment (*n*).

[134] H&M, pp. 139–141; Lewin, pp. 54–57; P&M, pp. 170–176; P&S pp. 166–167; Pettit pp. 117–118; T&H pp. 134–136; U&H, pp. 233–234; (1966) 30 Conv (NS) 286 (M.C. Cullity and H.A.J. Ford).

the future, have been developed and established by a line of well-known cases, of which *Holroyd v Marshall* (1862) 10 HL Cas 191; *Collyer v Isaacs* (1881) 19 Ch D 342; *Tailby v Official Receiver* (1888) 13 App Cas 523, and *Re Lind* [1915] 2 Ch 345 are the most important. 'And so', to use *Maitland's* words, 'lawyers easily slipped into the way of saying that in equity one could make an assignment of goods hereafter to be acquired though one could not do so at law. This was a compendious way of putting the matter and was not likely to deceive any equity lawyer': Maitland, *Equity,* 2nd edn (1936) p. 150.

Re Ellenborough
[1903] 1 Ch 697 (Ch D, **Buckley J**)

By a voluntary settlement, Miss Towry Law, a sister of Lord Ellenborough, purported to assign to the trustees the property to which she might become entitled under the wills of her brother and her sister. She received property under her sister's will and conveyed it to the trustees. On her brother's death in 1902, she received property under his will, and declined to transfer it to the trustees. The question was whether she was obligated to do so.

Held. She could not be compelled to hand over the property.

Buckley J: The question is whether a volunteer can enforce a contract made by deed to dispose of an expectancy. It cannot be and is not disputed that if the deed had been for value the trustees could have enforced it. If value be given, it is immaterial what is the form of assurance by which the disposition is made, or whether the subject of the disposition is capable of being thereby disposed of or not. An assignment for value binds the conscience of the assignor. A Court of Equity as against him will compel him to do that which *ex hypothesi* he has not yet effectually done. Future property, possibilities, and expectancies are all assignable in equity for value: *Tailby v Official Receiver* (1888) 13 App Cas 523 at 543. But when the assurance is not for value, a Court of Equity will not assist a volunteer. In *Meek v Kettlewell* (1842) 1 Hare 464, affirmed by Lord Lyndhust (1843) 1 Ph 342, the exact point arose which I have here to decide, and it was held that a voluntary assignment of an expectancy, even though under seal, would not be enforced by a Court of Equity. 'The assignment of an expectancy', says Lord Lyndhurst (1843) 1 Ph at 347, 'such as this is, cannot be supported unless made for a valuable consideration.' It is however suggested that that decision was overruled or affected by the decision of the Court of Appeal in *Kekewich v Manning* (1851) 1 De GM & G 176 at 187, and a passage in White and Tudor's *Leading Cases in Equity*, 7th edn, vol. ii, p. 851, was referred to upon the point. In my opinion *Kekewich v Manning* has no bearing upon that which was decided in *Meek v Kettlewell*. The assignment in *Kekewich v Manning* was not of an expectancy, but of property. 'It is on legal and equitable principles', said Knight Bruce LJ, 'we apprehend, clear that a person *sui juris*, acting freely, fairly, and with sufficient knowledge, ought to have and has it in his power to make, in a binding and effectual manner, a voluntary gift of any part of his property, whether capable or incapable of manual delivery, whether in possession or reversionary, and howsoever circumstanced.' The important words there are 'of his property'. The point of *Meek v Kettlewell* and of the case before me is that the assignment was not of property, but of a mere expectancy. On 22 December, 1893, that with which the grantor was dealing was not her property in any sense. She had nothing more than an expectancy. In *Re Tilt* (1896) 74 LT 163 there was again a voluntary assignment of an expectancy, and the point was not regarded as arguable. 'It was rightly admitted', said Chitty J 'that as, when this plaintiff executed the deed of 1880, she had no interest whatever in the fund in question, which was a mere expectancy, the deed was wholly inoperative both at law and in equity, being entirely voluntary.' By 'wholly inoperative' there the learned judge of course did not mean that if the voluntary settlor had handed over the funds the trustees would not have held them upon the trusts, but that the grantees under the deed could not enforce it as against the settlor in a Court of Equity or elsewhere. In my judgment the interest of the plaintiff as sole heiress-at-law and next-of-kin of the late Lord Ellenborough was not effectually assigned to the trustees by the deed, and the trustees cannot call upon her to grant, assign, transfer, or pay over to them his residuary real and personal estate.

In **Re Brooks' Settlement Trusts** [1939] Ch 993, property was held under a marriage settlement on trust for X for life, and after her death on trust for such of her issue as she might by deed or will appoint, and in default of appointment on trust for her children in equal shares. One child, A, conveyed to trustees 'all the part or share…and other interest whether vested or contingent to which the settlor is now or may at any time hereafter become entitled whether in default of appointment or under any appointment hereafter to be made'. X appointed the sum of £3,517 to A. The question was whether the trustees of the marriage settlement, who were also the trustees of A's settlement, should pay the money to A. FARWELL J held that they should pay. A could not settle property to which he might become entitled under a future appointment; for in that property he had only an expectancy. He could settle property to which he would become entitled in default of appointment; for in that property he had a vested interest subject to divestment.

This case does not appear to have been cited in *Re Ralli's Will Trusts* [1964] Ch 288 [p. 159, above].

In **Williams v Commissioner of Inland Revenue** [1965] NZLR 395,[135] Williams, who had a life interest under a trust, executed a voluntary deed, in which 'the assignor by way of gift hereby assigns to the assignee for the religious purposes of the Parish of the Holy Trinity Gisborne for the four years commencing on June 30, 1960 the first £500 of the net income which shall accrue to the assignor personally while he lives in each of the said four years from the Trust… And the assignor hereby declares that he is trustee for the sole use and benefit of the assignee for the purpose aforesaid of so much (if any) of the said income as may not be capable of assignment (or may come to his hands)'.

The question arose whether Williams had effectively divested himself of his interest in the £500 so as not to be liable for income tax on it. The New Zealand Court of Appeal held that he had not.

Turner J (delivering the judgment of **North P** and himself): Mr. Thorp, for the appellant, submitted that what was assigned by this document was a defined share in the existing life estate of the assignor in the trust property, and hence that the deed of assignment took effect, as at

---

[135] (1965) *Annual Survey of Commonwealth Law* 328 (J.D. Davies); see also *Shepherd v Federal Taxation Comr* (1965) 113 CLR 385.

its date, to divest the assignor of the annual sums of £500 so that he did not thereafter derive them for taxation purposes in the years under consideration. For the respondent Commissioner it was contended that the deed was ineffective to divest the assignor of the sums, and that its effect was no more than that of an order upon the trustees still revocable by the assignor until payment.

The life interest of the appellant in the trust was at the date of the execution of the deed an existing equitable interest. This cannot be doubted, and it was so conceded by the learned Solicitor-General. Being an existing interest, it was capable in equity of immediate effective assignment. Such an assignment could be made without consideration, if it immediately passed the equitable estate: *Kekewich v Manning* (1851) 1 De GM & G 176. There is no doubt that if the deed before us had purported to assign, not 'the first £500', but the whole of the appellant's life interest under the trust, such an assignment would have been good in equity.

But while equity will recognise a voluntary assignment of an existing equitable interest, it will refuse to recognise in favour of a volunteer an assignment of an interest, either legal or equitable, not existing at the date of the assignment, but to arise in the future. Not yet existing, such property cannot be owned, and what may not be owned may not be effectively assigned: *Holroyd v Marshall* (1862) 10 HL Cas 191 at 210, *per* Lord Westbury LC. If, not effectively assigned, it is made the subject of an agreement to assign it, such an agreement may be good in equity, and become effective upon the property coming into existence (ibid., 211) but if, and only if, the agreement is made for consideration (as in *Spratt v Comr of Inland Revenue* [1964] NZLR 272), for equity will not assist a volunteer: *Re Ellenborough* [1903] 1 Ch 697.

The deed on which this appeal is founded was not made for consideration. The simple question is therefore—was that which it purported to assign (*viz.* 'the first five hundred pounds of the net income which shall accrue') an existing property right, or was it a mere expectancy, a future right not yet in existence? If the former, counsel agree that the deed was effective as an immediate assignment: if the latter, it is conceded by Mr. Thorp that it could not in the circumstances of this case have effect.

What then was it that the assignor purported to assign? What he had was the life interest of a *cestui que trust* in a property or partnership adventure vested in or carried on by trustees for his benefit. Such a life interest exists in equity as soon as the deed of trust creating it is executed and delivered. Existing, it is capable of immediate assignment. We do not doubt that where it is possible to assign a right completely it is possible to assign an undivided interest in it. The learned Solicitor-General was therefore right, in our opinion, in conceding that if here, instead of purporting to assign 'the first £500 of the income', the assignor had purported to assign (say) an undivided one-fourth share in his life estate, then he would have assigned an existing right, and in the circumstances effectively.

But in our view, as soon as he quantified the sum in the way here attempted, the assignment became one not of a share or a part of his right, but of moneys which should arise from it. Whether the sums mentioned were ever to come into existence in whole or in part could not at the date of assignment be certain. In any or all of the years designated the net income might conceivably be less than five hundred pounds; in some or all of them the operations of the trust might indeed result in a loss. The first £500 of the net income, then, might or might not (judging the matter on the date of execution of the deed) in fact have any existence.

We accordingly reject Mr. Thorp's argument that what was here assigned was a part or share of the existing equitable right of the assignor. He did not assign part of his right to income; he assigned a right to a part of the income, a different thing. The £500 which was the subject of the purported assignment was five hundred pounds *out of the net income.* There could be no such income for any year until the operations of that year were complete, and it became apparent what debits were to be set off against the gross receipts. For these reasons we are of opinion that what was assigned here was money; and that was something which was not presently owned by the assignor. He had no more than an expectation of it, to arise, it is true, from an existing equitable interest—but that interest he did not purport to assign....

It was argued in the alternative by Mr. Thorp, but somewhat faintly, that if the document were not effective as an assignment it was effective as a declaration of trust, and that this result was sufficient to divest the appellant of the enjoyment of the annual sums so that he did not derive them as income. It will be recalled in this regard that the text of the deed includes an express declaration of trust. Mr. Thorp's submission was that this express declaration is effective even if the assignment fails. We agree that there may be circumstances in which a purported assignment, ineffective for insufficiency of form or perhaps through lack of notice, may yet perhaps be given effect by equity by reason of the assignor having declared himself to be a trustee; but it is useless to seek to use this device in the circumstances of the present case. Property which is not presently owned cannot presently be impressed with a trust any more than it can be effectively assigned; property which is not yet in existence may be the subject of a present agreement to impress it with a trust when it comes into the hands of the donor; but equity will not enforce such an agreement at the instance of the *cestui que trust* in the absence of consideration: *Ellison v Ellison* (1802) 6 Ves 656 at 662, *per* Lord Eldon LC; *Brennan v Morphett* (1908) 6 CLR 22 at 30 *per* Griffith CJ; cf. *Underhill's Law of Trusts and Trustees,* 11th edn 43. For the same reasons therefore as apply in this case to the argument on assignment, Mr. Thorp's second alternative submission must also fail.

Maudsley: *Perspectives of Law* (ed. R. Pound), p. 250

A contract for consideration to convey future property to trustees upon trust is valid[136] and, in most cases, specifically enforceable.[137] A gratuitous covenant under seal to convey property to trustees is actionable at the instance of the beneficiary, if the court finds, on a proper construction of the situation, that the promisee became trustee of the promise for the beneficiaries.[138] A purported assignment of an expectancy cannot be a conveyance because there is nothing to convey. If consideration is given for the purported conveyance, it will be construed as a contract to assign and enforceable as such.[139] But if it is made gratuitously it is a nullity.[140] In *Re Ellenborough,*[141] the sister of Lord Ellenborough purported to convey by voluntary settlement the property which she would receive under her brother's will. On his death she declined to transfer the property to the trustees, and Buckley J held that the trustees could not compel her to do so.

The question is whether such a gratuitous covenant or assignment in respect of future property can ever be effective as a declaration of trust, so that the trust will become effective when the property vests in the trustee. The situation can arise if the property, on falling in, is

---

[136] *Re Lind* [1915] 2 Ch 345; *Re Gillott's Settlement* [1934] Ch 97; *Re Haynes' Will Trusts* [1949] Ch 5.

[137] *Pullan v Koe* [1913] 1 Ch 9 [p. 171, above].

[138] *Fletcher v Fletcher* (1844) 4 Hare 67 [p. 179, above].

[139] Snell, *Equity* (26th edn), p. 91.

[140] *Meek v Kettlewell* (1842) 1 Hare 464; *Re Ellenborough* [1903] 1 Ch 697 [p. 182, above]; *Re Brooks' Settlement Trusts* [1939] Ch 993 [p. 183, above].   [141] Note 140 above [p. 182, above].

transferred to trustees without a further declaration of the trusts, or where the property vests in the settlor after he has declared the trusts on which he is to hold it.

We have seen that, in England, a covenant in a marriage settlement to settle after-acquired property is not enforceable at the suit of the next-of-kin because they are volunteers;[142] and it is clear that a deed purporting to grant future property on trust is ineffective.[143] But if, in either of these cases, the property found its way into the hands of the trustees, it would presumably be held upon the trusts declared in the relevant documents.[144] If the settlor, in either case, conveyed the property to the trustees, that action could be construed as a further declaration of the trusts; but if the property reaches the trustees by another route, being conveyed perhaps by the executors of the testator from whom the property came, or coming into the hands of the trustee in a different capacity,[145] the possibility of finding that there was a further declaration of trust is less strong. There appear to be three possible solutions to such a case: that the trustees take beneficially, that they hold on trust for the settlor, or that they hold on the trusts declared in the previous document. The first is obviously unsatisfactory; the second involves the proposition that the settlor could claim back in equity property which he had covenanted or purported to settle. The third avoids the necessity of making the ultimate destination of the property depend upon the route by which it reached the trustees; it is consistent with the expressed intention of the parties, and appears to be the most satisfactory solution.[146]

Where the property comes to the settlor himself, it is possible for the court to hold that a previous declaration of trust, followed by the vesting of the property in himself as trustee, constitutes the trust. The question is whether he will be treated as making the declaration at the moment he receives the property.[147] It is clear that a previous declaration is not of itself sufficient,[148] subsequent confirmation of a previous declaration is sufficient.[149] In less obvious cases it is no doubt a question of construction to determine whether or not the settlor is to be taken to have made a subsequent declaration or to have affirmed a previous one. If he made the declaration every day, the last declaration being made the moment before he received the property, this would no doubt be sufficient. But in the absence of authority, in England at least, it is unsafe to predict to what extent an argument on these lines might be acceptable. What is clear in these cases . . . is that the beneficiaries must show that the trust was properly declared and properly constituted. In connection with the declaration, there are again very difficult points of construction, the solution of which will largely depend on the view the court takes on the policy question whether or not trusts ought to be created in this way. There appears to be nothing intrinsically wrong in holding that the declaration of a trust may precede its constitution.

---

[142] *Re D'Angibau* (1879) 15 Ch D 228; *Re Plumptre's Marriage Settlement* [1910] 1 Ch 609.

[143] *Re Ellenborough*, note 140 above; *Re Brooks' Settlement Trusts*, note 140 above.

[144] *Re Ellenborough*, ibid; Miss Towry Law had already handed over to the trustees the property which she received under her sister's will and no attempt was made to recover it; *Re Adlard* [1954] Ch 29; *Re Ralli's Will Trusts* [1964] Ch 288 [p. 159, above].   [145] *Re Ralli's Will Trusts*, ibid.

[146] Ibid.

[147] Second Restatement of Trusts § 26, Comments k and l; § 86, Comment c.

[148] *Matter of Gurlitz* 105 Misc 30, 172 NY Supp 523 (1918); *Brennan v Morphett* (1908) 6 CLR 22.

[149] *Re Northcliffe* [1925] Ch 651.

QUESTIONS

1. What is the state of the rule in *Milroy v Lord?*

2. What was the nature of the trust recognised in *Pennington v Waine* [2002], [p. 164, above], EWCA Civ 227, [2002] 1 WLR 2075?

3. How useful is it to rely on a test of unconscionability to determine when equity will assist a volunteer?

4. What would be the result in *Re Ellenborough* [1903] 1 Ch 697 [p. 182, above], if, instead of purporting to assign what she would receive under her brother's will, Miss Towry Law had declared herself a trustee of it? *Matter of Gurlitz* 105 Misc 30, 172 NY Supp 523 (1918); *Brennan v Morphett* (1908) 6 CLR 22; *Williams v Comr of Inland Revenue* [1965] NZLR 395 [p. 183, above]; *Re Northcliffe* [1925] Ch 651; *Perspectives of Law,* pp. 257–258.

5. It appears that equity will not assist a volunteer (nor direct his trustees) to enforce a covenant to settle after-acquired property. Consider the effect of the House of Lords decision in *Beswick v Beswick* [1968] AC 58 on this; and, in particular, where the settlor has given valuable consideration, and an attempt to enforce the covenant is made by:

   (a) the settlor, or his estate,

   (b) the trustees,

   (c) a beneficiary who is a volunteer. What if the settlor had not given valuable consideration? Consider the potential application of the Contracts (Rights of Third Parties) Act 1999 [p. 169, above], especially where no consideration has been given.

   Re Cook's Settlement Trusts [1965] Ch 902 [p. 175, above]; *Coulls v Bagot's Executor and Trustee Co* (1967) 40 ALJR 471 at 477; cases in note 132 [p. 180, above]; H&M, pp. 137–138; Lewin, pp. 348–351; P&S pp. 183–184; Pettit pp. 110–111; U&H, pp. 225–226; [1967] *Annual Survey of Commonwealth Law* 387–396 (J.D. Davies); (1978) CLJ 301 (B. Coote).

6. After reading the articles quoted on p. 171, note 115, what do you think of *Re Pryce* and *Re Kay's Settlement?*

7. What exceptions exist to the rule that equity will not assist a volunteer? H&M, pp. 141–147; Lewin, pp. 57–67; P & M, pp. 147–160; P&S pp. 184–190; Pettit pp. 118–126; T & H pp. 136–140; U&H, pp. 213–231.

   On *donatio mortis causa,* see Borkowski, *Deathbed Gifts—The Law of Donatio Mortis Causa* (1999); *Sen v Headley* [1991] Ch 425; [1991] Conv 307 (M. Halliwell); (1991) 50 CLJ 404 (J. Thornley); [1991] All ER Rev 207 (P. Clarke); (1991) 1 *Caribbean Law Review* 100 (G. Kodilinye); (1993) 109 LQR 19 (P. Baker); *Woodard v Woodard* [1995] 3 All ER 980; [1992] Conv 53 (J. Martin).

8. What is the relationship between the rule in *Strong v Bird* (1874) LR 18 Eq 315 (whereby an incomplete gift made to a donee is constituted if the gift is vested in the donee as the donor's executor or administrator) and *Re Ralli's Will Trusts* [1964] Ch 288 [p. 159, above]? See *Re Gonin* [1979] Ch 16; (1977) 93 LQR 485; [1982] Conv 14 (G. Kodilinye); *Re Brooks' Settlement Trusts* [1939] Ch 993 [p. 183, above]; H&M, pp. 141–142; U&H, pp. 211–213; [2007] Conv 432 (J. Jaconelli).

5

BENEFICIARIES[1]

I NATURE OF ENTITLEMENT[2]

Under a trust, the beneficiaries are the owners of the property. If the beneficiary has a vested interest he may transfer it to another person.

Pettit, *Equity and the Law of Trusts* (10th edn, 2006), pp. 15–16

Once a trust has been established, as from the date of its establishment the beneficiary has, in equity, a proprietary interest in trust property,[3] which proprietary interest will be enforceable in equity against any subsequent holder of the property (whether the original property or substituted property into which it can be traced) other than a purchaser for value of the legal interest without notice. Moreover if the trustee has become bankrupt the trust property is not available to the trustee's creditors, but remains subject to the trust and unaffected by the bankruptcy.

Under a power, the objects own nothing; they merely have a hope that the power will be exercised in their favour. Until it is exercised, equitable ownership is in those who will take in default of the exercise of the power; their interest is subject to defeasance on such exercise. It is possible for an object of a power to release it and then 'the discretion or power is administered as if his name did not appear among the class of those entitled to be considered as objects of the exercise of the holder's discretion'.[4]

---

[1] P&M, pp. 711–720; P&S, pp. 118–120, 720–723; T&H, pp. 173–199.

[2] H&M, pp. 209–211; Lewin, pp. 5–10; P&S, p 100, 103–105; Pettit, pp. 14–15; Snell, p. 653; T&H, pp. 184–196; U&H, p. 4.   [3] See (2004) 120 LQR 108 (R. Nolan).

[4] P&M, p. 234, citing *Re Gulbenkian's Settlement Trusts (No 2)* [1970] Ch 408.

Lord Millett in *Equity in Commercial Law* (eds. Degeling and Edelman) (2005), p. 315[5]

The beneficiaries' interests in a trust fund are proprietary interests in the assets from time to time comprised in the fund subject to the trustees' overriding powers of managing and alienating the trust assets and substituting others. On an authorised sale of a trust investment, the beneficiaries' proprietary interests in the investment are overreached; that is to say, they are automatically transferred from the investment which is sold to the proceeds of sale and any new investment acquired with them. This is the 'fiction of persistence', except that it is not a fiction. The beneficiaries' interests in the new investment are exactly the same as their interest in the old. They have a continuing beneficial interest which persists in the substitute.

Now suppose that the disposal is unauthorised. The trustee sells a trust investment in breach of trust and uses the proceeds to buy shares for himself. The beneficiaries have a continuing proprietary interest in the original investment but they cannot recover it from the purchaser if he is a bona fide purchaser of the legal title without notice of the breach. But they can instead claim a proprietary interest in the shares which the trustee bought for himself...

The only difference between an unauthorised substitution of trust property and an authorised one is one of timing. If the substitution is authorised the beneficiaries' interest in the substituted property is automatically and fully vested at the moment of acquisition. If the substitution is unauthorised, their interest is inchoate, for they may reject it. Their interest in the substitute does not crystallise fully until they elect to accept it. Their right to accept it is a right given to them by the law of property. It is an incident of their property rights in the original asset. Unjust enrichment does not come into it.[6,7]

II ENFORCEMENT OF CLAIMS

In **Armitage v Nurse** [1998] Ch 241, 253 MILLETT LJ said: 'If the beneficiaries have no rights enforceable against the trustees there are no trusts.'

Parker and Mellows, *The Modern Law of Trusts* (8th edn, 2003), pp. 716–717

As part of his right to compel the due administration of the trust, a beneficiary can apply to the court if the trustees fail to take any action necessary to preserve the trust property.[8] A cause of action against a third party can itself be an item of trust property and the court may either direct the trustees to enforce that claim or allow the beneficiary to sue the third party directly for the benefit of the trust, where necessary using the name of the trustees.[9] Alternatively, a

---

[5] See also (2006) 1 *Journal of Equity* 18 (R. Nolan); (2006) 122 LQR 232 (R. Nolan); T. Honoré, 'Trusts: The Inessentials' in *Rationalizing Property, Equity and Trusts: Essays in Honour of Edward Burn* (ed. J. Getzler, 2003) pp. 17–20.

[6] For a fuller discussion see D. Fox, 'Overreaching' in *Breach of Trust* (eds. Birks and Pretto) (2002), chapter 4.   [7] See further Chapter 19 below.

[8] *Fletcher v Fletcher* (1844) 4 Hare 67.

[9] As in *Foley v Burnell* (1783) 1 Bro. CC 274, a case of trespass to trust land.

beneficiary can sue the trustees, making those who are alleged to be under obligations to the trust co-defendants.

III TERMINATION OF THE TRUST AT THE INSTANCE OF THE BENEFICIARIES[10]

A THE RULE IN SAUNDERS V VAUTIER

Under the rule in *Saunders v Vautier* (1841) 4 Beav 115,[11] below, an adult beneficiary, who is of sound mind and entitled to the whole beneficial interest under a trust, can direct the trustees to transfer the trust property to him, and thus put an end to the trust.[12]

The rule was extended during the nineteenth century to include cases where there are two or more beneficiaries,[13] and even where there are beneficiaries entitled in succession.[14] In both these cases all the beneficiaries must be of full age and of sound mind and together entitled to the whole beneficial interest, and must concur in the direction to the trustees.

Saunders v Vautier
(1841) 4 Beav 115 (Lord Langdale MR)

A testator bequeathed £2,000 East India Company stock to trustees on trust to accumulate the dividends until Vautier should attain the age of 25, and then to transfer the capital and accumulated dividends to Vautier. Vautier, having attained the age of 21,[15] claimed that he was entitled to have the whole fund transferred to him: 'he had a vested interest and as the accumulation and postponement of payment was for his benefit alone, he might waive it and call for an immediate transfer of the fund'.

Held. The whole fund was to be transferred to Vautier.

Lord Langale MR: I think that principle has been repeatedly acted upon; and where a legacy is directed to accumulate for a certain period, or where the payment is postponed, the legatee, if

---

[10] H&M, pp. 635–636; Lewin, pp. 845–859; P&M, pp. 234, 717–720; P&S, pp. 117–118; Pettit, pp. 405–408; Snell, pp. 652–653; T&H, pp. 175–177; U&H, pp. 899–912.

[11] Affd (1841) Cr & Ph 240; *IRC v Executors of Hamilton-Russell* [1943] 1 All ER 474; *Stephenson v Barclays Bank Trust Co Ltd* [1975] 1 WLR 882 [p. 192, below]. See (2006) 122 LQR 266 (P. Matthews).

[12] The rule applies even if the settlor purports to exclude it: *Stokes v Cheek* (1860) 28 Beav 620. It also applies in favour of a charity: *Wharton v Masterman* [1895] AC 186; cf. *Re Levy* [1960] Ch 346; *Re Jefferies* [1936] 2 All ER 626; *Re Beesty's Will Trusts* [1966] Ch 223.

[13] *Re Sandeman's Will Trusts* [1937] 1 All ER 368; *Re Smith* [1928] Ch 915, p. 193, below.

[14] *Brown v Pringle* (1845) 4 Hare 124; *Anson v Potter* (1879) 13 Ch D 141; *Re White* [1901] 1 Ch 570.

[15] The age of majority is now 18: Family Law Reform Act 1969, s. 1.

he has an absolute indefeasible interest in the legacy, is not bound to wait until the expiration of that period, but may require payment the moment he is competent to give a valid discharge.

On a subsequent hearing before LORD COTTENHAM LC (1841) Cr & Ph 240, it was argued on behalf of the testator's residuary legatees that Vautier's interest was contingent on his attaining 25 and therefore this rule did not apply. The Lord Chancellor held that the interest was vested, but that the enjoyment of it was merely postponed.

In **Stephenson v Barclays Bank Trust Co Ltd** [1975] 1 WLR 882, where, on the exercise of a deed of family arrangement, grandchildren became 'absolutely entitled as against the trustees' under the Finance Act 1965, section 22(5)[16] to the assets of the residuary estate, and therefore on its disposal by the trustees to them, Capital Gains Tax was chargeable, WALTON J said at 889:

Now it is trite law that the persons who between them hold the entirety of the beneficial interests in any particular trust fund are as a body entitled to direct the trustees how that trust fund is to be dealt with, and this is obviously the legal territory from which that definition derives. However, in view of the arguments advanced to me by Mr. Lawton, and more particularly that advanced by him on the basis of the decision of Vaisey J in *Re Brockbank* [1948] Ch 206, I think it may be desirable to state what I conceive to be certain elementary principles.

(1) In a case where the persons who between them hold the entirety of the beneficial interests in any particular trust fund are all *sui juris* and acting together, ('the beneficial interest holders'), they are entitled to direct the trustees how the trust fund may be dealt with.

(2) This does not mean, however, that they can at one and the same time override the pre-existing trusts and keep them in existence. Thus, in *Re Brockbank* itself the beneficial interest holders were entitled to override the pre-existing trusts by, for example, directing the trustees to transfer the trust fund to X and Y, whether X and Y were the trustees of some other trust or not, but they were not entitled to direct the existing trustee to appoint their own nominee as a new trustee of the existing trust. By so doing they would be pursuing inconsistent rights.

(3) Nor, I think, are the beneficial interest holders entitled to direct the trustees as to the particular investment they should make of the trust fund. I think this follows for the same reasons as the above. Moreover, it appears to me that once the beneficial interest holders have determined to end the trust they are not entitled, unless by agreement, to the further services of the trustees. Those trustees can of course be compelled to hand over the entire trust assets to any person or persons selected by the beneficiaries against a proper discharge, but they cannot be compelled, unless they are in fact willing to comply with the directions, to do anything else with the trust fund which they are not in fact willing to do.

(4) Of course, the rights of the beneficial interest holders are always subject to the right of the trustees to be fully protected against such matters as duty, taxes, costs or other outgoings; for example, the rent under a lease which the trustees have properly accepted as part of the trust property.[17]

---

[16] Now Taxation of Chargeable Gains Act 1992, s. 60.
[17] *Lloyds Bank plc v Duker* [1987] 1 WLR 1324; [1987] All ER Rev 262 (C.H. Sherrin).

B DISCRETIONARY TRUSTS

In **Re Smith** [1928] Ch 915, a fund was held by trustees upon trust 'to pay or apply the whole or any part of the annual income...thereof or if they shall think fit from time to time any part of the capital thereof unto and for the maintenance and personal support and benefit of...Lilian Aspinall'. There was provision for accumulation of the surplus, the accumulations and the remainder after her death to be held in trust for such of her sons as should attain the age of 21 and such of her daughters as should attain that age or marry.

Mrs. Aspinall had three children, all of whom attained 21, and one of whom had died. Mrs. Aspinall was past the age of bearing children. Mrs. Aspinall, her two surviving children, and the legal representatives of her deceased child, mortgaged their interests under the trust to the Legal and General Assurance Co. The question was whether the trustees should pay the income of the trust to the mortgagees, or whether they retained the discretion to pay to Mrs. Aspinall.

ROMER J held that the mortgage to the Legal and General Assurance Co. was valid. He said at 917:

The question I have to determine is whether the Legal and General Assurance Company are now entitled to call upon the trustees to pay the whole of the income to them. It will be observed from what I have said that the whole of this share is now held by the trustees upon trusts under which they are bound to apply the whole income and eventually pay over or apply the whole capital to Mrs. Aspinall and the three children or some or one of them. So far as the income is concerned they are obliged to pay it or apply it for her benefit or to pay it or apply it for the benefit of the children. So far as regards the capital they have a discretion to pay it and to apply it for her benefit and subject to that, they must hold it upon trust for the children. Mrs. Aspinall, the two surviving children and the representatives of the deceased child are between them entitled to the whole fund. In those circumstances it appears to me, notwithstanding the discretion which is reposed in the trustees, under which discretion they could select one or more of the people I have mentioned as recipients of the income, and might apply part of the capital for the benefit of Mrs. Aspinall and so take it away from the children, that the four of them, if they were all living, could come to the Court and say to the trustees: 'hand over the fund to us'. It appears to me that that is in accordance with the decision of the Court of Appeal in a case of *Re Nelson* [1928] Ch 920n, of which a transcript of the judgments has been handed to me, and is in accordance with principle. What is the principle? As I understand it it is this. Where there is a trust under which trustees have a discretion as to applying the whole or part of a fund to or for the benefit of a particular person, that particular person cannot come to the trustees and demand the fund; for the whole fund has not been given to him but only so much as the trustees think fit to let him have. But when the trustees have no discretion as to the amount of the fund to be applied, the fact that the trustees have a discretion as to the method in which the whole of the fund shall be applied for the benefit of the particular person does not prevent that particular person from coming and saying: 'hand over the fund to me'. That appears to be the result of the two cases which were cited to me: *Green v Spicer* (1830) 1 Russ & M 395 and *Younghusband v Gisborne* (1844) 1 Coll 400.

Now this third case arises. What is to happen where the trustees have a discretion whether they will apply the whole or only a portion of the fund for the benefit of one person, but are obliged to apply the rest of the fund, so far as not applied for the benefit of the first named person, to or for the benefit of a second named person? There, two people together are the sole objects of the discretionary trust and, between them, are entitled to have the whole fund applied to them or for their benefit. It has been laid down by the Court of Appeal in the case to which I have referred that, in such a case as that you treat all the people put together just as though they formed one person, for whose benefit the trustees were directed to apply the whole of a particular fund. The case before the Court of Appeal was this: a testator had directed his trustees to stand possessed of one-third of his residuary estate upon trust during the lifetime of the testator's son Arthur Hector Nelson: 'to apply the income thereof for the benefit of himself and his wife and child or children or of any such persons to the exclusion of the others or other of them as my trustees shall think fit'. What happened was something very similar to what happened in the case before me. Hector Nelson, his wife and the only existing child of the marriage joined together in asking the trustees to hand over the income to them, and it was held by the Court of Appeal that the trustees were obliged to comply with the request, in other words, to treat all those persons who were the only members of the class for whose benefit the income could be applied as forming together an individual for whose benefit a fund has to be applied by the trustees without any discretion as to the amount so to be applied.

PART III

IMPLIED AND
IMPUTED TRUSTS

PART III

IMPLIED AND IMPUTED TRUSTS

6

RESULTING TRUSTS[1]

I GENERAL

This chapter will deal with a miscellaneous group of situations in which the transferor has transferred property to other persons, but the beneficial interest returns, or 'results', to the transferor. Although such trusts have long been recognised, the theoretical foundation for them remains controversial, as does the functional importance of these trusts. Some consider that they are of profound importance as a method for securing restitution of enrichments which have been unjustly received.[2] The more traditional view, however, is that such trusts are of limited importance and operate within clearly defined categories.[3]

A   THE NATURE OF THE RESULTING TRUST

Two different theoretical bases for recognising resulting trusts can be identified.

---

[1] H&M, pp. 239–270; Lewin, pp. 232–235, 251–321; P&M, pp. 271–311; P&S, pp. 234–267, 549–563; Pettit, pp. 168–189; Snell, pp. 571–585; T&H, pp. 783–840; U&H, pp. 390–398, 401–403, 409–466; Chambers, *Resulting Trusts* (1997); Virgo, *The Principles of the Law of Restitution,* (2nd edn., 2006) pp. 595–604; *Restitution and Equity, Vol. 1: Resulting Trusts and Equitable Compensation* (ed. P. Birks and F. Rose) (2000).

[2] See P. Birks, Appendix 1 in *Restitution and Equity, Vol. 1,* ibid; Chambers, ibid, Part II.

[3] See C. Rickett and R. Grantham in *Restitution and Equity, Vol. 1,* ibid, pp. 39–59; A. Tettenborn in *Restitution and Insolvency* (ed. F. Rose) (2000), pp. 156–167.

(i) Positive Intent Analysis

According to this theory a resulting trust will only be recognised where the transferor of property can be considered to have intended that the property would be held on trust for him on the occurrence of certain events.[4] This intention can sometimes be presumed.

Westdeutsche Landesbank Girozentrale v Islington London Borough Council[5]
[1996] AC 669 (HL, **Lords Goff of Chieveley, Browne-Wilkinson, Slynn, Woolf** and **Lloyd**)

A local authority entered into an interest rate swaps agreement with a bank. This transaction involved an agreement between the parties by which each agreed to pay to the other an amount which was calculated by reference to the interest which would have accrued over a ten-year period from 1987, on a notional principal sum of £25 million. The rate of interest to be paid by each party was different. The bank's rate was fixed and the other was variable, being dependent on an identified fluctuating interest rate. The party which owed the highest amount of money paid the net difference to the other party every six months. In effect, this was a form of gambling on changes in the interest rate. In separate proceedings in 1990 the House of Lords held that local authorities lacked the capacity to make such contracts which were consequently ultra vires and null and void.[6] Westdeutsche Landesbank Girozentrale in the present case had paid more to the local authority than it had received and so it sought restitution from the local authority of the net difference. The key question for the House of Lords was whether any interest which was due was to be assessed as simple or as compound interest.

Held. The local authority was liable to make restitution by virtue of its unjust enrichment on the ground of failure of consideration. It was liable to pay interest to the bank but this could only be assessed as simple interest because, other than where there is fraud, compound interest is only available in equity against a fiduciary who is accountable for profits made from breach of the fiduciary duty,[7] and it was not possible to characterise the local authority as a fiduciary since it did not hold the bank's money on trust.

---

[4] *Tinsley v Milligan* [1994] 1 AC 340, 371 (Lord Browne-Wilkinson); *Westdeutsche Landesbank Girozentrale v Islington London Borough Council* [1996] AC 669, 708 (Lord Browne-Wilkinson). See also (1996) 16 LS 110 (W. Swadling); C. Rickett and R. Grantham in *Restitution and Equity, Vol. 1,* p. 53. Cp. E. Simpson in the same volume, pp. 1–21.

[5] (1996) 55 CLJ 432 (G. Jones); [1996] 4 *Restitution Law Review* 3 (P. Birks).

[6] *Hazell v Hammersmith and Fulham London Borough Council* [1992] 2 AC 1.

[7] See now *Sempra Metals Ltd. v IRC* [2007] UKHL 34, [2007] 3 WLR 354 [p. 968, below], where it was recognised that compound interest was generally available even if the claim was not equitable. Despite this *Westdeutsche* remains relevant for the analysis of the resulting trust.

Lord Browne-Wilkinson: Although the actual question in issue on the appeal is a narrow one, on the arguments presented it is necessary to consider fundamental principles of trust law. Does the recipient of money under a contract subsequently found to be void for mistake or as being ultra vires hold the moneys received on trust even where he had no knowledge at any relevant time that the contract was void? If he does hold on trust, such trust must arise at the date of receipt or, at the latest, at the date the legal title of the payer is extinguished by mixing moneys in a bank account:[8] in the present case it does not matter at which of those dates the legal title was extinguished. If there is a trust two consequences follow: (a) the recipient will be personally liable, regardless of fault, for any subsequent payment away of the moneys to third parties even though, at the date of such payment, the 'trustee' was still ignorant of the existence of any trust: see Burrows, 'Swaps and the Friction between Common Law and Equity' [1995] *Restitution Law Review* 15; (b) as from the date of the establishment of the trust (i.e. receipt or mixing of the moneys by the 'trustee') the original payer will have an equitable proprietary interest in the moneys so long as they are traceable into whomsoever's hands they come other than a purchaser for value of the legal interest without notice. Therefore, although in the present case the only question directly in issue is the personal liability of the local authority as a trustee, it is not possible to hold the local authority liable without imposing a trust which, in other cases, will create property rights affecting third parties because moneys received under a void contract are 'trust property'.

The practical consequences of the bank's argument

Before considering the legal merits of the submission, it is important to appreciate the practical consequences which ensue if the bank's arguments are correct. Those who suggest that a resulting trust should arise in these circumstances accept that the creation of an equitable proprietary interest under the trust can have unfortunate, and adverse, effects if the original recipient of the moneys becomes insolvent: the moneys, if traceable in the hands of the recipient, are trust moneys and not available for the creditors of the recipient. However, the creation of an equitable proprietary interest in moneys received under a void contract is capable of having adverse effects quite apart from insolvency. The proprietary interest under the unknown trust will, quite apart from insolvency, be enforceable against any recipient of the property other than the purchaser for value of a legal interest without notice.

Take the following example. T (the transferor) has entered into a commercial contract with R1 (the first recipient). Both parties believe the contract to be valid but it is in fact void. Pursuant to that contract: (i) T pays £1 million to R1 who pays it into a mixed bank account; (ii) T transfers 100 shares in X company to R1, who is registered as a shareholder. Thereafter R1 deals with the money and shares as follows: (iii) R1 pays £50,000 out of the mixed account to R2 otherwise than for value; R2 then becomes insolvent, having trade creditors who have paid for goods not delivered at the time of the insolvency; (iv) R1 charges the shares in X company to R3 by way of equitable security for a loan from R3.

If the bank's arguments are correct, R1 holds the £1 million on trust for T once the money has become mixed in R1's bank account. Similarly R1 becomes the legal owner of the shares in X company as from the date of his registration as a shareholder but holds such shares on a resulting trust for T. T therefore has an equitable proprietary interest in the moneys in the mixed account and in the shares.

---

[8] The legal title will be extinguished because it is not possible to trace at law into a mixed bank account. See p. 898, below.

T's equitable interest will enjoy absolute priority as against the creditors in the insolvency of R2 (who was not a purchaser for value) provided that the £50,000 can be traced in the assets of R2 at the date of its insolvency. Moreover, if the separation of title argument is correct, since the equitable interest is in T and the legal interest is vested in R2, R2 also holds as trustee for T. In tracing the £50,000 in the bank account of R2, R2 as trustee will be treated as having drawn out 'his own' moneys first,[9] thereby benefiting T at the expense of the secured and unsecured creditors of R2. Therefore in practice one may well reach the position where the moneys in the bank account of R2 in reality reflect the price paid by creditors for goods not delivered by R2: yet, under the tracing rules, those moneys are to be treated as belonging in equity to T.

So far as the shares in the X company are concerned, T can trace his equitable interest into the shares and will take in priority to R3, whose equitable charge to secure his loan even though granted for value will *pro tanto* be defeated.

All this will have occurred when no one was aware, or could have been aware, of the supposed trust because no one knew that the contract was void.

I can see no moral or legal justification for giving such priority to the right of T to obtain restitution over third parties who have themselves not been enriched, in any real sense, at T's expense and indeed have had no dealings with T. T paid over his money and transferred the shares under a supposed valid contract. If the contract had been valid, he would have had purely personal rights against R1. Why should he be better off because the contract is void?

My Lords, wise judges have often warned against the wholesale importation into commercial law of equitable principles inconsistent with the certainty and speed which are essential require- ments for the orderly conduct of business affairs: see *Barnes v Addy* (1874) LR 9 Ch App 244 at 251 and 255; *Scandinavian Trading Tanker Co AB v Flota Petrolera Ecuatoriana* [1983] 2 AC 694 at 703–704. If the bank's arguments are correct, a businessman who has entered into transactions relating to or dependent upon property rights could find that assets which appar- ently belong to one person in fact belong to another; that there are 'off balance sheet' liabilities of which he cannot be aware; that these property rights and liabilities arise from circumstances unknown not only to himself but also to anyone else who has been involved in the transactions. A new area of unmanageable risk will be introduced into commercial dealings. If the due applica- tion of equitable principles forced a conclusion leading to these results, your Lordships would be presented with a formidable task in reconciling legal principle with commercial common sense. But in my judgment no such conflict occurs. The resulting trust for which the bank contends is inconsistent not only with the law as it stands but with any principled development of it.

The relevant principles of trust law

(i) Equity operates on the conscience of the owner of the legal interest. In the case of a trust, the conscience of the legal owner requires him to carry out the purposes for which the property was vested in him (express or implied trust) or which the law imposes on him by reason of his unconscionable conduct (constructive trust).

(ii) Since the equitable jurisdiction to enforce trusts depends upon the conscience of the holder of the legal interest being affected, he cannot be a trustee of the property if and so long as he is ignorant of the facts alleged to affect his conscience, i.e. until he is aware that he is intended to hold the property for the benefit of others in the case of an express or implied

---

[9] By virtue of the rule in *Clayton's* case (1816) 1 Mer 572: see p. 935, below.

trust, or, in the case of a constructive trust, of the factors which are alleged to affect his conscience.

(iii) In order to establish a trust there must be identifiable trust property. The only apparent exception to this rule is a constructive trust imposed on a person who dishonestly assists in a breach of trust who may come under fiduciary duties even if he does not receive identifiable trust property.[10]

(iv) Once a trust is established, as from the date of its establishment the beneficiary has, in equity, a proprietary interest in the trust property, which proprietary interest will be enforceable in equity against any subsequent holder of the property (whether the original property or substituted property into which it can be traced) other than a purchaser for value of the legal interest without notice.

These propositions are fundamental to the law of trusts and I would have thought uncontroversial. However, proposition (ii) may call for some expansion. There are cases where property has been put into the name of X without X's knowledge but in circumstances where no gift to X was intended. It has been held that such property is recoverable under a resulting trust: *Birch v Blagrave* (1755) Amb 264; *Childers v Childers* (1857) 1 De G & J 482; *Re Vinogradoff* [1935] WN 68 [p. 258, below]; *Re Muller* [1953] NZLR 879. These cases are explicable on the ground that, by the time action was brought, X or his successors in title have become aware of the facts which gave rise to a resulting trust; his conscience was affected as from the time of such discovery and thereafter he held on a resulting trust under which the property was recovered from him. There is, so far as I am aware, no authority which decides that X was a trustee, and therefore accountable for his deeds, at any time before he was aware of the circumstances which gave rise to a resulting trust.

Those basic principles are inconsistent with the case being advanced by the bank. The latest time at which there was any possibility of identifying the 'trust property' was the date on which the moneys in the mixed bank account of the local authority ceased to be traceable when the local authority's account went into overdraft in June 1987. At that date, the local authority had no knowledge of the invalidity of the contract but regarded the moneys as its own to spend as it thought fit. There was therefore never a time at which both (a) there was defined trust property and (b) the conscience of the local authority in relation to such defined trust property was affected. The basic requirements of a trust were never satisfied.

I turn then to consider the bank's arguments in detail. They were based primarily on principle rather than on authority...

The retention of title point

It is said that, since the bank only intended to part with its beneficial ownership of the moneys in performance of a valid contract, neither the legal nor the equitable title passed to the local authority at the date of payment. The legal title vested in the local authority by operation of law when the moneys became mixed in the bank account but, it is said, the bank 'retained' its equitable title.

I think this argument is fallacious. A person solely entitled to the full beneficial ownership of money or property, both at law and in equity, does not enjoy an equitable interest in that property. The legal title carries with it all rights. Unless and until there is a separation of the

---

[10] See p. 982, below.

legal and equitable estates, there is no separate equitable title. Therefore to talk about the bank 'retaining' its equitable interest is meaningless. The only question is whether the circumstances under which the money was paid were such as, in equity, to impose a trust on the local authority. If so, an equitable interest arose for the first time under that trust.

  This proposition is supported by *Re Cook* [1948] Ch 212; *Vandervell v Inland Revenue Commissioners* [1967] 2 AC 291 at 311G, *per* Lord Upjohn, and at 317F, *per* Lord Donovan; *Commissioner of Stamp Duties (Queensland) v Livingston* [1965] AC 694 at 712B–E; Underhill and Hayton, *Law of Trusts and Trustees* (15th edn, 1995), p. 866.

His Lordship then considered whether the bank had a pre-existing equitable interest by virtue of which the local authority would be a trustee and concluded that no such interest could be identified. He continued:

Resulting trust
This is not a case where the bank had any equitable interest which pre-dated receipt by the local authority of the upfront payment. Therefore, in order to show that the local authority became a trustee, the bank must demonstrate circumstances which raised a trust for the first time either at the date on which the local authority received the money or at the date on which payment into the mixed account was made. Counsel for the bank specifically disavowed any claim based on a constructive trust. This was plainly right because the local authority had no relevant knowledge sufficient to raise a constructive trust at any time before the moneys, upon the bank account going into overdraft, became untraceable. Once there ceased to be an identifiable trust fund, the local authority could not become a trustee: *Re Goldcorp Exchange Ltd* [1995] 1 AC 74. Therefore, as the argument for the bank recognised, the only possible trust which could be established was a resulting trust arising from the circumstances in which the local authority received the upfront payment.

  Under existing law a resulting trust arises in two sets of circumstances:

  (A) Where A makes a voluntary payment to B or pays (wholly or in part) for the purchase of property which is vested either in B alone or in the joint names of A and B, there is a presumption that A did not intend to make a gift to B: the money or property is held on trust for A (if he is the sole provider of the money) or in the case of a joint purchase by A and B in shares proportionate to their contributions. It is important to stress that this is only a presumption, which presumption is easily rebutted either by the counter-presumption of advancement or by direct evidence of A's intention to make an outright transfer: see Underhill and Hayton, *Law of Trusts and Trustees,* pp. 317 et seq.; *Vandervell v Inland Revenue Commissioners* [1967] 2 AC 291 at 312 et seq; *Re Vandervell's Trusts (No 2)* [1974] Ch 269 at 288 et seq.

  (B) Where A transfers property to B on express trusts, but the trusts declared do not exhaust the whole beneficial interest: ibid. and *Quistclose Investments Ltd v Rolls Razor Ltd* [1970] AC 567 [p. 239, below]. Both types of resulting trust are traditionally regarded as examples of trusts giving effect to the common intention of the parties. A resulting trust is not imposed by law against the intentions of the trustee (as is a constructive trust) but gives effect to his presumed intention. Megarry J in *Re Vandervell's Trusts (No 2)* [1974] Ch 269 at 289 suggests that a resulting trust of type (B) does not depend on intention but operates automatically. I am not convinced that this is right. If the settlor has expressly, or by necessary implication, abandoned any beneficial interest in the trust property, there is in my view no resulting trust: the undisposed-of equitable interest vests in the Crown as *bona vacantia*: see *Re West*

Sussex Constabulary's Widows, Children and Benevolent (1930) Fund Trusts [1971] Ch 1
[p. 224, below].

Applying these conventional principles of resulting trust to the present case, the bank's
claim must fail. There was no transfer of money to the local authority on express trusts:
therefore a resulting trust of type (B) above could not arise. As to type (A) above, any presumption of resulting trust is rebutted since it is demonstrated that the bank paid, and the local
authority received, the upfront payment with the intention that the moneys so paid should
become the absolute property of the local authority. It is true that the parties were under a
misapprehension that the payment was made in pursuance of a valid contract. But that does
not alter the actual intentions of the parties at the date the payment was made or the moneys
were mixed in the bank account. As the article by William Swadling, 'A new role for resulting
trusts?' (1996) 16 LS 133 demonstrates the presumption of resulting trust is rebutted by
evidence of any intention inconsistent with such a trust, not only by evidence of an intention to
make a gift.

Professor Birks, 'Restitution and Resulting Trusts' (see *Equity: Contemporary Legal
Developments,* p. 335 at p. 360), whilst accepting that the principles I have stated represent 'a
very conservative form' of definition of a resulting trust, argues from restitutionary principles
that the definition should be extended so as to cover a perceived gap in the law of 'subtractive
unjust enrichment' (at p. 368) so as to give a plaintiff a proprietary remedy when he has transferred value under a mistake or under a contract the consideration for which wholly fails. He
suggests that a resulting trust should arise wherever the money is paid under a mistake (because
such mistake vitiates the actual intention) or when money is paid on a condition which is not
subsequently satisfied.

As one would expect, the argument is tightly reasoned but I am not persuaded. The search
for a perceived need to strengthen the remedies of a plaintiff claiming in restitution involves,
to my mind, a distortion of trust principles. First, the argument elides rights in property (which
is the only proper subject matter of a trust) into rights in 'the value transferred': see p. 361.
A trust can only arise where there is defined trust property: it is therefore not consistent with
trust principles to say that a person is a trustee of property which cannot be defined. Second,
Professor Birks's approach appears to assume (for example in the case of a transfer of value
made under a contract the consideration for which subsequently fails) that the recipient will be
deemed to have been a trustee from the date of his original receipt of money, i.e. the trust arises
at a time when the 'trustee' does not, and cannot, know that there is going to be a total failure of
consideration. This result is incompatible with the basic premise on which all trust law is built,
viz. that the conscience of the trustee is affected. Unless and until the trustee is aware of the
factors which give rise to the supposed trust, there is nothing which can affect his conscience.
Thus neither in the case of a subsequent failure of consideration nor in the case of a payment
under a contract subsequently found to be void for mistake or failure of condition will there be
circumstances, at the date of receipt, which can impinge on the conscience of the recipient,
thereby making him a trustee. Thirdly, Professor Birks has to impose on his wider view an
arbitrary and admittedly unprincipled modification so as to ensure that a resulting trust does
not arise when there has only been a failure to perform a contract, as opposed to total failure
of consideration: see pp. 356–359 and 362. Such arbitrary exclusion is designed to preserve
the rights of creditors in the insolvency of the recipient. The fact that it is necessary to exclude
artificially one type of case which would logically fall within the wider concept casts doubt on
the validity of the concept.

If adopted, Professor Birks's wider concepts would give rise to all the practical consequences and injustices to which I have referred. I do not think it right to make an unprincipled
alteration to the law of property (i.e. the law of trusts) so as to produce in the law of unjust
enrichment the injustices to third parties which I have mentioned and the consequential commercial uncertainty which any extension of proprietary interests in personal property is bound
to produce.

His Lordship considered *Sinclair v Brougham* [1914] AC 398, which had held that
money deposited with a building society, in circumstances where the building society
did not have capacity to borrow the money, was held on trust for the depositors. His
Lordship concluded that this decision should be overruled.[11] He also considered *Chase
Manhattan Bank NA v Israel-British Bank (London) Ltd* [1981] Ch 105 and *Re Ames'
Settlement* [1946] Ch 217 [p. 217, below], and continued.

Restitution and equitable rights
Those concerned with developing the law of restitution are anxious to ensure that, in certain
circumstances, the plaintiff should have the right to recover property which he has unjustly
lost. For that purpose they have sought to develop the law of resulting trusts so as to give the
plaintiff a proprietary interest. For the reasons that I have given, in my view such development
is not based on sound principle and in the name of unjust enrichment is capable of producing
most unjust results. The law of resulting trusts would confer on the plaintiff a right to recover
property from, or at the expense of, those who have not been unjustly enriched at his expense
at all, e.g. the lender whose debt is secured by a floating charge and all other third parties who
have purchased an equitable interest only, albeit in all innocence and for value.

Lord Goff of Chieveley: Ever since the law of restitution began, about the middle of this century,
to be studied in depth, the role of equitable proprietary claims in the law of restitution has been
found to be a matter of great difficulty. The legitimate ambition of restitution lawyers has been
to establish a coherent law of restitution, founded upon the principle of unjust enrichment; and
since certain equitable institutions, notably the constructive trust and the resulting trust, have
been perceived to have the function of reversing unjust enrichment, they have sought to embrace
those institutions within the law of restitution, if necessary moulding them to make them fit
for that purpose. Equity lawyers, on the other hand, have displayed anxiety that in this process
the equitable principles underlying these institutions may become illegitimately distorted; and
though equity lawyers in this country are nowadays much more sympathetic than they have been
in the past towards the need to develop a coherent law of restitution, and to identify the proper
role of the trust within that rubric of the law, they remain concerned that the trust concept
should not be distorted, and also that the practical consequences of its imposition should be
fully appreciated. There is therefore some tension between the aims and perceptions of these
two groups of lawyers, which has manifested itself in relation to the matters under consideration in the present case.

In the present case, however, it is not the function of your Lordships' House to rewrite the
agenda for the law of restitution, nor even to identify the role of equitable proprietary claims in
that part of the law. The judicial process is neither designed for, nor properly directed towards,

---

[11] Lords Slynn, at p. 718, and Lloyd, at 738, concurred. Lord Goff of Chieveley was simply prepared to
distinguish the case: at 688.

such objectives. The function of your Lordships' House is simply to decide the questions at issue before it in the present case; and the particular question now under consideration is whether, where money has been paid by a party to a contract which is ultra vires the other party and so void *ab initio*, he has the benefit of an equitable proprietary claim in respect of the money so paid....

As my noble and learned friend, Lord Browne-Wilkinson, observes, it is plain that the present case falls within neither of the situations which are traditionally regarded as giving rise to a resulting trust, *viz.* (1) voluntary payments by A to B, or for the purchase of property in the name of B or in his and A's joint names, where there is no presumption of advancement or evidence of intention to make an out-and-out gift; or (2) property transferred to B on an express trust which does not exhaust the whole beneficial interest. The question therefore arises whether resulting trusts should be extended beyond such cases to apply in the present case, which I shall treat as a case where money has been paid for a consideration which fails....

I conclude, in agreement with my noble and learned friend, that there is no basis for holding that a resulting trust arises in cases where money has been paid under a contract which is ultra vires and therefore void *ab initio*. This conclusion has the effect that all the practical problems which would flow from the imposition of a resulting trust in a case such as the present, in particular the imposition upon the recipient of the normal duties of trustee, do not arise. The dramatic consequences which would occur are detailed by Professor Burrows in his article on 'Swaps and the Friction between Common Law and Equity' [1995] *Restitution Law Review* 15 at 27: the duty to account for profits accruing from the trust property; the inability of the payee to rely upon the defence of change of position; the absence of any limitation period; and so on. Professor Burrows even goes so far as to conclude that the action for money had and received would be rendered otiose in such cases, and indeed in all cases where the payer seeks restitution of mistaken payments. However, if no resulting trust arises, it also follows that the payer in a case such as the present cannot achieve priority over the payee's general creditors in the event of his insolvency—a conclusion which appears to me to be just.

(ii) *Absence of Intention*

An alternative analysis of the resulting trust is that such trusts arise by virtue of the absence of any intention on the part of the transferor to pass a beneficial interest to the transferee. According to this theory the resulting trust arises by operation of law rather than by virtue of the claimant's positive intent. This theory was propounded by Birks[12] and developed by Chambers.[13] It has now been recognised by LORD MILLETT[14] in **Air Jamaica Ltd v Charlton** [1999] 1 WLR 1399 at 1412:[15]

Like a constructive trust, a resulting trust arises by operation of law, though unlike a constructive trust it gives effect to intention. But it arises whether or not the transferor intended to retain a beneficial interest—he almost always does not—since it responds to the absence of any intention on his part to pass a beneficial interest to the recipient. It may arise even where

[12] 'Restitution and Resulting Trusts' in *Equity: Contemporary Legal Developments* (ed. Goldstein, 1992), p. 335; [1996] *Restitution Law Review* 3.

[13] 'Resulting Trusts' p. 2; (2000) 38 *Alberta Law Review* 378; 'Resulting Trusts' in *Mapping the Law: Essays in Memory of Peter Birks* (eds. A. Burrows and Lord Rodger of Earlsferry, 2006), pp. 247–264.

[14] See also Millett LJ (as he then was) writing extra-judicially: (1998) 114 LQR 399, 400.

[15] (2000) 116 LQR 15 (C.E.F. Rickett and R. Grantham, p. 206, below); [2000] Conv 170 (C. Harpum).

the transferor positively wished to part with the beneficial interest, as in *Vandervell v Inland Revenue Commissioners* [1967] 2 AC 291.[16] In that case the retention of a beneficial interest by the transferor destroyed the effectiveness of a tax avoidance scheme which the transferor was seeking to implement. The House of Lords affirmed the principle that a resulting trust is not defeated by evidence that the transferor intended to part with the beneficial interest if he has not in fact succeeded in doing so. As Plowman J had said in the same case at first instance [1966] Ch 261 at 275, 'As I see it, a man does not cease to own property simply by saying "I don't want it". If he tries to give it away the question must always be, has he succeeded in doing so or not?' Lord Upjohn [1967] 2 AC 291 at 314 expressly approved this.

Similarly, in **Twinsectra Ltd v Yardley** [1999] Lloyd's Rep Bank 438. POTTER LJ said at 457:

Express trusts are fundamentally dependent upon the intention of the parties, whereas the role of intention in resulting trusts is a negative one, the essential question being whether or not the provider intended to benefit the recipient and not whether he or she intended to create a trust. The latter question is relevant to whether the provider succeeded in creating an express trust, but its relevance to the resulting trust is only as an indication of lack of intention to benefit the recipient: see the discussion in Chambers, *Resulting Trusts* (1997) at p 222.

(iii) Which Theory Represents English Law?

Analysis of the resulting trust based on absence of intent is consistent with a number of cases where a resulting trust was recognised, even though the intention of the transferor to create a trust could not be established, because, for example, it was clear that the transferor did not want a resulting trust.[17] But, despite this, the absence of intent analysis is inconsistent with the approaches of Lords Browne-Wilkinson and Goff in *Westdeutsche Landesbank Girozentrale v Islington London Borough Council*. Although Lord Millett has recognised the absence of intent analysis in the *Air Jamaica* case, he was giving the advice of the Privy Council; this is consequently persuasive but not binding authority.[18] The dictum of Potter LJ in *Twinsectra* is important, but it was given in the Court of Appeal. In the House of Lords in *Twinsectra Ltd v Yardley* [2002] UKHL 12, [2002] 2 AC 164 Lord Millett again referred to the absence of intent analysis as advocated by Chambers [see p. 249, below] but none of the other Law Lords considered it.

(iv) Presumed Intention

Perhaps the best approach to rationalising the law is to base resulting trusts on the presumed intention of the transferor or settlor.

(2000) 116 LQR 15, 18–19 (C.E.F. Rickett and R. Grantham)

The preferable view, and one entirely consistent with Lord Millett's analysis of the resulting trust... is that all resulting trusts are a response to the presumed intention of the transferor or

---

[16] See p. 209, below.   [17] *Vandervell v IRC* [1967] 2 AC 291 [p. 209, below].
[18] Although, increasingly opinions of the Privy Council are given greater weight in the English courts. See, for example, the interpretation of dishonesty for the purposes of the action of dishonest assistance [p. 983, below].

settlor. The fundamental inquiry . . . is whether the transfer of property to B is intended by A to be beneficial to B. It is *presumed* that A did not intend B to acquire a beneficial interest in the property. This presumption as to A's intention operates unless either the evidence establishes that A intended to make an outright gift to B, or the alternative presumption of advancement is invoked (and is not itself overtaken by actual evidence to the contrary) effectively to trump the presumption as to A's intention. . . .

All cases of resulting trusts therefore arise as a consequence of the transferor's or settlor's intention, even though that intention is established not by the actual evidence but by appeal to presumptions supplied by the law. Resulting trusts comprise a group of trusts that are founded on intention, although neither express nor implied. . . . All resulting trusts are more accurately termed 'presumed trusts'.

What then is their function? The resulting trust and its foundational presumptions operate as part of the law of property, simply as a series of default rules locating the beneficial interest in property when the transfer of the property is itself either ambiguous as to the location of that interest, or ineffective to dispose of the interest.

(v) *The Hybrid Theory*

(2008) 124 LQR 72 (W. Swadling)

Of the three trusts traditionally classified as resulting [voluntary-conveyance resulting trust, purchase-money resulting trust and failed-trust resulting trust], [the first] two arise because of a legal presumption that a trust was declared by the transferor in his own favour. Like the express trust, they are species of consensual trusts. The third, however, arises where there is no proof, by evidence or presumption, of a declaration of trust in favour of its beneficiary. In that respect, it arises by operation of law. But exactly why the law should impose a trust in such circumstances has yet to be satisfactorily explained, though one thing this cannot be is as a response to a 'non-beneficial transfer'.

(vi) *The Descriptive Characterisation of Resulting Trusts*

As an alternative to the theoretical debates about the characterisation of resulting trusts by reference to intention, there is a more straightforward characterisation of result- ing trusts which focuses simply on the factual circumstances when such trusts can arise. This was recognised by Lord Browne-Wilkinson in *Westdeutsche Landesbank Girozentrale v Islington London Borough Council* [1996] AC 669 at 708 [see p. 202, above] where he referred to category A and category B trusts. This broadly equates with the categorisation recommended by Megarry V-C, which distinguishes between 'automatic' and 'presumed' resulting trusts.[19]

The first category, which is Lord Browne-Wilkinson's category B, is that in which property has been conveyed to trustees, and the beneficial interest has not been wholly disposed of. The trustees cannot enjoy it, and inevitably a resulting trust arises in favour of the settlor, either because the settlor would have intended such a trust or because the settlor would not have intended the trustee to retain the property. Megarry V-C

---

[19] See *Re Vandervell's Trusts (No 2)* [1974] Ch 269 at 294; p. 212, below.

considered such trusts to arise automatically by operation of law,[20] as an automatic consequence of the failure to dispose of the beneficial interest, although Lord Browne-Wilkinson considered that they operated by virtue of what the settlor was presumed to have intended in such circumstances.

The second category, Lord Browne-Wilkinson's category A, arises where the transferor pays money to the defendant to purchase property or the transferor himself purchases property which is vested in the defendant or in their joint names. In such circumstances, by reason of certain presumptions established by the law, the legal owner is required to hold the property upon trust for the transferor.[21] These presumptions can be interpreted either as indicating that the transferor intended a trust to be created or that he did not want the legal owner to be the absolute owner. The presumptions are always rebuttable by evidence, and they may indeed give way to contrary, stronger presumptions, such as the presumption of advancement in favour of a person to whom the donor stands *in loco parentis*.[22] The presumptions were developed in earlier centuries; they are not always consistent with modern ideas of property ownership, and are easily displaced. As Lord UPJOHN said in *Vandervell v IRC*:[23] 'in reality the so-called presumption of a resulting trust is no more than a long-stop to provide the answer where the relevant facts and circumstances fail to reach a solution'. There is no difference between an 'automatic' and a 'presumed' resulting trust once the trust has been established.

B   THE DISTINCTION BETWEEN RESULTING AND CONSTRUCTIVE TRUSTS

If the positive intent analysis of the resulting trust is adopted, it follows that it is possible to draw a clear distinction between resulting and constructive trusts, since the former will only arise where the transferor of property can be considered to have intended that the property will be held on trust on the occurrence of certain events, whereas the constructive trust is imposed by operation of law regardless of the transferor's intent.

However, this clear-cut distinction is often confused in the cases, with sometimes the notions of the resulting and the constructive trust being used interchangeably. As LORD DENNING MR said in **Hussey v Palmer** [1972] 1 WLR 1286 at 1289:[24]

Although the plaintiff alleged that there was a resulting trust, I should have thought that the trust in this case, if there was one, was more in the nature of a constructive trust; but this is more a matter of words than anything else. The two run together.[25]

---

[20] Ibid, at 297.   [21] See pp. 257–263, below.
[22] See pp. 264–270, below.   [23] [1967] 2 AC 291 at 312–313.
[24] See p. 280, below.
[25] See also *Passee v Passee* [1988] 1 FLR 263 at 269, where Nicholls LJ suggested that a trust arising from a contribution to the acquisition of a matrimonial home could be called implied, constructive or resulting, the latter being not inappropriate. See p. 323, below.

This is unnecessarily confusing and the two types of trust should be kept distinct. The consequence of the confusion is especially apparent in the context of trusts relating to the purchase and occupation of a shared home. This is considered in Chapter 8.

QUESTIONS

1. Which of the theoretical bases for determining whether a resulting trust will be recognised do you prefer? Is the debate over the theoretical basis for recognising resulting trusts of any practical significance? See Virgo, *The Principles of the Law of Restitution* (2nd edn, 2006) pp. 595–599.

2. Should the recipient of money which has been paid under a void contract hold that money on resulting trust for the payer? See Chambers, pp. 111–142, Virgo, pp. 601–603, P&M, pp. 308–311. What if the money was mistakenly paid, as in these circumstances: the payer thought the money was due but, in fact, the money had been paid the previous week and the payer had forgotten this? See *Chase Manhattan Bank NA v Israel-British Bank (London) Ltd* [1981] Ch 105 [p. 281, below].

3. What are the duties of a resulting trustee? See Chambers, pp. 194–219.

II AUTOMATIC RESULTING TRUSTS[26]

A NO DECLARATION OF TRUST[27]

Vandervell v Inland Revenue Commissioners
[1967] 2 AC 291 (HL, **Lords Reid, Pearce, Upjohn, Donovan** and **Wilberforce**)

Re Vandervell's Trusts (No 2)
[1974] Ch 269 (CA, **Lord Denning MR, Stephenson** and **Lawton LJJ**)

Mr. Vandervell decided to make a gift of money to the Royal College of Surgeons for the purpose of founding a Chair of Pharmacology. His plan was to arrange the transfer to the Royal College of a block of shares in Vandervell Products Ltd., which were held by the National Provincial Bank as his nominee; to provide the bulk of the endowment by declaring dividends on those shares; and to enable Vandervell Trustees Ltd. (a private trustee company which acted as trustee for the Vandervell children's trust, among other private trusts) to repurchase the shares for £5,000. In this way the dividends

---

[26] H&M, pp. 243–256; Lewin, pp. 251–287; P&M, pp. 300–307; P&S, pp. 549–563; Pettit, pp. 168–175; Snell, pp. 580–585; T&H, pp. 792–812; U&H, pp. 409–424.

[27] *Restitution and Equity, Vol. 1* (ed. P. Birks and F. Rose) (2000), pp. 1–22 (E. Simpson).

would not be taxable in the hands of the charity; and the shares would return, after the payment of the dividends, into the family's control.

The shares were transferred in 1958, and dividends amounting to £266,000 gross were declared on them. But no express provision was made to declare the trusts on which Vandervell Trustees Ltd. held the option to repurchase the shares. If the option had been held on trust for Vandervell, the settlor, he would have been liable to pay Surtax upon the whole of the dividends paid to the Royal College, because he had failed to divest himself absolutely of all interest in the property within the Income Tax Act 1952, section 415(2).

On receiving an assessment to Surtax, Vandervell arranged, in October 1961, for Vandervell Trustees Ltd. to exercise the option. They did so, using £5,000 from the children's settlement for the purchase. The shares were transferred. Vandervell Trustees Ltd. treated them as being held on trust for the children's settlement, and paid to that settlement all dividends received during 1961–1965.

Vandervell was then assessed to Surtax on these dividends, on the ground that the shares were, like the option, held on resulting trust for him. At last, on 19 January, 1965, he executed a deed transferring to the trusts of the children's settlement any interest which he might have in the shares. He died in March 1967.

Before the assessment for 1961–1965 was settled, Vandervell's executors started an action against the trustee company, claiming that the dividends belonged to Vandervell. The Revenue asked to be joined as a party, but, on objection by the trustee company, was excluded: *Re Vandervell's Trusts* [1971] AC 912. The executors succeeded before Megarry J, but failed in the Court of Appeal.

In **Vandervell v IRC** [1967] 2 AC 291[28] the House of Lords, dealing with the position prior to the exercise of the option, examined three solutions: that the option was held on trust for the children's settlement; that Vandervell Trustees Ltd. held it beneficially; and that it was held on resulting trust for Vandervell. The third solution was chosen.

Lord Wilberforce: On these findings it was, in my opinion, at once clear that the appellant's contention that the option became subject to the trusts of the children's settlement of 1949 must fail, for the reason that it was not the intention of the settlor, or of his plenipotentiary, Mr. Robins, at the time the option was exercised that this should be so. I need not elaborate this point since I understand that there is no disagreement about it. This was the appellant's main (if not the sole) contention before the special commissioners and Plowman J and it remained his first contention on this appeal. The alternative which . . . is expressed in the printed case as being that the option was held by the trustee company in equity as well as in law as the absolute owner thereof for the purposes of its business, is, of course, one which the appellant is entitled to put forward, as a contention of law, at any stage, provided that it is consistent with the facts as found by the special commissioners. It is on that contention that the appellant ultimately fell back. For my part, I cannot find that it is so consistent . . .

Correspondingly, the evidence points clearly away from any conclusion that the trustee company held beneficially, or for the purpose of its business. It had no business, no function,

---

[28] (1964) 24 CLJ 19 (G.H. Jones); (1967) 31 Conv (NS) 175 (S.M. Spencer); (1967) 30 MLR 461 (N. Strauss).

except as a trustee; no assets, except as a trustee. The £5,000 to be paid if the option was to be exercised was, as a term of the arrangement between Mr. Vandervell and the college, part of the £150,000 benefaction; how could that come from the company's own resources? To extract from the findings a conclusion that the trustee company was to hold free from any trust but possibly subject to some understanding or gentleman's agreement seems to me, rather than even a benevolent interpretation of the evidence, a reconstruction of it. I may add that had this contention been put forward at the hearing before the special commissioners the Revenue might well have been tempted to explore, by cross-examination, the real control of the trustee company and to argue that the case came within section 415(2) of the Income Tax Act 1952.

If, then, as I think, both the first two alternatives fail, there remains only the third, which, to my mind, corresponds exactly with Mr. Robins' intentions, namely, that the option was held by the trustee company on trusts which were undefined, or in the air.

As to the consequences, there has been some difference and possibly lack of clarity below. The special commissioners held that the initially undefined trusts could be defined later in a way which might benefit the appellant, and they found the benefit to the appellant in this circumstance. The Court of Appeal, starting from the fact that the trustee company took the option as a volunteer, thought that this was a case where the presumption of a resulting trust arose and was not displaced. For my part, I prefer a slightly different and simpler approach. The transaction has been investigated on the evidence of the settlor and his agent and the facts have been found. There is no need, or room, as I see it, to invoke a presumption. The conclusion, on the facts found, is simply that the option was vested in the trustee company as a trustee on trusts, not defined at the time, possibly to be defined later. But the equitable, or beneficial interest, cannot remain in the air: the consequence in law must be that it remains in the settlor. There is no need to consider some of the more refined intellectualities of the doctrine of resulting trust, nor to speculate whether, in possible circumstances, the shares might be applicable for Mr. Vandervell's benefit: he had, as the direct result of the option and of the failure to place the beneficial interest in it securely away from him, not divested himself absolutely of the shares which it controlled.

In the later case, **Re Vandervell's Trusts (No 2)**, dealing with the position after the exercise of the option and prior to the 1965 deed, the width of the difference of the analysis of MEGARRY J [1974] Ch 269 and that of the Court of Appeal [1974] Ch 308 makes it necessary to include extracts from the judgments in both courts. On the executors' failure to recover the money representing the dividends for 1961–1965, the Revenue accepted the situation, and the assessment was withdrawn.

Megarry J: It seems to me that the relevant points on resulting trusts may be put in a series of propositions which, so far as not directly supported, appear at least to be consistent with Lord Wilberforce's speech, and reconcilable with the true intent of Lord Upjohn's speech, though it may not be with all his words on a literal reading. The propositions are the broadest of generalisations, and do not purport to cover the exceptions and qualifications that doubtless exist. Nevertheless, these generalisations at least provide a starting point for the classification of a corner of equity which might benefit from some attempt at classification. The propositions are as follows.

(1) If a transaction fails to make any effective disposition of any interest it does nothing. This is so at law and in equity, and has nothing to do with resulting trusts.

(2) Normally the mere existence of some unexpressed intention in the breast of the owner of the property does nothing: there must at least be some expression of that intention before it can effect any result. To yearn is not to transfer.

(3) Before any doctrine of resulting trust can come into play, there must at least be some effective transaction which transfers or creates some interest in property.

(4) Where A effectually transfers to B (or creates in his favour) any interest in any property, whether legal or equitable, a resulting trust for A may arise in two distinct classes of case. For simplicity, I shall confine my statement to cases in which the transfer or creation is made without B providing any valuable consideration, and where no presumption of advancement can arise; and I shall state the position for transfers without specific mention of the creation of new interests.

    (a) The first class of case is where the transfer to B is not made on any trust. If, of course, it appears from the transfer that B is intended to hold on certain trusts, that will be decisive, and the case is not within this category; and similarly if it appears that B is intended to take beneficially. But in other cases there is a rebuttable presumption that B holds on a resulting trust for A. The question is not one of the automatic consequences of a dispositive failure by A, but one of presumption: the property has been carried to B, and from the absence of consideration and any presumption of advancement B is presumed not only to hold the entire interest on trust, but also to hold the beneficial interest for A absolutely. The presumption thus establishes both that B is to take on trust and also what that trust is. Such resulting trusts may be called 'presumed resulting trusts'.

    (b) The second class of case is where the transfer to B is made on trusts which leave some or all of the beneficial interest undisposed-of. Here B automatically holds on a resulting trust for A to the extent that the beneficial interest has not been carried to him or others. The resulting trust here does not depend on any intentions or presumptions, but is the automatic consequence of A's failure to dispose of what is vested in him. Since *ex hypothesi* the transfer is on trust, the resulting trust does not establish the trust but merely carries back to A the beneficial interest that has not been disposed of. Such resulting trusts may be called 'automatic resulting trusts'.

(5) Where trustees hold property in trust for A, and it is they who, at A's direction, make the transfer to B, similar principles apply, even though on the face of the transaction the transferor appears to be the trustees and not A. If the transfer to B is on trust, B will hold any beneficial interest that has not been effectually disposed of on an automatic resulting trust for the true transferor, A. If the transfer to B is not on trust, there will be a rebuttable presumption that B holds on a resulting trust for A.

I turn to the speech of Lord Wilberforce [part of which is quoted on p. 210, above]...

Now as it seems to me this passage shows Lord Wilberforce as rejecting the application of what I have called the 'presumption' class of resulting trust and accepting that the case falls into what I have called the 'automatic' class. The grant of the option to the defendant company was, as he had held, on trust. There was thus no need, nor, indeed, any reason to consider whether the option was granted to the defendant company beneficially, or whether there was any presumption of a resulting trust, for that question had been foreclosed by the decision that the defendant company did not take beneficially but held on trust. The only question was whether Mr. Vandervell had ever effectually disposed of the beneficial interest that the defendant company, holding on trust, must hold on a resulting trust for him unless and until an effective trust for some other beneficiary was constituted. This had not been done, and so the defendant company continued to hold on a resulting trust for Mr. Vandervell.

If one bears in mind Lord Wilberforce's speech and the principles that I have tried to state it seems to me that when one looks again at Lord Upjohn's speech it is at least possible to read it as supporting what seems to me to be the right analysis of the case, namely, that the true grantor of the option was Mr. Vandervell, that the option was granted to the defendant company on trust, that no effective trusts were ever declared, and so the defendant company held the option on an automatic resulting trust for Mr. Vandervell. Indeed, that is what I think he was laying down. The question is whether, on the evidence before me, I ought to reach any other conclusion....

My conclusion is that there is nothing in the evidence before me that warrants any conclusion different from that reached in *Vandervell No 1*, namely, that the option was granted to the defendant company on trust, but that no effective trusts were ever established and so the defendant company held the option on a resulting trust for Mr. Vandervell.

(3) Effect of children's £5,000

The third issue is that of the effect of exercising the option with £5,000 of the moneys held by the defendant company on the trusts of the children's settlement. I shall deal with this main issue before I turn to estoppel and acquiescence. That issue is, in essence, whether trustees who hold an option on trust for X will hold the shares obtained by exercising that option on trust for Y merely because they used Y's money in exercising the option. Authority apart, my answer would be an unhesitating No. The option belongs to X beneficially, and the money merely exercises rights which belong to X. Let the shares be worth £50,000, so that an option to purchase those shares for £5,000 is worth £45,000, and it will at once be seen what a monstrous result would be produced by allowing trustees to divert from their beneficiary X the benefits of what they hold in trust for him merely because they used Y's money instead of X's...

I need only say that the consequences of recognising any rule to the effect that trustees of more than one trust can in effect transfer the assets of one trust to another trust simply by expending the money of that other trust on improving the assets seems to me to be incalculable... I merely add that, as I have already mentioned, Mr. Balcombe has throughout accepted what he has pleaded, namely, that the plaintiff's right to the shares is subject to a lien in favour of the children's settlement for the £5,000 paid for exercising the option with interest. This in effect will restore the status quo ante as regards this payment.

His Lordship then considered the effect of acquiescence and estoppel and concluded that the plaintiff's claim was not affected on either of these grounds.

In the Court of Appeal [1974] Ch 269 at 318.[29]

Lord Denning MR:

Summary of the claims
The root cause of all the litigation is the claim of the Revenue authorities.

The first period—1958–1961: The Revenue authorities claimed that Mr. Vandervell was the beneficial owner of the *option* and was liable for Surtax on the dividends declared from 1958 to

---

[29] (1974) 38 Conv (NS) 405 (P.J. Clarke); (1975) 38 MLR 557 (J.W. Harris); (1975) 7 *Ottawa Law Review* 483 (G. Battersby).

1961. This came to £250,000. The claim of the Revenue was upheld by the House of Lords: see *Vandervell v IRC* [1967] 2 AC 291 [p. 210, above].

The second period—1961–1965: The Revenue authorities claimed that Mr. Vandervell was the beneficial owner of the *shares*. They assessed him for Surtax in respect of the dividends from 11 October, 1961, to 19 January, 1965, amounting to £628,229. The executors dispute the claim of the Revenue. They appealed against the assessments. But the appeal was, by agreement, stood over pending the case now before us. The executors have brought this action against the trustee company. They seek a declaration that, during the second period, the dividends belonged to Mr. Vandervell himself, and they ask for an account of them. The Revenue asked to be joined as parties to the action. The court did join them (see *Re Vandervell's Trusts* [1970] Ch 44); but the House of Lords reversed the decision (see [1971] AC 912). So this action has continued—without the presence of the Revenue, whose claim to £628,229 has caused all the trouble.

The third period—1965–1967: The Revenue agreed that they have no claim against the estate for this period.

The law for the first period

The first period was considered by the House of Lords in *Vandervell v IRC* [1967] 2 AC 291. They held, by a majority of three to two, that, during this period, the trustee company held the option as a trustee. The terms of the trust were stated in two ways. Lord Upjohn (with the agreement of Lord Pearce) said that the proper inference was that 'the trustee company should hold as trustee upon such trusts as he [Mr. Vandervell] or the trust company should from time to time declare' (see at 309, 315, 317). Lord Wilberforce said 'that the option was held by the trustee company on trusts ... not at the time determined, but to be decided on a later date' (see at 328, 325).

The trouble about the trust so stated was that it was too uncertain. The trusts were not declared or defined with sufficient precision for the trustees to ascertain who the beneficiaries were. It is clear law that a trust (other than a charitable trust) must be for ascertainable beneficiaries: see *Re Gulbenkian's Settlements* [1970] AC 508 at 523–524, *per* Lord Upjohn. Seeing that there were no ascertainable beneficiaries, there was a resulting trust for Mr. Vandervell. But if and when Mr. Vandervell should declare any defined trusts, the resulting trust would come to an end. As Lord Upjohn said [1967] 2 AC 291 at 317: '... until these trusts should be declared, there was a resulting trust for [Mr. Vandervell]'.

During the first period, however, Mr. Vandervell did not declare any defined trusts. The option was, therefore, held on a resulting trust for him. He had not divested himself absolutely of the shares. He was, therefore, liable to pay Surtax on the dividends.

The law for the second period

In October and November 1961, the trustee company exercised the option. They paid £5,000 out of the children's settlement. The Royal College of Surgeons transferred the legal estate in the 100,000 'A' shares to the trustee company. Thereupon the trustee company became the legal owner of the shares. This was a different kind of property altogether. Whereas previously the trustee company had only a chose in action of one kind—an option—it now had a chose in action of a different kind—the actual shares. This trust property was not held by the trustee company beneficially. It was held by them on trust. On this occasion a valid trust was created at the time of the transfer. It was manifested in clear and unmistakable fashion. It was precisely defined. The shares were to be held on the trusts of the children's settlement. The evidence of intention is indisputable:

(i) The trustee company used the children's money—£5,000—with which to acquire the shares. This would be a breach of trust unless they intended the shares to be an addition to the children's settlement.

(ii) The trustee company wrote to the Revenue authorities the letter of 2 November, 1961, declaring expressly that the shares 'will henceforth be held by them upon the trusts of the [children's] settlement'.

(iii) Thenceforward all the dividends received by the trustees were paid by them to the children's settlement and treated as part of the funds of the settlement. This was all done with the full assent of Mr. Vandervell. Such being the intention, clear and manifest, at the time when the shares were conveyed to the trustee company, it is sufficient to create a trust.

Mr. Balcombe for the executors admitted that the intention of Mr. Vandervell and the trustee company was that the shares should be held on trust for the children's settlement. But he said that this intention was of no avail. He said that during the first period, Mr. Vandervell had an equitable interest in the property, namely, a resulting trust; that he never disposed of this equitable interest (because he never knew he had it): and that in any case it was the disposition of an equitable interest which, under section 53 of the Law of Property Act 1925, had to be in writing, signed by him or his agent, lawfully authorised by him in writing (and there was no such writing produced). He cited *Grey v IRC* [1960] AC 1 [p. 113, above], and *Oughtred v IRC* [1960] AC 206 [p. 118, above].

There is a complete fallacy in that argument. A resulting trust for the settlor is born and dies without any writing at all. It comes into existence whenever there is a gap in the beneficial ownership. It ceases to exist whenever that gap is filled by someone becoming beneficially entitled. As soon as the gap is filled by the creation or declaration of a valid trust, the resulting trust comes to an end. In this case, before the option was exercised, there was a gap in the beneficial ownership. So there was a resulting trust for Mr. Vandervell. But, as soon as the option was exercised and the shares registered in the trustees' name, there was created a valid trust of the shares in favour of the children's settlement. Not being a trust of land, it could be created without any writing. A trust of personalty can be created without any writing. Both Mr. Vandervell and the trustee company had done everything which needed to be done to make the settlement of these shares binding on them. So there was a valid trust: see *Milroy v Lord* (1862) 4 De GF & J 264 at 274, *per* Turner LJ.

The law as to the third period

The executors admit that from 19 January, 1965, Mr. Vandervell had no interest whatsoever in the shares. The deed of that date operated so as to transfer all his interest thenceforward to the trustee company to be held by them on trust for the children. I asked Mr. Balcombe: what is the difference between the events of October and November 1961, and the event of 19 January, 1965? He said that it lay in the writing. In 1965, Mr. Vandervell disposed of his equitable interest in writing: whereas in 1961 there was no writing. There was only conduct or word of mouth. That was insufficient. And, therefore, his executors were not bound by it.

The answer to this argument is what I have said. Mr. Vandervell did not dispose in 1961 of any equitable interest. All that happened was that his resulting trust came to an end—because there was created a new valid trust of the shares for the children's settlement.

Stephenson LJ: I have had more doubt than Lord Denning MR and Lawton LJ whether we can overturn the judgment of Megarry J [p. 211, above] in what I have not found an easy case. Indeed, treading a (to me) dark and unfamiliar path, I had parted from both my fellow travellers and following the windings of Mr. Balcombe's argument had nearly reached a different terminus before the light which they threw upon the journey enabled me to join them at the same conclusion.

To expound my doubts would serve no useful purpose; to state them shortly may do no harm. The cause of all the trouble is what the judge called [1974] Ch 269 at 298 'this ill-fated option' and its incorporation in a deed which was 'too short and simple' to rid Mr. Vandervell of the beneficial interest in the disputed shares, as a bare majority of the House of Lords held, not without fluctuation of mind on the part of one of them (Lord Upjohn), in *Vandervell v IRC* [1967] 2 AC 291 at 314–317. The operation of law or equity kept for Mr. Vandervell or gave him back an equitable interest which he did not want and would have thought he had disposed of if he had ever known it existed. It is therefore difficult to infer that he intended to dispose or ever did dispose of something he did not know he had until the judgment of Plowman J in *Vandervell v IRC* [1966] Ch 261 at 273, which led to the deed of 1965, enlightened him, or to find a disposition of it in the exercise by the trustee company in 1961 of its option to purchase the shares. And even if he had disposed of his interest, he did not dispose of it by any writing sufficient to comply with section 53(1)(c) of the Law of Property Act 1925.

But Lord Denning MR and Lawton LJ are able to hold that no such disposition is needed because (1) the option was held on such trusts as might thereafter be declared by the trustee company or Mr. Vandervell himself, and (2) the trustee company has declared that it holds the shares in the children's settlement. I do not doubt the first, because it was apparently the view of the majority of the House of Lords in *Vandervell v IRC* [1967] 2 AC 291. I should be more confident of the second if it had been pleaded or argued either here or below and we had had the benefit of Megarry J's views upon it. If counsel for the trustee company in the court below had thought that the evidence supported it, he would not, I think, have sought and obtained the amendment of the defence which he did to allege what the judge rejected as an unusual and improbable form of trust which was not supported by the evidence. If counsel for the trustee company in this court had accepted it, I do not think that he would have opened this appeal as he did with references to perfecting or completing the trust but none to declaring it. I see, as perhaps did counsel, difficulties in the way of a limited company declaring a trust by parole or conduct and without resolution of the board of directors, and difficulties also in the way of finding any declaration of trust by Mr. Vandervell himself in October or November 1961, or any conduct then or later which would in law or equity estop him from denying that he made one.

However, Lord Denning MR and Lawton LJ are of the opinion that these difficulties, if not imaginary, are not insuperable and that these shares went into the children's settlement in 1961 in accordance with the intention of Mr. Vandervell and the trustee company—a result with which I am happy to agree as it seems to me to be in accordance with the justice and the reality of the case.

B   WHERE AN EXPRESS TRUST FAILS

In **Essery v Cowlard** (1884) 26 Ch D 191, a marriage settlement of 1877 declared that certain property of the intended wife had been transferred to trustees to be held by them in trust for herself, her intended husband, and the issue of the marriage. The marriage never took place. The parties cohabited, and children were born. PEARSON J held that the contract for marriage had been rescinded. The trusts failed. Illegitimate children would not in those days have been able to take, nor could they be legitimated by the subsequent marriage of their parents. The trustees held on a resulting trust for the settlor (the intended wife), who could claim the return of the property.

Re Ames' Settlement
[1946] Ch 217 (Ch D, **Vaisey J**)

Mr. Ames and Miss Hamilton married in 1908. Ames' father transferred £10,000 to trustees to be held on the usual trusts of a marriage settlement. The parties lived together for a number of years in England and Kenya. In 1926, the Supreme Court of Kenya declared the marriage null and void on the ground of non-consummation. The wife surrendered all her interests under the settlement. There was no issue. On the death of Mr. Ames in 1945, the question was whether the £10,000 should be paid to those entitled under the settlement in default of issue, or to the representatives of the settlor.

Held. The marriage being void *ab initio*,[30] the fund was held on resulting trust for the settlor.

Vaisey J: I regard the contest as merely this: the plaintiffs hold certain funds in their hands, and they ask to which of the alternative claimants they ought to make those funds over. I think it would not be incorrect to say that the problem is really which of those parties has the better equity. The persons who constitute the hypothetical next-of-kin say 'Look at the deed of settlement. We are the persons there designated to take the fund, and there is no reason why we should not do so', and therefore claim to have the better equity. On the other hand it is said 'but that trust, with the other trusts, were all based on the consideration and contemplation of a valid marriage, and now that it has been judicially decided that there never was a marriage that trust cannot possibly form the foundation of a good equitable right'. The settlor's representatives say that theirs is the better equity because the money was only parted with by their testator on a consideration which was expressed but which in fact completely failed. It seems to me that the claim of the executors of the settlor in this case must succeed. I think that the case is, having regard to the wording of the settlement, a simple case of money paid on a consideration which failed. I do not think that that hypothetical class of next-of-kin (who were only brought in, so to speak, and given an interest in the fund on the basis and footing that there was going to be a valid marriage between John Ames and Miss Hamilton) have really any merits in equity, and I do not see how they can claim under the express terms of a document which, so far as regards the persons with whom the marriage consideration was concerned, has utterly and completely failed. If their claim be good, it is difficult to see at what precise period of time their interest became an interest in possession. But I hold that their claim is not good, and that they have not been able to establish it.[31]

---

[30] A decree of nullity in England granted after 31 July, 1971 in respect of a voidable marriage has prospective and not retrospective effect: Matrimonial Causes Act 1973, s. 16; see also s. 24, under which the court has power to make property adjustment orders.

[31] See also *Morice v Bishop of Durham* (1804) 9 Ves 399; on appeal (1805) 10 Ves 522, and *Chichester Diocesan Fund and Board of Finance Inc v Simpson* [1944] AC 341, being examples of resulting trusts arising

In **Air Jamaica v Charlton** [1999] 1 WLR 1399[32] a trust arising from the discontinuance of a pension scheme was held to be void since it infringed the perpetuity rule.[33] Contributions had been made equally by the members and the company. One question for the Privy Council was what should happen to the substantial surplus of the fund. It was held that the surplus should be held on resulting trust for those who had provided it (both existing members and the estates of deceased members) and the surplus was to be treated as provided as to one-half by the company and as to one-half by the members unless there was evidence to the contrary. As between the members themselves, their half of the surplus was to be divided pro rata in proportion to their contributions and regardless of any benefits they had received.[34] LORD MILLETT said at 1413:

Pension schemes in Jamaica, as in England, need the approval of the Inland Revenue if they are to secure the fiscal advantages that are made available. The tax legislation in both countries places a limit on the amount which can be paid to the individual employee. Allowing the employees to enjoy any part of the surplus by way of resulting trust would probably exceed those limits. This fact is not, however, in their Lordships' view a proper ground on which to reject the operation of a resulting trust in favour of the employees. The Inland Revenue had an opportunity to examine the pension plan and to withhold approval on the ground that some of its provisions were void for perpetuity. They failed to do so. There is no call to distort principle in order to meet their requirements. The resulting trust arises by operation of the general law, *dehors* the pension scheme and the scope of the relevant tax legislation.

Scott J was impressed by the difficulty of arriving at a workable scheme for apportioning the surplus funds among the members and the executors of deceased members. This was because he thought it necessary to value the benefits that each member had received in order to ascertain his share in the surplus. On the separate settlement with mutual insurance analysis which their Lordships have adopted in the present case, however, no such process is required. The members' share of the surplus should be divided pro rata among the members and the estates of deceased members in proportion to the contributions made by each member without regard to the benefits each has received and irrespective of the dates on which the contributions were made.

C   INCOMPLETE DISPOSAL OF BENEFICIAL INTEREST

(i) Surplus Funds

In **Re Cochrane** [1955] Ch 309 a marriage settlement provided for funds to be held on trust for the wife 'during her life so long as she shall continue to reside with the said W.J.B. Cochrane... and after [her] decease or the prior determination of the trust in her favour... upon trust to pay the said income to the said W.J.B.Cochrane (if then living)

---

where an intended charitable trust failed. Similarly, if a gift fails for lack of mental capacity: *Simpson v Simpson* [1989] *Family Law* 20.

[32] [2000] Conv 170 (C. Harpum); (2000) 116 LQR 15 (C.E.F. Rickett and R. Grantham).

[33] In England such schemes are exempt from the perpetuity rule: Pension Schemes Act 1993, s. 163.

[34] Cp. the authorities on the dissolution of clubs and associations [p. 223, below].

during his life and after the decease of the survivor of them…in trust for' such of their issue as they should jointly or as the survivor of them should appoint, and in default of appointment equally at the age of 21, or in the case of daughters, earlier marriage.

The wife ceased to reside with the husband. Her interest thus terminated and the income was paid to the husband. In 1953 the husband died. No appointment in favour of the children had been made. The question was whether the claim of the children was accelerated, or whether the fund was held on a resulting trust during the gap in the beneficial limitations following the husband's death.

HARMAN J, holding that a resulting trust arose, said at 315:

Is it clear not only that something has been left out, but what it is that ought to be put in?—the second, of course, being much the more difficult part. One can see that the limitations over do not marry with the prior trusts. It should have been obvious to the draftsman that the event might happen which in fact has happened. But is it clear that the gift over ought, so to speak, to be accelerated? I do not think so on this particular deed, and I base that decision on this: that I cannot see clearly what it is which should have been put in. There is a power for the spouses to appoint to issue; there is a power for the survivor to appoint. Now, it is clear and conceded that the wife, notwithstanding that she forfeited her interest in her husband's lifetime, still has for the rest of her life—or had, at any rate, after her husband's death—power to dispose of the fund as the survivor of the two, either by deed or by will. That power clearly did not stop with the cesser of her interest, so that she could alter the beneficial trust by appointing away from the children in favour of the grandchildren or by making an unequal division between her daughters; and it seems to me in the face of that that it is impossible to say that the gift over took effect at the date of the ceasing of her husband's interest.

It was admitted in fact before me that the fund could not be disturbed so long as the power of appointment was outstanding in the survivor of the two spouses, and that alone seems to me to show that it could not be true to say that the gift over could operate until the event had happened which is stated to be the event in the deed; namely, the death of the survivor of the husband and wife.

The result of that is that the draftsman has failed to provide for the event which has happened. A resulting trust is the last resort to which the law has recourse when the draftsman has made a blunder or failed to dispose of that which he has set out to dispose of, but that seems to have happened here, and until the death of the survivor I think that there is a resulting trust of the income of the fund in favour of the settlors in proportion to their several interests.

Re the Trusts of the Abbott Fund
[1900] 2 Ch 326 (ChD, **Stirling J**)

Dr. Abbott died in 1844, leaving ample funds for the support of his family, including two daughters who were deaf and dumb. But on the death of Dr. Abbott's surviving trustee in 1889, it was learned that all the money had disappeared.

Dr. Fawcett, and subsequently Mr. Smith, issued appeals to friends who subscribed money to a fund for the support of the two ladies. No provision was made for the disposal of the fund on the death of the survivor. This occurred in 1899, and there was then a surplus of £366 13s 9d.

Held. The fund was held upon a resulting trust for the subscribers.

Stirling J: It seems to me…that I may treat the fund which was collected by Dr. Fawcett as really applicable to the same purposes, for that is the effect of it, as that which was subscribed in response to the circular issued by Mr. Smith. The ladies are both dead, and the question is whether so far as this fund has not been applied for their benefit, there is a resulting trust of it for the subscribers. I cannot believe that it was ever intended to become the absolute property of the ladies so that they should be in a position to demand a transfer of it to themselves, or so that if they became bankrupt the trustee in the bankruptcy should be able to claim it. I believe it was intended that it should be administered by Mr. Smith, or the trustees who had been nominated in pursuance of the circular. I do not think the ladies ever became absolute owners of this fund. I think that the trustee or trustees were intended to have a wide discretion as to whether any, and if any what, part of the fund should be applied for the benefit of the ladies and how the application should be made. That view would not deprive them of all right in the fund, because if the trustees had not done their duty—if they either failed to exercise their discretion or exercised it improperly—the ladies might successfully have applied to the court to have the fund administered according to the terms of the circular. In the result, therefore, there must be a declaration that there is a resulting trust of the moneys remaining unapplied for the benefit of the subscribers to the Abbott fund.

In other cases it is possible to find that the gift, although expressed as applicable to a particular purpose only, was in fact intended to take effect as a gift to the beneficiary absolutely.

In **Re Osoba** [1979] 1 WLR 247[35] the testator left property to his widow on trust to be used 'for her maintenance and for the training of my daughter up to university grade and for the maintenance of my aged mother'. The mother predeceased the testator. The widow died in 1970, and the daughter completed her university education in 1975. The surplus was claimed by the testator's children by a previous marriage on intestacy. The Court of Appeal held that the testator's intention was to make absolute gifts to the beneficiaries, the references to maintenance and education being expressions of motive. BUCKLEY LJ said at 257:

If a testator has given the whole of a fund, whether of capital or income, to a beneficiary, whether directly or through the medium of a trustee, he is regarded, in the absence of any contra-indication, as having manifested an intention to benefit that person to the full extent of the subject matter, notwithstanding that he may have expressly stated that the gift is made for a particular purpose, which may prove to be impossible of performance or which may not exhaust the subject matter. This is because the testator has given the whole fund; he has not given so much of the fund as a trustee or anyone else should determine, but the whole fund. This must be reconciled with the testator's having specified the purpose for which the gift is made. This reconciliation is achieved by treating the reference to the purpose as merely a statement of the testator's motive in making the gift. Any other interpretation of the gift would frustrate the testator's expressed intention that the whole subject matter shall be applied for the benefit of the beneficiary. These considerations have, I think, added force where the subject matter is the

---

[35] (1978) CLJ 219 (C.E.F. Rickett). See also *Re Andrew's Trust* [1905] 2 Ch 48 (surplus from fund for education of children of a deceased clergyman held payable to the children. The gift was construed as a gift to them, applicable primarily for their education). See also *Re Foord* [1922] 2 Ch 519; *Re Denley's Trust Deed* [1969] 1 Ch 373 [p. 375, below]; *Re Lipinski's Will Trusts* [1976] Ch 235 [p. 372, below].

testator's residue, so that any failure of the gift would result in intestacy. The specified purpose is regarded as of less significance than the dispositive act of the testator, which sets the measure of the extent to which the testator intends to benefit the beneficiary.

His Lordship held that, in the absence of words of severance, the beneficiaries took as joint tenants, so that on the widow's death the daughter became entitled to the whole.

Re Gillingham Bus Disaster Fund
[1958] Ch 300 (ChD, Harman J)[36]

In 1951, a squad of Royal Marine cadets was marching through a street in Gillingham, when a bus, out of control, struck them, killing 24, and injuring several others. A memorial fund was established by the Mayors of Gillingham, Rochester, and Chatham, which was stated to be devoted 'among other things, to defraying the funeral expenses, caring for the boys who may be disabled, and then to such worthy cause or causes...as the Mayors may determine'.

The public contributed about £9,000, partly in identifiable sums from individual subscribers, but mainly from street collections and other untraceable sources. Various payments were made from the fund toward expenditure not covered by the common law liability accepted by the driver of the bus and his employers. There was a surplus, and the question arose as to its disposal.

Held. The surplus was held on a resulting trust for the donors.

Harman J: I have already decided that the surplus of this fund now in the hands of the plaintiffs as trustees ought not to be devoted to charitable purposes under a *cy-près* scheme.[37] There arises now a further question, namely, whether, as the Treasury Solicitor claims, this surplus should be paid to the Crown as *bona vacantia,* or whether there is a resulting trust in favour of the subscribers, who are here represented by the Official Solicitor. The general principle must be that where money is held upon trust and the trusts declared do not exhaust the fund it will revert to the donor or settlor under what is called a resulting trust. The reasoning behind this is that the settlor or donor did not part with his money absolutely out and out but only *sub modo* to the intent that his wishes as declared by the declaration of trust should be carried into effect. When, therefore, this has been done any surplus still belongs to him. This doctrine does not, in my judgment, rest on any evidence of the state of mind of the settlor, for in the vast majority of cases no doubt he does not expect to see his money back: he has created a trust which so far as he can see will absorb the whole of it. The resulting trust arises where that expectation is for some unforeseen reason cheated of fruition, and is an inference of law based on after-knowledge of the event.

Counsel for the Crown admitted that it was for him to show that this principle did not apply to the present case. Counsel for the subscribers cited to me *Re Abbott* [1900] 2 Ch 326 [p. 219, above]... Stirling J had no difficulty in coming to the conclusion that the ladies were not intended to become the absolute owners of the fund and therefore their personal representatives had no claim. It was never suggested in this case that any claim by the Crown to *bona vacantia* might arise. A similar result was reached in *Re Hobourn Aero Components Air Raid Distress Fund*

---

[36] Cf. *Re West Sussex Constabulary's Widows, Children and Benevolent (1930) Fund Trusts* [1971] Ch 1 [p. 224, below]. [37] For discussion of such schemes, see p. 544, below.

[1946] Ch 86 where the judge found that though the objects of the fund were charitable no general charitable intent was shown in the absence of any element of public benefit and decided that the money belonged to the subscribers upon a resulting trust. Here again no claim was made on behalf of the Crown that the surplus constituted *bona vacantia*.

I was referred to two cases where a claim was made to *bona vacantia* and succeeded. The first of these was *Cunnack v Edwards* [1896] 2 Ch 679. This was a case of a society formed to raise a fund by subscriptions and so forth from the members to provide for widows of deceased members. Upon the death of the last widow of a member it was found that there was a surplus. It was held by the Court of Appeal that no question of charity arose, that there was no resulting trust in favour of the subscribers, but that the surplus passed to the Crown as *bona vacantia*....

The ratio decidendi seems to have been that having regard to the constitution of the fund no interest could possibly be held to remain in the contributor who had parted with his money once and for all under a contract for the benefit of his widow. When this contract had been carried into effect the contributor had received all that he contracted to get for his money and could not ask for any more.

A similar result was reached in the case of *Smith v Cooke* [1891] AC 297, cited by A.L. Smith LJ [1896] 2 Ch 679 at 683, though it does not appear from the report what the result was. Another case cited to me was *Braithwaite v A-G* [1909] 1 Ch 510. Here again it was held that there was no room for a resulting trust and the claim to *bona vacantia* succeeded. The opponents there, it appears, were the last two surviving annuitants. Their claim was rejected on the ground that they had had or were having everything for which the contract provided. The claim of the Attorney-General on behalf of charity was rejected, it being held that there was no charity. A different result was reached by Kekewich J in *Re Buck* [1896] 2 Ch 727, but it was on the ground that the society was a charity and the money was therefore directed to be applied *cy-près*....

His Lordship referred to 'the three hospital cases': *Re Welsh Hospital (Netley) Fund* [1921] 1 Ch 655 [p. 227, below]; *Re Hillier's Trusts* [1954] 1 WLR 9,[38] and *Re Ulverston and District New Hospital Building Trusts* [1956] Ch 622 [p. 227, below] and continued:

It was argued for the Crown that the subscribers to this fund must be taken to have parted with their money out and out, and that there was here, as in *Cunnack v Edwards* [1896] 2 Ch 679 and *Braithwaite v A-G* [1909] 1 Ch 510, no room for a resulting trust. But there is a difference between those cases and this in that they were cases of contract and this is not. Further, it seems to me that the hospital cases are not of great help because the argument centred round general charitable intent, a point which cannot arise unless the immediate object be a charity. I have already held there is no such question here. In my judgment the nearest case is the *Hobourn* case [1946] Ch 86, which, however, is no authority for the present because no claim for *bona vacantia* was made.

In my judgment the Crown has failed to show that this case should not follow the ordinary rule merely because there was a number of donors who, I will assume, are unascertainable. I see no reason myself to suppose that the small giver who is anonymous has any wider intention than the large giver who can be named. They all give for the one object. If they can be found by inquiry the resulting trust can be executed in their favour. If they cannot I do not see how the money could then, with all respect to Jenkins LJ, change its destination and become *bona vacantia*. It will be

---

[38] On appeal [1954] 1 WLR 700 [p. 227, below].

merely money held upon a trust for which no beneficiary can be found. Such cases are common and where it is known that there are beneficiaries the fact that they cannot be ascertained does not entitle the Crown to come in and claim. The trustees must pay the money into court like any other trustee who cannot find his beneficiary. I conclude, therefore, that there must be an inquiry for the subscribers to this fund.[39]

(ii) Members' Clubs and Associations

Where members contribute to the funds or property of a club or society which is established for non-charitable purposes, the question arises as to the entitlement to its assets when the club or association is dissolved.[40] The various solutions are that the members are entitled under the doctrine of resulting trusts, or that the members are contractually entitled, or that the property is *bona vacantia,* to which the Crown is entitled.[41] It may be that persons other than the members have also contributed to the funds, as in *Re West Sussex Constabulary's Widows, Children and Benevolent (1930) Fund Trusts* [1971] Ch 1 [p. 224, below], in which case it must be decided whether they have any entitlement under a resulting trust. The earlier decisions display no uniformity of approach.[42] and should be read in the light of the analysis of Walton J in *Re Bucks Constabulary Widows' and Orphans' Fund Friendly Society (No 2)* [1979] 1 WLR 936 [p. 228, below]. His Lordship held that the surplus belonged to the members by contract, to the exclusion of any resulting trust or any entitlement of the Crown on the basis of *bona vacantia.* This decision was cited but not referred to in the judgment of Scott J in *Davis v Richards and Wallington Industries Ltd* [1990] 1 WLR 1511 [p. 231, below]. It was there considered that the contractual background did not preclude the finding of a resulting trust. However, any resulting trust for members was excluded by a contrary intention, so that their share would have devolved as *bona vacantia* had it not been held that the employers were entitled under the terms of the trust deed.[43] This conclusion is consistent with the positive intent analysis of the resulting trust,[44] but is inconsistent with the absence of intent analysis.[45] Indeed, the conclusion was criticised by the Privy Council in *Air Jamaica Ltd v Charlton*[46] for this reason.

---

[39] The fund was wound up in 1965, when the remainder of the money was paid into court. It was announced on 5 April, 1993 that this money (£7,300 uninvested) was to be spent on a memorial to the victims. Cf. Charities Act 1993, s. 14 [p. 572, below], which provides for the application *cy-près* of money given to charity, and obtained from gifts by unknown donors, even where it was given for a specific purpose only.

[40] As to when there is a dissolution so as to render the unspent assets distributable, see *Re William Denby & Sons Ltd Sick and Benevolent Fund* [1971] 1 WLR 973; *Re GKN Bolts and Nuts Ltd (Automotive Division) Birmingham Works Sports and Social Club* [1982] 1 WLR 774. See generally Warburton, *Unincorporated Associations: Law and Practice* (2nd edn, 1992).

[41] See Ing, *Bona Vacantia* (2nd edn, 1999).

[42] See (1973) 92 *Law Notes* 297, 330 (A. Cooklin).

[43] Criticised at [1991] Conv 366 (J. Martin); [1992] Conv 41 (S. Gardner); (1992) 6 *Trust Law International* 119 at 124 (Lord Browne-Wilkinson); (1994) 8 *Trust Law International* 35 (Vinelott J).

[44] See p. 198, above.   [45] See p. 205, above.

[46] [1999] 1 WLR 1399, 1412 [p. 234, below].

In **Cunnack v Edwards** [1896] 2 Ch 679, a society governed by the Friendly Societies Act 1829[47] was formed to raise funds, by the subscription, fines, and forfeitures of its members to provide annuities for the widows of those members who died. By 1879, all the members had died, and by 1892, the last widow died. There was then a surplus of £1,250.

The Court of Appeal, reversing Chitty J, held that the Crown took the fund as *bona vacantia*. There was no room for a resulting trust because each member had paid his contributions without reserving any beneficial interest to himself. A.L. SMITH LJ said, at 683:

As the member paid his money to the society, so he divested himself of all interest in this money for ever, with this one reservation, that if the member left a widow she was to be provided for during her widowhood. Except as to this he abandoned and gave up the money for ever.

The benefits were for the widows and not for the members.

Re West Sussex Constabulary's Widows, Children and Benevolent (1930) Fund Trusts[48]
[1971] Ch 1 (ChD, **Goff J**)

A fund was established for the purpose of providing payments to widows and certain dependants of deceased members of the West Sussex Constabulary. Clause 10 of the rules provided that, with exceptions, a member who resigned should forfeit all claims to the fund. Receipts to the fund came from members' subscriptions, the proceeds of entertainments, sweepstakes, raffles, and collecting boxes, and various donations and legacies. On the amalgamation of the constabulary with other police forces as from 1 January, 1968 the operation of the fund came to an end. The question arose as to the distribution of the fund.

Held. (i) Where a donation or legacy was made for the specific purpose of the fund, the donor was entitled under a resulting trust. (ii) Money received from all other sources passed to the Crown as *bona vacantia*.

Goff J: First, it was submitted that the fund belongs exclusively and in equal shares to all those persons now living who were members on 31 December, 1967, and the personal representatives of all the then members since deceased, to all of whom I will refer collectively as 'the surviving members'. That argument is based on the analogy of the members' club cases, and the decisions in *Re Printers and Transferrers Amalgamated Trades Protection Society* [1899] 2 Ch 184; *Re Lead Co's Workmen's Fund Society* [1904] 2 Ch 196 and the Irish case of *Tierney v Tough* [1914] 1 IR 142. The ratio decidendi of the first two of those cases was that there was a resulting trust, but that would not give the whole fund to the surviving members, unless rule 10 of the fund's rules could somehow be made to carry to them the contributions of the former members despite the failure of the purposes of the fund (as was pointed out by O'Connor MR in *Tierney v Tough* at 155), and unless indeed the moneys raised from outside sources also could

---

[47] On friendly societies, see Warburton, note 40 above, pp. 5–6.
[48] (1971) 87 LQR 464 (M.J. Albery).

somehow be made to accrue to the surviving members. I agree with Ungoed-Thomas J that the ratio decidendi of *Tierney v Tough* is to be preferred: see *Re St Andrew's Allotment Association* [1969] 1 WLR 229 at 238.

This brings one back to the principle of the members' clubs, and I cannot accept that as applicable for three reasons. First, it simply does not look like it; this was nothing but a pensions or dependent relatives fund not at all akin to a club; secondly, in all the cases where the surviving members have taken, with the sole exception of *Tierney v Tough,* the club society or organisation existed for the benefit of the members for the time being exclusively, whereas in the present case, as in *Cunnack v Edwards* [1896] 2 Ch 679, only third parties could benefit. Moreover, in *Tierney v Tough* the exception was minimal and discretionary and can, I think, fairly be disregarded. Finally, this very argument was advanced and rejected by Chitty J in *Cunnack v Edwards* at first instance [1895] 1 Ch 489 at 496, and was abandoned on the hearing of the appeal. That judgment also disposes of the further argument that the surviving members of the fund had power to amend the rules under rule 14 and could therefore have reduced the fund into possession, and so ought to be treated as the owners of it or the persons for whose benefit it existed at the crucial moment. They had the power but they did not exercise it, and it is now too late.

Then it was argued that there is a resulting trust, with several possible consequences. If this be the right view there must be a primary division of the fund into three parts, one representing contributions from former members, another contributions from the surviving members, and the third moneys raised from outside sources. The surviving members then take the second, and possibly by virtue of rule 10, the first also. That rule is as follows:

> 'Any member who voluntarily terminates his membership shall forfeit all claim against the fund, except in the case of a member transferring to a similar fund of another force, in which instance the contributions paid by the member to the West Sussex Constabulary's Widows, Children and Benevolent (1930) Fund may be paid into the fund of the force to which the member transfers.'

Alternatively, the first part may belong to the past members on the footing that rule 10 is operative so long only as the fund is a going concern, or may be *bona vacantia.* The third is distributable in whole or in part between those who provided the money, or again is *bona vacantia.*

In my judgment the doctrine of resulting trust is clearly inapplicable to the contributions of both classes. Those persons who remained members until their deaths are in any event excluded because they have had all they contracted for, either because their widows and dependants have received or are in receipt of the prescribed benefits, or because they did not have a widow or dependants. In my view that is inherent in all the speeches in the Court of Appeal in *Cunnack v Edwards* [1896] 2 Ch 679. Further, whatever the effect of the fund's rule 10 may be upon the contributions of those members who left prematurely, they and the surviving members alike are also in my judgment unable to claim under a resulting trust because they put their money on a contractual basis and not one of trust: see *per* Harman J in *Re Gillingham Bus Disaster Fund* [1958] Ch 300 at 314. The only case which has given me difficulty on this aspect of the matter is *Re Hobourn Aero Components Ltd's Air Raid Distress Fund* [1946] Ch 86, where in somewhat similar circumstances it was held there was a resulting trust. The argument postulated, I think, the distinction between contract and trust but in another connection, namely, whether the fund was charitable: see at 89 and 90. There was in that case a resolution to wind up but that was not, at all events as expressed, the ratio decidendi: see *per* Cohen J at 97, but, as Cohen J observed, there was no argument for *bona vacantia.* Moreover, no rules or regulations were ever made and although in fact £1 *per* month was paid or saved for each member serving with the forces, there was no prescribed contractual benefits. In my judgment that case is therefore distinguishable.

Accordingly, in my judgment all the contributions of both classes are *bona vacantia,* but I must make a reservation with respect to possible contractual rights. In *Cunnack v Edwards* [1895] 1 Ch 489 and *Braithwaite v A-G* [1909] 1 Ch 510 all the members had received, or provision had been made for, all the contractual benefits. Here the matter has been cut short. Those persons who died whilst still in membership cannot, I conceive, have any rights because in their case the contract has been fully worked out, and on a contractual basis I would think that members who retired would be precluded from making any claim by rule 10, although that is perhaps more arguable. The surviving members, on the other hand, may well have a right in contract on the ground of frustration or total failure of consideration, and that right may embrace contributions made by past members, though I do not see how it could apply to moneys raised from outside sources. I have not, however, heard any argument based on contract and therefore the declarations I propose to make will be subject to the reservation which I will later formulate. This will not prevent those parts of the fund which are *bona vacantia* from being paid over to the Crown as it has offered to give a full indemnity to the trustees.

I must now turn to the moneys raised from outside sources. Counsel for the Treasury Solicitor made an overriding general submission that there cannot be a resulting trust of any of the outside moneys because in the circumstances it is impossible to identify the trust property; no doubt something could be achieved by complicated accounting, but this, he submitted, would not be identification but notional reconstruction. I cannot accept that argument. In my judgment, in a case like the present, equity will cut the Gordian knot by simply dividing the ultimate surplus in proportion to the sources from which it has arisen. Chitty J in *Cunnack v Edwards* at first instance [1895] 1 Ch 489, particularly at 497 and 498, was prepared to order an inquiry, notwithstanding the difficulty that it involved, going back over many years, and despite the fact that the early records were not available; but that was a difficulty of ascertaining the original contributions, not of working out surpluses or interest calculations year by year. Similarly it was not suggested that any such operation ought to be carried out, or that the necessity for it prevented the doctrine of resulting trust being applied in the *Re Printers and Transferrers* case [1899] 2 Ch 184. Yet in both those cases, although the matter was not further complicated by outside contributions, the problem of interest on invested funds, and of contributions and expenditure made at different times, must have presented itself. Again, in the *Printers* case, fines and forfeitures were ignored: see at 189 and 190. There may be cases of tolerable simplicity where the court will be more refined, but in general, where a fund has been raised from mixed sources, interest has been earned over the years and income—and possibly capital— expenditure has been made indiscriminately out of the fund as an entirety, and then the venture comes to an end prematurely or otherwise, the court will not find itself baffled but will cut the Gordian knot as I have said.

Then counsel divided the outside moneys into three categories, first, the proceeds of enter- tainments, raffles and sweepstakes; secondly, the proceeds of collecting-boxes; and, thirdly, donations, including legacies if any, and he took particular objections to each.

I agree that there cannot be any resulting trust with respect to the first category. I am not certain whether Harman J in *Re Gillingham Bus Disaster Fund* [1958] Ch 300 meant to decide otherwise. In stating the facts at 304 he referred to 'street collections and so forth'. In the further argument at 309 there is mention of whist drives and concerts but the judge himself did not speak of anything other than gifts. If, however, he did, I must respectfully decline to follow his judgment in that regard, for whatever may be the true position with regard to collecting-boxes, it appears to me to be impossible to apply the doctrine of resulting trust to the proceeds of entertainments and sweepstakes and such-like money-raising operations for two reasons: first, the relationship is one of contract and not of trust; the purchaser of a ticket may have the motive of aiding the cause or he may not; he may purchase a ticket merely because he wishes to attend the particular entertainment or to try for the prize, but whichever it be, he pays his money as the price of what is offered and what he receives; secondly, there is in such cases no direct contribution to the fund at all; it is only the profit, if any, which is ultimately received and there may even be none.

In any event, the first category cannot be any more susceptible to the doctrine than the second to which I now turn. Here one starts with the well-known dictum of P.O. Lawrence J in *Re Welsh Hospital (Netley) Fund* [1921] 1 Ch 655 at 660, where he said:

> 'So far as regards the contributors to entertainments, street collections etc., I have no hesitation in holding that they must be taken to have parted with their money out-and-out. It is inconceivable that any person paying for a concert ticket or placing a coin in a collecting-box presented to him in the street should have intended that any part of the money so contributed should be returned to him when the immediate object for which the concert was given or the collection made had come to an end. To draw such an inference would be absurd on the face of it.'

This was adopted by Upjohn J in *Re Hillier's Trusts* [1954] 1 WLR 9, where the point was actually decided. . . .

[The analysis of Upjohn J] was approved by Denning LJ in the Court of Appeal [1954] 1 WLR 700 although it is true he went on to say that the law makes a presumption of charity. I quote from 714:

> 'Let me first state the law as I understand it in regard to money collected for a specified charity by means of a church collection, a flag day, a whist drive, a dance, or some such activity. When a man gives money on such an occasion, he gives it, I think, beyond recall. He parts with the money out-and-out . . .'

In *Re Ulverston and District New Hospital Building Trusts* [1956] Ch 622 at 633 Jenkins LJ threw out a suggestion that there might be a distinction in the case of a person who could prove that he put a specified sum in a collecting-box, and, in the *Gillingham* case [1958] Ch 300, Harman J after noting this, decided that there was a resulting trust with respect to the proceeds of collections. He said at 314: [quoting the last paragraph extracted, p. 222, above].

It will be observed that Harman J considered that *Re Welsh Hospital (Netley) Fund* [1921] 1 Ch 655; *Re Hillier's Trusts* and *Re Ulverston and District New Hospital Building Trusts* did not help him greatly because they were charity cases. It is true that they were, and, as will presently appear, that is in my view very significant in relation to the third category, but I do not think it was a valid objection with respect to the second, and for my part I cannot reconcile the decision of Upjohn J in *Re Hillier's Trusts* with that of Harman J in the *Gillingham* case. As I see it, therefore, I have to choose between them. On the one hand it may be said that Harman J had the advantage, which Upjohn J had not, of considering the suggestion made by Jenkins LJ. On the other hand that suggestion with all respect, seems to me somewhat fanciful and unreal. I agree that all who put their money into collecting-boxes should be taken to have the same intention, but why should they not all be regarded as intending to part with their money out and out absolutely in all circumstances? I observe that P.O. Lawrence J in *Re Welsh Hospital* [1921] 1 Ch 655 at 661 used very strong words. He said any other view was inconceivable and absurd on the face of it. That commends itself to my humble judgment, and I therefore prefer and follow the judgment of Upjohn J in *Re Hillier's Trusts*....[His Lordship referred to *Re Hillier's Trusts*, and continued:] Therefore, where, as in the present case, the object was neither equivocal nor charitable, I can see no justification for infecting the third category with the weaknesses of the first and second, and I cannot distinguish this part of the case from *Re Abbott Fund Trusts* [1900] 2 Ch 326 [p. 219, above].

[His Lordship directed certain inquiries, and continued:] And I make the following declarations: First, that the portion attributable to donations and legacies is held on a resulting trust for the donors or their estates and the estates of the respective testators; secondly, that the remainder of the fund is *bona vacantia*.

These declarations are, however, without prejudice to (1) Any claim which may be made in contract by any person or the personal representatives of any person who was at any time a member, and (2) Any right or claim of the trustees to be indemnified against any such claim out of the whole fund including the portion attributable to donations and legacies.

Finally there will, of course, be general liberty to apply.

Re Bucks Constabulary Widows' and Orphans' Fund Friendly Society (No 2)[49]
[1979] 1 WLR 936 (Ch D, **Walton J**)

The Bucks Constabulary Fund, which was registered under the Friendly Societies Act 1896, was established to provide, by voluntary contributions from its members, for the relief of widows and orphans of deceased members of the Bucks Constabulary. By section 49(1) of the 1896 Act, the property of such a society vested in its trustees for the benefit of the society and its members. In 1968 the Constabulary amalgamated with others and the society was wound up. Its rules did not provide for the distribution of its assets on dissolution. The main issue was whether the assets should be distributed among the persons who were members at the date of dissolution, or whether they should pass to the Crown as *bona vacantia*.

Held. As there were members in existence at the dissolution, the assets belonged to those members to the total exclusion of any claim by the Crown.

Walton J: Before I turn to a consideration of the authorities, it is I think pertinent to observe that all unincorporated societies rest in contract...but there is an implied contract between all of the members *inter se* governed by the rules of the society. In default of any rule to the contrary—and it will seldom, if ever, be that there is such a rule—when a member ceases to be a member of the association he ipso facto ceases to have any interest in its funds. Once again, so far as friendly societies are concerned, it is made very clear by section 49(1), that it is the members, the present members, who, alone, have any right in the assets. As membership always ceases on death, past members or the estates of deceased members therefore have no interest in the assets. Further, unless expressly so provided by the rules, unincorporated societies are not really tontine societies intended to provide benefits for the longest liver of the members. Therefore, although it is difficult to say in any given case precisely when a society becomes moribund, it is quite clear that if a society is reduced to a single member neither he, nor still

[49] (1980) 39 CLJ 88 (C.E.F. Rickett); (1980) 43 MLR 626 (B. Green).

less his personal representatives on his behalf, can say he is or was the society and therefore entitled solely to its fund. It may be that it will be sufficient for the society's continued existence if there are two members, but if there is only one the society as such must cease to exist. There is no association, since one can hardly associate with oneself or enjoy one's own society. And so indeed the assets have become ownerless.

His Lordship distinguished *Cunnack v Edwards* [1896] 2 Ch 679 [p. 224, above], on the ground that the combined effect of the rules of the society and the Friendly Societies Act 1892 precluded any argument in favour of distribution among the members' estates, and continued:

The next case to which I was referred was *Re Printers and Transferrers Amalgamated Trades Protection Society* [1899] 2 Ch 184. I am afraid that I get little assistance from that case. There, there was no claim by the Crown to the assets as *bona vacantia,* obviously correctly, but the distribution which was ordered was on the basis of a resulting trust apparently influenced by Chitty J's decision at first instance in the case just cited. With all respect to Byrne J who decided that case, I do not think that the method of distribution employed could, in the light of the judgment in the Court of Appeal in *Cunnack v Edwards* [1896] 2 Ch 679, ever have been correct.

The next case was *Braithwaite v A-G* [1909] 1 Ch 510. Although it is undeniably correct that no mention was made at any point in the case of the fact in express terms, the society there in question having been established as a friendly society in 1808 and actually registered under the Act of 1793, was, like the society in *Cunnack v Edwards* [1896] 2 Ch 679, governed by the provisions of the Act of 1829. It is therefore hardly surprising that, after deciding the new point namely that the contributions of honorary members were absolute gifts to the society and could not be recovered, it was held that the benefited members, of whom there were just two surviving both drawing annuities, did not take the fund. This was a straight following of *Cunnack v Edwards* on identical legislation. The rules made no further provision for benefited members and hence it is not to be wondered at that Swinfen Eady J summed the matter up in three pithy paragraphs, at 520:

> 'In the present case the two surviving benefited members are entitled to the annuities for which their contract of membership provides, but not to any other interest in the funds. The entire beneficial interest has been exhausted in respect of each deceased benefited member, and when the annuities to the two surviving members cease to be payable upon their respective deaths, they too will have exhausted all their beneficial interest in the funds. All possible claimants to the fund having now been disposed of, I decide that the surplus of the benefited members' fund and the children's fund belong to the Crown as *bona vacantia.*'

The next case is one from Ireland, *Tierney v Tough* [1914] 1 IR 142. O'Connor MR, though concurring in the decision, criticised the reasoning in the *Printers'* case [1899] 2 Ch 184 along the lines which appeal to me and which I have already noted. It is true that he did not in any way allude to the statutory provisions which appear to me to have played so large a part in *Cunnack v Edwards,* but the basis upon which he rested his decision is short, simple and wholly convincing. It must be borne in mind that this was simply the case of an unincorporated association. No question of the statutory provisions arose. O'Connor MR put it thus, at 155:

> 'The conclusion which I have arrived at in the present case is, that the fund belongs to the existing members, and I think that the true reason is to be found in the fact that the accumulated fund is the property of the society, which is composed of individual members. The society is only the

aggregation of those individuals, and the property of the former is the property of the latter. This is not a case in which all the members have disappeared, and their claims have been satisfied, or never arose, as in *Cunnack v Edwards*. There are here existing members with unsatisfied claims against the fund. As I said before, and I think this cannot be controverted, if the existing members, with the assent of their committee and their trustee, agreed to divide the fund among themselves, there is no person qualified to call them to account for so doing. The fund is a private one. On the authorities it is clear that there is no charitable trust attaching to it, and I think I have shown that the fund cannot be regarded as *bona vacantia*. The Attorney-General then has no claim.'

His Lordship considered *Re Customs and Excise Officers' Mutual Guarantee Fund* [1917] 2 Ch 18 and *Re St Andrew's Allotment Association* [1969] 1 WLR 229, and continued:

In *Re William Denby & Sons Ltd Sick and Benevolent Fund* [1971] 1 WLR 973, the main finding was that, as the substratum of the association had not gone, it continued, but Brightman J said, at 978:

> 'One matter is common ground. It is accepted by all counsel that a fund of this sort is founded in contract and not in trust. That is to say, the right of a member of the fund to receive benefits is a contractual right and the member ceases to have any interest in the fund if and when he has received the totality of the benefits to which he was contractually entitled. In other words, there is no possible claim by any member, founded on a resulting trust. I turn to the question whether the fund has already been dissolved or terminated so that its assets have already become distribut-able. If it has been dissolved or terminated, the members entitled to participate would *prima facie* be those persons who were members at the date of dissolution or termination...'

and he refers to the *Printers and Transferrers'* case [1899] 2 Ch 184; *Re Lead Co's Workmen's Fund Society* [1904] 2 Ch 196 at 207 and *Re St Andrew's Allotment Association* [1969] 1 WLR 229. Once again, this is fully in line with the principle of the cases as I see them.

Finally, although there is at any rate one later case, for the purpose of this review there comes a case which gives me great concern, *Re West Sussex Constabulary's Widows, Children and Benevolent (1930) Fund Trusts* [1971] Ch 1 [p. 224, above]. The case is indeed easily distinguishable from the present case in that what was there under consideration was a simple unincorporated association and not a friendly society, so that the provisions of section 49(1) of the Act of 1896 do not apply. Otherwise the facts in that case present remarkable parallels to the facts in the present case. Goff J decided that the surplus funds had become *bona vacantia*.

[His Lordship read extracts from the case and continued:] It will be observed that the first reason given by Goff J for his decision is that he could not accept the principle of the members' clubs as applicable. This is a very interesting reason because it is flatly contrary to the suc-cessful argument of Mr. Ingle Joyce in the case Goff J purported to follow, *Cunnack v Edwards* [1895] 1 Ch 489 at 494, where he said:

> 'This society was nothing more than a club, in which the members had no transmissible interest: *Re St James' Club* (1852) 2 De GM & G 383 at 387. Whatever the members, or even the surviving member, might have done while alive, when they died their interest in the assets of the club died with them.'

And in the Court of Appeal [1896] 2 Ch 679 he used the arguments he had used below. If all that Goff J meant was that the purposes of the fund before him were totally different from those of a members' club then of course one must agree, but if he meant to imply that there was some totally different principle of law applicable one must ask why that should be. His second reason is that in all the cases where the surviving members had taken, the organisation existed for the benefit of the members for the time being exclusively. This may be so, so far as actual decisions go, but what is the principle? Why are the members not in control, complete control, save as to any existing contractual rights, of the assets belonging to their organisation? One could understand the position being different if valid trusts had been declared of the assets in favour of third parties, for example charities, but that this was emphatically not the case was demonstrated by the fact that Goff J recognised that the members could have altered the rules prior to dissolution and put the assets into their own pockets. If there was no obstacle to their doing this, it shows in my judgment quite clearly that the money was theirs all the time. Finally, he purports to follow *Cunnack v Edwards* [1896] 2 Ch 679 and it will be seen from the analysis which I have already made of that case that it was extremely special in its facts, resting on a curious provision of the Act of 1829 which is no longer applicable. As I have already indicated, in the light of section 49(1) of the Act of 1896 the case before Goff J is readily distinguishable, but I regret that, quite apart from that, I am wholly unable to square it with the relevant principles of law applicable.

The conclusion therefore is that, as on dissolution there were members of the society here in question in existence, its assets are held on trust for such members to the total exclusion of any claim on behalf of the Crown. The remaining question under this head which falls now to be argued is, of course, whether they are simply held *per* capita, or, as suggested in some of the cases, in proportion to the contributions made by each.[50]

Davis v Richards and Wallington Industries Ltd
[1990] 1 WLR 1511 (Ch D, Scott J)

On the winding-up of a pension fund the question arose as to the entitlement to a surplus of some £3 million. The fund derived from contributions from employers and employees and from funds transferred from other schemes. There was some doubt as to the validity of the trust deed, which provided that the employers were entitled to any surplus.

Held. The trust deed was valid and so the employers were entitled to the surplus. Had the deed been invalid, any part of the surplus attributable to the contributions of the employees would have devolved as *bona vacantia*, as the resulting trust which would otherwise have arisen was excluded by a contrary intention.

Scott J: Finally I must address myself to the arguments on resulting trust. These arguments arise only if the definitive deed was ineffective and its inefficacy cannot be remedied by the execution of the executory trust.

Mr. Charles, arguing for *bona vacantia,* has drawn a distinction between payments made under contract and payments made under a trust. He suggested that rights arising under pension schemes were, basically, rights of a contractual character rather than equitable rights arising under a trust. As I understood the argument, if the context in which the rights arise is mainly or exclusively contractual, then a resulting trust will be excluded; but, if the context is mainly or exclusively that of trust, a resulting trust may apply. Unincorporated associations, he said, were based in contract, a pension scheme was a species of unincorporated association, the contributions to pension schemes by employees and employers alike were made under contract with one another; so there was no room for any resulting trust to apply to the surplus produced by the contributions.

His Lordship referred to *Kerr v British Leyland (Staff) Trustees Ltd* [1986] CA Transcript 286; *Mihlenstedt v Barclays Bank International Ltd* [1989] IRLR 522 and *Palmer v Abney Park Cemetery Co Ltd* (4 July 1985, unreported), and continued:

In my opinion, the contractual origin of rights under a pension scheme, although relevant to the question whether a resulting trust applies to surplus, is not conclusive. There are a number of authorities where the courts have had to deal with the question whether the assets of a defunct association or the surplus assets of a pension scheme had become *bona vacantia* or were held on resulting trusts for the subscribers or members.

His Lordship referred to *Re West Sussex Constabulary's Widows, Children and Benevolent (1930) Fund Trusts* [1971] Ch 1 [p. 224, above] and *Jones v Williams* (15 March 1988, unreported), where Knox J held that a resulting trust could be excluded by a clause in the trust deed, and continued:

I respectfully agree with Knox J's approach. I would, however, venture one qualification. The provision in a trust deed necessary to exclude a resulting trust need not, in my opinion, be express. In the absence of an express provision it would, I think, often be very difficult for a sufficiently clear intention to exclude a resulting trust to be established. But, in general, any term that can be expressed can also, in suitable circumstances, be implied. In my opinion, a resulting trust will be excluded not only by an express provision but also if its exclusion is to be implied. If the intention of a contributor that a resulting trust should not apply is the proper conclusion, it would not be right, in my opinion, for the law to contradict that intention.

In my judgment, therefore, the fact that a payment to a fund has been made under contract and that the payer has obtained all that he or she bargained for under the contract is not necessarily a decisive argument against a resulting trust.

I must apply these principles to the surplus in the present case. The fund was, as I have said, fed from three sources: employees' contributions, transfers from other pension schemes and employers' contributions. The employees' contributions were made under contract. Employees were obliged to contribute 5 per cent of salary. They were entitled, in return, to the specified pension and other benefits. The funds from other pension schemes, too, were transferred under contract. There would have been three parties to all these contracts, namely the trustees of the transferred scheme, the trustees of the 1975 scheme and the transferring members themselves. Perhaps the employer company would have been a party as well. The transfer would certainly have been made with its consent. Under these contracts, by implication if not expressly, the transferor trustees would have been discharged from liability in respect of the transferred funds, whether liability to the transferring employee members or liability to the employer company. Finally there are the employers. They, too, made their contributions under contract; they made them under the contracts of employment between themselves and their employees. But there is a very important difference between the contractual obligation of the employees and that of the employers. The employees' contractual obligation was specific in amount, 5 per cent of salary. The employers' contractual obligation was conceptually certain but the amount was inherently uncertain. The obligation was to pay whatever was necessary to fund the scheme. The terms of rule 3 of Part II of the 1975 rules describe accurately, in my opinion, the contractual obligation of the employers:

'The employer will pay to the trustees such amounts as may from time to time be required to enable the trustees to maintain the benefits...'

In practice, the amount of the employers' contributions in respect of each employee was actuarially calculated. The calculations were based on assumptions as to the time when the benefits would become payable and as to the amount of the employee's final salary at that time. If the scheme should terminate before that time, the amount paid would be bound to have been more than needed to have been paid in order to fund the employee's benefits as at the date of termination.

Two separate questions seem to me to require to be answered. First, to what extent should the surplus, the £3 million-odd, be regarded as derived from each of these three sources? One possible answer is that there should be a calculation of the total amount of employees' contributions, the total amount of funds transferred from other companies' pension schemes and the total amount of employers' contributions, and that the surplus should be regarded as derived from these three sources in the same proportions as the three totals bear to one another.

I do not accept that this is right. It ignores the different bases on which these contributions were paid. Since the employers' obligation was to pay whatever was from time to time necessary to fund the various scheme benefits and since the employees' 5 per cent contributions and the amount of the transferred funds constituted the base from which the amount of the employers' contributions would from time to time have to be assessed, it is logical, in my judgment, to treat the scheme benefits as funded first by the employees' contributions and the transferred funds, and only secondarily by the employers' contributions, and, correspondingly, to treat the surplus as provided first by the employers' contributions and only secondarily by the employees' contributions and the transferred funds.

There are two possible factual situations to be considered. It is possible (although, I think, very unlikely) that the employees' contributions and the funds transferred from the pension schemes of other companies would, without there having been any contribution at all from the employers, have been sufficient to provide in full for all the scheme benefits and, perhaps, still to have left some surplus. If that is the position, it would follow that, with the advantage of hindsight, the employers need not have made any contributions at all in order to have funded the benefits. This situation would, in my judgment, require that that surplus (which would be bound, I think, to be very small) should be regarded as derived from the employees' contributions and the transferred funds and that the balance of the surplus should be regarded as derived from the employers' contributions.

The much more likely situation is that some contribution at least was required from the employers in order to produce assets sufficient to provide all the scheme benefits to which employees became entitled on 31 July, 1982. In that event the whole of the surplus, in my judgment, should be regarded as derived from the employers' contributions. This conclusion is, to my mind, in accordance both with logic and with equity. The actuarial calculations on which the employers' actual contributions were based were themselves based upon a series of assumptions. The termination of the scheme invalidated the assumptions. The employers had, in the event, made payments exceeding the amount necessary to discharge their obligation to fund the benefits to which the employees eventually became entitled. There is a well-established equity that enables accounts drawn up under a mistake to be reopened (see Goff and Jones, *The Law of Restitution* (3rd edn, 1986), p. 199). In cases such as the present there was no mistake at the time the contributions were assessed and paid. The actuarial calculations were, I am sure, impeccable. But subsequent events having invalidated some of the assumptions underlying the calculations, the case is, in my opinion, strongly analogous to that of an account drawn up under a mistake. In my opinion, equity should treat the employers as entitled to claim the surplus, or so much of it as derived from the overpayments.

The second question is whether a resulting trust applies to the surplus, or to so much of the surplus as was derived from each of the three sources to which I have referred. As to the surplus derived from the employers' contributions, I can see no basis on which a resulting trust can be excluded. The equity to which I referred in the previous paragraph demands, in my judgment, the conclusion that the trustees hold the surplus derived from the employers' contributions upon trust for the employers. There is no express provision excluding a resulting trust and no circumstances from which, in my opinion, an implication to that effect could be drawn. On the other hand, in my judgment, the circumstances of the case seem to me to point firmly and clearly to the conclusion that a resulting trust in favour of the employees is excluded.

The circumstances are these.

(i) Each employee paid his or her contributions in return for specific financial benefits from the fund. The value of these benefits would be different for each employee, depending on how long he had served, how old he was when he joined and how old he was when he left. Two employees might have paid identical sums in contributions but have become entitled to benefits of a very different value. The point is particularly striking in respect of the employees, (and there were several of them), who exercised their option to a refund of contributions. How can a resulting trust work as between the various employees *inter se*? I do not think it can and I do not see why equity should impute to them an intention that would lead to an unworkable result.

(ii) The scheme was established to take advantage of the legislation relevant to an exempt approved scheme and a contracted-out scheme. The legislative requirements placed a maximum on the financial return from the fund to which each employee would become entitled. The proposed rules would have preserved the statutory requirements. A resulting trust cannot do so. In my judgment, the relevant legislative requirements prevent imputing to the employees an intention that the surplus of the fund derived from their contributions should be returned to them under a resulting trust

In my judgment, therefore, there is no resulting trust for the employees.

This conclusion was criticised by the Privy Council in **Air Jamaica Ltd v Charlton** [1999] 1 WLR 1399, where LORD MILLETT said at 1412:

In *Davis v Richards and Wallington Industries Ltd* [1990] 1 WLR 1511 Scott J held that the fact that a party has received all that he bargained for is not necessarily a decisive argument against a resulting trust, but that in the circumstances of the case before him a resulting trust in favour of the employees was excluded. The circumstances that impressed him were two-fold. He considered that it was impossible to arrive at a workable scheme for apportioning the employees' surplus among the different classes of employees and he declined, at 1544, to 'impute to them an intention that would lead to an unworkable result'. He also considered that he was precluded by statute from 'imputing to the employees an intention' that they should receive by means of a resulting trust sums in excess of the maximum permitted by the relevant tax legislation.

These formulations also adopt the approach to intention that their Lordships have already considered to be erroneous.[51] Their Lordships would observe that, even in the ordinary case of an actuarial surplus, it is not obvious that, when employees are promised certain benefits under a scheme to which they have contributed more than was necessary to fund them, they should not expect to obtain a return of their excess contributions.

(iii) Method of Distribution Among Members

If (as will usually be the case) the Crown cannot establish any entitlement to the surplus assets of a dissolved association, then the question arises as to the proper manner of distribution among the members. Some of the earlier cases have favoured the resulting trust solution but, as will be seen[52] the modern approach proceeds on the basis of a contractual entitlement. The question will not arise, however, if the rules of the association provide for the destination of the assets on a dissolution.

If the resulting trust solution is adopted the assets should be distributed among past and present members, in shares proportionate to their contributions, as in *Re Hobourn Aero Components Air Raid Distress Fund* [1946] Ch 86; affirmed [1946] Ch 194. Sometimes the distribution has been confined to those who were members at the dissolution, which is a more convenient solution where the ascertainment of the true entitlements would otherwise be too difficult. This was done in *Re Printers and Transferrers Amalgamated Trades Protection Society* [1899] 2 Ch 184.

If, as the modern cases show is more likely, the members' entitlement is based upon contractual rights, then the distribution will be per capita, and confined to those who were members at the time of the dissolution.

Re Sick and Funeral Society of St. John's Sunday School, Golcar[53]
[1973] Ch 51 (Ch D, **Megarry J**)

In 1866 a society was formed at a Sunday school near Huddersfield to provide for sickness and death benefits for its members. Teachers and children could join, and subscriptions were based on a sliding scale according to age; those under 13 paying ½d. per week (Rule 9) and those over 12 paying 1d. The benefits for those paying the full subscription were twice those of the smaller subscribers (Rules 12, 14).

On 12 December, 1966, a meeting unanimously decided to wind up the Society as from 31 December. No further subscriptions were paid. There was some £4,000 of surplus assets.

---

[51] See p. 205, above.   [52] See p. 386, below.

[53] Applied in *Re Bucks Constabulary Widows' and Orphans' Fund Friendly Society (No 2)* [1979] 1 WLR 936 [p. 228, above]; *Re GKN Bolts and Nuts Ltd (Automotive Division) Birmingham Works Sports and Social Club* [1982] 1 WLR 774; [1983] Conv 315 (R. Griffith); cf. *Davis v Richards and Wallington Industries Ltd* [1990] 1 WLR 1511 [p. 231, above]. Now see *Air Jamaica Ltd v Charlton* [1999] 1 WLR 1399 at 1412 [p. 234, above].

Before the assets were distributed among the current members, four ex-members, who had been excluded from membership for failure to pay subscriptions since 1963 (Rules 9, 17), claimed to pay up their arrears and to participate. A further meeting was held in September 1968 in which it was again resolved to wind up the Society and to distribute the assets among the persons who were members on 31 December, 1966, and the personal representatives of such members who had subsequently died.

Held. Distribution accordingly; with full shares for full members and half shares for the children. The ex-members were excluded.

Megarry J (having held that the resolution of December 1966 was a valid resolution to wind up the Society): In my judgment the substantive rights of all concerned crystallised on 31 December, 1966, when, in accordance with the resolution of 12 December, 1966, the society ceased all its activities...Accordingly, in my judgment the personal representatives of each deceased member are entitled to the share to which that member would have been entitled had he lived...

I turn to question 2. This relates to the basis of distribution. Is each member entitled to an equal share, or is there to be a division into full shares and half-shares, with those paying ½d. a week entitled only to a half-share, and those paying 1d. a week a full share? Or is the basis of distribution to be proportionate to the amounts respectively contributed by each member? The first step, in my view, is to decide between the first two contentions on the one hand and the third on the other: is the proper basis that of division per capita, whether in full or half-shares, or that of division in proportion to the amounts contributed? In discussing this, I speak, of course, in general terms, and subject to any other basis for division that is to be discerned in the rules or any other source.

The authorities are in a curious state. In *Re Printers and Transferrers Amalgamated Trades Protection Society* [1899] 2 Ch 184, Byrne J applied the amounts-contributed basis to a trade union, putting matters on the footing of a resulting trust, and directing division on that basis among the members existing at the time of the resolution for dissolution. In *Re Lead Company's Workmen's Fund Society* [1904] 2 Ch 196, Warrington J followed this decision in the case of an unregistered friendly society. In these cases payments for forfeitures, fines, sick benefits and so on, were disregarded. In *Tierney v Tough* [1914] 1 IR 142, another case of an unregistered friendly society, O'Connor MR was critical of the application of the law relating to resulting trusts to such cases. Despite his criticism, however, he directed division on the basis of the amounts contributed. On the other hand, in the case of clubs, *Brown v Dale* (1878) 9 Ch D 78 supports the per capita basis, though it is so shortly reported as to provoke more questions than it answers. *Feeney and Shannon v Macmanus* [1937] IR 23, another club case, also supports the same basis. The case is a little remarkable in that the headnote proclaims that *Tierney v Tough* [1914] 1 IR 142 was 'applied'; and it appears from p. 33 that the basis of the decision was not so much that equal division was right, but that equality was necessary because ascertaining the proportionate contributions was an impossibility. Finally, in *Re St Andrew's Allotment Association* [1969] 1 WLR 229, concerning an allotment association, Ungoed-Thomas J considered these cases, together with *Re Blue Albion Cattle Society* [1966] CLY 1274, (1996) The Guardian, May 28, where Cross J had applied the per capita basis to a cattle-breeding society. In the *St Andrew's* case Ungoed-Thomas J said at 238:

'If the true principle is that laid down in *Tierney v Tough* [1914] 1 IR 142 and that principle certainly seems to me preferable to the principle of the resulting trust adopted in *Re Printers and Transferrers Amalgamated Trades Protection Society* [1899] 2 Ch 184, then it would seem to me that *prima facie* the assets are distributable between members at the relevant date per capita. It is conceivable that a basis for distinguishing the friendly and mutual benefit society cases may be that, whereas in the club cases enjoyment *ab initio* and equality are contemplated, yet in the friendly and mutual benefit society cases what are contemplated are advantages related to contributions.'

The reference to the principle laid down in *Tierney v Tough* must, I think, be to the comments of O'Connor MR which rejected the concept of resulting trust, rather than to the actual decision, which was on the basis of the proportionate contributions that flow from the concept of resulting trust.

It seems to me, with all respect, that much of the difficulty arises from confusing property with contract. A resulting trust is essentially a property concept: any property that a man does not effectually dispose of remains his own. If, then, there is a true resulting trust in respect of an unexpended balance of payments made to some club or association, there will be a resulting trust in respect of that unexpended balance, and the beneficiaries under that trust will be those who made the payments. If any are dead, the trusts will be for their estates; death does not deprive a man of his beneficial interest. Yet in what I may call 'the resulting trust cases', the beneficiaries who were held to be entitled were the members living at the time of the dissolution, to the exclusion of those who died or otherwise ceased to be members. If, then, there were any resulting trust, it must be a trust modified in some way, perhaps by some unexplained implied term, that distinguishes between the quick and the dead. It cannot be merely an ordinary resulting trust.

On the other hand, membership of a club or association is primarily a matter of contract. The members make their payments, and in return they become entitled to the benefits of membership in accordance with the rules. The sums they pay cease to be their individual property, and so cease to be subject to any concept of resulting trust. Instead, they become the property, through the trustees of the club or association, of all the members for the time being, including themselves. A member who, by death or otherwise, ceases to be a member thereby ceases to be the part-owner of any of the club's property: those who remain continue owners. If, then, dissolution ensues, there must be a division of the property of the club or association among those alone who are owners of that property, to the exclusion of former members. In that division, I cannot see what relevance there can be in the respective amounts of the contributions. The newest member, who has made a single payment when he joined only a year ago, is as much a part-owner of the property of the club or association as a member who has been making payments for 50 years. Each has had what he has paid for: the newest member has had the benefits of membership for a year or so and the oldest member for 50 years. Why should the latter, who for his money has had the benefits of membership for 50 times as long as the former, get the further benefit of receiving 50 times as much in the winding-up?

I have, of course, been speaking in the broadest of outlines; but I must say that the view taken on principle by O'Connor MR in *Tierney v Tough* [1914] 1 IR 142 and by Ungoed-Thomas J in *Re St Andrew's Allotment Association* [1969] 1 WLR 229 seem to me to be preferable to the other view, despite certain difficulties in the basis of distinction between the club cases and the others tentatively suggested by Ungoed-Thomas J in the passage that I have read: at 238. Accordingly, I reject the basis of proportionate division in favour of equality, or division per capita. But then the second question arises, namely, whether the principle of equality prevails not only when there is no more than one class of members but when there are two or more classes. Is the proposed division into shares and half-shares sound, or ought it to be rejected in favour of equality throughout?

On the footing that the rules of a club or association form the basis of the contract between all the members, I must look at the rules of the society to see whether they indicate any basis other than that of equality. It seems to me that they do. Those aged from 5 to 12 years old pay contributions at half the rate (rule 9), and correspondingly their allowances (rule 12) and death benefit (rule 14) are also paid at half the rate. Where the rules have written into them the basis of inequality among different classes of members in relation to the principal contractual burdens and benefits of membership, it seems to me to follow that this inequality ought also to be applied to the surplus property of the society. A distinction between classes of members is quite different from a distinction between individual members of the same class based on the amounts contributed by each member. At any given moment one can say that the rights and liabilities of all the members of one class differ in the same way from the rights and liabilities of all the members of the other class, irrespective of the length of membership or anything else. It was indeed suggested that the words 'two classes of subscribers' in rule 9 did not mean that there were two classes of members, the word 'subscribers' being in contrast with the word 'member' used in the next sentence. But the rules are too ill-drafted for any such inferences to be drawn; and rule 5, providing for special meetings of the committee when requested by three 'subscribers', and a general meeting if required by twenty of the 'members', strongly suggests that the terms are used interchangeably. At any rate, I have heard no sensible explanations of the distinction...

His Lordship then rejected the claims of the ex-members.

D   THE *QUISTCLOSE* TRUST[54]

In some circumstances where, typically, money has been lent to a borrower for a particular purpose, the borrower will hold that money on trust for the payer. This enables the lender to convert what would otherwise be a debt into a trust, thereby avoiding the consequence of being an unsecured creditor if the borrower becomes insolvent. This trust has become known as the *Quistclose* trust, after the name of the case in which the House of Lords first recognised it.[55]

The essence of the *Quistclose* trust has been identified by LORD MILLETT in **Twinsectra Ltd v Yardley** [2002] UKHL 12, [2002] 2 AC 164:

68.   Money advanced by way of loan normally becomes the property of the borrower. He is free to apply the money as he chooses, and save to the extent to which he may have taken security for repayment the lender takes the risk of the borrower's insolvency. But it is well established that a loan to a borrower for a specific purpose where the borrower is not free to apply the money for any other purpose gives rise to fiduciary obligations on the part of the

---

[54] H&M, pp. 51–55; Lewin, pp. 267–279; P&M, pp. 291–300; P&S, pp. 556–561; Pettit, pp. 169–170; Snell, pp. 583–585; T&H, pp. 292–304, 812–814, 1542–1550; U&H, pp. 422–424; *The Quistclose Trust* (ed. W Swadling) (2004); [2004] Conv 418 (G. Watt).

[55] *Barclays Bank Ltd v Quistclose Investments Ltd* [1970] AC 567. See p. 239, below. For the background to this case see *The Quistclose Trust* (ed. W Swadling) (2004), Ch 1 (R. Stevens).

borrower which a court of equity will enforce. In the earlier cases the purpose was to enable the borrower to pay his creditors or some of them, but the principle is not limited to such cases.

69.   Such arrangements are commonly described as creating 'a Quistclose trust', after the well-known decision of the House in *Quistclose Investment Ltd v Rolls Razor Ltd* [1970] AC 567, below, in which Lord Wilberforce confirmed the validity of such arrangements and explained their legal consequences. When the money is advanced, the lender acquires a right, enforceable in equity, to see that it is applied for the stated purpose, or more accurately to prevent its application for any other purpose. This prevents the borrower from obtaining any beneficial interest in the money, at least while the designated purpose is still capable of being carried out. Once the purpose has been carried out, the lender has his normal remedy in debt. If for any reason the purpose cannot be carried out, the question arises whether the money falls within the general fund of the borrower's assets, in which case it passes to his trustee-in-bankruptcy in the event of his insolvency and the lender is merely a loan creditor; or whether it is held on a resulting trust for the lender. This depends on the intention of the parties collected from the terms of the arrangement and the circumstances of the case.

76.   . . . It is unconscionable for a man to obtain money on terms as to its application and then disregard the terms on which he received it. Such conduct goes beyond a mere breach of contract. As North J explained in *Gilbert v Gonard* (1884) 54 LJ Ch 439 at 440:

> 'It is very well known law that if one person makes a payment to another for a certain purpose, and that person takes the money knowing that it is for that purpose, he must apply it to the purpose for which it was given. He may decline to take it if he likes; but if he chooses to accept the money tendered for a particular purpose, it is his duty, and there is a legal obligation on him, to apply it for that purpose.'

The duty is not contractual but fiduciary. It may exist despite the absence of any contract at all between the parties, as in *Rose v Rose* (1986) 7 NSWLR 679; and it binds third parties as in the *Quistclose* case itself. The duty is fiduciary in character because a person who makes money available on terms that it is to be used for a particular purpose only and not for any other purpose thereby places his trust and confidence in the recipient to ensure that it is properly applied. This is a classic situation in which a fiduciary relationship arises, and since it arises in respect of a specific fund it gives rise to a trust.

(i) General Principle

Barclays Bank Ltd v Quistclose Investments Ltd
[1970] AC 567 (HL, **Lords Reid, Morris of Borth-y-Gest, Guest, Pearce** and **Wilberforce**)

Rolls Razor Ltd had declared a dividend upon their ordinary shares. They were in serious financial difficulties and were unable to pay the dividend without a loan of £209,719 8s. 6d., which the respondents Quistclose Investments Ltd agreed to make on the condition 'that it is used to pay the forthcoming dividend due on 24 July next'.

The cheque for £209,719 8s. 6d. was paid into a separate account at Barclays Bank Ltd, with whom it was agreed that the account would 'only be used to meet the dividend due on 24 July, 1964'. Before the dividend was paid, Rolls Razor Ltd went into liquidation. The question was whether Barclays Bank Ltd could set that sum against Rolls Razor's overdraft;[56] or whether they held it on trust for Quistclose.

Held. Barclays Bank held the money on trust for Quistclose. The fact that the transaction was a loan did not prevent there being also a trust.

Lord Wilberforce: Two questions arise, both of which must be answered favourably to the respondents if they are to recover the money from the bank. The first is whether as between the respondents and Rolls Razor Ltd the terms upon which the loan was made were such as to impress upon the sum of £209,719 8s. 6d. a trust in their favour in the event of the dividend not being paid. The second is whether, in that event, the bank had such notice of the trust or of the circumstances giving rise to it as to make the trust binding upon them.

It is not difficult to establish precisely upon what terms the money was advanced by the respondents to Rolls Razor Ltd. There is no doubt that the loan was made specifically in order to enable Rolls Razor Ltd to pay the dividend. There is equally, in my opinion, no doubt that the loan was made only so as to enable Rolls Razor Ltd to pay the dividend and for no other purpose. This follows quite clearly from the terms of the letter of Rolls Razor Ltd to the bank of 15 July, 1964, which letter, before transmission to the bank, was sent to the respondents under open cover in order that the cheque might be (as it was) enclosed in it. The mutual intention of the respondents and of Rolls Razor Ltd, and the essence of the bargain, was that the sum advanced should not become part of the assets of Rolls Razor Ltd, but should be used exclusively for payment of a particular class of its creditors, namely, those entitled to the dividend. A necessary consequence from this, by process simply of interpretation, must be that if, for any reason, the dividend could not be paid, the money was to be returned to the respondents: the word 'only' or 'exclusively' can have no other meaning or effect.

That arrangements of this character for the payment of a person's creditors by a third person, give rise to a relationship of a fiduciary character or trust, in favour, as a primary trust, of the creditors, and secondarily, if the primary trust fails, of the third person, has been recognised in a series of cases over some 150 years.

In *Toovey v Milne* (1819) 2 B & Ald 683 part of the money advanced was, on the failure of the purpose for which it was lent (*viz.* to pay certain debts), repaid by the bankrupt to the person who had advanced it. On action being brought by the assignee of the bankrupt to recover it, the plaintiff was nonsuited and the nonsuit was upheld on a motion for a retrial. In his judgment Abbot CJ said, at 684:

'I thought at the trial, and still think, that the fair inference from the facts proved was that this money was advanced for a special purpose, and that being so clothed with a specific trust, no property in it passed to the assignee of the bankrupt. Then the purpose having failed, there is an implied stipulation that the money shall be repaid. That has been done in the present case; and I am of opinion that the repayment was lawful, and that the nonsuit was right.'

The basis for the decision was thus clearly stated, *viz.* that the money advanced for the specific purpose did not become part of the bankrupt's estate. This case has been repeatedly followed and applied: see *Edwards v Glyn* (1859) 2 E & E 29; *Re Rogers, ex p Holland and Hannen* (1891) 8 Morr 243; *Re Drucker* [1902] 2 KB 237; *Re Hooley, ex p Trustee* [1915] HBR 181. *Re Rogers* (1891) 8 Morr 243 was a decision of a strong Court of Appeal. In that case, the money

---

[56] Insolvency Act 1986, s. 323; *Rolls Razor Ltd v Cox* [1967] 1 QB 552; *National Westminster Bank Ltd v Halesowen Presswork and Assemblies Ltd* [1972] AC 785.

provided by the third party had been paid to the creditors before the bankruptcy. Afterwards the trustee in bankruptcy sought to recover it. It was held that the money was advanced to the bankrupt for the special purpose of enabling his creditors to be paid, was impressed with a trust for the purpose and never became the property of the bankrupt. Lindley LJ decided the case on principle but said, at 248, that if authority was needed it would be found in *Toovey v Milne* (1819) 2 B & Ald 683 and other cases. Bowen LJ said at 248 that the money came to the bankrupt's hands impressed with a trust and did not become the property of the bankrupt divisible amongst his creditors, and the judgment of Kay LJ at 249 was to a similar effect.

These cases have the support of longevity, authority, consistency and, I would add, good sense. But they are not binding on your Lordships and it is necessary to consider such arguments as have been put why they should be departed from or distinguished...

The second, and main, argument for the appellant was of a more sophisticated character. The transaction, it was said, between the respondents and Rolls Razor Ltd, was one of loan, giving rise to a legal action of debt. This necessarily excluded the implication of any trust, enforceable in equity, in the respondents' favour: a transaction may attract one action or the other, it could not admit of both.

My Lords, I must say that I find this argument unattractive. Let us see what it involves. It means that the law does not permit an arrangement to be made by which one person agrees to advance money to another, on terms that the money is to be used exclusively to pay debts of the latter, and if, and so far as not so used, rather than becoming a general asset of the latter available to his creditors at large, is to be returned to the lender. The lender is obliged, in such a case, because he is a lender, to accept, whatever the mutual wishes of lender and borrower may be, that the money he was willing to make available for one purpose only shall be freely available for others of the borrower's creditors for whom he has not the slightest desire to provide.

I should be surprised if an argument of this kind—so conceptualist in character—had ever been accepted. In truth it has plainly been rejected by the eminent judges who from 1819 onwards have permitted arrangements of this type to be enforced, and have approved them as being for the benefit of creditors and all concerned. There is surely no difficulty in recognising the co-existence in one transaction of legal and equitable rights and remedies: when the money is advanced, the lender acquires an equitable right to see that it is applied for the primary designated purpose (see *Re Rogers* (1891) 8 Morr 243 where both Lindley LJ and Kay LJ recognised this): when the purpose has been carried out (i.e. the debt paid) the lender has his remedy against the borrower in debt; if the primary purpose cannot be carried out, the question arises if a secondary purpose (i.e. repayment to the lender) has been agreed, expressly or by implication: if it has, the remedies of equity may be invoked to give effect to it, if it has not (and the money is intended to fall within the general fund of the debtor's assets) then there is the appropriate remedy for recovery of a loan. I can appreciate no reason why the flexible interplay of law and equity cannot let in these practical arrangements, and other variations if desired: it would be to the discredit of both systems if they could not. In the present case the intention to create a secondary trust for the benefit of the lender, to arise if the primary trust, to pay the dividend, could not be carried out, is clear and I can find no reason why the law should not give effect to it.

I pass to the second question, that of notice. I can deal with this briefly because I am in agreement with the manner in which it has been disposed of by all three members of the Court of Appeal. I am prepared, for this purpose, to accept, by way of assumption, the position most favourable to the bank, i.e. that it is necessary to show that the bank had notice of the trust or of the circumstances giving rise to the trust, at the time when they received the money, *viz.* on 15 July, 1964, and that notice on a later date, even though they had not in any real sense given value when they received the money or thereafter changed their position, will not do. It is common ground, and I think right, that a mere request to put the money into a separate account is not sufficient to constitute notice. But on 15 July, 1964, the bank, when it received the cheque, also received the covering letter of that date which I have set out above; previously there had been the telephone conversation between Mr. Goldbart and Mr. Parker, to which I have also referred. From these there is no doubt that the bank was told that the money had been provided on loan by a third person and was to be used only for the purpose of paying the dividend. This was sufficient to give them notice that it was trust money and not assets of Rolls Razor Ltd: the fact, if it be so, that they were unaware of the lender's identity (though the respondent's name as drawer was on the cheque) is of no significance. I may add to this, as having some bearing on the merits of the case, that it is quite apparent from earlier documents that the bank were aware that Rolls Razor Ltd could not provide the money for the dividend and that this would have to come from an outside source and that they never contemplated that the money so provided could be used to reduce the existing overdraft. They were in fact insisting that other or additional arrangements should be made for that purpose. As was appropriately said by Russell LJ, [1968] Ch 540 at 563F, it would be giving a complete windfall to the bank if they had established a right to retain the money.

In my opinion, the decision of the Court of Appeal was correct on all points and the appeal should be dismissed.[57]

In **Twinsectra Ltd v Yardley** [2002] UKHL 12, [2002] 2 AC 164[58] the claimant lent money to Yardley for the purchase of property without specifying which property, after Sims, a solicitor, had given a personal undertaking that he would retain the money which had been lent until it was applied for the purchase of the property and that the money would not be used for any other purpose. The money was in fact used to discharge a debt owed by Sims to Yardley. Sims became bankrupt and the claimant wanted to recover the property. The only claim before the House of Lords was whether Leach, another solicitor acting for Yardley, was liable for dishonest assistance in a breach of trust [see p. 990, below]. Liability depended first on identifying that the money was held by Sims on trust. Lord Hoffmann (with whom Lords Slynn of Hadley,

---

[57] (1980) 43 MLR 489 (W. Goodhart and G. Jones); (1992) 12 LS 333 (M. Bridge); *Re Kayford Ltd* [1975] 1 WLR 279 (purchase money retained in separate account by mail-order company held in trust for customers); *Re Chelsea Cloisters Ltd* (1980) 41 P & CR 98 (tenants' damage deposit account moneys held on trust by company landlord in liquidation); *R v Clowes (No 2)* [1994] 2 All ER 316 (investment brochure indicated money would be kept separately, sufficient indication of trust); *Re Lewis's of Leicester* [1995] 1 BCLC 428; *Templeton Insurance Ltd v Penningtons Solicitors* [2006] EWHC 685 (Ch), [2007] WTLR 1103 (no need for the parties to have agreed that money would be applied for a sole or exclusive purpose); cf. *Re Multi Guarantee Co Ltd* [1987] BCLC 257 (no trust of insurance premium moneys transferred to solicitors' joint deposit account); *Re Farepak Food and Gifts Ltd* [2006] EWHC 3272 (Ch) (no trust where money paid to a savings organisation). See also (1988) 85 LS Gaz 14 (I.M. Hardcastle); *Aluminium Industrie Vaassen BV v Romalpa Aluminium Ltd* [1976] 1 WLR 676; (1976) 92 LQR 360, 528 (R.M. Goode); *Swiss Bank Corpn v Lloyds Bank Ltd* [1982] AC 584; (1980) 96 LQR 483 (proceeds of sale of foreign securities kept in separate account); cf. *Mac-Jordan Construction Ltd v Brookmount Erostin Ltd* [1992] BCLC 350. See also *Hussey v Palmer* [1972] 1 WLR 1286; *Re Sharpe* [1980] 1 WLR 219; *Rowlandson v National Westminster Bank Ltd* [1978] 1 WLR 798; *Borden (UK) Ltd v Scottish Timber Products Ltd* [1981] Ch 25, cf. *Potters v Loppert* [1973] Ch 399 (estate agent held entitled to retain interest earned by deposit held as stakeholder). See now Estate Agents Act 1979, s. 13.

[58] (2003) LQR 8 (T.M. Yeo and H. Tjio); (2002) CLJ 52 (R. Thornton); [2002] Conv 386 (J. Ross); [2002] All ER Rev 231 (P.J. Clarke).

Steyn and Hutton agreed) held, at 806, that a trust arose simply because the money was paid into a solicitor's client account. LORD MILLETT (with whom Lord Hutton also agreed) held that the money was held on a *Quistclose* trust. He said:

73.   A *Quistclose* trust does not necessarily arise merely because money is paid for a particular purpose. A lender will often inquire into the purpose for which a loan is sought in order to decide whether he would be justified in making it. He may be said to lend the money for the purpose in question, but this is not enough to create a trust; once lent the money is at the free disposal of the borrower. Similarly payments in advance for goods or services are paid for a particular purpose, but such payments do not ordinarily create a trust. The money is intended to be at the free disposal of the supplier and may be used as part of his cash-flow. Commercial life would be impossible if this were not the case.

74.   The question in every case is whether the parties intended the money to be at the free disposal of the recipient: *Re Goldcorp Exchange Ltd* [1995] 1 AC 74, 100, *per* Lord Mustill. His freedom to dispose of the money is necessarily excluded by an arrangement that the money shall be used *exclusively* for the stated purpose, for as Lord Wilberforce observed in the *Quistclose* case [1970] AC 567, 580:

> 'a necessary consequence from this, by a process simply of interpretation, must be that if, for any reason, [the purpose could not be carried out,] the money was to be returned to [the lender]: the word "only" or "exclusively" can have no other meaning or effect.'

[His Lordship considered the facts of the *Quistclose* case and continued:]

75.   In the present case paragraphs 1 and 2 of the undertaking are crystal clear. Mr. Sims undertook that the money would be used *solely* for the acquisition of property *and for no other purpose;* and was to be retained by his firm until so applied. It would not be held by Mr. Sims simply to Mr. Yardley's order; and it would not be at Mr. Yardley's free disposition. Any payment by Mr. Sims of the money, whether to Mr. Yardley or anyone else, otherwise than for the acquisition of property would constitute a breach of trust...

103.   In my opinion the Court of Appeal were correct to find that the terms of paragraphs 1 and 2 of the undertaking created a *Quistclose* trust. The money was never at Mr. Yardley's free disposal. It was never held to his order by Mr. Sims. The money belonged throughout to Twinsectra, subject only to Mr. Yardley's right to apply it for the acquisition of property. Twinsectra parted with the money to Mr. Sims, relying on him to ensure that the money was properly applied or returned to it.[59]

(ii) Antecedent Debt

In **Carreras Rothmans Ltd v Freeman Mathews Treasure Ltd** [1985] Ch 207 the plaintiff (CR) manufactured cigarettes and tobacco. This was advertised widely in the press by the defendants (FMT), who managed the advertising, and contracted as principals with production agencies and advertising media, thereby incurring substantial liabilities to media creditors (X). FMT paid the accounts, having been put in funds by CR. FMT was in financial difficulties, and CR became concerned that FMT might

---

[59] See also *Box v Barclays Bank* [1998] Lloyd's Rep Bank 185, 193 (*Quistclose* principle potentially applicable where money deposited for investing on the money market).

fail, leaving the debts to X unpaid. CR foresaw that X would have sufficient power to compel it to meet FMT's liabilities to X, even though CR was not legally responsible for them. As a result CR would have to pay the same sum twice, once to FMT and once to X. Accordingly in July 1983, CR agreed with FMT that a special bank account should be established in FMT's name, to be used 'only for the purposes of meeting the accounts of the media and production fees of third parties directly attributable to CR's involvement with the agency'. The bank was aware of this agreement.

FMT went into liquidation in August, at a time when there was a substantial sum in the special account which had not yet been paid over to X. As foreseen, X called upon CR to meet FMT's liabilities in full, threatening to interrupt CR's new advertising campaign if it did not pay. CR thereupon paid X's debts and took assignments from X of their rights against FMT.

CR sought a declaration that the moneys in the special bank account were held on trust for the sole purpose of paying X and for them to be repaid to CR. In holding that there was such a valid trust. PETER GIBSON J said at 220:

Mr. Millett and Mr. Higham for the plaintiff contended that the language of the contract letter was apt to create a trust and that such trust was fully constituted as to the moneys in the special account when the defendant agreed to the terms of the contract letter and received the moneys from the plaintiff. They relied on the line of cases of which *Barclays Bank Ltd v Quistclose Investments Ltd* [1970] AC 567 [p. 239, above], is the highest authority. Mr. Potts denied that any enforceable trust was created. He submitted that the language of the contract letter was apt to create obligations of a contractual nature only in relation to the moneys to be paid into the special account, that the *Quistclose* line of cases was distinguishable ...

The July agreement was plainly intended to vary the contractual position of the parties as to how, as the contract letter put it, payments made by the plaintiff to the defendant for purely onwards transmission, in effect, to the third party creditors, would be dealt with. If one looks objectively at the genesis of the variation, the plaintiff was concerned about the adverse effect on it if the defendant, which the plaintiff knew to have financial problems, ceased trading and the third party creditors of the defendant were not paid at a time when the defendant had been put in funds by the plaintiff. The objective was accurately described by Mr. Higgs in his informal letter of 19 July as to protect the interests of the plaintiff and the third parties. For this purpose a special account was to be set up with a special designation. The moneys payable by the plaintiff were to be paid not to the defendant beneficially but directly into that account so that the defendant was never free to deal as it pleased with the moneys so paid. The moneys were to be used only for the specific purpose of paying the third parties and as the cheque letter indicated, the amount paid matched the specific invoices presented by the defendant to the plaintiff. The account was intended to be little more than a conduit pipe, but the intention was plain that whilst in the conduit pipe the moneys should be protected. There was even a provision covering the possibility (though what actual situation it was intended to meet it is hard to conceive) that there might be a balance left after payment and in that event the balance was to be paid to the plaintiff and not kept by the defendant. It was thus clearly intended that the moneys once paid would never become the property of the defendant. That was the last thing the plaintiff wanted in view of its concern about the defendant's financial position. As a further precaution the bank was to be put on notice of the conditions and purpose of the account. I infer that this was to prevent the bank attempting to exercise any rights of set off against the moneys in the account.

Only two matters were relied on as indicating that no trust was intended. One was the consideration fee; but the presence of consideration does not negative a trust. The other was the express reference in the penultimate paragraph in relation to placements and forward media options with which was contrasted the absence of the word 'trust' in relation to the moneys in the account. But I regard that as of minimal significance when I consider all the other indications as to the capacity in which the defendant was to hold any moneys in the account. In my judgment even in the absence of authority it is manifest that the defendant was intended to act in relation to those moneys in a fiduciary capacity only...

There is of course ample authority that moneys paid by A to B for a specific purpose which has been made known to B are clothed with a trust. In the *Quistclose* case [1970] AC 567 at 580, Lord Wilberforce referred to the recognition, in a series of cases over some 150 years, that arrangements for the payment of a person's creditors by a third person gives rise to

'a relationship of a fiduciary character or trust, in favour, as a primary trust, of the creditors, and secondarily, if the primary trust fails, of the third person...'

Lord Wilberforce in describing the facts of the *Quistclose* case said a little earlier on at 580, that the mutual intention of the provider of the moneys and of the recipient of the moneys and the essence of the bargain was that the moneys should not become part of the assets of the recipient but should be used exclusively for payment of a particular class of its creditors. That description seems to me to be apt in relation to the facts of the present case too...

It is of course true that there are factual differences between the *Quistclose* case and the present case. The transaction there was one of loan with no contractual obligation on the part of the lender to make payment prior to the agreement for the loan. In the present case there is no loan but there is an antecedent debt owed by the plaintiff. I doubt if it is helpful to analyse the *Quistclose* type of case in terms of the constituent parts of a conventional settlement, though it may of course be crucial to ascertain in whose favour the secondary trust operates (as in the *Quistclose* case itself) and who has an enforceable right. In my judgment the principle in all these cases is that equity fastens on the conscience of the person who receives from another property transferred for a specific purpose only and not therefore for the recipient's own purposes, so that such person will not be permitted to treat the property as his own or to use it for other than the stated purpose. Most of the cases in this line are cases where there has been an agreement for consideration so that in one sense each party has contributed to providing the property. But if the common intention is that property is transferred for a specific purpose and not so as to become the property of the transferee, the transferee cannot keep the property if for any reason that purpose cannot be fulfilled. I am left in no doubt that the provider of the moneys in the present case was the plaintiff. True it is that its own witnesses said that if the defendant had not agreed to the terms of the contract letter, the plaintiff would not have broken its contract but would have paid its debt to the defendant, but the fact remains that the plaintiff made its payment on the terms of that letter and the defendant received the moneys only for the stipulated purpose. That purpose was expressed to relate only to the moneys in the account. In my judgment therefore the plaintiff can be equated with the lender in *Quistclose* as having an enforceable right to compel the carrying out of the primary trust.[60]

---

[60] Claims based on economic duress and fraudulent preference (see now Insolvency Act 1986, s. 239) were abandoned during the trial. (1985) 101 LQR 269 (P.J. Millett); [1985] All ER Rev 316 (P.J. Clarke); (1991) 107 LQR 608 (C. Rickett).

(iii) Loan Paid but Purpose Not Achieved

In **Re EVTR** [1987] BCLC 646, the company was in financial difficulties. The appellant (Barber), 'who had just won a very substantial prize on Premium Bonds', agreed to assist it in purchasing from Quantel Ltd some new equipment (the Encore System) to enable it to carry on business. To this end Barber deposited £60,000 with EVTR's solicitors (Knapp-Fisher's). EVTR also entered into a contract with Concord Leasing Company, whereby that company agreed to take over EVTR's obligations under the purchase agreement, to buy the Encore System itself, and to lease it to EVTR. Barber then authorised Knapp-Fisher's to release the £60,000 'for the sole purpose of buying new equipment'; £21,000 was paid to Contract Leasing Company, and £39,000 to Quantel Ltd. Before the Encore System was due for delivery, receivers were appointed in respect of EVTR, which then ceased trading. Since the equipment could no longer be delivered, the £60,000, less agreed deductions, was transferred to the receivers. The trial judge held that these moneys were part of the general assets of EVTR and were not impressed with a trust in favour of Barber.

In reversing the trial judge. DILLON LJ said, at 649:

In the forefront of the appellant's case counsel for the appellant (Mr. Jackson) refers to the decision of the House of Lords in *Barclays Bank Ltd v Quistclose Investments Ltd* [1970] AC 567 [p. 239, above]. There, Quistclose had lent money to a company (Rolls Razor Ltd.) on an agreed condition that the money be used only for the purpose of paying a particular dividend which the company had declared. In the event the company went into liquidation, after receiving Quistclose's money, but without having paid the dividend. It was held that Quistclose could claim the whole of the money back, as on a resulting trust, the specific purpose having failed, and Quistclose was not limited to proving as an unsecured creditor in the liquidation of the company.

In the present case the £60,000 was released by Knapp-Fisher's to the company on the appellant's instructions for a specific purpose only, namely the sole purpose of buying new equipment. Accordingly, I have no doubt, in the light of *Quistclose,* that, if the company had gone into liquidation, or the receivers had been appointed, and the scheme had become abortive before the £60,000 had been disbursed by the company, the appellant would have been entitled to recover his full £60,000, as between himself and the company, on the footing that it was impliedly held by the company on a resulting trust for him as the particular purpose of the loan had failed.

At the other end of the spectrum, if after the £60,000 had been expended by the company as it was, the Encore System had been duly delivered to, and accepted by, the company, there could be no doubt that the appellant's only right would have been as an unsecured creditor of the company for the £60,000. There would have been no question of the Encore System, or any interest in it, being held on any sort of trust for the appellant, and if, after it had been delivered and installed, the company had sold the system, the appellant could have had no claim whatsoever to the proceeds of sale as trust moneys held in trust for him.

The present case lies on its facts between those two extremes of the spectrum. Other scenarios between the extremes could equally be written, e.g. if, after the £60,000 had been paid by the company, Quantel had been injuncted by a third party from supplying the Encore System on the ground that the Encore System infringed patent rights or copyright of the third party and

Quantel had thereupon refunded the £60,000, or if the Encore system was supplied but proved totally useless for its purpose and was therefore rejected and the money was returned...

On *Quistclose* principles, a resulting trust in favour of the provider of the money arises when money is provided for a particular purpose only, and that purpose fails. In the present case, the purpose for which the £60,000 was provided by the appellant to the company was, as appears from the authority to Knapp-Fisher's, the purpose of [the company] buying new equipment. But in any realistic sense of the words that purpose has failed in that the company has never acquired any new equipment, whether the Encore System which was then in mind or anything else. True it is that the £60,000 was paid out by the company with a view to the acquisition of new equipment, but that was only at half-time, and I do not see why the final whistle should be blown at half-time. The proposed acquisition proved abortive and a large part of the £60,000 has therefore been repaid by the payees. The repayments were made because of, or on account of, the payments which made up the £60,000 and those were payments of trust moneys. It is a long-established principle of equity that, if a person who is a trustee receives money or property because of, or in respect of, trust property, he will hold what he receives as a constructive trustee on the trusts of the original trust property. An early application of this principle is the well-known case of *Keech v Sandford* (1726) Sel Cas Ch 61 [p. 791, below], but the instances in the books are legion. See also *Chelsea Estates Investment Trust Co Ltd v Marche* [1955] Ch 328 where somewhat similar reasoning applied to a mortgagee. It follows, in my judgment, that the repayments made to the receivers are subject to the same trusts as the original £60,000 in the hands of the company. There is now, of course, no question of the £48,536[61] being applied in the purchase of new equipment for the company, and accordingly, in my judgment, it is now held on a resulting trust for the appellant.

BINGHAM LJ said at 652:

It would, I think, strike most people as very hard if the appellant were in this situation to be confined to a claim as an unsecured creditor of the company. While it is literally true that the fund which he provided was applied to the stipulated purpose, the object of the payment was not achieved and that was why the balance was repaid to the respondents. My doubt has been whether the law as it stands enables effect to be given to what I can see as the common fairness of the situation. Our attention has not, I think, been drawn to any case closely analogous to the present. But the company certainly held the fund on trust in the first instance. The purpose for which the fund was paid out partially failed. The repayment to the respondents was a direct result of the company's original holding of the fund as trustee. The balance which was recovered may reasonably be regarded as not having been paid out at all. I am happy to be persuaded that the sums repaid are to be treated as held on the same trusts as the original £60,000 and, in present circumstances, on a resulting trust for the appellant.

I accordingly agree that the appeal should be allowed. I have had the advantage of reading in draft the judgment of Dillon LJ, and am in full agreement with both his reasoning and his conclusion.

In **Box v Barclays Bank** [1998] Lloyd's Rep Bank 185,[62] the plaintiffs had placed money with a company which was running a deposit-taking business. One of the company's

---

[61] £60,000 less agreed deductions.

[62] (1999) 14 *Banking and Finance Law Review* 613 (L. Smith); (1999) *Company Financial and Insolvency Law Review* 119 (G. Virgo).

directors had said that the money would be invested on the plaintiff's behalf with the defendant bank on the money market. However, the company deposited the money with the defendant bank in an account which was overdrawn. The company became insolvent and the plaintiffs sought restitution from the defendant on the basis that the money was held on an express *Quistclose* trust.

FERRIS J was prepared to consider whether a *Quistclose* trust could be identified on the facts even though it was clear that the purpose for which the money had been transferred, namely investment in a bank on the money market, could still be ful-filled.[63] The claim ultimately failed, however, because it could not be established that there was a common intention that the money would be held by the company on trust for the plaintiffs.

(iv) *Theoretical Analysis of the 'Quistclose Trust'*

Although the existence of the *Quistclose* trust is now well established, the ambit of this trust device remains unclear and whether this trust is properly characterised as an express trust, either for persons or purposes, or even whether it is a trust at all, have been matters of some controversy. It is possible to identify four distinct ways of characterising it.[64]

(a) Express trust for a non-charitable purpose

The orthodox analysis of the *Quistclose* trust is that it is an express trust which is created for a non-charitable purpose.[65] This analysis was adopted by Lord Wilberforce in *Quistclose* itself.[66] Once this primary trust fails it will be replaced by a secondary resulting trust for the lender. The problem with this analysis is that, since the trust is for purposes rather than persons, there is no beneficiary who can enforce the trust.[67] So where is the beneficial interest? It has been suggested that the beneficial interest is in suspense,[68] but this is not a satisfactory conclusion.

(b) Express trust for persons

To avoid the conclusion that the beneficial interest is in suspense, it might be prefer-able to characterise the *Quistclose* trust as a trust for persons, namely the lender, rather than a trust for purposes.[69] Throughout, the beneficial interest will be in the lender

---

[63] See also *Twinsectra Ltd v Yardley* [2002] UKHL 12, [2002] 2 AC 164 [p. 238, above], where the purpose for which the money had been lent, purchase of property, could still be satisfied.

[64] These are well summarised by J. Payne in '*Quistclose* and Resulting Trusts' in *Restitution and Equity: Resulting Trusts and Equitable Compensation* (2000) (ed. P. Birks and F. Rose), pp. 85–95.

[65] It is, therefore, an exception to the general rule that a non-charitable purpose trust is void since it infringes the rule that there must be a beneficiary to enforce the trust. See Chapter 9.

[66] [1970] AC 567 at 580 [p. 240, above].   [67] See Payne, note 64 above, pp. 85–88.

[68] *Carreras Rothman v Freeman Mathews Treasure* [1985] Ch 207, 223.

[69] (1986) 101 LQR 269 (P. Millett); *The Quistclose Trust* (ed. W Swadling, 2004), 'Lord Millett's Analysis' (J. Penner), pp. 41–66.

so that, where the purpose for which the money has been lent fails, there is no role for a resulting trust; the property will remain subject to the initial express trust.[70] This analysis of the *Quistclose* trust appears to have been adopted by Ferris J in *Box v Barclays Bank*.[71] But if·it is an express trust for the lender then this does not fit with the orthodox analysis of express trusts.

Payne: *Restitution and Equity, Volume 1: Resulting Trusts and Equitable Compensation* (2000) (ed. P. Birks and F. Rose), p. 89

[If] the lender takes a full beneficial interest in the trust property from the start then Quistclose ought to be able to wield all of the rights normally attached to full beneficial ownership (held by a person of full age and sound mind and so on) such as the right to compel Rolls Razor to use the money for the payment of the dividend, or to revoke the loan and require immediate repayment of the money, to prevent the payment of the dividend by Rolls Razor to the shareholders while the purpose remains capable of fulfilment, or to require the borrower to use the money for some other purpose. Quistclose does not seem to have had these rights.

(c) Contractual obligation

Chambers has suggested that, where money is lent for a specific purpose, there is no trust: the lender only has a contractual right, specifically enforceable in equity, to prevent the misapplication of the money.[72] According to this theory the borrower obtains the entire beneficial ownership of the money. If, however, the purpose for which the money was lent fails, the money is then held on resulting trust for the lender. This theory has been criticised as well.[73] primarily on the ground that it is inconsistent with many of the decided cases.

(d) *Sui generis* trust

As a result of the weaknesses of the other three theories it has been suggested that the only conclusion is that the *Quistclose* trust is a unique form of trust.[74]

(e) Resulting trust

An important analysis of the theoretical basis of the *Quistclose* trust, specifically concerning the location of the equitable interest while the purpose is capable of being carried out, has been provided by LORD MILLETT in **Twinsectra Ltd v Yardley** [2002] UKHL 12, [2002] 2 AC 164 [see p. 242, above]. Having referred to dicta of Lord

---

[70] Payne, note 64 above, p. 88.

[71] [1998] Lloyd's Rep Bank 185.

[72] Chambers, *Resulting Trusts* (1997), chap. 3. Some support for this theory can be found in the judgment of Potter LJ in *Twinsectra Ltd v Yardley* [1999] Lloyd's Rep Bank 438 at 456.

[73] (2001) OJLS 267 (L. Ho and P. St. J. Smart). See also Payne, in *Restitution and Equity: Resulting Trusts and Equitable Compensation* (ed. P. Birks and F. Rose), p. 95.

[74] *Restitution and Equity: Resulting Trusts and Equitable Compensation* (J. Payne) (ed. P. Birks and F. Rose), pp. 89–91. See also (1996) LS 110, 122 (W. Swadling).

Wilberforce in *Barclays Bank Ltd v Quistclose Investments Ltd* [1970] AC 567 [see p. 240, above], he said at 824:

79.   These passages suggest that there are two successive trusts, a primary trust for payment to identifiable beneficiaries, such as creditors or shareholders, and a secondary trust in favour of the lender arising on the failure of the primary trust. But there are formidable difficulties in this analysis, which has little academic support. What if the primary trust is not for identifiable persons, but as in the present case to carry out an abstract purpose? Where in such a case is the beneficial interest pending the application of the money for the stated purpose or the failure of the purpose? There are four possibilities: (i) in the lender; (ii) in the borrower; (iii) in the contemplated beneficiary; or (iv) in suspense.

80.   (i). *The lender.*

In 'The *Quistclose* Trust: Who Can Enforce It?' (1985) 101 LQR 269, I argued that the beneficial interest remained throughout in the lender. This analysis has received considerable though not universal academic support: see for example Priestley J 'The *Romalpa* Clause and the *Quistclose* Trust' in *Equity and Commercial Transactions,* ed. Finn (1987) 217, 237; and Professor M Bridge 'The *Quistclose* Trust in a World of Secured Transactions' (1992) 12 OJLS 333, 352; and others. It was adopted by the New Zealand Court of Appeal in *General Communications Ltd v Development Finance Corporation of New Zealand Ltd* [1990] 3 NZLR 406 and referred to with apparent approval by Gummow J in *Re Australian Elizabethan Theatre Trust* (1991) 102 ALR 681. Gummow J saw nothing special in the *Quistclose* trust, regarding it as essentially a security device to protect the lender against other creditors of the borrower pending the application of the money for the stated purpose.

81.   On this analysis, the *Quistclose* trust is a simple commercial arrangement akin (as Professor Bridge observes) to a retention of title clause (though with a different object) which enables the borrower to have recourse to the lender's money for a particular purpose without entrenching on the lender's property rights more than necessary to enable the purpose to be achieved. The money remains the property of the lender unless and until it is applied in accordance with his directions, and insofar as it is not so applied it must be returned to him. I am disposed, perhaps pre-disposed, to think that this is the only analysis which is consistent both with orthodox trust law and with commercial reality. Before reaching a concluded view that it should be adopted, however, I must consider the alternatives.

82.   (ii). *The borrower.*

It is plain that the beneficial interest is not vested unconditionally in the borrower so as to leave the money at his free disposal. That would defeat the whole purpose of the arrangements, which is to prevent the money from passing to the borrower's trustee-in-bankruptcy in the event of his insolvency. It would also be inconsistent with all the decided cases where the contest was between the lender and the borrower's trustee-in-bankruptcy, as well as with the *Quistclose* case itself: see in particular *Toovey v Milne* (1819) 2 B & Ald 683; *Re Rogers* (1891) 8 Morr 243.

83.   The borrower's interest pending the application of the money for the stated purpose or its return to the lender is minimal. He must keep the money separate; he cannot apply it except for the stated purpose; unless the terms of the loan otherwise provide he must return it to the lender if demanded; he cannot refuse to return it if the stated purpose cannot be achieved; and if he becomes bankrupt it does not vest in his trustee in bankruptcy. If there is any content to beneficial ownership at all, the lender is the beneficial owner and the borrower is not...

85.   (iii). *In the contemplated beneficiary.*

In the *Quistclose* case itself [1970] AC 567, as in all the reported cases which preceded it, either the primary purpose had been carried out and the contest was between the borrower's trustee-in-bankruptcy or liquidator and the person or persons to whom the borrower had paid the money; or it was treated as having failed, and the contest was between the borrower's trustee-in-bankruptcy and the lender. It was not necessary to explore the position while the primary purpose was still capable of being carried out and Lord Wilberforce's observations must be read in that light.

86.   The question whether the primary trust is accurately described as a trust for the creditors first arose in *Re Northern Developments Holdings Ltd* (unreported) 6 October 1978, where the contest was between the lender and the creditors. The borrower, which was not in liquidation and made no claim to the money, was the parent company of a group one of whose subsidiaries was in financial difficulty. There was a danger that if it were wound up or ceased trading it would bring down the whole group. A consortium of the group's banks agreed to put up a fund of more than £500,000 in an attempt to rescue the subsidiary. They paid the money into a special account in the name of the parent company for the express purpose of 'providing money for the subsidiary's unsecured creditors over the ensuing weeks' and for no other purpose. The banks' object was to enable the subsidiary to continue trading, though on a reduced scale; it failed when the subsidiary was put into receivership at a time when some £350,000 remained unexpended. Relying on Lord Wilberforce's observations in the passages cited above, Sir Robert Megarry V-C held that the primary trust was a purpose trust enforceable (*inter alios*) by the subsidiaries' creditors as the persons for whose benefit the trust was created.

87.   There are several difficulties with this analysis. In the first place, Lord Wilberforce's reference to *Re Rogers* (1891) 8 Morr 243 makes it plain that the equitable right he had in mind was not a mandatory order to compel performance, but a negative injunction to restrain improper application of the money; for neither Lindley LJ nor Kay LJ recognised more than this. In the second place, the object of the arrangements was to enable the subsidiary to continue trading, and this would necessarily involve it in incurring further liabilities to trade creditors. Accordingly the application of the fund was not confined to existing creditors at the date when the fund was established. The company secretary was given to understand that the purpose of the arrangements was to keep the subsidiary trading, and that the fund was 'as good as share capital'. Thus the purpose of the arrangements was not, as in other cases, to enable the debtor to avoid bankruptcy by paying off existing creditors, but to enable the debtor to continue trading by providing it with working capital with which to incur fresh liabilities. There is a powerful argument for saying that the result of the arrangements was to vest a beneficial interest in the subsidiary from the start. If so, then this was not a *Quistclose* trust at all.

88.   In the third place, it seems unlikely that the banks' object was to benefit the creditors (who included the Inland Revenue) except indirectly. The banks had their own commercial interests to protect by enabling the subsidiary to trade out of its difficulties. If so, then the primary trust cannot be supported as a valid non-charitable purpose trust: see *Re Grant's Will Trusts* [1980] 1 WLR 360 [see p. 392, below] and cf *Re Denley's Trust Deed* [1969] 1 Ch 373 [see p. 375, below].

89.   The most serious objection to this approach is exemplified by the facts of the present case. In several of the cases the primary trust was for an abstract purpose with no one but the lender to enforce performance or restrain misapplication of the money. In *Edwards v Glyn* (1859) 2 E & E the money was advanced to a bank to enable the bank to meet a run. In

Re EVTR [1987] BCLC 646 [p. 246, above], it was advanced 'for the sole purpose of buying new equipment'. In *General Communications Ltd v Development Finance Corporation of New Zealand Ltd* [1990] 3 NZLR 406 the money was paid to the borrower's solicitors for the express purpose of purchasing new equipment. The present case is another example. It is simply not possible to hold money on trust to acquire unspecified property from an unspecified vendor at an unspecified time. There is no reason to make an arbitrary distinction between money paid for an abstract purpose and money paid for a purpose which can be said to benefit an ascertained class of beneficiaries, and the cases rightly draw no such distinction. Any analysis of the *Quistclose* trust must be able to accommodate gifts and loans for an abstract purpose.

90. (iv). *In suspense.*

As Peter Gibson J pointed out in *Carreras Rothmans Ltd v Freeman Mathews Treasure Ltd* [1985] Ch 207 at 223 [p. 243, above] the effect of adopting Sir Robert Megarry V-C's analysis is to leave the beneficial interest in suspense until the stated purpose is carried out or fails. The difficulty with this (apart from its unorthodoxy) is that it fails to have regard to the role which the resulting trust plays in equity's scheme of things, or to explain why the money is not simply held on a resulting trust for the lender.

91.   Lord Browne-Wilkinson gave an authoritative explanation of the resulting trust in *Westdeutsche Landesbank Girozentrale v Islington Borough Council* [1996] AC 669 at 708 [see p. 198, above] and its basis has been further illuminated by Dr R Chambers in his book *Resulting Trusts* published in 1997. Lord Browne-Wilkinson explained that a resulting trust arises in two sets of circumstances. He described the second as follows:

'Where A transfers property to B *on express trusts,* but the trusts declared do not exhaust the whole beneficial interest.'

The *Quistclose* case [1970] AC 567 was among the cases he cited as examples. He rejected the argument that there was a resulting trust in the case before him because, unlike the situation in the present case, there was no transfer of money on express trusts. But he also rejected the argument on a wider and, in my respectful opinion, surer ground that the money was paid and received with the intention that it should become the absolute property of the recipient.

92.   The central thesis of Dr Chambers' book is that a resulting trust arises whenever there is a transfer of property in circumstances in which the transferor (or more accurately the person at whose expense the property was provided) did not intend to benefit the recipient. It responds to the absence of an intention on the part of the transferor to pass the entire beneficial interest, not to a positive intention to retain it. Insofar as the transfer does not exhaust the entire beneficial interest, the resulting trust is a default trust which fills the gap and leaves no room for any part to be in suspense. An analysis of the *Quistclose* trust as a resulting trust for the transferor with a mandate to the transferee to apply the money for the stated purpose sits comfortably with Dr Chambers' thesis, and it might be thought surprising that he does not adopt it.

93.   (v). *The Court of Appeal's analysis.*

The Court of Appeal were content to treat the beneficial interest as in suspense, or (following Dr Chambers' analysis) to hold that it was in the borrower, the lender having merely a contractual right enforceable by injunction to prevent misapplication. Potter LJ put it in these terms [1999] Lloyd's Rep 438 at 456, para 75:

'The purpose imposed at the time of the advance creates an enforceable restriction on the borrower's use of the money. Although the lender's right to enforce the restriction is treated as arising on the basis of a "trust", the use of that word does not enlarge the lender's interest in the fund. The borrower is entitled to the beneficial use of the money, subject to the lender's right to prevent its misuse; the lender's limited interest in the fund is sufficient to prevent its use for other than the special purpose for which it was advanced.'

This analysis, with respect, is difficult to reconcile with the court's actual decision insofar as it granted Twinsectra a proprietary remedy against Mr. Yardley's companies as recipients of the misapplied funds. Unless the money belonged to Twinsectra immediately before its misapplication, there is no basis on which a proprietary remedy against third party recipients can be justified.

94.   Dr Chambers' 'novel view' (as it has been described) is that the arrangements do not create a trust at all; the borrower receives the entire beneficial ownership in the money subject only to a contractual right in the lender to prevent the money being used otherwise than for the stated purpose. If the purpose fails, a resulting trust in the lender springs into being. In fact, he argues for a kind of restrictive covenant enforceable by negative injunction yet creating property rights in the money. But restrictive covenants, which began life as negative easements, are part of our land law. Contractual obligations do not run with money or a chose in action like money in a bank account.

95   Dr Chambers' analysis has attracted academic comment, both favourable and unfavourable. For my own part, I do not think that it can survive the criticism levelled against it by Lusina Ho and P St J Smart: 'Reinterpreting the *Quistclose* Trust: a Critique of Chambers' Analysis' (2001) 21 OJLS 267. It provides no solution to cases of non-contractual payment; is inconsistent with Lord Wilberforce's description of the borrower's obligation as fiduciary and not merely contractual; fails to explain the evidential significance of a requirement that the money should be kept in a separate account; cannot easily be reconciled with the availability of proprietary remedies against third parties; and while the existence of a mere equity to prevent misapplication would be sufficient to prevent the money from being available for distribution to the creditors on the borrower's insolvency (because the trustee-in-bankruptcy has no greater rights than his bankrupt) it would not prevail over secured creditors. If the bank in the *Quistclose* case [1970] AC 567 had held a floating charge (as it probably did) and had appointed a receiver, the adoption of Dr Chambers' analysis should have led to a different outcome.

96.   Thus all the alternative solutions have their difficulties. But there are two problems which they fail to solve, but which are easily solved if the beneficial interest remains throughout in the lender. One arises from the fact, well established by the authorities, that the primary trust is enforceable by the lender. But on what basis can he enforce it? He cannot do so as the beneficiary under the secondary trust, for if the primary purpose is fulfilled there is no secondary trust: the pre-condition of his claim is destructive of his standing to make it. He cannot do so as settlor, for a settlor who retains no beneficial interest cannot enforce the trust which he has created.

97.   Dr Chambers insists that the lender has merely a right to prevent the misapplication of the money, and attributes this to his contractual right to specific performance of a condition of the contract of loan. As I have already pointed out, this provides no solution where the arrangement is non-contractual. But Lord Wilberforce clearly based the borrower's obligation on an equitable or fiduciary basis and not a contractual one. He was concerned to justify the co-existence of equity's exclusive jurisdiction with the common law action for debt. Basing equity's intervention on its auxiliary jurisdiction to restrain a breach of contract would not have enabled the lender to succeed against the bank, which was a third party to the contract. There

is only one explanation of the lender's fiduciary right to enforce the primary trust which can be reconciled with basic principle: he can do so because he is the beneficiary.

98.   The other problem is concerned with the basis on which the primary trust is said to have failed in several of the cases, particularly *Toovey v Milne* 2 B & A 683 and the *Quistclose* case itself [1970] AC 567. Given that the money did not belong to the borrower in either case, the borrower's insolvency should not have prevented the money from being paid in the manner contemplated. A man cannot pay some only of his creditors once he has been adjudicated bankrupt, but a third party can. A company cannot pay a dividend once it has gone into liquidation, but there is nothing to stop a third party from paying the disappointed shareholders. The reason why the purpose failed in each case must be because the lender's object in making the money available was to save the borrower from bankruptcy in the one case and collapse in the other. But this in itself is not enough. a trust does not fail merely because the settlor's purpose in creating it has been frustrated: the trust must become illegal or impossible to perform. The settlor's motives must not be confused with the purpose of the trust; the frustration of the former does not by itself cause the failure of the latter. But if the borrower is treated as holding the money on a resulting trust for the lender but with power (or in some cases a duty) to carry out the lender's revocable mandate, and the lender's object in giving the mandate is frustrated, he is entitled to revoke the mandate and demand the return of money which never ceased to be his beneficially...

100.   As Sherlock Holmes reminded Dr Watson, when you have eliminated the impossible, whatever remains, however improbable, must be the truth. I would reject all the alternative analyses, which I find unconvincing for the reasons I have endeavoured to explain, and hold the *Quistclose* trust to be an entirely orthodox example of the kind of default trust known as a resulting trust. The lender pays the money to the borrower by way of loan, but he does not part with the entire beneficial interest in the money, and insofar as he does not it is held on a resulting trust for the lender from the outset. Contrary to the opinion of the Court of Appeal, it is the borrower who has a very limited use of the money, being obliged to apply it for the stated purpose or return it. He has no beneficial interest in the money, which remains throughout in the lender subject only to the borrower's power or duty to apply the money in accordance with the lender's instructions. When the purpose fails, the money is returnable to the lender, not under some new trust in his favour which only comes into being on the failure of the purpose, but because the resulting trust in his favour is no longer subject to any power on the part of the borrower to make use of the money. Whether the borrower is obliged to apply the money for the stated purpose or merely at liberty to do so, and whether the lender can countermand the borrower's mandate while it is still capable of being carried out, must depend on the circumstances of the particular case....

When the trust in favour of the lender arises

102.   Like all resulting trusts, the trust in favour of the lender arises when the lender parts with the money on terms which do not exhaust the beneficial interest. It is not a contingent reversionary or future interest. It does not suddenly come into being like an eighteenth-century use only when the stated purpose fails. It is a default trust which fills the gap when some part of the beneficial interest is undisposed-of and prevents it from being 'in suspense'.[75]

---

[75] See also *Templeton Insurance Ltd v Penningtons Solicitors* [2006] EWHC 685 (Ch), [2007] WTLR 1103.

(f) A Variety of Trusts

The Quistclose Trust (ed. W. Swadling, 2004): Foreword by Lord Millett, p. vii[76]

The so-called *Quistclose* trust probably represents the single most important application of equitable principles in commercial life. It has been well established for some two hundred years, at least in relation to insolvency, though it is now seen to be of more general application. Yet it has resisted attempts by academic lawyers to analyse it in terms of conventional equitable doctrine. Even that modern master of equity Sir Robert Megarry V-C was inclined to think that it was an aberrant creation of common law judges.

It was too much to hope that a single decision of the House of Lords would put an end to controversy. The nature of the trust and the location of the beneficial interest remain elusive and continue to be debated by distinguished academic lawyers. They demand to know whether the *Quistclose* trust is a form of express, implied, constructive or resulting trust. If the mere author of a foreword may venture to intrude in a private dispute (at the risk of exposing himself to derisive comment from all sides), I would say that it may be any of them, depending on the facts of the particular case and the boundaries between these various forms of trust, on which not everyone is agreed.

From a commercial point of view, however, the trust is simply a mechanism by which one person may allow the use of his money by another for a stated purpose without losing his right to the money more than necessary to achieve the purpose. The commercial need for such a mechanism is obvious. The problems which will face the courts are not likely to derive from any difficulty in analysing the nature of the trust, but from the need to distinguish the case where it arises from the ordinary case of the lender who naturally wishes to know why the borrower wants the money.

(g) Rejection of the 'Quistclose Trust'

The Quistclose Trust (ed. W. Swadling, 2004): Orthodoxy (W. Swadling), pp. 38–39

What seems to have worried Lord Wilberforce in *Quistclose* was the thought that Barclays could exercise its right of set-off and thereby evade a *Pari Passu* distribution of the loan monies. This would certainly not have been possible had Rolls Razor opened a special account with a different banker, and the real question, which will not be pursued here, is whether it is correct to say that set-off rights operate in an insolvency in the same way as when all parties are solvent. But in seeking to avoid the application of set-off by the finding of a trust, Lord Wilberforce departed from orthodox principles of trust law. It is impossible to say that the transfer was a transfer on trust because the restriction only referred to how the rights were to be applied, not for whom they were held. And even were we able to say that a trust was intended,

---

[76] See also *The Quistclose Trust* (ed. W Swadling, 2004), 'Restrictions on the Use of Money' (R Chambers), pp. 77–120; (2004) 63 CLJ 632 (J Glister); *Latimer v Commissioner of Inland Revenue* [2004] UKPC 13, [2004] 1 WLR 1466, para 41 (Lord Millett).

grave difficulties arise in identifying the objects of that trust. It could not be the creditors for a number of reasons, the most prominent of which is that it would allow them to be paid twice over. For almost identical reasons, it could not be the lender. Nor could it be the purpose, for the purpose was a private purpose and English law does not countenance trusts for private purposes. And the argument of Chambers, that there need be no primary trust, does not succeed either, because it fails to explain how a personal right to see that the fund is not misapplied can bind a stranger, including the borrower's trustee in bankruptcy, to the contract which creates that right. And given that Lord Wilberforce's secondary trust depends on the validity of the primary trust, the argument that there was a consensual trust of the loan monies in favour of the lender on the failure of the purpose cannot be sustained. For the same reasons, a secondary trust arising by not-consent on the subsequent failure of the primary trust is not arguable either. In short, the House of Lords was wrong in *Quistclose* to find a trust and thereby give priority to the lender. The funds should have been held to be part of Rolls Razor's general assets and treated accordingly.

QUESTIONS

1. How would you have decided *Re Vandervell's Trusts (No 2)* if it had gone on appeal to the House of Lords, and you had been sitting?

2. Re-examine the situations in which the court has found a solution based upon (i) a resulting trust, (ii) a contractual right, (iii) *bona vacantia*. Do you think that the choice was based upon logical analysis, or upon convenience of result, or upon chance?

3. Do you agree with the decisions in *Barclays Bank Ltd v Quistclose Investments Ltd* [1970] AC 567 [p. 239, above]; *Carreras Rothmans Ltd v Freeman Mathews Treasure Ltd* [1985] Ch 207 [p. 243, above]; *Re EVTR* [1987] BCLC 646 [p. 246, above]?

4. If a powerful lender was able to make a loan on the basis of its being for a particular purpose only, what would be the position of other, less powerful, creditors if the borrower subsequently becomes insolvent? See Heydon and Loughlan, *Cases and Materials on Equity and Trusts* (5th edn), p. 454 (suggesting that *Re Kayford Ltd* [1975] 1 WLR 279 and 'the *Quistclose* case provide startling opportunities for well-advised lenders to obtain protection against the prospect of the borrower's insolvency'); *Re EVTR* [1987] BCLC 646 at 652, *per* Bingham LJ [p. 246, above]).

5. Should the *Quistclose* principle be characterised as involving an express trust, a resulting trust, a *sui generis* trust or no trust at all? Does it matter? See J. Payne, p. 93 and C. Harpum, pp. 168–170, in *Restitution and Equity, Volume I: Resulting Trusts and Equitable Compensation* (ed. P. Birks and F. Rose, 2000); *The Quistclose Trust* (ed. W Swadling, 2004).

6. Do you agree with the analysis of Lord Millett in *Twinsectra Ltd v Yardley* [2002] UKHL 12, [2002] 2 AC 164 [p. 249, above]?

III THE PRESUMPTIONS[77]

A PRESUMPTION OF RESULTING TRUST

In **Stack v Dowden** [2007] UKHL 17, [2007] 2 AC 432, para. 60 BARONESS HALE said:

The presumption of resulting trust is not a rule of law. According to Lord Diplock in *Pettit v Pettit* [1970] AC 777, 823H, the equitable presumptions of intention are 'no more than a consensus of judicial opinion disclosed by reported cases as to the most likely inference of fact to be drawn in the absence of any evidence to the contrary'. Equity, being concerned with commercial realities, presumed against gifts and other windfalls (such as survivorship). But even equity was prepared to presume a gift where the recipient was the provider's wife or child. These days, the importance to be attached to who paid for what in a domestic context may be very different from its importance in other contexts or long ago.

(i) Voluntary Conveyances

Where property is transferred for no consideration to a stranger (that is, to a person who is not the wife or child of the transferor) a rebuttable presumption arises that the transferee holds on a resulting trust for the transferor. This presumption used to apply equally to land and personalty, but, as a result of section 60(3) of the Law of Property Act 1925, this is no longer so.

(a) Land

LAW OF PROPERTY ACT 1925

60. Abolition of technicalities in regard to conveyancing and deeds

(3) In a voluntary conveyance a resulting trust for the grantor shall not be implied merely by reason that the property is not expressed to be conveyed for the use or benefit of the grantee.

The effect of section 60(3) is that a voluntary conveyance of land takes effect as expressed, unless there is evidence of a contrary intention; in other words there is no longer a presumption of a resulting trust simply because the conveyance is not expressly made for the benefit of the person who receives the land. If, however, the transferor can establish that the transfer was not intended to be a gift then a resulting trust can still be recognised, regardless of section 60(3).[78]

---

[77] H&M, pp. 256–270; Lewin, pp. 290–309; P&M, pp. 274–290; P&S, pp. 237–264; Pettit, pp. 175–189; Snell, pp. 572–579; T&H, pp. 814–831; U&H, pp. 425–456; Chambers, pp. 11–39.

[78] Cp. W. Swadling in *Restitution and Equity, Vol 1: Resulting Trusts and Equitable Compensation* (ed. P. Birks and F. Rose, 2000), p. 74.

In **Hodgson v Marks** [1971] Ch 892[79] Mrs. Hodgson, a widow aged 83, was the owner of a house. Mr. Evans was her lodger. He gained her trust and affection and supervised the investment of her money. A nephew of Mrs. Hodgson was suspicious of Mr. Evans and tried to persuade her to turn him out. In order to protect Mr. Evans, she transferred the house to him, under an oral agreement that she would continue to be the beneficial owner.[80] Mr. Evans was registered as the absolute owner. He later sold it to Mr. Marks. The question was whether Mrs. Hodgson was entitled to protection against Mr. Marks. The Court of Appeal held that Mr. Evans had not been intended to have the property absolutely and so he held the house upon a resulting trust for Mrs. Evans.[81] She was, therefore, equitable owner of the house and her right to the house constituted an overriding interest under the Land Registration Act 1925, section 70(1)(g). (See Land Registration Act 2002, S.1, para. 2.)

(b) Personalty

In **Re Vinogradoff** [1935] WN 68[82] Mrs. Vinogradoff, in 1926, gratuitously transferred a sum of £800 War Loan into the joint names of herself and of her infant grand-daughter, Laura Jackson. The question was whether the stock was owned, on Mrs. Vinogradoff's death, by her estate or by Laura Jackson.

FARWELL J decided that it was held upon a resulting trust for the estate of Mrs. Vinogradoff. Section 20 of the Law Property Act 1925, under which the appointment of an infant as trustee is void, did not affect the presumption of a resulting trust. 'The stock was not the property of the infant, but formed part of the estate of the testatrix.'

Aroso v Coutts and Co
[2001] 1 WTLR 797[83] (Ch D. **Collins J**)

The defendant bank held investment and cash in a trusts account for the deceased, who was Portuguese. The deceased permitted his children to draw money from the account. After a family row, the deceased removed the power of the children to draw money from the account and transferred the assets to a new account in the names of himself and his nephew, Sr. Champalimaud. The mandate of this new bank account stated that the assets of the account would be held on trust for the benefit of the deceased and his nephew only, and that the survivor would be entitled to all the assets in the account. After their father's death, one of his children brought proceedings against the bank

---

[79] Ibid, pp. 61–75.

[80] This agreement was unenforceable because it had not been made in writing: LPA 1925, s. 53(1)(b). See p. 112, above.

[81] The creation of such a trust does not require writing to be valid: LPA 1925, s. 53(2) [p. 112, above].

[82] See also *Thavorn v Bank of Credit and Commerce International SA* [1985] 1 Lloyd's Rep 259 (resulting trust where aunt opened bank account in name of 15-year-old nephew).

[83] (2001) 31 *Trusts and Estates Law Journal* 9 (R. Walford).

claiming that the presumption of resulting trust applied, so that the property had been held on trust for the deceased.

Held. The terms of the mandate of the new bank account rebutted the presumption of resulting trust, so that the assets in the account belonged to the nephew.

Collins J: The starting point is that where a person transfers property, or directs a trustee for him to transfer property, otherwise than for valuable consideration, and where the presumption of advancement does not apply, it is a question of the intention of the transferor in making the transfer whether the transferee was to take beneficially or on trust, and if on trust, what trusts: *Vandervell v IRC* [1967] 2 AC 291 at 312, *per* Lord Hodson. If, as a matter of construction of the document making or directing the transfer, it is possible to discern the intentions of the transferor, that is an end of the matter and no extraneous evidence is admissible to correct and qualify his intentions so ascertained, but if the document is silent, then a resulting trust arises in favour of the transferor, but this is only a presumption and is easily rebutted. All the relevant facts and circumstances can be considered in order to ascertain the intentions of the transferor with a view to rebutting the presumption. Ibid. See also *Westdeutsche Landesbank Girozentrale v Islington London Borough Council* [1996] AC 669 at 708 . . .

A resulting trust will not arise where the relationship between the transferor and the transferee is such as to raise a presumption that a gift was intended and where the presumption is not rebutted, but in this case the relationship between the deceased and Sr. Champalimaud was not such as to raise a presumption of advancement. In this case Sr. Champalimaud gave no consideration for the transfer to him (and the deceased) of the interests of the deceased in the property standing to the credit of [the original bank account]. The question therefore is whether there is evidence of the intention of the deceased. That question has been considered in a number of cases relating to property, including bank accounts, in joint names, of which the most relevant for the purposes of this case are the decisions of Romer J in *Young v Sealey* [1949] Ch 278, Megarry J in *Re Figgis* [1969] 1 Ch 123 and of the High Court of Australia in *Russell v Scott* (1936) 55 CLR 440.

His Lordship considered *Russell v Scott* (1936) 55 CLR 440; *Marshal v Crutwell* (1875) LR 20 Eq 328; *Re Vinogradoff* [1935] WN 68 [p. 258, above]; *Young v Sealey* [1949] Ch 278; *Re Figgis* [1969] 1 Ch 123, and continued:

The essence of the claimant's case is that the investment account was in joint names purely for convenience. The essence of the bank's case is that the deceased put the account into joint names knowing and intending that Sr. Champalimaud should have a beneficial interest: and that the nature of the interest was such that each of them in theory had the immediate right to sever the beneficial joint tenancy, but that in practice it would not have been necessary because some or all of the assets could be dealt with by either of them in accordance with the mandate.

In my judgment the bank has adduced sufficient evidence to displace the presumption of resulting trust, and has proved that the deceased intended to give Sr. Champalimaud a beneficial interest in the assets in [the new bank account]. First, the terms of the mandate are absolutely clear. The deceased spoke English and was supplied with a translation of the mandate into Portuguese, and the words of the mandate are not capable of being other than an expression of intention that the beneficial interest is to be held jointly, and that the survivor is to take all beneficially. They are at least a representation to the bank that the assets in the account are in their joint beneficial ownership, and are not held on trust for any other person (which would include the deceased solely). Second, I do not think it is right to ignore the terms of the investment agreement which refer to the investments and cash being held for the account holders as beneficial joint tenants. Even if (which is doubtful, since a bank such as Coutts & Co is most unlikely to have operated an investment account without a written agreement from its customers) the bank omitted to obtain the signature of Sr. Champalimaud and it therefore has no contractual force, the deceased was prepared to sign it with this statement. Third, there is the uncontradicted and unchallenged evidence of Mr. Horsley (who speaks Portuguese) that he explained the effect of a joint account and that the deceased understood him, and that he intended to transfer a beneficial interest to Sr. Champalimaud, who would be free to deal with the assets in the account as he wished. Fourth, the surrounding circumstances corroborate that evidence. The discussions about a trust and the transfer to [the new bank account] followed what was rightly described by counsel for the bank as a monumental bust-up between the deceased and his children, and at a time when they were hardly on speaking terms. Fifth, I do not accept the argument for the claimant that the joint account was established for the convenience of the bank. When Mr. Horsley said in his witness statement that the bank 'was not in favour of accounts being held in a sole name as this caused complications on the death of the account holder' he plainly meant that it caused complications for the account holder's estate, which might have to obtain probate in the country of the domicile in order to claim the English account. Sixth, I do not consider that there is any subsequent conduct which is inconsistent with the intention to confer a beneficial interest, and even if there had been, the subsequent conduct of the deceased (except perhaps to the extent it may relate to property acquired after that conduct) is of little or no relevance. . . .

(ii) Purchase-Money Resulting Trusts

Where a purchaser buys property in the name of a third party or joins in the purchase of property with another party but in the name of that other party only, then, subject to the nature of the relationship between the parties, it is presumed that the property is held on resulting trust for the purchaser. This presumption, however, can be rebutted by the other party adducing evidence that the purchase was intended to be a gift.

In **Dyer v Dyer** (1788) 2 Cox Eq Cas 92. Eyre CB explained the principle at 93:

The clear result of all the cases, without a single exception, is, that the trust of a legal estate, whether freehold, copyhold, or leasehold; whether taken in the names of the purchasers and others jointly, or in the name of others without that of the purchaser; whether in one name or several; whether jointly or *successive*, results to the man who advances the purchase-money. This is a general proposition supported by all the cases, and there is nothing to contradict it; and it goes on a strict analogy to the rule of the common law, that where a feoffment is made without consideration, the use results to the feoffor.[84]

---

[84] LPA 1925, s. 60(3) does not apply, as the conveyance is not voluntary.

Fowkes v Pascoe[85]
(1875) 10 Ch App 343 (CA in Ch, **James** and **Mellish LJJ**)

Mrs. Baker made various purchases of 3¼ per cent annuities, amounting in all to £7,000 in the joint names of herself and Mr. Pascoe, who was the son of Mrs. Baker's daughter-in-law. By her will, Mrs. Baker gave her residuary estate to the daughter-in-law for life and after her death to Pascoe and his sister in equal shares. Pascoe claimed to be entitled both to the capital sum and to the dividends due at Mrs. Baker's death, and afterwards received by him.

Held. Pascoe was entitled to the capital, but not to the dividends.

Mellish LJ: Now, the presumption must, beyond all question, be of very different weight in different cases. In some cases it would be very strong indeed. If, for instance, a man invested a sum of stock in the name of himself and his solicitor, the inference would be very strong indeed that it was intended solely for the purpose of trust, and the Court would require very strong evidence on the part of the solicitor to prove that it was intended as a gift; and certainly his own evidence would not be sufficient. On the other hand, a man may make an investment of stock in the name of himself and some person, although not a child or wife, yet in such a position to him as to make it extremely probable that the investment was intended as a gift. In such a case, although the rule of law, if there was no evidence at all, would compel the Court to say that the presumption of trust must prevail, even if the Court might not believe that the fact was in accordance with the presumption, yet, if there is evidence to rebut the presumption, then, in my opinion, the Court must go into the actual facts. And if we are to go into the actual facts, and look at the circumstances of this investment, it appears to me utterly impossible, as the Lord Justice has said, to come to any other conclusion than that the first investment was made for the purpose of gift and not for the purpose of trust. It was either for the purpose of trust or else for the purpose of gifts; and therefore evidence which shows it was not for the purpose of trust is evidence to shew that it was for the purpose of gifts. We find a lady of considerable fortune, having no nearer connections than Mr. Pascoe, who was then a young man living in her house, and for whom she was providing. We find her, manifestly out of her savings, buying a sum of £250 stock in the joint names of herself and him, and at the same time buying another sum of £250 stock, on the very same day, in the joint names of herself and a lady who was living with her as a companion. Then, applying one's common sense to that transaction, what inference is it possible to draw, except that the purchases were intended for the purpose of gifts? If they were intended for the purpose of trusts, what possible reason was there why the two sums were not invested in the same names? Besides, at the very same time the lady had a large sum of stock in her own name, and could anything be more absurd than to suppose that a lady with £4,000 or £5,000 in her own name at that time in the same stock, and having a sum of £500 to invest out of her savings, should go and invest £250 in the name of herself and a young gentleman who was living in her house, and another £250 in the name of herself and her companion, and yet intend the whole to be for herself? I cannot come to any other conclusion than that it must have been intended by the way of a present after her death.

Then, when we have once arrived at the conclusion that the first investment was intended as a gift (and the second was exactly similar), and when we find that the account was opened for

[85] See also *Young v Sealy* [1949] Ch 278; (1969) 85 LQR 530 (M.C. Cullity).

the purpose of a gift, those facts appear to me to rebut the presumption altogether, because when an account is once found to be opened for the purpose of a gift there is very strong reason to suppose that everything added to that account was intended for the purpose of gift also. Assuming the testarix to know that she had made a gift, and had invested a sum of money in stock in the joint names of herself and Pascoe for the purpose of making a present to him, it would certainly be a very extraordinary thing that she should go and add other large sums to that account, not for the purpose of making a present to him, but for the purpose of his being a trustee. I cannot help coming to the conclusion that, as a matter of fact, these investments were intended for the purpose of gift.

There were one or two facts relied on against this conclusion. It was said that Mr. Pascoe kept the matter secret for a great number of years, and never revealed it. I do not greatly rely on that. Every one who has experience knows that some persons are very reticent about their affairs, and some persons are always talking about them. You cannot form any inference as to that. If he really and bona fide believed, and had no doubt that it was intended for a gift, and for his use, I do not see that there was anything extraordinary in his not mentioning it to the persons who now say it was not mentioned to them. The only fact that in the least degree, in my opinion, went against him was his not accounting for the dividend which was due at the death of the testatrix. I think it is not at all impossible that he might have honestly believed that that was his, although I entirely agree that in point of law it was not so; therefore on the whole I come to the same conclusion as the Lord Justice.[86]

In **Abrahams v Trustee in Bankruptcy of Abrahams** (1999) 31 LS Gaz R 38, [1999] BPIR 637, a wife paid her own share and that of her estranged husband in a National Lottery syndicate. It was held that there was nothing to rebut the presumption of resulting trust, so the wife was entitled to the winnings which were attributable to both shares.

In **Carlton v Goodman** [2002] EWCA Civ 545, [2002] 2 FLR 259[87] the defendant's father, Mr. Goodman, had purchased a house. He paid the deposit, but the mortgage was taken out with the Alliance & Leicester building society in the name of him and the claimant, Anita. The claimant argued that she had a beneficial interest in the house through a resulting trust. In holding that only Mr. Goodman has acquired a beneficial interest through a resulting trust by contributing to the purchase price, Lord Justice MUMMERY said:

22.   The main question raised by [counsel for the claimant] is whether the execution of a joint mortgage on jointly held property acquired for the sole use and occupation of one of them constituted the making of a contribution to the purchase price of the property, so as to entitle each party in all the circumstances, to a corresponding beneficial interest under a resulting trust of the property. In order to answer that question I turn to the fundamental principles described from over 200 years of case law . . . and apply them to the facts of this case. . . .

---

[86] See also *Crane v Davis* (1981) The Times, 13 May, where the defendant registered the title of a house in Oxford, in the name of his company, having purchased it with money given to him by the plaintiff for its purchase on her behalf. Falconer J held, following dicta in *Seldon v Davidson* [1968] 1 WLR 1083, that the house was held on a resulting trust for the plaintiff.

[87] See also *Curley v Parkes* [2004] EWCA Civ 1515; *McKenzie v McKenzie* [2003] 2 P and CR DG 6; [2005] Conv 79 (M. Dixon). See also *Stack v Dowden* [2007] UKHL 17, [2007] 2 AC 432 [p. 334, below].

v) Anita made no direct payment of the purchase price of the House. She claims contribution in the form of the liabilities undertaken by her in the Mortgage, which was jointly entered into in order to fund payment of a substantial part of the purchase price. In principle, I see no reason why such an arrangement cannot be treated as a contribution to the payment of the purchase price of property capable of giving rise to a resulting trust: see *Calverley v Green* (1984) 155 CLR 242 at 257–258 and 276–268.

vi) However, as observed by Laws LJ in the course of argument, the role in fact played by Anita was a different and lesser one than that of a contributor to the purchase price. She facilitated the purchase of the House by lending her name in order to secure the advance from the Alliance & Leicester. She thereby assisted Mr. Goodman in his purchase of the House. But that form of assistance was not, on the facts found by the judge, a contribution by her, or intended to be a contribution by her, to the purchase price of the House so as to give rise to a resulting trust in her favour.

vii) The fact is that Anita paid nothing towards the purchase price, and it was never intended, as between Mr. Goodman and her, that she should pay anything at all. Her involvement in the purchase was so circumscribed and temporary that it cannot fairly be described as a contribution to the purchase price, entitling her to an enduring beneficial interest in the House. She only became involved after Mr. Goodman found that he could not obtain a mortgage on his own in order to purchase the House as his home. On her own evidence the understanding was that she would 'come off' the mortgage after a year. The fact that she remained potentially liable to the Alliance & Leicester on the covenant in the mortgage does not assist her claim to a beneficial interest. What has to be considered is her contribution, as between Mr. Goodman and her, to the purchase price in the circumstances at the date of acquisition of the House. If she made no contribution at that time, subsequent enforcement of the covenant against her by the Alliance & Leicester would not be a contribution to the purchase price. It would be a contribution to the discharge of the mortgage liabilities.

viii) Nor could the making of such mortgage payments be relied on as a circumstance rebutting the resulting trust to Mr. Goodman as sole contributor to the purchase price. The position is that, as a trustee, she would be entitled to be indemnified out of the trust property for any expenses, such as mortgage repayments, incurred by her in respect of the trust property. She would not acquire a beneficial interest in the trust property simply as a result of making mortgage repayments to the building society.

ix) There were no other circumstances rebutting the presumption of resulting trust in favour of Mr. Goodman, such as purchasing the House as a family home for them both to live in, or discussions between the parties leading to an agreement, arrangement or understanding between them that the beneficial interests in the House were to be shared, or conduct from which an inference could be drawn that there was a common intention that Anita was to be given a beneficial interest in the House.[88]

Indirect contributions to the purchase price will not be sufficient to give rise to the presumption of a resulting trust. So, for example, payment of household bills by one party to enable the other to pay the mortgage will not suffice.[89]

---

[88] See p. 322, below. In *Springette v Defoe* [1992] 2 FLR 388 contribution of a 'right to buy' discount counted as a contribution to the purchase price. However, in *Buggs v Buggs* [2003] EWHC 1538 (Ch), [2004] WTLR 799 payment into a fund from which the mortgage was paid did not give rise to the presumption of resulting trust.

[89] *Gissing v Gissing* [1971] AC 886. Similarly with non-financial contributions to the running of the family home: *Burns v Burns* [1984] Ch 317.

B PRESUMPTION OF ADVANCEMENT

Where a voluntary conveyance is made to the wife[90] or a child of the father,[91] or to a person to whom he stands *in loco parentis,* the presumption is that a gift was intended. This is the presumption of advancement, but it can be rebutted by comparatively slight evidence of a contrary intention.[92] The burden of rebutting the presumption is placed on the transferor. In *Stack v Dowden*[93] LORD NEUBERGER OF ABBOTSBURY described the presumption of advancement as between man and wife as 'much weakened, although not quite to the point of disappearance.'[94]

In **Bennet v Bennet** (1879) 10 Ch D 474. JESSEL MR said at 476.[95]

The doctrine of equity as regards presumption of gifts is this, that where one person stands in such a relation to another that there is an obligation on that person to make a provision for the other, and we find either a purchase or investment in the name of the other, or in the joint names of the person and the other, of an amount which would constitute a provision for the other, the presumption arises of an intention on the part of the person to discharge the obligation to the other; and therefore, in the absence of evidence to the contrary, that purchase or investment is held to be in itself evidence of a gift.

In other words, the presumption of gift arises from the moral obligation to give.

That reconciles all the cases upon the subject but one, because nothing is better established than this, that as regards a child, a person not the father of the child may put himself in the position of one *in loco parentis* to the child, and so incur the obligation to make a provision for the child....

---

[90] *Tinker v Tinker* [1970] P 136. The presumption of advancement also applies in respect of transfers to a fiancée: Law Reform (Miscellaneous Provisions) Act 1970, s. 2 (1); *Mossop v Mossop* [1989] Fam 77; [1988] Conv 284 (J. Martin); cf. *Bernard v Josephs* [1982] Ch 391. But there is no presumption where a man puts property into the name of his mistress: *Lowson v Coombes* [1999] Ch 373; nor where a wife puts property into the name of her husband: *Mercier v Mercier* [1903] 2 Ch 98; *Heseltine v Heseltine* [1971] 1 WLR 342. The Law Commission Report: Matrimonial Property, 1988 (Law Com No. 175) considers that the law which presumes an advancement upon a transfer from husband to wife, but not vice versa, is out of date. It proposes that, where property other than land (or a life assurance policy) is purchased by one spouse for the joint use or benefit of both, it should be jointly owned in the absence of a contrary intention. Where land or other property is transferred by one spouse (whether husband or wife) to the other, it should be owned by the transferee, unless it was transferred for their joint use or benefit, in which case it should be jointly owned.

[91] *Antoni v Antoni* [2007] UKPC 10 (presumption not rebutted by statement in will that held on resulting trust). Cp. *Nelson v Nelson* (1995) 132 ALR 133 (High Court of Australia); [1996] Conv 274 (A. Dowling); [1996] 4 *Restitution Law Review* 78 (N. Enonchong) (presumption of advancement applied to mother/child relationship). See also *Re Cameron* [1999] Ch 386. In Canada the presumption of advancement has been abolished as regards transfers between parents and adult children, even where the adult child was dependent on the parent: *Pecore v Pecore* (2007) SCC 17 and *Madsen Estate v Saylor* (2007) SCC 18; [2007] Conv 370 (J. Glister).

[92] *McGrath v Wallis* [1995] 2 FLR 114; *Sulett v Meek* [2007] EWHC 1169 (Ch). Cf *Low Gim Siah v Low Geok Khim* [2007] 1 SLR 795 (Singapore Court of Appeal); (2007) 123 LQR 347 (K.F.K. Low) (presumption of advancement following transfer from father to son not easily rebutted, although rebutted on facts).

[93] [2007] UKHL 17, [2007] 2 AC 432, para. 101.

[94] For potential challenges by reference to the European Convention on Human Rights and the Equality Act 2006 see [2007] Conv 340 (G. Andrews).

[95] See also *Re Paradise Motor Co Ltd* [1968] 1 WLR 1125.

A person *in loco parentis* means a person taking upon himself the duty of a father of a child to make a provision for that child. It is clear that in that case the presumption can only arise from the obligation, and therefore in that case the doctrine can only have reference to the obligation of a father to provide for his child, and nothing else.

But the father is under that obligation from the mere fact of his being the father, and therefore no evidence is necessary to shew the obligation to provide for his child, because that is part of his duty. In the case of a father, you have only to prove the fact that he is the father, and when you have done that the obligation at once arises; but in the case of a person *in loco parentis* you must prove that he took upon himself the obligation.

Shephard v Cartwright
[1955] AC 431 (HL, Viscount Simonds, Lords Morton of Henryton, Reid, Tucker and Somervell of Harrow)

In 1929 Mr. Shephard established certain private companies which prospered. The shares in these companies were divided among his three children, the appellants, one of whom was an infant. One reason for so dividing the shares was to obtain certain tax advantages. In 1934 he formed a public company which took over the private companies, paying £300,000 in cash and £400,000 in shares. The Shephard children signed the necessary documents at the request of their father. Shephard in effect controlled the cash and the shares and obtained the children's signatures to all necessary documents, without their knowing what they were signing. By 1936 all the money properly due to the children was exhausted. On Shephard's death in 1949, the children sued the executors for an account. The defendants argued that the intention of the father since 1929 indicated clearly that he intended to treat the money and shares as his own.

Held. The estate was liable. The shares and money were owned beneficially by the children. Evidence of the activities of the father subsequent to the transfer of the shares to the children was not admissible in his favour.[96]

Viscount Simonds: I think it well to pause in this year 1929 and to ask what was the result in law or equity of the registration, in the names of his children of shares for which he supplied the cash, and I pause in order to examine the law, because it appears to me that the only two facts which are at this stage relied on to rebut the presumption of advancement, *viz.*, that the children were ignorant and that certificates were not given to them, are of negligible value.

My Lords, I do not distinguish between the purchase of shares and the acquisition of shares upon allotment, and I think that the law is clear that on the one hand where a man purchases shares and they are registered in the name of a stranger there is a resulting trust in favour of the purchaser; on the other hand, if they are registered in the name of a child or one to whom the purchaser then stood *in loco parentis*, there is no such resulting trust but a presumption of advancement. Equally it is clear that the presumption may be rebutted but should not, as Lord Eldon said, give way to slight circumstances: *Finch v Finch* (1808) 15 Ves 43.

It must then be asked by what evidence can the presumption be rebutted, and it would, I think, be very unfortunate if any doubt were cast (as I think it has been by certain passages in

---

[96] For criticism of this rule see E. Fung, 'The Scope of the Rule in *Shephard v Cartwright*' (2006) 122 LQR 651.

the judgments under review) upon the well settled law on this subject. It is, I think, correctly stated in substantially the same terms in every textbook that I have consulted and supported by authority extending over a long period of time. I will take, as an example, a passage from *Snell's Equity* (24th edn), p. 153, which is as follows:

> 'The acts and declarations of the parties before or at the time of the purchase, or so immediately after it as to constitute a part of the transaction, are admissible in evidence either for or against the party who did the act or made the declaration... But subsequent declarations are admissible as evidence only against the party who made them, and not in his favour.'

I do not think it necessary to review the numerous cases of high authority upon which this statement is founded. It is possible to find in some earlier judgments reference to 'subsequent' events without the qualifications contained in the textbook statement: it may even be possible to wonder in some cases how in the narration of facts certain events were admitted to consideration. But the burden of authority in favour of the broad proposition as stated in the passage I have cited is overwhelming and should not be disturbed.

But although the applicable law is not in doubt, the application of it is not always easy. There must often be room for argument whether a subsequent act is part of the same transaction as the original purchase or transfer, and equally whether subsequent acts which it is sought to adduce in evidence ought to be regarded as admissions by the party so acting, and if they are so admitted, further facts should be admitted by way of qualification of those admissions.

The first question, then, is whether any subsequent events are admissible as part of the original transaction to prove that the deceased had not in 1929 the intention of advancement which the law presumes. My Lords, for nearly five years nothing happened which could by any means be regarded as throwing light upon his original intention, but an event did happen which would amply explain a change in that intention. For within a short time of their promotion the businesses of the six companies were prosperous beyond all expectation. In the year 1931 their combined profits were £57,780, in 1932 £128, 525 and in 1933 £344,671. It is not surprising that in the light of this great success the deceased and his co-adventurer, Meyer, should form a public company to acquire all the shares of all the six companies. This they did.

[His Lordship reviewed the events subsequent to 1929, and continued:] I have omitted to state one fact subsequent to the original transaction which, whether or not it is to be regarded as part of it and admissible in evidence under that head, is clearly admissible as an admission by the deceased against interest. Shortly before the completion of the agreement with the new company and no doubt as part of the arrangement, one of the old companies, New Ideal Homesteads Ltd., declared and paid a dividend of £25 12s. per share. The deceased, acting presumably under the power of attorney to which I have referred, received the dividend attributable to the appellants' shares and, though retaining it for his own use, instructed the respondent Dunk, an accountant who acted for the deceased in the preparation of his income tax returns, that the dividend was the income of the appellants. It was so treated by Dunk, whose integrity has not been challenged. Similar information and instructions were given by the deceased to Dunk in regard to the sums placed to the deposit account of the appellants with Barclays Bank Ltd, and to the untaxed interest payable in respect of those sums, and were acted on by him.

I turn, then, again to ask how these facts which I have briefly narrated can be adduced in evidence by the deceased or his estate. And I think it convenient at this stage to refer to a matter in which, with great respect, I think the Master of the Rolls fell into an error and, moreover, into an error which largely influenced him in the conclusion to which he came. For he treated the appellants' claim merely as a claim against a dead man's estate, and therefore (as he says and reiterates) as a claim in which a heavy onus lay on the claimants. But that is not, in my opinion, the way in which the claim should be regarded. It starts with the fact that in 1929 certain shares were placed by their father in the names of the appellants, and, that fact being admitted or proved, a presumption at once arises which it is for the respondents to rebut. They as executors are in no stronger position than their testator would be in if he were alive.

My Lords, at the outset of this opinion I said that there must often be room for argument whether subsequent events can be regarded as forming part of the original transaction so as to be admissible evidence of intention and in this case it has certainly been vigorously argued that they can. But, though I know of no universal criterion by which a link can for this purpose be established between one event and another, here I see insuperable difficulty in finding any link at all. The time factor alone of nearly five years is almost decisive, but, apart from that, the events of 1934 and 1935, whether taken singly or in their sum, appear to me to be wholly independent of the original transaction. It is in fact fair to say that, so far from flowing naturally and inevitably from it, they probably never would have happened but for the phenomenal success of the enterprise. Nor can I give any weight to the argument much pressed upon us that the deceased was an honourable man and therefore could not have acted as he did, if he had in 1929 intended to give the shares outright to his children. I assume that he was an honourable man as well in the directions in regard to income tax that he gave to Mr. Dunk as otherwise, but I think that he may well have deemed it consistent with honourable conduct and with paternal benevolence to take back part of what he had given when the magnitude of the gift so far surpassed his expectation.

If, then, these events cannot be admitted in evidence as part of the original transaction, can they be admitted to rebut the presumption on the ground that they are admissions by the appellants against interest? I conceive it possible, and this view is supported by authority, that there might be such a course of conduct by a child after a presumed advancement as to constitute an admission by him of his parent's original intention, though such evidence should be regarded jealously. But it appears to me to be an indispensable condition of such conduct being admissible that it should be performed with knowledge of the material facts. In the present case the undisputed fact that the appellants under their father's guidance did what they were told without inquiry or knowledge precludes the admission in evidence of their conduct and, if it were admitted, would deprive it of all probative value. It is otherwise, however, with the conduct of the deceased. I have already made it clear that the respondents have failed to discharge the burden which rests on them of rebutting the presumption of advancement. The appellants, therefore, in my opinion, need no reinforcement from subsequent events. But, since inevitably in a complex case like this, either upon the footing of being examined *de bene esse* or because they have been admitted for some other purpose than the proof of intention, all the facts relevant or irrelevant have been reviewed, I do not hesitate to say that the only conclusion which I can form about the deceased's original intention is that he meant the provision he then made for his children to be for their permanent advancement. He may well have changed his mind at a later date, but it was too late. He may have thought that, having made an absolute gift, he could yet revoke it. This is something that no one will ever know. The presumption which the law makes is not to be thus rebutted. If it were my duty to speculate upon these matters, my final question would be why the deceased should have put these several parcels of shares in six different companies into the names of his wife and three children unless he meant to make provision for them, and since counsel have not been able to suggest any, much less any plausible, reason why he should have done so, I shall conclude that the intention which the law imputes to him was in fact his intention. The reasoning which made so strong an appeal to Mellish LJ in *Fowkes v Pascoe* (1875) 10 Ch App 343 has in this case also particular weight.

In my opinion, then, this appeal succeeds on the main question that has been argued before us.[97]

Warren v Gurney
[1944] 2 All ER 472 (CA, **Lord Greene MR, Finlay** and **Morton LJJ**)

In 1929, Mr. Gurney purchased a house, 'Fairview', for £300. It was conveyed to one of his daughters, Catherine, who was about to be married to Mr. Warren. Mr. Gurney retained the title deeds. In 1943 he signed a document headed 'my wish', in which he stated that the house was to be divided between his three daughters. No provision was made in his will. He died in 1944, and Catherine, claiming to be absolute owner of 'Fairview', sued Gurney's executors to recover possession of the deeds.

Held. Catherine held 'Fairview' on trust for her father. The presumption of advancement was rebutted by the contemporaneous declarations of Gurney. The document headed 'my wish' was inadmissible.

Morton LJ: It is well established that when a parent buys a property and has it conveyed into the name of his child, there arises a presumption that the parents intended to make a gift or advancement to the child of that property. Of course, that is a presumption which can be rebutted by evidence that that was not the father's intention. The father retained the title deeds of the property and he still had them in his possession when he died in the year 1944.

Three points were taken by counsel for the appellant. First of all, he contended that the judge was wrong in admitting as evidence a document headed 'my wish', which he held was signed by Elijah Gurney, which was dated 6 September, 1943. In my view counsel's contention under that heading was quite correct. The document headed 'my wish' was not admissible in evidence. It was in the nature of a subsequent declaration by the alleged donor, which was not against his own interest, and it is clearly established that subsequent declarations by the alleged donor are only admissible if they are against his interest. The reason for that is quite obvious. If the rule were otherwise it would be extremely easy for persons to manufacture evidence, even although at the time when they made the purchase they in fact intended the child to have the gift of property.

The second contention put forward by counsel for the appellants was that, on the admissible evidence, the judge was not justified in coming to the conclusion that the defendants had rebutted the presumption of advancement. In my view, there was ample evidence to justify that conclusion of the judge. In the first place, there is the fact that the father retained the title deeds from the time of purchase to the time of his death. I think that is a very significant fact, because title deeds, as it was said in *Coke on Littleton,* are 'sinews of the land'. One would

---

[97] For the operation of the principle of advancement in the case of a joint bank account, see *Marshal v Crutwell* (1875) LR 20 Eq 328; *Re Roberts* [1946] Ch 1; *Hoddinott v Hoddinott* [1949] 2 KB 406; *Jones v Maynard* [1951] Ch 572; *Re Bishop* [1965] Ch 450; *Re Figgis* [1969] 1 Ch 123; *Thompson v Thompson* (1970) 114 Sol Jo 455; *McHardy and Sons v Warren* [1994] 2 FLR 338; Lewin, pp. 333–336. The problem of housekeeping money was dealt with by the Married Women's Property Act 1964, under which equality of ownership is presumed in the absence of other evidence.

have expected the father to have handed them over, either to the plaintiff or her husband, if he had intended the gift. It is to be noted that the judge accepted the evidence given by the plaintiff's mother, Mary Ann Gurney, and by her brother, Meyrick George Gurney, and rejected the evidence of Denis Warren, the plaintiff's husband, where it conflicted with that given by those two witnesses.

I do not intend to travel all through the evidence given before the county court judge, but I wish to read one portion of it only, which, it seems to me, is of the utmost importance. Meyrick George Gurney gave evidence as follows:

'I am the son of Elijah Gurney and his executor. In 1929 father said he had thought of buying one of the properties for plaintiff: asked me which I thought best.'

Pausing there, the words, 'for plaintiff' might, if they had stood alone, seem to indicate that a gift was intended, but that possible meaning is displaced by what follows:

'I said 'Fairview'. Father said he had been talking to Warren. Father said Warren had said if father bought the house he would pay for the house as he could. I went with father to Wadeson, the solicitor. Father required property made in my sister's name, so that there could be no trouble at a later date, as Warren had to pay for it at a later date. Father said he should keep the deeds as security.'

There are other passages of importance in the evidence. There are passages in the evidence of Mary Ann Gurney, containing statements as to contemporaneous declarations by the testator. There are certain statements made by the plaintiff herself against her own interest: for instance, the statement that she had not enough money to pay any rent. But I need not go further into the evidence. It seems to me, on the passages which I have referred to alone, the county court judge was fully justified in coming to his conclusion. The passage I have read from the Evidence of Meyrick Gurney is a passage of the evidence of a witness whom the judge believed, and it seems to me that those contemporaneous declarations are quite sufficient to rebut the presumption even if they stood alone.

It is quite clear that contemporaneous declarations by the alleged donor are admissible in evidence. I am satisfied that there was ample evidence upon which the judge could found his conclusion, and, indeed, it is difficult to see how, on the evidence which he believed, he could have reached any other conclusion.

The last point raised by counsel for the appellant was this. He said that, on the evidence, and on the findings of the judge, his client was entitled to become the absolute owner of this property on the payment of a sum of £250 into the estate. I express no view as to whether that contention is or is not correct, because, even if it were correct, it would clearly not justify the plaintiff's claim to be handed the title deeds now. If that contention were correct she could only have them on payment of £250, which has never in fact been paid.

For these reasons, I think this appeal should be dismissed with costs.

Where a house has been acquired for joint occupation but conveyed into the name of one party, the presumption of advancement is a last resort, and is rebuttable by comparatively slight evidence whether the relationship is husband and wife or father and child.[98]

---

[98] But where the parties are cohabitants it is the common-intention constructive trust which will be used. See p. 322, below.

In **McGrath v Wallis** [1995] 2 FLR 114 a house was acquired as a family home for the occupation of the parents and their son and daughter. As the father was not employed, it was conveyed into the son's name, as only he was acceptable as a mortgagor. Solicitors drew up a declaration of trust indicating that the father had a share of 80 per cent and the son 20 per cent. This was never sent to the father for signature and was found in the solicitors' files. There was no reason why the father should have wished to give the house to the son. The Court of Appeal held that the evidence was ample to rebut the presumption. As the contributors were in fact 70 per cent and 30 per cent, the father's estate was entitled to a 70 per cent share. The observations in *Pettitt v Pettitt* [1970] AC 777 at 793, 811, 824, as to the weakness of the presumption with regard to the family home, applied equally to father and son.

C TRANSFERS FOR ILLEGAL PURPOSES[99]

Where property has been transferred for an illegal purpose, for example to keep it safe from the transferor's creditors, the question arises whether the transferor can invoke or rebut the presumptions in order to support his claim to beneficial ownership. It has long been established that the presumption of advancement cannot be rebutted by evidence of an unlawful purpose. Thus in **Gascoigne v Gascoigne** [1918] 1 KB 223 a husband who took a lease of land in his wife's name in order to keep it from his creditors could not rebut the presumption of advancement.

Tinsley v Milligan
[1994] 1 AC 340[100] (HL, Lords Keith of Kinkel, Goff of Chieveley, Jauncey of Tullichettle, Lowry and Browne-Wilkinson)

Two women purchased a house jointly but agreed that it should be in the name of the appellant in order to facilitate false claims to housing benefit by the respondent. Both were parties to the fraud, which was carried out over several years. Subsequently the parties fell out and the appellant moved out of the house. She brought an action seeking possession and the respondent counterclaimed for a declaration that the appellant held the house on trust for both parties equally, by virtue of the presumption of resulting trust. A majority of the House of Lords (Lords Jauncey of Tullichettle, Lowry and Browne-Wilkinson) upheld the counterclaim, Lords Keith of Kinkel and Goff of Chieveley dissented. The principle upheld by the majority was that a transferor was

---

[99] N. Enonchong, *Illegal Transactions* (1998); T&H, pp. 831–840; G. Virgo and J. O'Sullivan, 'Resulting Trusts and Illegality' in *Restitution and Equity, Vol 1: Resulting Trusts and Equitable Compensation* (ed. P. Birks and F. Rose) (2000), pp 97–118; [2004] Conv 439 (M. Halliwell).

[100] (1993) CLJ 394 (R. Thornton); (1993) 143 NLJ 1577 (B. Council); (1993) 7 *Trust Law International* 114 (M. Lunney); [1994] Conv 62 (M. Halliwell); (1994) 57 MLR 441 (H. Stowe); (1994) 110 LQR 3 (R. Buckley); (1995) 111 LQR 135 (N. Enonchong). G. Virgo 'The Effects of Illegality on Claims for Restitution in English Law' in *The Limits of Restitutionary Claims: A Comparative Analysis* (ed. W.J. Swadling) (1997), pp. 141–185.

entitled to succeed if he could establish his title without relying on his own illegality. The appellant could, therefore, rely on the presumption of resulting trust.

Lord Jauncey of Tullichettle: At the outset it seems to me to be important to distinguish between the enforcement of executory provisions arising under an illegal contract or other transaction and the enforcement of rights already acquired under the completed provisions of such a contract or transaction. Your Lordships were referred to a very considerable number of authorities, both ancient and modern, from which certain propositions may be derived.

First, it is trite law that the court will not give its assistance to the enforcement of executory provisions of an unlawful contract whether the illegality is apparent *ex facie* the document or whether the illegality of purpose of what would otherwise be a lawful contract emerges during the course of the trial; *Holman v Johnson* (1775) 1 Cowp 341 at 343, *per* Lord Mansfield CJ: *Pearce v Brooks* (1866) LR 1 Exch 213 at 217–218, *per* Pollock CB; *Alexander v Rayson* [1936] 1 KB 169 at 182, and *Bowmakers Ltd v Barnet Instruments Ltd* [1945] KB 65 at 70.

Second, it is well established that a party is not entitled to rely on his own fraud or illegality in order to assist a claim or rebut a presumption. Thus when money or property has been transferred by a man to his wife or children for the purpose of defrauding creditors and the transferee resists his claim for recovery he cannot be heard to rely on his illegal purpose in order to rebut the presumption of advancement; *Gascoigne v Gascoigne* [1918] 1 KB 223 at 226; *Chettiar v Chettiar* [1962] AC 294 at 302 and *Tinker v Tinker* [1970] P 136 at 143, *per* Salmon LJ.

Third, it has, however, for some years been recognised that a completely executed transfer of property or of an interest in property made in pursuance of an unlawful agreement is valid and the court will assist the transferee in the protection of his interest provided that he does not require to found on the unlawful agreement: *Ayerst v Jenkins* (1873) LR 16 Eq 275 at 283; *Alexander v Rayson* [1936] 1 KB 169 at 184–185; *Bowmakers Ltd v Barnet Instruments Ltd* [1945] KB 65; *Sajan Singh v Sardara Ali* [1960] AC 167 at 176. To the extent, at least, of his third proposition it would appear that there has been some modification over the years of Lord Eldon LC's principles.[101]

The ultimate question in this appeal is, in my view, whether the respondent in claiming the existence of a resulting trust in her favour is seeking to enforce unperformed provisions of an unlawful transaction or whether she is simply relying on an equitable proprietary interest that she has already acquired under such a transaction.

[His Lordship referred to *Gissing v Gissing* [1971] AC 886, and continued:] I find this a very narrow question but I have come to the conclusion that the transaction whereby the claimed resulting trust in favour of the respondent was created was the agreement between the parties that, although funds were to be provided by both of them, nevertheless the title to the house was to be in the sole name of the appellant for the unlawful purpose of defrauding the Department of Social Security. So long as that agreement remained unperformed, neither party could have enforced it against the other. However, as soon as the agreement was implemented by the sale to the appellant alone she became trustee for the respondent who can now rely on the equitable proprietary interest which has thereby been presumed to have been created in her favour and has no need to rely on the illegal transaction which led to its creation.

---

[101] 'To a fraudulent plaintiff seeking relief the court would say "Let the estate lie where it falls" ': *Muckleston v Brown* (1801) 6 Ves 52 at 68–69.

Lord Browne-Wilkinson: The presumption of a resulting trust is, in my view, crucial in considering the authorities. On that presumption (and on the contrary presumption of advancement) hinges the answer to the crucial question: does a plaintiff claiming under a resulting trust have to rely on the underlying illegality? Where the presumption of resulting trust applies, the plaintiff does not have to rely on the illegality. If he proves that the property is vested in the defendant alone but that the plaintiff provided part of the purchase money, or voluntarily transferred the property to the defendant, the plaintiff establishes his claim under a resulting trust unless either the contrary presumption of advancement displaces the presumption of resulting trust or the defendant leads evidence to rebut the presumption of resulting trust. Therefore, in cases where the presumption of advancement does not apply, a plaintiff can establish his equitable interest in the property without relying in any way on the underlying illegal transaction. In this case the respondent as defendant simply pleaded the common intention that the property should belong to both of them and that she contributed to the purchase price: she claimed that in consequence the property belonged to them equally. To the same effect was her evidence-in-chief. Therefore the respondent was not forced to rely on the illegality to prove her equitable interest. Only in the reply and the course of the respondent's cross-examination did such illegality emerge: it was the appellant who had to rely on that illegality.

Although the presumption of advancement does not directly arise for consideration in this case, it is important when considering the decided cases to understand its operation. On a transfer from a man to his wife, children or others to whom he stands *in loco parentis*, equity presumes an intention to make a gift. Therefore in such a case, unlike the cases where the presumption of resulting trust applies, in order to establish any claim the plaintiff has himself to lead evidence sufficient to rebut the presumption of gift and in so doing will normally have to plead, and give evidence of, the underlying illegal purpose.

[His Lordship reviewed the authorities and continued:] The majority of cases have been those in which the presumption of advancement applied: in those authorities the rule has been stated as being that a plaintiff cannot rely on evidence of his own illegality to rebut the presumption applicable in such cases that the plaintiff intended to make a gift of the property to the transferee. Thus in *Gascoigne v Gascoigne* [1918] 1 KB 223; *McEvoy v Belfast Banking Co Ltd* [1934] NI 67; *Re Emery's Investments' Trusts* [1959] Ch 410; *Chettiar v Chettiar* [1962] AC 294 and *Tinker v Tinker* [1970] P 136 at 141–142, the crucial point was said to be the inability of the plaintiff to lead evidence rebutting the presumption of advancement. In each case the plaintiff was claiming to recover property voluntarily transferred to, or purchased in the name of, a wife or child, for an illegal purpose. Although reference was made to Lord Eldon LC's principle, none of those cases was decided on the simple ground (if it were good law) that equity would not in any circumstances enforce a resulting trust in such circumstances. On the contrary in each case the rule was stated to be that the plaintiff could not recover because he had to rely on the illegality to rebut the presumption of advancement.

In my judgment, the explanation for this departure from Lord Eldon LC's absolute rule is that the fusion of the administration of law and equity has led the courts to adopt a single rule (applicable both at law and in equity) as to the circumstances in which the court will enforce property interests acquired in pursuance of an illegal transaction, *viz.* the *Bowmakers* rule: [1945] KB 65. A party to an illegality can recover by virtue of a legal or equitable property interest if, but only if, he can establish his title without relying on his own illegality. In cases where the presumption of advancement applies, the plaintiff is faced with the presumption of gift and therefore cannot claim under a resulting trust unless and until he has rebutted that presumption of gift: for those purposes the plaintiff does have to rely on the underlying illegality and therefore fails.[102]

In **Silverwood v Silverwood** (1997) 74 P & CR 453, a presumption of resulting trust arose despite the illegal purpose of the parties. The defendant sought to rebut this presumption by arguing that the plaintiff had intended the transfer of property to be a gift. It was held that the plaintiff was able to rely on his illegal purpose to defeat the defendant's argument.

Where property has been transferred for an illegal purpose in circumstances where the presumption of advancement applies, usually the transferor will not be able to recover the property because this would involve him pleading the illegality of the transaction to rebut the presumption and this is not allowed. An exception to this has, however, been recognised where no part of the illegal purpose has been fulfilled.

In **Tribe v Tribe** [1996] Ch 107[103] a father transferred shares to his son to conceal them from his creditors. This was an illegal purpose. Once the threat from his creditors had passed the father asked his son to return the shares to him. The son refused to do so. The son argued that, since there had been an apparent gift from father to son, the presumption of advancement applied and the father was unable to rebut this by pleading his actual unlawful purpose.

It was held that since none of the creditors had been aware of the transfer of shares, no part of the illegal purpose had been carried into effect so the father could rely on his actual purpose to rebut the presumption of advancement.

NOURSE LJ said at 117:

In both *Tinsley v Milligan* and the present case A transferred property into the name of B with the mutual intention of concealing A's interest in the property for a fraudulent or illegal purpose. Before *Tinsley v Milligan* the general rule that A could not recover the property was consistently applied irrespective of whether the presumption of advancement arose between A and B or not (see [1994] 1 AC 340 at 356, *per* Lord Goff and the authorities there cited). But now the majority of their Lordships have made a clear distinction between the two cases. In holding that the general rule does not apply where there is no presumption of advancement, they have necessarily affirmed its application to cases where there is. Thus Lord Browne-Wilkinson pointed out that, in a case where the presumption of advancement applies, in order to establish any claim, the plaintiff has himself to lead evidence sufficient to rebut the presumption of gift and in so doing will normally have to plead, and give evidence of, the underlying illegal purpose (see [1994] 1 AC 340 at 372 and 375).

At the end of his judgment in the court below, Judge Weeks QC said:

'Finally, it is not for me to criticise their Lordships' reasoning, but with the greatest respect I find it difficult to see why the outcome in cases such as the present one should depend to such a large

---

[102] See also *Lowson v Coombes* [1999] Ch 373; [1999] Conv 242 (M. Thompson); [1999] LMCLQ 465 (I. Cotterill); *Slater v Simm* [2007] EWHC 951 (Ch), [2007] WTLR 1043.

[103] (1996) CLJ 23 (G. Virgo); (1996) 26 *Family Law* 3 (S. Cretney); (1996) 112 LQR 386 (F. Rose); (1996) 10 *Trust Law International* 51 (P. Pettit); [1996] *Restitution Law Review* 78 (N. Enonchong); *Collier v Collier* [2002] EWCA Civ 1095. See also *Kohn v Wagschal* [2007] EWCA Civ 1022 (binding arbitration by Jewish law to the effect that there was no intent to make a gift despite an intent to evade tax)

extent on arbitrary factors, such as whether the claim is brought by a father against a son, or a mother against a son, or a grandfather against a grandson.'

I see much force in those observations. If the defendant had been his brother, grandson, nephew or son-in-law, the plaintiff would have succeeded without further inquiry. Moreover, in times when the presumption of advancement has for other purposes fallen into disfavour (see e.g. the observations of Lord Reid, Lord Hodson and Lord Diplock in *Pettitt v Pettitt* [1970] AC 777 at 793, 811, 824) there seems to be some perversity in its elevation to a decisive status in the context of illegality. Be that as it may, we are bound by *Tinsley v Milligan* for what it decided. It decided that where the presumption of advancement arises the general rule applies. It did not decide that there is no exception where the illegal purpose has not been carried into effect.

His Lordship considered *Gascoigne v Gascoigne* [1918] 1 KB 223; *Chettiar v Chettiar* [1962] AC 294; *Tinker v Tinker* [1970] P 136; *Perpetual Executors and Trustees Association of Australia Ltd v Wright* (1917) 23 CLR 185 and continued:

On this state of the authorities I decline to hold that the exception does not apply to a case where the presumption of advancement arises but the illegal purpose has not been carried into effect in any way. *Wright's* case, supported by the observations of the Privy Council in *Chettiar v Chettiar,* is clear authority for its application and no decision to the contrary has been cited. In the circumstances I do not propose to distinguish between law and equity, nor to become embroiled in the many irreconcilable authorities which deal with the exception in its application to executory contracts, nor even to speculate as to the significance, if any, of calling it a *locus poenitentiae,* a name I have avoided as tending to mislead. In a property transfer case the exception applies if the illegal purpose has not been carried into effect in any way.

I return to the facts of this case. The judge found that the illegal purpose was to deceive the plaintiff's creditors by creating an appearance that he no longer owned any shares in the company. He also found that it was not carried into effect in any way. Mr. Tunkel, for the defendant, attacked the latter finding on grounds which appeared to me to confuse the purpose with the transaction. Certainly the transaction was carried into effect by the execution and registration of the transfer. But *Wright's* case shows that that is immaterial. It is the purpose which has to be carried into effect and that would only have happened if and when a creditor or creditors of the plaintiff had been deceived by the transaction. The judge said there was no evidence of that and clearly he did not think it appropriate to infer it. Nor is it any objection to the plaintiff's right to recover the shares that he did not demand their return until after the danger had passed and it was no longer necessary to conceal the transfer from his creditors. All that matters is that no deception was practised on them. For these reasons the judge was right to hold that the exception applied.

MILLETT LJ said at 132:

In my opinion the weight of the authorities supports the view that a person who seeks to recover property transferred by him for an illegal purpose can lead evidence of his dishonest intention whenever it is necessary for him to do so provided that he has withdrawn from the transaction before the illegal purpose has been carried out. It is not necessary if he can rely on an express or resulting trust in his favour; but it is necessary (i) if he brings an action at law and (ii) if he brings proceedings in equity and needs to rebut the presumption of advancement....

At heart the question for decision in the present case is one of legal policy. The primary rule which precludes the court from lending its assistance to a man who founds his cause of action on an illegal or immoral act often leads to a denial of justice. The justification for this is that the rule is not a principle of justice but a principle of policy (see the much-quoted statement of Lord Mansfield CJ in *Holman v Johnson* (1775) 1 Cowp 341 at 343).[104] The doctrine of the *locus poenitentiae* is an exception which operates to mitigate the harshness of the primary rule. It enables the court to do justice between the parties even though, in order to do so, it must allow a plaintiff to give evidence of his own dishonest intent. But he must have withdrawn from the transaction while his dishonesty still lay in intention only. The law draws the line once the intention has been wholly or partly carried into effect.

Seen in this light the doctrine of the *locus poenitentiae,* although an exception to the primary rule, is not inconsistent with the policy which underlies it. It is, of course, artificial to think that anyone would be dissuaded by the primary rule from entering into a proposed fraud, if only because such a person would be unlikely to be a studious reader of the law reports or to seek advice from a lawyer whom he has taken fully into his confidence. But if the policy which underlies the primary rule is to discourage fraud, the policy which underlies the exception must be taken to be to encourage withdrawal from a proposed fraud before it is implemented, an end which is no less desirable. And if the former objective is of such overriding importance that the primary rule must be given effect even where it leads to a denial of justice, then in my opinion the latter objective justifies the adoption of the exception where this enables justice to be done.

To my mind these considerations are even more compelling since the decision in *Tinsley v Milligan*. One might hesitate before allowing a novel exception to a rule of legal policy, particularly a rule based on moral principles. But the primary rule, as it has emerged from that decision, does not conform to any discernible moral principle. It is procedural in nature and depends on the adventitious location of the burden of proof in any given case. Had Mr. Tribe transferred the shares to a stranger or distant relative whom he trusted, albeit for the same dishonest purpose, it cannot be doubted that he would have succeeded in his claim. He would also have succeeded if he had given them to his son and procured him to sign a declaration of trust in his favour. But he chose to transfer them to a son whom he trusted to the extent of dispensing with the precaution of obtaining a declaration of trust. If that is fatal to his claim, then the greater the betrayal, the less the power of equity to give a remedy.

In my opinion the following propositions represent the present state of the law.

(1) Title to property passes both at law and in equity even if the transfer is made for an illegal purpose. The fact that title has passed to the transferee does not preclude the transferor from bringing an action for restitution.

(2) The transferor's action will fail if it would be illegal for him to retain any interest in the property.

(3) Subject to (2) the transferor can recover the property if he can do so without relying on the illegal purpose. This will normally be the case where the property was transferred without consideration in circumstances where the transferor can rely on an express declaration of trust or a resulting trust in his favour.

(4) It will almost invariably be so where the illegal purpose has not been carried out. It may be otherwise where the illegal purpose has been carried out and the transferee can rely on the transferor's conduct as inconsistent with his retention of a beneficial interest.

[104] 'No Court will lend its aid to a man who founds his cause of action upon an immoral or illegal act.'

(5) The transferor can lead evidence of the illegal purpose whenever it is necessary for him to do so provided that he has withdrawn from the transaction before the illegal purpose has been wholly or partly carried into effect. It will be necessary for him to do so (i) if he brings an action at law or (ii) if he brings proceedings in equity and needs to rebut the presumption of advancement.

(6) The only way in which a man can protect his property from his creditors is by divesting himself of all beneficial interest in it. Evidence that he transferred the property in order to protect it from his creditors, therefore, does nothing by itself to rebut the presumption of advancement; it reinforces it. To rebut the presumption it is necessary to show that he intended to retain a beneficial interest and conceal it from his creditors.

(7) The court should not conclude that this was his intention without compelling circumstantial evidence to this effect. The identity of the transferee and the circumstances in which the transfer was made would be highly relevant. It is unlikely that the court would reach such a conclusion where the transfer was made in the absence of an imminent and perceived threat from known creditors.

As regards the so-called 'withdrawal exception', MILLETT LJ said at 135:

...I would hold that genuine repentance is not required. Justice is not a reward for merit; restitution should not be confined to the penitent. I would also hold that voluntary withdrawal from an illegal transaction when it has ceased to be needed is sufficient.

In 1999 the Law Commission published a Consultation Paper, *Illegal Transactions: The Effect of Illegality on Contract and Trusts*,[105] part of which considers the effect of illegality on resulting trusts. The Law Commission described the existing law as complex and criticised 'its potential to give rise to unjust decisions and its lack of certainty'.[106] The Law Commission provisionally recommended that the *Tinsley v Milligan* principle should be replaced by a structured statutory discretion.[107]

We therefore provisionally propose that, in exercising its discretion, a court should consider: (i) the seriousness of the illegality involved; (ii) the knowledge and intention of the party... seeking to recover benefits conferred under [the transaction]; (iii) whether refusing to allow standard rights and remedies would deter illegality; (iv) whether refusing to allow standard rights and remedies would further the purpose of the rule which renders the transaction illegal; and (v) whether refusing to allow standard rights and remedies would be proportionate to the illegality involved.[108]

The Law Commission has subsequently noted that the response to its proposals was mixed and that the matter was being reconsidered. In 2006 a paper contemplating the abolition of the presumption of advancement was published. The final report of the Law Commission is due in 2008.

---

[105] Law Com CP No. 154 (1999). See [2000] *Restitution Law Review* 82 (N. Enonchong); (2000) LS 156 (R. Buckley).　　　　　　　　　　　　　　　　　　　[106] Law Com CP No. 154 (1999), p. 81.

[107] See also the New Zealand Illegal Contracts Act 1970, ss. 6 and 7 of which permit restitution of property at the discretion of the court: (1992) 15 *New Zealand Universities Law Review* 80 (B. Coote). See also the Israeli Contract Law (General Part) 1973, s. 31.　　　　　　　　　　[108] Law Com CP No. 154, p. 9.

QUESTIONS

1. What part do presumptions play in this field today? What is their relevance where property has been transferred for an illegal purpose?

2. Should the presumption of advancement be abolished? See *Pettitt v Pettitt* [1970] AC 777; *McGrath v Wallis* [1995] 2 FLR 114; *Lowson v Coombes* [1999] Ch 373; G. Virgo and J. O'Sullivan in *Restitution and Equity, Volume 1: Resulting Trusts and Equitable Compensation* (ed. P. Birks and F. Rose, 2000), pp. 103–107.

3. Should a person who has transferred property to defeat his creditors be allowed to recover that property?

4. Is the creation of a statutory discretion an appropriate method for reforming the law of illegality in its application to resulting trusts? See G. Virgo and J. O'Sullivan in *Restitution and Equity, Volume 1: Resulting Trusts and Equitable Compensation* (ed. P. Birks and F. Rose, 2000), pp. 108–118.

7

CONSTRUCTIVE TRUSTS[1]

I GENERAL PRINCIPLES

A constructive trust arises by operation of law rather than by the intention of the parties[2] and it can arise in a wide variety of circumstances. But there is little agreement amongst the judiciary or academic writers as to when a constructive trust will be recognised and why it should be recognised. To make this area of the law even more complicated, there is no consistent use of terminology. Indeed, the term 'constructive trust' has been used in at least four different ways.

The institutional constructive trust.[3] According to this view of the constructive trust, it will only be recognised where the facts of the dispute fall within an existing category of cases where a constructive trust has previously been recognised.

The remedial constructive trust.[4] According to this view, a constructive trust will be recognised through the exercise of judicial discretion. This notion of the constructive trust has been recognised in a number of Commonwealth countries, including Australia, Canada, and New Zealand, but it has generally not been recognised in England.

The constructive trust as remedy.[5] Where a defendant has received property in which the claimant has an equitable proprietary right, it is possible for the court to vindicate

---

[1] H&M, pp. 301–343; Lewin, pp. 229–232; P&M, pp. 312–441; P&S, pp. 268–326; Pettit, pp. 139–150, 163–167; Snell, pp. 543–563, 587–593; T&H, pp. 768–773, 841–890; U&H, pp. 390–395, 398–408, 467–548. See generally (1913–14) 27 *Harvard Law Review* 125; (1955) 71 LQR 39 (A.W. Scott); Waters, *The Constructive Trust* (1964); Oakley, *Constructive Trusts* (3rd edn, 1997); Elias, *Explaining Constructive Trusts* (1990).
[2] *Air Jamaica Ltd v Charlton* [1999] 1 WLR 1399 at 1412, *per* Lord Millett [p. 205, above].
[3] See p. 280, below.   [4] See p. 315, below.   [5] See p. 944, below.

that right by requiring the defendant to hold the property on constructive trust for the claimant.[6] It is sometimes difficult to see the distinction between a constructive trust being imposed as a remedy and a duty to account. Where an agent has obtained illegal profits, should we say that he is a constructive trustee of those profits, or that he is simply under a duty to account to the claimant for their value? The former involves a proprietary claim by the claimant, the latter a personal claim. The difference may be considerable, but the terminology is indiscriminate.[7] So long as the defendant can pay, it makes little difference whether the claim is proprietary or personal. But if the defendant is insolvent, and the claimant will only be satisfied by a claim in priority over the general creditors, the distinction is crucial. By making a proprietary claim, the claimant can take any property in which it can be shown that he has an equitable proprietary interest; and he can make a claim in priority over the general creditors upon a mixed fund of money or investments. Further, if the investments have appreciated, the claimant may wish to claim a share of the fund at this higher value. A claim involving only the defendant's personal liability to account has nothing to do with a constructive trust. Where, however, the claimant brings a proprietary claim against a specific asset in the defendant's hands, whether that is the same asset which was taken from the claimant, or a product of, or a substitute for that asset, the claimant will want the court to decide that the asset (or a share of it where the asset has become mixed with property belonging to somebody else) is held on a constructive trust for him.[8]

Liability as if a constructive trustee.[9] Sometimes the language of the constructive trust is used even though the defendant does not hold property on trust at all. Rather, the language of the constructive trust is used simply as a device to hold the defendant personally liable to the claimant. The language of the constructive trust in this context, although still used, is inappropriate.[10] This area of the law is considered in Chapter 20 concerning personal liability arising from a breach of trust.

The constructive trust differs from the other types of trust which have been considered so far. Unlike the express trust, a constructive trust arises by operation of law and does not depend on the intention of the parties.[11] The distinction between constructive and resulting trusts is less clear than it used to be. Traditionally, resulting trusts arise where there is a failure to dispose of the whole beneficial interest, while constructive trusts are imposed to prevent unconscionable conduct.[12] Some of the

---

[6] See *Foskett v McKeown* [2001] 1 AC 102 [p. 915, below]. Cf Lord Millett in *Equity in Commercial Law* (eds. Degeling and Edelman) (2005), pp. 315–316 who says that the substitute property is held on the same trusts. So if the claimant was a beneficiary under an express trust, the substituted asset would be held on the same express trust.

[7] *Boardman v Phipps* [1967] 2 AC 46 [p. 801, below]; *A-G's Reference (No 1 of 1985)* [1986] QB 491 at 503.

[8] An alternative proprietary remedy is a charge on the fund held by the defendant. Such a remedy gives the claimant priority over the defendant's other creditors but does not involve a claim to any increase in the value of the asset. See p. 945, below.   [9] See p. 969, below.

[10] *Dubai Aluminium Co. Ltd. v Salaam* [2002] UKHL 48, [2003] 2 AC 366, 404. See also *Paragon Finance plc. v DB Thakerar and Co* [1999] 1 All ER 400, 408, *per* Millett LJ.

[11] *Westdeutsche Landesbank Girozentrale v Islington London Borough Council* [1996] AC 669 at 705; (Lord Browne-Wilkinson); *Air Jamaica Ltd v Charlton* [1999] 1 WLR 1399 at 1412, *per* Lord Millett.

[12] See (2006) 4 LS 475 (N. Hopkins).

more recent decisions have shown a tendency to merge the two concepts, as sometimes occurred in the context of family property disputes,[13] But the House of Lords has now ruled that only the constructive trust is available in that context.[14] This has little practical significance (for example, no formalities are required for the creation of either resulting or constructive trusts)[15] but adds to the existing difficulties in attempting to define the constructive trust.

Finally, we need to consider whether a general principle can be found which will determine the circumstances in which a constructive trust will be recognised. This would be a great improvement over the present miscellany. Some find this in the principle of unjust enrichment, arguing that where the defendant is unjustly enriched at the expense of the claimant, he should disgorge this enrichment, and, since the defendant should never have had the property, his creditors should not be entitled to share it. Some decisions in the era of Lord Denning MR. went further, treating a constructive trust as a doctrine which permits a desired result to be reached on a principle of justice and good conscience, regardless of the effect upon the rights of third parties of using a proprietary remedy to reach the solution.[16] Lord Browne-Wilkinson has sought to explain the constructive trust by reference to the unconscionable conduct of the potential trustee.[17] While this may explain some of the cases where a constructive trust has been recognised, it is a principle which is too uncertain to constitute a unifying theory of the constructive trust. Consequently, there appears to be no satisfactory general principle which explains when constructive trusts arise. Rather, we need to identify the particular categories where the constructive trust has previously been recognised.

II CATEGORIES OF CONSTRUCTIVE TRUST

A UNCONSCIONABLE CONDUCT[18]

The court may conclude that the defendant holds property on constructive trust where he received it from the claimant in circumstances where the defendant can be characterised as acting unconscionably.

---

[13] See Lord Denning MR in *Hussey v Palmer* [1972] 1 WLR 1286 at 1290. A resulting trust, however, creates a share proportionate to the contribution, which may not be the case with a constructive trust: p. 322, below.   [14] *Stack v Dowden* [2007] UKHL 17, [2007] 2 AC 432 [p. 334, below].

[15] See p. 112, above. See, however, *Macmillan Inc v Bishopsgate Investment Trust plc (No 3)* [1995] 1 WLR 978 (distinctions in the conflict of laws).

[16] [1973] CLP 17 (A.J. Oakley); (1977) 28 *Northern Ireland Law Quarterly* 123 (R.H. Maudsley).

[17] *Westdeutsche Landesbank Girozentrale v Islington London Borough Council* [1996] AC 669 at 705, p. 281, below. See also *Paragon Finance Ltd v D B Thakerar* [1999] 1 All ER 400 at 409 (Millett LJ).

[18] Lewin, pp. 242–245; P&M, pp. 410–418; P&S, pp. 271–272; Snell, pp. 587–588, 591–592; T&H, pp. 842–848;U&H, pp. 508–512.

This was recognised in **Westdeutsche Landesbank Girozentrale v Islington London Borough Council** [1996] AC 669[19] [p. 198, above]. In this case the plaintiff bank had paid money to the defendant local authority pursuant to an interest rate swap contract which was null and void. The bank sought restitution of the money. One question which was considered by LORD BROWNE-WILKINSON was whether the defendant held the money it had received on a constructive trust. His Lordship said at 705:

The relevant principles of trust law

(i) Equity operates on the conscience of the owner of the legal interest. In the case of a trust, the conscience of the legal owner requires him to carry out the purposes for which the property was vested in him (express or implied trust) or which the law imposes on him by reason of his unconscionable conduct (constructive trust).

(ii) Since the equitable jurisdiction to enforce trusts depends upon the conscience of the holder of the legal interest being affected, he cannot be a trustee of the property if and so long as he is ignorant of the facts alleged to affect his conscience, i.e. until he is aware ... in the case of a constructive trust, of the factors which are alleged to affect his conscience.

(iii) In order to establish a trust there must be identifiable trust property. The only apparent exception to this rule is a constructive trust imposed on a person who dishonestly assists in a breach of trust who may come under fiduciary duties even if he does not receive identifiable trust property.[20]

(iv) Once a trust is established, as from the date of its establishment the beneficiary has, in equity, a proprietary interest in the trust property, which proprietary interest will be enforceable in equity against any subsequent holder of the property (whether the original property or substituted property into which it can be traced) other than a purchaser for value of the legal interest without notice. . . .

This is not a case where the bank had any equitable interest which pre-dated receipt by the local authority of the upfront payment. Therefore, in order to show that the local authority became a trustee, the bank must demonstrate circumstances which raised a trust for the first time either at the date on which the local authority received the money or at the date on which payment into the mixed account was made. Counsel for the bank specifically disavowed any claim based on a constructive trust. This was plainly right because the local authority had no relevant knowledge sufficient to raise a constructive trust at any time before the moneys, upon the bank account going into overdraft, became untraceable. Once there ceased to be an identifiable trust fund, the local authority could not become a trustee: *Re Goldcorp Exchange Ltd* [1995] 1 AC 74.

His Lordship then considered whether the local authority held the money it received on a resulting trust for the bank: see p. 202, above. He considered various authorities including *Chase Manhattan Bank NA v Israel-British Bank (London) Ltd* [1981] Ch 105:

In that case Chase Manhattan, a New York bank, had by mistake paid the same sum twice to the credit of the defendant, a London bank. Shortly thereafter, the defendant bank went into

---

[19] [1996] *Restitution Law Review* 3 (P. Birks). See also *Pennington v Waine* [2002] EWCA Civ 227, [2002] 1 WLR 2075. See p. 164, above.

[20] But the better view is that there is no constructive trust in such a situation, but only a personal liability to the claimant. See p. 969, below.

insolvent liquidation. The question was whether Chase Manhattan had a claim *in rem* against the assets of the defendant bank to recover the second payment.

Goulding J was asked to assume that the moneys paid under a mistake were capable of being traced in the assets of the recipient bank: he was only concerned with the question whether there was a proprietary base on which the tracing remedy could be founded: at 116. He held that, where money was paid under a mistake, the receipt of such money without more constituted the recipient a trustee: he said that the payer 'retains an equitable property in it and the conscience of [the recipient] is subjected to a fiduciary duty to respect his proprietary right' at 119.

It will be apparent from what I have already said that I cannot agree with this reasoning. First, it is based on a concept of retaining an equitable property in money where, prior to the payment to the recipient bank, there was no existing equitable interest. Further, I cannot understand how the recipient's 'conscience' can be affected at a time when he is not aware of any mistake. Finally, the judge found that the law of England and that of New York were in substance the same. I find this a surprising conclusion since the New York law of constructive trusts has for a long time been influenced by the concept of a remedial constructive trust, whereas hitherto English law has for the most part only recognised an institutional constructive trust: see *Metall und Rohstoff AG v Donaldson Lufkin & Jenrette Inc* [1990] 1 QB 391 at 478–480. In the present context, that distinction is of fundamental importance. Under an institutional constructive trust, the trust arises by operation of law as from the date of the circumstances which give rise to it: the function of the court is merely to declare that such trust has arisen in the past. The consequences that flow from such trust having arisen (including the possibly unfair consequences to third parties who in the interim have received the trust property) are also determined by rules of law, not under a discretion. A remedial constructive trust, as I understand it, is different. It is a judicial remedy giving rise to an enforceable equitable obligation: the extent to which it operates retrospectively to the prejudice of third parties lies in the discretion of the court. Thus, for the law of New York to hold that there is a remedial constructive trust where a payment has been made under a void contract gives rise to different consequences from holding that an institutional constructive trust arises in English law.

However, although I do not accept the reasoning of Goulding J, Chase Manhattan may well have been rightly decided. The defendant bank knew of the mistake made by the paying bank within two days of the receipt of the moneys: see at 115. The judge treated this fact as irrelevant (at 114) but in my judgment it may well provide a proper foundation for the decision. Although the mere receipt of the moneys, in ignorance of the mistake, gives rise to no trust, the retention of the moneys after the recipient bank learned of the mistake may well have given rise to a constructive trust....[21]

The stolen bag of coins
The argument for a resulting trust was said to be supported by the case of a thief who steals a bag of coins. At law those coins remain traceable only so long as they are kept separate: as soon as they are mixed with other coins or paid into a mixed bank account they cease to be traceable at law.[22] Can it really be the case, it is asked, that in such circumstances the thief cannot be required to disgorge the property which, in equity, represents the stolen coins? Moneys can

---

[21] See *Bank of America v Arnell* [1999] Lloyd's Rep Bank 399; *Re Farepak Food and Gifts Ltd* [2006] EWHC 3272 (Ch), at para. 40 (Mann J).   [22] See p. 898, below.

only be traced in equity if there has been at some stage a breach of fiduciary duty, i.e. if either before the theft there was an equitable proprietary interest (e.g. the coins were stolen trust moneys) or such interest arises under a resulting trust at the time of the theft or the mixing of the moneys. Therefore, it is said, a resulting trust must arise either at the time of the theft or when the moneys are subsequently mixed. Unless this is the law, there will be no right to recover the assets representing the stolen moneys once the moneys have become mixed.

I agree that the stolen moneys are traceable in equity. But the proprietary interest which equity is enforcing in such circumstances arises under a constructive, not a resulting, trust. Although it is difficult to find clear authority for the proposition, when property is obtained by fraud equity imposes a constructive trust on the fraudulent recipient: the property is recoverable and traceable in equity. Thus, an infant who has obtained property by fraud is bound in equity to restore it: *Stocks v Wilson* [1913] 2 KB 235 at 244; *R Leslie Ltd v Sheill* [1914] 3 KB 607. Moneys stolen from a bank account can be traced in equity: *Bankers Trust Co v Shapira* [1980] 1 WLR 1274 at 1282: see also *McCormick v Grogan* (1869) LR 4 HL 82 at 97.[23]

The penultimate paragraph was considered by RIMER J in **Shalson v Russo** [2003] EWHC 1637 (Ch), [2005] Ch 281, at para. 110:

I do not find that an easy passage. As to the first paragraph, a thief ordinarily acquires no property in what he steals and cannot give a title to it even to a good faith purchaser: both the thief and the purchaser are vulnerable to claims by the true owner to recover his property. If the thief has no title in the property, I cannot see how he can become a trustee of it for the true owner: the owner retains the legal and beneficial title. If the thief mixes stolen money with other money in a bank account, the common law cannot trace into it. Equity has traditionally been regarded as similarly incompetent unless it could first identify a relevant fiduciary relationship, but in many cases of theft there will be none. The fact that, traditionally, equity can only trace into a mixed bank account if that precondition is first satisfied provides an unsatisfactory justification for any conclusion that the stolen money must necessarily be trust money so as to enable the precondition to be satisfied. It is either trust money or it is not. If it is not, it is not legitimate artificially to change its character so as to bring it within the supposed limits of equity's powers to trace: the answer is to develop those powers so as to meet the special problems raised by stolen money....

As to Lord Browne-Wilkinson's more general proposition in the second paragraph that property obtained by fraud is automatically held by the recipient on a constructive trust for the person defrauded, I respectfully regard the authorities he cites as providing less than full support for it. At any rate, they do not in my view support the proposition that property transferred under a voidable contract induced by fraud will immediately (and prior to any rescission) be held on trust for the transferor.[24]

---

[23] Other cases where a constructive trust has been recognised where the defendant has obtained property by fraud, include: *Halley v The Law Society* [2003] EWCA Civ 97, para [48] Carnwath LJ; *Papamichael v National Westminster Bank plc.* [2003] 1 Lloyd's Rep. 341, 374 (Judge Chambers QC); *Commerzbank AG v IMB Morgan plc* [2004] EWHC 2771 (Ch), [2004] All ER (D) 450 (Nov) at [36] (Lawrence Collins J); *Sinclair Investment Holdings SA v Versailles Trade Finance Ltd* [2005] EWCA Civ 722, [2006] 1 BCLC 60; *Campden Hill Ltd. v Chakrani* [2005] EWHC 911 (Ch.).

[24] See further p. 284, below.

QUESTIONS

1. Will a defendant hold money on constructive trust where that money was paid pursuant to a void contract and the defendant knew that the contract was void? See Virgo, *The Principles of the Law of Restitution* (2nd edn, 2006) p. 610. Cp. Chambers, *Resulting Trusts* (1997) chapter 7.

2. Will a defendant only be considered to have acted unconscionably where he knew of the relevant factors which affected his conscience, such as the claimant's mistake in making a payment? What if the defendant should have known of the mistake but this did not cross his mind? See *Westdeutsche Landesbank Girozentrale v Islington London Borough Council* [1996] AC 669 at 705; *Papamichael v National Westminster Bank plc* [2003] 1 Lloyd's Rep 341, 373 (Judge Chambers QC) (actual knowledge required); Virgo, *The Principles of the Law of Restitution*, (2nd edn, 2006) p.611; [1996] 4 *Restitution Law Review* 21 (P. Birks).

3. Should a defendant be considered to have acted unconscionably where she receives property innocently and only discovers subsequently that it was transferred, for example, by mistake? See Virgo, *The Principles of the Law of Restitution*, (2nd edn, 2006) pp. 611–612.

4. The victim of theft whose money has been stolen will retain title to that money in law. So how can the thief hold that money on constructive trust for the victim? See *Shalson v Russo* [2003] EWHC 1637 (Ch) [2005] Ch 281, at para. 110 (Rimer J) [p. 283, above]; Virgo, *The Principles of the Law of Restitution*, (2nd edn, 2006) p.609–610.

B   RESCISSION[25]

In **Twinsectra Ltd v Yardley**[26] [1999] Lloyd's Rep Bank 438 POTTER LJ said at 461:

There is also authority to be found in *El Ajou v Dollar Land Holdings plc* [1993] 3 All ER 717 that monies of the plaintiffs paid away by the plaintiffs in reliance on a fraudulent share selling scheme gave rise to an 'old fashioned institutional resulting trust' (see at 734). In that case, as in his earlier decision in *Lonrho plc v Fayed (No 2)* [1992] 1 WLR 1, Millett J held that a victim of fraud is entitled to rescind the transaction, thereby revesting his equitable title 'at least to the extent necessary to support an equitable tracing claim', later acknowledging in *Bristol and West Building Society v Mothew* [1998] Ch 1 at 23 that, in doing so, he:

'was concerned to circumvent the supposed rule that there must be a fiduciary relationship or retained beneficial interest before resort may be had to the equitable tracing remedy.'

---

[25] H&M, pp. 334–335; Lewin, p. 244; P&M, pp. 410–418; Snell, p. 592; T&H, pp. 857–858; U&H, pp. 538–539.

[26] (2000) 59 CLJ 444 (D. Fox). This point was not considered by the House of Lords.

In the *Lonhro* case, at 11–12, Millett J stated:

> 'A contract obtained by fraudulent misrepresentation is voidable, not void, even in equity. The representee may elect to avoid it, but until he does so, the representor is not a constructive trustee of the property transferred pursuant to the contract, and no fiduciary relationship exists between him and the representee, see *Daly v Sydney Stock Exchange Ltd* (1986) 160 CLR 371 at 387–390 *per* Brennan J. It may well be that if the representee elects to avoid the contract and set aside a transfer of property made pursuant to it, the beneficial interest in the property will be treated as having remained vested in him throughout, at least to the extent necessary to support any tracing claim.'

In the course of his submissions Mr. Tager sought to build upon a short passage of Lord Browne-Wilkinson's speech which I have quoted, an edifice which I do not think it was meant to support. He has argued (i) that the obtaining of monies by false pretences (at least in the circumstances of this case) should be regarded as 'theft', it having been long accepted, by whatever conceptual route, that theft, as such, immediately constitutes the thief a constructive trustee of the stolen money so that the victim may later trace in equity: see *Banque Belge pour L'Etranger v Hambrouck* [1921] 1 KB 321 *per* Bankes and Atkin LJJ, who held in the case of stolen cheques that the plaintiff bank could trace its money in law and equity, and *per* Scrutton LJ who considered that the bank could trace only in equity; (ii) that, even if that were not so, Lord Browne-Wilkinson's observation should be read at face value as recognising that a constructive trust is imposed upon the recipient at the moment of receipt.

I do not accept either argument. It seems to me that, whatever the legal distinctions between 'theft' and 'fraud' in other areas of the law, the distinction of importance here is that between non-consensual transfers and transfers pursuant to contracts which are voidable for misrepresentation. In the latter case, the transferor may elect whether to avoid or affirm the transaction and, until he elects to avoid it, there is no constructive (resulting) trust; in the former case, the constructive trust arises upon the moment of transfer. The result, so far as third parties are concerned, is that, before rescission, the owner has no proprietary interest in the original property; all he has is the 'mere equity' of his right to set aside the voidable contract. That equity binds volunteers and those taking with notice of the equity, but not purchasers for value without notice; see generally Worthington: *Proprietary Interests in Commercial Transactions* (1996) Clarendon Press at pp. 163–165 and 167. Despite dicta of Lord Mustill in *Re Goldcorp*[27] (a case in which the purchase monies sought to be traced were unidentifiable), which, if generally applied beyond the context of the facts in that case, would suggest that equitable title does not (or in appropriate circumstances may not) revest on rescission, the general position seems to me that summarised in *Underhill and Hayton* (15th edn) at p. 372(f). It is there stated that equity imposes a constructive trust on property where a transferor's legal and equitable title to his property has passed to the transferee according to basic principles of property law but in circumstances (e.g. involving fraud and misrepresentation) where the transferor has an equitable right (i.e. mere equity) to recover the property by having the transfer set aside, and the court declares that from the outset the transferee has held the property to transferor's order, though nowadays it seems better to regard a restitutionary resulting trust as arising.[28]

[27] *Re Goldcorp Exchange Ltd* [1995] 1 AC 74.

[28] See *Collings v Lee* [2001] 2 All ER 332 (trust arising from a non-consensual transfer to an agent); (2001) 117 LQR 381 (D. O'Sullivan); *Papamichael v National Westminster Bank plc.* [2003] 1 Lloyd's Rep. 341; *Shalson v Russo* [2004] EWHC 1637, [2005] Ch 281, paras. 120–127; *London Allied Holdings Ltd v Lee* [2007]

Lord Millett in *Equity in Commercial Law* (eds. Degeling and Edelman) (2005), p. 320

...I accepted the traditional view that rescission for fraud revested the legal title in the transferor: see *Car and Universe Finance Co Ltd v Caldwell* [1965] 1 QB 525. The proposition can be traced back to the judgment of Parke B in *Load v Green* (1846) 15 M and W 216...Since then, however, Mr. Swadling has convincingly demonstrated that Parke B invented the rule, which is difficult to justify in principle and is based on previous authority which does not support it:...(2005) 121 LQR 122. The better view, which he espouses and which is supported by authority before and since, is that a defrauded vendor should be able to rescind his contract of sale but this should not carry with it any revesting of title, at least in the case where title passed by delivery pursuant to the rescinded contract and not by the contract itself: see *Singh v Ali* [1960] AC 167. If this is right, then equity must follow the law by denying any revesting of title merely because the underlying transaction is set aside.[29]

C   UNAUTHORISED PROFIT BY A FIDUCIARY

A person in a fiduciary position may not make use of this position to gain a benefit for himself. Any profit which a fiduciary obtains in breach of this duty[30] can be claimed to be held on constructive trust for the principal to whom the duty is owed.[31] A fiduciary includes an express trustee and also, for example, personal representatives, company directors, partners, solicitors, and agents. The category of fiduciaries is not closed.[32]

D   FIDUCIARIES *DE SON TORT*[33]

Where a person who has not been properly appointed either as a trustee[34] or an executor,[35] or any other type of fiduciary, such as an agent,[36] intermeddles with trust or estate matters, or does acts which are characteristic of the fiduciary office, such a

---

EWHC 2061 (Ch). See also R. Nolan in *Restitution and Equity, Volume 1: Resulting Trusts and Equitable Compensation* (ed. P. Birks and F. Rose), pp. 119–146; [2002] 10 *Restitution Law Review* 28 (S. Worthington). Cp. Chambers, *Resulting Trusts*, chap. 7.

[29] See also [2002] *Restitution Law Review* 28 (S. Worthington). Cf [2006] *Restitution Law Review* 106 (B. Häcker).   [30] See Chapter 16.

[31] *Attorney-General for Hong Kong v Reid* [1994] 1 AC 324, see p. 815, below. See also *Clark v Cutland* [2003] EWCA Civ 810, [2004] 1 WLR 783; *Papamichael v National Westminster Bank plc.* [2003] 1 Lloyd's Rep. 341, 371 (Judge Chambers QC); *Smalley v Bracken Partners* [2003] EWCA Civ 1875, [2004] WTLR 599; *Daraydan Holdings Ltd v Solland* [2004] EWHC 622 (Ch), [2005] Ch. 119.

[32] *English v Dedham Vale Properties Ltd* [1978] 1 WLR 93, [1978] 1 All ER 382. See p. 780, n. 13, below.

[33] H&M, p. 303; Lewin, pp. 238, 1773–1776; P&M pp. 373–374; Pettit, pp. 151–152, 166–167; T&H, pp. 961–962; U&H, p. 473.

[34] *Blyth v Fladgate* [1891] 1 Ch 337; *Mara v Browne* [1896] 1 Ch 199; *Taylor v Davies* [1920] AC 636, 651 (Viscount Cave); *Dubai Aluminium Co Ltd v Salaam* [2002] UKHL 48, [2003] 2 AC 366, see p. 639, below.

[35] *James v Williams* [2000] Ch 1. See p. 287, below.

[36] *Lyell v Kennedy* (1889) 14 App. Cas. 437.

person can be considered to be a constructive trustee. Such fiduciaries *de son tort*[37] will be treated by operation of equity as though they had been properly appointed to the respective office and so will be subject to fiduciary duties in the ordinary way and will hold property on constructive trust.[38]

James v Williams
[2000] Ch 1 (CA, **Sir Stephen Brown P, Swinton Thomas** and **Aldous LJJ**)[39]

The plaintiff's mother ('the grandmother') died intestate. The family home was to be held on statutory trusts for the plaintiff and her brother (William Junior) and sister (Thirza), but the brother, although he knew that he was not solely entitled to it, did not take out letters of administration and took possession of the property as his own. The brother died. He left the property to Thirza. On her death the property was left to the defendant. The plaintiff claimed her one-third interest in the property. The defendant argued that the plaintiff's claim was time-barred under the Limitation Act 1980.[40]

Held. The brother was an executor *de son tort* since he knew that he was not solely entitled to the house and he held the property on constructive trust. Consequently, the plaintiff's claim was not time-barred.[41]

Aldous LJ: As a general rule a constructive trust attaches by law to property which is held by a person in circumstances where it would be inequitable to allow him to assert full beneficial ownership of the property. Is this such a case? . . .

In my view the circumstances of this case are such that the constructive trust arose in about 1972 on the death of the grandmother. William Junior knew that he was not solely entitled to the property. He took it upon himself to take possession of the property as if he owned it and assumed responsibility for its upkeep. In my view he was under an equitable duty to hold the property for himself and his sisters. Looking at the state of affairs as at the grandmother's death, the law envisaged that the property would be held upon a statutory trust for the children. It would be inequitable to allow William Junior and, through him the defendant, to take advantage of his decision not to take out letters of administration and to act as if he was the owner with the full knowledge that he was not. This is an unusual case and, as was made clear by Mr. Hinks in his article,[42] there are many cases where executors *de son tort* could not be constructive trustees. Each case will depend upon its own facts. But, in my view, this is a case where there was a constructive trust. It follows that the defendant's title is that of constructive trustee with the result that the plaintiff's case is not statute-barred.

---

[37] Perhaps better described simply as de facto trustees or executors. See *Dubai Aluminium Co Ltd v Salaam* [2002] UKHL 48, [2003] 2 AC 366, 403 (Lord Millett), p. 639, below.

[38] *Re Barney* [1892] 2 Ch 265, 273 (Kekewich J).

[39] [1999] All ER Rev 232 (P. Clarke).

[40] Section 15(1) (12-year limitation period).

[41] For discussion of limitation periods, see p. 876, below.

[42] [1974] Conv 176 (F. Hinks).

E MUTUAL WILLS[43]

Where two persons by agreement make wills which give the property of the first to die to the survivor, and after the survivor's death to agreed legatees, they are said to make mutual wills. The parties are commonly husband and wife, but not necessarily so. The survivor may be given a life interest with remainders over to the agreed legatees; or perhaps an absolute interest with a substitutionary gift to the agreed legatees.[44] It is now established that the doctrine of mutual wills applies even where no property is left to the survivor.

Assume that the husband is the first to die and he dies with a will which takes effect in the agreed form. The widow then remarries and decides to leave all her estate to her new husband. This would be a breach of the agreement. But, at least until recently, the agreed legatees cannot sue (even if they knew about the agreement) because they were not parties to the agreement.[45] Nor can the widow be prevented from making a new will, for an existing will is always revocable.[46] It is not right that the widow should be able to ignore the obligations of the contract, even if she has taken no benefit. Consequently, it has long been accepted that a trust is imposed in favour of the agreed legatees. But that simple solution leaves a number of questions unanswered.

1. Is this an express trust or a constructive trust? If an express trust, who declared it, and when, and in respect of which identifiable property? If a constructive trust, upon what ground?[47] The failure to carry out the contract is not a sufficient justification. The receipt of benefits under the first will would be sufficient justification; but it has been held that such receipt is not necessary.[48] Is fraud the basis?

2. To what property does the trust attach?[49] To that (if any) received by the survivor from the first to die? To that owned by the survivor at the date of the first death? To all property owned by the survivor at the date of the survivor's death?

---

[43] H&M pp. 324–331; Lewin, pp. 351–361; P&M, pp. 430–438; P&S , p. 280; Pettit, pp. 135–138; Snell, pp. 560–563; T&H, pp. 904–906; U&H, pp. 529–535; Oakley, *Constructive Trusts* (3rd edn), pp. 263–274; *Williams on Wills* (8th edn, 2002), chap. 2; *Theobald on Wills* (16th edn, 2001) pp. 27–28, 111–112; (1951) 14 MLR 136 (J.D.B. Mitchell); (1951) 15 Conv (NS) 28 (G.B. Graham); (1970) 34 Conv (NS) 230 (R. Burgess); (1977) 15 *Alberta Law Review* 211 (L.A. Sheridan); (1979) *University of Toronto Law Journal* 390 (T.G. Youdan); [1982] Conv 228 (K. Hodkinson); (1989) 105 LQR 534; (1991) 54 MLR 581 (C.E.F. Rickett); [1996] Conv 136 (C.E.F. Rickett); Conv Precedents 4–4.   [44] *Re Green* [1951] Ch 148.

[45] This may well be different following the enactment of the Contracts (Rights of Third Parties) Act 1999. See p. 169, above. By virtue of s. 1 of this Act a person who is not party to a contract is able to enforce terms of that contract in his own right either if it expressly provides that that party can enforce the contract or if the contract confers a benefit on him , save, in the latter case, where the parties did not intend the party to be able to enforce the terms of the contract.   [46] *Re Hey's Estate* [1914] P 192.

[47] In *Re Hobley* (1997) The Times, 16 June the trust was characterised as constructive. Similarly in *Healey v Brown* [2002] WTLR 849 [p. 301, below], where the trust was characterised as a common intention constructive trust. In *Thomas and Agnes Carvel Foundation v Carvel* [2007] EWHC 1314 (Ch), [2007] 4 All ER 81, the survivor was described simply as a trustee.   [48] *Re Dale* [1994] Ch 31 [p. 294, below].

[49] (1951) 14 MLR 136 at 139, 140 (J.D.B. Mitchell) [p. 289, below].

3. When does that trust come into effect? It is clear that the trust does not come into existence before the death of either testator.[50] So does it occur on the first death (which would prevent a lapse of the interest of one of the agreed beneficiaries)? Or on the second death, at which time the property which is the subject of the trust would be identifiable?

4. Could the estate of the first to die take proceedings to enforce the agreement on the principle of *Beswick v Beswick?* [1968] AC 58; H&M, p. 326; *Re Dale* [1994] Ch 31 [p. 294, below]. Alternatively, could the agreed legatees enforce the agreement under the Contracts (Rights of Third Parties) Act 1999 [p. 169, above]?

(1951) 14 MLR 136, 139–140 (J.D.B. Mitchell)

Scope of the Trust

The date of creation has important consequences on the scope of the trust. It is obvious that where the first testator's will only gives a life interest to the survivor, no question arises in relation to that estate. It must be held upon trust to give effect to the whole will including the ultimate dispositions. Similarly even if it apparently gives an absolute interest, yet the survivor holds all that he receives thereunder on trust for himself for life and then for the ultimate beneficiaries.[51] The trust, however, where the doctrine applies, affects not only the estate of the first testator but also that of the survivor. The question is as to the extent to which it does so. Is the entirety comprised in it and if so is it the entirety as at the first death or does the trust also comprise after-acquired property?

The short answer would simply be that the extent of the trust is defined by the agreement. Thus in *Re Green* the trust was to operate on property received from the other party and on property which was derived from another trust.[52] The definition might be express, as in that case, or implied, by reason, for example, of the fact that the ultimate gifts are set out in specific sums and not as residuary dispositions. This short answer is not, judging from the few reported cases, satisfactory since the agreement is often silent or ambiguous on the point. In one case[53] the trust apparently only affected property held by the survivor at the first death. That restriction was perhaps dictated by the fact that the mutual wills were only intended to deal with the assets of the two testators which resulted from a business they had carried on together. It was therefore reasonable to allow the survivor a free hand with the fruits of his unaided labour. In *Re Oldham*[54] Astbury J seemed disposed to hold that the trust only binds the property held by the survivor at the time of his death, thus leaving unimpaired the power of disposition *inter vivos*. This seems to conflict with the decision as to lapse in *Re Hagger,* which implies that the interest of the beneficiaries is vested during the lifetime of the survivor. Moreover a devise to A with a direction to settle 'so much as he shall die seised of' has, by reason of uncertainty, been held

---

[50] *Re Hobley* (1997), The Times, 16 June (the doctrine of mutual wills held not to apply once the first testator to die had altered his will in a way which was minor but not insignificant).

[51] *Re Green* [1951] Ch 148.

[52] In this respect *Re Green* does nothing more than make clear the effect of the agreement, which was implicit in earlier decisions, such as *Re Hagger* [1930] 2 Ch 190 at 195, or *Re Oldham* [1925] Ch 75, where, had the trust been regarded as effective, there would nevertheless have been some free property. The arrangement in *Dufour v Pereira* (1769) 1 Dick 419 seems only to have covered residue. See 2 Hargr Jurid Arg, p. 305.

[53] *Re Hagger* [1930] 2 Ch 190.   [54] [1925] Ch 75 at 88.

incapable of creating a trust.[55] Yet, in effect, that is what the view of Astbury J amounts to. The significance of this question lies of course in the powers of the survivor over his own property during his life. It would seem absurd if the court is prepared to prevent his breaking faith with the first testator only to the extent of preventing inconsistent testamentary dispositions thus allowing him to make the arrangement nugatory by dispositions *inter vivos*. It seems, therefore, that the two arguments of certainty and good faith lead to the conclusions that, in the absence of any definition, the trust of the survivor's property must be treated as embracing that which he holds at the death of the first testator together with subsequently acquired property; though clearly he will be entitled to deal freely with the income of the fund and accumulations of the income. Such indeed seems to be the implication to be drawn from Lord Camden's direction for accounts to be taken in *Dufour v Pereira,* and to have been the opinion of Lord Loughborough. It was one of his objections to finding an agreement in *Lord Walpole v Lord Orford*[56] that it would have resulted in an inability of the survivor to raise portions for his daughters by mortgage. This breadth of the scope of the trust, or at least the possibility of it, affords another reason for delimiting it in the agreement.

In **Re Hagger** [1930] 2 Ch 190, a husband and wife made a joint will (to which the same principles apply) by which, *inter alia*, the survivor was given a life interest in the whole of their estate, and after the survivor's death, their property at Wandsworth was to be held on trust for sale, with Eleanor Palmer as one of nine beneficiaries. The wife died in 1904, Eleanor Palmer in 1923, and the husband in 1928. By his will the husband left all his property on different trusts. The questions were whether the beneficiaries under the joint will could take on the husband's death; and, if so, whether Eleanor Palmer's interest lapsed by reason of her death before the husband. Clauson J held that all the beneficiaries, including Eleanor, could claim. He said at 195:

To my mind *Dufour v Pereira* (1769) 1 Dick 419 decides that where there is a joint will such as this, on the death of the first testator the position as regards that part of the property which belongs to the survivor is that the survivor will be treated in this Court as holding the property on trust to apply it so as to carry out the effect of the joint will. As I read Lord Camden's judgment in *Dufour v Pereira* that would be so, even though the survivor did not signify his election to give effect to the will by taking benefits under it. But in any case it is clear that Lord Camden has decided that if the survivor takes a benefit conferred on him by the joint will he will be treated as a trustee in this Court, and he will not be allowed to do anything inconsistent with the provisions of the joint will. It is not necessary for me to consider the reasons on which Lord Camden based his judgment. The case must be accepted in this Court as binding. Therefore I am bound to hold that from the death of the wife the husband held the property, according to the tenor of the will, subject to the trusts thereby imposed upon it, at all events if he took advantage of the provisions of the will. In my view he did take advantage of those provisions.

The effect of the will was that the husband and wife agreed that the property should on the death of the first of them to die pass to trustees to hold on trusts inconsistent with the right of survivorship, and therefore the will effected a severance of the joint interest of the husband and wife. By the will they made a provision which was inconsistent with the survivor taking by

[55] *Bland v Bland* (1745) 2 Cox Eq Cas 349. See also *Re Jones* [1898] 1 Ch 438.
[56] (1797) 3 Ves 402 at 417. For the opposed view see, however, Dixon J in *Birmingham v Renfrew* (1937) 57 CLR 666 at 689. See also *Re Cleaver* [1981] 1 WLR 939 [p. 292, below].

survivorship. Therefore the property at the moment when, on the wife's death, it came within the ambit of the will ceased to be held by the two jointly, and the husband had no title to the wife's interest on her dying in his lifetime, save in so far as he took a life interest under the joint will. From the moment of the wife's death the Wandsworth property was held on trust for the husband for life with a vested interest in remainder as to one-sixth in E. Palmer. So far as the husband's interest in the property is concerned the will operated as a trust from the date of the wife's death. There is, accordingly, no lapse by reason of Eleanor Palmer's death in the husband's lifetime, but after the wife's death.

Similar questions arise, where, as in **Ottaway v Norman** [1972] Ch 698, property is left to a legatee upon a secret trust to leave it by will to another. Brightman J, as has been seen,[57] upheld the trust.

(1973) 36 MLR 210, 212–214 (S.M. Bandali)

On the evidence [in *Ottaway v Norman*] Brightman J found that the residue was not intended to be subject to trust. However, he went on to state a new principle, while making clear that this was obiter. 'I am content to assume for present purposes but without so deciding that if property is given to the primary donee on the understanding that the primary donee will dispose by will of such assets, if any, as he may have at his command at his death in favour of the secondary donee, a valid trust is created in favour of the secondary donee which is in suspense during the lifetime of the primary donee, but attached to the estate of the primary donee at the moment of the latter's death.'[58] In the present case on the evidence there had been no such 'far-reaching undertaking' and, therefore, no trust arose as regards Eva's [the house-keeper's] residuary estate. Moreover, no obligation had been undertaken by Eva as regards the money she had received under H's will. Such an obligation could be binding provided the donor and donee had discussed and intended that the donee should keep the money distinct from her own money, but there was no such evidence here.[59] However, the above doctrine of a 'trust in suspense' calls for analysis, for apart from being a salutary, if bad, attempt at indicating the potential dynamism of equitable principles, the opinion ignores some difficulties.

There is no clear English authority on this concept. The court referred to *Birmingham v Renfrew*,[60] an Australian decision, as giving some support to the proposition. This was a case of mutual wills where the survivor-husband revoked his will in breach of the undertaking he had given to his wife, and the High Court held that the agreement between them had created a constructive trust not of any specific property but of any residue of property, of whatever character, at the time of the survivor's death. The obligation was a 'floating obligation, suspended, so to speak, during the lifetime of the survivor [and] can descend upon the assets at his death and crystallise into a trust'.[61] Let us consider theoretical difficulties.

First, there is the problem of determining the ownership of property in the interval. Is the property (i.e. which 'he may have at his command at his death') during the intervening period vested in the primary donee or the secondary donee? If the former, then the legal owner should

---

[57] See p. 132, above.   [58] *Ottaway v Norman* [1972] Ch 698 at 713.

[59] The absence of this intention to keep the money distinct was, according to Brightman J, the distinguishing factor from *Re Gardner* [1920] 2 Ch 523, where the half-secret trust clearly showed that the donee only had a life interest in the personal estate of the donor.   [60] (1937) 57 CLR 666.

[61] (1937) 57 CLR 666 at 689 *per* Dixon J.

logically be able to dispose of it subject to any possible remedy for a breach of contract which, again, would be subject to the rules of privity and consideration. If the ownership is vested in the secondary donee, then there is an immediate trust. But, according to Brightman J, the trust 'attaches...at the moment of the [primary donee's] death'. It is submitted that the difficulty cannot be avoided by holding that, in such circumstances, the primary donee has a life interest in such assets, for the fact is that the donor has been given a promise that property would be given 'if any' is left at the donee's death; this suggests that the donee is free to do what he likes with the property.[62] Moreover, if the trust attaches when the primary donee dies, what property could be subject to a life interest before that event?

Secondly, such an undertaking would in all probability fail to satisfy the requirement of certainty of the subject matter of a trust. This requirement has to be satisfied at the time the trust comes into operation. Brightman J's words that the trust is, during the intervening period, in suspense suggests that the trust has its existence at the time the donor dies, though it does not 'bite' until the primary donee dies. If so, such a trust would fail to meet the test of certainty. The primary donee should then take the property absolutely. Moreover, the trust is open to the charge of inconsistency of directions if the primary donee is entitled to do what he likes with the property during his lifetime (an absolute ownership) but is bound by a promise to leave any residue of that property in a particular way at his death.[63] It is therefore submitted that the trust concept cannot legitimately be extended to deal with the situation envisaged by Brightman J. It would be theoretically better if the situation is left to be dealt with by the law of contract, i.e. the estate of the promisor should be subject to contractual obligation undertaken by the promisor.

In **Re Cleaver** [1981] 1 WLR 939, an elderly couple married in 1967 and made wills in each other's favour, with a substitutionary gift to the husband's three children. After the husband's death, the wife made a new will, leaving the property to one child only. Nourse J held that, on the balance of probabilities, there had been an agreement to make mutual wills, and therefore a constructive trust had arisen. Following *Birmingham v Renfrew* (1937) 57 CLR 666, it was held that the trust attached to the survivor's assets, allowing her to enjoy the property subject to a fiduciary duty which crystallised on her death and disabled her only from voluntary dispositions *inter vivos* calculated to defeat the agreement. There would be no objection to ordinary gifts of small value.

Nourse J, having referred to *Dufour v Pereira* (1769) 1 Dick 419 and *Re Oldham* [1925] Ch 75, said at 945:

I do not find it necessary to refer to any other English case, but I have derived great assistance from the decision of the High Court of Australia in *Birmingham v Renfrew* (1937) 57 CLR 666. That was a case where the available extrinsic evidence was held to be sufficient to establish the necessary agreement between two spouses. It is chiefly of interest because both Sir John Latham CJ and more especially Dixon J examined with some care the whole nature of the legal theory on which these and other similar cases proceed. I would like to read three passages from the judgment of Dixon J which state, with all the clarity and learning for which the judgments of

---

[62] Presumably, if the trust arises at the death of the donee, and if the ultimate beneficiary predeceases the donee then, unlike in *Re Gardner* [1923] 2 Ch 230, the trust fails. Who would then be entitled to the property?

[63] Cf. *Re Golay's Will Trusts* [1965] 1 WLR 969 and *Re Jones* [1898] 1 Ch 438.

that most eminent judge are renowned, what I believe to be a correct analysis of the principles on which a case of enforceable mutual wills depends. The first passage reads, at 682–683:

'I think the legal result was a contract between husband and wife. The contract bound him, I think, during her lifetime not to revoke his will without notice to her. If she died without altering her will then he was bound after her death not to revoke his will at all. She on her part afforded the consideration for his promise by making her will. His obligation not to revoke his will during her life without notice to her is to be implied. For I think the express promise should be understood as meaning that if she died leaving her will unrevoked then he would not revoke his. But the agreement really assumes that neither party will alter his or her will without the knowledge of the other. It has long been established that a contract between persons to make corresponding wills gives rise to equitable obligations when one acts on the faith of such an agreement and dies leaving his will unrevoked so that the other takes property under its dispositions. It operates to impose upon the survivor an obligation regarded as specifically enforceable. It is true that he cannot be compelled to make and leave unrevoked a testamentary document and if he dies leaving a last will containing provisions inconsistent with his agreement it is nevertheless valid as a testamentary act. But the doctrines of equity attach the obligation to the property. The effect is, I think, that the survivor becomes a constructive trustee and the terms of the trust are those of the will which he undertook would be his last will.'

Next, at 689:

'There is a third element which appears to me to be inherent in the nature of such a contract or agreement, although I do not think it has been expressly considered. The purpose of an agreement for corresponding wills must often be, as in this case, to enable the survivor during his life to deal as absolute owner with the property passing under the will of the party first dying. That is to say, the object of the transaction is to put the survivor in a position to enjoy for his own benefit the full ownership so that, for instance, he may convert it and expend the proceeds if he choose. But when he dies he is to bequeath what is left in the manner agreed upon. It is only by the special doctrines of equity that such a floating obligation, suspended, so to speak, during the lifetime of the survivor can descend upon the assets at his death and crystallise into a trust. No doubt gifts and settlements, *inter vivos*, if calculated to defeat the intention of the compact, could not be made by the survivor and his right of disposition, *inter vivos*, is, therefore, not unqualified. But, substantially, the purpose of the arrangement will often be to allow full enjoyment for the survivor's own benefit and advantage upon condition that at his death the residue shall pass as arranged.'

Finally, at 690:

'In *Re Oldham* [1925] Ch 75 Astbury J pointed out, in dealing with the question whether an agreement should be inferred, that in *Dufour v Pereira* (1769) 1 Dick 419 the compact was that the survivor should take a life estate only in the combined property. It was therefore, easy to fix the corpus with a trust as from the death of the survivor. But I do not see any difficulty in modern equity in attaching to the assets a constructive trust which allowed the survivor to enjoy the property subject to a fiduciary duty which, so to speak, crystallised on his death and disabled him from voluntary dispositions *inter vivos*.'

I interject to say that Dixon J was there clearly referring only to voluntary dispositions *inter vivos* which are calculated to defeat the intention of the compact. No objection could normally be taken to ordinary gifts of small value. He went on:

'On the contrary, as I have said, it seems rather to provide a reason for the intervention of equity. The objection that the intended beneficiaries could not enforce a contract is met by the fact that a constructive trust arises from the contract and the fact that testamentary dispositions made upon the faith of it have taken effect. It is the constructive trust and not the contract that they are entitled to enforce.'

It is also clear from *Birmingham v Renfrew* that these cases of mutual wills are only one example of a wider category of cases, for example secret trusts, in which a court of equity will intervene to impose a constructive trust. A helpful and interesting summary of that wider category of cases will be found in the argument of Mr. Nugee in *Ottaway v Norman* [1972] Ch 698 at 701–702. The principle of all these cases is that a court of equity will not permit a person to whom property is transferred by way of gift, but on the faith of an agreement or clear understanding that it is to be dealt with in a particular way for the benefit of a third person, to deal with the property inconsistently with that agreement or understanding. If he attempts to do so after having received the benefit of the gift, equity will intervene by imposing a constructive trust on the property which is the subject matter of the agreement or understanding. I take that statement of principle, and much else which is of assistance in this case, from the judgment of Slade J in *Re Pearson Fund Trusts* (21 October, 1977 unreported). The statement of principle is at p. 52 of the official transcript. The judgment of Brightman J in *Ottaway v Norman* is to much the same effect.

I would emphasise that the agreement or understanding must be such as to impose on the donee a legally binding obligation to deal with the property in the particular way and that the other two certainties, namely, those as to the subject matter of the trust and the persons intended to benefit under it, are as essential to this species of trust as they are to any other. In spite of an argument by Mr. Keenan, who appears for Mr. and Mrs. Noble, to the contrary, I find it hard to see how there could be any difficulty about the second or third certainties in a case of mutual wills unless it was in the terms of the wills themselves. There, as in this case, the principal difficulty is always whether there was a legally binding obligation or merely what Lord Loughborough LC in *Lord Walpole v Lord Orford* (1797) 3 Ves 402 at 419, described as an honourable engagement.

Before turning in detail to the evidence which relates to the question whether there was a legally binding obligation on the testatrix in the present case or not I must return once more to *Birmingham v Renfrew*. It is clear from that case, if from nowhere else, that an enforceable agreement to dispose of property in pursuance of mutual wills can be established only by clear and satisfactory evidence. That seems to me to be no more than a particular application of the general rule that all claims to the property of deceased persons must be scrutinised with very great care. However, that does not mean that there has to be a departure from the ordinary standard of proof required in civil proceedings. I have to be satisfied on the balance of probabilities that the alleged agreement was made, but before I can be satisfied of that I must find clear and satisfactory evidence to that effect.

Re Dale[64]
[1994] Ch 31 (Ch D, **Morritt J**)

A husband and wife agreed that each would leave his or her estate to their son and daughter equally. The husband died first, leaving his estate of £18,500 accordingly. The

[64] (1993) 7 *Trust Law International* 18 (D. Brown); [1993] All ER Rev 415 (C. Sherrin); (1994) 144 NLJ 1272 (P. O'Hagan); (1995) 58 MLR 95 (A. Brierley).

wife made a new will leaving £300 to her daughter and the rest of her estate of £19,000 to her son.

Held. The son, as executor, held the estate on trust for himself and the daughter equally. Benefit by the survivor was not necessary to the doctrine of mutual wills.

Morritt J: There is no doubt that for the doctrine to apply there must be a contract at law. It is apparent from all the cases to which I shall refer later, but in particular from *Gray v Perpetual Trustee Co Ltd* [1928] AC 391, that it is necessary to establish an agreement to make and not revoke mutual wills, some understanding or arrangement being insufficient—'without such a definite agreement there can no more be a trust in equity than a right to damages at law': see *per* Viscount Haldane, at 400. Thus, as the defendant submitted, it is necessary to find consideration sufficient to support a contract at law. The defendant accepted that such consideration may be executory if the promise when performed would confer a benefit on the promisee or constitute a detriment to the promisor. But, it was submitted, the promise to make and not revoke a mutual will could not constitute a detriment to the first testator because he would be leaving his property in the way that he wished and because he would be able, on giving notice to the second testator, to revoke his will and make another if he changed his mind. Accordingly, it was argued, consideration for the contract had to take the form of a benefit to the second testator.

I do not accept this submission. It is to be assumed that the first testator and the second testator had agreed to make and not to revoke the mutual wills in question. The performance of that promise by the execution of the will by the first testator is in my judgment sufficient consideration by itself. But, in addition, to determine whether a promise can constitute consideration it is necessary to consider whether its performance would have been so regarded: cf. *Chitty on Contracts,* (26th edn, 1989), vol. 1, p. 160, para. 161. Thus it is to be assumed that the first testator did not revoke the mutual will notwithstanding his legal right to do so. In my judgment, this too is sufficient detriment to the first testator to constitute consideration. Thus mutual benefit is not necessary for the purpose of the requisite contract. What is necessary to obtain a decree of specific performance of a contract in favour of a third party is not, in my judgment, a relevant question when considering the doctrine of mutual wills. A will is by its very nature revocable: cf. *Re Heys' Estate* [1914] P 192. It seems to me to be inconceivable that the court would order the second testator to execute a will in accordance with the agreement at the suit of the personal representatives of the first testator or to grant an injunction restraining the second testator from revoking it. The principles on which the court acts in imposing the trust to give effect to the agreement to make and not revoke mutual wills must be found in the cases dealing with that topic, not with those dealing with the availability of the remedy of specific performance.

The origin of the doctrine of mutual wills is the decision of Lord Camden LC in *Dufour v Pereira* (1769) 1 Dick 419. . . . The case concerned a joint will made pursuant to an agreement between husband and wife whereby the residuary estate of each of them was to constitute a common fund to be held for the survivor for his or her life with remainders over. On the death of the husband the wife, who was one of his executors, proved the will. Thereafter she took possession of her husband's property and enjoyed the benefit of his residuary estate together with her separate property for many years, but on the death of the wife it was found that her last will disregarded the provisions of the joint will and left her estate to her daughter, the defendant, Mrs. Pereira. The plaintiffs were the beneficiaries under the joint will and claimed that the wife's personal estate was held in trust for them.

[His Lordship referred to the judgment of Lord Camden LC reported in Dickson's Reports and continued:] But in *Hargrave, Juridical Arguments and Collections,* vol. 2. . . . Mr. Hargrave quotes extensively from a manuscript copied from Lord Camden LC's own handwriting which he describes, at p. 306, as 'entered', seemingly in the decree. This source was described as authoritative by Viscount Haldane in *Gray v Perpetual Trustee Co Ltd* [1928] AC 391 at 399 and is, in my judgment, to be preferred because it is much fuller. In *Hargrave*, at pp. 304–306, the facts are set out. At p. 306, Lord Camden LC recorded that mutual wills were unknown in England but that the case must be decided in accordance with English law. He stated, at p. 307:

> 'And I trust, that the everlasting maxims of equity and conscience, upon which the jurisdiction of this court is built, are capacious enough, not only to comprehend this, but every other case that may happen; and that the justice of this court is co-extensive with every possible variety of human transactions. Consider it in two views. First, how far the mutual will shall operate as a binding engagement, independent of any confirmation by accepting the legacy under it. Secondly, whether the survivor can depart from this engagement, after she has accepted a benefit under it.'

Lord Camden LC's decision on the first point should be read in full. He said, at pp. 307–311:

> 'It was said upon the first point, and Mr. Skynner cited an authority to prove it, that where two had made a mutual will either of them might cheat his partner, *foeda machinatione*,[65] by a secret will to disappoint the joint disposition, because they are two distinct instruments. *Hall and Bickerstaff* to the same purpose.
>
>   The law of these countries then must be very defective, and totally destitute of the principles of equity and good conscience: for nothing can be more barbarous, than a law, which does permit in the very text of it one man to defraud another. The equity of this court abhors the principle. A mutual will is a mutual agreement. A mutual will is a revocable act. It may be revoked by joint consent clearly. By one only, if he give notice, I can admit. But to affirm, that the survivor (who has deluded his partner into this will upon the faith and persuasion that he would perform his part) may legally recall his contract, either secretly during the joint lives, or after at his pleasure; I cannot allow. The mutual will is in the whole and every part mutually upon condition, that the whole shall be the will. There is a reciprocity, that runs through the instrument. The property of both is put into a common fund and every devise is the joint devise of both. This is a contract. If not revoked during the joint lives by any open act, he that dies first dies with the promise of the survivor, that the joint will shall stand. It is too late afterwards for the survivor to change his mind: because the first to die's will is then irrevocable, which would otherwise have been differently framed, if that testator had been appraised of this dissent. Thus is the first testator drawn in and seduced by the fraud of the other, to make a disposition in his favour, which but for such a false promise he would never have consented to.
>
>   It was argued however, that the parties knowing that all testaments were in their nature revocable, were aware of this consequence, and must therefore be presumed to contract upon this hazard. There cannot be a more absurd presumption than to suppose two persons, while they are contracting, to give each a licence to impose upon the other. Though a will is always revocable, and the last must always be the testator's will; yet a man may so bind his assets by agreement, that his will shall be a trustee for performance of his agreement. A covenant to leave so much to his wife or daughter, etc. Or suppose he makes his will, and covenants not to revoke it. These cases are common; and there is no difference between promising to make a will in such a form and making his will with a promise not to revoke it. This court does not set aside the will but makes the devisee heir or executor trustee to perform the contract. Suppose the husband had so devised after the wife's promise, that he would devise in like manner. A man intends to devise for the benefit of A

---

[65] 'By a malicious plot'.

and B promises that if he will appoint him his executor, A shall have his legacy. *Thynn v Thynn* (1684) 1 Vern 296; *Devenish v Baines* (1689) Prec Ch 3, testator, persuaded by his wife to give his copyhold, which he intended to devise to his godson. *Chamberlaine's* case cited [(1678) 2 Eq Cas Abr 43]. A man persuaded his father not to make a will, promising his brother and sisters should have the provision intended. This court bound the will with the promise, and raised a trust in the devisee. The act done by one is a good consideration for the performance of the other.

This case stands upon the very same principle. The parties by the mutual will do each of them devise, upon the engagement of the other, that he will likewise devise in manner therein mentioned. The instrument itself is the evidence of the agreement; and he, that dies first, does by his death carry the agreement on his part into execution. If the other then refuses, he is guilty of a fraud, can never unbind himself, and becomes a trustee of course. For no man shall deceive another to his prejudice. By engaging to do something that is in his power, he is made a trustee for the performance, and transmits that trust to those that claim under him. The court is never deceived by the form of instruments. The actions of men here are stripped of their legal clothing, and appear in their first naked simplicity. Good faith and conscience are the rules, by which every transaction is judged in this court; and there is not an instance to be found since the jurisdiction was established, where one man has ever been released from his engagement, after the other has performed his part.'

Only in the sentence at p. 308 is there any reference to the first testator conferring a benefit on the second testator. The rest of the judgment on the first point emphasises more than once that there is a contract between the testators which, on the death of the first testator, is carried into effect by him, that the first testator dies with the promise of the second testator that the agreement will stand, and that it would be a fraud on the first testator to allow the second testator to disregard the contract which became irrevocable on the death of the first testator. In my judgment the essence of the decision is contained in the passage at p. 310:

'he, that dies first, does by his death carry the agreement on his part into execution. If the other then refuses, he is guilty of a fraud, can never unbind himself, and becomes a trustee of course. For no man shall deceive another to his prejudice.'

In my judgment, it is no part of the principle there expressed that the first testator must have conferred a benefit on the second testator by his will. If he has, the principle will apply *a fortiori*, but it may apply even if he has not.

Lord Camden LC's judgment on the second question appears at p. 311, in the following terms:

'I have perhaps given myself more trouble than was necessary upon this point; because, if it could be doubtful, whether after the husband's death his wife could be at liberty to revoke her part of the mutual will, it is most clear, that she has estopped herself to this defence by an actual confirmation of the mutual will, not only by proving it, but by accepting and enjoying an interest under it. She receives this benefit, takes possession of all her husband's estates, submits to the mutual will as long as she lives, and then breaks the agreement after her death. In this view the case falls within the rule of *Noys v Mordaunt* (1706) 2 Vern 581. She takes under the joint will and can take no otherwise.'

In my view the emphasis in this passage on proving the joint will and accepting and enjoying an interest under it underlines the fact that Lord Camden did not regard those matters as relevant to the application of the principle enunciated on the first question.

My conclusion on the defendant's submission based on this authority is that it does not establish that the doctrine of mutual wills can only apply if the testators confer mutual benefits on each other. In my judgment it establishes, subject to later authorities, that such mutual benefit is a sufficient but not a necessary condition.

His Lordship referred to *Lord Walpole v Lord Orford* (1797) 3 Ves 402; *Re Wilford's Estate* (1879) 11 Ch D 267; *Stone v Hoskins* [1905] P 194; *Re Heys' Estate* [1914] P 192; *Re Oldham* [1925] Ch 75; *Gray v Perpetual Trustee Co Ltd* [1928] AC 391; *Re Hagger* [1930] 2 Ch 190 [p. 290, above]; *Birmingham v Renfrew* (1937) 57 CLR 666; *Re Cleaver* [1981] 1 WLR 939 [p. 292, above]; *Re Basham* [1986] 1 WLR 1498, and continued:

> Having concluded the survey of the authorities to which I was so helpfully referred by counsel, I should now express my conclusion and my reasons for it. My conclusion is that I should answer the preliminary issue in the negative. It is clear from the decision of Lord Camden on the first question in *Dufour v Pereira* that there must be a legally binding contract to make and not to revoke mutual wills and that the first testator has died having performed his part of the agreement. The basis of the doctrine, at p. 310 in *Hargrave, Juridical Arguments and Collections*, vol. 2, is:
>
> > 'If the other then refuses, he is guilty of a fraud, can never unbind himself, and becomes a trustee of course. For no man shall deceive another to his prejudice. By engaging to do something that is in his power, he is made a trustee for the performance, and transmits that trust to those that claim under him.'
>
> As all the cases show, the doctrine applies when the second testator benefits under the will of the first testator. But I am unable to see why it should be any the less a fraud on the first testator if the agreement was that each testator should leave his or her property to particular beneficiaries, for example their children, rather than to each other. It should be assumed that they had good reason for doing so and in any event that is what the parties bargained for. In each case there is the binding contract. In each case it has been performed by the first testator on the faith of the promise of the second testator and in each case the second testator would have deceived the first testator to the detriment of the first testator if he, the second testator, were permitted to go back on his agreement. I see no reason why the doctrine should be confined to cases where the second testator benefits when the aim of the principle is to prevent the first testator from being defrauded. A fraud on the first testator will include cases where the second testator benefits, but I see no reason why the principle should be confined to such cases. In my judgment so to hold is consistent with all the authorities, supported by some of them, and is in furtherance of equity's original jurisdiction to intervene in cases of fraud.

In **Re Goodchild** [1997] 1 WLR 1216, a husband, Dennis, and wife, Joan, made wills at the same time in favour of the survivor of them and then in favour of their son, Gary. The wife died leaving her entire estate to her husband. He remarried and left his entire estate to his second wife, the defendant. On the husband's death Gary sought a declaration that the defendant held the husband's estate on trust for him.

It was held that the doctrine of mutual wills did not apply because there was no express agreement not to revoke the wills,[66] but the husband was under a moral obligation to provide for the plaintiff which meant that an order could be made under section 2 of the Inheritance (Provision for Family and Dependants) Act 1975.

---

[66] See also *Gillett v Holt* [2001] Ch 210; *Birch v Curtis* [2002] EWHC 1158 (Ch).

Leggatt LJ said at 1224:

'[T]he reason why, if mutual wills are to take effect, an agreement is necessary, is that without it the property of the second testator is not bound, whereas a secret trust concerns only the property of a person in the position of the first testator.... I am satisfied that for the doctrine to apply there must be a contract at law (see *Re Dale* [1994] Ch 31 at 38, *per* Morritt J).

Two wills may be in the same form as each other. Each testator may leave his or her estate to the other with a view to the survivor leaving both estates to their heir. But there is no presumption that a present plan will be immutable in future. A key feature of the concept of mutual wills is the irrevocability of the mutual intentions. Not only must they be binding when made, but the testators must have undertaken, and so must be bound, not to change their intentions after the death of the first testator. The test must always be, 'suppose that during the lifetime of the surviving testator the intended beneficiary did something which the survivor regarded as unpardonable, would he or she be free not to leave the combined estate to him?' The answer must be that the survivor is so entitled unless the testators agreed otherwise when they executed their wills. Hence the need for a clear agreement.

Dennis and Joan executed wills in the same terms save that each left his or her estate to the other. Thus the survivor was to have both estates. They wanted Gary to inherit the combined estates. But there was no express agreement not to revoke the wills. Nor could any such agreement be implied from the fact that the survivor was in a position to leave both estates to Gary. The fact that each expected that the other would leave them to him is not sufficient to impress the arrangement with a floating trust, binding in equity.[67] A mutual desire that Gary should inherit could not of itself prevent the survivor from resiling from the arrangement. What is required is a mutual intention that both wills should remain unaltered and that the survivor should be bound to leave the combined estates to the son. That is what is missing here. The judge found that Joan regarded the arrangement as irrevocable, but that Dennis did not. No mutual intention was proven that the survivor should be bound to leave the joint estate to Gary. That is what they meant to achieve. It could not happen unless they first left their respective estates to the survivor of them. But the fact that each was able to leave the combined estate to Gary does not without more mean that both were bound to do so.

The judge declined to infer any agreement between Dennis and Joan that would prevent the survivor of them from interfering with the succession. That was a conclusion to which he was entitled to come on the evidence. Mr. Gordon has helpfully marshalled the judge's references to what had to be shown to establish binding mutual wills. Though Joan believed that they mutually intended to leave their estates to Gary, Dennis was not shown to have shared it. So the intention was not in fact mutual. Hence the result that Dennis had no more than a moral obligation to give effect to Joan's belief at least in so far as it affected what had been her estate.

His Lordship then considered whether the court was able to make financial provision for Gary under section 2 of the Inheritance (Provision for Family and Dependants) Act 1975, and concluded:

When the court finds that the testator has been guilty in all the circumstances of a breach of moral obligation owed by a father towards his child, leaving the child in straitened financial circumstances, the court must ensure that adequate provision is made for the child out of the

---

[67] See *Ottaway v Norman* [1972] Ch 698.

estate, having regard to his need for maintenance and support (see *Bosch v Perpetual Trustee Co Ltd* [1938] AC 463). There was here the plainest possible basis for concluding that, whereas Dennis and Joan had not made a clear agreement for mutual wills, nonetheless Joan's understanding of the effect of the will she had made was such as to impose upon Dennis, free though he was of any legal obligation, a moral obligation, once Gary's need for reasonable financial provision was established, to devote to his son so much of his mother's estate as would have come to him if there had been mutual wills.

Morritt LJ said at 1229:

As Leggatt LJ has pointed out, a consistent line of authority requires that for the doctrine of mutual wills to apply there must be a contract between the two testators. In delivering the advice of the Privy Council in *Gray v Perpetual Trustee Co Ltd* [1928] AC 391 at 400 such requirement was made abundantly clear by Viscount Haldane. Counsel for Gary suggests that this test is too high. He does so by reference to the requirements for a secret trust or the imposition of a constructive trust. I do not accept that there is any justification to be found in those areas of equity such as would justify departing from the clear statement of Viscount Haldane.

The principles applicable to cases of a fully secret trust do, in substance, require the proof of a contract. Thus in *Ottaway v Norman* [1972] Ch 698 at 711, Brightman J recorded:

'The essential elements which must be proved to exist are: (i) the intention of the testator to subject the primary donee to an obligation in favour of the secondary donee; (ii) communication of that intention to the primary donee; and (iii) the acceptance of that obligation by the primary donee either expressly or by acquiescence.'

But if those principles do not require exactly the same degree of agreement as does a contract at law there is no reason to import that lesser requirement into the doctrine of mutual wills. Secret trusts affect the property of the donor not that of the primary donee. Where there are mutual wills the doctrine affects the property of both testators, in particular that of the second to die. If he is to be subjected to an obligation with regard to property of his own not derived from the other then an agreement should be required.

In the case of the imposition of a constructive trust[68] in cases like *Lloyds Bank plc v Rosset* [1991] 1 AC 107, on which counsel for Gary relied the court is considering the equitable interests in property acquired for joint use.

[His Lordship quoted from the judgment of Lord Bridge of Harwich at 132 [see p. 325, below], and continued:] In my view this principle has no operation in the case of mutual wills in regard to property already owned both legally and beneficially by the second testator to die. Even assuming that in the absence of an agreement a constructive trust may be imposed in relation to the property acquired by the second testator from the first there is no basis, in the absence of an agreement relating to the property of the second testator, to impose a constructive trust in relation to that property too.

The doctrine of mutual wills is anomalous. The bequest of his entire estate by a husband to his wife absolutely and beneficially with a gift over of whatever was left at her death could not take effect in accordance with its terms. Either the interest taken by the wife would be limited or the gift over would be void as repugnant to the absolute and beneficial nature of the gift.

---

[68] This is a particular form of the constructive trust known as the 'common-intention constructive trust', see p. 322, below.

Similarly the bare promise of the wife to leave her property by will in a particular manner would be unenforceable for any will she then made would be revocable under the Wills Act 1837. In my judgment if these principles are to be excluded in the case of mutual wills it is essential that there should be a contract to that effect. In my view that is what both principle and the authorities require.

In **Healey v Brown** [2002] WTLR 849[69] it was held that, where mutual wills related to land, section 2 of the Law Reform (Miscellaneous Provisions) Act 1989 required there to be a single document signed by both parties. It followed that the binding contract between the parties could not trigger the doctrine of mutual wills. However, the separate doctrine of common-intention constructive trust would apply,[70] by virtue of which it would be inequitable for the surviving testator to transfer the property during his lifetime otherwise than as they had agreed. However, this constructive trust could not be imposed upon the surviving testator's share of the property.

QUESTIONS

1. If the doctrine of mutual wills depends on a binding contract, should the trust be characterised as express or constructive? Does it matter?

2. You are a solicitor and are approached by a husband and wife who wish to make mutual wills. What advice should you give to them?

F SECRET TRUSTS[71]

It is unsettled whether secret trusts should be regarded as express or constructive trusts. The practical significance of the classification is that constructive trusts of land are exempted from the requirement of written evidence by section 53(2) of the Law of Property Act 1925.[72] If a secret trust is to be analysed as a declaration operating outside the will, then it looks like an express trust, particularly if it is a half-secret trust, where the intention to create a trust is expressed in the will. Fully secret trusts may be easier to classify as constructive, as they are enforceable on the ground of fraud (*McCormick v Grogan* (1869) LR 4 HL 82) which cannot be perpetrated by a half-secret trustee.[73] There is little authority on the point. In *Ottaway v Norman* [1972] Ch 698 [p. 132, above], an oral fully secret trust of land was upheld without discussing this

---

[69] [2003] Conv 238 (C. Davis).   [70] See p. 322, below.

[71] Pp. 131–150, above. See H&M, pp. 168–169; Lewin, pp. 77–78; P&M pp. 407–410; P&S, pp. 232–233; Pettit pp. 129–130; Snell, pp. 559–560; T&H, pp. 903–904; U&H, p. 535; Oakley, *Constructive Trusts* (3rd edn), pp. 260–263; (1972) 23 *Northern Ireland Law Quarterly* 263 (R. Burgess); (1951) 67 LQR 34 (L.A. Sheridan); *Brown v Pourau* [1995] 1 NZLR 352; [1996] Conv 302 (C. Rickett); (2004) 120 LQR 667 (B. McFarlane).

[72] See p. 112, above.

[73] Save in the sense of defeating the expectations of the testator. See [1980] Conv 341 (D.R. Hodge); *Re Dale* [1994] Ch 31 [p. 294, above].

matter,[74] whereas in *Re Baillie* (1886) 2 TLR 660 a half-secret trust of land was held to require written evidence. But if a fully secret trust of land were to fail for lack of writing on the ground that it was express, the secret trustee, having accepted the trust, would not hold for his own benefit, but for the residuary legatee or next-of-kin. Any other result would amount to using the statute as an instrument of fraud.

G   ACQUISITION OF PROPERTY BY A CRIMINAL[75]

It is a basic principle of public policy that no criminal should profit from his crime. This was recognised by FRY LJ in **Cleaver v Mutual Reserve Fund Life Association** [1892] 1 QB 147 at 156:

The principle of public policy invoked is in my opinion rightly asserted. It appears to me that no system of jurisprudence can with reason include amongst the rights which it enforces rights directly resulting to the person asserting them from the crime of that person. If no action can arise from fraud, it seems impossible to suppose that it can arise from felony or misdemeanour.... This principle of public policy, like all such principles, must be applied to all cases to which it can be applied without reference to the particular character of the right asserted or the form of its assertion.

One consequence of this principle is that where a killer obtains rights to property as a result of an unlawful killing, those rights are forfeited. This is called the Forfeiture Rule.

In **Dunbar v Plant** [1998] Ch 412, MUMMERY LJ recognised, at 422, that:

... this is a statement of a principle of public policy, the application of which may produce unfair consequences in some cases: it is not a statement of a principle of justice designed to produce a fair result in all cases: see the observations of Lord Goff of Chieveley on the principle of *in pari delicto* in *Tinsley v Milligan* [1994] 1 AC 340 at 355. (This principle of public policy is different from, for example, the equitable maxim that 'he who comes to equity must come with clean hands', which is a principle of justice designed to prevent those guilty of serious misconduct from securing a discretionary remedy, such as an injunction.) ...

[His Lordship then referred to the Forfeiture Act 1982 which recognises the forfeiture rule [see p. 305, below] and continued:] The following propositions relating to the scope of the principle enunciated by Fry LJ in *Cleaver v Mutual Reserve Fund Life Association* [1892] 1 QB 147 and recognised by section 1 of the Act of 1982 may be stated.

(1) The rule applies to a case where the benefit results from the commission of murder by the intended beneficiary. Dr. H.H. Crippen notoriously survived his wife. Between the date of his conviction for her murder and the carrying out of the death sentence passed on him,

---

[74] Although Brightman J did incorporate the plaintiff's pleadings into his judgment and these did base the claim upon a constructive trust.

[75] H&M, pp. 335–337; Lewin, pp. 245–247; P&M, pp. 407–410; P&S, pp. 273–279; Snell, p. 590; T&H, pp. 851–856; U&H, pp. 536–538. Oakley, *Constructive Trusts* (3rd edn), pp. 46–53; (1973) 89 LQR 235 (T. Youdan); [1998] *Restitution Law Review* 34, 46–61 (G. Virgo).

Dr. Crippen made a will naming Ethel Le Neve as the sole executrix and universal beneficiary. Not surprisingly Ethel Le Neve was passed over on a motion for the grant of an administration to Mrs. Crippen's intestate estate. In holding that there were special circumstances justifying this course Sir Samuel Evans P said:

> 'It is clear that the law is, that no person can obtain, or enforce, any rights resulting to him from his own crime; neither can his representative, claiming under him, obtain or enforce any such rights.' (See *Re Crippen* [1911] P 108 at 112.)

(2) The principle is not confined to murder cases, as was made clear by the Court of Appeal in *Re Hall* [1914] P 1. The court unanimously rejected the contention that a distinction should be drawn between cases of murder and manslaughter. Sir Herbert Cozens-Hardy MR. said, at 6, that he entirely failed to appreciate the supposed distinction: 'It was a case of felony and I see no reason to draw a distinction between murder and manslaughter in a case like this.' Hamilton LJ said, at 7–8, that the principle could only be expressed in a wide form:

> 'It is that a man shall not slay his benefactor and thereby take his bounty; and I cannot understand why a distinction should be drawn between the rule of public policy where the criminality consists in murder and the rule where the criminality consists in manslaughter.... The distinction seems to me either to rely unduly upon legal classification, or else to encourage what, I am sure, would be very noxious—a sentimental speculation as to the motives and degree of moral guilt of a person who has been justly convicted and sent to prison.'

His Lordship then considered whether the forfeiture rule only applied where the killing involved deliberate, intentional and unlawful violence and threats of violence, as had been suggested by the Court of Appeal in *Gray v Barr* [1971] 2 QB 554, and concluded:

In my judgment, however, the presence of acts or threats of violence is not necessary for the application of the forfeiture rule. It is sufficient that a serious crime has been committed deliberately and intentionally. The references to acts or threats of violence in the cases are explicable by the facts of those cases. But in none of those cases were the courts legislating a principle couched in specific statutory language. The essence of the principle of public policy is that (a) no person shall take a benefit resulting from a crime committed by him or her resulting in the death of the victim and (b) the nature of the crime determines the application of the principle. On that view the important point is that the crime that had fatal consequences was committed with a guilty mind (deliberately and intentionally). The particular means used to commit the crime (whether violent or non-violent) are not a necessary ingredient of the rule. There may be cases in which violence has been used deliberately without an intention to bring about the unlawful fatal consequences. Those cases will attract the application of the forfeiture rule. It does not follow, however, that when death has been brought about by a deliberate and intentional, but non-violent, act (e.g. poison or gas) the rule is inapplicable.

His Lordship held, on the facts of the case, that the forfeiture rule applied where the defendant was guilty of aiding and abetting suicide.

Where a killer has obtained property as a result of an unlawful killing this may be held on constructive trust since the killer is not entitled to benefit from the property. This is rare, because the usual effect of the forfeiture rule is to prevent the killer from obtaining the property in the first place. However, there is scope for greater use being made of the constructive trust in this context.

[1998] *Restitution Law Review* 57–58 (G. Virgo)[76]

A consequence of the principle that no criminal should profit from his or her crime is that title to the property which would otherwise accrue to the criminal, or to those claiming through him or her, cannot pass to the criminal. But this response is not free from difficulty. This is because in many cases, whether by virtue of statute or the common law, legal title should indeed pass to the criminal, and there is no provision in the statute or common law to the effect that an exception should be made where the passing of property is triggered by the criminal's own act. For the forfeiture rule to work it must be assumed that, for reasons of public policy, every legal rule contains an implied term to the effect that no criminal who, by the commission of the crime, has triggered the passing of property should be allowed to benefit from the crime.[77] It would be a much more honest response to apply the relevant statutory and judicial laws literally, without artificial interpretation. This would mean that title to property would pass to the criminal. But, because of the principle that no criminal should profit from his or her crime, equity should ensure that because of the killer's unconscionable conduct an equitable interest in the property is created in favour of the victim, with the result that the criminal should hold the property on a constructive trust for the victim's estate.[78] This would be consistent with Lord Browne-Wilkinson's interpretation of the constructive trust in *Westdeutsche Landesbank Girozentrale v Islington London Borough Council*.[79] Such an approach would have a number of advantages.

(i) The operation of the forfeiture rule would not conflict with the clear words of statute and judicial precedent but would continue to fulfil the policy that no criminal should profit from his or her crime.

(ii) If it is accepted that legal title to the victim's estate should pass to the killer, then a constructive trust will be imposed in favour of the people whom equity regards as entitled to the estate. Usually it will be clear who such people are, because the normal rules of succession will be applied, with the obvious qualification that the killer and those claiming through the killer will not have a beneficial interest. But in certain circumstances the flexibility of equity will enable the beneficial interest to be created in favour of another party. The most obvious example of this will be where there is clear evidence that the victim had intended to change his or her will, or to make a will, so as to leave the estate to a particular person, but was killed before he or she was able to do so.

(iii) If the property which had been acquired by or through the criminal had been received by a third party, then the victim of the crime, or the beneficiaries of the victim, would be able to recover the property. But this is subject to an important qualification, namely that the property could not be recovered from a third party who was a bona fide purchaser for value without notice.

This constructive trust analysis was not adopted, however, by the Court of Appeal in Re DWS [2001] Ch 568[80] where a son had murdered his parents who died intestate. The deceased's grandchild claimed that he was entitled to the estate, since his father could

---

[76] See also (1890) *Harvard Law Review* 394 (J.B. Ames); (2001) 117 LQR 371 (R. Kerridge).

[77] See e.g. *Re Royse* [1985] Ch 22, [1984] 3 All ER 339, where it was assumed that the application of the Inheritance (Provision for Family and Dependants) Act 1975 was subject to the forfeiture rule, even though the Act makes no provision for this rule. Similarly in *Re Sigsworth* [1935] Ch 89 the Administration of Estates Act 1925 was interpreted as though its provisions relating to intestacy were subject to the forfeiture rule.

[78] (1973) 89 LQR 235, 253 (T.G. Youdan).   [79] [1996] AC 669 at 716.

[80] (2001) 117 LQR 317 (R. Kerridge); (2004) 18 *Trust Law International* 194 (P. Smith).

not benefit by virtue of the forfeiture rule. However, the Court held that, by virtue of the Administration of Estates Act 1925, the grandson was not entitled to the estate since the Act specifically prevented him from succeeding to the estate if his parent was living. Instead, the Court held by a majority[81] that collateral relations were entitled to the estate. A preferable solution would have been to conclude that the forfeiture rule did not prevent the father from succeeding to the estate. Instead, it prevented him from taking the estate beneficially. So he should have held the estate on constructive trust for his son. An alternative solution is that recommended by the Law Commission,[82] namely that the Administration of Estates Act 1925 and Wills Act 1837 should be amended so that a murderer who, for example, has killed a parent should be deemed to have died immediately before the death of the parent. It would follow that the parent's estate in a case such as *Re DWS* would pass to the person next entitled, namely the murderer's own child.

The Forfeiture Act 1982[83] gives the court power to grant total or partial relief from forfeiture of inheritance and related rights to persons guilty of unlawful killing other than murder, where the court is satisfied that the justice of the case requires it.

FORFEITURE ACT 1982

1. The 'forfeiture rule'

(1) In this Act, the 'forfeiture rule' means the rule of public policy which in certain circumstances precludes a person who has unlawfully killed another from acquiring a benefit in consequence of the killing.

(2) References in this Act to a person who has unlawfully killed another include a reference to a person who has unlawfully aided, abetted, counselled or procured the death of that other and references in this Act to unlawful killing shall be interpreted accordingly.

2. Power to modify the rule

(1) Where a court determines that the forfeiture rule has precluded a person (in this section referred to as 'the offender') who has unlawfully killed another from acquiring any interest in property mentioned in subsection (4) below, the court may make an order under this section modifying the effect of that rule.

(2) The court shall not make an order under this section modifying the effect of the forfeiture rule in any case unless it is satisfied that, having regard to the conduct of the offender and of the deceased and to such other circumstances as appear to the court to be material, the justice of the case requires the effect of the rule to be so modified in that case.[84]

---

[81] Sedley LJ held that the estate should pass to the Crown as *bona vacantia* in the hope that the Crown would transfer all or some of it to the grandson.

[82] *The Forfeiture Rule and the Law of Succession* (Law Com No. 295, 2005).

[83] (1983) 46 MLR 66 (P.H. Kenny).

[84] See *Re K* [1986] Ch 180; *Re H* [1990] 1 FLR 441 (degree of moral blame significant); *Dunbar v Plant* [1998] Ch 412 [p. 307, below]; *Dalton v Latham* [2003] EWHC 796, [2003] WTLR 687 (refusal to grant relief from the forfeiture rule where the defendant had taken advantage of the victim's vulnerability).

(3) In any case where a person stands convicted of an offence of which unlawful killing is an element, the court shall not make an order under this section modifying the effect of the forfeiture rule in that case unless proceedings for the purpose are brought before the expiry of the period of three months beginning with his conviction.[85]

(4) The interests in property referred to in subsection (1) above are—

   (a) any beneficial interest in property which (apart from the forfeiture rule) the offender would have acquired—

      (i)   under the deceased's will...or the law relating to intestacy...;

      (ii) on the nomination of the deceased in accordance with the provisions of any enactment;

      (iii) as a *donatio mortis causa* made by the deceased;...

   (b) any beneficial interest in property which (apart from the forfeiture rule) the offender would have acquired in consequence of the death of the deceased, being property which, before the death, was held on trust for any person.

(5) An order under this section may modify the effect of the forfeiture rule in respect of any interest in property to which the determination referred to in subsection (1) above relates and may do so in either or both of the following ways, that is—

   (a) where there is more than one such interest, by excluding the application of the rule in respect of any (but not all) of those interests; and

   (b) in the case of any such interest in property, by excluding the application of the rule in respect of part of the property.

(6) On the making of an order under this section, the forfeiture rule shall have effect for all purposes (including purposes relating to anything done before the order is made) subject to the modifications made by the order.

(7) The court shall not make an order under this section modifying the effect of the forfeiture rule in respect of any interest in property which, in consequence of the rule, has been acquired before the coming into force of this section by a person other than the offender or a person claiming through him.[86]

(8) In this section—

   'property' includes any chose in action or incorporeal moveable property; and
   'will' includes codicil.

5. Exclusion of murderers

Nothing in this Act or in any order made under section 2 or referred to in section 3(1) of this Act [or in any decision made under section 4(1A) of this Act] shall affect the

---

[85] The doctrine does not require a criminal conviction: *Gray v Barr* [1971] 2 QB 554 (acquittal but lower standard of proof in civil action).

[86] *Re K*, note 84 above (property not 'acquired' if held by personal representatives who have not completed administration). Note also *Jones v Midland Bank Trust Co Ltd* [1998] 1 FLR 246 (the Forfeiture Act 1982 could not be used to rewrite the victim's will, so the property of the victim devolved on an intestacy).

application of the forfeiture rule in the case of a person who stands convicted of murder.

In **Dunbar v Plant** [1998] Ch 412, Plant and her fiancé, Dunbar, entered into a suicide pact. Dunbar killed himself but Plant survived. Dunbar's father, who was the administrator of his estate, sought a declaration as to the ownership, amongst other things, of a house jointly owned by his son and Plant, and the proceeds of an insurance policy on Dunbar's life for the benefit of Plant. The trial judge held that, since Plant had committed the crime of aiding and abetting a suicide, the forfeiture rule applied. The question for the Court of Appeal was whether the forfeiture rule could be modified in this case.

In holding that the forfeiture rule applied but could be modified on the facts, so that the defendant could take her fiancé's share of the house but she could not receive the proceeds of the insurance policy on his life, MUMMERY LJ said at 427:

> ... the relevant question for the court is: does 'the justice of the case require' that the effect of the forfeiture rule be modified? In my view, the judge erroneously regarded himself as under a duty to try and do 'justice between the parties'. That is not the approach required by section 2(2). The provision requires that the judge should look at the case in the round, pay regard to all the material circumstances, including the conduct of the offender and the deceased, and then ask whether 'the justice of the case requires' a modification of the effect of the forfeiture rule. Having taken the wrong approach, the judge failed, in my view, to give consideration in his reasons to all the factors material to the exercise of his discretion. In those circumstances it is open to this court to exercise the discretion afresh on the basis of the relevant material. On doing that, I have in fact reached the same conclusion as the judge on the limited scope of the modification order. It is difficult to draw the line with confidence. The point at which the judge drew it is not obviously wrong. The court is entitled to take into account a whole range of circumstances relevant to the discretion, quite apart from the conduct of the offender and the deceased: the relationship between them; the degree of moral culpability for what has happened; the nature and gravity of the offence; the intentions of the deceased; the size of the estate and the value of the property in dispute; the financial position of the offender; and the moral claims and wishes of those who would be entitled to take the property on the application of the forfeiture rule.

H THE VENDOR UNDER A CONTRACT FOR THE SALE OF LAND[87]

In **Rayner v Preston**[88] (1881) 18 Ch D 1, Preston agreed in 1878 to sell to Rayner for £3,100 a house which had been insured by Preston against fire. The contract did not

---

[87] H&M, pp. 331–335; Lewin, pp. 337–341; P&M pp. 438–440; P&S, pp. 279–280; Pettit pp. 163–164; Snell, pp. 544–546; T&H, pp. 879–880; U&H, p. 541–548; Farrand, *Contract and Conveyance* (4th edn, 1983), pp. 167–173; Oakley, *Constructive Trusts* (3rd edn), pp. 275–305; [1959] 23 Conv (NS) 173 (V.G. Wellings). The principle also applies to personalty if the contract is specifically enforceable. See further Law Commission Report: *Risk of Damage after Contract for Sale* (1990) (Law Com No. 191).

[88] *Lake v Bayliss* [1974] 1 WLR 1073; (1974) 38 Conv (NS) 357 (F.R. Crane); *Freevale Ltd v Metrostore (Holdings) Ltd* [1984] Ch 199; *Englewood Properties Ltd v Patel* [2005] EWHC 188 (Ch), [2005] 3 All ER 307;

refer to the insurance. After the date of the contract but before the time fixed for completion, the house was damaged by fire to the amount of £330, and this sum was paid
by the insurers to Preston. Rayner brought an action to establish his right to the sum,
or to have it applied in repairing the house. The Court of Appeal held that Rayner was
not entitled to the benefit of the insurance as against Preston.

The law on this point was changed by the Law of Property Act 1925, section 47,
under which, on completion, a purchaser may recover from the vendor any money
due under an insurance policy 'in respect of any damage or destruction of property
included in the contract'.

COTTON LJ[89] said at 6:

It was said that the vendor is, between the time of the contract being made and being completed
by conveyance, a trustee of the property for the purchaser, and that as, but for the fact of the
legal ownership of the building insured being vested in him, he could not have recovered on the
policy, he must be considered a trustee of the money recovered. In my opinion, this cannot be
maintained. An unpaid vendor is a trustee in a qualified sense only, and is so only because he has
made a contract which a Court of Equity will give effect to by transferring the property sold to
the purchaser, and so far as he is a trustee he is so only in respect of the property contracted
to be sold. Of this the policy is not a part. A vendor is in no way a trustee for the purchaser of
rents accruing before the time fixed for completion, and here the fire occurred and the right to
recover the money accrued before the day fixed for completion. The argument that the money is
received in respect of property which is trust property is, in my opinion, fallacious. The money
is received by virtue or in respect of the contract of insurance, and though the fact that the
insured had parted with all interest in the property insured would be an answer to the claim, on
the principle that the contract is one of indemnity only, this is very different from the proposition
that the money is received by reason of his legal interest in the property.

In **Shaw v Foster** (1872) LR 5 HL 321, LORD CAIRNS said at 338:

The vendor was a trustee of the property for the purchaser; the purchaser was the real beneficial owner in the eye of a Court of Equity of the property subject only to this observation, that
the vendor, whom I have called the trustee, was not a mere dormant trustee, he was a trustee
having a personal and substantial interest in the property, a right to protect that interest, and
an active right to assert that interest if anything should be done in derogation of it. The relation,
therefore, of trustee and *cestui que trust* subsisted, but subsisted subject to the paramount right
of the vendor and trustee to protect his own interest as vendor of the property.[90]

[2005] All ER Rev 273 (P.J. Clarke)(duty on vendor to protect the purchaser's interest and to take reasonable
care to preserve the property and not to damage it nor to prejudice purchaser's interest, but no duty to
impose covenants on adjoining property).

[89] Brett LJ and James LJ (who dissented) expressed different views.

[90] See also *Lysaght v Edwards* (1876) 2 Ch D 499 at 506, *per* Jessel MR. ('the position of the vendor is
something between what is called a naked or bare trustee, or a mere trustee (that is, a person without beneficial interest), and a mortgagee who is not, in equity (any more than a vendor), the owner of the estate, but
is, in certain events, entitled to what the unpaid vendor is, *viz.*, possession of the estate and a charge upon
the estate for his purchase-money.'); *Royal Bristol Permanent Building Society v Bomash* (1887) 35 Ch D 390
at 397, *per* Kekewich J ('of course we all know that he is only a trustee in a modified sense'); *Cumberland
Consolidated Holdings Ltd v Ireland* [1946] KB 264 at 269, *per* Lord Greene MR ('his position is that of a

In **Lloyds Bank plc v Carrick** [1996] 4 All ER 630,[91] the defendant, Mr. Carrick, had suggested to his sister-in-law, Mrs. Carrick, that she should sell her home, pay the proceeds to him and move into a property of which he was a lessee. She did this. He said that he would transfer the lease to her but did not do so. The title to the property was unregistered. The defendant charged the property to the plaintiff bank without informing it that his sister-in-law occupied the property. The bank brought proceedings for possession of the property. One of the issues for the court was whether the defendant was a bare trustee of the property. If he was, then the sister-in-law had an interest which did not need to be registered.

Held. As the sister-in-law had paid the purchase price the defendant was a bare trustee, but the existence of this bare trust prevented the court from concluding that there was a common intention constructive trust.

MORRITT LJ said at 637:

... it is accepted by Mrs. Carrick that if her only interest in the maisonette was derived from the contract which she accepts is void as against the bank as an unregistered estate contract then the appeal succeeds. Second, Mrs. Carrick accepts that the original contract between her and Mr. Carrick, as found by the recorder, was a valid open contract for the purchase of the maisonette; that it became enforceable by her when she partly performed it by entering into possession and paying the whole of the purchase price but that it remained executory, that is to say uncompleted, at the time of the legal charge to the bank granted in November 1986. Third, the bank accepts that if Mrs. Carrick had an interest in the maisonette not arising from but separate and distinct from the unregistered contract, it was and is binding on the bank for, as found by the recorder, the bank had notice of it.

Thus the issue argued on this appeal was whether Mrs. Carrick had an interest in the maisonette separate and distinct from that which arose under the unregistered estate contract which was capable of binding the bank as successor in title to Mr. Carrick. For Mrs. Carrick it was submitted that she did. It was contended that she was entitled to such an interest under a bare trust, a constructive trust and by virtue of a proprietary estoppel.

I shall consider each of these points in due course. But before doing so it is necessary to consider the position of Mr. Carrick and Mrs. Carrick before the charge to the bank was executed. At the time it was made the contract was valid but, as provided by section 40 of the Law of Property Act 1925, unenforceable for want of a memorandum in writing or part-performance. It became enforceable when in or about November 1982 Mrs. Carrick paid the purchase price to Mr. Carrick and went into possession. One consequence of the contract becoming enforceable was that it was specifically enforceable at the suit of Mrs. Carrick. Accordingly Mr. Carrick became a trustee of the maisonette for Mrs Carrick. Normally such trusteeship is of a peculiar kind because the vendor himself has a beneficial interest in the property as explained in *Megarry and Wade on The Law of Real Property* (5th edn, 1984), p 602. But in this case as Mrs. Carrick had paid the whole of the purchase price at the time the contract became

quasi-trustee for the purchaser'). The vendor owes no fiduciary duty to a sub-purchaser: *Berkley v Poulett* (1976) 242 Estates Gazette 39.

[91] [1996] Conv 295 (M. Thompson); (1997) 27 *Family Law* 95 (S. Cretney); (1998) 61 MLR 486 (N. Hopkins). See *Yaxley v Gotts* [2000] Ch 162 [p. 347, below] (no specifically enforceable contract so a constructive trust could be recognised).

enforceable, Mr. Carrick as the vendor had no beneficial interest. Thus he may properly be described as a bare trustee (cf. *Bridges v Mees* [1957] Ch 475 at 485). It follows that at all times after November 1982, Mrs. Carrick was the absolute beneficial owner of the maisonette and Mr. Carrick was a trustee of it without any beneficial interest in it.

His Lordship then concluded that, since this interest arose from the contract, it needed to be registered and was void for non-registration.[92]

> ### QUESTION
>
> Is it correct to say that a vendor of land who has entered into a contract of sale holds the land on a constructive trust? See H&M, pp. 332–333.

I UNDERTAKINGS BY A PURCHASER[93]

In certain exceptional circumstances where a purchaser has bought land and made an undertaking that he would respect the rights of a third party, the third party's rights are protected by means of a constructive trust.[94] This has proved to be important in respect of licences. In the context of contractual licences, the question whether a third party acquiring the land from the licensor holds on constructive trust for the licensee has been clarified by the Court of Appeal in *Ashburn Anstalt v Arnold* [1989] Ch 1 [below].

A licence to occupy land is traditionally regarded as creating a personal right only.[95] This is clearly so in the case of a gratuitous licence (unless the circumstances give rise to an estoppel, which is capable of binding third parties). Where the licence is contractual, the proper remedy is upon the contract. This may work hardship in cases where the land is sold to a third party, and the courts have sought to avoid the result that the purchaser, not being bound by the contract, can evict the licensee, by imposing a constructive trust on him.

In **Ashburn Anstalt v Arnold** [1989] Ch 1,[96] the question was whether the plaintiff purchaser took the land subject to the interest of the defendant. The Court of Appeal

---

[92] See Cheshire and Burn, *Modern Law of Real Property* (17th edn), pp. 112–113.

[93] H&M, pp. 340–432; Lewin, p. 248; P&M, pp.418–419, 422–423; P&S, pp.280–282; Pettit, pp. 165–166; Snell, pp. 590–591; T&H, pp. 887–890; U&H, pp. 511–512; Oakley, *Constructive Trusts* (3rd edn), pp. 53–63; B. McFarlane, 'Constructive Trusts Arising on a Receipt of Property *Sub Conditione*' (2004) 120 LQR 667; N. Hopkins, 'Conscience, discretion and the creation of property rights' (2006) 4 LS 475.

[94] Alternatively the third party may have a cause of action against the purchaser by virtue of the Contracts (Rights of Third Parties) Act 1999. See p. 169, above.

[95] *King v David Allen & Sons Billposting Ltd* [1916] 2 AC 54; *Clore v Theatrical Properties Ltd* [1936] 3 All ER 483. On licences generally, see Cheshire and Burn, *Modern Law of Real Property* (17th edn), chap. 23; H&M, chap. 27.

[96] (1988) 104 LQR 175 (P. Sparkes); (1988) 51 MLR 226 (J. Hill); [1988] Conv 201 (M.P. Thompson); (1988) CLJ 353 (A.J. Oakley); [1988] All ER Rev 177 (P.J. Clarke); *IDC Group Ltd v Clark* [1992] 1 EGLR 187 at 189 (not discussed on appeal at (1993) 65 P & CR 179).

held that the defendant had a lease which was binding on the plaintiff under the normal rules of property law.[97] The court, however, considered what the position would have been if the defendant had been only a contractual licensee. After concluding that such a licence could not bind a purchaser in the absence of a constructive trust, Fox LJ at 23 examined the circumstances in which a constructive trust could be imposed for the protection of the licensee:

We come then to four cases in which the application of the principle to particular facts has been considered.

In *Binions v Evans* [1972] Ch 359 the defendant's husband was employed by an estate and lived rent free in a cottage owned by the estate. The husband died when the defendant was 73. The trustees of the estate then entered into an agreement with the defendant that she could continue to live in the cottage during her lifetime as tenant at will rent free; she undertook to keep the cottage in good condition and repair. Subsequently the estate sold the cottage to the plaintiffs. The contract provided that the property was sold subject to the tenancy. In consequence of that provision the plaintiffs paid a reduced price for the cottage. The plaintiffs sought to eject the defendant, claiming that she was tenant at will. That claim failed. In the Court of Appeal Megaw and Stephenson LJJ decided the case on the ground that the defendant was a tenant for life under the Settled Land Act 1925. Lord Denning MR. did not agree with that. He held that the plaintiffs took the property subject to a constructive trust for the defendant's benefit. In our view that is a legitimate application of the doctrine of constructive trusts. The estate would certainly have allowed the defendant to live in the house during her life in accordance with their agreement with her. They provided the plaintiffs with a copy of the agreement they made. The agreement for sale was subject to the agreement, and they accepted a lower purchase price in consequence. In the circumstances it was a proper inference that on the sale to the plaintiffs, the intention of the estate and the plaintiffs was that the plaintiffs should give effect to the tenancy agreement. If they had failed to do so, the estate would have been liable in damages to the defendant.

In *DHN Food Distributors Ltd v Tower Hamlets Borough Council* [1976] 1 WLR 852 premises were owned by Bronze Investments Ltd. but occupied by an associated company (DHN) under an informal agreement between them—they were part of a group. The premises were subsequently purchased by the council and the issue was compensation for disturbance. It was said that Bronze was not disturbed and that DHN had no interest in the property. The Court of Appeal held that DHN had an irrevocable licence to occupy the land. Lord Denning MR. said, at 859:

'It was equivalent to a contract between the two companies whereby Bronze granted an irrevocable licence to DHN to carry on their business on the premises. In this situation Mr. Dobry cited to us *Binions v Evans* to which I would add *Bannister v Bannister* [1948] 2 All ER 133 and *Siew Soon Wah v Young Tong Hong* [1973] AC 836. Those cases show that a contractual licence (under which a person has a right to occupy premises indefinitely) gives rise to a constructive trust, under which the legal owner is not allowed to turn out the licensee. So, here. This irrevocable licence gave to DHN a sufficient interest in the land to qualify them for compensation for disturbance.'

Goff LJ made this a ground for his decision also.

[97] Overruled on this point in *Prudential Assurance Co Ltd v London Residuary Body* [1992] 2 AC 386.

On that authority, Browne-Wilkinson J in *Re Sharpe* [1980] 1 WLR 219 felt bound to conclude that, without more, an irrevocable licence to occupy gave rise to a property interest. He evidently did so with hesitation. For the reasons which we have already indicated, we prefer the line of authorities which determine that a contractual licence does not create a property interest. We do not think that the argument is assisted by the bare assertion that the interest arises under a constructive trust.

In *Lyus v Prowsa Developments Ltd* [1982] 1 WLR 1044 [p. 313, below], the plaintiffs contracted to buy a plot of registered land which was part of an estate being developed by the vendor company. A house was to be built which would then be occupied by the plaintiffs. The plaintiffs paid a deposit to the company, which afterwards became insolvent before the house was built. The company's bank held a legal charge, granted before the plaintiffs' contract, over the whole estate. The bank was under no liability to complete the plaintiffs' contract. The bank, as mortgagee, sold the land to the first defendant. By the contract of sale it was provided that the land was sold subject to and with the benefit of the plaintiffs' contract. Subsequently, the first defendant contracted to sell the plot to the second defendant. The contract provided that the land was sold subject to the plaintiffs' contract so far, if at all, as it might be enforceable against the first defendant. The contract was duly completed. In the action the plaintiffs sought a declaration that their contract was binding on the defendants and an order for specific performance. The action succeeded. This again seems to us to be a case where a constructive trust could justifiably be imposed. The bank were selling as mortgagees under a charge prior in date to the contract. They were therefore not bound by the contract and on any view could give a title which was free from it. There was, therefore, no point in making the conveyance subject to the contract unless the parties intended the purchaser to give effect to the contract. Further, on the sale by the bank a letter had been written to the bank's agents, Messrs. Strutt & Parker, by the first defendant's solicitors, giving an assurance that their client would take reasonable steps to make sure the interests of contractual purchasers were dealt with quickly and to their satisfaction. How far any constructive trust so arising was on the facts of that case enforceable by the plaintiffs against owners for the time being of the land we do not need to consider.

Re Sharpe seems to us a much more difficult case in which to imply a constructive trust against the trustee in bankruptcy and his successors, and we do not think it could be done. Browne-Wilkinson J did not, in fact, do so. He felt (understandably, we think) bound by authority to hold that an irrevocable licence to occupy was a property interest. In *Re Sharpe* although the aunt provided money for the purchase of the house, she did not thereby acquire any property interest in the ordinary sense, since the judge held that it was advanced by way of a loan, though, no doubt, she may have had some rights of occupation as against the debtor. And when the trustee in bankruptcy, before entering into the contract of sale, wrote to the aunt to find out what rights, if any, she claimed in consequence of the provision of funds by her, she did not reply. The trustee in bankruptcy then sold with vacant possession. These facts do not suggest a need in equity to impose constructive trust obligations on the trustee or his successors.

We come to the present case. It is said that when a person sells land and stipulates that the sale should be 'subject to' a contractual licence, the court will impose a constructive trust upon the purchaser to give effect to the licence: see *Binions v Evans* [1972] Ch 359 at 368, *per* Lord Denning MR. We do not feel able to accept that as a general proposition. We agree with the observations of Dillon J in *Lyus v Prowsa Developments Ltd* [1982] 1 WLR 1044 at 1051:

'By contrast, there are many cases in which land is expressly conveyed subject to possible incumbrances when there is no thought at all of conferring any fresh rights on third parties who may be entitled to the benefit of the incumbrances. The land is expressed to be sold subject to incumbrances to satisfy the vendor's duty to disclose all possible incumbrances known to him, and to protect the vendor against any possible claim by the purchaser.... So, for instance, land may be contracted to be sold and may be expressed to be conveyed subject to the restrictive covenants contained in a conveyance some 60 or 90 years old. No one would suggest that by accepting such a form of contract or conveyance a purchaser is assuming a new liability in favour of third parties to observe the covenants if there was for any reason before the contract or conveyance no one who could make out a title as against the purchaser to the benefit of the covenants.'

The court will not impose a constructive trust unless it is satisfied that the conscience of the estate owner is affected. The mere fact that that land is expressed to be conveyed 'subject to' a contract does not necessarily imply that the grantee is to be under an obligation, not otherwise existing, to give effect to the provisions of the contract. The fact that the conveyance is expressed to be subject to the contract may often, for the reasons indicated by Dillon J, be at least as consistent with an intention merely to protect the grantor against claims by the grantee as an intention to impose an obligation on the grantee. The words 'subject to' will, of course, impose notice. But notice is not enough to impose on somebody an obligation to give effect to a contract into which he did not enter. Thus, mere notice of a restrictive covenant is not enough to impose upon the estate owner an obligation or equity to give effect to it: *London County Council v Allen* [1914] 3 KB 642.

The material facts in the present case are as follows. (i) There is no finding that the plaintiff paid a lower price in consequence of the provision that the sale was subject to the 1973 agreement. (ii) The 1973 agreement was not contractually enforceable against Legal & General, which was not, therefore, exposed to the risk of any contractual claim for damages if the agreement was not complied with. The 1973 agreement was enforceable against Cavendish and it seems that in 1973 Cavendish was owned by Legal & General. There is no finding as to the relationship between Cavendish and Legal & General in August 1985, when Legal & General sold to the plaintiff. And there is no evidence before the deputy judge as to the circumstances or the arrangements attending the transfer by Cavendish to Legal & General. (iii) Whilst the letter of 7 February, 1985 is not precisely worded, it seems that Legal & General was itself prepared to give effect to the 1973 agreement.

In matters relating to the title to land, certainty is of prime importance. We do not think it desirable that constructive trusts of land should be imposed in reliance on inferences from slender materials. In our opinion the available evidence in the present case is insufficient. The deputy judge, while he did not have to decide the matter, was not disposed to infer a constructive trust, and we agree with him.

An important principle which can justify the use of the constructive trust against purchasers who have entered into undertakings in respect of third-party rights, is that a statute must not be used as an instrument of fraud.[98] So, for example, in **Lyus v Prowsa Developments Ltd** [1982] 1 WLR 1044[99] land was bought expressly subject to

---

[98] See *Rochefoucauld v Boustead* [1897] 1 Ch 196, where the trust that was recognised was an express trust. See W. Swadling, *Restitution and Equity, Vol 1: Resulting Trusts and Equitable Compensation* (ed. P. Birks and F. Rose), pp. 65–68.

[99] (1983) 46 MLR 96 (P.H. Kenny); [1983] Conv 64 (P. Jackson); (1983) CLJ 54 (C. Harpum); (1984) 47 MLR 476 (P. Bennett); (1985) CLJ 280 (M.P. Thompson). The decision was approved by CA in *Ashburn Anstalt v Arnold* [1989] Ch 1 [p. 310, above].

the plaintiff's contractual rights, but the defendants sought to defeat them by relying on the provisions of the Land Registration Act 1925. DILLON J, in imposing a constructive trust on the defendants on the ground that a statute is not to be used as an instrument of fraud, said at 1054:

It has been pointed out by Lord Wilberforce in *Midland Bank Trust Co Ltd v Green* [1981] AC 513 at 531, that it is not fraud to rely on legal rights conferred by Act of Parliament. Under section 20 [of the Land Registration Act 1925], the effect of the registration of the transferee of a freehold title is to confer an absolute title subject to entries on the register and overriding interests, but, 'free from all other estates and interests whatsoever, including estates and interests of His Majesty...'

[His Lordship considered *Miles v Bull (No 2)* [1969] 3 All ER 1585, and continued:] It seems to me that the fraud on the part of the defendants in the present case lies not just in relying on the legal rights conferred by an Act of Parliament, but in the first defendant reneging on a positive stipulation in favour of the plaintiffs in the bargain under which the first defendant acquired the land. That makes, as it seems to me, all the difference. It has long since been held, for instance, in *Rochefoucauld v Boustead* [1897] 1 Ch 196, that the provisions of the Statute of Frauds 1677, now incorporated in certain sections of the Law of Property Act 1925, cannot be used as an instrument of fraud, and that it is fraud for a person to whom land is agreed to be conveyed as trustee for another to deny the trust and relying on the terms of the statute to claim the land for himself. *Rochefoucauld v Boustead* was one of the authorities on which the judgment in *Bannister v Bannister* [1948] 2 All ER 133 was founded.

It seems to me that the same considerations are applicable in relation to the Land Registration Act 1925. If, for instance, the agreement of 18 October, 1979, between the bank and the first defendant had expressly stated that the first defendant would hold Plot 29 upon trust to give effect for the benefit of the plaintiffs to the plaintiffs' agreement with the vendor company, it would be difficult to say that that express trust was over-reached and rendered nugatory by the Land Registration Act 1925. The Land Registration Act 1925 does not, therefore, affect the conclusion which I would otherwise have reached in reliance on *Bannister v Bannister* and the judgment of Lord Denning MR. in *Binions v Evans* [1972] Ch 359 [p. 311, above], had Plot 29 been unregistered land.

Pettit: *Equity and the Law of Trusts* (10th edn, 2005), pp. 157–158

But there is no rule that the sale of land 'subject to' a contractual licence automatically gives rise to a constructive trust, rather the reverse. To establish a constructive trust very special circumstances must be proved showing that the transferee of the property undertook a new liability to give effect to provisions for the benefit of third parties. It is the conscience of the transferee which has to be affected and it has to be affected in a way which gives rise to an obligation to meet the legitimate expectations of the third party.[100] It has been suggested[101] that if a 'subject to' clause does create a trust the true analysis is that it arises because that is what the parties intended. It is therefore not a constructive trust at all, but rather an express trust.

---

[100]   *IDC Group Ltd v Clark* [1992] 1 EGLR 187; *Lloyd v Dugdale* [2001] EWCA Civ 1754, [2002] WTLR 863 noted [2002] Conv 584 (M Dixon).   [101]   (1983) 133 NLJ 798 (C.T. Emery and B. Smythe).

J THE REMEDIAL CONSTRUCTIVE TRUST[102]

A matter of particular controversy concerns whether the constructive trust should only be treated as an institutional mechanism or whether it can also be treated as a remedial mechanism. The 'institutional' constructive trust will be recognised where the dispute falls within one of the existing categories of case where such trusts are recognised. Being operative before the date of the court order which confirms it, this trust can affect third parties. This is the way in which the English cases have traditionally regarded the constructive trust.[103] The 'remedial' constructive trust is widely accepted in Australia, New Zealand, and Canada.[104] Such a trust can be imposed *de novo* as the foundation for the grant of an equitable remedy, and does not involve the vindication of some pre-existing proprietary right of the claimant. It may operate only from the date of the court order, and thus need not affect third parties.[105]

The crucial distinction between an institutional and a remedial constructive trust was recognised by LORD BROWNE-WILKINSON in **Westdeutsche Landesbank Girozentrale v Islington London Borough Council** [1996] AC 669 at 714:

Under an institutional constructive trust the trust arises by operation of law as from the date of the circumstances which give rise to it: the function of the court is merely to declare that such trust has arisen in the past. The consequences that flow from such trust having arisen (including the potentially unfair consequences to third parties who in the interim have received the trust property) are also determined by rules of law, not under a discretion. A remedial constructive trust, as I understand it, is different. It is a judicial remedy giving rise to an enforceable equitable obligation: the extent to which it operates retrospectively to the prejudice of third parties lies in the discretion of the court.

In England, the remedial constructive trust has never been formally recognised, although some judges have expressed a willingness to do so. In this case, Lord BROWNE-WILKINSON said at 716:

Although the resulting trust is an unsuitable basis for developing proprietary restitutionary remedies, the remedial constructive trust, if introduced into English law, may provide a more satisfactory road forward. The court by way of remedy might impose a constructive trust on a defendant who knowingly retains property of which the plaintiff has been unjustly deprived. Since the remedy can be tailored to the circumstances of the particular case, innocent third parties would not be prejudiced and restitutionary defences, such as change of position, are capable of being given effect. However, whether English law should follow the United States

---

[102] H&M, pp. 305–308; Lewin, pp. 236–238; P&M, pp. 322–330; P&S, pp. 318–326; Pettit, pp. 67–69; Snell, pp. 592–593; T&H, pp. 749–752; U&H, pp. 398–400; Oakley, *Constructive Trusts*, (3rd edn) pp. 34–35; Wright, *The Remedial Constructive Trust* (1998).

[103] See *Re Sharpe* [1980] 1 WLR 219.

[104] *Muschinski v Dodds* (1985) 160 CLR 583; *Powell v Thompson* [1991] 1 NZLR 597; *Pettkus v Becker* (1980) 117 DLR (3d) 257. See Wright, note 102 above.

[105] *Muschinski v Dodds*, ibid.

and Canada by adopting the remedial constructive trust will have to be decided in some future case when the point is directly in issue.[106]

More recently, however, the Court of Appeal specifically refused the opportunity to recognise the remedial constructive trust when it had the opportunity to do so.

In **Re Polly Peck International (No 2)** [1998] 3 All ER 812,[107] the issue for the Court of Appeal was whether the court had jurisdiction to hear a claim arising from the occupation of land in Cyprus by the subsidiaries of a company (PPI) which was insolvent and subject to an administration order. The plaintiffs sought restitution of a sum received by the administrators which the plaintiffs alleged represented the profits from the company's wrongdoing. The plaintiffs claimed, *inter alia*, that these profits were held on a remedial constructive trust.

MUMMERY LJ said at 826:

In my judgment, the intervening insolvency of PPI means that under English law there is no seriously arguable case for granting the applicants a remedial constructive trust on the basis of the allegations in the draft statement of claim. PPI is a massively insolvent company subject to an administration order. The administrators are bound to distribute the assets of PPI among the creditors on the basis of insolvency. Parliament has, in such an eventuality, sanctioned a scheme for *pari passu* distribution of assets designed to achieve a fair distribution of the insolvent company's property among the unsecured creditors. This scheme, now contained in the Insolvency Act of 1986, was described by Sir Donald Nicholls Vice-Chancellor in *Re Paramount Airways Ltd* [1993] Ch 223 at 230 as 'a coherent, modernised and expanded code'.

   The provisions of that code apply both to the case of an insolvent company which has gone into formal liquidation and to one in respect of which an administration order has been made. The essential characteristic of the statutory scheme is that the liquidator or administrator is bound to deal with the assets of the company as directed by statute for the benefit of all creditors who come in to prove a valid claim. There is a statutory obligation on the administrators of PPI to treat the general creditors in a particular way. A question may arise as to whether a particular asset was or was not the beneficial property of the company at the date of the commencement of the winding up (or administration). If it is established in a dispute that it is not an asset of the company then it never becomes subject of the statutory insolvency scheme: see *Chase Manhattan Bank NA v Israel-British Bank (London) Ltd* [1981] Ch 105. If, on the other hand, the asset is the absolute beneficial property of the company there is no general power in the liquidator, the administrators or the court to amend or modify the statutory scheme so as to transfer that asset or to declare it to be held for the benefit of another person. To do that would be to give a preference to another person who enjoys no preference under the statutory scheme.

   In brief, the position is that there is no prospect of the court in this case granting a remedial constructive trust to the applicants in respect of the proceeds of sale of the shares held by PPI

---

[106] See also *Metall und Rohstoff AG v Donaldson Lufkin & Jenrette Inc* [1990] 1 QB 391 at 479; *Re Goldcorp Exchange Ltd* [1995] 1 AC 74 at 104 (Lord Mustill); *London Allied Holdings v Lee* [2007] EWHC 2061 (Ch).

[107] [1999] All ER Rev 415–416 (P. Birks and W. Swadling). See also *Cobbold v Bakewell Management Ltd* [2003] EWHC 2289 (Ch), para. 17 (Rimer J); *Re Farepak Food and Gifts Ltd* [2006] EWHC 3272 (Ch), para 38 (Mann J).

in its subsidiaries, since the effect of the statutory scheme applicable on an insolvency is to shut out a remedy which would, if available, have the effect of conferring a priority not accorded by the provisions of the statutory insolvency scheme. In her eloquent address Miss Dohmann submitted that 'the law moves'. That is true. But it cannot be legitimately moved by judicial decision down a road signed 'No Entry' by Parliament. The insolvency road is blocked off to remedial constructive trusts, at least when judge-driven in a vehicle of discretion.

For those reasons alone I would refuse leave to the applicants to commence these proceedings. To a trust lawyer and, even more so to an insolvency lawyer, the prospect of a court imposing such a trust is inconceivable and, in my judgment, even the most enthusiastic student of the law of restitution would be forced to recognise that the scheme imposed by statute for a fair distribution of the assets of an insolvent company precludes the application of the equitable principles manifested in the remedial constructive trust developed by such courts as the Supreme Court of Canada.[108]

NOURSE LJ said at 830:

The formidable and continuing problems of terminology which afflict the consideration of many questions on constructive trusts make it desirable to start with definition. In referring to a remedial constructive trust, I mean an order of the court granting, by way of remedy, a proprietary right to someone who, beforehand, had no proprietary right.

The essential allegations the applicants seek leave to make were summarised by Mr. Justice Rattee towards the end of his judgment [1997] BCLC 648:

'(a) that the applicants remained at all material times entitled to possession of the applicants' properties, (b) that PPI knew that its subsidiaries were exploiting those properties, to which it knew the applicants claimed title and the right to possession, (c) that PPI actively encouraged such exploitation, (d) that it has benefited from that exploitation and should be bound to disgorge such profit, and (e) that the court should accordingly impose a remedial constructive trust on so much of the proceeds of the sale by PPI to Learned Ltd as represents such profit.'

Whatever other rights the applicants may have or may have had against the subsidiaries or PPI itself, it is plain that they have no proprietary right to any part of the proceeds of the sale of the shares in the subsidiaries. They could only get one by the imposition of a remedial constructive trust in their favour. So this case raises fairly and squarely the question whether the remedial constructive trust is part of English law.

Although...this court (Slade, Stocker and Bingham LJJ) in *Metall und Rohstoff AG v Donaldson, Lufkin & Jenrette Inc* [1990] 1 QB 391, Lord Mustill in *Re Goldcorp Exchange Ltd* [1995] 1 AC 74 and Lord Browne-Wilkinson in *Westdeutsche Landesbank Girozentrale v Islington London Borough Council* [1996] AC 669 have accepted the possibility that the remedial constructive trust may become part of English law, such observations, being both obiter and tentative, can only be of limited assistance when the question has to be decided, as it does here. There being no earlier decision, we must turn to principle. In doing so, we must recognise that the remedial constructive trust gives the court a discretion to vary proprietary rights. You cannot grant a proprietary right to A, who has not had one beforehand, without taking some proprietary right away from B. No English court has ever had the power to do that, except

---

[108] See *Pettkus v Becker* (1980) 117 DLR (3d) 257; *LAC Minerals Ltd v International Corona Resources Ltd* (1989) 61 DLR (4th) 14; and *Korkontzilas v Soulos* (1997) 146 DLR (4th) 214. See also (1989) 68 *Canadian Bar Review* 315 (D.M. Pacciocco).

with the authority of Parliament; cf. *Chapman v Chapman* [1954] AC 429. But it is said that, although that may be the law today, it may not be the law tomorrow. If the Supreme Court of Canada can develop the law so as to permit the court to vary proprietary rights without legislative authority, why cannot the House of Lords do likewise? At least, it is said, there must be a real prospect that they will, and so the applicants ought to be allowed to bring their action.

I agree with Mummery LJ that where, as here, there would be not simply a variation of proprietary rights but a variation of the manner in which the administrators are directed to deal with PPI's assets by the Insolvency Act 1986 it is not seriously arguable, even at the highest level, that a remedial constructive trust would be imposed. For myself, I would go further and hold that it would not be seriously arguable even if PPI was solvent. It is not that you need an Act of Parliament to prohibit a variation of proprietary rights. You need one to permit it; see the Variation of Trusts Act 1958 and the Matrimonial Causes Act 1973.

Partly because we were only referred to three of the Canadian decisions and partly because it appears that in none of them has the Supreme Court had to grapple with the insolvency of the party on whose assets the remedial constructive trust is to be imposed, this is not an appropriate occasion for a comparative inquiry into the jurisprudence of our two countries. Three points ought nevertheless to be made.

First, in Canada the remedial constructive trust, whose origin was in the dissenting judgment of Laskin J (as he then was) in *Murdoch v Murdoch* (1973) 41 DLR (3d) 367 (see also *Rathwell v Rathwell* (1978) 83 DLR (3d) 289), was developed through *Pettkus v Becker* (1980) 117 DLR (3d) 257 and *Sorochan v Sorochan* (1986) 29 DLR (4th) 1 as a remedy in property disputes between married and unmarried couples. Both *Murdoch v Murdoch* and, as I understand it, *Rathwell v Rathwell* were actually decided on the principles of *Gissing v Gissing* [1971] AC 886[109] and, subject to a rather surprising difference of opinion in the Supreme Court as to the findings of the trial judge, *Pettkus v Becker* could have been so decided and was so decided by the minority. *Sorochan v Sorochan,* on the other hand, could not have been decided according to those principles. In that case the Supreme Court had to rely for its decision on the remedial constructive trust. Although there must have been later family property cases which could have been decided on *Gissing v Gissing* principles, I believe that the remedial constructive trust has now become the accepted and perhaps the exclusive remedy in such cases.

Secondly, in Canada the application of the remedial constructive trust has not only been extended beyond family property cases (we were referred to *LAC Minerals Ltd v International Corona Resources Ltd* (1989) 61 DLR (4th) 14 and *Korkontzilas v Soulous* (1997) 146 DLR (4th) 214); in the other areas to which it has been extended there are also cases which could have been decided in exactly the same way according to principles well known to English law. For example, I would think that English notions of breach of confidential obligation and fiduciary duty were well up to leading to the same result as in *LAC Minerals Ltd v International Corona Resources Ltd.*

Thirdly, it is evident that some of the early Canadian decisions in family property cases were influenced by Lord Denning MR's constructive trust of a new model; cf. *Cooke v Head* [1972] 1 WLR 518; *Hussey v Palmer* [1972] 1 WLR 1286; and *Eves v Eves* [1975] 1 WLR 1338. However, in the 1980s this court, in particular in *Burns v Burns* [1984] Ch 317 and *Grant v Edwards* [1986] Ch 638 held that Lord Denning's approach was at variance with the principles stated in *Gissing v Gissing*. That is not to say that English law has remained static

---

[109] See p. 324, below.

in this area. In *Grant v Edwards* the court was able to achieve the same beneficial result as in *Eves v Eves,* although by adopting the approach, not of Lord Denning, but of Brightman J and Browne LJ. Since then the possibility of further developments through applying the principles of proprietary estoppel has been signalled by the House of Lords in *Lloyds Bank plc v Rosset* [1991] 1 AC 107 [p. 325, below].

It is appropriate that we on this side of the Atlantic should remind ourselves of some observations of Lord Simonds LC in *Chapman v Chapman* which were well known at the time but may have been forgotten. In holding that the court had no inherent jurisdiction to vary the beneficial interests of infants and unborn persons in settled property, he said at [1954] AC 429 at 444:

> 'It may well be that the result is not logical, and it may be asked why, if the jurisdiction of the court extends to this thing, it did not extend to that also. But, my Lords, that question is as vain in the sphere of jurisdiction as it is in the sphere of substantive law. We are as little justified in saying that a court has a certain jurisdiction, merely because we think it ought to have it, as we should be in declaring that the substantive law is something different from what it has always been declared to be, merely because we think it ought to be so. It is even possible that we are not wiser than our ancestors. It is for the legislature, which does not rest under that disability, to determine whether there should be a change in the law and what that change should be.'

Despite this the potential relevance of the remedial constructive trust remains a live issue. In **London Allied Holdings v Lee** [2007] EWHC 2061 (Ch) ETHERINGTON J, said, at para. 274, having referred to Professor Birks' criticism of this form of trust as 'a nightmare trying to be a noble dream' and 'rightlessness implicit in discretionary remedialism':

An equity lawyer might observe that such language is overly emphatic, having regard, for example, to the strong discretion in the Court to decide upon the appropriate form of relief for proprietary estoppel, including whether it should be personal or proprietary and whether it should be to protect the claimant's expectations or compensate for reliance loss. Moreover, there is no English authority, including *Polly Peck International plc (No 2)* (in which Mummery LJ, with whom Potter LJ agreed, concentrated on the fact of insolvency), which is binding authority against the remedial constructive trust in principle. Nevertheless, it seems realistic to assume that an English Court will be very slow indeed to adopt the US and Canadian model. On the other hand, there still seems scope for real debate about a model more suited to English jurisprudence, borrowing from proprietary estoppel; namely a constructive trust by way of discretionary restitutionary relief, the right to which is a mere equity prior to judgment, but which will have priority over the intervening rights of third parties on established principles, such as those relating to notice, volunteers and the unconscionability on the facts of a claim by the third party to priority.

QUESTIONS

1. '[*Re Polly Peck International*] cannot be taken to have excluded altogether the remedial constructive trust from the judicial armoury in England.' [1999] LMCLQ 111, 117 (C. Rickett and R. Grantham). Do you agree?

2. Should the remedial constructive trust be recognised in English law? See Virgo, *The Principles of the Law of Restitution* (2nd ed.), pp. 613–615; [1997] *New Zealand Law Review* 623, 641 (P. Birks); *Restitution: Past, Present and Future* (eds. W. Cornish, R. Nolan, J. O'Sullivan and G. Virgo), p. 199 (P. Millett). Cp. *Restitution and Insolvency* (ed. F. Rose), pp. 188–205 (C. Rickett), pp. 206–219 (D. Wright); [1999] *Restitution Law Review* 128 (D. Wright).

III THE NATURE OF CONSTRUCTIVE TRUSTEESHIP[110]

It is often assumed that a constructive trust, like any other trust, is a mechanism by virtue of which specific property is vested in a trustee on trust for ascertained beneficiaries. This is not always so; there are many differences between constructive trusts and other trusts. A constructive trustee may not know that he is a trustee.[111] Where the trust arises because a fiduciary has received a benefit in breach of a fiduciary obligation, it may be difficult to say what the trust property is. In many cases, the duty of a constructive trustee is less onerous than that of an express trustee; he is under no obligation to invest[112] nor to observe the usual duty of care. It would be unreasonable to impose such obligations in cases in which he did not know that he was a trustee.

Smith: *Privacy and Loyalty* (ed. P. Birks, 1997), p. 267

There is an obligation on the [constructive] trustee: to convey the trust property to or to the order of the beneficiary. A breach of this obligation would create a personal liability. But the trustee cannot, without fiction, be said to have assumed obligations of the utmost selflessness. The only way to reach the contrary conclusion would be to say that this is the technique of equity: to subject trustees, even unwilling ones, to the fiduciary standard, so as to generate the corresponding liabilities. That, however, would be using the fiduciary relationship in a wholly instrumental way.

[110] H&M, p. 304; P&M, pp. 312–315; T&H, pp .848–851.

[111] Cp. Lord Browne-Wilkinson's assertion in *Westdeutsche Landesbank Girozentrale v Islington London Borough Council* [1996] AC 669 at 705 that it is a fundamental principle of the law of trusts that a trustee must know that he is a trustee.

[112] *Lonrho plc v Fayed (No 2)* [1992] 1 WLR 1 at 12 (Millett J).

8

COMMON-INTENTION CONSTRUCTIVE TRUSTS[1]

I INTRODUCTION

One of the areas in which the constructive trust has had a vital role to play has been in the context of family property disputes, in particular as regards the ownership of the matrimonial home or of the home occupied by an unmarried cohabiting couple. In the case of spouses or civil partners, the dispute is likely to arise when the marriage or civil partnership has broken down. In such circumstances ascertaining the beneficial ownership of the home is only the first stage, as the court has a wide jurisdiction to make property adjustment orders under the Matrimonial Causes Act 1973.[2] No such jurisdiction exists in the case of unmarried couples; for them, entitlement is determined by the law of trusts.

---

[1] H&M, pp. 271–299; Lewin, pp. 309–333; P&M, pp. 422–429; P&S, pp. 282–318; Pettit, pp. 190–216; Snell, pp. 563–569; T&H, pp. 1693–1748; U&H, pp. 512–529; Oakley, *Constructive Trusts* (3rd edn, 1997), pp. 64–83; Bromley, *Family Law* (eds. N.Lowe and G. Douglas) (10th edn, 2007), chap. 4; Cretney, Masson and Bailey-Harris, *Principles of Family Law* (7th edn, 2003) chap. 5; Mee, *The Property Rights of Cohabitees* (1999).

[2] As to the interpretation of this statute see *White v White* [2001] 1 AC 596; *Miller v Miller* heard together with *McFarlane v McFarlane* [2006] UKHL 24, [2006] 2 AC 618. There are equivalent provisions for civil partners under the Civil Partnership Act 2004, sch, 5. A spouse or civil partner who has made a substantial contribution in money or money's worth to the improvement of property in which either or both of them has a beneficial interest, is treated by statute as having a share or an enlarged share in that beneficial interest: Matrimonial Proceedings and Property Act 1970, s. 37. This is subject to any contrary intention. See *Thomas v Fuller-Brown* [1988] 1 FLR 237 (where the claim failed because the inference was that the expenditure was in return for rent-free accommodation); *Cadman v Bell* [1988] EGCS 139 (licence for life); *Passee v Passee* [1988] 1 FLR 263; [1988] Conv 361 (J. Warburton). It is otherwise if the money was advanced as a loan: *Spence v Brown* [1988] Fam Law 291; cf *Hussey v Palmer* [1972] 1 WLR 1286.

If there is no express declaration of the beneficial interest,[3] beneficial ownership is ascertained by applying the principles of both resulting[4] and constructive trusts, but the constructive trust has proven to be more important in the form of what has been called 'the common-intention constructive trust'.[5] Sometimes the overlap with the doctrine of proprietary estoppel has been recognised,[6] although recently the courts have sought to distinguish more clearly between constructive trusts and estoppel.

Although the 'common-intention constructive trust' has been developed in the context of family property disputes, more recently this doctrine has been of growing importance in a purely commercial field. This raises difficult policy issues as to whether it is appropriate to adopt principles from one field and to apply them in another.

II FAMILY PROPERTY DISPUTES

A BASIC PRINCIPLES

When considering the allocation of beneficial interests in the family home it is important to distinguish clearly between issues concerning the identification of such interests and issues concerning the extent of such interests.

The principles relating to the beneficial ownership of the family home were reviewed by the House of Lords in *Lloyds Bank plc v Rosset* [1991] 1 AC 107 [p. 325, below].[7] It was considered that, in the absence of a declaration of trust evidenced in writing (p. 112, above), there are two ways of acquiring a beneficial interest in the home. The first is to establish that the parties expressed a common intention to share the beneficial interest,[8] followed by detrimental reliance by the claimant which is referable to the common intention.[9] It is this detrimental reliance which makes it unconscionable for the other party to deny the claimant's beneficial interest in the property.

---

[3] *Goodman v Gallant* [1986] Fam 106; *Rowe v Prance* [1999] 2 FLR 787; *Stack v Dowden* [2007] UKHL 17, [2007] 2 AC 432, at para.49 (Baroness Hale). See *Carlton v Goodman* [2002] EWCA Civ 545, [2002] 2 FLR 259, at para. 44 (Ward LJ); *Crossley v Crossley* [2005] EWCA Civ 1581, [2006] 1 FCR 655, at para. 15 (Sir Peter Gibson).   [4] See p. 257, above.

[5] Following the decision of the House of Lords in *Stack v Dowden* [2007] UKHL 17, [2007] 2 AC 432 [see p. 334, below], the resulting trust has little or no relevance to the identification of beneficial interests of cohabiting couples in the family home.

[6] See *Birmingham Midshires Mortgage Services Ltd v Sabherwal* (1999) 80 P & CR 256 at 263 (Robert Walker LJ). For analysis of the doctrine of proprietary estoppel, see *Gillett v Holt* [2001] Ch 210; *Jennings v Rice* [2003] 1 P and CR 100; *Cobbe v Yeoman's Row Management Ltd.* [2006] EWCA Civ 1139, [2006] 1 WLR 2964.

[7] (1990) 106 LQR 539 (J. Davies); [1990] Conv 314 (M. Thompson), [1990] All ER Rev 138 (S. Cretney); (1991) CLJ 38 (M. Dixon); (1991) 54 MLR 126 (S. Gardner); (1993) 23 *Family Law* 231 (J. Dewar). For the developments of the doctrine before that decision, see the judgment of Lord Walker in *Stack v Dowden* [2007] UKHL 17, [2007] 2 AC 432.

[8] *Grant v Edwards* [1986] Ch 638; *Eves v Eves* [1975] 1 WLR 1338.

[9] *Cox v Jones* [2004] EWHC 1486 (Ch), [2004] 2 FLR 1010.

Alternatively, the court can *infer* that the parties had a common intention to share the beneficial interest. Such an inference can be drawn, it was said, only where the claimant has contributed directly to the purchase price, either initially[10] or by payment of mortgage instalments. It was doubted whether indirect contributions would suffice.[11] Non-financial contributions to the running of the home will not be sufficient to infer a common intention.[12] Direct contributions were regarded as giving rise to a constructive trust, although traditionally such contributions give rise to a presumption of a resulting trust.[13] These financial contributions enable a common intention to be inferred and establish the detrimental reliance which makes it unconscionable for the other party to deny the claimant's beneficial interest. The practice, prevalent in the 1970s in particular, of recognising a constructive trust simply on the ground of justice and good conscience,[14] has now been rejected.[15]

The application of the law on common-intention constructive trusts has been subject to rigorous criticism, especially in its application to family property disputes.[16] The rejection of the view, expressed in cases before *Lloyds Bank v Rossett*,[17] that an indirect contribution can suffice to establish a proprietary interest in the home without the necessity of finding an express common intention to share, is capable of producing injustice, for example where the wife pays household bills, thereby enabling her husband to pay the mortgage instalments.[18] Some Commonwealth jurisdictions[19] have resolved this problem by legislation[20] or by applying the principles of unconscionability[21] or

---

[10] See, for example, *Parrott v Parkin* [2007] EWHC 210 (Admlty), [2007] 1 Lloyd's Rep 719.

[11] Although it has sometimes been recognised that indirect financial contributions will be enough to infer the common intention to share the beneficial interest if this enables the other party to be able to afford to make mortgage payments: *Le Foe v Le Foe Woolwich Building Society plc* [2001] 2 FLR 970. It seems that the other party must be aware of the claimant's contributions: *Lightfoot v Lightfoot-Brown* [2005] EWCA Civ 1201, [2005] 2 P and CR 22.

[12] *Lloyds Bank v Rosset* [1991] 1 AC 107, 132 (Lord Bridge) [see p. 325, below]. See also *Buggs v Buggs* [2003] EWHC 1538 (Ch), [2004] WTLR 799; *Mehra v Shah* [2004] EWCA Civ 632.

[13] Later payments of mortgage instalments, without any liability to make them, do not found a presumption of a resulting trust, although a constructive trust can arise: *Curley v Parkes* [2004] EWCA Civ 1515, [2005] 1 P & CR DG 15 [see p. 262, above]; *Stack v Dowden* [2007] UKHL 17, [2007] 2 AC 432 [see p. 334, below].

[14] See *Heseltine v Heseltine* [1971] 1 WLR 342; *Hussey v Palmer* [1972] 1 WLR 1286 and *Eves v Eves* [1975] 1 WLR 1338.

[15] See *Grant v Edwards* [1986] Ch 638 at 647 (Nourse LJ). *Eves v Eves* [1975] 1 WLR 1338 was approved by the House of Lords in *Lloyds Bank plc v Rosset* [1991] 1 AC 107 without reference to Lord Denning's approach. But query whether this old practice might be returning in the light of the decision of the House of Lords in *Stack v Dowden* [2007] UKHL 17, [2007] 2 AC 432 [see p. 334, below].

[16] See (1996) LS 325 (N. Glover and P. Todd); (1996) LS 218 (A. Lawson). The Law Commission has now prepared a report on the property rights of those who share homes. See p. 346, below. See also *Stack v Dowden* [2007] UKHL 17, [2007] 2 AC 432, para. 34 (Lord Walker), para. 63 (Baroness Hale) [see p. 334, below]; *Abbott v Abbott* [2007] UKPC 53.

[17] *Gissing v Gissing* [1971] AC 886; *Burns v Burns* [1984] Ch 317; *Grant v Edwards* [1986] Ch 638.

[18] Such a contribution may suffice under the 'reasonable expectation' approach in New Zealand: *Lankow v Rose* [1995] 1 NZLR 277.   [19] See (1998) LS 369 (S. Wong).

[20] De Facto Relationships Act 1984 (NSW); (1994) 8 *Trust Law International* 74 (M. Bryan). See also (1999) 19 LS 468 (A. Barlow and C. Lind), who recommend a legislative scheme creating statutory presumptions of co-ownership. See the recommendations of the Law Commission, p. 346, below.

[21] As in Australia: *Muschinski v Dodds* (1985) 160 CLR 583.

unjust enrichment,[22] and have rejected the view that domestic duties must be left out of account. A second approach is to invoke the more flexible principles of proprietary estoppel, where the act of detrimental reliance need not involve expenditure[23] and which does not require a search for an artificial common intention,[24] although it does require there to have been a representation or assurance by the owner of the property that the claimant has an interest in it.[25] The process of assimilating the doctrines of proprietary estoppel and constructive trust has begun, but is not complete.[26] A third view is that the relationship of the parties should itself generate the claim.[27]

The principles laid down in *Lloyds Bank plc v Rosset* have since been examined by the Court of Appeal in *Oxley v Hiscock* [2004] EWCA Civ 546, [2005] Fam 211 [p. 328, below], and reconsidered by the House of Lords in *Stack v Dowden* [2007] UKHL 17, [2007] 2 AC 432 [p. 334, below]. As regards the identification of a beneficial interest, these cases have distinguished between situations where property is registered in the name of one party and where it is registered in the name of both parties. In the former case a common-intention constructive trust needs to be established by means of an express or inferred common intent. Then the beneficial interest must be quantified. In the latter case there is a very strong presumption that the beneficial interest is shared equally and the only relevance of the constructive trust is to determine whether the claimant can establish a larger interest. There is some controversy over whether quantification of the claimant's interest should be achieved by reference to the parties' whole course of conduct, either to determine what would be a fair share or to determine what share the parties intended. The Court of Appeal in *Oxley v Hiscock* preferred the former approach,[28] focusing on fairness, whereas the House of Lords in *Stack v Dowden* have purported to prefer the latter approach, focusing on intention; see especially Baroness Hale, at para. 61 [p. 336, below]. But even the latter approach requires the court to consider a wide variety of factors.

B   PROPERTY REGISTERED IN THE NAME
OF ONE PARTY

Where the property is registered in the name of one party only, an opposing claimant needs first to establish a beneficial interest and then to prove the extent of that

---

[22]   As in Canada: *Peter v Beblow* (1993) 101 DLR (4th) 621. See also in Scotland: *Satchwel v McIntosh* 2006 SLT (Sh Ct) 117; *McKenzie v Nuller* 2007 SLT (Sh Ct) 17.

[23]   *Greasley v Cooke* [1980] 1 WLR 1306; *Campbell v Griffin* [2001] EWCA Civ 990, [2001] WTLR 981.

[24]   *Gillett v Holt* [2001] Ch 210; *Jennings v Rice* [2002] EWCA Civ 159, [2003] 1 P & CR 100; [1990] Conv 370 (D. Hayton); (1993) 109 LQR 114 (P. Ferguson) and 485 (D. Hayton); (1993) 3 *Caribbean Law Review* 96 (R. Smith); (2006) 122 LQR 492 (S. Gardner).

[25]   *Jennings v Rice* [2002] EWCA Civ 159, [2003] 1 P & CR 100.

[26]   *Grant v Edwards* [1986] Ch 638; *Lloyds Bank plc v Rosset* [1991] 1 AC 107; *Stokes v Anderson* [1991] 1 FLR 391; *S v S* [2006] EWHC 2892 (Fam), [2007] 1 FLR 1123; *Stack v Dowden* [2007] UKHL 17, [2007] 2 AC 432, para 34 (Lord Walker).   [27]   (1993) 109 LQR 263 (S. Gardner).

[28]   See also *Midland Bank plc v Cooke* [1995] 4 All ER 562 [see p. 329, below].

interest. The existence of the beneficial interest may be established by showing a direct financial contribution to the purchase of the property.

Lloyds Bank Plc v Rosset
[1991] 1 AC 107 (HL, **Lords Bridge of Harwich, Griffiths, Ackner, Oliver of Aylmerton** and **Jauncey of Tullichettle**)

A semi-derelict farmhouse was purchased as a family home with funds from the husband's family trust and (without the wife's knowledge) with a bank loan secured on the property, which was conveyed into the husband's sole name. The vendor permitted builders to enter and do works before completion. During this period the wife spent nearly every day at the property supervising the builders. She also helped her husband to plan the renovation and did some decorating. Subsequently the husband was unable to repay the bank loan and the bank took possession proceedings. The wife claimed that she had a share of the beneficial interest, and that this was enforceable against the bank.

Held. The wife had no beneficial interest. The question of priorities did not, therefore, arise.

Lord Bridge of Harwich: Even if there had been the clearest oral agreement between Mr. and Mrs. Rosset that Mr. Rosset was to hold the property in trust for them both as tenants in common, this would, of course, have been ineffective since a valid declaration of trust by way of gift of a beneficial interest in land is required by section 53(1) of the Law of Property Act 1925 to be in writing.[29] But if Mrs. Rosset had, as pleaded, altered her position in reliance on the agreement this could have given rise to an enforceable interest in her favour by way either of a constructive trust or of a proprietary estoppel.

Having rejected the contention that there had been any concluded agreement, arrangement or any common intention formed before contracts for the purchase of the property were exchanged on 23 November, 1982 that Mrs. Rosset should have any beneficial interest, the judge concentrated his attention on Mrs. Rosset's activities in connection with the renovation works as a possible basis from which to infer such a common intention.

His Lordship reviewed the trial judge's finding of fact and concluded that it was not possible to infer a common intention that the wife should have a beneficial interest in the property simply from her acts in renovating it, and continued:

These considerations lead me to the conclusion that the judge's finding that Mr. Rosset held the property as a constructive trustee for himself and his wife cannot be supported and it is on this short ground that I would allow the appeal. In the course of the argument your Lordships had the benefit of elaborate submissions as to the test to be applied to determine the circumstances in which the sole legal proprietor of a dwelling house can properly be held to have become a constructive trustee of a share in the beneficial interest in the house for the benefit of the partner with whom he or she has cohabited in the house as their shared home. Having in this case reached a conclusion on the facts which, although at variance with the views of the courts

---

[29] See p. 112, above.

below, does not seem to depend on any nice legal distinction and with which, I understand, all your Lordships agree, I cannot help doubting whether it would contribute anything to the illumination of the law if I were to attempt an elaborate and exhaustive analysis of the relevant law to add to the many already to be found in the authorities to which our attention was directed in the course of the argument. I do, however, draw attention to one critical distinction which any judge required to resolve a dispute between former partners as to the beneficial interest in the home they formerly shared should always have in the forefront of his mind.

The first and fundamental question which must always be resolved is whether, independently of any inference to be drawn from the conduct of the parties in the course of sharing the house as their home and managing the joint affairs, there has at any time prior to acquisition, or exceptionally at some later date, been any agreement, arrangement or understanding reached between them that the property is to be shared beneficially. The finding of an agreement or arrangement to share in this sense can only, I think, be based on evidence of express discussions between partners, however imperfectly remembered and however imprecise their terms may have been. Once a finding to this effect is made it will only be necessary for the partner asserting a claim to a beneficial interest against the partner entitled to the legal estate to show that he or she has acted to his or her detriment or significantly altered his or her position in reliance on the agreement in order to give rise to a constructive trust or proprietary estoppel.

In sharp contrast with this situation is the very different one where there is no evidence to support a finding of an agreement or arrangement to share, however reasonable it might have been for the parties to reach such an arrangement if they had applied their minds to the question, and where the court must rely entirely on the conduct of the parties both as the basis from which to infer a common intention to share the property beneficially and as the conduct relied on to give rise to a constructive trust. In this situation direct contributions to the purchase price by the partner who is not the legal owner, whether initially or by payment of mortgage instalments, will readily justify the inference necessary to the creation of a constructive trust. But, as I read the authorities, it is at least extremely doubtful whether anything less will do.

The leading cases in your Lordships' House are *Pettitt v Pettitt* [1970] AC 777 and *Gissing v Gissing* [1971] AC 886. Both demonstrate situations in the second category to which I have referred and their Lordships discuss at great length the difficulties to which these situations give rise. The effect of these two decisions is very helpfully analysed in the judgment of Lord MacDermott LCJ in *McFarlane v McFarlane* [1972] NI 59.

Outstanding examples on the other hand of cases giving rise to situations in the first category are *Eves v Eves* [1975] 1 WLR 1338 and *Grant v Edwards* [1986] Ch 638. In both these cases, where the parties who had cohabited were unmarried, the female partner had been clearly led by the male partner to believe, when they set up home together, that the property would belong to them jointly. In *Eves v Eves* the male partner had told the female partner that the only reason why the property was to be acquired in his name alone was because she was under 21 and that, but for her age, he would have had the house put into their joint names. He admitted in evidence that this was simply an 'excuse'. Similarly, in *Grant v Edwards* the female partner was told by the male partner that the only reason for not acquiring the property in joint names was because she was involved in divorce proceedings and that, if the property were acquired jointly, this might operate to her prejudice in those proceedings. As Nourse LJ put it [1986] Ch 638 at 649:

> 'Just as in *Eves v Eves*, these facts appear to me to raise a clear inference that there was an understanding between plaintiff and defendant, or a common intention, that the plaintiff was to have some sort of proprietary interest in the house; otherwise no excuse for not putting her name onto the title would have been needed.'

The subsequent conduct of the female partner in each of these cases, which the court rightly held sufficient to give rise to a constructive trust or proprietary estoppel supporting her claim to an interest in the property, fell far short of such conduct as would by itself have supported the claim in the absence of an express representation by the male partner that she was to have such an interest. It is significant to note that the share to which the female partners in *Eves v Eves* and *Grant v Edwards* were held entitled were one-quarter and one-half respectively. In no sense could these shares have been regarded as proportionate to what the judge in the instant case described as a 'qualifying contribution' in terms of the indirect contributions to the acquisition or enhancement of the value of the houses made by the female partners.

I cannot help thinking that the judge in the instant case would not have fallen into error if he had kept clearly in mind the distinction between the effect of evidence on the one hand which was capable of establishing an express agreement or an express representation that Mrs. Rosset was to have an interest in the property and evidence on the other hand of conduct alone as a basis for an inference of the necessary common intention....

For the reasons I have indicated I would allow the appeal....

(1998) 18 LS 369, 372–373 (S. Wong)

To some extent, *Rosset* has created a certain confusion about the type of trusts which the courts are dealing with in these disputes. In both instances, the courts have labelled them as constructive trusts. The first category, however, borders on an express trust. While the second, with its emphasis on direct financial contribution, appears to blur the distinction between traditional resulting and constructive trusts. The detrimental reliance requirement, therefore, appears necessary for overcoming the formality of section 53(1)(b) of the Law of Property Act 1925 and for bringing the matter out of the ambit of traditional resulting trusts. The requirement, however, is in itself problematic, as it is unclear what the exact nexus is between common intention and detrimental reliance. As a result, *Rosset* has been criticised on a number of grounds, the first of which is the common intention requirement. *Rosset* is less clear on the level of evidence required for finding the requisite intention. This has led the courts to fictionalise the intent and make contradictory findings in some cases.[30] Clarke argues that if the defendant finds some 'excuse' to fob off the claimant, this clearly evidences disagreement rather than agreement.[31] The contradictory findings of the courts effectively convert the unilateral intention of one party (the claimant) into an agreement. Gardner further argues that the courts' willingness to stretch the facts so as to find the necessary common intention to share ends up being nothing more than an exercise in 'inventing' agreement.[32] This has led one judge to describe it as being a 'phantom intent'.[33]

Another criticism of *Rosset* stems from the requirement that, in the absence of an express agreement, the contributions must be financial and directly referable to the acquisition of the

[30] In both *Eves v Eves* [1975] 1 WLR 1338 and *Grant v Edwards* [1986] Ch 638 the defendants had given excuses to the plaintiffs for not sharing the legal title in the properties and the plaintiffs had made indirect contributions rather than direct financial contributions. However, the courts construed the fact that excuses had to be given for not sharing the legal title as evidence of some intention to share. Although *Eves* and *Grant v Edwards* were decided prior to *Rosset* and therefore cannot be attributed to it *per se*, these cases were not expressly overruled in *Rosset*. Thus, it would seem that in both of these cases the courts' reasons for finding a common intention remain sound.   [31] (1992) 22 *Family Law* 72, 74 (P. Clarke).

[32] (1993) 109 LQR 263, 270 (S. Gardner).

[33] *Per* Dickson J, *Pettkus v Becker* (1980) 117 DLR (3d) 257 at 270.

property so as to give rise to an inference of common intention. This condition effectively places little significance on indirect contributions, even where such contributions are substantial. By ignoring indirect contributions, the main objection is that the principles effectively discriminate against women by making two basic assumptions.[34] The first is that the spouses and cohabitants are treated as strangers dealing with each other at arm's length, and will, therefore, 'bargain' for their respective shares over the family home. It imposes a commercial gloss to a relationship which is *prima facie* a personal one and the 'bargain' is interpreted as the first condition of common intention. The second assumption is that value cannot be attached to the domestic services provided by the claimant. The discriminatory effect of the law clearly manifests itself here, as it fails to take into account the effects of sexual division of labour in these relationships.[35]

Oxley v Hiscock[36]
[2004] EWCA Civ 546, [2005] Fam 211 (CA, **Chadwick, Mance** and **Scott Baker LJJ**)

In 1991 the claimant, Mrs. Oxley, bought 35 Dickens Close with the defendant, Mr. Hiscock, in which they cohabited. The property was registered in the sole name of the defendant. The purchase price of £127,000 was funded by the net proceeds of the sale of the claimant's property for £61,500, of which the defendant had contributed the full purchase price of £25,200; by £35,500 from the defendant and a mortgage loan of £30,000. The parties separated and the property was sold. The claimant sought a declaration that the proceeds were held by the defendant on trust for both of them in equal shares. The trial judge granted the declaration.

Held. There was no evidence from which a common intention to share equally could be inferred. Instead, the claimant would obtain 40 per cent of the proceeds.

Chadwick LJ:

21   The principal ground of appeal is that the judge misdirected herself in law in refusing to follow the decision of this court in *Springette v Defoe* [1992] 2 FLR 388. The basis of that decision is accurately summarised in the headnote to the report:

> 'If two or more persons purchased property in their joint names and there was no declaration of trusts on which they were to hold the property, they held the property on a resulting trust for the persons who provided the purchase money in the proportions in which they provided it, unless there was sufficient specific evidence of their common intention that they should be entitled in other proportions, that common intention being a shared intention communicated between them and made manifest at the time of the transaction itself.'

It was said that in the present case, as in *Springette v Defoe* [1992] 2 FLR 388, it was clear, notwithstanding any subjective intention each might have had, that there had been no discussion

---

[34] (1991) 17 *Monash University Law Review* 14 (M. Neave).

[35] K. O'Donovan, *Sexual Divisions in Law* (1985). Sexual division of labour refers to the system whereby the parties take on distinct roles of responsibility in which the female partner is the primary partner caring for the family and the male partner is the main wage-earner responsible for bringing home the family's income.

[36] (2004) 120 LQR 541 (J. Gardner); [2004] All ER Rev 247 (P.J. Clarke); [2004] Conv 496 (M. Thompson); [2005] Conv 79 (M.J. Dixon).

between the parties as to the extent of their respective beneficial interests at the time of the purchase of 35 Dickens Close. So it must follow that the presumption of resulting trust[37] was not displaced and the property was held for Mr. Hiscock and Mrs. Oxley in beneficial shares proportionate to their contributions....

24   The first question on this appeal, therefore, is whether the judge was required, by the decision of this court in *Springette v Defoe,* to find that, in the absence of some 'shared intention [as to the proportions in which they should be entitled] communicated between them and made manifest at the time of the transaction itself', the property was held upon a resulting trust for Mr. Hiscock and Mrs. Oxley in beneficial shares proportionate to the respective financial contributions which they had made to the acquisition cost. Or was the judge entitled and required—as she plainly thought—to follow the approach adopted by this court in *Midland Bank plc v Cooke* [1995] 4 All ER 562....

The law as understood before Midland Bank plc v Cooke

26   It is important to have in mind the underlying requirement, imposed by section 53(1) of the Law of Property Act 1925, (a) that no interest in land can be created orally and (b) that no declaration of trust respecting land can have effect if made orally.[38] But section 53(2) excludes from that requirement 'the creation or operation of resulting, implied or constructive trusts'. It is the requirement in section 53(1) of the 1925 Act—and the saving provision in section 53(2)— which has led to the need, in a case where one former co-habitee asserts against the other (in whose sole name the property is registered) a beneficial interest arising out of some informal arrangement or understanding (not evidenced in writing) or from subsequent conduct, to establish the existence of a constructive trust; or else to rely on a resulting trust arising from contributions.

His Lordship considered *Walker v Hall* [1984] FLR 126; *Turton v Turton* [1988] Ch 542; *Grant v Edwards* [1986] Ch 638; *Lloyds Bank plc v Rosset* [1991] 1 AC 107 [p. 325, above]; *Stokes v Anderson* [1991] 1 FLR 391; *Springette v Defoe* [1992] 2 FLR 388; *Huntingford v Hobbs* [1993] 1 FLR 736; *Evans v Hayward* [1995] 2 FLR 511; *Savill v Goodall* [1993] 1 FLR 755, and continued:

The decision in Midland Bank plc v Cooke

53   I have set out, at some length, the law in this area as it appears to have been understood in this court before the decision in *Midland Bank plc v Cooke* [1995] 4 All ER 562[39] because that decision must be examined in that context. The issue in that case—as to the extent of the wife's beneficial interest in the former matrimonial home—arose in proceedings brought by the bank to enforce a charge given by the husband to secure a business loan. The property had been purchased with the assistance of a mortgage advance (£6,450); the balance being found out of a wedding gift from the husband's parents (£1,100) and the husband's own moneys (£1,000 or thereabouts). The property was conveyed into the husband's sole name. There had been no discussion or agreement between husband and wife at the time of the acquisition as to the basis upon which the property was held by the husband, or as to the extent of their respective beneficial interests. Treating the wedding gift as made to husband and wife equally, it had been held in the county court that the wife was entitled to a beneficial interest on the basis of her contribution to the purchase price. But, following the approach in *Springette v Defoe,* the judge

---

[37] See p. 257, above.   [38] See p. 112, above.

[39] [1995] All ER Rev 286 (S. Cretney), 312 (P. Clarke); (1996) 112 LQR 378 (S. Gardner); (1996) 55 CLJ 194 (M. Oldham); [1997] Conv 66 (M. Dixon).

had held that the extent of that beneficial interest was limited to the proportion (6.47 per cent) which her contribution (equal to one-half of the wedding gift) bore to the whole. This court (Stuart-Smith, Waite and Schiemann LJJ) took a different view, holding that the wife was entitled to a half share in the property.

54   The leading judgment (with which the other two members of the court agreed) was given by Waite LJ. He endorsed, at p. 569b, the view of the County Court judge that, in the absence of any discussion or agreement at the time of the purchase, the wife's claim to have a beneficial interest in the property depended on her being held to have made a monetary contribution. But if she had made a contribution equal to one-half of the wedding gift—as the judge had been entitled to hold on the evidence—then this was a case within the second of the categories identified by Lord Bridge in *Lloyds Bank plc v Rosset*.[40] Waite LJ then addressed the question: '(B) Is the proportion of Mrs Cooke's beneficial interest to be fixed solely by reference to the percentage of the purchase price which she contributed directly, so as to make all other conduct irrelevant?' He accepted the submission on behalf of the bank that

> 'in determining (in the absence of evidence of express agreement) whether a party unnamed in the deeds has any beneficial interest in the property at all the test is the stringent one stated by Lord Bridge of Harwich in *Lloyds Bank plc v Rosset* . . .'

—that is to say that (for a case to fall within the second of Lord Bridge's categories) it was, at the least, extremely doubtful whether anything less than direct contributions to the purchase price by the partner who is not the legal owner, whether initially or by payment of mortgage instalments, will 'justify the inference necessary to the creation of a constructive trust'. He summarised the further submission advanced on behalf of the bank in these terms [1995] 4 All ER 562, 571:

> 'By parity of reasoning, in cases where a direct contribution has been duly proved by the partner who is not the legal owner (thus establishing a resulting trust in his or her favour of some part of the beneficial interest) the proportion of that share will be fixed at the proportion it bears to the overall price of the property. Although the proportion may be enlarged by subsequent contribution to the purchase price, such contributions must be direct—i.e. further cash payments or contribution to the capital element in instalment repayments of any mortgage under which the unpaid proportion of the purchase remains secured. Nothing less will do.'

As he pointed out that submission was based on the decision of this court in *Springette v Defoe* [1992] 2 FLR 388 . . .

57   Waite LJ . . . continued, at 574:

> 'The general principle to be derived from *Gissing v Gissing* [1971] AC 886 and *Grant v Edwards* [1986] Ch 638 can in my judgment be summarised in this way. When the court is proceeding, in cases like the present where the partner without legal title has successfully asserted an equitable interest through direct contribution, to determine (in the absence of express evidence of intention) what proportions the parties must be assumed to have intended for their beneficial ownership, the duty of the judge is to undertake a survey of the whole course of dealing between the parties relevant to their ownership and occupation of the property and their sharing of its burdens and advantages. That scrutiny will not confine itself to the limited range of acts of direct contribution of the sort that are needed to found a beneficial interest in the first place. It will

[40] See p. 326, above.

take into consideration all conduct which throws light on the question what shares were intended. Only if that search proves inconclusive does the court fall back on the maxim that "equality is equity".'

58   On the basis of that analysis he concluded that the question posed under (B) should be answered in the negative. The court is not bound to deal with the matter on the strict basis of the trust resulting from the cash contribution to the purchase price, and is free to attribute to the parties an intention to share the beneficial interest in some different proportions. He then addressed a further submission advanced on behalf of the bank in that case, which he put as question (C): 'Can an agreement be attributed by inference of law to parties who have expressly stated that they reached no agreement?' After referring, again, to the passages from the judgments of Dillon LJ and Steyn LJ in *Springette v Defoe* [1992] 2 FLR 388, 393d–h, 395f–g.... Waite LJ concluded that that question should be answered in the affirmative [1995] 4 All ER 562, 575:

> 'I would therefore hold that positive evidence that the parties neither discussed nor intended any agreement as to the proportions of their beneficial interest does not preclude the court, on general equitable principles, from inferring one.'....

60   I return, therefore, to the first question on this appeal—whether the judge was required by the decision of this court in *Springette v Defoe* [1992] 2 FLR 388 to find that, in the absence of some shared intention as to the proportions in which they should be entitled to the property communicated between them at the time of the purchase, the property was held upon a resulting trust for Mr. Hiscock and Mrs. Oxley in beneficial shares proportionate to the respective financial contributions which they had made to the acquisition cost. In my view the judge was not so required. For my part, I doubt whether the observations in *Springette v Defoe* upon which the defendant relies did, in truth, reflect the state of the law at the time when that appeal was decided. Be that as it may, they have not done so since the decision of this court in *Midland Bank plc v Cooke* [1995] 4 All ER 562. I reject the submission, in so far as it was pursued in argument, that *Midland Bank plc v Cooke* was wrongly decided. But I think that the law has moved on since that decision.

Developments since the decision in Midland Bank plc v Cooke

61   The judgments of this court in *Midland Bank plc v Cooke* were handed down in July 1995. Within a few months the familiar question—'what is the interest of one unmarried cohabitee in the house purchased in the name of the other as a home in which they intend to live as man and wife?'—was before this court, again, in *Drake v Whipp* [1996] 1 FLR 826[41]....

65   It is very difficult, if not impossible, to find anything in the facts in *Drake v Whipp* [1996] 1 FLR 826 to suggest that either of the parties ever gave thought to an arrangement under which the property should be shared in the proportions two-thirds and one-third; let alone that that was ever their common intention. Nor do I think that Peter Gibson LJ approached the matter on that basis. As he said, at p 830, 'in constructive trust cases, the court can adopt a broad brush approach to determining the parties' respective shares... I would approach the matter more broadly, looking at the parties' entire course of conduct together.' That approach, as it seems to me, had received the approval of the House of Lords some 35 years earlier, in *Gissing v Gissing* [1971] AC 886, 909e, *per* Lord Diplock; had been endorsed, at least by

---

[41] [1997] Conv 467 (A. Dunn).

Sir Nicolas Browne-Wilkinson V-C, in *Grant v Edwards* [1986] Ch 638, 657h; and had been acknowledged and accepted by Nourse LJ in *Stokes v Anderson* [1991] 1 FLR 391, 399f. If these problems are to be solved by an analysis based on constructive trust, which requires the imputation of some common intention at the time of acquisition, then, as Nourse LJ observed in *Stokes v Anderson,* at p 400c, 'the court must supply the common intention by reference to that which all the material circumstances have shown to be fair'. That is, I think, what Waite LJ had in mind when he referred, in *Midland Bank plc v Cooke* [1995] 4 All ER 562, 575, to 'equity's assistance in formulating a fair presumed basis for the sharing of the beneficial title' in a case where the parties 'had been honest enough to admit they never gave ownership a thought...'

66   Once it is recognised that what the court is doing, in cases of this nature, is to supply or impute a common intention as to the parties' respective shares (in circumstances in which there was, in fact, no common intention) on the basis of that which, in the light of all the material circumstances (including the acts and conduct of the parties after the acquisition), is shown to be fair, it seems to me very difficult to avoid the conclusion that an analysis in terms of proprietary estoppel will, necessarily, lead to the same result; and that it may be more satisfactory to accept that there is no difference, in cases of this nature, between constructive trust and proprietary estoppel. It is clear that Sir Nicolas Browne-Wilkinson V-C in *Grant v Edwards* thought that there was much to be said for that view. In *Stokes v Anderson,* Nourse LJ seems to have thought the same. More recently, in *Yaxley v Gotts* [2000] Ch 162, 176 [see p. 347, below], Robert Walker LJ observed that 'in the area of a joint enterprise for the acquisition of land (which may be, but is not necessarily, the matrimonial home) the two concepts [estoppel and constructive trust] coincide'; and, at p 180, that 'the species of constructive trust based on "common intention" ... is closely akin to, if not indistinguishable from, proprietary estoppel'. He found support for those observations in the three cases to which much reference has been made in this judgment: *Gissing v Gissing, Grant v Edwards* and *Lloyds Bank plc v Rosset....*

Summary

68   I have referred, in the immediately preceding paragraphs, to 'cases of this nature'. By that, I mean cases in which the common features are: (i) the property is bought as a home for a couple who, although not married, intend to live together as man and wife; (ii) each of them makes some financial contribution to the purchase; (iii) the property is purchased in the sole name of one of them; and (iv) there is no express declaration of trust. In those circumstances the first question is whether there is evidence from which to infer a common intention, communicated by each to the other, that each shall have a beneficial share in the property. In many such cases—of which the present is an example—there will have been some discussion between the parties at the time of the purchase which provides the answer to that question. Those are cases within the first of Lord Bridge's categories in *Lloyds Bank plc v Rosset* [1991] 1 AC 107 [see p. 326, above]. In other cases—where the evidence is that the matter was not discussed at all—an affirmative answer will readily be inferred from the fact that each has made a financial contribution. Those are cases within Lord Bridge's second category. And, if the answer to the first question is that there was a common intention, communicated to each other, that each should have a beneficial share in the property, then the party who does not become the legal owner will be held to have acted to his or her detriment in making a financial contribution to the purchase in reliance on the common intention.

69   In those circumstances, the second question to be answered in cases of this nature is: 'what is the extent of the parties' respective beneficial interests in the property?' Again, in many such cases, the answer will be provided by evidence of what they said and did at the time of the

acquisition. But, in a case where there is no evidence of any discussion between them as to the amount of the share which each was to have—and even in a case where the evidence is that there was no discussion on that point—the question still requires an answer. It must now be accepted that (at least in this court and below) the answer is that each is entitled to that share which the court considers fair having regard to the whole course of dealing between them in relation to the property. And, in that context, 'the whole course of dealing between them in relation to the property' includes the arrangements which they make from time to time in order to meet the outgoings (for example, mortgage contributions, council tax and utilities, repairs, insurance and housekeeping) which have to be met if they are to live in the property as their home.

70   As the cases show, the courts have not found it easy to reconcile that final step with a traditional, property-based, approach. It was rejected, in unequivocal terms, by Dillon LJ in *Springette v Defoe* [1992] 2 FLR 388, 393 when he said: 'the court does not as yet sit, as under a palm tree, to exercise a general discretion to do what the man in the street, on a general overview of the case, might regard as fair'. Three strands of reasoning can be identified.

(1)   That suggested by Lord Diplock in *Gissing v Gissing* [1971] AC 886, 909d and adopted by Nourse LJ in *Stokes v Anderson* [1991] 1 FLR 391, 399g, 400b–c. The parties are taken to have agreed at the time of the acquisition of the property that their respective shares are not to be quantified then, but are left to be determined when their relationship comes to an end or the property is sold on the basis of what is then fair having regard to the whole course of dealing between them. The court steps in to determine what is fair because, when the time came for that determination, the parties were unable to agree.

(2)   That suggested by Waite LJ in *Midland Bank plc v Cooke* [1995] 4 All ER 562, 574d–g. The court undertakes a survey of the whole course of dealing between the parties 'relevant to their ownership and occupation of the property and their sharing of its burdens and advantages' in order to determine 'what proportions the parties must be assumed to have intended [from the outset] for their beneficial ownership'. On that basis the court treats what has taken place while the parties have been living together in the property as evidence of what they intended at the time of the acquisition.

(3)   That suggested by Sir Nicolas Browne-Wilkinson V-C in *Grant v Edwards* [1986] Ch 638, 656g–h, 657h and approved by Robert Walker LJ in *Yaxley v Gotts* [2000] Ch 162, 177c–e. The court makes such order as the circumstances require in order to give effect to the beneficial interest in the property of the one party, the existence of which the other party (having the legal title) is estopped from denying. That, I think, is the analysis which underlies the decision of this court in *Drake v Whipp* [1996] 1 FLR 826, 831e–g.

71   For my part, I find the reasoning adopted by this court in *Midland Bank plc v Cooke* to be the least satisfactory of the three strands. It seems to me artificial—and an unneces- sary fiction—to attribute to the parties a common intention that the extent of their respect- ive beneficial interests in the property should be fixed as from the time of the acquisition, in circumstances in which all the evidence points to the conclusion that, at the time of the acquisition, they had given no thought to the matter. The same point can be made—although with less force—in relation to the reasoning that, at the time of the acquisition, their common intention was that the amount of the respective shares should be left for later determination. But it can be said that, if it were their common intention that each should have some beneficial interest in the property—which is the hypothesis upon which it becomes necessary to answer the second question—then, in the absence of evidence that they gave any thought to the amount

of their respective shares, the necessary inference is that they must have intended that question would be answered later on the basis of what was then seen to be fair. But, as I have said, I think that the time has come to accept that there is no difference in outcome, in cases of this nature, whether the true analysis lies in constructive trust or in proprietary estoppel.

His Lordship applied these principles to the facts and concluded that, since there was no evidence as to any discussion about the parties' shares in the property, it was necessary to have regard to what would be a fair share having regard to the whole course of dealing between the parties in relation to the property. This was 60 per cent to Mr. Hiscock and 40 per cent to Mrs. Oxley.

C PROPERTY REGISTERED IN THE NAMES OF BOTH PARTIES

Where the property is registered in the names of both parties they clearly both have a beneficial interest, so the only remaining question concerns the extent of that interest.

Stack v Dowden[42]

[2007] UKHL 17, [2007] 2 AC 432 (**Lords Hoffmann, Hope of Craighead, Walker of Gestingthorpe, Neuberger of Abbotsbury** and **Baroness Hale of Richenard**)

In 1993 Mr. Stack and Ms. Dowden purchased 114 Chatsworth Road as the family home, which was conveyed into their joint names. Two-thirds of the purchase price came from Ms. Dowden's account and one-third from a mortgage in their joint names, to which they both contributed. The parties separated in 2002. The trial judge ordered that the property be sold and the net proceeds be divided equally between them. Ms. Dowden appealed and the Court of Appeal ordered that the net proceeds be divided 65 per cent to 35 per cent in her favour. Mr. Stack appealed.

   Held: (Lord Neuberger dissenting) Appeal dismissed.

Lord Hope:

3   The key to simplifying the law in this area lies in the identification of the correct starting point. Each case will, of course, turn on its own facts. But law can, and should, provide the right framework. Traditionally, English law has always distinguished between legal ownership in land and its beneficial ownership. The trusts under which the land is held will determine the extent of each party's beneficial ownership. Where the parties have dealt with each other at arm's length it makes sense to start from the position that there is a resulting trust according to how much each party contributed. Then there is the question whether the trust is truly a constructive trust. This may be helpful in their case but in others may seem to be a distinctly academic exercise, as my noble and learned friend Lord Walker of Gestingthorpe points out. But cohabiting couples

are in a different kind of relationship. The place where they live together is their home. Living together is an exercise in give and take, mutual co-operation and compromise. Who pays for what in regard to the home has to be seen in the wider context of their overall relationship. A more practical, down-to-earth, fact-based approach is called for in their case. The framework which the law provides should be simple, and it should be accessible.

4   The cases can be broken down into those where there is a single legal ownership and those where there is joint legal ownership. There must be consistency of approach between these two cases, a point to which my noble and learned friend Lord Neuberger of Abbotsbury has drawn our attention. I think that consistency is to be found by deciding where the onus lies if a party wishes to show that the beneficial ownership is different from the legal ownership. I agree with Baroness Hale that this is achieved by taking sole beneficial ownership as the starting point in the first case and by taking joint beneficial ownership as the starting point in the other. In this context joint beneficial ownership means that the shares are presumed to be divided between the beneficial owners equally. So in a case of sole legal ownership the onus is on the party who wishes to show that he has any beneficial interest at all, and if so what that interest is. In a case of joint legal ownership it is on the party who wishes to show that the beneficial interests are divided other than equally.

5   The advantage of this approach is that everyone will know where they stand with regard to the property when they enter into their relationship. Parties are, of course, free to enter into whatever bargain they wish and, so long as it is clearly expressed and can be proved, the court will give effect to it. But for the rest the state of the legal title will determine the right starting point. The onus is then on the party who contends that the beneficial interests are divided between them otherwise than as the title shows to demonstrate this on the facts. . . .

11   In a case such as this, where the parties had already been living together for about eighteen years and had four children when 114 Chatsworth Road was purchased in joint names and payments on the mortgage secured on that property were in effect contributed to by each of them equally, there would have been much to be said for adhering to the presumption of English law that the beneficial interests were divided between them equally. But I do not think that it is possible to ignore the fact that the contributions which they made to the purchase of that property were not equal. The relative extent of those contributions provides the best guide as to where their beneficial interests lay, in the absence of compelling evidence that by the end of their relationship they did indeed intend to share the beneficial interests equally. The evidence does not go that far. On the contrary, while they pooled their resources in the running of the household, in larger matters they maintained their financial independence from each other throughout their relationship. . . .

12   I think that indirect contributions, such as making improvements which added significant value to the property, or a complete pooling of resources in both time and money so that it did not matter who paid for what during their relationship, ought to be taken into account as well as financial contributions made directly towards the purchase of the property. I would endorse Chadwick LJ's view in *Oxley v Hiscock* [2005] Fam 211, para 69 [see p. 332, above] that regard should be had to the whole course of dealing between them in relation to the property. But the evidence in this case shows that there never was a stage when both parties intended that their beneficial interests in the property should be shared equally. Taking a broad view of the matter, therefore, I agree that the order that the Court of Appeal provides the fairest result that can be achieved in the circumstances.

Baroness Hale of Richmond:

40   The issue before us is the effect of a conveyance into the joint names of a cohabiting couple, but without an explicit declaration of their respective beneficial interests, of a dwelling

house which was to become their home. This is, so far as I am aware, the first time that this issue has come before the House, whether the couple be married or, as in this case, unmarried. The principles of law are the same, whether or not the couple are married, although the inferences to be drawn from their conduct may be different: *Bernard v Josephs* [1982] Ch 391, 402, *per* Griffith LJ . . .

54   . . . It should only be expected that joint transferees would have spelt out their beneficial interests when they intended them to be different from their legal interests. Otherwise, it should be assumed that equity follows the law and that the beneficial interests reflect the legal interests in the property. I do not think that this proposition is controversial, even in old-fashioned unregistered conveyancing. It has even more force in registered conveyancing in the consumer context.

55   Of course, it is something of an over-simplification. All joint legal owners must hold the land on trust . . . Section 53(1)(b) of the Law of Property Act 1925[43] requires that a declaration of trust respecting any land or any interest therein be manifested and proved by signed writing; but section 53(2)[44] provides that this 'does not affect the creation or operation of resulting, implied or constructive trusts'. The question is, therefore, what are the trusts to be deduced in the circumstances?

56   Just as the starting point where there is sole legal ownership is sole beneficial ownership, the starting point where there is joint legal ownership is joint beneficial ownership. The onus is upon the person seeking to show that the beneficial ownership is different from the legal ownership. So in sole ownership cases it is upon the non-owner to show that he has any interest at all. In joint ownership cases, it is upon the joint owner who claims to have other than a joint beneficial interest . . . . . .

58   The issue as it has been framed before us is whether a conveyance into joint names indicates only that each party is intended to have some beneficial interest but says nothing about the nature and extent of that beneficial interest, or whether a conveyance into joint names establishes a *prima facie* case of joint and equal beneficial interests until the contrary is shown. For the reasons already stated, at least in the domestic consumer context, a conveyance into joint names indicates both legal and beneficial joint tenancy, unless and until the contrary is proved.

59   The question is, how, if at all, is the contrary to be proved? Is the starting point the presumption of resulting trust, under which shares are held in proportion to the parties' financial contributions to the acquisition of the property, unless the contributor or contributors can be shown to have had a contrary intention? Or is it that the contrary can be proved by looking at all the relevant circumstances in order to discern the parties' common intention? . . . .

60   The law has indeed moved on in response to changing social and economic conditions. The search is to ascertain the parties' shared intentions, actual, inferred or imputed, with respect to the property in the light of their whole course of conduct in relation to it.

[Her Ladyship considered *Oxley v Hiscock* [2004] EWCA Civ 546, [2005] Fam 211, and continued:] . . .

61   The view of the Law Commission in *Sharing Homes* (2002, No. 278, para 4.27) on the quantification of beneficial entitlement [is]:

' If the question really is one of the parties' "common intention", we believe that there is much to be said for adopting what has been called a "holistic approach" to quantification, undertaking a survey of the whole course of dealing between the parties and taking account of all conduct which throws light on the question what shares were intended.'

[43] See p. 112, above.   [44] Ibid.

That may be the preferable way of expressing what is essentially the same thought, for two reasons. First, it emphasises that the search is still for the result which reflects what the parties must, in the light of their conduct, be taken to have intended. Second, therefore, it does not enable the court to abandon that search in favour of the result which the court itself considers fair....

62 Furthermore, although the parties' intentions may change over the course of time, producing what my noble and learned friend, Lord Hoffmann, referred to in the course of argument as an 'ambulatory' constructive trust, at any one time their interests must be the same for all purposes. They cannot at one and the same time intend, for example, a joint tenancy with survivorship should one of them die while they are still together, a tenancy in common in equal shares should they separate on amicable terms after the children have grown up, and a tenancy in common in unequal shares should they separate on acrimonious terms while the children are still with them.

63 We are not in this case concerned with the first hurdle.[45] There is undoubtedly an argument for saying, as did the Law Commission in *Sharing Homes, A Discussion Paper* (2002, No. 278, para 4.23) that the observations, which were strictly obiter dicta, of Lord Bridge of Harwich in *Lloyd's Bank plc v Rossett* [1991] 1 AC 107 have set that hurdle rather too high in certain respects. But that does not concern us now. It is common ground that a conveyance into joint names is sufficient, at least in the vast majority of cases, to surmount the first hurdle. The question is whether, that hurdle surmounted, the approach to quantification should be the same.

64 The majority of cases reported since *Pettitt* and *Gissing* have concerned homes conveyed into the name of one party only and it is in that context that the more flexible approach to quantification identified by Chadwick LJ in *Oxley v Hiscock* has emerged: see, in particular, *Grant v Edwards* [1986] Ch 638, described by Chadwick LJ as ' an important turning point' and referred to with ' obvious approval' in *Lloyds Bank plc v Rosset* [1991] 1 AC 107, *Stokes v Anderson* [1991] 1 FLR 391, *Midland Bank plc v Cooke* [1995] 4 All ER 562, and *Drake v Whipp* [1996] 1 FLR 826.

65 Curiously, it is in the context of homes conveyed into joint names but without an express declaration of trust that the courts have sometimes reverted to the strict application of the principles of the resulting trust...

[Her Ladyship referred to *Walker v Hall* [1984] FLR 126, *Springette v Defoe* [1992] 2 FLR 388, *Huntingford v Hobbs* [1993] 1 FLR 736, and continued:] The approach to quantification in cases where the home is conveyed into joint names should certainly be no stricter than the approach to quantification in cases where it has been conveyed into the name of one only. To the extent that *Walker v Hall, Springette v Defoe* and *Huntingford v Hobbs* hold otherwise, they should not be followed.... But the questions in a joint names case are not simply 'what is the extent of the parties' beneficial interests?' but 'did the parties intend their beneficial interests to be different from their legal interests?' and 'if they did, in what way and to what extent?' There are differences between sole and joint names cases when trying to divine the common intentions or understanding between the parties. I know of no case in which a sole legal owner (there being no declaration of trust) has been held to hold the property on a beneficial joint tenancy. But a court may well hold that joint legal owners (there being no declaration of trust) are also beneficial joint tenants. Another difference is that it will almost always have been a conscious decision to put the house into joint names. Even if the parties have not executed

---

[45] Referring to the need to establish a beneficial interest.

the transfer, they will usually, if not invariably, have executed the contract which precedes it. Committing oneself to spend large sums of money on a place to live is not normally done by accident or without giving it a moment's thought.

67   This is not to say that the parties invariably have a full understanding of the legal effects of their choice: there is recent empirical evidence from a small-scale qualitative study to confirm that they do not (see Gillian Douglas, Julie Pearce and Hilary Woodward, 'Dealing with Property Issues on Cohabitation Breakdown' [2007] *Family Law* 36). But that is so whether or not there is an express declaration of trust and no-one thinks that such a declaration can be overturned, except in cases of fraud or mistake.... Nor do they always have a completely free choice in the matter. Mortgagees used to insist upon the home being put in the name of the person whom they assumed would be the main breadwinner. Nowadays, they tend to think that it is in their best interests that the home be jointly owned and both parties assume joint and several liability for the mortgage. (It is, of course, a matter of indifference to the mortgagees where the beneficial interests lie.) Here again, this factor does not invalidate the parties' choice if there is an express declaration of trust, nor should it automatically count against it where there is none.

68   The burden will therefore be on the person seeking to show that the parties did intend their beneficial interests to be different from their legal interests, and in what way. This is not a task to be lightly embarked upon. In family disputes, strong feelings are aroused when couples split up. These often lead the parties, honestly but mistakenly, to reinterpret the past in self-exculpatory or vengeful terms. They also lead people to spend far more on the legal battle than is warranted by the sums actually at stake. A full examination of the facts is likely to involve disproportionate costs. In joint names cases it is also unlikely to lead to a different result unless the facts are very unusual. Nor may disputes be confined to the parties themselves. People with an interest in the deceased's estate may well wish to assert that he had a beneficial tenancy in common. It cannot be the case that all the hundreds of thousands, if not millions, of transfers into joint names using the old forms are vulnerable to challenge in the courts simply because it is likely that the owners contributed unequally to their purchase.

69   In law, 'context is everything' and the domestic context is very different from the commercial world. Each case will turn on its own facts. Many more factors than financial contributions may be relevant to divining the parties' true intentions. These include: any advice or discussions at the time of the transfer which cast light upon their intentions then; the reasons why the home was acquired in their joint names; the reasons why (if it be the case) the survivor was authorised to give a receipt for the capital moneys; the purpose for which the home was acquired; the nature of the parties' relationship; whether they had children for whom they both had responsibility to provide a home; how the purchase was financed, both initially and subsequently; how the parties arranged their finances, whether separately or together or a bit of both; how they discharged the outgoings on the property and their other household expenses. When a couple are joint owners of the home and jointly liable for the mortgage, the inferences to be drawn from who pays for what may be very different from the inferences to be drawn when only one is owner of the home. The arithmetical calculation of how much was paid by each is also likely to be less important. It will be easier to draw the inference that they intended that each should contribute as much to the household as they reasonably could and that they would share the eventual benefit or burden equally. The parties' individual characters and personalities may also be a factor in deciding where their true intentions lay. In the cohabitation context, mercenary considerations may be more to the fore than they would be in marriage, but it should not be assumed that they always take pride of place over natural love and affection. At the end of the

day, having taken all this into account, cases in which the joint legal owners are to be taken to have intended that their beneficial interests should be different from their legal interests will be very unusual.

70   This is not, of course, an exhaustive list. There may also be reason to conclude that, whatever the parties' intentions at the outset, these have now changed. An example might be where one party has financed (or constructed himself) an extension or substantial improvement to the property, so that what they have now is significantly different from what they had then.

Lord Walker of Gestingthorpe:

33   In the ordinary domestic case where there are joint legal owners there will be a heavy burden in establishing to the court's satisfaction that an intention to keep a sort of balance sheet of contributions actually existed, or should be inferred, or imputed to the parties. The presumption will be that equity follows the law. In such cases the court should not readily embark on the sort of detailed examination of the parties' relationship and finances that was attempted (with limited success) in this case. I agree with Lady Hale that this is, on its facts, an exceptional case.

34   In those cases (it is to be hoped, a diminishing number) in which such an examination is required the Court should in my opinion take a broad view of what contributions are to be taken into account. In *Gissing v Gissing* [1971] AC 886, 909G Lord Diplock referred to an adjustment of expenditure 'referable to the acquisition of the house'. 'Referable' is a word of wide and uncertain meaning. It would not assist the development of the law to go back to the sort of difficulties that arose in connection with the doctrine of part performance, where the act of part performance relied on had to be 'uniquely referable' to a contract of the sort alleged (see *Steadman v Steadman* [1976] AC 536). Now that almost all houses and flats are bought with mortgage finance, and the average period of ownership of a residence is a great deal shorter than the contractual term of the mortgage secured on it, the process of buying a house does very often continue, in a real sense, throughout the period of its ownership. The law should recognise that by taking a wide view of what is capable of counting as a contribution towards the acquisition of a residence, while remaining sceptical of the value of alleged improvements that are really insignificant, or elaborate arguments (suggestive of creative accounting) as to how the family finances were arranged.

37   I add a brief comment as to proprietary estoppel. In paragraphs 70 and 71 of his judgment in *Oxley v Hiscock* [2005] Fam 211 [see p. 333, above], Chadwick LJ considered the conceptual basis of the developing law in this area, and briefly discussed proprietary estoppel, a suggestion first put forward by Sir Nicolas Browne-Wilkinson V-C in *Grant v Edwards* [1986] Ch 638, 656. I have myself given some encouragement to this approach (*Yaxley v Gotts* [2000] Ch 162, 177 [see p. 347, below]) but I have to say that I am now rather less enthusiastic about the notion that proprietary estoppel and 'common-interest' constructive trusts can or should be completely assimilated. Proprietary estoppel typically consists of asserting an equitable claim against the conscience of the 'true' owner. The claim is a 'mere equity'. It is to be satisfied by the minimum award necessary to do justice (*Crabb v Arun District Council* [1976] Ch 179, 198), which may sometimes lead to no more than a monetary award. A 'common-intention' constructive trust, by contrast, is identifying the true beneficial owner or owners, and the size of their beneficial interests.

Lord Neuberger of Abbotsbury (dissenting):

107   ... while the domestic context can give rise to very different factual considerations from the commercial context, I am unconvinced that this justifies a different approach in principle to the issue of the ownership of the beneficial interest in property held in joint names. In the

absence of statutory provisions to the contrary, the same principles should apply to assess the apportionment of the beneficial interest as between legal co-owners, whether in a sexual, platonic, familial, amicable or commercial relationship. In each type of case, one is concerned with the issue of the ownership of the beneficial interest in property held in the names of two people, who have contributed to its acquisition, retention or value.

108   It appears to me helpful for present purposes to consider the issue in a structured way. First, to consider how the beneficial interest is owned at the date of acquisition, which involves identifying the nature and effect of the relevant features of what transpired between the parties up to, and at, the date of acquisition of the property. Then to consider the position at the date of the hearing, which involves identifying the relevant features of what subsequently transpired between the parties, and deciding whether they justify a change in the way in which the beneficial ownership is held. As already explained, I believe that the proper approach to these highly fact-sensitive enquiries should be in accordance with established legal principles and, as far as is consistent with those principles, as simple as possible.

Beneficial ownership on acquisition: where there is no evidence

109   In the absence of any relevant evidence other than the fact that the property, whether a house or a flat, acquired as a home for the legal co-owners is in joint names, the beneficial ownership will also be joint, so that it is held in equal shares. This can be said to result from the maxims that equity follows the law and equality is equity. On a less technical, and some might say more practical, approach, it can also be justified on the basis that any other solution would be arbitrary or capricious.

Beneficial ownership on acquisition: differential contributions

110   Where the only additional relevant evidence to the fact that the property has been acquired in joint names is the extent of each party's contribution to the purchase price, the beneficial ownership at the time of acquisition will be held, in my view, in the same proportions as the contributions to the purchase price. That is the resulting trust solution. The only realistic alternative in such a case would be to adhere to the joint ownership solution. There is an argument to support the view that equal shares should still be the rule in cohabitation cases, on the basis that it may be what many parties may expect if they purchase a home in joint names, even with different contributions. However, I consider that the resulting trust solution is correct in such circumstances....

113   There are also practical reasons for rejecting equality and supporting the resulting trust solution. The property may be bought in joint names for reasons which cast no light on the parties' intentions with regard to beneficial ownership. It may be the solicitor's decision or assumption, the lender's preference for the security of two borrowers, or the happenstance of how the initial contact with the solicitor was made.....

114   There is also an important point about consistency of approach with a case where the purchase of a home is in the name of one of the parties. As Baroness Hale observes, where there is no evidence of contributions, joint legal ownership is reflected in a presumption of joint beneficial ownership just as sole legal ownership is reflected in a presumption of sole beneficial ownership. Where there is evidence of the parties' respective contributions to the purchase price (and no other relevant evidence) and one of the parties has contributed X%, the fact that the purchase is in the sole name of the other does not prevent the former owning X% of the beneficial interest on a resulting trust basis. Indeed, it is because of the resulting trust presumption that such ownership arises. It seems to me that consistency suggests that the party

who contributed X% of the purchase price should be entitled to X% (no more and no less) of the beneficial interest in the same way if he is a co-purchaser. The resulting trust presumption arises because it is assumed that neither party intended a gift of any part of his own contribution to the other party. That would seem to me to apply to contributions irrespective of the name or names in which the property concerned is acquired and held, as a matter of both principle and logic.

115   It may be asked why the bigger contributor agreed to the property being taken in joint names, unless he intended joint beneficial ownership. There are four answers to that. The first is that the question sets out to justify what it assumes, namely that, in the absence of any discussion, the parties must have assumed an equal split. Secondly, if the other party was a contributor, he would often want to be a co-owner, and the only way real property can be held in law by two persons is as joint owners. Thirdly, the converse point can be made where a property is acquired in the name of one party: if the other party has contributed to the purchase, his absence from the title is not evidence that he was not intended to have an interest. (In this connection, it seems to me that, where a home is taken in the name of only one party, this is almost as likely to have been a conscious decision as where it is acquired in joint names: where both have contributed to the purchase, it is unlikely that either will have been unaware of the fact that the home was being acquired in the name of only one of them). Fourthly, there are the practical considerations to which I have already alluded.

116   Having said that, the fact that a property is taken in joint names is some evidence that both parties were intended to have some beneficial interest....

122   So, in the absence of any relevant evidence other than the parties' respective contributions, I would favour the resulting trust solution as at the date of acquisition.... Application of the resulting trust approach in the present case would justify Mr. Stack's appeal being dismissed. On the figures summarised by Baroness Hale, Mr. Stack could not possibly establish more than a 36% interest in the house as a result of all his contributions. Indeed, on the basis of the evidence, I would put his contribution at around 30%, but, as Ms. Dowden is prepared to concede 35%, it is unnecessary to consider that aspect further. Thus, on a resulting trust basis, Mr. Stack had no more than a 35% share of the beneficial interest at the date of acquisition.

Beneficial ownership on acquisition: constructive trust

123   Accordingly, in my judgment, where there are unequal contributions, the resulting trust solution is the one to be adopted. However, it is no more than a presumption, albeit an important one....

124   In many cases, there will, in addition to the contributions, be other relevant evidence as at the time of acquisition. Such evidence would often enable the court to deduce an agreement or understanding amounting to an intention as to the basis on which the beneficial interests would be held. Such an intention may be express (although not complying with the requisite formalities) or inferred, and must normally be supported by some detriment, to justify intervention by equity. It would be in this way that the resulting trust would become rebutted and replaced, or (conceivably) supplemented, by a constructive trust.

125   While an intention may be inferred as well as express, it may not, at least in my opinion, be imputed. That appears to me to be consistent both with normal principles and with the majority view of this House in *Pettitt v Pettitt* [1970] AC 777, as accepted by all but Lord Reid in *Gissing v Gissing* [1971] AC 886, 897H, 898B–D, 900E–G, 901B–D, and 904E–F, and reiterated by the Court of Appeal in *Grant v Edwards* [1986] Ch 638 at 651F–653A. The distinction between inference and imputation may appear a fine one (and in *Gissing* at 902G–H,

Lord Pearson, who, on a fair reading I think rejected imputation, seems to have equated it with inference), but it is important.

126   An inferred intention is one which is objectively deduced to be the subjective actual intention of the parties, in the light of their actions and statements. An imputed intention is one which is attributed to the parties, even though no such actual intention can be deduced from their actions and statements, and even though they had no such intention. Imputation involves concluding what the parties would have intended, whereas inference involves concluding what they did intend.

127   To impute an intention would not only be wrong in principle and a departure from two decisions of your Lordships' House in this very area, but it also would involve a judge in an exercise which was difficult, subjective and uncertain. (Hence the advantage of the resulting trust presumption). It would be difficult because the judge would be constructing an intention where none existed at the time, and where the parties may well not have been able to agree. It would be subjective for obvious reasons. It would be uncertain because it is unclear whether one considers a hypothetical negotiation between the actual parties, or what reasonable parties would have agreed. The former is more logical, but would redound to the advantage of an unreasonable party. The latter is more attractive, but is inconsistent with the principle, identified by Baroness Hale at paragraph 61, that the court's view of fairness is not the correct yardstick for determining the parties' shares (and see *Pettitt* at 801C–F, 809C–G and 826C).

128   A constructive trust does not only arise from an express or implied agreement or understanding. It can also arise in a number of circumstances in which it can be said that the conscience of the legal owner is affected. For instance, it may well be that facts which justified a proprietary estoppel against one of the parties in favour of the other would give rise to a constructive trust. However, in agreement with Lord Walker, I do not consider it necessary or appropriate to discuss proprietary estoppel further in this case.

129   It is hard to identify, particularly in the abstract, the factors which can be taken into account to infer an agreement or understanding, and the effect of such factors. Each case will be highly fact-sensitive, and what is relevant, and how, may be contentious, whether one is considering actions, discussions or statements, even where there is no dispute as to what was done or said....

131   Any assessment of the parties' intentions with regard to the ownership of the beneficial interest by reference to what they said and did must take into account all the circumstances of their relationship, in the same way as the interpretation of a contract must be effected by reference to all the surrounding circumstances. However, that does not mean that all the circumstances of the relationship are of primary or equal relevance to the issue.

132   I am unimpressed, for instance, by the argument that, merely because they have already lived together for a long time sharing all regular outgoings, including those in respect of the previous property they occupied, the parties must intend that the beneficial interest in the home they are acquiring, with differently sized contributions, should be held in equal shares. Particularly where the parties have chosen not to marry, their close and loving relationship does not by any means necessarily imply an intention to share all their assets equally. There is a large difference between sharing outgoings and making a gift of a valuable share in property; outgoings are relatively small regular sums arising out of day-to-day living, but an interest in the home is a capital asset, with a substantial value. I am similarly unconvinced that the ownership of the beneficial interest in a home acquired in joint names is much affected by whether the parties have children at the time of acquisition. While it justifies the obvious inference that

it is to be used for the children as well as the parties, it says nothing on its own as to the intended ownership of the beneficial interest.

133 The fact that the parties operated their day-to-day financial affairs through a joint bank account, into which both their wages were paid and from which all family outgoings were paid, could fairly be said to be strong evidence that they intended the sums in that account to be owned equally. Accordingly, it would normally be easy to justify the contention that a home acquired with money from that account (often together with a mortgage in joint names) should be treated as acquired with jointly owned money and therefore as beneficially owned jointly. However, I am unhappy with the suggestion that, because parties share or pool their regular income and outgoings, it can be assumed that they intended that the beneficial interest in their home, acquired in joint names but with significantly different contributions, should be shared equally. There is a substantial difference, in law, in commercial terms, in practice, and almost always in terms of value and importance, between the ownership of a home and the ownership of a bank account or, indeed, furniture, furnishings and other chattels.

134 The fact that the parties keep assets such as bank accounts and financial investments separate and in separate names could be said to indicate that the parties do not intend to pool their resources. But it could equally be said that the fact that they choose, exceptionally, to acquire the home in joint names indicates that it is to be treated differently from their other assets, namely that it is to be jointly owned beneficially. In my view, however, such evidence is again of little value on its own, as it relates to a very different category of assets, in terms of nature and value, from the home they are buying.

135 The factors I have been discussing in the previous three paragraphs will often, however, have some significance. If there is other, possibly contested, evidence which is said to support the contention that the parties intended a different result from that indicated by a resulting trust analysis, those factors may make it easier for the court to accept, or even to interpret, that evidence as justifying such a different result.

136 For instance, the fact that the parties are in a close and loving relationship would render it easier, than in a normal contractual context, to displace the resulting trust solution with, say, an equal division of the beneficial ownership. That is because a departure from the resulting trust solution normally involves a gratuitous transfer of value from one party to the other....

Beneficial ownership: events after the acquisition of the house

138 The fact that the ownership of the beneficial interest in a home is determined at the date of acquisition does not mean that it cannot alter thereafter. My noble and learned friend Lord Hoffmann suggested during argument that the trust which arises at the date of acquisition, whether resulting or constructive, is of an ambulatory nature. That elegant characterisation does not justify a departure from the application of established legal principles any more than such a departure is justified at the time of acquisition. It seems to me that 'compelling evidence', to use Lord Hope's expression in paragraph 11, is required before one can infer that, subsequent to the acquisition of the home, the parties intended a change in the shares in which the beneficial ownership is held. Such evidence would normally involve discussions, statements or actions, subsequent to the acquisition, from which an agreement or common understanding as to such a change can properly be inferred...

139 There are, however, one or two aspects I should like to mention. I agree with Lord Walker that, subject of course to other relevant facts justifying a different conclusion, the fact

that one party carries out significant improvements to the home will justify an adjustment of the apportionment of the beneficial interest in his favour. In such a case, the cost could be seen as capital expenditure which differs from regular outgoings relating to the use of the home, and is not dissimilar in financial effect, from the cost of acquiring the home in the first place. To qualify, any work must be substantial: decoration or repairs (at least unless they were very significant) would not do.

140   There is also the question of repayments of the mortgage, and payments of other outgoings. I have already discussed the effect of the parties taking a mortgage in joint names, and suggested that, in some cases, repayments of capital could have the effect of adjusting the shares in the beneficial interest. (It is conceivable that that could apply to payments of interest as well). In many cases, the repayments of capital, even if effected wholly by one party, should not be interpreted as indicating an intention to alter the way in which the beneficial interest is apportioned. Thus, the fact that one party is the home-maker (and, often, child-carer) and the other is the wage-earner would probably not justify the former having his share decreased simply because the other party repays the mortgage by instalments, but it may be different where both parties earn and share the home-making, but one of them repays the mortgage by a single capital sum.

141   Consistently with what has already been discussed, I am unconvinced that the original ownership of the beneficial interest could normally be altered merely by the way in which the parties conduct their personal and day-to-day financial affairs. I do not see how the facts that they have lived together for a long time, have been in a loving relationship, have children, operated a joint bank account, and shared the outgoings of the household, including in respect of use and occupation of the home, can, of themselves, indicate an intention to equalise their originally unequal shares any more than they would indicate an intention to equalise their shares on acquisition, as discussed earlier. So, too, the facts that they both earn and share the home-making, or that one party has a well-paid job and the other is the home-maker, seem to me to be irrelevant at least on their own. Even the fact that one party pays all the outgoings and the other does nothing would not seem to me to justify any adjustment to the original ownership of the beneficial interest (subject to the possible exception of mortgage repayments).

142   In many cases, these points may result in an outcome which would seem unfair at least to some people. However (unless and until the legislature decides otherwise) fairness is not the guiding principle as Baroness Hale says, and, at least without legislative directions, it would be a very subjective and uncertain guide. Further, it is always important to bear in mind the need for clarity and certainty.

143   It is worth repeating that one is concerned with the ownership of what will normally be the most important and valuable asset of the parties, and the way they conduct their day-to-day living and finances is, in my view, at least of itself, not a reliable guide to their intentions in relation to that ownership. Even payments on decoration, repairs, utilities and Council Tax, although related to the home, are concerned with its use and enjoyment, as opposed to its ownership as a capital asset. It is also worth repeating that these factors are not irrelevant to the issue of whether there has been a change in the shares in which the beneficial interest in the home is held. They provide part of the vital background against which any alleged discussion, statement or action said to give rise to a change in the beneficial ownership is to be assessed, in relation to both whether it occurred and what its effect was.

144   I am unhappy with the formulation of Chadwick LJ in *Oxley v Hiscock* [2005] Fam 211 at paragraph 69 [see p. 333, above]...namely that the beneficial ownership should be

apportioned by reference to what is 'fair having regard to the whole course of dealing between [the parties] in relation to the property'. First, fairness is not the appropriate yardstick. Secondly, the formulation appears to contemplate an imputed intention. Thirdly, 'the whole course of dealing ... in relation to the property' is too imprecise, as it gives insufficient guidance as to what is primarily relevant, namely dealings which cast light on the beneficial ownership of the property, and too limited, as all aspects of the relationship could be relevant in providing the context by reference to which any alleged discussion, statement and actions must be assessed. As already explained, I also disagree with Chadwick LJ's implicit suggestion in the same paragraph that 'the arrangements which [the parties] make with regard to the outgoings' (other than mortgage repayments) are likely to be of primary relevance to the issue of the ownership of the beneficial interest in the home.

145   I am rather more comfortable with the formulation of the Law Commission in Sharing Hanes, A Discussion Paper (Law Com No. 278), para 4.27, also quoted in para 61 of Baroness Hale's opinion, that the court should 'undertak[e] a survey of the whole course of dealing between the parties ... taking account of all conduct which throws light on the question what shares were intended'. It is perhaps inevitable that this formulation begs the difficult questions of what conduct throws light, and what light it throws, as those questions are so fact-sensitive. 'Undertaking a survey of the whole course of dealings between the parties' should not, I think, at least normally, require much detailed or controversial evidence. That is not merely for reasons of practicality and certainty. As already indicated, I would expect almost all of 'the whole course of dealing' to be relevant only as background: it is with actions discussions and statements which relate to the parties' agreement and understanding as to the ownership of the beneficial interest in the home with which the court should, at least normally, primarily be concerned. Otherwise, the enquiry is likely to be trespassing into what I regard as the forbidden territories of imputed intention and fairness.

146   In other words, where the resulting trust presumption (or indeed any other basis of apportionment) applies at the date of acquisition, I am unpersuaded that (save perhaps in a most unusual case) anything other than subsequent discussions, statements or actions, which can fairly be said to imply a positive intention to depart from that apportionment, will do to justify a change in the way in which the beneficial interest is owned. To say that factors such as a long relationship, children, a joint bank account, and sharing daily outgoings of themselves are enough, or even of potential central importance, appears to me not merely wrong in principle, but a recipe for uncertainty, subjectivity, and a long and expensive examination of facts. It could also be said to be arbitrary, as, if such factors of themselves justify a departure from the original apportionment, I find it hard to see how it could be to anything other than equality. If a departure from the original apportionment was solely based on such factors, it seems to me that the judge would almost always have to reach an 'all or nothing' decision. Thus, in this case, he would have to ask whether, viewed in the round, the personal and financial characteristics of the relationship between Mr. Stack and Ms. Dowden, after they acquired the house, justified a change in ownership of the beneficial interest from 35–65 to 50–50, even though nothing they did or said related to the ownership of that interest (save, perhaps, the repayments of the mortgage). In my view, that involves approaching the question in the wrong way. Subject, perhaps, to exceptional cases, whose possibility it would be unrealistic not to acknowledge, an argument for an alteration in the way in which the beneficial interest is held cannot, in my opinion, succeed, unless it can be shown that there was a discussion, statement or action which, viewed in its context, namely the parties' relationship, implied an actual agreement or understanding to effect such an alteration.

In **Abbott v Abbott** [2007] UKPC 53[46] the Privy Council applied the principles in *Stack v Dowden* to a case where the property had been registered in the name of one party only, in that case the husband. Since the wife was jointly liable for the mortgage repayments, a common-intention constructive trust was inferred. As regards quantification of the beneficial interest BARONESS HALE considered the parties' course of conduct concerning the property, including that the couple organised their finances jointly, and concluded that the beneficial ownership was split equally between the husband and wife.

In **Ritchie v Ritchie**, unreported (CC Leeds, 17 August, 2007), the principles recognised in *Stack v Dowden* were applied to ascertain the beneficial interests of a deceased mother and her son. In that case property had been conveyed into the joint names of the mother and son but, because of the very unusual circumstances of the case, it was held that they did not share the beneficial interest equally. These circumstances included that the property had been purchased by the mother from a local authority at a substantial discount, and that the mother could not have funded the mortgage without the assistance of her son, who also lived in the property. That explained why the property was purchased in their joint names. However, the primary purpose of the acquisition was to provide a home for the mother and the judge concluded that there was no intent that their interests in the property should be equal. The discount obtained by the mother was more than 50 per cent of the purchase price and the son's financial contribution was significantly less. Consequently, the son was held to have a one-third share of the beneficial interest.[47]

D   LAW REFORM

The Law Commission in *Cohabitation: the Financial Consequences of Relationship Breakdown* (Law Com. No. 307, 2007) has considered the law involving cohabitants generally and specifically as regards their property rights in the family home. The Law Commission has recommended that cohabitants should not have the same rights and remedies as married couples or civil partners. Instead, the Law Commission has recommended the creation of a new scheme which would apply specifically to cohabiting couples who separate. The scheme would apply, save where it was specifically disapplied by the couple, where two key conditions were satisfied:

(i)   the couple had a child together or had lived together as a couple in a joint household for a specified period (possibly between two to five years) and

(ii)   the applicant for relief had made 'qualifying contributions to the relationship giving rise to certain enduring consequences at the point of separation'.[48]

---

[46] [2007] Conv. 456 (M. Dixon); (2008) LQR 209 (R. Lee). See also *Holman v Howes* [2007] EWCA Civ 877.

[47] See also *Laskar v Laskar* [2008] EWCA Civ 347.   [48] Law Com, No. 307 (2007), p. 3.

1.19   In broad terms, the scheme would seek to ensure that the pluses and minuses of the relationship were shared between the couple. The applicant would have to show that the respondent retained a benefit, or that the applicant had a continuing economic disadvantage, as a result of contributions made to the relationship. The value of any award would depend on the extent of the retained benefit or continuing economic disadvantage. The court would have discretion to grant such financial relief as might be appropriate to deal with these matters, and in doing so would be required to give first consideration to the welfare of any dependent children.

As regards the application of this new scheme to property interests in the family home, the court would be given a discretion to make orders including financial awards, transfer of property, and property settlements. Crucially, if this new scheme applies, the law of implied trusts, estoppel, and contract would be excluded.

III COMMERCIAL PROPERTY DISPUTES

In **Yaxley v Gotts** [2000] Ch 162[49] the plaintiff and second defendant (Brownie Gotts) informally agreed that the latter would purchase a house which the plaintiff would convert into flats. The plaintiff would own the ground floor and would act as the second defendant's managing agent for the four flats in the rest of the house. The house was in fact purchased by the first defendant, the second defendant's son (Alan Gotts), but the plaintiff assumed that the father had bought it. The plaintiff converted the property and acted as managing agent for two-and-a-half years. The plaintiff and the father fell out. The son refused to allow the plaintiff to manage the flats and denied that the plaintiff had any interest in the ground floor. The plaintiff commenced proceedings against the defendants. The trial judge held that the plaintiff had a leasehold interest in the ground floor by virtue of proprietary estoppel. On appeal, the defendants argued that the oral agreement between the plaintiff and the father was void by virtue of section 2 of the Law of Property (Miscellaneous Provisions) Act 1989, which requires contracts of sale of land to be in writing, and that it could not be made effective by the doctrine of proprietary estoppel.

Held. If there was an oral agreement between the parties, the plaintiff was entitled to a leasehold interest under a constructive trust which was expressly saved by section 2(5) of the 1989 Act.

ROBERT WALKER LJ said at 176:

At a high level of generality, there is much common ground between the doctrines of proprietary estoppel and the constructive trust, just as there is between proprietary estoppel and part-performance. All are concerned with equity's intervention to provide relief against unconscionable conduct, whether as between neighbouring landowners, or vendor and purchaser, or

---

[49] (2000) CLJ 23 (L. Tee); (2000) 116 LQR 11 (R.J. Smith); (2000) 63 MLR 912 (I. Moore); [2000] Conv 245 (M. Thompson); [2000] All ER Rev 242 (P.J. Clarke).

relatives who make informal arrangements for sharing a home, or a fiduciary and the beneficiary or client to whom he owes a fiduciary obligation....

The overlap between estoppel and the constructive trust...seems to me to be of central
importance to the determination of this appeal. Plainly there are large areas where the two
concepts do not overlap: when a landowner stands by while his neighbour mistakenly builds
on the former's land the situation is far removed (except for the element of unconscionable
conduct) from that of a fiduciary who derives an improper advantage from his client. But in the
area of a joint enterprise for the acquisition of land (which may be, but is not necessarily, the
matrimonial home) the two concepts coincide. Lord Diplock's very well-known statement in
Gissing v Gissing [1971] AC 886 at 905 brings this out:

> 'A resulting, implied or constructive trust—and it is unnecessary for present purposes to distin-
> guish between these three classes of trust—is created by a transaction between the trustee and the
> *cestui que trust* in connection with the acquisition by the trustee of a legal estate in land, whenever
> the trustee has so conducted himself that it would be inequitable to allow him to deny to the *cestui
> que trust* a beneficial interest in the land acquired. And he will be held so to have conducted himself
> if by his words or conduct he has induced the *cestui que trust* to act to his own detriment in the
> reasonable belief that by so acting he was acquiring a beneficial interest in the land.'

His Lordship also referred to the dicta of Lord Bridge in *Lloyds Bank plc v Rosset* [1991]
1 AC 107 at 132 [p. 325, above] and Sir Nicolas Browne-Wilkinson V-C in *Grant v
Edwards* [1986] Ch 638 at 656, and continued:

In this case the judge did not make any finding as to the existence of a constructive trust. He
was not asked to do so, because it was not then seen as an issue in the case. But on the findings
of fact which the judge did make it was not disputed that a proprietary estoppel arose, and that
the appropriate remedy was the grant to Mr. Yaxley, in satisfaction of his equitable entitlement,
of a long leasehold interest, rent free, of the ground floor of the property. Those findings do in
my judgment equally provide the basis for the conclusion that Mr. Yaxley was entitled to such an
interest under a constructive trust. The oral bargain which the judge found to have been made
between Mr. Yaxley and Mr. Brownie Gotts, and to have been adopted by Mr. Alan Gotts, was
definite enough to meet the test stated by Lord Bridge in *Lloyds Bank v Rosset*....

To recapitulate briefly: the species of constructive trust based on 'common intention' is
established by what Lord Bridge in *Rosset* called an 'agreement, arrangement or understanding' actually reached between the parties, and relied on and acted on by the claimant. A constructive trust of that sort is closely akin to, if not indistinguishable from, proprietary estoppel.
Equity enforces it because it would be unconscionable for the other party to disregard the
claimant's rights. Section 2(5) [of the Law of Property (Miscellaneous Provisions) Act 1989]
expressly saves the creation and operation of a constructive trust.

In **Banner Homes Group plc v Luff Developments Ltd** [2000] Ch 372[50] the plaintiff,
Banner Homes, and the defendant, Luff Development, commenced negotiations to
form a joint venture to purchase a site for development. The parties reached an agreement in principle to acquire a site through a company which they would own equally.
The defendant incorporated S Ltd for this purpose. The defendant had second thoughts

---

[50] [2000] All ER Rev 245; [2002] Conv 35 (N. Hopkins). See also *Cox v Jones* [2004] EWHC 1486 (Ch);
[2005] Conv 168 (R. Probert).

about the arrangement with the plaintiff and began looking for a new partner, but the plaintiff was not informed of this because the defendant thought that the plaintiff might acquire the site for itself. S Ltd acquired the site, with funds provided by the defendant. The defendant then informed the plaintiff that it was withdrawing from the proposed joint venture. The plaintiff commenced proceedings alleging that the defendant held half the shares in S Ltd on constructive trust. The trial judge found that the parties had not made a binding contract; that the defendant could not be estopped from denying the existence of a binding contract; and that the defendant did not hold any shares on a constructive trust. The plaintiff appealed against the last finding.

Held: Since there was an understanding that the property would be acquired, and the defendant had obtained an advantage by keeping the plaintiff out of the market, the defendant held half the shares on constructive trust for the plaintiff.

CHADWICK LJ said at 383:

The judge was referred—as we have been—to a number of cases at first instance which illustrate the circumstances in which equity will impose a constructive trust on property acquired by one person, say A, in furtherance of some pre-acquisition arrangement or understanding with another, say B, that, upon the acquisition of the property by A in circumstances in which B kept out of the market, B would be granted some interest in the property; notwithstanding that the arrangement or understanding falls short of creating contractual obligations enforceable at law.

His Lordship considered dicta from *Paragon Finance plc v D B Thakerar & Co* [1999] 1 All ER 400 at 408–409 (Millett LJ) [p. 878, below]; *Yaxley v Gotts* [2000] Ch 162 at 176 (Robert Walker LJ) [p. 347, above]; *Lloyds Bank plc v Rosset* [1991] 1 AC 107 at 132 (Lord Bridge of Harwich) [p. 325, above]; *Grant v Edwards* [1986] Ch 638 at 656 (Sir Nicolas Browne-Wilkinson V-C) and continued:

With those principles in mind, I turn to examine the first instance decisions in which equity has imposed a constructive trust on property acquired by one person in furtherance of some arrangement or understanding with another that, by keeping out of the market, that other would, nevertheless, be able to acquire some interest in the property.

His Lordship considered *Chattock v Muller* (1878) 8 Ch D 177; *Pallant v Morgan* [1953] Ch 43; *Holiday Inns Inc v Broadhead* (1974) 232 Estates Gazette 951; *Time Products Ltd v Combined English Stores Group Ltd* (2 December, 1974, unreported) and *Island Holdings Ltd v Birchington Engineering Ltd* (7 July, 1981, unreported), and continued:

I have thought it appropriate to analyse the decisions at first instance in more detail than might otherwise have been necessary in the circumstances that the present appeal provides the first opportunity, so far as I am aware, for this court to consider the basis and scope of what may be called the *Pallant v Morgan* equity in a case in which reliance has to be placed upon it by the appellant. In my view there is no doubt that such an equity does exist and is firmly based. It is an example of the wider equity to which Millett J referred in *Lonrho plc v Fayed (No 2)* [1992] 1 WLR 1 at 9–10:

'Equity will intervene by way of constructive trust, not only to compel the defendant to restore the plaintiff's property to him, but also to require the defendant to disgorge property which he should have acquired, if at all, for the plaintiff. In the latter category of case, the defendant's wrong lies not in the acquisition of the property, which may or may not have been lawful, but in his subsequent denial of the plaintiff's beneficial interest. For such to be the case, however, the defendant must either have acquired property which but for his wrongdoing would have belonged to the plaintiff, or he must have acquired property in circumstances in which he cannot conscientiously retain it as against the plaintiff.'

Or, as the same judge was to say in this court, in the passage in *Paragon Finance plc v D B Thakerar & Co* [1999] 1 All ER 400 at 408–409. . . . :

'His [the defendant's] possession of the property is coloured from the first by the trust and confidence by means of which he obtained it, and his subsequent appropriation of the property to his own use is a breach of that trust.'

It is important, however, to identify the features which will give rise to a *Pallant v Morgan* equity and to define its scope; while keeping in mind that it is undesirable to attempt anything in the nature of an exhaustive classification. As Millett J pointed out in *Lonrho plc v Fayed (No 2)* [1992] 1 WLR 1 at 9, in a reference to the work of distinguished Australian commentators, equity must retain its 'inherent flexibility and capacity to adjust to new situations by reference to mainsprings of the equitable jurisdiction'. Equity must never be deterred by the absence of a precise analogy, provided that the principle invoked is sound. Mindful of this caution, it is, nevertheless, possible to advance the following propositions.

(1) A *Pallant v Morgan* equity may arise where the arrangement or understanding on which it is based precedes the acquisition of the relevant property by one of those parties to that arrangement. It is the pre-acquisition arrangement which colours the subsequent acquisition by the defendant and leads to his being treated as a trustee if he seeks to act inconsistently with it. Where the arrangement or understanding is reached in relation to property already owned by one of the parties, he may (if the arrangement is of sufficient certainty to be enforced specifically) thereby constitute himself trustee on the basis that 'equity looks on that as done which ought to be done'; or an equity may arise under the principles developed in the proprietary estoppel cases. As I have sought to point out, the concepts of constructive trust and proprietary estoppel have much in common in this area. . . .

(2) It is unnecessary that the arrangement or understanding should be contractually enforceable. Indeed, if there is an agreement which is enforceable as a contract, there is unlikely to be any need to invoke the *Pallant v Morgan* equity; equity can act through the remedy of specific performance and will recognise the existence of a corresponding trust. . . . In particular, it is no bar to a *Pallant v Morgan* equity that the pre-acquisition arrangement is too uncertain to be enforced as a contract—see *Pallant v Morgan* itself, and *Time Products Ltd v Combined English Stores Group Ltd*—nor that it is plainly not intended to have contractual effect—see *Island Holdings Ltd v Birchington Engineering Ltd* (7 July, 1981, unreported).

(3) It is necessary that the pre-acquisition arrangement or understanding should contemplate that one party (the acquiring party) will take steps to acquire the relevant property; and that, if he does so, the other party (the non-acquiring party) will obtain some interest in that property. Further, it is necessary that (whatever private reservations the acquiring party may have) he has not informed the non-acquiring party before the acquisition (or, more accurately, before it is too late for the parties to be restored to a position of no advantage/no detriment) that he no longer intends to honour the arrangement or understanding.

(4) It is necessary that, in reliance on the arrangement or understanding, the non-acquiring party should do (or omit to do) something which confers an advantage on the acquiring party in relation to the acquisition of the property; or is detrimental to the ability of the non-acquiring party to acquire the property on equal terms. It is the existence of the advantage to the one, or detriment to the other, gained or suffered as a consequence of the arrangement or understanding, which leads to the conclusion that it would be inequitable or unconscionable to allow the acquiring party to retain the property for himself, in a manner inconsistent with the arrangement or understanding which enabled him to acquire it.... In many cases the advantage/detriment will be found in the agreement of the non-acquiring party to keep out of the market. That will usually be both to the advantage of the acquiring party—in that he can bid without competition from the non-acquiring party—and to the detriment of the non-acquiring party—in that he loses the opportunity to acquire the property for himself. But there may be advantage to the one without corresponding detriment to the other.

(5) That leads, I think, to the further conclusions: (i) that, although, in many cases, the advantage/detriment will be found in the agreement of the non-acquiring party to keep out of the market, that is not a necessary feature; and (ii) that, although there will usually be advantage to the one and co-relative disadvantage to the other, the existence of both advantage and detriment is not essential—either will do. What is essential is that the circumstances make it inequitable for the acquiring party to retain the property for himself in a manner inconsistent with the arrangement or understanding on which the non-acquiring party has acted. Those circumstances may arise where the non-acquiring party was never 'in the market' for the whole of the property to be acquired; but (on the faith of an arrangement or understanding that he shall have a part of that property) provides support in relation to the acquisition of the whole which is of advantage to the acquiring party. They may arise where the assistance provided to the acquiring party (in pursuance of the arrangement or understanding) involves no detriment to the non-acquiring party; or where the non-acquiring party acts to his detriment (in pursuance of the arrangement or understanding) without the acquiring party obtaining any advantage therefrom....

In my view the judge misunderstood the principles upon which equity intervenes in cases of this nature when he held that 'Banner's hope and expectation, however much Luff may have encouraged it, that a formal agreement would be entered into following which Banner would discharge the obligations and take the benefits arising under the joint venture' could not 'give rise to the common arrangement or understanding which is a necessary foundation for the establishment of the equity'. He was wrong to reject the constructive trust claim on the grounds that Banner was seeking to invoke the assistance of equity in order to 'turn a common arrangement or understanding, which is implicitly qualified by the right of either side to withdraw, into an unqualified arrangement or undertaking which denied any such right'. The *Pallant v Morgan* equity does not seek to give effect to the parties' bargain—still less to make for them some bargain which they have not themselves made—as the cases to which I have referred make clear. The equity is invoked where the defendant has acquired property in circumstances where it would be inequitable to allow him to treat it as his own; and where, because it would be inequitable to allow him to treat the property as his own, it is necessary to impose on him the obligations of a trustee in relation to it. It is invoked because there is no bargain which is capable of being enforced. If there were an enforceable bargain there would have been no need for equity to intervene in the way that it has done in the cases to which I have referred.

I am satisfied, also, that the judge was wrong to reject the constructive trust claim on the grounds that Banner had failed to show that it had acted to its detriment in reliance on the arrangement agreed on 14 July, 1995. There was evidence, to which I have referred, that the existence of the arrangement led Banner to regard the site as 'out of play'; that is to say, the existence of the arrangement made it unnecessary, and inappropriate, for Banner to consider the site as a potential acquisition for its own commercial portfolio. But, as the judge himself recognised, one of the reasons why Luff wanted Banner kept 'on board'—and so did not disclose its own doubts as to the future of the joint venture—was that, 'if dropped, Banner might emerge as a rival for the site'. In other words, Luff saw it as an advantage that Banner's belief that the site was out of play should be maintained. Luff wanted to keep Banner out of the market. In those circumstances, it does not lie easily in Luff's mouth to say that Banner suffered no detriment. But whether or not Banner suffered detriment from the fact that it never regarded itself as free to consider the site as a potential acquisition of its own does not seem to me conclusive. Luff obtained the advantage which it sought. Further, Luff obtained the advantage of knowing that it had Banner's support, as a potential joint venturer whose commitment was not in doubt, in an acquisition on which it had not been willing to embark on its own.

As I have sought to show, the *Pallant v Morgan* equity is invoked where it would be inequitable to allow the defendant to treat the property acquired in furtherance of the arrangement or understanding as his own. It may be just as inequitable to allow the defendant to treat the property as his own when it has been acquired by the use of some advantage which he has obtained under the arrangement or understanding as it is to allow him to treat the property as his own when the plaintiff has suffered some detriment under the arrangement or understanding. That, as it seems to me, is this case.

In **Cobbe v Yeoman's Row Management Ltd** [2006] EWCA Civ 1139, [2006] 1 WLR 2964 the claimant had entered into an oral agreement to purchase flats belonging to the defendant, with a view to redeveloping them. Believing that the property would be sold to him, the claimant spent the next 18 months obtaining planning permission. Once planning permission had been obtained the defendant withdrew from the agreement. The value of the property increased as a result of the grant of planning permission. Following a finding that the defendant had led the claimant to believe that the agreement would be binding in honour and that it would not withdraw from it, the trial judge held both that the defendant was estopped from denying that the claimant had a beneficial interest in the property and alternatively that the property was held on constructive trust for the claimant. He awarded the claimant a share of one-half of the increased value of the property following the grant of planning permission. The Court of Appeal affirmed the decision of the trial judge both as regards the identification of proprietary estoppal and the award of a share in the increased value of the property to satisfy the claimant's equity.

QUESTIONS

1. Is the 'common-intention constructive trust' a misnomer?

2. When will a common-intention constructive trust be recognised? Is the resulting trust still of any relevance when determining whether a cohabiting party should get a beneficial interest in property? If so, when is it relevant?

Does it really matter whether the trust is characterised as constructive or resulting?

3. What event triggers the common-intention constructive trust? Can it be considered to be triggered by a wrong, by unjust enrichment, or something else? See (2007) 123 LQR 511, 518 (W. Swadling).

4. Is it appropriate to distinguish between common-intention constructive trusts in domestic and commercial contexts?

5. Is there any difference today between the common-intention constructive trust and proprietary estoppel? See (2000) LQR 11 (R.J.M. Smith); (1998) 18 LS 369, 378 (S. Wong); *Oxley v Hiscock* [2004] EWCA Civ 546, [2005] Fam 211. para. 66 (Chadwick LJ) [p. 332, above]. Compare *Re Basham* [1986] 1 WLR 1498 (constructive trust imposed where stepfather failed to leave property to stepdaughter as he had promised) and *Gillett v Holt* [2001] Ch 210, (2000) CLJ 453 (M. Dixon) (proprietary estoppel established where defendant led the plaintiff to believe that he would succeed to a farm business). See also (1999) 115 LQR 438 (S. Gardner); *Jennings v Rice* [2002] EWCA Civ 159, [2003] 1 P and CR 100; *Ottey v Grundy* [2003] EWCA Civ 11776; [2004] Conv 135 (M.P.Thompson); *Cobbe v Yeoman's Row Management Ltd* [2006] EWCA Civ 1139, [2006] 1 WLR 2964; [2005] Conv 247 (M. Dixon); *Kinane v Mackie-Conteh* [2005] EWCA Civ 45; [2005] Conv 501 (B. McFarlane); *Stack v Dowden* [2007] UKHL 17, [2007] AC 432, para. 37 (Lord Walker) [p. 339, above].

6. After the decision of the House of Lords in *Stack v Dowden* [2007] UKHL 17, [2007] AC 432, to what extent is the identification of beneficial interests dependent on the judge's view as to what is fair and just?

7. Is legislation required to determine how beneficial interests of a cohabiting couple who have separated should be identified? If so, should that legislation focus on the identification of the parties' intentions or, instead, be explicitly re-distributive?

PART IV

PURPOSE TRUSTS

9

NON-CHARITABLE
PURPOSE TRUSTS[1]

I THE REQUIREMENT OF ASCERTAINABLE
BENEFICIARIES

As has already been seen,[2] it is a fundamental feature of the law relating to express trusts that there are ascertainable beneficiaries who are able to enforce the trust. It follows that trusts for purposes rather than persons are generally not recognised in English law because of the absence of an ascertainable beneficiary. This is, however, subject to the significant exception that charitable purpose trusts have long been recognised

---

[1] H&M, pp. 371–372; Lewin, pp. 102–111; P&M, pp. 74–78; P&S pp. 378–380; Pettit pp. 56–57; Snell p. 471; T&H pp. 154–155; U&H, p. 145–170; Baxendale-Walker, *Purpose Trusts* (1999); Matthews in *Trends in Contemporary Trust Law* (ed. A.J. Oakley) (1996) chap. 1; Maudsley, *Modern Law of Perpetuities* (1979), pp. 166–178; Morris and Leach, *Rule Against Perpetuities* (2nd edn, 1962 and Supplement), chap. 12; Gray, *Rule against Perpetuities* (4th edn, 1942), Appendix H § 894–909; Scott, *Trusts* (4th edn) § 119, 123–124; (1892) 5 HLR 389 (J.B. Ames); (1953) 17 Conv (NS) 46 (L.A. Sheridan); (1953) 6 CLP 151 (O.R. Marshall); (1958) 4 *University of Western Australia Law Review* 235 (L.A. Sheridan); (1970) 34 Conv (NS) 77 (P.A. Lovell); (1971) 87 LQR 31 (J.W. Harris); (1973) 37 Conv (NS) 420 (L. McKay); [2007] Conv 274 (P. Luxton).

[2] See p. 108, above.

despite the absence of ascertainable beneficiaries.[3] Instead the Attorney-General has the function of enforcing such trusts.

The reasons given for disallowing non-charitable purpose trusts can all be challenged.[4] Supporters of such trusts point out that enforcement should be no problem; for in every case which has been litigated, the trustees have been willing to perform. Those entitled in default could complain in a case of misapplication. If a question of enforcement should arise, this is no more of a problem than the enforcement of charitable trusts; if it is a matter of social importance to enforce a particular purpose trust, an officer or Department of State could be instructed to undertake it.[5] Further, the requirement of ascertainable beneficiaries is a rule of *private* trusts in favour of *beneficiaries.* That rule should not be relevant to a purpose trust. If it is insisted that, charitable trusts always excepted, a trust *must* have a beneficiary who can enforce the trust, then purpose trusts could be treated as fiduciary powers.[6] It is not asking very much to suggest that a disposition which calls itself a trust but fails to provide persons capable of enforcing the obligation should be treated as a power. To say that trustees cannot be *compelled* to perform, is not to say that they *must not* perform.[7]

It must not, however, be assumed that it is always a simple matter to *classify* a trust as being a trust for persons or a trust for purposes. This problem will be seen in the later discussion[8] of unincorporated associations. A gift of property to an unincorporated association raises the question of the identification of the beneficial ownership. Such a gift may be construed as a gift to the present members beneficially, or to those persons who may be members at any particular time; and the claim of each member may be based upon the contractual rights controlling his membership, or upon rights arising under trusts on which the property is held. If the rights are based upon a trust, there are problems relating to the nature of the ownership among the members; whether each member can sever and claim his share[9] and problems of perpetuity. The real problem arises, however, where the gift cannot be construed as one to which the members are entitled; as where the gift was not intended to be for their personal benefit,[10] or where there is no list kept of the members; or, more especially, where the object of the association is the promotion of a purpose, as opposed to the benefit of the members. Then the problem is the same as that of an express trust for purposes. 'It is at this point that the cases on gifts to unincorporated associations become relevant to the question whether there can be a trust without a *cestui que trust*. It would certainly seem strange if a testator could give property to an unincorporated anti-vivisection

---

[3] See p. 410, below.

[4] See Morris and Leach, p. 307, note 1; (1977) 40 MLR 397 (N.P. Gravells).

[5] Note the use of the 'protector' in offshore purpose trusts. See D.W.M. Waters in *Trends in Contemporary Trust Law* (ed. A.J. Oakley), pp. 63–122.

[6] Ames, *Lectures on Legal History* (1913), p. 285; Morris and Leach, pp. 319–321.

[7] Scott, *Trusts* (4th edn), §§ 123, 124. *IRC v Broadway Cottages Trust* [1955] Ch 20 is Court of Appeal authority against this view.   [8] See pp. 378–399, below.

[9] See p. 380, below; *Neville Estates Ltd v Madden* [1962] Ch 832.

[10] *Leahy v A-G for New South Wales* [1959] AC 457 [p. 381, below]; *Re Smith* [1914] 1 Ch 937; *R v District Auditor, ex p West Yorkshire Metropolitan County Council* [1986] RVR 24 [p. 000, above].

society to be applied for its purposes, but could not give property to an individual trustee to be applied by him for the purpose of anti-vivisection.'[11] But a gift to an anti-vivisection society may be construed as a gift to its members.[12] Also a gift which is to benefit specified persons by the use of property in a particular manner may be construed as a trust for those persons and not a trust for purposes.[13] This question is discussed in Section V. The law relating to non-charitable purpose trusts will be examined first.

Re Astor's Settlement Trusts[14]
[1952] Ch 534 (Ch D, **Roxburgh J**)

An *inter vivos* settlement was made in 1945, expressly limited to the perpetuity period, under which substantially all the issued shares in The Observer Ltd were held by the trustees upon trust for various non-charitable purposes, which included, among others: '1. The maintenance...of good understanding sympathy and co-operation between nations; 2. The preservation of the independence and integrity of newspapers; 4. The control publication... financing or management of any newspapers periodicals books pamphlets or publications; 5. The protection of newspapers... from being absorbed... by combines or being tied by finance or otherwise to special... views... inconsistent with the highest integrity and independence.' It was conceded that the trusts were not charitable.

Held. The trusts were invalid, because (i) they were non-charitable purpose trusts which no one could enforce; (ii) the trusts included objects which were too uncertain.

Roxburgh J: The question upon which I am giving this reserved judgment is whether the non-charitable trusts of income during 'the specified period' declared by clause 5 and the third schedule of the settlement of 1945 are void. Mr. Jennings and Mr. Buckley have submitted that they are void on two grounds: (1) that they are not trusts for the benefit of individuals; (2) that they are void for uncertainty.

Lord Parker considered the first of these two questions in his speech in *Bowman v Secular Society Ltd* [1917] AC 406 and I will cite two important passages. The first is at 437: 'The question whether a trust be legal or illegal or be in accordance with or contrary to the policy of the law, only arises when it has been determined that a trust has been created, and is then only part of the larger question whether the trust is enforceable. For, as will presently appear, trusts may be unenforceable and therefore void, not only because they are illegal or contrary to the policy of the law, but for other reasons.' The second is at 441: 'A trust to be valid must be for the

11 Morris and Leach, p. 317.

12 *Re Recher's Will Trusts* [1972] Ch 526 [p. 386, below].

13 *Re Denley's Trust Deed* [1969] 1 Ch 373 (recreation ground for benefit of employees); [1968] *Annual Survey of Commonwealth Law* 437 (J.D. Davies); (1969) 32 MLR 96 (J.M. Evans); (1970) 34 Conv (NS) 77 (P.A. Lovell); *Re Lipinski's Will Trusts* [1976] Ch 235 [p. 372, below] (buildings for Jewish Association for benefit of members); (1977) 93 LQR 167; cf. *Re Grant's Will Trusts* [1980] 1 WLR 360 [p. 392, below].

14 (1952) 68 LQR 449 (R.E.M.); (1953) 6 CLP 151 (O.R. Marshall); (1953) 17 Conv (NS) 46 (L.A. Sheridan); (1955) 18 MLR 120 (L.H. Leigh).

benefit of individuals, which this is certainly not, or must be in that class of gifts for the benefit of the public which the courts in this country recognize as charitable in the legal as opposed to the popular sense of that term.'

Commenting on those passages Mr. Gray observed that *Bowman v Secular Society Ltd* arose out of a will and he asked me to hold that Lord Parker intended them to be confined to cases arising under a will. But they were, I think, intended to be quite general in character. Further, Mr. Gray pointed out that Lord Parker made no mention of the exceptions or apparent exceptions which undoubtedly exist, and from this he asked me to infer that no such general principle can be laid down. The question is whether those cases are to be regarded as exceptional and anomalous or whether they are destructive of the supposed principle. I must later analyse them. But I will first consider whether Lord Parker's propositions can be attacked from a base of principle.

The typical case of a trust is one in which the legal owner of property is constrained by a court of equity so to deal with it as to give effect to the equitable rights of another. These equitable rights have been hammered out in the process of litigation in which a claimant on equitable grounds has successfully asserted rights against a legal owner or other person in control of property. *Prima facie*, therefore, a trustee would not be expected to be subject to an equitable obligation unless there was somebody who could enforce a correlative equitable right, and the nature and extent of that obligation would be worked out in proceedings for enforcement. This is what I understand by Lord Parker's first proposition. At an early stage, however, the courts were confronted with attempts to create trusts for charitable purposes which there was no equitable owner to enforce. Lord Eldon explained in *A-G v Brown* (1818) 1 Swan 265 at 290 how this difficulty was dealt with:

> 'It is the duty of a court of equity, a main part, originally almost the whole, of its jurisdiction, to administer trusts; to protect not the visible owner, who alone can proceed at law, but the individual equitably, though not legally, entitled. From this principle has arisen the practice of administering the trust of a public charity: persons possessed of funds appropriate to such purposes are within the general rule; but no one being entitled by an immediate and peculiar interest to prefer a complaint, who is to compel the performance of their obligations, and to enforce their responsibility? It is the duty of the King, as *parens patriae*, to protect property devoted to charitable uses; and that duty is executed by the officer who represents the Crown for all forensic purposes. On this foundation rests the right of the Attorney-General in such cases to obtain by information the interposition of a court of equity. ...'

But if the purposes are not charitable, great difficulties arise both in theory and in practice. In theory, because having regard to the historical origins of equity it is difficult to visualise the growth of equitable obligations which nobody can enforce, and in practice, because it is not possible to contemplate with equanimity the creation of large funds devoted to non-charitable purposes which no court and no department of state can control, or in the case of maladministration reform. Therefore, Lord Parker's second proposition would *prima facie* appear to be well founded. Moreover, it gains no little support from the practical considerations that no officer has ever been constituted to take, in the case of non-charitable purposes, the position held by the Attorney-General in connexion with charitable purposes,[15] and no case has been found in the reports in which the court has ever directly enforced a non-charitable purpose against a trustee. Indeed where, as in the present case, the only beneficiaries are purposes and an at

---

[15] See p. 581, below for consideration of the Attorney-General's function in enforcing charitable trusts.

present unascertainable person, it is difficult to see who could initiate such proceedings. If the purposes are valid trusts, the settlors have retained no beneficial interest and could not initiate them. It was suggested that the trustees might proceed *ex parte* to enforce the trusts against themselves. I doubt that, but at any rate nobody could enforce the trusts against them. This point, in my judgment, is of importance, because in most of the cases which are put forward to disprove Lord Parker's propositions the court had indirect means of enforcing the execution of the non-charitable purpose.

These cases I must now consider. First of all, there is a group relating to horses, dogs, graves and monuments,[16] among which I was referred to *Pettingall v Pettingall* (1842) 11 LJ Ch 176; *Mitford v Reynolds* (1848) 16 Sim 105; *Re Dean* (1889) 41 Ch D 552; *Pirbright v Salwey* [1896] WN 86, and *Re Hooper* [1932] 1 Ch 38.

[His Lordship examined these cases, and also *Re Thompson* [1934] Ch 342, and *Re Price* [1943] Ch 422, and continued:] Let me then sum up the position so far. On the one side there are Lord Parker's two propositions with which I began. These were not new, but merely re-echoed what Sir William Grant had said as Master of the Rolls in *Morice v Bishop of Durham* (1804) 9 Ves 399 at 405 as long ago as 1804: 'there must be somebody, in whose favour the court can decree performance'. The position was recently restated by Harman J in *Re Wood* [1949] Ch 498 at 501: 'a gift on trust must have a *cestui que trust*', and this seems to be in accord with principle. On the other side is a group of cases relating to horses and dogs, graves and monuments—matters arising under wills and intimately connected with the deceased—in which the courts have found means of escape from these general propositions and also *Re Thompson* [1934] Ch 342 and *Re Price* [1943] Ch 422 which I have endeavoured to explain. *Re Price* belongs to another field. The rest may, I think, properly be regarded as anomalous and exceptional and in no way destructive of the proposition which traces descent from or through Sir William Grant through Lord Parker to Harman J. Perhaps the late Sir Arthur Underhill was right in suggesting that they may be concessions to human weakness or sentiment (see *Law of Trusts*, 8th edn, p. 79). They cannot, in my judgment, of themselves (and no other justification has been suggested to me) justify the conclusion that a Court of Equity will recognise as an equitable obligation affecting the income of large funds in the hands of trustees a direction to apply it in furtherance of enumerated non-charitable purposes in a manner which no court or department can control or enforce. I hold that the trusts here in question are void on the first of the grounds submitted by Mr. Jennings and Mr. Buckley.

The second ground upon which the relevant trusts are challenged is uncertainty. If (contrary to my view) an enumeration of purposes outside the realm of charities can take the place of an enumeration of beneficiaries, the purposes must, in my judgment, be stated in phrases which embody definite concepts and the means by which the trustees are to try to attain them must also be prescribed with a sufficient degree of certainty. The test to be applied is stated by Lord Eldon in *Morice v Bishop of Durham* (1805) 10 Ves 522 at 539 as follows:

'As it is a maxim, that the execution of a trust shall be under the control of the court, it must be of such a nature, that it can be under that control; so that the administration of it can be reviewed by the court; or, if the trustee dies, the court itself can execute the trust: a trust therefore, which, in case of maladministration could be reformed; and a due administration directed; and then, unless the subject and the objects can be ascertained, upon principles, familiar in other cases, it must be decided, that the court can neither reform maladministration, nor direct a due administration.'

---

16 See p. 366, below.

See also *Re Macduff* [1896] 2 Ch 451 at 463.

Mr. Gray argued that this test was not properly applicable to trusts declared by deed, but I can see no distinction between a will and a deed in this respect.

Applying this test, I find many uncertain phrases in the enumeration of purposes, for example, 'different sections of people in any nation or community' in paragraph 1 of the third schedule, 'constructive policies' in paragraph 2, 'integrity of the press' in paragraph 3, 'combines' in paragraph 5, 'the restoration... of the independence of... writers in newspapers' in paragraph 6, and 'benevolent schemes' in paragraph 7. Mr. Gray suggested that in view of the unlimited discretion bestowed upon the trustees (subject only to directions from the settlors) the trustees would be justified in excluding from their purview purposes indicated by the settlors but insufficiently defined by them. But I cannot accept this argument. The purposes must be so defined that if the trustees surrendered their discretion, the court could carry out the purposes declared, not a selection of them arrived at by eliminating those which are too uncertain to be carried out. If, for example, I were to eliminate all the purposes except those declared in paragraph 4, but to decree that those declared in paragraph 4 ought to be performed, should I be executing the trusts of this settlement?

But how in any case could I decree in what manner the trusts applicable to income were to be performed? The settlement gives no guidance at all. Mr. Hunt suggested that the trustees might apply to the court *ex parte* for a scheme. It is not, I think, a mere coincidence that no case has been found outside the realm of charity in which the court has yet devised a scheme of ways and means for attaining enumerated trust purposes. If it were to assume this (as I think) novel jurisdiction over public but not charitable trusts it would, I believe, necessarily require the assistance of a custodian of the public interest analogous to the Attorney-General in charity cases, who would not only help to formulate schemes but could be charged with the duty of enforcing them and preventing maladministration. There is no such person. Accordingly, in my judgment, the trusts for the application of income during 'the specified period' are also void for uncertainty.

But while I have reached my decision on two separate grounds, both, I think, have their origin in a single principle, namely, that a court of equity does not recognise as valid a trust which it cannot both enforce and control. This seems to me to be good equity and good sense.

Re Endacott
[1960] Ch 232 (CA, **Lord Evershed MR**, **Sellers** and **Harman LJJ**)

The testator gave his residuary estate 'to North Tawton Devon Parish Council for the purpose of providing some useful memorial to myself...' The value of the residuary estate was approximately £20,000. The question was whether the gift was valid.

Held. The gift, not being beneficial to the Council, nor to the inhabitants, and not being charitable, was void.

LORD EVERSHED MR [having held that the language of the will showed an intention to impose a trust; and that the trust was not charitable]:

I now turn to Mr. Arnold's alternative argument based on the view that there is here a trust and a trust of a public character, but not a charitable trust. What he says is, that the trust is in line with the trusts which were rendered effective in those cases which I have called 'anomalous', and many of which are referred to in Roxburgh J's decision, beginning with *Pettingall v Pettingall* (1842) 11 LJ Ch 176. I include in that list cases such as the three to which we have had our attention particularly drawn today. The argument is that assuming the non-charitable but public nature of this trust, still it is of a character which the court can efficiently, and will, enforce. It must be said that these cases are of a somewhat anomalous kind. They are classified in the recent book written by Mr. J.H.C. Morris and Professor Barton Leach, *The Rule Against Perpetuities* (1956) (p. 298). 'We proceed', say the authors, 'to examine these "anomalous" exceptions. It will be found that they fall into the following groups: (1) trusts for the erection or maintenance of monuments or graves; (2) trusts for the saying of masses, in jurisdictions where such trusts are not regarded as charitable; (3) trusts for the maintenance of particular animals; (4) trusts for the benefit of unincorporated associations (though this group is more doubtful); (5) miscellaneous cases.' I am prepared to accept, for the purposes of the argument, that it does not matter that the trusts here are attached to residue and not to a legacy; that is to say, it does not matter that the persons who would come to the court and either complain if the trusts were not being carried out, or claim the money on the footing that they had not been carried out, are next-of-kin rather than residuary legatees. Still, in my judgment, the scope of these cases... ought not to be extended. So to do would be to validate almost limitless heads of non-charitable trusts, even though they were not (strictly speaking) public trusts, so long only as the question of perpetuities did not arise; and, in my judgment, that result would be out of harmony with the principles of our law. No principle perhaps has greater sanction of authority behind it than the general proposition that a trust by English law, not being a charitable trust, in order to be effective, must have ascertained or ascertainable beneficiaries. These cases constitute an exception to that general rule. The general rule, having such authority as that of Lord Eldon, Lord Parker and my predecessor, Lord Greene MR, behind it, was most recently referred to in the Privy Council in *Leahy v A-G for New South Wales* [1959] AC 457. I add also that, in my judgment, the proposition stated in Mr. Morris and Professor Barton Leach's book (p. 308) that if these trusts should fail as trusts they may survive as powers, is not one which I think can be treated as accepted in English law.[17]

I therefore, so far as this case is concerned, conclude (having already stated my view of the meaning of the words) that, though this trust is specific, in the sense that it indicates a purpose capable of expression, yet it is of far too wide and uncertain a nature to qualify within the class of cases cited. It would go far beyond any fair analogy to any of those decisions.

Harman LJ: I cannot think that charity has anything to do with this bequest. As for establishing it without the crutch of charity, I applaud the orthodox sentiments expressed by Roxburgh J in the *Astor* case [1952] Ch 534, and I think, as I think he did, that though one knows there have been decisions at times which are not really to be satisfactorily classified, but are perhaps merely occasions when Homer has nodded, at any rate these cases stand by themselves and ought not to be increased in number, nor indeed followed, except where the one is exactly like another. Whether it would be better that some authority now should say those cases were wrong, this perhaps is not the moment to consider. At any rate, I cannot think a case of this kind, the case of providing outside a church an unspecified and unidentified memorial, is the kind of instance which should be allowed to add to those troublesome, anomalous and aberrant cases.

In my judgment, Danckwerts J came to the right conclusion, and this appeal ought to be dismissed.

---

[17] See p. 43, above for discussion of the distinction between trusts and powers.

In **Re Shaw** [1957] 1 WLR 729 the question arose as to the validity of a residuary gift under the will of George Bernard Shaw, which provided that the residue of his estate should be applied towards the institution of a 40-letter alphabet in the place of the present 26-letter alphabet. HARMAN J decided that the trusts were not charitable; nor could they be enforced as purpose trusts or as powers.[18]

By way of background, HARMAN J said at 731:

All his long life Bernard Shaw was an indefatigable reformer. He was already well known when the present century dawned, as novelist, critic, pamphleteer, playwright, and during the ensuing half-century he continued to act as a kind of itching powder to the British public, to the English-speaking peoples, and, indeed to an even wider audience, castigating their follies, their foibles and their fallacies, and bombarding them with a combination of paradox and wit that earned him in the course of years the status of an oracle: the Shavian oracle; and the rare distinction of adding a word to the language. Many of his projects he lived to see gain acceptance and carried into effect and become normal. It was natural that he should be interested in English orthography and pronunciation. These are obvious targets for the reformer. It is as difficult for the native to defend the one as it is for the foreigner to compass the other. The evidence shows that Shaw had for many years been interested in the subject. Perhaps his best known excursion in this field is *Pygmalion,* in which the protagonist is a professor of phonetics: this was produced as a play in 1914 and has held the stage ever since and invaded the world of the film. It is, indeed, a curious reflection that this same work, tagged with versicles which I suppose Shaw would have detested, and tricked out with music which he would have eschewed (see the preface to the 'Admirable Bashville'), is now charming huge audiences on the other side of the Atlantic and has given birth to the present proceedings. I am told that the receipts from this source have enabled the executor to get on terms with the existing death duties payable on the estate, thus bringing the interpretation of the will into the realm of practical politics.

The testator, whatever his other qualifications, was the master of a pellucid style, and the reader embarks on his will confident of finding no difficulty in understanding the objects which the testator had in mind. This document, moreover, was evidently originally the work of a skilled equity draftsman. As such I doubt not it was easily to be understood if not of the vulgar at any rate by the initiate. Unfortunately the will bears ample internal evidence of being in part the testator's own work. The two styles, as ever, make an unfortunate mixture. It is always a marriage of incompatibles: the delicate testamentary machinery devised by the conveyancer can but suffer when subjected to the *cacoethes scribendi*[19] of the author, even though the latter's language, if it stood alone, might be a literary masterpiece.

[And on purpose trusts:] The principle has been recently restated by Roxburgh J in *Re Astor's Settlement Trusts* [1952] Ch 534, where the authorities are elaborately reviewed. An object cannot complain to the court, which therefore cannot control the trust, and, therefore, will not allow it to continue. I must confess that I feel some reluctance to come to this conclusion. I agree at once that, if the persons to take in remainder are unascertainable, the court is deprived of any means of controlling such a trust, but if, as here, the persons taking the ultimate residue are ascertained, I do not feel the force of this objection. They are entitled to the estate except in so far as it has been devoted to the indicated purposes, and in so far as it is not devoted to

---

[18] Mrs. Shaw's will was held to be valid [p. 446, below].
[19] Literally 'bad habit of writing'.

those purposes, the money being spent is the money of the residuary legatees of the ultimate remaindermen, and they can come to the court and sue the executor for a *devastavit*, or the trustee for a breach of trust, and thus, though not themselves interested in the purposes, enable the court indirectly to control them. This line of reasoning is not, I think, open to me. See, for instance, the statement by Lord Greene MR in *Re Diplock* [1941] Ch 253 at 259.

> 'Those principles,' he says, dealing with uncertainty, 'I apprehend are really nothing more than the application of a fundamental principle of the law relating to trusts. In order that a trust may be properly constituted, there must be a beneficiary. The beneficiary must be ascertained or must be ascertainable. In the case of what I may call impersonal trusts, such as a gift to charitable purposes, or to benevolent purposes, there is no class of beneficiary which can be defined in the same sense as a class of beneficiaries such as a class of relatives. In the latter case, although no particular person in the class may be able to say that at any given moment he is entitled to anything out of the trust, the class as a whole can enforce the trust. Now in the case of charitable trusts in which no defined class is specified, nevertheless owing to the particular principles which have come to be applied to charitable gifts, the courts have not treated the trust as failing for that reason. There is a very good ground for that, namely that the Crown, as *parens patriae* taking all charities under its protection, is in a position to enforce the trust; and therefore, although there may be no specified charitable beneficiary who can come to the court and insist on having the trust performed, nevertheless the Attorney-General can appear and is entitled to insist on the trust being carried out, if necessary, by a scheme *cy-près*.[20] But that exception to the general rule, that there must be beneficiaries ascertained or ascertainable—if I may call it an exception—does not extend beyond what falls within the legal class of charity. It does not extend to other public spirited purposes.'

The same view is taken in the judgment of Jenkins LJ in *IRC v Broadway Cottages Trusts* [1955] Ch 20.

I should have wished to regard this bequest as a gift to the ultimate residuary legatees subject to a condition by which they cannot complain of income during the first 21 years after the testator's death being devoted to the alphabet project. This apparently might be the way in which the matter would be viewed in the United States, for I find in Morris and Leach's work on the *Rule against Perpetuities* (1956), at p. 308, the following passage quoted from the American Law Institute's Restatement of Trusts.[21] 'Where the owner of property transfers it upon an intended trust for a specific non-charitable purpose, and there is no definite or definitely ascertainable beneficiary designated, no trust is created; but the transferee has power to apply the property to the designated purpose, unless he is authorized so to apply the property beyond the period of the rule against perpetuities, or the purpose is capricious.' As the authors point out, this is to treat a trust of this sort as a power, for clearly there is no one who can directly enforce the trust, and if the trustees choose to pay the whole moneys to the residuary legatees, no one can complain. All that can be done is to control the trustees indirectly in the exercise of their power. In my judgment, I am not at liberty to validate this trust, by treating it as a power. (See *per* Jenkins LJ in *Sunnylands* case above [1955] Ch 20 at 36. 'We do not think that a valid power is to be spelt out of an invalid trust'. This also was the view of the learned author of Gray on Perpetuities (4th edn), the leading work on the subject . . . , and I feel bound to accept it).

The result is that the alphabet trusts are, in my judgment, invalid, and must fail. It seems that their begotter suspected as much, hence his jibe about failure by judicial decision. I answer that

---

[20] See p. 544, below. [21] 1st edn. For 2nd edn § 124, see p. 401, below.

it is not the fault of the law, but of the testator, who failed almost for the first time in his life to grasp the legal problem or to make up his mind what he wanted.[22]

II ANOMALOUS CASES OF TRUSTS FOR PURPOSES BEING VALID

There are certain anomalous cases where purpose trusts have been recognised as valid. Most of these have been concerned with the care of particular animals,[23] and a few for the erection or maintenance of tombs or monuments.[24] Even though they are anomalous trusts, because they fail to satisfy the beneficiary principle, they must comply with other rules relating to trusts, including the perpetuity rules.[25] Although there are no beneficiaries to enforce such trusts, the significance of their recognition as being valid is that the trustees are able to apply the fund for the valid purpose if they wish.[26]

Re Dean
(1889) 41 Ch D 552 (Ch D, **North J**)

A testator charged his freehold estates with the payment of £750 per annum to his trustees for the period of 50 years if any of his horses and hounds should live so long, and declared that the trustees should apply the money in the maintenance of his horses and hounds; but without imposing upon them any obligation to render any account.

Held. This was a valid non-charitable trust, although there was no one who could enforce it.

North J: The first question is as to the validity of the provision made by the testator in favour of his horses and dogs. It is said that it is not valid; because (for this is the principal ground upon which it is put) neither a horse nor a dog could enforce the trust; and there is no person who could enforce it. It is obviously not a charity, because it is intended for the benefit of the particular animals mentioned and not for the benefit of animals generally, and it is quite distinguishable from the gift made in a subsequent part of the will to the *Royal Society for the Prevention of Cruelty to Animals,* which may well be a charity.[27] In my opinion this provision for the particular horses and hounds referred to in the will is not, in any sense, a charity, ...

Then it is said, that there is no *cestui que trust* who can enforce the trust, and that the Court will not recognise a trust unless it is capable of being enforced by some one. I do not assent to

---

[22] 'It is understood that the case was compromised on appeal and that the alphabet trusts are being carried out; see [1958] 1 All ER 245.' Morris and Leach, p. 310. See (1957) 73 LQR 305 (R.E.M.). See Holroyd, *The Shaw Companion* (1992), vol. 4, pp. 3–26 and Appx. B for a detailed discussion of the compromise and the full text of the will.

[23] *Pettingall v Pettingall* (1842) 11 LJ Ch 176; *Re Dean* (1889) 41 Ch D 552; *Re Haines* (1952) The Times, 7 November; (1983) 80 LSG 2451 (P. Matthews). See also *Re Thompson* [1934] Ch 342 [p. 369, below].

[24] *Trimmer v Danby* (1856) 25 LJ Ch 424 [p. 368, below]; *Mussett v Bingle* [1876] WN 170 [p. 368, below]; *Pirbright v Salwey* [1896] WN 86; *Re Hooper* [1932] 1 Ch 38 [p. 367, below].   [25] See p. 110, above.

[26] *Trimmer v Danby* (1856) 25 LJ Ch 424.   [27] The RSPCA is a charity. See p. 600, below.

that view. There is not the least doubt that a man may if he pleases, give a legacy to trustees, upon trust to apply it in erecting a monument to himself, either in a church or in a churchyard, or even in unconsecrated ground, and I am not aware that such a trust is in any way invalid, although it is difficult to say who would be the *cestui que trust* of the monument. In the same way I know of nothing to prevent a gift of a sum of money to trustees, upon trust to apply it for the repair of such a monument. In my opinion such a trust would be good, although the testator must be careful to limit the time for which it is to last, because, as it is not a charitable trust, unless it is to come to an end within the limits fixed by the rule against perpetuities, it would be illegal. But a trust to lay out a certain sum in building a monument, and the gift of another sum in trust to apply the same to keeping that monument in repair, say, for ten years, is in my opinion, a perfectly good trust, although I do not see who could ask the Court to enforce it. If persons beneficially interested in the estate could do so, then the present Plaintiff can do so; but, if such persons could not enforce the trust, still it cannot be said that the trust must fail because there is no one who can actively enforce it.

Is there then anything illegal or obnoxious to the law in the nature of the provision, that is, in the fact that it is not for human beings, but for horses and dogs? It is clearly settled by authority that a charity may be established for the benefit of horses and dogs, and, therefore, the making of a provision for horses and dogs, which is not a charity, cannot of itself be obnoxious to the law, provided, of course, that it is not to last for too long a period. Then there is what I consider an express authority upon this point in *Mitford v Reynolds* (1848) 16 Sim 105.

Re Hooper
[1932] 1 Ch 38 (Ch D, **Maugham J**)

A testator gave a sum of money to trustees for the care and upkeep of certain family graves and monuments, and a tablet and a window in a church for 'so far as [the trustees] legally can do so'. The question was whether the gift was valid.

Held. The trust for the upkeep of the graves and monuments, not being charitable, was valid for 21 years.

Maugham J: This point is one to my mind of doubt, and I should have felt some difficulty in deciding it if it were not for *Pirbright v Salwey* [1896] WN 86, a decision of Stirling J, which unfortunately is reported, as far as I know, only in the Weekly Notes. The report is as follows: 'A testator, after expressing his wish to be buried in the inclosure in which his child lay in the churchyard of E., bequeathed to the rector and church-wardens for the time being of the parish church 800l. Consols, to be invested in their joint names, the interest and dividends to be derived therefrom to be applied, so long as the law for the time being permitted, in keeping up the inclosure and decorating the same with flowers: *Held,* that the gift was valid for at least a period of 21 years from the testator's death, and *semble* that it was not charitable.'

That was a decision arrived at by Stirling J, after argument by very eminent counsel. The case does not appear to have attracted much attention in text-books, but it does not appear to have been commented upon adversely, and I shall follow it.

The trustees here have the sum of 1,000l. which they have to hold upon trust to 'invest the same and to the intent that so far as they legally can do so and in any manner that they may in their discretion arrange they will out of the annual income thereof' do substantially four things: first, provide for the care and upkeep of the grave and monument in the Torquay cemetery; secondly, for the care and upkeep of a vault and monument there in which lie the remains of the testator's wife and daughter; thirdly, for the care and upkeep of a grave and monument in

Shotley churchyard near Ipswich, where the testator's son lies buried; and, fourthly, for the care and upkeep of the tablet in Saint Matthias' Church at Ilsham to the memories of the testator's wife and children and the window in the same church to the memory of his late father. All those four things have to be done expressly according to an arrangement made in the discretion of the trustees and so far as they legally can do so. I do not think that is distinguishable from the phrase 'so long as the law for the time being permits', and the conclusion at which I arrive, following the decision I have mentioned, is that this trust is valid for a period of 21 years from the testator's death so far as regards the three matters which involve the upkeep of graves or vaults or monuments in the churchyard or in the cemetery. As regards the tablet in St. Matthias' Church and the window in the same church there is no question but that that is a good charitable gift, and, therefore, the rule against perpetuities does not apply.

Something has been said with regard to apportionment. To my mind there is no room for a legal apportionment, because it is left to the discretion of the trustees to arrange how much they will out of this income apply during the 21 years to the four objects in question. At the end of the 21 years any part which is not applied for the upkeep of the tablet and the window in St. Matthias' Church will, of course, be undisposed-of and will fall, unless some other event happens, into residue.

In **Trimmer v Danby** (1856) 25 LJ Ch 424, the testator gave £1,000 to his executors, 'and I do direct them to lay out and expend the same to erect a monument to my memory in St. Paul's Cathedral, among those of my brothers in art'. The bequest was upheld by KINDERSLEY V-C, who said at 427:

I do not suppose that there would be anyone who could compel the executors to carry out this bequest and raise the monument; but if the residuary legatees or the trustees insist upon the trust being executed, my opinion is that this Court is bound to see it carried out. I think, therefore, that as the trustees insist upon the sum of 1,000l. being laid out according to the directions in the will, that sum must be set apart for the purpose.

In **Mussett v Bingle** [1876] WN 170, the testator gave £300 to be applied in the erection of a monument to his wife's first husband, and £200 the interest of which was to be applied in keeping up the monument. It was admitted that the latter direction was void for perpetuity. The former was upheld; HALL V-C saying that the direction was one which the executors 'were ready to perform, and it must be performed accordingly'.

PARISH COUNCILS AND BURIAL AUTHORITIES (MISCELLANEOUS PROVISIONS) ACT 1970

1. Maintenance of private graves

(1) A burial authority or a local authority may agree with any person in consideration of the payment of a sum by him, to maintain—

...

(b) a monument or other memorial to any person situated in any place within the area of the authority to which the authority have a right of access;

so, however, that no agreement...made under this subsection by any authority with respect to a particular monument or other memorial may impose on the authority an obligation with respect to maintenance for a period exceeding 99 years from the date of that agreement.

In **Re Thompson** [1934] Ch 342, the testator, an alumnus of Trinity Hall, Cambridge, gave a legacy of £1,000 to a friend Mr. Lloyd, to be applied by him towards the promotion and furthering of fox-hunting. Trinity Hall was the residuary legatee. Both parties desired to carry out the testator's wishes, so far as they could legally do so, but Trinity Hall felt obligated, as a charity, to make objections to the enforcement of the trust. CLAUSON J upheld the gift; 'following the example of Knight Bruce V-C in *Pettingall v Pettingall* (1842) 11 LJ Ch 176, to order that, upon the defendant Mr. Lloyd giving an undertaking (which I understand he is willing to give) to apply the legacy when received by him towards the object expressed in the testator's will, the plaintiffs do pay to the defendant Mr. Lloyd the legacy of 1,000*l.*; and that, in case the legacy should be applied by him otherwise than towards the promotion and furthering of fox-hunting, the residuary legatees are to be at liberty to apply.'

Law Commission Report *The Rules Against Perpetuities and Excessive Accumulations*, 1998 (Law Com No. 251), p. 7

This is the rule against inalienability, often called the rule against perpetual trusts. This rule does not restrict the future vesting of estates or interests, but the duration of trusts established for non-charitable purposes. Non-charitable purpose trusts are usually void because there is no beneficiary who can enforce them, but they are also objectionable because they may be perpetual.[28] Even in those exceptional circumstances where such purpose trusts are recognised notwithstanding the absence of any person who can enforce them (such as trusts for the upkeep of tombs), they are restricted to the perpetuity period.[29] However, we note that the courts view non-charitable purpose trusts with some suspicion, given the very real difficulties that exist in enforcing and policing them.[30] The rule against inalienability is, in reality, just one of the devices that is employed to keep the development of such trusts in check. In the light of this, any consideration of the rule against inalienability belongs more properly in a review of the law governing non-charitable purpose trusts and unincorporated associations.

Consequently the Law Commission has not made any recommendation about reform of the rule against inalienability.

There seems to be no reason why purpose trusts should not be drafted so as to continue for the full period of lives in being plus 21 years. No English case, however, has upheld a purpose trust for more than 21 years.[31] The trust in *Re Astor's Settlement Trusts*[32] was designed to continue for lives in being plus 21 years; and, though the trust failed, no objection was taken on this point; indeed, counsel pointed out that

---

[28] See *Thomson v Shakespear* (1860) 1 De GF & J 399; *Carne v Long* (1860) 2 De GF & J 75, 80.

[29] See, eg *Re Denley's Trust Deed* [1969] 1 Ch 373 [p. 375, below], where the perpetuity period was for specified lives in being plus 21 years. Cf *Re Hooper* [1932] 1 Ch 38 [p. 367, above] (trust for the upkeep of a monument so long as the trustees might legally do so, held to be valid for 21 years only).

[30] Cf. *Re Astor's Settlement Trusts* [1952] Ch 534 at 547 where this policy consideration is clearly stated.

[31] See *Re Khoo Cheng Teow* [1932] Straits Settlement Reports 226 [p. 370, below].

[32] [1952] Ch 534 [p. 359, above].

'such a trust could continue for 100 years'. If the trust provides for its continuation 'so long as the law allows', or for some similar period, it will be valid for 21 years.[33] In *Re Dean*,[34] a trust for the maintenance of the testator's horses and hounds 'for the period of 50 years if any should so long live' was upheld, presumably on the ground that it must end within 21 years. Certainly, the animals could not be used as lives in being: as MEREDITH J said in *Re Kelly*:[35]'There can be no doubt that "lives" means lives of human beings, not animals or trees in California.'

In **Re Khoo Cheng Teow** [1932] Straits Settlement Reports 226, a Chinese testator devised No. 56 Church Street, Singapore to the British Malaya Trustee and Executor Co Ltd as trustees, with a direction to let the premises and to apply the net rents 'in the performance of the religious ceremonies according to the custom of the Chinese called *Sin Chew* to perpetuate my memory'. The period specified was 'during the lives of Her Majesty Queen Victoria and her descendants now living and during the lives and life of the survivors and survivor of them and during the period of twenty-one years after the death of such survivor.' TERRELL J, in declaring the trust valid, held that the rule against perpetuities applied to the Straits Settlements, and that the gift for Sin Chew ceremonies was not charitable, and said at 228: 'it is clear that the devise does not offend the rule against perpetuities'.

PERPETUITIES AND ACCUMULATIONS ACT 1964

15. Short title, interpretation and extent

(4) Nothing in this Act shall affect the operation of the rule of law rendering void for remoteness certain dispositions under which property is limited to be applied for purposes other than the benefit of any person or class of persons in cases where the property may be so applied after the end of the perpetuity period.

Hanbury & Maudsley: *Modern Equity* (11th edn, 1981), p. 439

The provision is susceptible of two constructions. First, the orthodox view, that it means, in short, that the Act is to make no change to the law relating to the duration of purpose trusts. On the other hand, under the terms of the section, what is unaffected is the "operation of the rule of law rendering void...certain dispositions...where the property may be so applied after the end of the perpetuity period". In short, a purpose trust still remains void if it may last beyond the perpetuity period. But, what is the perpetuity period? Section 1 says that the perpetuity period "applicable to [a] disposition...shall be of a duration equal to such number of years not exceeding eighty as is specified...in the instrument".

So construed, the subsection means that purpose trusts existing beyond the perpetuity period are void; but the perpetuity period may be either the usual period measured by life in being plus 21 years; or a period of years not exceeding 80 as may be specified in the instrument; and

---

[33] *Re Hooper* [1932] 1 Ch 38 [p. 367, above].   [34] (1889) 41 Ch D 552 [p. 366, above].
[35] [1932] IR 255 at 260–261; Maudsley and Burn, *Land Law: Cases and Materials* (8th edn, 2004), p. 380.

it would seem therefore that a testator could specify such a period. Eighty years is of course longer than many would think to be the ideal period. But it is an improvement on royal lives; and it is submitted that the second interpretation is open to the courts, and that it should be applied.[36]

P. Matthews: *Trends in Contemporary Trust Law* (ed. A.J. Oakley, 1996), p. 12

We must remember first of all that the Act was primarily designed to reform the rules against remoteness of vesting.[37] This subsection, by contrast, deals with a certain other 'rule of law', which it then goes on to describe. If the only rule with which the subsection is intended to deal is the precise one mentioned, the difficulty is that there is no such rule. But if (as we must suppose) the rule concerned is intended to be the rule against inalienability which we are discussing, then it is not very well described by the draftsman. In particular, the expression 'void for remoteness' is not apt. But section 15(4) only bars the operation of the Act in cases where the rule apples to *pure purpose* trusts. So it seems that the settlor or testator *can* select an 80-year period even for the purposes of the rule against inalienability if the trust is for *beneficiaries,* but not where the trust is for pure purposes.[38]

NEW ZEALAND PERPETUITIES ACT 1964[39]

20. Rule against inalienability

(1) Except as provided in subsection (2) of this section, nothing in this Act shall affect the operation of the rule of law rendering non-charitable purpose trusts void for remoteness in cases where the trust property may be applied for the purposes of the trusts after the end of the perpetuity period.

(2) If any such trust is not otherwise void, the provision of section 8 of this Act [necessity to wait and see] shall apply to it, and the property subject to the trust may be applied for the purposes of the trust during the perpetuity period, but not thereafter.

III TRUSTS FOR PERSONS OR PURPOSES

A gift which is to benefit specified persons by the use of property in a particular manner may be construed as a trust for persons and not for purposes.

---

[36] Maudsley, *Modern Law of Perpetuities* (1979), pp. 177–178; (1965) 29 Conv (NS) 165 (J.A. Andrews).
[37] See p. 110, above.
[38] See also H&M (17th edn, 2005), p. 386; U&H, p. 158; Law Com No. 258, (1999) para. 8.35; Morris and Leach, p. 21.
[39] See also Victoria Perpetuities and Accumulations Act 1968, s.18.

Re Lipinski's Will Trusts[40]
[1976] Ch 235 (Ch D, **Oliver J**)

In 1967 the testator bequeathed his residuary estate to trustees on trust as to one-half for the Hull Judeans (Maccabi) Association 'in memory of my late wife to be used solely in the work of constructing the new buildings for the association and/or improvements to the said buildings'. The objects of the Association included '(a) To promote the interest, and the active participation of Anglo-Jewish youth, of both sexes, in amateur sports, in all forms of cultural, and in non-political, communal activities. (b) To inculcate within its ranks a team spirit, a conception of fair play, good citizenship and self-discipline ... (d) To promote and foster the interest to cultivate a knowledge of Jewish history, of the Hebrew language and national traditions'. On a summons to determine the effect of the trust.

Held. It was valid. It was a trust for the members of the Association, who were ascertained or ascertainable.

Oliver J: I approach question 1 of the summons, therefore, on the footing that this is a gift to an unincorporated non-charitable association. Such a gift, if it is an absolute and beneficial one, is of course perfectly good: see, for instance, the gift to the Corps of Commissionaires in *Re Clarke* [1901] 2 Ch 110. What I have to consider, however, is the effect of the specification by the testator of the purposes for which the legacy was to be applied.

The principles applicable to this type of case were stated by Cross J in *Neville Estates Ltd v Madden* [1962] Ch 832 at 849 [p. 380, below], and they are conveniently summarised in Tudor, *Charities*, 6th edn (1967), p. 150, where it is said:

'In *Neville Estates Ltd v Madden* Cross J expressed the opinion (which is respectfully accepted as correct) that every such gift might, according to the actual words used, be construed in one of three quite different ways:

(a) As a gift to the members of the association at the date of the gift as joint tenants so that any member could sever his share and claim it whether or not he continued to be a member.

(b) As a gift to the members of the association at the date of the gift not as joint tenants, but subject to their contractual rights and liabilities towards one another as members of the association. In such a case a member cannot sever his share. It will accrue to the other members on his death or resignation, even though such members include persons who become members after the gift took effect. If this is the effect of the gift, it will not be open to objection on the score of perpetuity or uncertainty unless there is something in its terms or circumstances or in the rules of the association which precludes the members at any given time from dividing the subject of the gift between them on the footing that they are solely entitled to it in equity.

(c) The terms or circumstances of the gift or the rules of the association may show that the property in question—i.e., the subject of the gift—is not to be at the disposal of the members

---

[40] [1976] *Annual Survey of Commonwealth Law* 419 (J. Hackney); (1977) 93 LQR 167; (1977) 41 Conv (NS) 139 (F.R. Crane), 179 (K. Widdows); (1977) 40 MLR 231 (N.P. Gravells); (1977) 9 *Victoria University of Wellington Law Review* R 1 (L. McKay); cf. *R v District Auditor, ex p West Yorkshire Metropolitan County Council* [1986] RVR 24 [p. 102, above] (no ascertained or ascertainable beneficiaries); (1986) CLJ 391 (C. Harpum).

for the time being but is to be held in trust for or applied for the purposes of the association as a quasi-corporate entity. In this case the gift will fail unless the association is a charitable body.'

That summary may require, I think, a certain amount of qualification in the light of subsequent authority, but for present purposes I can adopt it as a working guide. Mr. Blackburne, for the next-of-kin, argues that the gift in the present case clearly does not fall within the first category, and that the addition of the specific direction as to its employment by the association prevents it from falling into the second category. This is, therefore, he says, a purpose trust and fails both for that reason and because the purpose is perpetuitous. He relies upon this passage from the judgment of the Board in *Leahy v A-G for New South Wales* [1959] AC 457 at 478:

'If the words "for the general purposes of the association" were held to import a trust, the question would have to be asked, what is the trust and who are the beneficiaries? A gift can be made to persons (including a corporation) but it cannot be made to a purpose or to an object: so also, a trust may be created for the benefit of persons as *cestuis que trust* but not for a purpose or object unless the purpose or object be charitable. For a purpose or object cannot sue, but, if it be charitable, the Attorney-General can sue to enforce it.' ...

I accept Mr. Blackburne's submission that the designation of the sole purpose of the gift makes it impossible to construe the gift as one falling into the first of Cross J's categories, even if that were otherwise possible. But I am not impressed by the argument that the gift shows an intention of continuity. Mr. Blackburne prays in aid *Re Macaulay's Estate* [1943] Ch 435n which is reported as a note to *Re Price* [1943] Ch 422, where the gift was for the 'maintenance and improvement of the Theosophical Lodge at Folkestone'. The House of Lords held that it failed for perpetuity, the donee being a non-charitable body. But it is clear from the speeches of both Lord Buckmaster and Lord Tomlin that their Lordships derived the intention of continuity from the reference to 'maintenance'. Here it is quite evident that the association was to be free to spend the capital of the legacy. As Lord Buckmaster said in *Re Macaulay's Estate* at 436:

'In the first place it is clear that the mere fact that the beneficiary is an unincorporated society in no way affects the validity of the gift... The real question is what is the actual purpose for which the gift is made. There is no perpetuity if the gift were for the individual members for their own benefit, but that, I think, is clearly not the meaning of this gift. Nor again is there a perpetuity if the society is at liberty in accordance with the terms of the gift, to spend both capital and income as they think fit.'

Re Price itself is authority for the proposition that a gift to an unincorporated non-charitable association for objects upon which the association is at liberty to spend both capital and income will not fail for perpetuity, although the actual conclusion in that case has been criticised—the point that the trust there (the carrying on of the teachings of Rudolf Steiner) was a 'purpose trust' and thus unenforceable on that ground was not argued.[41] It does not seem to me, therefore, that in the present case there is a valid ground for saying that the gift fails for perpetuity.

---

[41] See *Re Grant's Will Trusts* [1980] 1 WLR 360 at 369 [p. 392, below].

But that is not the end of the matter. If the gift were to the association *simpliciter*, it would, I think, clearly fall within the second category of Cross J's categories. At first sight, however, there appears to be a difficulty in arguing that the gift is to members of the association subject to their contractual rights *inter se* when there is a specific direction or limitation sought to be imposed upon those contractual rights as to the manner in which the subject matter of the gift is to be dealt with. This, says Mr. Blackburne, is a pure 'purpose trust' and is invalid on that ground, quite apart from any question of perpetuity. I am not sure, however, that it is sufficient merely to demonstrate that a trust is a 'purpose' trust. With the greatest deference, I wonder whether the dichotomy postulated in the passage which I have referred to in the judgment of the Board in *Leahy's* case [1959] AC 457 at 478 is not an over-simplification. Indeed, I am not convinced that it was intended as an exhaustive statement or to do more than indicate the broad division of trusts into those where there are ascertainable beneficiaries (whether for particular purposes or not) and trusts where there are none...

There would seem to me to be, as a matter of common sense, a clear distinction between the case where a purpose is prescribed which is clearly intended for the benefit of ascertained or ascertainable beneficiaries, particularly where those beneficiaries have the power to make the capital their own, and the case where no beneficiary at all is intended (for instance, a memorial to a favourite pet) or where the beneficiaries are unascertainable: as in the case, for instance, of *Re Price* [1943] Ch 422. If a valid gift may be made to an unincorporated body as a simple accretion to the funds which are the subject matter of the contract which the members have made *inter se*—and *Neville Estates Ltd v Madden* [1962] Ch 832, and *Re Recher's Will Trusts* [1972] Ch 526 [p. 386, below], show that it may—I do not really see why such a gift, which specifies a purpose which is within the powers of the association and of which the members of the association are the beneficiaries, should fail. Why are not the beneficiaries able to enforce the trust or, indeed, in the exercise of their contractual rights, to terminate the trust for their own benefit? Where the donee association is itself the beneficiary of the prescribed purpose, there seems to me to be the strongest argument in common sense for saying that the gift should be construed as an absolute one within the second category—the more so where, if the purpose is carried out, the members can by appropriate action vest the resulting property in themselves, for here the trustees and the beneficiaries are the same persons.

Is such a distinction as I have suggested borne out by the authorities? The answer is, I think, 'not in terms', until recently. But the cases appear to me to be at least consistent with this. For instance *Re Clarke* [1901] 2 Ch 110 (the case of the Corps of Commissionaires); *Re Drummond* [1914] 2 Ch 90 (the case of the Old Bradfordians)[42] and *Re Taylor* [1940] Ch 481 (the case of the Midland Bank Staff Association), in all of which the testator had prescribed purposes for which the gifts were to be used, and in all of which the gifts were upheld, were all cases where there were ascertainable beneficiaries; whereas in *Re Wood* [1949] Ch 498, and *Leahy's* case (where the gifts failed) there were none. *Re Price* is perhaps out of line, because there was no ascertained beneficiary and yet Cohen J was prepared to uphold the gift even on the supposition that (contrary to his own conclusion) the purpose was non-charitable. But, as I have mentioned, the point about the trust being a purpose trust was not argued before him.

A striking case which seems to be not far from the present is *Re Turkington* [1937] 4 All ER 501, where the gift was to a masonic lodge 'as a fund to build a suitable temple in Stafford'. The

---

[42] The reasons given for this decision were doubted by Vinelott J in *Re Grant's Will Trusts* [1980] 1 WLR 360 at 369.

members of the lodge being both the trustees and the beneficiaries of the temple, Luxmoore J construed the gift as an absolute one to the members of the lodge for the time being.

Directly in point is the more recent decision of Goff J in *Re Denley's Trust Deed* [1969] 1 Ch 373, where the question arose as to the validity of a deed under which land was held by trustees as a sports ground:

> 'primarily for the benefit of employees of [a particular company] and secondarily for the benefit of such other person or persons...as the trustees may allow to use the same...'

The latter provision was construed by Goff J as a power and not a trust. The same deed conferred on the employees a right to use and enjoy the land subject to regulations made by the trustees. Goff J held that the rule against enforceability of non-charitable 'purpose or object' trusts was confined to those which were abstract or impersonal in nature where there was no beneficiary or *cestui que trust*. A trust which, though expressed as a purpose, was directly or indirectly for the benefit of an individual or individuals was valid provided that those individuals were ascertainable at any one time and the trust was not otherwise void for uncertainty. Goff J said at 382:

> 'I think there may be a purpose or object trust, the carrying out of which would benefit an individual or individuals, where that benefit is so indirect or intangible or which is otherwise so framed as not to give those persons any *locus standi* to apply to the court to enforce the trust, in which case the beneficiary principle would, as it seems to me, apply to invalidate the trust, quite apart from any question of uncertainty or perpetuity. Such cases can be considered if and when they arise. The present is not, in my judgment, of that character, and it will be seen that clause 2(d) of the trust deed expressly states that, subject to any rules and regulations made by the trustees, the employees of the company shall be entitled to the use and enjoyment of the land. Apart from this possible exception, in my judgment the beneficiary principle of *Re Astor's Settlement Trusts* [1952] Ch 534, which was approved in *Re Endacott* [1960] Ch 232—see particularly by Harman LJ, at 250—is confined to purpose or object trusts which are abstract or impersonal. The objection is not that the trust is for a purpose or object *per se*, but that there is no beneficiary or *cestui que trust*.... Where, then, the trust, though expressed as a purpose, is directly or indirectly for the benefit of an individual or individuals, it seems to me that it is in general outside the mischief of the beneficiary principle.'

I respectfully adopt this, as it seems to me to accord both with authority and with common sense.

If this is the right principle, then on which side of the line does the present case fall? Mr. Morritt has submitted in the course of his argument in favour of charity that the testator's express purpose 'solely in the work of constructing the new buildings for the association' referred and could only refer to the youth centre project, which was the only project for the erection of buildings which was under consideration at the material time. If this is right, then the trust must, I think, fail, for it is quite clear that the project as ultimately conceived embraced not only the members of the association, but the whole Jewish community in Hull, and it would be difficult to argue that there was any ascertainable beneficiary. I do not, however, so construe the testator's intention. The evidence is that the testator knew the association's position and that he took a keen interest in it. I infer that he was kept informed of its current plans. The one thing that is quite clear from the minutes is that from 1965 right up to the testator's death there was great uncertainty about what was going to be done. There was a specific project for the purchase of a house in 1965. By early 1966 the youth centre was back in favour. By October 1966 it was being suggested that the association should stay where they were in their rented premises. The meeting of 21 March is, I think, very significant because it shows that they were again thinking in terms of their own exclusive building and that the patrons (of whom the testator was one) would donate the money when it was needed. At the date of the will, the association had rejected the youth centre plans and were contemplating again the purchase of premises of their own; and thereafter interest shifted to the community centre. I am unable to conclude that the testator had any specific building in mind; and, in my judgment, the reference to 'the' buildings for the association means no more than whatever buildings the association may have or may choose to erect or acquire. The reference to improvements reflects, I think, the testator's contemplation that the association might purchase or might, at his death, already have purchased an existing structure which might require improvement or conversion, or even that they might, as had at one time been suggested, expend money in improving the premises which they rented from the Jewish Institute. The association was to have the legacy to spend in this way for the benefit of its members.

I have already said that, in my judgment, no question of perpetuity arises here, and accordingly the case appears to me to be one of the specification of a particular purpose for the benefit of ascertained beneficiaries, the members of the association for the time being. There is an additional factor. This is a case in which, under the constitution of the association, the members could, by the appropriate majority, alter their constitution so as to provide, if they wished, for the division of the association's assets among themselves. This has, I think, a significance. I have considered whether anything turns in this case upon the testator's direction that the legacy shall be used 'solely' for one or other of the specified purposes. Mr. Rossdale has referred me to a number of cases where legacies have been bequeathed for particular purposes and in which the beneficiaries have been held entitled to override the purpose, even though expressed in mandatory terms.

Perhaps the most striking in the present context is Re Bowes [1896] 1 Ch 507, where money was directed to be laid out in the planting of trees on a settled estate. That was a 'purpose' trust, but there were ascertainable beneficiaries, the owners for the time being of the estate; and North J held that the persons entitled to the settled estate were entitled to have the money whether or not it was laid out as directed by the testator. . . .

I can see no reason why the same reasoning should not apply in the present case simply because the beneficiary is an unincorporated non-charitable association. I do not think the fact that the testator has directed the application 'solely' for the specified purpose adds any legal force to the direction. The beneficiaries, the members of the association for the time being, are the persons who could enforce the purpose and they must, as it seems to me, be entitled not to enforce it or, indeed, to vary it.

Thus, it seems to me that whether one treats the gift as a 'purpose' trust or as an absolute gift with a superadded direction or, on the analogy of Re Turkington [1937] 4 All ER 501 as a gift where the trustees and the beneficiaries are the same persons, all roads lead to the same conclusion.

In my judgment, the gift is a valid gift.[43]

---

[43] See Re Grant's Will Trusts [1980] 1 WLR 360 [p. 392, below], where Vinelott J held, as a second ground for his decision, that the gift was a trust for non-charitable purposes and therefore void for perpetuity; (1980) 43 MLR 459 (B. Green).

IV USELESS OR CAPRICIOUS PURPOSES

If there is a theory upon which purpose trusts are valid, will this cover trusts for every purpose? Or will there be exceptions for illegal, immoral, wasteful, or useless purposes?

In **Brown v Burdett** (1882) 21 Ch D 667, the testatrix devised a freehold house upon trust to block up all the rooms of the house,[44] except four which were to be set aside for a house-keeper and his wife for 20 years, and subject thereto upon trust for Mr. Burdett for life and after his death to Mr. Baxter in fee. BACON V-C had no difficulty in holding that the provisions for blocking up the house were void. The whole judgment states: 'I think I must "unseal" this useless, undisposed-of property. There will be a declaration that the house and premises were undisposed-of by the will, for the term of 20 years from the testatrix's death.'

The M'Caigs of Oban could not resist the attractions of posthumous greatness. Mr. M'Caig provided in his will that the income of his whole estate should be used for the purpose of building statues of himself and his family and the building of 'artistic towers' at prominent points on his estates. Miss M'Caig, who was his sister and also his heir, succeeded in having the trust set aside on the ground that, under Scots law, an heir can only be disinherited by a beneficial gift to someone else: **M'Caig v University of Glasgow** (1907) SC 231. On the question whether the doctrine of public policy would have destroyed the trust, LORD KYLLACHY said at 242:

I have, I confess, much sympathy with that argument. For I consider that if it is not unlawful, it ought to be unlawful, to dedicate by testamentary disposition, for all time, or for a length of time, the whole income of a large estate—real and personal—to objects of no utility, private or public, objects which benefit nobody, and which have no other purpose or use than that of perpetuating at great cost, and in an absurd manner, the idiosyncracies of an eccentric testator. I doubt much whether a bequest of that character is a lawful exercise of the *testamenti factio*. Indeed, I suppose it would be hardly contended to be so if the purposes, say of the trust here, were to be slightly varied, and the trustees were, for instance, directed to lay the truster's estate waste, and to keep it so; or to turn the income of the estate into money, and throw the money yearly into the sea; or to expend income in annual or monthly funeral services in the testator's memory; or to expend it in discharging from prominent points upon the estate, salvoes of artillery upon the birthdays of the testator, and his brothers and sisters. Such purposes would hardly, I think, be alleged to be consistent with public policy; and I am by no means satisfied that the purposes which we have here before us are in a better position.

In her turn, Miss M'Caig provided in her will for the erection of eleven bronze statues of her parents and their nine children, each to cost not less than £1,000. This failed in

---

44 The method is described in some detail at pp. 668–670 of the report.

M'Caig's Trustees v Kirk-Session of United Free Church of Lismore (1915) SC 426. LORD SALVESEN declared it void on grounds of public policy and said at 434:

In the first place, I think it is so because it involves a sheer waste of money, and not the less so that the expenditure would give employment to a number of sculptors and workmen, for it must be assumed that their labour could be usefully employed in other ways. I think, further, that it would be a dangerous thing to support a bequest of this kind which can only gratify the vanity of testators, who have no claim to be immortalised, but who possess the means by which they can provide for more substantial monuments to themselves than many that are erected to famous persons by public subscription. A man may, of course, do with his money what he pleases while he is alive, but he is generally restrained from wasteful expenditure by a desire to enjoy his property, or to accumulate it, during his lifetime. The actings of the two M'Caigs form an excellent illustration of this principle of human conduct. For many years they had apparently contemplated the erection of similar statues, but they could not bring themselves to part with the money during their own lifetimes... The prospect of Scotland being dotted with monuments to obscure persons who happened to have amassed a sufficiency of means, and cumbered with trusts for the purposes of maintaining these monuments in all time coming, appears to me to be little less than appalling...[45]

V THE PECULIAR PROBLEM OF UNINCORPORATED ASSOCIATIONS[46]

A GENERAL

A corporation, like a human being, is a legal person,[47] and can own property. An unincorporated association is not a legal person; but many unincorporated associations exist and operate, and have done so for many years. In **Conservative and Unionist Central Office v Burrell** [1982] 1 WLR 522 at 525 [p. 395, below] LAWTON LJ defined an unincorporated association as:

two or more persons bound together for one or more common purposes, not being business purposes, by mutual undertakings each having mutual duties and obligations, in an organisation

---

[45] See also *Aitken's Trustees v Aitken* (1927) SC 374 (massive bronze equestrian statue of artistic merit); *Mackintosh's Judicial Factor v Lord Advocate* (1935) SC 406 (erection of vault); *Lindsay's Executor v Forsyth* 1940 SC 568 (£1,000 on trust to provide 'a weekly supply of fresh flowers on the grave of my mother and my own').

[46] H&M, pp. 379–388; Lewin, pp. 108–111; P&M, pp. 85–86, 88–94; P&S, pp. 653–660; Pettit, pp. 60–63; T&H, pp. 157–158; U&H, pp. 162–170. See Morris and Leach, *Rule Against Perpetuities* (2nd edn, 1962), pp. 313–318; Maudsley, *Modern Law of Perpetuities* (1979), pp. 171–176; Ford, *Unincorporated Non-Profit Associations* (1977), pp. 1–49; Warburton, *Unincorporated Associations: Law and Practice* (2nd edn, 1992); Baxendale-Walker, *Purpose Trusts* (2001), pp. 153–163; [1985] Conv 415; Conv Prec 15–4; [1992] Conv 41 (S. Gardner); [1995] Conv 302 (P. Matthews).   [47] *Salomon v Salomon & Co Ltd* [1897] AC 22.

which has rules which identify in whom control of it and its funds rests and on what terms and which can be joined or left at will.

Hence an organisation which is not incorporated may fail to satisfy the requirements of an unincorporated association.[48] The question which must be investigated now is this: what is the proper legal analysis of the way in which such associations hold property?

The variety of unincorporated associations is limitless. In order to determine into which category any particular association fits, it is necessary for the court to construe the language of its constitution or rules or of the instrument which created it. Certain types may be categorised in order to show some of the possibilities.

1. An unincorporated association which holds property for charitable purposes; as, for example, on trust for the relief of poverty. This is valid. It is exempt from most forms of taxation, and may continue for ever. Charitable trusts are discussed in Chapter 10.

2. An unincorporated association whose funds are required by its rules to be applied for non-charitable purposes; for example: a trust for the preservation of the independence and integrity of newspapers. As has been seen, generally speaking, a trust for non-charitable purposes is void.

3. An unincorporated association whose committee or officers hold property on trust for the members of the association; for example, to the Treasurer for the time being of a school old boys' society.[49] This may be construed as an ordinary trust for beneficiaries. But difficulties can arise in connection with the following questions: whether beneficiaries are sufficiently ascertainable; whether such a beneficial interest under a trust can be obtained or released by joining or leaving an association; and whether the rule against perpetuities applies so as to render void the beneficial interest of any member who joins outside the perpetuity period.

4. An unincorporated association in which the members have a right based upon contract to claim a share of the property. For example, a members' club, such as a golf club. This situation is outside the law of trusts, but it is mentioned here in order to complete the categories by including an explanation of the most common type of unincorporated association. Legal difficulties can of course arise in this analysis, including, for example, if the members are minors. In many cases the members of the association will be unaware of the existence or the terms of the contract. A consequence of this analysis is that individual members may be personally liable, as for example in *Howells v Dominion Insurance Co Ltd*[50] where 32 named members of a football club were held liable for repayment of an insurance payment which had been mistakenly made to the club, amounting to £76,000.

---

[48] The case was concerned with the meaning of 'unincorporated association' for the purposes of ICTA 1970, but it would seem that the definition is of general application: H&M p. 379. See also *Re Koeppler's Will Trust* [1986] Ch 423 at 431, *per* Slade LJ: 'an association of persons bound together by identifiable rules and having an identifiable membership'. See also *J H Rayner (Mincing Lane) Ltd v Department of Trade and Industry* [1989] Ch 72 (International Tin Council).

[49] See *Re Drummond* [1914] 2 Ch 90, as discussed in *Leahy v A-G for New South Wales* [1959] AC 457 at 479 [p. 383, below]. [50] [2005] EWHC 552 (QB).

The subject of unincorporated associations is included in this book because, in some of the categories, especially categories 2. and 3., questions arise relating to the requirements of a trust. Prior to the decision of the Privy Council in *Leahy v A-G for New South Wales* [1959] AC 457 [p. 381, below], the courts did not analyse the theoretical basis of property holding by unincorporated associations in terms of category 3., and in consequence did not put such an unincorporated association 'at risk' of invalidity by reason of failure to comply with the requirements of a trust for beneficiaries. Before 1959, the courts seemed satisfied so long as the society, by its rules, could alienate its property and did not create a perpetuity.[51] This issue, and the earlier cases,[52] are discussed in relation to *Leahy*, below.

But the analysis of an unincorporated association on the basis of a trust was sometimes made in the context of a resulting trust arising upon the *dissolution* of the society, and the disposal of the surplus funds. This question is related to the one under discussion here, but its detailed implications were considered in Chapter 6 on Resulting Trusts.[53] It was seen there that the disposal of the surplus can depend on whether the situation is analysed as being one where the property is held on trust, or whether it is held subject to the contractual rights of the members. Where a friendly society, a mutual insurance society, a golf club, or whatever, is wound up, and there is a surplus, should the surplus be paid out to the existing members? Or to past and present members? Or to those who contributed the funds, whether they are members or not? And whether they can be identified or not? Or, should the surplus be treated as one without a claimant, and paid to the Crown as *bona vacantia*? It was seen that each of these solutions has at times been applied. Again, much depends on whether the situation is analysed as one of contract or trust.

B   THEORETICAL BASIS OF PROPERTY HOLDING

In **Neville Estates Ltd v Madden** [1962] Ch 832[54] the trustees of Catford Synagogue entered into a contract to sell some land. The question arose whether the consent of the Charity Commissioners was required. Consent would be required if the land was held upon charitable trusts and if the Charitable Trusts Act 1853, section 62[55] did not apply. The members of the Synagogue claimed that they were entitled to the purchase money.

CROSS J decided that the land was held on charitable trusts and that consent was required. In considering the claim of the members, he discussed the question of the nature of gifts in favour of unincorporated associations. He said at 849:

---

[51] *Carne v Long* (1860) 2 De GF & J 75.

[52] *Re Drummond* [1914] 2 Ch 90; *Re Patten* [1929] 2 Ch 276; *Re Prevost* [1930] 2 Ch 383; (1937) 53 LQR 24 at p. 46 (W.O. Hart); *Re Price* [1943] Ch 422; *Re Macaulay's Estate,* [1943] Ch 435n.

[53] See p. 223, above.

[54] See also *Re Recher's Will Trusts* [1972] Ch 526 at 538 [p. 386, below].

[55] Which exempts charities which are wholly or partly maintained by voluntary subscription.

I turn now at last to the legal issues involved. The question of the construction and effect of gifts to or in trust for unincorporated associations was recently considered by the Privy Council in *Leahy v A-G for New South Wales* [1959] AC 457. The position, as I understand it, is as follows. Such a gift may take effect in one or other of three quite different ways. In the first place, it may, on its true construction, be a gift to the members of the association at the relevant date as joint tenants, so that any member can sever his share and claim it whether or not he continues to be a member of the association. Secondly, it may be a gift to the existing members not as joint tenants, but subject to their respective contractual rights and liabilities towards one another as members of the association. In such a case a member cannot sever his share. It will accrue to the other members on his death or resignation, even though such members include persons who became members after the gift took effect. If this is the effect of the gift, it will not be open to objection on the score of perpetuity or uncertainty unless there is something in its terms or circumstances or in the rules of the association which precludes the members at any given time from dividing the subject of the gift between them on the footing that they are solely entitled to it in equity.

Thirdly, the terms or circumstances of the gift or the rules of the association may show that the property in question is not to be at the disposal of the members for the time being, but is to be held in trust for or applied for the purposes of the association as a quasi-corporate entity. In this case the gift will fail unless the association is a charitable body. If the gift is of the second class, i.e., one which the members of the association for the time being are entitled to divide among themselves, then, even if the objects of the association are in themselves charitable, the gift would not, I think, be a charitable gift. If, for example, a number of persons formed themselves into an association with a charitable object—say the relief of poverty in some district—but it was part of the contract between them that, if a majority of the members so desired, the association should be dissolved and its property divided between the members at the date of dissolution, a gift to the association as part of its general funds would not, I conceive, be a charitable gift.

(i) Property Held on Trust for Members

Leahy v Attorney-General for New South Wales[56]
[1959] AC 457 (PC, Viscount Simonds, Lords Morton of Henryton, Cohen, Somervell of Harrow and Denning)

An Australian testator provided by clause 3 of his will, *inter alia*, that his property, known as 'Elmslea', should be held upon trust for 'such order of nuns of the Catholic Church or the Christian Brothers as my executors and trustees shall select'. The gift was not a valid charitable trust, because such orders included some purely contemplative orders, which were not 'charitable' in law.[57]

The New South Wales Conveyancing Act 1919–54, section 37D provided that a trust should not be invalid on the ground that the property might be applicable to objects some of which were charitable and some of which were not.

---

[56] See *Bacon v Pianta* (1966) 114 CLR 634 ('The Communist Party of Australia'); (1971) 8 *Melbourne Law Review* 1, (P.W. Hogg). [57] See p. 471, below.

The question was whether the property could be applied, as being a valid private trust, in favour of the individual members of contemplative orders; or whether it should be treated as an endowment of the orders selected; and valid only, as a charitable trust, under the New South Wales Conveyancing Act 1919–54, section 37D;[58] and, as such, applicable only in favour of such orders as were charitable.

Held. The trust was intended as an endowment of the orders selected. It could not take effect as a private trust, but was validated by the New South Wales Conveyancing Act.

Viscount Simonds: The disposition made by clause 3 must now be considered. As has already been pointed out, it will in any case be saved by the section so far as Orders other than Contemplative Orders are concerned, but the trustees are anxious to preserve their right to select such Orders. They can only do so if the gift is what is called an absolute gift to the selected Order, an expression which may require examination.

Upon this question there has been a sharp division of opinion in the High Court. Williams and Webb JJ agreed with Myers J that the disposition by clause 3 was valid. They held that it provided for an immediate gift to the particular religious community selected by the trustees and that it was immaterial whether the Order was charitable or not because the gift was not a gift in perpetuity. 'It is given', they said (and these are the significant words) 'to the individuals comprising the community selected by the trustees at the date of the death of the testator. It is given to them for the benefit of the community.' Kitto J reached the same conclusion. He thought that the selected Order would take the gift immediately and absolutely and could expend immediately the whole of what it received. 'There is', he said, 'no attempt to create a perpetual endowment.' A different view was taken by the Chief Justice and McTiernan J. After an exhaustive examination of the problem and of the relevant authorities they concluded that the provision made by clause 3 was intended as a trust operating for the furtherance of the purpose of the Order as a body of religious women or, in the case of the Christian Brothers, as a teaching Order. 'The membership of any Order chosen', they said, 'would be indeterminate and the trust was intended to apply to those who should become members at any time. There was no intention to restrain the operation of the trust to those presently members or to make the alienation of the property a question for a Governing Body of the Order chosen or any section or part of that Order.' They therefore held that unless the trust could be supported as a charity it must fail.

The brief passages that have been cited from the judgments in the High Court sufficiently indicate the question that must be answered and the difficulty of solving it. It arises out of the artificial and anomalous conception of an unincorporated society which, though it is not a separate entity in law, is yet for many purposes regarded as a continuing entity and, however inaccurately, as something other than an aggregate of its members. In law a gift to such a society *simpliciter* (i.e., where, to use the words of Lord Parker in *Bowman v Secular Society Ltd* [1917] AC 406 at 437, neither the circumstances of the gift nor the directions given nor the objects expressed impose on the donee the character of a trustee) is nothing else than a gift to its members at the date of the gift as joint tenants or tenants in common. It is for this reason that the prudent conveyancer provides that a receipt by the treasurer or other proper officer of the recipient society for a legacy to the society shall be a sufficient discharge to executors. If it

---

[58] See p. 542, below.

were not so, the executors could only get a valid discharge by obtaining a receipt from every member. This must be qualified by saying that by their rules the members might have authorised one of themselves to receive a gift on behalf of them all.

It is in the light of this fundamental proposition that the statements, to which reference has been made, must be examined. What is meant when it is said that a gift is made to the individuals comprising the community and the words are added 'it is given to them for the benefit of the community'? If it is a gift to individuals, each of them is entitled to his distributive share (unless he has previously bound himself by the rules of the society that it shall be devoted to some other purpose). It is difficult to see what is added by the words 'for the benefit of the community'. If they are intended to import a trust, who are the beneficiaries? If the present members are the beneficiaries, the words add nothing and are meaningless. If some other persons or purposes are intended, the conclusion cannot be avoided that the gift is void. For it is uncertain, and beyond doubt tends to a perpetuity.

The question then appears to be whether, even if the gift to a selected Order of Nuns is *prima facie* a gift to the individual members of that Order, there are other considerations arising out of the terms of the will, or the nature of the society, its organisation and rules, or the subject matter of the gift which should lead the court to conclude that, though *prima facie* the gift is an absolute one (absolute both in quality of estate and in freedom from restriction) to individual nuns, yet it is invalid because it is in the nature of an endowment and tends to a perpetuity or for any other reason. This raises a problem which is not easy to solve, as the divergent opinions in the High Court indicate.

The *prima facie* validity of such a gift (by which term their Lordships intend a bequest or devise)[59] is a convenient starting point for the examination of the relevant law. For as Lord Tomlin (sitting at first instance in the Chancery Division) said in *Re Ogden* [1933] Ch 678, a gift to a voluntary association of persons for the general purposes of the association is an absolute gift and *prima facie* a good gift. He was echoing the words of Lord Parker in *Bowman's* case [1917] AC 406 at 442, that a gift to an unincorporated association for the attainment of its purposes 'may...be upheld as an absolute gift to its members'. These words must receive careful consideration, for it is to be noted that it is because the gift can be upheld as a gift to the individual members that it is valid, even though it is given for the general purposes of the association. If the words 'for the general purposes of the association' were held to import a trust, the question would have to be asked, what is the trust and who are the beneficiaries? A gift can be made to persons (including a corporation) but it cannot be made to a purpose or to an object: so also, a trust may be created for the benefit of persons as *cestuis que trust* but not for a purpose or object unless the purpose or object be charitable.

His Lordship referred to *Cocks v Manners* (1871) LR 12 Eq 574 (a share of residue to the 'Dominican Convent at Carisbrooke payable to the Superior for the time being'); *Re Smith* [1914] 1 Ch 937 (bequest to 'the society or institution known as the Franciscan Friars of Clevedon County of Somerset'); *Re Clarke* [1901] 2 Ch 110 (bequest to 'the committee for the time being of the Corps of Commissionaires in London'); *Re Drummond* [1914] 2 Ch 90 (residuary testamentary gift upon trust for 'the Old Bradfordians Club, London'); *Re Taylor* [1940] Ch 481 (residuary testamentary gift upon trust for 'the Midland Bank Staff Association, Liverpool and District Centre');

[59] The report says demise; but presumably devise is intended.

Re Price [1943] Ch 422 (residuary testamentary gift to 'the Anthroposophical Society in Great Britain'); *Re Prevost* [1930] 2 Ch 383 (residuary testamentary gift to 'the trustees of the London Library'); *Re Ray's Will Trusts* [1936] Ch 520 (bequest to 'the person who, at the time of my death, shall be or shall act as the abbess of the Franciscan Convent, Woodchester, Gloucestershire') and continued:

The cases that have been referred to (and many others might have been referred to in the courts of Australia, England and Ireland) are all cases in which gifts have been upheld as valid either on the ground that, where a society has been named as legatee, its members could demand that the gift should be dealt with as they should together think fit; or on the ground that a trust had been established (as in *Re Drummond* [1914] 2 Ch 90) which did not create a perpetuity. It will be sufficient to mention one only of the cases in which a different conclusion has been reached, before coming to a recent decision of the House of Lords which must be regarded as of paramount authority. In *Carne v Long* (1860) 2 De GF & J 75 the testator devised his mansion-house after the death of his wife to the trustees of the Penzance Public Library to hold to them and their successors for ever for the use, benefit, maintenance and support of the said library. It appeared that the library was established and kept on foot by the subscriptions of certain inhabitants of Penzance, that the subscribers were elected by ballot and the library managed by officers chosen from amongst themselves by the subscribers, that the property in the books and everything else belonging to the library was vested in trustees for the subscribers and that it was provided that the institution should not be broken up so long as ten members remained. It was urged that the gift was to a number of private persons and there were in truth no other beneficiaries. But Campbell LC rejected the plea in words which, often though they have been cited, will bear repetition (ibid., at 79):

> 'If the devise had been in favour of the existing members of the society, and they had been at liberty to dispose of the property as they might think fit, then it might, I think, have been a lawful disposition and not tending to a perpetuity. But looking to the language of the rules of this society, it is clear that the library was intended to be a perpetual institution, and the testator must be presumed to have known what the regulations were.'

This was perhaps a clear case where both from the terms of the gift and the nature of the society a perpetuity was indicated.

Their Lordships must now turn to the recent case of *Re Macaulay's Estate,* which appears to be reported only in a footnote to *Re Price* [1943] Ch 422 at 435. There the gift was to the Folkestone Lodge of the Theosophical Society absolutely for the maintenance and improvement of the Theosophical Lodge at Folkestone. It was assumed that the donee, 'the Lodge', was a body of persons. The decision of the House of Lords in July 1933, to which both Lord Buckmaster and Lord Tomlin were parties, was that the gift was invalid. A portion of Lord Buckmaster's speech may well be quoted. He had previously referred to *Re Drummond* [1914] 2 Ch 90 and *Carne v Long* (1860) 2 De GF & J 75.

> 'A group of people,' he said, 'defined and bound together by rules and called by a distinctive name can be the subject of gift as well as any individual or incorporated body. The real question is what is the actual purpose for which the gift is made. There is no perpetuity if the gift is for the individual members for their own benefit, but that, I think, is clearly not the meaning of this gift. Nor again is there a perpetuity if the society is at liberty in accordance with the terms of the gift to spend both capital and income as they think fit... If the gift is to be for the endowment of the

society to be held as an endowment and the society is according to its form perpetual, the gift is bad: but, if the gift is an immediate beneficial legacy, it is good.'

In the result he held the gift for the maintenance and improvement of the Theosophical Lodge at Folkestone to be invalid. Their Lordships respectfully doubt whether the passage in Lord Buckmaster's speech in which he suggests the alternative ground of validity: *viz.*, that the society is at liberty in accordance with the terms of the gift to spend both capital and income as they think fit, presents a true alternative. It is only because the society, i.e., the individuals constituting it, are beneficiaries, that they can dispose of the gift. Lord Tomlin came to the same conclusion. He found in the words of the will 'for the maintenance and improvement' a sufficient indication that it was the permanence of the Lodge at Folkestone that the testatrix was seeking to secure and this, he thought, necessarily involved endowment. Therefore a perpetuity was created. A passage from the judgment of Lord Hanworth MR (which has been obtained from the records) may usefully be cited. He said:

'The problem may be stated in this way. If the gift is in truth to the present members of the society described by their society name so that they have the beneficial use of the property and can, if they please, alienate and put the proceeds in their own pocket, then there is a present gift to individuals which is good: but if the gift is intended for the good not only of the present but of future members so that the present members are in the position of trustees and have no right to appropriate the property or its proceeds for their personal benefit then the gift is invalid. It may be invalid by reason of there being a trust created, or it may be by reason of the terms that the period allowed by the rule against perpetuities would be exceeded.'

It is not very clear what is intended by the dichotomy suggested in the last sentence of the citation, but the penultimate sentence goes to the root of the matter. At the risk of repetition their Lordships would point out that, if a gift is made to individuals, whether under their own names or in the name of their society, and the conclusion is reached that they are not intended to take beneficially, then they take as trustees. If so, it must be ascertained who are the beneficiaries...[60]

It must now be asked, then, whether in the present case there are sufficient indications to displace the *prima facie* conclusion that the gift made by clause 3 of the will is to the individual members of the selected Order of Nuns at the date of the testator's death so that they can together dispose of it as they think fit. It appears to their Lordships that such indications are ample.

In the first place, it is not altogether irrelevant that the gift is in terms upon trust for a selected Order. It is true that this can in law be regarded as a trust in favour of each and every member of the Order. But at least the form of the gift is not to the members, and it may be questioned whether the testator understood the niceties of the law. In the second place, the members of the selected Order may be numerous, very numerous perhaps, and they may be spread over the world. If the gift is to the individuals it is to all the members who were living at the death of the testator, but only to them. It is not easy to believe that the testator intended an 'immediate beneficial legacy' (to use the words of Lord Buckmaster) to such a body of beneficiaries. In the third place, the subject matter of the gift cannot be ignored. It appears from the evidence filed in the suit that Elmslea is a grazing property of about 730 acres, with a furnished homestead

---

[60] Which would now be decided according to the test laid down in *McPhail v Doulton* [1971] AC 424 [p. 91, above].

containing 20 rooms and a number of outbuildings. With the greatest respect to those judges who have taken a different view, their Lordships do not find it possible to regard all the individual members of an Order as intended to become the beneficial owners of such a property. Little or no evidence has been given about the organisation and rules of the several Orders, but it is at least permissible to doubt whether it is a common feature of them, that all their members regard themselves or are to be regarded as having the capacity of (say) the Corps of Commissionaires (see *Re Clarke* [1901] 2 Ch 110) to put an end to their association and distribute its assets. On the contrary, it seems reasonably clear that, however little the testator understood the effect in law of a gift to an unincorporated body of persons by their society name, his intention was to create a trust, not merely for the benefit of the existing members of the selected Order, but for its benefit as a continuing society and for the furtherance of its work.

Different views have been held upon the question whether the legal title remains in the will trustees after they have selected an Order. Kitto J (expressly) and Williams and Webb JJ (by implication) held that 'when a body is selected by the trustees the property will be at home' and will vest presumably in some authorised person or persons. (The Roman Catholic Charities Land Act of 1942 was not invoked in the High Court and becomes irrelevant if the chosen Order is not a charity.) The Chief Justice and McTiernan J were of opinion that the trustees were intended, subject to the power of sale, to remain the repository of the whole legal title and to administer the trust by affording the enjoyment to the selected Order. The latter view is attractive if only because of the difficulty of transferring title when the above-mentioned Act does not apply. But their Lordships do not think it necessary for the purpose of this case to decide the question. No difficulty will arise if only a charitable body can be selected. If the choice is wider, the question will not arise. The dominant and sufficiently expressed intention of the testator is in their opinion (again in the words of Lord Buckmaster) that 'the gift is to be an endowment of the society to be held as an endowment', and that 'as the society is according to its form perpetual' the gift must, if it is to a non-charitable body, fail.

Their Lordships, therefore, humbly advise her Majesty that the appeal should be dismissed, but that the gift made by clause 3 of the will is valid by reason only of the provisions of section 37D of the Conveyancing Act, 1919–54, and that the power of selection thereby given to the trustees does not extend to Contemplative Orders of Nuns.

(ii) *Ownership by Members on Contractual Basis*[61]

In **Re Recher's Will Trusts** [1972] Ch 526,[62] one question was whether a gift to the London and Provincial Anti-Vivisection Society was valid. The society was unincorporated.[63] Its main object[64] was to secure the total abolition of vivisection. It consisted of ordinary and life members, and the constitution was laid down in its Rules.

---

[61] Whether a gift is made to the members or a gift to the members which takes effect as an accretion to the association's funds depends on the construction of the contract which binds the members: [1995] Conv 302 (P. Matthews).

[62] (1971) 35 Conv (NS) 381 (J. Mummery); (1971) 8 *Melbourne University Law Review* 1 (P.W Hogg); (1973) 47 ALJ 305 (R. Baxt); *Re Bucks Constabulary Widows' and Orphans' Fund Friendly Society (No 2)* [1979] 1 WLR 936 [p. 228, above]. See also [1995] Conv 302 (P. Matthews).

[63] In 1963 it was incorporated as The National Anti-Vivisection Society Ltd.

[64] Which is not charitable: *National Anti-Vivisection Society v IRC* [1948] AC 31 [p. 511, below].

BRIGHTMAN J considered the various ways in which the property of the society could be held, and continued at 538:

Having reached the conclusion that the gift in question is not a gift to the members of the London & Provincial Society at the date of death, as joint tenants or tenants in common, so as to entitle a member as of right to a distributive share, nor an attempted gift to present and future members beneficially, and is not a gift in trust for the purposes of the society, I must now consider how otherwise, if at all, it is capable of taking effect.

As I have already mentioned, the rules of the London & Provincial Society do not purport to create any trusts except in so far as the honorary trustees are not beneficial owners of the assets of the society, but are trustees upon trust to deal with such assets according to the directions of the committee.

A trust for non-charitable purposes, as distinct from a trust for individuals, is clearly void because there is no beneficiary. It does not, however, follow that persons cannot band themselves together as an association or society, pay subscriptions and validly devote their funds in pursuit of some lawful non-charitable purpose. An obvious example is a members' social club. But it is not essential that the members should only intend to secure direct personal advantages to themselves. The association may be one in which personal advantages to the members are combined with the pursuit of some outside purpose. Or the association may be one which offers no personal benefit at all to the members, the funds of the association being applied exclusively to the pursuit of some outside purpose. Such an association of persons is bound, I would think, to have some sort of constitution; that is to say, the rights and liabilities of the members of the association will inevitably depend on some form of contract *inter se*, usually evidenced by a set of rules. In the present case it appears to me clear that the life members, the ordinary members and the associate members of the London & Provincial Society were bound together by a contract *inter se*. Any such member was entitled to the rights and subject to the liabilities defined by the rules. If the committee acted contrary to the rules, an individual member would be entitled to take proceedings in the courts to compel observance of the rules or to recover damages for any loss he had suffered as a result of the breach of contract. As and when a member paid his subscription to the association, he would be subjecting his money to the disposition and expenditure thereof laid down by the rules. That is to say, the member would be bound to permit, and entitled to require, the honorary trustees and other members of the society to deal with that subscription in accordance with the lawful directions of the committee. Those directions would include the expenditure of that subscription, as part of the general funds of the association, in furthering the objects of the association. The resultant situation, on analysis, is that the London & Provincial society represented an organisation of individuals bound together by a contract under which their subscriptions became, as it were, mandated towards a certain type of expenditure as adumbrated in rule 1. Just as the two parties to a bi-partite bargain can vary or terminate their contract by mutual assent, so it must follow that the life members, ordinary members and associated members of the London & Provincial Society could, at any moment of time, by unanimous agreement (or by majority vote, if the rules so prescribe), vary or terminate their multi-partite contract. There would be no limit to the type of variation or termination to which all might agree. There is no private trust or trust for charitable purposes or other trust to hinder the process. It follows that if all members agreed, they could decide to wind up the London & Provincial Society and divide the net assets among themselves beneficially. No one would have any *locus standi* to stop them so doing. The contract is the same as any other contract and concerns only those who are parties to it, that is to say, the members of the society.

The funds of such an association may, of course, be derived not only from the subscriptions of the contracting parties but also from donations from non-contracting parties and legacies from persons who have died. In the case of a donation which is not accompanied by any words which purport to impose a trust, it seems to me that the gift takes effect in favour of the existing members of the association as an accretion to the funds which are the subject matter of the contract which such members have made *inter se*, and falls to be dealt with in precisely the same way as the funds which the members themselves have subscribed. So, in the case of a legacy. In the absence of words which purport to impose a trust, the legacy is a gift to the members beneficially, not as joint tenants or as tenants in common so as to entitle each member to an immediate distributive share, but as an accretion to the funds which are the subject matter of the contract which the members have made *inter se*.

In my judgment the legacy in the present case to the London & Provincial Society ought to be construed as a legacy of that type, that is to say, a legacy to the members beneficially as an accretion to the funds subject to the contract which they had made *inter se*. Of course, the testatrix did not intend the members of the society to divide her bounty between themselves, and doubtless she was ignorant of that remote but theoretical possibility. Her knowledge or absence of knowledge of the true legal analysis of the gift is irrelevant. The legacy is accordingly in my view valid, subject only to the effect of the events of 1 January, 1957.[65]

A strong argument has been presented to me against this conclusion and I have been taken through most, if not all, of the cases which are referred to in *Leahy*'s case [1959] AC 457, as well as later authorities. It has been urged upon me that if the gift is not a purpose gift, there is no halfway house between, on the one hand, a legacy to the members of the London & Provincial Society at the date of death, as joint tenants beneficially, or as tenants in common beneficially, and, on the other hand, a trust for members which is void for perpetuity because no individual member acting by himself can ever obtain his share of the legacy. I do not see why the choice should be confined to these two extremes. If the argument were correct it would be difficult, if not impossible, for a person to make a straightforward donation, whether *inter vivos* or by will, to a club or other non-charitable association which the donor desires to benefit. This conclusion seems to me contrary to common sense.[66]

In **Artistic Upholstery Ltd v Art Forma (Furniture) Ltd** [1999] 4 All ER 277 the claimant was a member of a guild of furniture manufacturing companies which was an unincorporated association. The claimant sued the defendant, on behalf of the association, for a declaration that the registration of a trademark by the defendant was invalid. The issue for the court was whether an unincorporated association could own the goodwill in a name to found an action in passing off. In holding that an unincorporated association could own the goodwill in a name, LAWRENCE COLLINS QC said at 285:

---

[65] When the London & Provincial Society merged with the National Society.

[66] *Re Lipinski's Will Trusts* [1976] Ch 235 [p. 372, above]; *Universe Tankships Inc of Monrovia v International Transport Workers Federation* [1983] 1 AC 366 (payment by ship owners of sum into the Federation fund held not to be a contribution on trust and therefore void and so returnable to the shipowners by way of resulting trust, but to be an accretion to the fund by way of outright gift). See also the CA judgment in [1981] ICR 129; (1980) 45 MLR 564; (1983) 46 MLR 36 (B. Green); (1983) 133 NLJ 15 (J. McMullen and A. Grubb).

Since there are substantial associations with a large (and changing) membership, holding property in the form of subscriptions or donations or association premises, it has been necessary to develop a legal analysis which will provide a practical solution to the problem that an unincorporated association, as such, has no capacity to hold property. Several solutions have been developed, including treating the members as holding as joint tenants, or having trustees holding on trust for the members or for the purposes of the association. But the prevailing view is that, at least where there are no appointed trustees to hold the property of the association, or where a transfer of property has not been accompanied by a valid declaration of trust, personal property will be held under the express or implied terms of the contract of the members *inter se*. Thus in *Re Recher's Will Trusts,* when the association received a donation which was not accompanied by words which purported to impose a trust, the gift took effect 'in favour of the existing members of the association as an accretion to the funds which are the subject matter of the contract which such members have made *inter se*' (see [1972] Ch 526 at 539). Brightman J followed the decision of Cross J in *Neville Estates Ltd v Madden* [1962] Ch 832 at 849, who had analysed the proprietary effects of a gift to an unincorporated association; one of the ways in which it could take effect was as a gift to the members not as joint tenants, but subject to their rights and liabilities towards one another as members of the association: in such a case the member could not sever his share.

In the *Bucks Constabulary* case [*Bucks Constabulary Widows' and Orphans' Fund Friendly Society*][1979] 1 WLR 936 at 943, Walton J applied *Re Recher's Will Trusts* in the context of a friendly society and said:

> '...all unincorporated societies rest in contract to this extent, that there is an implied contract between all the members *inter se* governed by the rules of the society. In default of any rule to the contrary, and it will seldom if ever be that there is such a rule, when a member ceases to be a member of the association he *ipso facto* ceases to have any interest in its funds.'

Consequently, even though an unincorporated association as such cannot hold property because it is not a legal person, property can be held by the members subject to the express or implied terms of the contract into which they enter with one another upon becoming members. The constitution and rules of the guild are consistent with that analysis. The objects of the guild include the selection and adoption of a trade mark to be used *by the guild* to identify the products of its members; to acquire and take over by purchase or otherwise any property, etc. of similar bodies; to purchase, lease, exchange, hire or otherwise acquire any real or personal property; to invest moneys of the guild not immediately required; to apply for and take out, etc. any trade marks, etc. which may be useful for the guild's objects. Clause 4 provides that the income and property of the guild is to be applied solely towards the promotion of the objects of the guild. The rules deal expressly with property of the guild in the following respects: the members are to keep books of account with respect to the assets and liabilities of the guild (r. 8.1); provision is made for the payment of subscriptions, and for the payment of expenses of the members out of the funds of the guild (rr. 9.1, 9.3). A member who resigns or is expelled forfeits any rights or claims (r. 10.3).

It follows from the authorities to which I have referred, and from the constitution and rules of the guild, that if the goodwill which is the foundation of a claim in passing-off is to be regarded as property...then an unincorporated association, such as the guild, through its members, may own goodwill which could found an action in passing-off. The goodwill is held by the members as their property in that capacity in accordance with the constitution and rules.

In **Re Horley Town Football Club** [2006] EWHC 2386 (Ch), [2006] WTLR 1817[67] the issue for the court concerned which class of members of an unincorporated association owned the association's assets. In holding that only the adult and senior members of the club did so, LAWRENCE COLLINS J said:

113   Since the members of an unincorporated association own its assets subject to the contractual obligations owed by them to each other, they can vary the contractual arrangements between each other. A change of the rules changes the contract between the members: *Re Recher* [1972] Ch 526 at 539. A change of rules need not simultaneously effect an assignment by the members beneficially entitled under the previous set of rules to the members beneficially entitled under the new set of rules. It is a question of construction of the rules.

114   I am satisfied that the Deed should be construed as a gift to the Club, as a 'contract-holding' gift to the Club and its members for the time being within category (2) in *Neville Estates v Madden*...

118   The next question is the identity of the persons who hold the beneficial interest. I am satisfied that the beneficial ownership is in the current full members (and not the temporary or associate members), and is held on bare trust for them. The members hold subject to the current rules, and could unanimously or by AGM call for the assets to be transferred. Adult and senior members are entitled to share in distribution on per capita basis.

119   In *Re GKN Bolts & Nuts Ltd etc Work Sports and Social Club* [1982] 1 WLR 774 the question was whether a social club formed for the benefit of employees had ceased to exist in 1975 when, following financial difficulties, it resolved to sell the sports ground, and the basis on which there should be distribution of the assets.

120   Sir Robert Megarry V-C said at 776:

'As is common in club cases, there are many obscurities and uncertainties, and some difficulty in the law. In such cases, the court usually has to take a broad sword to the problems, and eschew an unduly meticulous examination of the rules and regulations... I think that the courts have to be ready to allow general concepts of reasonableness, fairness and common sense to be given more than their usual weight when confronted by claims to the contrary which appear to be based on any strict interpretation and rigid application of the letter of the rules.'

121   He held that the club had ceased to exist. It was held that where, as in that case, there was nothing in the rules or anything else to indicate a different basis, distribution of the assets should be on the basis of equality among the members, irrespective of the length of membership or the amount of subscriptions paid. There was no possible nexus between the length of membership or the amount of subscriptions paid and the property rights of members on a dissolution. Each member was entitled to one equal share.

122   The club's rules provided that the club would consist of 'ordinary and honorary members and, in special cases, of temporary members as hereinafter provided'. The rules also referred to 'full members' who were the same as 'ordinary members, 'associates', 'temporary members' and spouses and children who were 'entitled to membership without voting rights'.

123   'Associates' were employees of a group company club having similar objects who, if they wrote their name in a book with the names of their clubs, would have the same rights as ordinary members, except that they could not vote at meetings or take away alcoholic drinks.

---

[67] [2007] Conv 274 (P. Luxton).

'Temporary members' were those invited by the committee to participate in the amenities of the club on the day of a sporting or social event. Spouses and children of members were thought by Sir Robert Megarry to fall within the same category as associates and temporary members. The object in each case was to confer the right to use the club premises and facilities without imposing the powers and responsibilities of full members, for whom alone the rule provided for the payment of subscriptions....

125   The result was a holding that no members except those who were properly called 'full members' or 'ordinary members' were entitled to any interest in the assets of the club.

126   I accept that in certain respects the distinction between 'full' members and other types of membership was somewhat clearer in *Re GKN* than it is in the present case. It appears that (with the exception of honorary members, some of whom paid a subscription but none of whom were entitled to vote or to an interest in the club's assets) in *Re GKN* there was a correspondence between members who paid subscriptions and members who were entitled to vote. In the present case, the voting rights do not correspond with the obligation to subscribe. There is a subscription for Youth Membership (under 18) and for Junior Membership (under 16), but Junior and Youth Members are not entitled to vote: Rule 5 (although Adult Membership includes non-playing children under 18 and attracts one vote).

127   In my judgment I should adopt the same approach as Sir Robert Megarry in taking a 'broad sword' and applying fairness and common sense. In my judgment it does not make a difference that in the present case the Rules say in Rule 4 that the Club shall consist of 'members and temporary members'; or in Rule 5 provide that Associate Members will enjoy the same rights as full members except those relating to voting rights; or that Rule 15 gives a right to vote to 'independently constituted clubs enjoying Associate Membership'. I would accept that a mere inequality in voting rights would not mean that a category of members is excluded altogether from any entitlement to the surplus assets of the association upon its dissolution. But the associate members in the present case have no effective rights and it would be wholly unrealistic to treat the introduction of Associate Members by amendment of the Rules as a transfer of the Club's property to them.

128   The consequence would be that the beneficial ownership is held on bare trust for the members, who could either unanimously or at an AGM call for the assets to be transferred.

129   All the sets of Rules, including the 2004 Rules, provide for amendment of the Rules by AGM. The members may agree to dissolve the Club and to distribute the assets amongst themselves or the association may be wound up by the court: *Re Lead Co's Workmen's Fund Society* [1904] 2 Ch 196; *Neville Estates Ltd v Madden* [1962] Ch 832, 849; *Re Recher* [1972] Ch 526, 538–539. The Rules do not specify how the Club's assets are to be distributed following dissolution. In the absence of any rule to the contrary, there is to be implied into the rules of the Club a rule to the effect that the surplus funds of the Club should be divided on a dissolution amongst the members of the Club, and this distribution will normally be per capita among the members (irrespective of length of membership or the amount of subscriptions paid) but may reflect different classes of membership: *Re Sick and Funeral Society of St John's Sunday School, Golcar* [1973] Ch 51, at 60; *Re Bucks Constabulary Widows' and Orphans' Fund Friendly Society (No 2)* [1979] 1 WLR 936, at 952; *Re GKN Bolts & Nuts Ltd etc Work Sports and Social Club* [1982] 1 WLR 774, at 778.

130   In the light of these decisions and in the light of my conclusion on Temporary and Associate Members, the persons entitled to share in a distribution would be the adult and senior members of the Club on a per capita basis.

(iii) Requirements for Validity of Gift

In **Re Grant's Will Trusts** [1980] 1 WLR 360[68] a testator left all his real and personal
estate 'to the Labour Party property committee for the benefit of the Chertsey headquarters of the Chertsey and Walton Constituency Labour Party'. In holding that the
gift failed and devolved as on intestacy, VINELOTT J said at 364:

The question raised by the summons is whether the gift in the will of the testator's real and
personal estate is a valid gift, or is void for uncertainty or for perpetuity or otherwise; and if it
is a valid gift, who are the persons entitled to benefit thereunder?

Before turning to this question, it will be convenient to explain what are in my judgment the
principles which govern the validity of a gift to an unincorporated association. A convenient
starting point is a passage in the decision of Cross J in *Neville Estates Ltd v Madden* [1962]
Ch 832 at 849 which is often cited. [His Lordship quoted the extract set out at p. 381, above,
and continued:] This statement, though it may require amplification in the light of subsequent
authorities, is still, as I see it, an accurate statement of the law.

In a case in the first category, that is a gift which, on its true construction, is a gift to members
of an association who take as joint tenants, any member being able to sever his share, the association is used in effect as a convenient label or definition of the class which is intended to take;
but, the class being ascertained, each member takes as joint tenant free from any contractual
fetter. So, for instance, a testator might give a legacy or share of residue to a dining or social
club of which he had been a member with the intention of giving to each of the other members an
interest as joint tenant, capable of being severed in the subject matter of the gift. Cases within
this category are relatively uncommon. A gift to an association will be more frequently found to
fall within the second category. There the gift is to members of an association, but the property
is given as an accretion to the funds of the association so that the property becomes subject to
the contract (normally evidenced by the rules of the association) which govern[s] the rights of
the members *inter se*. Each member is thus in a position to ensure that the subject matter of the
gift is applied in accordance with the rules of the association, in the same way as any other funds
of the association. This category is well illustrated by the decision of Brightman J in *Re Recher's
Will Trusts* [1972] Ch 526. There a share of residue was given to 'The Anti-Vivisection Society,
76 Victoria Street, London, S.W.1.' The society in fact ceased to exist, being amalgamated with
another society, during the testatrix's lifetime. Brightman J first examined whether the gift
would have been valid if the society had continued to exist. He said at 538:

[His Lordship quoted the extract set out at p. 387, above, and continued:]

Two points should be noted. First, as Brightman J pointed out, it is immaterial in considering
whether a gift falls within this category that the members of an association have not joined
together for a social and recreational purpose, or to secure some personal advantage, but in
pursuit of some altruistic purpose. The motive which led the testator to make the gift may have
been, indeed most frequently will have been, a desire to further that purpose. It may be said that
in that sense the gift is made for the furtherance of the purpose. But the testator has chosen
as the means of furthering the purpose to make a gift to an association formed for the pursuit
of that purpose in the expectation that the subject matter of the gift will be so used, without
imposing or attempting to impose any trust or obligation on the members, or the trustees, or
the committee of the association. Indeed, there are cases where the gift has been expressed as

---

[68]   (1980) 43 MLR 459 (B. Green); [1980] Conv 80 (G.A. Shindler).

a gift for the purposes, or one of the purposes, of the association, and nonetheless has been held not to impose any purported trust. Two examples will suffice.

His Lordship referred to *Re Turkington* [1937] 4 All ER 501 (gift expressed as a gift to the Staffordshire Knot Masonic Lodge as a fund to build a suitable temple in Stafford was construed by Luxmoore J as a gift to the members of the Lodge) and to *Re Lipinski's Will Trusts* [1976] Ch 235 [p. 372, above], and continued:

That leads to the second point. It must, as I see it, be a necessary characteristic of any gift within the second category that the members of the association can by an appropriate majority, if the rules so provide, or acting unanimously if they do not, alter their rules so as to provide that the funds, or part of them, should be applied for some new purpose, or even distributed amongst the members for their own benefit. For the validity of a gift within this category rests essentially upon the fact that the testator has set out to further a purpose by making a gift to the members of an association formed for the furtherance of that purpose in the expectation that although the members at the date when the gift takes effect will be free, by a majority if the rules so provide or acting unanimously if they do not, to dispose of the fund in any way they may think fit, they and any future members of the association will not in fact do so but will employ the property in the furtherance of the purpose of the association and will honour any special condition attached to the gift.

Turning to the third category, the testator may seek to further the purpose by giving a legacy to an association as a quasi-corporate entity, that is, to present and future members indefinitely, or by purporting to impose a trust. In the former case the gift will fail for perpetuity unless confined within an appropriate period; though if it is so confined and if the members for the time being within the perpetuity period are free to alter the purposes for which the property is to be used and to distribute the income amongst themselves it will not, as I see it, fail upon any other ground. In the latter case, the gift will fail upon the ground that the court cannot compel the use of the property in furtherance of a stated purpose unless, of course, the purpose is a charitable one. As Viscount Simonds said in *Leahy v A-G for New South Wales* [1959] AC 457 at 478:

'If the words "for the general purposes of the association" were held to import a trust, the question would have to be asked, what is the trust and who are the beneficiaries? A gift can be made to persons (including a corporation) but it cannot be made to a purpose or to an object: so also, a trust may be created for the benefit of persons as *cestuis que trust* but not for a purpose or object unless the purpose or object be charitable. For a purpose or object cannot sue, but, if it be charitable, the Attorney-General can sue to enforce it. (Upon this point something will be said later.) It is therefore by disregarding the words "for the general purposes of the association" (which are assumed not to be charitable purposes) and treating the gift as an absolute gift to individuals that it can be sustained.'

There are two cases in which, if this analysis is correct, the reasons given for the decision, though possibly not the decision itself, are not well-founded. [His Lordship referred to *Re Drummond* [1914] 2 Ch 90, and *Re Price* [1943] Ch 422, and continued:]

I have been referred to the recent decision of Goff J in *Re Denley's Trust Deed* [1969] 1 Ch 373.[69] There by clause 2 of a trust deed trustees were given powers of sale over land held

---

[69] See (1977) 41 Conv (NS) 179 (K. Widdows); (1980) 39 CLJ 88 (C.E.F. Rickett); [1985] Conv 318 (J. Warburton).

by them and were directed to hold the land while unsold during a defined perpetuity period on trust, that

> '(c)   The said land shall be maintained and used as and for the purpose of a recreation or sports ground primarily for the benefit of the employees of the company and secondarily for the benefit of such other person or persons (if any) as the trustees may allow to use the same...'

Goff J, having held that the words 'secondarily for the benefit of such other person or persons if any as the trustees may allow to use the same', conferred on the trustees a power operating in partial defeasance of a trust in favour of the employees, held that the trust deed created a valid trust for the benefit of the employees, the benefit being the right to use the land subject to and in accordance with the rules made by the trustees. That case on a proper analysis, in my judgment, falls altogether outside the categories of gifts to unincorporated associations and purpose trusts. I can see no distinction in principle between a trust to permit a class defined by reference to employment to use and enjoy land in accordance with rules to be made at the discretion of trustees on the one hand, and, on the other hand, a trust to distribute income at the discretion of trustees amongst a class, defined by reference to, for example, relationship to the settlor. In both cases the benefit to be taken by any member of the class is at the discretion of the trustees, but any member of the class can apply to the court to compel the trustees to administer the trust in accordance with its terms. As Goff J pointed out, at 388:

> 'The same kind of problem is equally capable of arising in the case of a trust to permit a number of persons—for example, all the unmarried children of a testator or settlor—to use or occupy a house or to have the use of certain chattels; nor can I assume that in such cases agreement between the parties concerned would be more likely, even if that be a sufficient distinction, yet no one would suggest, I fancy, that such a trust would be void.'

With those principles in mind, I return to the testator's will...

Reading the gift in the will in the light of the rules governing the Chertsey and Walton CLP, it is, in my judgment, impossible to construe the gift as a gift made to the members of the Chertsey and Walton CLP at the date of the testator's death with the intention that it should belong to them as a collection of individuals, though in the expectation that they and any other members subsequently admitted would ensure that it was in fact used for what in broad terms has been labelled 'headquarters' purposes' of the Chertsey and Walton CLP.

I base this conclusion on two grounds. First, the members of the Chertsey and Walton CLP do not control the property, given by subscription or otherwise, to the CLP. The rules which govern the CLP are capable of being altered by an outside body which could direct an alteration under which the general committee of the CLP would be bound to transfer any property for the time being held for the benefit of the CLP to the National Labour Party for national purposes. The members of the Chertsey and Walton CLP could not alter the rules so as to make the property bequeathed by the testator applicable for some purpose other than that provided by the rules; nor could they direct that property to be divided amongst themselves beneficially.

Brightman J observed in *Re Recher's Will Trusts* [1972] Ch 526 at 536:

> 'It would astonish the layman to be told there was a difficulty in his giving a legacy to an unincorporated non-charitable society which he had, or could have, supported without trouble during his lifetime.'

The answer to this apparent paradox is, it seems to me, that subscriptions by members of the Chertsey and Walton CLP must be taken as made upon terms that they will be applied by the general committee in accordance with the rules for the time being including any modifications imposed by the Annual Party Conference or the National Executive Committee. In the event of the dissolution of the Chertsey and Walton CLP any remaining fund representing subscriptions would (as the rules now stand) be held on a resulting trust for the original subscribers. Thus, although the members of the CLP may not be able themselves to alter the purposes for which a fund representing subscriptions is to be used or to alter the rules so as to make such a fund divisible amongst themselves, the ultimate proprietary right of the original subscribers remains. There is, therefore, no perpetuity and no non-charitable purpose trust. But if that analysis of the terms on which subscriptions are held is correct, it is fatal to the argument that the gift in the testator's will should be construed as a gift to the members of the Chertsey and Walton CLP at the testator's death, subject to a direction not amounting to a trust that it be used for headquarters' purposes. Equally it is in my judgment impossible, in particular having regard to the gift over to the National Labour Party, to read the gift as a gift to the members of the National Labour Party at the testator's death, with a direction not amounting to a trust, for the National Party to permit it to be used by the Chertsey and Walton CLP for headquarters' purposes.

That first ground is of itself conclusive, but there is another ground which reinforces this conclusion. The gift is not in terms a gift to the Chertsey and Walton CLP, but to the Labour Party property committee, who are to hold the property for the benefit of, that is in trust for, the Chertsey headquarters of the Chertsey and Walton CLP. The fact that a gift is a gift to trustees and not in terms of an unincorporated association, militates against construing it as a gift to the members of the association at the date when the gift takes effect, and against construing the words indicating the purposes for which the property is to be used as expressing the testator's intention or motive in making the gift and not as imposing any trust. This was, indeed, one of the considerations which led the Privy Council in *Leahy*'s case to hold that the gift '...upon trust for such Order of Nuns of the Catholic Church or the Christian Brothers as my executors and trustees should elect' would, apart from the Australian equivalent of the Charitable Trusts (Validation) Act [1954], have been invalid.

I am therefore, compelled to the conclusion that the gift of the testator's estate fails, and that his estate accordingly devolves as on intestacy.

(iv) The Mandate or Agency Theory

In **Conservative and Unionist Central Office v Burrell** [1982] 2 All ER 1,[70] BRIGHTMAN LJ said at 6:

The issue is whether or not the investment income of the Conservative Party Central Office funds during the relevant years was the income of an unincorporated association.[71] The assertion is that Central Office funds are held for the purposes of an organisation known as the Conservative Party, or more fully as the Conservative and Unionist Party, that such organisation has all the necessary requirements for qualifying as an unincorporated association and that the Special Commissioners were justified in finding that it is such an association. The members of the association are said to be (i) all the persons who are members of the local constituency

---

[70] (1983) 133 NLJ 87 (C.T. Emery); [1983] Conv 150 (P. Creighton); [1987] Conv 415 (P.St.J. Smart).
[71] And so chargeable to corporation tax as an 'unincorporated association' within the meaning of ICTA 1970, s. 526 (5).

associations (which local associations are themselves unincorporated associations) and (ii) the members of both Houses of Parliament who accept the Conservative Party whip. The contract which is alleged to bind together the members of this unincorporated association known as the Conservative Party is said to consist of the rules forming the constitution of the National Union of Conservative and Unionist Associations, the rules regulating 'party meetings' at which the candidate chosen by the Parliamentary Conservative Party as leader of the party is presented for election as party leader and the rules forming the respective constitutions of the local constituency associations. I agree, for the reasons given by Lawton LJ, that no such overall unincorporated association exists.[72]

Before, however, that conclusion is accepted, I think that a critical observer is entitled to ask the question what, on that hypothesis, would be the legal relationship between a contributor to Central Office funds and the recipient of the contributions so made.

Strictly speaking, this court does not have to answer that question; it has only to decide the issue whether the Special Commissioners were entitled to find that the Conservative Party is an unincorporated association. But, if no realistic legal explanation of the relationship is forthcoming except the existence of an unincorporated association, one might justifiably begin to entertain doubts as to the credibility of the hypothesis on which the question is asked. I will therefore attempt an answer.

If the Conservative Party is rightly described as an unincorporated association with an identifiable membership bound together by identifiable rules, and Central Office funds are funds of the Conservative Party, no problem arises. In that event, decided cases say that the contribution takes effect in favour of the members of the unincorporated association known as the Conservative Party as an accretion to the funds which are the subject matter of the contract which such members have made *inter se*: see, for example, *Re Recher's Will Trusts* [1972] Ch 526 [p. 386, above]. If, however, the Conservative Party is not an unincorporated association, that easy answer is not available.

I will consider the hypothesis by stages. No legal problem arises if a contributor (as I will call him) hands to a friend (whom I will call the recipient) a sum of money to be applied by the recipient for political purposes indicated by the contributor, or to be chosen at the discretion of the recipient. That would be a simple case of mandate or agency. The recipient would have authority from the contributor to make use of the money, in the indicated way. So far as the money is used within the scope of the mandate, the recipient discharges himself *vis-à-vis* the contributor. The contributor can at any time demand the return of his money so far as not spent, unless the mandate is irrevocable, as it might be or become in certain circumstances. But once the money is spent, the contributor can demand nothing back, only an account of the manner of expenditure. No trust arises, except the fiduciary relationship inherent in the relationship of principal and agent. If, however, the recipient were to apply the money for some purpose outside the scope of the mandate, clearly the recipient would not be discharged. The recipient could be restrained, like any other agent, from a threatened misapplication of the money entrusted to him, and like any other agent could be required to replace any money misapplied.

The next stage is to suppose that the recipient is the treasurer of an organisation which receives and applies funds from multifarious sources for certain political purposes. If the contributor pays money to that treasurer, the treasurer has clear authority to add the contribution to the mixed fund (as I will call it) that he holds. At that stage I think the mandate becomes

---

[72] See p. 378, above.

irrevocable. That is to say, the contributor has no right to demand his contribution back, once it has been mixed with other money under the authority of the contributor. The contributor has no legal right to require the mixed fund to be unscrambled for his benefit. This does not mean, however, that all contributors lose all rights once their cheques are cashed, with the absurd result that the treasurer or other officers can run off with the mixed fund with impunity. I have no doubt that any contributor has a remedy against the recipient (i.e. the treasurer, or the officials at whose direction the treasurer acts) to restrain or make good a misapplication of the mixed fund *except* so far as it may appear on ordinary accounting principles that the plaintiff's own contribution was spent before the threatened or actual misapplication. In the latter event the mandate given by the contributor will not have been breached. A complaining contributor might encounter problems under the law of contract after a change of the office holder to whom his mandate was originally given. Perhaps only the original recipient can be sued for the malpractices of his successors. It is not necessary to explore such procedural intricacies.

So in the present case it seems to me that the status of a contribution to the Conservative Party central funds is this. The contributor draws a cheque (for example) in favour of, or hands it to, the treasurers. The treasurers are impliedly authorised by the contributor to present the cheque for encashment and to add the contribution to Central Office funds. Central Office funds are the subject matter of a mandate which permits them to be used for the purposes of the Conservative Party as directed by the leader of the party. The contributor cannot demand his money back once it has been added to Central Office funds. He could object if Central Office funds were used or threatened to be used otherwise than in accordance with their declared purposes, unless it is correct to say, on ordinary accounting principles, that his contribution has already passed out of Central Office funds.

This discussion of mandates, and complaining contributors, is all very remote and theoretical. No contributor to Central Office funds will view his contribution in this way, or contemplate even the remotest prospect of legal action on his part. He believes he is making an out-and-out contribution or gift to a political party. And so he is in practical terms. The only justification for embarking on a close analysis of the situation is the challenge, which was thrown down by counsel for the Crown in opening, to suggest any legal framework which fits the undoubted fact that funds are held by the Central Office and are administered for the use and benefit of the Conservative Party, except the supposition that the Conservative Party is an unincorporated association.

I see no legal difficulty in the mandate theory. It is not necessary to invent an unincorporated association in order to explain the situation. The only problem which might arise in practice under the mandate theory would be the case of an attempted bequest to Central Office funds, or to the treasurers thereof, or to the Conservative Party, since no agency could be set up at the moment of death between a testator and his chosen agent. A discussion of this problem is outside the scope of this appeal and, although I think that the answer is not difficult to find, I do not wish to prejudge it.

I would dismiss the appeal.

Compare the analysis given by VINELOTT J at first instance [1980] 3 All ER 42 at 62:[73]

It appears to me that if someone invites subscriptions on the representation that he will use the fund subscribed for a particular purpose, he undertakes to use the fund for that purpose and for

---

[73] The CA judgments, although affirming the decision, do not refer to this analysis.

no other and to keep the subscribed fund and any accretions to it (including any income earned by investing the fund pending its application in pursuance of the stated purpose) separate from his own moneys. I can see no reason why if the purpose is sufficiently well defined, and if the order would not necessitate constant and possibly ineffective supervision by the court, the court should not make an order directing him to apply the subscribed fund and any accretions to it for the stated purpose... Apart from the possible remedy of specific performance I can see no reason why the court should not restrain the recipient of such a fund from applying it (or any accretions to it such as income of investments made with it) otherwise than in pursuance of the stated purpose. If that is so, then it appears to me that the recipient of the fund is clearly not the beneficial owner of it and that the income of it is not part of his total income for tax purposes. Equally, whilst the purpose remains unperformed and capable of performance the subscribers are clearly not the beneficial owners of the fund or of the income (if any) derived from it. If the stated purpose proves impossible to achieve or if there is any surplus remaining after it has been accomplished there will be an implied obligation to return the fund and any accretions thereto to the subscribers in proportion to their original contributions, save that a proportion of the fund representing subscriptions made anonymously or in circumstances in which the subscribers receive some benefit (for instance, by subscription to a whist drive or raffle) might then devolve as *bona vacantia*... A testamentary gift to a named society which is not an incorporated body must fail unless it can be construed as a gift to the members of an unincorporated association either as joint tenants or as an accretion to the funds of the association to be applied in accordance with its rules (commonly with a view to the furtherance of its objects). But in the case of a testamentary gift there is no room for the implication of any contract between the testator and the persons who are to receive the bequest. In the case of an *inter vivos* subscription the intention of the subscriber can be given effect by the implication of contractual undertakings of the kind I have described. On further consideration that seems to me to be the proper explanation of the status of the subscriptions made by members of the Chertsey and Walton Constituency Labour Party on which I made some observations in *Re Grant's Will Trusts* [1980] 1 WLR 360 [p. 392, above]. The right of subscribers to the return of their subscriptions so far as not used for the purposes for which they were subscribed rests on an implied contractual term and not on a resulting trust.

[1983] Conv 150, 154 (P. Creighton)

It remains to be considered whether and how the mandate analysis is likely to be utilised in the future. For example, should a gift to an unincorporated association be construed as creating in the members a mandate to apply the property for the association's purposes? Brightman LJ would evidently discourage such a development, preferring the solution he pioneered in *Re Recher*. But what of cases like *Re Gillingham* [1959] Ch 62 [p. 221, above], or *Re Denley* [1969] 1 Ch 373 [p. 375, above], where property was donated for particular purposes, quite independent of any association? In principle, whether the recipient is a trustee or agent depends upon the intention of the donor. So, for example, if the terms of the gift describe the recipient as a trustee, or title to land is vested in his name (as in *Re Denley*), then the likely inference is that a trust is intended. But in circumstances where the donor's precise intention is not evident, a court will have some flexibility in determining which analysis to apply. It would still seem preferable to treat the recipients as trustees for the relevant purpose, provided that such a trust would not be void. Where that construction would only lead to invalidating the gift, it might be possible to salvage the disposition by treating it as a power. But where the donor's intention appears obligatory rather than merely permissive, excluding the possibility of a mere power, *Re Endacott* [1960] Ch 232 [p. 362, above], it might then be appropriate to resort to the mandate analysis, at least where the gift was made *inter vivos*. A valid agency might be spelled out to allow funds to be applied towards a purpose where a trust for that purpose would have failed. To the extent that it prevents the initial invalidity of such a gift, the mandate concept might be considered a useful alternative to the purpose trust. But consideration of the limited scope of its possible application, and the measure of control over the funds that it permits, suggests that it cannot provide a general framework for explaining gifts for non-charitable purposes. Indeed, as an explanation, it seems scarcely adequate to save the Conservative Party from corporation tax.[74]

> ## QUESTION
>
> Take as an example any club that you know; or of which you are a member. Then consider who is the legal owner of the land or premises occupied by the club, of any investments held, and of its current bank account. Could each member claim a share now? On the ground that he is a beneficial owner? Or on a basis of a contract? Could each member claim a share of the assets on a dissolution? If so, on what basis? See p. 223, above.

VI   HOW TO ACHIEVE A NON-CHARITABLE PURPOSE

A   BY INCORPORATION

Report of the Goodman Committee on Charity Law and Voluntary Organisations 1976, para. 24

Purpose Trusts

24. The point made about those trusts whose purposes are held not to be charitable because they fail on grounds of legal uncertainty is one of substance. The legal argument is that these trusts fail because the beneficiaries are a fluctuating class and therefore uncertain, or because their objects are uncertain. This can in fact be obviated by careful drafting through the medium of a company. A simple and common course is to form a company limited by guarantee with

---

[74] And for the possible use of the mandate analysis in *Universe Tankships Inc of Monrovia v International Transport Workers Federation* [1983] 1 AC 366 [p. 388, n. 66, above], see (1983) 133 NLJ 515 (J. McMullen and A. Grubb). See also *Roche v Sherrington* [1982] 1 WLR 599, where Slade J held that a special fiduciary relationship could in principle exist between a contributing member of an unincorporated association and the recipient members for the time being at the date of a transaction challenged on the ground of undue influence (Opus Dei).

the desired non-charitable objects and this will be perfectly valid. The long-standing invalidity of non-charitable purpose trusts now serves as a trap for the unwary and has led to much litigation. A will which provides money for the fulfilment of a purpose the testator has in mind may be attacked by disappointed beneficiaries on the grounds that the gift is void. The question before the court is whether the declared purpose is charitable, or whether the testator has declared a charitable intent. If so, the gift is valid but, if not, void. This involves the trustees in much expense and if the gift is held invalid, the clearly stated intentions of the testator will have been defeated. Since the testator's object could have been achieved by adopting a different technique, there seems no purpose in maintaining the rule as it stands. Accordingly, our recommendation is that further consideration be given by government to the validation of such 'purpose trusts'.[75]

B   BY LEGISLATION

ONTARIO PERPETUITIES ACT 1966[76]

16. Specific non-charitable trusts

(1) A trust for a specific non-charitable purpose that creates no enforceable equitable interest in a specific person shall be construed as a power to appoint the income or the capital, as the case may be, and, unless the trust is created for an illegal purpose or a purpose contrary to public policy, the trust is valid so long as and to the extent that it is exercised either by the original trustee or his successor, within a period of twenty-one years, notwithstanding that the limitation creating the trust manifested an intention, either expressly or by implication, that the trust should or might continue for a period in excess of that period, but, in the case of such a trust that is expressed to be of perpetual duration, the court may declare the limitation to be void if the court is of opinion that by so doing the result would more closely approximate the intention of the creator of the trust than the period of validity provided by this section.

(2) To the extent that the income or capital of a trust for a specific non-charitable purpose is not fully expended within a period of twenty-one years, or within any annual or other recurring period within which the limitation creating the trust provided for the expenditure of all or a specified portion of the income or the capital, the person or persons, or his or their successors, who would have been entitled to the property comprised in the trust if the trust had been invalid from the time of its creation, are entitled to such unexpended income or capital.[77]

---

[75] Baxendale-Walker, *Purpose Trusts*, p. 223 does not consider that incorporation is an effective alternative to a purpose trust.

[76] See [1967] *Annual Survey of Commonwealth Law*, pp. 378–380 (J.D. Davies).

[77] See also New Zealand Perpetuities Act 1964, s.20, see p. 371, above; Belize Trusts Act 1992.

C CONSTRUE OR DRAFT AS A POWER

American Law Institute: *Restatement of the Law of Trusts* (2d) (1959) §124

Where the owner of property transfers it in trust for a specific non-charitable purpose, and there is no definite or definitely ascertainable beneficiary designated, no enforceable trust is created; but the transferee has power to apply the property to the designated purpose, unless such application is authorized or directed to be made beyond the period of the rule against perpetuities, or the purpose is capricious.

Although the courts have ruled[78] that 'a valid power is not to be spelt out of an invalid trust', there appears to be no objection to drafting the purpose as a power instead of as a trust, i.e. by giving the property not to a trustee upon trust, but to the ultimate beneficiary subject to a power in a third party to apply the property for the non-charitable purpose for the perpetuity period.

Morris and Leach: *Rule Against Perpetuities* (2nd edn, 1962), p. 320

No case decides that a power to apply property towards a specific non-charitable purpose must be treated as void. Such authority as exists suggests that it may well be valid. It is now clear that the law recognises the validity of powers of appointment which cannot be described as either general or special powers. Moreover, a power to appoint to such charitable institutions (including two named unincorporated associations) as the donee should nominate has been upheld, notwithstanding that the two named institutions were not charitable.[79] It is not a long step from this to hold that a power to appoint for a specific non-charitable purpose is valid, even though a trust for such a purpose is void . . . It may well be, therefore, that if testators or settlors express their wishes in the form of a power and not in the form of a trust, they may be able to accomplish their non-charitable purposes. No question of enforcement would arise, for to the extent that the power was not exercised, there would be a resulting trust for the persons entitled in default of appointment. Of course the power, being more analogous to a special than to a general power of appointment, would have to be exercisable only within the limits of perpetuity. But subject to this, the only question would be one of policy. It is not desirable that eccentric or vainglorious testators should be allowed to give large sums of money for the purpose of erecting costly monuments to themselves or to seal up their houses for 20 years or to order their property to be thrown into the sea. But is there anything contrary to public policy in permitting testators to indulge such human desires as to bequeath a moderate sum of money for the maintenance of their pet animals or the repair of their graves within the period of perpetuities? The present authors conclude that there is not.

---

[78] *IRC v Broadway Cottages Trust* [1955] Ch 20, *per* Jenkins LJ. See also *Re Shaw* [1957] 1 WLR 729 at 746 [p. 364, above], where Harman J followed the Court of Appeal with apparent reluctance; Scott, *Trusts* §§ 124 where this question is asked: 'should the failure of the duty drag down with it the power?'

[79] *Re Douglas* (1887) 35 Ch D 472; (1902) 15 *Harvard Law Review* 67 (J.C. Gray); (1958) 4 *University of Western Australia Law Review* 235 at p. 260 (L.A. Sheridan).

D DRAFT AS A GIFT TO A GROUP OF PERSONS, SUCH AS AN UNINCORPORATED ASSOCIATION, AND NOT FOR PURPOSES ONLY

Re Recher's Will Trusts [1972] Ch 526 [p. 386, above].
Re Denley's Trust Deed [1969] 1 Ch 373 [p. 375, above].
Re Lipinski's Will Trusts [1976] Ch 235 [p. 372, above].

E CONVEYANCING DEVICE

If there is a gift to one charity followed by a gift over to another charity upon an event which might happen outside the perpetuity period, the gift over to the second charity is valid. Advantage was taken of this rule to achieve a non-charitable purpose in *Re Tyler*.[80]

Re Tyler
[1891] 3 Ch 252 (CA, **Lindley, Fry** and **Lopes LJJ**)

Sir James Tyler, who died in 1890, bequeathed £42,000 Russian 5 per cent stock to the trustees of the London Missionary Society and committed to their care and charge the keys of his family vault at Highgate Cemetery 'the same to be kept in good repair, and name legible, and to rebuild when it shall require: failing to comply with this request, the money to go to the Blue Coat School, Newgate Street, London'.

Held. The gift and gift over were valid.

Fry LJ: In this case the testator has given a sum of money to one charity with a gift over to another charity upon the happening of a certain event. That event, no doubt, is such as to create an inducement or motive on the part of the first donee, the *London Missionary Society,* to repair the family tomb of the testator. Inasmuch as both the donees of this fund, the first donee and the second, are charitable bodies, and are created for the purposes of charity, the rule of law against perpetuities has nothing whatever to do with the donees. Does the rule of law against perpetuities create any objection to the nature of the condition? If the testator had required the first donee, the *London Missionary Society,* to apply any portions of the fund towards the repair of the family tomb, that would, in all probability, at any rate, to the extent of the sum required, have been void as a perpetuity which was not charity. But he has done nothing of the sort. He has given the first donee no power to apply any part of the money. He has only created a condition that the sum shall go over to *Christ's Hospital* if the *London Missionary Society* do not keep the tomb in repair. Keeping the tomb in repair is not an illegal object. If it were, the condition tending to bring about an illegal act would itself be illegal; but to repair the tomb is a perfectly lawful thing. All that can be said is that it is not lawful to tie up property for that purpose. But the rule of law against perpetuities applies to property, not motives; and I know of no rule which

---

[80] See also [1987] Conv 415 (P.St. J. Smart).

says that you may not try to enforce a condition creating a perpetual inducement to do a thing which is lawful. That is this case.

Then it is said by Mr. *Buckley*, 'but if the gift had been to the *London Missionary Society* simply, they might have spent the money; by imposing this condition you require them to keep that invested, because it may have to go over at any moment to *Christ's Hospital.*' What is the harm of that? Being a charity, and not affected by the rule against perpetuities, whether you direct them to keep the money invested in plain words, or whether you impose the condition which renders it necessary to keep it invested, seems to me the same thing and to be equally harmless, and not affected by the law against perpetuities.

I think the learned Judge in the Court below was quite right, and that this appeal must be dismissed.

In **Re Dalziel** [1943] Ch 277, a testatrix gave £20,000 to the governors of St. Bartholomew's Hospital 'subject to the condition that they shall use the income' for the upkeep and repair of the mausoleum and surrounding garden in Highgate Cemetery, with a gift over to another charity 'subject to the above conditions' if they failed to do so.

COHEN J held that both the gift and the gift over were void, and said at 282:

Lady Dalziel has not only given power, but directed the trustees to apply part of this gift or, if necessary, the whole of this gift in the maintenance of the tomb.

F   CREATE AN OFFSHORE TRUST[81]

To attract trust business a number of overseas jurisdictions have enacted statutes which provide for the possibility of creating non-charitable purpose trusts.[82] Such provision is becoming particularly important for international trust planning.

P. Matthews in *Trends in Contemporary Trust Law* (ed. A.J. Oakley) (1996), pp. 19, 23–24, 31

The characteristic of the true non-charitable purpose trust is that it has no beneficiaries. This means that the beneficial ownership is not in the trustees—it is after all a trust, not for their benefit—and there is no one else in whom it can be located. So—it is said—the property the subject of the trust cannot, in strict law, be said to belong beneficially to *anyone*. Now there are many estate-planning exercises and commercial transactions that can make good use of this phenomenon....

A curiosity is that non-charitable-purpose trust legislation in general has not purported to answer explicitly the question where the 'beneficial' ownership of the trust property lies.

[81] H&M, pp. 394–395; T&H, pp. 1239–1289; Baxendale-Walker, *Purpose Trusts*, Part II; P. Matthews in *Trends in Contemporary Trust Law* (ed. A.J. Oakley), pp. 18–31.

[82] For example: Bermuda (Trusts (Special Provisions) Act 1989, as amended by the Trusts (Special Provisions) Amendment Act 1998), British Virgin Islands (Trustee (Amendment) Act 1993, as amended by the Trustee (Amendment) Act 2003), Cyprus (International Trusts Law 1992, s. 7(3)), Isle of Man (Purposes Trusts Act 1996) and Jersey (Trusts (Jersey) Law 1984, as amended).

But—safety in numbers—it has tended to follow a certain model. There are five main features, although it must be emphasized that not every example of such legislation makes provision for each of these features.

The five features are as follows:

1. Restrictions on the purposes for which the trust can be established; typically the legislation says that the purposes must be both *workable,* i.e. specific or certain and possible to carry out, and *beneficial,* i.e. not immoral or contrary to public policy.

2. Enforcement mechanism: typically there must be a person whose job it is to keep an eye on the trust and to enforce it. For this purpose he will have rights to information about the trust. He may be called the 'enforcer' or the 'protector', or something else, but he will have certain obligations to blow the whistle, apply to the Court, or notify an official (typically the Attorney-General) if he thinks something wrong is going on, or if there is no enforcer in office. Sometimes these duties are backed up by criminal sanctions.[83]

3. Restrictions on the trustees: it is common to provide that at least one of the trustees must be resident in the jurisdiction concerned, and/or must be a professionally qualified person or body, for example a lawyer or accountant. Also, usually a trustee may not be the enforcer.

4. Restrictions on the trust property: often such trusts are not allowed to own land in the jurisdiction concerned.

5. Duration and termination of the trust: most of the jurisdictions have perpetuity periods or maximum duration periods, and provision for what is to happen to the property at the determination of the trust...

We must see trusts—and the purpose trust in particular—in this light. It is a product, serving a commercial need. To some extent, like all law and legal institutions, it is a conjuring trick. It is a way of making another legal institution—ownership—disappear, or half-disappear. First it is refracted into legal ownership and beneficial enjoyment, and then beneficial enjoyment seems to dissolve into thin air.

There is nothing wrong in any of this, provided that we understand what we are doing, and that we are doing it deliberately. Unlike the laws of physics, the laws of man are fully mutable. But what we must *not* do—and we are in danger of doing it—is to misunderstand and to misuse a doctrine, to think we have achieved an object when we have not. The statutory purpose trust is, or can be, a good thing. But it is not the entirely autonomous vehicle that its promoters think. It is not the Holy Grail. There are obligations—no one doubts that—but also there are rights. If the trust has background beneficiaries, like *Re Denley*[84] then *they* have rights. If the trust is a sham, then again there will be real beneficiaries, able to exercise rights and—more seriously— saddled with the beneficial ownership. Even if—and it is a big if—it is a genuine, substantive purpose statutory non-charitable-purpose trust, the enforcer has rights. If there is a trust, there is a benefit. And, like the *damnosa hereditas* of the classical Roman law, the question can still be asked, to whom does it belong in the end?

---

[83] See generally D.W.M. Waters in *Trends in Contemporary Trust Law* (ed. A.J. Oakley), pp. 63–122.

[84] [1969] 1 Ch 373 [p. 375, above].

CAYMAN ISLANDS SPECIAL TRUSTS (ALTERNATIVE REGIME) LAW 1997[85]

2. (1) In this Law, unless the context otherwise requires—

'beneficiary' means a person who will or may derive a benefit or advantage, directly or indirectly, from the execution of a special trust;

'enforcer' means a person who has standing to enforce a special trust;

'ordinary', in reference to a trust or power, signifies that it is a trust or power which is not subject to this Law;

'power' includes an administrative power as well as a dispositive power;

'special', in reference to a trust or power, signifies that it is a trust or power which is subject to this Law;

'standing to enforce' means the right or duty to bring an enforcement of a special trust; and

'trust' includes a trust of a power, as well as a trust of property, and 'trustee' has a correspondingly extended meaning.

3. (1) A trust or power is subject to this Law, and is described as special, if—

(a) it is created by or on the terms of a written instrument, testamentary or inter vivos; and

(b) the instrument contains a declaration to the effect that this Law is to apply.

(2) If a trust or power is created by written instrument in exercise of a special power, and the instrument contains no declaration as to the application of this Law, this Law shall, subject to evidence of a contrary intention, be deemed to be intended to apply; and for the purpose of subsection (1) the instrument shall be deemed to contain a declaration to that effect.

(3) A trust or power which does not meet the requirements of subsection (1), and is not deemed to do so by virtue of subsection (2), is an ordinary trust or power and is not subject to this Law.

4. Nothing in this Law affects an ordinary trust or power directly or by inference.

5. The law relating to special trusts and powers is the same in every respect as the law relating to ordinary trusts and powers, save as provided in this Law.

6. (1) The objects of a special trust or power may be persons[86] or purposes or both.

(2) The persons may be of any number.

(3) The purposes may be of any number or kind, charitable or non-charitable, provided that they are lawful and not contrary to public policy.

---

[85] See (1998) 12 *Trust Law International* 107 for full text. Commentary: (1997) 11 *Trust Law International* 67 (P. Matthews); (1998) 12 *Trust Law International* 16 (A. Duckworth); (1998) 12 *Trust Law International* 98 (P. Matthews).   [86] The inclusion of a trust for persons is unusual in the offshore trust business.

7. (1) A beneficiary of a special trust does not as such have standing to enforce the trust, or an enforceable right against a trustee or an enforcer, or an enforceable right to the trust property.

   (2) The only persons who have standing to enforce a special trust are such persons, whether or not beneficiaries, as are appointed to be enforcers—

   (a) by or pursuant to the terms of the trust; or

   (b) by order of the court.

   (3) A right or a duty to enforce a trust is presumed, subject to evidence of a contrary intention, to extend to every trust which is created by or on the terms of the same instrument, or pursuant to a power so created.

8. (1) Standing to enforce a special trust may be granted or reserved as a right or as a duty.

   (2) Subject to evidence of a contrary intention, an enforcer is deemed to have a fiduciary duty to act responsibly with a view to the proper execution of the trust.

   (3) A trustee or another enforcer, or any person expressly authorised by the terms of the special trust has standing to bring an action for the enforcement of the duty (if any) of an enforcer.

9. Subject to the terms of his appointment—

   (a) an enforcer has the same rights as a beneficiary of an ordinary trust

   (i) to bring administrative and other actions, and make applications to the court concerning the trust; and

   (ii) to be informed of the terms of the trust, to receive information concerning the trust and its administration from the trustee, and to inspect and take copies of trust documents;

   (b) in the performance of his duties, if any, an enforcer has the rights of a trustee of an ordinary trust to protection and indemnity and to make applications to the court for an opinion, advice or direction or for relief from personal liability; and

   (c) in the event of a breach of trust an enforcer has, on behalf of the trust, the same personal and proprietary remedies against the trustee and against third parties as a beneficiary of an ordinary trust.

10. (1) Subject to subsection (4), a special trust is not rendered void by uncertainty as to its objects or mode of execution.

   (2) The terms of a special trust may give the trustee or any other person power to resolve an uncertainty as to its objects or mode of execution.

   (3) If a special trust has multiple objects and there is no allocation of the trust property between them, the trustee, subject to evidence of contrary intention, has discretion to allocate the trust property.

(4) If an uncertainty as to the objects or mode of execution of a special trust cannot be resolved, or has not been resolved pursuant to the terms of the trust, the court—

    (a) may resolve the uncertainty—

        (i) by reforming the trust;

        (ii) by settling a plan for its administration; or

        (iii) in any other way which the court deems appropriate; or

    (b) insofar as the objects of the trust are uncertain and the general intent of the trust cannot be found from the admissible evidence as a matter of probability, may declare the trust void.

(5) This section applies to powers as to trusts.

11. (1) If the execution of a special trust in accordance with its terms is or becomes in whole or in part—

    (a) impossible or impracticable;

    (b) unlawful or contrary to public policy; or

    (c) obsolete in that, by reason of changed circumstances, it fails to achieve the general intent of the special trust,

the trustee shall, unless the trust is reformed pursuant to its own terms, apply to the court to reform the trust *cy-près* or, if or insofar as the court is of the opinion that it cannot be reformed consistently with the general intent of the trust, the trustees shall dispose of the trust property, as though the trust or the relevant part of it has failed.

QUESTIONS

1. What would you say of the following purpose in *Re Astor's Settlement Trusts* [1952] Ch 534: '7. The establishment...or support of any charitable public or benevolent schemes...for or in connection with (a) the improvement of newspapers or journalism or (b) the relief or benefit of persons (or the families or dependants of persons) actually or formerly engaged in journalism or in the newspaper business'? See p. 426, below on charitable purposes.

2. Consider *Oppenheim v Tobacco Securities Trust Co Ltd* [1951] AC 297 [p. 455, below]. Must such a gift be void, whether as a charitable or a non-charitable purpose trust?

3. Assuming that purpose trusts are enforceable upon one theory or another, do you consider that it will be necessary to determine a dividing line between those which are useful to the public and those which are useless or harmful? How would you draw such a line? Is the theory of *Brown v Burdett* (1882) 21 Ch D 667 [p. 377, above], adequate? Before finally reaching a conclusion on this, read the material on the definition of legal charity [p. 426, below], and observe the difficulties that have been experienced in drawing a line

between 'charitable purposes' and 'useful' or 'benevolent purposes'. Royal Commission on the Taxation of Profits and Income, paras. 168–175 (1955) Cmd 9474; (1956) 72 LQR 187 (G. Cross); *Dingle v Turner* [1972] AC 601 [p. 432, below], *per* Lord Cross of Chelsea.

4. Consider the perpetuity problem raised in *Re Dean* (1889) 41 Ch D 552 [p. 366, above]. How would this be affected by the Perpetuities and Accumulations Act 1964? Morris and Leach, p. 322; *Re Kelly* [1932] IR 255; *Re Searight's Estate*, 95 NE 2d 779, 87 Ohio App 417 (1950); Scott, *Cases on Trusts* (5th edn), p. 351; H&M, pp. 367–368, 380–383; Maudsley, *Modern Law of Perpetuities*, (1979) pp. 166–178.

5. Consider the Cayman Islands Special Trusts (Alternative Regime) Law 1997 [p. 405, above]. Can the special trust which is recognised by that law be properly characterised as a trust? Does it matter? Compare (1997) 11 *Trust Law International* 67 (P. Matthews) and (1998) 12 *Trust Law International* 98 (P. Matthews) with (1998) 12 *Trust Law International* 16 (A. Duckworth).

6. Should we adopt a statutory scheme in this country to recognise and enforce purpose trusts? See [2007] Conv 148 (J. Brown); [2007] Conv 440 (M. Pawlowski and J. Summers).

10

CHARITABLE TRUSTS: CHARACTERISTICS AND PURPOSES[1]

---

[1] H&M, pp. 397–476; P&M, pp. 442–502; P&S pp. 479–547; Pettit pp. 240–346; Snell pp. 511–542; Hill, Smith and Holmes *The Charities Act 2006*; Maclennan, *Blackstone's Guide to the Charities Act 2006*; Current Law Statutes Annotated, Charities Act 2006 (A. and P. Kenny). See generally *Tudor on Charities* (9th edn, 2003); Cairns, *Charities: Law and Practice* (3rd edn, 1997); Luxton, *The Law of Charities* (2001); Picarda, *The Law and Practice Relating to Charities* (3rd edn, 1999); Chesterman, *Charities, Trusts and Social Welfare* (1979); Gladstone, *Charity Law and Social Justice* (1982). See also the Annual Reports of the Charity Commission for England and Wales (formerly of the Charity Commissioners); the Decisions of the Charity Commission (which began in 1993) and its Publications; the Annual Charity and Appeals Supplements of the Solicitor's Journal and the Annual Charities Review and Christmas Appeals Supplements of the New Law Journal; and the *Charity Law & Practice Review* (which began in 1992). For information about the Charity Commission and details of Commission publications including recent decisions of the Charity Commission, see the website: <http://www.charity-commission.gov.uk/>.

For important reviews of the law and practice, *Charities: A Framework for the Future* (1989) Cm 694 (White Paper by the Secretary of State for the Home Department); *Meeting the Challenge of Change: Voluntary*

I THE ESSENTIAL CHARACTERISTICS
OF A CHARITY

A trust which provides that income is to be applied exclusively for charitable purposes is treated with special favour by the law. Charitable trusts operate in a very different legal, fiscal, and social context to family and commercial trusts.[2] Such a trust is valid, even though it is a purpose trust. The Attorney-General is charged with the duty of enforcing it in the name of the Crown, although the general administration of charitable trusts is carried out by the Charity Commission.[3] Charitable purposes can be satisfied without resorting to a trust device. So, for example, it is possible to incorporate a charitable corporation or to use the devices of an unincorporated association, a friendly society or an industrial or provident society.[4] There are 190,000 charities registered with the Charity Commission, which have an annual income of £36 billion, almost 600,000 paid staff, and 900,000 trustees.[5]

The essential features of a charity were recognised by MUMMERY LJ in **Gaudiya Mission v Brahmachary** [1998] Ch 341 at 350:

Under English law charity has always received special treatment. It often takes the form of a trust; but it is a public trust for the promotion of purposes beneficial to the community, not a trust for private individuals. It is therefore subject to special rules governing registration, administration, taxation and duration. Although not a state institution, a charity is subject to the constitutional protection of the Crown as *parens patriae,* acting through the Attorney-General, to the state supervision of the Charity Commissioners and to the judicial supervision of the High Court. This regime applies whether the charity takes the form of a trust or of an incorporated body.

The key characteristics of a charity were also identified by MUMMERY LJ at 349:

A charity does not have to take any particular legal form; it may be a trust or an undertaking; it may be incorporated or unincorporated. But it must satisfy both requirements for the definition in section 96(1).[6] It must be 'established for charitable purposes'. It will be noted that 'charitable purposes' is a defined term, meaning those 'purposes which are exclusively charitable according to the law of England and Wales'; and it must be 'subject

---

Action into the 21st Century (The Deakin Report) (1996) (Report of the Commission on the Future of the Voluntary Sector). On the history of charity, see Jones, *History of the Law of Charity* (1969). See also (1979) 38 CLJ 118 (C. Rickett).

  [2] [1999] 63 Conv 20, 21–22 (J. Warburton). See also Luxton, pp. 16–17.

  [3] Charities Act 1993, s.1A, as inserted by Charities Act 2006, s. 6 [p. 580, below].

  [4] The Charities Act 2006, s. 34 and Sched. 7 creates a separate form of incorporation specifically for charities which is called a 'Charitable Incorporated Organisation'.

  [5] Charity Commission *Consultation on Draft Public Benefit Guidance* (February 2007).

  [6] Charities Act 1993. See now Charities Act 2006, p. 415 below.

to the control of the High Court in the exercise of the court's jurisdiction with respect to charities'.

A charitable trust has a number of advantages over other types of express trust.[7]

1. Such a trust may exist perpetually;[8] indeed, some charitable trusts currently in existence were founded some 500 years ago.

2. It is no objection that the trust fails to provide with reasonable certainty what are the charitable purposes for which the money must be applied; certainty of intention to apply it for charitable purposes is sufficient, but the purposes must be wholly and exclusively charitable.[9] If there is doubt as to the particular charitable purposes, the Charity Commissioners, or the court, or in some cases the Crown, will prepare a scheme.

3. There are numerous fiscal advantages for charities and donors.[10] The more significant these advantages become, the more insistent is the Revenue in challenging particular claims to relief.

There are also disadvantages which arise from charitable status such as restrictions on permitted activities and application of funds.[11] Sometimes the balance of advantage and disadvantage is a fine one, meaning that an institution may determine that it does not wish to avail itself of charitable status.[12]

The attitude of the courts to gifts for charitable purposes has varied. In 1908, LORD LOREBURN said: 'Now there is no better rule than that a benignant construction will be placed upon charitable bequests.'[13] But since the 1940s, when taxation became punitive, the courts have been astute in restricting the scope of charity, especially by emphasising the requirement of public benefit.[14] In 1982, however, LORD HAILSHAM OF ST. MARYLEBONE referred to Lord Loreburn's dictum and said 'in construing trust

---

[7] Luxton, pp. 61–72.

[8] Although such trusts are subject to the rule against remoteness of vesting: *Re Lord Stratheden and Campbell* [1894] 3 Ch 265. See p. 110, above. See also *The Rules Against Perpetuities and Excessive Accumulations*, Law Com No. 251 (1998), para. 10.21.

[9] See p. 536, below. *Gibbs v Harding* [2007] EWHC 3 (Ch); [2008] 2 WLR 361.

[10] For a review and criticism of fiscal advantages, see Goodman Committee, chap. 5; [1972] BTR 346 (G.N. Glover); [1989] Conv 28, 37–38, (S. Bright); (1999) 62 MLR 333, 336–343 (M. Chesterman). See generally Tudor, chap. 8; Picarda, chaps. 49 and 50 and Luxton, chap. 3.

[11] See p. 521, below.

[12] See *IRC v Oldham Training and Enterprise Council* [1996] STC 1218, 1230 (Lightman J). See also (1999) LS 380, 394 (I. McLean and M. Johnes).

[13] *Weir v Crum-Brown* [1908] AC 162 at 167.

[14] The Royal Commission on the Taxation of Profits and Income (1955) Cmnd. 9474, recommended (paras. 168–175) that some charitable trusts should be subject to tax liability, and others, measured by a stricter definition, should be entitled to the present exemptions. See the different views expressed in the House of Lords on this question in *Dingle v Turner* [1972] AC 601, p. 432 below. A major review of charity taxation was undertaken in 1997 which resulted in the publication of 'Review of Charity Taxation: Consultation Document' in 1999 and this provided the foundation for a fundamental reform of charity taxation in 2000.

deeds the intention of which is to set up a charitable trust, and in others too, where it can be claimed that there is an ambiguity, a benignant construction should be given if possible'.[15] Similarly, the Government's intention is to encourage the liberality of the donor, and within the present financial restraints, the development of the voluntary sector as a whole.

A study of the material in this Chapter will indicate the many problems which are faced in keeping this area of the law in line with modern developments. Much of the work previously done by voluntary bodies is now undertaken by the Government.[16] It is no small problem to make the law of charity adjust to the pattern of the modern welfare state.

QUESTION

Is it appropriate to consider the law relating to charitable trusts as part of the general law of trusts or are such trusts unique? See [1999] 63 Conv 20 (J. Warburton) and Luxton, pp. 16–17.

II THE DEFINITION OF CHARITY[17]

With so much at stake, one would hope for a precise definition of charity. Instead, the courts have sought a satisfactory one for 400 years. The scope of charity is based upon a large number of decisions, themselves based on the spirit and intentions of the preamble to the Charitable Uses Act 1601. These decisions may be either those of the courts or those of the Charity Commission on an application for registration under the Charities Act 1993.[18] The enactment of the Charities Act 2006 has, however,

---

[15] *IRC v McMullen* [1981] AC 1 at 14 [p. 450, below]; *Re Koeppler Will Trusts* [1986] Ch 423 at 438 [p. 448, below]; *Re Hetherington* [1990] Ch 1 [p. 476, below]; *Guild v IRC* [1992] 2 AC 310 [p. 496, below]. In *IRC v Oldham Training and Enterprise Council* [1996] STC 1218, 1235 Lightman J held that this principle of benignant construction only applies where a gift or provision would be void and fail unless it was held to be charitable.

[16] But note the recent policy of encouraging government and charities to work together. Increasingly this involves charities entering into contracts with public bodies whereby the charity provides a service in exchange for payment. The difficulties which this relationship creates are considered by D. Morris (2000) 20 LS 409. See also Charity Commission, 'Charities and Public Service Delivery' (CC37) (February 2007) and Charity Commission, 'The Independence of Charities from the State' (RR7) (February 2001).

[17] H&M, pp. 405–407; Luxton, pp. 3–16, 111–113; P&M, pp. 448–451; P&S pp. 484–489; Pettit pp. 250–287; Picarda, pp. 3–12; Snell pp. 514–515; Tudor, pp. 1–17. See also (1945) 61 LQR 268 (J. Brunyate); (1956) 72 LQR 187 (G. Cross).

[18] Charities Act 1993, s. 3, as amended by Charities Act 2006, s. 9; p. 583, below.

provided a statutory definition of charity for the first time.[19] The key provisions of that Act came into force in April 2008.

A THE PREAMBLE TO THE CHARITABLE USES ACT 1601

43 Eliz. I, c. 4: The Preamble

WHEREAS Lands, Tenements, Rents, Annuities, Profits, Hereditaments, Goods, Chattels, Money and Stocks of Money, have been heretofore given, limited, appointed and assigned, as well by the Queen's most excellent Majesty, and her most noble Progenitors, as by sundry other well disposed Persons; some for Relief of aged, impotent and poor People, some for Maintenance of sick and maimed Soldiers and Mariners, Schools of Learning, Free Schools, and Scholars in Universities, some for Repair of Bridges, Ports, Havens, Causeways, Churches, Sea-Banks and Highways, some for Education and Preferment of Orphans, some for or towards Relief, Stock or Maintenance for Houses of Correction, some for Marriages of poor Maids, some for Supportation, Aid and Help of young Tradesmen, Handicraftsmen and Persons decayed, and others for Relief or Redemption of Prisoners or Captives, and for Aid or Ease of any poor Inhabitants concerning Payments of Fifteens,[20] setting out of Soldiers and other Taxes; which Lands, Tenements, Rents, Annuities, Profits, Hereditaments, Goods, Chattels, Money and Stocks of Money, nevertheless have not been employed according to the charitable Intent of the givers and Founders thereof, by reason of Frauds, Breaches of Trust, and Negligence in those that should pay, deliver and employ the same: For Redress and Remedy whereof, Be it enacted...

Tudor on Charities (6th edn, 1967) p. 2

The Charitable Uses Act, 1601[21] will usually be referred to in this work as 'the Statute of Elizabeth I'. The Statute of Elizabeth I was not directed so much to the definition of charity as to the correction of abuses which had grown up in the administration of trusts of a charitable nature. But the Court of Chancery used the preamble to the statute in order to simplify its task of determining what purposes were charitable and what were not. The preamble to the statute contained a comprehensive list of objects which in 1601 were recognised as charitable. The court never regarded the list as exhaustive. It treated the objects enumerated in the preamble

---

[19] There had been calls for a statutory definition of charity for many years. See the Report of the Committee on the Law and Practice Relating to Charitable Trusts (the Nathan Committee) (1952, Cmd. 8710), paras. 120–140; the Report for the Commission on the Future of the Voluntary Sector (the Deakin Report) (1996), para. 3.2.6.

[20] A tax on movable property originating in the twelfth century and last heard of in the reign of James I. See I Bl Com. 309; Jowitt, *Dictionary of English Law* (1977) Vol. I, p. 789.　　[21] 43 Eliz. I, c. 4.

as particular instances to which additions might properly be made from time to time. It became the practice of the court to refer to the preamble as a sort of index or chart[22] in order to determine whether or not a given purpose was charitable. That which began as a rule of practice became in course of time a rule of law, and in 1805 Sir William Grant MR was able to declare that 'those purposes are charitable which that Statute enumerates or which by analogies are deemed within its spirit and intendment'.[23] But objects which are neither enumerated in the preamble nor by analogy deemed to be within its spirit and intendment are not charitable, even though such objects are beneficial to the public.[24]

The preamble to 43 Eliz. I, c. 4, was repealed by section 38(1)[25] of the Charities Act 1960; however, for a trust to be charitable, its purposes had to still fall within the spirit and 'intendment' of the preamble.

B   THE FOUR HEADS OF CHARITY

In **Commissioners for Special Purposes of Income Tax v Pemsel** [1891] AC 531, LORD MACNAGHTEN summarised the scope of charity[26] at 583:

No doubt the popular meaning of the words 'charity' and 'charitable' does not coincide with their legal meaning;[27] and no doubt it is easy enough to collect from the books a few decisions which seem to push the doctrine of the court to the extreme, and to present a contrast between the two meanings in an aspect almost ludicrous. But still it is difficult to fix the point of divergence, and no one as yet has succeeded in defining the popular meaning of the word 'charity'.... How far then, it may be asked, does the popular meaning of the word 'charity' correspond with its legal meaning? 'Charity' in its legal sense comprises four principal divisions: trusts for the relief of poverty; trusts for the advancement of education; trusts for the advancement of religion; and trusts for other purposes beneficial to the community, not falling under any of the preceding heads.

In **Scottish Burial Reform and Cremation Society v Glasgow Corpn** [1968] AC 138, LORD WILBERFORCE spoke of the legal test of charitable purposes at 154:

---

[22] *Income Tax Special Purposes Comrs v Pemsel* [1891] AC 531 at 581, *per* Lord Macnaghten.

[23] *Morice v Bishop of Durham* (1804) 9 Ves 399 at 405.

[24] *Gilmour v Coats* [1949] AC 426 at 443, *per* Viscount Simonds; *A-G v National Provincial and Union Bank of England* [1924] AC 262 at 265, *per* Viscount Cave LC; *Houston v Burns* [1918] AC 337; *Re Macduff* [1896] 2 Ch 451 at 466, *per* Lindley LJ; *Dunne v Byrne* [1912] AC 407 at 411, *per* Lord Macnaghten; *Farley v Westminster Bank Ltd* [1939] AC 430. This is only a selection from among the many cases that might have been cited.

[25] Itself repealed as spent by Education Act 1973, Sch. 2, Part I.

[26] The classification originated in the argument of Sir Samuel Romilly in *Morice v Bishop of Durham* (1805) 10 Ves 522 at 523; *Ashfield Municipal Council v Joyce* [1978] AC 122.

[27] 'The words "charity" and "charitable" bear, for the purposes of English law and equity, meanings totally different from the senses in which they are used in ordinary educated speech, or, for instance, in the Authorised Version of the Bible'; *IRC v McMullen* [1981] AC 1 at 15, *per* Lord Hailsham of St. Marylebone.

On this subject, the law of England, though no doubt not very satisfactory and in need of ration-alisation, is tolerably clear. The purposes in question, to be charitable, must be shown to be for the benefit of the public, or the community, in a sense or manner within the intendment of the preamble to the statute 43 Eliz. I, c.4. The latter requirement does not mean quite what it says; for it is now accepted that what must be regarded is not the wording of the preamble itself, but the effect of decisions given by the courts as to its scope, decisions which have endeavoured to keep the law as to charities moving according as new social needs arise or old ones become obso-lete or satisfied. Lord Macnaghten's grouping of the heads of recognised charity in *Pemsel's* case[28] is one that has proved to be of value and there are many problems which it solves. But three things may be said about it, which its author would surely not have denied: first that, since it is a classification of convenience, there may well be purposes which do not fit neatly into one or other of the headings; secondly, that the words used must not be given the force of a statute to be construed; and thirdly, that the law of charity is a moving subject which may well have evolved even since 1891.[29]

So, for a trust to be charitable, it needed to fall within the spirit and 'intendment' of the preamble to the Act of 1601 and satisfy the requirement for public benefit.[30] Each[31] of the four heads of Lord Macnaghten's classification involved two elements; that of benefit, and that of public benefit. There was no need to prove that the relief of poverty, the advancement of education, or the advancement of religion were beneficial; they were always considered to be so. The question of proving that the purposes of a trust were beneficial arose only under the fourth head. But under each of the heads it was necessary to determine the proper test for the identification of the public; or that part of the public which the law required to be benefited.

C   THE CHARITIES ACT 2006

The Charities Act 2006 received the Royal Assent on 8 November, 2006. It came fully into force in April 2008. The main thrust of the Act is to increase the powers of the Charity Commission to protect charities and the obligations of charities to account to the public. The effect of the Act is to increase the duty of trustees to prepare and submit annual accounts, to disqualify certain persons from trusteeship, to control

---

[28] [1891] AC 531 at 583.

[29] See also Lord Reid at 146 and Lord Upjohn at 153; and Russell LJ in *Incorporated Council of Law Reporting for England and Wales v A-G* [1972] Ch 73 at 88–89 [p. 517, below].

[30] H&M, pp. 432–442; Luxton, pp. 16–29; P&M, pp. 452–457; P&S, pp. 525–543; Pettit, pp. 276–284; Picarda, pp. 12–34; Snell, pp. 521–523; Tudor, pp. 7–12; (1953) 31 *Canadian Bar Review* 537 (G.H.L. Fridman); (1956) 72 LQR 187 (G. Cross); (1958) 21 MLR 138 (P.S. Atiyah); (1974) CLJ 63 (G. Jones); (1975) 39 Conv (NS) 183 (S. Plowright); (1976) 27 *Northern Ireland Legal Quarterly* 198 (J.C. Brady); (1977) 40 MLR 397 (N.P. Gravells); (1983) 36 CLP 241 (H. Cohen); [1989] Conv 28 (S. Bright); (1990) 64 *Australian Law Journal* 404 (P.L. Hemphill).

[31] There are many charitable purposes which overlap; for example, a gift for 'the preparation of poor students for the Ministry' might come under all four of Lord Macnaghten's divisions: H&M, p. 405, n. 66.

fundraising and public charitable collections, and to provide more effective means to enforce charitable trusts. However, the Act also provides a new definition of 'charity'.

(i) The Meaning of Charity

CHARITIES ACT 2006

1. Meaning of 'charity'

(1) For the purposes of the law of England and Wales, 'charity' means an institution which—

    (a) is established for charitable purposes only, and

    (b) falls to be subject to the control of the High Court in the exercise of its jurisdiction with respect to charities.

(2) The definition of 'charity' in subsection (1) does not apply for the purposes of an enactment if a different definition of that term applies for those purposes by virtue of that or any other enactment.

(3) A reference in any enactment or document to a charity within the meaning of the Charitable Uses Act 1601 (c. 4) or the preamble to it is to be construed as a reference to a charity as defined by subsection (1).

(ii) Charitable purposes

CHARITIES ACT 2006

2. Meaning of 'charitable purpose'

(1) For the purposes of the law of England and Wales, a charitable purpose is a purpose which—

    (a) falls within subsection (2), and

    (b) is for the public benefit (see section 3).

(2) A purpose falls within this subsection if it falls within any of the following descriptions of purposes—

    (a) the prevention or relief of poverty;

    (b) the advancement of education;

    (c) the advancement of religion;

    (d) the advancement of health or the saving of lives;

    (e) the advancement of citizenship or community development;

    (f) the advancement of the arts, culture, heritage or science;

    (g) the advancement of amateur sport;

(h)   the advancement of human rights, conflict resolution or reconciliation or the promotion of religious or racial harmony or equality and diversity;

(i)   the advancement of environmental protection or improvement;

(j)   the relief of those in need by reason of youth, age, ill-health, disability, financial hardship or other disadvantage;

(k)   the advancement of animal welfare;

(l)   the promotion of the efficiency of the armed forces of the Crown, or of the efficiency of the police, fire and rescue services or ambulance services;

(m)   any other purposes within subsection (4).

(5)   Where any of the terms used in any of paragraphs (a) to (l) of subsection (2), or in subsection (3), has a particular meaning under charity law, the term is to be taken as having the same meaning where it appears in that provision.

(6)   Any reference in any enactment or document (in whatever terms)—

(a)   to charitable purposes, or

(b)   to institutions having purposes that are charitable under charity law,

is to be construed in accordance with subsection (1).

(7)   Subsection (6)—

(a)   applies whether the enactment or document was passed or made before or after the passing of this Act, but

(b)   does not apply where the context otherwise requires.

(8)   In this section—

'charity law' means the law relating to charities in England and Wales; and 'existing charity law' means charity law as in force immediately before the day on which this section comes into force.

Charity Commission, *Charities and Public Benefit* (January 2008), C2

New charitable purposes may be recognised in the future, by the Charity Commission or the Charity Tribunal or the courts, as charity law continues to develop.

(iii) Public benefit

CHARITIES ACT 2006

3 The 'public benefit' test

(1)   This section applies in connection with the requirement in section 2(1)(b) that a purpose falling within section 2(2) must be for the public benefit if it is to be a charitable purpose.

(2) In determining whether that requirement is satisfied in relation to any such purpose, it is not to be presumed that a purpose of a particular description is for the public benefit.

(3) In this Part any reference to the public benefit is a reference to the public benefit as that term is understood for the purposes of the law relating to charities in England and Wales.

(4) Subsection (3) applies subject to subsection (2).

4. Guidance as to operation of public benefit requirement

(1) The Charity Commission for England and Wales (see section 6 of this Act) must issue guidance in pursuance of its public benefit objective.

(2) That objective is to promote awareness and understanding of the operation of the requirement mentioned in section 3(1)....

(3) The Commission may from time to time revise any guidance issued under this section.

(4) The Commission must carry out such public and other consultation as it considers appropriate—

(a) before issuing any guidance under this section, or

(b) (unless it considers that it is unnecessary to do so) before revising any such guidance.

(5) The Commission must publish any guidance issued or revised under this section in such manner as it considers appropriate.

(6) The charity trustees of a charity must have regard to any such guidance when exercising any powers or duties to which the guidance is relevant.

The effect of this provision is that all charities, new and existing, will have to satisfy the test of public benefit. This is a test which has been developed over many years through the courts and is not a new test under the 2006 Act. Different tests of public benefit were developed for each of the four recognised heads of charity. Public benefit was presumed[32] for those charities with purposes to relieve poverty, advance education, and advance religion (or, more precisely, benefit was presumed and most of the cases were concerned with whether this was for the public). These presumptions have been abolished, which means that in each case an organisation will have to demonstrate that its purposes do benefit the public. If this cannot be established then a new charity will not be registered and an existing charity will cease to be registered. Once a charity has been registered charity trustees are under a statutory duty to ensure that the charity acts for the public benefit, and to avoid making decisions which adversely affect the charity's public benefit.

The Charities Act 2006 does not provide any definition of public benefit. That definition is derived from previous cases and decisions of the Charity Commission. However,

---

[32] *National Anti-Vivisection Society v IRC* [1948] AC 31, 56 (Lord Simonds). See p. 511, below.

the Charity Commission is required to produce guidance as to the interpretation of public benefit, having undertaken a public consultation. The Charity Commission, having undertaken such consultation, published its guidance in January 2008.[33] This involves the identification of two key principles with a number of factors which need to be considered. These principles and factors have been distilled from the myriad of cases on the interpretation of public benefit, extracts from many of which are included later in this chapter.

Charity Commission, *Charities and Public Benefit* (January 2008)

C3. What are the principles of public benefit?

There are two key principles both of which must be met in order to show that an organisation's aims are for the public benefit. Within each principle there are some important factors that must be considered in all cases. These are:

Principle 1: There must be an identifiable benefit or benefits

Principle 1a   It must be clear what the benefits are (see section E2)

[E2:... The benefits to the public should be capable of being recognised, identified, defined or described but that does not mean that they also have to be capable of being quantified or measured....]

Principle 1b   The benefits must be related to the aims (see section E3)

[E3...Some charities carry out incidental activities that are not related to achieving their charitable aims. Such activities may be permitted, on the basis that they are a small or incidental part of what the charity does, but any benefit arising from such activities would not count towards any public benefit assessment of the charity's aims....]

Principle 1c   Benefits must be balanced against any detriment or harm (see section E4)

[E4...The existence of detriment or harm does not necessarily mean that the organisation cannot be charitable. It is a question of balancing the benefits against the detriment or harm.

If the detrimental or harmful consequences are greater than the benefits, the overall result is that the organisation would not be charitable....]

Principle 2: Benefit must be to the public, or a section of the public

Principle 2a   The beneficiaries must be appropriate to the aims (see section F2) [F2...Who constitutes 'the public, or a section of the public' is not a simple matter of numbers, but the number of people who can potentially benefit (now or in the future) must not be negligible. What is important is who could benefit, as well as who is benefiting. The class of people who can benefit must be a public class. In general, the public class must be sufficiently large or open in nature given the charitable aim that is to be carried out. The actual number of people who can benefit at one time can be quite small provided that anyone who qualifies as a beneficiary is eligible to be considered. A charity is for the public benefit if the benefits it offers are made widely available, even though in practice only a few people from time to time are able to benefit...]

---

[33] *Charities and Public Benefit* (January 2008), below; (2008) 4 *Solicitors Journal* 8 (A. Holt); (2008) 158 NLJ 286 (S. Claus). In February and March 2008 the Charity Commission published draft supplementary guidance for consultation on 'Public Benefit and the Prevention or Relief of Poverty', 'Public Benefit and the Advancement of Education', 'Public Benefit and the Advancement of Religion' and 'Public Benefit and Fee-Charging'.

Principle 2b   Where benefit is to a section of the public, the opportunity to benefit must not
be unreasonably restricted: . . .
    by geographical or other restrictions (see sections F4–F9) or
    [F4: . . . It is generally reasonable for a charity's aims to be intended to benefit people living
in a particular geographical area, such as a village, town, city, county or country. Restricting
benefit to people living in a particular street, or a few named houses, is likely to be too small an
area to be considered a 'section of the public'. In some cases, restricting benefit to a ward or
parish may be acceptable; it depends on the charity's aims. . . .]
    by ability to pay any fees charged (see section F10)
    [F10. . . . Charities can charge for the services or facilities they provide. They can also charge
fees that more than cover the cost of those services or facilities, provided that the charges are
reasonable and necessary in order to carry out the charity's aims, for example in maintaining
or developing the service being provided. However, where, in practice, the charging restricts
the benefits to only those who can afford to pay the fees charged, this may result in the benefits
not being available to a sufficient section of the public. . . . In considering the extent to which
charging by a charity might affect its ability to meet the public principle of the public benefit
requirement, the following broad principles apply:

in deciding whether an organisation has aims that are for the 'public' benefit, different types
     of benefits to the intended beneficiaries are taken into account;

the fact that the charitable facilities or services will be charged for, and will be provided
     mainly to people who can afford to pay the charges, does not necessarily mean that the
     organisation does not have aims that are for the public benefit;

however, an organisation that excluded people from the *opportunity* to benefit because of
     their inability to pay any fees charged would not have aims that are for the public benefit.

In assessing the overall public benefit provided by a fee-charging charity we will take into
     account the totality of the benefits arising from carrying out its aims. However, where
     the people the aims are intended to benefit are not a sufficient section of the public, the
     organisation's aims will not be for the public benefit.

'Not excluding' people who are unable to pay the fees from the opportunity to benefit does
not mean providing some sort of 'token' benefit to such people. It should be more than minimal
or nominal benefit and does not include benefit that occurs merely by chance. But neither does
it mean there have to be no financial barriers to accessing benefits . . .]
    Principle 2c   People in poverty must not be excluded from the opportunity to benefit (see
section F11)
    [F11. . . . In practice this is most likely to be an issue for high-fee-charging charities, but it
is something that all charities should consider. This does not mean, in effect, introducing an
element of relieving poverty into all charitable aims. It is not the case that people in poverty
actually have to benefit. Or, that charitable aims have to be limited or confined to people in
poverty, although the founders of charities can choose to do that if they wish. It merely means
that people in poverty must not be excluded from the *opportunity* to benefit.
    Although 'poverty' can sometimes be interpreted to mean people who are financially and/
or socially disadvantaged, the legal meaning of poverty in charity law means people who are
financially disadvantaged. The Oxford English Dictionary defines 'poor' as 'of a person or
people; having few, or no, material possessions; lacking the means to procure the comforts or
necessities of life, or to live at a standard considered comfortable or normal in society; needy,

necessitous, indigent, destitute'. Whilst this is not an absolute definition of what 'people in poverty' might mean, it does reflect well the circumstances of people regarded in charity law terms as being 'poor'.

The meaning of 'people in poverty' in individual cases will be considered in the context of the organisation's aims, whom those aims are intended to benefit and where it carries out its aims.

For example, for a charity carrying out its aims in the poorest areas in developing countries, 'people in poverty' might typically mean people who lack even the most basic essentials to sustain life, such as adequate clean water, food and shelter. But, for a charity carrying out its aims in England and Wales for example, 'people in poverty' might typically mean households living on less than 60% of average income or people living on or below the level of 'income support'. However, even then, 'poverty' is a relative term that may be interpreted differently depending upon the organisation's aims.

The context and aims of each organisation are therefore all important in deciding who 'people in poverty' are and whether those people are excluded from the opportunity to benefit.]

Principle 2d Any private benefits must be incidental (see section F12)

[F12...'Private benefits' are benefits that people, or organisations, may receive other than as a beneficiary... Private benefits will be incidental if it can be shown that they directly contribute towards achieving the charity's aims and/or are a necessary result or by-product of carrying out those aims...]

D2. What is the legal standing of the Charity Commission's public benefit guidance?

The Charity Commission's public benefit guidance is guidance on what the law says on public benefit. It does not create new public benefit law. Nor does it create a new legal definition of public benefit. Our guidance sets out a framework of factors to consider when assessing public benefit based on the principles of public benefit contained in existing case law.

We have expressed the principles of public benefit as legal requirements, as we believe they are required by existing case law. But we recognise that this guidance is, of necessity, a summary of the underlying law, rather than a detailed statement of the law with all the fine distinctions that can apply in diverse, individual cases.

(iv) Charitable purposes overseas[34]

Charity Commission, *Charities and Public Benefit* (January 2008)

F4:...Where the aims are intended to benefit people who are defined by reference to geographical areas then those areas should be defined clearly. The geographical areas do not have to be in England and Wales. An organisation can be a charity that is set up and registered in England and Wales whose beneficiaries are entirely outside that area. Charities can operate locally, nationally or internationally.

[34] H&M, pp. 406–407; Luxton, pp. 194–199; P&S, pp. 517–518; Picarda, pp. 27–29; (1965) 29 Conv (NS) 123 (D.M. Emrys Evans); Goodman Report, paras. 86–88 (International Activity), 89–92 (Foreign Charities); [1993–94] 2 *Charity Law & Practice Review* 1 (L. Sheridan).

Decisions of the Charity Commissioners 1993, vol 1, pp. 16–17

Charities Operating Overseas: Charities for Fourth Head Purposes

In our Annual Report for 1963 we reproduced extracts from a letter of advice we had sent to major charities concerned with overseas relief work. Part of that advice was that we had entertained no doubt that the advancement of religion, the advancement of education and the relief of poverty (the first three heads of charity as classified in the well known judgment *Income Tax Special Purposes Comrs v Pemsel* [1891] AC 531) were charitable in whatever part of the world they are carried out, but that charities within the fourth head of the classification in the *Pemsel* case, i.e. for other purposes beneficial to the community, would be charitable only if of benefit to the community of the United Kingdom. We have taken a fresh look at the basis upon which we should consider the charitable status of charities operating overseas.

We take the view that jurisdiction is not an issue. An institution can only be a charity if it is subject to the jurisdiction of the English Courts and only such an institution can be registered by us.[35] That has one important consequence—we are considering only the status of institutions based in the United Kingdom and whether they are charitable or not depends upon English law—see Evershed MR in *Camille and Henry Dreyfus Foundation Incorporated v IRC* [1954] Ch 672 at pages 683, 685 and 687. To be charitable all institutions must be for the public benefit. That test of public benefit has to be the same for all charities whether they operate in the United Kingdom or elsewhere as the Courts cannot judge what is for the public benefit in a foreign country and cannot recognise as charitable an institution which is contrary to the public benefit in the United Kingdom but is for the public benefit elsewhere.

When considering the charitable status of institutions whose purposes are to be carried out abroad, the first question must still be 'Would the objects of the institution be charitable according to English law if its purposes were to be carried out in England?' Having established that the objects of the institution are ostensibly charitable the Courts will then look at the overseas dimension. That approach seems to us to be implicit in both *Keren Kayemeth Le Jisroel Ltd v IRC* [1932] AC 650 and in the *Dreyfus Foundation* case.....

The criteria of public benefit must be [those] adopted by the Courts in respect of charities operating in the United Kingdom. We consider, however, that rather than try to develop complex concepts of tangible and intangible benefit to the community of the United Kingdom, there is a simpler approach which is equally consistent with the cited cases. We consider that in determining the charitable status of institutions operating abroad, one should first consider whether they would be regarded as charities if their operations are confined to the United Kingdom. If they would, then they should be presumed also to be charitable even though operating abroad unless it would be contrary to public policy to recognise them. (See *Re Vagliano* (1905) 75 LJ Ch 119; *Armstrong v Reeves* (1890) 25 LR Ir 325; *Re Jackson* (1910) The Times, 11 June; *Mitford v Reynolds* (1841) 1 Ph 185 and *Re Jacobs* (1970) 114 Sol Jo 515 and also the Canadian case of *Re Levy Estate* (1989) 58 DLR (4th) 375 and the Australian cases of *Re Stone* (1970) 91 WNNSW 704 and *Lander v Whitbread* (1982) 2 NSWLR 530.) We consider that this approach reconciles the decision in *Keren Kayemeth Le Jisroel Ltd* and the comments made in the *Dreyfus Foundation* case. In particular, we noted the words of Lord Evershed MR in the *Dreyfus Foundation* case that 'to such cases the argument of public policy [meaning the

---

[35] Now see *Gaudiya Mission v Bramachary* [1998] Ch 341 [see p. 423, below].

United Kingdom public policy] might be the answer' and of Jenkins LJ in that case that 'it is here only necessary for me to observe that it cannot be maintained that no purpose is recognised as charitable under our law unless it is carried out in and for the benefit of the public, or some section of the public, of the United Kingdom'. Illustrations of that principle are provided by *A-G v Guise* (1692) 2 Vern 266 (gift for application in Scotland contrary to Scottish law) and *Habershon v Vardon* (1851) 4 De G & Sm 467 (a trust to restore Jews to Jerusalem then under Turkish rule, held as tending to promote revolution in a friendly state. A similar trust has been upheld when Palestine was no longer under Turkish rule, see *Re Rosenblum* (1924) 131 LT 21). We further consider that it is necessary to distinguish carefully between the objects of a charity and the means by which that object is to be carried out. If the object itself is contrary to the laws of the foreign state in which it would operate then the trust will not be charitable. On the other hand, if only the means of carrying out the object is contrary to such laws then there will be a failure in the trusts and a case for a *cy-près* application.

In **Re Robinson** [1931] 2 Ch 122, MAUGHAM J held that a gift 'to the German Government for the time being for the benefit of its soldiers disabled in the late war' was charitable. He said at 126:

It is abundantly clear that, whatever the construction which might have been placed upon the Statute of Elizabeth when that statute was passed in the forty-third year of the Queen's reign, for at least 200 years the Courts have been in the habit of treating the phrase 'charitable purposes' as not confined to charitable purposes within this realm.[36]

In **Gaudiya Mission v Brahmachary** [1998] Ch 341, the Court of Appeal held that the English courts' charitable jurisdiction was not exercisable in respect of a charity which was established under a foreign legal system. LEGGATT LJ said at 355–356:

Charities provide a prime example of institutions which it is in the English public interest to regulate and control. But that is only so if they are English charities. Any attempt to control foreign charities would represent something akin to encroachment upon the sovereignty of a foreign state. I am quite satisfied that . . . the mission is not established in England for charitable purposes and is not subject to the control of the High Court in the exercise of its jurisdiction in respect to charities . . .

---

[36] See also *Re Vagliano* [1905] WN 179 (trust for the establishment of . . . or aids to churches, hospitals and schools, and assistance to poor and aged persons for the time being resident in or natives of Cephalonia held charitable); *Keren Kayemeth Le Jisroel Ltd v IRC* [1932] AC 650 [p. 491, below] (trust for the purchase of land in 'Palestine, Syria, or other parts of Turkey, in Asia and the peninsula of Sinai for the purpose of settling Jews on such lands' held not charitable); *Re Jacobs* (1970) 114 Sol Jo 515 (trust 'for the purpose of planting a grove of trees in Israel to perpetuate my name on the eternal soil of the Holy Land' held charitable; Annual Report for 1970, para. 78); *Re Niyazi's Will Trusts* [1978] 1 WLR 910 [p. 430, below] (trust for 'the construction of a working men's hostel' in Famagusta, Cyprus, held charitable; *McGovern v A-G* [1982] Ch 321 [p. 526, below]; *Lander v Whitbread* [1982] 2 NSWLR 530 (trust 'for the Government of the State of Israel for the advancement of education in that State' held charitable in New South Wales); *Re Levy Estate* (1989) 58 DLR (4th) 375 held valid in Ontario; *Re Gray* (1990) 73 DLR (4th) 161; (1990) 4 *Trust Law & Practice* 74 (G. Kodiline); *Re Stone* (1970) 91 WNNSW 704 at 707. See also Annual Report for 1990, paras. 32–34 (Gdansk Hospice Fund; Nairobi Hospice Trust; Kuwaiti Support Fund); 1991, paras. 69–70 (Kurdish Charitable Trust; Amar Trust; Independent Iran Fund).

(v) The Impact of the Human Rights Act 1998[37]

The incorporation of the European Convention on Human Rights into English law by the Human Rights Act 1998, which came into force on 2 October, 2000, is likely to have an important impact on the law of charities, although it is still unclear how dramatic this impact will be.[38] To the extent that the Charity Commissioners and the courts have so far considered the effect of the European Convention on Human Rights on charitable status, the Convention does not appear to have had any dramatic effect on the law.[39]

Charity Commission: *Operational Guidance: Human Rights Act 1998: Charities and Human Rights* (OG 71 B3–September 2000)

The Human Rights Act makes it unlawful for public authorities, including private bodies that carry out public functions, to act in a manner that is incompatible with the rights and freedoms that are guaranteed by the European Convention on Human Rights.

This will include some charities and voluntary organisations.

Although the term 'public authority' is not defined by the Human Rights Act it covers three broad categories:

- obvious public authorities such as a Minister, a Government Department or Agency (including the Charity Commission)...[40]

- courts and tribunals.[41]

- any person or organisation which carries out some functions of a public nature.[42]

Charities do not fall within the definition of a public authority for the purpose of the Human Rights Act by virtue of their being charities. Some charities that appear to be aimed at the individual may in fact be carrying out a public function if they are doing work that would normally be the responsibility of central government or a local or health authority. Many charities and voluntary organisations carry out public functions, either on behalf of, or in partnership with, other authorities. In many cases local authorities have stopped carrying out certain public functions themselves and have entered into contracts with private organisations to carry them out for them. Many of these organisations are charities.

---

[37] Luxton, pp. 36–53.

[38] See Charity Commission: *Operational Guidance: Human Rights Act 1998: Charities and Human Rights.* OG 71 B3 (September 2000) below.

[39] See, for example, the decision of the Charity Commissioners to refuse to register the Church of Scientology (England and Wales) despite Article 9 of the European Convention which protects the right to freedom of religion [see p. 466, below]. See also *RSPCA v A-G* [2002] 1 WLR 448 [p. 600, below] where the charity's policy of excluding members who wished to join the charity for an ulterior purpose was held to be consistent with Article 11 (freedom of association).

[40] It follows that the Charity Commissioners must have regard to the European Convention when determining whether a trust has charitable status. See Luxton. pp. 39–40.

[41] It follows that the courts must have regard to the European Convention when determining whether a trust has charitable status.

[42] Such as the National Trust: *Scott v National Trust* [1998] 2 All ER 705.

The work a charity does for or on behalf of another authority will be considered a public function for the purposes of the Human Rights Act. Such work must be carried out in a way that is compatible with human rights. As it appears likely that local government work will continue to be entrusted to charities in this way, more and more voluntary and charitable activity will fall within the scope of the Human Rights Act.

Examples of charities with public functions might include:

- residential homes;
- hospices;
- healthcare and advice centres;
- child care agencies;
- housing associations;
- family planning, abortion advice centres.

Although it is the functions, i.e. the legal powers and duties of the organisations, which are important in determining whether a person or body is a public authority for the purposes of the Human Rights Act, it is their relationship with the individual which will come under scrutiny when the Human Rights Act is applied because it gives *human* rights.

If everything that a charity does can be regarded as public functions, then it will all have to be done in a way that is compatible with human rights. More commonly though, charities falling within the definition of a public authority will have some public and some private functions. Private acts are not covered by the Human Rights Act....

If a charity does breach the Human Rights Act it would be liable to the remedies available in the courts. Someone may bring a freestanding case against the charity under the Human Rights Act and could apply to the courts for damages against it.

Convention rights most likely to affect charities
The Human Rights Act is about human dignity above all else. This approach must be central to a charity's considerations about human rights. Some Convention rights are likely to have more impact on charities and voluntary organisations than others do. Examples of those that are likely to affect such organisations are:

Article 3—Right not to be subjected to torture or inhuman treatment
This includes the right not to be subjected to degrading treatment and so could apply to organisations providing care, such as hospitals, residential homes etc.

Article 6—Right to a fair trial
This right might affect procedures for case reviews, complaints hearings, tribunals and appeals conducted by charities. It ensures that everyone has a right to a fair hearing.[43]

Article 8—Right to respect for private and family life
This has relevance for organisations providing care homes or domiciliary care and to any organisation with a public function that holds personal information.

---

[43] This will also affect the procedures adopted by the Charity Commission, especially when determining whether a trust has charitable status.

Article 9—Freedom of thought, conscience and religion[44]
This might affect, for example a charity running a care home where one of the patients is a Muslim and wishes to wear the *chadoor*. The home may find this inconvenient and contrary to its policies but it could not force compliance with the policy because under Article 9 the patient has a right to manifest her religion. (On the other hand in a privately run prison a rule about what clothing could be worn would be seen as being in accordance with the law. A sensible rule on prisoners' clothing could be justified as having a legitimate aim and being necessary in a democratic society.)

Article 2 of the First Protocol—Right to education
This may be relevant for issues involving special educational needs provision, access to, or expulsion or exclusion of children from, schools, and (when taken together with Article 14: Prohibition of discrimination) the provision of education which is discriminatory between sexes, races or other categories (although this is likely to mainly be an issue where adequate educational provision is not available elsewhere locally for children excluded from schools that do discriminate), such as single sex schools.

> **QUESTION**
>
> Is it appropriate that the definition of such a key concept as 'public benefit' is left to be determined by the Charity Commission and the Charity Tribunal [see p. 581, below]?

III CHARITABLE PURPOSES AND DESCRIPTIONS

A GENERAL PRINCIPLES

Although the Charities Act 2006 has formally recognised a number of new heads of charity, they are all consistent with the earlier development of the law, either by the courts or through the interpretation and application of the law by the Charity Commission, which expanded the notion of charitable purpose by analogy with the four recognised heads of charitable purposes in *Pemsel's* case and the Preamble to the Charitable Uses Act 1601. Section 2(4) of the Charities Act 2006 recognises that the notion of charitable purpose is not static and can be developed by analogy with the old heads of charitable purpose or the new ones.

---

[44] See p. 464, below.

B PREVENTION OR RELIEF OF POVERTY[45]

(i) Charitable purpose

Under the old law of charity, the first of the four heads of charitable purpose recognised in *Pemsel's* case[46] was the relief of aged, impotent, and poor people. This head has now been divided into the relief of the poor in section 2(2)(a) of the Charities Act 2006, with 'relief of those in need' now covered by section 2(2)(j). It is important to note that section 2(2)(a) covers both the relief and the prevention of poverty.

Tudor on Charities (9th edn, 2003), pp. 37–38

'Poor' is a relative term[47] and an individual need not be destitute in order to qualify as a poor person within the meaning of the preamble to the Statute of Charitable Uses 1601.[48] The Courts have never defined 'poor': its meaning has to be ascertained from the reported cases, which show that an individual is considered to be poor if he is in genuinely straitened circumstances and unable to maintain a very modest standard of living for himself and the persons (if any) dependent upon him.[49]

Charity Commission: *Charities for the Relief of Financial Hardship* (CC4, August 2003), paras 4–5

4.   Many older charities for the relief of financial hardship, particularly those which were originally set up before the advent of the State welfare system, have objects which refer directly to 'the poor' or to 'poverty'. However, a person does not have to be destitute to qualify as 'poor'. Nor do people necessarily have to be 'poor' over a long period of time to qualify; someone suffering a temporary period of financial hardship due to a sudden change in circumstances (for example an accident or a death in the family) might also be eligible for assistance. Generally speaking, anyone who does not have access to the normal things of life which most people take for granted would probably qualify for help.

5.   People may qualify for assistance from a charity whether or not they are eligible for State benefits. Some people who already receive their full entitlement of State benefits may need additional help. Equally, some people who are not entitled to State benefits may sometimes need help because of particular circumstances (where, say, they encounter some gap in an acceptable standard of living which they would [find] it difficult to fill from resources available to them). Each person's actual needs and financial circumstances must be assessed individually.

---

[45] H&M, pp. 408–409, 433–434; Luxton, pp. 16–29; P&M, pp. 457–459; P&S, pp. 489–492; Pettit, pp. 253–255; Picarda, pp. 35–46; Snell, p. 515; Tudor, pp. 38–47. For an analysis of the reasons why trusts for the relief of poverty are enforced see (2000) 20 LS 222 (A. Dunn).

[46] *Income Tax Special Purposes Comrs v Pemsel* [1891] AC 531. See p. 414, above.

[47] *Mary Clark Home Trustees v Anderson* [1904] 2 KB 645 at 655 *per* Channell J; *Re Clarke* [1923] 2 Ch 407 at 411, 412 *per* Romer J.

[48] *Re de Carteret* [1933] Ch 103 at 108 *per* Maugham J. See also (1956) 72 LQR 182, 206 (G. Cross).

[49] *Mary Clark Home Trustees v Anderson*, note 47 above; *Re Gardom* [1914] 1 Ch 662 (reversed, but not on this point, by the House of Lords (1915) 84 LJ Ch 749); *Shaw v Halifax Corpn* [1915] 2 KB 170; *Re Clarke* [1923] 2 Ch 407; *Re de Carteret*, ibid [p. 429, below].

In **Re Coulthurst** [1951] Ch 661, SIR RAYMOND EVERSHED said at 665:

It is quite clearly established that poverty does not mean destitution; it is a word of wide and somewhat indefinite import; it may not unfairly be paraphrased for present purposes as meaning persons who have to 'go short' in the ordinary acceptation of that term, due regard being had to their status in life, and so forth.

Tudor on Charities (9th edn, 2003), pp. 39–41

A charitable gift for the poor may be expressed in general and indefinite language,[50] or may be for the poor of a particular defined area (parish, town or other place),[51] or poor persons of a particular religious denomination attending a specified chapel or chapels,[52] or the poor of a particular regiment,[53] or families of men or women (not being commissioned) in the armed forces,[54] or a particular class of poor people, such as poor gentlewomen,[55] distressed gentlefolk,[56] or persons of moderate[57] or limited[58] means, who are not self-supporting,[59] or housekeepers,[60] or tradesmen of a particular kind,[61] or unsuccessful literary men,[62] or servants,[63] or 'poor struggling youths of merit',[64] or poor pious persons,[65] or poor emigrants,[66] or persons descended from residents of a named borough in a particular year needing assistance to improve their

---

[50] *A-G v Peacock* (1676) Cas temp Finch 245 (for the good of poor people for ever); *A-G v Rance* (1728) cited in (1762) Amb 422; *Nash v Morley* (1842) 5 Beav 177; *Re Darling* [1896] 1 Ch 50 (to the poor and the service of God, following *Powerscourt v Powerscourt* (1824) 1 Mol 616).

[51] *Woodford Inhabitants v Parkhurst* (1639) Duke 70; *A-G v Pearce* (1740) 2 Atk 87; *A-G v Clarke* (1762) Amb 422; *A-G v Exeter Corpn* (1826) 2 Russ 45; (1827) 3 Russ 395; *A-G v Wilkinson* (1839) 1 Beav 370; *A-G v Bovill* (1840) 1 Ph 762; *Salter v Farey* (1843) 7 Jur 831; *Re Lambeth Charities* (1853) 22 LJ Ch 959; *A-G v Blizard* (1855) 21 Beav 233; *Russell v Kellett* (1855) 3 Sm & G 264; *Re Lousada* (1887) 82 LT Jo 358 (London poor); *Re St Alphage, London Wall* (1888) 59 LT 614; *Re Lucas* [1922] 2 Ch 52 (poor inhabitants of Gunville, a small town); *Re Monk* [1927] 2 Ch 197 (gift of income of a fund set aside out of residue to buy coal for distribution among poor and deserving inhabitants of a particular parish and to apply the rest of the residue, capital and income, in making loans of interest to poor and deserving inhabitants of that parish); *Re Roadley* [1930] 1 Ch 524 (poor of two named parishes); *Guinness Trust (London Fund) Founded 1890, Registered 1902 v West Ham Corpn* [1959] 1 WLR 233; *Re Lepton's Charity* [1972] Ch 276. The place may be abroad; *Re Niyazi's Will Trusts* [1978] 1 WLR 910 [p. 430, below] (Famagusta).

[52] *Re Wall* (1889) 42 Ch D 510.   [53] *Re Donald* [1909] 2 Ch 410.

[54] *Soldiers', Sailors' and Airmen's Families Association v A-G* [1968] 1 WLR 313.

[55] *A-G v Power* (1809) 1 Ball & B 145; *Mary Clark Home Trustees v Anderson* [1904] 2 KB 645; *Re Gardom* [1914] 1 Ch 662; *Shaw v Halifax Corpn* [1915] 2 KB 170.   [56] *Re Young* [1951] Ch 344.

[57] *Re Clarke* [1923] 2 Ch 407.

[58] *Re de Carteret* [1933] Ch 103.

[59] *Re Central Employment Bureau for Women and Students' Careers Association* [1942] 1 All ER 232.

[60] *A-G v Pearce* (1740) 2 Akt 87. 'Housekeeper' is a word now used to denote a domestic servant who looks after the house of another, but in the case of old charities it sometimes means a person who is housebound, and sometimes a householder.

[61] *Re White's Trusts* (1886) 33 Ch D 449.

[62] *Thompson v Thompson* (1844) 1 Coll 381 at 395.

[63] *Reeve v A-G* (1843) 3 Hare 191; *Loscombe v Wintringham* (1850) 13 Beav 87.

[64] *Milne's Executors v Aberdeen University Court* (1905) 7 F 642.

[65] *Nash v Morley* (1842) 5 Beav 177.

[66] *Barclay v Maskelyne* (1858) 32 LTOS 205. But a gift 'for emigration uses' is not charitable: see *Re Sidney* [1908] 1 Ch 488.

condition in life by emigrating,[67] or inmates of a workhouse,[68] or patients in a hospital,[69] or debtors,[70] or fifty needy and deserving old men and fifty needy and deserving old women of a particular place,[71] or widows and orphans of poor clergymen,[72] or seamen of a particular port,[73] or victims of a particular disaster,[74] or widows and orphans of a particular parish,[75] or indigent bachelors and widowers 'who have shown sympathy with science',[76] or the relief of domestic distress.[77]

In **Re de Carteret** [1933] Ch 103, a trust, created by the will of a Bishop of Jamaica, provided for the payment of 'annual allowances of forty pounds each to widows or spinsters in England whose income otherwise shall not be less than eighty or more than one hundred and twenty pounds per annum'. Preference was to 'be given to widows with young children dependent on them'. This was held to be a valid charitable trust for the relief of poverty. It was no objection that there was a minimum income qualification for the persons to be benefited.[78] Emphasis was placed by MAUGHAM J on the fact that the preference was to be given to widows with young children dependent upon them. 'I should have hesitated to hold that it was a good charitable gift had it merely been for "widows and spinsters"; but I think that, in confining it, as I do, in effect, to widows with young children dependent on them, I am within the decisions to which I have referred.'

In **Re Sanders' Will Trusts** [1954] Ch 265, a codicil gave money 'to provide or assist in providing dwellings for the working classes and their families resident in the area of Pembroke Dock... or within a radius of five miles therefrom...'

HARMAN J held that the gift was not a charitable trust because the expression 'the working classes' did not indicate poor persons.[79]

[67] *Re Tree* [1945] Ch 325 (Hastings). For the grounds on which Evershed J distinguished *Re Compton* [1945] Ch 123, see [1945] Ch 325 at 328–332; and see (1956) 72 LQR 182 (G. Cross), at p. 190, n. 8. In *Re Tree* the element of poverty was present. It is doubtful whether the decision could have been justified if that element had been absent: see *Davies v Perpetual Trustee Co Ltd* [1959] AC 439 at 456.

[68] *A-G v Vint* (1850) 3 De G & Sm 704.

[69] *Reading Corpn v Lane* (1601) Toth 32; see also *Re Roadley* [1930] 1 Ch 524.

[70] *A-G v Painter-Stainers' Co* (1788) 2 Cox Eq Cas 51; *A-G v Ironmongers' Co* (1834) 2 My & K 576.

[71] *Re Reed* (1893) 10 TLR 87; and see also *Re Wall* (1889) 42 Ch D 510.

[72] *Waldo v Caley* (1809) 16 Ves 206; and see *Re Friend of the Clergy's Charters* [1921] 1 Ch 409, where this was assumed without argument.   [73] *Powell v A-G* (1817) 3 Mer 48.

[74] *Pease v Pattinson* (1886) 32 Ch D 154; *Re Hartley Colliery Accident Relief Fund* (1908) 102 LT 165n; *Cross v Lloyd-Greame* (1909) 102 LT 163 (where there were only six victims); *Re North Devon and West Somerset Relief Fund Trusts* [1953] 1 WLR 1260 (flood disaster). It is suggested, however, that disaster relief funds fall more naturally under the fourth head of charities, as those relieved need not necessarily be poor. The emphasis of such a fund is need for 'relief'. See generally [p. 508, below].

[75] *A-G v Comber* (1824) 2 Sim & St 93; *Russell v Kellett* (1855) 3 Sm & G 264.

[76] *Weir v Crum-Brown* [1908] AC 162 (on appeal from the Court of Session).

[77] *Kendall v Granger* (1842) 5 Beav 300 at 303.

[78] Following *Spiller v Maude* (1881) 32 Ch D 158n ('incapacitated actors'); *Re Lacy* [1899] 2 Ch 149; *Re Gardom* [1914] 1 Ch 662 (where the gift was 'for the maintenance of a temporary house of residence for ladies of limited means'); cf. *Over Seventies Housing Association v Westminster City Council* [1974] RA 247.

[79] The case was settled on appeal; (1954) The Times, 22 July. Some homes for working classes have been registered as charities, where there were other factors which indicated a requirement of poverty: Annual Report for 1965, Appendix C, para. I. A. 9; Goodman Report, paras. 75–78 (Housing).

In **Re Niyazi's Will Trusts** [1978] 1 WLR 910, the testator gave his residuary estate worth about £15,000 for 'the construction of or as a contribution towards the cost of a working men's hostel' to be created in Famagusta, Cyprus. MEGARRY V-C held that this was a charitable trust and said at 915:

The word 'hostel' has to my mind a strong flavour of a building which provides somewhat modest accommodation for those who have some temporary need for it and are willing to accept accommodation of that standard in order to meet the need. When 'hostel' is prefixed by the expression 'working men's', then the further restriction is introduced of the hostel being intended for those with a relatively low income who work for their living, especially as manual workers.[80] The need, in other words, is to be the need of working men, and not of students or battered wives or anything else. Furthermore, the need will not be the need of the better-paid working men who can afford something superior to mere hostel accommodation, but the need of the lower end of the financial scale of working men, who cannot compete for the better accommodation but have to content themselves with the economies and shortcomings of hostel life. It seems to me that the word 'hostel' in this case is significantly different from the word 'dwellings' in *Re Sanders' Will Trusts* [1954] Ch 265, a word which is appropriate to ordinary houses in which the well-to-do may live, as well as the relatively poor.

Has the expression 'working men's hostel' a sufficient connotation of poverty in it to satisfy the requirements of charity? On any footing the case is desperately near the border-line, and I have hesitated in reaching my conclusion. On the whole, however, for the reasons that I have been discussing, I think that the trust is charitable, though by no great margin. This view is in my judgment supported by two further considerations. First, there is the amount of the trust fund, which in 1969 was a little under £15,000. I think one is entitled to assume that a testator has at least some idea of the probable value of his estate. The money is given for the purpose 'of the construction of or as a contribution towards the cost of the construction of a working men's hostel'. £15,000 will not go very far in such a project...

The other consideration is that of the state of housing in Famagusta. Where the trust is to erect a building in a particular area, I think it is legitimate, in construing the trust, to have some regard to the physical conditions existing in that area. Quite apart from any question of the size of the gift, I think that a trust to erect a hostel in a slum or in an area of acute housing need may have to be construed differently from a trust to erect a hostel in an area of housing affluence or plenty. Where there is a grave housing shortage, it is plain that the poor are likely to suffer more than the prosperous, and that the provision of a 'working men's hostel' is likely to help the poor and not the rich.

In the result, then, I hold that the trust is charitable.

In **IRC v Oldham Training and Enterprise Council** [1996] STC 1218, LIGHTMAN J said at 1233:

So far as the object of Oldham TEC is to set up in trade or business the unemployed and enable them to stand on their own feet, that is charitable as a trust for the improvement of the conditions in life of those 'going short' in respect of employment and providing a fresh start in life for those in need of it, and accordingly are for the relief of poverty.

---

[80] On the meaning of 'working classes', see *Westminster City Council v Duke of Westminster* [1991] 4 All ER 136 (reversed (1992) 24 HLR 572).

In **Biscoe v Jackson** (1887) 35 Ch D 460, the testator gave a sum of money out of his residuary estate to be applied in the establishment of a soup kitchen[81] for the parish of Shoreditch and of a cottage hospital adjoining thereto. This was held to be a charitable trust for the relief of poverty.

In **Re Coulthurst** [1951] Ch 661, a testator provided a fund to be applied 'to or for the benefit of such...of the...widows and orphaned children of deceased officers and deceased ex-officers of Coutts & Co...as the bank shall in its absolute discretion consider by reason of his her or their financial circumstances to be most deserving of such assistance'. This was held by the Court of Appeal to create a valid trust for the relief of poverty.[82]

In **Re Gwyon** [1930] 1 Ch 255, the testator established a fund, to be called 'Gwyon's Boys Clothing Foundation'. The income of the fund was to be applied in providing knickers ('loose fitting breeches, gathered in at the knee'[83]) for boys of Farnham and district, with certain qualifications expressed by Eve J in the extract below. No preference was indicated in favour of children of poor parents. In holding that the trust was not charitable but void, EVE J said at 260:

The question is whether the testator has effectively created such a charity as he contemplated, a charity in the legal sense of the word. Is the object of his benefaction the relief of poverty, are the gifts for the benefit of the poor and needy? I do not think they are. Apart from residential and age qualifications, the only conditions imposed on a recipient are (1) that he shall not belong to or be supported by any charitable institution, (2) that neither he nor his parents shall be in receipt of parochial relief, (3) that he shall not be black,[84] (4) that on a second or subsequent application he shall not have disposed of any garment received within the then-preceding year from the Foundation and that when he comes for a new pair of knickers or trousers the legend 'Gwyon's Present' shall still be decipherable on the waistband of his old ones.

None of these conditions necessarily imports poverty nor could the recipients be accurately described as a class of aged, impotent or poor persons. The references to the receipt of parochial relief and to the possibility of last year's garment having been disposed of show, no doubt, that the testator contemplated that candidates might be forthcoming from a class of society

[81] Mrs Beeton's recipe for 'Benevolent Soup, suitable for a Soup Kitchen, at any time, average cost 2d *per* pint', included 'half an ox cheek; four onions, two turnips, one cabbage, a bunch of herbs, one and a half pints of lentils, 10 quarts of water. Simmer for four hours'. See The Times for 2 January, 1800, 5 January and 7 January, 1985.

[82] On the element of public benefit in the definition of the class to be benefited, cf. *Re Compton* [1945] Ch 123; *Oppenheim v Tobacco Securities Trust Co Ltd* [1951] AC 297 [p. 455, below]; *Gibson v South American Stores (Gath and Chaves) Ltd* [1950] Ch 177 (necessitous and deserving employees, ex-employees and their dependents); *Dingle v Turner* [1972] AC 601 [p. 432, below]; *Re Denison* (1974) 42 DLR (3d) 652 ('relief of impoverished or indigent members of the Law Society of Upper Canada and of their wives, widows and children' held charitable).

[83] *Shorter Oxford English Dictionary*. See *The Ballad of the Reverend John Gwyon*, by P. Hawkins; (1990) 109 Law Notes 166.

[84] The Race Relations Act 1976, s. 34(1) states that a provision contained in any charitable instrument which provides for conferring benefits on people in a class defined by reference to colour shall be interpreted as conferring the benefits on the class without the restriction by reference to colour. See *Gibbs v Harding* [2007] EWHC 3 (Ch), [2008] 2 WLR 361.

where incidents of this nature might occur, but although a gift to or for the poor other than those who were in receipt of parochial relief—that is, paupers—would be a good charitable gift, it does not follow that a gift to all and sundry in a particular locality and not expressed to be for the poor ought to be construed as evidencing an intention to relieve poverty merely because the testator is minded to exclude paupers. I think that according to the true construction of these testamentary documents the benevolence of the testator was intended for all eligible boys other than paupers, and I cannot spell out of them any indication which would justify the Foundation Trustees refusing an applicant otherwise eligible on the ground that his material circumstances were of too affluent a character. In these circumstances I cannot hold this trust to be within the description of a legal charitable trust.

In **AITC Foundation's Application for Registration as a Charity** [2005] WTLR 1265 the Charity Commission registered a charity to relieve poverty, need, hardship, and distress suffered by people who had invested in split-capital investment companies which had collapsed. These investors, possibly fewer than 300, might have been eligible for compensation, but only after an investigation had been concluded and liability determined.

(ii) Public benefit

The presumption that trusts for the relief of the poor would satisfy the test of public benefit was removed by the Charities Act 2006, section 3(2), so that it will be necessary to establish in each case that such trusts do indeed satisfy the public benefit test. The old law remains relevant, however, in determining what the public benefit might be for this type of charitable object.

Dingle v Turner[85]
[1972] AC 601, (HL. **Viscount Dilhorne, Lords MacDermott, Hodson, Simon of Glaisdale** and **Cross of Chelsea**)

Mr. Dingle, the testator, directed the trustees of his will to pay the income of his residuary estate to his wife for her life, and after her death to invest a capital sum in the names of the 'pension fund trustees' upon trust 'to apply the income thereof in paying pensions to poor employees of E. Dingle and Co Ltd' who were aged or incapacitated. The ultimate residue of the estate was to be held on similar trusts. At the date of the testator's death in 1950, the company had over 600 employees and there was a substantial number of ex-employees. The widow died in 1966.

Held (affirming Megarry J): The will created a valid charitable trust.

Lord Cross of Chelsea: By his judgment given on 2 April, 1971, Megarry J held *inter alia*, following the decision of the Court of Appeal in *Gibson v South American Stores (Gath and Chaves) Ltd* [1950] Ch 177, that the trust declared by clause 8(e) was a valid charitable trust but, on the application of the appellant Betty Mary Dingle, one of the persons interested under an

---

[85] (1974) CLJ 3 (G.H. Jones); (1972) 36 Conv (NS) 209 (D.J. Hayton); (1973) 36 MLR 532 (S.E.A. Johnson); [1978] Conv 277 (T.G. Watkin).

intestacy, he granted a certificate under section 12 of the Administration of Justice Act 1969 enabling her to apply to this House directly for leave to appeal against that part of his judgment and on 17 May, 1971, the House gave her leave to appeal.

Your Lordships, therefore, are now called upon to give to the old 'poor relations' cases and the more modern 'poor employees' cases that careful consideration which, in his speech in *Oppenheim v Tobacco Securities Trust Co Ltd* [1951] AC 297 at 313 [p. 455, below], Lord Morton of Henryton said that they might one day require.

The contentions of the appellant and the respondents may be stated broadly as follows. The appellant says that in the *Oppenheim* case this House decided that in principle a trust ought not to be regarded as charitable if the benefits under it are confined either to the descendants of a named individual or individuals or to the employees of a given individual or company and that though the 'poor relations' cases may have to be left standing as an anomalous exception to the general rule because their validity has been recognised for so long the exception ought not to be extended to 'poor employees' trusts which had not been recognised for long before their status as charitable trusts began to be called in question. The respondents, on the other hand, say, first, that the rule laid down in the *Oppenheim* case with regard to educational trusts ought not to be regarded as a rule applicable in principle to all kinds of charitable trust, and, secondly, that in any case it is impossible to draw any logical distinction between 'poor relations' trusts and 'poor employees' trusts, and that, as the former cannot be held invalid today after having been recognised as valid for so long, the latter must be regarded as valid also....

Most of the cases on the subject were decided in the eighteenth or early nineteenth centuries and are very inadequately reported, but two things at least were clear. First, that it never occurred to the judges who decided them that in the field of 'poverty' a trust could not be a charitable trust if the class of beneficiaries was defined by reference to descent from a common ancestor. Secondly, that the courts did not treat a gift or trust as necessarily charitable because the objects of it had to be poor in order to qualify, for in some of the cases the trust was treated as a private trust and not a charity. The problem in *Re Scarisbrick's Will Trusts* [1951] Ch 622 [p. 436, below], was to determine on what basis the distinction was drawn.... The Court of Appeal... held that in this field the distinction between a public or charitable trust and a private trust depended on whether as a matter of construction the gift was for the relief of poverty amongst a particular description of poor people or was merely a gift to particular poor persons, the relief of poverty among them being the motive of the gift. The fact that the gift took the form of a perpetual trust would no doubt indicate that the intention of the donor could not have been to confer private benefits on particular people whose possible necessities he had in mind; but the fact that the capital of the gift was to be distributed at once did not necessarily show that the gift was a private trust.

His Lordship reviewed the earlier cases, referring to *Spiller v Maude* (1881) reported at (1886) 32 Ch D 158n; *Pease v Pattinson* (1886) 32 Ch D 154; *Re Buck* [1896] 2 Ch 727; *Re Gosling* (1900) 48 WR 300; *Re Drummond* [1914] 2 Ch 90; *Re Sir Robert Laidlaw*, unreported, but explained at [1950] Ch 177 at 195; *Re Compton* [1945] Ch 123; *Re Hobourn Aero Components Ltd's Air Raid Distress Fund* [1946] Ch 194; *Gibson v South American Stores (Gath and Chaves) Ltd* [1950] Ch 177; *Oppenheim v Tobacco Securities Trust Co Ltd* [1951] AC 297; *Re Cox* [1955] AC 627; *Re Young* [1955] 1 WLR 1269 and *Davies v Perpetual Trustee Co Ltd* [1959] AC 439, and continued:

After this long—but I hope not unduly long—recital of the decided cases, I turn to consider the arguments advanced by the appellant in support of the appeal. Even on [the assumption that the 'poor relations' cases, the 'poor members' cases, and the 'poor employees' cases are all anomalous] the appeal must fail. The status of some of the 'poor relations' trusts as valid charitable trusts was recognised more than 200 years ago and a few of those then recognised are still being administered as charities today. In *Re Compton* Lord Greene MR said, at 139, at 206, that it was 'quite impossible' for the Court of Appeal to overrule such old decisions and in *Oppenheim* Lord Simonds in speaking of them remarked, at 309, on the unwisdom of casting doubt on 'decisions of respectable antiquity in order to introduce a greater harmony into the law of charity as a whole'. Indeed, counsel for the appellant hardly ventured to suggest that we should overrule the 'poor relations' cases. His submission was that which was accepted by the Court of Appeal for Ontario in *Re Cox* [1951] OR 205—namely that while the 'poor relations' cases might have to be left as long-standing anomalies there was no good reason for sparing the 'poor employees' cases which only date from *Re Gosling* (1900) 48 WR 300 and which have been under suspicion ever since the decision in *Re Compton* [1945] Ch 123. But the 'poor members' and the 'poor employees' decisions were a natural development of the 'poor relations' decisions and to draw a distinction between different sorts of 'poverty' trusts would be quite illogical and could certainly not be said to be introducing 'greater harmony' into the law of charity. Moreover, though not as old as the 'poor relations' trusts 'poor employees' trusts have been recognised as charities for many years; there are now a large number of such trusts in existence; and assuming, as one must, that they are properly administered in the sense that benefits under them are only given to people who can fairly be said to be, according to current standards, 'poor persons', to treat such trusts as charities is not open to any practical objection. So as it seems to me it must be accepted that wherever else it may hold sway the *Compton* rule has no application in the field of trusts for the relief of poverty and that there the dividing line between a charitable trust and a private trust lies where the Court of Appeal drew it in *Re Scarisbrick's Will Trusts* [1951] Ch 622.

Oppenheim [1951] AC 297 was a case of an educational trust and though the majority evidently agreed with the view expressed by the Court of Appeal in the *Hoboum Aero* case [1946] Ch 194 that the *Compton* rule was of universal application outside the field of poverty it would no doubt be open to this House without overruling *Oppenheim* to hold that the scope of the rule was more limited. If ever I should be called upon to pronounce on this question—which does not arise in this appeal—I would as at present advised be inclined to draw a distinction between the practical merits of the *Compton* rule and the reasoning by which Lord Greene MR sought to justify it. That reasoning—based on the distinction between personal and impersonal relationships—has never seemed to me very satisfactory and I have always—if I may say so—felt the force of the criticism to which my noble and learned friend Lord MacDermott subjected it in his dissenting speech in *Oppenheim*. For my part I would prefer to approach the problem on far broader lines. The phrase a 'section of the public' is in truth a vague phrase which may mean different things to different people. In the law of charity judges have sought to elucidate its meaning by contrasting it with another phrase: 'a fluctuating body of private individuals'. But I get little help from the supposed contrast for as I see it one and the same aggregate of persons may well be describable both as a section of the public and as a fluctuating body of private individuals. The ratepayers of the Royal Borough of Kensington and Chelsea, for example, certainly constitute a section of the public; but would it be a misuse of language to describe them as a 'fluctuating body of private individuals'? After all, every part of the public is composed of individuals and being susceptible of increase or decrease is fluctuating. So at the end of the day one is left where one started with the bare contrast between 'public' and 'private'. No doubt some classes are more naturally describable as sections of the public than as private classes while other classes are more naturally describable as private classes than as sections of the public. The blind, for example, can naturally be described as a section of the public; but what they have in common—their blindness—does not join them together in such a way that they could be called a private class. On the other hand, the descendants of Mr. Gladstone might more reasonably be described as a 'private class' than as a section of the public, and in the field of common employment the same might well be said of the employees in some fairly small firm. But if one turns to large companies employing many thousands of men and women most of whom are quite unknown to one another and to the directors the answer is by no means so clear. One might say that in such a case the distinction between a section of the public and a private class is not applicable at all or even that the employees in such concerns as I.C.I. or G.E.C. are just as much 'sections of the public' as the residents in some geographical area. In truth the question whether or not the potential beneficiaries of a trust can fairly be said to constitute a section of the public is a question of degree and cannot be by itself decisive of the question whether the trust is a charity. Much must depend on the purpose of the trust. It may well be that, on the one hand, a trust to promote some purpose, *prima facie* charitable, will constitute a charity even though the class of potential beneficiaries might fairly be called a private class and that, on the other hand, a trust to promote another purpose, also *prima facie* charitable, will not constitute a charity even though the class of potential beneficiaries might seem to some people fairly describable as a section of the public. In answering the question whether any given trust is a charitable trust the courts—as I see it—cannot avoid having regard to the fiscal privileges accorded to charities. As counsel for the Attorney-General remarked in the course of the argument the law of charity is bedevilled by the fact that charitable trusts enjoy two quite different sorts of privilege. On the one hand, they enjoy immunity from the rules against perpetuity and uncertainty and though individual potential beneficiaries cannot sue to enforce them the public interest arising under them is protected by the Attorney-General. If this was all there would be no reason for the courts not to look favourably on the claim of any 'purpose' trust to be considered as a charity if it seemed calculated to confer some real benefit on those intended to benefit by it whoever they might be and if it would fail if not held to be a charity. But that is not all. Charities automatically enjoy fiscal privileges which with the increased burden of taxation have become more and more important and in deciding that such and such a trust is a charitable trust the court is endowing it with a substantial annual subsidy at the expense of the taxpayer.[86] Indeed, claims of trusts to rank as charities are just as often challenged by the Revenue as by those who would take the fund if the trust was invalid. It is, of course, unfortunate that the recognition of any trust as a valid charitable trust should automatically attract fiscal privileges, for the question whether a trust to further some purpose is so little likely to benefit the public that it ought to be declared invalid and the question whether it is likely to confer such great benefits on the public that it should enjoy fiscal immunity are really two quite different questions. The logical solution would be to separate them and to say—as the Radcliffe Commission[87] proposed—that only some charities should enjoy fiscal privileges. But, as things are, validity

[86] See at p. 610, where counsel for the Attorney-General stated that in 1972 the annual estimated income of trusts for poor employees, poor members of associations, or professional groups was £4,690,000, and the income for poor relations was £3,400.

[87] Royal Commission on the Taxation of Profits and Income (1955) Cmd. 9474, chap. 7; see also (1956) 72 LQR 187 (G. Cross); (1977) 40 MLR 397 (N.P. Gravells).

and fiscal immunity march hand in hand and the decisions in the *Compton* [1945] Ch 123 and *Oppenheim* [1951] AC 297 cases were pretty obviously influenced by the consideration that if such trusts as were there in question were held valid they would enjoy an undeserved fiscal immunity. To establish a trust for the education of the children of employees in a company in which you are interested is no doubt a meritorious act; but however numerous the employees may be the purpose which you are seeking to achieve is not a public purpose.[88] It is a company purpose and there is no reason why your fellow taxpayers should contribute to a scheme which by providing 'fringe benefits' for your employees will benefit the company by making their conditions of employment more attractive. The temptation to enlist the assistance of the law of charity in private endeavours of this sort is considerable—witness the recent case of the Metal Box scholarships—*IRC v Educational Grants Association Ltd* [1967] Ch 993 [p. 460, below]—and the courts must do what they can to discourage such attempts. In the field of poverty the danger is not so great as in the field of education—for while people are keenly alive to the need to give their children a good education and to the expense of doing so they are generally optimistic enough not to entertain serious fears of falling on evil days much before they fall on them. Consequently the existence of company 'benevolent funds' the income of which is free of tax does not constitute a very attractive 'fringe benefit'. This is a practical justification—though not, of course, the historical explanation—for the special treatment accorded to poverty trusts in charity law. For the same sort of reason a trust to promote some religion among the employees of a company might perhaps safely be held to be charitable provided that it was clear that the benefits were to be purely spiritual. On the other hand, many 'purpose' trusts falling under Lord Macnaghten's fourth head (*Income Tax Special Purposes Comrs v Pemsel* [1891] AC 531 at 583) if confined to a class of employees would clearly be open to the same sort of objection as educational trusts. As I see it, it is on these broad lines rather than for the reasons actually given by Lord Greene MR that the *Compton* rule [1945] Ch 123 can best be justified.

My Lords, for the reasons given earlier in this speech I would dismiss this appeal; but as the view was expressed in the *Oppenheim* case [1951] AC 297 that the question of the validity of trusts for poor relations and poor employees ought some day to be considered by this House and as the fund in dispute in this case is substantial your Lordships may perhaps think it proper to direct that the cost of all parties to the appeal be paid out of it.

Lord Hodson: My Lords, I agree with my noble and learned friend, Lord Cross of Chelsea, that this appeal should be dismissed and with his reasons for that conclusion. With this reservation: that I share the doubts expressed by my noble and learned friends, Lord MacDermott and Viscount Dilhorne, as to the relevance of fiscal considerations in deciding whether a gift or trust is charitable.

A trust may be charitable even though the trustees may distribute the capital and even though the persons to be benefited are selected at the discretion of the trustees.

In **Re Scarisbrick** [1951] Ch 622, a testatrix provided that, after the death of her children, the residue of her estate should be held upon trust 'for such relations of my said son and daughters as in the opinion of the survivor of my said son and daughters shall be in needy circumstances and for such charitable objects either in Germany

---

[88] For criticism of this approach, see [1978] Conv 277 (T.G. Watkin).

or...Great Britain...for such interests and in such proportions...as the survivor of my said son and daughters shall by deed or will appoint'.

The parties agreed that one-half of the fund was effectively devoted to charity. The question arose in respect of the gifts in favour of the relations. No appointment was ever made by the survivor of the children. The Court of Appeal (reversing Roxburgh J) upheld the gift.

JENKINS LJ, after laying down a number of general propositions relating to the requirement of public benefit in charitable trusts, and referring to the exceptional case of a trust for poor relations, said at 650:

Applying these general propositions to the present case, I ask myself whether the trust in cl. 11 for 'such relations...as in the opinion of the survivor of' the testatrix's 'son and daughters shall be in needy circumstances for such interests and in such proportions...as the survivor...shall by deed or will appoint' is a trust for the relief of poverty. If it is such a trust, then, as I understand the exception above referred to, it matters not that the potential objects of such trust are confined to relations of the son and daughters. If language means anything, a person in needy circumstances is a person who is poor and as such a proper object of charity, and no one can take under this trust who is not in needy circumstances. I do not think that the effect of the expression in 'needy circumstances' is materially altered by the qualifying words 'in the opinion of the survivor....'

'Poverty' is necessarily to some extent a relative matter, a matter of opinion, and it is not to be assumed that the person made the judge of 'needy circumstances' in the present case would have acted otherwise than in accordance with an opinion fairly and honestly formed as to the circumstances, needy or otherwise, of anyone coming into consideration as a potential object of the power. Under a similar trust which did not expressly make the appointor's opinion the test of eligibility, the appointor would in practice have to make the selection according to the best of his or her opinion or judgment. The express reference to the appointor's opinion merely serves to reduce the possibility of dispute as to the eligibility or otherwise of any particular individual on the score of needy circumstances. Accordingly, I dismiss the words 'in the opinion of the survivor' as having no material bearing on the character of this trust. In so doing, I am fortified by the similar conclusion reached in this court as to the effect of the words 'in the opinion of the London Board' in *Gibson v South American Stores (Gath and Chaves) Ltd* [1950] Ch 177 at 185.

[His Lordship discussed the cases relating to the requirement of public benefit in relation to gifts in favour of poor relations, and continued:] Accordingly, in the view I take, this is a trust for the relief of poverty in the charitable sense amongst the class of relations described, and, being a trust for the relief of poverty, is in view of the exception above stated, not disqualified from ranking as a legally charitable trust by the circumstances that its application is confined to a class of relations (albeit a wide class), with the result that its potential beneficiaries do not comprise the public or a section thereof under the decisions to which I have referred.

I am accordingly of opinion that as the law now stands the trust in question should be upheld as a valid charitable trust for the relief of poverty.

The judge took a different view...

I find myself unable to accept the judge's view as to the effect of the authorities. I think the true question in each case has really been whether the gift was for the relief of poverty amongst a class of persons, or rather, as Sir William Grant MR put it,[89] a particular description of poor,

[89] In *A-G v Price* (1810) 17 Ves 371 at 374.

or was merely a gift to individuals, albeit with relief of poverty amongst those individuals as the motive of the gift, or with a selective preference for the poor or poorest amongst those individuals. If the gift is perpetual in character, that no doubt is an important circumstance as demonstrating that the intention cannot have been merely to benefit the statutory next of kin of the *propositus* or other particular individuals identified by the gift. Moreover, the gift, if perpetual, can only be supported on the footing that it is charitable—an illogical though in past practice probably a persuasive reason for holding it such.

But I see no sufficient ground in the authorities for holding that a gift for the benefit of poor relations qualifies as charitable only if it is perpetual in character. I do not think that the observation of Sir William Grant MR above referred to goes by any means as far as that. It is fully satisfied if taken as meaning that an immediate bequest of a sum to be distributed among poor relations may on its true construction be no more than a gift to particular individuals (i.e., the next of kin of the *propositus*), whereas a gift having perpetual continuance cannot be so confirmed. If a gift or trust on its true construction does extend to those in need amongst relations in every degree, even though it provides for immediate distribution, then, inasmuch as the class of potential beneficiaries becomes so wide as to be incapable of exhaustive ascertainment, the impersonal quality, if I may so describe it, supplied in continuing gifts by the element of perpetuity, is equally present.[90]

In **Re Segelman**[91] [1996] Ch 171, the testator left his residuary estate on trust for 21 years to be used for the benefit of the poor and needy members of a designated group of his family and their issue, as identified in the second schedule which was attached to his will. The issue for the court was whether this created a charitable trust. In holding that it did CHADWICK J said at 190:

The position, therefore, is that there are at present 26 members of the second-schedule class. Of those, 11 are in the third generation of descent from the testator's parents and 10 are in the fourth generation. Their ages are such that it is reasonable to assume that, by the end of the period of 21 years from the testator's death... the second-schedule class will be substantially larger. On the other hand, there are at present at least 10 living descendants of the testator's parents who are not members of the second-schedule class. It is clear that the testator has made a considered selection of those who are to be the members of the class from amongst the descendants of his parents. He has not included all those descendants, nor all the descendants in any particular line of descent... nor all those descendants who have been named as pecuniary legatees.

It is clear, also, that the testator has not selected the members of the second-schedule class on the basis that they are all poor. The evidence which has been filed on the construction summons by or on behalf of members of that class does not suggest uniform poverty. Rather, it suggests that most members of the class are comfortably off, in the sense that they are able to meet their day-to-day expenses out of income, but not affluent. Like many others in similar circumstances, they need a helping hand from time to time in order to overcome an unforeseen crisis: the failure of a business venture, urgent repairs to a dwelling house or expenses brought on by reason of failing health. Further, the second-schedule class includes the issue of named individuals, many

[90] *Re Cohen* [1973] 1 WLR 415 (trust 'for or towards the maintenance and benefit of any relative of mine whom any trustees shall consider to be in special need' held charitable).
[91] [1996] Conv 379, 383–386 (E.B. Histed).

of whom are still minors. It is impossible to conclude that the minors have been selected because they are, or are likely to be, poor. No doubt, in common with most of their contemporaries, they will experience relative poverty as students. There will be periods when their income from grants or parental resources fails to cover expenditure on their actual or perceived needs. But they are not as a class 'poor persons' within any ordinarily accepted meaning of that expression. The conclusion that I draw from the evidence is that the testator selected the members of the second-schedule class on the basis that they were persons who might need financial help from time to time in the future—as had been the case, at least in relation to some of them, in the past—and that they were persons who, by reasons of ties of blood or affection, he would wish to help after his death, as he had done from time to time during his lifetime.

[His Lordship considered *Re Scarisbick* [1951] Ch 622 [p. 436, above], and *Dingle v Turner* [1972] AC 601 [p. 432, above], and continued:] Wherever the line is to be drawn, it is clear that the present gift is nearer to it than that which the Court of Appeal had to consider in *Re Scarisbrick* [1951] Ch 622. The second-schedule class is narrower than a class of relations of every degree on both sides of the family. The question is whether the class is so narrow that the gift must be disqualified as a trust for the relief of poverty in the charitable sense... Is this properly to be regarded as a gift to such of a narrow class of near relatives as at the testator's death shall be in needy circumstances?

The basis for disqualification as a charitable gift must be that the restricted nature of the class leads to the conclusion that the gift is really a gift to the individual members of the class. In my view, the gift in clause 11 of the will is not of that character. The gift with which I am concerned has, in common with the gift which the Court of Appeal had to consider in *Re Scarisbrick*, the feature that the class of those eligible to benefit was not closed upon the testator's death. It remained open for a further period of 21 years. During that period issue of the named individuals born after the death of the testator will become members of the class. It is, in my view, impossible to attribute to the testator an intention to make a gift to those after-born issue as such. His intention must be taken to have been the relief of poverty amongst the class of which they would become members.

It follows that I am satisfied that the gift to the poor and needy of the class of persons set out in the second schedule to the will falls on the charitable side of the line, wherever that line has to be drawn.

Charity Commission Consultation on Draft Public Benefit Guidance (February 2007)

B10 *Exceptions for the relief of poverty*

46. In the case of charities for the relief of poverty, the pool from which the intended beneficiaries may be chosen may be more narrowly drawn than for other charitable purposes.

47. The case of *Re Scarisbrick*[92] is the principal authority establishing that charities for the relief of poverty, are excepted from the general principle that there must not be a personal family connection or tie within the definition for the pool from which the beneficiaries may be drawn.

48. The court concluded that the exception was established by a series of long-standing authorities which must accept as valid, not withstanding the general principle that

---

[92] [1951] Ch 622, p. 436, above.

applied to the other heads of charity, that a personal connection or tie would affect public benefit.

49.   This was confirmed in *Dingle v Turner*,[93] concerning a gift to pay pensions to poor employees of a family company, where Lord Cross reviewed and confirmed the poor relations cases as well as cases on poor employees. The 'poor relations' and 'poor employees' exceptions are well established and have been confirmed and applied by the court and by the Commission.

50.   Our provisional view is that the legal position will not be affected by the provisions in the Charities Act 2006, with its statutory requirement for public benefit. This is on the basis that *Dingle v Turner* still regards 'poor relations' and 'poor employees' charities as providing some public benefit. We shall return to this issue in more detail when we prepare and consult on the sub-sector guidance about public benefit and the relief of poverty.

QUESTIONS

1. Can you formulate a satisfactory definition of poverty?

	Should this be sought in terms of persons who pay no income tax, receive public assistance, or are entitled to legal aid? (Tudor, p. 29; (1956) 72 LQR 187 at pp. 206–207 (G. Cross); Nathan Report, paras. 120–140).

	Or should it be limited to persons who, for one reason or another, are ineligible to obtain relief from the State? See Charity Commission 'Public Benefit and the Prevention or Relief of Poverty' (February 2008).

2. Why are trusts for the relief of poverty enforced? See (2000) 20 LS 222 (A. Dunn).

C   ADVANCEMENT OF EDUCATION[94]

(i)   *Charitable purpose*

The concept of education has progressed a long way since the Preamble to the Charitable Uses Act 1601 spoke of 'the maintenance of schools of learning, free schools and scholars in universities' and 'the education and preferment of orphans'. As BUCKLEY LJ said in *Incorporated Council of Law Reporting for England and Wales v A-G*, it now extends 'to the improvement of a useful branch of human knowledge and its public dissemination'.[95] Education was, however, given a wide interpretation under the old law to include the promotion of the arts and culture. This has now been separated from the advancement of education to form a new head of charity, with the promotion of

---

[93] [1972] AC 601. See p. 432, above.

[94] H&M, pp. 409–416, 434–438; Luxton, pp. 117–124, 176–178; P&M, pp. 459–463; P&S, pp. 492–494; Pettit, pp. 255–259; Picarda, pp. 47–71; Snell, pp. 515–517; Tudor, pp. 47–73.

[95] [1972] Ch 73 at 102. In *IRC v Oldham Training and Enterprise Council* [1996] STC 1218, 1233 Lightman J recognised that the promotion and provision of vocational education and training and retraining of the public were charitable objects.

heritage and science.[96] In the light of this it is likely that education as a head of charity will be given a narrower interpretation, although what this interpretation is or should be remains controversial. It is clear that the concept of education includes 'satellite' purposes such as the payment of teachers and administrative staff,[97] and an educational institution may be charitable, even though it is a private company, so long as it does not operate for profit.[98] It has also been recognised that education is not limited to teaching. The charitable purpose may take place abroad.[99]

In **Royal Choral Society v Inland Revenue Commissioners** [1943] 2 All ER 101, the question was whether the appellants were a society 'established for charitable purposes only' and thus entitled to exemption from Income Tax. The objects of the society were 'to form and maintain a choir in order to promote the practice and performance of choral works, whether by way of concerts or choral pageants in the Royal Albert Hall or as otherwise decided from time to time'.

The Court of Appeal held that the Society was charitable as being established for the purposes of the advancement of aesthetic education.[100] LORD GREENE MR said at 104:

Dealing with the educational aspect from the point of view of the public who hear music, the Solicitor-General argued that nothing could be educational which did not involve teaching—as I understood him, teaching in the sense of a master teaching a class. He said that in the domain of art the only thing that could be educational in a charitable sense would be the education of the executants: the teaching of the painter, the training of the musician, and so forth. I protest against that narrow conception of education when one is dealing with aesthetic education. Very few people can become executants, or at any rate executants who can give pleasure either to themselves or to others; but a very large number of people can become instructed listeners with a trained and cultivated taste. In my opinion, a body of persons established for the purpose of raising the artistic taste of the country and established by an appropriate document which confines them to that purpose, is established for educational purposes, because the education of artistic taste is one of the most important things in the development of a civilised human being.

In **Re Dupree's Deed Trusts** [1945] Ch 16, a trust with capital of £5,000 was established for the purpose of providing an annual chess tournament for boys and young men under the age of 21 resident in the city of Portsmouth.[101] In spite of the argument of

---

[96] See p. 485, below.

[97] *Case of Christ's College, Cambridge* (1757) 1 Wm Bl 90.

[98] *Abbey Malvern Wells Ltd v Ministry of Local Government and Planning* [1951] Ch 728; *Re Girls' Public Day School Trust* [1951] Ch 400, where a girls' school carried on by a private company was held not to be a charity because profits could benefit the shareholders. See *Butterworth v Keeler* 219 NY 446, 114 NE 308 (1916); Scott and Scott, *Cases on Trusts* (5th edn), pp. 678–679.

[99] *Manoogian v Sonsino* [2002] EWHC 1304, [2002] WTLR 989 ('education and advancement in life of Armenian children').

[100] Presumably today this would be recognised as a charity under paragraph (f), being a charity for the promotion of arts or culture.

[101] This is not contrary to the Sex Discrimination Act 1975. Charities are expressly excepted: s. 43; Sex Discrimination Act 1975 (Amendment of Section 43) Order 1977, S.I. 1977 No. 528. In 1976 a Phyllis Loe

counsel for the next-of-kin that the encouragement of 'the playing of chess in schools would not be altogether desirable. It might take pupils away from cricket, football and athletic pursuits generally', the trust was upheld as an educational charitable trust. VAISEY J however had some anxiety as to the problem of drawing the right line in these cases. He said at 20:

One feels, perhaps, that one is on rather a slippery slope. If chess, why not draughts? If draughts, why not bezique, and so on, through to bridge and whist, and, by another route, to stamp collecting and the acquisition of birds' eggs? Those pursuits will have to be dealt with if and when they come up for consideration...

Re Hopkins' Will Trusts[102]
[1965] Ch 669 (Ch D, **Wilberforce J**)

The testatrix gave one third part of her estate to 'the Francis Bacon Society Inc.... to be earmarked and applied towards finding the Bacon–Shakespeare manuscripts and in the event of the same having been discovered by the date of my death then for the general purposes of the work and propaganda of the society'.

The objects of the Society were: '(1) To encourage the study of the works of Francis Bacon as philosopher, lawyer, statesman and poet; also his character, genius and life; his influence on his own and succeeding times, and the tendencies and results of his writings. (2) To encourage the general study of evidence in favour of Francis Bacon's authorship of the plays commonly ascribed to Shakespeare, and to investigate his connection with other works of the Elizabethan period.' The Society was registered as a charity under the Charities Act 1960.

Held. A valid educational charitable trust.[103]

Wilberforce J [after commenting that the Society was a registered charity under Charities Act 1960 and so was conclusively presumed to be a charity]:[104] Miss Hopkins could have given the money to the Society during her life and the Society under its constitution could have spent it for the purposes stated in the will. But the validity of her testamentary disposition is questioned. The basis for the challenge is that this is a gift to the Society not absolutely but upon a stated trust, so that it is necessary to see whether the trust is valid. It cannot be upheld as a gift upon valid but non-charitable trusts, and the Society does not seek so to uphold it. It can only be supported if it is a valid charitable trust. Whether it is so is what the court has to decide...

Let me say at once that no determination of the authorship of the 'Shakespeare' plays, or even of any subsidiary question relating to it, falls to be made in the present proceedings. The court is only concerned, at this point, with the practicability and later with the legality of carrying Miss Hopkins' wishes into effect, and it must decide this, one way or the other, upon the evidence of the experts which is before it.

Chess Tournament for Girls Trust was established for girls below the age of 18 educated in Portsmouth. See (1977) 41 Conv (NS) 8.

[102] (1965) 29 Conv (NS) 368 (M. Newark and A. Samuels).

[103] The trust was also held to be charitable for other purposes beneficial to the community, and would presumably be valid today as a trust for the advancement of art and culture under pagaraph (f). See p. 485, below.   [104] See Charities Act 1993, s. 4(1) [p. 585, below].

[His Lordship reviewed the evidence and continued:] On this evidence, should the conclusion be reached that the search for the Bacon–Shakespeare manuscripts is so manifestly futile that the court should not allow this bequest to be spent upon it as upon an object devoid of the possibility of any result? I think not. The evidence shows that the discovery of any manuscript of the plays is unlikely; but so are many discoveries before they are made (one may think of the Codex Sinaiticus, or the Tomb of Tutankhamen, or the Dead Sea Scrolls); I do not think that that degree of improbability has been reached which justifies the court in placing an initial interdict on the testatrix's benefaction.

I come, then, to the only question of law: is the gift of a charitable character? The society has put its case in the alternative under the two headings of education and of general benefit to the community and has argued separately for each. This compartmentalisation is derived from the accepted classification into four groups of the miscellany found in the Statute of Elizabeth (43 Eliz. I, c. 4). That Statute, preserved as to the preamble only by the Mortmain and Charitable Uses Act, 1888, lost even that precarious hold on the Statute Book when the Act of 1888 was repealed by the Charities Act, 1960, but the somewhat ossificatory classification to which it gave rise survives in the decided cases. It is unsatisfactory because the frontiers of 'educational purposes' (as of the other divisions) have been extended and are not easy to trace with precision, and because, under the fourth head, it has been held necessary for the court to find a benefit to the public within the spirit and intendment of the obsolete Elizabethan statute. The difficulty of achieving that, while at the same time keeping the law's view of what is charitable reasonably in line with modern requirements, explains what Lord Simonds accepted as the case-to-case approach of the courts: see *National Anti-Vivisection Society v IRC* [1948] AC 31. There are, in fact, examples of accepted charities which do not decisively fit into one rather than the other category. Examples are institutes for scientific research (see the *National Anti-Vivisection* case, *per* Lord Wright at 42, museums (see *Re Pinion* [1965] Ch 85 at 104), the preservation of ancient cottages (*Re Cranstoun* [1932] 1 Ch 537), and even the promotion of Shakespearian drama (*Re Shakespeare Memorial Trust* [1923] 2 Ch 398). The present may be such a case.

Accepting, as I have the authority of Lord Simonds for so doing, that the court must decide each case as best it can, on the evidence available to it, as to benefit, and within the moving spirit of decided cases, it would seem to me that a bequest for the purpose of search, or research, for the original manuscripts of England's greatest dramatist (whoever he was) would be well within the law's conception of charitable purposes. The discovery of such manuscripts, or of one such manuscript, would be of the highest value to history and to literature. It is objected, against this, that as we already have the text of the plays, from an almost contemporary date, the discovery of a manuscript would add nothing worth while. This I utterly decline to accept. Without any undue exercise of the imagination, it would surely be a reasonable expectation that the revelation of a manuscript would contribute, probably decisively, to a solution of the authorship problem, and this alone is benefit enough. It might also lead to improvements in the text. It might lead to more accurate dating.

Is there any authority, then, which should lead me to hold that a bequest to achieve this objective is not charitable? By Mr. Fox, for the next-of-kin, much reliance was placed on the decision on Bernard Shaw's will, the '*British Alphabet*' case (*Re Shaw* [1957] 1 WLR 729 [p. 364, above]). Harman J held that the gift was not educational because it merely tended to the increase of knowledge and that it was not within the fourth charitable category because it was not itself for a beneficial purpose but for the purpose of persuading the public by propaganda that it was beneficial. The gift was very different from the gift here. But the judge did say this at 737: 'if the object be merely the increase of knowledge, that is not in itself a charitable object unless it be combined with teaching or education'; and he referred to the House of Lords decision, *Whicker v Hume* (1858) 7 HL Cas 124, where, in relation to a gift for advancement of education and learning, two of the Lords read 'learning' as equivalent to 'teaching', thereby in his view implying that learning, in its ordinary meaning, is not a charitable purpose.

This decision certainly seems to place some limits upon the extent to which a gift for research may be regarded as charitable. Those limits are that either it must be 'combined with teaching or education', if it is to fall under the third head, or it must be beneficial to the community in a way regarded by the law as charitable, if it is to fall within the fourth category. The words 'combined with teaching or education', though well explaining what the judge had in mind when he rejected the gift in *Shaw's* case [1957] 1 WLR 729, are not easy to interpret in relation to other facts. I should be unwilling to treat them as meaning that the promotion of academic research is not a charitable purpose unless the researcher were engaged in teaching or education in the conventional meaning; and I am encouraged in this view by some words of Lord Greene MR in *Re Compton* [1945] Ch 123 at 127. The testatrix there had forbidden the income of the bequest to be used for research, and Lord Greene MR treated this as a negative definition of the education to be provided. It would, he said, exclude a grant to enable a beneficiary to conduct research on some point of history or science. This shows that Lord Greene MR considered that historic research might fall within the description of 'education'. I think, therefore, that the word 'education' as used by Harman J in *Re Shaw* must be used in a wide sense, certainly extending beyond teaching, and that the requirement is that, in order to be charitable, research must either be of educational value to the researcher or must be so directed as to lead to something which will pass into the store of educational material, or so as to improve the sum of communicable knowledge in an area which education may cover—education in this last context extending to the formation of literary taste and appreciation (compare *Royal Choral Society v IRC* [1943] 2 All ER 101 [p. 441, above]). Whether or not the test is wider than this, it is, as I have stated it, amply wide enough to include the purposes of the gift in this case.

As regards the fourth category, Harman J is evidently leaving it open to the court to hold, on the facts, that research of a particular kind may be beneficial to the community in a way which the law regards as charitable, 'beneficial' here not being limited to the production of material benefit (as through medical or scientific research) but including at least benefit in the intellectual or artistic fields.

So I find nothing in this authority to prevent me from finding that the gift falls under either the third or fourth head of the classification of charitable purposes.

On the other side there is *Re British School of Egyptian Archaeology* [1954] 1 WLR 546, also a decision of Harman J, a case much closer to the present. The trusts there were to excavate, to discover antiquities, to hold exhibitions, to publish works and to promote the training and assistance of students—all in relation to Egypt. Harman J held that the purposes were charitable, as being educational. The society was one for the diffusion of a certain branch of knowledge, namely, knowledge of the ancient past of Egypt; and it also had a direct educational purpose, namely, to train students. The conclusion reached that there was an educational charity was greatly helped by the reference to students, but it seems that Harman J must have accepted that the other objects—those of archaeological research—were charitable, too. They were quite independent objects on which the whole of the society's funds could have been spent, and the language 'the school has a direct educational purpose, namely, to train students' seems to show that the judge was independently upholding each set of objects.

Mr. Fox correctly pointed out that in that case there was a direct obligation to diffuse the results of the society's research and said that it was this that justified the finding that the archaeological purposes were charitable. I accept that research of a private character, for the benefit only of the members of a society, would not normally be educational—or otherwise charitable—as did Harman J [1954] 1 WLR 546 at 551, but I do not think that the research in the present case can be said to be of a private character, for it is inherently inevitable, and manifestly intended, that the result of any discovery should be published to the world. I think, therefore, that the *British School of Egyptian Archaeology* case supports the Society's contentions.

A number of other authorities were referred to as illustrating the wide variety of objects which have been accepted as educational or as falling under the fourth category but, since none of them is close to the present, I shall not refer to them. They are well enough listed in the standard authorities.

One final reference is appropriate: to *Re Shakespeare Memorial Trust* [1923] 2 Ch 398. The scheme there was for a number of objects which included the performance of Shakespearian and other classical English plays, and stimulating the art of acting. I refer to it for two purposes, first as an example of a case where the court upheld the gift either as educational or as for purposes beneficial to the community—an approach which commends itself to me here—and secondly as illustrative of the educational and public benefit accepted by the court as flowing from a scheme designed to spread the influence of Shakespeare as the author of the plays. This gift is not that, but it lies in the same field, for the improving of our literary heritage, and my judgment is for upholding it.

In **Re Besterman's Will Trusts** (1980) The Times, 21 January,[105] SLADE J, in upholding a trust for completing research on Voltaire and Rousseau, said:

(1) A trust for research will ordinarily qualify as a charitable trust if, but only if (a) the subject matter of the proposed research is a useful subject of study; and (b) it is contemplated that knowledge acquired as a result of the research will be disseminated to others; and (c) the trust is for the benefit of the public, or a sufficiently important section of the public.

(2) In the absence of a contrary context, however, the court will be readily inclined to construe a trust for research as importing subsequent dissemination of the results thereof.

(3) Furthermore, if a trust for research is to constitute a valid trust for the advancement of education, it is not necessary either (a) that a teacher/pupil relationship should be in contemplation, or (b) that the persons to benefit from the knowledge to be acquired should be persons who are already in the course of receiving 'education' in the conventional sense.

(4) In any case where the court has to determine whether a bequest for the purposes of research is or is not of a charitable nature, it must pay due regard to any admissible extrinsic evidence which is available to explain the wording of the will in question or the circumstances in which it was made.

---

[105] Applied in *McGovern v A-G* [1982] Ch 321 at 352 [p. 526, below] (research into the maintenance and observance of human rights).

In **Re Shaw's Will Trusts** [1952] Ch 163,[106] the testatrix, who was the widow of George Bernard Shaw, bequeathed the residue of her estate upon the following trusts: 'The making of grants contributions and payments to any foundation…having for its objects the bringing of the masterpieces of fine art within the reach of the people of Ireland of all classes in their own country.… The teaching promotion and encouragement in Ireland of self control, elocution, oratory, deportment, the arts of personal contact, of social intercourse, and the other arts of public, private, professional and business life…'

VAISEY J upheld the gift as an educational charitable trust. It was 'a sort of finishing school for the Irish people'. 'I think' he said at 172, at 55, 'that "education" includes…not only teaching, but the promotion or encouragement of these arts and graces of life which are, after all, perhaps the finest and best part of the human character…It is education of a desirable sort, and which, if corrected and augmented and amplified by other kinds of teaching and instruction, might have most beneficial results.'

In **Incorporated Council of Law Reporting for England and Wales v Attorney-General**[107] [1972] Ch 73, the Court of Appeal unanimously held that the Council was charitable under the head of other purposes beneficial to the community.[108] Two of the judges, Sachs and Buckley LJJ, held that it was charitable also as being for the advancement of education. BUCKLEY LJ said at 101:

Foster J declined to accept the view that the council's objects are educational, mainly, I think, upon the ground that in many respects they are not used for instructional purposes. He did, however, take the view that they are charitable on the ground that the purpose of the publication of The Law Reports is to enable judge-made law to be properly developed and administered by the courts, a purpose beneficial to the community and within the spirit of the preamble.

What then does the evidence establish about the need for reliable law reports and the reasons for publishing them? As the uncontradicted evidence of Professor Goodhart makes clear, in a legal system such as ours, in which judges' decisions are governed by precedents, reported decisions are the means by which legal principles (other than those laid down by statutes) are developed, established and made known, and by which the application of those legal principles to particular kinds of facts are illustrated and explained. Reported decisions may be said to be the tissue of the body of our non-statutory law. Whoever, therefore, would carry out any anatomical researches upon our non-statutory *corpus juris* must do so by research amongst, and study of, reported cases.

Professor Goodhart recalls that Sir Frederick Pollock in his paper entitled *The Science of Case Law* published in 1882 pointed out that the study of law is a science in the same sense as physics or chemistry are sciences, and that the material with which it is concerned consists of individual cases which must be analysed and measured as carefully as is the material in the other sciences. At about the same time the 'case system' of teaching law was introduced at the Harvard Law School, which has since become generally adopted. Accurate and authoritative

---

[106] See Holroyd, *The Shaw Companion* (1992), vol. 4, pp. 6–9 for a discussion of the case and a full text of the will.   [107] See p. 517, below.

[108] See also *Incorporated Council of Law Reporting of the State of Queensland v Comr of Taxation* (1971) 45 *Australian Law Journal*R 552; (1972) 88 LQR 171.

law reports are thus seen to be essential both for the advancement of legal education and the proper administration of justice. As Professor Goodhart says: 'accuracy in The Law Reports is, therefore, as important for the science of law as is the accuracy of instruments in the physical sciences'.

The legal profession has from times long past been termed a learned profession, and rightly so, for no man can properly practise or apply the law who is not learned in that field of law with which he is concerned. He must have more than an aptitude and more than a skill. He must be learned in a sense importing true scholarship. In a system of law such as we have in this country this scholarship can only be acquired and maintained by a continual study of case law.

I agree with Foster J in thinking that, when counsel in court cites a case to a judge, counsel is not in any real sense 'educating' the judge, counsel performing the role of a teacher and the judge filling the role of a pupil; but I do not agree with him that the process should not be regarded as falling under the charitable head of 'the advancement of education'.

In a number of cases learned societies have been held to be charitable. Sometimes the case has been classified under Lord Macnaghten's fourth head, sometimes under the second. It does not really matter under which head such a case is placed, but for my own part I prefer to treat the present case as falling within the class of purposes for the advancement of education rather than within the final class of other purposes for the benefit of the community. For the present purpose the second head should be regarded as extending to the improvement of a useful branch of human knowledge and its public dissemination.

His Lordship referred to *Beaumont v Oliveira* (1869) 4 Ch App 309, where bequests to the Royal Society whose object is 'improving natural knowledge' and the Royal Geographical Society for 'the improvement and diffusion of geographical knowledge' were held charitable under the fourth head of charity; *Royal College of Surgeons of England v National Provincial Bank Ltd* [1952] AC 631, where the objects were 'the encouragement of the study and practice of the art and science of surgery'; *Re Lopes* [1931] 2 Ch 130, a gift to the Zoological Society of London whose objects are 'the advancement of Zoology and animal physiology and the introduction of new and curious subjects of the animal kingdom'; and *Re British School of Egyptian Archaeology* [1954] 1 WLR 546 [p. 444, above], where gifts were upheld as being for the advancement of education; and continued:

The fact that the council's publications can be regarded as a necessary part of a practising lawyer's equipment does not prevent the council from being established exclusively for charitable purposes. The practising lawyer and the judge must both be lifelong students in that field of scholarship for the study of which The Law Reports provide essential material and a necessary service. The benefit which the council confers upon members of the legal profession in making accurate reports available is that it facilitates the study and ascertainment of the law. It also helps the lawyer to earn his livelihood, but that is incidental to or consequential on the primary scholastic function of advancing and disseminating knowledge of the law, and does not detract from the exclusively charitable character of the council's objects: compare *Royal College of Surgeons of England v National Provincial Bank Ltd* [1952] AC 631 and *Royal College of Nursing v St Marylebone Corpn* [1959] 1 WLR 1077.

The service which publication of The Law Reports provides benefits not only those actively engaged in the practice and administration of the law, but also those whose business it is to study and teach law academically, and many others who need to study the law for the purposes of their trades, businesses, professions or affairs. In all these fields, however, the nature of the service is the same: it enables the reader to study, and by study to acquaint himself with and instruct himself in the law of this country. There is nothing here which negatives an exclusively charitable purpose.

Although the objects of the council are commercial in the sense that the council exists to publish and sell its publications, they are unself-regarding. The members are prohibited from deriving any profit from the council's activities, and the council itself, although not debarred from making a profit out of its business, can only apply any such profit in the further pursuit of its objects. The council is consequently not prevented from being a charity by reason of any commercial element in its activities.

I therefore reach the conclusion that the council is a body established exclusively for charitable purposes and is entitled to be registered under the Act of 1960.

In **Re South Place Ethical Society** [1980] 1 WLR 1565, the objects of the Society were 'the study and dissemination of ethical principles and the cultivation of a rational religious sentiment'. DILLON J held that the trust was for the advancement of education, and said at 1576:

The first part of the objects is the study and dissemination of ethical principles. Dissemination, I think, includes dissemination of the fruits of the study, and I have no doubt that that part of the objects satisfies the criterion of charity as being for the advancement of education. The second part, the cultivation of a rational religious sentiment, is considerably more difficult. As I have already said, I do not think that the cultivation is limited to cultivation of the requisite sentiment in the members of the Society and in no one else. In the context the Society is outward looking, and the cultivation would extend to all members of the public whom the Society's teachings may reach. The sentiment or state of mind is to be rational, that is to say founded in reason. As I see it, a sentiment or attitude of mind founded in reason can only be cultivated or encouraged to grow by educational methods, including music, and the development of the appreciation of music by performances of high quality. The difficulty in this part of the Society's objects lies in expressing a very lofty and possibly unattainable ideal in a very few words, and the difficulty is compounded by the choice of the word 'religious', which while giving the flavour of what is in mind, is not in my view used in its correct sense.[109]

In **Re Koeppler Will Trusts** [1986] Ch 423,[110] the testator left a share of his residuary estate 'for the warden and the chairman of the academic advisory council... of the institution known as Wilton Park... for the benefit at their discretion of the said institution as long as Wilton Park remains a British contribution to the formation of an

---

[109] P. 466, below; [1993] Charity Commissioners' Report 1 (Cult Information Centre, for the education of the public, mainly students, about techniques used for recruitment into alternative or unconventional religious or contemporary sects sometimes known as 'new religious movements' held to be charitable). Cp. *Human Life International in Canada Inc v Canada (Minister of National Revenue)* [1998] 3 FC 202 (Federal Court of Canada held a trust to 'promote true Christian family values, encourage chastity and teach natural family planning' by lectures and literature was not charitable because, rather than constituting a formal training of the mind or improving human knowledge, the trust was aimed at swaying public opinion on a social matter). In *Living in Radiance's Application for Registration as a Charity* [2007] WTLR 683 an institution which provided information, services, and education about the science of meditation and peace education was not registered because it failed to add to the participants' factual knowledge or skills base.

[110] [1985] Conv 412 (T.G. Watkin).

informed international public opinion and to the promotion of greater co-operation in Europe and the West in general'. In holding that the gift in favour of Wilton Park was charitable, SLADE LJ said at 435:

Concluding, therefore, as I do, that the gift falls to be construed as a 'purpose trust' for the furtherance of the work of the Wilton Park project, in the form which that work took at the date of the death, were those purposes of an exclusively charitable nature? The evidence as to the nature of the work of the Wilton Park project is to be found summarised fully and accurately in the judge's judgment [1984] Ch 243 and I propose merely to draw attention to certain particular points.

The organisation and conduct of the conferences which had been held since 1950 at Wiston House were clearly the central features of the Wilton Park project. The 'specific aspects' dealt with at each conference covered a wide range of topics. Examples of these specific aspects are to be found in the programmes for the four conferences immediately preceding the date of the testator's will and those for the four conferences immediately preceding his death. They were:

'(1) An inquiry into the "quality of life", ecology and the environment; participation in government and industry; tensions in free societies; (2) Europe and the emergent patterns and super-power relationships; (3) the unification of Europe; a balance sheet; (4) the requirements of Western defence and the possibilities of arms control; (5) the European Community and its external relations; (6) the media, public opinion and the decision-making process in government; (7) security issues as a factor in domestic and international politics; (8) labour and capital and the future of industrial society.'

As the judge observed, those specific themes are self-evidently matters on which persons of differing political persuasions might have differing views and some of the speakers invited to speak at plenary sessions of the conferences were politicians. However, he found, at 251d, that 'it is clear that Wilton Park has taken pains to avoid inculcating any particular political viewpoint'. There is therefore no question of the Wilton Park conferences being intended to further the interests of a particular political party.

No one would suggest that the mere organisation and conduct of conferences, albeit dealing with topics of public interest, would necessarily constitute a charitable activity. If such activities are to be charitable, they must be shown to be for the benefit of the public, or the community, in a sense or manner within the intendment of the preamble to the statute 43 Eliz. 1, c.4. The possibly relevant head of charity in the present case is that of the advancement of education.

In the context of the activities of the Wilton Park project, the judge had this to say, at 261f–g:

'Let me consider first whether the Wilton Park process can properly be described as educational. Mr. McCall submitted, and I accept, that the following salient points emerged from the evidence: (i) the conferences sought to improve the minds of participants, not necessarily by adding to their factual knowledge but by expanding their wisdom and capacity to understand; (ii) the subjects discussed at conferences were recognised academic subjects in higher education; (iii) the conferences operated by a process of discussion designed to elicit an exchange of views in a manner familiar in places of higher education; (iv) the conferences were designed to capitalise on the expertise of participants who were there both to learn and to instruct.'

Having considered certain arguments to the contrary submitted by Mr. Farrow on behalf of the second defendant, the judge concluded, at p. 262f: 'the Wilton Park process can be described as educational' and, I think, by necessary inference, that when looked at on its own it can properly be described as charitable.

As I understood Mr. Farrow's argument, he did not seek to challenge this conclusion before this court. He conceded that if, on the true construction of the will, the purpose of the gift is the furtherance of the Wilton Park project, then that is an educational purpose and the gift is of a charitable nature. The essential point of his argument was that the purpose of the gift is furtherance of the formation end and the promotion end—an argument which, for the reasons already given, I would reject.

I think that this concession made on behalf of the second defendant was rightly made. As the judge said, at 262: 'the concept of education is now wide enough to cover the intensive discussion process adopted by Wilton Park in relation to a somewhat special class of adults, persons influencing opinion in their own countries, designed (as I was told Sir Heinz put it) to dent opinions and to cross-fertilise ideas.'

Mr. McCall referred us to what was said by Lord Hailsham of St. Marylebone LC in *IRC v McMullen* [1981] AC 1 at 15: 'both the legal conception of charity, and within it the educated man's ideas about education, are not static, but moving and changing'. As to the element of public benefit, the participants in the courses appear to have been selected from widely drawn categories, as persons likely to influence opinion in their own country. Like the judge, I find little difficulty in inferring that not only they themselves are likely to benefit from the courses, but are likely to pass on such benefits to others.

Some activities, not otherwise educational, are treated as being for the advancement of education if they are carried out as part of school or university activities.[111]

Inland Revenue Commissioners v McMullen
[1981] AC 1 (HL, **Lord Hailsham of St Marylebone LC, Lords Diplock, Salmon, Russell of Killowen** and **Keith of Kinkel**)

In 1972 the Football Association created a trust, the objects of which were stated in clause 3(a) of the deed to be, *inter alia*, 'to organise or provide or assist in the organisation and provision of facilities which will enable and encourage pupils of schools and universities in any part of the United Kingdom to play association football or other games or sports and thereby to assist in ensuring that due attention is given to the physical education and development of such pupils as well as to the development and occupation of their minds'. There were then set out various methods to be adopted to further these objects.

The Charity Commissioners registered the trust as a charity under the Charities Act 1960, section 4. An appeal against registration was allowed by Walton J [1978] 1 WLR 664, and the Court of Appeal by a majority (Stamp and Orr LJJ, Bridge LJ dissenting) [1979] 1 WLR 130. On appeal by the trustees.

Held (reversing Court of Appeal): A valid educational charitable trust.

Lord Hailsham of St Marylebone LC: Four questions arose for decision below. In the first place neither the parties nor the judgment below were in agreement as to the proper construction

[111] Similarly *Re Gray* [1925] Ch 362 [p. 513, below] (sport in the Army). See also *Re Lipinski's Will Trusts* [1976] Ch 235 at 242.

of the trust deed itself. Clearly this is a preliminary debate which must be settled before the remaining questions are even capable of decision. In the second place the appellants contend and the respondents dispute that, on the correct construction of the deed, the trust is charitable as being for the advancement of education. Thirdly, the appellants contend and the respondents dispute that if they are wrong on the second question the trust is charitable at least because it falls within the fourth class of Lord Macnaghten's categories as enumerated in *Income Tax Special Purposes Comrs v Pemsel* [1891] AC 531 at 583 [p. 414, above], as a trust beneficial to the community within the spirit and intendment of the preamble to the statute 43 Eliz. 1, c.4. Fourthly the appellants contend and the respondents dispute that, even if not otherwise charitable, the trust is a valid charitable trust falling within section 1 of the Recreational Charities Act 1958 [p. 496, below], that is a trust to provide or to assist in the provision of facilities for recreation or other leisure time occupation provided in the interests of social welfare....

Since we have reached the view that the trust is a valid educational charity their Lordships have not sought to hear argument nor, therefore, to reach a conclusion on any but the first two disputed questions in the dispute. Speaking for myself, however, I do not wish my absence of decision on the third or fourth points to be interpreted as an indorsement of the majority judgments in the Court of Appeal nor as necessarily dissenting from the contrary views contained in the minority judgment of Bridge LJ.[112] For me at least the answers to the third and fourth questions are still left entirely undecided.

I now turn to the question of construction.

His Lordship held that the deed meant that the 'purpose of the settlor is to promote the physical education and development of pupils at schools and universities as an addition to such part of their education as relates to their mental education by providing the facilities and assistance to games and sports in the manner set out at greater length and in greater detail in the enumerated subclauses of clause 3(a) of the deed', and continued:

On a proper analysis, therefore, I do not find clause 3(a) ambiguous. But, before I part with the question of construction, I would wish to express agreement with a contention made on behalf of the appellants and of the Attorney-General, but not agreed to on behalf of the respondents, that in construing trust deeds the intention of which is to set up a charitable trust, and in others too, where it can be claimed that there is an ambiguity, a benignant construction should be given if possible.[113] This was the maxim of the civil law: *semper in dubiis benigniora praeferenda sunt*. There is a similar maxim in English law: *ut res magis valeat quam pereat*. It certainly applies to charities when the question is one of uncertainty (*Weir v Crum-Brown* [1908] AC 162, 167), and, I think, also where a gift is capable of two constructions one of which would make it void and the other effectual (cf. *Bruce v Deer Presbytery* (1867) LR 1 Sc & Div 96, 97; *Houston v Burns* [1918] AC 337, *per* Lord Finlay LC, at 341–2, and cf. also *Re Bain* [1930] 1 Ch 224, 230). In the present case I do not find it necessary to resort to benignancy in order to construe the clause, but, had I been in doubt, I would certainly have been prepared to do so.

I must now turn to the deed, construed in the manner in which I have found it necessary to construe it, to consider whether it sets up a valid charitable trust for the advancement of education.

[112] Now upheld in *Guild v IRC* [1992] 2 AC 496 [p. 496, below].
[113] See p. 411, above.

It is admitted, of course, that the words 'charity' and 'charitable' bear, for the purposes of English law and equity, meanings totally different from the senses in which they are used in ordinary educated speech or, for instance, in the Authorised Version of the Bible (contrast, for instance, the expression 'cold as charity' with the Authorised Version of I Corinthians xiii and both of these with the decisions in *Incorporated Council of Law Reporting for England and Wales v A-G* [1972] Ch 73 [p. 446, above]; *IRC v Yorkshire Agricultural Society* [1928] 1 KB 611; *Brisbane City Council v A-G for Queensland* [1979] AC 411; but I do not share the view, implied by Stamp LJ and Orr LJ in the instant case [1979] 1 WLR 130, 139, that the words 'education' and 'educational' bear, or can bear, for the purposes of the law of charity, meanings different from those current in present-day educated English speech. I do not believe that there is such a difference. What has to be remembered, however, is that, as Lord Wilberforce pointed out in *Re Hopkins' Will Trusts* [1965] Ch 669, 678, and in *Scottish Burial Reform and Cremation Society Ltd v Glasgow City Corpn* [1968] AC 138, especially at 154, both the legal conception of charity, and within it the educated man's ideas about education, are not static, but moving and changing. Both change with changes in ideas about social values. Both have evolved with the years. In particular in applying the law to contemporary circumstances it is extremely dangerous to forget that thoughts concerning the scope and width of education differed in the past greatly from those which are now generally accepted.

In saying this I do not in the least wish to cast doubt on *Re Nottage* [1895] 2 Ch 649 [p. 514, below], which was referred to in both courts below and largely relied on by the respondents here. Strictly speaking *Re Nottage* was not a case about education at all. The issue there was whether the bequest came into the fourth class of charity categorised in Lord Macnaghten's classification of 1891. The mere playing of games or enjoyment of amusement or competition is not *per se* charitable, nor necessarily educational, though they may (or may not) have an educational or beneficial effect if diligently practised. Neither am I deciding in the present case even that a gift for physical education *per se* and not associated with persons of school age or just above would necessarily be a good charitable gift. That is a question which the courts may have to face at some time in the future. But in deciding what is or is not an educational purpose for the young in 1980 it is not irrelevant to point out what Parliament considered to be educational for the young in 1944 when, by the Education Act of that year, in sections 7 and 53 (which are still on the statute book), Parliament attempted to lay down what was then intended to be the statutory system of education organised by the state, and the duties of the local education authorities and the minister in establishing and maintaining the system. Those sections are so germane to the present issue that I cannot forbear to quote them both. Section 7 provides (in each of the sections the emphasis being mine):

'The statutory system of public education shall be organised in three progressive stages to be known as primary education, secondary education, and further education; and it shall be the duty of the local education authority for every area, so far as their powers extend, to contribute towards the *spiritual, moral, mental, and physical development of the community by secur- ing that efficient education throughout those stages shall be available to meet the needs of the population of their area*.'

[His Lordship quoted section 53(1) and (2) of the same Act and continued:]

There is no trace in these sections of an idea of education limited to the development of mental, vocational or practical skills, to grounds or facilities the special perquisite of particular schools, or of any schools or colleges, or term-time, or particular localities, and there is express recognition of the contribution which extra-curricular activities and voluntary societies or bod- ies can make even in the promotion of the purely statutory system envisaged by the Act. In the light of section 7 in particular I would be very reluctant to confine the meaning of education to formal instruction in the classroom or even the playground, and I consider it sufficiently wide to cover all the activities envisaged by the settlor in the present case. One of the affidavits filed on the part of the respondent referred to the practices of ancient Sparta. I am not sure that this particular precedent is an entirely happy one, but from a careful perusal of Plato's *Republic* I doubt whether its author would have agreed with Stamp LJ in regarding 'physical education and development' as an elusive phrase, or as other than an educational charity, at least when used in association with the formal education of the young during the period when they are pupils of schools or *in statu pupillari* at universities.

It is, of course, true that no authority exactly in point could be found which is binding on your Lordships in the instant appeal. Nevertheless, I find the first instance case of *Re Mariette* [1915] 2 Ch 284, a decision of Eve J, both stimulating and instructive. Counsel for the respondents properly reminded us that this concerned a bequest effectively tied to a particular institution. Nevertheless, I cannot forbear to quote a phrase from the judgment, always bearing in mind the danger of quoting out of context. Eve J said at 288:

> 'No one of sense could be found to suggest that between those ages [10 and 19] any boy can be properly educated unless at least as much attention is given to the development of his body as is given to the development of his mind.'[114]

Apart from the limitation to the particular institution I would think that these words apply as well to the settlor's intention in the instant appeal as to the testator's in *Re Mariette,* and I regard the limitation to the pupils of schools and universities in the instant case as a sufficient association with the provision of formal education to prevent any danger or vagueness in the object of the trust or irresponsibility or capriciousness in application by the trustees. I am far from suggesting that the concept either of education or of physical education even for the young is capable of indefinite extension. On the contrary, I do not think that the courts have as yet explored the extent to which elements of organisation, instruction, or the disciplined inculcation of information, instruction or skill may limit the whole concept of education. I believe that in some ways it will prove more extensive, in others more restrictive than has been thought hitherto. But it is clear at least to me that the decision in *Re Mariette* is not to be read in a sense which confines its application for ever to gifts to a particular institution. It has been extended already in *Re Mellody* [1918] 1 Ch 228 to gifts for annual treats for schoolchildren in a particular locality (another decision of Eve J); to playgrounds for children (*Re Chesters* 25 July, 1934, unreported), and possibly *not* educational, but referred to in *IRC v Baddeley* [1955] AC 572, 596); to a children's outing (*Re Ward's Estate* (1937) 81 Sol Jo 397); to a prize for chess to boys and young men resident in the city of Portsmouth (*Re Dupree's Deed Trusts* [1945] Ch 16 [p. 441, above], a decision of Vaisey J) and for the furthering of the Boy Scouts movement by helping to purchase sites for camping, outfits, etc. (*Re Webber* [1954] 1 WLR 1500; another decision of Vaisey J). In that case Vaisey J is reported as saying, at 1501:

> 'I am bound to say that I am surprised to hear that anyone suggests that the Boy Scouts movement,[115] as distinguished from the Boy Scout Association, or the Boy Scouts organisation,

---

[114] Bequest of £1,000 to the Governing Body of Aldenham School for the purpose of building Eton fives courts or squash rackets courts held to be valid charitable gift. Eve J added: 'to leave 200 boys at large and to their own devices during their leisure hours would be to court catastrophe; it would not be educating them, but would probably result in their quickly relapsing into something approaching barbarism'.

[115] Its purpose is stated in its charter to be the instruction of 'boys of all classes in the principles of discipline, loyalty and good citizenship'.

or any other form of words, is other than an educational charity. I should have thought that it was well settled and well understood that the objects of the organisation of boy scouts is an education of a very special kind no doubt, but still, none the less, educational.'

It is important to remember that in the instant appeal we are dealing with the concept of physical education and development of the young deliberately associated by the settlor with the status of pupillage in schools or universities (of which, according to the evidence, about 95 per cent are within the age group 17 to 22). We are not dealing with adult education, physical or otherwise, as to which some considerations may be different. Whether one looks at the statute or the cases, the picture of education when applied to the young which emerges is complex and varied, but not, to borrow Stamp LJ's epithet [1979] 1 WLR 130, 134h, 'elusive'. It is the picture of a balanced and systematic process of instruction, training and practice containing, to borrow from section 7 of the Act of 1944, both spiritual, moral, mental and physical elements, the totality of which in any given case may vary with, for instance, the availability of teachers and facilities, and the potentialities, limitations and individual preferences of the pupils. But the totality of the process consists as much in the balance between each of the elements as in the enumeration of the things learned or the places in which the activities are carried on. I reject any idea which would cramp the education of the young within the school or university syllabus, confine it within the school or university campus, limit it to formal instruction, or render it devoid of pleasure in the exercise of skill. It is expressly acknowledged to be a subject in which the voluntary donor can exercise his generosity, and I can find nothing contrary to the law of charity which prevents a donor providing a trust which is designed to improve the balance between the various elements which go into the education of the young. That is what in my view the object of the instant settlement seeks to do.

I am at pains to disclaim the view that the conception of this evolving, and therefore not static, view of education is capable of infinite abuse or, even worse, proving void for uncertainty....

I also wish to be on my guard against the 'slippery slope' argument of which I see a reflection in Stamp LJ's reference to 'hunting, shooting and fishing'. It seems to me that that is an argument with which Vaisey J dealt effectively in *Re Dupree's Deed Trusts* [1945] Ch 16, in which he validated the chess prize.

[His Lordship quoted from Vaisey J at 20, set out at p. 442, above, and continued:] My Lords, for these reasons I reach the conclusion that the trust is a valid charitable gift for the advancement of education, which, after all, is what it claims to be. The conclusion follows that the appeal should be allowed, the judgments appealed from be reversed and the order for registration made by the commissioners be restored.

(ii) Public benefit

It was in the area of education that the modern emphasis on the necessity for 'public benefit' first came to the fore. The question was hardly material in the low-tax days before 1939. If it was charitable to advance education among the many, why was it not charitable to advance education among the few? Indeed, the highly selective system of British education assumed this. Scholarships for boys born in particular villages, or for boys to be educated at particular schools, have been upheld for centuries, as have 'closed' scholarships to individual Colleges at Oxford or Cambridge. The fiscal exemptions which charities enjoy, the dramatic increase in the rates of taxation from 1939 and the emphasis upon equality in education rather than selectivity prompt the asking of a different question: even if the provision of money for the education of a

CHARITABLE PURPOSES & DESCRIPTIONS

selected few is to be encouraged, how is it possible to justify the tax-free status of such money? In short, the law of charity must not be allowed to develop into a tax-planning device for the tax-free education of the children of the wealthy;[116] nor must employers, by setting up educational trusts for the children of their employees, be able to use it for commercial advantage.[117] The same sort of concept relating to public benefit carried over to religious trusts. We have seen that the problem has been avoided in the case of trusts for the relief of poverty [see p. 432, above]. The presumption that trusts for the advancement of education were presumed to satisfy the test of public benefit was removed by the Charities Act 2006, section 3(2). The old law remains relevant, however, in determining what the public benefit might be for this type of charitable object. In March 2008 the Charity Commission published draft supplementary guidance on 'Public Benefit and the Advancement of Education'.

Oppenheim v Tobacco Securities Trust Co Ltd[118]
[1951] AC 297 (HL, **Lords Simonds, Normand, Oaksey, Morton of Henryton** and **MacDermott**)

The income of a trust fund was directed to be applied 'in providing for...the education of children of employees or former employees of the British-American Tobacco Co Ltd...or any of its subsidiary or allied companies in such manner...as the acting trustees shall in their absolute discretion...think fit' with power also to apply the capital for the like purposes.

The number of employees of the company and their subsidiary and allied companies exceeded 110,000. The question was whether the class to be benefited was a sufficient section of the public.

Held. (Lord MacDermott dissenting): Because the qualification to benefit was based upon a personal nexus, the class of beneficiaries was not a section of the public and the trust was void.

[116] Goodman Report, paras. 47 (Costly Services), 60–61 (Education), p. 145; House of Commons Report, vol. I, paras. 45–52, vol. II, pp. 39–43, 93, 164–165, 249–271. See [1996] 60 Conv 24 (J. Jaconelli). See also p. 411, above.

[117] See *Wicks v Firth* [1983] 2 AC 214 (scholarships paid by trustees of Imperial Chemical Industries Educational Trust to children of higher-paid employees of ICI held (Lord Templeman dissenting) not taxable as emoluments of the fathers' employments). The effect of the decision was reversed by Finance Act 1983, s.20, in respect of scholarships awarded after 15 March, 1983. *Glynn v IRC* [1990] 2 AC 298 (school fees of taxpayer's daughter at Roedean paid directly by employer pursuant to taxpayer's contract of service held to be perquisite of employment and therefore taxable). See also *Sherdley v Sherdley* [1988] AC 213 (taxpayer held entitled to apply against himself for an order under Matrimonial Causes Act 1973, s.23(1)(d) that he pay school fees for the benefit of his infant children; the sole purpose of the application was to obtain tax advantages).

[118] (1951) 67 LQR 162 (R.E.M.), 164 (A.L.G.); *Caffoor v Income Tax Comr, Colombo* [1961] AC 584 at 602, *per* Lord Radcliffe. See also *Davies v Perpetual Trustee Co Ltd* [1959] AC 439 (a gift of land in Sydney, New South Wales 'to the Presbyterians the descendants of those settled in the Colony hailing from or born in the North of Ireland to be held in trust for the purpose of establishing a college for the education and tuition of their youth in the standards of the Westminster Divines as taught in the Holy Scriptures' held void by Privy Council. The class of persons was 'a fluctuating body of private individuals', and in no sense 'a section of the community'). See also *Southwood v A-G* (2000) 80 P & CR D34 [see p. 525, below].

Lord Simonds: My Lords, once more your Lordships have to consider the difficult subject of charitable trusts, and this time a question is asked to which no wholly satisfactory answer can be given.

Before I turn to the authorities I will make some preliminary observations. It is a clearly established principle of the law of charity that a trust is not charitable unless it is directed to the public benefit. This is sometimes stated in the proposition that it must benefit the community or a section of the community. Negatively it is said that a trust is not charitable if it confers only private benefits. In the recent case of *Gilmour v Coats* [1949] AC 426 [p. 471, below], this principle was reasserted. It is easy to state and has been stated in a variety of ways, the earliest statement that I find being in *Jones v Williams* (1767) Amb 651 in which Lord Hardwicke LC is briefly reported as follows: 'Definition of charity: a gift to a general public use, which extends to the poor as well as to the rich...'. With a single exception, to which I shall refer, this applies to all charities. We are apt now to classify them by reference to Lord Macnaghten's division in *Income Tax Special Purposes Comrs v Pemsel* [1891] AC 531 at 538, and, as I have elsewhere pointed out, it was at one time suggested that the element of public benefit was not essential except for charities falling within the fourth class, 'other purposes beneficial to the community'. This is certainly wrong except in the anomalous case of trusts for the relief of poverty with which I must specifically deal. In the case of trusts for educational purposes the condition of public benefit must be satisfied. The difficulty lies in determining what is sufficient to satisfy the test, and there is little to help your Lordships to solve it.

If I may begin at the bottom of the scale, a trust established by a father for the education of his son is not a charity. The public element, as I will call it, is not supplied by the fact that from that son's education all may benefit. At the other end of the scale the establishment of a college or university is beyond doubt a charity. 'Schools of learning and free schools and scholars of universities' are the very words of the preamble to the Statute of Elizabeth. So also the endowment of a college, university or school by the creation of scholarships or bursaries is a charity and none the less because competition may be limited to a particular class of persons. It is upon this ground, as Lord Greene MR pointed out in *Re Compton* [1945] Ch 123 at 136 that the so-called Founder's Kin cases can be rested. The difficulty arises where the trust is not for the benefit of any institution either then existing or by the terms of the trust to be brought into existence, but for the benefit of a class of persons at large. Then the question is whether that class of persons can be regarded as such a 'section of the community' as to satisfy the test of public benefit. These words 'section of the community' have no special sanctity, but they conveniently indicate first, that the possible (I emphasize the word 'possible') beneficiaries must not be numerically negligible, and secondly, that the quality which distinguishes them from other members of the community, so that they form by themselves a section of it, must be a quality which does not depend on their relationship to a particular individual. It is for this reason that a trust for the education of members of a family or, as in *Re Compton*, of a number of families cannot be regarded as charitable. A group of persons may be numerous but, if the nexus between them is their personal relationship to a single *propositus* or to several *propositi*, they are neither the community nor a section of the community for charitable purposes.

I come, then, to the present case where the class of beneficiaries is numerous but the difficulty arises in regard to their common and distinguishing quality. That quality is being children of employees of one or other of a group of companies. I can make no distinction between children of employees and the employees themselves. In both cases the common quality is found in employment by particular employers. The latter of the two cases by which the Court of Appeal held itself to be bound, *Re Hobourn Aero Components Ltd's Air Raid Distress Fund* [1946] Ch 194, is a direct authority for saying that such a common quality does not constitute its possessors a section of the public for charitable purposes. In the former case, *Re Compton,* Lord Greene MR had by way of illustration placed members of a family and employees of a particular employer on the same footing, finding neither in common kinship nor in common employment the sort of nexus which is sufficient. My Lords, I am so fully in agreement with what was said by Lord Greene in both cases and by my noble and learned friend, then Morton LJ in the *Hobourn* case, that I am in danger of repeating without improving upon their words. No one who has been versed for many years in this difficult and very artificial branch of the law can be unaware of its illogicalities, but I join with my noble and learned friend in echoing the observations which he cited [1946] Ch 194 at 208 from the judgment of Russell LJ in *Re Grove-Grady* [1929] 1 Ch 557 at 582, and I agree with him that the decision in *Re Drummond* [1914] 2 Ch 90 'imposed a very healthy check upon the extension of the legal definition of "charity"'. It appears to me that it would be an extension, for which there is no justification in principle or authority, to regard common employment as a quality which constitutes those employed a section of the community. It must not, I think, be forgotten that charitable institutions enjoy rare and increasing privileges, and that the claim to come within that privileged class should be clearly established. With the single exception of *Re Rayner* (1920) 89 LJ Ch 369, which I must regard as of doubtful authority, no case has been brought to the notice of the House in which such a claim as this has been made, where there is no element of poverty in the beneficiaries, but just this and no more, that they are the children of those in a common employment.

Learned counsel for the appellant sought to fortify his case by pointing to the anomalies that would ensue from the rejection of his argument. For, he said, admittedly those who follow a profession or calling, clergymen, lawyers, colliers, tobacco-workers and so on, are a section of the public; how strange then it would be if, as in the case of railwaymen, those who follow a particular calling are all employed by one employer. Would a trust for the education of railwaymen be charitable, but a trust for the education of men employed on the railways by the Transport Board not be charitable? And what of service of the Crown whether in the civil service or the armed forces? Is there a difference between soldiers and soldiers of the King? My Lords, I am not impressed by this sort of argument and will consider on its merits, if the occasion should arise, the case where the description of the occupation and the employment is in effect the same, where in a word, if you know what a man does, you know who employs him to do it. It is to me a far more cogent argument, as it was to my noble and learned friend in the *Hobourn* case, that if a section of the public is constituted by the personal relation of employment, it is impossible to say that it is not constituted by 1,000 as by 100,000 employees, and, if by 1,000, then by 100, and, if by 100, then by 10. I do not mean merely that there is a difficulty in drawing the line, though that too is significant: I have it also in mind that, though the actual number of employees at any one moment might be small, it might increase to any extent, just as, being large, it might decrease to any extent. If the number of employees is the test of validity, must the court take into account potential increase or decrease, and, if so, as at what date? ...

I would also, as I have previously indicated, say a word about the so called 'poor relations' cases. I do so only because they have once more been brought forward as an argument in favour of a more generous view of what may be charitable. It would not be right for me to affirm or to denounce or to justify these decisions: I am concerned only to say that the law of charity, so far as it relates to 'the relief of aged, impotent and poor people' (I quote from the statute) and to poverty in general, has followed its own line, and that it is not useful to try to harmonize decisions on that branch of the law with the broad proposition on which the determination of this case must rest. It is not for me to say what fate might await those cases if in a poverty case this House had to consider them . . . [119]

The appeal should in my opinion be dismissed with costs.

Lord MacDermott (dissenting): My Lords, it is not disputed that this trust is for the advancement of education. The question is whether it is of a public nature, whether, in the words of Lord Wrenbury in *Verge v Somerville* [1924] AC 496 at 499, 'it is for the benefit of the community or of an appreciably important class of the community'. The relevant class here is that from which those to be educated are to be selected. The appellant contends that this class is public in character; the respondent bank (as personal representative of the last surviving settlor) denies this and says that the class is no more than a group of private individuals.

Until comparatively recently the usual way of approaching an issue of this sort, at any rate where educational trusts were concerned, was, I believe, to regard the facts of each case and to treat the matter very much as one of degree. No definition of what constituted a sufficient section of the public for the purpose was applied, for none existed; and the process seems to have been one of reaching a conclusion on a general survey of the circumstances and considerations regarded as relevant rather than of making a single, conclusive test. The investigation left the course of the dividing line between what was and what was not a section of the community unexplored, and was concluded when it had gone far enough to establish to the satisfaction of the court whether or not the trust was public; and the decision as to that was, I think, very often reached by determining whether or not the trust was private.

If it is still permissible to conduct the present inquiry on these broad if imprecise lines, I would hold with the appellant. The numerical strength of the class is considerable on any showing. The employees concerned number over 110,000, and it may reasonably be assumed that the children, who constitute the class in question, are no fewer. The large size of the class is not, of course, decisive but in my view it cannot be left out of account when the problem is approached in this way. Then it must be observed that the *propositi* are not limited to those presently employed. They include former employees (not reckoned in the figure I have given) and are, therefore, a more stable category than would otherwise be the case. And, further, the employees concerned are not limited to those in the service of the 'British-American Tobacco Co Ltd or any of its subsidiary or allied companies'—itself a description of great width—but include the employees, in the event of the British-American Tobacco Co Ltd being reconstructed or merged on amalgamation, of the reconstructed or amalgamated company or any of its subsidiary companies. No doubt the settlors here had a special interest in the welfare of the class they described, but, apart from the fact that this may serve to explain the particular form of their bounty, I do not think it material to the question in hand. What is material, as I regard the matter, is that they have chosen to benefit a class which is, in fact, substantial in point of size and importance and have done so in a manner which, to my mind, manifests an intention to advance the interests of the class described as a class rather than as a collection or succession of particular individuals. . . .

The respondent bank, however, contends that the inquiry should be of quite a different character to that which I have been discussing. It advances as the sole criterion a narrower test derived from the decisions of the Court of Appeal in *Re Compton* [1945] Ch 123, and *Re Hobourn Aero Components Ltd's Air Raid Distress Fund* [1946] Ch 194.

---

[119] Their fate was decided in favour of charity in *Dingle v Turner* [1972] AC 601 [p. 432, above].

The test [there] propounded focuses upon the common quality which unites those within the class concerned and asks whether that quality is essentially impersonal or essentially personal. If the former, the class will rank as a section of the public and the trust will have the element common to and necessary for all legal charities; but, if the latter, the trust will be private and not charitable. It is suggested in the passage just quoted, and made clear beyond doubt in *Re Hobourn* that in the opinion of the Court of Appeal employment by a designated employer must be regarded for this purpose as a personal and not as an impersonal bond of union. In this connexion and as illustrating the discriminating character of what I may call 'the *Compton* test' reference should be made to that part of the judgment of the learned Master of the Rolls in *Re Hobourn* [1946] Ch 194 at 206 in which he speaks of the decision in *Hall v Derby Borough Urban Sanitary Authority* (1885) 16 QBD 163. The passage runs thus:

> 'That related to a trust for railway servants. It is said that if a trust for railway servants can be a good charity, so too a trust for railway servants in the employment of a particular railway company is a good charity. That is not so. The reason, I think, is that in the one case the trust is for railway servants in general and in the other case it is for employees of a particular company, a fact which limits the potential beneficiaries to a class ascertained on a purely personal basis.'

My Lords, I do not quarrel with the result arrived at in the *Compton* and *Hobourn* cases, and I do not doubt that the *Compton* test may often prove of value and lead to a correct determination. But, with the great respect due to those who have formulated this test, I find myself unable to regard it as a criterion of general applicability and conclusiveness. In the first place I see much difficulty in dividing the qualities or attributes, which may serve to bind human beings into classes, into two mutually exclusive groups, the one involving individual status and purely personal, the other disregarding such status and quite impersonal. As a task this seems to me no less baffling and elusive than the problem to which it is directed, namely, the determination of what is and what is not a section of the public for the purposes of this branch of the law. After all, what is more personal than poverty or blindness or ignorance? Yet none would deny that a gift for the education of the children of the poor or blind was charitable; and I doubt if there is any less certainty about the charitable nature of a gift for, say, the education of children who satisfy a specified examining body that they need and would benefit by a course of special instruction designed to remedy their educational defects.

But can any really fundamental distinction, as respects the personal or impersonal nature of the common link, be drawn between those employed, for example, by a particular university and those whom the same university has put in a certain category as the result of individual examination and assessment? Again, if the bond between those employed by a particular railway is purely personal, why should the bond between those who are employed as railway men be so essentially different? Is a distinction to be drawn in this respect between those who are employed in a particular industry before it is nationalized and those who are employed therein after that process has been completed and one employer has taken the place of many? Are miners in the service of the National Coal Board now in one category and miners at a particular pit or of a particular district in another? Is the relationship between those in the service of the Crown to be distinguished from that obtaining between those in the service of some other employer? Or, if not, are the children of, say, soldiers or civil servants to be regarded as not constituting a sufficient section of the public to make a trust for their education charitable?

It was conceded in the course of the argument that, had the present trust been framed so as to provide for the education of the children of those engaged in the tobacco industry in a named county or town, it would have been a good charitable disposition, and that even though the class to be benefited would have been appreciably smaller and no more important than is the class here. That concession follows from what the Court of Appeal has said. But if it is sound and a personal or impersonal relationship remains the universal criterion I think it shows, no less than the queries I have just raised in indicating some of the difficulties of the problem, that the *Compton* test is a very arbitrary and artificial rule. This leads me to the second difficulty that I have regarding it. If I understand it aright it necessarily makes the quantum of public benefit a consideration of little moment; the size of the class becomes immaterial and the need of its members and the public advantage of having that need met appear alike to be irrelevant. To my mind these are considerations of some account in the sphere of educational trusts for, as already indicated, I think the educational value and scope of the work actually to be done must have a bearing on the question of public benefit.

Finally, it seems to me that, far from settling the state of the law on this particular subject, the *Compton* test is more likely to create confusion and doubt in the case of many trusts and institutions of a character whose legal standing as charities has never been in question. I have particularly in mind gifts for the education of certain special classes such, for example, as the daughters of missionaries, the children of those professing a particular faith or accepted as ministers of a particular denomination, or those whose parents have sent them to a particular school for the earlier stages of their training. I cannot but think that in cases of this sort an analysis of the common quality binding the class to be benefited may reveal a relationship no less personal than that existing between an employer and those in his service. Take, for instance, a trust for the provision of university education for boys coming from a particular school. The common quality binding the members of that class seems to reside in the fact that their parents or guardians all contracted for their schooling with the same establishment or body. That the school in such a case may itself be a charitable foundation seems altogether beside the point and quite insufficient to hold the *Compton* test at bay if it is well founded in law.

My Lords, counsel for the appellant and for the Attorney-General adumbrated several other tests for establishing the presence or absence of the necessary public element. I have given these my careful consideration and I do not find them any more sound or satisfactory than the *Compton* test. I therefore return to what I think was the process followed before the decision in *Compton's* case, and, for the reasons already given, I would hold the present trust charitable and allow the appeal. I have only to add that I recognize the imperfections and uncertainties of that process. They are as evident as the difficulties of finding something better. But I venture to doubt if it is in the power of the courts to resolve those difficulties satisfactorily as matters stand. It is a long cry to the age of Elizabeth and I think what is needed is a fresh start from a new statute.

Inland Revenue Commissioners v Educational Grants Association Ltd
[1967] Ch 123 (Ch D, **Pennycuick** J)

The Educational Grants Association Ltd was an association established for the advancement of education. It had a close relation with the Metal Box Co Ltd, and the bulk of its income came from a deed of covenant executed in its favour by the Metal Box Co Ltd.

In the years relevant to the present claim for repayment of Income Tax, between 76 per cent and 85 per cent of the income of the Association was applied for the education of children of persons connected with the Metal Box Co Ltd.

The claim for repayment raised the question whether the Association was established for charitable purposes only, and whether the income was applied 'for charitable purposes only' within section 447(1)(b) of the Income Tax Act 1952.

Held. The claim failed because the income was not applied for charitable purposes only.

Pennycuick J: ... The objects of the corporation, in order that they may be exclusively charitable, must be confined to objects for the public benefit. Equally, the application of the income, if it is to be within those objects, must be for the public benefit. Conversely, the application of income otherwise than for the public benefit must be outside the objects and ultra vires. For example, under an object for the advancement of education, once that is accepted as an exclusively charitable object, the income must be applied for the advancement of education by way of public benefit. An application of income for the advancement of education by way of private benefit would be ultra vires, and nonetheless so by reason that, in the nature of things, the members of a private class are included in the public as a whole. This may perhaps explain the repetition of the words 'for charitable purposes only' in the second requirement of the subsection.

Mr. Talbot, for the association, advanced a simple and formidable argument: namely, (i) the association is established for specified educational purposes; (ii) those purposes are admittedly charitable purposes, so the first requirement is satisfied; (iii) the income has been applied for the specified educational purposes; and (iv) therefore the income has been applied for charitable purposes, and the second requirement is satisfied. It seems to me that this argument leaves out of account the element of public benefit. It is true that it is claimed by the association and admitted by the Revenue that the educational purposes specified in the association's memorandum are charitable purposes, but this by definition implies that the purposes are for the public benefit. In order that the second requirement may be satisfied, it must equally be shown that its income has been applied not merely for educational purposes as expressed in the memorandum, but for those educational purposes by way of public benefit. An application of income by way of private benefit would be ultra vires. It is not open to the association first to set up a claim which can only be sustained on the basis that the purposes expressed in the memorandum are for the public benefit, and then, when it comes to the application of income, to look only to the purposes expressed in the memorandum, leaving the element of public benefit out of account. This point may be illustrated by considering the familiar example of a case in which a fund is settled upon trust for the advancement of education in general terms and the income is applied for the education of the settlor's children. Mr. Talbot does not shrink from the conclusion that such an application comes within the terms of the trust and satisfies the second requirement of the subsection. I think it does neither.

I understand from Mr. Talbot that he advanced the foregoing contention—and, I think, only this contention—before the Special Commissioners, although it is not very clearly reflected in their findings. The Special Commissioners were evidently much pre-occupied by *Re Koettgen's Will Trusts* [1954] Ch 252, to which I shall refer in a moment. It was substantially the only argument which Mr. Talbot advanced before me as to the construction of the section.

Mr. Goulding, for the Inland Revenue Commissioners, based his argument upon construction broadly on the lines which I have indicated above as being correct. He devoted much of his argument to repelling the application of the *Koettgen* case to the present one. The headnote in the *Koettgen* case is as follows:

'a testatrix bequeathed her residuary estate on trust "for the promotion and furtherance of commercial education..." The will provided that "the persons eligible as beneficiaries under the fund shall be persons of either sex who are British-born subjects and who are desirous of educating themselves or obtaining tuition for a higher commercial career but whose means are insufficient or will not allow of their obtaining such education or tuition at their own expense...." She further directed that in selecting the beneficiaries "it is my wish that the...trustees shall give a preference to any employees of John Batt & Co (London) Ltd or any members of the families of such employees; failing a sufficient number of beneficiaries under such description then the persons eligible shall be any persons of British birth as the...trustees may select Provided that the total income to be available for benefiting the preferred beneficiaries shall not in any one year be more than 75 per cent of the total available income for that year". In the event of the failure of those trusts there was a gift over to a named charity. It was admitted that the trust was for the advancement of education, but it was contended for the charity that having regard to the direction to prefer a limited class of persons the trusts were not of a sufficiently public nature to constitute valid charitable trusts:—

Held, that the gift to the primary class from whom the trustees could select beneficiaries contained the necessary element of benefit to the public, and that it was when that class was ascertained that the validity of the trust had to be determined; so that the subsequent direction to prefer, as to 75 per cent of the income, a limited class did not affect the validity of the trust, which was accordingly a valid and effective charitable trust. *Oppenheim v Tobacco Securities Trust Co Ltd* [1951] AC 297 distinguished.'

That headnote, I think, accurately represents the effect of what the judge decided.

The other case considered by the special commissioners was *Caffoor v Income Tax Comr, Colombo* [1961] AC 584, in the Privy Council. The headnote, so far as now relevant, is as follows:

'By the terms of a trust deed executed in Ceylon in 1942 the trust income after the death of the grantor was to be applied by the board of trustees, the appellants, in their absolute discretion for all or any of a number of purposes which included "(2)...(b) the education instruction or training in England or elsewhere abroad of deserving youths of the Islamic Faith" in any department of human activity. "The recipients of the benefits...shall be selected by the board from the following classes of persons and in the following order:—(i) male descendants along either the male or female line of the grantor or of any of his brothers or sisters failing whom" youths of the Islamic faith born of Moslem parents of the Ceylon Moorish community permanently resident in Colombo or elsewhere in Ceylon...

Held,...(2) that in view of what was in effect the absolute priority to the benefit of the trust income which was conferred on the grantor's own family by clause (2)(b)(i) of the trust deed this was a family trust and not a trust of a public character solely for charitable purposes, and the income thereof was accordingly not entitled to the exemption claimed....' *Re Compton* [1945] Ch 123, *Oppenheim v Tobacco Securities Trust Co Ltd* [1951] AC 297 and *Re Koettgen's Will Trusts* [1954] Ch 252 considered....

I think it right, however, to add that for myself I find considerable difficulty in the *Koettgen* decision. I should have thought that a trust for the public with preference for a private class comprised in the public might be regarded as a trust for the application of income at the discretion of the trustees between charitable and non-charitable objects. However, I am not concerned here to dispute the validity of the *Koettgen* decision. I only mention the difficulty I feel as affording some additional reason for not applying the *Koettgen* decision by analogy in connection with the second requirement of the subsection.

I return now to the present case. The association has claimed that the purposes of the association are exclusively charitable, which imports that the purposes must be for the public benefit. The Revenue have admitted that claim. I have then to consider whether the association has applied its income within its expressed objects and by way of public benefit. There is no doubt that the application has been within its expressed objects, but has it been by way of public benefit? In order to answer this question, I must, I think, look at the individuals and institutions for whose benefit the income has been applied, and seek to discern whether these individuals and institutions possess any, and, if so, what, relevant characteristics by virtue of which the income has been applied for their benefit. One may for this purpose look at the minutes of the council, circular letters and so forth. Mr. Goulding at one time appeared to suggest that one might look at the actual intention of the members of the council. I do not think that is so.

When one makes this inquiry, one finds that between 75 per cent and 85 per cent of the income of the association has been expended upon the education of children connected with Metal Box. The association is intimately connected with Metal Box in the many respects found in the case stated. It derives most of its income from Metal Box. The council of management, as the Special Commissioners found, has followed a policy of seeking applications for grants from employees and ex-employees of Metal Box, though these applications are not, of course, always successful. The inference is inescapable that this part of the association's income—i.e. 75 per cent to 85 per cent—has been expended for the benefit of these children by virtue of a private characteristic; i.e. their connection with Metal Box. Such an application is not by way of public benefit. It is on all fours with an application of 75 per cent to 85 per cent of the income of a trust fund upon the education of a settlor's children. It follows, in my judgment, that, as regards the income which has been applied for the education of children connected with Metal Box, the association has failed to satisfy the second requirement in the subsection, and that the claim for relief fails. No reason has been suggested why the association should not obtain relief in respect of income applied for the benefit of institutions and outside individuals: see the words 'so far as' in the section.

I recognise that this conclusion involves a finding that the council of management has acted ultra vires in applying the income of the association as it has done, albeit within the expressed objects of the association memorandum. This conclusion follows from the basis on which the association has framed its objects and based its claim. It is of course open to a comparable body to frame its objects so as to make clear that its income may be applied for private as well as public purposes, but in that case it may not obtain tax relief. It does not seem to me that such a body can have it both ways. I propose, therefore, to allow this appeal.[120]

---

[120] The decision was affirmed by the Court of Appeal [1967] Ch 993. See Annual Report for 1976, paras. 45–49 (The Cowen Charitable Trust); Annual Report for 1978, paras. 86–89 (where the Charity Commissioners followed *Re Koettgen's Will Trusts* [1954] Ch 252 in three cases; 75 per cent, 65 per cent and 75 per cent); *Re Martin* (1977) 121 Sol Jo 828, The Times, 17 November.

QUESTIONS

1. Consider the difficulties with which a court is faced when compelled to make a value judgment upon educational matters. What would you say of a gift:

   (a) to the Plantagenet Society for the purpose of establishing that Henry VII was responsible for the deaths of the Princes in the Tower of London?

   (b) for sex education in primary schools?

   (c) for the provision in schools of instruction on driving cars?

2. The disagreement between Lord Simonds and Lord MacDermott on the question of the ascertainment of the test of public benefit was discussed by Lord Cross of Chelsea in *Dingle v Turner* [p. 434, above]. Where do you stand on this controversy? How would *Oppenheim v Tobacco Securities Trust Co Ltd* [p. 455, above] be decided if it arose today? (1974) CLJ 63 (G.H. Jones); Annual Report for 1971, para. 21; (1993–94) 2 *Charity Law & Practice Review* 203 (J. Callman).

3. (After reading pp. 470–478, below) Compare the test of public benefit in trusts for the advancement of education and trusts for the advancement of religion.

4. What would be the legal consequences of removing charitable status from independent schools? Consider [1996] 60 Conv 24 (J. Jaconelli) and Chapter 9, above and Chapter 11, below.

D ADVANCEMENT OF RELIGION[121]

(i) Charitable purpose

The recognition of the advancement of religion derives from nothing more specific than the inclusion in the Preamble to the Charitable Uses Act 1601 of 'the repair of churches'.[122] The concept has widened with the spread of religious toleration, so that it was not confined to the Established Church, or even to the Christian religion.[123] It has been widened even further with the enactment of the Charities Act 2006.

---

[121] H&M, pp. 416–419, 438–440; Luxton, pp. 125–135, 178–179; P&M, pp. 464–467; P&S, pp. 494–498; Pettit, pp. 259–264; Picarda, pp. 72–116; Snell, pp. 517–518; Tudor, pp. 73–97. Goodman Report, paras. 40–41, 51–57; House of Commons Report, vol. 1, paras. 53–58, vol II, pp. 191–217, 313–316, 362–364; White Paper, paras. 2.18–2.36. [1999] *Juridical Review* 303 (C.R. Barber); (1995/6) 3 *Charity Law & Practice Review* 29 (P. Edge). See generally Crowther, *Religious Trusts* (1954). On the history, see Holdsworth, *H.E.L.* viii, pp. 402–410; (1930) 45 LQR 293, at p. 305 (Sir F. Pollock).

[122] On the use of church halls for other charitable purposes see Charity Commission CC18 (July 2001).

[123] *Gilmour v Coats* [1949] AC 426 at 457, 458, *per* Lord Reid; *Neville Estates Ltd v Madden* [1962] Ch 832 at 853, *per* Cross J.

CHARITIES ACT 2006

2. (3) In subsection (2)—

    (a) in paragraph (c) 'religion' includes—

        (i) a religion which involves belief in more than one god, and

        (ii) a religion which does not involve belief in a god.

EQUALITY ACT 2006

58 Charities relating to religion or belief

(1) Nothing in this Part shall make it unlawful for a person to provide benefits only to persons of a particular religion or belief, if—

    (a) he acts in pursuance of a charitable instrument, and

    (b) the restriction of benefits to persons of that religion or belief is imposed by reason of or on the grounds of the provisions of the charitable instrument.

The extracts which follow are chosen as illustrations of significant issues which have arisen in this field, but they must be read in the light of the recent expansion of the notion of what constitutes a religion. It will also be seen that the courts have been concerned with what constitutes *advancement* of religion.

Tudor on Charities (9th edn, 2003), p. 74

'Religion' has been defined as meaning 'a particular system of faith and worship' and 'recognition on the part of man of some higher unseen power as having control of his destiny, and as being entitled to obedience, reverence, and worship';[124] and numerous cases concerned with gifts and trusts for the advancement of religion show that this is the meaning accepted by the court. Hence the advancement or promotion of religion means, according to Lord Hanworth MR in *Keren Kayemeth Le Jisroel Ltd v IRC*[125] 'the promotion of spiritual teaching in a wide sense, and the maintenance of the doctrines on which it rests, and the observances that serve to promote and manifest it'. In *United Grand Lodge of Ancient Free and Accepted Masons of England v Holborn Borough Council*[126] Donovan J said: 'to advance religion means to promote it, to spread its message ever wider among mankind; to take some positive steps to sustain and increase religious belief; and these things are done in a variety of ways which may be comprehensively described as pastoral and missionary'.

In the **United Grand Lodge** case [1957] 1 WLR 1080, Donovan J, in holding that the objects of freemasonry were not 'charitable or otherwise concerned with the advancement of religion' within the Rating and Valuation (Miscellaneous Provisions) Act 1955, said at 1090:

Accordingly, one cannot really begin to argue that the main object of freemasonry is to advance religion, except perhaps by saying that religion can be advanced by example as well as by precept,

---

[124] *Oxford English Dictionary*, 1979 (Compact) ed.
[125] [1931] 2 KB 465 at 477 (affd [1932] AC 650).   [126] [1957] 1 WLR 1080 at 1090, below.

so that the spectacle of a man leading an upright moral life may persuade others to do likewise. The appellants did not in fact advance this argument, but even if it were accepted, it leads to no useful conclusion here. For a man may persuade his neighbour by example to lead a good life without at the same time leading him to religion. And there is nothing in the constitution, nor, apparently, in the evidence tendered to the appeals committee, to support the view that the main object of masonry is to encourage masons to go out in the world and by their example lead persons to some religion or another.

When one considers the work done by organizations which admittedly do set out to advance religion, the contrast with masonry is striking. To advance religion means to promote it, to spread its message ever wider among mankind; to take some positive steps to sustain and increase religious belief; and these things are done in a variety of ways which may be comprehensively described as pastoral and missionary. There is nothing comparable to that in masonry. This is not said by way of criticism. For masonry really does something different. It says to a man, 'whatever your religion or your mode of worship, believe in a Supreme Creator and lead a good moral life'. Laudable as this precept is, it does not appear to us to be the same thing as the advancement of religion. There is no religious instruction, no programme for the persuasion of unbelievers, no religious supervision to see that its members remain active and constant in the various religions they may profess, no holding of religious services, no pastoral or missionary work of any kind.

In **Re South Place Ethical Society** [1980] 1 WLR 1565,[127] the objects of the Society were 'the study and dissemination of ethical principles and the cultivation of a rational religious sentiment'. DILLON J held that these were not for the advancement of religion, and said at 1571:

In a free country—and I have no reason to suppose that this country is less free than the United States of America—it is natural that the court should desire not to discriminate between beliefs deeply and sincerely held, whether they are beliefs in a god or in the excellence of man or in ethical principles or in Platonism or some other scheme of philosophy. But I do not see that that warrants extending the meaning of the word 'religion' so as to embrace all other beliefs and philosophies. Religion, as I see it, is concerned with man's relations with God, and ethics are concerned with man's relations with man. The two are not the same, and are not made the same by sincere inquiry into the question: what is God? If reason leads people not to accept Christianity or any known religion, but they do believe in the excellence of qualities such as truth, beauty and love, or believe in the Platonic concept of the ideal, their beliefs may be to them the equivalent of a religion, but viewed objectively they are not religion. The ground of the opinion of the court, in the United States Supreme Court, that any belief occupying in the life of its possessor a place parallel to that occupied by belief in God in the minds of theists prompts the comment that parallels, by definition, never meet.

In 1999 the Charity Commissioners considered whether the Church of Scientology for England and Wales (CoS) should be registered as a charity (17 November, 1999). The Commissioners decided that it should not be registered.[128]

---

[127] [1981] Conv 150 (St.J. Robilliard). Cf. *United States v Seeger* 380 US 163 (1965); (1978) 91 *Harvard Law Review* 1056.

[128] Cp. *Church of the New Faith v Comr of Pay-Roll Tax (Victoria)* (1982) 154 CLR 120, where the High Court of Australia held that Scientology was a religion and was therefore exempt from pay-roll tax.

The Commissioners concluded as follows:

CoS is not charitable as an organisation established for the advancement of religion because having regard to the relevant law and evidence:

(a) Scientology is not a religion for the purposes of English charity law. That religion for the purposes of charity law constitutes belief in a supreme being and worship of that being. That it is accepted that Scientology believes in a supreme being. However, the core practices of Scientology, being auditing[129] and training,[130] do not constitute worship as they do not display the essential characteristic of reverence or veneration for a supreme being.

(b) That even were CoS otherwise established for the advancement of religion, public benefit should not be presumed given the relative newness of Scientology and public and judicial concern expressed—i.e. the presumption of public benefit available to religious organisations as charities was rebutted; and that

(c) Public benefit arising from the practice of Scientology and/or the purposes of CoS had not been established.

CoS is not charitable as an organisation established to promote the moral or spiritual welfare or improvement of the community because having regard to the relevant law and evidence:

(a) The practice of Scientology and the purposes of CoS are not analogous to the legal authorities establishing the moral or spiritual welfare or improvement of the community as a charitable purpose, and in taking a broader view of the authorities, would not be likely to achieve such a purpose.

(b) That even were CoS otherwise established for the promotion of the moral or spiritual welfare or improvement of the community, public benefit arising out of the practice of Scientology and/or the purposes of CoS had not been established.

(2001) 21 LS 36, 46–47 (P. Edge and J.M. Loughrey)

The decision in the Scientology decision turned upon the concept of worship, which the Commissioners stated was an essential element of religion, and defined as conduct which indicated reverence or veneration for the supreme being and submission to the object worshipped.[131] They rejected defining worship as 'formal observation of the tenets of the belief system or canons of conduct giving effect to the belief in question'.[132] The central practices of auditing and training by the Church of Scientology did not include reverence or veneration of a supreme being and were not akin to acts of worship recognised by English case law. Consequently, despite a belief in a supreme being, Scientology was not a religion in English law.[133]

There are a number of problems with this approach. First, as already indicated, the Commissioners are inconsistent in the application of these principles: it is unclear that worship in such a sense is always a feature of Buddhism. Secondly, as argued before the Commissioners,

---

[129] This involves 'a series of gradient steps that Hubbard [the founder of Scientology] developed to address past painful experiences…'. [130] This involves the intensive study of Scientology Scripture.

[131] CoS 15.

[132] CoS 24 citing from and rejecting *Fellowship of Humanity v County of Alameda* 153 Cal App 2d 673, 315 P 2d 394 (1957) and *Church of the New Faith v Comr for Pay-Roll Tax (Vic)* (1983) 49 ALR 65 respectively.

[133] CoS 25.

the requirement of and definition of worship is heavily reliant on Judaeo-Christian concepts.[134] Although the Commissioners indicated that this requirement was a clear and objective criteri[on],[135] they can be criticised for an inarticulate drawing upon the traditions of a subset of religious systems in order to formulate a requirement applicable to all. Thirdly, by shifting one way in which religion can be advanced to the definition of religion the Commissioners emphasised one type of religious practice over others without clearly indicating why worship is so paramount. The Commissioners considered the requirement of worship to be necessary as it maintained the distinction between trusts registrable under the third and fourth heads of charity. This was desirable as, in their opinion, the presumption of public benefit was appropriate only to the former. This suggests that there is something in the nature of worshipping which attracts the presumption although no explanation is given for this.[136] Finally, and perhaps most germane to this paper, the emphasis on worship in the case law is rather weaker than the emphasis on monotheism, which the Commissioners have been prepared to disregard.

In relation to the definition of religion, then, it would appear that the Commissioners have taken their strong law-making role seriously, being prepared not only to develop themes from persuasive authorities, but also to disregard the ratio decidendi of elderly cases they regard as outmoded. This activism has not been matched by development of a clear, coherent ground for their findings.

Pettit: *Equity and the Law of Trusts* (10th edn, 2006), pp. 259–261

It is generally accepted that 'the Court of Chancery makes no distinction between one religion and another...[or] one sect and another...[unless] the tenets of a particular sect inculcate doctrines adverse to the very foundations of all religion and...subversive of all morality...If the tendency were not immoral and although this Court might consider the opinions sought to be propagated foolish or even devoid of foundation' the trust would nevertheless be charitable.[137] 'As between different religions the law stands neutral, but it assumes that any religion is at least likely to be better than none.'[138] The courts are understandably reluctant to judge the relative worth of different religions or the truth of competing religious doctrines, all of which may have a place in a tolerant and culturally diverse society.

These propositions are undoubtedly true so far as the various Christian denominations are concerned; there is no doubt as to the charitable character of religious trusts not only for the established church, but also for nonconformist bodies,[139] Unitarians,[140] Roman Catholics,[141]

---

[134] See discussion at CoS 22–23.   [135] CoS 24.   [136] Ibid.

[137] *Per* Romilly MR in *Thornton v Howe* (1862) 31 Beav 14 at 19; *Gilmour v Coats* [1949] AC 426 [p. 471, below]; *Re Watson* [1973] 1 WLR 1472 [p. 470, below].

[138] *Per* Cross J in *Neville Estates Ltd v Madden* [1962] Ch 832 at 853. See (1992/93) 1 *Charity Law & Practice Review* 87 (A. Longley); (1996) 8 *Auckland University Law Review* 25 (S.T. Woodfield). P. Edge argues, in (1995/96) 3 *Charity Law & Practice Review* 29, that this head of charity should be abolished, to which M. King responded in (1995/96) 3 *Charity Law & Practice Review* 179.

[139] Since the Toleration Act 1688. See eg *Re Strickland's Will Trusts* [1936] 3 All ER 1027; appeal dismissed by consent [1937] 3 All ER 676 (Baptist); *Re Manser* [1905] 1 Ch 68 (Quakers).

[140] Since the Doctrine of Trinity Act 1813. Eg *Re Nesbitt's Will Trusts* [1953] 1 WLR 595.

[141] Since the Roman Catholic Charities Act 1832. Eg *Dunne v Byrne* [1912] AC 407, PC; *Re Flinn* [1948] Ch 241. As to whether there has been, or now is, an anti-Roman Catholic bias, see (1981) 2 *Journal of Legal History* 207 (M. Blakeney); [1990] Conv 34 (C.E.F. Rickett).

and the Exclusive Brethren.[142] More controversially two trusts associated with the Unification Church[143] have been registered as charitable, as has a trust for the publication of the works of Joanna Southcote.[144] Similarly with regard to organizations which exist for the advancement of religion, such as the Church Army,[145] the Salvation Army,[146] the Church Missionary Society,[147] the Society for the Propagation of the Gospel in Foreign Parts,[148] the Sunday School Association,[149] the Protestant Alliance and kindred institutions,[150] and even, it has been held, a society of clergymen, in connection with a trust to provide dinners, on the ground that the free meals would increase the usefulness of the society by attracting a greater number of clergymen to the meetings.[151] Also a faith-healing movement of a religious nature.[152] But not, it has been decided, the Oxford Group Movement.[153]

Beyond the Christian religion, trusts for the advancement of the Jewish religion are undoubtedly charitable.[154] So far as wholly distinct religions such as Islam or Buddhism are concerned, there are clear dicta[155] in favour of charitable status, and this is assumed in regulations[156]

[142] *Holmes v A-G* (1981) The Times, 12 February; *Broxtowe Borough Council v Birch* [1981] RA 215. See also *Radmanovich v Nedeljkovic* (2001) 52 HSWCR 641.

[143] Popularly known as the Moonies. The Attorney-General appealed against the refusal of the Charity Commissioners to accede to his request to remove the trusts from the register, but the appeal was eventually discontinued; see the statement of the Attorney-General in Hansard, 3 February 1988, 977ff, and the debate in the Lords, 10 February 1988, 247ff.

[144] *Thornton v Howe* (1862) 31 Beav 14; Joanna Southcote claimed that she was with child by the Holy Ghost, and would give birth to a second Messiah. As the law then was, the effect of holding the gift charitable was that, being given out of land, it failed by reason of the Statute of Mortmain 1736 and went to the heir-at-law.   [145] *Re Smith* (1938) 54 TLR 851.

[146] *Re Fowler* (1914) 31 TLR 102; *Re Smith*, ibid.   [147] *Re Clergy Society* (1856) 2 K & J 615.

[148] *Re Maguire* (1870) LR 9 Eq 632.

[149] *R v Income Tax Special Comrs, ex p Essex Hall* [1911] 2 KB 434, CA.

[150] *Re Delmar Charitable Trust* [1897] 2 Ch 163 (societies having as their object 'to maintain and defend the doctrines of the Reformation, and the principles of civil and religious liberty against the advance of Popery').   [151] *Re Charlesworth* (1910) 26 TLR 214.

[152] *Funnell v Stewart* [1996] 1 WLR 288 noted [1996] *Liverpool Law Review* 63 (D. Morris); (1996) 112 LQR 557 (R. Fletcher). See p. 477, below.

[153] *Re Thackrah* [1939] 2 All ER 4; *Oxford Group v IRC* [1949] 2 All ER 537, CA (the movement is probably a social movement founded on Christian ethics rather than a movement for the advancement of religion).

[154] Since the Religious Disabilities Act 1846, according, inter alia, to *Neville Estates Ltd v Madden* [1962] Ch 832. But a Jewish religious trust was held charitable in *Straus v Goldsmid* (1837) 8 Sim 614. See (1993/94) 2 *Charity Law & Practice Review* 155 (H. Picarda).

[155] *Re South Place Ethical Society* [1980] 1 WLR 1565, where two of the essential attributes of religion were said to be faith and worship—faith in a god and worship of that god. This was said, it is submitted rightly, to be too narrow a test by the High Court of Australia in *Church of the New Faith v Comrs for Pay Roll Tax* (1983) 57 *Australian Law Journal Report* 785, noted (1984) 100 LQR 340; (1984) 14 *Melbourne University Law Review* 539 (M. Darian Smith); [1984] Conv 449 (St. J. Robilliard), where Scientology was held to be a religion in Victoria, and it may well be inconsistent with the Human Rights Act 1998. It is accepted that Buddhism is a religion, though it does not have the attributes stated in *Re South Place Ethical Society*, supra. The wider Australian view has been applied in New Zealand—*Centrepoint Community Growth Trust v IRC* [1985] 1 NZLR 673. See (1981) 131 NLJ 436 (H. Picarda); (1989) 63 *Australian Law Journal* 834 (W. Sadurski); (1999) 5 *Charity Law & Practice Review* 153 (F. Quint and T. Spring).

[156] S.I. 1962 No. 1421; S.I. 1963 No. 2074. See the Interpretation Act 1978, s. 17(2)(b). [Many non-Christian religious organisations have been recognised as charitable. However, 'many Hindu, Sikh, and Moslem organisations which are basically religious also have social, cultural and educational functions which have a greater importance than is the case with comparable Christian communities': Annual Report for 1976, para. 109. For the position of Rastafarians, see *Crown Suppliers (PSA) Ltd v Dawkins* [1993] ICR 517; S.I. 1996 No. 180.]

made under the Charities Act 1993. Moreover the Charity Commissions have registered trusts for the advancement of the Hindu, Sikh, Islamic and Buddhist religions. Neither the objects of the Theosophical Society[157] nor those of the South Place Ethical Society[158] or the Church of Scientology[159] are for the advancement of religion, and it has not been thought arguable that gifts for the maintenance of a masonic temple[160] or a college for training spiritualistic mediums[161] are charitable on this ground, and the same must surely be true of an atheistic society.[162]

In **Re Watson** [1973] 1 WLR 1472,[163] PLOWMAN J had to consider the validity of a gift in a will 'for the continuance of the work of God as it has been maintained by Mr. H.G. Hobbs and myself since 1942 by God's enabling...in propagating the truth as given in the Holy Bible'. The testatrix and Mr. Hobbs were members of a very small group of undenominational Christians, who met at Long Melford, Suffolk, and which apparently contained no member outside their immediate families. Mr. Hobbs had written and distributed a large number of religious books and tracts mainly at the expense of the testatrix. Expert evidence was given that their intrinsic worth was nil. The trust was upheld.

(ii) Public benefit

Again, it is necessary to show a benefit to the public or a section of the public. This must be proved by evidence which is acceptable to the court; the faith of a particular religion that prayer and intercession will confer a benefit on the public is not sufficient. It seems that the concept of public benefit under this head is similar to that in the case of education, but not identical,[164] for while the pupils of a private school form a section of the public for the purposes of education, the same is not true of the members of a cloistered order in the context of religion. The presumption that trusts for the advancement of religion satisfy the test of public benefit was removed by the Charities Act 2006, section 3(2). The old law remains relevant, however, in determining what the public benefit might be for this type of charitable object. In March 2008 the Charity Commission published draft supplementary guidance for consultation on 'Public Benefit and the Advancement of Religion'.

---

[157] *Re Macaulay's Estate* [1943] Ch 435n, HL ('to form a nucleus of Universal Brotherhood of Humanity without distinction of race, creed, caste or colour'). Cf *Re Price* [1943] Ch 422 (Anthroposophical Society).

[158] *Re South Place Ethical Society* [1980] 1 WLR 1565 ('the study and dissemination of ethical principles' and 'the cultivation of a rational religious sentiment'—society concerned with man's relations with man, not man's relations with God). See (1981) 131 NLJ 761 (A. Hoffer). See p. 466, above.

[159] *R v Registrar General, ex p Segerdal* [1970] 2 QB 697, and see p. 466, above.

[160] *Re Porter* [1925] Ch 746.

[161] *Re Hummeltenberg* [1923] 1 Ch 237.

[162] The point did not arise in *Bowman v Secular Society Ltd* [1917] AC 406, HL, where it was held that there is nothing contrary to law in an attack on or a denial of the truth of Christianity unaccompanied by vilification, ridicule, or irreverence. Christianity is not part of the law of England.

[163] (1974) 90 LQR 4; [1973] *Annual Survey of Commonwealth Law* 468 (J. Hackney). On fringe religious organisations, see Annual Report for 1976, paras 103–108; and on Exorcism, paras 65–67.

[164] See *Dingle v Turner* [1972] AC 601 at 625 [p. 432, above], *per* Lord Cross of Chelsea.

Gilmour v Coats
[1949] AC 426, (HL, **Lords Simonds, du Parcq, Normand, Morton of Henryton** and **Reid**)

A gift of £500 was made in trust for the purposes of the Carmelite Priory, St Charles' Square, London, if those purposes were charitable.

The Priory was a community of strictly cloistered nuns, who devoted their lives to prayer, contemplation, penance, and self-sanctification. They engaged in no works outside the convent. An affidavit of Cardinal Griffin, Roman Catholic Archbishop of Westminster, stated that, according to the doctrine of the Roman Catholic Church, the work of such a community conferred benefits, not only upon the participants, but upon the public generally.

Held. The purposes of the Priory lacked the element of public benefit which was necessary to make them charitable.

Lord Simonds: It is the established belief of the Roman Catholic Church, as appears from the Apostolic Constitution *Umbratilem,* that the prayers and other spiritual penances and exercises, in which the nuns engage for the benefit of the public, in fact benefit the public by drawing down upon them grace from God, which enables those who are not yet Christians to embrace the Christian religion and those who are already Christians to practise Christianity more fully and fruitfully, and, further that the prayers and other spiritual exercises of the nuns are the more efficacious by virtue of the fact that they devote their lives with especial devotion to the service of God. It is this benefit to all the world, arising from the value of their intercessory prayers, that the appellant puts in the forefront of her case in urging the charitable purpose of the trust.

Nor is it only on the intercessory value of prayer that the appellant relies for the element of public benefit in their lives. For it is the evidence of Cardinal Griffin—and I do not pause to ask whether it is evidence of fact or opinion—that the practice of the religious life by the Carmelite nuns and other religions is a source of great edification to other Catholics—and indeed in innumerable cases to non-Catholics—leading them to a higher estimation of spiritual things and to a greater striving after their own spiritual perfection and that the knowledge that there are men and women who are prepared to sacrifice all that the worldly in man holds dear in order to attain a greater love of God and union with Him inculcates in them a greater estimation of the value and importance of the things which are eternal than they would have if they had not these examples before them. Here then is the second element of public benefit on which the appellant relies, the edification of a wider public by the example of lives devoted to prayer.

I will reserve for final consideration an argument which was not urged in the courts below; that the trusts declared by the settlement are beneficial to the public, in that qualification for admission to the community is not limited to any private group of persons but any person being a female Roman Catholic may be accepted, and therefore those trusts provide facilities for the intensified and most complete practice of religion by those members of the public who have a vocation for it. Your Lordships were reluctant to listen to an argument on which you have not the advantage of the opinions of the learned judges in the courts below, but in the special circumstances of this case thought fit to admit it.

I turn then to the question whether, apart from this final consideration, the appellant has established that there is in the trusts which govern this community the element of public benefit which is the necessary condition of legal charity...

I need not go beyond the case of *Cocks v Manners* (1871) LR 12 Eq 574 which was decided nearly 80 years ago by Wickens V-C. In that case the testatrix left her residuary estate between a number of religious institutions, one of them being the Dominican Convent at Carisbrooke, a community not differing in any material respect from the community of nuns now under consideration. The learned judge who was, I suppose, as deeply versed in this branch of the law as any judge before or since (for he had been for many years junior counsel to the Attorney-General in equity cases), used these words, which I venture to repeat, though they have already been cited in the courts below (1871) LR 12 Eq 574 at 585:

'On the Act [the Statute of Elizabeth I] unaffected by authority I should certainly hold that the gift to the Dominican Convent is neither within the letter nor the spirit of it; and no decision has been referred to which compels me to adopt a different conclusion. A voluntary association of women for the purpose of working out their own salvation by religious exercises and self denial seems to me to have none of the requisites of a charitable institution, whether the word 'charitable' is used in its popular sense or in its legal sense. It is said, in some of the cases, that religious purposes are charitable, but that can only be true as to religious services tending directly or indirectly towards the instruction or the edification of the public; an annuity to an individual, so long as he spent his time in retirement and constant devotion, would not be charitable, nor would a gift to ten persons, so long as they lived together in retirement and performed acts of devotion, be charitable. Therefore the gift to the Dominican Convent is not, in my opinion, a gift on a charitable trust.'

No case, said the learned Vice-Chancellor, had been cited to compel him to come to a contrary conclusion, nor has any such case been cited to your Lordships. Nor have my own researches discovered one. But since that date the decision in *Cocks v Manners* has been accepted and approved in numerous cases. They are referred to in the judgment of Jenkins J and I need only remind your Lordships, first, that Lindsey LJ in *Re White* [1893] 2 Ch 41 at 51 used these words: 'a society for the promotion of private prayer and devotion by its own members, and which has no wider scope, no public element, no purposes of general utility would be a "religious" society, but not a "charitable" one: see *Cocks v Manners*', and, secondly, that in *Dunne v Byrne* [1912] AC 407 at 410 Lord Macnaghten in delivering the judgment of the Privy Council refers to *Cocks v Manners* as the exemplar of a case in which the purpose would be considered by a devout Catholic to be conducive to the good of religion but which is 'certainly not charitable'. I have thus stated the law as it was universally accepted in case-law (except some recent Irish cases) and also in all text-books of authority at the date when these proceedings were begun, and I now ask what is the argument upon which your Lordships are invited to unsettle it.

Apart from what I have called the final argument, which I will deal with later, the contention of the appellant rests not on any change in the lives of the members of such a community as this nor, from a wider aspect, on the emergence of any new conception of the public good, but solely on the fact that for the first time certain evidence of the value of such lives to a wider public together with new arguments based upon that evidence has been presented to the court. Never before, it was urged, has the benefit to be derived from intercessory prayer and from edification been brought to the attention of the court; if it had been, the decision in *Cocks v Manners* (1871) LR 12 Eq 574 would, or at least should, have been otherwise. I have examined the records of *Cocks v Manners* which were supplied to me by the Record Office and I find that the case has been fully and accurately reported. There was no such evidence as was adduced in this case by the appellant and Cardinal Griffin. Nor, as appears from the report, was any argument addressed to this specific point nor any judgment on it. What weight is to be attributed to this, which is the mainstay of the appellant's case? To me, my Lords, despite the admirable argument of Mr. Charles Russell, the weight is negligible. True it is that Wickens V-C emphasised that aspect of the religious life which is admittedly its more important aim, 'the love and contemplation of divine things' (1871) LR 12 Eq 574 at 585. But 'its secondary aim the apostolate, particularly all that pertains to our neighbour's salvation' (I use the appellant's words) is no new thing and I cannot suppose that it was absent from the learned judge's mind that those, who devote their lives to prayer, pray not for themselves alone, or that they believe that their prayers are not in vain. Nor, as I think, can he have been unaware of the effect which the example of their lives may have upon others. As I venture to think, these aspects of the case were neither insisted on in evidence or argument nor discussed by the learned judge because they do not afford any real support for the contention that there is in the purpose of the community the element of public benefit which is the condition of legal charity.

My Lords, I would speak with all respect and reverence of those who spend their lives in cloistered piety, and in this House of Lords Spiritual and Temporal, which daily commences its proceedings with intercessory prayers, how can I deny that the Divine Being may in His wisdom think fit to answer them? But, my Lords, whether I affirm or deny, whether I believe or disbelieve, what has that to do with the proof which the court demands that a particular purpose satisfies the test of benefit to the community? Here is something which is manifestly not susceptible of proof. But, then it is said, this is a matter not of proof but of belief: for the value of intercessory prayer is a tenet of the Catholic faith, therefore in such prayer there is benefit to the community. But it is just at this 'therefore' that I must pause. It is, no doubt, true that the advancement of religion is, generally speaking, one of the heads of charity. But it does not follow from this that the court must accept as proved whatever a particular church believes. The faithful must embrace their faith believing where they cannot prove; the court can act only on proof. A gift to two or ten or a hundred cloistered nuns in the belief that their prayers will benefit the world at large does not from that belief alone derive validity any more than does the belief of any other donor for any other purpose. The importance of this case leads me to state my opinion in my own words but, having read again the judgment of the learned Master of the Rolls, I will add that I am in full agreement with what he says on this part of the case.[165]

I turn to the second of the alleged elements of public benefit, edification by example. And I think that this argument can be dealt with very shortly. It is in my opinion sufficient to say that this is something too vague and intangible to satisfy the prescribed test. The test of public benefit has, I think, been developed in the last two centuries. To-day it is beyond doubt that that element must be present. No court would be rash enough to attempt to define precisely or exhaustively what its content must be. But it would assume a burden which it could not discharge if now for the first time it admitted into the category of public benefit something so indirect, remote, imponderable and, I would add, controversial as the benefit which may be derived by others from the example of pious lives. The appellant called in aid the use by Wickens V-C of the word 'indirectly' in the passage that I have cited from his judgment in *Cocks v Manners* (1871) LR 12 Eq 574 at 585, but I see no reason to suppose that that learned judge had in mind any such question as your Lordships have to determine....

It remains finally to deal with an argument which, as I have said, was not presented to the Court of Appeal but appears in the appellant's formal case. It is that the element of public benefit is supplied by the fact that qualification for admission to membership of the community

---

[165] [1948] Ch 340. 'They are to be paid, not to do good, but to be good', at 353, *per* Greene MR. See Annual Report for 1990, para. 56 (Society of the Precious Blood).

is not limited to any group of persons but is open to any woman in the wide world who has the necessary vocation. Thus, it is said, just as the endowment of a scholarship open to public competition is a charity, so also is a gift to enable any woman (or, presumably, any man) to enter a fuller religious life a charity. To this argument which, it must be admitted, has a speciously logical appearance, the first answer is that which I have indicated earlier in this opinion. There is no novelty in the idea that a community of nuns must, if it is to continue, from time to time obtain fresh recruits from the outside world. That is why a perpetuity is involved in a gift for the benefit of such a community and it is not to be supposed that, to mention only three masters of this branch of the law, Wickens V-C, Lord Lindsey, or Lord Macnaghten failed to appreciate the point. Yet by direct decision or by way of emphatic example a community such as this is by them regarded as the very type of religious institution which is not charitable. I know of no considera-tion applicable to this case which would justify this House in unsettling a rule of law which has been established so long and by such high authority. But that is not the only, nor indeed the most cogent, reason why I cannot accede to the appellant's argument. It is a trite saying that the law is life, not logic. But it is, I think, conspicuously true of the law of charity that it has been built up not logically but empirically. It would not, therefore, be surprising to find that, while in every category of legal charity some element of public benefit must be present, the court had not adopted the same measure in regard to different categories, but had accepted one standard in regard to those gifts which are alleged to be for the advancement of education and another for those which are alleged to be for the advancement of religion, and it may be yet another in regard to the relief of poverty. To argue by a method of syllogism or analogy from the category of education to that of religion ignores the historical process of the law. Nor would there be lack of justification for the divergence of treatment which is here assumed. For there is a legislative and political background peculiar to so-called religious trusts, which has I think influenced the development of the law in this matter. Thus, even if the simple argument that, if education is a good thing, then the more education the better, may appear to be irrefutable, to repeat that argument substituting 'religion' for 'education' is to ignore the principle which I understand to be conceded that not all religious purposes are charitable purposes. It was, no doubt, this con-sideration which led Wickens V-C to say (1871) LR 12 Eq 574 at 585 that a gift to a Dominican convent was 'one of the last gifts which the legislature which passed the Act would have thought of including in it'. Upon this final argument I would add this observation. I have stressed the empirical development of the law of charity and your Lordships may detect some inconsistency in an attempt to rationalise it. But it appears to me that it would be irrational to the point of absurdity on the one hand to deny to a community of contemplative nuns the character of a charitable institution but on the other to accept as a charitable trust a gift which had no other object than to enable it to be maintained in perpetuity by recruitment from the outside world.

Finally I would say this. I have assumed for the purpose of testing this argument that it is a valid contention that a gift for the advancement of education is necessarily charitable if it is not confined within too narrow limits. But that assumption is itself difficult to justify. It may well be that the generality of the proposition is subject to at least two limitations. The first of them is implicit in the decision of Russell J in *Re Hummeltenberg* [1923] 1 Ch 237: the second is one that is not in the nature of things likely to occur, but, if it can be imagined that it was made a condition of a gift for the advancement of education that its beneficiaries should lead a cloistered life and communicate to no one, and leave no record of, the fruits of their study, I do not think that the charitable character of the gift could be sustained.

For the reasons that I have given I am of opinion that this appeal should be dismissed.

In **Neville Estates Ltd v Madden** [1962] Ch 832, the trustees of the Catford Synagogue entered into a contract to sell two plots of land to the plaintiffs for £10,000. The plaintiffs obtained detailed planning permission for the building thereon of flats and garages. The value of the land increased and the Charity Commissioners refused their permission to sell.

The plaintiffs brought an action for specific performance arguing, *inter alia*, that the land was not held on charitable trusts, and that the permission of the Charity Commissioners was not therefore necessary. The argument was that the trustees held the land upon trust for the advancement of religion among a private group of persons only. In holding that the purposes were charitable, CROSS J said at 852:

I turn now to the argument that this is a private, not a public trust... The trust with which I am concerned resembles that in *Gilmour v Coats* [1949] AC 426 in this, that the persons immediately benefited by it are not a section of the public but the members of a private body. All persons of the Jewish faith living in or about Catford might well constitute a section of the public, but the members for the time being of the Catford Synagogue are no more a section of the public than the members for the time being of a Carmelite Priory. The two cases, however, differ from one another in that the members of the Catford Synagogue spend their lives in the world, whereas the members of a Carmelite Priory live secluded from the world. If once one refuses to pay any regard—as the courts refused to pay any regard—to the influence which these nuns living in seclusion might have on the outside world, then it must follow that no public benefit is involved in a trust to support a Carmelite Priory. As Lord Greene said in the Court of Appeal [1948] Ch 340 at 345: 'having regard to the way in which the lives of the members are spent, the benefit is a purely private one'. But the court is, I think, entitled to assume that some benefit accrues to the public from the attendance at places of worship of persons who live in this world and mix with their fellow citizens. As between different religions the law stands neutral, but it assumes that any religion is at least likely to be better than none.

But then it is said—and it is this part of the argument that has caused me the greatest difficulty: 'but this is a case of self-help'. Suppose that a body of persons, being dissatisfied with the facilities for the education of small children provided in their district, form an association for the education of the children of members. A committee is formed; each member pays a subscription; the funds of the society are employed in hiring premises and paying a teacher; and the rules provide that the association cannot be dissolved by the members at any given moment but is to continue for the benefit of the members existing from time to time. No doubt the public benefits by the fact that the children of the members receive an education. But could it possibly be argued that the association was a charity and was entitled to the great fiscal advantages which a charity enjoys? Or would it make any difference if the committee allowed the children of non-members to attend the classes free of charge if there was room for them, in the same way as members of the public, though having no right to enter the synagogue, are not in practice refused admission?

I feel the force of this analogy; but, as Lord Simonds pointed out in *Gilmour v Coats* [1949] AC 426 at 449, it is dangerous to reason by analogy from one head of charity to another. After the passing of the Toleration Acts, dissenting chapels sprang up all over the country. As can be deduced from the language of section 1 of the Trustees Appointment Act, 1850 (see Sir Morton Peto's Act), the chapel was normally vested in trustees for the particular congregation or society of dissenters in question. In course of time disputes sometimes arose between rival groups, some members alleging that others had ceased to hold the tenets laid down in the trust deed and were not entitled to its benefits. A typical example of such a dispute is to be found in *A-G v Bunce* (1868) LR 6 Eq 563. No one, so far as I know, ever questioned that trusts for such dissenting bodies were charitable trusts provided that the members for the time being could not put an end to them. What the position would be if the members for the time being could divide the property among themselves was expressly left open by Sir George Jessel MR in *Bunting v Sargent* (1879) 13 Ch D 330 at 337.

Section 4 of the Religious Disabilities Act, 1846, provided that Her Majesty's subjects professing the Jewish religion in respect of their schools, places of religious worship, education and charitable purposes and the property held therewith, should be subject to the same laws as Her Majesty's Protestant subjects dissenting from the Church of England were subject to and not further or otherwise. From that time it has, I think, always been assumed by lawyers that trusts for the benefit of a congregation of Jews attending a synagogue were charitable trusts. It is, for example, obvious that Parliament and the Charity Commissioners assumed in 1870 that the four synagogues which became the constituent synagogues of the United Synagogue were charitable bodies. Yet it is equally clear from clause 6a of this scheme that the constituent synagogues have not been open to all persons of the Jewish faith, but were unincorporated associations with a list of members.

Generally speaking, no doubt, an association which is supported by its members for the purposes of providing benefits for themselves will not be a charity. But I do not think that this principle can apply with full force in the case of trusts for religious purposes. As Lord Simonds pointed out, the law of charity has been built up not logically but empirically, and there is a political background peculiar to religious trusts which may well have influenced the development of the law with regard to them.

In my judgment, this trust with which I am concerned in this case is a charitable trust.

In **Re Hetherington** [1990] Ch 1,[166] the testatrix left £2,000 to 'the Roman Catholic Church Bishop of Westminster for the repose of the souls of my husband and my parents and my sisters and also myself when I die', and her residuary estate 'to the Roman Catholic Church St Edwards Golders Green for Masses for my soul'. In holding that both gifts were charitable, SIR NICOLAS BROWNE-WILKINSON V-C said at 12:

The grounds on which the trust in the present case can be attacked are that there is no *express* requirement that the Masses for souls which are to be celebrated are to be celebrated in public. The evidence shows that celebration in public is the invariable practice but there is no requirement of Canon law to that effect. Therefore it is said the money could be applied to saying Masses in private which would not be charitable since there would be no sufficient element of public benefit.

In my judgment the cases establish the following propositions.

(1) A trust for the advancement of education, the relief of poverty or the advancement of religion is *prima facie* charitable and assumed to be for the public benefit. *National Anti-vivisection Society v IRC* [1948] AC 31, 42 and 65 [p. 511, below]. This assumption of public benefit can be rebutted by showing that in fact the particular trust in question cannot operate

---

[166] (1989) CLJ 373 (J. Hopkins); [1989] Conv 453 (N.D.M. Parry); [1989] All ER Rev 181 (P.J. Clarke); (1989) 139 NLJ 1767 (J.M.Q. Hepworth); (1990) 22 *Malaya Law Review* 114 (C.H. Sherrin).

so as to confer a legally recognised benefit on the public, as in *Gilmour v Coats* [1949] AC 426 [p. 471, above].

(2) The celebration of a religious rite in public does confer a sufficient public benefit because of the edifying and improving effect of such celebration on the members of the public who attend. As Lord Reid said in *Gilmour v Coats* at 459:

'A religion can be regarded as beneficial without it being necessary to assume that all its beliefs are true, and a religious service can be regarded as beneficial to all those who attend it without it being necessary to determine the spiritual efficacy of that service or to accept any particular belief about it.'

(3) The celebration of a religious rite in private does not contain the necessary element of public benefit since any benefit by prayer or example is incapable of proof in the legal sense, and any element of edification is limited to a private, not public, class of those present at the celebration: see *Gilmour v Coats; Yeap Cheah Neo v Ong Cheng Neo* (1875) LR 6 PC 381 and *Hoare v Hoare* (1886) 56 LT 147.

Where there is a gift for a religious purpose which could be carried out in a way which is beneficial to the public (i.e. by public Masses) but could also be carried out in a way which would not have sufficient element of public benefit (i.e. by private masses) the gift is to be construed as a gift to be carried out only by the methods that are charitable, all non-charitable methods being excluded: see *Re White* [1893] 2 Ch 41, 52–53; and *Re Banfield* [1968] 1 WLR 846.[167]

Applying those principles to the present case, a gift for the saying of Masses is *prima facie* charitable, being for a religious purpose. In practice, those Masses will be celebrated in public which provides a sufficient element of public benefit. The provision of stipends for priests saying the Masses, by relieving the Roman Catholic Church *pro tanto* of the liability to provide such stipends, is a further benefit. The gift is to be construed as a gift for public Masses only on the principle of *Re White*, private Masses not being permissible since it would not be a charitable application of the fund for a religious purpose.

I will therefore declare that both gifts are valid charitable trusts for the saying of Masses in public. The pecuniary legacy should be paid to the Archbishop of Westminster who is plainly the person referred to as the Bishop of Westminster, to be held by him on those trusts. Since the will appoints no trustee of the residuary gift, the residuary gift will be dealt with by the Crown under a scheme made under the Sign Manual.[168]

In **Funnell v Stewart** [1996] 1 WLR 288,[169] HAZEL WILLIAMSON QC said at 297:

The only question left is, therefore, whether this spiritual healing work itself, in the form of the faith-healing part of the group's work, which I find to be the substance of the group's work, is indeed charitable. On this point I have again come to the conclusion that Mr. Henderson is right. I accept his argument that it is charitable, and I so hold either on the basis that faith healing has by the present time (although this would not necessarily have been the case when *Re Hummeltenberg* [1923] 1 Ch 237 was decided) become a recognised activity of public benefit or, in any event, on the basis that the religious element in the present case, and the religious nature

---

[167] Alternatively, the non-charitable purpose may be characterised as subsidiary to the public benefit and this will not prevent the charitable purpose from being recognised: *Funnell v Stewart* [1996] 1 WLR 288, below (private religious services ancillary to public faith healing).

[168] On Sign Manual generally, see Tudor, pp. 368–370.   [169] (1996) 112 LQR 557 (R. Fletcher).

of the faith-healing movement in question, renders this work a charitable purpose within which a sufficient element of public benefit is assumed so as to enable the charity to be recognised by law as being such unless there is contrary evidence. There is no such contrary evidence.

Accordingly, I find that this is a charitable trust. It follows that it is unnecessary for me to consider the question whether the evidence of actual public benefit in the form of the demonstrable efficaciousness of the healing work of the group is actually required.

QUESTIONS

1. What are the key characteristics of a religion?

2. Now compare the differences in the requirements of public benefit between religious and educational trusts.
   What would you say of:
   (a) a trust for the provision of a private chapel in an independent school?
   (b) a trust to provide religious services for long-term prisoners in the maximum-security wing of a prison?
   (c) a trust to provide a church for Methodists and for persons likely to become Methodists in West Ham? (see *IRC v Baddeley* [1955] AC 572 [p. 492, below]).

3. Would there have been a different result in *Gilmour v Coats* if it had been shown that a number of nuns retired periodically and returned to life outside the convent? See Cross J in *Neville Estates Ltd v Madden* [1962] Ch 832 at 853.

4. In the light of the expanded definition of religion in the Charities Act 2006 should the following be treated as religious charities:
   (a) a trust for the advancement of Scientology?
   (b) a trust for the advancement of atheism?
   (c) a trust for the advancement of science?

E   ADVANCEMENT OF HEALTH OR THE SAVING OF LIVES[170]

CHARITIES ACT 2006

2. (3) In subsection 2—
   (a) in paragraph (d) 'the advancement of health' includes the prevention or relief of sickness, disease or human suffering; . . .

---

[170] Charity Commission Publication 6 (Charities for the Relief of Sickness), March 2000; [1995] Ch Com Rep. 35 (Funds Raised and Donated to NHS Hospitals); Goodman Report, paras. 47 (Costly Services), 48–49 (Hospitals). Criticised (1999) 62 MLR 333 (M. Chesterman).

Re Resch's Will Trusts
[1969] 1 AC 514 (PC, **Lords Hodson, Guest, Donovan, Wilberforce** and **Sir Alfred North**)

A number of questions arose under the will of Mr. Resch, who died in 1963, leaving a residuary estate worth A\$8 million. The relevant question was whether a gift to a private non-profit-making hospital was a charitable gift. The gift was of income 'to the Sisters of Charity for a period of 200 years or for so long as they shall conduct St Vincent's Private Hospital whichever shall be the shorter period, to be applied for the general purposes of such hospital and upon the expiration of the said period of 200 years or upon the said Sisters of Charity ceasing to conduct such hospital' to pay the income to named charities.

Held. a valid charitable gift.

Lord Wilberforce: St Vincent's Private Hospital was inaugurated in 1909, when the present building, called by that name, was converted to that purpose, having previously been used as a Hospice for the Dying. The hospital was established and has since 1909 been conducted by the Sisters of Charity, a voluntary association or congregation of women, governed by their constitution under which they devote themselves without reward to good works. The Sisters also conducted in 1909 and still conduct the adjacent St Vincent's Hospital which is a public hospital within the Public Hospitals Act, 1929–59. The evidence shows that the reason for the establishment of the private hospital was to relieve the pressing demand of the public for admission to the general hospital which was quite inadequate to the demand upon it. Another reason was that there were many persons who needed hospital nursing and attention who were not willing to enter a public hospital but were willing and desirous of having hospital accommodation with more privacy and comfort than would be possible in the general hospital. The establishment of an adjacent private hospital would enable the honorary medical staff in the general hospital to admit for treatment under their care in the private hospital patients who were reluctant to enter the general hospital and were able and willing to pay reasonable and proper fees for admission and treatment in a private hospital. The private hospital has 82 beds as compared with over 500 in the general hospital....

A gift for the purposes of a hospital is *prima facie* a good charitable gift. This is now clearly established both in Australia and in England, not merely because of the use of the word 'impotent' in the Preamble to 43 Eliz. c.4, though the process of referring to the Preamble is one often used for reassurance, but because the provision of medical care for the sick is, in modern times, accepted as a public benefit suitable to attract the privileges given to charitable institutions. This has been recognised in the High Court in Australia in *Taylor v Taylor*[171] and *Kytherian Association of Queensland v Sklavos* (1958) 101 CLR 56: in England in *Re Smith* [1962] 1 WLR 763.

In spite of this general proposition, there may be certain hospitals, or categories of hospitals, which are not charitable institutions (see *Re Smith*). Disqualifying indicia may be either that the hospital is carried on commercially, i.e., with a view to making profits for private individuals, or that the benefits it provides are not for the public, or a sufficiently large class of the public to satisfy the necessary tests of public character. Each class of objection is taken in

---

[171] (1910) 10 CLR 218 at 227, *per* Griffith CJ.

the present case. As regards the first, it is accepted that the private hospital is not run for the profit, in any ordinary sense, of individuals. Moreover, if the purposes of the hospital are otherwise charitable, they do not lose this character merely because charges are made to the recipients of benefits—see *IRC v Falkirk Temperance Café Trust* 1927 SC 261; *Salvation Army (Victoria) Property Trust v Fern Tree Gully Corpn* (1951) 85 CLR 159 at 173. But what is said is that surpluses are made and are used for the general purposes of the Sisters of Charity. This association, while in a broad sense philanthropic, has objects which may not be charitable in the legal sense. Furthermore its purposes, though stated in its 'constitutions' are not limited by law, other than the canon law of the Roman Catholic Church, and under this, they are empowered, and may be obliged, to alter their purposes so as to include other objects which may not be strictly charitable.

Their Lordships do not consider it necessary to enter upon these latter considerations. For whatever the Sisters of Charity may be empowered to do with regard to their general property, as regards the share of income of the residuary estate, given to them as trustees, they are bound by the trusts declared in the will under which any money received by them must be applied exclusively for the general purposes of the private hospital as above defined. As regards these purposes, it appears, from the evidence already summarised, that the making of profits for the benefit of individuals is not among them. The most that is shown is that, on a cash basis, and without making such adjustments as would be required for commercial accounting, a net surplus is produced over the years which in fact has been applied largely, though not exclusively for hospital purposes. The share of income given by the will must be devoted entirely to the purposes of the private hospital. The character, charitable or otherwise, of the general activities of the Sisters, is not therefore a material consideration...

Their Lordships turn to the second objection. This, in substance, is that the private hospital is not carried on for purposes 'beneficial to the community' because it provides only for persons of means who are capable of paying the substantial fees required as a condition of admission.

In dealing with this objection, it is necessary first to dispose of a misapprehension. It is not a condition of validity of a trust for the relief of the sick that it should be limited to the poor sick. Whether one regards the charitable character of trusts for the relief of the sick as flowing from the word 'impotent' ('aged, impotent and poor people') in the Preamble to 43 Eliz. c.4 or more broadly as derived from the conception of benefit to the community, there is no warrant for adding to the condition of sickness that of poverty. As early as *Income Tax Special Comrs v Pemsel* Lord Herschell was able to say [1891] AC 531 at 571:

> 'I am unable to agree with the view that the sense in which "charities" and "charitable purpose" are popularly used is so restricted as this. I certainly cannot think that they are limited to the relief of wants occasioned by lack of pecuniary means. Many examples may, I think, be given of endowments for the relief of human necessities, which would be as generally termed charities as hospitals or almshouses, where, nevertheless, the necessities to be relieved do not result from poverty in its limited sense of the lack of money.'

Similarly in *Verge v Somerville* [1924] AC 496 Lord Wrenbury, delivering the judgment of this Board on an appeal from New South Wales, pointed out that trusts for education and religion do not require any qualification of poverty to be introduced to give them validity and held generally that poverty is not a necessary qualification in trusts beneficial to the community. The proposition that relief of sickness was a sufficient purpose without adding poverty was accepted by the Court of Appeal in *Re Smith* [1962] 1 WLR 763. The appellants did not really contest this. They based their argument on the narrower proposition that a trust could not be charitable which excluded the poor from participation in its benefits. The purposes of the private hospital were, they said, to provide facilities for the well-to-do: an important section of the community was excluded: the trusts could not therefore be said to be for the benefit of the community. There was not sufficient 'public element'.

To support this, they appealed to some well-known authorities. [His Lordship referred to *Jones v Williams* (1767) Amb 651 and *Re Macduff* [1896] 2 Ch 451 where, in a general discussion of such expressions as 'charitable' or 'philanthropic', Lindley LJ said at 464:

> 'I am quite aware that a trust may be charitable though not confined to the poor; but I doubt very much whether a trust would be declared to be charitable which excluded the poor.'

... Their Lordships accept the correctness of what has been said in those cases, but they must be rightly understood. It would be a wrong conclusion from them to state that a trust for the provision of medical facilities would necessarily fail to be charitable merely because by reason of expense they could only be made use of by persons of some means. To provide, in response to public need, medical treatment otherwise inaccessible but in its nature expensive, without any profit motive, might well be charitable: on the other hand to limit admission to a nursing home to the rich would not be so. The test is essentially one of public benefit, and indirect as well as direct benefit enters into the account. In the present case, the element of public benefit is strongly present. It is not disputed that a need exists to provide accommodation and medical treatment in conditions of greater privacy and relaxation than would be possible in a general hospital and as a supplement to the facilities of a general hospital. This is what the private hospital does and it does so at, approximately, cost price. The service is needed by all, not only by the well-to-do. So far as its nature permits it is open to all: the charges are not low, but the evidence shows that it cannot be said that the poor are excluded: such exclusion as there is, is of some of the poor—namely, those who have (a) not contributed sufficiently to a medical benefit scheme or (b) need to stay longer in the hospital than their benefit will cover or (c) cannot get a reduction of or exemption from the charges. The general benefit to the community of such facilities results from the beds and medical staff of the general hospital, the availability of a particular type of nursing and treatment which supplements that provided by the general hospital and the benefit to the standard of medical care in the general hospital which arises from the juxtaposition of the two institutions...

[Their Lordships]...hold...that the gift in favour of the Sisters of Charity is a valid charitable bequest.[172]

Report of the Charity Commissioners for England and Wales for the year 1975, para. 70

Charities engaged in fringe medicine

70. As a result of our considerations of the New Age Healing Trust mentioned in paragraphs 68 and 69 above[173] we considered the practical difficulties involved and the principles which should be followed in considering applications for the registration of institutions set up

---

[172] *Joseph Rowntree Memorial Trust Housing Association Ltd v A-G* [1983] Ch 159 [p. 502, below].

[173] An application to register a trust for 'the practising for the public benefit of New Age Healing for the relief of the sick and persons in ill-health' was rejected. But the Yoga for Health Foundation is a registered charity; the trust is 'for the purpose of research into the therapeutic benefits to be obtained by the practice of Yoga both mentally and physically and the promotion of such benefits': *Yoga for Health Foundation v Customs and Excise Comrs* [1984] STC 630.

to promote and/or practice unorthodox methods of healing. The main problem was the need to make value judgements in such cases. For this purpose we would require evidence to satisfy us that an unusual form of treatment had some merit, in the same way as the court would require evidence if the case had been brought before them. An organisation proposing to engage in such well-known therapeutic activities as acupuncture, osteopathy and faith healing[174] would not necessarily be required to submit evidence concerning the effectiveness of its activities. In other cases, however, evidence would be required concerning the nature of the healing method proposed and the therapeutic result of that method. The effectiveness of proposed treatment could be a matter of special knowledge derived from a study of cases or from other sources. It could also be provided by evidence that the treatment was generally acceptable to the medical profession. This did not mean that every institution practising in the field of fringe medicine must necessarily use methods acceptable to the generality of the medical profession if it were to obtain charitable status, but there might be grounds for reasonable doubt if no medically quali-fied persons were prepared to testify to the beneficial results of the treatment. We concluded that where therapeutic methods and results were common knowledge evidence on these points would not be required before registration but, where they were not, the applicant should be required to submit evidence, and a decision whether to register the institution should be based on a study of that evidence as well as of the stated objects.[175]

F ADVANCEMENT OF CITIZENSHIP OR COMMUNITY DEVELOPMENT

CHARITIES ACT 2006

2. (3) In subsection (2)—

    (c) paragraph (e) includes—

        (i)   rural or urban regeneration, and

        (ii) the promotion of civic responsibility, volunteering, the voluntary sec-tor or the effectiveness or efficiency of charities; . . .

Charity Commission: *Review of the Register: Promotion of Urban and Rural Regeneration* (RR2) (March 1999), paras 6–8 and Annex A5, A6 and A18

Urban and rural regeneration

    6.   Following public consultation, the Charity Commissioners have recognised the promotion of urban and rural regeneration for public benefit in areas of social and economic deprivation

---

[174] See *Funnell v Stewart* [1996] 1 WLR 288. See p. 477, above.

[175] *NFSH Charitable Trust Ltd's Application for Registration as a Charity* [2006] WTLR 629 (charity for the promotion of spiritual healing registered on condition that the healers did not claim to diagnose illness, did not make unfounded claims to cure illness, and the purpose of healing was to relieve illness and to promote wellbeing in healthy people).

as a charitable purpose in its own right. Charitable regeneration organisations can achieve this by the maintenance or improvement of the physical, social and economic infrastructure and by assisting people who are at a disadvantage because of their social and economic circumstances. This guidance does not cover organisations set up solely for the purpose of community development.

7. Regeneration organisations might do some, or all, of the following:

- provide financial or other assistance to people who are poor;
- provide housing for those in need and help to improve housing standards generally in those parts of an area of deprivation where poor housing is a problem;
- help unemployed people find employment;
- provide education, training and re-training opportunities and work experience, especially for unemployed people;
- provide financial or technical assistance or advice to new businesses or existing businesses where it would lead to training and employment opportunities for unemployed people;
- provide land and buildings on favourable terms to businesses in order to create training and employment opportunities for unemployed people;
- provide, maintain and improve roads and accessibility to main transport routes;
- provide, maintain and improve recreational facilities;
- preserve buildings in the area which are of historic or architectural importance;
- provide public amenities.

They may, of course, undertake other activities as well.

Tests for charitable status

8. Broadly speaking in order to be charitable a regeneration organisation will normally need to demonstrate that:

- it has effective criteria to determine whether or not an area is in need of regeneration;
- it will undertake at least 3 or 4 of the activities listed in paragraph 7 above, and that these activities cover a broad spectrum of regeneration work;
- the public benefit from its activities outweighs any private benefit which might be conferred on individuals or companies. This means it must have clear criteria by which to determine this; and
- its objects are exclusively charitable....

Public and private benefit

A5. A charity must confer a benefit on the public as a whole or on a sufficient section of the public. Most of the tangible benefits of urban or rural regeneration would normally seem to go, in the first place, to individuals and individual businesses rather than the wider public.

A6. If an organisation is to be a charity its purposes and activities must therefore be restricted so that any private benefits arise only as a necessary means of achieving the overall charitable purpose and are incidental to it. It would not be acceptable if the private benefits were an end in themselves. The status of the organisation will therefore depend on its poise in this respect. This will have to be determined in each particular case.[176] ...

Area of benefit

A18.   The area to be regenerated must be large enough to encompass a sufficiently large beneficial class. This would normally rule out organisations set up to regenerate particular roads.

Report of the Charity Commissioners for England and Wales for the year 1981, paras. 68–70[177]

The Earl Mountbatten of Burma Statue Appeal Trust

68.   Following the assassination in 1979 of Admiral of the Fleet, The Earl Mountbatten of Burma, a charitable trust (The Mountbatten Memorial Trust) having wide charitable objects was established. In addition, in July 1981 an appeal was made, including a letter in *The Times* signed by the Prime Minister and other eminent people, for a public memorial to take the form of a statue of the Earl, in naval uniform, to be sited on the Foreign Office green overlooking Horse Guards Parade and the Admiralty, with a maintenance fund for its upkeep and repair. The project was estimated to cost £100,000 and any surplus was to be used for charitable purposes.

69.   The law on the charitable status of public memorials is scanty and imprecise. The decision of Mr. Justice Clauson in *Murray v Thomas* [1937] 4 All ER 545 indicated that a war memorial of a substantial kind (in that case a memorial hall) intended not only to commemorate the dead but to serve a useful purpose for the benefit of the community could be charitable; but the Judge reserved the question whether funds collected to provide a non-utilitarian object such as a statue might be charitable. We had registered as charities one or two funds for the upkeep and maintenance of statues but we had not previously considered whether a fund for the provision of a statue was charitable. In Halsbury's *Laws of England*, Fourth Edition, Volume 5, page 339, it is stated that 'the erection of a monument, not of the donor, or memorial, may perhaps be charitable' and the footnote numbered 17 adds that 'the Charity Commissioners have treated some such cases as charitable, e.g. the Wellington Monument in Somerset and the Cobden Obelisk at Midhurst'. However, the Wellington Monument was erected on land belonging to the National Trust so that there were other amenity aspects, which made for charitability, and we were unable to trace any papers relating to the Cobden Obelisk.

70.   After due consideration, and reference to the law in the U.S.A. (where statues have been accepted as charitable in some States) we concluded that the provision of a statue might be held to have a sufficient element of public benefit where the person being commemorated was

---

[176] After referring to the *Oldham Training and Enterprise Council* case [p. 520, below], the publication continues: 'Conversely, in the case of *ViRSA Educational Trust*, the Commissioners decided that registration could proceed. This organisation was established to carry out research into the availability of retail and other services in villages, *to provide training and guidance to rural communities on establishing and maintaining those services and to promote trades and crafts connected with the rural economy as a whole.* The organisation was charitable because it provided support to rural communities generally. (An organisation which promoted particular village shops would confer too high a degree of private benefit on the proprietors to be charitable.)'

[177] See (1999) 19 LS 380, 383–384 (I. McLean and M. Johnes) (a memorial for the victims of the Aberfan Disaster).

nationally, and perhaps internationally, respected and could be said to be a figure of historical importance. In such a case the provision and maintenance of a statue can be held to be charitable as likely to foster patriotism and good citizenship, and to be an incentive to heroic and noble deeds. The Earl Mountbatten of Burma Statue Appeal Trust established by a declaration of trust dated 9 October 1981 came into this category, its object being 'the commemoration for the benefit of the public of the life and works of (the late Earl) by the erection of a statue... and by maintaining that memorial', and has been registered as a charity.[178]

G ADVANCEMENT OF THE ARTS, CULTURE, HERITAGE, OR SCIENCE

Before the Charities Act 2006 recognised a distinct head of charity involving the advancement of arts, culture, heritage, or science, trusts for such purposes would only be upheld as charitable if they were considered to be for the advancement of education or for other purposes beneficial to the community. Indication as to whether a purpose could be considered to be for the advancement of culture was considered in some cases.

In **Commissioners of Inland Revenue v White** [1980] TR 155, the principal object of the Clerkenwell Green Association for Craftsmen was 'to promote any charitable purpose which will encourage the exercise and maintain the standards of crafts both ancient and modern, preserve and improve craftsmanship and foster, promote and increase the interest of the public therein'. The Association had converted two buildings for use as workshops by craftsmen, who included a hand engraver, antique furniture restorer, clock maker, silversmith, polisher and plater, musical instrument maker, glass polisher, manufacturing jeweller, diamond mounter, watch repairer, general engraver, printer, and fashion designer. Fox J held that the purpose was charitable and said at 158:

The word 'craftsmanship', in its general use in the English language, suggests a degree of quality of workmanship... There is, in my opinion, a substantial range of activity which would foster, promote and increase the interest of the public in craftsmanship and which would itself be charitable.... It seems to me that there is a wide field of high-quality craftsmanship where there could be no doubt as to the educative value to the public of increased information.

Even when artistic purposes were considered to be charitable under the head of the advancement of education it was necessary to determine whether aesthetic and artistic subjects could be described as educational. Today it is not necessary to treat an artistic purpose as educational for it to be charitable, but it is still necessary to consider whether it can even be considered to be artistic. Not all noise-making qualifies as music; not every collection of junk as a museum of art. And what qualifies in one age

---

[178] (1983) 133 NLJ 1107 (H. Picarda). For private memorials which are for non-charitable purposes, see *Re Endacott* [1960] Ch 232 [p. 362, above]; *M'Caig v University of Glasgow* 1907 SC 231 [p. 377, above].

may fail in the next, and vice versa. The policy of the law is to encourage the promotion of artistic work of quality; but it is an extreme step to permit the promotion, free of tax and permanently, of the work of a particular artist. How should the selection be determined, and by whom?

Re Delius
[1957] Ch 299 (Ch D, Roxburgh J)

The widow of the composer Frederick Delius gave her residuary estate upon various trusts for the advancement of Delius's musical works. The most significant clause was clause 12 by which the trustees were to 'apply the royalties income and the income of my residuary trust fund for or towards the advancement...of the musical works of my late husband...under conditions in which the making of profit is not the object to be attained and which might be economically impossible by any concert operatic or other organisation...' and then suggested ways in which this should be achieved. The question was whether the will created a charitable trust.

Held. A valid charitable trust for the advancement of education.

Roxburgh J: First of all, I have to decide what is the purpose of this trust. In arriving at a conclusion on that point, I must have regard not only to the language in which the purpose is expressed (and, indeed, that is of itself reasonably clear) but also to the means which are indicated for achieving that purpose, which make the position even clearer. It seems to me that in very truth the purpose is the spreading and establishment of knowledge and appreciation of Delius's works amongst the public of the world. It is, indeed, remarkable to what extent that objective has been achieved in the 21 years or so since the widow died. The copyrights in Delius's works were valued at the date of her death at £1,483, and at that time formed a comparatively small portion of his residuary estate. The royalties received in the year ending 5 April, 1936, amounted to £103, in the year 1946 they amounted to £2,233, and in the year 1956 they amounted to £7,278; which is no doubt largely to be attributed to Sir Thomas Beecham.

The position is now that certain of Delius's works are so well known that no guarantee is required by the recording companies in respect thereof, but the trustees are now advised that some of the lesser-known works which were recorded in the early history of the trust should be re-recorded if the work of the trust can continue to be carried on. Sir Thomas Beecham has been engaged for some years on the task of editing the whole of the compositions of Delius, with a view to the publication and issue of a uniform edition of the whole body of his musical works in accordance with the provisions of clause 12 of the will, but the printing and publication of the major portion of this edition has been held in abeyance pending the decision of this court whether after the period of 21 years from the death of the testatrix the trusts declared in clause 12 constitute valid and effectual charitable trusts, or are void as infringing the rule against perpetuities or otherwise.

I have stated what I understand to be the purpose of the trusts, and the question is whether that purpose is charitable in the eye of the law? I can do no better in this connexion than to read certain passages from the judgment of Lord Greene MR in *Royal Choral Society v IRC* [1943] 2 All ER 101. There are, of course, certain points which necessarily occur to the mind in connexion with a musical composition. It might be suggested as regards some music, at any rate, that its purpose was limited to giving pleasure, and as regards all music it must be said that it gives pleasure. That is a feature about music. When I say 'all music', I mean all that can be truly called music. Indeed, a lot of pleasure is derived by some from something which can hardly be truly called music, but, at any rate, pleasure is a circumstance intimately connected with music. But that in itself does not operate to destroy the charitable character of a bequest for the advancement of the art of music. I adopt, with great satisfaction, the words of Lord Greene [1943] 2 All ER 101 at 104: 'Curiously enough, some people find pleasure in providing education. Still more curiously, some people find pleasure in being educated: but the element of pleasure in those processes is not the purpose of them, but what may be called a by-product which is necessarily there.' That seems to me to be all that need be said about the aspect of pleasure connected with the music of Delius.

Lord Greene proceeded: [His Lordship quoted the extract at p. 441, above; and continued:] Those words have been freely adopted in subsequent cases, and I adopt them and also hold that they are directly applicable to this trust.

I do not find it necessary to consider what the position might be if the trusts were for the promotion of the works of some inadequate composer. It has been suggested that perhaps I should have no option but to give effect even to such a trust. I do not know, but I need not investigate that problem, because counsel who have argued before me have been unanimous in the view that the standard of Delius's work is so high that that question does not arise in the present case.

The point which has been made—and it is one of interest and importance—is, that first of all this trust is not a trust for the promotion of music in general but the music of a particular individual composer. That could not of itself vitiate the charitable nature of the trust, because, after all, aesthetic appreciation of music in a broad sense can only be derived from aesthetic appreciation of the works of a large number of composers. It is the aggregate of the work of a large number of composers which is the basis of the aesthetic appreciation, and, therefore, if it is charitable to promote music in general it must be charitable to promote the music of a particular composer, presupposing (as in this case I can assume) that the composer is one whose music is worth appreciating.

In order to make that plain, I would refer to *Re Shakespeare Memorial Trust* [1923] 2 Ch 398, where the charitable trust was, to put it shortly, to promote the works of Shakespeare. I cannot conceive that anybody would doubt that a trust to promote the works of Beethoven would be charitable, but the real strength of the point put in this case arises from the fact that this trust was created by the widow of Delius, and nobody would doubt that, amongst the many motives which actuated her, affection for her deceased husband was to be found. But one must be careful to distinguish motive from purpose, because motive is not relevant in these cases except in so far as it is incorporated into the purpose. Considering the purposes, it is possible to approach the purposes upon the hypothesis that their intention was, as Mr. Browne-Wilkinson put it, to enhance her husband's reputation.

This is, of course, rather subtle. It is a question which is the cart and which is the horse, because, of course, the more aesthetic appreciation of Delius's music is achieved the more Delius's reputation will necessarily be enhanced. The two things fit together, and there is no doubt whatever that both objects have in fact already been to a large extent achieved. But, in my judgment, it is not fair to approach the problem from that point of view. I think that there is every reason to suppose that the testatrix took the view, and was well advised to take it, that if the work of Delius was brought before the public in an efficient manner, the aesthetic appreciation of the public would grow and, inherent in that growth, would be the enhancement of Delius's reputation, which was in itself a desirable thing, and I for my part refuse to disentangle it. There is no reliable evidence on which I can disentangle it. What is quite clear to me is that these purposes would plainly be charitable if for the name 'Delius' the name 'Beethoven' were substituted and, in my judgment, they do not cease to be charitable because in this context the name is 'Delius' and not 'Beethoven'.

Re Pinion
[1965] Ch 85 (CA, **Harman, Davies** and **Russell LJJ**)

By his will, the testator, Mr. Pinion, gave the income of the residue of his estate to his sister for her life and after her death provided that his studio and contents, which included pictures, furniture, china, glass, and *objets d'art* should be offered to the National Trust, kept intact in the studio, and displayed to the public. A custodian was appointed, the post to be offered to the sister and after her death to a blood relation. Goods and chattels not of an antique nature could be disposed of. By a codicil he revoked his sister's life interest and provided that if, as happened, the National Trust was not prepared to observe the provisions of the will, his executors should maintain the studio and contents as a museum.

Held (reversing Wilberforce J). The trust was not for the advancement of education and was void.

Harman LJ: This appeal concerns the testamentary dispositions of Arthur Watson Hyde Pinion, who died in the year 1961, having, by his will made in 1956 as varied by a codicil made in 1961, sought to devote almost the whole of his not inconsiderable estate to a project designed to keep himself and his family for all time before the public eye by allowing the public to view without cost his studio, situate at 22a Pembridge Villas, Notting Hill, intact with its entire contents. These treasures are to be entrusted to a custodian, first his sister and subsequently a blood relation of his, who are to be paid and housed out of his estate. The question is whether he was entitled to saddle his property with this chimaera to the deprivation of his next-of-kin and this, the judge has held, he was entitled to do at the instance of the Attorney-General, who persuaded him, though hardly, that the testator has created a valid charitable trust.

The will and codicil are rambling and half-coherent documents reduced to some semblance of order by the judge but his summary is, I think, perhaps too neat and logical and the actual words should be read to convey its authentic flavour. It starts by conferring a life interest in the whole estate on his sister, the first defendant, who is also his sole next-of-kin, and proceeds. [His Lordship then read passages of the will and codicils and continued:] I construe this farrago as meaning that the entire contents of the studio, which housed all the articles referred to, are to be exhibited as a whole and, as he says, 'to be kept intact in the studio'. The only exception is that articles 'not of an antique nature' may be disposed of. I assume that the revocation of the sister's life interest accelerated the gift to the National Trust, which has refused the bequest, and that the authority to his executors to appoint a trust to carry out the bequest is in fact mandatory, the contrary not having been argued.

In this court the Attorney-General did not seek to support the gift as being beneficial in a general sense to the public, but confined his pleas to that head of charity which is characterised as the advancement of education. He argued both here and below that no evidence was receivable on this subject. A museum, he said, is a place which the law assumes to have an educational value and purpose. The cases on this subject to be found in *Tudor on Charities*, 5th edition

(1929), are not very satisfactory. It would appear that a gift to an established museum is charitable: see *British Museum Trustees v White* (1826) 2 Sim & St 594. In *Re Holburne* (1885) 53 LT 212 a gift to trustees of objects of art to form an art museum in Bath open to the public and a fund to endow it was held a valid charitable gift as being of public utility or benefit. No question was there raised as to the merit of the collection. It must have been agreed that such merit existed, for everyone assumed it, including the judge. I conclude that a gift to found a public museum may be assumed to be charitable as of public utility if no one questions it. So in a case about religion, such as *Thornton v Howe* (1862) 31 Beav 14, the case about Joanna Southcote, the court will assume without inquiry that the teaching may do some good if not shown to be subversive of morality. Where the object is to found a school the court will not study the methods of education provided that on the face of them they are proper: *Re Shaw's Will Trusts* [1952] Ch 163. A school for prostitutes or pickpockets would obviously fail. A case about education is *Re Hummeltenberg* [1923] 1 Ch 237, where the headnote reads: 'To be valid a charitable bequest must be for the public benefit, and the trust must be capable of being administered and controlled by the court. The opinion of the donor of a gift or the creator of a trust that the gift or trust is for the public benefit does not make it so, the matter is one to be determined by the court on the evidence before it.'

The bequest in that case was connected with spiritualism and the point to which I draw attention is that the judge (the late Lord Russell of Killowen, then Russell J) said it must be decided on the evidence. There is a passage in his judgment as follows [1923] 1 Ch 237 at 242:

> 'It was contended' (says he) 'that the court was not the tribunal to determine whether a gift or trust was or was not a gift or a trust for the benefit of the public. It was said that the only judge of this was the donor of the gift or the creator of the trust. For this view reliance was placed on the views expressed by the Master of the Rolls [Porter MR] and by some members of the Court of Appeal in Ireland in *Re Cranston* [1898] 1 IR 431 at 446. Reliance was also placed on a sentence in the judgment of Chitty J in *Re Foveaux* [1895] 2 Ch 501. So far as the views so expressed declare that the personal or private opinion of the judge is immaterial, I agree; but so far as they lay down or suggest that the donor of the gift or the creator of the trust is to determine whether the purpose is beneficial to the public, I respectfully disagree. If a testator by stating or indicating his view that a trust is beneficial to the public can establish that fact beyond question, trusts might be established in perpetuity for the promotion of all kinds of fantastic (though not unlawful) objects, of which the training of poodles to dance might be a mild example. In my opinion the question whether a gift is or may be operative for the public benefit is a question to be answered by the court by forming an opinion upon the evidence before it.'

Where a museum is concerned and the utility of the gift is brought in question it is, in my opinion, and herein I agree with the judge, essential to know at least something of the quality of the proposed exhibits in order to judge whether they will be conducive to the education of the public. So I think with a public library, such a place if found to be devoted entirely to works of pornography or of a corrupting nature, would not be allowable. Here it is suggested that education in the fine arts is the object. For myself a reading of the will leads me rather to the view that the testator's object was not to educate anyone, but to perpetuate his own name and the repute of his family, hence perhaps the direction that the custodian should be a blood relation of his. However that may be, there is a strong body of evidence here that as a means of education this collection is worthless. The testator's own paintings, of which there are over 50, are said by competent persons to be in an academic style and 'atrociously bad' and the other pictures without exception worthless. Even the so-called 'Lely' turns out to be a 20th-century copy.

Apart from pictures there is a haphazard assembly—it does not merit the name collection, for no purpose emerges, no time nor style is illustrated—of furniture and objects of so-called 'art' about which expert opinion is unanimous that nothing beyond the third-rate is to be found. Indeed one of the experts expresses his surprise that so voracious a collector should not by hazard have picked up even one meritorious object. The most that skilful cross-examination extracted from the expert witnesses was that there were a dozen chairs which might perhaps be acceptable to a minor provincial museum and perhaps another dozen not altogether worthless, but two dozen chairs do not make a museum and they must, to accord with the will, be exhibited stifled by a large number of absolutely worthless pictures and objects.

It was said that this is a matter of taste, and *de gustibus non est disputandum*, but here I agree with the judge that there is an accepted canon of taste on which the court must rely, for it has itself no judicial knowledge of such matters, and the unanimous verdict of the experts is as I have stated. The judge with great hesitation concluded that there was that scintilla of merit which was sufficient to save the rest. I find myself on the other side of the line. I can conceive of no useful object to be served in foisting upon the public this mass of junk. It has neither public utility nor educative value. I would hold that the testator's project ought not to be carried into effect and that his next-of kin is entitled to the residue of his estate.

The public benefit requirement also applies to trusts for the advancement of art and culture etc.

Williams' Trustees v Inland Revenue Commissioners
[1947] AC 447 (HL, **Viscount Simon, Lords Wright, Porter, Simonds** and **Normand**)

A trust was established for the purpose of promoting Welsh interests in London by various methods: by social contacts, the study of the Welsh language, literature, and art, and the maintenance of a library of literature on the Welsh language or relating to Wales. The trustees were also empowered to maintain an institute for the benefit of the Welsh people in London 'with a view to creating a centre in London for promoting the moral social spiritual and educational welfare of Welsh people and fostering the study of the Welsh language and of Welsh history literature music and art'. No alcoholic liquor was to be sold or consumed on any part of the premises.

The question was whether the trust was exempt from income tax.

Held. Not being charitable, the trust was liable to pay income tax.

Lord Simonds: My Lords, I must mention another aspect of this case, which was discussed in the Court of Appeal and in the argument at your Lordships' bar. It is not expressly stated in the preamble to the statute, but it was established in the Court of Chancery, and, so far as I am aware, the principle has been consistently maintained, that a trust in order to be charitable must be of a public character. It must not be merely for the benefit of particular private individuals: if it is, it will not be in law a charity though the benefit taken by those individuals is of the very character stated in the preamble. The rule is thus stated by Lord Wrenbury in *Verge v Somerville* [1924] AC 496 at 499: 'To ascertain whether a gift constitutes a valid charitable trust so as to escape being void on the ground of perpetuity, a first inquiry must be whether it is public—whether it is for the benefit of the community or of an appreciably important class of the community. The inhabitants of a parish or town, or any particular class of such inhabitants, may for instance, be the objects of such a gift, but private individuals, or a fluctuating body of private individuals, cannot.' It is, I think, obvious that this rule, necessary as it is, must often be difficult of application and so the courts have found. Fortunately perhaps, though Lord Wrenbury put it first, the question does not arise at all, if the purpose of the gift whether for the benefit of a class of inhabitants or of a fluctuating body of private individuals is not itself charitable. I may however refer to a recent case in this House which in some aspects resembles the present case. In *Keren Kayemeth le Jisroel Ltd v IRC* [1932] AC 650 a company had been formed which had as its main object (to put it shortly) the purchase of land in Palestine, Syria or other parts of Turkey in Asia and the peninsula of Sinai for the purpose of settling Jews on such lands. In its memorandum it took numerous other powers which were to be exercised only in such a way as should in the opinion of the company be conducive to the attainment of the primary object. No part of the income of the company was distributable among its members. It was urged that the company was established for charitable purposes for numerous reasons, with only one of which I will trouble your Lordships, namely, that it was established for the benefit of the community or of a section of the community, namely, Jews, whether the association was for the benefit of Jews all over the world or of the Jews repatriated in the Promised Land. Lord Tomlin dealing with the argument that I have just mentioned upon the footing that, if benefit to 'a community' could be established the purpose might be charitable, proceeded to examine the problem in that aspect and sought to identify the community. He failed to do so, finding it neither in the community of all Jews throughout the world nor in that of the Jews in the region prescribed for settlement. It is perhaps unnecessary to pursue the matter. Each case must be judged on its own facts and the dividing line is not easily drawn. But the difficulty of finding the community in the present case, when the definition of 'Welsh people' in the first deed is remembered, would not I think be less than that of finding the community of Jews in *Keren's case*.[179]

QUESTION

Consider the difficulties with which a court is faced when compelled to make a value judgment upon artistic matters. What would you say of a gift to promote the music of D.J. Blithe Spirit (an unknown but promising disc jockey)?

H ADVANCEMENT OF AMATEUR SPORT

Before the enactment of the Charities Act 2006 trusts for the provision of sporting facilities were not charitable *per se*.[180] However, if the facilities were for pupils of

[179] See, however, Annual Report for 1977, para 79, where the Charity Commissioners, when subsequently registering the trust as a charity under Validation of Trusts Act 1954, held, citing *Idle v Tree* [1945] Ch 325, that the definition of the beneficiary class in *Williams' Trustees v IRC* nevertheless did comprise a sufficient section of the public [p. 543, below].

[180] *Re Nottage* [1895] 2 Ch 649 [p. 514, below] (prize for a yacht race); *Re Clifford* (1912) 106 LT 14 (Oxford Angling and Preservation Society); *Re Patten* [1929] 2 Ch 276 (Sussex County Cricket Club); *IRC v City of Glasgow Police Athletic Association* [1953] AC 380; *Re North Taunton Rugby Union Football Club* [1995] Ch Com Rep 22; cf. *Re Laidlaw Foundation* (1985) 13 DLR (4th) 491 (foundation to promote amateur

schools or universities, or if the game itself was of an educational nature, the trusts would be charitable for the advancement of education; and if the facilities were within the armed forces, they would contribute to the safety and protection of the country and so would be charitable under the fourth head of other purposes beneficial to the community, but only if the public benefit requirement was satisfied.

Inland Revenue Commissioners v Baddeley
[1955] AC 572 (HL, **Viscount Simonds, Lords Porter, Reid, Tucker** and **Somervell of Harrow**)

Two conveyances of land were made to the respondent trustees on similar but not identical terms. In the first deed land, on which were a mission church, lecture room, and store, was conveyed upon trust to permit the property to be 'used by the leaders for the time being of the Stratford Newtown Methodist Mission for the promotion of the religious social and physical well-being of persons resident in the County Boroughs of West Ham and Leyton...by the provision of facilities for religious services and instruction and for the social and physical training and recreation of such aforementioned persons who for the time being are in the opinion of such leaders members or likely to become members of the Methodist Church and of insufficient means otherwise to enjoy the advantages provided...and by promoting and encouraging all forms of such activities as are calculated to contribute to the health and well-being of such persons' (Clause 2(a)). In the second deed four pieces of land laid out as playing fields were conveyed upon similar trusts, the main difference being that the trustees were to permit them to be used for the moral (instead of religious), social, and physical well-being of the same class of persons.

The question was whether the conveyances could be stamped at the reduced rate on the ground that the purposes were charitable.

Held (Lord Reid dissenting). The purposes were not charitable, because: (i) the purposes were wide enough to include non-charitable purposes; (ii) (Lords Tucker and Porter expressing no opinion) the requirement of public benefit was not satisfied.

Viscount Simonds: I find it convenient, my Lords, to examine the two deeds separately, and take first a deed of conveyance to the respondents as trustees of certain land at Stratford, in the county of Essex, of an area of about 680 square yards with a mission church, lecture room and store erected on some part thereof. So far as relevant (omitting certain words which admittedly were inserted in error) the trusts of this property were as follows: [His Lordship read clause 2(a) and continued:] This main trust is followed by certain ancillary provisions which cannot, I think, affect the question whether it is a charitable trust. It is at once apparent that the document is not skilfully drawn. It is presumably *all* the persons resident in the specified boroughs whose religious, social and physical well-being is to be promoted, but this is to be achieved by providing certain facilities for religious services and instruction and for the social

athletic sports held charitable as promoting health); doubted in Annual Report 1989, para. 53, where Birchfield Harriers Athletic Club was refused registration. See (1956) CLP 39 (O.R. Marshall); (1988) 52 NLJ Annual Charities Review iv (H. Picarda); (2008) LQR 202 (M. McInnes) *Amateur Youth Soccer Association (AYSA) v Canada* 2007 SCC 42.

and physical training and recreation of 'such aforementioned persons', i.e., such residents, as are for the time being 'in the opinion of such leaders members or likely to become members of the Methodist Church and of insufficient means...to enjoy the advantages provided by these presents'. This awkward phraseology leaves me in doubt whether the beneficiaries under this trust are to be all the residents in a certain area or only such of the residents as satisfy two conditions, first that they are Methodists or in the opinion of the leaders potential Methodists, and secondly, that they are of limited means. It might even be that upon a true interpretation of the deed some benefits are open to all the residents, others to a more limited class. Fortunately I do not find it necessary to determine this question, for I think that, whatever view may be taken of it, this case is governed by the recent decision of this House in *Williams' Trustees v IRC* [1947] AC 447 [p. 490, above]....

Other aspects of the trust established by the first deed were discussed and it is right that I should make some observations upon them, but before doing so I will turn to the second deed....

[His Lordship held that this trust also failed for vagueness and generality, and continued:]

This brings me to another aspect of the case, which was argued at great length and to me at least presents the most difficult of the many difficult problems in this branch of the law. Suppose that, contrary to the view that I have expressed, the trust would be a valid charitable trust, if the beneficiaries were the community at large or a section of the community defined by some geographical limits, is it the less a valid trust if it is confined to members or potential members of a particular church within a limited geographical area?

The starting point of the argument must be, that this charity (if it be a charity) falls within the fourth class in Lord Macnaghten's classification. It must therefore be a trust which is, to use the words of Sir Samuel Romilly in *Morice v Bishop of Durham* (1805) 10 Ves 522 at 532, of 'general public utility', and the question is what these words mean. It is, indeed, an essential feature of all 'charity' in the legal sense that there must be in it some element of public benefit, whether the purpose is educational, religious or eleemosynary:[181] see the recent case of *Oppenheim v Tobacco Securities Trust Co Ltd* [1951] AC 297 [p. 455, above], and, as I have said elsewhere, it is possible, particularly in view of the so-called 'poor relations' cases', the scope of which may one day have to be considered, that a different degree of public benefit is requisite according to the class in which the charity is said to fall. But it is said that if a charity falls within the fourth class, it must be for the benefit of the whole community or at least of all the inhabitants of a sufficient area. And it has been urged with much force that, if as Lord Greene said in *Re Strakosch* [1949] Ch 529 [p. 500, below], this fourth class is represented in the Preamble to the Statute of Elizabeth by the repair of bridges, etc., and possibly by the maintenance of Houses of Correction, the class of beneficiaries or potential beneficiaries cannot be further narrowed down. Some confusion has arisen from the fact that a trust of general public utility, however general and however public, cannot be of equal utility to all and may be of immediate utility to few. A sea wall, the prototype of this class in the Preamble, is of remote, if any, utility to those who live in the heart of the Midlands. But there is no doubt that a trust for the maintenance of sea walls generally or along a particular stretch of coast is a good charitable trust. Nor, as it appears to me, is the validity of a trust affected by the fact that by its very nature only a limited number of people are likely to avail themselves, or are perhaps even capable of availing themselves, of its benefits. It is easy, for instance, to imagine a charity which has for its

---

[181] 'Of or pertaining to alms or almsgiving: charitable': *The Oxford English Dictionary.*

object some form of child welfare, of which the immediate beneficiaries could only be persons of tender age. Yet this would satisfy any test of general public utility. It may be said that it would satisfy the test because the indirect benefit of such a charity would extend far beyond its direct beneficiaries, and that aspect of the matter has probably not been out of sight. Indirect benefit is certainly an aspect which must have influenced the decision of the 'cruelty to animals' cases. But, I doubt whether this sort of rationalisation helps to explain a branch of the law which has developed empirically and by analogy upon analogy.

It is, however, in my opinion, particularly important in cases falling within the fourth category to keep firmly in mind the necessity of the element of general public utility, and I would not relax this rule. For here is a slippery slope. In the case under appeal the intended beneficiaries are a class within a class; they are those of the inhabitants of a particular area who are members of a particular church: the area is comparatively large and populous and the members may be numerous. But, if this trust is charitable for them, does it cease to be charitable as the area narrows down and the numbers diminish? Suppose the area is confined to a single street and the beneficiaries to those whose creed commands few adherents: or suppose the class is one that is determined not by religious belief but by membership of a particular profession or by pursuit of a particular trade. These were considerations which influenced the House in the recent case of *Oppenheim* [1951] AC 297. That was a case of an educational trust, but I think that they have even greater weight in the case of trusts which by their nominal classification depend for their validity upon general public utility.

It is pertinent, then, to ask how far your Lordships might regard yourselves bound by authority to hold the trusts now under review valid charitable trusts, if the only question in issue was the sufficiency of the public element. I do not repeat what I said in the case of *Williams' Trustees v IRC* [1947] AC 447 about *Goodman v Mayor of Saltash* (1882) 7 App Cas 633 and the cases that closely followed it.[182] Further consideration of them does not change the view that I then expressed, which in effect endorsed the opinion of the learned editor of the last edition of *Tudor on Charities*. More relevant is the case of *Verge v Somerville* [1924] AC 496. In that case, in which the issue was as to the validity of a gift 'to the trustees of the Repatriation Fund or other similar fund for the benefit of New South Wales returned soldiers', Lord Wrenbury, delivering the judgment of the Judicial Committee, said at 499 that, to be a charity, a trust must be 'for the benefit of the community or of an appreciably important class of the community. The inhabitants', he said, 'of a parish or town or any particular class of such inhabitants, may, for instance, be the objects of such a gift, but private individuals, or a fluctuating body of private individuals, cannot.' Here, my Lords, are two expressions: 'an appreciably important class of the community' and 'any particular class of such inhabitants', to which in any case it is not easy to give a precise quantitative or qualitative meaning. But I think that in the consideration of them the difficulty has sometimes been increased by failing to observe the distinction, at which I hinted earlier in this opinion, between a form of relief extended to the whole community yet by its very nature advantageous only to the few and a form of relief accorded to a selected few out of a larger number equally willing and able to take advantage of it. Of the former type repatriated New South Wales soldiers would serve as a clear example. To me it would not seem arguable that they did not form an adequate class of the community for the purpose of the particular charity that was being established. It was with this type of case that Lord Wrenbury was dealing, and

---

[182] *Peggs v Lamb* [1994] Ch 172. On trusts for the benefit of a locality, see *A-G of the Cayman Islands v Wahr-Hansen* [2001] 1 AC 75 [see p. 541, below]. See also H&M, pp. 443–444; Luxton, pp. 155–157; Picarda, 145–146; Tudor, pp. 113–116.

his words are apt to deal with it. Somewhat different considerations arise if the form, which the purporting charity takes, is something of general utility which is nevertheless made available not to the whole public but only to a selected body of the public—an important class of the public it may be. For example, a bridge which is available for all the public may undoubtedly be a charity and it is indifferent how many people use it. But confine its use to a selected number of persons, however numerous and important: it is then clearly not a charity. It is not of general public utility: for it does not serve the public purpose which its nature qualifies it to serve.

Bearing this distinction in mind, though I am well aware that in its application it may often be very difficult to draw the line between public and private purposes, I should in the present case conclude that a trust cannot qualify as a charity within the fourth class in *Income Tax Special Purposes Comrs v Pemsel* [1891] AC 531 if the beneficiaries are a class of persons not only confined to a particular area but selected from within it by reference to a particular creed. The Master of the Rolls in his judgment cites a rhetorical question asked by Mr. Stamp in argument [1953] Ch 504 at 519. 'Who has ever heard of a bridge to be crossed only by impecunious Methodists?' The *reductio ad absurdum* is sometimes a cogent form of argument, and this illustration serves to show the danger of conceding the quality of charity to a purpose which is not a public purpose. What is true of a bridge for Methodists is equally true of any other public purpose falling within the fourth class and of the adherents of any other creed.

The passage that I have cited from *Verge v Somerville* [1924] AC 496 at 499 refers also (not, I think, for the first time) to 'private individuals' or a 'fluctuating body of private individuals' in contradistinction to a class of the community or of the inhabitants of a locality. This is a difficult conception to grasp: the distinction between a class of the community and the private individuals from time to time composing it is elusive. But, if it has any bearing on the present case, I would suppose that the beneficiaries, a body of persons arbitrarily chosen and impermanent, fall more easily into the latter than the former category.

I conclude that on this ground also I should decide this case against the respondents even if I were otherwise in their favour ...

The Charities Act 2006 has clarified the meaning of sport as follows:

CHARITIES ACT 2006

Meaning of 'charitable purpose'

2. (3) In subsection (2)—

    (a) in paragraph (g) 'sport' means sports or games which promote health by involving physical or mental skill or exertion; ...

The charitable status of trusts for the provision of sporting facilities was sought to be clarified by the Recreational Charities Act 1958. Aspects of this Act have been updated and clarified by the Charities Act 2006.

RECREATIONAL CHARITIES ACT 1958[183]

(subsection 2 and 2A substituted by Charities Act 2006, section 5)

---

[183] (1959) 23 Con (NS) 15 (S.G. Maurice); (1958) 21 MLR 534 (L. Price); [1980] Conv 173 (J. Warburton); Goodman Report, paras. 69–71 (Sport).

1. General provision as to recreational and similar trusts, etc.

(1) Subject to the provisions of this Act, it shall be and be deemed always to have been charitable to provide, or assist in the provision of, facilities for recreation or other leisure-time occupation, if the facilities are provided in the interests of social welfare:

Provided that nothing in this section shall be taken to derogate from the principle that a trust or institution to be charitable must be for the public benefit.

(2) The requirement in subsection (1) that the facilities are provided in the interests of social welfare cannot be satisfied if the basic conditions are not met.

(2A) The basic conditions are—

(a) that the facilities are provided with the object of improving the conditions of life for the persons for whom the facilities are primarily intended; and

(b) that either—

(i) those persons have need of the facilities by reason of their youth, age, infirmity or disability, poverty, or social and economic circumstances,[184] or

(ii) the facilities are to be available to members of the public at large or to male, or to female, members of the public at large.

(3) Subject to the said requirement, subsection (1) of this section applies in particular to the provision of facilities at village halls, community centres and women's institutes, and to the provision and maintenance of grounds and buildings to be used for purposes of recreation or leisure-time occupation, and extends to the provision of facilities for those purposes by the organising of any activity.

CHARITIES ACT 2006

Special provisions about recreational charities, sports clubs, etc.

5 (4) A registered sports club established for charitable purposes is to be treated as not being so established, and accordingly cannot be a charity.

(5) In subsection (4) a 'registered sports club' means a club for the time being registered under Schedule 18 to the Finance Act 2002 (c. 23) (relief for community amateur sports club).

In **Guild v Inland Revenue Commissioners**[185] [1992] 2 AC 310, the House of Lords held that a bequest 'to the town council of North Berwick for the use in connection with the sports centre in North Berwick or some similar purpose in connection with sport' was charitable under section 1(1) and (2) of the Recreational Charities Act 1958, and therefore exempt from Capital Transfer Tax. LORD KEITH OF KINKEL said at 318:

---

[184] In 1995 the Charity Commissioners decided that it would be charitable to establish a 'community organisation or other recreational organisation primarily for the use of some identifiable racial minority group': see Review of the Register (RR1) (March 1999), para. B2.

[185] [1992] Conv 361 (H. Norman); (1992) 51 CLJ 429 (J. Hopkins); [1992] All ER Rev 213 (P.J. Clarke); [1992–93] 1 *Charity Law & Practice Review* 45 (D. Morris).

In the course of his argument in relation to the first branch of the bequest counsel for the Commissioners accepted that it assisted in the provision of facilities for recreation or other leisure time occupation within the meaning of subsection (1) of section 1 of the Act, and also that the requirement of public benefit in the proviso to the subsection was satisfied. It was further accepted that the facilities of the sports centre were available to the public at large so that the condition of subsection (2)(b)(ii) was satisfied. It was maintained, however, that these facilities were not provided 'in the interests of social welfare' as required by subsection (1), because they did not meet the condition laid down in subsection (2)(a), namely that they should be 'provided with the object of improving the conditions of life for the persons for whom the facilities are primarily intended'. The reason why it was said that this condition was not met was that on a proper construction it involved that the facilities should be provided with the object of meeting a need for such facilities in people who suffered from a position of relative social disadvantage. Reliance was placed on a passage from the judgment of Walton J in *IRC v McMullen* [1978] 1 WLR 664. That was a case where the Football Association had set up a trust to provide facilities to encourage pupils of schools and universities in the United Kingdom to play association football and other games and sports. Walton J held that the trust was not valid as one for the advancement of education nor did it satisfy section 1 of the Act of 1958. He said, at 675, in relation to the words 'social welfare' in subsection (1):

'In my view, however, these words in themselves indicate that there is some kind of deprivation— not, of course, by any means necessarily of money—which falls to be alleviated; and I think that this is made even clearer by the terms of subsection (2)(a). The facilities must be provided with the object of improving the conditions of life for persons for whom the facilities are primarily intended. In other words, they must be to some extent and in some way deprived persons.'

When the case went to the Court of Appeal [1979] 1 WLR 130 the majority (Stamp and Orr LJJ) affirmed the judgment of Walton J on both points, but Bridge LJ dissented. As regards the Recreational Charities Act 1958 point he said, at 142–143:

'I turn therefore to consider whether the object defined by clause 3(a) is charitable under the express terms of section 1 of the Recreational Charities Act 1958. Are the facilities for recreation contemplated in this clause to be 'provided in the interests of social welfare' under section 1(1)? If this phrase stood without further statutory elaboration, I should not hesitate to decide that sporting facilities for persons undergoing any formal process of education are provided in the interests of social welfare. Save in the sense that the interests of social welfare can only be served by the meeting of some social need, I cannot accept the judge's view that the interests of social welfare can only be served in relation to some 'deprived' class. The judge found this view reinforced by the requirement of subsection (2)(a) of section 1 that the facilities must be provided 'with the object of improving the conditions of life for the persons for whom the facilities are primarily intended; . .' Here again I can see no reason to conclude that only the deprived can have their conditions of life improved. Hyde Park improves the conditions of life for residents in Mayfair and Belgravia as much as for those in Pimlico or the Portobello Road, and the village hall may improve the conditions of life for the squire and his family as well as for the cottagers. The persons for whom the facilities here are primarily intended are pupils of schools and universities, as defined in the trust deed, and these facilities are in my judgment unquestionably to be provided with the object of improving their conditions of life. Accordingly the ultimate question on which the application of the statute to this trust depends, is whether the requirements of section 1(2) (b)(i) are satisfied on the grounds that such pupils as a class have need of facilities for games or sports which will promote their physical education and development by reason either of their youth or of their social and economic circumstances, or both. The overwhelming majority of pupils within the definition are young persons and the tiny minority of mature students can be ignored as *de minimis*. There cannot surely be any doubt that young persons as part of their education do need facilities for organised games and sports both by reason of their youth and by reason of their social and economic circumstances. They cannot provide such facilities for themselves but are dependent on what is provided for them.

In the House of Lords [1981] AC 1 the case was decided against the Crown upon the ground that the trust was one for the advancement of education, opinion being reserved on the point under the Recreational Charities Act 1958. **Lord Hailsham of St Marylebone LC** said, at 11:

...I do not wish my absence of decision on the third or fourth points to be interpreted as an endorsement of the majority judgments in the Court of Appeal nor as necessarily dissenting from the contrary views contained in the minority judgment of Bridge LJ.

His Lordship referred to *National Deposit Friendly Society Trustees v Skegness Urban District Council* [1959] AC 293; *Valuation Comr for Northern Ireland v Lurgan Borough Council* [1968] NI 104, and continued:

The fact is that persons in all walks of life and all kinds of circumstances may have their conditions of life improved by the provision of recreational facilities of suitable character. The proviso requiring public benefit excludes facilities of an undesirable nature. In my opinion the view expressed by Bridge LJ in *IRC v McMullen* is clearly correct and that of Walton J in the same case is incorrect. I would therefore reject the argument that the facilities are not provided in the interests of social welfare unless they are provided with the object of improving the conditions of life for persons who suffer from some form of social disadvantage. It suffices if they are provided with the object of improving the conditions of life for members of the community generally. The Lord President, whose opinion contains a description of the facilities available at the sports centre which it is unnecessary to repeat, took the view that they were so provided. I respectfully agree, and indeed the contrary was not seriously maintained.

It remains to consider the point upon which the executor was unsuccessful before the First Division, namely whether or not the second branch of the bequest of residue, referring to 'some similar purpose in connection with sport', is so widely expressed as to admit of the funds being applied in some manner which falls outside the requirements of section 1 of the Act of 1958....

The matter for decision turns upon the ascertainment of the intention of the testator in using the words he did. The adjective 'similar' connotes that there are points of resemblance between one thing and another. The points of resemblance here with the sports centre cannot be related only to location in North Berwick or to connection with sport. The first of these is plainly to be implied from the fact of the gift being to the town council of North Berwick and the second is expressly stated in the words under construction. So the resemblance to the sports centre which the testator had in mind must be ascertained by reference to some other characteristics possessed by it. The leading characteristics of the sports centre lie in the nature of the facilities which are provided there and the fact that those facilities are available to the public at large. These are the characteristics which enable it to satisfy section 1 of the Act of 1958. Adopting so far as necessary a benignant construction, I infer that the intention of the testator was that any other purpose to which the town council might apply the bequest or any part of it should also display those characteristics. In the result I am of opinion, the first part of the bequest having been found to be charitable within the meaning of section 1 of the Act of 1958, that the same is true of the second part, so that the funds in question qualify for exemption from Capital Transfer Tax.

The Charity Commission has provided guidance on the scope of section 1 of the Recreational Charities Act 1958.

Charity Commission: *Review of the Register: The Recreational Charities Act 1958* (RR4) (August 2000), paras 8 and 14

8. . . . the range of recreational activities available, and of organisations existing to provide them, is now significantly greater than when the Act was passed. Additionally, the importance and value of leisure-time activity is increasingly accepted. As a result, we receive many applications for the registration of recreational organisations, including types which did not exist when the Act was passed. . . .

- In determining whether an organisation providing facilities or organising activities for recreation or other leisure-time occupation is charitable under section 1 of the Act we would need to be certain that:[186]
- it provides facilities for recreation or other leisure-time occupation;
- it meets the social welfare requirement. That requires that:
  - the facilities are provided with the object of improving the conditions of life.[187] That requires that the facilities:
  - are provided solely with that object, and
  - are capable, on an objective basis, of improving conditions of life;
  - the facilities are available to the public at large or to a restricted class of persons who may be regarded as having special need of those facilities;
  - the organisation is altruistic in nature;
  - the facilities are set up to meet certain social needs, i.e. needs which must be met if people's conditions of life are not to be inadequate; and
- it meets the public benefit requirement. That requires that:
  - the organisation benefits the public or a sufficient section of the public and any benefit to private individuals is no more than incidental or ancillary to that public benefit;
  - its overall effect is not harmful;
  - if the organisation adopts a membership structure, it does so only as a matter of administrative convenience for the better delivery of benefits rather than to restrict them, and membership is in practice open to all who wish to join; and
  - it is not set up substantially for the benefit of its members;
  - there is no legally binding preference regarding the use of the facilities in favour of a non-charitable body or class of people.

[186] More detailed explanations of these interpretations can be found in the Annex to the publication.
[187] See *Guild v IRC* [1992] 2 AC 310 [p. 496, above].

Other major points of interpretation

14.   In considering the scope and extent of section 1 of the Act we have further concluded that:

- Providing facilities and organising events for specific social contact or entertainment purposes (as opposed to the provision of recreational facilities to be used for any purpose, including entertainment) is not generally capable of falling within the Act. The exception to this is where facilities meet a clear social need which needs to be met if people's conditions of life are not to be inadequate.

- The provision of facilities for a single sport is less likely to meet the social welfare requirement than the provision of facilities for a range of sports.

QUESTIONS

1. What is the effect of the Recreational Charities Act 1958 on the *Baddeley* case? H&M, pp. 424–427.

2. Which sports or games promote health by involving physical or mental skill or exertion?

I ADVANCEMENT OF HUMAN RIGHTS

CHARITIES ACT 2006

Meaning of 'charitable purpose'

2. (2) (h) the advancement of human rights,[188] conflict resolution or reconciliation or the promotion of religious or racial harmony or equality and diversity; ...

In **Re Strakosch** [1949] Ch 529, a testator provided a fund 'for any purpose which in [the trustees'] opinion is designed to strengthen the bonds of unity between the Union of South Africa and the Mother Country, and which incidentally will conduce to the appeasement of racial feeling between the Dutch and English speaking sections of the South African community'.

The Court of Appeal held that this was not a charitable trust. LORD GREENE said at 536:

Roxburgh J held that it was not a good charitable gift. Before us further evidence was produced consisting of an affidavit by Field Marshal Smuts. We have given this affidavit most careful consideration but we are unable to regard it as affording a reason for coming to a conclusion different from that at which Roxburgh J arrived. We realize the truth of the contention that the objects to which the gift is to be devoted are matters of great public concern both in the Union

---

[188] See *McGovern v Attorney-General* [1982] Ch 321 [p. 526, below]. See also Annual Report for 1987, para 12 (trusts for research into human rights registered).

of South Africa and in the Mother Country. In particular the appeasement of racial feeling in the Union cannot but benefit all inhabitants of the Union, not merely the members of the two sections of the community expressly referred to. But the very wide and vague scope of the gift and the unrestricted latitude of application which its language permits make it impossible in our opinion to find that it falls within the spirit and intendment of the Preamble to the Statute of Elizabeth.

... Field Marshal Smuts (than whom no one can speak with greater authority on this subject) expresses a strong opinion that the proper method for the appeasement of racial feeling is education in its widest sense—'students' education, journalistic training, interchange of young men and women between Britain and South Africa, and between young South Africans of different racial origin'. It is unfortunate if, as may well be, these methods were in the testator's mind that he did not seek to constitute a trust which might well have been valid as an educational trust notwithstanding that the education had the ultimate aim as set out in the will. We, however, find it impossible to construe this trust as one confined to educational purposes.

Promotion of racial harmony is now recognised by the Charities Act 2006 as a legitimate charitable purpose, although a trust in the same terms as that in *Re Strakosch* may still fail for being too wide and vague in scope.

Whilst the advancement of human rights is a legitimate charitable purpose, charities can engage in political activities to fulfil this purpose, but cannot engage in political purposes.[189] The distinction between political purposes and activities may sometimes be a fine one.

Charity Commission *Consultation on Draft Public Benefit Guidance* (February 2007)

E5.   *Benefit must not be concerned with fulfilling a political purpose*

Charities can legitimately undertake political activities and campaigning in carrying out their charitable purposes, but a charity's purposes cannot be political.

A 'political purpose' means any purpose directed at furthering the interests of any political party; or securing, or opposing, any change in the law or in the policy or decisions of central government or local authorities, whether in this country or abroad.

'Political' has a particular meaning within charity law and is covered in more detail in our separate guidance *Political Activities and Campaigning by Charities*.[190]

Charity law draws a distinction between political purposes and political activities. Charities cannot undertake political purposes because neither the courts nor the Charity Commission is in a position to judge whether a political purpose is or is not for the benefit of the public. However, a charity can undertake political activities and campaigning as a way of carrying out its charitable purposes, provided that:

- it is not the dominant means by which the charity carries out its charitable purposes; and there is a reasonable expectation that the extent to which the political activities will further the charity's purposes justifies the resources the charity commits to those activities.

---

[189] See p. 521, below. See *R v Radio Authority, ex p Bull* [1998] QB 294 (promotion of awareness of human rights with the object of bringing pressure to bear on a government is a political objective). See [1997] PL 615 (J. Stevens and D. Feldman).   [190] See p. 531, below.

For example, a charity for the relief of poverty abroad could campaign in favour of the adoption of human rights in a particular country if it could be shown that the adoption of those rights would tend to relieve poverty in that country. Or, a charity concerned with relieving the victims of human rights abuse, in the course of doing so, may identify measures which might be taken by the government in question (or by other governments) to prevent that abuse.

However, an organisation which was set up for the purpose of seeking the repeal of the Human Rights Act 1998, or which used political means as the dominant way of carrying out its purposes of preventing and relieving poverty, for example, would not be charitable.

J   ADVANCEMENT OF ENVIRONMENTAL PROTECTION

CHARITIES ACT 2006
Meaning of 'charitable purpose'

2. (2) (i) the advancement of environmental protection or improvement;...

K   RELIEF OF THOSE IN NEED

CHARITIES ACT 2006
Meaning of 'charitable purpose'

2. (2) (j) the relief of those in need by reason of youth, age, ill-health, disability, financial hardship or other disadvantage

   (3) In subsection (2)—

      (e) paragraph (j) includes relief given by the provision of accommodation or care to the persons mentioned in that paragraph...

(i) Aged

Joseph Rowntree Memorial Trust Housing Association Ltd v Attorney-General[191]
[1983] Ch 159 (Ch D, **Peter Gibson J**)

A charitable housing association wished to build small self-contained dwellings for sale to elderly people on long leases in consideration of a capital payment. Five schemes were designed to provide accommodation to meet the disabilities and requirements of the elderly. All applicants were required to be 65 if male, and 60 if female, to be able

---

[191] (1983) 46 MLR 782 (R. Nobles); [1983] All ER Rev 356 (P.J. Clarke). Joseph Rowntree was the Quaker philanthropist and cocoa manufacturer.

to pay the service charge, to lead an independent life, and to be in need of the type of accommodation provided.

The schemes were based on the National Federation of Housing Associations' standard scheme called 'The Leasehold Scheme for the Elderly'. They differed in detail. In one scheme, the tenant would pay a premium of 70 per cent of the cost of the premises, the remaining 30 per cent being met by Housing Association Grant under the Housing Act 1980. On death the lease was assignable to the tenant's spouse or relative if living at the premises when the tenant died. Failing such assignment, or if the tenant became incapable, the lease would revert to the Association, and the tenant or his estate would receive 70 per cent of the then value of the property.

The question was whether the schemes were charitable.

Held (reversing the Charity Commissioners). This was a valid charitable scheme for the aged.

Peter Gibson J: I hope I summarise the objections of the Charity Commissioners fairly as being the following: (1) the schemes provide for the aged only by way of bargain on a contractual basis rather than by way of bounty. (2) The benefits provided are not capable of being withdrawn at any time if the beneficiary subsequently ceases to qualify. (3) The schemes are for the benefit of private individuals, not for a charitable class. (4) The schemes are a commercial enterprise capable of producing profit for the beneficiary.

Before I deal with these objections it is appropriate to consider the scope of the charitable purpose which the plaintiffs claim the scheme carries out, that is to say in the words of the Preamble to the Statute of Elizabeth I (1601) 'the relief of aged persons'. That purpose is indeed part of the very first set of charitable purposes contained in the Preamble: 'the relief of aged, impotent and poor people.' Looking at those words without going to authority and attempting to give them their natural meaning, I would have thought that two inferences therefrom were tolerably clear. First, the words 'aged, impotent and poor' must be read disjunctively. It would be as absurd to require that the aged must be impotent or poor as it would be to require the impotent to be aged or poor, or the poor to be aged or impotent. There will no doubt be many cases where the objects of charity prove to have two or more of the three qualities at the same time. Second, essential to the charitable purpose is that it should relieve aged, impotent and poor people. The word 'relief' implies that the persons in question have a need attributable to their condition as aged, impotent or poor persons which requires alleviating, and which those persons could not alleviate, or would find difficulty in alleviating, themselves from their own resources. The word 'relief' is not synonymous with 'benefit'.

Those inferences are in substance what both Mr. Nugee for the plaintiffs and Mr. McCall for the Attorney-General submit are the true principles governing the charitable purpose of the relief of aged persons. Mr. Nugee stresses that any benefit provided must be related to the needs of the aged. Thus a gift of money to the aged millionaires of Mayfair would not relieve a need of theirs as aged persons.[192] Mr. McCall similarly emphasises that to relieve a need of the aged attributable to their age would be charitable only if the means employed are appropriate to the need. He also points out that an element of public benefit must be found if the purpose is to be charitable. I turn then to authority to see if there is anything that compels a different conclusion.

[192] (1955) 71 LQR 16 (R.E. Megarry); (1958) 21 MLR at pp. 140–141 (P.S. Atiyah).

His Lordship referred to *Re Lucas* [1922] 2 Ch 52 (bequest to the oldest respect-able inhabitants of Gunville of the amount of 5s *per* week); *Re Glyn* (1950) 66 (pt 2) TLR 510 (bequest for building cottages for old women of the working classes of the age of 60 years or upwards)[193]; *Re Bradbury* [1950] 2 All ER 1150n (bequest to pay sums for the maintenance of an aged person or persons in a nursing home approved by 'my trustees'); *Re Robinson* [1951] Ch 198 (bequest to the old people over 65 years of Hazel Slade near Hednesford to be given 'as my trustees think best'); *Re Cottam* [1955] 1 WLR 1299 (gift to provide flats for persons over 65 to be let at economic rents)[194]; *Re Lewis* [1955] Ch 104 (gift to ten blind girls and ten blind boys, Tottenham residents if possible, the sum of £100 each) and continued:

In *Re Neal* (1966) 110 Sol Jo 549, a testator provided a gift for the founding of a home for old persons. Further directions provided for fees to be charged sufficient to maintain the home with sufficient staff to run it and cover the costs of the trustees. Goff J, in a very briefly reported judgment, said that in order to conclude whether a trust was charitable or not it was not neces-sary to find in it an element of relief against poverty, but it was sufficient to find an intention to relieve aged persons. The form of the gift and directions were a provision for succouring and supplying such needs of old persons as they had because they were old persons. Therefore he held it was a charitable bequest.

[His Lordship referred to *Re Resch's Will Trusts* [1969] 1 AC 514 and quoted from Lord Wilberforce at 542, 544, cited p. 479, above, and continued:]

These authorities convincingly confirm the correctness of the proposition that the relief of the aged does not have to be relief for the aged poor. In other words the phrase 'aged, impotent and poor people' in the Preamble must be read disjunctively. The decisions in *Re Glyn*, *Re Bradbury*, *Re Robinson*, *Re Cottam* and *Re Lewis* give support to the view that it is a sufficient charitable purpose to benefit the aged, or the impotent, without more. But these are all deci-sions at first instance and with great respect to the judges who decided them they appear to me to pay no regard to the word 'relief'. I have no hesitation in preferring the approach adopted in *Re Neal* and *Re Resch's Will Trusts* that there must be a need which is to be relieved by the charitable gift, such need being attributable to the aged or impotent condition of the person to be benefited. My attention was drawn to Picarda, *The Law and Practice Relating to Charities* (1977), p. 79 where a similar approach is adopted by the author.

In any event in the present case, as I have indicated, the plaintiffs do not submit that the pro-posed schemes are charitable simply because they are for the benefit of the aged. The plaintiffs have identified a particular need for special housing to be provided for the elderly in the ways proposed and it seems to me that on any view of the matter that is a charitable purpose, unless the fundamental objections of the Charity Commissioners to which I have referred are correct. To these I now turn.

The first objection is, as I have stated, that the scheme makes provision for the aged on a contractual basis as a bargain rather than by way of bounty. This objection is sometimes

---

[193] In *Re Wall* (1889) 42 Ch D 510, the age of 50 years was accepted as a qualification for 'aged'.
[194] *Re Payling's Will Trusts* [1969] 1 WLR 1595, where Buckley J upheld a gift of a house 'to be used as a home for aged persons…as Mansfield Corporation in their absolute discretion may decide'. The accom-modation was to be free, but the occupiers had to provide for their own maintenance. Cf. *Re Martin* (1977) 121 Sol Jo 828; The Times, 17 November.

expressed in the form that relief is charitable only where it is given by way of bounty and not by way of bargain: see *Halsbury's Laws of England,* 4th edn, vol. 5 (1974), para. 516. But as the editors recognise this does not mean that a gift cannot be charitable if it provides for the beneficiaries to contribute to the cost of the benefits they receive. There are numerous cases where beneficiaries only receive benefits from a charity by way of bargain. *Re Cottam* [1955] 1 WLR 1299 and *Re Resch's Will Trusts* [1969] 1 AC 514 provide examples. Another class of cases relates to fee-paying schools: see for example *Abbey Malvern Wells Ltd v Ministry of Local Government and Planning* [1951] Ch 728. Another example relates to a gift for the provision of homes of rest for lady teachers at a rent: *Re Estlin* (1903) 89 LT 88. It is of course crucial in all these cases that the services provided by the gift are not provided for the private profit of the individuals providing the services.

The source of the statement that charity must be provided by way of bounty and not bargain is to be found in some remarks of Rowlatt J in *IRC v Society for the Relief of Widows and Orphans of Medical Men* (1926) 11 TC 1. This was a case relating to the statutory provisions allowing tax relief for income applicable to charitable purposes only of trusts or bodies established for charitable purposes only. Rowlatt J said, at 22:

'It seems to me that when it is said that the relief of poverty is a charity within the meaning of the rule which we are discussing that does mean the relief of poverty by way of bounty; it does not mean the relief of poverty by way of bargain. A purely mutual society among very poor people whose dependants would quite clearly always be very poor would not, I think, be a charity; it would be a business arrangement as has been said in one of the cases, whereby contractual benefits accrued to people whose poverty makes them very much in need of them. That would not be a charity. I think, therefore, that the crux of this case is whether this is a case of that sort.'

He went on to hold that the case before him was not that of a mutual society: the beneficiaries had no right to anything.

In my judgment Rowlatt J's remarks must be understood in their limited context. They are entirely appropriate in determining whether a mutual society conferring rights on members is charitable. If a housing association were a co-operative under which the persons requiring the dwellings provided by the housing association had by the association's constitution contractual rights to the dwellings, that would no doubt not be charitable, but that is quite different from bodies set up like the trust and the association. The applicants for dwellings under the schemes which I am considering would have no right to any dwelling when they apply. The fact that the benefit given to them is in the form of a contract is immaterial to the charitable purpose in making the benefit available. I see nothing in this objection of the Charity Commissioners.[195]

The second objection was that the schemes do not satisfy the requirement that the benefits they provide must be capable of being withdrawn at any time if the beneficiary ceases to qualify. No doubt charities will, so far as practical and compatible with the identified need which they seek to alleviate, try to secure that their housing stock becomes available if the circumstances of the persons occupying the premises change. But it does not seem to me to be an essential part of the charitable purpose to secure that this should always be so. The nature of some benefits may be such that it will endure for some time, if benefits in that form

---

[195] See (1990) 134 SJ 946 (R. Venables); [1991] Conv 419 (J. Warburton and D. Morris); [1993] 1 Charity Commissioners' Report 18.

are required to meet the particular need that has been identified. Thus in *Re Monk* [1927] 2 Ch 197, a testatrix set up a loan fund whereby loans for up to nine years were to be made available to the poor. This was held to be charitable. No doubt the circumstances of the borrower might change whilst the loan was outstanding. If the grant of a long-term leasehold interest with the concomitant security of tenure that such an interest would give to the elderly is necessary to meet the identified needs of the elderly then in my judgment that is no objection to such a grant. The plaintiffs have put in evidence that they oppose the inclusion in a lease of any provision entitling the plaintiffs to determine the lease in the event of a change in financial circumstances of the tenant. Their main reason—which to my mind is a cogent one—is the unsettling effect it could have on aged tenants. In any event the distinction between what *prima facie* is a short-term letting and a long lease has been rendered somewhat illusory by statute. A charity may find it no less difficult to recover possession from weekly tenants whose circumstances have changed than it would to recover possession from a tenant under a long lease.

The third objection was that the schemes were for the benefit of private individuals and not for a charitable class. I cannot accept that. The schemes are for the benefit of a charitable class, that is to say the aged having certain needs requiring relief therefrom. The fact that, once the association and the trust have selected individuals to benefit from the housing, those individuals are identified private individuals does not seem to me to make the purpose in providing the housing a non-charitable one any more than a trust for the relief of poverty ceases to be a charitable purpose when individual poor recipients of bounty are selected.

The fourth objection was that the schemes were a commercial enterprise capable of producing a profit for the beneficiary. I have already discussed the cases which show that the charging of an economic consideration for a charitable service that is provided does not make the purpose in providing the service non-charitable, provided of course that no profits accrue to the provider of the service. It is true that a tenant under the schemes may recover more than he or she has put in, but that is at most incidental to the charitable purpose. It is not a primary objective. The profit—if it be right to call the increased value of the equity a profit as distinct from a mere increase avoiding the effects of inflation, as was intended—is not a profit at the expense of the charity, and indeed it might be thought improper, if there be a profit, that it should accrue to the tenant which has provided no capital and not to the tenant which has provided most if not all the capital. Again, I cannot see that this objection defeats the charitable character of the schemes.

[His Lordship considered the schemes and continued:] In my judgment the trustees may provide accommodation in the form of small self-contained dwellings for aged persons in need of such accommodation by granting it to them in consideration of the payment to the trustees of the whole or a substantial part of the cost or market value of such dwellings in accordance with the schemes. The presence or absence of the following provisions is not essential to the charitable nature of the scheme, that is to say (1) the H.A.G. contribution; (2) the provision of warden services, provided that the accommodation is designed to meet the special needs of the elderly tenants; (3) the prohibition of any assignment except on the death of the tenant to his spouse or qualified member of the family or household; (4) the right of the landlords to determine the lease on the death of the tenant or on the tenant becoming incapable of managing his or her own affairs; (5) the right of the tenant to surrender the lease.

(ii) Others in need

Under the old law of charity, the first of the four heads of charitable purpose recognised in *Pemsel's* case[196] included the relief of the impotent. This word is no longer used in the Charities Act 2006, but it is important to be aware of how 'impotent' was interpreted to understand how wide the new head of the relief of those in need is likely to be.

Tudor on Charities (9th edn, 2003), pp. 35–36

The word 'impotent' has never been defined by the Court, but it has been interpreted fairly liberally. It is defined in the Oxford English Dictionary as meaning 'physically weak, without bodily strength; unable to use one's limbs; helpless, decrepit', a definition sufficiently wide to cover not only those suffering from permanent disability, whether of body or mind, but those temporarily incapacitated by injury or illness, or in need of rest, and young children incapable of protecting themselves from the consequences of cruelty or neglect. The cases show that this definition, or something like it, has guided the Courts. Thus gifts for the benefit of the blind,[197] the sick and wounded,[198] including former enemies who have been wounded,[199] the prevention of cruelty to children,[200] and faith-healing,[201] have been held to be charitable.

Although in *Re Roadley*[202] a trust to apply income in payment of the expenses and maintenance of patients in a hospital was upheld on the ground that it was for the relief of persons who were both impotent and poor, it is now clear[203] that (given always the necessary element of public benefit) gifts for the establishment or support of hospitals and nursing homes are charitable as being for the relief of impotent persons who need not necessarily be poor. Furthermore, a gift to provide accommodation for relations coming from a distance to visit patients critically ill in hospital is charitable.[204]

Gifts for the establishment or support of homes of rest are also charitable. The term 'home of rest' connotes not primarily a home for persons who are old or worn out and so permanently in need of rest, but rather a convalescent home to which persons ordinarily actively employed in their various pursuits are enabled to retire.[205]

---

[196] *Income Tax Special Purposes Comrs v Pemsel* [1891] AC 531 [see p. 414, above].

[197] *Re Fraser* (1883) 22 Ch D 827; *Re Lewis* [1955] Ch 104 and see *Re Elliott* (1910) 102 LT 528, 530; *Barber v Chudley* (1922) 128 LT 766; see also *Re Spence's Will Trusts* [1979] Ch 483.

[198] *Re Hillier* [1944] 1 All ER 480. The sick or wounded may be abroad: Annual Report for 1990, para. 32 (The Gdansk Hospice Fund).

[199] *Re Robinson* [1931] 2 Ch 122 (gift for disabled German Soldiers).

[200] *Comrs for the Special Purposes of Income Tax v Pemsel* [1891] AC 531 at 572. It may be that the prevention of cruelty to children is also charitable on another ground, namely, that such gifts are calculated to promote public morality by encouraging kindness, discouraging cruelty and stimulating humane sentiments for the benefit of mankind: see and compare *Re Wedgwood* [1915] 1 Ch 113; *Re Moss* [1949] 1 All ER 495 [p. 508, below].

[201] *Re Kerin* (1966) The Times, 24 May: Goff J held that faith healing was for the relief of impotent persons, or for the advancement of religion, or for both purposes.   [202] [1930] 1 Ch 524.

[203] See *Re Adams* [1968] Ch 80, (reversing in part [1967] 1 WLR 162); *Re Resch's Will Trusts* [1969] 1 AC 514 [p. 479, above]; see also *Liverpool and District Hospital for Diseases of the Heart v A-G* [1981] Ch 193.

[204] *Re Dean's Will Trusts* [1950] 1 All ER 882.

[205] *Re White's Will Trusts* [1951] 1 All ER 528 at 529. See also *IRC v Roberts Marine Mansions Trustees* (1927) 11 TC 425.

QUESTION

What advice would you give for the drawing up of a public appeal and trust deed following a tragic accident or disaster? CC40: Disaster Appeals: Atttorney-General's Guidelines (2002); (1982) 132 NLJ 223 (H. Picarda); Cairns, *Charities: Law and Practice* (3rd edn, 1997), pp. 191–196, H&M, pp. 449–450; Luxton, chap. 25. See also (1999) 19 LS 380 (I. McLean and M. Johnes).

L ADVANCEMENT OF ANIMAL WELFARE

Before the enactment of the Charities Act 2006 trusts for the advancement of animal welfare could only be charitable within the fourth head of *Pemsel's* case, being another purpose beneficial to the community. Now animal welfare is identified as a specific charitable head. It is still necessary to show that there is a public benefit in the charitable purpose and the absence of such a benefit has proved decisive in decisions of the court not to recognise such trusts as charitable. Purposes connected with animals may also be charitable if expressed in terms of education[206] or of environmental protection.[207] As FARWELL J said in **Re Lopes** [1931] 2 Ch 130 at 136: 'a ride on an elephant may be educational.'

In **Re Wedgwood** [1915] 1 Ch 113, the testatrix gave the residue of her estate to her brother upon an oral understanding that he would apply it for the protection and benefit of animals. One aspect of such work—and one in which the testatrix was particularly interested—was the improvement of methods of slaughtering animals.

The Court of Appeal held this to be a valid charitable trust. The protection of animals was calculated to protect public morality by checking the innate tendency to cruelty.

In **Re Moss** [1949] 1 All ER 495, the testatrix made gifts to a friend 'for her to use at her discretion for her work for the welfare of cats and kittens needing care and attention'. ROMER J held this to be a valid charitable trust.[208]

Re Grove-Grady[209]
[1929] 1 Ch 557 (CA, Lord Hanworth MR, Lawrence and Russell LJJ)

The testatrix gave her residuary estate upon trust to found the 'Beaumont Animals Benevolent Society', whose objects included (object No. 1) the acquisition of land 'for

---

[206] *Re Lopes* [1931] 2 Ch 130.   [207] *Re Verrall* [1916] 1 Ch 100 (National Trust). See p. 502, above.

[208] *Re Douglas* (1887) 35 Ch D 472 (home for lost dogs); *Re Cranston* [1898] 1 IR 431 (to promote vegetarianism); *Marsh v Means* (1857) 3 Jur NS 790 (to finance propaganda against cruelty to animals); *Tatham v Drummond* (1864) 4 De GJ & Sm 484 (Royal Society for the Prevention of Cruelty to Animals); *University of London v Yarrow* (1857) 1 De G & J 72 (hospital for animals useful to mankind); *National Anti-Vivisection Society v IRC* [1948] AC 31 at 45, *per* Lord Wright; *Re Green's Will Trust* [1985] 3 All ER 455 (rescue, maintenance, and benefit of cruelly treated animals and the prevention of cruelty to animals).

[209] Compromised in the House of Lords sub nom *A-G v Plowden* [1931] WN 89.

the purpose of providing a refuge or refuges for the preservation of all animals birds or other creatures not human...and so that all such animals birds or other creatures not human shall there be safe from molestation or destruction by man...'

Held (Lawrence LJ dissenting; and reversing Romer J). The trust was not charitable because it lacked the necessary element of benefit to the community.

Russell LJ: There can be no doubt that upon the authorities as they stand a trust in perpetuity for the benefit of animals may be a valid charitable trust if in the execution of the trust there is necessarily involved benefit to the public; for if this be a necessary result of the execution of the trust, the trust will fall within Lord Macnaghten's fourth class in *Pemsel's* case [1891] AC 531 at 583—namely, 'trusts for other purposes beneficial to the community'.

So far as I know there is no decision which upholds a trust in perpetuity in favour of animals upon any other ground than this, that the execution of the trust in the manner defined by the creator of the trust must produce some benefit to mankind. I cannot help feeling that in some instances matters have been stretched in favour of charities almost to bursting point: and that a decision benevolent to one doubtful charity has too often been the basis of a subsequent decision still more benevolent in favour of another.

The cases have accordingly run to fine distinctions, and speaking for myself I doubt whether some dispositions in favour of animals held to be charitable under former decisions would be held charitable today. For instance, anti-vivisection societies, which were held to be charities by Chitty J in *Re Foveaux*,[210] and were described by him as near the border line, might possibly in the light of later knowledge in regard to the benefits accruing to mankind from vivisection be held not to be charities.

The difficulty arises when you apply the test of benefit to the public to each particular case. The will of Mrs. Grove-Grady is no exception, for it presents a very difficult problem....

Assuming that I have correctly interpreted object No. 1, it comes down to this, that the residuary estate may be applied in acquiring a tract of land, in turning it into an animal sanctuary, and keeping a staff of employees to ensure that no human being shall ever molest or destroy any of the animals there. Is that a good charitable trust within the authorities?

In my opinion it is not. It is merely a trust to secure that all animals within the area shall be free from molestation or destruction by man. It is not a trust directed to ensure absence or diminution of pain or cruelty in the destruction of animal life. If this trust is carried out according to its tenor, no animal within the area may be destroyed by man no matter how necessary that destruction may be in the interests of mankind or in the interests of the other denizens of the area or in the interests of the animal itself; and no matter how painlessly such destruction may be brought about. It seems to me impossible to say that the carrying out of such a trust necessarily involves benefit to the public. Beyond perhaps hearing of the existence of the enclosure the public does not come into the matter at all. Consistently with the trust the public could be excluded from entering the area or even looking into it. All that the public need know about the matter would be that one or more areas existed in which all animals (whether good or bad from mankind's point of view) were allowed to live free from any risk of being molested or killed by man; though liable to be molested and killed by other denizens of the area. For myself I feel quite

---

[210] [1895] 2 Ch 501 at 507; overruled in *National Anti-Vivisection Society v IRC* [1948] AC 31 [p. 511, below].

unable to say that any benefit to the community will necessarily result from applying the trust fund to the purposes indicated in the first object.

If then benefit to the community as a necessary result of the execution of the trust is essential, this trust is not charitable. It is well settled that if consistently with the trust the funds may be applied for a purpose not charitable, the trust will fail for perpetuity notwithstanding that the funds might under the trust have been applied for purposes strictly charitable.

[His Lordship referred to *Re Wedgwood* [1915] 1 Ch 113 and continued:] It was a peculiar case in this, that the trust was a secret trust declared orally. To ascertain the scope of the trust all the verbal statements made by the testatrix had to be regarded. The testatrix had explained the nature of the methods by which she desired her estate to be applied for the protection and benefit of animals—namely, in obtaining for them the benefit of humane slaughtering, i.e. avoidance of cruelty. All the members of the Court refer to that fact in their judgments; and from that they were able to spell out public benefit. Except for that purpose, there was no occasion to refer to that fact at all. Lord Cozens-Hardy says [1915] 1 Ch 113 at 117: 'it tends to promote public morality by checking the innate tendency to cruelty'. Kennedy LJ at 120, 121, in reviewing what he calls the particularly pertinent decisions, relies on those in which it is pointed out that the prevention of cruelty to animals is for the benefit of the public. Swinfen Eady LJ seems quite clear on the point. After referring to the explanation of the testatrix above mentioned he uses this language at 122: 'The object of the trust being thus ascertained and defined, the question arises, is this a valid charitable trust?' He says that it is, because it is a gift for a general public purpose beneficial to the community. He arrives at that view, because (amongst other things) the discouragement of cruelty promotes humane sentiments in man towards the lower animals and elevates the human race. It seems to me that the decision in *Re Wedgwood* is definitely based on the view that the object of the trust being discouragement of cruelty to lower animals, that, upon the existing authorities, involved benefit to the community.

The Court in *Re Wedgwood* was certainly not purporting to lay down any new law. It is not, in my opinion, a decision either (1) that every trust for the benefit of animals necessarily involves benefit to the community, or (2) that a trust for the benefit of animals which involves no such benefit is a charitable trust.

In my opinion, the Court must determine in each case whether the trusts are such that benefit to the community must necessarily result from their execution.

In the present case I cannot persuade myself that the trusts described by the testatrix under the head of the first object fulfil that description. To do so would go beyond any decided case. The authorities have, in my opinion, reached the furthest admissible point of benevolence in construing, as charitable, gifts in favour of animals, and for myself, I am not prepared to go any further.

In **Re Murawski's Will Trust** [1971] 1 WLR 707, a gift to the Bleakholt Animal Sanctuary, whose objects were 'the provision of care and shelter for stray, neglected and unwanted animals of all kinds and the protection of animals from ill-usage, cruelty and suffering' was held to be charitable.[211]

---

[211] See Annual Report for 1971, para. 26 (Home of Rest for Horses); [1994] 2 Charity Commissioners' Report 1 (Animal Abuse, Injustice and Defence Society).

National Anti-Vivisection Society v Inland Revenue Commissioners
[1948] AC 31, (HL, **Viscount Simon**, **Lords Wright**, **Simonds**, **Normand** and **Porter**)

The appellants were a society whose object was the suppression of vivisection, and which had been registered as a charity in 1895.[212] They claimed exemption from Income Tax on the ground that they were 'a body of persons... established for charitable purposes only' within the Income Tax Act 1918, section 37(1)(b).

Held (Lord Porter dissenting). The Society was not established for charitable purposes only, and was not therefore within this exemption.[213]

Lord Simonds: My Lords, the question raised in this appeal is whether the National Anti-Vivisection Society, which I will call 'the society', is a body of persons established for charitable purposes only within the meaning of section 37 of the Income Tax Act, 1918, and, accordingly, entitled to exemption from income tax on the income of its investments. Before I refer to the cases and to the judgments in the courts below I will state the two questions which appear to me to be raised in this appeal. The first and shorter point is whether a main purpose of the society is of such a political character that the court cannot regard it as charitable. To this point little attention was directed in the courts below. It is mentioned only in the judgment of the learned Master of the Rolls. As will appear in the course of this opinion, it is worthy of more serious debate [p. 522, below]. The second point is fundamental. It is at the very root of the law of charity as administered by the Court of Chancery and its successor, the Chancery Division of the High Court of Justice. It is whether the court, for the purpose of determining whether the object of the society is charitable may disregard the finding of fact that any assumed public benefit in the direction of the advancement of morals and education was far outweighed by the detriment to medical science and research and consequently to the public health which would result if the society succeeded in achieving its object, and that on balance, the object of the society, so far from being for the public benefit, was gravely injurious thereto. The society says that the court must disregard this fact, arguing that evidence of disadvantages or evils which would or might result from the stopping of vivisection is irrelevant and inadmissible.

The second question raised in this appeal, which I have already tried to formulate, is of wider importance, and I must say at once that I cannot reconcile it with my conception of a court of equity that it should take under its care and administer a trust, however well-intentioned its creator, of which the consequence would be calamitous to the community. I would not weary your Lordships with a historical excursion into the origin of the equitable jurisdiction in matters of charity, one of the 'heads of equity' as Lord Macnaghten called it in *Pemsel*'s case [1891] AC 531...

My Lords, this then being the position, that the court determined 'one by one' whether particular named purposes were charitable, applying always the overriding test whether the purpose was for the public benefit, and that the King as *parens patriae* intervened *pro bono publico* for the protection of charities, what room is there for the doctrine which has found favour with the learned Master of the Rolls and has been so vigorously supported at the bar of the House, that the court may disregard the evils that will ensue from the achievement by the society of its ends?

212 *Re Foveaux* [1895] 2 Ch 501.
213 This case illustrates that charitable purposes for the benefit of the public can change over time, so that what was once charitable may cease to be charitable subsequently.

It is to me a strange and bewildering idea that the court must look so far and no farther, must see a charitable purpose in the intention of the society to benefit animals and thus elevate the moral character of men but must shut its eyes to the injurious results to the whole human and animal creation. I will readily concede that, if the purpose is within one of the heads of charity forming the first three classes in the classification which Lord Macnaghten borrowed from Sir Samuel Romilly's argument in *Morice v Bishop of Durham* (1805) 10 Ves 522, the court will easily conclude that it is a charitable purpose. But even here to give the purpose the name of 'religious' or 'educational' is not to conclude the matter. It may yet not be charitable, if the religious purpose is illegal or the educational purpose is contrary to public policy. Still there remains the overriding question: Is it *pro bono publico*? It would be another strange mis-reading of Lord Macnaghten's speech in *Pemsel's* case [1891] AC 531 (one was pointed out in *Re Macduff* [1896] 2 Ch 451) to suggest that he intended anything to the contrary. I would rather say that, when a purpose appears broadly to fall within one of the familiar categories of charity, the court will assume it to be for the benefit of the community and, therefore, charitable, unless the contrary is shown, and further that the court will not be astute in such a case to defeat on doubtful evidence the avowed benevolent intention of a donor. But, my Lords, the next step is one that I cannot take. Where on the evidence before it the court concludes that, however well-intentioned the donor, the achievement of his object will be greatly to the public disadvantage, there can be no justification for saying that it is a charitable object. If and so far as there is any judicial decision to the contrary, it must, in my opinion, be regarded as inconsistent with principle and be overruled. This proposition is clearly stated by Russell J in *Re Hummeltenberg* [1923] 1 Ch 237 at 242. 'In my opinion,' he said, 'the question whether a gift is or may be operative for the public benefit is a question to be answered by the court forming an opinion upon the evidence before it.' This statement of that very learned judge follows immediately upon some observations on the cases of *Re Foveaux* [1895] 2 Ch 501 and *Re Cranston* [1898] 1 IR 431 which were the mainstay of the appellant's argument...

[His Lordship examined these cases and *A-G v Marchant* (1866) LR 3 Eq 424 and *Re Campden Charities* (1881) 18 Ch D 310, and continued:] My Lords, what I have said is enough to conclude this case. But there is an important passage in the judgment of the Master of the Rolls, which I ought not to ignore.

> 'I do not see,' he says [1946] KB 185, 205, 'how at this time of day it can be asserted that a particular exemplification of those objects is not beneficial merely because in that particular case the achievement of those objects would deprive mankind of certain consequential benefits however important those benefits may be. If this were not so, it would always be possible, by adducing evidence which was not before the court on the original occasion to attack the status of an established charitable object to the great confusion of trustees and all others concerned. Many existing charities would no doubt fall if such a criterion were to be adopted.'

I venture with great respect to think that this confuses two things. A purpose regarded in one age as charitable may in another be regarded differently. I need not repeat what was said by Jessel MR in *Re Campden Charities* (1881) 18 Ch D 310. A bequest in the will of a testator dying in 1700 might be held valid on the evidence then before the court but on different evidence held invalid if he died in 1900. So, too, I conceive that an anti-vivisection society might at different times be differently regarded. But this is not to say that a charitable trust, when it has once been established, can ever fail. If by a change in social habits and needs, or, it may be, by a change in the law the purpose of an established charity becomes superfluous or even illegal, or if with increasing knowledge it appears that a purpose once thought beneficial is truly detrimental to the community, it is the duty of trustees of an established charity to apply to the court or in suitable cases to the Charity Commissioners... and ask that a *cy-près* scheme may be established.[214] And I can well conceive that there might be cases in which the Attorney-General would think it his duty to intervene to that end. A charity once established does not die, though its nature may be changed. But it is wholly consistent with this that in a later age the court should decline to regard as charitable a purpose, to which in an earlier age that quality would have been ascribed, with the result that (unless a general charitable intention could be found) a gift for that purpose would fail. I cannot share the apprehension of the Master of the Rolls that great confusion will be caused if the court declines to be bound by the beliefs and knowledge of a past age in considering whether a particular purpose is today for the benefit of the community. But if it is so, then I say that it is the lesser of two evils.

M PROMOTION OF EFFICIENCY OF PUBLIC SERVICES

CHARITIES ACT 2006

Meaning of 'charitable purpose'

2. (2) (1) the promotion of the efficiency of the armed forces of the Crown,[215] or of the efficiency of the police,[216] fire[217] and rescue services or ambulance services;...

(3) In subsection (2)—

(f) in paragraph (1) 'fire and rescue services' means services provided by fire and rescue authorities under Part 2 of the Fire and Rescue Services Act 2004 (c. 21).

In **Re Gray** [1925] Ch 362, the testator gave sums of money for the establishment of a regimental fund for the Carabiniers to be called 'the Gray Fund'. Its objects were 'the promotion of sport (including in that term only shooting fishing cricket football and polo)'.

---

[214] See p. 544, below.

[215] *Re Stephens* (1892) 8 TLR 792 (gift to the National Rifle Association 'for the teaching of shooting at moving objects so as to prevent as far as possible a catastrophe similar to that at Majuba Hill' held charitable); *Re Lord Stratheden and Campbell* [1894] 3 Ch 265 ('an annuity of £100 to be provided to the Central London Rangers on the appointment of the next lieutenant-colonel'. The gift was held to be charitable but void for perpetuity); *Re Good* [1905] 2 Ch 60 (trust for the 'maintenance of a library for the officers' mess of the 2nd Battalion 14th Regiment of Foot now at Natal' held charitable); *Re Donald* [1909] 2 Ch 410 (gift 'to the officer commanding the Northamptonshire Militia for the mess of that regiment or for the poor of the regiment' held charitable); *Re Barker* (1909) 25 TLR 753 (gift to the Royal Engineers' Institute to provide prizes for competition among Royal Engineer cadets or officers held charitable); *Re Corbyn* [1941] Ch 400 (trust for the benefit of boys from the training ship *Exmouth* 'to be trained to become officers in His Majesty's Navy (Britannic) or the British Mercantile Marine' held charitable); *Re Driffill* [1950] Ch 92 (trust to be applied 'in whatever manner the trustees may consider desirable to promote the defence of the United Kingdom against the attack of hostile aircraft' held charitable).

[216] *IRC v City of Glasgow Police Athletic Association* [1953] AC 380, 391 (Lord Normand). See also Annual Report for 1984, para. 17 (Police Memorial Trust to commemorate officers killed on duty).

[217] *Re Wokingham Fire Brigade Trusts* [1951] Ch 373.

ROMER J held that the gifts were charitable, as they promoted the physical efficiency of the Army. His Lordship said at 365:

It is contended on behalf of the persons entitled to the residue that those two legacies were given on trusts which are not charitable. It is said that the object of the testator was merely to encourage sport. If that were so the gifts would no doubt be given on trusts which were not charitable: see *Re Nottage* [1895] 2 Ch 649, where a gift for purposes of encouraging yacht racing was held not to be a charitable legacy. But in my opinion it was not the object of the testator in the present case to encourage or promote either sport in general or any sport in particular. I think it is reasonably clear that it was his intention to benefit the officers and men of the Carabiniers by giving them an opportunity of indulging in healthy sport. It is to be observed that the particular sports specified were all healthy outdoor sports, indulgence in which might reasonably be supposed to encourage physical efficiency. That I think was his object even though he refers to the fund as the 'Sporting Fund'. This case, therefore, does not, in my opinion, fall within *Re Nottage*.

I realise the truth of what Eve J said in *Re Mariette* [1915] 2 Ch 284 [p. 453, above], as to the natural inclination of the Court, if possible, to give effect to a gift of this sort and the danger of allowing that natural inclination to induce one to disregard established principles. But I am glad to find that there is an established principle enabling me to give effect to the gifts in the present case. This principle was established by Farwell J in *Re Good* [1905] 2 Ch 60 at 66, 67, a case that as far as I know has never been questioned in any way. In that case the testator gave his residuary personalty upon trust for the officers' mess of his regiment, to be invested and the income to be applied in maintaining a library for the officers' mess for ever, any surplus to be expended in the purchase of plate for the mess. According to the headnote of the report of that case it was held that the gift to maintain the library and to purchase plate for the officers' mess, being for a general public purpose tending to increase the efficiency of the army and aid taxation, was a good charitable bequest. It was also held that the gift might be supported as a 'setting out of soldiers' within the meaning of those words in the statute of Elizabeth. But the judgment of Farwell J was based primarily on the ground that the gift on trust for the maintenance of the library was a gift tending to increase the efficiency of the army, and he referred, only as a possible alternative ground, to the fact that the trust tended to aid taxation.

In the course of his judgment he said, referring to the argument, for the Attorney-General:

'Now Mr. Parker has put his argument on two grounds. First, he says that anything that improves the efficiency of the army is charitable within the meaning of the Act, because it is for a public purpose—a purpose in which the public are interested. Secondly, he says that it also comes within the last clause of the Preamble of the Statute of Elizabeth: "the aid or ease of any poor inhabitants concerning payments of fifteens, setting out of soldiers and other taxes", because it will relieve the taxation of the public...I think it would be difficult to say that money given to be expended in terms in some specific way in order to increase the efficiency of a regiment in a particular mode is not a good charity. This gift, to my mind, does tend to increase the efficiency of the army by giving the officers greater opportunities of providing themselves with literature.'

Then, after dealing with the suggestion that the money might conceivably be applied in the purchase of books which were unlikely to increase the efficiency of the army, he says:

'An officer is all the better equipped if he can speak several languages, and if he knows the history and geography of his own nation as well as many other nations, as well as being instructed in the military art, I should be sorry to have to hold that any gift which tends to educational equipment in that way is not a charitable gift.'...

In the case before Farwell J the efficiency was mental efficiency, and the only distinction between that case and the present case is that in the present case the efficiency is physical as opposed to mental efficiency. But it is obviously for the benefit of the public that those entrusted with the defence of the realm should be not only mentally but also physically efficient, and I think I am justified in coming to the conclusion that there is no difference between mental and physical efficiency for the present purpose.[218]

In **Re City of London Rifle and Pistol Club and Burnley Rifle Club**[219] (1993) Decisions of the Charity Commissioners, vol. 1, p. 4, the Charity Commissioners held that the Clubs were not entitled to charitable status. Their objects were 'to encourage skill in shooting by providing instruction and practice in the use of firearms to Her Majesty's subjects so that they will be better fitted to serve their country in the Armed Forces, Territorial Army or any other organisation in which their services may be required in the defence of the Realm in times of peril'.

In holding that the activities of the Clubs did not promote the security of the nation and the defence of the realm, the Commissioners distinguished *Re Stephens* [1892] 8 TLR 792, where KEKEWICH J upheld as charitable a gift under the will of Mr. Stephens to the National Rifle Association to form a fund to be called The Stephens' Prize Fund, 'to be expended by the Council for the teaching of shooting at moving objects in any manner they may think fit, so as to prevent as far as possible a catastrophe similar to that at Majuba Hill'.

They referred to *Re Good* [1905] 2 Ch 60; *Re Driffill* [1950] Ch 92; *Re Lord Stratheden and Campbell* [1894] 3 Ch 265; *Re Gray* [1925] Ch 362; *Re Corbyn* [1941] Ch 400 [p. 513, n. 215, above] and continued:

Two particular aspects of the judgment of Kekewich J served to underline the distinction between the purposes of the gift in *Re Stephens* and the purposes of the City Club and Burnley Clubs:

(1) Kekewich J found that the object in the testator's mind was clear. He desired that Englishmen should be taught to shoot with those particular weapons which were used in war for the destruction of their enemies and the protection of themselves.

(2) Kekewich J found that what the testator meant was that accurate shooting was to be taught among Englishmen in general—an object which would be promoted directly or indirectly in the Army—and so a repetition of the catastrophe at Majuba Hill would be adverted.

The answers provided by the City and Burnley Clubs to a questionnaire established that the purpose of the Clubs was not to teach members of the public *in general* to shoot. The answers

---

[218] Annual Report for 1965, Appendix E; 1977, paras. 123–124 (Old Contemptibles Association, founded in 1925 to foster the spirit of 'The Contemptible Little Army of 1914'—a purpose analogous to promoting the efficiency of the Army—wound up in 1977). Cf. Annual Report for 1983, paras. 35–36 (trust to eliminate waste in the public service so as to increase its efficiency not analogous to promotion of efficiency of the armed forces and of the police and so not registered).

[219] See also *The Review of the Register of Charities* (RR1), paras. B3, B4. (March 1999). [1992–93] 2 *Charity Law & Practice Review* 97 (P.J. Clarke), criticising this unduly restrictive view of the law.

also established that the purpose of the Clubs was not to teach members of the public in general to shoot with *those particular weapons which were used in times of war.* Evidence revealed that whilst firearms used by the Armed Forces might bear some resemblance to firearms used by civilian shooting clubs, there was nevertheless a substantial difference in equipment and style between military and civilian shooting disciplines.

We concluded that if *Re Stephens* was still to be considered a good authority, it could be only for the proposition that it was charitable to promote the teaching of the general public in the use of weapons used by the Armed Forces and not that institutions in the form of the City and Burnley Clubs were necessarily charitable. That would depend upon the inherent nature of the Clubs themselves.

Even if we were wrong in our view that *Re Stephens* was not authority for the proposition that the City and Burnley Clubs were charitable, we considered that there had been such a radical change in circumstances since the decision in *Re Stephens* that the City and Burnley Clubs could not be regarded as charities for promoting the security of the nation and the defence of the Realm. On the evidence before us, we concluded that that charitable purpose was not carried out in the modern day by the provision of facilities for the instruction and practice in shooting through the medium of rifle and pistol clubs in the form adopted by the City and Burnley Clubs.

It has been judicially recognised that changes in social habits and needs might subsequently lead to reconsideration of the question whether a particular object continued to be charitable in law. (See *National Anti-Vivisection Society v IRC* [1948] AC 31, Lord Simonds at p. 74, and *Gilmour v Coats* [1949] AC 426, Lord Simonds at p. 143).

We considered that the following factors had rendered the decision in *Re Stephens* obsolete in the sense indicated by Lord Simonds in *National Anti-Vivisection Society v IRC* and *Gilmour v Coats:*

(1) The strength of the modern British Army no longer depended on the expert shooting skills of soldiers in the way that it did at the time of the Boer War (and the Battle of Majuba Hill). The tactical and technological advances that had taken place in modern warfare (as exemplified in the recent Falklands and Gulf conflicts) had substantially increased the gulf between fully trained service personnel familiar with the latest communications equipment and technical weaponry and the competent single-shot competition shooter.

(2) The social and organisational changes affecting the recruitment and training of men and women for the Armed Forces had rendered it anachronistic to view rifle and pistol clubs as fulfilling the role of a semi-trained third-line reserve for the Armed Forces. There was no reason to believe that rifle and pistol clubs would be used as a manpower reserve in times of war or other national emergency...

We also considered that the main purpose of each of the Clubs was to benefit their members by providing them with facilities for the enjoyment of shooting as a recreation and the practice of shooting as a sport. In our opinion, any benefit to the public by way of promoting the security of the nation and the defence of the realm was incidental to the benefits to members in the way of affording them recreational and sporting facilities. We concluded, therefore, that the Clubs fell clearly within the decision in *IRC v City of Glasgow Police Athletic Association* [1953] AC 380 and were not established for exclusively charitable purposes.

We also considered that the Clubs could not be regarded as charities either for the advancement of education, or the promotion of public recreation because they lacked the essential element of public benefit. Furthermore, they did not satisfy the condition of section 1(2)(b) (ii)[220]of the Recreational Charities Act 1958 [p. 496, above], that the facilities for recreation and other leisure-time occupation should be available to the members or female members of the public at large.

N OTHER PURPOSES

CHARITIES ACT 2006

Meaning of 'charitable purpose'

2. (2)(m) any other purposes within subsection (4).

   (4) The purposes within this subsection (see subsection (2)(m)) are—

   (a) any purposes not within paragraphs (a) to (l) of subsection (2) but recognised as charitable purposes under existing charity law or by virtue of section 1 of the Recreational Charities Act 1958;

   (b) any purposes that may reasonably be regarded as analogous to, or within the spirit of, any purposes falling within any of those paragraphs or paragraph (a) above; and

   (c) any purposes that may reasonably be regarded as analogous to, or within the spirit of, any purposes which have been recognised under charity law as falling within paragraph (b) above or this paragraph.

The test of whether a charitable purpose is analogous to another purpose or falls within the spirit of a previously recognised purpose has been considered in the context of a purpose falling within the spirit of the Preamble to the Charitable Uses Act 1601.

Incorporated Council of Law Reporting for England and Wales v Attorney-General[221]
[1972] Ch 73 (CA, **Russell, Sachs** and **Buckley LJJ**)

The Incorporated Council of Law Reporting for England and Wales was incorporated in 1870 with the primary object of 'the preparation and publication in a convenient form, at a moderate price, and under gratuitous professional control, of reports of judicial decisions of the superior and appellate courts in England'. All income and property were to be applied solely towards the promotion of the Council's objects, and

---

[220] Now s. 2A(b)(ii).

[221] (1972) 88 LQR 171; *Incorporated Council of Law Reporting of the State of Queensland v Comr of Taxation* (1971) 45 *Australian Law Journal Report* 552, where the High Court of Australia held that the council was a charitable institution within the Income Tax and Social Services Contribution Assessment Act 1936–62, s.23(e). Barwick CJ said at 555: 'the production of law reports is clearly beneficial to the whole community because of the universal importance of maintaining the socially sustaining fabric of the law'. See also Annual Report for 1980, paras. 78–79 (National Law Library Trust, which is concerned with a computer-assisted information retrieval system for legal information).

no portion could be paid by way of profit to its members. Payment of remuneration was authorised for editors, reporters, and other persons for services rendered.

In 1966 the Council applied to be registered as a charity. In 1967 the Charity Commissioners refused to register it as a charity. The Council appealed to the High Court, joining as parties the Commissioners of Inland Revenue and the Attorney-General.

Held. The Council was entitled to be registered as a charity under the head of other purposes beneficial to the community; and also (Russell LJ dissenting) as a trust for the advancement of education.[222]

Russell LJ: I come now to the question whether, if the main purpose of the council is, as I think it is, to further the sound development and administration of the law in this country, and if, as I think it is, that is a purpose beneficial to the community or of general public utility, that purpose is charitable according to the law of England and Wales.

On this point the law is rooted in the Statute of Elizabeth I, a statute the object of which was the oversight and reform of abuses in the administration of property devoted by donors to purposes which were regarded as worthy of such protection as being charitable. The Preamble to the Statute listed certain examples of purposes worthy of such protection. These were from an early stage regarded merely as examples, and have through the centuries been regarded as examples or guideposts for the courts in the differing circumstances of a developing civilisation and economy. Sometimes recourse has been had by the courts to the instances given in the Preamble in order to see whether in a given case sufficient analogy may be found with something specifically stated in the Preamble, or sufficient analogy with some decided case in which already a previous sufficient analogy has been found. Of this approach perhaps the most obvious example is the provision of crematoria by analogy with the provisions of burial grounds by analogy with the upkeep of churchyards by analogy with the repair of churches. On other occasions a decision in favour or against a purpose being charitable has been based in terms upon a more general question whether the purpose is or is not within 'the spirit and intendment' of the Statute of Elizabeth I and in particular its Preamble. Again (and at an early stage in development) whether the purpose is within 'the equity' or within 'the mischief' of the Statute. Again whether the purpose is charitable 'in the same sense' as purposes within the preview of the Statute. I have much sympathy with those who say that these phrases do little of themselves to elucidate any particular problem. 'Tell me', they say, 'what you define when you speak of spirit, intendment, equity, mischief, the same sense, and I will tell you whether a purpose is charitable according to law. But you never define. All you do is sometimes to say that a purpose is none of these things. I can understand it when you say that the preservation of sea walls is for the safety of lives and property, and therefore by analogy the voluntary provision of lifeboats and fire brigades are charitable. I can even follow you as far as crematoria. But these other generalities teach me nothing.'

I say I have much sympathy for such approach: but it seems to me to be unduly and improperly restrictive. The Statute of Elizabeth I was a statute to reform abuses: in such circumstances and in that age the courts of this country were not inclined to be restricted in their implementation of Parliament's desire for reform to particular examples given by the Statute; and they deliberately kept open their ability to intervene when they thought necessary in cases not

[222] See p. 446, above.

specifically mentioned, by applying as the test whether any particular case of abuse of funds or property was within the 'mischief' or the 'equity' of the Statute.

For myself I believe that this rather vague and undefined approach is the correct one, with analogy its handmaid, and that when considering Lord Macnaghten's fourth category in *Pemsel's* case [1891] AC 531 at 583 of 'other purposes beneficial to the community' (or as phrased by Sir Samuel Romilly (then Mr. Romilly) in argument in *Morice v Bishop of Durham* (1805) 10 Ves 522 at 531: 'objects of general public utility') the courts, in consistently saying that not all such are necessarily charitable in law, are in substance accepting that if a purpose is shown to be so beneficial or of such utility it is *prima facie* charitable in law, but have left open a line of retreat based on the equity of the Statute in case they are faced with a purpose (e.g., a political purpose) which could not have been within the contemplation of the Statute even if the then legislators had been endowed with the gift of foresight into the circumstances of later centuries.

In a case such as the present, in which in my view the object cannot be thought otherwise than beneficial to the community and of general public utility, I believe the proper question to ask is whether there are any grounds for holding it to be outside the equity of the Statute[223] and I think the answer to that is here in the negative. I have already touched upon its essential importance to our rule of law. If I look at the somewhat random examples in the Preamble to the Statute I find in the repair of bridges, havens, causeways, sea banks and highways examples of matters which if not looked after by private enterprise must be a proper function and responsibility of government, which would afford strong ground for a statutory expression by Parliament of anxiety to prevent misappropriation of funds voluntarily dedicated to such matters. It cannot I think be doubted that if there were not a competent and reliable set of reports of judicial decisions, it would be a proper function and responsibility of government to secure their provision for the due administration of the law. It was argued that the specific topics in the Preamble that I have mentioned are all concerned with concrete matters, and that so also is the judicially accepted opinion that the provision of a court house is a charitable purpose. But whether the search be for analogy or for the equity of the Statute this seems to me to be too narrow or refined an approach. I cannot accept that the provision, in order to facilitate the proper administration of the law, of the walls and other physical facilities of a court house is a charitable purpose, but that the dissemination by accurate and selective reporting of knowledge of a most important part of the law to be there administered is not.

Accordingly the purpose for which the association is established is exclusively charitable in the sense of Lord Macnaghten's fourth category. I would not hold that the purpose is purely the advancement of education: but in determining that the purpose is within the equity of the Statute I by no means ignore the function of the purpose in furthering knowledge in legal science.

I would dismiss the appeal.

---

[223] The approach of Russell LJ was commended by the Privy Council in *A-G of the Cayman Islands v Wahr-Hansen* [2001] 1 AC 75 at 82–83. In determining whether a specified purpose falls within the spirit and 'intendment' of the Preamble to the Statute of Elizabeth I, 'general' words should not be artificially restricted to purposes within the preamble. See p. 541, below. Cf. the approach of the High Court of Australia in *Incorporated Council of Law Reporting of the State of Queensland v Comr of Taxation* (1971) 45 ALJR 552 at 555; *Royal National Agricultural and Industrial Association v Chester* (1974) 48 ALJR 304 at 305 ('improving the breeding and racing of Homer pigeons' held not charitable); (1975) 91 LQR 167 (F.A. Mann).

Report of the Charity Commissioners for England and Wales for the year 1973, paras. 69–70

Council of Industrial Design

The object of the Council of improving the design of industrial products was in our view clearly of benefit to the public not only in the general sense of making industry more efficient and competitive but also more directly in encouraging the production of safer, more effective and more pleasing articles. The spread of knowledge of such articles was also of public benefit. On the other hand the Council's activities, through its design centres with their catalogues describing approved products and displaying goods with the manufacturer's name attached, must provide some commercial benefit to the individual firms concerned. Moreover, the advantage was something more than mere advertisement in the sense of publicity: there was the additional publicised advantage of approval by the Council, a body subsidised by public funds and so semi-official. However, the industrial firms whose products were exhibited were not members of the institution. Moreover the members of the Council were not self-regarding industrialists but the nominees of a Minister of the Crown who had an absolute power to remove them from office. It accordingly appeared to us that it was not a purpose of the Council to benefit the firms concerned and we decided that the Council was a charity and should be registered.

[The Commissioners referred in para. 70 to the judgment of Russell LJ in *Incorporated Council of Law Reporting for England and Wales v A-G* and continued:] We were satisfied that in the case of the Council of Industrial Design there was a substantial public benefit which raised a *prima facie* assumption of charitability and that, applying Lord Justice Russell's test mentioned above, there was nothing in the circumstances of the case to negative the assumption.

In **IRC v Oldham Training and Enterprise Council** [1996] STC 1218 the objects of the Oldham Training and Enterprise Council included the promotion of vocational education, and training and retraining of the public,[224] and to promote industry, commerce, and enterprise for the benefit of the public in and around Oldham. The Council was assessed to pay Corporation Tax and challenged this assessment on the ground that its objects were wholly and exclusively charitable. LIGHTMAN J said at 1234–1235:

To fall within the fourth category, it is necessary (but not sufficient) that the object is of general public utility. The public to be benefited for this purpose may be a section of the public and this includes the inhabitants of an area such as Oldham (see e.g. *Re Smith* [1932] 1 Ch 153). The object must be to promote a purpose beneficial to the community, and not to the interests of individual members of the community. But an object may none the less be charitable as beneficial to the community though its fulfilment either directly or indirectly incidentally may benefit such individuals. Beyond such general public utility it is necessary that the object comes within the spirit and intendment, even if not within the words, of the Statute of Elizabeth 43 Eliz I c 4. As an example, if the object of setting up the unemployed in trade or business was not charitable as being for the relief of poverty, it would fall within the fourth head of charity.

---

[224] By themselves these were charitable educational objects. See p. 440, n. 95, above. See also *Vancouver Society of Immigrant and Visible Minority Women v Minister of National Revenue* (1999) 169 DLR (4th) 34 (Supreme Court of Canada) (educative programme to get immigrant and visible minority women out of unemployment was charitable, but the trust failed because of further non-charitable objects such as creating a job-skills directory and establishing a support group for professionals.)

It is a matter of general public utility that the unemployed should be found gainful activity and that the state should be relieved of the burden of providing them with unemployment and social security benefits, and this object is within the spirit, if not the words, of the Statute of Elizabeth, which includes amongst its list of charitable objects the 'supportation, aid and help of young tradesmen [and] handicraftsmen'. . . .

I turn now to the objects of Oldham TEC. There are certain indicia of charity. Oldham TEC is an altruistic organisation, in the sense that no profit or benefit can be conferred on its members, and its *raison d'être* is to assist others; its objects clauses place stress on its overall objective of benefiting the public or community in or around Oldham; and it is substantially publicly funded, financed by government grants. Further, certain of its objects are indisputably charitable. The question raised is whether the remaining objects viewed in this context can and should be construed as subject to the implicit limitation 'so far as charitable'. There is of course no such express limitation. In my judgment on a careful examination of the objects clauses no such limitation can be implied or is compatible with the range of benefits and of the eligible recipients of such benefits which it is the object of Oldham TEC to provide.

To ascertain the objects of an institution such as Oldham TEC, where the objects are comprehensively set out in a document, it is necessary to refer to that document (in this case the memorandum of association) and to that alone. It is irrelevant to inquire into the motives of the founders or how they contemplated or intended that Oldham TEC should operate or how it has in fact operated. To determine whether the object, the scope of which has been ascertained by due process of construction, is a charitable purpose, it may be necessary to have regard to evidence to discover the consequences of pursuing that object (see *Incorporated Council of Law Reporting for England and Wales v A-G* [1972] Ch 73 at 99 *per* Buckley LJ. What the body has done in pursuance of its objects may afford graphic evidence of the potential consequences of the pursuit of its objects.

Under the unamended objects clause, the second main object, namely promoting trade, commerce and enterprise, and the ancillary object, of providing support services and advice to and for new businesses, on any fair reading must extend to enabling Oldham TEC to promote the interests of individuals engaged in trade, commerce or enterprise and provide benefits and services to them. Paragraph 4.2 of the statement of agreed facts shows that Oldham TEC in the form of the provision of enterprise services does exactly this. Such efforts on the part of Oldham TEC may be intended to make the recipients more profitable and thereby, or otherwise, to improve employment prospects in Oldham. But the existence of these objects, in so far as they confer freedom to provide such private benefits, regardless of the motive or the likely beneficial consequences for employment, must disqualify Oldham TEC from having charitable status. The benefits to the community conferred by such activities are too remote.

O POLITICAL PURPOSES[225]

Charities must not have political objects. Indeed the rule appears to be that an activity whose objective is to change the law is thereby disabled from being a charity. How, it is

[225] Goodman Report, chap. 4; House of Commons Report, vol. I, paras. 35–44, vol. II, pp. 23, 25–26, 48–83, 117–119, 129–154, 156–159, 214–215, 313–314, 316–317, 349–350, 361–362; Luxton, pp. 221–248; White Paper, paras. 2.37–2.46. (1999) CLP 255 (G.F.K. Santow).

said, can a trust to change the law be regarded by the law as so beneficial to the community that it deserves the privileges of charity? However, with the recognition in section 2(2)(h) of the Charities Act 2006 that the advancement of human rights is a legitimate charitable purpose, it is necessary to distinguish clearly between political and human rights objectives. The attitude of the government and the Charity Commission has been increasingly in favour of charities becoming more involved in reform debates, with a distinction emerging between campaigning and political activities.

(i) Political Objectives

In **National Anti-Vivisection Society v Inland Revenue Commissioners** [1948] AC 31 [p. 511, above], LORD SIMONDS said at 61:

The learned Master of the Rolls cites in his judgment [1946] KB 185 at 207, a passage from the speech of Lord Parker in *Bowman v Secular Society Ltd* [1917] AC 406 at 442: 'a trust for the attainment of political objects has always been held invalid, not because it is illegal . . . but because the court has no means of judging whether a proposed change in the law will or will not be for the public benefit'. Lord Parker is here considering the possibility of a valid charitable trust and nothing else and when he says 'has always been held invalid' he means 'has always been held not to be a valid charitable trust'. The learned Master of the Rolls found this authoritative statement upon a branch of the law, with which no one was more familiar than Lord Parker, to be inapplicable to the present case for two reasons, first, because he felt difficulty in applying the words to 'a change in the law which is in common parlance a "non-political" question', and secondly, because he thought they could not in any case apply, when the desired legislation is 'merely ancillary to the attainment of what is *ex hypothesi* a good charitable object'.

My Lords, if I may deal with this second reason first, I cannot agree that in this case an alteration in the law is merely ancillary to the attainment of a good charitable object. In a sense no doubt, since legislation is not an end in itself, every law may be regarded as ancillary to the object which its provisions are intended to achieve. But that is not the sense in which it is said that a society has a political object. Here the finding of the Commissioners is itself conclusive. 'We are satisfied,' they say, 'that the main object of the society is the total abolition of vivisection . . . and (for that purpose) the repeal of the Cruelty to Animals Act, 1876, and the substitution of a new enactment prohibiting vivisection altogether.' . . . Coming to the conclusion that it is a main object, if not the main object, of the Society, to obtain an alteration of the law, I ask whether that can be a charitable object, even if its purposes might otherwise be regarded as charitable.

My Lords, I see no reason for supposing that Lord Parker in the cited passage used the expression 'political objects' in any narrow sense or was confining it to objects of acute political controversy. On the contrary he was, I think, propounding familiar doctrine, nowhere better stated than in a textbook, which has long been regarded as of high authority but appears not to have been cited for this purpose to the courts below (as it certainly was not to your Lordships), *Tyssen on Charitable Bequests,* 1st edn. The passage which is at p. 176, is worth repeating at length:

'It is a common practice for a number of individuals amongst us to form an association for the purpose of promoting some change in the law, and it is worth our while to consider the effect of a gift to such an association. It is clear that such an association is not of a charitable nature.

However desirable the change may really be, the law could not stultify itself by holding that it was for the public benefit that the law itself should be changed. Each court in deciding on the validity of a gift must decide on the principle that the law is right as it stands. On the other hand, such a gift could not be held void for illegality.'

Lord Parker uses slightly different language but means the same thing, when he says that the court has no means of judging whether a proposed change in the law will or will not be for the public benefit. It is not for the court to judge and the court has no means of judging. The same question may be looked at from a slightly different angle. One of the tests, and a crucial test, whether a trust is charitable, lies in the competence of the court to control and reform it. I would remind your Lordships that it is the King as *parens patriae* who is the guardian of charity and that it is the right and duty of his Attorney-General to intervene and inform the court, if the trustees of a charitable trust fall short of their duty. So too it is his duty to assist the court, if need be, in the formulation of a scheme for the execution of a charitable trust. But, my Lords, is it for a moment to be supposed that it is the function of the Attorney-General on behalf of the Crown to intervene and demand that a trust shall be established and administered by the court, the object of which is to alter the law in a manner highly prejudicial, as he and His Majesty's Government may think, to the welfare of the state? This very case would serve as an example, if upon the footing that it was a charitable trust it became the duty of the Attorney-General on account of its maladministration to intervene. There is undoubtedly a paucity of judicial authority on this point. It may fairly be said that *de Themmines v de Bonneval* (1828) 5 Russ 288, to which Lord Parker referred in *Bowman's* case [1917] AC 406, turned on the fact that the trust there in question was held to be against public policy. In *IRC v Temperance Council of the Christian Churches of England and Wales* (1926) 136 LT 27, the principle was clearly recognised by Rowlatt J, as it was in *Re Hood* [1931] 1 Ch 240 at 250, 252. But in truth the reason of the thing appears to me so clear that I neither expect nor require much authority. I conclude upon this part of the case that a main object of the Society is political and for that reason the Society is not established for charitable purposes only. I would only add that I would reserve my opinion on the hypothetical example of a private enabling Act, which was suggested in the course of the argument. I do not regard *Re Villers-Wilkes* (1895) 72 LT 323 as a decision that a legacy which had for its main purpose the passing of such an Act is charitable.[226]

(ii) Political propaganda masquerading as education

A trust for a political party is not charitable. Attempts have been made to establish trusts for political purposes in the form of educational trusts. The dividing line between education in certain political principles and support of a political party is sometimes difficult to draw. A trust for 'the furtherance of Conservative principles and religious and mental improvement' was upheld as charitable in *Re Scowcroft* [1898] 2 Ch 638. Since then, however, the courts have been quick to find a political object disguised as education. The courts have at least been consistent between the parties.[227]

---

[226] Lord Porter thought that the rule should apply only to trusts which are purely political. Lord Normand would have excluded only trusts whose predominant purpose was political. See also *Re Shaw* [1957] 1 WLR 729.

[227] *Bonar Law Memorial Trust v IRC* (1933) 49 TLR 220 (Conservative); *Re Ogden* [1933] Ch 678 (Liberal); *Re Hopkinson* [1949] 1 All ER 346 (Labour). See also Annual Report for 1982, paras 45–51 (refusal to register Youth Training because of its political purpose to assist the work of the Workers Revolutionary Party); 1991,

In **Re Hopkinson** [1949] 1 All ER 346, the testator gave his residuary estate to found an educational fund 'for the advancement of adult education with particular reference to... the education of men and women of all classes (on the lines of the Labour Party's memorandum headed "A Note on Education in the Labour Party"...) to a higher conception of social, political and economic ideas and values and of the personal obligations of duty and service which are necessary for the realisation of an improved and enlightened social civilisation'.

VAISEY J held that the trust was not charitable. He said at 348:

In my judgment, there are two ways of reading the words which I have quoted. They may be read, first, as equivalent to a general trust for the advancement of adult education which, standing alone, would admittedly be charitable, the super-added purpose being treated merely as a rough guide to be followed or as a hint to be taken as to the kind of adult education which the testator had in mind, the strictly educational main purpose always being adhered to, or, secondly, they may be read as indicating that the first part is to be taken as a general direction and the second part beginning with the words 'with particular reference to' as the particular direction dominating the whole of the trust. The second of these alternative views seems to me to be the right one. I think that the particular purpose is the main purpose of the trust, that is to say, while every or any kind of adult education is within the discretion reposed in the residuary legatees, the particular purpose referred to is, so to speak, the overriding and essential purpose, on the nature of which the validity of the whole trust depends...

  Political propaganda masquerading—I do not use the word in any sinister sense—as education is not education within the Statute of Elizabeth (43 Eliz., c.4). In other words, it is not charitable.

In **Re Bushnell** [1975] 1 WLR 1596[228] a testator who died in 1941 gave the residue of his estate, subject to a life interest for his wife, who died in 1972, on trust to apply the income towards 'furthering the knowledge of the socialised application of medicine to public and personal health and well-being and to demonstrating that the full advantage of socialised medicine can only be enjoyed in a socialist state' by means of lectures, and by publishing and distributing books and literature on socialised medicine. GOULDING J held that the dominant and essential object of the trust was a political one and that it did not constitute a charitable trust.

In **Re Koeppler Will Trusts** [1986] Ch 423 [p. 448, above], where the facts are given, SLADE LJ said at 437:

However, in the present case, as I have already mentioned, the activities of Wilton Park are not of a party-political nature. Nor, so far as the evidence shows, are they designed to procure changes in the laws or governmental policy of this or any other country: even when they touch

para. 75 (refusal to register Margaret Thatcher Foundation, as it was concerned with arguing and advancing a particular political viewpoint).

[228] (1975) 38 MLR 471 (R.M.B. Cotterrell). In *Baldry v Feintuck* [1972] 1 WLR 552 the students' union of Sussex University was restrained from making payment to a publicity campaign against the abolition of free milk. See also *A-G v Ross* [1986] 1 WLR 252 [p. 541, below].

on political matters, they constitute, so far as I can see, no more than genuine attempts in an objective manner to ascertain and disseminate the truth. In these circumstances I think that no objections to the trust arise on a political score, similar to those which arose in the *McGovern* case [1982] Ch 321 [p. 526, below]. The trust is, in my opinion, entitled to what is sometimes called 'benignant construction', in the sense that the court is entitled to presume that the trustees will only act in a lawful and proper manner appropriate to the trustees of a charity and not, for example, by the propagation of tendentious political opinions, any more than those running the Wilton Park project so acted in the 33 years preceding the testator's death: compare *McGovern v A-G*, at 353.

In **Webb v O'Doherty** (1991) The Times, 11 February, a students' union was restrained from making payments to the National Student Committee to Stop War in the Gulf. HOFFMANN J said:

'The Student Union is an educational charity. Its purposes are wholly charitable and its funds can be devoted to charitable purposes only. Charitable educational purposes undoubtedly include discussion of political issues: *A-G v Ross* [1986] 1 WLR 252 at 263, *per* Scott J. There is, however, a clear distinction between the discussion of political matters, or the acquisition of information which may have a political content, and a campaign on a political issue. There is no doubt that campaigning, in the sense of seeking to influence public opinion on political matters, is not a charitable activity.[229] It is, of course, something which students are, like the rest of the population, perfectly at liberty to do in their private capacities, but it is not a proper object of the expenditure of charitable money.

In **Southwood v Attorney-General** (2000) 80 P & CR D34[230] a trust ('Prodem') was established for the 'advancement of the education of the public in the subject of militarism and disarmament and related fields'. The Court of Appeal refused to recognise this trust as charitable because the dominant purpose was considered to be political rather than educational. CHADWICK LJ said:

There is no objection on public benefit grounds to an educational programme which begins from the premise that peace is generally preferable to war. For my part, I would find it difficult to believe that any court would refuse to accept, as a general proposition, that it promotes public benefit for the public to be educated to an acceptance of that premise. That does not lead to the conclusion that the promotion of pacifism is necessarily charitable. The premise that peace is generally preferable to war is not to be equated with the premise that peace at any price is always preferable to any war....

I would have no difficulty in accepting the proposition that it promotes public benefit for the public to be educated in the differing means of securing a state of peace and avoiding a state of war. The difficulty comes at the next stage. There are differing views as to how best to secure peace and avoid war. To give two obvious examples: on the one hand it can be contended that war is best avoided by bargaining through strength; on the other hand it can be argued, with equal passion, that peace is best secured by disarmament if necessary, by unilateral disarmament. The court is in no position to determine that promotion of the one view rather than the other is for the public benefit. Not only does the court have no material on which to make that

---

[229] See now Charity Commission: *Campaigning and Political Activities by Charities* (Publication CC 9), (2004) [p. 531, below].   [230] (2000) 14 *Trust Law International* 233 (J. Gorton).

choice; to attempt to do so would be to usurp the role of government. So the court cannot recognise as charitable a trust to educate the public to an acceptance that peace is best secured by demilitarisation in the sense in which that concept is used in the Prodem background paper and briefing documents. Nor, conversely, could the court recognise as charitable a trust to educate the public to an acceptance that war is best avoided by collective security through the membership of a military alliance say, NATO.

... Prodem's object is not to educate the public in the differing means of securing a state of peace and avoiding a state of war. Prodem's object is to educate the public to an acceptance that peace is best secured by demilitarisation.... It is because the court cannot determine whether or not it promotes the public benefit for the public to be educated to an acceptance that peace is best secured by demilitarisation that Prodem's object cannot be recognised as charitable.

(iii) Reform of the law or governmental practices of a foreign country

McGovern v Attorney-General
[1982] Ch 321, (Ch D, Slade J)[231]

In 1977 a pilot trust was created by Amnesty International, the purposes of which were set out in clause 2 of the trust deed:

A. The relief of needy persons within any of the following categories:

(i)   Prisoners of Conscience

(ii) persons who have recently been Prisoners of Conscience

(iii) persons who would in the opinion of the Trustees be likely to become Prisoners of Conscience if they returned to their country of ordinary residence

(iv) relatives and dependents of the foregoing persons

by the provision of appropriate charitable (and in particular financial educational or rehabilitational) assistance.

B. Attempting to secure the release of Prisoners of Conscience.

C. Procuring the abolition of torture or inhuman or degrading treatment or punishment.

D. The undertaking promotion and commission of research into the maintenance and observance of human rights.

E. The dissemination of the results of such research...

F. The doing of all other such things as shall further the charitable purposes set out above.

The Charity Commissioners refused to register the trust as a charity. On appeal. *Held.* Trust not charitable. Its main purpose was political.

Slade J: As a broad proposition, I would accept that a trust for the relief of human suffering and distress would *prima facie* be capable of being of a charitable nature, within the spirit and intendment of the Preamble to the Statute of Elizabeth, as being what Mr. Hoffmann termed a 'charity of compassion'. It does not, however, follow that a trust established for good

[231] [1982] Conv 387 (T.G. Watkin); (1982) 45 MLR 704 (R. Nobles); (1982) 10 *New Zealand Universities Law Review* 169 (C.E.F. Rickett); (1983) 46 MLR 385 (F. Weiss); [1984] Conv 263 (C.J. Forder).

compassionate purposes will necessarily qualify as a charity according to English law, any more than it necessarily follows that such a qualification will attach to a trust for the relief of poverty or for the advancement of education or for the advancement of religion.

His Lordship referred to *Bowman v Secular Society Ltd* [1917] AC 406 at 442, [p. 522, above], *per* LORD PARKER OF WADDINGTON, and to *National Anti-Vivisection Society v IRC* [1948] AC 31 at 49–50, 62–63, [1947] 2 All ER 217 at 224, 232, [p. 522, above], *per* Lords Wright and Simonds, and continued:

From the passages from the speeches of Lord Parker, Lord Wright and Lord Simonds which I have read I extract the principle that the court will not regard as charitable a trust of which a main object is to procure an alteration of the law of the United Kingdom for one or both of two reasons: first, the court will ordinarily have no sufficient means of judging as a matter of evidence whether the proposed change will or will not be for the public benefit. Secondly, even if the evidence suffices to enable it to form a *prima facie* opinion that a change in the law is desirable, it must still decide the case on the principle that the law is right as it stands since to do otherwise would usurp the functions of the legislature...

I now turn to consider the status of a trust of which a main object is to secure the alteration of the laws of a *foreign* country. The mere fact that the trust was intended to be carried out abroad would not by itself necessarily deprive it of charitable status. A number of trusts to be executed outside this country have been upheld as charities, though the judgment of Sir Raymond Evershed MR in *Camille and Henry Dreyfus Foundation Inc v IRC* [1954] Ch 672, 684–685 illustrates that certain types of trust—for example, trusts for the setting out of soldiers or the repair of bridges or causeways—might be acceptable as charities only if they were to be executed in the United Kingdom. The point with which I am at present concerned is whether a trust of which a direct and main object is to secure a change in the laws of a foreign country can *ever* be regarded as charitable under English law. Though I do not think that any authority cited to me precisely covers the point, I have come to the clear conclusion that it cannot.

I accept that the dangers of the court encroaching on the functions of the legislature or of subjecting its political impartiality to question would not be nearly so great as when similar trusts are to be executed in this country. I also accept that on occasions the court will examine and express an opinion upon the quality of a foreign law. Thus, for example, it has declined to enforce or recognise rights conferred or duties imposed by a foreign law, in certain cases where it has considered that, on the particular facts, enforcement or recognition would be contrary to justice or morality. I therefore accept that the particular point made by Mr. Tyssen (about the law stultifying itself) has no application in this context. There is no obligation on the court to decide on the principle that any foreign law is *ex hypothesi* right as it stands; it is not obliged for all purposes to blind itself to what it may regard as the injustice of a particular foreign law.

In my judgment, however, there remain overwhelming reasons why such a trust still cannot be regarded as charitable. All the reasoning of Lord Parker of Waddington in *Bowman v Secular Society Ltd* [1917] AC 406 seems to me to apply *a fortiori* in such a case. *A fortiori* the court will have no adequate means of judging whether a proposed change in the law of a foreign country will or will not be for the public benefit. Sir Raymond Evershed MR in *Camille and Henry Dreyfus Foundation Inc v IRC* [1954] Ch 672, 684 expressed the *prima facie* view that the community which has to be considered in this context, even in the case of a trust to be executed abroad, is the community of the United Kingdom. Assuming that this is the right test, the court in applying it would still be bound to take account of the probable effects of attempts to procure the proposed legislation, or of its actual enactment, on the inhabitants of the country concerned, which would doubtless have a history and social structure quite different from that of the United Kingdom. Whatever might be its view as to the content of the relevant law from the standpoint of an English lawyer, it would, I think, have no satisfactory means of judging such probable effects upon the local community.

Furthermore, before ascribing charitable status to an English trust of which a main object was to secure the alteration of a foreign law, the court would also, I conceive, be bound to consider the consequences for this country as a matter of public policy. In a number of such cases there would arise a substantial *prima facie* risk that such a trust, if enforced, could prejudice the relations of this country with the foreign country concerned: compare *Habershon v Vardon* (1851) 4 De G & Sm 467. The court would have no satisfactory means of assessing the extent of such risk, which would not be capable of being readily dealt with by evidence and would be a matter more for political than for legal judgment. For all these reasons, I conclude that a trust of which a main purpose is to procure a change in the laws of a foreign country is a trust for the attainment of political objects within the spirit of Lord Parker of Waddington's pronouncement and, as such, is non-charitable.

Thus, far, I have been considering trusts of which a main purpose is to achieve changes in the law itself or which are of a party-political nature. Under any legal system, however, the government and its various authorities, administrative and judicial, will have wide discretionary powers vested in them, within the framework of the existing law. If a principal purpose of a trust is to procure a reversal of government policy or of particular administrative decisions of governmental authorities, does it constitute a trust for political purposes falling within the spirit of Lord Parker's pronouncement? In my judgment it does. If a trust of this nature is to be executed in England, the court will ordinarily have no sufficient means of determining whether the desired reversal would be beneficial to the public, and in any event could not properly encroach on the functions of the executive, acting intra vires, by holding that it should be acting in some other manner. If it is a trust which is to be executed abroad, the court will not have sufficient means of satisfactorily judging, as a matter of evidence, whether the proposed reversal would be beneficial to the community in the relevant sense, after all its consequences, local and international, had been taken into account. It may be added that Lord Normand, in the *National Anti-Vivisection Society* case [1948] AC 31, specifically equated legislative change and changes by way of government administration in the present context. As he said, at 77:

'The Society seems to me to proclaim that its purpose is a legislative change of policy toward scientific experiments on animals, the consummation of which will be an Act prohibiting all such experiments. I regard it as clear that a society professing these purposes is a political association and not a charity. If for legislative changes a change by means of government administration was substituted the result would be the same.'

If the crucial test whether a trust is charitable formulated by Lord Simonds in the same case, at 62—namely, the competence of the court to control and reform it—is applied, I think one is again driven to the conclusion that trusts of the nature now under discussion, which are to be executed abroad, cannot qualify as charities any more than if they are to be executed in this country. The court, in considering whether particular methods of carrying out or reforming them would be for the public benefit, would be faced with an inescapable dilemma, of which a hypothetical example may be given. It appears from the Amnesty International Report 1978,

p. 270, that Islamic law sanctions the death penalty for certain well-defined offences, namely, murder, adultery and brigandage. Let it be supposed that a trust were created of which the object was to secure the abolition of the death penalty for adultery in those countries where Islamic law applies, and to secure a reprieve for those persons who have been sentenced to death for this offence. The court, when invited to enforce or to reform such a trust, would either have to apply English standards as to public benefit, which would not necessarily be at all appropriate in the local conditions, or would have to attempt to apply local standards, of which it knew little or nothing. An English court would not, it seems to me, be competent either to control or reform a trust of this nature, and it would not be appropriate that it should attempt to do so.

Summary of conclusions relating to trusts for political purposes

Founding them principally on the House of Lords decisions in the *Bowman* case [1917] AC 406 and the *National Anti-Vivisection Society* case [1948] AC 31, I therefore summarise my conclusions in relation to trusts for political purposes as follows. (1) Even if it otherwise appears to fall within the spirit and intendment of the Preamble to the Statute of Elizabeth, a trust for political purposes falling within the spirit of Lord Parker's pronouncement in *Bowman's* case can never be regarded as being for the public benefit in the manner which the law regards as charitable. (2) Trusts for political purposes falling within the spirit of this pronouncement include, *inter alia*, trusts of which a direct and principal purpose is either (i) to further the interests of a particular political party; or (ii) to procure changes in the laws of this country; or (iii) to procure changes in the laws of a foreign country; or (iv) to procure a reversal of government policy or of particular decisions of governmental authorities in this country; or (v) to procure a reversal of governmental policy or of particular decisions of governmental authorities in a foreign country.

This categorisation is not intended to be an exhaustive one, but I think it will suffice for the purposes of this judgment; I would further emphasise that it is directed to trusts of which the *purposes* are political. As will appear later, the mere fact that trustees may be at liberty to employ political *means* in furthering the non-political purposes of a trust does not necessarily render it non-charitable...

[His Lordship then considered the requirement that trust purposes must be wholly and exclusively charitable, and continued:] From all these authorities, I think that two propositions follow in the present case. First, if any one of the main objects of the trusts declared by the trust deed is to be regarded as 'political' in the relevant sense, then, the trusts of the trust deed cannot qualify as being charitable. Secondly, however, if all the main objects of the trust are exclusively charitable, the mere fact that the trustees may have incidental powers to employ political means for their furtherance will not deprive them of their charitable status.

After this introduction I now turn to examine these trusts themselves....

It will not be necessary to consider the trusts declared by clause 2A, since it is common ground that, if read in isolation, these trusts are of a charitable nature. Of the remaining subclauses, I shall begin by considering the construction and legal effect of clause 2B....

Expressed in one sentence, the main object of the broadly-defined trust contained in clause 2B must in my judgment be regarded as being the procurement of the reversal of the relevant decisions of governments and governmental authorities in those countries where such authorities have decided to detain 'prisoners of conscience', whether or not in accordance with the local law. The procurement of the reversal of such decisions cannot, I think, be regarded merely as one possible method of giving effect to the purposes of clause 2B, any more than in the *National*

Anti-Vivisection Society case [1948] AC 31 the alteration of the law could be regarded as merely one method of giving effect to the purpose of abolishing vivisection. On the construction which I place on clause 2B, it is the principal purpose itself. On this view of the matter, the trust declared by clause 2B cannot in my judgment qualify as a charitable trust. It is a trust for political purposes, within the fifth of the categories listed above....

For these reasons it must in my judgment follow that the trusts of clause 2B are not charitable. Unlike those of clause 2A, they cannot be regarded as purely eleemosynary. It must also follow from this that the trusts of the trust deed as a whole are invalid as not being for exclusively charitable purposes. Nevertheless, having heard full argument as to clause 2C, D and E, I will express my conclusions in relation to them, in case this may be of assistance either to the parties or to a higher court....

I prefer to base my conclusion in relation to the trusts of clause 2C on the wider grounds that they include the procurement not only of changes in the law of the United Kingdom but also of changes in the laws of foreign countries and the reversal of particular decisions of governmental authorities in foreign countries. They are therefore political trusts within the second, third and fifth of the heads categorised above. For these reasons, it must follow that in my judgment the trusts of clause 2C are not charitable....

If sub-clauses D and E had been the only trust purposes contained in the trust deed, I would have held them to be of a charitable nature. The subject matter of the proposed research seems to me manifestly a subject of study which is capable of adding usefully to the store of human knowledge.... It appears that the study of human rights has become an accepted academic discipline; the subject is taught in many universities, and is part of the curriculum in departments of many schools. I think that sub-clauses D and E when read together make it clear that it is contemplated that the knowledge acquired as a result of the research would be disseminated to others. Furthermore, if these two sub-clauses had stood in isolation I would have felt little difficulty in holding that the trusts thereby declared were for the benefit of the public. The mere theoretical possibility that the trustees might have implemented them in a political manner would not have rendered them non-charitable; the two sub-clauses would have been entitled to a benignant construction and to the presumption, referred to by Gray J in *Jackson v Phillips* (1867) 96 Mass (14 Allen) 539, that the trustees would only act in lawful and proper manner appropriate to the trustees of a charity and not, for example, by the propagation of tendentious political opinions.

As things are, the trusts of sub-clauses D and E, just as much as the trusts of sub-clauses A and F, must in my judgment fail along with sub-clauses B and C. None of the trusts of this trust deed can be regarded as being charitable.

Conclusion

In eloquent passages at the end of their addresses, Mr. Knox and Mr. Hoffmann made reference to the classic problem facing Antigone, who believed that there are certain laws of men which a higher law may require them to disregard. Mr. Hoffmann, by reference to the various international conventions to which this country has been a party, submitted that it is committed to the elimination of unjust laws and actions wherever these may exist or occur throughout the world.

Indisputably, laws do exist both in this country and in many foreign countries which many reasonable persons consider unjust. No less indisputably, laws themselves will from time to time be administered by governmental authorities in a manner which many reasonable persons consider unjust, inhuman or degrading. Amnesty International, in striving to remedy what it considers to be such injustices, is performing a function which many will regard as being of great value to humanity. Fortunately, the laws of this country place very few restrictions on the rights of philanthropic organisations such as this, or of individuals, to strive for the remedy of what they regard as instances of injustice, whether occurring here or abroad. However, for reasons which I think adequately appear from Lord Parker of Waddington's pronouncement in *Bowman's* case [1917] AC 406, the elimination of injustice has not as such ever been held to be a trust purpose which qualifies for the privileges afforded to charities by English law. I cannot hold it to be a charitable purpose now.

For all these reasons, I must decline to make the declaration sought by the originating summons, namely, that the trust constituted by the trust deed ought to be registered as a charity.

(iv) Guidelines

(a) Political Activities by Charities

Charity Commission: *Campaigning and Political Activities by Charities* (Publication CC 9) (September 2004), paras 3, 12–15, 22–24, 50–51, 55–56, 61–62

Meaning of words and expressions used

3. In this guidance: ...

Political purpose means in essence any purpose directed at:

- furthering the interests of any political party; or
- securing, or opposing, any change in the law or in the policy or decisions of central government or local authorities, whether in this country or abroad.

Campaigning covers a wide range of activities. It is used to refer to:

- public awareness raising and education on a particular issue;
- influencing and changing public attitudes; and
- political activities which are intended to influence Government policy or legislation, and which may involve contact with political parties.

Much campaigning work by charities involves acting as an advocate for their service users or beneficiaries. Like campaigning, advocacy covers a wide range of activities, which can range from general awareness-raising activities through to direct engagement in political activities. It may, or may not, involve political campaigning.

Political activity means any activity that is directed at securing, or opposing, any change in the law or in the policy or decisions of central government or local authorities, whether in this country or abroad.

The scope of charity

12. Although organisations that are established to pursue political purposes cannot be charities, campaigning and political activity may be carried out by recognised charities as a means of furthering their charitable purposes.

13. Consequently, an organisation set up for a purpose (or which includes a purpose) of advocating or opposing changes in the law or public policy (in this country or abroad) or supporting a political party cannot be a charity. This is because the question of whether the

organisation is established for the benefit of the public, an essential feature of all charities, cannot be assessed by the Charity Commission.

14. Organisations established for exclusively charitable purposes may carry out campaigning and political activities to the extent outlined below, provided that the activities pursued are a legitimate means of furthering those purposes. A charity may quite properly be established with charitable purposes which can be carried out either wholly or partly by campaigning methods.

15. Campaigning and political campaigning are distinct activities—the latter confined only to campaigns and activities which advocate or oppose changes in the law or public policy. Apart from the question of the proportion of charitable resources which may be applied (see below), expenditure on both are governed by the same legal rules.

What proportion of its resources can a charity properly devote to campaigning and political activity?

22. As noted above, campaigning is a broad term that can include public awareness-raising and education, or seeking to influence and change public attitudes. Provided it complies with the requirements set out above, a charity may choose to devote up to all its resources to non-political campaigning to further its purposes.

23. However, where the campaign or other activity is of a political nature (i.e. seeking to advocate or oppose a change in the law or public policy), charity trustees must ensure that these activities do not become the dominant means by which they carry out the purposes of the charity. These activities must remain incidental or ancillary to the charity's purposes. What is dominant is a question of scope and degree upon which trustees must make a judgement. In making this judgement trustees should take into account factors such as the amount of resources applied and the period involved, the purposes of the charity and the nature of the activity.

24. Where political activities do begin to dominate the activities of the charity, an issue will arise as to whether the charity trustees are acting outside their trusts. In exceptional cases this might also lead us to reconsider whether the organisation should ever have been registered as a charity, or whether it was in fact established for non-charitable political purposes.

PART B: Campaigning And Political Activities—Some Practical Examples

50. This list is not exhaustive or exclusive, and does not mean or imply that charities are prevented from engaging in other types of political activity.

Influencing Government or local authorities

51. A charity can seek to influence Government, local authorities, or public opinion on issues either relating to the achievement of the charity's own stated purposes, or on issues of relevance to the well-being of the charitable sector.

Responding to proposed legislation

55. A charity may provide and publish comments on possible or proposed changes in the law or government policy, whether contained in a Green or White Paper, draft Parliamentary Bill or elsewhere. A charity may also supply to Members of either House relevant information about the implications of a Parliamentary Bill, for use in debate.

Supporting, opposing and promoting new legislation and public policy, and changes to existing legislation and public policy

56. A charity can support or oppose the passage of a Parliamentary Bill if such support or opposition can reasonably be expected to further its charitable purposes. On the same basis a charity can also promote the need for a particular piece of legislation.

Commenting on public issues

61.   A charity can make public comment on social, economic and political issues if these relate to its purpose or the way in which the charity is able to carry out its work.

Supporting political parties

62.   As explained in paragraphs 47–49, to support a political party, or its doctrine, is not, in itself, a charitable purpose. However, it may further a charity's purposes to support a policy which is also advocated by a political party. In supporting a policy that a political party also advocates the charity should seek to stress and make clear its independence, both to its supporters and to those people whose views its is seeking to influence.

(b) Expenditure by Student Unions

Report of the Charity Commissioners for England and Wales for the year 1983, Appendix A

Attorney-General's Guidance on Expenditure by Student Unions:

The Attorney-General, as protector of charities, frequently receives complaints about the use of Student Union funds for purposes which go beyond those permitted for such funds, and he is greatly concerned about those cases in which the complaints turn out to be well founded because the funds have been used for a purpose incompatible with the charitable objects of the Student Union in question.

It has been held in the Courts that a Student Union has charitable objects if it exists to represent and foster the interests of the students at an educational establishment in such a way as to further the educational purposes of the establishment itself. The Attorney-General believes that that will be the case with the great majority of Student Unions, including those provided for in the constitutions of their parent establishments (unless those establishments do not themselves have charitable objects). If a Student Union has charitable objects it follows as a matter of law that, whatever may be stated in its constitution, those objects cannot be changed, even by unanimous vote of its members, so as to include non-charitable objects; and Union funds may be spent only on those charitable objects or for properly incidental purposes.

The Attorney-General recognises the difficult position in which officers of Student Unions with charitable objects may find themselves. They may have no experience of charity law, and their members may believe that Union funds can be spent on anything that they think to be of general interest. However, the officers are trustees of the funds, and they have a duty to see that the funds are used only for purposes permitted by charity law. The complaints which have been made in recent years contain allegations of considerable expenditure of an improper nature. Such investigation as has been undertaken confirms that there are grounds for concern. Although perhaps the items taken individually appear not to be very great, they represent in total a major abuse of charitable funds.

In the circumstances the Attorney-General considers it right that he should issue guidelines to assist Union officers in the discharge of their responsibility for Union funds. In the event of wrongful application of funds, such officers would potentially be at personal risk to a claim that they have been party to a breach of trust, and might well find themselves bound to make good any loss to the funds of their Union at their own expense. It is therefore important that they should be aware of their responsibilities.

The Attorney-General considers that expenditure of a Student Union's charitable funds is proper if it can be said to be appropriate for the purpose of representing and furthering the interests of the students at the relevant college (and 'college' here includes 'university') in such a way as to assist in the educational aims of the college—for example, by providing channels for the representation of student views within the college, or by improving the conditions of life of the students and in particular providing facilities for their social and physical well-being.

It is clear, for example, that if a college is to function properly, there is a need for the normal range of clubs and societies so as to enable each student to further the development of his abilities, mental and physical. Equally, it is likely that the college will gain from the fact that the students hold meetings to debate matters of common concern, and publish some form of campus newspaper. Reasonable expenditure on such purposes is, in the view of the Attorney-General, plainly permissible for a Student Union.

On the other hand, for the students to offer financial support to a political cause in a foreign country—as opposed to merely debating the merits of that cause—is, in the Attorney-General's view, irrelevant to the educational purpose of the college. Such expenditure must accordingly be rejected as improper.

Between these extremes there is a wide range of cases for which the Attorney-General believes the best touchstone to be the question: does the matter in issue affect the interests of either students *as such* or the affairs of the college *as such?* If the answer is 'no', then the case is likely to be one on which the students may hold debates and express views but not charge expenditure to the charitable funds of the Union.

A major area of difficulty appears to be that of political issues. While the Attorney-General recognises that it is entirely natural that students will wish to express their views on political matters, the law sets strict limits to the expenditure of charitable funds for political purposes. Such expenditure is permissible only if the political purposes are merely *incidental* to the necessarily non-political objects of the charity. Thus, for a Union to expend its charitable funds in supporting a political campaign or demonstration is extremely unlikely to be justifiable unless the issue directly affects students as students. It may be helpful to mention that in this context politics is not to be limited to party politics, but extends essentially to all aspects of the making and changing of laws. Thus it would be no less improper, in the view of the Attorney-General, for charitable funds of a Union to be devoted to a campaign for or against the legalisation of drugs, even though this is not a matter of party-political debate, than it would be for such funds to be used either in support of or opposition to a campaign concerning, say, nuclear weapons or some controversial parliamentary debate not concerned with the interests of students as such.

Another area of difficulty appears to be that of industrial disputes. The Attorney-General accepts that students may often wish to express a view on a current dispute, particularly if it be centred upon the neighbourhood of the college of which they are students. There is, however, in his view no justification for applying charitable funds in support of either side to the dispute. It would be as wrong for charitable funds to be spent on the hire of coaches, say, for the purpose of taking demonstrators to the scene of the dispute as it would be to hire coaches to take students to a demonstration in respect of the political issues referred to in the last paragraph.

There is, of course, no objection whatsoever to students joining together to collect their own moneys for a particular purpose for which Union funds cannot be used. The Attorney-General wishes to stress that the objection is not to student participation in activities outside the educational sphere, but to the use of charitable funds for purposes for which they cannot properly be applied according to the law.

In issuing these guidelines the Attorney-General is anxious solely to assist those who may find themselves called to account for their actions as trustees of charitable moneys. Officers should, of course, bear in mind that it will be amongst their most important duties to identify and keep proper accounts of all Union funds (including, for example, not merely subscriptions to the Union, but income from Union investments, and profits from Union activities, such as the running of a bar or dance at the expense of the Union and with the assistance of its employees). They have a further duty to ensure that expenditure not only is within the proper bounds within which the funds of their Union can be used, but also has been approved and recorded as the Constitution of the Union requires.

They should also bear in mind that a trustee is at all times entitled to seek advice, if necessary at the expense of the trust fund, on any aspect of his trust which causes him doubt or concern; in particular, under Section 24 of the Charities Act 1960 [now see Charities Act 1993, s. 29, p. 594, below] the Charity Commissioners are empowered on the written application of a charity trustee to give him their opinion or advice on any matter affecting the performance of his duties as such.

The Attorney-General would add that he hopes that the senior members of the college concerned will always be willing to assist Student Union officers in considering doubtful items of expenditure. It must be borne in mind that where the parent body is itself a charitable body and thus has a duty to ensure that its funds are properly applied for purposes within, or incidental to, its own charitable educational purposes, it might well be that upon becoming aware of major items of improper expenditure by the Union it ought properly to cease to fund the Union until the position had been rectified.

(v) Critique of the Law

The refusal to grant charitable status to trusts which predominantly have political purposes has been subject to much criticism.[232]

[1997] PL 615, 622 (J. Stevens and D. Feldman)

Those cases which established that charitable status could not extend to purposes which are political belong to an earlier social era. The fundamental objection to according such status, namely that the law is incapable of judging whether a change in the law or government policy is good or bad, is plainly spurious. In a relativistic age and a mature democracy the law should be able to uphold as charitable objects which are diametrically opposed to each other, provided that they are for the 'public benefit' in the view of a sizeable body of adherents. Religious purposes which are diametrically opposed are already upheld as equally charitable. A Christian missionary organisation seeking to convert Muslims would be just as charitable as a Muslim organisation seeking to convert Christians. There is no reason why a body seeking to promote research into the benefits of vegetarianism should not be charitable alongside a body to promote research into the health benefits of meat consumption. As Lord Wilberforce observed in *Scottish Burial Reform and Cremation Society Ltd v Glasgow City Corpn*[233] the law of charities

---

[232] See, for example, M. Chesterman, pp. 333, 343–349 and A. Dunn, in 'Foundations of Charity' (ed. C. Mitchell and S.R. Moody), p. 57. On the question of whether the Human Rights Act 1998 compels the English courts and the Charity Commissioners to accord charitable status to trusts whose objects are political, see Luxton, pp. 49–53 and (1999) 5 *Charity Law & Practice Review* 219 (D. Morris). This argument largely turns on the interpretation of Article 10 of the European Convention on Human Rights which concerns the 'right to freedom of expression'. The preferable view is, as Luxton recognises at p. 51, that 'such restrictions are nothing to do with freedom of speech, and everything to do with ensuring that funds given for charitable purposes are not misapplied by those who undertook to apply them for such charitable purposes, in fraud of the contributors'. [233] [1968] AC 138.

is not static. It should be allowed to evolve so as to encompass the promotion of the observance of human rights, whether in this country or overseas, and the honouring of international obligations which have been entered into. The very fact that the UK has acceded to such international conventions is indicative that the pursuit of such objectives should be conclusive evidence of benefit to the community. If, as Lord Woolf accepts, it is regrettable that the laws and policies of many countries do not comply with the Charter of the United Nations of which they are members, and that campaigning to change incompatible laws and policies is commendable[234] the law of charities should be allowed to treat such campaigns as charitable notwithstanding their political character.

QUESTIONS

1. Should trusts for political purposes be charitable?

2. Is a trust to reform the law of charitable trusts valid?

3. If you were reviewing the register of charities are there any types of charity which you would register which are not currently registered and are there any types of charity which are presently on the register which you would wish to remove? Why?

4. Does the Charity Commission have too much power in determining whether a trust's purpose is charitable? See (2001) 21 LS 36 (P. Edge and J.M.L. Loughrey).

5. Does fiscal immunity play too large a part in the law of charities? Should provision be made to validate certain useful and beneficial trusts without giving them tax-free status? Consider what is said by the House of Lords in *Dingle v Turner* [1972] AC 601 [p. 432, above]; (1956) 72 LQR 187 (G. Cross); Royal Commission on the Taxation of Profits and Income (1955) Cmd. 9474, chap. 7; (1977) 40 MLR 397 (N.P. Gravells); and tie this in with your thoughts on non-charitable purpose trusts in Chapter 9.

IV THE TRUST MUST BE EXCLUSIVELY CHARITABLE[235]

To be charitable, the purpose of a trust must not merely include purposes which are charitable. The purposes must be exclusively charitable.[236] This requirement has appeared in cases previously discussed. It appears dramatically in cases where the

---

[234] *R v Radio Authority, ex p Bull* [1998] QB 294 at 306 (Lord WOOLF MR).
[235] H&M, pp. 444–449; Luxton, pp. 201–220; P&M, pp. 476–482; P&S, pp. 544–547; Pettit, pp. 240–246; Picarda, pp. 212–264; Snell, pp. 523–527; Tudor, pp. 12–13, 141–147. See *Latimer v Commissioner of Inland Revenue* [2004] 1 WLR 1446.   [236] See Charities Act 2006, s. 1(1)(a) [p. 416, above].

purposes are for charitable or some alternative purpose which is wider than legal charity. Thus, 'charitable *or* benevolent' purposes are wider than legal charity, because 'benevolent' is not a charitable purpose and the trustee may apply funds for that purpose rather than a charitable purpose. However, 'charitable *and* benevolent purposes' are charitable, because, even though 'benevolent' is wider than 'charitable',[237] the purposes here must be not only 'benevolent' but 'charitable' as well.

Where the purposes of a trust extend beyond the limits of legal charity, the court may, on construing the language, reach one of several possible solutions.

1. That the trust is void. This result seems inevitable if it is possible, consistently with the terms of the trust, to apply the whole of the fund to non-charitable purposes. The assets will then be held on resulting trust for the settlor unless the trust can be validated as a non-charitable purpose trust. See Chapter 9.

2. That the non-charitable purposes are incidental only, and so do not prevent the whole of the fund from being applied to a charitable purpose.

3. That the fund should be divided into parts; some being applicable to charity and some not. Such a solution can only be reached where the language of the trust instrument can be construed as directing such a division.

A   AND/OR CASES[238]

Chichester Diocesan Fund and Board of Finance Incorporated v Simpson
[1944] AC 341 (HL, Viscount Simon LC, Lords Macmillan, Wright, Porter and Simonds)

Mr. Diplock, the testator, directed his executors to apply the residue of his estate, amounting to more than £250,000, 'for such charitable institution or institutions or

---

[237] See also *Re Atkinson's Will Trusts* [1978] 1 WLR 586 ('worthy causes' held not to be exclusively charitable).

[238] (a) Cases of *Or*: *Blair v Duncan* [1902] AC 37 ('such charitable or public purposes as my trustee thinks proper'); *Houston v Burns* [1918] AC 337 ('public, benevolent or charitable purposes'); *Re Macduff* [1896] 2 Ch 451 ('some one or more purposes, charitable, philanthropic or...'); *A-G of Cayman Islands v Wahr-Hansen* [2001] 1 AC 75 (PC) ('to any one or more religious, charitable or educational institution or institutions or any organisations or institutions operating for the public good'). These purposes were all held not to be charitable. Cf. *Re Bennett* [1920] 1 Ch 305 ('charity, or any other public objects in the parish of Faringdon'); *Guild v IRC* [1992] 2 AC 310 [p. 496, above] (gift to specified charitable purpose 'or some similar purpose in connection with it').

(b) Cases of *And*: *Blair v Duncan*, above, at 44, *per* Lord Davey: 'If the words were "charitable and public purposes", I think effect might be given to them, the words... being construed to mean charitable purposes of a public character.'; *Re Sutton* (1885) 28 Ch D 464 ('charitable and deserving objects'); *Re Best* [1904] 2 Ch 354 ('charitable and benevolent institutions'). These purposes were held to be charitable. Cf. *Williams v Kershaw* (1835) 5 Cl & Fin 111n ('benevolent, charitable and religious purposes'); *Re Eades* [1920] 2 Ch 353 ('such religious, charitable and philanthropic objects as X Y and Z shall jointly appoint'). See also *A-G v National Provincial and Union Bank of England* [1924] AC 262 ('such patriotic purposes or objects and such charitable

other charitable or benevolent object or objects in England' as they should in their absolute discretion select.

Held. The gift was void.[239]

Lord Simonds: My Lords, the words for your consideration are 'charitable or benevolent'. The question is whether, in the context in which they are found in this will, these words give to the executors a choice of objects extending beyond that which the law recognizes as charitable. If they do not, that is the end of the matter. The trust is a good charitable trust. If they do, it appears to be conceded by counsel for the appellant institution that the trust is invalid, but, in deference to the argument of the Attorney-General, who invited your Lordships to take a different view, I must say a few words at a later stage. My Lords, of those three words your Lordships will have no doubt what the first, 'charitable', means. It is a term of art with a technical meaning and that is the meaning which the testator must be assumed to have intended. If it were not so, if in this will 'charitable' were to be given, not its legal, but some popular, meaning, it would not be possible to establish the validity of the bequest. The last of the three words 'benevolent' is not a term of art. In its ordinary meaning it has a range in some respects far less wide than legal charity, in others somewhat wider. It is, at least, clear that the two words, the one here used in its technical meaning, the other having only, and, accordingly, here used in, a popular meaning, are by no means coterminous. These two words are joined or separated by the word 'or', a particle, of which the primary function is to co-ordinate two or more words between which there is an alternative. It is, I think, the only word in our language apt to have this effect. Its primary and ordinary meaning is the same, whether or not the first alternative is preceded by the word 'either'.

My Lords, averting my mind from the possible ill effects of an alternative choice between objects 'charitable' and objects 'benevolent', I cannot doubt that the plain meaning of the testator's words is that he has given this choice, and that, if he intended to give it, he could have used no words more apt to do so. Is there, then, anything in the context which narrows the area of choice by giving to the words 'or benevolent' some other meaning than that which they primarily and naturally have? And if so, what is the other meaning which is to be given to them? Let me examine the second question first. Since the test of validity depends on the area of choice not being extended beyond the bounds of legal charity, a meaning must be given to the words 'or benevolent' which retains them within these bounds. This result, it has been contended, may be reached by giving to the word 'or' not its primary disjunctive meaning but a secondary meaning which may, perhaps, be called exegetical or explanatory. Undoubtedly 'or' is capable of this meaning. So used, it is equivalent to 'alias' or 'otherwise called'. The dictionary examples of this use will generally be found to be topographical, as 'Papua or New Guinea', but, my Lords, this use of the word 'or' is only possible if the words or phrases which it joins connote the same thing and are interchangeable the one with the other. In this case the testator is assumed to use the word 'charitable' in its legal sense. I see no possible ground for supposing that he proceeds to explain it by another word which has another meaning and by no means can have that meaning. I must reject the exegetical 'or'. Then it was suggested that the words 'or benevolent' should be construed as equivalent to 'provided such objects are also of a benevolent character', that is to say, the objects must be charitable but of that order of charity which is

institution or institutions or charitable object or objects in the British Empire as my trustees may select' held void); *A-G of the Bahamas v Royal Trust Co* [1986] 1 WLR 1001 ('for any purposes for and/or connected with the education and welfare of Bahamian children and young people'); [1986] All ER Rev 202 (P.J. Clarke).

[239] For the sequel, see *Ministry of Health v Simpson* [1951] AC 251 [p. 904, below].

commonly called benevolent. I think that this is only a roundabout way of saying that 'or' should be read as 'and,' that the objects of choice must have the two characteristics of charitable and benevolent. It is possible that a context may justify so drastic a change as that involved in reading the disjunctive as conjunctive. I turn then to the context to see what justification it affords for reading the relevant words in any but their natural meaning. Reading and re-reading them, as your Lordships have so often done in the course of this case, I can find nothing which justifies such a departure. It is true that the word 'other' introduces the phrase 'charitable or benevolent object or objects' and to this the appellants attached some importance, suggesting that since 'other' looked back to 'charitable institution or institutions', so all that followed must be of the genus charitable. There can be no substance in this, for in the phrase so introduced the word 'charitable' is itself repeated and is followed by the alternative 'or benevolent'. Apart from this slender point it seemed that the appellants relied on what is called a general, a dominant, an overriding, charitable intention, giving charitable content to a word or phrase which might otherwise not have that quality. That such a result is possible there are cases in the books to show. Some of them have been cited to your Lordships, but here again I look in vain for any such context. On the plain reading of this will I could only come to the conclusion that the testator intended exclusively to benefit charitable objects if I excised the words 'or benevolent' which he has used. That I cannot do.

B   MAIN AND SUBSIDIARY OBJECTS[240]

In **Oxford Group v Inland Revenue Commissioners** [1949] 2 All ER 537,[241] the question was whether the Oxford Group, a company limited by guarantee, was exempt from Income Tax. The objects of the movement, as laid down in its memorandum of association, included—

3 (A) The advancement of the Christian religion, and, in particular, by the means and in accordance with the principles of the Oxford Group Movement, founded in or about the year 1921 by Frank Nathan Daniel Buchman.

  (B) The maintenance, support, development and assistance of the Oxford Group Movement in every way...

  (C) (9) To establish and support or aid in the establishment and support of any charitable or benevolent associations or institutions, and to subscribe or guarantee money for charitable or benevolent purposes in any way connected with the purposes of the association or calculated to further its objects.

    (10) To do all such other things as are incidental, or the association may think conducive, to the attainment of the above objects or any of them.

No question arose under 3(A). The Court of Appeal held however that 3(B) and 3(C) (9) and (10) included purposes which were outside the scope of legal charity, and that the Company was not exempt from Income Tax.

---

240 [1978] Conv 92 (N.P. Gravells).
241 See also *IRC v Oldham Training and Enterprise Council* [1996] STC 1218 [p. 520, above].

In **General Nursing Council for England and Wales v St Marylebone Borough Council** [1959] AC 540, the House of Lords, by a majority of 3–2, decided that the General Nursing Council for England and Wales, a body whose main object was the regulation of the nursing profession, was not a charity, nor was it 'otherwise concerned with the advancement of...social welfare'. (Rating and Valuation (Miscellaneous Provisions) Act 1955, section 8(1)(a)). It was not therefore entitled to rating relief under section 8(2).

There may, however, be incidental non-charitable purposes.

In **Re Bernstein's Will Trusts** (1971) 115 Sol Jo 808, the testator, after a life interest to his widow, gave his residuary estate on trust for the Eye, Ear and Throat Infirmary, Liverpool, one-quarter of which was to form a nursing staff fund 'for the purpose of providing extra comforts at Christmas time for the nursing staff'. Ungoed-Thomas J held that the trust for the nursing staff was charitable, being subservient to the gift to the hospital.

In **Royal College of Surgeons of England v National Provincial Bank Ltd** [1952] AC 631, the House of Lords decided, by a majority of 3–2, that the Royal College of Surgeons was a charity. Its object was 'the due promotion and encouragement of the study and practice of the...art and science [of surgery]'. The other activities, which included the professional protection of the members of the profession, were merely ancillary.

In **Re Coxen** [1948] Ch 747, a trust fund, amounting to some £200,000, was held upon trust for medical charities and provided expressly for the payment of £100 towards a dinner for the Court of Aldermen of the City of London upon their meeting upon the business of the trust, and the payment of one guinea to each Alderman who attended during the whole of a Committee meeting. The trust was upheld on the ground, either that such payments should be treated as being made for the better administration of the trust; or as being incidental and ancillary to it.

In **Incorporated Council of Law Reporting for England and Wales v Attorney-General**[242] [1972] Ch 73 [p. 517, above], the Court of Appeal held that the activities of the Council were charitable. Buckley LJ said at 103:

The subsidiary objects, such as printing and publishing statutes, the provision of a noting-up service and so forth, are ancillary to this primary object and do not detract from its exclusively charitable character. Indeed, the publication of the statutes of the realm is itself, I think, a charitable purpose for reasons analogous to those applicable to reporting judicial decisions.

In **London Hospital Medical College v Inland Revenue Commissioners** [1976] 1 WLR 613, a students' union was held to be a charitable trust where its predominant

---

[242] Followed by the Charity Commissioners, in deciding that the Commonwealth Magistrates Association should be entered on the register of charities: Annual Report for 1975, para. 63.

object was to further the educational purposes of the college, even though one of its objects was to confer private and personal benefits on union members.[243]

In **A-G v Ross** [1986] 1 WLR 252, a students' union was also held to be a charitable trust, even though one of its objects was affiliation to a non-charitable organisation, the National Union of Students. SCOTT J said at 265:

The union was formed and exists for the charitable purpose of furthering the educational function of the [North London] Polytechnic. The non-charitable activities which the union is, under its constitution, authorised to carry on and has carried on are, in my judgment, as a matter of degree no more than ancillary means by which the charitable purpose may be pursued.[244]

C SEVERANCE

In **Salusbury v Denton** (1857) 3 K & J 529, Mr. Burrows bequeathed a fund to his widow to be applied by her in her will, 'part to the foundation of a charity school, or such other charitable endowment for the benefit of the poor of Offley as she may prefer…and the remainder…to be at her disposal among my relatives, in such proportions as she may be pleased to direct'. The widow died without having made a will or appointment. One question was whether the fund was divisible. PAGE-WOOD V-C held that the fund was divisible into two equal parts, one for charitable purposes, and the other for the plaintiff absolutely, as the only person entitled under the Statute of Distribution 1670. He said at 539:

Here there is a plain direction to the widow to give a part to the charitable purposes referred to in the will as she may think fit, and the remainder among the testator's relatives as she may direct. And the widow having died without exercising that discretion, the moiety in question must be divided equally.

Equal division may however be inappropriate: *Re Coxen* [1948] Ch 747 [p. 540, above].

D LOCALITY CASES

In **A-G of the Cayman Islands v Wahr-Hansen** [2001] 1 AC 75 (PC),[245] LORD BROWNE-WILKINSON said at 81 that the 'locality cases'—

---

243 See also *IRC v City of Glasgow Police Athletic Association* [1953] AC 380; *Re Lipinski's Will Trusts* [1976] Ch 235 [p. 372, above]; *Re South Place Ethical Society* [1980] 1 WLR 1565 [p. 466, above] (social activities held to be ancillary to objects of ethical humanist society); *Funnell v Stewart* [1996] 1 WLR 288 [p. 477, above] (private religious services confined to a closed group held to be subsidiary to public spiritual or faith-healing part of the group's work); *McGovern v A-G* [1982] Ch 321 at 340–343 [p. 526, above]; *IRC v White* [1980] TR 155 [p. 485, above]. See also *Re City of London Rifle and Pistol Club and the Burnley Rifle Club* (1993) Decisions of the Charity Commissioners, Vol 1, p 4 [p. 515, above].

244 [1985] All ER Rev 320 (P.J. Clarke).

245 See p. 537, n. 238, above. See also *Gibbs v Harding* [2007] EWHC 3 (Ch); [2008] 2 WLR 361.

are cases where the gift is made, for example, to a parish (*West v Knight* (1669) 1 Cas in Ch 134) or 'for the good of' a specific county (*A-G v Lord Lonsdale* (1827) 1 Sim. 105) or for 'charitable, beneficial, and public works' (*Mitford v Reynolds* (1841) 1 Ph 185) or for 'the benefit and advantage of Great Britain' (*Nightingale v Goulbourn* (1847) 5 Hare 484) or 'unto my country England': *Re Smith* [1932] 1 Ch 153. In all these cases the gifts were held to be valid charitable trusts, even though the breadth of the words used, literally construed, would certainly have authorised the applications of the funds for non-charitable purposes in the speci-fied locality. The courts have held that such purposes are to be impliedly limited to charitable purposes in the specified community....

There is a limited class of cases where gifts in general terms are made for the benefit of a named locality or its inhabitants. For reasons which are obscure, such cases have been benevo-lently construed. They are now so long established that in cases falling within the very circum-scribed description of gifts for the benefit of a specified locality they remain good law. But they have been widely criticised and indeed have been said to be wrongly decided: see, for example, Michael Albery, 'Trusts for the Benefit of the Inhabitants of a Locality' (1940) 56 LQR 49. To apply the same principle to all cases where there are general statements of benevolent or philanthropic objects so as to restrict the meaning of the general words to such objects as are in law charitable would be inconsistent with the overwhelming body of authority which decides that general words are not to be artificially construed so as to be impliedly limited to charitable purposes only.

NEW SOUTH WALES CHARITABLE TRUSTS ACT 1993

23. Inclusion of non-charitable purpose not to invalidate trust:

(1) A trust is not invalid merely because some non-charitable and invalid purpose as well as some charitable purpose is or could be taken to be included in any of the purposes to or for which an application of the trust property or of any part of it is directed or allowed by the trust.

(2) Any such trust is to be construed and given effect to in the same manner in all respects as if no application of the trust property or of any part of it to or for any such non-charitable and invalid purpose had been or could be taken to have been so directed or allowed.

E   LIMITED REFORM

The Charitable Trusts (Validation) Act 1954[246] provided retrospective validation for instruments coming into effect before 16 December, 1952,[247] where, 'consistently with the terms of the [trust] provision, the property could be used exclusively for charitable purposes, but could nevertheless be used for purposes which are not charitable'. The

---

[246] (1954) 18 Conv (NS) 532; (1962) 26 Conv (NS) 200 (S.G. Maurice).

[247] The date of the publication of the Report of the Committee on the Law and Practice relating to Charitable Trusts (1952 Cmd. 8710), see Chapter 14.

Act is complex, and produced much litigation.[248] It has no application upon trusts coming into effect after 15 December, 1952. More comprehensive legislation has been enacted in some Commonwealth countries.[249]

[248] *Vernon v IRC* [1956] 1 WLR 1169; *Re Gillingham Bus Disaster Fund* [1959] Ch 62; (1958) 74 LQR 190, 489 (P.S. Atiyah); (1959) CLJ 41 (S.J. Bailey); *Re Wykes* [1961] Ch 229; *Re Mead's Trust Deed* [1961] 1 WLR 1244; *Re Harpur's Will Trusts* [1962] Ch 78; *Re Chitty's Will Trusts* [1970] Ch 254; *Re South Place Ethical Society* [1980] 1 WLR 1565 [p. 466, above] (imperfect trust provision validated); *Ulrich v Treasury Solicitor* [2005] EWHC 67 (Ch), [2005] 1 All ER 1059; [2005] All ER Rev 274 (P.J. Clarke). The trust in *Williams' Trustees v IRC* [1947] AC 447 [p. 491, above], was eventually saved by the Act and registered by the Charity Commissioners in 1977; Annual Report for 1977, paras. 71–80.

[249] (New South Wales) Conveyancing Act 1919–1954, s.37D; (New Zealand) Trustee Act 1956, s.82; (Victoria) Property Law Act 1958, s.131; (Western Australia) Trustee Act 1962, s.102; (1940) 14 *Australian Law Journal* 58; (1946) 62 LQR 23; (1950) 24 *Australian Law Journal* 239 (E.H. Coghill); (1967) 16 ICLQ 464 (M.C. Cullity); (1973) 47 *Australian Law Journal* 68 (I.J. Hardingham); Charities Act (Northern Ireland) 1964, s.24.

11

CHARITABLE TRUSTS: FAILURE OF PURPOSES

I *CY-PRÈS*[1]

A GENERAL

If it should be impossible or impracticable to apply funds for the precise charitable purpose intended by the donor, the question arises whether the trust should fail or whether the funds should be applied for a slightly different charitable purpose.[2] Where the *cy-près* doctrine operates it makes possible the application of funds to purposes as near as possible to those selected by the donor.

Before the Charities Act 1960 came into force, the *cy-près* doctrine could only be applied if it was 'impossible or impracticable' to carry out the purposes of the trust. Although the word 'impossible' was widely construed, this requirement caused a number of difficulties; for nothing could be done in cases where the continued administration of the trust was highly inconvenient, but not 'impossible'; nor where, perhaps

---

[1] H&M, pp. 450–464; Luxton, pp. 543–601; P&M, pp. 482–493; P&S, pp. 568–579; Pettit, pp. 325–328; Picarda, pp. 295–400; Snell, pp. 530–536; Tudor, pp. 435–489; *Theobald on Wills* (16th edn, 2001) pp. 489–496. See, generally, Sheridan and Delany, *The Cy-près Doctrine* (1959); (1968) 6 *Alberta Law Review* 16; (1972) 1 *Anglo-American Law Review* 101 (L.A. Sheridan); Report of the Committee on the Law and Practice relating to Charitable Trusts (1952 Cmd. 8710), chap. 9; Goodman Report, paras. 188–192; House of Commons Report, vol I, paras. 63–71, vol. II, pp. 122, 177–178, 200–201; (1987) 50 NLJ Annual Charities Review 34 (P. Luxton); Annual Report for 1989, paras. 73–80 [p. 562, below] containing guidelines.

[2] Where gifts were made to a company which had been incorporated to carry out charitable purposes at a time when the company had gone into insolvent liquidation but had not been formally dissolved, the gifts would be valid gifts for the company beneficially unless the company was intended to take the gift as trustee: *Re ARMS (Multiple Sclerosis Research) Ltd* [1997] 1 WLR 877. Presumably, if the company was intended to take the gift as a trustee but was in insolvent liquidation at the time this will constitute an initial failure of the trust. See p. 545, below.

through changes in the needs of society or the value of money, an old charity served no useful purpose in modern times. The whole matter was modernised by the Charities Act 1960, now Charities Act 1993, sections 13 and 14, as amended and expanded by the Charities Act 2006.

Before that matter is examined in detail, however, it will be convenient to look at another requirement for the application of the *cy-près* doctrine, namely that, in a case where the problem arises *at the commencement* of the trust, the language of the instrument must show that there was a paramount charitable intention. There is no such requirement in a case of subsequent failure.

In the case of initial failure, the gift will lapse and result to the donor or to his estate, unless there is, on the construction of the instrument, a paramount intention to benefit charity. In the case of failure after the trust has been in operation, there can be no such resulting trust. As ROMER LJ said in *Re Wright* [1954] Ch 347 at 362:

Once money is effectually dedicated to charity, whether in pursuance of a general or particular charitable intent, the testator's next-of-kin or residuary legatees are for ever excluded.

If, however, the donor wants the property to return to himself or to his estate or to pass to a third party, he must expressly so provide by a gift over to take effect within the perpetuity period.[3]

B INITIAL FAILURE[4]

Where a charitable trust fails at the commencement of the trust, the destiny of the property depends on the width of charitable intent manifested by the donor. If the intention was that the property should be applied to the one purpose or institution selected by the donor, and that alone, then the gift will lapse and will be held on resulting trust for the donor. But if the intention was to benefit charity generally, then the property may be applied *cy-près*.

(i) Width of Charitable Intent

Re Rymer
[1895] 1 Ch 19 (CA, **Lord Herschell LC, Lindley** and **A.L. Smith LJJ**)

Mr. Rymer bequeathed a legacy of £5,000 'to the rector for the time being of St. Thomas' Seminary for the education of priests in the diocese of Westminster'. The testator died in 1893.

---

[3] *Re Peel's Release* [1921] 2 Ch 218; *Re Randell* (1888) 38 Ch D 213; *Re Cooper's Conveyance Trusts* [1956] 1 WLR 1096; Perpetuities and Accumulations Act 1964, ss.3, 12; Maudsley, *Modern Law of Perpetuities* (1979), p. 190.
[4] See generally (1969) 32 MLR 283 (J.B.E. Hutton).

At the date of the will St. Thomas' Seminary was in existence and provided education for priests for the diocese of Westminster. But at the date of the testator's death,
the seminary ceased to exist, and the students were transferred to a seminary near
Birmingham.

The question was whether the legacy lapsed or whether it should be applied
cy-près.

Held (affirming Chitty J). There being no general charitable intent, the legacy lapsed
and fell into the testator's estate.

Lindley LJ: I think the result at which Mr. Justice Chitty has arrived is right. I have attended
to and followed the arguments both of Mr. *Cozens-Hardy* and of Mr. *Ingle Joyce,* and in a great
many of those arguments I concur. I think, with Mr. *Joyce,* that it does not do to approach a
will of this kind by a short cut by saying there is a lapse, and there is an end of it. It is begging
the question whether there is a lapse or not. You must construe the will and see what the real
object of the language which you have to interpret is. I will not read the words of this gift again;
I have read them very often, and studied them with care. I cannot arrive at the conclusion at
which the Appellant's counsel ask me to arrive, that this is in substance and in truth a bequest of
£5,000 for the education of the priests in the diocese of *Westminster.* I do not think it is. It is a
gift of £5,000 to a particular seminary for the purposes thereof, and I do not think it is possible
to get out of that. I think the context shews it. I refer to the masses, the choice of candidates,
and so on. If once you get thus far the question arises, does that seminary exist? The answer
is, it does not. Then you arrive at the result that there is a lapse; and if there is a lapse, is there
anything in the doctrine of *cy-près* to prevent the ordinary doctrine of lapse from applying? I
think not. Once you arrive at the conclusion that there is a lapse, then all the authorities which
are of any value shew that the residuary legatee takes the lapsed gift. We are asked to overrule
that doctrine, laid down by Vice-Chancellor Kindersley in *Clark v Taylor* (1853) 1 Drew 642 and
followed in *Fisk v A-G* (1867) LR 4 Eq 521. I think that the doctrine is perfectly right. There
may be a difficulty in arriving at the conclusion that there is a lapse. But when once you arrive at
the conclusion that a gift to a particular seminary or institution, or whatever you may call it, is
'for the purposes thereof', and for no other purpose—if you once get to that, and it is proved that
the institution or seminary, or whatever it is, has ceased to exist in the lifetime of the testator,
you are driven to arrive at the conclusion that there is a lapse, and then the doctrine of *cy-près*
is inapplicable. That is in accordance with the law, and in accordance with all the cases that can
be cited. I quite agree that in coming to that conclusion you have to consider whether the mode
of attaining the object is only machinery, or whether the mode is not the substance of the gift.
Here it appears to me the gift to the seminary is the substance of the whole thing. It is the object
of the testator. I think that is plain from the language used.

Those are the short grounds of my judgment. I do not comment upon the decisions, because
the Lord Chancellor has done that sufficiently.[5]

In **Re Wilson** [1913] 1 Ch 314, a testator, who died in 1870, provided a sum of money
as a salary for a schoolmaster, who was to teach at a school to be erected by voluntary

---

[5] *Re Crowe* (1979) unreported; Annual Report for 1979 paras. 40–45, where SLADE J found no general
charitable intention in the case of a trust for a scholarship at the Royal Naval School in the Spanish and
Russian languages. 'The court could not construct a general charitable intention from mere guess work.'

subscriptions from landowners in the neighbourhood. There was no reasonable likelihood of such a school being established.

PARKER J was unable to find any general charitable intent. The particular purpose failed, and the gift fell into residue.

In **Re Packe** [1918] 1 Ch 437, the testatrix gave to the Poor Clergy Relief Corporation a cottage and £1,000 upon trust to provide 'a holiday home or house of rest for clergymen of the Church of England and their wives'; and provided that, if the Corporation should refuse the gift, then the property was to be given to any other society selected by her executors 'as a holiday home or house of rest for ladies or gentlemen of limited means'. The Corporation renounced the gift, and it was not possible to find any other society willing to carry out the wishes of the testatrix. NEVILLE J held that the gift failed.

In **Re Good's Will Trusts** [1950] 2 All ER 653, the testator provided funds for the purpose of purchasing land, erecting thereon 'six or more rest homes each home consisting of a living room, sleeping apartment and usual outside domestic conveniences, all to be on the ground floor and all on one level', and money for paying for the upkeep of the homes. The money was insufficient for the purpose. WYNN-PARRY J held that the language was so particular as to exclude the possibility of finding a general charitable intention. The gift failed.

Biscoe v Jackson

(1887) 35 Ch D 460 (CA, **Cotton, Lindsey** and **Fry LJJ**)

A testator provided that his trustees should set aside, out of such of his personal estate as might by law be bequeathed for charitable purposes, a sum of £10,000, of which £4,000 was to be applied 'in the establishment of a soup kitchen for the parish of *Shoreditch*, and of a cottage hospital adjoining thereto ...' and the provision of various related services. It was impossible to obtain the land necessary to carry out the provisions of the will. The next of kin claimed the fund.

Held. The will showed a general charitable intention. A scheme for the application of the funds *cy-près* was directed.

Cotton LJ: This is an appeal from an order made in November by Mr. Justice *Kay*, which directed a reference to settle a scheme to apply a sum of £10,000. For the purpose of this appeal we must assume that the bequest contained in the will could not be carried into effect in accordance with the particular directions contained in the will as was found by the certificate. That certificate was excepted to, and Mr. Justice *Kay* disallowed the exception. For the present purpose the Attorney-General does not press his appeal against the decision of Mr. Justice *Kay*. The real question, therefore, is whether or not the Court can, in a legacy like this, apply the doctrine of *cy-près*? It is clear that when there is a legacy given to a particular legatee, and that legatee fails before the death of the testator—there being only the gift to the particular legatee, even though that legatee is an institution—the legacy fails. But the question which we have now to consider is this, is this to be considered as a legacy to a particular institution which cannot be carried into effect, or do we see here an expressed intention by the testator to benefit the poor of the parish of *Shoreditch,* pointing out a particular mode in which he desires that benefit to be effected? For if the latter be the true view, then if that particular mode cannot have effect given to it, the Court will take hold of the charitable intention to benefit the poor of the parish and will apply the legacy in the best way *cy-près* for their benefit.

Now, in my opinion, notwithstanding the argument which has been addressed to us, I think there is that general intention. It is very true that the testator leaves certain things to be done by the trustees to whom he is giving the sum of £10,000, and if that is to be considered as a gift to an existing institution, or as a gift for that purpose only, it has failed. But then, in my opinion, looking at this whole clause, we see an intention on the part of the testator to give £10,000 to the sick and poor of the parish of *Shoreditch,* pointing out how he desires that to be applied; and that particular mode having failed, as we must for the purposes of this appeal assume to be the case, then the intention to benefit the poor of *Shoreditch,* being a good charitable object, will have effect given to it according to the general principle laid down long ago by this Court, by applying it *cy-près.* If the will had said that the trustees must build the particular building within the parish of *Shoreditch* there might be some difficulty, but what the testator desires to do is to provide a particular kind of hospital and a soup kitchen for the poor of the parish of *Shoreditch.* To my mind that shows that he intends not that it is to be located in a particular place, though that would be a proper mode of giving effect to the particular directions contained, if a place in the parish could be found; but that it is for the benefit of the parish, that is of the poor in the parish of *Shoreditch.* The testator directs that this shall be done by providing them with soup in this kitchen, by providing them with relief in a cottage hospital, and then by a direction that there is to be a woman living in the hospital to look after the inmates in the hospital, and that a sum of money is to be paid to a medical man to attend to them; and then he directs his trustees 'to apply the residue of such annual income towards the necessities and for the benefit thereof, and of the patients who shall from time to time be taken into such hospital in such manner in all respects as my trustees or trustee in their or his absolute discretion think fit'. Of course we have to determine what is the effect, looking fairly at the words used by the testator, to see what his intention was. To my mind the clear result is that he intended here to provide for the benefit of the poor, which is a good charitable bequest, and to provide for that primarily in the particular way he points out. If that fails then the doctrine applies, and Mr. Justice *Kay* was right in directing a reference to ascertain what was the best means for giving effect to his intentions, having regard to what the testator has said in the will as to the particular mode in which he desires his intentions should have effect given to them. In my opinion this appeal must fail; and that being our decision the other appeal is of course abandoned by the Attorney-General.

(ii) *Defunct or Non-Existent Charity*

In **Re Harwood** [1936] Ch 285, a testatrix, by a will made in 1925, left *inter alia* £200 to the Wisbech Peace Society, Cambridge, and £300 to the Peace Society of Belfast. She died in 1934. The Wisbech Peace Society had existed before 1934 but had ceased to exist by that date; there was no evidence that the Peace Society of Belfast had ever existed. FARWELL J held the second legacy was applicable *cy-près*, but not the first legacy. He said at 286:

The first question that I have to determine is whether a gift of 200l. 'to the Wisbech Peace Society, Cambridge' fails. The evidence is that this particular society ceased to exist in the testatrix's lifetime. It is said that it is being still carried on as part of the work of the Peace Committee of the Society of Friends. The onus is upon them to show that they are the persons entitled to take. The evidence in this case is so unsatisfactory that I cannot say that that onus has been discharged.

That leaves the question whether there is any general charitable intent, so as to admit of the application of the *cy-près* doctrine. In that will there is a long list of various charitable societies including charities whose work is devoted to peace. It is said that as this is one of a long list of charitable legacies there is a general charitable intent. On the other hand, it is said that where there is a gift to a particular society, which once existed but ceased to exist before the death of the testator or testatrix, the gift lapses and there is no room for the *cy-près* doctrine. I have been referred to *Re Davis* [1902] 1 Ch 876. In that case the learned judge was able to come to the conclusion that as to one particular gift there was a general charitable intent; but in that case no such society as that named in the will had ever existed. It was not a case of a society which had been in existence and had ceased to exist. I do not propose to decide that it can never be possible for the Court to hold that there is a general charitable intent in a case where the charity named in the will once existed but ceased to exist before the death. Without deciding that, it is enough for me to say that, where the testator selects as the object of his bounty a particular charity and shows in the will itself some care to identify the particular society which he desires to benefit, the difficulty of finding any general charitable intent in such case if the named society once existed, but ceased to exist before the death of the testator, is very great. Here the testatrix has gone out of her way to identify the object of her bounty. In this particular case she has identified it as being 'the Wisbech Peace Society Cambridge (which is a branch of the London Peace Society)'. Under those circumstances, I do not think it is open to me to hold that there is in this case any such general charitable intent as to allow the application of the *cy-près* doctrine.

Accordingly, in my judgment, the legacy of 200*l.* fails and is undisposed of.

Then there is the gift to the 'Peace Society of Belfast'.

The claimant for this legacy is the Belfast Branch of the League of Nations Union. I am quite unable on the evidence to say that that was the society which this lady intended to benefit, and I doubt whether the lady herself knew exactly what society she did mean to benefit. I think she had a desire to benefit any society which was formed for the purpose of promoting peace and was connected with Belfast. Beyond that, I do not think that she had any very clear idea in her mind. That is rather indicated by the pencil note which was found after her death. At any rate I cannot say that by the description, 'the Peace Society of Belfast', the lady meant the Belfast Branch of the League of Nations Union; but there is enough in this case to enable me to say that, although there is no gift to any existing society, the gift does not fail. It is a good charitable gift and must be applied *cy-près*. The evidence suggests that at some time or other, possibly before the late War, there may have been a society called the Peace Society of Belfast. It is all hearsay evidence; there is nothing in the least definite about it, and it does not satisfy me that there ever was any society in existence which exactly fits the description in this case, and there being a clear intention on the part of the lady, as expressed in her will, to benefit societies whose object was the promotion of peace, and there being no such society as that named in her will, in this case there is a general charitable intent, and, accordingly, the doctrine of *cy-près* applies.

In **Re Spence** [1979] Ch 483, a testatrix, who made her will in 1968 and died in 1972, left one moiety of her residue to 'the Old Folks Home at Hillworth Lodge Keighley for the benefit of the patients'. Hillworth Lodge, originally built as a workhouse, had from 1948 to 1971 been an aged persons' home under the National Assistance Act 1948. It was closed down in 1971 and had since then been used as government offices. The question arose whether the gift was a valid charitable gift. MEGARRY V-C held that the gift failed, and said at 492:

[*Re Harwood* [1936] Ch 285 and cases which apply it, such as *Re Stemson's Will Trusts* [1970] Ch 16, [1969] 2 All ER 517] have been concerned with gifts to institutions, rather than gifts for purposes. The case before me, on the other hand, is a gift for a purpose, namely, the benefit of the patients at a particular Old Folks Home. It therefore seems to me that I ought to consider the question, of which little or nothing was said in argument, whether the principle in *Re Harwood,* or a parallel principle, has any application to such case. In other words, is a similar distinction to be made between, on the one hand, a case in which the testator has selected a particular charitable purpose, taking some care to identify it, and before the testator dies that purpose has become impracticable or impossible of accomplishment, and on the other hand a case where the charitable purpose has never been possible or practicable?

As at present advised I would answer Yes to that question. I do not think that the reasoning of the *Re Harwood* line of cases is directed to any feature of institutions as distinct from purposes. Instead, I think the essence of the distinction is in the difference between particularity and generality. If a particular institution or purpose is specified, then it is that institution or purpose, and no other, that is to be the object of the benefaction. It is difficult to envisage a testator as being suffused with a general glow of broad charity when he is labouring, and labouring successfully, to identify some particular specified institution or purpose as the object of his bounty. The specific displaces the general. It is otherwise where the testator has been unable to specify any particular charitable institution or practicable purpose, and so, although his intention of charity can be seen, he has failed to provide any way of giving effect to it. There, the absence of the specific leaves the general undisturbed. It follows that in my view in the case before me, where the testatrix has clearly specified a particular charitable purpose which before her death became impossible to carry out, Mr. Mummery has to face that level of great difficulty in demonstrating the existence of a general charitable intention which was indicated by *Re Harwood*....

From what I have said it follows that I have been quite unable to extract from the will, construed in its context, any expression of a general charitable intention which would suffice for the moiety to be applied *cy-près*. Instead, in my judgment, the moiety was given for a specific charitable purpose which, though possible when the will was made, became impossible before the testatrix died. The gift of the moiety accordingly fails, and it passes as on intestacy.[6]

(iii) Continuation of Charity in Another Form

Although a particular charity no longer exists in its original form, the court may find that it continues elsewhere.

---

[6] See also pp. 554, 556, below; *Re Finger's Will Trusts* [1972] Ch 286 at 299 [p. 552, below].

Re Faraker[7]
[1912] 2 Ch 488 (CA, Cozens-Hardy MR, Farwell and Kennedy LJJ)

Mrs. Faraker, the testatrix, who died in 1911, bequeathed a legacy of £200 to 'Mrs. Bailey's Charity, Rotherhithe'.

A charity, known as Hannah Bayly's Charity, had been founded in 1756 by a Mrs. Hannah Bayly for the benefit of poor widows who were resident in and parishioners of Rotherhithe. A scheme had been made in 1905 by the Charity Commissioners which had consolidated this and a number of charities in Rotherhithe. The funds were to be held upon various trusts for the benefit of the poor of Rotherhithe, no mention being made of widows.

No question was raised as to the spelling of the name Bayly, and it was admitted that the testatrix referred to Hannah Bayly's Charity. The question was whether the legacy lapsed.

Held (reversing Neville J). The consolidated charities were entitled to the legacy.

Farwell LJ: ... Neville J has held that Hannah Bayly's Charity is no longer in existence. If that be so, I ask myself, how did it come to an end? and the answer suggested is, by the scheme of the Charity Commissioners. The jurisdiction given to the Charity Commissioners is given by the [Charitable Trusts] Act of 1860, and they have amongst other authorities the same power that the Court of Chancery had and the Chancery Division has for establishing schemes for the administration of any charity. That administration may, under proper circumstances, be *cy-près*, but the jurisdiction is for the establishment, encouragement, and continuance of a charity—even going beyond the actual words of the will, if there be an impossibility of carrying out literally the trusts—and a jurisdiction to administer *cy-près*. In the present case there is no question of a *cy-près* execution. Nobody suggests that there has been a failure of poor widows in Rotherhithe, and unless and until that happy event happens there will be no case for any *cy-près* administration. What is said is this: the Commissioners have in fact destroyed this trust because in the scheme which they have issued dealing with the amalgamation of the several charities the objects are stated to be poor persons of good character resident in Rotherhithe, not mentioning widows in particular—not of course excluding them, but not giving them that preference which I agree with the Master of the Rolls in thinking ought to have been given. But to say that this omission has incidentally destroyed the Bayly Trust is a very strained construction of the language and one that entirely fails, because the Charity Commissioners had no jurisdiction whatever to destroy the charity. Suppose the Charity Commissioners or this Court were to declare that a particular existing charitable trust was at an end and extinct, in my opinion they would go beyond their jurisdiction in so doing. They cannot take an existing charity and destroy it; they are obliged to administer it. To say that this pardonable slip (I use the word with all respect to the draftsman) has the effect of destroying the charity appears to me extravagant. In all these cases one has to consider not so much the means to the end as the charitable end which is in view, and so long as that charitable end is well established the means are only machinery, and no alteration of the machinery can destroy the charitable trust for the benefit of which the machinery is provided.

7 *Re Lucas* [1948] Ch 424; cf. *Re Stemson's Will Trusts* [1970] Ch 16; *Re Slatter's Will Trusts* [1964] Ch 512; (1964) 28 Conv (NS) 313 (J.T. Farrand).

In my opinion it is quite impossible to say here that the widows are excluded, or even if they were in terms excluded, that that would destroy the trust: it could only give grounds for an application to set right that which in any event could only be put in *per incuriam*. I agree that the appeal must be allowed.

(iv) Unincorporated and Incorporated Charities[8]

In **Re Finger's Will Trusts** [1972] Ch 286,[9] a testatrix left shares of her residuary estate to eleven named charities, of which two were the National Radium Commission, an unincorporated charity, and the National Council for Maternity and Child Welfare, an incorporated charity. Both charities had ceased to exist between the date of the will and the date of death.

GOFF J held that (i) the first gift was valid as a purpose trust and ordered a scheme for its administration; (ii) the second gift failed, but, since there was a general charitable intention, it was applicable *cy-près*. He said at 294:

Both gifts therefore fail unless they can be supported as purpose gifts, in which case they will be applicable by way of scheme for the indicated purpose, and if either or both cannot so stand there remains a final question, whether the will discloses a general charitable intention, in which case of course the share or shares will be applicable by scheme *cy-près*, failing which there is an intestacy.

If the matter were *res integra* I would have thought that there would be much to be said for the view that the status of the donee, whether corporate or unincorporate, can make no difference to the question whether as a matter of construction a gift is absolute or on trust for purposes. Certainly drawing such a distinction produces anomalous results.

In my judgment, however, on the authorities a distinction between the two is well established, at all events in this court. I refer first to *Re Vernon's Will Trusts* [1972] Ch 300n where Buckley J said at 303:

'Every bequest to an unincorporated charity by name without more must take effect as a gift for a charitable purpose. No individual or aggregate of individuals could claim to take such a bequest beneficially. If the gift is to be permitted to take effect at all, it must be as a bequest for a purpose, *viz.*, that charitable purpose which the named charity exists to serve. A bequest which is in terms made for a charitable purpose will not fail for lack of a trustee but will be carried into effect either under the Sign Manual or by means of a scheme. A bequest to a named unincorporated charity, however, may on its true interpretation show that the testator's intention to make the gift at all was dependent upon the named charitable organisation being available at the time when the gift takes effect to serve as the instrument for applying the subject matter of the gift to the charitable purpose for which it is by inference given. If so and the named charity ceases to exist in the lifetime of the testator, the gift fails: *Re Ovey* (1885) 29 Ch D 560. A bequest to a corporate body, on the other hand, takes effect simply as a gift to that body beneficially,

---

[8] For the difference between an unincorporated and an incorporated association, see p. 378, above.

[9] (1972) 36 Conv (NS) 198 (R.B.M. Cotterrell); (1974) 38 Conv (NS) 187 (J. Martin); *Re Edis's Declaration of Trust* [1972] 1 WLR 1135; *Re Koeppler Will Trusts* [1986] Ch 423 [pp. 448, 524, above]. See also *Liverpool and District Hospital for Diseases of the Heart v A-G* [1981] Ch 193; [1984] Conv 112 (J. Warburton).

unless there are circumstances which show that the recipient is to take the gift as a trustee. There is no need in such a case to infer a trust for any particular purpose. The objects to which the corporate body can properly apply its funds may be restricted by its constitution, but this does not necessitate inferring as a matter of construction of the testator's will a direction that the bequest is to be held in trust to be applied for those purposes: the natural construction is that the bequest is made to the corporate body as part of its general funds, that is to say, beneficially and without the imposition of any trust. That the testator's motive in making the bequest may have undoubtedly been to assist the work of the incorporated body would be insufficient to create a trust.'

As I read the dictum in *Re Vernon's Will Trusts,* the view of Buckley J was that in the case of an unincorporated body the gift is *per se* a purpose trust, and provided that the work is still being carried on will have effect given to it by way of scheme notwithstanding the disappearance of the donee in the lifetime of the testator, unless there is something positive to show that the continued existence of the donee was essential to the gift. Then Buckley J put his dictum into practice and decided *Re Morrison* (1967) 111 Sol Jo 758 on that very basis, for there was nothing in that case beyond the bare fact of a gift to a dissolved unincorporated committee. In the case of a corporation, however, *Re Vernon* shows that the position is different as there has to be something positive in the will to create a purpose trust at all.

[His Lordship referred to *Re Meyers* [1951] Ch 534; *Re Roberts* [1963] 1 WLR 406; and *Re Morrison* (1967) 111 Sol Jo 758, and continued:] Accordingly I hold that the bequest to the National Radium Commission being a gift to an unincorporated charity is a purpose trust for the work of the commission which does not fail but is applicable under a scheme, provided (1) there is nothing in the context of the will to show—and I quote from *Re Vernon's Will Trusts*—that the testatrix's intention to make a gift at all was dependent upon the named charitable organisation being available at the time when the gift took effect to serve as the instrument for applying the subject matter of the gift to the charitable purpose for which it was by inference given; (2) *that* charitable purpose still survives; but that the gift to the National Council for Maternity and Child Welfare, 117 Piccadilly, London being a gift to a corporate body fails, notwithstanding the work continues, unless there is a context in the will to show that the gift was intended to be on trust for that purpose and not an absolute gift to the corporation.

I take first the National Radium Commission and I find in this will no context whatever to make that body of the essence of the gift....

In my judgment, therefore, this is a valid gift for the purposes of the Radium Commission as specified in article 7 of the supplemental charter of 20 July, 1939, and I direct that a scheme be settled for the administration of the gift.

I turn to the other gift and here I can find no context from which to imply a purpose trust. Counsel for the Attorney-General relied on *Re Meyers* [1951] Ch 534, but there the context was absolutely compelling. There were many gifts to hospitals and the case dealt only with the hospitals, and whilst hospitals are not identical, this did mean that all were of the same type and character. Moreover, not only were those gifts both to incorporated and unincorporated hospitals but in some of the corporate cases the name used by the testator was that by which the hospital was generally known to the public but was not the exact title of the corporation. In the present case there are at best three different groups of charities not one; they are not in fact grouped in the order in which they appear in the will, and the particular donees within the respective groups are not all of the same type or character. Further, and worse, two do not fit into any grouping at all, and for what it is worth they come first in the list. In my judgment, therefore, this case is not comparable with *Re Meyers* and I cannot find a context unless I am prepared—which I am not—to say that the mere fact that residue is given to a number of charities, some of which are incorporated and others not, is of itself a sufficient context to fasten a purpose trust on the corporation.

In my judgment, therefore, the bequest to the National Council for Maternity and Child Welfare fails.

Finally, I must consider, however, whether the share passes on intestacy or whether the will discloses a general charitable intention. Here, of course, I was at once presented with *Re Harwood* [1936] Ch 285 [p. 548, above], and I feel the force of the argument on behalf of the next-of-kin based on that case, although I confess I have always felt the decision in that case to be rather remarkable. However, Farwell J did not say that it was impossible to find a general charitable intention where there is a gift to an identifiable body which has ceased to exist but only that it would be very difficult. Moreover, I observe that in *Re Roberts* [1963] 1 WLR 406, 416, Wilberforce J said this about *Re Harwood:*

'Lastly, there is *Re Harwood,* a decision of Farwell J, where there was a gift to a very particular society for a very special purpose, the Wisbech Peace Society, where it was not difficult to come to the conclusion that that society having disappeared, the gift lapsed. Though of course I accept—and gladly accept—what Farwell J said, that where the gift is to a particular charity carefully identified it would be very difficult for the court to find a general charitable intent if the named society had ceased to exist at the testator's death, one must consider that in relation to the circumstance of the charity and the information which can be found whether in fact the particular charity has ceased to exist.'

In the present case the circumstances are very special. First, of course, apart from the life interest given to the mother and two small personal legacies, the whole estate is devoted to charity and that is, I think, somewhat emphasised by the specific dedication to charity in the preface:

'and after payment of the said legacies my trustees shall hold the balance then remaining of my residuary estate upon trust to divide the same in equal shares between the following charitable institutions and funds.'

Again, I am I think entitled to take into account the nature of the council, which as I have said was mainly, if not exclusively, a co-ordinating body. I cannot believe that this testatrix meant to benefit that organisation and that alone.

Finally, I am entitled to place myself in the armchair of the testatrix and I have evidence that she regarded herself as having no relatives.

Taking all these matters into account, in my judgment I can and ought to distinguish *Re Harwood* and find—as I do—a general charitable intention. Accordingly, this share is applicable *cy-près,* and I understand the Attorney-General is willing that it should be paid to the association. That seems to me manifestly the proper thing to do, and therefore I shall order by way of scheme, the Attorney-General not objecting, that this share be paid to the proper officer of the association to be held on trust to apply the same for its general purposes.

In **Re Spence** [1979] Ch 483 [p. 549, above], MEGARRY V-C, in holding that there was no general charitable intent, distinguished *Re Finger's Will Trusts.* He referred to the three 'very special circumstances' mentioned by Goff J in respect of the gift to the incorporated charity, and said at 493:

In the case before me neither of these last two circumstances applies, nor have any substitute special circumstances been suggested. As for the first, the will before me gives 17 pecuniary legacies to relations and friends, amounting in all to well over one-third of the net estate. Further, in *Re Rymer* [1895] 1 Ch 19, which does not appear to have been cited, the will had prefaced the disputed gift by the words 'I give the following charitable legacies to the following institutions and persons respectively'. These words correspond to the direction which in *Re Finger's Will Trusts* was regarded as providing emphasis, and yet they did not suffice to avoid the conclusion of Chitty J and the Court of Appeal that a gift to an institution which had ceased to exist before the testator's death lapsed and could not be applied *cy-près*. I am not sure that I have been able to appreciate to the full the cogency of the special circumstances that appealed to Goff J; but however that may be, I can see neither those nor any other special circumstances in the present case which would suffice to distinguish *Re Harwood*.

(v) Charity by Association

In **Re Jenkins's Will Trusts** [1966] Ch 249, the testatrix bequeathed her residuary estate to be divided into seven equal parts, one of which was to be held in trust for six charitable institutions and the seventh in trust for 'the British Union for the Abolition of Vivisection to do all in its power to urge and get an Act passed prohibiting unnecessary cruelty to animals'. The question was whether the seventh share should be held upon charitable trusts on the ground that the will disclosed a general charitable intention. BUCKLEY J held that the gift of the seventh share failed. He said at 256:

The principle of *noscitur a sociis* does not in my judgment entitle one to overlook self-evident facts. If you meet seven men with black hair and one with red hair you are not entitled to say that here are eight men with black hair. Finding one gift for a non-charitable purpose among a number of gifts for charitable purposes the court cannot infer that the testator or testatrix meant the non-charitable gift to take effect as a charitable gift when in the terms it is not charitable, even though the non-charitable gift may have a close relation to the purposes for which the charitable gifts are made.

In **Re Satterthwaite's Will Trusts**[10] [1966] 1 WLR 277, the testatrix announced to an official of the Bond Street branch of the Midland Bank that she hated the whole human race and wished to leave her estate to animal charities. Nine were selected, apparently from the London telephone directory. Seven of them were animal charities, and the other two were an anti-vivisectionist society and the London Animal Hospital. It was not possible to identify an institution of that name which was in existence at the date of the will. The Court of Appeal (Harman, Diplock and Russell LJJ) held that the share for the hospital was to be applied *cy-près*. RUSSELL LJ said at 286:

What is the result in law of this? I have already indicated that [the testatrix] is to be taken as intending to benefit a charitable activity. But the organisation picked by name was not such.

---

[10] Decided twelve days earlier than, but apparently not cited in, *Re Jenkins's Will Trusts* [above].

Prima facie, therefore, the bequest would fail and there would be a lapse, with the result in this case in fact—owing to the incidence of liabilities and death duties—of mere relief of other residuary objects. But my assumption is that the testatrix was pointing to a particular charitable application of this one-ninth of residue. If a particular mode of charitable application is incapable of being performed as such, but it can be discerned from his will that the testator has a charitable intention (commonly referred to as a general charitable intention) which transcends the particular mode of application indicated, the court has jurisdiction to direct application of the bequest to charitable purposes *cy-près.* Here I have no doubt from the nature of the other dispositions by this testatrix of her residuary estate that a general intention can be discerned in favour of charity through the medium of kindness to animals. I am not in any way deterred from this conclusion by the fact that one-ninth of residue was given to an anti-vivisection society which in law—unknown to the average testator—is not charitable.

In **Re Spence** [1979] Ch 483 [p. 549, above], MEGARRY V-C held that the doctrine of charity by association was not applicable and said at 494:

The other way in which Mr. Mummery sought to meet his difficulty was by relying on *Re Satterthwaite's Will Trusts* (which he said was his best case), and on *Re Knox* [1937] Ch 109, which I think may possibly be better. The doctrine may for brevity be described as charity by association. If the will gives the residue among a number of charities with kindred objects, but one of the apparent charities does not in fact exist, the court will be ready to find a general charitable intention and so apply the share of the non-existent charity *cy-près.* I have not been referred to any explicit statement of the underlying principle, but it seems to me that in such cases the court treats the testator as having shown the general intention of giving his residue to promote charities with that type of kindred objects, and then, when he comes to dividing the residue, as casting around for particular charities with that type of objects to name as donees. If one or more of these are non-existent, then the general intention will suffice for a *cy-près* application. It will be observed that, as stated, the doctrine depends, at least to some extent, upon the detection of 'kindred objects' (a phrase which comes from the judgment of Luxmoore J in *Re Knox* at 113) in the charities to which the shares of residue are given; in this respect the charities must in some degree be *ejusdem generis.*

[His Lordship referred to *Re Satterthwaite's Will Trusts, Re Knox,* and *Re Hartley* (1978) unreported, and continued:] It will be observed that these are all cases of gifts to bodies which did not exist. In such cases, the court is ready to find a general charitable intention: see *Re Davis* [1902] 1 Ch 876, especially at 884. The court is far less ready to find such an intention where the gift is to a body which existed at the date of the will but ceased to exist before the testator died, or, as I have already held, where the gift is for a purpose which, though possible and practicable at the date of the will, has ceased to be so before the testator's death. The case before me is, of course, a case in this latter category, so that Mr. Mummery has to overcome this greater difficulty in finding a general charitable intention.

Not only does Mr. Mummery have this greater difficulty: he also has, I think, less material with which to meet it. He has to extract the general charitable intention for the gift which fails from only one other gift: the residue, of course, was simply divided into two. In *Re Knox* and *Re Hartley* the gifts which failed were each among three other gifts, and in *Re Satterthwaite's Will Trusts* there were seven or eight other gifts. I do not say that a general charitable intention or a genus cannot be extracted from a gift of residue equally between two: but I do say that larger numbers are likely to assist in conveying to the court a sufficient conviction both of the genus and of the generality of the charitable intention.

C SUBSEQUENT FAILURE[11]

As has been seen, once money is absolutely and effectively dedicated to charity, the next-of-kin are for ever excluded. Thus, *cy-près* may apply even if a general charitable intention is lacking.

Re Slevin
[1891] 2 Ch 236 (CA, **Lindley, Bowen** and **Kay LJJ**)

The testator by his will bequeathed 'the pecuniary legacies following', one of which was a legacy of £200 to the Orphanage of St. Dominic's, Newcastle-on-Tyne. That Orphanage was in existence at the testator's death; but it came to an end soon afterwards, and before the legacy was paid.

Held (reversing Stirling J). The money was applicable *cy-près*.

Kay LJ: The orphanage did come to an end before the legacy was paid over. In the case of a legacy to an individual, if he survived the testator it could not be argued that the legacy would fall into the residue. Even if the legatee died intestate and without next-of-kin, still the money was his, and the residuary legatee would have no right whatever against the Crown. So, if the legatee were a corporation which was dissolved after the testator's death, the residuary legatee would have no claim.

Obviously it can make no difference that the legatee ceased to exist immediately after the death of the testator. The same law must be applicable whether it was a day, or month, or year, or, as might well happen, ten years after; the legacy not having been paid either from delay occasioned by the administration of the estate or owing to part of the estate not having been got in. The legacy became the property of the legatee upon the death of the testator, though he might not, for some reason, obtain the receipt of it till long after. When once it became the absolute property of the legatee, that is equivalent to saying that it must be provided for; and the residue is only what remains after making such provision. It does not for all purposes cease to be part of the testator's estate until the executors admit assets and appropriate and pay it over; but that is merely for their convenience and that of the estate. The rights as between the particular legatee and the residue are fixed at the testator's death.

These positions are so obvious that it would seem impossible to dispute some authority to the contrary. Is there any such authority?

[Having found no such authority, his Lordship continued:] In the present case we think that the Attorney-General must succeed, not on the ground that there is such a general charitable intention that the fund should be administered *cy-près* even if the charity had failed in the testator's lifetime, but because, as the charity existed at the testator's death, this legacy became the property of that charity, and on its ceasing to exist its property falls to be administered by the Crown, who will apply it, according to custom, for some analogous purpose of charity: *A-G v Ironmongers' Co* (1834) 2 My & K 576; *Wilson v Barnes* (1886) 38 Ch D 507; *Tyssen on Charitable Bequests* (at p. 440).

---

[11] See generally [1983] Conv 107 (P. Luxton).

In **Re Wright**[12] [1954] Ch 347, the testatrix, who died in 1933, provided that her residuary estate, subject to a life interest, should be held on trust to provide and maintain a convalescent home. This would have been practicable in 1933. But, on the death of the life tenant in 1942, the balance of probabilities was against it. The question was whether the test of practicability should be applied at the date of the testatrix's death or at the date when the funds became available. The Court of Appeal (Denning and Romer LJJ), following *Re Slevin* [1891] 2 Ch 236, held that the material date was that of the death of the testatrix. ROMER LJ said at 359:

Mr. Dillon's argument, on behalf of the testatrix's next-of-kin, was to the effect that the gift in the will was for a special charitable purpose: namely, for the establishment and maintenance of the convalescent home which the testatrix had in mind and which she described with such particularity; and that the gift was dependent and conditional upon it being practicable to carry the purpose, as so described, into effect when the death of the life tenant, Mrs. Webb, made the fund available for the home. It is not so much a question of lapse, he said, as a condition of practicability being attached to the gift, so that if the condition could not be satisfied the bequest would fail. Mr. Buckley, on the other hand, contended that no such condition or contingency as suggested attached to the bequest. He argued that in the case of any charitable gift by will, whether immediate or future, no question of impracticability supervening after the testator's death is of any materiality, provided that the object or purpose to which the gift is to be applied is practicable when the testator died. That is the time, he argued, when the rights of the parties, charity on the one hand and the next-of-kin or other persons taking in default on the other, are to be ascertained and they are to be ascertained at that time once and for all.

In the present case Roxburgh J followed, on the point now under consideration, his earlier decision in *Re Moon* [1948] 1 All ER 300. In that case a testator directed that after the death of his wife his trustees should pay a legacy of '£3,000 to the Trustees of the Gloucester Street Wesleyan Methodist Church at Devonport on trust to invest the same in some Government security and to apply the income thereof to mission work in the district served by the said Gloucester Street Wesleyan Methodist Church including particularly John Street and Moon Street'. When the testator's widow died, it had become impracticable to carry out the mission work which the testator envisaged. Roxburgh J held that the gift was charitable and held further that, although the legacy was a future legacy, the question whether or not the charitable purpose lapsed for impracticability had to be ascertained at the moment when the charity trustees became absolutely entitled to the legacy, that was, at the moment of the testator's death and not at the moment when it became payable. The judge was guided to this conclusion by the reasoning of the judgment of this court in *Re Slevin* [1891] 2 Ch 236, which was delivered by Kay LJ. The testator in that case bequeathed, amongst other 'charitable legacies', a legacy to an orphanage which was in existence at the time of the testator's death but which was discontinued before his assets had been administered and therefore before the legacy was or properly could be paid. The question was whether, in those circumstances, the legacy failed and fell into residue. In the course of the argument Kay LJ rhetorically asked at 237; ... 'where the charity, the legatee, is in existence at the death of the testator, and has received, or might have received the legacy, does not the legacy by that very fact become impressed with charity which the residuary legatee cannot get rid of?' The judgment of the court gave an affirmative answer to that question.

[12] *Re Tacon* [1958] Ch 447; *Harris v Sharp* (1987) unreported; [1988] Conv 288 (D. Partington).

In **Re King** [1923] 1 Ch 243, a testatrix left residue for the purpose of providing a stained-glass window in the church of Irminster to the memory of herself and her relatives. The net residue was £1,094 14*s*. 4*d*. and the estimate for the window was between £750 and £800. ROMER J held that the whole residue had been dedicated to charity and directed that the surplus be applied *cy-près*. He said at 246:

In cases of a gift to a charitable institution, where such institution ceases to exist before the death of the testator the *cy-près* doctrine does not apply unless a general charitable intention can be found, and it is contended by the next-of-kin that there is not any difference between such a case and the present case, where the sum is left over after a particular intention has been fulfilled, there being no general charitable intention shown. But in the case of a legacy to a charitable institution that exists at the death of the testator, but ceases to exist after his death and before the legacy is paid over, the legacy is applied *cy-près*, even in the absence of a general charitable intention: see *Re Slevin* [1891] 2 Ch 236. In *Tyssen's Charitable Bequests*, 2nd edn, p. 202, I find the following statement: 'where a gift is made for a particular charitable purpose which is sufficiently provided for without the gift, the gift will be applied *cy-près*', and various authorities are cited in support of this principle. Such authorities and the other authorities cited to me show that the contention of the Attorney-General is well founded, and I therefore hold that the contention on behalf of the next-of-kin fails, and that the surplus must be applied *cy-près*. The Attorney-General consenting, this surplus will be applied in the erection of a further stained-glass window or windows in the same church.

D ALTERATION OF THE ORIGINAL PURPOSES

Before the enactment of the Charities Act 1960 the *cy-près* doctrine could only be applied if the object of the trust became impossible or impracticable in whole or in part. If it became impossible or impracticable to apply the whole of the fund for the charitable purpose, the surplus might be applied *cy-près*.[13] *Cy-près* application was not available where the fund could be more usefully or conveniently applied for other purposes,[14] nor where the objects were outmoded in the sense that they concerned purposes which were once of significance, but which are unrelated to present conditions; or for purposes for which other sources of provision exist. In order to move with the times, the test of impossibility or impracticability was given an increasingly wide construction.[15]

---

[13] See, for example, *A-G v City of London* (1790) 3 Bro CC 171 (trust for 'the advancement and propagation of the Christian religion among the Infidels in Virginia' could be applied *cy-près* since there were no longer infidels); *Ironmongers' Co v A-G* (1844) 10 Cl & Fin 908; *Re Robinson* [1923] 2 Ch 332 (requiring preacher to wear a black gown in an evangelical church was impracticable); *Re Dominion Students' Hall Trust* [1947] Ch 183 (confining benefit of charity to Dominion students 'of European origin' fell within a broad description of impossibility); *Re Lysaght* [1966] Ch 191 (deletion of religious disqualification attached to a gift to the Royal College of Surgeons).

[14] See, for example, *Re Weir Hospital* [1910] 2 Ch 124 (use of property as a hospital even though it was not a suitable site).

[15] See, especially, *Re Dominion Students' Hall Trust* [1947] Ch 183.

The Nathan Committee[16] recommended the relaxation of the requirements of impracticability. Far-reaching reforms were introduced by the Charities Act 1960, now section 13 of the Charities Act 1993, as amended by the Charities Act 2006.

CHARITIES ACT 1993 (as amended by Charities Act 2006, s. 15)

13. Occasions for applying property *cy-près*.[17]

(1) Subject to subsection (2) below, the circumstances in which the original purposes of a charitable gift can be altered to allow the property given or part of it to be applied *cy-près* shall be as follows:—

(a) where the original purposes, in whole or in part,—

(i) have been as far as may be fulfilled; or

(ii) cannot be carried out, or not according to the directions given and to the spirit of the gift;[18] or

(b) where the original purposes provided a use for part only of the property available by virtue of the gift;[19] or

(c) where the property available by virtue of the gift and other property applicable for similar purposes can be more effectively used in conjunction, and to that end can suitably, regard being had to the appropriate considerations, be made applicable to common purposes;[20] or

(d) where the original purposes were laid down by reference to an area which then was but has since ceased to be a unit for some other purpose, or by reference to a class of persons or to an area which has for any reason since ceased to be suitable, regard being had to the appropriate considerations, or to be practical in administering the gift;[21] or

(e) where the original purposes, in whole or in part, have, since they were laid down—

(i) been adequately provided for by other means; or

(ii) ceased, as being useless or harmful to the community or for other reasons, to be in law charitable;[22] or

---

[16] Report of the Committee on the Law and Practice relating to Charitable Trusts (1952 Cmd. 8710), para. 365.

[17] See Annual Report for 1970, paras. 37–46; 1989, paras. 73–80 [p. 561, below].

[18] See *Re Robinson* [1923] 2 Ch 332; *Re Dominion Students' Hall Trust* [1947] Ch 183; *Re Lysaght* [1966] Ch 191.   [19] See *Re North Devon and West Somerset Relief Fund* [1953] 1 WLR 1260.

[20] For the previous powers concerning amalgamation, see Trustee Act 1925, s. 57; *Re Harvey* [1941] 3 All ER 284.

[21] *Peggs v Lamb* [1994] Ch 172 (gift for benefit of freemen of ancient borough of Huntingdon, whose qualifying members had been substantially reduced to 15, and whose income had been increased to £13,700 each; scheme ordered to enlarge class to cover inhabitants of borough as a whole).

[22] See *National Anti-Vivisection Society v IRC* [1948] AC 31. In 1993 the Charity Commissioners ruled that, as there had been a radical change in circumstances relating to shooting, the activities pursued by rifle and pistol clubs could no longer be regarded as charitable: Decisions of the Charity Commissioners (1993), p. 4.

(iii) ceased in any other way to provide a suitable and effective method of using the property available by virtue of the gift, regard being had to the appropriate considerations.[23]

(1A) In subsection (1) above 'the appropriate considerations' means—

(a) (on the one hand) the spirit of the gift concerned, and

(b) (on the other) the social and economic circumstances prevailing at the time of the proposed alteration of the original purposes.[24]

(2) Subsection (1) above shall not affect the conditions which must be satisfied in order that property given for charitable purposes may be applied *cy-près*, except in so far as those conditions require a failure of the original purposes.

(3) References in the foregoing subsections to the original purposes of a gift shall be construed, where the application of the property given has been altered or regulated by a scheme or otherwise, as referring to the purposes for which the property is for the time being applicable.

(4) Without prejudice to the power to make schemes in circumstances falling within subsection (1) above, the court may by scheme made under the court's jurisdiction with respect to charities, in any case where the purposes for which the property is held are laid down by reference to any such area as is mentioned in the first column in Schedule 3[25] to this Act, provide for enlarging the area to any such area as is mentioned in the second column in the same entry in that Schedule.

(5) It is hereby declared that a trust for charitable purposes places a trustee under a duty, where the case permits and requires the property or some part of it to be applied *cy-près*, to secure its effective use for charity by taking steps to enable it to be so applied.[26]

Report of the Charity Commissioners for England and Wales for the year 1970, paras. 42–43

42.   The relaxation of the rule relating to failure has enabled us over the last 10 years to assist many charities which wish to serve the local community in more modern and effective ways. As we have indicated above, this process had started 100 years before the Charities Act; but many of the schemes which our predecessors made during that time have in their turn grown out-of-date. The process of modifying the objects of charities, whether local or national, is an ever-continuing process. Thus the original terms of a charitable gift of the 18th century or earlier may have required the trustees to distribute to poor persons loaves of bread, candles or particular kinds of clothing. Even by the end of the 19th century many such trusts had failed, but the schemes which we then made prescribed in narrow terms the amounts of income which

---

23 *Re JW Laing Trust* [1984] Ch 143 [p. 568, below]; Annual Report for 1985, App. B.
24 Inserted by Charities Act 2006, s. 15(3).
25 As amended by Local Government Act 1972, s. 210(9)(f).
26 See *National Anti-Vivisection Society v IRC* [1948] AC 31 at 74 *per* Lord Simonds.

could be given in direct grants, or the particular institutions (e.g. a hospital or a clothing club) to which subscriptions might be granted, or the particular purposes (e.g. the cost of an outfit on entering a trade or the provision of passage money to aid emigration) to which contributions might be made. The amount of money which might be granted by way of temporary relief in cases of unexpected loss or sudden destitution was always most carefully limited as our predecessors were concerned lest the indiscriminate distribution of gift by a charity might have the effect of pauperizing the beneficiaries. Only too often neither the terms of the original gift nor the terms of the subsequent scheme appear to us to be achieving the basic intention of the donor, which was usually to make a real contribution towards relieving distress. In such cases we substitute more general provisions allowing the trustees to use the charity's resources in ways which will relieve need in whatever form it may still be found to exist. It is therefore our practice to make the provisions of the scheme as wide as possible, but we also add an explanatory note, which is strictly not part of the scheme, to draw the trustees' attention to those ways which we know of at present in which the income may be usefully applied.

43.   We have made good use of the power contained in section 13(1)(e)(i) which makes it clear that a *cy-près* scheme can be made where the original purposes in whole or in part have, since they have been laid down, been adequately provided for by other means. For example, we have made schemes for a number of charities established for the repair of roads and bridges, substituting for those purposes other general purposes for the benefit of local inhabitants which could include, for instance, the promotion of the arts, the provision of seats or shelters, the preservation of old buildings, or the improvement of local amenities.

Report of the Charity Commissioners for England and Wales for the year 1989, paras. 74–75

74.   The application of the *cy-près* doctrine is a legal process involving the establishment of a scheme. The determination of the new purposes to be conferred is essentially a practical issue in which usefulness and practicality as well as proximity to the existing trusts must be taken into account. In determining the appropriate *cy-près* application, regard must first be had to the trusts of the charity. With these in mind the nearest practicable charitable purpose needs to be ascertained. Consideration must be given to whether that purpose is suitable and effective, bearing in mind the situation of the charity in the community and the needs of that community. If the view is taken that the nearest practical purpose is not suitable or effective, then other purposes may be selected. To choose a purpose which may be the nearest practicable purpose to the original purposes of the charity, but which is already adequately provided for, or which cannot provide a suitable and effective method of using the charity's property, would be to impose purposes which will have already failed within the circumstances laid down in section 13.... Thus, for example, the proceeds of sale of an almshouse or a school might not be appropriated solely for the relief of poverty or for educational purposes respectively if the area of benefit were already adequately provided with poor or educational charities. Similarly, there would be no point in extending the area of benefit of a charity if the adjoining areas to which it might be extended already had adequate provision in the terms of the charity's purposes. Instead, the purposes might be extended within the existing area of benefit. The physical location of the charity within its existing area of benefit might also be a factor in determining a practical *cy-près* application: adjoining areas might not be readily combined with the existing area of benefit.

75.   In determining the new purposes, it is essential not to erect artificial barriers to a flexible use of the doctrine. Factors which are relevant but not overriding should not be rigidly

applied as immutable legal rules or principles. In the course of consultation following the Woodfield Report the following areas were mentioned as giving rise to problems:

(i) The elevation of the Macnaghten classification[27] into a rigid legal definition which creates four distinct and mutually exclusive types of charity.
The Macnaghten classification is not a definition and there is no rule of law which prohibits the charity whose purposes fall within one part of the classification from being schemed so that its new purposes include other areas of the classification. The extent to which a charity's purposes can be altered would depend upon the circumstances pertaining to the charity mentioned in the preceding paragraph. The degree of flexibility which can be applied in altering the purposes of a charity is all the greater when the existing purposes already include elements of more than one part of the classification, for instance trusts for the education of poor persons or a trust for the poor and for the public benefit. Whilst closed schools would normally, on *cy-près* principles, be schemed for educational purposes, there may be cases where the local nature of the trust is clearly present and the circumstances warrant consideration being given to widening the objects rather than altering the area of benefit.

(ii) The pursuit of ostensible legal points at the expense of practical consideration.
It is claimed that schemes proposing mutually beneficial amalgamations of charities have in the past been turned down because the purposes of the charities were not wholly coincidental. There is no legal rule which restricts amalgamations of charities to those whose purposes are identical. 'Similar' in section 13(1)(c) of the 1960 Act does not mean 'the same'. There is no reason why adjustments cannot be made to beneficiary classes and areas of benefit where the practical considerations are clearly in favour of it.

(iii) The automatic placing of greater weight on one part of a charity's objects than another.
Where the beneficiary class of the charity is defined by reference to a number of components, for instance poor women resident in the parish of X, care should be taken not to attach undue importance to one component as against the remainder. It may be that other factors in the charity's foundation or trust deed will indicate that one element is more important than another but in the absence of any such indication, rules should not be created which would inhibit flexibility.

(iv) The concept that a charity's objects can never be changed so as to exclude any part of its existing purposes.
As a matter of general practice this is a sound rule but if taken to excessive lengths it can effectively frustrate radical reorganisations of trusts where such reorganisation would be appropriate. It is, for instance, sensible when making regulating schemes for schools to amalgamate the varied and various prize funds into a single fund so that the identity of the separate fund is lost. Such an amalgamation may be administratively and practically sound as the individual prize funds established many years ago may now be insufficient to provide the prizes intended. The process can be applied to other groupings of charities.

(v) The idea that certain elements of a trust are sacrosanct, for instance the age limit included in educational schemes, religious qualifications in essentially secular charities, sex qualifications particularly in relation to schools.
We take the view that no part of a charity's trust is unalterable.

[27] From *Pemsel's* case [see p. 414, above].

Varsani v Jesani
[1999] Ch 219 (CA, **Sir Stephen Brown P, Morritt** and **Chadwick LJJ**)[28]

A Hindu religious sect split into two factions. The majority continued to recognise the authority and divine status of the successor to the founder of the sect, whereas the minority did not recognise the successor. As a result neither group was able to worship together in the same temple. Both groups sought a scheme under section 13(1)(e)(iii) of the Charities Act 1993 and a declaration as to which group was the true proponent of the faith and so able to worship in the temple.

Held. It was sufficient that the claim fell within one of the heads of section 13(1) without showing that the original purpose was impossible or impracticable. Since the claim did fall within section 13(1)(e)(iii), a scheme as to the division of the charity's funds would be directed.[29]

Morritt LJ: It is convenient to start by considering the nature of the *cy-près* jurisdiction and how it has developed in relation to indefinite gifts to charity which have once taken effect. In such a case the directions given by the donor as to how, that is to say the purpose for which, the property was to be applied were regarded as subsidiary to the charitable intention so as to justify overriding them when appropriate. But the circumstances in which it was considered appropriate to do so were originally confined to those where it was demonstrated that the original purpose had become impossible or impractical to carry out. In the 19th century, at least, impossibility or impracticality were narrowly defined. In cases where impossibility or impracticality was shown then the court had jurisdiction to alter the original purpose indicated by the donor to another, charitable, purpose as close as possible to the original purpose. The Committee on the Law and Practice relating to Charitable Trusts (1952) (Cmd 8710) reported that the witnesses who had appeared before them were practically unanimous on the need to relax the rigour of the *cy-près* doctrine and themselves recommended a relaxation.

The relaxation was effected by section 13 of the Charities Act 1960...

It is common ground that the faith the charity was established to promote is that of Swaminarayan according to the teaching and tenets of Muktajivandasji. It is also common ground that until 1984 both the majority and minority groups professed that faith. It is the case for the minority group that the majority group no longer does so because, so it is alleged, the 1969 constitution provided that no successor should be treated as divine, that the successor claims to possess divine attributes and the majority group continue to give him their allegiance, notwithstanding that claim. The majority group consider that the minority group have departed from the true faith because they do not accept as a fundamental tenet the authority and divine attributes of the successor....

Now the jurisdiction to make a *cy-près* scheme depends on whether the case falls within one or other of the paragraphs of section 13(1). The relevant test in this case is now whether the

---

[28] [1998] All ER Rev 277 (P.J. Clarke).

[29] The Scheme which was proposed by the Charity Commissioners was also challenged. In *Varsani v Jesani* (2001) unreported, PATTEN J held that 'when exercising its discretion to make a scheme under the Charities Act 1993, s. 13(1)(e)(iii) whereby the assets of a religious charity would be divided between two opposing factions, the court should assume an agnostic role and treat both factions as adherents to a branch of faith which justified recognition and support'.

original purpose has ceased to provide a suitable and effective method of using the property, regard being had to the spirit of the gift.

In my view that test is satisfied in this case. First, there is no doubt what the original purpose of the charity was and is. It was and is the promotion of the faith of Swaminarayan according to the teachings and tenets of Muktajivandasji. Second, until the problems disclosed by the events of 1984 arose those original purposes were both suitable and effective as a method of using the property for both the majority and minority group were agreed on all relevant matters and therefore able to worship together in the temples provided by the charity. Third, the exposure of differing beliefs by the events of 1984 has produced a situation in which neither group is able to worship in the same temple as the other so that the minority group has been excluded from the facilities for the worship the charity was established to provide. Fourth, unless the impasse can be resolved as a matter of faith, so that both groups reunite to embrace the faith the charity was established to promote, the impasse will remain so long as the original purpose remains. Fifth, the impasse cannot be resolved as a matter of faith because the teachings and tenets of Muktajivandasji did not deal with whether a belief in a particular successor to Muktajivandasji or in the divine attributes of a successor were or are essential tenets of the faith. I do not accept that the parts of the 1969 Constitution on which counsel for the minority group relied resolve the question. And a decision of the Helping Committee or this court is not binding as a matter of faith. Thus the impasse and the original purpose of the charity go together. If the original purpose leads in the present circumstances to such an impasse then in my view it is self-evident that the original purpose has ceased to be a suitable and effective method of using the available property.

The court is enjoined by section 13(1)(e)(iii) of the Charities Act 1993 to have regard to the spirit of the gift. In my view it does not matter whether the origin of that concept is to be found in *Re Campden Charities* (1881) 18 Ch D 310 at 333, as suggested by counsel for the Attorney-General in *Re Lepton's Charity* [1972] Ch 276 at 283 [see p. 567, below], or in section 15 of the Educational Endowments Act 1882 (45 & 46 Vict c. 59) as indicated in the Report of the Committee on the Law and Practice relating to Charitable Trusts to which I have already referred and suggested by counsel for the majority group in this case. Either way the concept is clear enough, namely, the basic intention underlying the gift or the substance of the gift rather than the form of the words used to express it or conditions imposed to effect it. It is noteworthy that the phrase is used in section 13(1) only in contexts which require the court to make a value judgment. Thus it does not appear in paragraphs (a)(i), (b), (e)(i) or (ii). Moreover, when it is used, in each case except one it appears in the context of suitability. The exception, paragraph (a)(ii), whilst not actually using the word 'suitable', requires a similar value judgment. The court is not bound to follow the spirit of the gift but it must pay regard to it when making the value judgments required by some of the provisions of section 13(1).

For my part I have no hesitation in concluding that the spirit of the gift supports the submission that the court should accept and exercise the jurisdiction conferred by section 13(1)(e)(iii), of the Charities Act 1993 by directing a scheme for the division of the property of the charity between the majority and minority groups. The choice lies between directing such a scheme for the benefit of all those who down to 1984 shared the belief for the promotion of which the charity was established and, no doubt, in many cases supported the charity financially as well, even though some of them may no longer do so, and requiring a substantial proportion of the trust property to be spent in litigation which can never finally resolve the problems which divide the two groups. I do not minimise the strength of feeling which arises in connection with disputes such as this. In such cases either or both groups often litigate in preference to permitting a benefit to be conferred on the other. But the spirit of the gift to which the court is to have regard is that which prevailed at the time of the gift when the two groups were in harmony.

Accordingly I would reject the submissions of both the minority group and the Attorney-General. First, it is not necessary to ascertain the precise limits of the purpose of the charity before deciding whether the case comes within section 13(1) of the Charities Act 1993. The purpose of this charity is clear; it is the promotion of the faith of Swaminarayan according to the teaching and tenets of Muktajivandasji. It is the expression of that purpose in the light of subsequent events which has given rise to the schism with the result that the original purpose has ceased to be a suitable and effective method of using the trust property. Second, it is not a necessary condition for the application of the section that the original purposes have become impossible or impractical, only that the circumstances come within one or other paragraph of section 13(1). Thus even if the inquiries sought were ordered and pursued and ultimately demonstrated that the minority group but not the majority group still embraced the relevant faith that does not now preclude the application of the section for the outcome of the inquiries would merely demonstrate that the original purpose was not impossible or impractical.

If, as I would hold, there is jurisdiction to make a scheme under section 13(1)(e)(iii) of the Charities Act 1993 that is good reason for not ordering the inquiries suggested by the minority group. Such inquiries would show either that one of the groups no longer professed the relevant faith or both of them still did. For the reasons I have tried to explain the former alternative is irrelevant to the question of jurisdiction to make a *cy-près* scheme. But if the answer were that both groups still professed the relevant faith then it would be permissible to make an administrative scheme for no alteration of the purpose of the charity would arise. The justification for such a scheme would remain the same, namely to resolve the impasse and avoid the expenditure on costs. Therefore whatever the answers to the proposed inquiries there would be jurisdiction to make the proposed scheme and the same factual justification for doing so. . . .

In rejecting the submission for the Attorney-General I do not seek to undermine or belittle in any way the concerns expressed by his counsel to which I have already referred. First, there is his concern that potential donors should not be deterred by a belief that their intentions will be overridden by a too ready use of the *cy-près* jurisdiction. I agree; but that problem has to be set beside the equal but opposite problem that in circumstances unforeseen by the donor his or her bounty may not achieve all that was intended or was reasonably feasible. The balance between those two considerations has to be struck and was struck by Parliament in 1960 when, following the Report of the Committee on Law and Practice of Charitable Trusts to which I have referred, it enacted section 13 of the Charities Act 1960. Since then it has been the duty of the court fairly to apply the provisions of that section to the circumstances of each case without any predilection either to making or to refusing to make a scheme altering the original purposes of the charity.

Chadwick LJ: I agree with Morritt LJ that, if the underlying question which, if either, of the views now held by the majority group and the minority group respectively do truly reflect the teachings and tenets of Muktajivandasji in the circumstances which have arisen were to be resolved in favour of one group and against the other, the position would be that the original purposes had ceased to provide a suitable and effective method of using the property available by virtue of the gift. It is not, of course, the case that the property could not be used in accordance with the original purposes. Clearly it could be so used by the group who were found, on this hypothesis, to be the followers of the true faith. But to appropriate the property to the sole use of one group, to the exclusion of the other, would not—in a case like the present—be a suitable and effective method of using that property, regard being had to the spirit of the gift.

The need to have regard to the spirit of the gift requires the court to look beyond the original purposes as defined by the objects specified in the declaration of trust and to seek to identify the spirit in which the donors gave property upon trust for those purposes. That can be done, as it seems to me, with the assistance of the document as a whole and any relevant evidence as to the circumstances in which the gift was made. In the present case I have no doubt that the spirit in which property was given in 1967 was a desire to provide facilities for a small but united community of the followers of Muktajivandasji in and around Hendon to worship together in the faith of Swaminarayan. The original purposes specified in the declaration of trust—that is to say the promotion of the faith of Swaminarayan as practised in accordance with the teachings and tenets of Muktajivandasji—are no longer a suitable and effective method of using the property given in 1967, or added property held upon the same trusts, because the community is now divided and cannot worship together. Nothing that the court may decide will alter that. To hold that one group has adhered to the true faith and that the other group has not will not alter the beliefs of that other group. The position will remain that the community cannot worship together. To appropriate the use of the property to the one group to the exclusion of the other would be contrary to the spirit in which the gift was made.

It follows that there would be jurisdiction to make a scheme *cy-près* even if the underlying question which, if either, of the views now held by the majority group and the minority group respectively do truly reflect the teachings and tenets of Muktajivandasji in the circumstances which have arisen were to be resolved in favour of one group and against the other. Given jurisdiction, it would plainly be appropriate to make a scheme. To refuse to do so would be to perpetuate a position in which the property of the charity is no longer being used in a suitable and effective manner.

In **Re Lepton's Charity** [1972] Ch 276, Mr. Lepton, in 1715, had devised land known as 'Dickroyd' in Pudsey, Yorkshire, to trustees upon trust to pay £3 per annum 'unto such Protestant dissenting minister whether he be Presbiterian or Independant as shall statedly preach at the Protestant dissenting meeting place at Pudsey soe long as such minister shall preach there' and to distribute 'the overplus of the profitts... unto such poor aged and necessitouse people legally settled within the town of Pudsey as shall subsist without the town allowance' at the discretion of the trustees. Lepton died in 1716 when the total income from the rents and profits was £5 per annum. The land was sold and the income in 1970 was £791 14s. 6d. There was one Protestant dissenting meeting place, the Pudsey Congregational Chapel.

The question arose whether the court had jurisdiction to vary the will by scheme under the Charities Act 1960, section 13 so as to raise the annual payment to £100.

PENNYCUICK V-C ordered a scheme to be made and said at 285:

One must next consider whether in relation to a trust for payment of a fixed annual sum out of the income of a fund to charity A and payment of the residue of that income to charity B the expression 'the original purposes of a charitable gift' in section 13(1) should be construed as referring to the trusts as a whole or must be related severally to the trust for payment of the fixed annual sum and the trust for payment of residuary income. Mr. Browne-Wilkinson contends that the former is the correct view. Mr. Griffith contends that the latter is the correct view.

It seems to me that the words 'the original purposes of a charitable gift' are apt to apply to the trusts as a whole in such a case. Where a testator or settlor disposes of the entire income of a fund for charitable purposes, it is natural to speak of the disposition as a single charitable gift, albeit the gift is for more than one charitable purpose. Conversely, it would be rather unnatural to speak of the disposition as constituting two or more several charitable gifts each for a single purpose. Nor, I think, is there any reason why one should put this rather artificial construction on the words. The point can, so far as I can see, only arise as a practical issue in regard to a trust of the present character. A trust for division of income between charities in *aliquot* shares would give rise to different considerations, inasmuch as even if one treats it as a single gift the possibility or otherwise of carrying out the trusts of one share according to the spirit of the gift could hardly react upon the possibility or otherwise of carrying out the trusts of the other share according to the spirit of the gift. The same is true, *mutatis mutandis*, of trusts for charities in succession. But in a trust of the present character there is an obvious interrelation between the two trusts in that changes in the amount of the income and the value of money may completely distort the relative benefits taken under the respective trusts. The point is familiar in other instances of fixed annuity and residual income.

Once it is accepted that the words 'the original purposes of a charitable gift' bear the meaning which I have put upon them it is to my mind clear that in the circumstances of the present case the original purposes of the gift of Dickroyd cannot be carried out according to the spirit of the gift, or to use the words of paragraph (e)(iii) 'have ceased...to provide a suitable and effective method of using the property... regard being had to the spirit of the gift'. The intention underlying the gift was to divide a sum which, according to the values of 1715, was modest but not negligible, in such a manner that the minister took what was then a clear three-fifths of it. This intention is plainly defeated when in the conditions of today the minister takes a derisory £3 out of a total of £791....

I conclude that the new conditions for *cy-près* applications introduced by section 13 of the Act of 1960 have been satisfied. Mr. Griffith concedes that if it is legitimate to alter the purposes at all then £100 a year is a reasonable amount to be paid to the minister. There was some expert evidence on the value of money into which, for this reason, it is unnecessary to enter.

I propose to make an order by way of scheme accordingly. I should perhaps add, to avoid misunderstanding—and this is not in dispute—that should there cease to be a minister at the chapel with the consequence that the income becomes applicable in accordance with the provisions of the will, limited to take effect upon that event, section 13 will have no application as between the poor of Pudsey and the heirs of the testator.

In **Re J W Laing Trust** [1984] Ch 143,[30] a settlor in 1922 transferred shares worth £15,000 to the plaintiff company as trustee to hold on a charitable trust. Both capital and income were to be wholly distributed in the lifetime of the settlor or within ten years of his death. The settlor died in 1978. By 1982 the capital as yet undistributed was worth £24 million. The plaintiff company applied to the court for the settlement of a scheme enabling the trustee to be discharged from the obligation to distribute capital within ten years of the settlor's death. PETER GIBSON J refused the application under

---

[30] [1984] Conv 319 (J. Warburton); [1984] All ER Rev 305 (P.J. Clarke); [1985] Conv 313 (P. Luxton). See also *Re Woodhams* [1981] 1 WLR 493 (restrictions limiting scholarships to absolute orphans from Dr Barnardo's homes or the Church of England Children's Society homes deleted).

section 13(1)(e)(ii) on the ground that the obligation was an administrative provision and not an 'original purpose of a charitable gift'. He went on, however, to approve a scheme for the discharge of the obligation in the exercise of the court's inherent jurisdiction. He said at 149:

It is necessary to identify the original purposes of the gift. I venture to suggest that, as a matter of ordinary language, those purposes in the present case should be identified as general charitable purposes and nothing further. I would regard it as an abuse of language to describe the requirement as to distribution as a purpose of the gift. Of course, that requirement was one of the provisions which the settlor intended to apply to the gift, but it would, on any natural use of language, be wrong to equate all the express provisions of a gift, which *ex hypothesi* the settlor intended to apply to the gift, with the purposes of a gift. To my mind the purposes of a charitable gift would ordinarily be understood as meaning those charitable objects on which the property given is to be applied. It is not meaningful to talk of the requirement as to distribution being either charitable or non-charitable. The purposes of a charitable gift correspond to the beneficiaries in the case of a gift by way of a private trust....

I confess that from the outset I have found difficulty in accepting that it is meaningful to talk of a *cy-près* application of property that has from the date of the gift been devoted both as to capital and income to charitable purposes generally, albeit subject to a direction as to the timing of the capital distributions. No case remotely like the present had been drawn to my attention...

In the result, despite all the arguments that have been ably advanced, I remain unpersuaded that such a gift is capable of being applied *cy-près* and, in particular, I am not persuaded that the requirement as to distribution is a purpose within the meaning of section 13. Rather, it seems to me to fall on the administrative side of the line, going, as it does, to the mechanics of how the property devoted to charitable purposes is to be distributed. Accordingly, I must refuse the application so far as it is based on section 13.

In my judgment, the plaintiff has made out a very powerful case for the removal of the requirement as to distribution, which seems to me to be inexpedient in the very altered circumstances of the charity since that requirement was laid down 60 years ago. I take particular account of the fact that this application is one that has the support of the Attorney-General. Although the plaintiff is not fettered by the express terms of the gift as to the charitable purposes for which the charity's funds are to be applied, it is, in my view, proper for the plaintiff to wish to continue to support the causes which the settlor himself wished the charity to support from its inception, and which would suffer if that support was withdrawn as a consequence of the distribution of the charity's assets. I have no hesitation in reaching the conclusion that the court should, in the exercise of its inherent jurisdiction, approve a scheme under which the trustees for the time being of the charity will be discharged from the obligation to distribute the capital within ten years of the death of the settlor.

In **Oldham Borough Council v Attorney-General** [1993] Ch 210[31] land was conveyed in 1962 to the Oldham Borough Council upon trust 'to preserve and manage it at all times hereafter as playing fields to be known as "the Clayton Playing Fields" for the benefit and enjoyment of the inhabitants of Oldham Chadderton and Royton'.

[31] [1993] All ER Rev 260 (P.J. Clarke).

The question was whether the court had power to authorise the Council to sell the land to developers for a very large price, and to use the proceeds for the acquisition of playing fields with much better facilities than the existing site. The Court of Appeal held that it had power to authorise the sale under its inherent jurisdiction, even though none of the requirements of section 13(1) was satisfied.

DILLON LJ said at 219:

Broadly, the effect of that section is that an alteration of the 'original purposes' of a charitable gift can only be authorised by a scheme for the *cy-près* application of the trust property and such a scheme can only be made in the circumstances set out in paragraphs (a) to (e) of section 13(1).

It follows that if the retention of a particular property is part of the 'original purposes' of a charitable trust, sale of that property would involve an alteration of the original purposes even if the proceeds of the sale were applied in acquiring an alternative property for carrying out the same charitable activities. If so, a sale of the original property could only be ordered as part of a *cy-près* scheme, and then only if circumstances within one or other of paragraphs (a) to (e) are made out. The particular bearing of that in the present case is that the council accepts, and the Attorney-General agrees, that the circumstances of this charity do not fall within any of these paragraphs. If, therefore, on a true appreciation of the deed of gift and of section 13, the retention of the existing site is part of the original purposes of the charity, the court cannot authorise any sale. It is necessary, therefore, to look first at the terms of the deed of gift...

[His Lordship examined the terms and continued:] On that wording, I have no doubt at all that the original purpose, in ordinary parlance, of the donor was, in one sense, that the particular land conveyed should be used for ever as playing fields for the benefit and enjoyment of the inhabitants of Oldham, Chadderton and Royton...

As Lord Cranworth LC said in *President and Scholars of the College of St Mary Magdalen, Oxford v A-G* (1857) 6 HL Cas 189, 205:

> 'it is plain that persons who give lands to a charity, devote them for ever to the purposes of that charity, and such is always the expression used in such gifts, the gifts being made to the charitable object "for ever". With the belief that the charity will endure for ever, it is extremely improbable that they can have contemplated the sale of the lands...'

I come then to what I regard as the crux of this case, *viz.*, the true construction of the words 'original purposes of a charitable gift' in section 13 of the Act of 1960. Do the 'original purposes' include the intention and purpose of the donor that the land given should be used for ever for the purposes of the charity, or are they limited to the purposes of the charity, in the sense in which Lord Cranworth LC was using these words in the passage just cited?

Certain of the authorities cited to us can be put on one side. Thus in *Re JW Laing Trust* [1984] Ch 143 at 153 [p. 568, above], Peter Gibson J said, plainly correctly:

> 'It cannot be right that any provision, even if only administrative, made applicable by a donor to his gift should be treated as a condition and hence as a purpose.'

In that case, however, the provision, which was held to be administrative and was plainly not a 'purpose', was a provision that the capital was to be wholly distributed within the settlor's lifetime or within 10 years of his death.

Conversely, there are cases where the donor has imposed a condition, as part of the terms of his gift, which limits the main purpose of the charity in a way which, with the passage of time, has come to militate against the achievement of that main purpose. The condition is there part of the purpose, but the court has found itself able on the facts to cut out the condition by way of a *cy-près* scheme under the *cy-près* jurisdiction, on the ground that the subsistence of the condition made the main purpose impossible or impracticable of achievement: see *Re Dominion Students' Hall Trust* [1947] Ch 183, where a condition of a trust for the maintenance of a hostel for male students of the overseas dominions of the British Empire restricted the benefits to dominion students of European origin; and see, also *Re Robinson* [1923] 2 Ch 332, where it was a condition of the gift of an endowment for an evangelical church that the preacher should wear a black gown in the pulpit. But unlike those conditions, the intention or purpose in the present case that the actual land given should be used as playing fields is not a condition qualifying the use of that land as playing fields.

It is necessary, in my judgment, in order to answer the crucial question of the true construction of section 13, to appreciate the legislative purpose of section 13. Pennycuick V-C said in *Re Lepton's Charity* [1972] Ch 276, 284f [p. 567, above], that the section 'in part restates the principles applied under the existing law, but also extends those principles'. But the principles with which it is concerned are the principles for applying property *cy-près* and nothing else. The stringency of those principles, as stated in *Re Weir Hospital* [1910] 2 Ch 124, has been somewhat mitigated, but to nothing like the extent contended for by the unsuccessful parties in *Re Weir Hospital*. But there is nothing to suggest any legislative intention, in enacting section 13, to extend the cases where a *cy-près* scheme is necessary, if anything is to be done, to cases where before the Act of 1960 no scheme was required.

The cases seem to be consistent, before the Act of 1960, that mere sale of charitable property and reinvestment of the proceeds in the acquisition of other property to be held on precisely the same charitable trusts, or for precisely the same charitable purposes, did not require a scheme.

[His Lordship referred to *Re Ashton's Charity* (1856) 22 Beav 288; *Re Parke's Charity* (1842) 12 Sim 329 and *Re North Shields Old Meeting House* (1859) 7 WR 541 and continued:] This seems to have been the standard practice in the 19th century and I see no reason why Parliament should have intended to alter it by section 13 of the Act of 1960. That section is concerned with the *cy-près* application of charitable funds, but sales of charitable lands have, in so far as they have been dealt with by Parliament, always been dealt with by other sections not concerned with the *cy-près* doctrine.

There are, of course, some cases where the qualities of the property which is the subject matter of the gift are themselves the factors which make the purposes of the gift charitable, e.g. where there is a trust to retain for the public benefit a particular house once owned by a particular historical figure or a particular building for its architectural merit or a particular area of land of outstanding natural beauty. In such cases, sale of the house, building or land would necessitate an alteration of the original charitable purposes and, therefore, a *cy-près* scheme because after a sale the proceeds or any property acquired with the proceeds could not possibly by applied for the original charitable purpose. But that is far away from cases such as the present, where the charitable purpose—playing fields for the benefit and enjoyment of the inhabitants of the districts of the original donees, or it might equally be a museum, school or clinic in a particular town—can be carried on on other land.

Accordingly, I would allow this appeal, set aside the declaration made by the judge, and substitute a declaration to the opposite effect.

(i) Charity Collections

Charities Act 1993 (as amended by Charities Act 2006, s. 16)

14. Application *cy-près* of gifts of donors unknown or disclaiming

(1) Property given for specific charitable purposes which fail shall be applicable *cy-près* as if given for charitable purposes generally, where it belongs—

   (a) to a donor who after—

   (i)   the prescribed advertisements and inquiries have been published and made,[32] and

   (ii) the prescribed period beginning with the publications of those advertisements has expired, cannot be identified or cannot be found;[33]

   (b) to a donor who has executed a disclaimer in the prescribed form of his right to have the property returned.[34]

(2) Where the prescribed advertisements and inquiries have been published and made by or on behalf of trustees with respect to any such property, the trustees shall not be liable to any person in respect of the property if no claim by him to be interested in it is received by them before the expiry of the period mentioned in subsection (1)(a)(ii) above.

(3) For the purposes of this section property shall be conclusively presumed (without any advertisement or inquiry) to belong to donors who cannot be identified, in so far as it consists—

   (a) of the proceeds of cash collections made by means of collecting boxes or by other means not adapted for distinguishing one gift from another; or

   (b) of the proceeds of any lottery, competition, entertainment, sale or similar money-raising activity, after allowing for property given to provide prizes or articles for sale or otherwise to enable the activity to be undertaken.

(4) The court or the Commission may by order direct that property not falling within sub-section (3) above shall for the purposes of this section be treated (without any advertisement or inquiry) as belonging to donors who cannot be identified, where it appears to the court [or Commission] either—

   (a) that it would be unreasonable, having regard to the amounts likely to be returned to the donors, to incur expense with a view to returning the property; or

   (b) that it would be unreasonable, having regard to the nature, circumstances and amounts of the gifts, and to the lapse of time since the gifts were made, for the donors to expect the property to be returned.

---

[32] Charities (*Cy-près* Advertisements Inquiries and Disclaimers) Regulations 1993.
[33] *Re Henry Wood National Memorial Trust* [1966] 1 WLR 1601; Annual Report for 1965, paras. 19–21.
[34] Annual Report for 1980, paras. 135–136 (South Scarborough Swimming Pool Association); 1981, paras. 62–63 (South Petherton Swimming Pool Fund, Somerset).

(5) Where property is applied *cy-près* by virtue of this section, the donor shall be deemed to have parted with all his interest at the time when the gift was made; but where property is so applied as belonging to donors who cannot be identified or cannot be found, and is not so applied by virtue of subsection (3) or (4) above,—

(a) the scheme shall specify the total amount of that property; and

(b) the donor of any part of that amount shall be entitled, if he makes a claim not later than six months after the date on which the scheme is made, to recover from the charity for which the property is applied a sum equal to that part, less any expenses properly incurred by the charity trustees after that date in connection with claims relating to his gift; and

(c) the scheme may include directions as to the provision to be made for meeting any such claim.

(6) Where—

(a) any sum is, in accordance with any such directions, set aside for meeting any such claims, but

(b) the aggregate amount of any such claims actually made exceeds the relevant amount,

then, if the Commission so directs, each of the donors in question shall be entitled only to such proportion of the relevant amount as the amount of his claim bears to the aggregate amount referred to in paragraph (b) above; and for this purpose 'the relevant amount' means the amount of the sum so set aside after deduction of any expenses properly incurred by the charity trustees in connection with claims relating to the donors' gifts.

(7) For the purposes of this section, charitable purposes shall be deemed to 'fail' where any difficulty in applying property to those purposes makes that property or the part not applicable *cy-près* available to be returned to the donors.

(10) In this section, except in so far as the context otherwise requires, references to a donor include persons claiming through or under the original donor, and references to property given include the property for the time being representing the property originally given or property derived from it.

(11) This section shall apply to property given for charitable purposes, notwithstanding that it was so given before the commencement of this Act.

14A Application *cy-près* of gifts made in response to certain solicitations[35]

(1) This section applies to property given—

(a) for specific charitable purposes, and

(b) in response to a solicitation within subsection (2) below.

[35] Inserted by the Charities Act 2006, s. 17.

(2) A solicitation is within this subsection if—

    (a) it is made for specific charitable purposes, and

    (b) it is accompanied by a statement to the effect that property given in response to it will, in the event of those purposes failing, be applicable *cy-près* as if given for charitable purposes generally, unless the donor makes a relevant declaration at the time of making the gift.

(3) A 'relevant declaration' is a declaration in writing by the donor to the effect that, in the event of the specific charitable purposes failing, he wishes the trustees holding the property to give him the opportunity to request the return of the property in question (or a sum equal to its value at the time of the making of the gift).

(4) Subsections (5) and (6) below apply if—

    (a) a person has given property as mentioned in subsection (1) above,

    (b) the specific charitable purposes fail, and

    (c) the donor has made a relevant declaration.

(5) The trustees holding the property must take the prescribed steps for the purpose of—

    (a) informing the donor of the failure of the purposes,

    (b) enquiring whether he wishes to request the return of the property (or a sum equal to its value), and

    (c) if within the prescribed period he makes such a request, returning the property (or such a sum) to him.

(6) If those trustees have taken all appropriate prescribed steps but—

    (a) they have failed to find the donor, or

    (b) the donor does not within the prescribed period request the return of the property (or a sum equal to its value),

section 14(1) above shall apply to the property as if it belonged to a donor within paragraph (b) of that subsection (application of property where donor has disclaimed right to return of property).

(7) If—

    (a) a person has given property as mentioned in subsection (1) above,

    (b) the specific charitable purposes fail, and

    (c) the donor has not made a relevant declaration,

section 14(1) above shall similarly apply to the property as if it belonged to a donor within paragraph (b) of that subsection.

(8) For the purposes of this section—

    (a) 'solicitation' means a solicitation made in any manner and however communicated to the persons to whom it is addressed,

(b) it is irrelevant whether any consideration is or is to be given in return for the property in question, and

(c) where any appeal consists of both solicitations that are accompanied by statements within subsection (2)(b) and solicitations that are not so accompanied, a person giving property as a result of the appeal is to be taken to have responded to the former solicitations and not the latter, unless he proves otherwise.

(9) In this section 'prescribed' means prescribed by regulations made by the Commission, and any such regulations shall be published by the Commission in such manner as it thinks fit.

(10) Subsections (7) and (10) of section 14 shall apply for the purposes of this section as they apply for the purposes of section 14.

(ii) Cy-près schemes

CHARITIES ACT 1993

14B Cy-près schemes[36]

(1) The power of the court or the Commission to make schemes for the application of property *cy-près* shall be exercised in accordance with this section.

(2) Where any property given for charitable purposes is applicable *cy-près*, the court or the Commission may make a scheme providing for the property to be applied—

(a) for such charitable purposes, and

(b) (if the scheme provides for the property to be transferred to another charity) by or on trust for such other charity,

as it considers appropriate, having regard to the matters set out in subsection (3).

(3) The matters are—

(a) the spirit of the original gift,

(b) the desirability of securing that the property is applied for charitable purposes which are close to the original purposes, and

(c) the need for the relevant charity to have purposes which are suitable and effective in the light of current social and economic circumstances.

The 'relevant charity' means the charity by or on behalf of which the property is to be applied under the scheme.

(4) If a scheme provides for the property to be transferred to another charity, the scheme may impose on the charity trustees of that charity a duty to secure that

---

36 Inserted by the Charities Act 2006, s. 18.

the property is applied for purposes which are, so far as is reasonably practicable, similar in character to the original purposes.

(5) In this section references to property given include the property for the time being representing the property originally given or property derived from it.

(6) In this section references to the transfer of property to a charity are references to its transfer—

(a) to the charity, or

(b) to the charity trustees, or

(c) to any trustee for the charity, or

(d) to a person nominated by the charity trustees to hold it in trust for the charity,

as the scheme may provide.

(iii) Small Charities

The Charities Act 1993 makes specific provision to enable trustees of certain small charities in effect to determine their own *cy-près* application with the concurrence of the Charity Commissioners.

CHARITIES ACT 1993
74. Small charities: power to transfer all property, modify objects etc.

(1) This section applies to a charity if—

(a) its gross income in its last financial year did not exceed £5,000, and

(b) it does not hold any land on trusts which stipulate that the land is to be used for the purposes, or any particular purposes, of the charity,

and it is neither an exempt charity nor a charitable company.

(2) Subject to the following provisions of this section, the charity trustees of a charity to which this section applies may resolve for the purposes of this section—

(a) that all the property of the charity should be transferred to such other charity as is specified in the resolution, being either a registered charity or a charity which is not required to be registered;

(b) that all the property of the charity should be divided, in such manner as is specified in the resolution, between such two or more other charities as are so specified, being in each case either a registered charity or a charity which is not required to be registered;

(c) that the trusts of the charity should be modified by replacing all or any of the purposes of the charity with such other purposes, being in law charitable, as are specified in the resolution;

(d) that any provision of the trusts of the charity—

    (i) relating to any of the powers exercisable by the charity trustees in the administration of the charity, or

    (ii) regulating the procedure to be followed in any respect in connection with its administration,

should be modified in such manner as is specified in the resolution.

(3) Any resolution passed under subsection (2) must be passed by a majority of not less than two-thirds of such charity trustees as vote on the resolution.

(4) The charity trustees of a charity to which this section applies ('the transferor charity') shall not have power to pass a resolution under subsection (2)(a) or (b) unless they are satisfied—

    (a) that the existing purposes of the transferor charity have ceased to be conducive to a suitable and effective application of the charity's resources; and

    (b) that the purposes of the charity or charities specified in the resolution are as similar in character to the purposes of the transferor charity as is reasonably practicable;

and before passing the resolution they must have received from the charity trustees of the charity, or (as the case may be) of each of the charities, specified in the resolution written confirmation that those trustees are willing to accept a transfer of property under this section.

(5) The charity trustees of any such charity shall not have power to pass a resolution under subsection (2)(c) unless they are satisfied—

    (a) that the existing purposes of the charity (or, as the case may be, such of them as it is proposed to replace) have ceased to be conducive to a suitable and effective application of the charity's resources; and

    (b) that the purposes specified in the resolution are as similar in character to those existing purposes as is practical in the circumstances.

75. Small charities: power to spend capital

(1) This section applies to a charity if—

    (a) it has a permanent endowment which does not consist of or comprise any land, and

    (b) its gross income in its last financial year did not exceed £1,000, and it is neither an exempt charity nor a charitable company.

(2) Where the charity trustees of a charity to which this section applies are of the opinion that the property of the charity is too small, in relation to its purposes, for any useful purpose to be achieved by the expenditure of income alone, they may resolve for the purposes of this section that the charity ought to be freed from the restrictions with respect to expenditure of capital to which its permanent endowment is subject.

(3) Any resolution passed under subsection (2) must be passed by a majority of not less than two-thirds of such charity trustees as vote on the resolution.

(4) Before passing such a resolution the charity trustees must consider whether any reasonable possibility exists of effecting a transfer or division of all the charity's property under section 43 (disregarding any such transfer or division as would, in their opinion, impose on the charity an unacceptable burden of costs).

Under both sections, the trustees must give public notice of their resolution, a copy of which must be sent to the Charity Commissioners for their approval.[37] Neither section applies to an exempt or corporate charity.

QUESTIONS

1. Would it now be possible for gifts such as those in *National Anti-Vivisection Society v IRC* [1948] AC 31 [p. 511, above], and *Oppenheim v Tobacco Securities Trust Co Ltd* [1951] AC 297 [p. 455, above], to be saved by Charities Act 1993, section 13(1)(e)(ii)? H&M, p. 462; (1974) 38 Conv (NS) at p. 233.

2. In what circumstances is proof of a general charitable intent still necessary? Charities Act 1993, section 13(2), section 14; Pettit, pp. 329–332.

3. How do you distinguish between the following trusts?
   (a) *Re Finger's Will Trusts* [1972] Ch 286 [p. 552, above], where the gift to the incorporated charity failed and there was a *cy-près* scheme, and where the gift to the unincorporated charity did not fail and there was a scheme, but not *cy-près*; and *Re Faraker* [1912] 2 Ch 488 [p. 551, above], where the gift did not fail and there was no scheme.
   (b) *Re Jenkins's Will Trusts* [1966] Ch 249 [p. 555, above] and *Re Satterthwaite's Will Trusts* [1966] 1 WLR 277 [p. 555, above].

4. Now consider *Re Spence* [1979] Ch 483 [p. 557, above], where the gift failed and there was no *cy-près* scheme. Could the gift have been saved by applying *Re Finger's Will Trusts* [p. 552, above], *Re Faraker* [p. 551, above], or *Re Satterthwaite's Will Trusts* [p. 555, above]? (1972) 36 Conv NS 198 (R.B.M. Cotterell); (1974) 38 Conv (NS) 187 (J. Martin); Luxton, pp. 575–583.

---

[37] See CC 44 (Small Charities: Transfer of Property, Alteration of Trusts, Expenditure of Capital (2004)).

I REGULATION OF CHARITIES[1]

A THE REGULATORY AUTHORITIES

(i) *The Charity Commission*

The role of the Charity Commission is all-important and all-pervasive.[2] It produces an annual Report on its activities and important decisions about registration and

---

[1] H&M, pp. 464–472; Luxton, pp. 251–687; P&M, pp. 493–502; Pettit, pp. 288–325, 338–346; Picarda, pp. 403–685; Snell, pp. 536–547; Tudor, pp. 333–433.

[2] Previously this role was carried out by the Charity Commissioners, but this office was abolished by s. 6(3), Charities Act 2006.

administration of charities are published on the Charity Commission website. The objectives, general functions, and duties of the Charity Commission are set out in the Charities Act 1993, as inserted by the Charities Act 2006.

CHARITIES ACT 1993 (as inserted by Charities Act 2006, ss. 6 and 7)

1A. The Charity Commission

(1) There shall be a body corporate to be known as the Charity Commission for England and Wales (in this Act referred to as 'the Commission').

(3) The functions of the Commission shall be performed on behalf of the Crown.

1B. The Commission's objectives

(1) The Commission has the objectives set out in subsection (2).

(2) The objectives are—

1. The public confidence objective.
2. The public benefit objective.
3. The compliance objective.
4. The charitable resources objective.
5. The accountability objective.

(3) Those objectives are defined as follows—

1. The public confidence objective is to increase public trust and confidence in charities.
2. The public benefit objective is to promote awareness and understanding of the operation of the public benefit requirement.[3]
3. The compliance objective is to promote compliance by charity trustees with their legal obligations in exercising control and management of the administration of their charities.
4. The charitable resources objective is to promote the effective use of charitable resources.
5. The accountability objective is to enhance the accountability of charities to donors, beneficiaries and the general public.

1C. The Commission's general functions

(1) The Commission has the general functions set out in subsection (2).

(2) The general functions are—

1. Determining whether institutions are or are not charities.
2. Encouraging and facilitating the better administration of charities.

---

[3] See p. 418, above.

3. Identifying and investigating apparent misconduct or mismanagement in the administration of charities and taking remedial or protective action in connection with misconduct or mismanagement therein.

4. Determining whether public collections certificates should be issued, and remain in force, in respect of public charitable collections.

5. Obtaining, evaluating and disseminating information in connection with the performance of any of the Commission's functions or meeting any of its objectives.

6. Giving information or advice, or making proposals, to any Minister of the Crown on matters relating to any of the Commission's functions or meeting any of its objectives.

(3) The Commission's fifth general function includes (among other things) the maintenance of an accurate and up-to-date register of charities under section 3 below.[4]

(ii) The Charity Tribunal

CHARITIES ACT 1993 (as inserted by Charities Act 2006, s. 8)

2A. The Charity Tribunal

(1) There shall be a tribunal to be known as the Charity Tribunal (in this Act referred to as 'the Tribunal').

(4) The Tribunal shall have jurisdiction to hear and determine—

(a) such appeals and applications as may be made to the Tribunal in accordance with Schedule 1C[5] to this Act, or any other enactment, in respect of decisions, orders or directions of the Commission, and

(b) such matters as may be referred to the Tribunal in accordance with Schedule 1D[6] to this Act by the Commission or the Attorney-General.

(iii) The Attorney-General[7]

The Attorney-General is responsible for enforcing the charitable trust in the name of the Crown.[8] The Attorney-General's function, therefore, is as protector of the charity. He or she is the 'representative of the beneficial interest'.[9] There is a need for the

---

[4] See p. 583, below.

[5] Concerning matters such as the decision to register or not to register a charity, or to remove an institution from the register of charities.

[6] Concerning matters such as the powers of the Charity Commission and the 'operation of charity law'.

[7] Or the Solicitor-General: The Law Officers Act 1997, s. 1.

[8] *Gaudiya Mission v Brahmachary* [1998] Ch 341 at 350 (Mummery LJ).

[9] *Weth v A-G* [1999] 1 WLR 686, 691 (Nourse LJ).

Attorney-General to protect the property of the charitable trust because such trusts are matters which concern the public and because no private individual has a beneficial interest in the trust's property.[10]

(iv) *The Visitor*[11]

The Visitor of an ecclesiastical[12] or eleemosynary corporation[13] has exclusive jurisdiction over matters of internal management, such as the admission and removal of students,[14] and the award of degrees and prizes.[15] There is no appeal from his or her decisions, unless the statutes of the corporation so provide, but he or she is subject to judicial review, if he or she has acted outside his jurisdiction, or in breach of the rules of natural justice, or has abused his or her powers.[16] The Visitor will also be subject to the European Convention on Human Rights. Article 6 is especially relevant referring as it does to a right to a 'fair and public hearing'.[17]

The Education Reform Act 1988 abolished the visitor's jurisdiction in relation to the appointment, employment and dismissal of academic staff.[18]

In **Re Christ Church** (1866) 1 Ch App 526, LORD CRANWORTH LC, representing the Queen as the Visitor of Christ Church, Oxford, sanctioned the appropriation of part of the revenues of the college to augment the stipend of the Regius Professorship of Greek, which was on the same foundation as the college. He said at 527:

The study of Greek is an important and material element of education, and it is most desirable that a stipend larger than the very inadequate one of £40 per annum should be provided for the professorship. The present application is highly honourable to the Dean and Chapter, and not only receives my ready sanction, but also my hearty approval.

---

[10] [1999] 63 Conv 20, 22 (J. Warburton).

[11] Luxton, chap. 12; Pettit, pp. 307–313; Picarda, chap. 42; Tudor, pp. 412–430; Mitcheson, *Opinion on the Visitation of Charities* (1887); (1970) 86 LQR 531 (J.W. Bridge); (1981) 97 LQR 610 (P.M. Smith); (1986) 136 NLJ 484, 519, 567, 665 (P.M. Smith).

[12] Corporations which exist for the furtherance of religion and the perpetuation of the rites of the church.

[13] Originally a corporation whose object was the distribution of free alms, or the relief of individual distress: *Re Armitage* [1972] Ch 438. For the purpose of visitatorial powers, corporate schools, certain universities, and the Inns of Court are included.

[14] *Patel v University of Bradford Senate* [1979] 1 WLR 1066.

[15] *R v HM the Queen in Council, ex p Vijayatunga* [1990] 2 QB 444; *Oakes v Sidney Sussex College, Cambridge* [1988] 1 WLR 431.

[16] *R v Lord President of the Privy Council, ex p Page* [1993] AC 682; (1993) 109 LQR 155 (H.W.R. Wade); *R v Visitors to the Inns of Court, ex p Calder* [1994] QB 1. See also [1992–93] *Charity Law & Practice Review* 63 (H. Picarda); [1993–94] *Charity Law & Practice Review* 103 (P.M. Smith).

[17] See Luxton, pp. 41–44; Pettit, p. 313. See *Elijah Jemchi v The Visitor, Brunel University* (25 July 2001, unreported).

[18] S. 206. The Act applies to publicly funded universities and similar institutions: s. 202; (1991) 54 MLR 137 (P. Pettit).

B THE REGISTER

CHARITIES ACT 1993 (as amended by Charities Act 2006, s. 9)

3. Register of charities

(1) There shall continue to be a register of charities, which shall be kept by the Commission.

(2) The register shall be kept by the Commission in such manner as it thinks fit.

(3) The register shall contain—

(a) the name of every charity registered in accordance with section 3A below (registration), and

(b) such other particulars of, and such other information relating to, every such charity as the Commission thinks fit.

(4) The Commission shall remove from the register—

(a) any institution which it no longer considers is a charity, and

(b) any charity which has ceased to exist or does not operate.

(5) If the removal of an institution under subsection (4)(a) above is due to any change in its trusts, the removal shall take effect from the date of that change.

(6) A charity which is for the time being registered under section 3A(6) below (voluntary registration) shall be removed from the register if it so requests.

(7) The register (including the entries cancelled when institutions are removed from the register) shall be open to public inspection at all reasonable times.

3A Registration of charities

(1) Every charity must be registered in the register of charities unless subsection (2) below applies to it.

(2) The following are not required to be registered—

(a) any exempt charity (see Schedule 2 to this Act);

(b) any charity which for the time being—

(i) is permanently or temporarily excepted by order of the Commission, and

(ii) complies with any conditions of the exception,

and whose gross income does not exceed £100,000;

(c) any charity which for the time being—

(i) is, or is of a description, permanently or temporarily excepted by regulations made by the Secretary of State, and

(ii) complies with any conditions of the exception,

and whose gross income does not exceed £100,000; and

(d) any charity whose gross income does not exceed £5,000.

(3) For the purposes of subsection (2)(b) above—

    (a) any order made or having effect as if made under section 3(5)(b) of this Act (as originally enacted) and in force immediately before the appointed day has effect as from that day as if made under subsection (2)(b) (and may be varied or revoked accordingly); and

    (b) no order may be made under subsection (2)(b) so as to except on or after the appointed day any charity that was not excepted immediately before that day.

(4) For the purposes of subsection (2)(c) above—

    (a) any regulations made or having effect as if made under section 3(5)(b) of this Act (as originally enacted) and in force immediately before the appointed day have effect as from that day as if made under subsection (2)(c) (and may be varied or revoked accordingly);

    (b) such regulations shall be made under subsection (2)(c) as are necessary to secure that all of the formerly specified institutions are excepted under that provision (subject to compliance with any conditions of the exception and the financial limit mentioned in that provision); but

    (c) otherwise no regulations may be made under subsection (2)(c) so as to except on or after the appointed day any description of charities that was not excepted immediately before that day.

(5) In subsection (4)(b) above 'formerly specified institutions' means—

    (a) any institution falling within section 3(5B)(a) or (b) of this Act as in force immediately before the appointed day (certain educational institutions); or

    (b) any institution ceasing to be an exempt charity by virtue of section 11 of the Charities Act 2006 or any order made under that section.

5. Status of registered charity (other than small charity) to appear on official publications etc.

(1) This section applies to a registered charity if its gross income in its last financial year exceeded £10,000.[19]

(2) Where this section applies to a registered charity, the fact that it is a registered charity shall be stated in English in legible characters—

    (a) in all notices, advertisements and other documents issued by or on behalf of the charity and soliciting money or other property for the benefit of the charity;

    (b) in all bills of exchange, promissory notes, endorsements, cheques and orders for money or goods purporting to be signed on behalf of the charity; and

    (c) in all bills rendered by it and in all its invoices, receipts and letters of credit.

---

[19] Charities Act 1993 (Substitution of Sums) Order 1995 (S.I. 1995 No. 2696, art. 2 (1), (2)).

CHARITIES ACT 1993

4. Effect of, and claims and objections to, registration[20]

(1) An institution shall for all purposes other than rectification of the register be conclusively presumed to be or to have been a charity at any time when it is or was on the register of charities.

(2) Any person who is or may be affected by the registration of an institution as a charity may, on the ground that it is not a charity, object to its being entered by the Commissioners in the register, or apply to them for it to be removed from the register; and provision may be made by regulations made by the Secretary of State as to the manner in which any such objection or application is to be made, prosecuted or dealt with.

(5) Any question affecting the registration or removal from the register of an institution may, notwithstanding that it has been determined by a decision on appeal under subsection (3) above, be considered afresh by the Commissioners and shall not be concluded by that decision, if it appears to the Commissioners that there has been a change of circumstances or that the decision is inconsistent with a later judicial decision.

C SCHEME-MAKING POWERS[21]

CHARITIES ACT 1993

16. Concurrent jurisdiction with High Court for certain purposes[22]

(1) Subject to the provisions of this Act, the Commission may by order exercise the same jurisdiction and powers as are exercisable by the High Court in charity proceedings for the following purposes—

(a) establishing a scheme for the administration of a charity;[23]

---

[20] As amended by the Charities Act 2006, Sch. 9, which has removed the right to appeal to the High Court against any decision not to register an institution as a charity.

[21] See Charities Act 1993, ss.15 (schemes for charities established or regulated by Royal Charter), 17 (schemes for charities established by statute) 20 (publicity for proceedings), 24 (schemes to establish common investment funds [p. 612, below]). For examples, see Annual Report for 1975, paras. 51–61; 1976, paras. 76–95; 1977, paras. 86–153; 1978, paras. 99–145; 1979, paras. 86–113; 1980, paras. 113–149; 1981, paras. 79–93; 1982, paras. 58–74 (including the Armitt Trust, Ambleside, for the exhibition of watercolour drawings by Beatrix Potter); 1983, paras. 45–72 (Guide Dogs for the Blind Association); 1984, paras. 32–34 (Hospital of St. Cross, Winchester); 1985, paras. 36–48; 1986, paras. 22–25, App. B (Royal Academy of Music—John Retson Bequest including three named Stradivarius instruments); 1987, para. 48 (sale of 30 Greek manuscripts by Highgate School); 1988, paras. 49–68; White Paper 1989, paras. 6.14–6.16; Annual Report for 1993, paras 39–49 (schemes approved for Holloway and Bedford New College to sell three paintings by Gainsborough, Turner, and Constable) and for Bridge House Estate to spend surplus income for maintenance and repair of bridges over the River Thames on transport, and access to it for elderly and disabled people in Greater London, or for charitable purposes for the general benefit of its inhabitants.

[22] As amended by the Charities Act 2006, Sch. 8.

[23] No alteration of the purposes of a charity can be made unless the cy-près doctrine is satisfied. See ss.13 and 14, Charities Act 1993 [pp. 560, 572 above].

(b) appointing, discharging or removing a charity trustee or trustee for a charity, or removing an officer or employee;

(c) vesting or transferring property, or requiring or entitling any person to call for or make any transfer of property or any payment.

(2) Where the court directs a scheme for the administration of a charity to be established, the court may by order refer the matter to the Commission for it to prepare or settle a scheme in accordance with such directions (if any) as the court sees fit to give, and any such order may provide for the scheme to be put into effect by order of the Commission as if prepared under subsection (1) above and without any further order of the court.

(3) The Commission shall not have any jurisdiction under this section to try or determine the title at law or in equity to any property as between a charity or trustee for a charity and a person holding or claiming the property or an interest in it adversely to the charity, or to try or determine any question as to the existence or extent of any charge or trust.

(4) Subject to the following subsections the Commission shall not exercise its jurisdiction under this section as respects any charity, except—

(a) on the application of the charity; or

(b) on an order of the court under subsection (2) above; or

(c) on the application of the Attorney-General.

(5) In the case of a charity whose gross income does not exceed £500 a year, the Commission may exercise its jurisdiction under this section on the application—

(a) of any one or more of the charity trustees; or

(b) of any person interested in the charity; or

(c) of any two or more inhabitants of the area of the charity if it is a local charity.

(6) Where in the case of a charity, other than an exempt charity, the Commission is satisfied that the charity trustees ought in the interests of the charity to apply for a scheme, but have unreasonably refused or neglected to do so and the Commission has given the charity trustees an opportunity to make representations to them, the Commission may proceed as if an application for a scheme had been made by the charity but the Commission shall not have power in a case where it acts by virtue of this subsection to alter the purposes of a charity, unless 40 years have elapsed from the date of its foundation.

(8) The Commission may on the application of any charity trustee or trustee for a charity, exercise its jurisdiction under this section for the purpose of discharging him from his trusteeship.

(10) The Commission shall not exercise its jurisdiction under this section in any case (not referred to them by order of the court) which, by reason of its contentious

character, or of any special question of law or of fact which it may involve, or for other reasons, the Commission may consider more fit to be adjudicated on by the court.

Annual Report of the Charity Commissioners for England and Wales (1999–2000), para. 3.7

The Charities Act 1993 gives the Commission powers to act in certain circumstances in place of the High Court. In general it exercises this legal authority in two ways:

- to enable charities to keep their purposes up to date in a modern environment; and
- to authorise transactions which are in the interests of charities.

When it registers a charity, the Commission will ensure it has a relevant and workable governing document. However over time some charities encounter problems in operating effectively on the basis of their original governing documents.

The difficulty is often that social changes have made the original objects no longer relevant or achievable. The Commission's role here is to facilitate a change to the objects that will allow the charity's funds to be applied more effectively. The Commission has to abide by what is known as the *cy-près* principle.[24] This requires that any change to a charity's objects keeps faith with the spirit of its original trusts.

St Dunstan's

St Dunstan's is a charity with an annual expenditure of over £11 million. It was established in 1915 to care for ex-Service personnel blinded in 'war or warlike' conflict. Recently, the trustees became aware that these limitations meant that many ex-Service personnel who urgently needed help, but who could not prove that their condition was directly caused by their service, and those whose sight became impaired for other reasons, could not be helped by the charity.

In 1999, in order to meet the needs of all blind ex-Service men and women, St Dunstan's sought approval from the Charity Commission to widen the charity's objects to enable it to benefit all blind ex-Service personnel, irrespective of the cause of their visual impairment. The Commission therefore approved this change to the charity's objects, which will enable the charity to make the most effective use of its funds.

Charities can also find that the administrative structure provided in their governing document becomes unworkable. Again the Commission's role is to facilitate appropriate changes so that the charity can be more effectively governed.[25]

In addition to authorising administrative changes for a particular charity, the Commission uses its powers to facilitate mergers between charities where this will enable funds to be applied more effectively.[26]

---

[24] See chapter 11, above. The court has power to order a *cy-près* scheme for a charitable company: *Liverpool and District Hospital for Diseases of the Heart v A-G* [1981] Ch 193 [p. 552, n. 9, above], [1984] Conv 112 (J. Warburton). On the alteration of its objects clause by a charitable company, see Charities Act 1993, s. 64.

[25] For a scheme extending the trustees' power of investment, see Annual Report for 1979, para. 166 (Investment in the Pooh Properties. 'Pooh is a great money-spinner and has so far withstood the test of time.').

[26] Annual Report for 1978, paras. 132–136 (amalgamation of Cuddesdon and Ripon Theological Colleges). See also Annual Report (2000–2001), p. 11.

The Most Venerable Order of the Hospital of St John of Jerusalem (Order of St John)
This charity runs ambulance and first-aid services in many countries and also an eye hospital in Jerusalem. In 1998 the charity decided to improve its service delivery to beneficiaries by restructuring its operations in England to make them more streamlined, and by re-aligning its relationship with its overseas partners so that it could carry out an international co-ordinating role most effectively. The Commission worked closely with the charity to advise on the best way to achieve this end. A scheme was established to make the necessary changes to the Royal Charter, in conjunction with the Privy Council.

In England, a new charity was created and decided to conduct most of its charitable work through a separate charitable company, now registered as St John Ambulance. A further scheme was made to transfer over 600 properties from the Order of St John Ambulance, which saved the charity about £60,000 in legal costs.

In addition to authorising long-term changes to the objects or governance structure of a charity, the Commission will often be asked to authorise particular one-off transactions which the trustees judge to be in the charity's interests, but which are outside their own powers. Provided it agrees that the proposal is in the best interests of the charity and that it is inappropriate to amend the governing document, the Commission will issue an order to authorise the transaction.

D   POWER TO AUTHORISE DEALINGS AND DIRECT APPLICATION OF CHARITY PROPERTY

Section 26 of the Charities Act 1993 empowers the Charity Commissioners to authorise transactions beneficial to a charity.

CHARITIES ACT 1993

26. Power to authorise dealings with charity property etc.[27]

(1) Subject to the provisions of this section, where it appears to the Commission that any action proposed or contemplated in the administration of a charity is expedient in the interests of the charity, the Commission may by order sanction that action, whether or not it would otherwise be within the powers exercisable by the charity trustees in the administration of the charity; and anything done under the authority of such an order shall be deemed to be properly done in the exercise of those powers.[28]

(2) An order under this section may be made so as to authorise a particular transaction, compromise or the like, or a particular application of property, or so as to give a more general authority, and (without prejudice to the generality of subsection (1)

---

[27] Annual Report for 1989, paras. 112–14; 1992, paras. 54–57 (Central Young Men's Christian Association). On decisions under the earlier law, see Annual Report for 1982, paras. 75–80 (sale of the Old Vic Theatre); 1983 (sale of the Mermaid and Roundhouse Theatres).

[28] *Seray-Wurie v Charity Commissioners for England and Wales* [2006] EWHC 3181 (Ch), [2007] 1 WLR 3242 (exercise of powers under s. 26 preferable to court proceedings because cheaper and quicker).

above) may authorise a charity to use common premises, or employ a common staff, or otherwise combine for any purpose of administration, with any other charity.

CHARITIES ACT 1993 (as inserted by Charities Act 2006, s. 21)

19B Power to direct application of charity property

(1) This section applies where the Commission is satisfied—

    (a) that a person or persons in possession or control of any property held by or on trust for a charity is or are unwilling to apply it properly for the purposes of the charity, and

    (b) that it is necessary or desirable to make an order under this section for the purpose of securing a proper application of that property for the purposes of the charity.

(2) The Commission may by order direct the person or persons concerned to apply the property in such manner as is specified in the order.

(3) An order under this section—

    (a) may require action to be taken whether or not it would otherwise be within the powers exercisable by the person or persons concerned in relation to the property, but

    (b) may not require any action to be taken which is prohibited by any Act of Parliament or expressly prohibited by the trusts of the charity.

(4) Anything done by a person under the authority of an order under this section shall be deemed to be properly done in the exercise of the powers mentioned in subsection (3)(a) above.

(5) Subsection (4) does not affect any contractual or other rights arising in connection with anything which has been done under the authority of such an order.

E RESTRICTIONS ON DISPOSITIONS OF LAND[29]

Part V of the Charities Act 1993 provides that the consent of the Charity Commission is not required by charity trustees to sell charity land, provided that the statutory requirements are satisfied.[30] There are less stringent requirements for leases for seven years or less.

---

[29] All charity land is held on a trust of land: s. 2(5) Trusts of Land and Appointment of Trustees Act 1996. See generally on restrictions on the disposition of charity land, Cheshire and Burn, *Modern Law of Real Property* (17th edn, 2006), pp. 926–928; [2006] Conv 219 (D. Dennis).

[30] A disposition not complying with s. 36 is valid in favour of a purchaser in good faith for money or money's worth: Charities Act 1993, s. 37(4); *Bayoumi v Women's Total Abstinence Educational Union Ltd* [2004] Ch 46.

F *EX GRATIA* PAYMENTS

Section 27 of the Charities Act 1993 extends to the Commission the power of the Attorney-General to permit a charity to make an *ex gratia* payment under his or her supervision. Guidance as to the circumstances under which this power may be exercised is given in *Re Snowden* [1979] Ch 528[31] and *Re Henderson* [1970] Ch 700.[32]

CHARITIES ACT 1993

27. Power to authorise *ex gratia* payments etc.

(1) Subject to subsection (3) below, the Commission may by order exercise the same power as is exercisable by the Attorney-General to authorise the charity trustees of a charity—

  (a) to make any application of property of the charity, or

  (b) to waive to any extent, on behalf of the charity, its entitlement to receive any property,

in a case where the charity trustees—

  (i) (apart from this section) have no power to do so, but

  (ii) in all the circumstances regard themselves as being under a moral obligation to do so.

(2) The power conferred on the Commission by subsection (1) above shall be exercisable by the Commission under the supervision of, and in accordance with such directions as may be given by, the Attorney-General; and any such directions may in particular require the Commission, in such circumstances as are specified in the directions—

  (a) to refrain from exercising that power; or

  (b) to consult the Attorney-General before exercising it.

(3) Where—

  (a) an application is made to the Commission for it to exercise that power in a case where it is not precluded from doing so by any such directions, but

  (b) the Commission considers that it would nevertheless be desirable for the application to be entertained by the Attorney-General rather than by the Commission,

the Commission shall refer the application to the Attorney-General.

(4) It is hereby declared that where, in the case of any application made to the Commission as mentioned in subsection (3)(a) above, the Commission determines the application by refusing to authorise charity trustees to take any action

---

[31] See p. 591, below.

[32] See also Charity Commission, '*Ex Gratia* Payments by Charities' (CC7) (2001).

falling within subsection (1)(a) or (b) above, that refusal shall not preclude the Attorney-General, on an application subsequently made to him by the trustees, from authorising the trustees to take that action.

Report of the Charity Commissioners for England and Wales for the year 1969, paras. 27–29

27.　Briefly summarised the facts in the *Snowden* case were that a testator gave to close relatives all his shares in certain companies with which he had been connected and, after making other legacies, left his residuary estate to a number of charities. Those companies were, however, taken over by a much larger company and all the testator's shares were sold and at the date of his death were represented in his estate by cash. The result was that nothing passed under the gift to the relatives, but the legacies received by the charities under the residuary gift were enhanced to an extent that the testator obviously had not anticipated. Most, but not all, of the charities felt that they were under an obligation to make a payment out of the residuary legacies to the relatives to go some way towards achieving the obvious intention of the testator. It was argued on their behalf that since charities rely for their subscriptions on the recognition by the public of a moral duty to support charities, so also charities cannot and must not ignore moral obligations that are laid on them and should behave in this respect at least as well as a responsible individual.

28.　The facts in the *Henderson* case were different because there were no specific named charities which benefited and which could consider whether or not an *ex gratia* payment should be made. In this case the testatrix made a holograph will[33] to which certain words had been added in her handwriting but in a different colour. It was uncertain whether these words had been added before execution and they were not admitted to probate; but in the circumstances they would have had a considerable effect in increasing the size of legacies that were payable to a nephew and niece. The will ended with the words: 'anything over to *Charitys*'. The proceedings were brought by the executrix who asked that she might be allowed to make some reasonable payment to provide increased legacies for the nephew and niece to meet the wishes expressed in the written words even though this would reduce the size of the residue falling to be distributed to charities.

29.　Mr. Justice Cross delivered a considered judgment in which he reviewed other instances in which persons under disability are expected to recognise moral obligations and considered some old cases where charities were authorised not to press to their full legal claims arising from breaches of trust. He then reached the important conclusion that the court and the Attorney-General had power to give authority to charity trustees to make *ex gratia* payments out of funds held on charitable trusts. It is to be noted, however, that the Judge did not suggest that trustees have any power themselves to make such payments without authority. The Judge emphasised that the power to give this authority is not to be exercised on slender grounds but only in cases where it can be fairly said that if the charity were an individual it would be morally wrong for him to refuse to make the payment. He drew the distinction between cases like those which were before him in which the testator never intended the charity to receive so large a gift as it did receive and other cases in which the testator did intend the charity to receive exactly what came to it but the testator's relatives considered that he was not morally justified

---

[33] A will which is in the testator's handwriting.

in leaving his money to a charity rather than to them. In the latter case there would as a rule be no moral obligation resting on the charity and no authority should be given for it to make a payment. There might be some cases where an *ex gratia* payment could be justified even though the intentions of the testator had been carried out; for instance the testator in making the gift to the charity might have been breaking a solemn, though not legally enforceable, promise to leave a legacy to someone else. The judge, however, said he thought that instances in which an *ex gratia* payment would be justified would be rarer in the cases where the testator clearly intended to leave the money to charity and not to the claimant, than in those in which the testator's obvious intention to benefit the claimant had been frustrated through some oversight or legal technicality.[34]

G INQUIRIES

Section 8 of the Charities Act 1993 gives powers to the Commission to institute inquiries. An inquiry is necessary before it can exercise its wide powers for the protection of a charity under section 18.[35]

CHARITIES ACT 1993

8. General power to institute inquiries[36]

(1) The Commission may from time to time institute inquiries with regard to charities or a particular charity or class of charities, either generally or for particular purposes, but no such inquiry shall extend to any exempt charity.

(2) The Commission may either conduct such an inquiry itself or appoint a person to conduct it and make a report to the Commission.

(6) Where an inquiry has been held under this section, the Commission may either—

   (a) cause the report of the person conducting the inquiry, or such other statement of the results of the inquiry, as the Commission thinks fit, to be printed and published, or

   (b) publish any such report or statement in some other way which is calculated in the Commission's opinion to bring it to the attention of persons who may wish to make representations to the Commission about the action to be taken.

---

[34] See Annual Report for 1970, para. 84; 1976, paras. 114–116; 1977, paras. 154–156.

[35] See p. 603, below.

[36] See also ss. 9 (power to call for documents, and search records), 18 (power to act for protection of charities) [p. 603, below]; CC47 (Inquiries into Charities) (2003); and generally [1992–93] 1 *Charity Law & Practice Review* 127 (E. Cairns).

Report of the Charity Commissioners for England and Wales for the year 1986, para. 44

44. Allegations of abuse cover a wide range of problems: alleged misappropriation of funds forms only a small proportion of the cases examined. Complaints cover such matters as unconstitutional behaviour, inadequate financial control, weak administration, unduly high administration or fund-raising costs, factional disputes or personality clashes, political activities, deficiencies in the treatment of beneficiaries, and dubious fund-raising methods.[37] Many complaints are based on misapprehension about trustees' powers; some are trivial or obsessive. All allegations and complaints, whether pointing to a weakness in administration or a breach of trust, are investigated unless they are clearly mistaken, vindictive or repetitive; if they are substantiated, action is taken to remedy the situation if it is possible to do so.

CHARITIES ACT 1993 (as inserted by Charities Act 2006, s. 20)

19A Power to give specific directions for protection of charity

(1) This section applies where, at any time after the Commission has instituted an inquiry under section 8 above with respect to any charity, it is satisfied as mentioned in section 18(1)(a) or (b) above.[38]

(2) The Commission may by order direct—

   (a) the charity trustees,

   (b) any trustee for the charity,

   (c) any officer or employee of the charity, or

   (d) (if a body corporate) the charity itself,

   to take any action specified in the order which the Commission considers to be expedient in the interests of the charity.

(3) An order under this section—

   (a) may require action to be taken whether or not it would otherwise be within the powers exercisable by the person or persons concerned, or by the charity, in relation to the administration of the charity or to its property, but

   (b) may not require any action to be taken which is prohibited by any Act of Parliament or expressly prohibited by the trusts of the charity or is inconsistent with its purposes.

(4) Anything done by a person or body under the authority of an order under this section shall be deemed to be properly done in the exercise of the powers mentioned in subsection (3)(a) above.

(5) Subsection (4) does not affect any contractual or other rights arising in connection with anything which has been done under the authority of such an order.

---

[37] Now see the Charities Act 2006, Part 3. See also See Part II of the Charities Act 1992 (Control of Fund-Raising for Charitable Institutions), which introduced a new regime aimed at professional fund-raisers.

[38] See p. 603, below.

H   PROVISION OF ADVICE AND DETERMINING MEMBERSHIP

CHARITIES ACT 1993 (as inserted by Charities Act 2006, ss. 24 and 25)

29   Power to give advice and guidance

(1) The Commission may, on the written application of any charity trustee or trustee for a charity, give that person its opinion or advice in relation to any matter—

    (a) relating to the performance of any duties of his, as such a trustee, in relation to the charity concerned, or

    (b) otherwise relating to the proper administration of the charity.

(2) A charity trustee or trustee for a charity who acts in accordance with any opinion or advice given by the Commission under subsection (1) above (whether to him or to another trustee) is to be taken, as regards his responsibility for so acting, to have acted in accordance with his trust.

(3) But subsection (2) above does not apply to a person if, when so acting, either—

    (a) he knows or has reasonable cause to suspect that the opinion or advice was given in ignorance of material facts, or

    (b) a decision of the court or the Tribunal has been obtained on the matter or proceedings are pending to obtain one.

(4) The Commission may, in connection with its second general function mentioned in section 1C(2) above,[39] give such advice or guidance with respect to the administration of charities as it considers appropriate.

(5) Any advice or guidance so given may relate to—

    (a) charities generally,

    (b) any class of charities, or

    (c) any particular charity,

and may take such form, and be given in such manner, as the Commission considers appropriate.

29A   Power to determine membership of charity

(1) The Commission may—

    (a) on the application of a charity, or

    (b) at any time after the institution of an inquiry under section 8 above[40] with respect to a charity,

determine who are the members of the charity.

---

[39] See p. 580, above.   [40] See p. 592, above.

I LEGAL PROCEEDINGS RELATING TO CHARITIES

CHARITIES ACT 1993

32. Proceedings by the Commission

(1) Subject to subsection (2) below, the Commission may exercise the same powers with respect to—

(a) the taking of legal proceedings with reference to charities or the property or affairs of charities, or

(b) the compromise of claims with a view to avoiding or ending such proceedings, as are exercisable by the Attorney-General acting *ex officio*.

(5) The powers exercisable by the Commission by virtue of this section shall be exercisable by the Commission of its own motion, but shall be exercisable only with the agreement of the Attorney-General on each occasion.

33. Proceedings by other persons

(1) Charity proceedings may be taken with reference to a charity either by the charity, or by any of the charity trustees, or by any other person interested[41] in the charity, or by any two or more inhabitants of the area of the charity if it is a local charity,[42] but not by any other person.

(2) Subject to the following provisions of this section, no charity proceedings relating to a charity shall be entertained or proceeded with in any court unless the taking of the proceedings is authorised by order of the Commission.

(3) The Commission shall not, without special reasons, authorise the taking of charity proceedings where in its opinion the case can be dealt with by the Commission under the powers of this Act other than those conferred by section 32 above.

(5) Where the foregoing provisions of this section require the taking of charity proceedings to be authorised by an order of the Commission, the proceedings may nevertheless be entertained or proceeded with if, after the order had been applied for and refused, leave to take the proceedings was obtained from one of the judges of the High Court attached to the Chancery Division.

(6) Nothing in the foregoing subsections shall apply to the taking of proceedings by the Attorney-General, with or without a relator, or to the taking of proceedings by the Commissioners in accordance with section 32 above.

---

[41] Defined in *Scott v National Trust for Places of Historical Interest or Natural Beauty* [1998] 2 All ER 705 as where a person has an interest which is materially greater than or different from that possessed by ordinary members of the public in securing the due administration of the charity. See p. 596, below. See also *Brooks v Richardson* [1986] 1 WLR 385; *Bradshaw v University College of Wales* [1988] 1 WLR 190; *Re Hampton Fuel Allotment Charity* [1989] Ch 484; *Gunning v Buckfast Abbey Trustees Registered* (1994) The Times, 9 June; (1995) 9 *Trust Law International* 13 (R. Nolan).

[42] See Charities Act 1993, s. 96 (1).

(7) Where it appears to the Commission, on an application for an order under this section or otherwise, that it is desirable for legal proceedings to be taken with reference to any charity or its property or affairs, and for the proceedings to be taken by the Attorney-General, the Commission shall so inform the Attorney-General, and send him such statements and particulars as the Commission thinks necessary to explain the matter.

(8) In this section 'charity proceedings' means proceedings in any court in England or Wales brought under the court's jurisdiction with respect to charities, or brought under the court's jurisdiction with respect to trustees in relation to the administration of a trust for charitable purposes.[43]

In **Muman v Nagasena** [2000] 1 WLR 299, Mummery J said at 305:

This . . . is a trust for charitable purposes, and it is clear that there are now issues in the possession proceedings which relate to the administration of those trusts, namely: (i) who are the trustees of the charity; and (ii) who is the patron of the charity. There is a possible third issue as to who are the members. Those are matters of internal or domestic dispute and are not a dispute with an outsider to the charity. These are charity proceedings within section 33(8). That means that they cannot be continued without the authorisation either of the order of the Charity Commissioners or of a judge of the High Court of Justice, Chancery Division. No such authorisation has been obtained. To allow the proceedings to continue without authorisation would be to offend the whole purpose of requiring authorisation for the charity proceedings. That is to prevent charities from frittering away money subject to charitable trusts in pursuing litigation relating to internal disputes.

Scott v National Trust for Places of Historic Interest or Natural Beauty
[1998] 2 All ER 705 (Ch **Robert Walker J**)

The National Trust had decided not to renew licenses to hunt deer on its land in the south-west of England. Members of various hunts which were affected by this decision and tenant farmers on the relevant land belonging to the Trust sought judicial review of the decision. The Charity Commissioners refused to authorise a judicial review application so the plaintiffs commenced 'charity proceedings' under section 33 by originating summons. The issue before the court concerned *locus standi* of the plaintiffs and the relationship between judicial review and charity proceedings.

Held. The plaintiffs could bring charity proceedings but not an application for judicial review.[44]

Robert Walker J: It is easy to recognise a public element in charitable institutions, and especially in a charitable institution which is regulated by Act of Parliament and is of such great

---

[43] The court only has jurisdiction over a charity which is established under English law: *Gaudiya Mission v Brahmachary* [1998] Ch 341 [see p. 410, above].

[44] The charity proceedings were not successful because the decision-making process of the National Trust was considered to be reasonable.

national importance as the National Trust. Charitable trusts were being commonly referred to as 'public' trusts long before the expression 'public law' was in common use. As long ago as 1767 Lord Camden LC began his definition of charity as a 'gift to the general public use': see *Jones v Williams* (1767) Amb 651. In *IRC v Educational Grants Association Ltd* [1967] Ch 993 at 1011 Harman LJ quoted that definition and commented that the 'word "public" there runs through all the charity cases'.

The questions of how the law should monitor charities, and of how the law should monitor those public officers and non-charitable bodies which are obviously amenable to judicial review, raise similar problems, to which the law has, it seems to me, provided similar although by no means identical solutions.

The way in which these entities exercise their powers and discretions may affect directly or indirectly many different sections of the public; and even members of the general public who are not personally affected financially or otherwise in any way, may still have very strong and sincerely held views about the rights or wrongs of decisions, whether by a charity or a local authority on a subject such as hunting. The court has jurisdiction to prevent misuse of public powers either by judicial review or (in the case of a charity) by charity proceedings (as that expression is defined in section 33(8) of the Charities Act 1993). In each case the complainant must have a sufficient interest, either under section 33(1) of the Charities Act 1993 or under section 31(3) of the Supreme Court Act 1981....

Moreover, in each case there is a 'protective filter'—as Nicholls LJ put it in one case that I shall come back to—of the need to get over the preliminary threshold of consent under Order 53, rule 3, of a judge taking the Crown Office List (for judicial review) or of the Charity Commissioners or a judge of the Chancery Division under section 33(2) or (5) of the Charities Act 1993 (for charity proceedings). This protective filter is intended to protect public officers, public bodies and charities from being harassed by a multiplicity of hopeless challenges (as has nevertheless occurred, in one series of cases which will be well known to the Attorney-General's counsel, in connection with the trusts of the Royal Masonic Hospital). The efficacy of the protective screen is, of course, enhanced by the need for the complainant to have a sufficient interest or an interest in the charity.

Just as the 'sufficient interest' referred to in section 31(3) of the Supreme Court Act 1981 reflects an old (but developing) body of law on prerogative writs and orders...so section 33(1) of the Charities Act 1993 reflects law that goes back at least to sections 17 and 43 of the Charitable Trusts Act 1853. In the old days when education and healthcare was more generally provided through charities, the question whether a schoolmaster or resident medical officer appointed and paid by charity trustees had lawfully been dismissed could be seen either as a matter of employment law or as a matter of the proper administration of charitable trusts. In some nineteenth-century cases referred to by Miss Judith Jackson, QC (for the Attorney-General) the Court of Appeal decided that whether the litigation constituted charity proceedings (or rather, the equivalent phrase in the 1853 Act) depended on the nature of the relief sought—see *Benthall v Earl of Kilmourey* (1883) 25 Ch D 39 and *Rendall v Blair* (1890) 45 Ch D 139. It is rightly conceded that the originating summons proceedings are charity proceedings. No such concession is made in relation to the writ proceedings. A similar concession seems to have been made in a much more recent case before Arden J, *Gunning v Buckfast Abbey Trustees Registered* (1994) The Times, 9 June. Those were proceedings brought by parents complaining of the closure of a fee-paying boarding-school run by charity trustees. On a preliminary issue as to the parents' interest the trustees submitted, unsuccessfully, that because their relationship with the parents was founded in contract, the parents' only interest in the charity was an interest adverse to the charity and that they were therefore not persons interested in the relevant sense. As I say, that submission failed.

The *Buckfast Abbey* case is the most recent case in which the court has had to grapple with the phrase 'interested in the charity' in section 33(1) and its predecessor, section 28(1) of the Charities Act 1960. The court (including the Court of Appeal) has shown a marked reluctance to embark on any comprehensive definition or explanation of that difficult phrase. But *Re Hampton Fuel Allotment Charity* [1989] Ch 484—the one recent case which has gone to the Court of Appeal—does, in the judgment of Nicholls LJ, give some guidance. The whole passage in Nicholls LJ's judgment ([1989] Ch 484 at 490–494) calls for careful study, but I will read some crucial passages:

> 'The words "interest" and "interested" are words which bear widely differing meanings according to their context. Although section 28 of the Act of 1960 contains no definition, the context does provide a little guidance on what Parliament must have had in mind. First, the context is that of standing to bring charity proceedings with reference to a particular charity. So that the person needs to have some good reason for bringing the matter before the court. Second, whilst there may be special historical reasons for this, it is to be noted that in the case of local charities, any two or more inhabitants of the area of the charity are competent plaintiffs. So there the net is spread widely. Third, a protective filter exists in respect of charity proceedings, in that persons competent to bring charity proceedings under section 28(1) generally require approval from the Charity Commissioners or the court, under section 28(2) [or] (5). So that concern to avoid charities being vexed with frivolous and ill-founded claims does not dictate that "person interested" must be given a narrow meaning. Fourth and importantly, the historic role of the Attorney-General, representing the Crown, is preserved in relation to charity proceedings by section 28(6).' [See [1989] Ch 484 at 493–494.]

Then, after a reference to some observations by Lord Macnaghten, Nicholls LJ continued (at 494):

> 'Again, as Lord Simonds observed in *National Anti-Vivisection Society v IRC* ([1948] AC 31 at 62), it is the right and duty of the Attorney-General to intervene and inform the court if the trustees of a charitable trust fall short of their duty. Thus the interest which ordinary members of the public, whether or not subscribing to a charity, and whether or not potential beneficiaries of a charity, have in seeing that a charity is properly administered is a matter in respect of which the Attorney-General remains charged with responsibilities. He can institute proceedings *ex officio* or *ex relatione*. This suggests, therefore, that to qualify as a plaintiff in his own right a person generally needs to have an interest materially greater than or different from that possessed by ordinary members of the public such as we have described. In our view that may be as near as one can get to identifying what is the nature of the interest which a person needs to possess to qualify under this heading as a competent plaintiff. It is not a definition. But charitable trusts vary so widely that to seek a definition here is, we believe, to search for a will-o'-the-wisp. If a person has an interest in securing the due administration of a trust materially greater than, or different from, that possessed by ordinary members of the public as described above, that interest may, depending on the circumstances, qualify him as a "person interested". It may do so because that may give him, to echo the words of Sir Robert Megarry V-C in *Haslemere Estates Ltd v Baker* ([1982] 3 All ER 525 at 537): "some good reason for seeking to enforce the trusts of a charity or secure its due administration..." We appreciate that this is imprecise, even vague, but we can see

no occasion or justification for the court attempting to delimit with precision a boundary which Parliament has left undefined.'

As to Nicholls LJ's fourth point, I would, with diffidence, comment that although the power (and on appropriate occasions the duty) of the Attorney-General to intervene is beyond question, there may often be occasions when (on grounds of expense to public funds, or uncertainty as to the outcome or otherwise) the Attorney-General may perfectly properly decide not to intervene. By enacting section 33 of the Charities Act 1993 and its predecessors, Parliament has plainly intended not to give the Attorney-General a monopoly of proceedings for judicial monitoring of charities. As Nicholls LJ said in his second and third points, the net is spread widely and there is a protective filter (though perhaps those metaphors do not, with great respect, sit very happily together). The purpose of the filter is, as I have said, to protect charities from being harassed and put to expense by a multiplicity of claims, which may or may not be well-founded, by persons who may or may not fairly be described as 'busybodies'....

The Court of Appeal in the *Hampton* case emphasised...that the question of interest is not simply a bare question of law, but depends on all the circumstances of the particular case. Counsel for the National Trust (Mr. Michael Douglas QC, with Mr. Simon Henderson) rely on the decision of Megarry V-C in *Haslemere Estates Ltd v Baker,* for excluding as a sufficient interest that of a person claiming adversely to the charity. That case was a claim by a property developer against the trustees of Dulwich College. It was a wholly commercial dispute which had no real connection with the internal or functional administration of charitable trusts. The nineteenth-century cases about schoolmasters and medical officers, and the *Buckfast Abbey* case, show that the position may be different when the complainant, although having some sort of contractual link with the charity trustees which might, on analysis, be described as adverse, is really complaining about the way in which the charity is performing its essential functions. In the *Hampton* case [1989] Ch 484 at 492 it is recognised that if land is functional land of a charity, that may make an important difference.

In this case the Devon and Somerset staghounds and the Quantock staghounds have been hunting deer on Exmoor and the Quantocks since long before the National Trust owned land there. Whether their activities are regarded as laudable or deplorable, the affidavit evidence makes out a strong case that they are an important part of the rural economy in contributing to deer culling, in providing a service in destroying and removing sick and injured beasts, and generally in deer management—the need for which was recognised and strongly emphasised in the Savage working party recommendations. They contribute to the local economy through livery stables, bed-and-breakfast accommodation and in other ways. They freely co-operated with the research carried out over an 18-month period by Professor Bateson and Dr. Bradshaw on behalf of the National Trust. Their co-operation is clearly still needed, and hoped for, by the National Trust in any modified schemes of deer management which may be needed as a result of deer-hunting ceasing on National Trust land (except for the 750 hectares or thereabouts of the Dunkery Estate).

I find it quite impossible to equate the plaintiffs' position with that of the commercial property developer in the *Haslemere Estates* case. It seems to me that until this year and for many years the hunts and the tenant farmers have been in a loose, but nevertheless, a real sense, partners with the National Trust in the management of its land on Exmoor and the Quantocks, and in the successful preservation of the red deer population, whose preservation can fairly be regarded as one of the National Trust's statutory purposes under section 4(1) of the National Trust Act 1907.

For those reasons I conclude that the plaintiffs in the originating summons proceedings have a sufficient interest (within the meaning of section 33(1) of the Charities Act 1993) to bring charity proceedings in the form of the originating summons. I need not decide whether the fact that individuals pay ordinary annual subscriptions as members of the National Trust (as Mrs. Scott and Mr. Fewings do) would by that alone give them a sufficient interest. There are about two million members of the National Trust, so that would be to cast the net very wide indeed, and what Nicholls LJ said in the *Hampton* case [1989] Ch 484 at 493 seems to me to be fairly definitely against it....

I do not think it is helpful, or even possible, to consider the broad question of whether any charity, or even any charity specially established by statute, is subject to judicial review. Charities are, as Nicholls LJ said, many and various. But the National Trust is a charity of exceptional importance to the nation, regulated by its own special Acts of Parliament. Its purposes and functions are of high public importance, as is reflected by the special statutory provisions (in the fields of taxation and compulsory acquisition) to which I have already referred. It seems to me to have all the characteristics of a public body which is, *prima facie*, amenable to judicial review, and to have been exercising its statutory public functions in making the decision which is challenged.

However, it is well established that judicial review will not normally be granted where an alternative remedy is available, whether by way of appeal or otherwise—see *R v Chief Constable of the Merseyside Police, ex p Calveley* [1986] QB 424 at 433–434, at 435–437 and 440, *per* Donaldson MR, May LJ and Glidewell LJ respectively. There are exceptions to the general rule, as that case shows. But it seems to me that Parliament has laid down a special procedure—charity proceedings in the Chancery Division—for judicial monitoring of charities, and that in all but the most exceptional cases that is the procedure which should be followed. A possible exception (and this is mere speculation) might be where a local authority held land on charitable trusts and questions about its dealings with that land were caught up with other questions about its dealings with land which it owned beneficially (though subject, of course, to statutory constraints). But I can see no good reason for making an exception in this case. The plaintiffs, whatever false starts they made, are now some considerable way down the road of their originating summons proceedings and I have held that they have a sufficient interest to do so. It seems to me that it would be less convenient, not more, if they were now to have to go through the double filter of section 33 of the Charities Act 1933 and section 31 of the Supreme Court Act 1981 in order to bring the substance of their complaint before the High Court. I can readily understand why, after their unsuccessful application in the Crown Office List, the plaintiffs have thought it right to take every precaution against what they may regard as being thwarted again by a technicality. But it seems to me that the right course is for the plaintiffs to proceed with their charity proceedings—that is the originating summons—and that to have parallel judicial review proceedings would simply be wasteful duplication. I do not however, for myself, regard the protective filter and the need for a sufficient interest as matters of technicality, but (for reasons which I have tried to explain) as a sensible and necessary requirement in the public law field, including the law of public (or charitable) trusts.

In **Royal Society for the Prevention of Cruelty to Animals v Attorney-General** [2002] 1 WLR 448 there was a challenge to the charity's policy of excluding existing members and preventing new members from joining if their reason for joining was to change the charity's policy against hunting with dogs. Before considering the validity of the policy, LIGHTMAN J had first to consider whether those who had challenged the policy were interested in the charity under section 33. After concluding that an existing member of the charity was so interested he went on to say, at 458:

But I do not think that a disappointed applicant for membership has any such sufficient interest. Any member of the public is free to apply for membership: the exercise of that liberty cannot elevate the status of a non-member into that of a person interested. To extend the right of suit to any such applicant would be to cast the net too wide (consider *Scott v National Trust for Places of Historic Interest or Natural Beauty* [1998] 2 All ER 705 at 715). I should add, in view of the suggestion by Mr. Martin QC [for the added defendants] to the contrary, that it does not seem to me to be a factor of any significance on the issue of the status of the added defendants that in 1932, by a private Act, the Society was transformed from being an unincorporated association into a corporate body. The fact that the Society is now constituted by an Act of Parliament does not give a member or prospective member any greater right of access to the court.

The second issue is whether Baron Vinson and Ms. Atkinson are able to challenge the Society's decision on their applications for membership in judicial review proceedings in the Administrative Court. It is well established that judicial review proceedings are inappropriate where the issue can be the subject matter of charity proceedings. The question raised is whether Baron Vinson and Ms. Atkinson are able to bring judicial review proceedings if they do not have the necessary interest to bring charity proceedings. The answer to this question is in the negative. There is a serious question whether the Society is the sort of public body which is amenable to judicial review, most particularly in respect of decisions made in relation to its membership (consider *Scott's* case (at 716)). The fact that a charity is by definition a public, as opposed to a private, trust means that the trustees are subject to public law duties and judicial review is in general available to enforce performance of such duties. There is therefore a theoretical basis for allowing recourse to judicial review. It is also true that the Society is a very important charity and its activities (in particular, the inspectorate and its prosecutions for cruelty to animals) are of great value to society. In particular, its inspectorate is the largest non-governmental law enforcement agency in England and Wales. But in carrying out these activities the Society is in law in no different position from that of any citizen or other organisation. Unlike the National Trust, the subject of consideration by Walker J in *Scott's* case, the Society has no statutory or public law role. All I will say is that, though theoretically and in a proper case an application for judicial review may lie, it would not (at any rate in any ordinary case) lie at the instance of disappointed applicants for membership whose interest was insufficient to meet the statutory standard for the institution of charity proceedings. The statutory standard is laid down as a form of protection of charity trustees and the Administrative Court would rarely (if ever) be justified in allowing that protection to be circumvented by the expedient of commencing (in place of charity proceedings) judicial review proceedings. That does not mean that a disappointed applicant for membership is without recourse, for he can complain to the Charity Commission or the Attorney-General and request them to take action.

His Lordship then went on to hold that it was appropriate for a charity to adopt a policy of excluding from its membership those people whom it honestly believed would be damaging to its interest, since such exclusion was consistent with the right to freedom of association under Article 11 of the European Convention on Human Rights. However, the particular method of exclusion adopted by the RSPCA was draconian since it did not give the prospective member the opportunity to argue that he or she did not have an ulterior motive for joining the Society.

It is possible for the court to require internal disputes arising within a charity to be resolved by mediation before legal proceedings are pursued: **Muman v Nagasena** [2000] 1 WLR 299 at 305. A combined mediation service for charities has been established by the Centre for Dispute Resolution jointly with the National Council for Voluntary Organisations. MUMMERY LJ recognised that the purpose of this service is to 'achieve, by voluntary action confidentially conducted, a healing process under which disputes within a charity can be resolved at a modest fee and without diminishing the funds which have been raised for charitable purposes'.

II CHARITY TRUSTEES[45]

A DEFINITION

CHARITIES ACT 1993

General interpretation

97 (1) In this Act, except in so far as the context otherwise requires—
  'charity trustees' means the persons having the general control and management of the administration of a charity;[46] ...

B NUMBER

TRUSTEE ACT 1925

34. Limitation of the number of trustees

  (3) This section only applies to settlements and dispositions of land, and the restrictions imposed on the number of trustees do not apply—
    (a) in the case of land vested in trustees for charitable, ecclesiastical, or public purposes.

It follows that there is no maximum number of trustees of a charitable trust.

---

[45] See CC3(a)(The Essential Trustee: An Introduction) (2007). For the personal liability of charity trustees and their right to be indemnified out of the trust fund, see (1979) 95 LQR 99 (A.J. Hawkins).
[46] On the use of beneficiaries as trustees, see CC24 (Users on Board: Beneficiaries who become Trustees) (2000).

C APPOINTMENT

CHARITIES ACT 1993

18. Power to act for protection of charities

(5) The Commission may by order made of its own motion appoint a person to be a charity trustee—

    (a) in place of a charity trustee removed by the Commission under this section or otherwise;

    (b) where there are no charity trustees, or where by reason of vacancies in their number or the absence or incapacity of any of their number the charity cannot apply for the appointment;

    (c) where there is a single charity trustee, not being a corporation aggregate, and the Commission is of opinion that it is necessary to increase the number for the proper administration of the charity;

    (d) where the Commission is of opinion that it is necessary for the proper administration of the charity to have an additional charity trustee because one of the existing charity trustees who ought nevertheless to remain a charity trustee either cannot be found or does not act or is outside England and Wales.

(6) The powers of the Commission under this section to remove or appoint charity trustees of its own motion shall include power to make any such order with respect to the vesting in or transfer to the charity trustees of any property as the Commission could make on the removal or appointment of a charity trustee by it under section 16 above.[47]

D RETIREMENT

Charity trustees may retire in the same way as trustees of private trusts.[48]

E REMOVAL AND SUSPENSION

CHARITIES ACT 1993

18. Power to act for protection of charities

(1) Where, at any time after it has instituted an inquiry under section 8 above[49] with respect to any charity, the Commission is satisfied—

    (a) that there is or has been any misconduct or mismanagement in the administration of the charity; or

---

[47] See p. 585, above.   [48] See p. 640, below.   [49] See p. 592, above.

(b) that it is necessary or desirable to act for the purpose of protecting the property of the charity or securing a proper application for the purposes of the charity of that property or of property coming to the charity

the Commission may of its own motion do one or more of the following things—

(i) by order suspend any trustee, charity trustee, officer, agent or employee of the charity from the exercise of his office or employment pending consideration being given to his removal (whether under this section or otherwise);

(ii) by order appoint such number of additional charity trustees as they consider necessary for the proper administration of the charity;

(iii) by order vest any property held by or in trust for the charity in the official custodian, or require the persons in whom any such property is vested to transfer it to him, or appoint any person to transfer any such property to him;

(iv) order any person who holds any property on behalf of the charity, or of any trustee for it, not to part with the property without the approval of the Commission;

(v) order any debtor of the charity not to make any payment in or towards the discharge of his liability to the charity without the approval of the Commission;

(vi) by order restrict (notwithstanding anything in the trusts of the charity) the transactions which may be entered into, or the nature or amount of the payments which may be made, in the administration of the charity without the approval of the Commission;

(vii) by order appoint (in accordance with section 19 below) an interim manager, who shall act as receiver and manager in respect of the property and affairs of the charity.

(2) Where, at any time after it has instituted an inquiry under section 8 above with respect to any charity, the Commission is satisfied—

(a) that there is or has been any misconduct or mismanagement in the administration of the charity; and

(b) that it is necessary or desirable to act for the purpose of protecting the property of the charity or securing a proper application for the purposes of the charity of that property or of property coming to the charity

the Commission may of its own motion do either or both of the following things—

(i) by order remove any trustee, charity trustee, officer, agent or employee of the charity who has been responsible for or privy to the misconduct or mismanagement or has by his conduct contributed to it or facilitated it

(ii) by order establish a scheme for the administration of the charity.

(3) The references in subsection (1) or (2) above to misconduct or mismanagement shall (notwithstanding anything in the trusts of the charity) extend to the employment for the remuneration or reward of persons acting in the affairs of the charity, or for other administrative purposes, of sums which are excessive in relation to the property which is or is likely to be applied or applicable for the purposes of the charity.

(4) The Commission may also remove a charity trustee by order made of its own motion—

    (a) where, within the last five years, the trustee—

        (i) having previously been adjudged bankrupt or had his estate seques-trated, has been discharged, or

        (ii) having previously made a composition or arrangement with, or granted a trust deed for, his creditors, has been discharged in respect of it;

    (b) where the trustee is a corporation in liquidation;

    (c) where the trustee is incapable of acting by reason of mental disorder within the meaning of the Mental Health Act 1983;

    (d) where the trustee has not acted, and will not declare his willingness or unwillingness to act;

    (e) where the trustee is outside England and Wales or cannot be found or does not act, and his absence or failure to act impedes the proper administration of the charity.

(5) (6) p. 603, above.

(11) The power of the Commission to make an order under subsection (1)(i) above shall not be exercisable so as to suspend any person from the exercise of his office or employment for a period of more than 12 months; but (without prejudice to the generality of section 89(1) below), any such order made in the case of any person may make provision as respects the period of his suspension for matters arising out of it, and in particular for enabling any person to execute any instrument in his name or otherwise act for him and, in the case of a charity trustee, for adjusting any rules governing the proceedings of the charity trustees to take account of the reduction in the number capable of acting.[50]

The Charities Act 2006 creates a new power for the Charity Commission to remove a person from membership of a charity.

---

[50] On disqualification for acting as a charity trustee, see Charities Act 1993, ss. 72 and 73, as amended by Insolvency Act 2000, s. 8, Sch. 4, para. 18. On application for waiver under s. 22(1), see [1993] 1 Charity Commissioners' Report 26; [1994] 2 Charity Commissioners' Report 11. The Commission has power to waive a trustee's disqualification: s. 72(4A), Charities Act 1993, as inserted by Charities Act 2006.

CHARITIES ACT 1993 (as inserted by Charities Act 2006, ss. 19)

18A Power to suspend or remove trustees etc. from membership of charity

(1) This section applies where the Commission makes—

  (a) an order under section 18(1) above suspending from his office or employment any trustee, charity trustee, officer, agent or employee of a charity, or

  (b) an order under section 18(2) above removing from his office or employment any officer, agent or employee of a charity,

  and the trustee, charity trustee, officer, agent or employee (as the case may be) is a member of the charity.

(2) If the order suspends the person in question from his office or employment, the Commission may also make an order suspending his membership of the charity for the period for which he is suspended from his office or employment.

(3) If the order removes the person in question from his office or employment, the Commission may also make an order—

  (a) terminating his membership of the charity, and

  (b) prohibiting him from resuming his membership of the charity without the Commission's consent.

(4) If an application for the Commission's consent under subsection (3)(b) above is made five years or more after the order was made, the Commission must grant the application unless satisfied that, by reason of any special circumstances, it should be refused.

F   ACTING BY MAJORITY

In **Re Whiteley** [1910] 1 Ch 600, one question was whether a decision of the majority of charitable trustees was binding on the whole. Earlier cases[51] had held that the decision of the majority was binding in matters of a public nature. EVE J held that the rule covered decisions of charitable trustees generally, and said at 608:

It is true that the authorities referred to by the applicants are both concerned with the appointment of a person to discharge the duties of an office of a public nature, but I cannot read the observations of Lord Lyndhurst[52] as limiting the principle there stated to the particular class of case with which he was there dealing; and I think when he speaks of a 'trust of a public nature' he is using an expression equivalent for all practical purposes to 'a trust of a charitable nature'. In other words, I regard the words 'public' and 'charitable' in this connection as synonymous, and, so regarding them, I think that the rule on which the applicants rely is of general application.

---

[51] *Wilkinson v Malin* (1832) 2 Tyr 544; *Perry v Shipway* (1859) 4 De G & J 353.
[52] *Wilkinson v Malin*, ibid, at 571.

III POWERS AND DUTIES OF CHARITABLE TRUSTEES

Trustees of charitable trusts are subject to the same duties as trustees of other types of trust,[53] and have many of the same powers.[54] The Trustee Act 2000 applies to charitable trustees.[55] Certain aspects of the general duties of trustees become especially important as regards charitable trustees. For example, charitable trustees must preserve their independence, by ensuring that they are not directly controlled by others,[56] and there are additional statutory requirements relating to accountability.[57] Also, some of the general powers and duties are interpreted in a different way because of the peculiar nature of a charitable trustee.

A REGISTRATION

CHARITIES ACT 1993 (as inserted by Charities Act 2006, s. 9)

3B Duties of trustees in connection with registration

(1) Where a charity required to be registered by virtue of section 3A(1)[58] above is not registered, it is the duty of the charity trustees—

   (a) to apply to the Commission for the charity to be registered, and

   (b) to supply the Commission with the required documents and information.

(3) Where an institution is for the time being registered, it is the duty of the charity trustees (or the last charity trustees)—

   (a) to notify the Commission if the institution ceases to exist, or if there is any change in its trusts or in the particulars of it entered in the register, and

   (b) (so far as appropriate), to supply the Commission with particulars of any such change and copies of any new trusts or alterations of the trusts.

B INVESTMENT POWERS[59]

There is no statutory definition of investment. The Charity Commissioners stated that they considered an investment to be:

an asset which is purchased with the hope of maintaining or enhancing its value, but with the main purpose of obtaining an incoming resource derived from ownership of the asset. An

---

[53] See Ch. 14, below.   [54] See Ch. 15, below.   [55] See p. 687, below.
[56] See Charity Commission, 'The Hall-marks of an Effective Charity' (CC60) (2004) and 'The Independence of Charities from the State' (RR7) (2001).   [57] See p. 614, below.
[58] See p. 583, above.
[59] Luxton, chap. 16; (2001) NLJ (Ch. App. Supp) 15 (A. Paines). On investment powers generally see p. 691, below.

incoming resource need not necessarily take the form of interest or dividends. It might take the form of an assured capital appreciation—such as where interests or earning are not distributed and are, therefore, reflected in the intrinsic capital value of the asset itself, or where loan stock is issued to or purchased by trustees at a discount to its repayment value.[60]

There used to be a special statutory regime which related to the powers of investment of charitable trustees. Most of this special regime was removed by the Trustee Act 2000. It follows that the general powers of investment under the Trustee Act 2000 also apply to charitable trustees.[61] The essential feature of this statutory regime is that trustees are authorised to make any kind of investments which they would be able to make if they were absolutely entitled to the assets which are the subject matter of the trust.[62]

It follows that charitable trustees are generally not subject to any special considerations when they consider the nature of their investments.[63] However, it has been accepted that charitable trustees should not invest in investments which directly contradict the purpose of the trust, even though this may involve a financial detriment.

In **Harries v Church Commissioners for England**[64] [1992] 1 WLR 1241, the Bishop of Oxford and other clergy claimed that the Church Commissioners, whose purpose was to promote the Christian faith through the Church of England, should not select investments in a manner incompatible with that purpose, even if this involved a risk of significant financial detriment. SIR DONALD NICHOLLS V-C, in holding that ethical considerations could be taken into account only in so far as the profitability of investments was not jeopardised, said at 124:

The Church Commissioners for England administer vast estates and large funds. At the end of 1990 their holdings of land were valued at about £1.7bn., their mortgages and loans at about £165m., and their stock exchange investments at about £780m. In 1990 these items yielded altogether an investment income of £164m. The Commissioners' income included also some £66m. derived principally from parish and diocesan contributions to clergy stipends. So the Commissioners' total income last year was £230m.

The needs which the Commissioners seek to satisfy out of this income are daunting. In 1990 they provided almost one-half of the costs of the stipends of the Church of England serving clergy, much of their housing costs, and almost all their pension costs. These items absorbed over 85 per cent of the Commissioners' income: that is, a sum of almost £200m. Unfortunately, this does not mean that the clergy are well remunerated or that the retired clergy receive good pensions. Far from it. The Commissioners' income has to be spread widely, and hence thinly, over 11,400 serving clergy and 10,100 clergy pensioners and widows. So, as is well known, the

---

[60] (1995) 3 *Decisions* 18–19. See Luxton, p. 605.

[61] See p. 692, below. See generally the Charity Commission's guidance, 'Investment of Charitable Funds: Basic Principles' (CC14) (2004).

[62] Trustee Act 2000, s. 3(1). See p. 692, below. This includes investment in freehold or leasehold land, subject to any restriction or exclusion in the charity's governing document: Trustee Act 2000, s. 8 (1).

[63] Save where Charities Act 1993, ss. 24 and 25 apply. See p. 612, below.

[64] [1992] Conv 115 (R. Nobles); (1992) 55 MLR 587 (P. Luxton); (1992) 6 *Trust Law International* 119, 1253 (Lord Browne-Wilkinson); [1993] All ER Rev 258 (P.J. Clarke).

amount each receives is not generous. In 1990–1991 the national average stipend of incumbents was only £11,308. The full-service pension from April 1991 was £6,700 per year.

For some time there have been voices in the Church of England expressing disquiet at the investment policy of the Commissioners. They do not question either the good faith or the investment expertise of the Commissioners. Their concern is not that the Commissioners have failed to get the best financial return from their property and investments. Their concern is that, in making investment decisions, the Commissioners are guided too rigorously by purely financial considerations, and that the Commissioners give insufficient weight to what are now called 'ethical' considerations. They contend, moreover, that the Commissioners have fallen into legal error. The Commissioners attach overriding importance to financial considerations, and that is a misapprehension of the approach they ought properly to adopt when making investment decisions. The Commissioners ought to have in mind that the underlying purpose for which they hold their assets is the promotion of the Christian faith through the Church of England. The Commissioners should not exercise their investment functions in a manner which would be incompatible with that purpose even if that involves a risk of incurring significant financial detriment.

Before going further into the criticism made of the Commissioners I will consider the general principles applicable to the exercise of powers of investment by charity trustees. It is axiomatic that charity trustees, in common with all other trustees, are concerned to further the purposes of the trust of which they have accepted the office of trustee. That is their duty. To enable them the better to discharge that duty, trustees have powers vested in them. Those powers must be exercised for the purpose for which they have been given: to further the purposes of the trust. That is the guiding principle applicable to the issues in these proceedings. Everything which follows is no more than the reasoned application of that principle in particular contexts.

Broadly speaking, property held by charitable trustees falls into two categories. First, there is property held by trustees for what may be called functional purposes. The National Trust owns historic houses and open spaces. The Salvation Army owns hostels for the destitute. And many charities need office accommodation in which to carry out essential administrative work. Second, there is property held by trustees for the purpose of generating money, whether from income or capital growth, with which to further the work of the trust. In other words, property held by trustees as an investment. Where property is so held, *prima facie* the purposes of the trust will be best served by the trustees seeking to obtain therefrom the maximum return, whether by way of income or capital growth, which is consistent with commercial prudence. That is the starting point for all charity trustees when considering the exercise of their investment powers. Most charities need money; and the more of it there is available, the more the trustees can seek to accomplish.

In most cases this *prima facie* position will govern the trustees' conduct. In most cases the best interests of the charity require that the trustees' choice of investments should be made solely on the basis of well-established investment criteria, having taken expert advice where appropriate and having due regard to such matters as the need to diversify, the need to balance income against capital growth, and the need to balance risk against return.

In a minority of cases the position will not be so straightforward. There will be some cases, I suspect comparatively rare, when the objects of the charity are such that investments of a particular type would conflict with the aims of the charity. Much-cited examples are those of cancer research companies and tobacco shares, trustees of temperance charities and brewery and distillery shares, and trustees of charities of the Society of Friends and shares in companies engaged in production of armaments. If, as would be likely in those examples, trustees were satisfied that investing in a company engaged in a particular type of business would conflict with the very objects their charity is seeking to achieve, they should not so invest. Carried to its logical conclusion the trustees should take this course even if it would be likely to result in significant financial detriment to the charity. The logical conclusion, whilst sound as a matter of legal analysis, is unlikely to arise in practice. It is not easy to think of an instance where in practice the exclusion for this reason of one or more companies or sectors from the whole range of investments open to trustees would be likely to leave them without an adequately wide range of investments from which to choose a properly diversified portfolio.

There will also be some cases, again I suspect comparatively rare, when trustees' holdings of particular investments might hamper a charity's work either by making potential recipients of aid unwilling to be helped because of the source of the charity's money, or by alienating some of those who support the charity financially. In these cases, the trustees will need to balance the difficulties they would encounter, or likely financial loss they would sustain, if they were to hold the investments against the risk of financial detriment if those investments were excluded from their portfolio. The greater the risk of financial detriment, the more certain the trustees should be of countervailing disadvantages to the charity before they incur that risk. Another circumstance where trustees would be entitled, or even required, to take into account non-financial criteria would be where the trust deed so provides.

No doubt there will be other cases where trustees are justified in departing from what should always be their starting point. The instances I have given are not comprehensive. But I must emphasise that of their very nature, and by definition, investments are held by trustees to aid the work of the charity in a particular way: by generating money. That is the purpose for which they are held. That is their *raison d'être*. Trustees cannot properly use assets held as an investment for other, *viz.*, non-investment, purposes. To the extent that they do they are not properly exercising their powers of investment. This is not to say that trustees who own land may not act as responsible landlords or those who own shares may not act as responsible shareholders. They may. The law is not so cynical as to require trustees to behave in a fashion which would bring them or their charity into disrepute (although their consciences must not be too tender: see *Buttle v Saunders* [1950] 2 All ER 193 [p. 685, below]). On the other hand, trustees must act prudently. They must not use property held by them for investment purposes as a means for making moral statements at the expense of the charity of which they are trustees. Those who wish may do so with their own property, but that is not a proper function of trustees with trust assets held as an investment.

I should mention one other particular situation. There will be instances today when those who support or benefit from a charity take widely different views on a particular type of investment, some saying that on moral grounds it conflicts with the aims of the charity, others saying the opposite. One example is the holding of arms-industry shares by a religious charity. There is a real difficulty here. To many questions raising moral issues there are no certain answers. On moral questions widely differing views are held by well-meaning, responsible people. This is not always so. But frequently, when questions of the morality of conduct are being canvassed, there is no identifiable yardstick which can be applied to a set of facts so as to yield one answer which can be seen to be 'right' and the other 'wrong'. If that situation confronts trustees of a charity, the law does not require them to find an answer to the unanswerable. Trustees may, if they wish, accommodate the views of those who consider that on moral grounds a particular investment would be in conflict with the objects of the charity, so long as the trustees are satisfied that course would not involve a risk of significant financial detriment. But when they are not so satisfied trustees should not make investment decisions on the basis of preferring one view of whether on moral grounds in investment conflicts with the objects of the charity over another. This is so even when one view is more widely supported than the other.

I have sought above to consider charity trustees' duties in relation to investment as a matter of basic principle. I was referred to no authority bearing directly on these matters. My attention was drawn to *Cowan v Scargill* [1985] Ch 270 [p. 705, below], a case concerning a pension fund. I believe the views I have set out accord with those expressed by Sir Robert Megarry V-C in that case, bearing in mind that he was considering trusts for the provision of financial benefits for individuals. In this case I am concerned with trusts of charities, whose purposes are multifarious.

[His Lordship considered the Commissioners' objects and their investment policy, and continued:] The statement of policy records that the Commissioners do not invest in companies whose main business is in armaments, gambling, alcohol, tobacco or newspapers. Of these, newspapers fall into a category of their own. The Commissioners' policy regarding newspapers is based on the fact that many newspapers are associated, to a greater or lesser extent, with a particular political party or political view. Leaving aside newspapers, the underlying rationale of the Commissioners' policy on these items is that there is a body of members of the Church of England opposed to the businesses in question on religious or moral grounds. There are members who believe these business activities are morally wrong, and that they are in conflict with Christian teaching and its moral values. But this list has only to be read for it to be obvious that many committed members of the Church of England take the contrary view. To say that not all members of the Church of England eschew gambling, alcohol or tobacco would be an understatement. As to armaments, the morality of war, and the concepts of a 'just war', are issues which have been debated for centuries. These are moral questions on which no single view can be shown to be 'right' and the others 'wrong'. As I understand the position, the Commissioners have felt able to exclude these items from their investments despite the conflicting views on the morality of holding these items as investments because there has remained open to the Commissioners an adequate width of alternative investments.

I have already indicated that at the heart of the plaintiffs' case is a contention that the Commissioners' policy is erroneous in law in that the Commissioners are only prepared to take non-financial considerations into account to the extent that such considerations do not significantly jeopardise or interfere with accepted investment principles. I think it is implicit, if not explicit, in the Commissioners' evidence that they do regard themselves as constrained in this way. So far as I have been able to see, this is the only issue identifiable as an issue of law raised in these proceedings. In my view this self-constraint applied by the Commissioners is not one which in practice has led to any error of law on their part, nor is it likely to do so. I have already indicated that the circumstances in which charity trustees are bound or entitled to make a financially disadvantageous investment decision for ethical reasons are extremely limited. I have noted that it is not easy to think of a practical example of such a circumstance. There is no evidence before me to suggest that any such circumstance exists here. . . .

[His Lordship considered the relief claimed, and continued:] I add only this. In bringing these proceedings the Bishop of Oxford and his colleagues are actuated by the highest moral concern. But, as I have sought to show, the approach they wish the Commissioners to adopt to investment decisions would involve a departure by the Commissioners from their legal obligations. Whether such a departure would or would not be desirable is, of course, not an issue in these proceedings. That is a matter to be pursued, if at all, elsewhere than in this court.

The Trustee Act 2000 does not remove the special regime under the Charities Act 1993 relating to the creation of common investment and deposit funds.[65] This gives power to the court or the Charity Commission to create common investment schemes under which property transferred to the fund can be invested by trustees appointed to manage the fund. The participating charities are entitled to shares related to their contributions.

A common investment fund which excluded investment in tobacco stocks was approved by the Charity Commissioners in 1997 for NHS- and cancer-related charities, since such investments would have directly contradicted the objects of the charities.[66]

CHARITIES ACT 1993

24. Schemes to establish common investment funds

(1) The court or the Commission may by order make and bring into effect schemes (in this section referred to as 'common investment schemes') for the establishment of common investment funds under trusts which provide—

  (a) for property transferred to the fund by or on behalf of a charity participating in the scheme to be invested under the control of trustees appointed to manage the fund; and

  (b) for the participating charities to be entitled (subject to the provisions of the scheme) to the capital and income of the fund in shares determined by reference to the amount or value of the property transferred to it by or on behalf of each of them and to the value of the fund at the time of the transfers.

(2) The court or the Commission may make a common investment scheme on the application of any two or more charities.[67]

(3) A common investment scheme may be made in terms admitting any charity to participate, or the scheme may restrict the right to participate in any manner.

(4) A common investment scheme may make provision for, and for all matters connected with, the establishment, investment, management and winding up of the common investment fund, and may in particular include provision—

  (a) for remunerating persons appointed trustees to hold or manage the fund or any part of it, with or without provision authorising a person to receive the remuneration notwithstanding that he is also a charity trustee of or trustee for a participating charity;

  (b) for restricting the size of the fund, and for regulating as to time, amount or otherwise the right to transfer property to or withdraw it from the fund, and

---

[65] Trustee Act 2000, s. 38.   [66] [1999] 62 Conv. 20, 23 (J. Warburton).

[67] Even though the trustees of the trust funds are the same: *Re London University's Charitable Trust* [1964] Ch 282.

for enabling sums to be advanced out of the fund by way of loan to a participating charity pending the withdrawal of property from the fund by the charity;

(c) for enabling income to be withheld from distribution with a view to avoiding fluctuations in the amounts distributed, and generally for regulating distributions of income;

(d) for enabling moneys to be borrowed temporarily for the purpose of meeting payments to be made out of the fund;

(e) for enabling questions arising under the scheme as to the right of a charity to participate, or as to the rights of participating charities, or as to any other matter, to be conclusively determined by the decision of the trustees managing the fund or in any other manner;

(f) for regulating the accounts and information to be supplied to participating charities.

(5) A common investment scheme, in addition to the provision for property to be transferred to the fund on the basis that the charity shall be entitled to a share in the capital and income of the fund, may include provision for enabling sums to be deposited by or on behalf of a charity on the basis that (subject to the provisions of the scheme) the charity shall be entitled to repayment of the sums deposited and to interest thereon at a rate determined by or under the scheme; and where a scheme makes any such provision it shall also provide for excluding from the amount of capital and income to be shared between charities participating otherwise than by way of deposit such amounts (not exceeding the amounts properly attributable to the making of deposits) as are from time to time reasonably required in respect of the liabilities of the fund for the repayment of deposits and for the interest on deposits, including amounts required by way of reserve.

25. Schemes to establish common deposit funds

(1) The court or the Commission may by order make and bring into effect schemes (in this section referred to as 'common deposit schemes') for the establishment of common deposit funds under trusts which provide—

(a) for sums to be deposited by or on behalf of a charity participating in the scheme and invested under the control of trustees appointed to manage the fund; and

(b) for any such charity to be entitled (subject to the provisions of the scheme) to repayment of any sums so deposited and to interest thereon at a rate determined under the scheme.

Annual Report of the Charity Commissioners for England and Wales (1999–2000), para. 3.8.1

3.8.1   Review of Common Investment Funds
Following public consultation, the Commission proposed changes to the regulation of charitable common investment funds (charities which comprise the pooled funds of a number of

participating charities), in particular to improve the protection of the charitable assets invested in them. Parliament agreed this in December 1999. The new structure, and the requirement from June 2000 that trustees of common investment funds must be authorised by IMRO if they are carrying out investment management business, has increased the protection available for charities who invest their assets in these funds.

C   ACCOUNTS, REPORTS, AND RETURNS

Part VI of the Charities Act 1993, as amended by Charities Act 2006, imposes strict duties on trustees to keep annual accounting records, prepare annual accounts, arrange for their audit, and send annual reports to the Commissioners on their activities, with a statement of the accounts and the auditor's report. There are criminal penalties for failure to submit reports and returns.[68]

D   REMUNERATION[69]

CHARITIES ACT 1993 (as inserted by Charities Act 2006, s. 36)

73A Remuneration of trustees etc. providing services to charity

(1) This section applies to remuneration for services provided by a person to or on behalf of a charity where—

   (a) he is a charity trustee or trustee for the charity, or

   (b) he is connected[70] with a charity trustee or trustee for the charity and the remuneration[71] might result in that trustee obtaining any benefit.[72]

   This is subject to subsection (7) below.

(2) If conditions A to D are met in relation to remuneration within subsection (1), the person providing the services ('the relevant person') is entitled to receive the remuneration out of the funds of the charity.

(3) Condition A is that the amount or maximum amount of the remuneration—

   (a) is set out in an agreement in writing between—

      (i) the charity or its charity trustees (as the case may be), and

      (ii) the relevant person,

      under which the relevant person is to provide the services in question to or on behalf of the charity, and

---

[68] See Statement of Recommended Practice (SORP 2000) on accounts by charities: CC61b ('Charity Accounts: The framework') (2007). See also CC8 ('Internal Financial Controls for Charities') (2003).

[69] See Charity Commission, 'Payment of Charity Trustees' (CC11) (2004) for published guidance on best practice as regards paying trustees.

[70] Including spouse, child, parent, company: Charities Act 1993, s. 73B(5).

[71] Including benefits in kind: Charities Act 1993, s. 73B(4).

[72] Meaning direct or indirect benefit: Charities Act 1993, s. 73B(4).

(b) does not exceed what is reasonable in the circumstances for the provision by that person of the services in question.

(4) Condition B is that, before entering into that agreement, the charity trustees decided that they were satisfied that it would be in the best interests of the charity for the services to be provided by the relevant person to or on behalf of the charity for the amount or maximum amount of remuneration set out in the agreement.

(5) Condition C is that if immediately after the agreement is entered into there is, in the case of the charity, more than one person who is a charity trustee and is—

(a) a person in respect of whom an agreement within subsection (3) above is in force, or

(b) a person who is entitled to receive remuneration out of the funds of the charity otherwise than by virtue of such an agreement, or

(c) a person connected with a person falling within paragraph (a) or (b) above,

the total number of them constitute a minority of the persons for the time being holding office as charity trustees of the charity.

(6) Condition D is that the trusts of the charity do not contain any express provision that prohibits the relevant person from receiving the remuneration.

(7) Nothing in this section applies to—

(a) any remuneration for services provided by a person in his capacity as a charity trustee or trustee for a charity or under a contract of employment, or

(b) any remuneration not within paragraph (a) which a person is entitled to receive out of the funds of a charity by virtue of any provision or order within subsection (8).

(8) The provisions or orders within this subsection are—

(a) any provision contained in the trusts of the charity,

(b) any order of the court or the Commission,

(c) any statutory provision contained in or having effect under an Act of Parliament other than this section.

73B Supplementary provisions for purposes of section 73A

(1) Before entering into an agreement within section 73A(3) the charity trustees must have regard to any guidance given by the Commission concerning the making of such agreements.

(2) The duty of care in section 1(1) of the Trustee Act 2000[73] applies to a charity trustee when making such a decision as is mentioned in section 73A(4).

---

[73] See p. 687, below.

E POWER TO EMPLOY AGENTS, NOMINEES, AND CUSTODIANS

The Trustee Act 2000, Part IV regulates the appointment of agents,[74] nominees[75] and custodians[76] by trustees.[77] These provisions apply to charitable trustees as well, with the following modifications:

TRUSTEE ACT 2000

11. Power to employ agents

...

(3) In the case of a charitable trust, the trustees' delegable functions are—

(a) any function consisting of carrying out a decision that the trustees have taken;

(b) any function relating to the investment of assets subject to the trust (including, in the case of land held as an investment, managing the land and creating or disposing of an interest in the land);

(c) any function relating to the raising of funds for the trust otherwise than by means of profits of a trade which is an integral part of carrying out the trust's charitable purpose;

(d) any other function prescribed by an order made by the Secretary of State.[78]

TRUSTEE ACT 2000

19. Persons who may be appointed as nominees or custodians

(4) The trustees of a charitable trust which is not an exempt charity must act in accordance with any guidance given by the Charity Commission[79] concerning the selection of a person for appointment as a nominee or custodian under section 16, 17 or 18.

The Official Custodian for Charities holds investments and property in his or her name on behalf of many charity trustees.[80] The Official Custodian is only allowed to buy or sell investments or property on behalf of a charity if the trustees instruct him or her to do so. He or she has no power to manage investments.[81] Charity trustees can bring

---

[74] Trustee Act 2000, s. 11. See p. 695, below.   [75] Trustee Act 2000, s. 16. See p. 698, below.
[76] Trustee Act 2000, s. 17. See p. 698, below.   [77] See p. 755, below.
[78] So far, no regulations have been promulgated.
[79] See Charity Commission, 'Appointing Nominees and Custodians: Guidance under s. 19 (4) of the Trustee Act 2000' (CC42) (2001).
[80] See *The Official Custodian for Charities Annual Report 2006–07*, the Foreword of which contains a description of the role of the Official Custodian for Charities.   [81] Charities Act 1993, s. 22.

proceedings in their own name to recover the charity's property without obtaining the permission of the Official Custodian or joining him or her to the proceedings.[82]

The purpose of the Official Custodian for Charities was identified by Mummery LJ in **Muman v Nagasena** [2000] 1 WLR 299 at 304:

The vesting of a legal estate of charity property in the Official Custodian for Charities is done to avoid the necessity of periodical transfers of charity property upon the successive appointments of new trustees of the charity.

CHARITIES ACT 1993

2. The official custodian for charities

(1) There shall continue to be an officer known as the official custodian for charities (in this Act referred to as 'the official custodian'), whose function it shall be to act as trustee for charities in the cases provided for by this Act,[83] and the official custodian for charities shall be by that name a corporation sole having perpetual succession and using an official seal, which shall be officially and judicially noticed.

F RELIEF FROM LIABILITY

CHARITIES ACT 1993 (inserted by Charities Act 2006, ss. 38 and 39)

73D Power to relieve trustees, auditors etc. from liability for breach of trust or duty

(1) This section applies to a person who is or has been—

(a) a charity trustee or trustee for a charity,

(b) a person appointed to audit a charity's accounts (whether appointed under an enactment or otherwise), or

(c) an independent examiner, reporting accountant or other person appointed to examine or report on a charity's accounts (whether appointed under an enactment or otherwise).

(2) If the Commission considers—

(a) that a person to whom this section applies is or may be personally liable for a breach of trust or breach of duty committed in his capacity as a person within paragraph (a), (b) or (c) of subsection (1) above, but

(b) that he has acted honestly and reasonably and ought fairly to be excused for the breach of trust or duty,

the Commission may make an order relieving him wholly or partly from any such liability.

---

[82] *Muman v Nagasena* [2000] 1 WLR 299.   [83] See ss. 21 and 22.

(3) An order under subsection (2) above may grant the relief on such terms as the Commission thinks fit.

(4) Subsection (2) does not apply in relation to any personal contractual liability of a charity trustee or trustee for a charity.

73F Trustees' indemnity insurance

(1) The charity trustees of a charity may arrange for the purchase, out of the funds of the charity, of insurance designed to indemnify the charity trustees or any trustees for the charity against any personal liability in respect of—

    (a) any breach of trust or breach of duty committed by them in their capacity as charity trustees or trustees for the charity, or

    (b) any negligence, default, breach of duty or breach of trust committed by them in their capacity as directors or officers of the charity (if it is a body corporate) or of any body corporate carrying on any activities on behalf of the charity.

(2) The terms of such insurance must, however, be so framed as to exclude the provision of any indemnity for a person in respect of—

    (a) any liability incurred by him to pay—

        (i) a fine imposed in criminal proceedings, or

        (ii) a sum payable to a regulatory authority by way of a penalty in respect of non-compliance with any requirement of a regulatory nature (however arising);

    (b) any liability incurred by him in defending any criminal proceedings in which he is convicted of an offence arising out of any fraud or dishonesty, or wilful or reckless misconduct, by him; or

    (c) any liability incurred by him to the charity that arises out of any conduct which he knew (or must reasonably be assumed to have known) was not in the interests of the charity or in the case of which he did not care whether it was in the best interests of the charity or not.

(4) The charity trustees of a charity may not purchase insurance under this section unless they decide that they are satisfied that it is in the best interests of the charity for them to do so.

(5) The duty of care in section 1(1) of the Trustee Act 2000[84] applies to a charity trustee when making such a decision.

(8) This section—

    (a) does not authorise the purchase of any insurance whose purchase is expressly prohibited by the trusts of the charity, but

    (b) has effect despite any provision prohibiting the charity trustees or trustees for the charity receiving any personal benefit out of the funds of the charity.

---

[84] See p. 687, below.

G   DUTIES AS REGARDS THE PUBLIC
BENEFIT REQUIREMENT

Charity Commission, *Charities and Public Benefit* (January 2008)

C4.   Charity trustees' public benefit duties
Charity trustees must:

- ensure that they carry out their charity's aims for the public benefit;
- have regard to guidance we publish on public benefit (when they exercise any powers or duties where that may be relevant); and
- report on their charity's public benefit in their Trustees' Annual Report.

Charity trustees are not legally required to follow this guidance but they must have regard to it when it is relevant for their charity. . . .

Charity trustees have a new duty to regularly report in their Trustees' Annual Report on how they are carrying out their charity's aims for the public benefit.

PART V

TRUSTEES

13

GENERAL PRINCIPLES
RELATING TO TRUSTEES[1]

I APPOINTMENT[2]

A BY DONEE OF POWER TO APPOINT

(i) *Number of Trustees*

There is no restriction on the number of trustees of a trust of personalty, but there are restrictions on the number of trustees of a trust of land.

---

[1] For a general commentary on the Trustee Act 1925, see Wolstenholme & Cherry, *Conveyancing Statutes* (13th edn, 1972) vol. 4. For a general commentary on the Trustee Act 2000, see C. Whitehouse and N. Hassall, *Trusts of Land, Trustee Delegation and the Trustee Act 2000* (2nd edn) (2001).

[2] H&M, pp. 516–522; Lewin, pp. 467–509; P&M, pp. 549–561; P&S, pp. 674–677; Pettit, pp. 347–362; Snell, pp. 597–604; T&H, pp. 671–685; U&H, pp. 926–955.

TRUSTEE ACT 1925

34. Limitation of the number of trustees

(2) In the case of settlements and dispositions creating trusts of land³ made or coming into operation after the commencement of this Act—

   (a) the number of trustees thereof shall not in any case exceed four, and where more than four persons are named as such trustees, the four first named (who are able and willing to act) shall alone be the trustees, and the other persons named shall not be trustees unless appointed on the occurrence of a vacancy;

   (b) the number of the trustees shall not be increased beyond four.

(3) This section only applies to settlements and dispositions of land, and the restrictions imposed on the number of trustees do not apply—

   (a) in the case of land vested in trustees for charitable, ecclesiastical, or public purposes; or

   (b) where the net proceeds of the sale of the land are held for like purposes; or

   (c) to the trustees of a term of years absolute limited by a settlement on trusts for raising money, or of a like term created under the statutory remedies relating to annual sums charged on land.

Law Reform Committee 23rd Report, *The Powers and Duties of Trustees*, 1982 Cmnd 8733, para. 9.1.II.1

1.   Where the settlor makes no specific provision about the number of trustees, they should be limited to four regardless of the nature of the trust property, subject to the existing restrictions in the case of trusts for sale of land and settled land and to the exceptions presently contained in section 34(3)(a) of the Trustee Act 1925.

(ii) Appointment of new or additional trustees

TRUSTEE ACT 1925

36. Power of appointing new or additional trustees

(1) Where a trustee, either original or substituted, and whether appointed by a court or otherwise, is dead, or remains out of the United Kingdom for more than twelve months, or desires to be discharged from all or any of the trusts or powers reposed in or conferred on him, or refuses or is unfit to act therein, or is incapable of acting therein, or is an infant, then, subject to the restrictions imposed by this Act on the number of trustees,—

   (a) the person or persons nominated for the purpose of appointing new trustees by the instrument, if any, creating the trust; or

---

³ Words substituted by Trusts of Land and Appointment of Trustees Act (TLATA) 1996, s. 25 (1), Sch. 3, para. 3(9).

(b) if there is no such person, or no such person able and willing to act, then the surviving or continuing trustees or trustee for the time being, or the personal representatives of the last surviving or continuing trustee,[4]

may, by writing, appoint one or more other persons (whether or not being the persons exercising the power) to be a trustee or trustees in the place of the trustee so deceased, remaining out of the United Kingdom, desiring to be discharged, refusing, or being unfit or being incapable, or being an infant, as aforesaid.

(2) Where a trustee has been removed under a power contained in the instrument creating the trust, a new trustee or new trustees may be appointed in the place of the trustee who is removed, as if he were dead, or, in the case of a corporation, as if the corporation desired to be discharged from the trust, and the provisions of this section shall apply accordingly, but subject to the restrictions imposed by this Act on the number of trustees.

(3) Where a corporation being a trustee is or has been dissolved, either before or after the commencement of this Act, then, for the purposes of this section and of any enactment replaced thereby, the corporation shall be deemed to be and to have been from the date of the dissolution incapable of acting in the trusts or powers reposed in or conferred on the corporation.

(4) The power of appointment given by subsection (1) of this section or any similar previous enactment to the personal representatives of a last surviving or continuing trustee shall be and shall be deemed always to have been exercisable by the executors for the time being (whether original or by representation) of such surviving or continuing trustee who have proved the will of their testator or by the administrators for the time being of such trustee without the concurrence of any executor who has renounced or has not proved.

(5) But a sole or last surviving executor intending to renounce, or all the executors where they all intend to renounce, shall have and shall be deemed always to have had power, at any time before renouncing probate, to exercise the power of appointment given by this section, or by any similar previous enactment, if willing to act for that purpose and without thereby accepting the office of executor.

(6) Where, in the case of any trust, there are not more than three trustees—[5]

(a) the person or persons nominated for the purpose of appointing new trustees by the instrument, if any, creating the trust; or

(b) if there is no such person, or no such person able and willing to act, then the trustee or trustees for the time being;

---

[4] Or the executor of a deceased sole trustee: *Re Shafto's Trusts* (1885) 29 Ch D 247. A personal representative may exercise the power without having obtained probate: *Re Crowhurst Park* [1974] 1 WLR 583; but a trustee so appointed will be unable to prove his title unless a grant is obtained. Apart from the circumstances covered by the sub-paragraph, executors do not have power to appoint new trustees; see *Re King's Will Trusts* [1964] Ch 542.

[5] As substituted by TLATA 1996, s. 25 (1), Sch. 3, para. 3(11).

may, by writing appoint another person or other persons[6] to be an additional trustee or additional trustees, but it shall not be obligatory to appoint any additional trustee, unless the instrument, if any, creating the trust, or any statutory enactment provides to the contrary, nor shall the number of trustees be increased beyond four by virtue of any such appointment.[7]

(7) Every new trustee appointed under this section as well before as after all the trust property becomes by law, or by assurance, or otherwise, vested in him, shall have the same powers, authorities, and discretions, and may in all respects act as if he had been originally appointed a trustee by the instrument, if any, creating the trust.

(8) The provisions of this section relating to a trustee who is dead include the case of a person nominated trustee in a will but dying before the testator, and those relative to a continuing trustee include a refusing or retiring trustee, if willing to act in the execution of the provisions of this section.[8]

(9) Where a trustee lacks capacity to exercise his functions as trustee and is also entitled in possession to some beneficial interest in the trust property, no appointment of a new trustee in his place shall be made by virtue of paragraph (b) of subsection (1) of this section unless leave to make the appointment has been given by the Court of Protection.[9]

(iii) 'Surviving' or 'continuing'

The Trustee Act 1925, section 36(8) enables a retiring sole trustee or a retiring group of trustees to appoint their successors.[10] It is usual for retiring trustees to participate in the appointment of new trustees, but it is not essential.

In **Re Coates to Parsons** (1886) 34 Ch D 370, the title to a Methodist chapel at Thrapston, Northamptonshire, was vested in eleven trustees. One died, and another,

---

[6] And not therefore himself: *Re Power's Settlement Trusts* [1951] Ch 1074. Under sub-s.(1) the donee may appoint himself.

[7] This section was further amended by the Trustee Delegation Act 1999 (which inserted new s. 36(6A)–(6D)), as itself amended by the Mental Capacity Act 2005, to give a power to appoint additional trustees to the donee of an enduring or lasting power of attorney, to whom trustee functions relating either to land or the proceeds of sale of land have been delegated.

[8] See Trustee Act 1925, s. 37 (1) (c) (as amended by TLATA 1996, s. 25 (1), Sch. 3, para. 3(12)), which provides that a trustee shall not be discharged unless there is a trust corporation or at least two individuals (meaning natural persons and not companies: *Jasmine Trustees Ltd v Wells and Hind* [2007] EWHC 38 (ch), [2007] 3 WLR 810) act as trustees to perform the trust. There is an exception where only one trustee was appointed and a sole trustee will be able to give a receipt for capital money. In *Mettoy Pension Trustees Ltd v Evans* [1990] 1 WLR 1587 at 1607, Warner J doubted whether the express terms of the settlement can override these provisions.

[9] As amended by Mental Capacity Act 2005.

[10] But two retiring trustees cannot be replaced by one trustee which is not a trust corporation: *Adam & Company International Trustees Ltd v Theodore Goddard* [2000] 13 LS Gaz R 44; [2003] Conv 15 (F. Barlow).

W.R. Dearlove, remained out of the United Kingdom for twelve months. The nine remaining trustees purported to appoint T.M. Coleman a trustee, acting under the statutory power.[11]

A purchaser under a contract for sale of the land by the trustees objected to the title, one of the grounds being that W.R. Dearlove had not participated in the appointment of new trustees. NORTH J upheld the appointment, saying at 377:

I hold, therefore, that under the terms of the Act the nine trustees, who were clearly continuing trustees were competent to make the appointment, unless it was shewn that the person who had been absent for so long, and in whose place there was a clear right to substitute a new trustee, was willing and competent to act. This has not been shewn, and it seems to me, therefore, that the first objection, *viz.* that *W.R. Dearlove* ought to have concurred in making the appointment, is not established.

In **Re Stoneham's Settlement Trusts** [1953] Ch 59, one trustee, Stoneham, who had absented himself from the United Kingdom for over 12 months, was willing to continue to act. His co-trustee, intending to retire, appointed two others in place of Stoneham and himself. Stoneham wished to continue. DANCKWERTS J held that the appointments were valid. The co-trustee could make them as a retiring trustee. Stoneham's participation was not necessary. 'I come to the conclusion quite plainly that a trustee who is removed against his will is not a refusing or retiring trustee, not, at any rate, in the case of a trustee removed because of his absence outside the United Kingdom for consecutive periods of more than 12 months.'

(iv) Direction of beneficiaries

TRUSTS OF LAND AND APPOINTMENT OF TRUSTEES ACT 1996

19. Appointment and retirement of trustee at instance of beneficiaries[12]—

(1) This section applies in the case of a trust where—

   (a) there is no person nominated for the purpose of appointing new trustees by the instrument, if any, creating the trust, and

   (b) the beneficiaries under the trust are of full age and capacity and (taken together) are absolutely entitled to the property subject to the trust.

(2) The beneficiaries may give a direction or directions of either or both of the following descriptions—

   (a) a written direction to a trustee or trustees to retire from the trust, and

   (b) a written direction to the trustees or trustee for the time being, (or, if there are none, to the personal representative of the last person who was

---

11 Given by Conveyancing Act 1881, s. 31(1).
12 (1996) 146 NLJ 1779 (M. Keppel-Palmer); [1996] Conv 411, 428–430 (N. Hopkins).

a trustee) to appoint by writing to be a trustee or trustees the person or persons specified in the direction.[13]

(5) This section has effect subject to the restrictions imposed by the Trustee Act 1925 on the number of trustees.

21. Supplementary

(1) For the purposes of section 19 or 20[14] a direction is given by beneficiaries if—

    (a) a single direction is jointly given by all of them, or

    (b) (subject to subsection (2)) a direction is given by each of them (whether solely or jointly with one or more, but not all, of the others),

and none of them by writing withdraws the direction given by him before it has been complied with.[15]

(2) Where more than one direction is given each must specify for appointment or retirement the same person or persons.

(3) Subsection (7) of section 36 of the Trustee Act 1925 (powers of trustees appointed under that section)[16] applies to a trustee appointed under section 19 or 20 as if he were appointed under that section....

(5) Sections 19 and 20 do not apply in relation to a trust created by a disposition in so far as provision that they do not apply is made by the disposition.

(6) Sections 19 and 20 do not apply in relation to a trust created before the commencement of this Act by a disposition in so far as provision to the effect that they do not apply is made by a deed executed—

    (a) in a case in which the trust was created by one person and he is of full capacity, by that person, or

    (b) in a case in which the trust was created by more than one person, by such of the persons who created the trust as are alive and of full capacity.

(7) A deed executed for the purposes of subsection (6) is irrevocable.

(8) Where a deed is executed for the purposes of subsection (6)—

    (a) it does not affect anything done before its execution to comply with a direction under section 19 or 20, but

    (b) a direction under section 19 or 20 which has been given but not complied with before its execution shall cease to have effect.

(1996) 146 NLJ 1779, 1786 (M. Keppel-Palmer)

In itself, s. 19 poses considerable problems, the answers to which may be provided by the courts of chancery in due course. Indeed, I fully expect that practitioners will exclude s. 19 as a matter of course in creating trusts in the future. However, in general policy terms this may be the

[13] For sub-ss. (3) and (4) see p. 640, below.
[14] For s. 20 (appointment of substitute for incapable trustee) [see p. 629, below].
[15] So unanimity is required.   [16] See p. 626, above.

moment when the family trust starts to become divorced from the more commercial trusts such as pensions, which clearly require a different agenda from their forebears.

To allow beneficiaries the whip hand over trustees, by threatening to and replacing them on a whim, surely undermines the basis of trusteeship, especially in its stakeholding between the interests of the beneficiaries. With so many of the powers of trustees being discretionary, are we going to discover that the concept of trusteeship is under attack. As Vaisey J articulated:[17]'a discretionary power . . . in my opinion is no longer exercisable and, indeed, can no longer exist if it has become one of which the exercise can be dictated by others'.

(v) 'Incapable' or 'unfit'

In **Re Wheeler and de Rochow** [1896] 1 Ch 315,[18] a marriage settlement gave to the husband and wife, or the survivor of them, the power to appoint new trustees in certain specified circumstances, including that of a trustee becoming 'incapable'. One of the trustees became bankrupt. This rendered him 'unfit' but not 'incapable'. The question was whether a new trustee should be appointed by the husband (as the survivor), under paragraph (a) of section 36(1), or by the continuing trustees under paragraph (b).[19] KEKEWICH J held that the husband and wife (or the survivor) were the 'persons nominated for the purpose of appointing new trustees by the instrument' only in the circumstances specified in the settlement. No such circumstances had occurred, and the new trustee must therefore be appointed by the continuing trustees.

TRUSTS OF LAND AND APPOINTMENT OF TRUSTEES ACT 1996

20. Appointment of substitute for trustee who lacks capacity[20]

(1) This section applies where—

    (a) a trustee lacks capacity (within the meaning of the Mental Capacity Act 2005) to exercise,

    (b) there is no person who is both entitled and willing and able to appoint a trustee in place of him under section 36(1) of the Trustee Act 1925, and

    (c) the beneficiaries under the trust are of full age and capacity and (taken together) are absolutely entitled to the property subject to the trust.

(2) The beneficiaries may give to—

    (a) a deputy appointed for the trustee by the Court of Protection,

    (b) an attorney acting for him under the authority of an enduring power of attorney or lasting power of attorney under the Mental Capacity Act 2005

    (c) a person authorised for the purpose by the Court of Protection

    a written direction to appoint by writing the person or persons specified in the direction to be a trustee or trustees in place of the incapable trustee.[21]

---

[17] *Re Brockbank* [1948] Ch 206 at 208.

[18] Followed reluctantly in *Re Sichel's Settlements* [1916] 1 Ch 358.

[19] The section applicable was the Trustee Act 1893, s. 10(1), which was substantially the same as TA 1925, s. 36(1).　　　　　[20] As amended by the Mental Capacity Act 2005.

[21] For supplementary provisions see s. 21, p.628, above.

(vi) Selection of trustees

The selection of the right trustees is a matter of the greatest importance. Modern settlements usually give many discretionary powers to the trustees. In selecting the original trustees, the settlor will select persons who can be relied on to exercise these powers in a manner of which he would himself approve. He cannot, however, control the trustees in the exercise of their powers and discretions. Nor, unless he retains the power to appoint new trustees, can he determine future appointments. Where beneficiaries give directions as to the appointment of trustees[22] it seems that there is no restriction in the choice of person they direct to be appointed.[23]

The question has been raised whether the statutory power enables a donee of the power to appoint a person outside the United Kingdom.[24]

In **Richard v The Hon A.B. Mackay** (14 March, 1987) (1997) 11 *Trust Law International* 23, the English trustees of a settlement made in 1965 by Lord Tanlaw, on trusts governed by English law, sought a declaration that transfer of part of the trust fund (the fund was worth £7.5 million) to a new settlement to be established in Bermuda was valid. The beneficiaries under the proposed new settlement were the infant children of Lord Tanlaw, and, although the family had international connections, Lord Tanlaw was domiciled and resident in the United Kingdom. In holding that the transfer was valid MILLETT J said:

In *Re Whitehead's Will Trusts* [1971] 1 WLR 833 Sir John Pennycuick, the Vice-Chancellor, was asked to declare that an appointment of foreign trustees of an English trust was effective to discharge the English trustees.

At 837, he said:

'...the law has been quite well established for upwards of a century that there is no absolute bar to the appointment of persons resident abroad as trustees of an English trust. I say "no absolute bar", in the sense that such an appointment would be prohibited by law and would consequently be invalid. On the other hand, apart from exceptional circumstances, it is not proper to make such an appointment, that is to say, the court would not, apart from exceptional circumstances, make such an appointment; nor would it be right for the donees of the power to make such an appointment out of court. If they did, presumably the court would be likely to interfere at the instance of the beneficiaries. There do, however, exist exceptional circumstances in which such an appointment can properly be made. The most obvious exceptional circumstances are those in which the beneficiaries have settled permanently in some country outside the United Kingdom and what is proposed to be done is to appoint new trustees in that country. In those exceptional circumstances it has, I believe, almost uniformly been accepted as the law that trustees in the country where the beneficiaries have settled can properly be appointed.'

---

[22] See p. 627, above.   [23] H&M, p. 521.

[24] Once made, however, such an appointment, whether made under an express or statutory power, is valid: *Meinertzhagen v Davis* (1844) 1 Coll 335; *Re Smith's Trusts* (1872) 26 LT 820; (1969) 85 LQR 15 (P.V.B.); (1976) 40 Conv (NS) 295 (T.G. Watkin).

At 838, the learned Vice-Chancellor added:

'...It cannot, I think, make any difference whether the court is asked under the Variation of Trusts Act 1958 to transfer a fund to a new settlement in a foreign country or whether one is concerned merely with the appointment of new trustees of the existing settlement.'

This is not a case where the family concerned or the beneficiaries have become resident abroad. The settlor and his two children live in England. Nor is it a case where the proposed new settlement is to be formed in the country where the beneficiaries reside or may be expected to reside in the future. The possibility which is envisaged is that they may well wish to live in the Far East, whereas the seat of the proposed settlement is to be Bermuda.

But in my judgment the language of Sir John Pennycuick, which is narrowly drawn, is too restrictive for the circumstances of the present day if, at least, it is intended to lay down any rule of practice. Nor in my view is it accurate to equate the approach that the court adopts to exercise its own discretion with the approach it adopts when asked to authorise the trustees to exercise theirs.

Where the court is invited to exercise an original discretion of its own, whether by appointing trustees under the Trustee Act 1925 or by approving a scheme under the Variation of Trust Act 1958, or where the trustees surrender their discretion to the court, the court will require to be satisfied that the discretion should be exercised in the manner proposed. The applicants must make out a positive case for the exercise of the discretion, and the court is unlikely to assist them where the scheme is nothing more than a device to avoid tax and has no other advantages of any kind.

Where, however, the transaction is proposed to be carried out by the trustees in exercise of their own discretion, entirely out of court, the trustees retaining their discretion and merely seeking the authorisation of the court for their own protection, then in my judgment the question that the court asks itself is quite different. It is concerned to ensure that the proposed exercise of the trustees' power is lawful and within the power and that it does not infringe the trustees' duty to act as ordinary, reasonable and prudent trustees might act, but it requires only to be satisfied that the trustees can properly form the view that the proposed transaction is for the benefit of beneficiaries or the trust estate.

[His Lordship referred to *Re Kay, MacKinnon v Stringer* [1927] VLR 66 and continued:] Certainly in the conditions of today, when one can have an international family with international interests, and where they are as likely to make their home in one country as in another and as likely to choose one jurisdiction as another for the investment of their capital, I doubt that the language of Sir John Pennycuick is really in tune with the times. In my judgment, where the trustees retain their discretion, as they do in the present case, the court should need to be satisfied only that the proposed transaction is not so inappropriate that no reasonable trustee could entertain it.

I have evidence before me that the proposed trustee is the leading trustee corporation in Bermuda, that the trust law of Bermuda is similar to and based upon and derived from English law, and that there are no restrictions upon the free movement of capital. I think I can take judicial notice of the fact that Bermuda has a stable regime within the United States' sphere of influence and that many wealthy families, acting in their own interests and in a businesslike way, have been in the habit in recent years of entrusting substantial portions of their fortunes to trustees in that jurisdiction.

There are obvious potential advantages in diversification. What is proposed is only the removal from the jurisdiction of 25 per cent of a very substantial fund. There is great force in the submission that what is proposed is positively a prudent step, and I have no doubt at all that it cannot possibly be stigmatised as imprudent or unreasonable.

So far as the appropriateness of what is proposed is concerned, as I have already indicated the family have a strong connection with the Far East; there is a considerable likelihood that the children, when they grow up, may wish to live or make the basis of their careers in the Far East; and to have some proportion at least of the trust funds out of the United Kingdom in an appropriate but stable area may properly be considered to be to their advantage.

Accordingly I consider that there is no reason why the trustees should not take the view that the proposed transaction is for the benefit of the principal beneficiaries, and I will give the direction sought.

In **Re Beatty's WT (No 2)** (4 March, 1987) (1997) 11 *Trust Law International* 77, executors and trustees wished to appoint Jersey resident trustees, since having overseas trustees would bring tax advantages. There were three principal beneficiaries of the trust. One was resident in Australia, one was about to emigrate to Spain, and the third was resident in the United Kingdom. VINELOTT J said at 80:

Turning again to the instant case, there are, in my judgment, clearly circumstances which the executors can properly regard as justifying the appointment of the proposed new trustees as trustees of the will. Lord Brooke is and Lady Charlotte is about to become resident outside the United Kingdom. It is impractical to appropriate the whole residuary estate into one-third shares and impractical, therefore, to appoint trustees resident in and to administer the trusts in a single jurisdiction where all the beneficiaries are domiciled and resident. Mrs. Thompson-Jones is herself willing that trustees resident outside the United Kingdom should be appointed, and she is the only beneficiary now ascertainable who is resident in the United Kingdom. It would, I think, be unjust to the non-resident beneficiaries that because Mrs. Thompson-Jones is resident here they should be exposed to heavy fiscal liabilities which will not arise if non-resident trustees are appointed.

There can be no question but that the proposed individual new trustees are responsible persons and the proposed corporate trustee is a well-established and well-known trust corporation.

The trustees all reside in a stable jurisdiction in which many English trusts are now administered and in which the assets and the future administration of the trusts will be fully safeguarded.

In these circumstances, I have no hesitation in giving the direction and making the order sought.

(vii) Vesting of the property in the trustees[25]

TRUSTEE ACT 1925

40. Vesting of trust property in new or continuing trustees

(1) Where by a deed a new trustee is appointed to perform any trust, then—

   (a) if the deed contains a declaration by the appointor to the effect that any estate or interest in any land subject to the trust, or in any chattel so subject, or the right to recover or receive any debt or other thing in action so subject,

[25] H&M, pp. 522–524; Lewin, pp. 529–546; P&M, p. 564; P&S, pp. 686–687; Pettit, pp. 370–372; Snell, pp. 604–606; T&H, pp. 690–699; U&H, pp. 955–967.

shall vest in the persons who by virtue of the deed become or are the trustees for performing the trust, the deed shall operate, without any conveyance or assignment, to vest in those persons as joint tenants and for the purposes of the trust the estate interest or right to which the declaration relates; and

(b) if the deed is made after the commencement of this Act and does not contain such a declaration, the deed shall, subject to any express provision to the contrary therein contained, operate as if it had contained such a declaration by the appointor extending to all the estates interests and rights with respect to which a declaration could have been made.

(2) Where by a deed a retiring trustee is discharged under section 39 of this Act[26] or section 19 of the Trusts of Land and Appointment of Trustees Act 1996[27] without a new trustee being appointed, then—

(a) if the deed contains such a declaration as aforesaid by the retiring and continuing trustees, and by the other person, if any, empowered to appoint trustees, the deed shall, without any conveyance or assignment, operate to vest in the continuing trustees alone, as joint tenants, and for the purposes of the trust, the estate, interest, or right to which the declaration relates; and

(b) if the deed is made after the commencement of this Act and does not contain such a declaration, the deed shall, subject to any express provision to the contrary therein contained, operate as if it had contained such a declaration by such persons as aforesaid extending to all the estates, interests and rights with respect to which a declaration could have been made.

(3) An express vesting declaration, whether made before or after the commencement of this Act, shall, notwithstanding that the estate, interest or right to be vested is not expressly referred to, and provided that the other statutory requirements were or are complied with, operate and be deemed always to have operated (but without prejudice to any express provision to the contrary contained in the deed of appointment or discharge) to vest in the persons respectively referred to in subsections (1) and (2) of this section, as the case may require, such estate, interests and rights as are capable of being and ought to be vested in those persons.

(4) This section does not extend—

(a) to land conveyed by way of mortgage for securing money subject to the trust, except land conveyed on trust for securing debentures or debenture stock;

(b) to land held under a lease which contains any covenant, condition or agreement against assignment or disposing of the land without licence or consent, unless, prior to the execution of the deed containing expressly or impliedly the vesting declaration, the requisite licence or consent has been obtained, or

---

26 See p. 640, below.
27 As added by TLATA 1996, s. 25(1), Sch. 3, para. 3(14). See p. 627, above and p. 640, below.

CHAPTER 13: TRUSTEES—GENERAL PRINCIPLES

unless, by virtue of any statute or rule of law, the vesting declaration, express or implied, would not operate as a breach of covenant or give rise to a forfeiture;

(c) to any share, stock, annuity or property which is only transferable in books kept by a company or other body, or in a manner directed by or under an Act of Parliament.[28]

In this subsection 'lease' includes an underlease and an agreement for a lease or underlease.

(5) For purposes of registration of the deed in any registry, the person or persons making the declaration expressly or impliedly, shall be deemed the conveying party or parties, and the conveyance shall be deemed to be made by him or them under a power conferred by this Act.

(6) This section applies to deeds of appointment or discharge executed on or after the first day of January, eighteen hundred and eighty-two.

B   BY THE COURT

(i) *The power to appoint*

TRUSTEE ACT 1925

41. Power of court to appoint new trustees

(1) The court may, whenever it is expedient to appoint a new trustee or new trustees, and it is found inexpedient difficult or impracticable so to do without the assistance of the court,[29] make an order appointing a new trustee or new trustees either in substitution for or in addition to any existing trustee or trustees, or although there is no existing trustee.

In particular and without prejudice to the generality of the foregoing provision, the court may make an order appointing a new trustee in substitution for a trustee who lacks capacity to exercise his functions as trustee or is a bankrupt, or is a corporation which is in liquidation or has been dissolved.[30]

(4) Nothing in this section gives power to appoint an executor or administrator.

43. Powers of new trustee appointed by the court

Every trustee appointed by a court of competent jurisdiction shall, as well before as after the trust property becomes by law, or by assurance, or otherwise, vested in him,

---

[28] See (1992) 142 NLJ 541 (M. Russell).

[29] If the power of appointment given by TA 1925, s. 36, [see p. 624, above] can be exercised, the court should not be asked to make an appointment: *Re Gibbon's Trusts* (1882) 30 WR 287; see also *Re May's Will Trusts* [1941] Ch 109.　　　　　　　　　　　　　　[30] As amended by Mental Capacity Act 2005, Sch. 6.

have the same powers, authorities, and discretions, and may in all respects act as if he had been originally appointed a trustee by the instrument, if any, creating the trust.

In **Polly Peck International plc v Henry** [1999] 1 BCLC 407, BUCKLEY J refused to appoint a new trustee to a pension trust under section 41 because the proposed trustee lacked expertise and the appointment would not have been cost-effective for the trust.

(ii) Selection of trustees[31]

Re Tempest
(1866) 1 Ch App 485 (CA in Ch, **Turner** and **Knight-Bruce** LJJ)

A family settlement was created by the will of Sir Charles Tempest, Bart., appointing the Hon. T.E. Stoner and Mr. J. Fleming as trustees. Mr. Stoner predeceased the testator. The persons to whom the power of appointing new trustees was given were unable to agree upon a selection. A petition was presented, asking the court to appoint the Hon. Edward Petre. One beneficiary opposed, on the ground that Mr. Petre was connected with, and proposed by, a branch of the family with which the testator was not on friendly terms, and which he had excluded from participation in the management of his property. The Master of the Rolls appointed Mr. Petre and Lord Camoys 'hoping to satisfy both parties'.

Held. Mr. Petre was not a person whom the Court would appoint.

Turner LJ: There are two questions raised by this appeal. First, whether the order of the Master of the Rolls ought to be reversed in so far as it appoints Mr. *Petre* to be a trustee of the testator's will; and secondly, whether assuming that the order ought to be reversed in this respect, Lord *Camoys* ought to be appointed the trustee. The first of these questions has not seemed to me to be altogether free from difficulty, and in my view of this case it is by no means an unimportant question. It involves, as I think, to no inconsiderable extent the principles on which this Court ought to act in the appointment of new trustees.

It was said in argument, and has been frequently said, that in making such appointments the Court acts upon and exercises its discretion; and this, no doubt, is generally true; but the discretion which the Court has and exercises in making such appointments, is not, as I conceive, a mere arbitrary discretion, but a discretion in the exercise of which the Court is, and ought to be, guided by some general rules and principles, and, in my opinion, the difficulty which the Court has to encounter in these cases lies not so much in ascertaining the rules and principles by which it ought to be guided, as in applying those rules and principles to the varying circumstances of each particular case. The following rules and principles may, I think, safely be laid down as applying to all cases of appointments by the Court of new trustees.

First, the Court will have regard to the wishes of the persons by whom the trust has been created, if expressed in the instrument creating the trust, or clearly to be collected from it. I think this rule may be safely laid down, because if the author of the trust has in terms declared

[31] H&M, pp. 524- 526; Lewin, pp. 505–506; P&M, p. 560; P&S, pp. 690–691; Pettit, pp. 362–364; Snell, pp. 602–604; T&H, pp. 679–682; U&H, pp. 948–954.

that a particular person, or a person filling a particular character, should not be a trustee of the instrument, there cannot, as I apprehend, be the least doubt that the Court would not appoint to the office a person whose appointment was so prohibited, and I do not think that upon a question of this description any distinction can be drawn between express declarations and demonstrated intention. The analogy of the course which the Court pursues in the appointment of guardians affords, I think, some support to this rule. The Court in those cases attends to the wishes of the parents, however informally they may be expressed.

Another rule which may, I think, safely be laid down is this—that the Court will not appoint a person to be trustee with a view to the interest of some of the persons interested under the trust, in opposition either to the wishes of the testator or to the interests of others of the *cestui que trusts*. I think so for this reason, that it is of the essence of the duty of every trustee to hold an even hand between the parties interested under the trust. Every trustee is in duty bound to look to the interests of all, and not of any particular member or class of members of his *cestui que trusts*.

A third rule which, I think, may safely be laid down is,—that the Court in appointing a trustee will have regard to the question, whether his appointment will promote or impede the execution of the trust, for the very purpose of the appointment is that the trust may be better carried into execution.

These are the principles by which, in my judgment, we ought to be guided in determining whether Mr. *Petre* ought to be appointed to be a trustee of this will, and, in my opinion, there are substantial objections to his appointment on each of the three grounds to which I have referred. There is not, of course, and cannot be, any possible objection to Mr. *Petre* in point of character, position, or ability, and I desire most anxiously to be understood as not intending, in disapproving his appointment, to cast the slightest possible reflection upon him. I have not for one moment doubted that he is a gentleman of most unexceptionable character, and well qualified in every respect to fill the office of trustee; but I think that the principles to which I have referred are opposed to his appointment.

First, as to the wishes of this testator, it is impossible, I think, to read this will without being fully satisfied that the great object and purpose of the testator was to exclude Mr. *Charles Henry Tempest* not only from all interest in, but from all connection with his estate. A more complete exclusion of him, both from any interest in and from any power over the estate, could not, as it seems to me, have been devised. Is it then consistent with this purpose of the testator that a trustee should be appointed who, upon the evidence before us, I cannot doubt is the nominee of Mr. *Charles Henry Tempest*, and is proposed for the purpose of carrying into effect his wishes and intentions? The facts, I think, prove that this is the position of Mr. *Petre*. He is proposed by Mr. *Washington Hibbert*, the father-in-law of Mr. *C.H. Tempest*, and the very person the connection with whom led to the making of this will, by which he was excluded. He is supported, and I desire not to be understood as saying, in any other than a legal sense, improperly, by Mr. *A.C. Tempest* his brother, who it appears upon the evidence declined to attend the testator's funeral on account of the dispositions of the will; and one of the principal witnesses in support of his appointment, and the person most active in these proceedings is Mr. *Broadbent*, the solicitor of Sir *C.H. Tempest*, under whose advice we find that Mr. *Petre* adopted that most unfortunate and, I must say, ill-advised step of declining to meet his co-trustees. Looking to all these circumstances, and to the whole of the evidence before us, I have as little doubt as to what led to the proposal of Mr. *Petre* as I have as to the intentions of this testator, and upon this ground, therefore, I think that Mr. *Petre* ought not to be appointed to be a trustee of this will.

It was said for the respondents, that the testator's dispositions were captious and absurd, and ought not therefore to be regarded, but much as we may regret that such dispositions were made, we cannot disregard them.

Then, as to the second ground, the objection to the appointment of Mr. *Petre* seems to me to be still more decisive. The evidence, in my opinion, very plainly shews that Mr. *Petre* has been proposed as a trustee, and has accepted that office, with a view to his acting in the trust in the interests of some only of the objects of it, and in opposition to the wishes of the testator, and not with a view to his acting as an independent trustee for the benefit of all the objects of the trusts, and I do not hesitate to say that, in my opinion, this fact is alone sufficient to prevent us from confirming his appointment. It was objected on the part of the respondents, that the proof of this fact rests upon evidence of what has occurred since the order under appeal was pronounced, and ought not, therefore, to be attended to; but this is a rehearing of the Petition under which Mr. *Petre* has been appointed. The question before us, therefore, is, whether he ought now to be appointed or not—a question of his present fitness or unfitness—and I am aware of no rule which precludes us from receiving upon such a question evidence of what has occurred since the original hearing. Supposing, however, that there was any difficulty upon that point, I apprehend there can be no doubt that the evidence of what has so occurred ought to be looked at as shewing the purpose for which he was proposed, and that it was not proper that he should be appointed at the time when the order appointing him was made.

It was also argued on the part of the respondents, that their interests ought to be considered in the appointment to be made by the Court, and there would have been great force in this argument, if it could have been considered that Mr. *Petre* was proposed as an independent trustee to act on behalf of, and with a view to, the interests of all the *cestui que trusts;* but when the purpose for which he is proposed is seen, this argument loses all weight and cannot be attended to. It is the appointment of a trustee for the benefit of all, and not with a view to the interests of some, that the wishes of *cestui que trusts* are to be consulted, for the trustee to be appointed must represent and consult the interests of all, and not of some only of the *cestui que trusts*. It was indeed with this view, that in the course of the argument I suggested to the parties the expediency of their agreeing upon the appointment of an independent trustee.

The third and remaining ground of objection to the appointment of Mr. *Petre* is, I think, open to more difficulty. On the one hand, there cannot, I think, be any doubt that the Court ought not to appoint a trustee whose appointment will impede the due execution of the trust; but, on the other hand, if the continuing or surviving trustee refuses to act with a trustee who may be proposed to be appointed—and I make this observation with reference to what appears to have been said by Mr. *Fleming*, as to Mr. *Petre* having come forward in opposition to his wishes—I think it would be going too far to say that the Court ought, on that ground alone, to refuse to appoint the proposed trustee; for this would, as suggested in the argument, be to give the continuing or surviving trustee a veto upon the appointment of the new trustee. In such a case, I think it must be the duty of the Court to inquire and ascertain whether the objection of the surviving or continuing trustee is well founded or not, and to act or refuse to act upon it accordingly. If the surviving or continuing trustee has improperly refused to act with the proposed trustee, it might be a ground for removing him from the trust. Upon the facts of this case, however, it seems to me that the objections taken by Mr. *Fleming* to the appointment of Mr. *Petre* were and are well founded, and upon the whole case, therefore, my opinion is, that the order under appeal, so far as it appoints Mr. *Petre,* ought to be discharged....

The order upon this appeal should, I think, be to discharge the order at the Rolls, to appoint Lord *Camoys* to be the trustee in the place of Mr. *Stoner,* and to vest the estate in him and Mr. *Fleming*.

(iii) Vesting orders

TRUSTEE ACT 1925

44. Vesting orders of land

In any of the following cases, namely:—

(i)   Where the court appoints or has appointed a trustee, or where a trustee has been appointed out of court under any statutory or express power;

(ii)   Where a trustee entitled to or possessed of any land or interest therein, whether by way of mortgage or otherwise, or entitled to a contingent right therein, either solely or jointly with any other person—

(a)   is under disability; or

(b)   is out of the jurisdiction of the High Court; or

(c)   cannot be found, or being a corporation, has been dissolved;

(iii)   Where it is uncertain who was the survivor of two or more trustees jointly entitled to or possessed of any interest in land;

(iv)   Where it is uncertain whether the last trustee known to have been entitled to or possessed of any interest in land is living or dead;

(v)   Where there is no personal representative of a deceased trustee who was entitled to or possessed of any interest in land, or where it is uncertain who is the personal representative of a deceased trustee who was entitled to or possessed of any interest in land;

(vi)   Where a trustee jointly or solely entitled to or possessed of any interest in land, or entitled to a contingent right therein, has been required, by or on behalf of a person entitled to require a conveyance of the land or interest or a release of the right, to convey the land or interest or to release the right, and has wilfully[32] refused or neglected to convey the land or interest or release the right for twenty-eight days after the date of the requirement;

(vii)   Where land or any interest therein is vested in a trustee whether by way of mortgage or otherwise, and it appears to the court to be expedient;

the court may make an order (in this Act called a vesting order) vesting the land or interest therein in any such person in any such manner and for any such estate or interest as the court may direct, or releasing or disposing of the contingent right to such person as the court may direct:

Provided that—

(a)   Where the order is consequential on the appointment of a trustee the land or interest therein shall be vested for such estate as the court may direct in the persons who on the appointment are the trustees; and

---

[32] Law Reform Committee 23rd Report (*The Powers and Duties of Trustees*) 1982 Cmnd 8733, paras. 5–8, recommended the removal of the word 'wilfully'; cf. TA 1925, s. 51(1)(ii)(d).

(b) Where the order relates to a trustee entitled or formerly entitled jointly with another person, and such trustee is under disability or out of the jurisdiction of the High Court or cannot be found, or being a corporation has been dissolved, the land interest or right shall be vested in such other person who remains entitled, either alone or with any other person the court may appoint.[33]

C TRUSTEE DE SON TORT

In **Dubai Aluminium Co Ltd v Salaam** [2002] UKHL 48, [2003] 2 AC 366, LORD MILLETT considered *Mara v Browne* [1896] 1 Ch 199:

136   The case concerned a marriage settlement. The first defendant, whom I shall call HB, was a solicitor. He advised the persons who were acting as trustees, though not yet formally appointed as such. He suggested a series of investments for the trust funds. They were not proper investments for trustees to make. The money was to be lent on building property of a speculative character and the margin was unsatisfactory. The investments were made and the money was lost. Lord Herschell considered that, if the claimants had charged HB with negligence as a solicitor and brought the action in time, they might well have succeeded, in which case both HB and his partner would have been liable. But any such action was barred by the Statute of Limitations. Accordingly the claimants alleged that HB had intermeddled with the trust and was liable as a *trustee de son tort*. They alleged that he had laid out the trust moneys at a time when there were no trustees, and therefore must be taken to have acted as a principal in the matter and not as a mere agent for the trustees. Such a claim was not statute-barred. The judge agreed with this analysis and held that both HB and his partner were liable.

137   The Court of Appeal took a different view of the facts. They held that it was not correct to say that at the relevant dates there were no trustees. But even if there had been none HB would not have been liable. He did not intend or purport to act as a trustee, and no one supposed that he was so acting. He purported to act throughout only as solicitor to the trustees and was understood by all concerned to be acting as such.

138   This summary is sufficient to show what Lord Herschell and Rigby LJ meant by 'constructive trustee'. They meant 'trustee de son tort'; that is to say, a person who, though not appointed to be a trustee, nevertheless takes it upon himself to act as such and to discharge the duties of a trustee on behalf of others. In *Taylor v Davies* [1920] AC 636, 651, Viscount Cave described such persons as follows:

'though not originally trustees, [they] had taken upon themselves the custody and administration of property on behalf of others; and though sometimes referred to as constructive trustees, they were, in fact, actual trustees, though not so named.'

Substituting dog Latin for bastard French, we would do better today to describe such persons as *de facto* trustees. In their relations with the beneficiaries they are treated in every respect as if they had been duly appointed. They are true trustees and are fully subject to fiduciary obligations. Their liability is strict; it does not depend on dishonesty. Like express trustees they could not plead the Limitation Acts as a defence to a claim for breach of trust. Indeed, for the

[33] For further provisions relating to orders made by the court, see also ss. 45–56, as amended by the Mental Capacity Act 2005.

purposes of the relevant provision (section 25(3) of the Supreme Court of Judicature Act 1873 (36 & 37 Vict c 66)), which distinguished between property held on express trusts and other trusts, they were treated by the courts as express trustees. That is why the action in *Mara v Browne* was not statute-barred.

II RETIREMENT[34]

TRUSTEE ACT 1925

39. Retirement of trustee without a new appointment

(1) Where a trustee is desirous of being discharged from the trust, and after his discharge there will be either a trust corporation or at least two persons[35] to act as trustees to perform the trust, then, if such trustee as aforesaid by deed declares that he is desirous of being discharged from the trust, and if his co-trustees and such other person, if any, as is empowered to appoint trustees, by deed consent to the discharge of the trustee, and to the vesting in the co-trustees alone of the trust property, the trustee desirous of being discharged shall be deemed to have retired from the trust, and shall, by the deed, be discharged therefrom under this Act, without any new trustee being appointed in his place.[36]

(2) Any assurance or thing requisite for vesting the trust property in the continuing trustees alone shall be executed or done.[37]

TRUSTS OF LAND AND APPOINTMENT OF TRUSTEES ACT 1996

19. Appointment and retirement of trustee at instance of beneficiaries[38]

(3) Where—

(a) a trustee has been given a direction under subsection (2) (a),[39]

(b) reasonable arrangements have been made for the protection of any rights of his in connection with the trust,

(c) after he has retired there will be either a trust corporation or at least two persons to act as trustees to perform the trust, and

---

[34] H&M, pp. 526–528; Lewin, pp. 443–459; P&M, pp. 565–568; P&S, pp. 677–678; Pettit, pp. 376–380; Snell, p. 609; T&H, pp. 660–668; U&H, pp. 916–922.

[35] A sole trustee other than a trust corporation does not suffice, even if he has power to give a valid receipt for capital money: (1986) 1 *Trust Law & Practice* 16 (M. Jacobs). See also (1987) 2 *Trust Law & Practice* 43 (J. Hayes); (1990) 106 LQR 87 at 94 (D. Hayton). The word 'persons' was inserted by TLATA 1996, Sch. 3, para. 3(13). This replaces the word 'individuals'. It follows that a corporate trustee (as distinct from a trust corporation [see p. 000, below]) is now included as a relevant trustee.

[36] It is unlikely that these conditions can be avoided by the terms of the settlement: (1986) 1 *Trust Law & Practice* 95 (M. Jacobs); *Mettoy Pension Trustees Ltd v Evans* [1990] 1 WLR 1587.

[37] See TA 1925, s. 40(2). See p. 653, below.   [38] For sub-ss. (1) and (2) see p. 627, above.

[39] A written direction by the beneficiaries to a trustee or trustees to retire from the trust.

(d) either another person is to be appointed to be a new trustee on his retirement (whether in compliance with a direction under subsection (2) (b) or otherwise) or the continuing trustees by deed consent to his retirement,

he shall make a deed declaring his retirement and shall be deemed to have retired and be discharged from the trust.[40]

(4) Where a trustee retires under subsection (3) he and the continuing trustees (together with any new trustee) shall (subject to any arrangements for the protection of his rights) do anything necessary to vest the trust property in the continuing trustees (or the continuing and new trustees).

A trustee who retires, whether by replacement under TA 1925 section 36[41] or section 39 or TLATA 1996, section 19 should seek from the beneficiaries a formal discharge from liability. Even without this, he will incur no liability in respect of future breaches of trust, unless he resigned in order to facilitate a breach.[42]

Law Reform Committee 23rd Report (*The Powers and Duties of Trustees*) 1982 Cmnd 8733, para. 9.1. VII.43

43.   Both executors and administrators should be able to retire:—

(i) where the demands of the office are such as to impose unreasonable and unforeseen burdens; and

(ii) where the personal representative is suffering from serious supervening ill health;

with, in each case, the leave of the court.

III REMOVAL[43]

TRUSTEE ACT 1925

36. Power of appointing new or additional trustees: see p. 624, above.

41. Power of court to appoint new trustees: see p. 634, above.

In **Letterstedt v Broers** (1884) 9 App Cas 371,[44] the Privy Council had to consider whether, independently of statute, it should remove the Board of Executors of Cape Town, the sole surviving executors and trustees of the will of Mr. Letterstedt, against

---

[40] It is not clear what would happen if the trustee refused to retire. One consequence may be that the beneficiaries would terminate the trust under the rule in *Saunders v Vautier* (1841) 4 Beav 115 [see p. 191, above].

[41] See p. 624, above.   [42] *Head v Gould* [1898] 2 Ch 250 at 272 [p. 866, below].

[43] H&M, pp. 528–529; Lewin, pp. 459–466; P&M, pp. 568–570; P&S, pp. 695–696; Pettit, pp. 376–380; Snell, p. 610; T&H, pp. 668–671; U&H, p. 922. On removal of executors, see *Re Clore* [1982] Ch 456. Under the Administration of Justice Act 1985, s.50, the High Court has power to appoint a substitute for, or to remove, a personal representative: *Practice Direction* [1948] WN 273 (evidence on removal of trustee under disability).

[44] See also *Thomas and Agnes Carvel Foundation v Carvel* [2007] EWHC 1314 (Ch), [2007] 4 All ER 81.

whom the appellant, a beneficiary, made allegations of misconduct in the administration of the trust. The Board was removed; but the allegations were not substantiated, and no costs were awarded. LORD BLACKBURN described at 385 the principles upon which the court's discretion should be exercised:

The whole case has been argued here, and, as far as their Lordships can perceive, in the Court below, as depending on the principles which should guide an English Court of Equity when called upon to remove old trustees and substitute new ones. It is not disputed that there is a jurisdiction 'in cases requiring such a remedy', as is said in *Story's Equity Jurisprudence*, s.1287, but there is very little to be found to guide us in saying what are the cases requiring such a remedy; so little that their Lordships are compelled to have recourse to general principles.

Story says, s.1289, 'But in cases of positive misconduct, Courts of Equity have no difficulty in interposing to remove trustees who have abused their trust; it is not indeed every mistake or neglect of duty, or inaccuracy of conduct of trustees, which will induce Courts of Equity to adopt such a course. But the acts or omissions must be such as to endanger the trust property or to shew a want of honesty, or a want of proper capacity to execute the duties, or a want of reasonable fidelity'.

It seems to their Lordships that the jurisdiction which a Court of Equity has no difficulty in exercising under the circumstances indicated by Story is merely ancillary to its principal duty, to see that the trusts are properly executed. This duty is constantly being performed by the substitution of new trustees in the place of original trustees for a variety of reasons in non-contentious cases. And therefore, though it should appear that the charges of misconduct were either not made out, or were greatly exaggerated, so that the trustee was justified in resisting them, and the Court might consider that in awarding costs, yet if satisfied that the continuance of the trustee would prevent the trusts being properly executed, the trustee might be removed. It must always be borne in mind that trustees exist for the benefit of those to whom the creator of the trust has given the trust estate.

The reason why there is so little to be found in the books on this subject is probably that suggested by Mr. Davey in his argument. As soon as all questions of character are as far settled as the nature of the case admits, if it appears clear that the continuance of the trustee would be detrimental to the execution of the trusts, even if for no other reason than that human infirmity would prevent those beneficially interested, or those who act for them, from working in harmony with the trustee, and if there is no reason to the contrary from the intentions of the framer of the trust to give this trustee a benefit or otherwise, the trustee is always advised by his own counsel to resign, and does so. If, without any reasonable ground, he refused to do so, it seems to their Lordships that the Court might think it proper to remove him; but cases involving the necessity of deciding this, if they ever arise, do so without getting reported. It is to be lamented that the case was not considered in this light by the parties in the Court below, for, as far as their Lordships can see, the Board would have little or no profit from continuing to be trustees, and as such coming into continual conflict with the appellant and her legal advisers, and would probably have been glad to resign, and get out of an onerous and disagreeable position. But the case was not so treated.

In exercising so delicate a jurisdiction as that of removing trustees, their Lordships do not venture to lay down any general rule beyond the very broad principle above enunciated, that their main guide must be the welfare of the beneficiaries. Probably it is not possible to lay down any more definite rule in a matter so essentially dependent on details often of great nicety. But they proceed to look carefully into the circumstances of the case...

It is quite true that friction or hostility between trustees and the immediate possessor of the trust estate is not of itself a reason for the removal of the trustees. But where the hostility is grounded on the mode in which the trust has been administered, where it has been caused wholly or partially by substantial overcharges against the trust estate, it is certainly not to be disregarded.

Looking therefore at the whole circumstances of this very peculiar case, the complete change of position, the unfortunate hostility that has arisen, and the difficult and delicate duties that may yet have to be performed, their Lordships can come to no other conclusion than that it is necessary, for the welfare of the beneficiaries, that the Board should no longer be trustees.

Probably if it had been put in this way below they would have consented. But for the benefit of the trust they should cease to be trustees, whether they consent or not.

Their Lordships think therefore that the portion of the final judgment which is, 'that the prayer for removal of the executors be refused', should be reversed, and that in lieu of it the Court below should be directed to remove the Board from the further execution of the trusts created by the will, and to take all necessary and proper proceedings for the appointment of other and proper persons to execute such trusts in future, and to transfer to them the trust property in so far as it remains vested in the Board. The rest of the judgment should stand.

In **Re Wrightson** [1908] 1 Ch 789, the trustees had been guilty of a breach of trust, in connection with an advance of a part of the trust funds upon mortgage. In an administration action, one question was whether the trustees should be removed. WARRINGTON J said at 800:

The next question is, ought I to make an order for the removal of the trustees upon the materials which were before the Court at the trial, which, in my judgment, are the only materials at which I can look? That raises a somewhat troublesome question. The trustees admitted that they were guilty of a breach of trust. The statement to which I have already referred, together with the proposals of the trustees, was remarked upon in strong language by the judge at the trial, and I desire to associate myself with the remarks which he made without further explanation that that statement is one which the trustees ought not to have made, and I think that the learned judge intended that an application for the removal of the trustees founded on that statement should *prima facie* be one which would at all events receive the favourable attention of the Court. But I have now before me not only the plaintiffs, but other beneficiaries representing somewhere about one-half of the estate. The plaintiffs' interest, if you are to count heads, predominates to some extent, but I have a very substantial proportion of the beneficiaries who object to the removal of the trustees, and who say there is no ground for it. Now, what are the grounds on which the Court removes trustees? The only case that I can find which helps one at all in this matter is the case of *Letterstedt v Broers* (1884) 9 App Cas 371, in the Privy Council. There some very valuable remarks were made by Lord Blackburn, who delivered the judgment of the Judicial Committee at 385. [His Lordship quoted from the extract on p. 642, above, and continued:] And then [Lord Blackburn] thus sums up what he regards as expressing the general principle guiding the Court in these cases at 387: 'In exercising so delicate a jurisdiction as that of removing trustees, their Lordships do not venture to lay down any general rule beyond the very broad principle enunciated, that their main guide must be the welfare of the beneficiaries. Probably it is not possible to lay down any more definite rule in a matter so essentially dependent on details often of great nicety. But they proceed to look carefully into the circumstances of the case.' Is it necessary here, having regard to the welfare of the beneficiaries and for the protection of this trust, to remove the trustees? At the present moment nothing remains for the trustees to do except to wind up the estate; the testator's widow is dead; the whole of the estate is divisible amongst a number of persons who are *sui juris*. But the summons was taken out on 27 February, 1906, two years ago, at a time when the widow was alive and the estate was not immediately divisible, and therefore I must, with a view at any rate of dealing with the costs, look at the state of things as they existed at the date when the summons was issued. Is it necessary for the welfare of the trust now to remove the trustees on the grounds alleged in the statement of claim? There is one contention on the part of the plaintiffs to which I think I ought to refer. Mr. Cave as one argument, or as one reason for the removal of the trustees, said, in effect, 'we do not like to have these persons who have been charged with a breach of trust and have admitted it, and who have made that statement which is set out in the pleadings, in custody of our trust estate'. That is not enough, especially when there are other *cestuis que trust* entitled. A somewhat similar question arose in the case of *Forster v Davies* (1861) 4 De GF & J 133 at 139, in which Turner LJ expressed the view, which I have just expressed, that disagreement between the *cestuis que trust* and the trustees, or the disinclination on the part of the *cestuis que trust* to have the trust property remain in the hands of a particular individual, is not a sufficient ground for the removal of the trustees. You must find something which induces the court to think either that the trust property will not be safe, or that the trust will not be properly executed in the interests of the beneficiaries. Is that so here, and is it for the welfare of the trust generally, and not merely of the plaintiffs, that these trustees should be removed? I think it is not. The trustees were undoubtedly guilty of a breach of trust, and they undoubtedly in the statement to which I have referred expressed views which have occasioned the blame which has been attached to the trustees both by Buckley J and myself, but, having regard to the fact that the Court has now the power of seeing that the trust is properly executed, to the fact that a large proportion of the beneficiaries do not require the trustees to be removed, and further (and this is of great importance), to the extra expense and loss to the trust estate which must be occasioned by the change of trustees, I think it would not be for the welfare of the *cestuis que trust* generally, or necessary for the protection of the trust estate, that these trustees should be removed. I must therefore refuse the application for their removal as well as the application for the further accounts and inquiries.

In **Moore v M'Glynn** [1894] 1 IR 74, William M'Glynn appointed his brother Edward and his son Patrick as trustees of his estate for the benefit of his widow and children. After his death, Edward managed the testator's business of shopkeeper and local postmaster. Subsequently Edward was appointed postmaster, and later started his own business which was similar to that of the trust. CHATTERTON V-C held that Edward had committed no breach of trust; but that the conflict required that he should be discharged from his office as trustee.[45]

CHARITIES ACT 1993

18. Power to act for protection of Charities

(2) (b) (i): see p. 604, above.

---

[45] *Re Edwards' Will Trusts* [1982] Ch 30, where Buckley LJ, in upholding removal of a trustee, said at 42: 'such an order should only be made on cogent grounds, but the jurisdiction is undoubtedly discretionary'; *Clarke v Heathfield* [1985] ICR 203; *Clarke v Heathfield (No 2)* [1985] ICR 606, where, in an interlocutory application, an order was made to remove the three trustees of the National Union of Mineworkers 'who were in flagrant breach of an order of the High Court' and to appoint a receiver.

Report of the Charity Commissioners for England and Wales for the year 1976, paras. 25–29

Sanctuary

25.   In paragraphs 90 to 96 of our report for 1971 we mentioned that, following an inquiry and report under section 6 of the Charities Act 1960, we had made an order removing Mr. Robert Jones and his sister from being trustees of the charity called Sanctuary, that Mr. Jones' appeal to the High Court against our order had been dismissed by Mr. Justice Ungoed-Thomas and that Mr. Jones was appealing to the Court of Appeal. In 1973 the Court of Appeal resolved that the case should be remitted for a rehearing in the Court of first instance on the grounds that the Judge might have attributed too little weight to the appellant's affidavit evidence in which he sought to challenge some of the findings in the report of the inquiry. The Court of Appeal held that it was for an appellant who appeals against such an order to show that it had been wrongly made, but the report of the inquiry, to the extent that it was not challenged by him, should be treated as evidence in the appeal (*Jones v A-G* [1974] Ch 148).

26.   The rehearing took place before Mr. Justice Brightman, and Mr. Jones' application was dismissed. In his Judgment dated 9 November, 1976 the Judge noted that out of a sum exceeding £10,000 collected from the public over a period of some three years not one penny was ever spent on any charitable purpose; that collecting boxes left in public places were frequently abandoned because it was uneconomic to collect them; that most of the personal collectors for the charity, but not Mr. Jones himself, received a percentage remuneration sometimes as high as 35 per cent, and probably even as high as 50 per cent; and that the administrative expenses of the charity were so high that between January 1970 and May 1971 only 11 pennies out of each pound remained available for charitable purposes.

27.   The Judge commented on the fact that during the three years that Mr. Jones ran the charity he was living on social security and had indicated that he would probably have tried to stay on social security for the rest of his life so as to carry on the charity. The Judge found it disturbing that a person could draw public funds for his maintenance while engaged in charitable activities selected by himself.

28.   Another point which troubled Mr. Justice Brightman was the legality of commissions charged by people who took round charity collecting boxes. A collecting box which named a charity as the recipient of a donation represented that money placed in the box went to the charity, and if the collector retained commission this was contrary to the representation on the collecting box and to the belief of most contributors. Furthermore, a person who solicited money for a charity was a trustee of the contribution and unless he made it known to the donor that he intended to retain a percentage of the contribution for himself it seemed to the Judge that he had no title to that percentage.

29.   The Judge also referred to the use of deceptive labels and letter headings, failure to check the credentials of area organisers, an untruthful application for a licence under the House to House Collections Act [1939], a failure to maintain proper books of account over part of the period, misuse of charity money, and lack of security in regard to the issue and sealing of collecting boxes. In his judgment there was overwhelming evidence to support the allegations of misconduct and mismanagement which had been made against Mr. Jones, and he found the allegations proved. In his judgment it was out of the question to set aside our order removing Mr. Jones from the trusteeship of Sanctuary.[46]

---

[46] CA upheld the decision of Brightman J as 'wholly unassailable': Annual Report for 1977, paras. 31–33.

IV PARTICULAR TRUSTEES[47]

A JUDICIAL TRUSTEES

JUDICIAL TRUSTEES ACT 1896

1. Power of court on application to appoint judicial trustee

(1) Where application is made to the court by or on behalf of the person creating or intending to create a trust, or by or on behalf of a trustee or beneficiary, the court may, in its discretion, appoint a person (in this Act called a judicial trustee) to be a trustee of that trust, either jointly with any other person or as sole trustee, and, if sufficient cause is shown, in place of all or any existing trustees.

(2) The administration of the property of a deceased person, whether a testator or intestate, shall be a trust, and the executor or administrator a trustee, within the meaning of this Act.

(3) Any fit and proper person nominated for the purpose in the application may be appointed a judicial trustee, and, in the absence of such nomination, or if the court is not satisfied of the fitness of a person so nominated, an official of the court may be appointed, and in any case a judicial trustee shall be subject to the control and supervision of the court as an officer thereof.

(4) The court may, either on request or without request, give to a judicial trustee any general or special directions in regard to the trust or the administration thereof.

(5) There may be paid to a judicial trustee out of the trust property such remuneration, not exceeding the prescribed limits, as the court may assign in each case, subject to any rules under this Act respecting the application of such remuneration where the judicial trustee is an official of the court, and the remuneration so assigned to any judicial trustee shall, save as the court may for special reasons otherwise order, cover all his work and personal outlay.

(6) In any case where the court shall so direct, an inquiry into the administration by a judicial trustee of any trust, or into any dealing or transaction of a judicial trustee, shall be made in the prescribed manner.[48]

---

[47] H&M, pp. 511–515; Lewin, pp. 547–574; P&M, pp. 542–549; P&S, pp. 693–695; Pettit, pp. 381–388; Snell, pp. 606–608; T&H, pp. 701–716; U&H, pp. 969–989.

[48] As amended by AJA 1982, s. 57(1). On the auditing of accounts, see Judicial Trustees Act 1896, s. 4(1), paras. 11 and 12, as added by AJA 1982, s. 57(2) and Judicial Trustee Rules 1983 (S.I. 1983 No. 370). A new category of corporate judicial trustee was created by r. 2, for whose accounts separate provision is made, and exemption granted from automatic audit by the court; r. 13. A corporate trustee 'means the Official Solicitor, the Public Trustee, or a corporation either appointed by the Court in any particular case to be a trustee or entitled by rules made under section 4(3) of the Public Trustee Act 1906 to act as custodian trustee'. Cf the definition of a trust corporation [p. 653, below].

(7) Where an application relating to the estate of a deceased person is made to the court under this section, the court may, if it thinks fit, proceed as if the application were, or included an application under section 50 of the Administration of Justice Act 1985 (power of High Court to appoint substitute for, or to remove, personal representative).[49]

In **Re Ridsdel** [1947] Ch 597, the question arose whether rule 12 of the Judicial Trustee Rules 1897,[50] under which the judicial trustee may at any time request the court to give him directions as to the trust or its administration, by implication deprived him of the power of compromise under section 15 of the Trustee Act 1925.[51] JENKINS J held that it did not, and said at 605:

I cannot think that that is the effect of this rule. After all, the object of the Judicial Trustees Act 1896, as I understand it, was to provide a middle course in cases where the administration of the estate by the ordinary trustees had broken down and it was not desired to put the estate to the expense of a full administration. In those circumstances, a solution was found in the appointment of a judicial trustee, who acts in close concert with the court and under conditions enabling the court to supervise his transactions. I cannot think that it was intended to complicate the matter by prohibiting such a trustee from exercising any discretion without first going to the court and asking for directions. That, as Mr. Stamp points out, involves this, that whenever the trustee wanted to exercise some discretion, such as the power of compromise under section 15 of the Trustee Act 1925, he would perforce have to come to the court for directions; but (to give only one instance) the court would give no directions without summoning before it all persons interested in the exercise of the discretion in order that the matter might be argued and decided in the presence of all parties. One would thus reduce the administration of an estate by a judicial trustee to very much the same position as where an estate is being administered by the court and every step has to be taken in pursuance of the court's directions. It does not seem to me to be right or necessary to construe the Judicial Trustee Rules 1897, as having any such effect.

B THE PUBLIC TRUSTEE

PUBLIC TRUSTEE ACT 1906

1. Office of public trustee

(1) There shall be established the office of public trustee.

(2) The public trustee shall be a corporation sole under that name, with perpetual succession and an official seal, and may sue and be sued under the above name like any other corporation sole, but any instruments sealed by him shall not, by

---

[49] As added by AJA 1985, s. 50 (6).
[50] See now Judicial Trustee Rules 1983, r. 8 (S.I. 1983 No. 370).   [51] See p. 750, below.

reason of his using a seal, be rendered liable to a higher stamp duty than if he were an individual.

2. General powers and duties of public trustee

(1) Subject to and in accordance with the provisions of this Act and rules made thereunder, the public trustee may, if he thinks fit—

(a) act in the administration of estates of small value;

(b) act as custodian trustee;[52]

(c) act as an ordinary trustee;

(d) be appointed to be a judicial trustee;[53] ...

(2) Subject to the provisions of this Act, and to the rules made thereunder, the public trustee may act either alone or jointly with any person or body of persons in any capacity to which he may be appointed in pursuance of this Act, and shall have all the same powers, duties, and liabilities, and be entitled to the same rights and immunities and be subject to the control and orders of the court, as a private trustee acting in the same capacity.

(3) The public trustee may decline, either absolutely or except on the prescribed conditions, to accept any trust, but he shall not decline to accept any trust on the ground only of the small value of the trust property.

(4) The public trustee shall not accept any trust which involves the management or carrying on of any business, except in the cases in which he may be authorised to do so by rules made under this Act, nor any trust under a deed of arrangement for the benefit of creditors, nor the administration of any estate known or believed by him to be insolvent.[54]

(5) The public trustee shall not accept any trust exclusively for religious or charitable purposes,[55] and nothing in this Act contained, or in the rules to be made under the powers in this Act contained, shall abridge or affect the powers or duties of the official trustee of charity lands or official trustees of charitable funds.[56]

(1) In the Administration of Small Estates

3. Administration of small estates

(1) Any person who in the opinion of the public trustee would be entitled to apply to the court for an order for the administration by the court of an estate, the gross

---

[52] See p. 650, below.   [53] See p. 646, above.

[54] Such matters will instead be dealt with by the Official Solicitor acting as such: <http://www.officialsolicitor.gov.uk/os/offsol.htm>.

[55] The Public Trustee accepted the trusts of the will of George Bernard Shaw under which he left the residue of his estate to be applied to the reform of the alphabet: *Re Shaw* [1957] 1 WLR 729 [p. 364, above]. Harman J held that the gift was not charitable. The Official Solicitor can accept trusts which are exclusively for religious or charitable purposes: see above, n. 54.

[56] Now the Official Custodian for Charities.

capital value whereof is proved to the satisfaction of the public trustee to be less than one thousand pounds, may apply to the public trustee to administer the estate, and, where any such application is made and it appears to the public trustee that the persons beneficially entitled are persons of small means, the public trustee shall administer the estate, unless he sees good reason for refusing to do so....

(2) *As Custodian Trustee*

4. Custodian trustee

(1) Subject to rules[57] under this Act the public trustee may, if he consents to act as such, and whether or not the number of trustees has been reduced below the original number, be appointed to be custodian trustee of any trust—

    (a) by order of the court made on the application of any person on whose application the court may order the appointment of a new trustee; or

    (b) by the testator, settlor, or other creator of any trust; or

    (c) by the person having power to appoint new trustees.

(3) *As an Ordinary Trustee*

5. Appointment of public trustee to be trustee, executor, &c

(1) The public trustee may by that name, or any other sufficient description, be appointed to be trustee of any will or settlement or other instrument creating a trust or to perform any trust or duty belonging to a class which he is authorised by the rules made under this Act to accept, and may be so appointed whether the will or settlement or instrument creating the trust or duty was made or came into operation before or after the passing of this Act, and either as an original or as a new trustee, or as an additional trustee, in the same cases, and in the same manner, and by the same persons or court, as if he were a private trustee, with this addition, that, though the trustees originally appointed were two or more, the public trustee may be appointed sole trustee.[58]

ADMINISTRATION OF ESTATES ACT 1925

9. Vesting of estate in Public Trustee where intestacy or lack of executors[59]

(1) Where a person dies intestate, his real and personal estate shall vest in the Public Trustee until the grant of administration.

---

[57] Public Trustee Rules 1912, rr. 6–11 (r. 10 as amended by S.R.&O. 1916 No. 489).

[58] *Re Moxon* [1916] 2 Ch 595; *Re Duxbury's Settlement Trusts* [1995] 1 WLR 425 (appointment as sole trustee of discretionary settlement valid, in spite of express clause prohibiting exercise of trustees' powers by fewer than two trustees); [1996] Conv 50 (J. Snape).

[59] As substituted by Law of Property (Miscellaneous Provisions) Act 1994, s. 14(1); Public Trustee (Notices Affecting Land) (Title on Death) Regulations 1995 (S.I. 1995 No. 1330). See Law Commission Report: *Title on Death* 1989 (Law Com No. 184), paras. 2.20–2.26.

(2) Where a testator dies and—

    (a) at the time of his death there is no executor with power to obtain probate of the will, or

    (b) at any time before probate of the will is granted there ceases to be any executor with power to obtain probate,

the real and personal estate of which he disposes by the will shall vest in the Public Trustee until the grant of representation.

(3) The vesting of real or personal estate in the Public Trustee by virtue of this section does not confer on him any beneficial interest in, or impose on him any duty, obligation or liability in respect of, the property.

In May 2007 the Lord Chancellor approved proposals for the Official Solicitor and Public Trustee to retire from the bulk of their existing caseload of trust and estate work. A private sector corporate trustee has been appointed to take on this work. The Official Solicitor and Public Trustee will continue to act and accept new cases where nobody else is suitable, able, and willing to act and an injustice would result if the Official Solicitor and Public Trustee did take on this work. The office of the Official Solicitor and Public Trustee estimates that only about 1,600 trusts are managed in the public sector.

C CUSTODIAN TRUSTEES[60]

PUBLIC TRUSTEE ACT 1906

4. Custodian Trustee

(1) See p. 649, above.

PUBLIC TRUSTEE RULES 1912[61]

30. Corporate Bodies as Custodian Trustees

(1) The following corporations shall be entitled to act as custodian trustees:—

    (a) the Treasury Solicitor;

    (b) any corporation which:—

        (i) is constituted under the law of the United Kingdom or of any part thereof, or under the law of any other Member State of the European Economic Community or of any part thereof;

---

[60] See generally (1960) 24 Conv (NS) 196 (S.G. Maurice).

[61] SR & O 1912 No. 348, as substituted by the Public Trustee (Custodian Trustee) Rules 1975 (S.I. 1975 No. 1189), r. 2, and as added by S.I. 1976 No. 836; S.I. 1981 No. 358; S.I. 1984 No. 109; S.I. 1985 No. 132; S.I. 1987 No. 1891; S.I. 1994 No. 2519.

(ii) is empowered by its constitution to undertake trust business (which for the purpose of this rule means the business of acting as trustee under wills and settlements and as executor and administrator) in England and Wales;[62]

(iii) has one or more places of business in the United Kingdom; and

(iv) is—

a company incorporated by special Act of Parliament or Royal Charter, or

a company registered (with or without limited liability) in the United Kingdom under the Companies Act 1985 or in another Member State of the European Economic Community and having a capital (in stock or shares) for the time being issued of not less than £250,000 (or its equivalent in the currency of the State where the company is registered), of which not less than £100,000 (or its equivalent) has been paid up in cash, or

a company which is registered without limited liability in the United Kingdom under the Companies Act 1985 or in another member State of the European Economic Community and of which one of the members is a company within any of the classes defined in this sub-paragraph;

The Rules refer to a number of other corporations including health authorities and local authorities.

In **Re Brooke Bond & Co Ltd's Trust Deed** [1963] Ch 357[63] the Welfare Insurance Co Ltd were custodian trustee under a trust deed which secured the pension fund of the employees of Brooke Bond & Co Ltd. Its managing trustees had powers to take out a group insurance policy and they desired to take it out with Welfare Insurance Co Ltd, the custodian trustee. The question was whether, without leave of the court, the custodian trustee could enter into the policy with the managing trustees, and retain for their own benefit any profit which they might make. Cross J held that they could not and said at 363:

It is apparent that the duties of a custodian trustee differ substantially from those of an ordinary trustee. If the trust instrument or the general law gives the trustee power to do this, that or the other, it is not for the custodian trustee to consider whether it should be done. The exercise of powers or discretions is a matter for the managing trustees with which the custodian trustee has no concern, and he is bound to deal with the trust property so as to give effect to the decisions and actions taken by the managing trustees unless what he is requested to do by them would be a breach of trust or would involve him in personal liability. On the other hand, it is plain that he

[62] *Re Bigger* [1977] Fam 203 (Bank of Ireland).

[63] (1963) 79 LQR 177 (R.E.M.). See also *Forster v Williams Deacon's Bank Ltd* [1935] Ch 359 (bank may not be appointed both managing trustee and custodian trustee in order to allow it to charge fees as custodian trustee).

is a trustee holding the trust property and its income on trust for the beneficiaries according to the terms of the trust instrument and he is *prima facie* liable to the beneficiaries for any dealing with capital or income which is a breach of trust. In practice this liability may be considerably qualified as regards income by the provisions of subsection (2)(e)[64] and as regards capital or income by the provisions of subsection (2)(h); but subject to the protection provided by those subsections the custodian trustee, as I understand the matter, is as liable as an ordinary trustee to be sued by a beneficiary for the misapplication of the trust property. His position is quite unlike that of a third party—a bailee of the trust property, for instance—who is in contractual relationship with the trustee but owes no duty to the beneficiaries.

It is, however, argued that the fact that a custodian trustee is not concerned with the management of the trust makes the rule that a trustee may not make a profit out of his trust inapplicable to him. If trustees have power to sell or lease the trust property or to invest it in some way, the custodian trustee is not concerned with the question whether the power should be exercised and is not concerned with any negotiations which take place between the managing trustees and the other contracting parties. All the custodian trustee is concerned to do is to be satisfied that the managing trustees have the power to enter into the transaction which they call on him to carry out.

That being the position, it is said how can there be any conflict between his interest and duty if he himself is the other contracting party? He must indeed satisfy himself that the proposed transaction is one which the managing trustees have power to enter into just as he would have to do if they had contracted with a third party, but once he is satisfied as to that, his duty in the matter is at an end and he can properly look only to his own interests in negotiating the terms of the contract in question with the managing trustees.

This argument is ingenious but in my judgment it is unsound. In the first place, it presupposes that a hard and fast line can always be drawn between the power to enter into a contract of a certain character and the terms of the contract. I do not think that this is always the case. For example, the managing trustees may have power to lease the trust property but only on the terms that they obtain the best rent reasonably obtainable. In such a case if the proposal was to grant a lease to a nominee of the custodian trustee, the custodian trustee would be under a duty to see that the best rent was obtained so that no breach of trust was committed, but it would be to his interest as the prospective lessee to have the rent fixed at as low a figure as possible. Again it is *prima facie* the duty of a trustee to place at the disposal of the beneficiaries any special knowledge he has of the value of the trust property or of any advantages or disadvantages of any contract which is in contemplation with regard to it. It may be that if the contract is being made by the managing trustees with a third party, a custodian trustee is under no positive duty to communicate any such knowledge which he may have to the managing trustees. I do not say whether that is so or not, but assuming it is so it does not follow by any means that if the custodian trustee was himself the other contracting party he could properly refrain from disclosing any such special knowledge to the managing trustees as a third party would be entitled to refrain from disclosing it. I appreciate that it may well be that the chances of there being a conflict between interest and duty are less in the case of transactions between a custodian trustee and managing trustees than they are in the case of transactions between an ordinary trustee and his co-trustees. But the possibility of conflict is still there and the rule, as Lord Herschell pointed out in *Bray v Ford* [1896] AC 44, is an inflexible one unless the trust instrument provides for a profit being made by the trustees or the court makes a special order in a particular case.

[64] Public Trustee Act 1906, s. 4 (2).

For the reasons I have tried to give, I can see no sound reason for saying that the rule does not apply to a custodian trustee as much as to an ordinary trustee.

D   TRUSTEES OF CHARITABLE TRUSTS

TRUSTEE ACT 1925

34(3). Limitation of the number of trustees: see p. 602, above.

CHARITIES ACT 1993

16(8). Concurrent jurisdiction with High Court for certain purposes: see p. 586, above.

18. Power to act for protection of charities: see pp. 603, above.

E   TRUST CORPORATIONS

TRUSTEE ACT 1925[65]

68(18). Definitions

(1) In this Act, unless the context otherwise requires, the following expressions have the meanings hereby assigned to them respectively, that is to say:— ...

(xxx) 'Trust corporation' means the Public Trustee[66] or a corporation either appointed by the court in any particular case to be a trustee or entitled by rules made under subsection (3) of section four of the Public Trustee Act 1906, to act as a custodian trustee ...

LAW OF PROPERTY (AMENDMENT) ACT 1926

3. Meaning of 'trust corporation'

(1) For the purposes of the Law of Property Act, 1925, the Settled Land Act 1925, the Trustee Act 1925, the Administration of Estates Act 1925, and the Supreme Court Act 1981,[67] the expression 'Trust Corporation' includes the Treasury Solicitor, the Official Solicitor and any person holding any other official position prescribed by the Lord Chancellor, and, in relation to the property of a bankrupt and property subject to a deed of arrangement, includes the trustee in bankruptcy and the trustee under the deed respectively, and, in relation to charitable ecclesiastical and public trusts,

---

[65] See also Settled Land Act 1925, s. 117(1)(xxx); Law of Property Act 1925, s. 205(1)(xxviii); Administration of Estates Act 1925, s. 55(1)(xxvi); Supreme Court Act 1981, s. 128.   [66] See p. 647, above.
[67] As substituted by Supreme Court Act 1981, s. 152 (1), Sch. 5.

also includes any local or public authority so prescribed, and any other corporation constituted under the laws of the United Kingdom or any part thereof which satisfies the Lord Chancellor that it undertakes the administration of any such trusts without remuneration, or that by its constitution it is required to apply the whole of its net income after payment of outgoings for charitable, ecclesiastical or public purposes, and is prohibited from distributing, directly or indirectly, any part thereof by way of profits amongst any of its members, and is authorised by him to act in relation to such trusts as a trust corporation.

V   INVOLVEMENT OF THE COURTS[68]

Although the court will compel a trustee to carry out a specific duty, there are difficulties in determining what is the right course to take in respect of powers and discretions. Generally the court will not intervene, in the absence of *mala fides*, in the exercise of a power. But, as in the case of a discretionary trust, the trustee may be under an obligation to exercise a discretion. If the trustee does not exercise it, as has been seen, in appropriate circumstances the court may exercise it for him.[69] But if the trustee does exercise it within the terms of the power or discretion, how can the court interfere? The discretion is that of the trustee, not that of the court. The court can interfere in the case of fraud; or if the trustees show that they reached a conclusion for wrong reasons. But if they say nothing, there is little that the court can do. The problem is particularly acute if a complainant suspects fraud or *mala fides* on the part of the trustees; but cannot prove this unless the trustees disclose their deliberations.[70]

A   BONA FIDE EXERCISE OF THE POWER

Tempest v Lord Camoys
(1882) 21 Ch D 571 (CA, **Jessel MR**, **Brett** and **Cotton LJJ**)

Under the will of Sir Charles Robert Tempest, Bart., Mr. James Fleming and Mr. Wilfred Tempest, the trustees, had power at their absolute discretion to sell land, to apply the purchase money in the purchase of other land, and to raise money by mortgage for the purpose.

---

[68]   H&M, pp. 529–535; Lewin, pp. 1001–1012, 1075–1083; P&M, pp. 212–220; P&S, pp. 699–705; Pettit, pp. 496–502; Snell, pp. 654–657; T&H, pp. 613–632; U &H, pp. 852–860.
[69]   *McPhail v Doulton* [1971] AC 424 [p. 44, above]; *Re Locker's Settlement* [1977] 1 WLR 1323 [p. 97, n. 53, above].
[70]   As to whether beneficiaries can obtain information about trustees' deliberations see p. 739, below.

Some of the family wished to purchase Bracewell Hall for £60,000, using £30,000 of available money, and raising the balance by mortgage. Tempest supported the suggestion, Fleming opposed. Tempest brought this petition, asking that the purchase might be ordered.

Held (affirming CHITTY J). The Court would not interfere with the bona fide exercise of his discretion by a trustee.

Jessel MR: It is very important that the law of the Court on this subject should be understood. It is settled law that when a testator has given a pure discretion to trustees as to the exercise of a power, the Court does not enforce the exercise of the power against the wish of the trustees, but it does prevent them from exercising it improperly. The Court says that the power, if exercised at all, is to be properly exercised. This may be illustrated by the case of persons having a power of appointing new trustees. Even after a decree in a suit for administering the trusts has been made they may still exercise the power, but the Court will see that they do not appoint improper persons.

But in all cases where there is a trust or duty coupled with the power the Court will then compel the trustees to carry it out in a proper manner and within a reasonable time. In the present case there was a power which amounts to a trust to invest the fund in question in the purchase of land. The trustees would not be allowed by the Court to disregard that trust, and if Mr. *Fleming* had refused to invest the money in land at all the Court would have found no difficulty in interfering. But that is a very different thing from saying that the Court ought to take from the trustees their uncontrolled discretion as to the particular time for the investment and the particular property which should be purchased. In this particular case it appears to me that the testator in his will has carefully distinguished between what is to be at the discretion of his trustees and what is obligatory on them.

There is another difficulty in this case. The estate proposed to be purchased will cost £60,000, and only £30,000 is available for the purchase, and the trustees will have to borrow the remaining £30,000. There is power to raise money by mortgage at the absolute discretion of the trustees, and assuming that such a transaction as this is within the power, and that the trustees can mortgage the estate before they have actually bought it, there is no trust to mortgage, it is purely discretionary. The Court cannot force Mr. *Fleming* to take the view that it is proper to mortgage the estate in this way; he may very well have a different opinion from the other trustee. Here again the Court cannot interfere with his discretion. The appeal must therefore be dismissed.

Re Beloved Wilkes' Charity
(1851) 3 Mac & G 440 (**Lord Truro LC**)

Trustees of a charitable trust were to select a boy to be educated at Oxford in preparation for him to become a Minister of the Church of England. Preference was to be given to boys from four named parishes if, in the judgment of the trustees, a fit and proper candidate therefrom could be found.

In 1848 the trustees selected Charles Joyce, who did not come from one of the four parishes. They gave no reasons for their choice, but stated that they had considered the candidates impartially. It appeared, however, that Joyce's brother was a Minister, who had sought the assistance of one of the trustees in favour of Charles. The court was asked to set aside the selection, and to select William Gale, whose father was a respectable farmer residing in one of the specified parishes.

Held. In the absence of evidence that the trustees had exercised their discretion unfairly or dishonestly, the Court would not interfere.

Lord Truro LC: The question, therefore, is, whether it was the duty of the trustees to enter into particulars, or whether the law is not, that trustees who are appointed to execute a trust according to discretion, that discretion to be influenced by a variety of circumstances (as, in this instance, by those particular circumstances which should be connected with the fitness of a lad to be brought up as a minister of the Church of England), are not bound to go into a detail of the grounds upon which they come to their conclusion, their duty being satisfied by shewing that they have considered the circumstances of the case, and have come to their conclusion accordingly. Without occupying time by going into a lengthened examination of the decisions, the result of them appears to me so clear and reasonable, that it will be sufficient to state my conclusion in point of law to be, that in such cases as I have mentioned it is to the discretion of the trustees that the execution of the trust is confided, that discretion being exercised with an entire absence of indirect motive, with honesty of intention, and with a fair consideration of the subject. The duty of supervision on the part of this Court will thus be confined to the question of the honesty, integrity, and fairness with which the deliberation has been conducted, and will not be extended to the accuracy of the conclusion arrived at, except in particular cases. If, however, as stated by Lord Ellenborough in *R v Archbishop of Canterbury* (1812) 15 East 117, trustees think fit to state a reason, and the reason is one which does not justify their conclusion, then the Court may say that they have acted by mistake and in error, and that it will correct their decision; but if, without entering into details, they simply state, as in many cases it would be most prudent and judicious for them to do, that they have met and considered and come to a conclusion, the Court has then no means of saying that they have failed in their duty, or to consider the accuracy of their conclusion.[71] It seems, therefore, to me, that having in the present case to look to the motives of the trustees as developed in the affidavits, no ground exists for imputing bad motives. The Petitioners, indeed, candidly state, on the face of their petition, that they do not impute such motives, they merely charge the trustees with a miscarriage as regards the duty which they had to perform. I cannot, therefore, deal with the case as if the petition had contained a statement of a different kind, and if I could, still I should say, having read the affidavits, that I see nothing whatever which can lay the foundation for any judicial conclusion that the trustees intentionally and from bad motives failed in their duty, if they failed at all.

Klug v Klug
[1918] 2 Ch 67 (Ch D, **Neville J**)

Madame Moro (as Frida Klug) became entitled, on attaining the age of 21 in August, 1915, to a share in her father's estate. Legacy duty had to be paid, and it was agreed with the Inland Revenue that this should be paid by four equal instalments. After the First World War, income from the investments fell and the cost of living rose, and she was unable to make the payments out of income, and asked the trustees of her father's will to make an advancement to her out of the capital of her share, as they had power to do under the advancement clause of the will.

[71] See *Re Londonderry's Settlement* [1965] Ch 918 [p. 740, below].

The trustees were the Public Trustee, and Mrs. Klug, the mother of Madame Moro. The Public Trustee wished to make an advancement; but Mrs. Klug refused, on the ground that Madame Moro had married without her approval.

Held. Payment out of the capital was ordered.

Neville J: In this case Madame Moro is entitled to a life interest in one-third of her father's residuary estate with remainder to her children, and has to pay a legacy duty of 10 per cent because, according to English law, she is to be considered a stranger to her father. But that is not material, the real question here being when and how far the Court will interfere with the discretion given to trustees. I should be sorry by anything I may say to be thought to diminish the jurisdiction and control which the Court has over trustees in exercising their discretion, but on the other hand I should be loth to say that, where trustees have honestly exercised their discretion, the Court will interfere in the absence of special circumstances. Here the trustees are the Public Trustee and the testator's widow, and they have power to advance not more than a moiety of the capital of Madame Moro's settled share for her advancement and benefit, and the question is whether it will be for her benefit that the instalments of the legacy duty that have been paid and the two remaining instalments that are due should be paid out of the corpus instead of out of the income of her settled share. She is in difficulties owing to the times in which we are living. When the summons was previously before me I decided that the trustees could in the exercise of their discretion under the powers of advancement, if they thought fit, advance out of capital a sum sufficient to pay this legacy duty. The Public Trustee thinks that their discretion should be so exercised, but his co-trustee, the mother, declines to join him in so doing, not because she has considered whether or not it would be for her daughter's welfare that the advance should be made, but because her daughter has married without her consent, and her letters show, in my opinion, that she has not exercised her discretion at all. What, then, ought the Court to do when one trustee very properly desires to exercise his discretion under a power for the benefit of a beneficiary and his co-trustee will not exercise her discretion? I think that in such circumstances it is the duty of the Court to interfere and, in the exercise of its control over the discretion given to the trustees, to direct a sum to be raised out of the capital sufficient to pay off the mortgage of 250l and two remaining instalments of the legacy duty, and that is the order I now make.

In **Wilson v Law Debenture Trust Corporation** [1995] 2 All ER 337[72] it was recognised that, even in a pension trust, where a trustee has a discretion to perform he is not required to give reasons for its exercise.[73] Further, in the absence of evidence that the trustees had acted improperly, the court would not interfere with the exercise of the discretion.

B TRUSTEE MISTAKES

Where trustees make a decision which has an adverse effect on the beneficiaries it is sometimes possible to reverse this decision by means of the rule in *Hastings-Bass*.[74] The ambit of this rule has proved to be a matter of particular uncertainty, as has the

[72] (1994) 8 *Trust Law International* 118 (D. Schaffer); [1995] All ER Rev 321 (P.J. Clarke): (1995) 145 NLJ 1414 (P. O'Hagan). [73] See p. 740, below.
[74] [1975] Ch 25.

justification for it.[75] It is clear, however, that the existence of the rule is motivated by the need to protect beneficiaries from trustees' mistakes.

Sieff v Fox[76]
[2005] EWHC 1312 (Ch), [2005] 1 WLR 3811 (Lloyd LJ)

Trustees of a settlement, having received advice concerning potential Inheritance and Capital Gains Tax liability, exercised their power of appointment in favour of the second defendant. The advice was incorrect and the second defendant was liable for a substantial sum of Capital Gains Tax, amounting possibly to over £1 million. The trustees sought a declaration that the appointment was not valid because, had they known the true tax position, they would not have made it.

Held: The trustees' decision was vitiated and the appointment set aside.

Lloyd LJ:

33   As a general proposition, English law affords relief against the consequences of a mistake on the part of a person who executes a document as to the nature, terms or effect of that document, but only in circumstances which are quite strictly limited. At common law the defence of *non est factum,* if established, results in the document being void, and for this reason the doctrine is strictly limited: see *Saunders v Anglia Building Society* [1971] AC 1004. In that case the document was held to be voidable, having been obtained by fraud, but that meant that the innocent mortgagee's interest in the property was effective despite the fraud; the plaintiff's attempt to recover the property free from the mortgage failed.

34   In equity, rectification or rescission may be available in cases of mistake, but these are discretionary remedies, granted only on equitable principles, which enable the court to ensure that relief is not granted in circumstances in which it would lead to injustice. Moreover the courts have developed principles which limit the availability of the remedy.

35   Voluntary dispositions by an individual may be set aside for mistake, or may be rectified, in appropriate circumstances. Rectification of a unilateral instrument may be available if it is shown that, by mistake, it does not accord with the intention of the party making it. The mistake must be either as to the words used or as to their legal effect.

[His Lordship considered *Gibbon v Mitchell* [1990] 1 WLR 1304 and continued:]

37   So far as acts by trustees in the exercise of a discretionary power are concerned, traditionally the courts are reluctant to interfere. It has been said that, when a power has been exercised in good faith and within its terms, the court will not interfere: see *Gisborne v Gisborne* (1877) 2 App Cas 300. This judicial reticence is further emphasised by the well established entitlement of trustees not to give reasons for their exercise of discretionary distributive powers.[77] That has not been a feature of the recent cases from the *Hastings-Bass* case [1975] Ch 25, as the trustees have been open with the court and the beneficiaries about the circumstances of the appointment or other relevant act. Nevertheless, if the trustees do not vouchsafe their reasons it is the more difficult for a beneficiary to challenge the exercise of their discretions unless a

---

[75] [2002] *Private Client Business* 226 (R. Walker); (2002) 16 *Trust Law International* 202 (J. Hilliard); [2003] *Private Client Business* 173 (E. Nugee); [2004] Conv 208 (J. Hilliard); (2007) 21 *Trust Law International* 62 (H. W. Tang).

[76] (2006) 122 LQR 35 (C. Mitchell); [2006] Conv 91 (M. Thomas and B. Dowrick); (2006) CLJ 15 (R. Nolan and M. Conaglen); [2005] All ER Rev 269 (P.J. Clarke).   [77] See p. 740, below.

defect is apparent from the documents. In *Tempest v Lord Camoys* (1882) 21 Ch D 571 [p. 654, above], the court would not override the refusal of one of two trustees to agree with a course of action proposed by the other involving the purchase of particular land and the raising of some of the purchase money on mortgage. Conversely, in *Klug v Klug* [1918] 2 Ch 67 [p. 656, above], the refusal of one of two trustees (the mother of the relevant beneficiary) to agree to an advance to a beneficiary to provide funds for the payment of legacy duty, which the other trustee, the Public Trustee, considered would be a proper exercise of a power, was overridden where it appeared that the mother's refusal to agree was due to the daughter having married without her consent. The mother's refusal to exercise the power in her daughter's favour was disregarded because of her irrelevant motivation.

38   There are several different categories of case where an exercise by trustees of a discretionary power may be held to be invalid.

(i) There may be a formal or procedural defect, such as the failure to use the stipulated form of document, for example a document under hand instead of a deed, or to obtain a necessary prior consent. (In some such cases, and for the benefit of some interested persons, equity may relieve against such a formal or procedural defect.)

(ii) The power may have been exercised in a way which it does not authorise, for example with an unauthorised delegation, or by the inclusion of beneficiaries who are not objects of the power.

(iii) The exercise may infringe some rule of the general law, such as the rule against perpetuities.[78]

(iv) The trustees may have exercised the power for an improper purpose, in cases known as fraud on the power.[79] *Cloutte v Storey* [1911] 1 Ch 18, among the cases cited to me, is an example of this, where the power was exercised in favour of one of the objects, but under a private arrangement whereby he passed the benefit back to his parents, who had made the appointment. Another example, in a different context, was *Hillsdown Holdings plc v Pensions Ombudsman* [1997] 1 All ER 862. I take it that references, for example in *Gisborne v Gisborne* 2 App Cas 300 (and in the *Hastings-Bass* case [1975] Ch 25 itself, see para 44 below), to good faith are to be understood in this context, so that an exercise which is not in good faith is, or at any rate includes, a case where the exercise is a fraud on the power.

(v) The trustees may have been unaware that they had any discretion to exercise: see *Turner v Turner* [1984] Ch 100, an extreme and highly unusual case on the facts, which has been described as equitable *non est factum*.

(vi) To these categories, of which the first four are clear and well established, the rule or principle in the *Hastings-Bass* case is said to add a further class of case, namely where the trustees have failed to have regard to some relevant consideration which they ought to have taken into account.

39   In the *Hastings-Bass* case [1975] Ch 25 itself the appointment was held to be valid, despite the fact that it was partly void for perpetuity. In that respect the result differed from the rather similar case of *Re Abrahams' Will Trusts* [1969] 1 Ch 463, the difference being accounted for by factual differences as regards what was left of the appointment once that which was void had been eliminated.

---

[78] See p. 110, above.   [79] See p. 58, above.

His Lordship considered *Re Baron Vestey's Settlement* [1951] Ch 209; *Re Pilkington's Will Trust* [1959] Ch 699; *Re Abrahams' Will Trusts* [1969] 1 Ch 463, *Re Hastings-Bass* [1975] Ch 25, and continued:

44   The Court of Appeal [in *Re Hasting-Bass*] found that the object of saving Estate Duty was a primary consideration in the minds of the trustees when they exercised the power of advancement, and that to the extent that the advancement could be effective, notwithstanding the rule against perpetuities, it was so plainly for William's benefit that the trustees, if they had realised the effect of the rule, could not have thought that the invalidity of the ulterior trusts would render the exercise something that was other than for William's benefit. They held that the trustees believed themselves to be exercising, of their own choice, a discretion under section 32 of the Trustee Act 1925,[80] and doing it because they considered that to do so would benefit William. They observed that, if trustees intend to make an advancement by way of sub-settlement, they must apply their minds to the question whether the sub-settlement as a whole will be for the benefit of the person to be advanced. If the true effect of the exercise were such that it could not reasonably be regarded as beneficial to the person to be advanced, then the exercise cannot stand, because it would not be within the powers under section 32. In the *Hastings-Bass* case [1975] Ch 25, 41c 'in any other case', they said, 'the advancement should...be permitted to take effect in the manner and to the extent that it is capable of doing so'..... They summarised their conclusion on this aspect of the case in the following terms, at p 41:

> 'where by the terms of a trust (as under section 32) a trustee is given a discretion as to some matter under which he acts in good faith, the court should not interfere with his action notwithstanding that it does not have the full effect which he intended, unless (1) what he has achieved is unauthorised by the power conferred upon him, or (2) it is clear that he would not have acted as he did (a) had he not taken into account considerations which he should not have taken into account, or (b) had he not failed to take into account considerations which he ought to have taken into account.'...

46   The statement set out at para 44 is in negative form. A positive formulation was first put forward by Warner J in *Mettoy Pension Trustees Ltd v Evans* [1990] 1 WLR 1587. That case concerned the exercise by pension trustees of a power to amend the rules applying to the pension scheme. In most respects no issue arose as to the terms of the amended rules, but the amendments did change the position as regards the allocation of any surplus in a winding-up, which had been at the disposition of the trustees, but which, after the amendments, was to be decided on by the company. The evidence was that the trustees were unaware of this particular point in the new rules. The judge held that the discretion conferred on the company was fiduciary. Nevertheless, the representatives of employees and pensioners argued that the power of amendment had not been validly exercised to the extent of the change in the power over any surplus, and relied on *Re Hastings-Bass* [1975] Ch 25 as authority for this. At the outset of the passage in his judgment in which he deals with the submissions on this point, Warner J set out the proposition as the positive converse of what the Court of Appeal had said in the *Hastings-Bass* case itself [1990] 1 WLR 1587, 1621h:

> 'where a trustee acts under a discretion given to him by the terms of the trust, the court will interfere with his action if it is clear that he would not have acted as he did had he not failed to take into account considerations which he ought to have taken into account.'

---

[80] See p. 769, below.

47   He then considered the submissions made to him, as to whether there was any such rule, and if so what it amounted to. He held that such a rule did exist, and was not limited to cases of invalidity for, so to speak, external reasons (such as the rule against perpetuities), and that it could invalidate part only of a disposition in an appropriate case. He then said, at p 1624:

'I have come to the conclusion that there is a principle which may be labelled "the rule in *Hastings-Bass*". I do not think that the application of that principle is confined, as Mr. Nugee suggested, to cases where an exercise by trustees of a discretion vested in them is partially ineffective because of some rule of law or because of some limit on their discretion which they overlooked. If, as I believe, the reason for the application of the principle is the failure of the trustees to take into account considerations that they ought to have taken into account, it cannot matter whether that failure is due to their having overlooked (or to their legal advisers having overlooked) some relevant rule of law or limit on their discretion, or is due to some other cause.

For the principle to apply, however, it is not enough that it should be shown that the trustees did not have a proper understanding of the effect of their act. It must also be clear that, had they had a proper understanding of it, they would not have acted as they did.'

48   Applying these principles to the facts, the judge said that three questions arose. (1) What were the trustees under a duty to consider? (2) Did they fail to consider it? (3) If so, what would they have done if they had considered it? Having reviewed the evidence, and in the light of his finding that the company's power over surplus was fiduciary, he held that the new rules were not in any respect invalidated under the rule in *Re Hastings-Bass*.

49   Mr. Herbert pointed out that Warner J's positive formulation in the *Mettoy* case [1990] 1 WLR 1587 omitted one element in the principle, namely that which the Court of Appeal in the *Hastings-Bass* case [1975] Ch 25, 41g expressed in the words 'notwithstanding that it does not have the full effect which he intended'. He submitted that, accepting that there is a positive principle established by the *Mettoy* case, its expression ought to include words corresponding to those. Of course, those words referred to the invalidating effect of the rule against perpetuities, which cut down to the life interest in favour of William the effect which the advancement could have. There is no difficulty in principle in adapting that phrase to the facts of other types of case. In the *Mettoy* case itself, for example, where the trustees did not appreciate that the amended rules would alter the powers of distribution in relation to surplus, the phrase used in the Court of Appeal does not fit literally. It could easily be adapted to cover that sort of case as well as a *Hastings-Bass* type of case, for example, using words such as 'notwithstanding that its effect is different from that which he intended'. In the light of that, (and expanding it to cover expressly a point which would no doubt be implied) what one might call the *Mettoy* case formulation of the principle could be fully expressed as follows:

'Where a trustee acts under a discretion given to him by the terms of the trust, but the effect of the exercise is different from that which he intended, the court will interfere with his action if it is clear that he would not have acted as he did had he not failed to take into account considerations which he ought to have taken into account, or taken into account considerations which he ought not to have taken into account.'

His Lordship considered *Stannard v Fisons Pension Trust Ltd* [1991] PLR 225, *Kerr v British Leyland (Staff) Trustees Ltd* [2001] WTLR 1071, and continued:

55   The *Kerr* case [2001] WTLR 1071 is thus a rather different kind of case, where the trustees are the arbiters of a beneficiary's entitlement to a particular benefit under the rules of

the pension scheme, and that entitlement is derived not from pure bounty, as would be the case in a family trust, but from the contract of employment. In those circumstances, and given the inadequate information provided to the trustees on which to take their decision, it seems to me logical that a relatively low threshold of relevance ('might') should have been adopted by the court as the test of whether the deficiency of information entitles the beneficiary to have his case, in effect, reconsidered....

56   Likewise in the *Stannard* case [1991] PLR 225 the trustees were under an obligation to act, by appropriating an amount to be applied for the benefit of the transferring employees, though they had to decide, after consulting the actuary, what amount should be appropriated, as being the amount which they decided to be just and equitable. Although on its facts the *Stannard* case is a different kind of case from the *Kerr* case [2001] WTLR 1071, it seems to me that the analogy is fair. Both were pension cases, so that the rights of the members or beneficiaries arose in the context of the contract of employment. Both were cases in which the trustees were under a duty to act, though with some freedom as to how they proceeded. It is true that even outside this type of case, if trustees have a discretionary power, they are under obligations in relation to it, including to consider from time to time whether to exercise it, and if they do decide to exercise it they are under duties in respect of that process, but it seems to me that there is a real distinction between such a case (which *Re Abraham's Will Trusts* [1969] 1 Ch 463, *Re Hastings-Bass* [1975] Ch 25 and the present case are) and cases such as the *Kerr* case and the *Stannard* case where the trustees are under a duty to act, not merely a duty to consider from time to time whether to. I consider, therefore, that Mr Herbert's submissions in this respect are well founded....

His Lordship considered *Green v Cobham* [2002] STC 820, *Breadner v Granville-Grossman* [2001] Ch 523, *AMP (UK) plc v Barker* [2001] PLR 77, *Abacus Trust Co (Isle of Man) Ltd v National Society for the Prevention of Cruelty to Children* [2001] STC 1344, and continued:

In [the latter] case trustees had had advice as to a scheme for avoiding a substantial charge to Capital Gains Tax on underlying trust assets, which required certain steps to be taken before the end of the current tax year, and others not until after the beginning of the next. Despite clear advice as to the timing, the trustees took all the relevant steps before the end of the tax year, thereby giving rise to a large charge to Capital Gains Tax on the settlor, with a possible right of recovery against the trust property. The judge was satisfied that, if the trustees had been aware of the fiscal consequences of what they were doing, they would not have taken one of the steps in the sequence until on or after 6 April, instead of doing everything on 3 April. He held, on the basis of *Green v Cobham* [2002] STC 820 that trustees when exercising powers of appointment are bound to have regard to the fiscal consequences of their actions, and that if it can be shown that, had they considered those consequences properly, they would not have proceeded as they did, the appointment should be declared void as an invalid exercise of the power of appointment. He observed that the time might come when the limits of the *Hastings-Bass* principle fall to be determined by a higher court, but as regards the relevance of fiscal consequences he said [2001] STC 1344, 1353:

'16.   The financial consequences for the beneficiaries of any intended exercise of a fiduciary power cannot be assessed without reference to their fiscal implications. The two seem to me inseparable. Therefore if the effect of an intended appointment is likely to be to expose the fund or its beneficiaries to a significant charge to tax that is something which the trustees have an obligation to consider when deciding whether it is proper to proceed with the appointment. Once relevance is established then a failure to take those matters into account must vitiate the exercise of the power unless (as in *Re Hastings-Bass* [1975] Ch 25 itself) it is clear that on a proper consideration of all relevant matters the decision would still have been the same.'

His Lordship considered *Hearn v Younger* [2002] WTLR 1317; *Abacus Trust Co (Isle of Man) v Barr* [2003] Ch 409[81] and *Burrell v Burrell* [2005] STC 569, and continued:

76   One element introduced in the *Hastings-Bass* formulation is whether the trustees took into account matters which they ought not to have done, or failed to take into account matters which they ought to have. This is reminiscent of public law and the *Wednesbury* test (see *Associated Provincial Picture Houses Ltd v Wednesbury Corpn* [1948] 1 KB 223), though that case does not seem to have been cited in the *Hastings-Bass* case itself. That is now established as a relevant test in relation to the exercise of a discretion by trustees, as a result of *Edge v Pensions Ombudsman* [2000] Ch 602. In that case the Court of Appeal...held that trustees to whom the exercise of a discretionary power is entrusted were under a duty to exercise that power (if they chose to exercise it) only for the purpose for which it is given, giving proper consideration to the matters which are relevant and excluding from consideration matters which are irrelevant: see *Edge v Pensions Ombudsman* [2000] Ch 602, 627e. The introduction into trust law of what might seem to be a public law concept has been criticised, at any rate in relation to private family trusts as distinct from pension funds (see Underhill and Hayton, *Law of Trusts and Trustees,* 16th ed (2003), p 696), but it seems to me that this formulation respects the traditional view, that it is for the trustees to exercise the power, and to decide whether or not to do so (unless they have an obligation to do so, as in the *Kerr* [2001] WTLR 1071 or the *Stannard* [1991] PLR 225 type cases), and is at the same time consistent with the cases about fraud on the power or other examples of caprice or bad faith, such as *Clouette v Storey* [1911] 1 Ch 18 or *Klug v Klug* [1918] 2 Ch 67 [see p. 656, above]. In those cases the defaulting trustee was motivated by irrelevant considerations in deciding whether or not to exercise the power, and if so how: the advantage of a non-object in cases such as the *Cloutte* case (or *Hillsdown Holdings plc v Pensions Ombudsman* [1997] 1 All ER 862) or an irrelevant consideration in relation to an object in the *Klug* case.

77   It seems to me that, for the purposes of a case where the trustees are not under a duty to act, the relevant test is still that stated in the *Hastings-Bass* case [1975] Ch 25, namely whether, if they had not misunderstood the effect that their actual exercise of the discretionary power would have, they *would* have acted differently. In my judgment that is correct both on authority, starting with the *Hastings-Bass* case itself, and on principle. Only in a case where the beneficiary is entitled to require the trustees to act, such as the *Kerr* case [2001] WTLR 1071 or the *Stannard* case [1991] PLR 225, should it suffice to vitiate the trustees' decision to show that they *might* have acted differently... If an act by trustees is set aside, where the trustees have acted under an obligation, then the beneficiaries can require the trustees to start again, on the correct basis. It seems to me that the lower test of 'might' is appropriate in such cases: see para 55 above. If the trustees' act was voluntary, so that they cannot be compelled to act again

---

[81]   (2004) CLJ 283 (M. Conaglen).

if the act is set aside, the more demanding test of 'would' is justified in order to decide whether the trustees' act can be set aside.

78   Another unresolved question on the cases is whether, if the trustees' exercise is vitiated on this principle, the result is that the trustees' act is void or voidable. Lightman J in *Abacus Trust Co (Isle of Man) v Barr* [2003] Ch 409 held that it was voidable, and adjourned the question whether it should be avoided. In *Re Abraham's Will Trusts* [1969] 1 Ch 463 Cross J held that the defective appointment in that case was void. Since it was the Inland Revenue that sought this result, it was only on the basis of it being void that the submission could have been accepted. That body would not have standing to seek to have a voidable act set aside. If the exercise of a power is vitiated by the doctrine of fraud on a power, the result appears to be that the exercise is declared void: see *Topham v Duke of Portland* (1869) LR 5 Ch App 40... This may be because the appointment is treated as having been, in effect, to a non-object, and plainly a direct appointment to such a person would be void. On the other hand, if, as Warner J held in the *Mettoy* case [1990] 1 WLR 1587, the principle could result in part of a document being set aside but not the rest, the process would come close to rectification, and it would be difficult to say that a part of it was altogether void. He did not have to consider that aspect, since on the facts he held that no part was to be set aside.

79   Lightman J held that the exercise was voidable, rather than void, because its being set aside resulted from a breach of the trustees' duty. Some acts of trustees which are set aside for breach of duty are voidable; they will not be set aside if no one with the right to do so applies for that remedy, and such an application may be defeated on discretionary and equitable grounds which would not be available if the disposition was void, such as affirmation or *laches*. It is also fair to say (as Lightman J clearly bore in mind, and as Park J mentioned in *Breadner v Granville-Grossman* [2001] Ch 523) that if the consequence of the doctrine is that the exercise is void, this might have dramatic and potentially unfair disruptive consequences for the trustees and the beneficiaries. To hold that the defect makes the appointment voidable, rather than void, is therefore attractive.

80   Nevertheless it seems to be questionable whether the application of the doctrine should be regarded as depending on a breach of duty, and whether its consequences should be aligned with those of a breach of trust...

82   I do not need to decide between 'void' and 'voidable' in order to decide this case: all counsel agreed that nothing turned on that distinction in this instance. It seems to me, however, that on authority, the main ways at present open to the court to control the application of the principle are: (a) to insist on a stringent application of the tests as they have been laid down, (b) to take a reasonable and not over-exigent view of what it is that the trustees ought to have taken into account, and (c) to adopt a critical approach to contentions that the trustees would have acted differently if they had realised the true position, perhaps especially so in cases (unlike the present) where it is in the interests of all who are before the court that the appointment should be set aside. As Park J said in *Breadner v Granville-Grossman* [2001] Ch 523, 543, para 61: 'It cannot be right that whenever trustees do something which they later regret and think that they ought not to have done, they can say that they never did it in the first place.'

83   The position would also be more flexible if equitable considerations can be taken into account in deciding whether or not to grant any and if so what relief. The court's task might be easier in some cases if the Inland Revenue did not always decline the invitation to take part in cases of this kind, but there are no doubt policy reasons of one kind or another for that attitude, of which the court is not aware....

'I have no doubt that fiscal consequences may be relevant considerations which the trustees ought to take into account, and that a material difference between the intended and actual fiscal consequences of the act may be sufficient to bring the principle into play.'

His Lordship went on to consider whether the appointment could also be set aside on the alternative ground of mistake and concluded that it could.

114   Looking at the appointment, therefore, it seems to me that, on the part of the trustees, it is vitiated by the failure of the trustees to take into account the true consequences of the appointment as regards Capital Gains Tax, which they failed to take account of because they had been wrongly advised. In my judgment the consequences of the appointment as regards tax (in particular Inheritance Tax and Capital Gains Tax) were matters which the trustees were under a duty to consider, which they did in fact consider, and to which they failed to give proper consideration because they were provided by their advisers with wrong advice on the point. I find that, if they had had the correct advice, they would not have made the 2001 appointment. Applying the *Mettoy* test [1990] 1 WLR 1587 as I have reformulated it above (para 49) I find that the effect of the trustees' exercise of their discretion was different from that which they intended, that they failed to take into account considerations which they ought to have taken into account, and that they would not have acted as they did had they known the correct position as regards the charge to Capital Gains Tax which would result from the appointment....

119   I will, however, summarise the *Hastings-Bass* principle as I see it, as follows.

(i)   The best formulation of the principle seems to me to be this. Where trustees act under a discretion given to them by the terms of the trust, in circumstances in which they are free to decide whether or not to exercise that discretion, but the effect of the exercise is different from that which they intended, the court will interfere with their action if it is clear that they would not have acted as they did had they not failed to take into account considerations which they ought to have taken into account, or taken into account considerations which they ought not to have taken into account.

(ii)   I have expanded the formula from that set out at para 49 above to include expressly the proposition that the trustees are not acting under an obligation, so as to distinguish cases such as the *Kerr* case [2001] WTLR 1071 and the *Stannard* case [1991] PLR 225. It is only in cases, such as those, where the trustees are obliged to act, that the 'might' test applies. The *Stannard* case should not be treated as applying or endorsing the *Hastings-Bass* principle, but as being in the same line as cases such as the *Kerr* case.

(iii)   It does not seem to me that the principle applies only in cases where there has been a breach of duty by the trustees, or by their advisers or agents, despite what Lightman J said in *Abacus Trust Co (Isle of Man) v Barr* [2003] Ch 409.

(iv)   His conclusion that, if the principle is satisfied, the act in question is voidable rather than void is attractive, but seems to me to require further consideration, in the light of earlier authority.

(v)   I am in no doubt that, as a general proposition, fiscal consequences are among the matters which may be relevant for the purposes of the principle.[82]

---

[82]   See also *Gallaher Ltd v Gallaher Pensions Ltd* [2005] EWHC 42; *Betafence Ltd v Veys* [2006] EWHC 999 (Ch), [2006] All ER (D) 91; *Donaldson v Smith* [2006] All ER (D) 293; (2006) 65 CLJ 499 (M Congalen and R Nolan); *Smithson v Hamilton* [2007] EWHC 2900 (ch); *Ogden v Trustees of the RHS Griffiths 2003 Settlement* [2008] EWHC 11.

VI POWER OF DECISION[83]

A settlor or testator sometimes gives to his trustees express power to make decisions concerning issues relating to the trust. The dividing line between what is permitted and what is not is very obscure. Certainly, 'a testator cannot confide to another the right to make a will for him'.[84] Nor can the jurisdiction of the court be excluded.

Re Coxen
[1948] Ch 747 (Ch D, **Jenkins J**)

The testator devised a dwelling-house to trustees upon trust to permit his wife to reside therein; and he declared that, 'if in the opinion of my trustees she shall have ceased permanently to reside therein', the house was to fall into residue. The question was whether this proviso constituted a valid limitation upon the gift.

Held. The condition was not void for uncertainty. The decision of the trustees would be sufficient to determine the widow's interest.

Jenkins J: I have so far treated the condition as if it was simply in the terms 'if she shall have ceased permanently to reside', whereas its actual terms are 'if in the opinion of my trustees she shall have ceased permanently to reside'. That I think makes a very material difference. The opinion of the trustees that the double event has happened, and not simply the happening of the double event, is what brings about the cesser of Lady Coxen's interest. If the testator had insufficiently defined the state of affairs on which the trustees were to form their opinion, he would not I think have saved the condition from invalidity on the ground of uncertainty merely by making their opinion the criterion, although the declaration by the trustees of this or that opinion would be an event about which in itself there could be no uncertainty. But as I have already indicated, I think the relevant double event is sufficiently defined to make it perfectly possible for the trustees (as the judges of fact for this purpose) to decide whether it has happened or not, and in my view the testator by making the trustees' opinion the criterion has removed the difficulties which might otherwise have ensued from a gift over in a double event the happening of which, though in itself sufficiently defined, may necessarily be a matter of inference involving nice questions of fact and degree.

In **Re Wynn** [1952] Ch 271, the question was whether a clause in a will in the following terms was valid: 'I authorise and empower my trustees to determine what articles pass under any specific bequest contained in this my will...and whether any moneys are to be considered as capital or income and how valuations are to be made and or value determined for any purpose in connexion with the trusts and provisions of this my will...and to apportion blended trust funds and to determine all questions and matters of doubt arising in the execution of the trusts of this my will...and I declare that every such determination whether made upon a question actually raised or only

---

[83] H&M, p. 534–535; Lewin, pp. 126–127; P&M, pp. 70–71; P&S, pp. 402–403; Pettit, p. 493; Snell, p. 657; T&H, pp. 120–123.

[84] *Per* Lord Penzance in *In Bonis Smith's Goods* (1869) LR 1 P & D 717; (1953) 69 LQR 334 (D.M. Gordon).

implied in the acts and proceedings of ... my trustees shall be conclusive and binding upon all persons interested under this my will.'

DANCKWERTS J held it void. He said at 279:

No doubt it may be said that it is convenient to have matters regarding the apportionment of capital moneys and the application of moneys in the payment of expenses referred to some informal decision, and that in that way expense may be saved which would be necessarily incurred if the matters had to be referred to the court; but in my view a clause of this kind has no effect if it is attempted to use it so as to prevent the beneficiaries requiring the matter to be decided by the court. As long as the clause is not contested, it may be that the beneficiaries will be content to have the matters dealt with by the trustees in the course of their operations in the administration of the estate; and it may, of course, be that the trustees have applied their minds and carried out their duties in a perfectly proper manner in the way in which they deal with matters connected with the estate; but it seems to me that the result is that any beneficiary is entitled to go to the court to have his rights considered and, if necessary, upheld; and that a testator may not by the provisions of his will exclude the right of the court to decide the matters, even though the trustees have considered them and reached a certain decision.

In **Re Jones** [1953] Ch 125, a testator directed his trustees to hold his residuary trust fund after the death of his wife upon trust to purchase an annuity for his daughter, and he directed that 'if at any time ... my ... daughter Doris ... shall in the uncontrolled opinion of the company [the trustees] have social or other relationship with [a certain named person] ... then in such case as from the occurrence of such event my said daughter ... shall absolutely forfeit and lose one half of the annuity payments hereinbefore directed to be paid to her ...'

On the question whether the forfeiture clause was valid, DANCKWERTS J held (a) that it was void for uncertainty and (b) that the reference to the opinion of the trustees did not prevent that invalidity. He said at 128:

Unless [the difficulty] is cured by reference to the opinion of the trustees, it seems to me that this clause cannot be regarded as sufficiently certain to be upheld as a forfeiture clause or a condition subsequent. The words in the present case are 'shall in the uncontrolled opinion of the company have social or other relationship'. Mr. Albery has submitted that that surmounts the difficulty, because the guiding factor is not the existence of 'social or other relationship', but the existence of 'the uncontrolled opinion' on the part of the executor company, the bank.

He has referred me to a decision of the House of Lords, which certainly is of great interest in regard to the matter: *Dundee General Hospitals Board of Management v Walker* [1952] 1 All ER 896 at 898. In that case, in order that a named body should qualify for a legacy, the trustees had to be satisfied as regarded a certain hospital, the Dundee Royal Infirmary, that 'the said infirmary has not been taken over wholly or partly by or otherwise placed under the control of the State or of a local authority or of a body directly or indirectly responsible to the State and/or a local authority'. As Mr. Albery perfectly correctly said, after quoting a well-known observation of Bowen LJ that the state of a man's mind was as much a fact as the state of his digestion,[85]

---

[85] *Edgington v Fitzmaurice* (1885) 29 Ch D 459 at 483.

it is the existence of an opinion or the non-existence of a particular opinion on the part of the company, the trustees, which is the test of forfeiture or otherwise in the present case.

In the present case, however, the opinion of the trustees is substituted for the opinion of the court, and it is the trustees who have to decide whether or not a certain obscure and difficult state of facts has occurred; the trustees might be unable to decide the question just as the court might be unable to decide it, and further the court might have to decide the matter or to attempt to decide the matter upon a reference to it by the trustees.

In **Re Tuck's Settlement Trusts** [1978] Ch 49,[86] the settlor provided an income for the holder for the time being of the family baronetcy if and when and so long as he should be of the Jewish faith, and married and living with 'an approved wife' or, if separated, being so separated through no fault of his. An 'approved wife' was defined as a wife of Jewish blood by one or both of her parents, who had been brought up in the Jewish faith, had never departed from it, and, who, at the date of the marriage, continued to worship according to the Jewish faith. The Chief Rabbi in London of either the Portuguese or the Anglo-German community was designated to decide any question as to who was an approved wife, and whether any separation was or was not due to the fault of the baronet.

The question was whether the trusts were void for uncertainty; and whether the reference to the Chief Rabbi was effective, or void as an ouster of the jurisdiction of the court. The Court of Appeal held that the condition was sufficiently certain. On the question whether, if it had been void for uncertainty, the trust would have been saved by the provision making the Chief Rabbi's decision conclusive,LORD DENNING MR referred to *Dundee General Hospitals Board of Management v Walker* [1952] 1 All ER 896 as being a decision 'of the highest persuasive value', and continued at 61:

I see no reason why a testator or settlor should not provide that any dispute or doubt should be resolved by his executors or trustees, or even by a third person. To prove this, I will first state the law in regard to contracts. Here the general principle is that whenever persons agree together to refer a matter to a third person for decision, and further agree that his decision is to be final and binding upon them, then, so long as he arrives at his decision honestly and in good faith, the two parties are bound by it....

If two contracting parties can by agreement leave a doubt or difficulty to be decided by a third person, I see no reason why a testator or settlor should not leave the decision to his trustees or to a third party. He does not thereby oust the jurisdiction of the court. If the appointed person should find difficulty in the actual wording of the will or settlement, the executors or trustees can always apply to the court for directions so as to assist in the interpretation of it. But if the appointed person is ready and willing to resolve the doubt or difficulty, I see no reason why he should not do so. So long as he does not misconduct himself or come to a decision which is wholly unreasonable, I think his decision should stand. After all, that was plainly the intention of the testator or settlor.[87]

---

[86] [1978] Conv 242 (F.R. Crane).

[87] *Re Tepper's Will Trusts* [1987] Ch 358 (gift by a devout and practising Jewish testator to children provided that 'they shall not marry outside the Jewish faith': Scott J was reluctant to find the condition

VII PAYMENTS TO A TRUSTEE[88]

A REIMBURSEMENT OF EXPENSES

TRUSTEE ACT 2000

31. Trustees' expenses

(1) A trustee—

    (a) is entitled to be reimbursed from the trust funds, or

    (b) may pay out of the trust funds,

expenses properly incurred by him when acting on behalf of the trust.

(2) This section applies to a trustee who has been authorised under a power conferred by Part IV[89] or any other enactment or any provision of subordinate legislation, or by the trust instrument—

    (a) to exercise functions as an agent of the trustees, or

    (b) to act as a nominee or custodian,

as it applies to any other trustee.[90]

In **Hardoon v Belilios** [1901] AC 118, the plaintiff was employed by a firm of share brokers. In order to assist a syndicate speculating in shares, fifty £10 shares in the Bank of China, Japan and the Straits Ltd were placed in his name. The defendant was the absolute beneficial owner of the shares.

On the liquidation of the Bank, the liquidator made calls upon the plaintiff for over £400. The Privy Council held that the defendant was personally liable to reimburse him. LORD LINDLEY said at 124:

Where the only *cestui que trust* is a person *sui juris*, the right of the trustee to indemnity by him against liabilities incurred by the trustee by his retention of the trust property has never been limited to the trust property; it extends further, and imposes upon the *cestui que trust* a personal obligation enforceable in equity to indemnify his trustee. This is no new principle, but is as old as trusts themselves.[91]

---

subsequent void for uncertainty and adjourned the case for further evidence of the Jewish faith as practised by the testator and his family); [1987] All ER Rev 159 (P.J. Clarke), 260 (C.H. Sherrin).

[88] H&M, pp. 607–612; Lewin, pp. 647–670; P&M, pp. 721–740; P&S, pp. 785–787; Pettit, pp. 443–448; Snell, pp. 162–171; T&H, pp. 633–647; U&H, pp. 794–804.

[89] See p. 695, below.

[90] This section applies in respect of expenses incurred after 1 February, 2001, regardless of when the trust was created: TA 2000, s. 33 (1). Cases on TA 1925, s. 30, which was replaced by TA 2000, s. 31, include *Stott v Milne* (1884) 25 Ch D 710; *Re Chapman* (1894) 72 LT 66; *Holding and Management Ltd v Property Holding and Investment Trust plc* [1989] 1 WLR 1313.

[91] See *JW Broomhead (Vic) Pty Ltd v JW Broomhead Pty Ltd* [1985] VR 891; (1990) 64 *Australian Law Journal* 567 (R.A. Hughes).

In **Foster v Spencer** [1996] 2 All ER 672 trustees' claims for reimbursement were successful. However, JUDGE PAUL BAKER QC refused to award interest on the amount of out-of-pocket expenses. He said at 678:

These proceedings are not proceedings for the recovery of a debt or damages. No party can be ordered to pay them. The trustees are entitled to the expenses out of the trust estate, and only out of the trust estate. They come to court simply to gain approval of their exercise of their right of retainer so as to forestall any future allegations of breach of trust.

A related problem is whether the trustees can recover the costs of litigation. The trustee will be reimbursed costs on the indemnity basis,[92] but only if the costs were reasonably and properly incurred for the benefit of the trust.

In **Re Beddoe** [1893] 1 Ch 547,[93] BOWEN LJ said at 562:

The principle of law to be applied appears unmistakably clear. A trustee can only be indemnified out of the pockets of his *cestuis que trust* against costs, charges, and expenses properly incurred for the benefit of the trust—a proposition in which the word 'property' means reasonably as well as honestly incurred. While I agree that the trustees ought not to be visited with personal loss on account of mere errors in judgment, which fall short of negligence or unreasonableness, it is on the other hand essential to recollect that mere bona fides is not the test, and that it is no answer in the mouth of a trustee who has embarked in idle litigation to say that he honestly believed what his solicitor told him, if his solicitor has been wrong-headed and perverse. Costs, charges, and expenses which in fact have been unreasonably incurred, do not assume in the eye of the law the character of reasonableness simply because the solicitor is the person who was in fault. No more disastrous or delusive doctrine could be invented in a Court of Equity than the dangerous idea that a trustee himself might recover over from his own *cestuis que trust* costs which his own solicitor has unreasonably and perversely incurred merely because he had acted as his solicitor told him.

If there be one consideration again more than another which ought to be present to the mind of a trustee, especially the trustee of a small and easily dissipated fund, it is that all litigation should be avoided, unless there is such a chance of success as to render it desirable in the interests of the estate that the necessary risk should be incurred. If a trustee is doubtful as to the wisdom of prosecuting or defending a lawsuit, he is provided by the law with an inexpensive method of solving his doubts in the interest of the trust. He has only to take out an originating summons, state the point under discussion, and ask the Court whether the point is one which should be fought out or abandoned. To embark in a lawsuit at the risk of the fund without this salutary precaution might often be to speculate in law with money that belongs to other people.

In **Alsop Wilkinson v Neary** [1996] 1 WLR 1220, the plaintiff firm of solicitors had commenced proceedings against the defendant trustees in respect of shares which it was alleged had illegally been transferred to the trust. The trustees sought a direction

---

[92] CPR 1998, Pt. 48.4.

[93] See also *Re Yorke* [1911] 1 Ch 370; *Holding and Management Ltd v Property Holding and Investment Trust plc* [1989] 1 WLR 1313; *Singh v Bhasin* (1998) The Times, 21 August. In *McDonald v Horn* [1995] 1 All ER 961 it was held that the court had power to order costs to be paid out of a pension fund.

as to whether they should defend the action and they also sought a pre-emptive costs order. LIGHTMAN J held that the trustees were not under a duty to defend actions and, on the facts of the case, a pre-emptive costs order would not be made. He said at 1223:

Trustees may be involved in three kinds of dispute.

(1) The first (which I shall call 'a trust dispute') is a dispute as to the trusts on which they hold the subject matter of the settlement. This may be 'friendly' litigation involving e.g. the true construction of the trust instrument or some other question arising in the course of the administration of the trust: or 'hostile' litigation e.g. a challenge in whole or in part to the validity of the settlement by the settlor on grounds of undue influence or by a trustee in bankruptcy or a defrauded creditor of the settlor, in which case the claim is that the trustees hold the trust funds as trustees for the settlor, the trustee in bankruptcy or creditor in place of or in addition to the beneficiaries specified in the settlement. The line between friendly and hostile litigation, which is relevant as to the incidence of costs, is not always easy to draw: see *Re Buckton* [1907] 2 Ch 406.

(2) The second (which I shall call a 'beneficiaries dispute') is a dispute with one or more of the beneficiaries as to the propriety of any action which the trustees have taken or omitted to take or may or may not take in the future. This may take the form of proceedings by a beneficiary alleging breach of trust by the trustees and seeking removal of the trustees and/or damages for breach of trust.

(3) The third (which I shall call 'a third-party dispute') is a dispute with persons, otherwise than in the capacity of beneficiaries, in respect of rights and liabilities e.g. in contract or tort assumed by the trustees as such in the course of administration of the trust.

Trustees (express and constructive) are entitled to an indemnity against all costs, expenses and liabilities properly incurred in administering the trust and have a lien on the trust assets to secure such indemnity. Trustees have a duty to protect and preserve the trust estate for the benefit of the beneficiaries and accordingly to represent the trust in a third-party dispute. Accordingly their right to an indemnity and lien extends in the case of a third-party dispute to the costs of proceedings properly brought or defended for the benefit of the trust estate. Views may vary whether proceedings are properly brought or defended, and to avoid the risk of a challenge to their entitlement to the indemnity, (a beneficiary dispute), trustees are well advised to seek court authorisation before they sue or defend. The right to an indemnity and lien will ordinarily extend to the costs of such an application. The form of application is a separate action to which all the beneficiaries are parties (either in person or by a representative defendant). With the benefit of their views the judge thereupon exercising his discretion determines what course the interests of justice require to be taken in the proceedings: see *Evans v Evans* [1986] 1 WLR 101, considered by Hoffmann LJ in *McDonald v Horn* [1995] ICR 685. So long as the trustees make full disclosure of the strengths and weaknesses of their case, if the trustees act as authorised by the court, their entitlement to an indemnity and lien is secure.

A beneficiaries dispute is regarded as ordinary hostile litigation in which costs follow the event and do not come out of the trust estate: see *per* Hoffmann LJ in *McDonald v Horn* [1995] ICR 685 at 696.

The role of trustees in case of a trust dispute was considered by Kekewich J in two cases.

[His Lordship considered *Merry v Pownall* [1898] 1 Ch 306 and *Ideal Bedding Co Ltd v Holland* [1907] 2 Ch 157, and continued:] I do not think that the view expressed by Kekewich J in the *Ideal Bedding* case that in case of a trust dispute (as was the dispute in that case) a trustee has a duty to defend the trust is correct or in accordance with modern authority. In a case where the dispute is between rival claimants to a beneficial interest in the subject matter of the trust, rather the duty of the trustee is to remain neutral and (in the absence of any court direction to the contrary and substantially as happened in *Merry's* case [1898] 1 Ch 306) offer to submit to the court's directions leaving it to the rivals to fight their battles. If this stance is adopted, in respect of the costs necessarily and properly incurred e.g. in serving a defence agreeing to submit to the courts direction and in making discovery, the trustees will be entitled to an indemnity and lien. If the trustees do actively defend the trust and succeed, e.g. in challenging a claim by the settlor to set aside for undue influence, they may be entitled to their costs out of the trust, for they have preserved the interests of the beneficiaries under the trust: consider *Re Holden, ex p Official Receiver* (1887) 20 QBD 43. But if they fail, then in particular in the case of hostile litigation although in an exceptional case the court may consider that the trustees should have their costs (see *Bullock v Lloyds Bank Ltd* [1955] Ch 317) ordinarily the trustees will not be entitled to any indemnity, for they have incurred expenditure and liabilities in an unsuccessful effort to prefer one class of beneficiaries e.g. the express beneficiaries specified in the trust instrument, over another e.g. the trustees in bankruptcy or creditors, and so have acted unreasonably and otherwise than for the benefit of the trust estate: consider RSC Ord. 62, r. 6; and see *National Anti-Vivisection Society v Duddington* (1989) The Times, 23 November and *Snell's Equity:* (29th edn, 1990), p. 258.

In X v A [2000] 1 All ER 490, a sole trustee sought directions as to whether it had a lien over the trust fund for liabilities, including future and contingent liabilities, in respect of the land which was held on trust. ARDEN J held that the trustee did have a lien for proper costs and expenses and that such a lien extended to an indemnity against future liabilities.

B   REMUNERATION AUTHORISED BY TRUST INSTRUMENT

A professional trustee will always insist upon provision being made for the payment of proper fees for his work.

Encyclopedia of Forms and Precedents (5th edn) vol. 40 (1), p. 443

Any trustee other than the settlor and any spouse of the settlor being a solicitor or other person engaged in any profession or business shall be entitled to charge and be paid all usual professional or other charges for business done by him or his firm in relation to the trusts of this settlement and also his reasonable charges in addition to disbursements for all other work and business done and all time spent by him or his firm in connection with matters arising in the premises including matters which might or should have been attended to in person by a trustee not being a solicitor or other person so engaged but which such a Trustee might reasonably require to be done by a solicitor or other person so engaged.

TRUSTEE ACT 2000

28. Trustees' entitlement to payment under trust instrument

(1) Except to the extent (if any) to which the trust instrument makes inconsistent provisions, subsections (2) to (4) apply to a trustee if—

    (a) there is a provision in the trust instrument entitling him to receive payment out of trust funds in respect of services provided by him to or on behalf of the trust, and

    (b) the trustee is a trust corporation or is acting in a professional capacity.

(2) The trustee is to be treated as entitled under the trust instrument to receive payment in respect of services even if they are services which are capable of being provided by a lay trustee.

(3) Subsection (2) applies to a trustee of a charitable trust who is not a trust corporation only—

    (a) if he is not a sole trustee, and

    (b) to the extent that a majority of the other trustees have agreed that it should apply to him.

(4) Any payments to which the trustee is entitled in respect of services are to be treated as remuneration for services (and not as a gift) for the purposes of—

    (a) section 15 of the Wills Act 1837 (gifts to an attesting witness to be void), and

    (b) section 34 (3) of the Administration of Estates Act 1925 (order in which estate to be paid out).

(5) For the purposes of this Part, a trustee acts in a professional capacity if he acts in the course of a profession or business which consists of or includes the provision of services in connection with—

    (a) the management or administration of trusts generally or a particular kind of trust, or

    (b) any particular aspect of the management or administration of trusts generally or a particular kind of trust,

and the services he provides to or on behalf of the trust fall within that description.

(6) For the purposes of this Part, a person acts as a lay trustee if he—

    (a) is not a trust corporation, and

    (b) does not act in a professional capacity.[94]

---

[94] This section applies in respect of services provided after 1 February, 2001, regardless of when the trust was created: TA 2000, s. 33(1).

C   REMUNERATION AUTHORISED BY STATUTE[95]

TRUSTEE ACT 2000

29. Remuneration of certain trustees

(1) Subject to subsection (5), a trustee who—

    (a) is a trust corporation, but

    (b) is not a trustee of a charitable trust,

is entitled to receive reasonable remuneration out of the trust funds for any services that the trust corporation provides to or on behalf of the trust.

(2) Subject to subsection (5), a trustee who—

    (a) acts in a professional capacity, but

    (b) is not a trust corporation, a trustee of a charitable trust or a sole trustee,

is entitled to receive reasonable remuneration out of the trust funds for any services that he provides to or on behalf of the trust if each other trustee has agreed in writing that he may be remunerated for the services.

(3) 'Reasonable remuneration' means, in relation to the provision of services by a trustee, such remuneration as is reasonable in the circumstances for the provision of those services to or on behalf of that trust by that trustee and for the purposes of subsection (1) includes, in relation to the provision of services by a trustee who is an authorised institution under the Banking Act 1987 and provides the services in that capacity, the institution's reasonable charges for the provision of such services.

(4) A trustee is entitled to remuneration under this section even if the services in question are capable of being provided by a lay trustee.

(5) A trustee is not entitled to remuneration under this section if any provision about his entitlement to remuneration has been made—

    (a) by the trust instrument, or

    (b) by any enactment or any provision of subordinate legislation.

(6) This section applies to a trustee who has been authorised under a power conferred by Part IV[96] or the trust instrument—

    (a) to exercise functions as an agent of the trustees, or

    (b) to act as a nominee or custodian,

as it applies to any other trustee.[97]

---

[95] See Law Com. No. 260, *Trustees' Powers and Duties* (1999), pp. 72–80. See also TA 1925, s. 42 (corporation appointed as trustee by court, the court may authorise the corporation to charge remuneration as the court thinks fit); see *Re Masters* [1953] 1 WLR 81; Public Trustee Act 1906, ss. 4, 9; Public Trustee (Fees) Act 1957; Public Trustee (Fees) Order 1999 (S.I. 1999 No. 855), as amended S.I. 2002.2232, S.I. 2003/690, S.I. 2005/799, S.I. 2005/351; Judicial Trustees Act 1896, s. 1 [p. 646, above] (under which a corporation appointed to act as custodian trustee, the Public Trustee and a judicial trustee are authorised to charge fees); (1952) 16 Conv (NS) 13 (G. Boughen Graham). On the remuneration of charity trustees [see p. 614, above].   [96] See p. 695, above.

[97] This section applies in respect of services provided after 1 February, 2001, regardless of when the trust was created: TA 2000, s. 33(1).

32. Remuneration and expenses of agents, nominees and custodians

(1) This section applies if, under a power conferred by Part IV[98] or any other enactment or any provision of subordinate legislation, or by the trust instrument, a person other than a trustee has been—

    (a) authorised to exercise functions as an agent of the trustees, or

    (b) appointed to act as a nominee or custodian.

(2) The trustees may remunerate the agent, nominee or custodian out of the trust funds for services if—

    (a) he is engaged on terms entitling him to be remunerated for those services, and

    (b) the amount does not exceed such remuneration as is reasonable in the circumstances for the provision of those services by him to or on behalf of that trust.

(3) The trustees may reimburse the agent, nominee or custodian out of the trust funds for any expenses properly incurred by him in exercising functions as an agent, nominee or custodian.[99]

D   REMUNERATION AUTHORISED BY THE COURT IN SPECIAL CASES[100]

In **Re Duke of Norfolk's Settlement Trusts** [1982] Ch 61,[101] a trustee company was entitled under a settlement made in 1958 to remuneration in accordance with its usual scale of fees then in force. In 1966 further property was added to the settlement, involving the trustee company in exceptionally burdensome work in connection with the development of Arundel Court in the Strand; this was entirely outside anything which could reasonably have been foreseen when the trustee company accepted office. The introduction of Capital Transfer Tax in 1975 also involved further work. The trustee company sought extra remuneration for this extra work done, and also a general review of its fees for the future.

At first instance [1979] Ch 37, Walton J awarded the company additional remuneration in respect of the development, but not in respect of Capital Transfer Tax. He further held that the court had no inherent jurisdiction to authorise any general

---

[98]   See p. 695, above.

[99]   This section applies in respect of services provided after 1 February, 2001, regardless of when the trust was created: TA 2000 s. 33(1).

[100]   See also the equitable allowance awarded to a fiduciary who has breached his fiduciary duty: p. 822, below.

[101]   (1981) 98 LQR 181 (P.V.B.); (1981) CLJ 243 (C.M.G. Ockleton); [1982] Conv 231 (K. Hodkinson); (1982) 45 MLR 211 (B. Green). See *Re Keeler's Settlement Trusts* [1981] Ch 156 [p. 797, below]. On the powers of the court to reduce trustees' remuneration, see (1984) 128 SJ 41 (A.M. Kenny).

increase in fees for the future. The Court of Appeal reversed the latter part of Walton J's decision. BRIGHTMAN LJ said at 80:

In this appeal we are concerned with the power of the High Court to authorise a trust corporation, which has been in office for some 20 years, to charge fees for its future services in excess of those laid down in the trust instrument. In his admirable submissions in the unwelcome role of *advocatus diaboli* which this court imposed upon him, Mr. Romer confined himself to that narrow issue. He did not dispute that the High Court can, in the exercise of its inherent jurisdiction, authorise a trustee to retain remuneration where none is provided by the terms of the trust. What the court has no jurisdiction to do, he submitted, was to authorise an increase in the general level of remuneration of a paid trustee by way of addition to the remuneration which is allowed by the trust, once the trust has been unconditionally accepted.

Where the court appoints a trust corporation to be a trustee, it has a statutory power to authorise it to charge remuneration: Trustee Act 1925, section 42. The inherent power of the court to authorise a prospective trustee to charge remuneration is exemplified by such cases as *Re Freeman's Settlement Trusts* (1887) 37 Ch D 148. The inherent power to authorise an unpaid trustee to charge remuneration, notwithstanding prior acceptance of the unpaid office, was regarded by Lord Langdale MR in *Bainbrigge v Blair* (1845) 8 Beav 588 as undoubted.

If the court has an inherent power to authorise a prospective trustee to take remuneration for future services, and has a similar power in relation to an unpaid trustee who has already accepted office and embarked upon his fiduciary duties on a voluntary basis, I have some difficulty in appreciating the logic of the principle that the court has no power to increase or otherwise vary the future remuneration of a trustee who has already accepted office. It would mean that, if the remuneration specified in the trust instrument were lower than was acceptable to the incumbent trustee or any substitute who could be found, the court would have jurisdiction to authorise a substitute to charge an acceptable level of remuneration, but would have no jurisdiction to authorise the incumbent to charge precisely the same level of remuneration. Such a result appears to me bizarre, and to call in question the validity of the principle upon which it is supposedly based.

Two foundations for the principle are suggested. One is that the right to remuneration is based upon contract, and the court has no power to vary the terms of a contract. The contractual conception suffers from the difficulties explained in the judgment of Fox LJ.[102] It also seems to me, in the context of the present debate, to give little weight to the fact that a trustee, whether paid or unpaid, is under no obligation, contractual or otherwise, to provide future services to the trust. He can at any time express his desire to be discharged from the trust and in that case a new trustee will in due course be appointed under section 36 or section 41 of the Trustee Act 1925 [pp. 624, 634, above]. The practical effect therefore of increasing the remuneration of the trustee (if the contractual conception is correct) will merely be to amend for the future, in favour of a trustee, the terms of a contract which the trustee has a unilateral right to determine. The interference of the court in such circumstances can hardly be said, in any real sense, to derogate from the contractual rights of the settlor or the beneficiaries if he or they are to be regarded as entitled to the benefit of the contract.

---

[102] Fox LJ considered the contractual analysis to be artificial since it would often be unclear with whom the trustee was contracting and often the trustee knows nothing of the terms of the settlement until the settlor is dead: [1982] Ch 61 at 76.

The other foundation suggested for the supposed principle is that the remuneration allowed to a trustee under the terms of the trust is a beneficial interest, and the court has no inherent jurisdiction to vary that beneficial interest save in special circumstances not here material: see *Chapman v Chapman* [1954] AC 429 [p. 826, below]. I agree that the remuneration given to a trustee by a will is an interest within the meaning of section 15 of the Wills Act 1837; that it is a gift upon a condition for the purposes of the legislation which formerly charged legacy duty upon testamentary gifts; and that an executor or trustee remunerated by the will cannot retain such remuneration against creditors if the estate turns out to be insolvent. There are obvious arguments why a testator should not be able to circumvent the provisions of the Wills Act, or avoid legacy duty, or defeat his creditors, by the award of remuneration to his executors or trustees. It does not follow that a remunerated trustee is to be considered as a *cestui que trust* for the purposes of the principles laid down in the *Chapman* case. If he were it is difficult, as Fox LJ says, to see what right the court would have to authorise remuneration to be charged by a prospective trustee, since such authority will have the inevitable effect of adding a new beneficiary to the trust at the expense of the existing beneficiaries.

I would allow the appeal.

The matter was remitted to the Chancery Division to enable the trustees to make such application and upon such further evidence as they thought fit.[103]

In **Foster v Spencer** [1996] 2 All ER 672, JUDGE PAUL BAKER QC awarded remuneration to the trustees of a cricket club for their past, but not future, services.[104] As regards remuneration for past services His Honour said at 681:

Where, as in this case, there were no funds out of which to pay remuneration at the time of their appointment, nor was a true appreciation of the extent of the task possible, a prospective application would be impracticable, if not impossible. The refusal of remuneration...would result in the beneficiaries being unjustly enriched at the expense of the trustees.

The right of the trustee to remuneration for past services cannot depend upon the circumstances that at the time he seeks it, his services are further required so that he is in a position to demand remuneration for the past as a condition of continuing in office.

The services rendered by the trustees were wholly outside their contemplation when appointed. They were appointed as trustees of a cricket club which had its own ground. They found themselves obliged by unforeseen circumstances to dispose of the ground. This proved far more difficult than would normally be expected and made great demands on the expertise of Mr. Sealy and of Mr. Foster, and on the time of all of them. I have no doubt that if they had realised what they were in for, they would have declined to act unless remunerated in some way.

The authorities provide little or no guidance on the issue of quantum. As might be expected, it is left to the discretion of the court. The size of the trust fund is one obvious factor. The cost of engaging outside professional help, the amount of time spent are all relevant. In the end, however, the judge must try to assess what is reasonable in all the circumstances...

[His Honour then considered what was reasonable remuneration for each trustee and continued:] Finally I come to the application for future remuneration, which is sought on behalf of

---

[103] See also *Re Berkeley Applegate (Investment Consultants)* [1989] Ch 32 (liquidators remunerated out of assets held on trust by company for investors). See Virgo, *The Principles of the Law of Restitution* (2006, 2nd ed.) p. 76.   [104] The trustees were also reimbursed for past expenses. See p. 670, above.

all three trustees. The suggestion here is that I should make an order in the form of the normal wide professional charging clause.

I am unable to do that. The present position is that owing to the efforts of the trustees, the trust assets are now in the form of cash and deposits. The tasks remaining are quite different from those leading to the disposal of the ground. They consist of restoring the originating summons to determine the beneficial interests. I do not see that that calls for any special expertise on the part of the trustees. They have said that they are not willing to continue if not allowed to charge. It was submitted in reply that the experience of the trustees is very important and difficult to replace with anybody who would not charge. I am not persuaded of this. It may be that the knowledge of the trustees is important for the purpose of placing evidence before the court in determining the beneficial interest, but the duties of the trustees at this stage would not appear to be onerous. The burden will fall on solicitors who will be paid. There may be other beneficiaries who could be persuaded to take over if the plaintiffs insist on resigning. I do not say that if the burden proves too onerous than at present seems likely, a further application would be excluded. But as things stand, I cannot say that the continued services of these trustees is necessary for the good administration of the trusts, whether these take the form of a distribution among the contributors or the refounding of the cricket club elsewhere.

E REMUNERATION FOR LITIGATION WORK BY SOLICITOR-TRUSTEES

There is an exception to the rule that, in the absence of an enabling clause, a solicitor-trustee cannot charge profit costs, which is known as the rule in *Cradock v Piper*.[105] Under the rule a solicitor-trustee may charge costs if he has acted for a co-trustee as well as himself in respect of business done in an action or matter in court, except in so far as the costs have been increased by his being one of the parties.

VIII LIABILITY OF TRUSTEES TO CREDITORS[106]

A party who enters into a contract with a trustee is able to enforce his rights against the trustee, but cannot obtain payment from the trust assets.[107] This is because a trust is not a legal entity and so it cannot be a principal and have an agent.[108] The trustee, however, is entitled to be indemnified from the trust fund for all liabilities which have been properly incurred. But the trust fund might not be sufficient and it is not possible to

---

[105] (1850) 1 Mac & G 664; (1998) 19 *Legal History* 189 (C. Stebbings).
[106] H&M, pp. 509–510; Pettit, pp. 410–411.
[107] *Perring v Draper* [1997] EGCS 109 and *Marston Thompson and Evershed plc v Bend* (19 September 1997, unreported).
[108] Trust Law Committee Report, *Rights of Creditors Against Trustees and Trust Funds* (1999), p. 2.

indemnify the trustee where the liability was not properly incurred, whether because of lack of capacity, lack of authorisation, or breach of duty.[109]

The creditor may be subrogated[110] to the trustee's right to an indemnity from the trust fund, but only to the extent that the trustee could have made a claim against the fund, so if the trustee had committed a breach of trust it follows that the creditor cannot be indemnified.

The Trust Law Committee has recommended statutory reform of the law in this area.

Trust Law Committee: *Rights of Creditors Against Trustees and Trust Funds* (1999), paras 10.3, 10.4

10.3 (a) Subject to any contrary intention in the trust instrument, where a trustee's entry into a contract with a creditor was in breach of his equitable duties this shall not prevent such creditor having a right of indemnity out of the trust fund unless he was dishonest.

(b) Where a trustee's conduct as trustee makes him a tortfeasor and such conduct amounted to a breach of his equitable duties this shall not prevent the victim of the tortious conduct from having a right of indemnity out of the trust fund.

10.4 Where an individual, who is a trustee or an executor or an administrator or a personal representative, contracts with a person 'as trustee' or 'as executor' or 'as administrator' or 'as personal representative', he shall be rebuttably presumed not to contract otherwise than in such capacity and be liable personally no further than the value of the trust fund or the deceased's estate at the time the other person requests payment; provided that, if such representative individual knew of a liquidated sum that is due or will become payable at a future date but reduced the value of the trust fund, by making distributions to beneficiaries or by incurring further obligations that were not reasonably necessary for the preservation of trust assets, he shall also be personally liable to the extent of such reduction in value.

The Law Commission will commence a project to review the law of the rights of creditors against trustees and trust funds when it has completed its work on *Capital and Income on Trusts: Classification and Appointment* [see p. 735, below].

QUESTIONS

1. Assume that you are:
   (a) the owner of £100,000 more than you can ever need, and you decide to make a settlement. Whom would you choose as your trustees?
   (b) the trustee of a family trust, whose value has quadrupled since 1985. The beneficiaries wish you to resign from the trust, so that some Jersey-resident trustees can be appointed, and the trust managed in Jersey. The beneficiaries are all resident in England. What would you do?

[109] Ibid, pp. 3–5.   [110] For subrogation generally see p. 945, below.

2. Consider the dilemma of a disappointed beneficiary, such as the plaintiff in *Re Beloved Wilkes' Charity* (1851) 3 Mac & G 440 [p. 655, above], who suspects that the trustees' discretion has been wrongly, or even fraudulently, exercised, but can only establish such fact if he can compel the trustees to give their reasons.

   Is this problem insoluble? Compare *Re Londonderry's Settlement* [1965] Ch 918 [p. 740, below].

3. Is it appropriate to allow the courts to unravel appointments when it is discovered that they have adverse tax consequences? What if this arose from mistaken legal advice from a solicitor? If this is appropriate in the trust context, should a similar principle apply to mistakes about tax consequences of transactions in other contexts?

4. Should the rule in *Re Hastings-Bass* [1975] Ch 25, [p. 657, above] be analysed as a doctrine based on the trustees' duty to act on the proper basis, or on the trustees' mistake? See Tang (2007) 21 *Trust Law International* 62.

14

DUTIES OF TRUSTEES

I DUTY ON BECOMING A TRUSTEE[1]

**Parker and Mellows: *Modern Law of Trusts*
(8th edn, 2003), p. 562**

When a person accepts a trusteeship, he should do four things: first, acquaint himself with the terms of the trust; secondly, inspect the trust instrument and any other trust deeds; thirdly, procure that all the property subject to the trust is vested in the joint names of himself and

---

[1] H&M, pp. 537–540; Lewin, pp. 437–439; P&M, pp. 562–565; Pettit, pp. 391–393; Snell, pp. 637–639; T&H, pp. 308–309; U&H, pp. 602–612; *Re Strahan* (1856) 8 De GM & G 291; *Harvey v Olliver* (1887) 57 LT

his co-trustees, and that all title deeds are placed under their joint control; and, fourthly, in the case of an appointment as a new trustee of an existing trust, to investigate any suspicious circumstances which indicate a prior breach of trust, and to take action to recoup the trust fund if any breach has in fact taken place. If he fails to do these things, he may make himself liable in an action for breach of trust.

Re Brogden[2]
(1888) 38 Ch D 546 (Ch D, **North J**; CA, **Cotton, Fry** and **Lopes LJJ**)

By his will, Mr. Brogden, a successful contractor in Manchester, left substantial legacies to members of his family, and provided that none of them should be payable until five years after his death, nor should money be paid out of the partnership between him and his sons for five years thereafter, unless his sons so required. He also covenanted to pay £10,000 to the trustees of his daughter's (Mrs. Billing's) marriage settlement, within five years of his death. This sum and the legacies were to carry interest meanwhile. Brogden died on 9 December, 1869.

Mr. Budgett was one of the trustees of Mrs. Billing's marriage settlement. He pressed the Brogden brothers on many occasions for payment, before and after the expiry of the five-year period. On several occasions security for the payment was given, one of these being in response to an action started by Budgett for the administration of the estate.

The Brogden partnership became less prosperous. Throughout Budgett was trying to avoid disturbance within the family, and any crisis which would upset the solvency of the firm. Eventually the firm became insolvent, and the securities were inadequate. The question was whether Budgett was liable to Mrs. Billing for breach of trust.

Held. Budgett was liable, as he had not taken all possible steps to obtain payment of the £10,000.

Cotton LJ: Now what was the duty of the trustee, Mr. *Budgett?* It was his duty, in my opinion, at the expiration of five years, to call for payment and to take reasonable means of enforcing payment if the executors did not pay the debt and the legacy. And there having been a postponed period during which no steps were to be taken against the partners or against the executors, it was the more his duty at the expiration of that period to assume that the executors had done what it was their duty to do by preparing for paying the debts and paying the legacies of the testator.... And, in my opinion, in the case here, it became the duty of Mr. *Budgett* to take active measures immediately after the expiration of the five years—that is immediately the legacy became payable and immediately the debt became payable.

We must therefore consider what he did. The five years expired in the beginning of December, 1874. I do not suggest that during the remaining of that month of December he should have taken any legal proceedings. That would hardly be expected, but what in my opinion he ought to have done, if not in December, 1874, early in the year 1875, was to have demanded payment,

239; *Hallows v Lloyd* (1888) 39 Ch D 686; *Re Chapman* (1894) 72 LT 66; *Re Lucking's Will Trusts* [1968] 1 WLR 866.

2 Cf. *Ward v Ward* (1843) 2 HL Cas 777n. See also *Harris v Black* (1983) 46 P & CR 366.

and if payment was not made, then he ought to have taken effectual proceedings in order to recover payment both of the legacy and of the debt. I do not say it was his duty to recover them, because that assumes that he could have done so: but in my opinion it was his duty to demand payment of them, and to take effectual proceedings for the purpose of recovering them.

Now, what did he do? On 12 December, 1874, Mr. *Billing*, who was anxious, subject to what I shall hereafter mention, to recover payment of the sum settled on his wife and children, wrote to him urging him to see about getting payment of these sums of money. That was on 12 December, 1874, and he did nothing as far as one can see—nothing in the way of taking any proceedings at all, till some time in March, 1875. On 18 March, 1875, he had an interview with Mr. *Alexander Brogden,* who was the eldest son, and was the senior surviving partner in the firm, and who apparently had the command which his position gave him. Then there is a letter from Mr. *Holmes....* Mr. *Holmes* of Messrs. *Ingle, Cooper & Holmes,* writes a letter on 18 March, 1875, to Mr. *Alexander Brogden,* he says this:—[His Lordship read the letter and proceeded:] In my opinion this points to what was the great blot in the proceedings taken by Mr. *Budgett.* He did not say 'you must pay'. He was willing to enter into negotiations for the purpose of getting security. And what seems to have been proposed—we have not got very satisfactory evidence as to what took place at the interview—was that they should have a charge upon certain shares in order to secure the money. I gather from that letter that he did not direct Mr. *Holmes* to demand the payment: he did not say 'do not make any doubt about it: have payment. If you cannot have payment, then let the partners see that I am determined, as being the only independent trustee, to do my duty, and to enforce payment from them by such means as are open to me.'

Then we come to two other letters, which are the only other ones I shall read, namely, those from Mr. *Budgett* to Mrs. *Billing* of 27 May, 1875, and from Mr. *Budgett* to his solicitors of 29 June, 1875:—[His Lordship read portions of these letters.] I do not at all say that I have any suspicion that Mr. *Budgett* acted from any self-interested motives, I think it was suggested that his wife had a legacy left to her, and her interests were looked after better than Mrs. *Billing's* interests. I have no such suspicion. What I think is this: it was natural that he should be unwilling to take any active proceedings against his brother-in-law; he trusted him in the belief that this firm, which then stood in good credit, was a perfectly solvent firm, and that the money was safe; and that being so he did not take those proceedings which he ought to have taken to make them understand that it was his duty to obtain payment, and that he must obtain payment from them. He did not take that course, and he takes the risk of whatever the consequences may be.

To proceed with the story. In October, 1875, proceedings were taken, but they were not taken by him. They were taken by his brother, who was a trustee for Mrs. *Budgett.* As I say, I do not at all suggest that that was done to get her any benefit rather than Mrs. *Billing,* but that left the control of the proceedings not in Mr. *Budgett's* hands, and when a settlement was made in March of the following year, it was a settlement only to give security for the legacy and the debt which was due to his brother, the trustee for his wife.

Then, again in May, 1876, he does take proceedings, and does not get any security which can excuse him for the loss of the money, because he took in September, 1876, the security of a leasehold colliery, and although it is possible that if he had at once realised that security in the then state of the market he might have got money enough to pay everything of which he was trustee, yet, it was a leasehold colliery; coals went down; there was a difficulty about the rent; the landlord took proceedings; there had to be a large sum paid in order to get that colliery; and when it was realised it realised a sum insufficient to provide for the payment of these sums for which Mr. *Budgett* was trustee. That being so it is said that a trustee who is acting as he was, and not without consulting his solicitor, has never been held liable for what must be considered as an error of judgement.

In my opinion that is not the true way to state the case. If he had determined to get payment for this—if he had applied for payment in such a way as to shew that he meant to have it, and had consulted solicitors as to the best mode of proceedings, that might have been an error of judgement. But the conclusion to which I come, having regard to those letters, is this, that he did not do his duty in requiring payment—demanding it, and taking what he was advised were the best means of enforcing payment at least till the period of October, 1876—a late period, when we consider the state of the market as regards coal and iron. In regard to that the evidence is this; that in 1874 coal was in a very good state, collieries were very valuable property. But, although they were good in 1875, and not quite so good in 1876, both coal and iron then went rapidly down; and although in 1874 and 1875 there was a good state of coal and iron, unhappily at a later period that was not the case.

That decides the first question, with regard to which the rule is well laid down by Lord *Cottenham* in the case of *Clough v Bond* (1838) 3 My & Cr 490 at 496, that where a trustee does not do that which it is his duty to do, *prima facie* he is answerable for any loss occasioned thereby.

Then comes this question, if any loss is occasioned, on whom does it lie to shew whether any good would have resulted if the trustee had taken proceedings? Is that for the *cestuis que trust*, who are seeking to make Mr. *Budgett* liable, or is it for Mr. *Budgett* to shew that no good would have resulted? Is it for the *cestuis que trust* to shew that he could have got the money, or for Mr. *Budgett* to shew that he could not have got it if he had taken such proceedings as it was his duty to take?

In my opinion it is not for the *cestuis que trust* seeking to make the trustee liable, to shew that if he had done his duty he would have got the money for which they are seeking to make him answerable. It is the trustee who is seeking to excuse himself for the consequences of his breach of duty. It was his duty to take active proceedings if necessary earlier—to take active proceedings by way of action at law, if necessary; and if the trustee is to excuse himself, it is for him to shew that if he had taken proceedings no good would have resulted from it. Once shew that he has neglected his duty and *prima facie* he is answerable for all the consequences of that neglect; and in this case the result has been that only a very small sum could be recovered from the security which he took in the year 1876. That being so, has the trustee made out that if he had taken proceedings against the executors—against those who were carrying on the business, he would not have got any good from it? In my opinion he has not made that out, and my reason for thinking so is this—that at the time of the expiration of the five years, and certainly during the early part of the year 1875—probably up to the autumn of that year, the firm of *Brogden & Sons* was in very good credit. Immediately before the expiration of the five years, as I say, coal and iron had both been, as regards vendors, in a very satisfactory state. Coal was at an extraordinarily high price, and iron was good in the market....

I have therefore come to the conclusion that the decision of Mr. Justice *North* must be affirmed. It is an unfortunate position no doubt for Mr. *Budgett,* and I quite think that he believed that the firm were perfectly solvent, and that he was incurring no risk in letting the money remain with them. He ought not to have trusted them; as he did that and his expectations and those of the family have turned out to be wrong, and he has not shewn that no good would have resulted from his performing his duty by pressing for payment, and if necessary by taking proceedings to enforce payment, he must be held liable.

In **Buttle v Saunders** [1950] 2 All ER 193,[3] trustees for the sale of land had orally agreed to sell it to Mrs. Simpson for £6,142. One of the beneficiaries, Canon Buttle, wished to purchase it for a charity. After all the documents had been prepared for the sale to Mrs. Simpson, but before the contract was signed, Canon Buttle offered £6,500. The trustees felt that they had reached a stage in the negotiation with Mrs. Simpson from which they could not honourably withdraw. Canon Buttle brought this action to restrain the trustees from selling for any price below that which he had offered. By a counterclaim, the trustees asked for the directions of the court. WYNN-PARRY J held that the trustees must accept Canon Buttle's offer. He said at 195:

It has been argued on behalf of the trustees that they were justified in the circumstances in not pursuing the offer made by Canon Buttle and in deciding to go forward with the transaction with Mrs. Simpson. It is true that persons who are not in the position of trustees are entitled, if they so desire, to accept a lesser price than that which they might obtain on the sale of property, and not infrequently a vendor, who has gone some lengths in negotiating with a prospective purchaser, decides to close the deal with that purchaser, notwithstanding that he is presented with a higher offer. It redounds to the credit of a man who acts like that in such circumstances. Trustees, however, are not vested with such complete freedom. They have an overriding duty to obtain the best price which they can for their beneficiaries. It would, however, be an unfortunate simplification of the problem if one were to take the view that the mere production of an increased offer at any stage, however late in the negotiations, should throw on the trustees a duty to accept the higher offer and resile from the existing offer. For myself, I think that trustees have such a discretion in the matter as will allow them to act with proper prudence. I can see no reason why trustees should not pray in aid the common-sense rule underlying the old proverb: 'a bird in the hand is worth two in the bush'. I can imagine cases where trustees could properly refuse a higher offer and proceed with a lower offer. Each case must, of necessity, depend on its own facts. In regard to the case now before me, my view is that the trustees and their solicitors acted on an incorrect principle. The only consideration which was present to their minds was that they had gone so far in the negotiations with Mrs. Simpson that they could not properly, from the point of view of commercial morality, resile from those negotiations. That being so, they did not, to any extent, probe Canon Buttle's offer as, in my view, they should have done. It was urged on me that, by pausing to probe his offer, they ran the risk of losing the contract with Mrs. Simpson. On the view of the facts which I take, I do not consider that that was much of a risk. Mrs. Simpson had bought the leasehold term, which was nearing its end, and she was a very anxious purchaser. Equally, Canon Buttle had demonstrated beyond a peradventure that he was a very anxious buyer, and, as it seems to me, the least the trustees should have done would have been to have said to him: 'You have come on the scene at a late stage. You have made this offer well past the eleventh hour. We have advanced negotiations with Mrs. Simpson which can be concluded within a matter of hours. If you are really serious in your offer, you must submit in the circumstances to somewhat stringent terms, and you must be prepared to bind yourself at once to purchase the property for the sum of £6,500 on the terms, so far as applicable, of the draft

---

[3] (1950) 14 Conv (NS) 228 (E.H. Bodkin); (1975) 39 Conv (NS) 177 (A. Samuels). See *Cowan v Scargill* [1985] Ch 270 at 288, p. 705, below; *Sargeant v National Westminster Bank* (1990) 61 P & CR 518. As to whether trustees can sell at a valuation to be determined by a third party, see [1985] Conv 44 (G. Lightman). For the duty of charitable trustees when selling under the Charities Act 1993, ss. 26, 36, p. 588, above.

contract which otherwise would be entered into with Mrs. Simpson.' I have not the slightest doubt but that in the circumstances Canon Buttle would have agreed to those stringent terms and that the matter would have been carried out. The trustees, however, perfectly bona fide, maintained their attitude...[4]

> ### QUESTION
>
> What would you have done in Mr. Budgett's place in 1875–76? To what extent would his position have been eased if the Trustee Act 1925, section 15 (or its predecessor) had been in operation at that time? See p. 750, below. *Re Greenwood* (1911) 105 LT 509; *Re Ezekiel's Settlement Trusts* [1942] Ch 230.

II DUTIES AND DISCRETIONS[5]

A trustee's duties are imperative. Equity requires strict compliance. The standard required is that of *exacta diligentia*. Failure to comply may render a trustee liable for breach of trust; even though the trustee thought that what he did was right, and even if it was done with the intention of benefiting the beneficiaries. However, onerous though the duties of a trustee are, a clause may be inserted in the trust instrument exempting a trustee from liability (the extent of its effectiveness is discussed below),[6] and section 61 of the Trustee Act 1925 gives the court a discretion to excuse a trustee who has acted honestly and reasonably and ought fairly to be excused.[7]

A THE STATUTORY DUTY OF CARE[8]

Prior to the enactment of the Trustee Act 2000, the general standard of care of a trustee in the performance of his administrative powers and duties, as opposed to fiduciary duties,[9] was that he should exercise the same due diligence and care as an ordinary prudent man of business would use in the management of his own affairs.[10] A higher standard of care was expected of a professional trustee.[11] The Trustee Act

---

[4] The property was subsequently ordered to be sold to Mrs. Simpson for £6,600.

[5] H&M, pp. 505–507; Lewin, pp. 1213–1221; P&M, pp. 573–577; P&S, p. 697; Pettit, pp. 389–391; Snell, pp. 639–651; T&H, p. 308; U&H, pp. 601–844; J. Getzler, 'Duty of Care' in *Breach of Trust* (eds. P. Birks and A. Pretto, 2002), pp. 41–74.   [6] See p. 867, below.

[7] See p. 871, below.

[8] H&M, pp. 505–507; Lewin, pp. 1216–1221; P&M, pp. 573–577; P&S, pp. 621–622; Pettit, pp. 393–395; Snell, pp. 637–640; T&H, pp. 310–323; U&H, pp. 708–732. See generally Law Com. No. 260, *Trustees' Powers and Duties* (1999), pp. 33–43.   [9] See Chapter 16 for examination of fiduciary duties.

[10] *Speight v Gaunt* (1883) 9 App Cas 1.

[11] *Bartlett v Barclays Bank Trust Co Ltd* [1980] Ch 515. See also *Re Waterman's Will Trusts* [1952] 2 All ER 1054.

2000 creates a new statutory duty of care which applies to the exercise of those powers and duties which are provided for under the 2000 Act and other statutory provisions. It follows that the common law duty of care remains relevant in respect of other powers and duties.

TRUSTEE ACT 2000

1. The duty of care

(1) Whenever the duty under this subsection applies to a trustee, he must exercise such care and skill as is reasonable in the circumstances, having regard in particular—

    (a) to any special knowledge or experience that he has or holds himself out as having, and

    (b) if he acts as trustee in the course of a business or profession, to any special knowledge or experience that it is reasonable to expect of a person acting in the course of that kind of business or profession.

(2) In this Act the duty under subsection (1) is called 'the duty of care'.

2. Application of duty of care

Schedule 1 makes provision about when the duty of care applies to a trustee.

SCHEDULE 1
APPLICATION OF DUTY OF CARE

Investment

1 The duty of care applies to a trustee—

    (a) when exercising the general power of investment or any other power of investment, however conferred;[12]

    (b) when carrying out a duty to which he is subject under section 4 or 5 (duties relating to the exercise of a power of investment or to the review of investments).[13]

Acquisition of land

2 The duty of care applies to a trustee—

    (a) when exercising the power under section 8 to acquire land;[14]

    (b) when exercising any other power to acquire land, however conferred;

    (c) when exercising any power in relation to land acquired under a power mentioned in sub-paragraph (a) or (b).

---

[12] See p. 692, below.   [13] See p. 692, below.   [14] See p. 694, below.

Agents, nominees and custodians

3 (1) The duty of care applies to a trustee—

  (a) when entering into arrangements under which a person is authorised under section 11 to exercise functions as an agent;[15]

  (b) when entering into arrangements under which a person is appointed under section 16 to act as a nominee;[16]

  (c) when entering into arrangements under which a person is appointed under section 17 or 18 to act as a custodian;[17]

  (d) when entering into arrangements under which, under any other power, however conferred, a person is authorised to exercise functions as an agent or is appointed to act as a nominee or custodian;

  (e) when carrying out his duties under section 22 (review of agent, nominee or custodian, etc).[18]

  (2) For the purposes of sub-paragraph (1), entering into arrangements under which a person is authorised to exercise functions or is appointed to act as a nominee or custodian includes, in particular—

  (a) selecting the person who is to act,

  (b) determining any terms on which he is to act, and

  (c) if the person is being authorised to exercise asset management functions, the preparation of a policy statement under section 15.[19]

Compounding of liabilities

4 The duty of care applies to a trustee—

  (a) when exercising the power under section 15 of the Trustee Act 1925 to do any of the things referred to in that section;[20]

  (b) when exercising any corresponding power, however conferred.

Insurance

5 The duty of care applies to a trustee—

  (a) when exercising the power under section 19 of the Trustee Act 1925 to insure property;[21]

  (b) when exercising any corresponding power, however conferred.

Reversionary interests, valuations and audit

6 The duty of care applies to a trustee—

  (a) when exercising the power under section 22(1) or (3) of the Trustee Act 1925 to do any of the things referred to there;[22]

  (b) when exercising any corresponding power, however conferred.

---

[15] See p. 695, below.   [16] See p. 698, below.   [17] See p. 698, below.
[18] See p. 700, below.   [19] See p. 697, below.   [20] See p. 750, below.
[21] See p. 751, below.   [22] See p. 753, below.

Exclusion of duty of care

7 The duty of care does not apply if or in so far as it appears from the trust instrument that the duty is not meant to apply.[23]

Whitehouse and Hassall: *Trusts of Land, Trustee Delegation and the Trustee Act 2000* (2nd edn, 2001), pp. 203–206

What is the duty of care?

The duty is laid down in s 1. It is akin to the standard used in the tort of negligence: it depends on what is 'reasonable in all the circumstances'. The higher standard expected of the professional (set out in sub clauses (a) and (b)) applies whether or not the professional charges for his services.[24] A number of further matters are worthy of note:

(a) The Law Commission rejected the more familiar (at least to trust lawyers) test based on the prudent man of business. This preference for the reasonable man test was, at the end of the day arrived at because:

— to retain the prudent man test would be no more than a restatement of the traditional common law rule;[25]

— the standard adopted permits express regard to be had to the particular skill and position of the trustee (see TA 2000, s. 1(a) and (b));[26]

— 'the standard of care must be a robust and, within reason, a demanding one'; and

— 'there may, in fact, be little difference between the two alternatives'.

The case in favour of replacing the prudent man of business with the reasonable man test is therefore hardly persuasive;[27]

---

[23] See p. 867, below.

[24] The wording is similar to that in the Insolvency Act 1986, s. 214 (4), which deals with the duty of care owed by a director in the context of wrongful trading and is as follows:

'the facts which a director of a company ought to know or ascertain, the conclusions which he ought to reach and the steps which he ought to take are those which would be known or ascertained or reached or taken, by a reasonably diligent person having both: (a) the general knowledge, skill and experience that may reasonably be expected of a person carrying out the same functions as are carried out by that director in relation to the company, and (b) the general knowledge, skill and experience that that director has'.

The relationship between limbs (a) and (b) is far from clear. Take the example of a solicitor in a small high-street practice with limited experience of trusts and compare him with a private client partner in a leading practice. Both are professional and both will charge (doubtless at very different rates!) but are they both subject to the same standard of care? It is thought that there must be a minimum standard required of all solicitor-trustees but that the private client partner will presumably be subject to a higher standard by reference to his special skills. Remuneration is not expressly mentioned in the legislation and it is curious that a professional appears to attract a higher standard even though he may not be remunerated (as, for instance, might be the case with a retired solicitor acting as trustee or with a professional but who acts on the basis of being a family friend).

[25] See LC No 260 at para. 3.24. The prudent man of business standard is, of course, adopted in the Pensions Act 1995, s. 34(4) in relation to the delegation of investment decisions to a fund manager (it is also employed by the Uniform Prudent Investor Act in the USA).

[26] The existing common law, of course, did permit such an allowance to be made.

[27] The authors were tempted to add a fifth reason as follows: '(5) Er...that's it.'

(b) How far is the test subjective? It is intended to be a standard which increases when a professional trustee is involved *but* 'this does not mean that an incompetent trustee should be absolved from responsibility just because he or she was plainly unsuited to the task. Every trustee should be required to exercise such care and skill as is reasonable in the circumstances. However, the level of care and skill which is reasonable may increase if the trustee has special knowledge or skills...[28] Taking the ignorant missionary trustee as an example[29] what standard does he owe under s. 1? He is not a professional so that the special features in s. 1(a) and (b) can be ignored which leaves the question of what is a reasonable standard to apply to him in the circumstances? The phrase 'in the circumstances' with its heavily subjective connotations may suggest that regard must be had to his ignorance so that, provided he has acted honestly, he will have satisfied the test.[30] The prudent man of business test offered an idealised figure against which to measure the performance of particular trustees.

(c) Is the statutory test different from the standard adopted by the common law? From the foregoing discussion it will be appreciated that the answer would appear to be yes which raises interesting questions about the relationship between the two tests and the extent to which the common law test is now redundant.

Nature of the statutory duty of care

It is not thought that what has occurred is a statutory codification of the common law: rather a new test has been introduced. So what is the position of the common law test?[31] The Explanatory Notes published with the Act state that:

'[t]he duty will take effect in addition to the existing fundamental duties of trustees (for example to act in the best interests of the beneficiaries and to comply with the terms of the trust) but will exclude any common law duty of care which might otherwise have applied'.[32]

---

[28] Law Com No. 260 at para. 3.24. Contrast the original wording produced by the Law Commission for option (5) in CP No. 146 at para. 111, which was subsequently rejected on the basis of excessive subjectivity: '(5) act with the care and diligence that may reasonably be expected having regard to the nature, composition and purposes of the particular trust, the skills which the trustees actually have, or if they are employed as professional trustees, those which they either ought to have or hold themselves out as having'.

[29] See Maugham J commenting on the trustee in *Re Vickery* [1931] 1 Ch 572 at 573 that he 'had spent his life as a missionary in the city of London and...was completely ignorant of business affairs'.

[30] In the context of the similar wrongful trading test in *Re DKG Contractors Ltd* [1990] BCC 903 it was noted that 'Patently, (the Directors') own knowledge, skill and expertise were hopelessly inadequate for the task they undertook. That is not sufficient to protect them.' It should, however, be noted that IA 1986, s. 214 is couched in more objective terms than the Trustee Act (TA) 2000 duty; in particular: (i) in s. 214(3) the Director is required to take 'every step' with a view to 'minimising' the potential loss to the company's creditors; (ii) s. 214(4)(a) refers to the knowledge, skill, and experience to be expected of a person carrying out the same functions as are carried out by the director in relation to the same company.

[31] The prudent businessman test will continue to apply to certain situations not falling within the s. 1 test; e.g. to trustees in exercising a power to carry on business.

[32] See para. 10. Speaking at the STEP London Central Conference in October 2000 Charles Harpum (the Law Commissioner) commented on the duty of care as follows:
'When it applies, it requires a trustee to exercise such skill and care as is reasonable in the circumstances, having regard to two factors. The first is any special knowledge or experience that he has or holds himself out to have. The second, which only applies where he acts as a trustee in the course of a business or profession, is any special knowledge or experience that it is reasonable to expect of a person acting in the course of that kind of business or profession. This duty is, therefore, in part objective and in part subjective. It was an attempt to codify the common law duty of care that has been applied to trustees in relation (for example) to investment or trust management.'

Nowhere, however, has the common law been abolished which suggests that the two duties must coexist: if the statutory duty is excluded, for instance, the common law may still apply. There is also some uncertainty about the position of a trustee who breaches the new statutory duty: is that a straightforward breach of trust or a breach of statutory duty? If the latter will there be important differences in terms of causation, remoteness and applicable limitation periods? Pending resolution of these problems it may be attractive to frame any claims for breach of duty under alternative heads. Of course a court is likely to be heavily influenced by what the Law Commission intended to do (and believes that it has succeeded in doing) and it would therefore be no great surprise for the robust view to be taken that in the circumstances listed in Sch. 1 the common law duty has been wholly superseded!

QUESTION

To what extend does the statutory duty of care differ from the common law duty of care?

III DUTY TO INVEST[33]

A INTRODUCTORY

Trustees are under a duty to invest the trust fund and so make it productive.[34] For many years it has been usual to give to trustees a wide power of investment in the trust instrument setting up the trust.[35] Otherwise their powers were limited to those which were provided by statute. Until recently the relevant statute was the Trustee Investment Act 1961, the operation of which was described by the Law Commission as 'positively detrimental to most trusts to which it applies'.[36] Much of this Act was repealed by the Trustee Act 2000,[37] Part II of which creates a regime which is more in keeping with modern investment practice.[38] This Act substantially widened the investment powers of trustees. It is, however, still possible either to limit these statutory powers of investment in the trust instrument,[39] or to expand them.[40]

---

[33] H&M, pp. 540–557; Lewin, pp. 1255–1334; P&M, pp. 592–611; P&S, pp. 605–629; Pettit, pp. 412–427; Snell, pp. 643–644; T&H, pp. 327–337; U&H, pp. 733–762.

[34] *Re Wragg* [1919] 2 Ch 58 at 64, per P.O. Lawrence J.

[35] Such clauses are construed strictly: *Re Harari's Settlement Trusts* [1949] WN 79.

[36] *Trustees' Powers and Duties*, 1999 (Law Com No. 260), p. 16.

[37] Following the recommendations of the Law Commission: *Trustees' Powers and Duties*, ibid.

[38] Most notably 'portfolio theory' by virtue of which investment decisions are to be made by reference to the whole portfolio of investments. See P&S, pp. 619–620; (1995) *Trust Law International* 71 (Lord Nicholls of Birkenhead); (1996) 10 *Trust Law International* 102 (E. Ford); (2000) 14 *Trust Law International* 75 (I. Legair); (2001) 15 *Trust Law International* 203 (A. Hicks). See also Law Com. No. 260 (1999), p. 23; H&M, p. 545–546.   [39] TA 2000, s. 6(1)(b).

[40] To include, for example, investment in land situated abroad. See TA 2000, s. 8 at p. 694, below.

B   GENERAL POWER OF INVESTMENT

TRUSTEE ACT 2000[41]

PART II[42]

INVESTMENT

3. General power of investment

(1) Subject to the provisions of this Part, a trustee may make any kind of investment[43] that he could make if he were absolutely entitled to the assets of the trust.

(2) In this Act the power under subsection (1) is called 'the general power of investment'.

(3) The general power of investment does not permit a trustee to make investments in land other than in loans secured on land (but see also section 8).[44]

(4) A person invests in a loan secured on land if he has rights under any contract under which—

(a) one person provides another with credit, and

(b) the obligation of the borrower to repay is secured on land.

(5) 'Credit' includes any cash loan or other financial accommodation.

(6) 'Cash' includes money in any form.

4. Standard investment criteria

(1) In exercising any power of investment, whether arising under this Part or otherwise, a trustee must have regard to the standard investment criteria.

(2) A trustee must from time to time review the investments of the trust and consider whether, having regard to the standard investment criteria, they should be varied.

(3) The standard investment criteria, in relation to a trust, are—

(a) the suitability to the trust of investments of the same kind as any particular investment proposed to be made or retained and of that particular investment as an investment of that kind, and

(b) the need for diversification of investments of the trust, in so far as is appropriate to the circumstances of the trust.

---

[41] See Whitehouse and Hassall, *Trusts of Land, Trustee Delegation and the Trustee Act 2000* (2nd edn, 2001), pp. 209–237.

[42] This Part of the Act does not apply to: the investment powers of trustees of pension schemes: TA 2000, s. 36(3) (these powers are governed by the Pensions Act 1995); the investment powers of trustees of authorised unit trusts: TA 2000, s. 37(1); and to charitable trustees who are managing common investment or common deposit schemes: TA 2000, s. 38 [see p. 612, above].

[43] This word is not defined. The Law Commission considered that it was an evolving concept which should be defined by the courts: Law Com No. 260 (1999), para. 2.58, n. 56.

[44] See p. 694, below.

5. Advice

(1) Before exercising any power of investment, whether arising under this Part or otherwise, a trustee must (unless the exception applies) obtain and consider proper advice about the way in which, having regard to the standard investment criteria, the power should be exercised.

(2) When reviewing the investments of the trust, a trustee must (unless the exception applies) obtain and consider proper advice about whether, having regard to the standard investment criteria, the investments should be varied.

(3) The exception is that a trustee need not obtain such advice if he reasonably concludes that in all the circumstances it is unnecessary or inappropriate to do so.

(4) Proper advice is the advice of a person who is reasonably believed by the trustee to be qualified to give it by his ability in and practical experience of financial and other matters relating to the proposed investment.

6. Restriction or exclusion of this Part etc.

(1) The general power of investment is—

(a) in addition to powers conferred on trustees otherwise than by this Act, but

(b) subject to any restriction or exclusion imposed by the trust instrument or by any enactment or any provision of subordinate legislation.

7. Existing trusts

(1) This Part applies in relation to trusts whether created before or after its commencement.

(2) No provision relating to the powers of a trustee contained in a trust instrument made before 3rd August 1961 is to be treated (for the purposes of section 6(1)(b)) as restricting or excluding the general power of investment.

(3) A provision contained in a trust instrument made before the commencement of this Part which—

(a) has effect under section 3(2) of the Trustee Investments Act 1961[45] as a power to invest under that Act, or

(b) confers power to invest under that Act,

is to be treated as conferring the general power of investment on a trustee.

Schedule 1, paragraph 1

The duty of care[46] applies to a trustee—

(a) when exercising the general power of investment or any other power of investment, however conferred;

---

[45] This provision applied the Trustee Investment Act 1961 to investment powers which had been conferred before that Act was passed.

[46] This is the statutory duty to exercise 'such care and skill as is reasonable in the circumstances': TA 2000, s. 1: see p. 687, above.

(b) when carrying out a duty to which he is subject under section 4 or 5 (duties relating to the exercise of a power of investment or to the review of investments).

C PURCHASE OF LAND

TRUSTEE ACT 2000

PART III

ACQUISITION OF LAND

8. Power to acquire freehold and leasehold land

(1) A trustee may acquire freehold or leasehold land in the United Kingdom—
  (a) as an investment,
  (b) for occupation by a beneficiary, or
  (c) for any other reason.

(2) 'Freehold or leasehold land' means—
  (a) in relation to England and Wales, a legal estate in land ...

(3) For the purpose of exercising his functions as a trustee, a trustee who acquires land under this section has all the powers of an absolute owner in relation to the land.

9. Restriction or exclusion of this Part etc.

The powers conferred by this Part are—

(a) in addition to powers conferred on trustees otherwise than by this Part, but
(b) subject to any restriction or exclusion imposed by the trust instrument or by any enactment or any provision of subordinate legislation.

10. Existing trusts

(1) This Part does not apply in relation to—
  (a) a trust of property which consists of or includes land which (despite section 2 of the Trusts of Land and Appointment of Trustees Act 1996) is settled land ... [47]

(2) Subject to subsection (1), this Part applies in relation to trusts whether created before or after its commencement.

Schedule 1, paragraph 2

Acquisition of land

The duty of care[48] applies to a trustee—

(a) when exercising the power under section 8 to acquire land;
(b) when exercising any other power to acquire land, however conferred;

---

[47] See Maudsley and Burn's *Land Law: Cases and Materials* (8th edn, 2004), Ch. 6.
[48] TA 2000, s. 1. See p. 687, above.

(c) when exercising any power in relation to land acquired under a power mentioned in sub-paragraph (a) or (b).

D DELEGATION OF INVESTMENT POWERS

Before the enactment of the Trustee Act 2000 it was not possible for trustees to delegate their powers of investment unless this was provided for by the trust instrument. Instead, the trustees had to apply to the court for an extension of their powers of investment. Following the enactment of the Trustee Act 2000, it is now possible for trustees to delegate these powers.

TRUSTEE ACT 2000

PART IV[49]
AGENTS, NOMINEES AND CUSTODIANS

Agents

11. Power to employ agents

(1) Subject to the provisions of this Part, the trustees of a trust may authorise any person to exercise any or all of their delegable functions as their agent.

(2) In the case of a trust other than a charitable trust, the trustees' delegable functions consist of any function other than—

(a) any function relating to whether or in what way any assets of the trust should be distributed,

(b) any power to decide whether any fees or other payment due to be made out of the trust funds should be made out of income or capital,

(c) any power to appoint a person to be a trustee of the trust, or

(d) any power conferred by any other enactment or the trust instrument which permits the trustees to delegate any of their functions or to appoint a person to act as a nominee or custodian.

(3) In the case of a charitable trust, the trustees' delegable functions are—

(a) any function consisting of carrying out a decision that the trustees have taken;

(b) any function relating to the investment of assets subject to the trust (including, in the case of land held as an investment, managing the land and creating or disposing of an interest in the land);

---

[49] See Whitehouse and Hassall, *Trusts of Land, Trustee Delegation and the Trustee Act 2000* (2nd edn, 2001), pp. 239–270. See p. 754, below.

(c) any function relating to the raising of funds for the trust otherwise than by means of profits of a trade which is an integral part of carrying out the trust's charitable purpose;

(d) any other function prescribed by an order made by the Secretary of State.

(4) For the purposes of subsection (3)(c) a trade is an integral part of carrying out a trust's charitable purpose if, whether carried on in the United Kingdom or elsewhere, the profits are applied solely to the purposes of the trust and either—

(a) the trade is exercised in the course of the actual carrying out of a primary purpose of the trust, or

(b) the work in connection with the trade is mainly carried out by beneficiaries of the trust.

12. Persons who may act as agents

(1) Subject to subsection (2), the persons whom the trustees may under section 11 authorise to exercise functions as their agent include one or more of their number.

(2) The trustees may not authorise two (or more) persons to exercise the same function unless they are to exercise the function jointly.

(3) The trustees may not under section 11 authorise a beneficiary to exercise any function as their agent (even if the beneficiary is also a trustee).

(4) The trustees may under section 11 authorise a person to exercise functions as their agent even though he is also appointed to act as their nominee or custodian (whether under section 16, 17 or 18 or any other power).

13. Linked functions etc.

(1) Subject to subsections (2) and (5), a person who is authorised under section 11 to exercise a function is (whatever the terms of the agency) subject to any specific duties or restrictions attached to the function.

For example, a person who is authorised under section 11 to exercise the general power of investment is subject to the duties under section 4[50] in relation to that power.

(2) A person who is authorised under section 11 to exercise a power which is subject to a requirement to obtain advice is not subject to the requirement if he is the kind of person from whom it would have been proper for the trustees, in compliance with the requirement, to obtain advice.

(3) Subsections (4) and (5) apply to a trust to which section 11(1) of the Trusts of Land and Appointment of Trustees Act 1996 (duties to consult beneficiaries and give effect to their wishes) applies.

---

[50] The standard investment criteria. See p. 692, above.

(4) The trustees may not under section 11 authorise a person to exercise any of their functions on terms that prevent them from complying with section 11(1) of the 1996 Act.

(5) A person who is authorised under section 11 to exercise any function relating to land subject to the trust is not subject to section 11(1) of the 1996 Act.

14. Terms of agency

(1) Subject to subsection (2) and sections 15(2) and 29 to 32,[51] the trustees may authorise a person to exercise functions as their agent on such terms as to remuneration and other matters as they may determine.

(2) The trustees may not authorise a person to exercise functions as their agent on any of the terms mentioned in subsection (3) unless it is reasonably necessary for them to do so.

(3) The terms are—

(a) a term permitting the agent to appoint a substitute;

(b) a term restricting the liability of the agent or his substitute to the trustees or any beneficiary;

(c) a term permitting the agent to act in circumstances capable of giving rise to a conflict of interest.

15. Asset management: special restrictions

(1) The trustees may not authorise a person to exercise any of their asset management functions as their agent except by an agreement which is in or evidenced in writing.

(2) The trustees may not authorise a person to exercise any of their asset management functions as their agent unless—

(a) they have prepared a statement that gives guidance as to how the functions should be exercised ('a policy statement'),[52] and

(b) the agreement under which the agent is to act includes a term to the effect that he will secure compliance with—

(i) the policy statement, or

(ii) if the policy statement is revised or replaced under section 22, the revised or replacement policy statement.

(3) The trustees must formulate any guidance given in the policy statement with a view to ensuring that the functions will be exercised in the best interests of the trust.

(4) The policy statement must be in or evidenced in writing.

---

51 See p. 674, above.
52 This may, for example, identify ethical considerations in managing the assets.

(5) The asset management functions of trustees are their functions relating to—

    (a) the investment of assets subject to the trust,

    (b) the acquisition of property which is to be subject to the trust, and

    (c) managing property which is subject to the trust and disposing of, or creating or disposing of an interest in, such property.

Nominees and custodians

16. Power to appoint nominees

(1) Subject to the provisions of this Part, the trustees of a trust may—

    (a) appoint a person to act as their nominee in relation to such of the assets of the trust as they determine (other than settled land), and

    (b) take such steps as are necessary to secure that those assets are vested in a person so appointed.

(2) An appointment under this section must be in or evidenced in writing.

(3) This section does not apply to any trust having a custodian trustee[53] or in relation to any assets vested in the official custodian for charities.[54]

17. Power to appoint custodians

(1) Subject to the provisions of this Part, the trustees of a trust may appoint a person to act as a custodian in relation to such of the assets of the trust as they may determine.

(2) For the purposes of this Act a person is a custodian in relation to assets if he undertakes the safe custody of the assets or of any documents or records concerning the assets.

(3) An appointment under this section must be in or evidenced in writing.

(4) This section does not apply to any trust having a custodian trustee[55] or in relation to any assets vested in the official custodian for charities.[56]

18. Investment in bearer securities

(1) If trustees retain or invest in securities payable to bearer, they must appoint a person to act as a custodian of the securities.

(2) Subsection (1) does not apply if the trust instrument or any enactment or provision of subordinate legislation contains provision which (however expressed) permits the trustees to retain or invest in securities payable to bearer without appointing a person to act as a custodian.

(3) An appointment under this section must be in or evidenced in writing.

(4) This section does not apply to any trust having a custodian trustee or in relation to any securities vested in the official custodian for charities.

---

[53] See p. 650, above.   [54] See p. 617, above.   [55] See p. 650, above.
[56] See p. 617, above.

19. Persons who may be appointed as nominees or custodians

(1) A person may not be appointed under section 16, 17 or 18 as a nominee or custodian unless one of the relevant conditions is satisfied.

(2) The relevant conditions are that—

    (a) the person carries on a business which consists of or includes acting as a nominee or custodian;

    (b) the person is a body corporate which is controlled by the trustees;

    (c) the person is a body corporate recognised under section 9 of the Administration of Justice Act 1985.

(3) The question whether a body corporate is controlled by trustees is to be determined in accordance with section 840 of the Income and Corporation Taxes Act 1988.[57]

(4) The trustees of a charitable trust which is not an exempt charity must act in accordance with any guidance given by the Charity Commission concerning the selection of a person for appointment as a nominee or custodian under section 16, 17 or 18.[58]

(5) Subject to subsections (1) and (4), the persons whom the trustees may under section 16, 17 or 18 appoint as a nominee or custodian include—

    (a) one of their number, if that one is a trust corporation, or

    (b) two (or more) of their number, if they are to act as joint nominees or joint custodians.

(6) The trustees may under section 16 appoint a person to act as their nominee even though he is also—

    (a) appointed to act as their custodian (whether under section 17 or 18 or any other power), or

    (b) authorised to exercise functions as their agent (whether under section 11 or any other power).

(7) Likewise, the trustees may under section 17 or 18 appoint a person to act as their custodian even though he is also—

    (a) appointed to act as their nominee (whether under section 16 or any other power), or

    (b) authorised to exercise functions as their agent (whether under section 11 or any other power).

[57] This includes the power to secure that the affairs of a company are conducted in accordance with the wishes of the controller by virtue of holding shares or possessing voting power or by virtue of powers contained in the articles of association or any other document.

[58] *Appointing Nominees and Custodians: Guidance under S. 19(4) of the Trustee Act 2000* (CC42) (February 2001).

20. Terms of appointment of nominees and custodians

(1) Subject to subsection (2) and sections 29 to 32,[59] the trustees may under section 16, 17 or 18 appoint a person to act as a nominee or custodian on such terms as to remuneration and other matters as they may determine.

(2) The trustees may not under section 16, 17 or 18 appoint a person to act as a nominee or custodian on any of the terms mentioned in subsection (3) unless it is reasonably necessary for them to do so.

(3) The terms are—
   (a) a term permitting the nominee or custodian to appoint a substitute;
   (b) a term restricting the liability of the nominee or custodian or his substitute to the trustees or to any beneficiary;
   (c) a term permitting the nominee or custodian to act in circumstances capable of giving rise to a conflict of interest.

Review of and liability for agents, nominees and custodians etc

21. Application of sections 22 and 23

(1) Sections 22 and 23 apply in a case where trustees have, under section 11, 16, 17 or 18—
   (a) authorised a person to exercise functions as their agent, or
   (b) appointed a person to act as a nominee or custodian.

(2) Subject to subsection (3), sections 22 and 23 also apply in a case where trustees have, under any power conferred on them by the trust instrument or by any enactment or any provision of subordinate legislation—
   (a) authorised a person to exercise functions as their agent, or
   (b) appointed a person to act as a nominee or custodian.

(3) If the application of section 22 or 23 is inconsistent with the terms of the trust instrument or the enactment or provision of subordinate legislation, the section in question does not apply.

22. Review of agents, nominees and custodians etc.

(1) While the agent, nominee or custodian continues to act for the trust, the trustees—
   (a) must keep under review the arrangements under which the agent, nominee or custodian acts and how those arrangements are being put into effect,
   (b) if circumstances make it appropriate to do so, must consider whether there is a need to exercise any power of intervention that they have, and
   (c) if they consider that there is a need to exercise such a power, must do so.

---

[59] See p. 674, above.

(2) If the agent has been authorised to exercise asset management functions, the duty under subsection (1) includes, in particular—

(a) a duty to consider whether there is any need to revise or replace the policy statement made for the purposes of section 15,

(b) if they consider that there is a need to revise or replace the policy statement, a duty to do so, and

(c) a duty to assess whether the policy statement (as it has effect for the time being) is being complied with.

(3) Subsections (3) and (4) of section 15 apply to the revision or replacement of a policy statement under this section as they apply to the making of a policy statement under that section.

(4) 'Power of intervention' includes—

(a) a power to give directions to the agent, nominee or custodian;

(b) a power to revoke the authorisation or appointment.

23. Liability for agents, nominees and custodians etc.

(1) A trustee is not liable for any act or default of the agent, nominee or custodian unless he has failed to comply with the duty of care applicable to him, under paragraph 3 of Schedule 1[60]—

(a) when entering into the arrangements under which the person acts as agent, nominee or custodian, or

(b) when carrying out his duties under section 22.

(2) If a trustee has agreed a term under which the agent, nominee or custodian is permitted to appoint a substitute, the trustee is not liable for any act or default of the substitute unless he has failed to comply with the duty of care applicable to him, under paragraph 3 of Schedule 1—[61]

(a) when agreeing that term, or

(b) when carrying out his duties under section 22 in so far as they relate to the use of the substitute.

Supplementary

24. Effect of trustees exceeding their powers

A failure by the trustees to act within the limits of the powers conferred by this Part—

(a) in authorising a person to exercise a function of theirs as an agent, or

(b) in appointing a person to act as a nominee or custodian,

does not invalidate the authorisation or appointment.

[60] See p. 687, above.   [61] See p. 687, above.

25. Sole trustees

(1) Subject to subsection (2), this Part applies in relation to a trust having a sole trustee as it applies in relation to other trusts (and references in this Part to trustees—except in sections 12(1) and (3) and 19(5)—are to be read accordingly).

(2) Section 18 does not impose a duty on a sole trustee if that trustee is a trust corporation.

26. Restriction or exclusion of this Part etc.

The powers conferred by this Part are—

(a) in addition to powers conferred on trustees otherwise than by this Act, but

(b) subject to any restriction or exclusion imposed by the trust instrument or by any enactment or any provision of subordinate legislation.

27. Existing trusts

This Part applies in relation to trusts whether created before or after its commencement.

Schedule 1, paragraph 3

[Application of the statutory duty of care[62] to trustees who appoint agents, nominees and custodians. See p. 687, above.]

E SELECTING INVESTMENTS

(i) General Duty[63]

Nestlé v National Westminster Bank Plc[64]
[1993] 1 WLR 1260 (CA, **Dillon, Staughton** and **Leggatt LJJ**)

Miss Nestlé's grandfather, who died in 1922, appointed the National Provincial Bank Ltd (which later merged with the National Westminster Bank plc) as his executor and trustee. Under his will his widow had a life interest in 'Winterbourne', the family home, and an annuity. On her death their two sons each had an annuity from the ages of 21 to 25, and then a half-interest in the residue. When the sons died, their shares went to their children.

In 1986 Miss Nestlé, who then became absolutely entitled to the capital, claimed that the trust fund which was then valued at £269,203 should have been worth well over £1 million. She brought an action against the trustee bank for default in the management of the fund.

Held. For the bank.

---

[62] See TA 2000, s. 1. See p. 687, above.

[63] In *X v A* [2000] 1 All ER 490 Arden J held that trustees were not under a duty to consult beneficiaries on the selection of investments, but should take beneficiaries' comments into account as appropriate.

[64] (1992) 142 NLJ 1279 (J.E. Martin); [1993] Conv 61 (A. Kenny).

Leggatt LJ: When trusts came into their own in Victorian times they were no doubt intended to preserve capital while assuring beneficiaries of a steady, if conservative, income. Little was demanded of a trustee beyond the safeguarding of the trust fund by refraining from improvident investment. This process was no doubt also intended to save beneficiaries from trouble and anxiety, or what is now called 'hassle'. But during the 64 years for which the trust set up by the plaintiff's grandfather endured, the contentment of his descendants declined. The plaintiff's uncle and father conducted with the respondent bank vigorous campaigns designed to improve their respective incomes, which, if the bank had not resisted them, would have worked to the ultimate detriment of the plaintiff, while the plaintiff herself is now locked in mortal financial combat with the bank.

George and John Nestlé saw the bank, or said they saw the bank, as unfairly looking out for the plaintiff at their expense. In fact John turns out to have had a fortune of his own, which was invested in equities. So to the extent that he was successful in getting the bank to invest in gilts he was achieving a balance between his funds. The plaintiff, on the other hand, with whom her father was latterly at odds, has become obsessed with the idea that the bank over the years has failed to look after her interests. She claims that the sum of £269,203 which she inherited should have been larger than it was. It will not be of any consolation to her to reflect that, if since 1986 she had in that period done for the fund what she claims that the bank ought to have done for it previously, and it had grown at the same rate as the cost of living, it would probably now be worth over £400,000.

There is no dispute about the nature of the bank's duty. It was, as Lindley LJ has expressed it, a duty 'to take such care as an ordinary prudent man would take if he were minded to make an investment for the benefit of other people for whom he felt morally bound to provide': *Re Whiteley* (1886) 33 Ch D 347 at 355.[65] The trustee must have regard 'not only to the interests of those who are entitled to the income, but to the interests of those who will take in future': *per* Cotton LJ, at 350. 'A trustee must not choose investments other than those which the terms of his trust permit': *Speight v Gaunt* (1883) 9 App Cas 1 at 19, *per* Lord Blackburn. So confined, the trustee must also 'avoid all investments of that class which are attended with hazard': *Learoyd v Whiteley* (1887) 12 App Cas 727 at 733, *per* Lord Watson. The power of investment

> 'must be exercised so as to yield the best return for the beneficiaries, judged in relation to the risks of the investments in question; and the prospects of the yield of income and capital appreciation both have to be considered in judging the return from the investment': *Cowan v Scargill* [1985] Ch 270 at 287 [p. 705, below].

Since the Trustee Investments Act 1961 came into force a trustee has been required by section 6(1) to have regard in the exercise of his powers of investment 'to the need for diversification of investments of the trust, in so far as is appropriate to the circumstances of the trust'.[66] It is common ground that a trustee with a power of investment must undertake periodic reviews of the investments held by the trust. In relation to this trust, that would have meant a review carried out at least annually, and whenever else a reappraisal of the trust portfolio was requested or was otherwise requisite. It must also be borne in mind that, as expressed by the Report of the Scarman Committee on the Powers and Duties of Trustees (1982) (Law Reform Committee: 23rd Report Cmnd. 8733), at para. 2.15, 'professional trustees, such as banks, are under a special duty to display expertise in every aspect of their administration of the trust'.

[65] Now see the statutory duty of care: TA 2000, s. 1, see p. 687, above.
[66] Now see the standard investment criteria; TA 2000, s. 4(3), p. 692, above.

The plaintiff alleges that the bank is in breach of trust because over the years since her grandfather set up the trust the bank has supposed that its power of investment was more limited than it was; has failed to carry out periodic reviews of the portfolio, and to maintain a proper balance between equities and gilts, and to diversify the equity investments; and has unduly favoured the interests of her father and her uncle as life-tenants at the expense of her own interest as remainderman. She says that in consequence the trust fund was worth less in 1986 than it should have been.

The essence of the bank's duty was to take such steps as a prudent businessman would have taken to maintain and increase the value of the trust fund. Unless it failed to do so, it was not in breach of trust. A breach of duty will not be actionable, and therefore will be immaterial, if it does not cause loss. In this context I would endorse the concession of Mr. Nugee for the bank that "loss" will be incurred by a trust fund when it makes a gain less than would have been made by a prudent businessman. A claimant will therefore fail who cannot prove a loss in this sense caused by breach of duty. So here in order to make a case for an inquiry, the plaintiff must show that loss was caused by breach of duty on the part of the bank.

On the plaintiff's behalf Mr. Lyndon-Stanford seeks to rely on a presumption against a wrongdoing trustee. He invokes Brightman J's dictum in *Bartlett v Barclays Bank Trust Co Ltd (No 2)* [1980] Ch 515 at 545 that: 'the trustee's obligation is to restore to the trust estate the assets of which he has deprived it'. But that presupposes deprivation.

The plaintiff alleges, and I am content to assume, that the bank was at all material times under a misapprehension about the meaning of the investment clause in the will, with the result that the bank believed that the scope of its powers of investment was more confined than it was. I also regard it as unlikely that the bank conducted any reviews of the portfolio between 1922 and 1959. If any were conducted, they were unplanned, sporadic and indecisive. Mr. Lyndon-Stanford argues that it should be presumed that, had there been a better balance between gilts and equities and had the equity investment been more diversified, the fund would ultimately have been worth more than it was. The fallacy is that it does not follow from the fact that a wider power of invest- ment was available to the bank than it realised either that it would have been exercised or that, if it had been, the exercise of it would have produced a result more beneficial to the bank than actually was produced. Loss cannot be presumed, if none would necessarily have resulted. Until it was proved that there was a loss, no attempt could be made to assess the amount of it.

[His Lordship referred to *Guerin v R* (1984) 13 DLR (4th) 321, and continued:] In my judg- ment either there was a loss in the present case or there was not. Unless there was a loss, there was no cause of action. It was for the plaintiff to prove on balance of probabilities that there was, or must have been, a loss. If proved, the court would then have had to assess the amount of it, and for the purpose of doing so might have had recourse to presumptions against the bank. In short, if it were shown that a loss was caused by breach of trust, such a presumption might avail the plaintiff in quantifying the loss. The plaintiff's difficulty is in reaching that stage.

The plaintiff therefore had to prove that a prudent trustee, knowing of the scope of the bank's investment power and conducting regular reviews, would so have invested the trust funds as to make it worth more than it was worth when the plaintiff inherited it. That was a matter for expert evidence. In the result there was evidence which the judge was entitled to accept and did accept that the bank did no less than expected of it up to the death of the testator's widow in 1960.

The proportion of the fund already invested in equities at the time when 'Winterbourne' was sold makes it impossible in my judgment to impugn the decision to put the proceeds of sale into conversion stock.

After 1960 investment of the trust funds preponderantly in tax-exempt gilts for the benefit of life tenants resident abroad is not shown to have produced a less satisfactory result for the remainderman than an investment in equities after taking into account savings in Estate Duty and Capital Transfer Tax, because this policy had the effect of preserving the capital. By the time that John Nestlé died the equities to replace the tax-exempt gilts would have had to be worth more than twice as much as the gilts in order to achieve the same benefit net of tax.

It is true that the calculations upon which the bank relied in making these comparisons were based on the assumptions that the whole fund was subject to Estate Duty, and that the bank did not contemplate that it might be able to take advantage of a late switch into gilts, especially in relation to Mrs. Elsie Nestlé. But even if a less favourable assumption were made in relation to Estate Duty, the result would not have been so inferior as to demonstrate failure to look out for the remainderman amounting to a breach of trust. Similarly, although the fact that Mrs. Elsie Nestlé returned to live in this country now indicates that it might have been advantageous if a switch into equities had been made after George's death, the bank cannot in my judgment be reproached for failing to anticipate that she would outlive her husband by ten years, and that she would destroy the benefit of investment in tax-exempt gilts by resuming her domicile in England. Had she not done so, it would have been impossible for the bank to assess with any accuracy the timing of a switch back into gilts. In any event, without having pleaded any defect in the management of Mrs. Elsie Nestlé's fund, the plaintiff cannot now rely on this argument.

No testator, in the light of this example, would choose this bank for the effective management of his investment. But the bank's engagement was as a trustee; and as such, it is to be judged not so much by success as by absence of proven default. The importance of preservation of a trust fund will always outweigh success in its advancement. Inevitably, a trustee in the bank's position wears a complacent air, because the virtue of safety will in practice put a premium on inactivity. Until the 1950s active management of the portfolio might have been seen as speculative, and even in these days such dealing would have to be notably successful before the expense would be justified. The very process of attempting to achieve a balance, or (if that be old-fashioned) fairness, as between the interests of life tenants and those of a remainderman inevitably means that each can complain of being less well served than he or she ought to have been. But by the undemanding standard of prudence the bank is not shown to have committed any breach of trust resulting in loss.

I am therefore constrained to agree that the appeal must be dismissed.[67]

(ii) Ethical Considerations

Cowan v Scargill[68]
[1985] Ch 270 (Ch D, **Sir Robert Megarry V-C**)

A mineworkers' pension fund, with assets of some £3,000 million and very wide powers of investment, was managed by a committee of ten trustees, of whom five were

[67] See also *Martin v City of Edinburgh District Council* (1988) SLT 329 (declaration granted by Scottish Court that policy to oppose apartheid by disinvesting in companies with South Africa was a breach of duty, even though no loss occurred).

[68] [1984] All ER Rev 306 (P.J. Clarke); (1984) 81 *Scottish Law Gazette* 2291 (S.C. Butler); (1986) 102 LQR 32 (J.H. Farrar and J.K. Maxton). For the position as regards ethical considerations on investment by charitable trustees, see *Harries v Church Comrs for England* [1992] 1 WLR 1241, p. 608, above.

appointed by the National Coal Board, and five, including the defendant, by the National Union of Mineworkers. They were assisted in their investment decisions by an advisory panel of experts. Prior to 1982 the plan for investment included overseas investment and investment in oil and gas. In 1982 when a revised plan was considered, the five union trustees, on the basis of union policy determined at the annual conference, refused to accept the revised plan, unless it was amended so that there would be no increase in overseas investment; that overseas investment already made would be withdrawn at the most opportune time; and that there would be no investment in energies competing with coal. The five Board trustees applied to the court for directions.

Held. The five union trustees were in breach of their duties as members of the committee of management in refusing to concur in adopting the revised plan for investment.

Sir Robert Megarry V-C: The main issue (and I put it very shortly) is whether the defendants are in breach of their fiduciary duties in refusing approval of an investment plan for the scheme unless it is amended so as to prohibit any increase in overseas investment, to provide for the withdrawal of existing overseas investments at the most opportune time, and to prohibit investment in energies which are in direct competition with coal....

I turn to the law. The starting point is the duty of the trustees to exercise their powers in the best interests of the present and future beneficiaries of the trust, holding the scales impartially between different classes of beneficiaries. This duty of the trustees towards their beneficiaries is paramount. They must, of course, obey the law; but subject to that, they must put the interests of their beneficiaries first. When the purpose of the trusts is to provide financial benefits for the beneficiaries, as is usually the case, the best interests of the beneficiaries are normally their best financial interests. In the case of a power of investment, as in the present case, the power must be exercised so as to yield the best return for the beneficiaries, judged in relation to the risks of the investments in question; and the prospects of the yield of income and capital appreciation both have to be considered in judging the return from the investment.

The legal memorandum that the union obtained from their solicitors is generally in accord with these views. In considering the possibility of investment for 'socially beneficial reasons which may result in lower returns to the fund', the memorandum states that 'the trustees' only concern is to ensure that the return is the maximum possible consistent with security'; and then it refers to the need for diversification. However, it continues by saying:

> 'Trustees cannot be criticised for failing to make a particular investment for social or political reasons, such as in South African stock for example, but may be held liable for investing in assets which yield a poor return or for disinvesting in stock at inappropriate times for non-financial criteria.'

This last sentence must be considered in the light of subsequent passages in the memorandum which indicate that the sale of South African securities by trustees might be justified on the ground of doubts about political stability in South Africa and the long-term financial soundness of its economy, whereas trustees could not properly support motions at a company meeting dealing with pay levels in South Africa, work accidents, pollution control, employment conditions for minorities, military contracting and consumer protection. The assertion that trustees could not be criticised for failing to make a particular investment for social or political reasons is one that I would not accept in its full width. If the investment in fact made is equally beneficial to the beneficiaries, then criticism would be difficult to sustain in practice, whatever the position in theory. But if the investment in fact made is less beneficial, then both in theory and in practice the trustees would normally be open to criticism.

This leads me to the second point, which is a corollary of the first. In considering what investments to make trustees must put on one side their own personal interests and views. Trustees may have strongly held social or political views. They may be firmly opposed to any investment in South Africa or other countries, or they may object to any form of investment in companies concerned with alcohol, tobacco, armaments or many other things. In the conduct of their own affairs, of course, they are free to abstain from making any such investments. Yet under a trust, if investments of this type would be more beneficial to the beneficiaries than other investments, the trustees must not refrain from making the investments by reason of the views that they hold.

Trustees may even have to act dishonourably (though not illegally) if the interests of their beneficiaries require it. Thus where trustees for sale had struck a bargain for the sale of trust property but had not bound themselves by a legally enforceable contract, they were held to be under a duty to consider and explore a better offer that they received, and not to carry through the bargain to which they felt in honour bound: *Buttle v Saunders* [1950] 2 All ER 193 [p. 685, above]. In other words, the duty of trustees to their beneficiaries may include a duty to 'gazump', however honourable the trustees. As Wynn-Parry J said at 195, trustees 'have an overriding duty to obtain the best price which they can for their beneficiaries'. In applying this to an official receiver in *Re Wyvern Developments Ltd* [1974] 1 WLR 1097 at 1106, Templeman J said that he 'must do his best by his creditors and contributories. He is in a fiduciary capacity and cannot make moral gestures, nor can the court authorise him to do so.' In the words of Sir James Wigram V-C in *Balls v Strutt* (1841) 1 Hare 146 at 149:

> 'It is a principle in this court, that a trustee shall not be permitted to use the powers which the trust may confer upon him at law, except for the legitimate purposes of his trust; . . .'

Powers must be exercised fairly and honestly for the purposes for which they are given and not so as to accomplish any ulterior purpose, whether for the benefit of the trustees or otherwise: see *Duke of Portland v Lady Topham* (1864) 11 HL Cas 32, a case on a power of appointment that must apply *a fortiori* to a power to trustees as such.

Thirdly, by way of caveat I should say that I am not asserting that the benefit of the beneficiaries which a trustee must make his paramount concern inevitably and solely means their financial benefit, even if the only object of the trust is to provide financial benefits. Thus if the only actual or potential beneficiaries of a trust are all adults with very strict views on moral and social matters, condemning all forms of alcohol, tobacco and popular entertainment, as well as armaments, I can well understand that it might not be for the 'benefit' of such beneficiaries to know that they are obtaining rather larger financial returns under the trust by reason of investments in those activities than they would have received if the trustees had invested the trust funds in other investments. The beneficiaries might well consider that it was far better to receive less than to receive more money from what they consider to be evil and tainted sources. 'Benefit' is a word with a very wide meaning, and there are circumstances in which arrangements which work to the financial disadvantage of a beneficiary may yet be for his benefit: see, for example, *Re T's Settlement Trusts* [1964] Ch 158 and *Re CL* [1969] 1 Ch 587. But I would emphasise that such cases are likely to be very rare, and in any case I think that under a trust for the provision of financial benefits the burden would rest, and rest heavily, on him who asserts that it is for the benefit of the beneficiaries as a whole to receive less by reason of the exclusion of some of the possibly more profitable forms of investment. Plainly the present case is not one of this rare type of cases. Subject to such matters, under a trust for the provision of financial benefits, the paramount duty of the trustees is to provide the greatest financial benefits for the present and future beneficiaries.

Fourth, the standard required of a trustee in exercising his powers of investment is that he must

'take such care as an ordinary prudent man would take if he were minded to make an investment for the benefit of other people for whom he felt morally bound to provide:'

per Lindley LJ in Re Whiteley (1886) 33 Ch D 347 at 355; see also at 350, 358; and see Learoyd v Whiteley (1887) 12 App Cas 727.[69] That duty includes the duty to seek advice on matters which the trustee does not understand, such as the making of investments, and on receiving that advice to act with the same degree of prudence. This requirement is not discharged merely by showing that the trustee has acted in good faith and with sincerity. Honesty and sincerity are not the same as prudence and reasonableness. Some of the most sincere people are the most unreasonable; and Mr. Scargill told me that he had met quite a few of them. Accordingly, although a trustee who takes advice on investments is not bound to accept and act on that advice, he is not entitled to reject it merely because he sincerely disagrees with it, unless in addition to being sincere he is acting as an ordinary prudent man would act.

Fifth, trustees have a duty to consider the need for diversification of investments. [His Lordship read section 6(1) of the Trustee Investments Act 1961. See now section 4(3) of the Trustee Act 2000 [p. 692, above], and continued:] The reference to the 'circumstances of the trust' plainly includes matters such as the size of the trust funds: the degree of diversification that is practicable and desirable for a large fund may plainly be impracticable or undesirable (or both) in the case of a small fund.

In the case before me, it is not in issue that there ought to be diversification of the investments held by the fund. The contention of the defendants, put very shortly, is that there can be a sufficient degree of diversification without any investment overseas or in oil, and that in any case there is no need to increase the level of overseas investments beyond the existing level. Other pension funds got on well enough without overseas investments, it was said, and in particular the NUM's own scheme had, in 1982, produced better results than the scheme here in question. This was not so, said Mr. Jenkins, if you compared like with like, and excluded investments in property, which figure substantially in the mineworkers' scheme but not at all in the NUM scheme: and in any case the latter scheme was much smaller, being of the order of £7 million.

I shall not pursue this matter. Even if other funds in one particular year, or in many years, had done better than the scheme which is before me, that does not begin to show that it is beneficial to this scheme to be shorn of the ability to invest overseas. The main difference between the 1980 and the 1982 plans, I may say, is that although the target for overseas investments remains at 15 per cent the 1982 plan increases the percentage of the cash flow that can be invested in overseas realty from 7½ to 10 per cent, and relaxes the overall limit of 15 per cent in this respect. It should be added that, in addition, something like 10 per cent of the assets of British companies in which the fund has invested consist of overseas holdings, so

[69] Now see the statutory duty of care: TA 2000, s. 1. See p. 687, above.

that there is this additional foreign element. As for oil, the 1982 plan made no real difference: the existing holdings of just under 12 per cent could have been maintained if that plan had been implemented.

Sixth, there is the question whether the principles that I have been stating apply, with or without modification, to trusts of pension funds. Mr. Stamler asserted that they applied without modification, and that it made no difference that some of the funds came from the members of the pension scheme, or that the funds were often of a very substantial size. Mr. Scargill did not in terms assert the contrary. He merely said that this was one of the questions to be decided, and that pension funds may be subject to different rules. I was somewhat unsuccessful in my attempts to find out from him why this was so, and what the differences were. What it came down to, I think, was that the rules for trusts had been laid down for private and family trusts and wills a long time ago; that pension funds were very large and affected large numbers of people; that in the present case the well-being of all within the coal industry was affected; and that there was no authority on the point except *Evans v London Co-operative Society Ltd* (1976) The Times, 6 July, and certain overseas cases.

I shall refer to the authorities in a moment, and consider the question of principle first. I can see no reason for holding that different principles apply to pension fund trusts from those which apply to other trusts. Of course, there are many provisions in pension schemes which are not to be found in private trusts, and to these the general law of trusts will be subordinated. But subject to that, I think that the trusts of pension funds are subject to the same rules as other trusts. The large size of pension funds emphasises the need for diversification, rather than lessening it, and the fact that much of the fund has been contributed by the members of the scheme seems to me to make even more important that the trustees should exercise their powers in the best interests of the beneficiaries. In a private trust, most, if not all, of the beneficiaries are the recipients of the bounty of the settlor, whereas under the trusts of a pension fund many (though not all) of the beneficiaries are those who, as members, contributed to the funds so that in due time they would receive pensions. It is thus all the more important that the interests of the beneficiaries should be paramount, so that they may receive the benefits which in part they have paid for. I can see no justification for holding that the benefits to them should run the risk of being lessened because the trustees were pursuing an investment policy intended to assist the industry that the pensioners have left, or their union.

His Lordship referred to *Evans v London Co-operative Society Ltd* (1976) The Times, 6 July; *Blankenship v Boyle* 329 F Supp 1089 (1971) in the US District Court for the District of Columbia; *Withers v Teachers' Retirement System of the City of New York* 444 F Supp 1248 (1978) and continued:

I can see no escape from the conclusion that the NUM trustees were attempting to impose the prohibitions in order to carry out union policy; and mere assertions that their sole consideration was the benefit of the beneficiaries do not alter that conclusion. If the NUM trustees were thinking only of the benefit of the beneficiaries, why all the references to union policy instead of proper explanations of how and why the prohibitions would bring benefits to the beneficiaries? No doubt some trustees with strong feelings find it irksome to be forced to submerge those feelings and genuinely put the interests of the beneficiaries first. Indeed, there are some who are temperamentally unsuited to being trustees, and are more fitted for campaigning for changes in the law. This, of course, they are free to do; but if they choose to become trustees they must accept that the rules of equity will bind them in all they do as trustees.

QUESTION

Would *Nestlé v National Westminster Bank plc* [1993] 1 WLR 1260 [p. 702, above] and *Cowan v Scargill* [1985] Ch 270 [p. 705, above], be decided differently following the enactment of Parts I (the statutory duty of care [see p. 687, above]) and II of the Trustee Act 2000 (see pp. 691–694, above)? See H&M, pp. 551; P&M, pp. 593–595; P&S, pp. 621–622; Pettit, p. 420; T&H, pp. 334–335; U&H, pp. 739–740.

F TRUSTEES HOLDING CONTROLLING INTEREST IN A COMPANY

Bartlett v Barclays Bank Trust Co Ltd (No 1)[70]
[1980] Ch 515 (Ch D, **Brightman J**)

The bank was trustee of the Bartlett Trust, of which the sole asset was a holding of 99.8 per cent of shares in a private property company. The beneficiaries were the settlor's family and issue. By 1960 no beneficiary or member of the settlor's family was on the board of the company, and none of the directors was a nominee of the bank. Money being required to pay Estate Duty, the bank and the board considered a public flotation of the company's shares. Merchant bankers advised the board that this would be more likely to succeed if the company invested in land development. The bank agreed to this so long as the beneficiaries were not left short of income. Investment was made in two projects, without consulting the bank, one at Guildford, which was successful, and the other, opposite the Old Bailey, which was not. The profit from the former was used to finance the latter, which resulted in a substantial loss. The bank was content with information issued at annual general meetings; it was not aware of the hazardous nature of the projects and did not intervene to prevent them. The beneficiaries sued the bank as trustee for breach of trust.

Held. The bank was liable for the loss.

Brightman J: I turn to the question, what was the duty of the bank as the holder of shares? ... The bank, as trustee, was bound to act in relation to the shares and to the controlling position which they conferred, in the same manner as a prudent man of business. The prudent man of business will act in such manner as is necessary to safeguard his investment. He will do this in two ways. If facts come to his knowledge which tell him that the company's affairs are not being conducted as they should be, or which put him on inquiry, he will take appropriate action. Appropriate action will no doubt consist in the first instance of inquiry of and consultation with the directors, and in the last but most unlikely resort, the convening of a general meeting to replace one or more directors. What the prudent man of business will *not* do is to content himself with the

---

[70] [1980] Conv 155 (G.A. Shindler); [1983] Conv 127 (R. Pearce and A. Samuels). See also *Walker v Stones* [2001] QB 902 [p. 869, below].

receipt of such information on the affairs of the company as a shareholder ordinarily receives at annual general meetings. Since he has the power to do so, he will go further and see that he has sufficient information to enable him to make a responsible decision from time to time either to let matters proceed as they are proceeding, or to intervene if he is dissatisfied. This topic was considered by Cross J in *Re Lucking's Will Trusts* [1968] 1 WLR 866, more fully reported in [1967] 3 All ER 726.[71] In that case nearly 70 per cent of the shares in the company were held by two trustees, L and B, as part of the estate of a deceased; about 29 per cent belonged to L in his own right, and 1 per cent belonged to L's wife. The directors in 1954 were Mr. and Mrs. L and D, who was the manager of the business. In 1956 B was appointed trustee to act jointly with L. The company was engaged in the manufacture and sale of shoe accessories. It had a small factory employing about twenty people, and one or two travellers. It also had an agency in France. D wrongfully drew some £15,000 from the company's bank account in excess of his remuneration, and later became bankrupt. The money was lost. Cross J said, at 874:

> 'The conduct of the defendant trustees is, I think, to be judged by the standard applied in *Speight v Gaunt* (1883) 9 App Cas 1, namely, that a trustee is only bound to conduct the business of the trust in such a way as an ordinary prudent man would conduct a business of his own.[72] Now what steps, if any, does a reasonably prudent man who finds himself a majority shareholder in a private company take with regard to the management of the company's affairs? He does not, I think, content himself with such information as to the management of the company's affairs as he is entitled to as shareholder, but ensures that he is represented on the board. He may be prepared to run the business himself as managing director or, at least, to become a non-executive director while having the business managed by someone else. Alternatively, he may find someone who will act as his nominee on the board and report to him from time to time as to the company's affairs. In the same way, as it seems to me, trustees holding a controlling interest ought to ensure so far as they can that they have such information as to the progress of the company's affairs as directors would have. If they sit back and allow the company to be run by the minority shareholder and receive no more information than shareholders are entitled to, they do so at their risk if things go wrong.'

I do not understand Cross J to have been saying that in every case where trustees have a controlling interest in a company it is their duty to ensure that one of their number is a director or that they have a nominee on the board who will report from time to time on the affairs of the company. He was merely outlining convenient methods by which a prudent man of business (as also a trustee) with a controlling interest in a private company, can place himself in a position to make an informed decision whether any action is appropriate to be taken for the protection of his asset. Other methods may be equally satisfactory and convenient, depending upon the circumstances of the individual case. Alternatives which spring to mind are the receipt of copies of the agenda and minutes of board meetings if regularly held, the receipt of monthly management accounts in the case of a trading concern, or quarterly reports. Every case will depend on its own facts. The possibilities are endless. It would be useless, indeed misleading, to seek to lay down a general rule. The purpose to be achieved is not that of monitoring every move of the directors, but of making it reasonably probable, so far as circumstances permit, that the trustee or (as in the *Lucking* case) one of them will receive an adequate flow of information in time to enable the trustees to make use of their controlling interest should this be necessary for the protection of their trust asset, namely, the shareholding. The obtaining of information

---

[71] See [1979] Conv 345, 358 (J.E. Stannard).
[72] Now see the statutory duty of care: TA 2000, s. 1. See p. 687, above.

is not an end in itself, but merely a means of enabling the trustees to safeguard the interests of their beneficiaries.

The principle enunciated in the *Lucking* case appears to have been applied in *Re Miller's Deed Trusts* (21 March, 1978, unreported), a decision of Oliver J. No transcript of the judgment is available but the case is briefly noted in the Law Society's Gazette published on 3 May, 1978. There is also a number of American decisions proceeding upon the same lines, to which counsel has helpfully referred me....

It was not proper for the bank to confine itself to the receipt of the annual balance sheet and profit and loss account, detailed annual financial statements and the chairman's report and statement, and to attendance at the annual general meetings and the luncheons that followed, which were the limits of the bank's regular sources of information. Had the bank been in receipt of more frequent information it would have been able to step in and stop, and ought to have stopped, the board embarking on the Old Bailey project. That project was imprudent and hazardous and wholly unsuitable for a trust whether undertaken by the bank direct or through the medium of its wholly-owned company. Even without the regular flow of information which the bank ought to have had, it knew enough to put it upon inquiry. There were enough obvious points at which the bank should have intervened and asked questions.

G   ENLARGEMENT OF INVESTMENT
POWERS BY THE COURT

Although the powers of investment under the Trustee Act 2000 are very wide, there may be exceptional circumstances where trustees wish to have these powers extended by the courts.[73] Alternatively, the trust instrument may have restricted the powers of investment and the trustees may wish this restriction to be removed. Whether the courts are prepared to enlarge the investment powers in such circumstances and, if so, when they are prepared to do so, has been considered by the courts in the context of the Trustee Investment Act 1961.

In **Trustees of the British Museum v Attorney-General** [1984] 1 WLR 418,[74] SIR ROBERT MEGARRY V-C, in approving a scheme to give the trustees wider powers of investment, said at 419:

In this case the Trustees of the British Museum have issued an originating summons relating to charitable funds held by them... The object of the summons is to obtain the approval of the court to a scheme that will give the trustees wider powers of investment than those that they have at present under a scheme approved by Pennycuick J on 18 July, 1960... The main point of importance is whether the court should continue to apply the principle that was laid down in cases such as *Re Kolb's Will Trusts* [1962] Ch 531 (a case in which an appeal was compromised: see (1962) 106 Sol Jo 669); *Re Cooper's Settlement* [1962] Ch 826 and *Re Porritt's Will*

---

[73]   Either under s. 57 of the Trustee Act 1925 [see p. 749, below], or under the Variation of Trusts Act 1958 [see p. 832, below].

[74]   [1984] Conv 373 (H.E. Norman). See also *Steel v Wellcome Custodian Trustees Ltd* [1988] 1 WLR 167.

Trusts (1961) 105 Sol Jo 931, and was recognised in *Re Clarke's Will Trusts* [1961] 1 WLR 1471 and *Re University of London Charitable Trusts* [1964] Ch 282.

As is well known, the instrument establishing a trust may prescribe powers of investment which are either narrower or wider than those laid down by the general law: see Trustee Act 1925, section 69(2); Trustee Investments Act 1961, section 1(3).[75] [His Lordship considered what constituted authorised investments by statute and continued:] The [Trustee Investments] Act was passed on 3 August, 1961; and in October of that year the first three cases that I have cited, *Kolb, Cooper* and *Porritt,* all fell for decision. In each case an application had been made, doubtless before the Act was passed, for an extension of the powers of investment. Each case seems to have been decided without either of the others being cited; but in each the judge (Cross, Buckley and Pennycuick JJ respectively) reached the same conclusion. In the words of Cross J: 'the powers given by the Act must, I think, be taken to be *prima facie* sufficient and ought only to be extended if, on the particular facts, a special case for extending them can be made out': *Re Kolb* at 540....

That was in 1961; and no doubt for some time that doctrine remained soundly based. However, in recent years the court, usually in chambers, has become ready to authorise extensions of the power of investment, often by an increased willingness to accept circumstances as being 'special'. Further, it has become increasingly common for draftsmen of wills and settlements to insert special investment powers which are far wider than those conferred by the Act of 1961....

The evidence before me establishes that over the last twenty years significant changes in investment practice have occurred, especially in the case of large trust funds.... I feel no doubt that it is in the best interests of the trustees and the trusts that there should be relaxation of the terms of the 1960 scheme which will take account of these changes. At the same time, any scheme must have appropriate safeguards. The main features of the scheme put forward in this case, as it stands revised after discussion, may be stated as follows.

[His Lordship stated the main features of the scheme and continued:] I am conscious that such a scheme gives extremely wide powers of investment to the trustees. At the same time I consider that it is proper and desirable that such powers should be given, and I have made an order accordingly. There are four factors that I should mention in particular. First, there is the eminence and responsibility of the trustees, the machinery for obtaining highly skilled advice, and the success that this machinery has achieved over the past twenty years. Second, there are the changed conditions of investment, conditions which require great liberty of choice if, upon skilled advice, advantage is to be taken of opportunities which often present themselves upon short notice and for short periods; and for this, the provision for delegation is plainly advantageous. Third, there is obvious advantage in there being freedom to invest in any part of the world. At the same time, there is due recognition of prudence of maintaining a solid core of relatively safe investments while setting free a substantial part for investment which, though less 'safe', offer greater opportunities for a substantial enhancement of value. Opinions may vary about the precise percentages; certainly my views have fluctuated. However, in the end I have reached the conclusion that the percentages put forward are reasonable...

Fourth, I bear in mind the large size of the trust fund.[76] From the point of view of powers of investment, this carries the matter out of the realm of the ordinary private trust into the field of pension funds and large institutional investors; and for success in this field a wide flexibility of the powers of investment is plainly desirable, if not essential.

---

[75] Now see TA 2000, s. 6(1)(b), p. 693, above.　　[76] Between £5 million and £6 million.

From what I have said it will be seen that much of what I say depends to a greater or lesser extent upon the special position of the trustees and the trust funds in the case before me. On the other hand, there is much that is of more general application, and it may be convenient if I attempt to summarise my views.

1. In my judgment, the principle laid down in the line of cases headed by *Re Kolb's Will Trusts* [1962] Ch 531 is one that should no longer be followed, since conditions have changed so greatly in the last twenty years. Though authoritative, those cases were authorities only *rebus sic stantibus;* and in 1983 they bind no longer. However, if Parliament acts on the recommendation of the Law Reform Committee and replaces the Act of 1961 with revised powers of investment, the *Kolb* principle may well become applicable once more. Until then, the court should be ready to grant suitable applications for the extension of trustees' powers of investment, judging each application on its merits, and without being constrained by the provisions of the Act of 1961.

2. In determining what extended powers of investment should be conferred, there are many matters which will have to be considered. I shall refer to five, without in any way suggesting that this list is exhaustive, or that anything I say is intended to fetter the discretion that the court has to exercise in each case.

(i)   The court is likely to give great weight to the width and efficacy of any provisions for advice and control. The wider the powers, the more important these provisions will be. An existing system of proven efficacy, as here, is likely to be especially cogent.

(ii)   Where the powers are of great width, as in the present case, there is much to be said for some scheme of fractional division, confining part of the fund to relatively safe investments, and allowing the other part to be used for investments in which the greater risks will be offset by substantial prospects of a greater return. On the other hand, when the powers are appreciably less wide than they are in the present case, I would in general respectfully concur with the views expressed by the Law Reform Committee that no division of the fund into fractions should be required, and that the only division should be into investments which require advice and those which do not. Nevertheless, although a division of the fund into fractions should not be essential, there may well be cases where such a division may be of assistance in obtaining the approval of the court.

(iii) The width of the powers in the present scheme seems to me to be at or near the extreme limit for charitable funds. Without the fractional division of the fund and the assurance of effective control and advice I very much doubt whether such a scheme could have been approved. What the court has to judge is the combined effect of width, division, advice and control, which all interact, together with the standing of the trustees.

(iv)   The size of the fund in question may be very material. A fund that is very large may well justify a latitude of investment that would be denied to a more modest fund; for the spread of investments possible for a larger fund may justify the greater risks that wider powers will permit to be taken.

(v)   The object of the trust may be very material. In the present case, the desirability of having an increase of capital value which will make possible the purchase of desirable acquisitions for the museum despite soaring prices does something to justify the greater risks whereby capital appreciation may be obtained.

Since writing this judgment I have been referred to the very recent decision in *Mason v Farbrother* [1983] 2 All ER 1078 [p. 828, below]; and counsel on both sides sent me a helpful joint note on the subject. Much of the judgment is directed to questions of jurisdiction and the details of the revised investment clause there under consideration. Of these matters I need say nothing. However, in considering whether the jurisdiction to approve the revised clause ought to be exercised, Judge Blackett-Ord, the Vice-Chancellor of Lancaster, appears to have treated the *Kolb* line of cases as still being binding authorities, saying (as indeed is the case) that the rule was not absolute but applied in the absence of special circumstances. He then said at 1086 that 'the special circumstances in the present case are manifest: in a word, inflation since 1961'. He added that the trust in question was unusual in that it was not a private or family trust but a trust of a pension fund with perhaps something of a public element in it.

For my part, I would hesitate to describe inflation since 1961 as amounting to 'special circumstances'; it is, unhappily, a very general circumstance. With all respect, I can see little virtue (judicial comity and humility apart) in seeking to preserve the rule and yet establishing universal special circumstances that will engulf the rule. I do not, of course, know what arguments on this point were addressed to the court, but for the reasons that I have given I would prefer to say that the rule has gone, and with it any question of what circumstances are special. However, the ultimate result is much the same, and although the reasoning in the two cases differs, I am happy to think that there is this support for my conclusion in the present case.

Hanbury and Martin, *Modern Equity* (17th edn, 2005), p. 557

...the Trustee Act 2000 has revolutionised investment powers, making it unlikely that trustees will have much need to apply to court for extended powers. Should they do so, for example if they should wish to purchase land abroad (which the new Act does not permit), the *Re Kolb* principle[77] would again be relevant. It is more likely that applications to court after the commencement of the new Act will involve attempts to lift specific restrictions and exclusions imposed by the settlor. In such cases the *Re Kolb* principle would not apply, as the trustees would not be seeking powers beyond those contained in the Trustee Act 2000. The issue for the court would be whether it would be justified in overturning the wishes of the settlor.

IV DUTY TO INFORM POTENTIAL BENEFICIARIES

D. Hayton in *Trends in Contemporary Trust Law* (ed. A.J. Oakley) (1996), p. 49

As a necessary incident of the trustee–beneficiary relationship at the core of the trust the trustee is under a duty to find and pay a beneficiary entitled to an income or capital

---

[77] Namely 'that special circumstances have to be shown to justify an extension beyond the powers conferred by a modern statute': H&M, p. 556.

payment, thereby making such beneficiary aware that he is a beneficiary.[78] In the case
of a discretionary trust, since the beneficiary's entitlement to put his case to the trustees
for the exercise of their discretion in his favour is of no effect unless he is aware of it, and
since he cannot be expected to become aware of it unless the trustees draw it to his attention it must surely be a necessary incident of the trustee–beneficiary relationship that the
trustee must be under a duty to take reasonable steps[79] to make a discretionary beneficiary
aware that he be such.[80] Knowledge of the trust is necessary to make the trust effectual
with the trustees being accountable to the beneficiaries for their stewardship of the property: unaccountability to the beneficiaries arising from the trustees not letting them know
that they are beneficiaries is inconsistent with, and repugnant to, the purposes for which
the settlor transferred the trust property to the trustees or the fundamental requirement of
accountability to beneficiaries before there can be duties of trusteeship.[81] Thus beneficiaries,
even if discretionary, have a right to information revealing what the trustees have done with
the trust property,[82] though not the reasons[83] for the exercise of distributive powers in favour
of beneficiaries.

V DUTY TO DISTRIBUTE[84]

A beneficiary can compel a trustee to pay to him what he is entitled to under the trust.
Usually this gives rise to no difficulties. But situations might arise where the trustees'
duty is not clear; either because there is doubt as to the beneficiaries' entitlement, or
because known beneficiaries cannot be found. In doubtful cases, a trustee may seek
the directions of the court; and is of course safe in following them. There are various
ways in which the trustee may seek protection.

---

[78] *Hawkesley v May* [1956] 1 QB 304 at 322; *Burrows v Walls* (1855) 5 De G M & G 233 at 253; *Brittlebank v Goodwin* (1868) LR 5 Eq 545 at 550.
[79] These will require a businesslike approach depending on the size of the class and the extent to which a sub-class may be regarded as the primary object of the settlor's bounty cf. *Re Manisty's Settlement* [1974] Ch 17 at 25; *Hartigan Nominees Pty Ltd v Rydge* (1992) 29 NSWLR 405 at 432; *Re Baden's Deed Trusts (No 2)* [1973] Ch 9 at 20, 27.
[80] Cf. *Scally v Southern Health and Social Services Board* [1992] 1 AC 294 at 306–307.
[81] Cf. *Hawkins v Clayton* (1988) 164 CLR 539 at 553. A clause directing the trustees not to inform any discretionary beneficiary that he be such unless so directed by the settlor or the protector should either negate the trust or more likely, be regarded as repugnant to the trust: such a person should only be made the object of a power.
[82] *Re Londonderry's Settlement* [1964] Ch 594; *Chaine-Nickson v Bank of Ireland* [1976] IR 393; *Spellson v George* (1987) 11 NSWLR 300 at 315; *Lemos v Coutts & Co* [1992–3] CILR 460; *West v Lazard Bros (Jersey) Ltd* [1987–8] JLR 414; *A-G of Ontario v Stavro* (1994) 119 DLR (4th) 750.
[83] *Re Londonderry's Settlement*, ibid; *Wilson v Law Debenture Trust Corpn* [1995] 2 All ER 337; *Hartigan Nominees Pty Ltd v Rydge*, note 79, above.
[84] H&M, pp. 557–560; Lewin, pp. 917–979; P&M, pp. 616–617; Pettit, pp. 400–404; Snell, pp. 731–742; T&H, pp. 337–341; U&H, pp. 762–772.

A RELEASE ON COMPLETION

Lewin on Trusts 18th edn, 2008, pp. 946–947

A trustee, upon making final distribution of the trust fund and thus depriving himself of the security previously afforded to him by his retention of the trust property, naturally and reasonably wishes to procure for himself the maximum security against future litigation. In practice it is common for a trustee to seek a release under seal. But a trustee has in general no right to insist upon a release.[85] If the case is altogether clear, as to the assets to be distributed and as to the proper recipient, he may be entitled to no more than a receipt;[86] if the case is complicated, or if the beneficiary behaves in such a way as to raise an apprehension that at some future time he may challenge the propriety of the proposed distribution, the trustee is entitled to insist that accounts be settled between them, either voluntarily or by the court.[87]

In particular circumstances, a release may be required. A trustee who is asked to depart from the strict terms of the trust may demand a release.[88] [...] And if a beneficiary has settled his share, it seems that the trustee making the distribution is entitled to a release under seal from the beneficiary, though merely to a receipt from the trustees of the beneficiary's settlement.[89]

B ADVERTISEMENT FOR CLAIMANTS

TRUSTEE ACT 1925

27. Protection by means of advertisements

(1) With a view to the conveyance to or distribution among the persons entitled to any real or personal property, the trustees of a settlement, trustees of land, trustees for sale of personal property or personal representatives[90] may give notice by advertisement in the Gazette, and in a newspaper[91] circulating in the district in which the land is situated, and such other like notices, including notices elsewhere than in England and Wales, as would, in any special case, have been directed by a court of competent jurisdiction in an action for administration, of their intention to make such conveyance or distribution as aforesaid, and requiring any person interested to send to the trustees or personal representatives within the time, not being less than two months, fixed in the notice or,

[85] *Chadwick v Heatley* (1845) 2 Coll 137; *King v Mullins* (1852) 1 Drew 308; *Warter v Anderson* (1853) 11 Hare 301; *Re Roberts' Trusts* (1869) 38 LJ Ch 708. [...] Nor in general can he apply trust money in effecting insurance against liability for his own breach of duty: *Kemble v Hicks* [1999] PLR 287.

[86] *King v Mullins*, ibid; *Re Hoskin's Trusts* (1877) 5 Ch D 229 (on appeal (1877) 6 Ch D 281); *Re Ruddock* (1910) 102 LT 89.

[87] *Chadwick v Heatley*, note 85 above; *Re Wright's Trusts* (1857) 3 K & J 419 (queried *arguendo* in *Re Ruddock*, ibid). [88] *King v Mullins*, note 85 above.

[89] *Re Cater's Trusts (No 2)* (1858) 25 Beav 366.

[90] As amended by Trusts of Land and Appointment of Trustees Act (TLATA) 1996, s. 25(1), Sch. 3, para. 3 (7). [91] As amended by Law of Property (Amendment) Act (LP(A)A) 1926, Sch.

where more than one notice is given, in the last of the notices, particulars of his claim in respect of the property or any part thereof to which the notice relates.

(2) At the expiration of the time fixed by the notice the trustees or personal representatives may convey or distribute the property or any part thereof to which the notice relates, to or among the persons entitled thereto, having regard only to the claims, whether formal or not, of which the trustees or personal representatives then had notice and shall not, as respects the property so conveyed or distributed, be liable to any person of whose claim the trustees or personal representatives have not had notice at the time of conveyance or distribution; but nothing in this section—

(a) prejudices the right of any person to follow the property, or any property representing the same, into the hands of any person, other than a purchaser, who may have received it; or

(b) frees the trustees or personal representatives from any obligation to make searches or obtain official certificates of search similar to those which an intending purchaser would be advised to make or obtain.

(3) This section applies notwithstanding anything to the contrary in the will or other instrument, if any, creating the trust.

Law Reform Committee 23rd Report (*The Powers and Duties of Trustees*) 1982 Cmnd 8733, para. 5.1

Adverse Claims

5.1 We have considered the suggestion that trustees should be protected from liability from claims arising after a distribution if they have obtained counsel's opinion that a distribution should be made which has been sent to the beneficiaries. However, difficulties could arise where trustees have notice of a possible claim by creditors. The trustees could not safely distribute in such circumstances and they should be able to set some sort of time limit for positive action failing which distribution can proceed. We recommend that a provision be introduced to the effect that trustees should be empowered to write to any potential creditors, enclosing a copy of counsel's opinion, informing them that they should make their claim within three months of receiving the opinion and if no claim is made within that time they will proceed with the distribution. Then if no claim is made, they should be free to make the distribution proposed without incurring liability to the creditor concerned, but without prejudice to the latter's right to follow the trust assets.

C SETTING ASIDE A FUND TO MEET CLAIMS IN RESPECT OF RENTS AND COVENANTS

TRUSTEE ACT 1925

26. Protection against liability in respect of rents and covenants

(1) Where a personal representative or trustee liable as such for—

(a) any rent, covenant, or agreement reserved by or contained in any lease; or

(b) any rent, covenant or agreement payable under or contained in any grant made in consideration of a rent charge; or

(c) any indemnity given in respect of any rent, covenant or agreement referred to in either of the foregoing paragraphs;

satisfies all liabilities under the lease or grant which may have accrued and been claimed,[92] up to the date of the conveyance hereinafter mentioned, and, where necessary, sets apart a sufficient fund to answer any future claim that may be made in respect of any fixed and ascertained sum which the lessee or grantee agreed to lay out on the property demised or granted, although the period for laying out the same may not have arrived, then and in any such case the personal representative or trustee may convey the property demised or granted to a purchaser, legatee, devisee, or other person entitled to call for a conveyance thereof and thereafter—

(i) he may distribute the residuary real and personal estate of the deceased testator or intestate, or, as the case may be, the trust estate (other than the fund, if any, set apart as aforesaid) to or amongst the persons entitled thereto, without appropriating any part, or any further part, as the case may be, of the estate of the deceased or of the trust estate to meet any future liability under the said lease or grant;

(ii) notwithstanding such distribution, he shall not be personally liable in respect of any subsequent claim under the said lease or grant.

(1A) Where a personal representative or trustee has as such entered into, or may as such be required to enter into, an authorised guarantee agreement with respect to any lease comprised in the estate of a deceased testator or intestate or a trust estate (and, in a case where he has entered into such an agreement, he has satisfied all liabilities under it which may have accrued and been claimed up to the date of distribution)—

(a) he may distribute the residuary real and personal estate of the deceased testator or intestate, or the trust estate, to or amongst the persons entitled thereto—

(i) without appropriating any part of the estate of the deceased, or the trust estate, to meet any future liability (or, as the case may be, any liability) under such agreement, and

(ii) notwithstanding any potential liability of his to enter into any such agreement; and

(b) notwithstanding such distribution, he shall not be personally liable in respect of any subsequent claim (or, as the case may be, any claim) under any such agreement.

In this subsection 'authorised guarantee agreement' has the same meaning as in the Landlord and Tenant (Covenants) Act 1995.[93]

---

[92] As amended by LP(A)A 1926, Sch.

[93] Inserted by the Landlord and Tenant (Covenants) Act 1995, s. 30(1), Sch. 1, para. 1. For the meaning of 'authorised guarantee agreement', see ss. 16 and 28(1) of the Landlord and Tenant (Covenants) Act 1995.

(2) This section operates without prejudice to the right of the lessor or grantor, or the persons deriving title under the lessor or grantor, to follow the assets of the deceased or the trust property into the hands of the persons amongst whom the same may have been respectively distributed, and applies notwithstanding anything to the contrary in the will or other instrument, if any, creating the trust.

(3) In this section 'lease' includes an underlease and an agreement for a lease or underlease and any instrument giving any such indemnity as aforesaid or varying the liabilities under the lease; 'grant' applies to a grant whether the rent is created by limitation, grant, reservation, or otherwise, and includes an agreement for a grant and any instrument giving any such indemnity as aforesaid or varying the liabilities under the grant; 'lessee' and 'grantee' include persons respectively deriving title under them.

D BENJAMIN ORDER

In **Re Benjamin** [1902] 1 Ch 723, Philip Benjamin was entitled, if he was living on 25 June, 1893, the date of his father's death, to a share (about £30,000) in his father's estate. He had disappeared in September 1892, and searching enquiries failed to produce any news of him. JOYCE J said at 725:

I think in this case that Philip David Benjamin must be presumed to be dead...The question is as to when he died. If he is to be presumed to be dead, I think the case of *Re Walker* (1871) 7 Ch App 120 distinctly applies, and the onus of proof is on his administrator. He has failed to adduce any evidence to shew that P.D. Benjamin survived the testator. I myself consider it highly probable that he died on 1 September, 1892, or at all events shortly after. I am clearly of opinion that the onus is on those claiming under him to prove that he survived the testator. In my opinion, therefore, the trustees are at liberty to distribute. I am anxious, however, not to do anything which would prevent his representative from making any claim if evidence of his death at any other time should be subsequently forthcoming. I shall not, therefore, declare that he is dead, but I will make an order in the following form:—

In the absence of any evidence that the said P.D. Benjamin survived the testator, let the trustees of the testator's will be at liberty to divide the share of the testator's estate devised and bequeathed in favour of the said P.D. Benjamin, his wife and children, upon the footing that P.D. Benjamin was unmarried and did not survive the testator.[94]

E INSURANCE

In **Re Evans** [1999] 2 All ER 777,[95] the defendant had been appointed the administrator of her deceased father's estate, which was held on statutory trusts for herself and her brother, the plaintiff. The defendant had not heard from her brother for thirty years and

---

[94] See *Ministry of Health v Simpson* [1951] AC 251; *Re Lowe's Will Trusts* [1973] 1 WLR 882 at 887; *Re Green's Will Trusts* [1985] 3 All ER 455; [1986] Conv 138 (P. Luxton).
[95] See also *Re Yorke* [1997] 4 All ER 907 (reliance on deceased's reinsurance policy).

TO DISTRIBUTE 721

assumed that he was dead. She consequently distributed the estate to herself once she had taken out a missing beneficiary insurance policy. Her brother reappeared and issued proceedings in respect of certain matters concerning the administration of the estate, including the purchase of the insurance policy. RICHARD McCOMBE QC said at 785:

In my view, personal representatives, particularly of small estates, should not be discouraged from seeking practical solutions to difficult administration problems, without the expense of resort to the court. Further, in small intestate administrations, where frequently the representative will have a personal interest, sizeable sums should not have to be tied up indefinitely for fear of the re-emergence of a long-lost beneficiary. The missing beneficiary policy does provide, at relatively small cost, a practical answer to such problems. Such a policy provides a fund to meet the claim of such a beneficiary in exoneration of the representative and of the overpaid beneficiary. The policy is to the advantage of all and is to some extent more effective than the limited protection provided by the more costly application to court for a *Benjamin* order. I am disinclined, therefore, to draw a distinction in this case between cases where the personal representative is beneficially entitled and those where he or she is not. It may be that circumstances will differ in future cases, but in my view the defendant was advised to take a practical course in circumstances where the beneficiary had been unheard of for nearly thirty years and to my mind the premium was a sensible and proper expense of this administration.

F   PERSONAL INDEMNITY

Lewin on Trusts (18th edn, 2008), p. 944

Sometimes where there is only a shadow of a doubt as to the parties interested and the chance of an adverse claim being made is extremely remote, a trustee may be willing to distribute in reliance on an indemnity, especially if he is a member of the family interested under the settlement; but it should be realised that an indemnity (especially from an individual) is an unsatisfactory safeguard: when the danger arises, the person who granted the indemnity may be insolvent or his assets may have been distributed. An outstanding indemnity may also prove extremely inconvenient to his personal representatives when the estate of the person who granted it is being wound up. Sometimes an insurance company will issue an indemnity policy. In fixing the amount of the policy the impact of inheritance tax and of any rise in the value of investments which may have to be replaced should be borne in mind.

G   PAYMENTS BY PERSONAL REPRESENTATIVES TO MINORS

ADMINISTRATION OF ESTATES ACT 1925

42. Power to appoint trustees of infants' property

(1) Where an infant is absolutely entitled under the will or on the intestacy of a person dying before or after the commencement of this Act (in this subsection called 'the deceased') to a devise or legacy, or to the residue of the estate of the deceased, or any share therein, and such devise, legacy, residue or share is not

under the will, if any, of the deceased, devised or bequeathed to trustees for the infant, the personal representatives of the deceased may appoint a trust corporation or two or more individuals not exceeding four (whether or not including the personal representatives or one or more of the personal representatives), to be the trustee or trustees of such devise, legacy, residue or share for the infant, and to be trustees of any land devised or any land being or forming part of such residue or share for the purposes of the Settled Land Act, 1925, and of the statutory provisions relating to the management of land during a minority, and may execute or do any assurance or thing requisite for vesting such devise, legacy, residue or share in the trustee or trustees so appointed.

On such appointment the personal representatives, as such, shall be discharged from all further liability in respect of such devise, legacy, residue, or share, and the same may be retained in its existing condition or state of investment, or may be converted into money, and such money may be invested in any authorised investment.

H   APPLICATION TO THE COURT

Trustees may make an application to the court for directions as to the claims of beneficiaries.[96]

(1966) 82 LQR 306 (R.E.M.)

The facts in *Re Allen-Meyrick's Will Trusts* [1966] 1 WLR 499 were simple and elegant. A testatrix gave her residue to trustees in trust to apply the income thereof 'in their absolute discretion for the maintenance of my ... husband', and subject to the exercise of this discretion, she gave the residue in trust for her two godchildren equally. The trustees had made certain payments for the benefit of the husband, who was bankrupt, but had been unable to agree whether any further income should be so applied. In these circumstances, the trustees sought to surrender their discretion to the court, and also sought to have it determined whether their discretion still existed in relation to past accumulations of income.

It is well settled that trustees confronted by a particular problem may surrender their discretion to the court, and so be relieved both of the agony of decision and the responsibility for the result.[97] But it is another matter where it is sought to surrender discretion which is not merely present and confined but prospective and indefinite. The Court of Chancery had a long history of administrative jurisdiction; but it exercised this jurisdiction not on its own investigations but on facts duly put before it in evidence by those concerned. It is not surprising, therefore, that Buckley J refused to accept the proffered general surrender of discretion. Whenever a specific problem arose upon specific facts, the aid of the court could be sought; but that was all. As regards past accumulations of income, the position was simple. The whole of the property, capital and income, belonged to the two godchildren except in so far as the trustees had effectually exercised their discretionary power to apply income to the husband. Trustees must, of course, be unanimous in exercising any

[96] See CPR 1998, Part 64, replacing RSC Order 85.
[97] See *Marley v Mutual Security Merchant Bank and Trust Co Ltd* [1991] 3 All ER 198.

powers vested in them, and so if within a reasonable time of receiving any income they had failed to exercise their discretion in favour of the husband, it ceased to be exercisable, and the godchildren became entitled to it.[98] The principles are old, the facts new, and the result satisfactory.

In **RSPCA v Attorney-General** [2002] 1 WLR 448, LIGHTMAN J said at 462:

There is a stream of authority to the effect there is a distinction between cases where trustees seek the approval by the court of a proposed exercise by them of their discretion and where they surrender their discretion to the court (see e.g. *Re Allen-Meyrick's Will Trusts,* [1966] 1 WLR 499 at 503). In cases where there is a surrender, the court starts with a clean sheet and has an unfettered discretion to decide what it considers should be done in the best interests of the trust. In cases where there is no surrender, the primary focus of the court's attention must be on the views of the trustees and the exercise of discretion proposed by the trustees. Though not fettered by those views, the court is bound to lend weight to them unless tested and found wanting and it will not, without good reason, substitute its own view for those of the trustees. Mr. Henderson, for the Attorney-General, however, submitted that there is no difference between the two situations and that, in both cases, the court is vested with the discretion previously vested in the trustees. In support of this proposition he relies on the speech of Lord Oliver in *Marley v Mutual Security Merchant Bank and Trust Co Ltd* [1991] 3 All ER 198. In that case the trustees entered into a contract for sale whose binding effect was made conditional upon obtaining the prior approval of the court. The question raised for judicial guidance was, rather, the question of fact whether the price agreed was the best price reasonably obtainable than how a discretion should be exercised. Lord Oliver (giving the opinion of the Privy Council) held that, in that case, the trustees had surrendered their discretion to the court and that the court in such a situation was engaged solely in considering what ought to be done in the best interests of the trust and the beneficiaries, and that for that purpose the parties were obliged to put before the court all the material appropriate to enable it to exercise that discretion. By the terms of the contract, the trustees reposed in the court the decision whether the price was such that the contract should become unconditional and be completed. No question arose as to the distinction between a case where there was a surrender of discretion (as was held to have occurred in that case) and a case where there is no such surrender. My view that Lord Oliver's speech lends no support to Mr. Henderson's proposition accords with that expressed by Hart J in *Public Trustees v Cooper* (20 December 1999, unreported).

Law Reform Committee 23rd Report (*The Powers and Duties of Trustees*) 1982 Cmnd 8733, para. 9.1.V.36

36. Where it appears that the cost of taking out a summons is out of all proportion to the amount at stake, trustees should be empowered to take the advice of counsel (in the case of trusts having adult beneficiaries only) or Queen's Counsel practising in the Chancery Division of the High Court or conveyancing counsel of the court (where there are infant beneficiaries) and to distribute on the basis of that advice if no adult beneficiary starts proceedings within 3 months of being sent a copy of the relevant opinion. (paragraph 5.4)[99]

---

[98] Cf. *Re Locker's Settlement Trusts* [1977] 1 WLR 1323, where the trustees' discretion was not extinguished on the lapse of a reasonable time for distribution under an exhaustive discretionary trust.

[99] Cf. a similar use of counsel's advice recommended to deal with possible adverse claims by creditors [p. 718, above]. See Administration of Justice Act (AJA) 1985, s. 48 (power of High Court to authorise

I PAYMENT INTO COURT

TRUSTEE ACT 1925

63. Payment into court by trustees

(1) Trustees, or the majority of trustees, having in their hands or under their control money or securities belonging to a trust, may pay the same into court.[100]

(2) The receipt or certificate of the proper officer shall be a sufficient discharge to trustees for the money or securities so paid into court.

(3) Where money or securities are vested in any persons as trustees, and the majority are desirous of paying the same into court, but the concurrence of the other or others cannot be obtained, the court may order the payment into court to be made by the majority without the concurrence of the other or others.

(4) Where any such money or securities are deposited with any banker, broker, or other depositary, the court may order payment or delivery of the money or securities to the majority of the trustees for the purpose of payment into court.

(5) Every transfer payment and delivery made in pursuance of any such order shall be valid and take effect as if the same had been made on the authority or by the act of all the persons entitled to the money and securities so transferred, paid, or delivered.

(1968) 84 LQR 65 (A.J. Hawkins)

Payment into court, no matter how unjustified, was always effective, to give the trustees a good discharge. As Kindersley V-C said in *Re Lloyd's Trust*,[101] 'the intention of the Trustee Act was for the present relief of trustees'. Relief might prove expensive, but it appears to have been effective to the extent that trustees were relieved of the burden of future administration. The sanction against unjustifiable payment into court was a disallowance of the costs incurred in paying in. Trustees were later condemned in the costs incurred in the payment out to the beneficiaries. In the early cases they were not entitled to costs of the payment in if their actions had been vexatious.[102] Later, they had to justify their actions by showing doubt as to the identity of the beneficiaries, the extent of their interest or their inability to give receipts.[103] 'The legislature did not intend that where the trust was clear, a trustee should pay the fund into court. A trustee cannot pay money into court merely to get rid of a trust he has undertaken to perform, and the Act would lead to greater oppression if it were otherwise.'[104] Furthermore the trustees' doubts should be bona fide. This appears to have meant such doubts as would assail and disturb a practical lawyer, rather than ruffle the academic conscience of eminent conveyancers.[105]

---

action to be taken in reliance on counsel's opinion where any question has arisen out of the terms of a will or a trust).

[100] As amended by AJA 1965, s. 36(4) and Sch. 3.   [101] (1854) 2 WR 371.

[102] *Re Lane's Trust* (1854) 3 WR 134.   [103] *Re Knight's Trusts* (1859) 27 Beav 45.

[104] *Re Knight's Trusts* ibid, at 49, *per* Romilly MR.

[105] In *Re Knight's Trusts* ibid, the fact that trustees acted on counsel's opinion was regretted but made no difference to their liability. In *Re Cull's Trusts* (1875) LR 20 Eq 561 the particular trustees were protected having taken counsel's opinion, but Jessel MR added 'the next set of trustees who come before me having so acted must pay costs'.

What is the effect of payment in? Clearly, payment into court does operate as a discharge of trustees. In other words, by paying in the trustees retire from the trust.[106] They will, of course, still be liable for any breaches of trust in the past[107] and responsible for any money that should come into their hands in the future.[108] Apparently, they also remain trustees for the purposes of receiving notices relating to dealings with the trust funds.[109] Subject to these two matters, however, new trustees can be appointed, either by the persons nominated as appointors in the trust instrument,[110] or by the Court.[111]

VI DUTY TO ACT IMPARTIALLY BETWEEN LIFE TENANT AND REMAINDERMAN[112]

It is the duty of a trustee to act in the interests of all the beneficiaries. Where there are beneficiaries whose interests conflict, as in the case of life tenant and remainderman, the trustee, acting in the general interests of all, must act impartially between them.[113]

Nowhere is this duty of greater significance than in the selection of investments. Some investments, for example, will produce a good income stream but with poor capital growth. These investments would be preferred by the life tenant. The remainderman, however, would benefit more from those investments which have a prospect of substantial future growth rather than producing a good income stream in the short term, such as a new and developing business.

A GENERAL DUTY

In the Court of Appeal in **Nestlé v National Westminster Bank plc** [1993] 1 WLR 1260 [p. 702, above], STAUGHTON LJ said at 1279:

The obligation of a trustee is to administer the trust fund impartially, or fairly (I can see no significant difference), having regard to the different interests of beneficiaries. Wilberforce J said in *Re Pauling's Settlement Trusts (No 2)* [1963] Ch 576, 586:

'The new trustees would be under the normal duty of preserving an equitable balance, and if at any time it was shown they were inclining one way or the other, it would not be a difficult matter to bring them to account.'

---

[106] *Re Williams' Settlement* (1858) 4 K & J 87.   [107] *Barker v Peile* (1865) 2 Drew & Sm 340.
[108] *Re Nettlefold's Trusts* (1888) 59 LT 315.
[109] *Thompson v Tomkins* (1862) 2 Drew & Sm 8, and see also *Warburton v Hill* (1854) Kay 470.
[110] *Re Bailey's Trust* (1854) 3 WR 31.
[111] 13 & 14 Vict. c.60, ss. 32 and 33, replaced with significant changes by ss. 25 and 37 of the Trustee Act 1893. See now ss. 41 and 43 of the Trustee Act 1925. See p. 634, above.
[112] H&M, pp. 561–569; Lewin, pp. 861–916; P&M, pp. 653–671; P&S, pp. 388–393, 594–596; Pettit, pp. 428–441; Snell, pp. 644–649; T&H, pp. 313–319; U&H, pp. 656–694.
[113] On the general duty to act impartially, see *Lloyds Bank plc v Duker* [1987] 1 WLR 1324; *Nestlé v National Westminster Bank plc* (29 June 1988, unreported) (Hoffmann J) (1996) [2000] WTLR 795, below].

At times it will not be easy to decide what is an equitable balance. A life tenant may be anxious to receive the highest possible income, whilst the remainderman will wish the real value of the trust fund to be preserved. If the life tenant is living in penury and the remainderman already has ample wealth, common sense suggests that a trustee should be able to take that into account, not necessarily by seeking the highest possible income at the expense of capital but by inclining in that direction. However, before adopting that course a trustee should, I think, require some verification of the facts. In this case the trustees did not, so far as I am aware, have any reliable information as to the relative wealth of the life tenants and the plaintiff. They did send an official to interview Mr. John Nestlé[114] in Cyprus on one occasion; but the information which they obtained was conflicting and (as it turned out) incomplete.

Similarly I would not regard it as a breach of trust for the trustees to pay some regard to the relationship between Mr. George Nestlé and the plaintiff. He was merely her uncle, and she would have received nothing from his share of the fund if he had fathered a child who survived him. The trustees would be entitled, in my view, to incline towards income during his life tenancy and that of his widow, on that ground. Again common sense suggests to me that such a course might be appropriate, and I do not think that it would be a breach of the duty to act fairly, or impartially.

The dominant consideration for the trustees, however, was that George's fund from 1960, and John's from 1969, would not be subject to United Kingdom Income Tax in so far as it was invested in exempt gilts. That was a factor which the trustees were entitled—and I would say bound—to take into account. A beneficiary who has been left a life interest in a trust fund has an arguable case for saying that he should not be compelled to bear tax on the income if he is not lawfully obliged to do so.

It was no more than a factor for the trustees to bear in mind, and would rarely justify more than a modest degree of preference for income paid gross over capital growth.

A trustee should also bear in mind, as the trustees did, that Estate Duty or Capital Transfer Tax is likely to be reduced in such a case if part of the fund is invested in tax-exempt gilts. That may provide a compensating benefit for the remainderman. Of course it is by no means certain that the benefit will materialise; the life tenant may return to this country, as happened in the case of Mrs. Elsie Nestlé. It has been said that nothing in this world is certain except death and taxes. But even the tax benefit was imponderable, since it could not be forecast what rate of tax would be applicable on the death of a life tenant.

At first instance in **Nestlé v National Westminster Bank plc** (29 June, 1988, [2000] WTLR 795, HOFFMANN J said:

There was no dispute over the general principles to be applied. First, there is the prudence principle. The classic statement is that of Lindley LJ (*Re Whiteley* (1886) 33 Ch D 347 at 355):

> 'The duty of a trustee is not to take such care only as a prudent man would take if he had only himself to consider, the duty rather is to take such care as the ordinary prudent man would take if he were minded to make an investment for the benefit of other people for whom he felt morally bound to provide.'[115]

This is an extremely flexible standard capable of adaptation to current economic conditions and contemporary understanding of markets and investments, for example, investments which

---

[114] A life tenant.   [115] Now see the statutory duty of care: TA 2000, s. 1, see p. 687, above.

were imprudent in the days of the gold standard may be sound and sensible in times of high inflation. Modern trustees acting within their investment powers are entitled to be judged by the standards of current portfolio theory, which emphasises the risk level of the entire portfolio rather than the risk attaching to each investment taken in isolation. (This is not to say that losses on investments made in breach of trust can be set off against gains in the rest of the portfolio but only that an investment which in isolation is too risky and therefore in breach of trust may be justified when held in conjunction with other investments. See Jeffrey N. Gordon, 'The Puzzling Persistence of the Constrained Prudent Man Rule' (1987) 62 *New York University Law Review* 52). But in reviewing the conduct of trustees over a period of more than 60 years, one must be careful not to endow the prudent trustee with prophetic vision or expect him to have ignored the received wisdom of his time.

Mr. Gerard Wright, who appeared for Miss Nestlé, referred me to another passage in *Re Whiteley* at 350 in which Cotton LJ said:

> 'Trustees are bound to preserve the money for those entitled to the corpus in remainder, and they are bound to invest it in such a way as will produce a reasonable income for those enjoying the income for the present.'

In 1886 what Cotton LJ had in mind was the safety of the capital in purely monetary terms. But Mr. Wright submitted that in the conditions which prevail a century later, the trustees were under an overriding duty to preserve the real value of the capital. In my judgment this cannot be right. The preservation of the monetary value of the capital requires no skill or luck. The trustees can discharge their duties, as they often did until 1961, by investing the whole fund in gilt-edged securities. Preservation of real values can be no more than an aspiration which some trustees may have the good fortune to achieve. Plainly they must have regard to the interests of those entitled in the future to capital and such regard will require them to take into consideration the potential effects of inflation, but a rule that real capital values must be maintained would be unfair to both income beneficiaries and trustees.

This brings me to the second principle on which there was general agreement, namely that the trustee must act fairly in making investment decisions which may have different consequences for different classes of beneficiaries. There are two reasons why I prefer this formulation to the traditional image of holding the scales equally between tenant for life and remainderman. The first is that the image of the scales suggests a weighing of known quantities whereas investment decisions are concerned with predictions of the future. Investments will carry current expectations of their future income yield and capital appreciation and these expectations will be reflected in their current market price, but there is always a greater or lesser risk that the outcome will deviate from those expectations. A judgment on the fairness of the choices made by the trustees must have regard to these imponderables. The second reason is that the image of the scales suggests a more mechanistic process than I believe the law requires. The trustees have in my judgment a wide discretion. They are for example entitled to take into account the income needs of the tenant for life or the fact that the tenant for life was a person known to the settlor or a stranger. Of course these cannot be allowed to become the overriding considerations but the concept of fairness between classes of beneficiaries does not require them to be excluded. It would be an inhuman law which required trustees to adhere to some mechanical rule for preserving the real value of the capital when the tenant for life was the testator's widow who had fallen upon hard times and the remainderman was young and well-off.

Where trustees have a discretionary power to choose between different classes of beneficiary than the duty to act impartially is not applicable. In **Edge v Pensions Ombudsman** [2000] Ch 602, CHADWICK LJ said at 627:

Properly understood, the so-called duty to act impartially—on which the ombudsman placed such reliance—is no more than the ordinary duty which the law imposes on a person who is entrusted with the exercise of a discretionary power: that he exercises the power for the purpose for which it is given, giving proper consideration to the matters which are relevant and excluding from consideration matters which are irrelevant. If pension fund trustees[116] do that, they cannot be criticised if they reach a decision which appears to prefer the claims of one interest—whether that of employers, current employers or pensioners—over others. The preference will be the result of a proper exercise of the discretionary power.

(1943) 7 Conv (NS) 128 (S.J. Bailey)

In ordinary circumstances, when property has been settled upon trust for A for life, and thereafter for B absolutely, the whole of the net income derived from the property until A dies is payable to him. Such is his right, neither more nor less. Though this income be abnormally high, nothing of it is held back for the benefit of B. Though it be abnormally low or non-existent, neither A nor his executors after him has any right to claim a compensation out of the capital value of the property or out of any enhanced income it may yield after he dies. So long as the trust comprises property which produces an abnormally low or high income, any incidental hardship to A or B must be borne. But if the trustees have the power to dispose of that particular property and reinvest in something which will produce a more fair and steady income, this inequitable state of affairs will cease if and when they choose to do so.[117] It is perhaps surprising that equity has not cast upon trustees, in every such case, a duty to convert the trust property as soon as practicable into something more likely to produce an equitable result. One might have expected further, perhaps, that in every such case equity would require the trustees to make some financial adjustment, as between the beneficiaries, to cover the intervening period during which the desired conversion is delayed. In fact, however, equity does not ordinarily intervene in these cases; but to this there are three celebrated exceptions. The three exceptions have much in common: they apply only where the trust is created by will, and only in so far as the property comprised in the trust is the residuary personal estate of the testator; and they are said to rest upon his presumed intention to deal evenly with the beneficiaries under the trust. This is no doubt the reason why they are often grouped together, and described as the rule in *Howe v Lord Dartmouth*.[118] In origin, however, they are three distinct rules: (i) the rule in *Gibson v Bott*,[119] (ii) the rule in *Howe v Lord Dartmouth*; and (iii) the rule in *Re Chesterfield's Trusts*.[120] Of these,

---

[116] The case concerned pension fund trustees, but the principle is of general application.

[117] The so-called equitable duty of trustees 'to hold the scales evenly between the beneficiaries' does not ordinarily appear to compel them to realise and reinvest in such a case: see *Re Courtier* (1886) 34 Ch D 136; *Re Searle* [1900] 2 Ch 829 at 834 ('if the estate produces nothing, the tenant for life can get nothing'), *per* Kekewich J. On the other hand, when trustees do exercise a power to invest they must not allow themselves to be persuaded into an investment prejudicial to one beneficiary, in order to benefit another of their beneficiaries: *Raby v Ridehalgh* (1855) 7 De GM & G 104.

[118] (1802) 7 Ves 137. See, e.g., *Macdonald v Irvine* (1878) 8 Ch D 101 at 112, *per* Baggallay LJ.

[119] (1802) 7 Ves 89.

[120] (1883) 24 Ch D 643. Note that the judgment of Simonds J in *Re Woodhouse* [1941] Ch 332, which finally decided that this rule has no application to trusts of real estate, was based in part on the fact that the other two rules do not apply to real estate. And the learned Judge, throughout his judgment, treated the three rules

rules (i) and (ii) operate chiefly to prevent a life tenant from obtaining an unjust advantage to the detriment of the remainderman,[121] whilst rule (iii) operates in the reverse direction in order to prevent an injustice to the tenant for life.

B   THE RULE IN *HOWE V LORD DARTMOUTH*[122]

(i) *Duty to convert*

A duty to convert the trust fund into authorised investments by sale and reinvestment may be imposed by statute;[123] or by the trust instrument; or by the Rule in *Howe v Lord Dartmouth.*

Lewin on Trusts (18th edn, 2008), p. 894

The first branch of the rule in *Howe v Lord Dartmouth* may be stated in outline as follows:
  'If a testator gives his residuary personal estate in trust for, or directly to, persons in succession without imposing a trust for sale and it comprises wasting assets or unauthorised investments then, unless the tenant for life can show that the testator meant him to enjoy the income of those assets or investments in specie, they must be sold and the proceeds invested in authorised securities.'
  A trustee who breaks the rule is liable for breach of trust.[124] The first branch of the rule therefore imposes an implied trust for sale.

(ii) *Duty of apportionment pending conversion*
Lewin on Trusts (18th edn, 2008), pp. 902–903, 905, 906[125]

The rule in *Howe v Lord Dartmouth* has a second branch. This applies, in the absence of a contrary intention, where for any reason (be it a trust for sale expressed in the trust instrument or imposed by statute or implied by the first branch of the rule) personal property which is held on trust for persons in succession ought to have been sold. When the second branch of the rule applies then, as between tenant for life and remainderman, the property concerned must be treated as if it had been sold and the proceeds reinvested in authorised investments; the life tenant is entitled to the fair equivalent of the income he would have received if that had been done, but no more. . . .[126]

as distinct from one another. 'This is an equitable rule established by this Court in order to deal fairly in the administration of estates between persons having successive interests in a residuary estate. It is a rule of administration which, in my judgment, is to be regarded as complementary to other rules of administration established also to do justice as between persons entitled to successive interests, as, for example, the rule in *Howe v Earl of Dartmouth*': *Re Woodhouse* [1941] Ch 332 at 334–335.

[121] 'It has recently been made clear, in *Re Fawcett* [1940] Ch 402, that these two rules may also operate to prevent injustice to the life tenant.'
[122] (1802) 7 Ves 137. See (1943) 7 Conv (NS) 128, 191 (S.J. Bailey); (1952) 16 Conv (NS) 349 (L.A. Sheridan); (1981) 59 *Canadian Bar Review* 687 (J. Smith).
[123] Administration of Estates Act 1925, s. 33. as amended by TLATA 1996, Sch. 2, (now a power, rather than a duty, to sell an intestate's assets).   [124] Footnotes omitted.
[125] See also Trust Law Commission, *Capital and Income of Trusts* (Consultation Paper) (1998), pp. 8–9.
[126] Footnotes omitted.

Calculation of the 'fair equivalent'

Where the second branch of the rule applies, the life tenant is entitled before conversion to the fair equivalent of the income he would have enjoyed if conversion had taken place, that is, he is given interest on the value of the unconverted property....

The interest is to be calculated on the value of the assets on the first anniversary of the testator's death[127] unless they are sold within that year, when the interest is calculated on the amount they fetched,[128] or unless there is a power to postpone sale, when for want of any better date the assets are to be valued at the date of death.[129]

Whenever the interest is calculated it runs from the testator's death to the date on which the asset is sold.[130]

In **Re Fawcett**[131] [1940] Ch 402, a testatrix bequeathed her residuary estate, which contained unauthorised investments, upon trust to pay the income to her nieces and nephews in equal shares for their lives, and after their death to divide the capital money among their children on attaining the age of 21. In holding that the rule in *Howe v Lord Dartmouth* applied, FARWELL J made an order as follows:

In answer to question 2 of the summons I will make a declaration that (a) in the case of unauthorised investments which were still retained unsold at the end of one year from the death of the testatrix the life tenants were and are entitled to interest at the rate of 4 per cent per annum on the value of such investments taken at the end of such year but commencing from the date of the death and running on until the realisation of such investments respectively; (b) in the case of unauthorised investments realised during the first year after the death of the testatrix the life tenants are entitled to interest at the rate aforesaid on the net proceeds of such realisation respectively from the date of the death down to the respective dates of completions of such realisations; (c) the unauthorised investments for the time being unsold ought to be taken *en bloc* as one aggregate for the purposes of the rule in *Howe v Lord Dartmouth* (1802) 7 Ves 137; (d) in applying that rule the Apportionment Act, 1870, ought not to be applied in the income accounts at the death of the testatrix or at the beginning or end of any accounting period with reference to the income of unauthorised investments; (e) any excess of income from unauthorised investments beyond the interest payable in respect of such investments to the life tenants ought to be invested in authorised investments as part of the capital with the other authorised investments, and accordingly the whole of the actual subsequent income of such invested excess income is payable as income; (f) the interest so payable in respect of unauthorised investments was and is payable out of moneys being income from unauthorised investments or, so far as such income is insufficient, being proceeds of realisation of such investments, and any interest so payable for the time being in arrears is payable (but calculated as simple interest only) out of subsequent income from unauthorised investments which are for the time being retained and out of the proceeds of sale of such investments as and when realised, but neither any excess income from unauthorised investments, which at the end of any accounting period is available under head (e) for investment in authorised investments, nor any proceeds of realisation of

---

[127] *Re Fawcett* [1940] Ch 402, especially at 407 and 409, para. (a).

[128] *Re Fawcett*, ibid, especially at 409, para. (b).   [129] *Re Parry* [1947] Ch 23.

[130] *Re Fawcett*, note 128 above; *Re Parry*, ibid.

[131] For details of calculation and accounting, see Josling, *Apportionments for Executors and Trustees* (4th edn, 1976) pp. 34–39.

unauthorised investments not required at the date of realisation to pay interest payable as aforesaid for the time being in arrears and accordingly available to be invested in authorised investments, were or are applicable towards payment of subsequently accruing interest as aforesaid in respect of unauthorised investments then still retained.

(iii) Exclusion

The duty to convert or to apportion may be excluded by appropriate language in the will. The exclusion of the duty to convert necessarily excludes the duty to apportion. But the testator might desire the property to be converted, but still allow the life tenant the whole income pending conversion. There has been much litigation to determine these questions.[132] It is usual now to provide expressly for the exclusion of both duties.

Key & Elphinstone: *Precedents in Conveyancing* (15th edn, 1953), vol. 2, p. 926

CONVERSION AND INVESTMENT

1.   UPON trust that my trustees shall sell, call in, collect and convert into money the said real and personal property at such time or times, and in such manner as they shall think fit (but as to reversionary property not until it falls into possession, unless it shall appear to my trustees that an earlier sale would be beneficial), with power to postpone the sale, calling in or conversion of the whole or any part or parts of the said property [including leaseholds or other property of a terminable hazardous or wasting nature] during such period as they shall think proper, and to retain the same or any part thereof in its actual form of investment, without being responsible for loss. And I direct that the income of such of the same premises as for the time being shall remain unsold shall as well during the first year after my death as afterwards be applied as if the same were income arising from investments hereinafter directed to be made of the proceeds of sale thereof, and that no reversionary or other property not actually producing income shall be treated as producing income for the purposes of this my will.[133]

(iv) The rule today

Hanbury & Martin: *Modern Equity* (17th edn, 2005), p. 560

The rules relating to conversion and apportionment demonstrate basic principles of equity. But they should be understood in their proper perspective.

   (a) *Exclusion of Duty to Apportion*. The duty to apportion is in practice nearly always excluded, both in respect of income from unauthorised securities and in respect of reversionary interests. The duty to convert, where it exists, thus appears in the context of a duty to change the investments.

---

[132] Pettit, pp. 428–429; Snell, pp. 645–646; [1999] Conv 84, 98–103 (R. Mitchell).
[133] Footnotes omitted.

(b) *Effect of Current Investment Situation.* The utility of the rules of conversion and apportionment varies according to the current investment situation:

'The dividend yield on the shares in the most regarded index of 100 leading equities has for years been far less than the interest yield obtainable on medium-dated fixed-interest government stock. In present-day circumstances, retaining unauthorised equities therefore tends to depress the life tenant's income, whereas when *Howe v Dartmouth* was decided the effect was the opposite. It no longer makes sense to say that the income of a life tenant from a fund of unauthorised equities ought to be limited to the yield of government stocks, since that would usually be higher, not lower.'[134]

Thus the life tenant wants fixed interest investments when they provide a high income; the remainderman wants unauthorised securities for the preservation of the real value of the capital. It is the life tenant who will be pressing the trustees to convert urgently into gilt-edged securities at times when they can bring an income in excess of the mere four per cent allowed to the life tenant by the rule of apportionment.

C REVERSIONARY INTERESTS

The problem which has been considered so far related to wasting and hazardous securities which may be expected to produce too high an income for the life tenant, and to leave unprotected the remainderman's interest in the capital. The converse problem is that of a reversionary interest; that is to say one which is not yet an interest in possession.

Assume that a fund of £500,000 is held on trust for A for life, remainder to B absolutely. A is entitled to the income, and B, on A's death, to the capital. B dies before A, leaving his estate to Mrs. B for life with remainder to his children. The capital of B's testamentary trust is a valuable reversionary interest, its value depending, of course, on A's age and state of health, and also upon the total value of other transfers of capital made by A *inter vivos* or upon his death.

However that may be, the corpus of B's testamentary trust is a valuable reversionary interest which is producing no income. It could of course be sold, and the proceeds of sale invested. But it is obvious, because of all the uncertainties involved, that it is difficult for the trustees to obtain a satisfactory price; usually it is uneconomical to sell a reversionary interest. If Mrs. B needs the income, something will have to be done, whether by selling, or by borrowing against the security of the fund, or by some other method.

Unless the reversionary interest is immediately sold and the proceeds reinvested the problem arises of apportioning the value of the reversionary interest. The solution is to take the value of the reversionary interest when it falls in (or when it is sold), and then calculate backwards to see what sum, if available at B's death, and if used to pay a reasonable income to Mrs. B until the date when the reversionary interest actually

---

[134] Trust Law Committee Consultation Paper, *Capital and Income of Trusts* (1998).

becomes available, would have produced the capital sum now available. That sum is notionally the capital of the fund. The children are entitled to that. Mrs. B, who has had no income in the meantime, is entitled to the balance.

In **Re Earl of Chesterfield's Trusts** (1883) 24 Ch D 643, CHITTY J ordered the apportionment of a reversionary interest between life tenant and remainderman as follows:

Upon the petition &c, this Court is of opinion that the [reversionary] moneys are apportionable between principal and income by ascertaining the respective sums which, put out at 4 per cent per annum on the [date of death of the testator] and accumulating at compound interest calculated at that rate with yearly rests, and deducting Income Tax, would, with the accumulations of interest, have produced, at the respective dates of receipt, the amounts actually received; and that the aggregate of the sums so ascertained ought to be treated as principal and be applied accordingly, and the residue should be treated as income.

Trust Law Committee: *Capital and Income of Trusts* (Consultation Paper) (1998), p. 9

The Rule in *Re Chesterfield's Trusts*[135] is another equitable apportionment rule, in this case apportioning capital receipts between capital and income beneficiaries. It applies where a testator is entitled to future or reversionary property, pure personalty, not currently yielding income, and directs it to be sold, but leaves the time of sale to the discretion of the trustees, who decline to sell until it falls into possession. The rule requires a calculation to be made to ascertain the sum which, put out at interest on the day of the testator's death, and accumulating at compound interest with yearly rests, would, together with such interest and accumulations, after deducting income tax, amount on the day when the reversion falls in or is realised to the sum actually received. Only the sum so ascertained is treated as capital, and the balance of the amount actually received goes to the income beneficiary. Again, in the latest authority the rate of interest used was 4 per cent. The rule has been applied to arrears of an annuity with interest, money payable on a life policy,[136] stock in a gas company at a premium,[137] a reversionary interest which had been retained unconverted although it happened to be expectant on the death of the tenant for life of residue,[138] instalments of purchase-money payable over a number of years,[139] a debt recovered without interest,[140] and where settlement income went back on a resulting trust to the settlor's estate.[141] The rule does not apply to settlements by deed, and probably only applies to gifts by will of residuary personal estate as one fund to be enjoyed by persons in succession.[142] It can be excluded by an appropriate declaration in the will....

Turning now to consider the way in which the Rules in *Howe v Lord Dartmouth* and *Re Chesterfield's Trusts* operate in practice at the present day, perhaps the first thing to note is that the sums involved are small. They are often, perhaps usually, so small as not to be worth

---

135 (1883) 24 Ch D 643.
136 *Re Morley* [1895] 2 Ch 738.
137 *Re Eaton* [1894] WN 95.
138 *Re Hobson* (1885) 55 LJ Ch 422.
139 *Re Hollebone* [1919] 2 Ch 93.
140 *Re Duke of Cleveland's Estate* [1895] 2 Ch 542.
141 *Re Guinness's Settlement* [1966] 1 WLR 1355.
142 *Re Van Straubenzee* [1901] 2 Ch 779 at 782; *Re Woodhouse* [1941] Ch 332.

the cost of the professional time involved in the calculations needed for the trustees or personal representatives to carry out their duties of apportionment.

A particular defect of the Rules in *Howe v Dartmouth* and *Re Chesterfield's Trusts* is that, though the rate of interest to be used is a vitally important factor, trustees, personal representatives and beneficiaries are left in doubt as to what rate of interest should be used... in the latest authorities on each of the Rules the rate of interest used was 4 per cent. But the latest authority on *Howe v Dartmouth* was in decided in 1961[143] and the latest authority on *Re Chesterfield's Trusts* was decided in 1940,[144] the rate had been changed before, most recently from 4 to 3 per cent in 1895[145] and back to 4 per cent in 1920[146] and Romer J indicated in 1947 that, if at the relevant time interest rates generally had changed so materially and for so long as to justify an alteration in the rate, the rate used would be altered.[147] The interest rates obtainable on government stocks have stood well above 4 per cent for decades, so it seems clear that an increase in the rate, even to as much as 6 per cent,[148] would be justified, but no one has apparently sought a decision on the point, presumably because the amounts involved have not justified the cost. Trustees, personal representatives and beneficiaries are left in doubt, but the expense of applying to the court to determine the proper rate for trustees and personal representatives to use in carrying out their duty to make an apportionment cannot be justified in view of the smallness of the sums involved.

D   THE RULE IN *ALLHUSEN V WHITTELL*[149]

Where the testator leaves debts which are not paid immediately out of his estate, the tenant for life receives interest on capital in fact required for the payment of those debts. In a calculation often involving minute amounts of money, that part of his income so required has to be deducted. The rule may be excluded by contrary intention, or when its application would be inappropriate in the circumstances.[150]

In **Corbett v Inland Revenue Commissioners** [1938] 1 KB 567, ROMER LJ said at 584:

For the purpose of adjusting rights as between the tenant for life and the remainderman of a residuary estate, debts, legacies, estate duties, probate duties and so forth are to be deemed to have been paid out of such capital of the testator's estate as will be sufficient for that purpose, when to that capital is added interest on that capital from the date of the testator's death to the date of the payment of the legacy or debt, or whatever it may have been, interest being calculated at the average rate of interest[151] earned by the testator's estate during the relevant period.

---

[143] *Re Berry* reported at [1962] Ch 97.   [144] *Re Fawcett* [1940] Ch 402. See p. 730, above.
[145] *Re Goodenough* [1895] 2 Ch 537.   [146] *Re Beech* [1920] 1 Ch 40; *Re Baker* [1924] 2 Ch 271.
[147] *Re Parry* [1947] Ch 23 at 46, 47.
[148] The rate of interest on legacies under RSC Ord. 44, r. 10 [now see CPR, Sch. 1] since 1983, cf. Trustee Act 1925, s. 31(3)—where 5 per cent is used for a not very different purpose.
[149] (1867) LR 4 Eq 295. See Trust Law Committee, *Capital and Income of Trusts* (Consultation Paper) (1998), pp. 12–14.   [150] *Re McEuen* [1913] 2 Ch 704; *Re Darby* [1939] Ch 905.
[151] *Re Wills* [1915] 1 Ch 769; *Re Oldham* (1927) 71 Sol Jo 491.

E LAW REFORM

Law Commission, *Capital and Income in Trusts: Classification and Apportionment* (Law Com. C.P., 175, 2004): Executive Summary, paras. 7–18[152]

Allocating receipts and expenses to balance competing interests

7.   The current duty of trustees to balance the competing interests of income and capital beneficiaries ('the duty to balance') rests on the fundamental equitable principle of impartiality. The existing equitable rules of apportionment are underpinned by this fundamental principle and exist in order to achieve a balance in the limited circumstances in which they apply.

8.   We consider that the duty to balance should continue to be recognised as fundamental and we ask consultees whether or not the duty should be placed on a statutory footing. By this we mean whether its existence should be laid down in statute: we do not propose that statute should set out a list of factors relevant to the meaning of 'balance'. We propose that the duty to balance should, in any event, continue to be capable of exclusion or modification by the terms of the trust (either expressly or by necessary implication).

9.   Under the law as it stands, the duty to balance is of primary significance to trustees when they exercise their powers of investment. In order to discharge the duty to balance, trustees must select investments which they reasonably expect to deliver investment returns in a form which balances the interests of income and capital beneficiaries. Trustees would, in many cases, be able to achieve increased investment returns (to the advantage of all the beneficiaries) if they could select investments without concern for the form which returns were likely to take (that is to say, whether those returns would be classified as income or capital).

10.   This 'total return' approach to investment can be achieved by giving trustees the power to allocate investment returns, subsequent to their receipt, between income and capital. We therefore propose that a new statutory power of allocation should be made available to trustees, exercisable by them insofar as it is necessary to discharge the duty to balance (and for no other purpose).

11.   We recognise that some settlors and trustees might be concerned about the administrative burdens inherent in such a power and also that, if the power were implied into all trusts by default, some trustees might not be aware of its availability. We therefore ask consultees whether the power of allocation should be available on an 'opt-in' or 'opt-out' basis.

12.   Where the power of allocation is available the rules of classification would only operate by default. A power of allocation would therefore also have the advantage of allowing trustees to adjust the classification of trust receipts and expenses if the proposed rules of classification produced an unjust or illogical result.

13.   The effect of trustees exercising the statutory power would be to allocate particular receipts or expenses to income or capital. The power of allocation would only be available for a specified period after the date of the particular receipt or expense. If trustees failed to make a decision to allocate within that time limit, then the default classification, based upon the rules we have outlined above, would become final and conclusive.

---

[152] See also Law Reform Committee 23rd Report (1982); Trust Law Committee Consultation Paper, *Capital and Income of Trusts* (1998).

14.   The proposed power of allocation would be an administrative power. It is intended to facilitate the internal administration of the trust and to enable trustees to discharge their over-riding duty to balance. We therefore consider that trustees should not be entitled to take into account the personal circumstances of the beneficiaries when deciding where a proper balance lies in order to exercise the power of allocation. We believe that allowing the meaning of bal-ance to be influenced by personal circumstances would provoke legal uncertainty, increase the likelihood of litigation by beneficiaries against trustees and have a potentially adverse impact on the tax treatment of trusts containing the power of allocation.

15.   We accept that this approach to the personal circumstances of beneficiaries sits some-what uneasily with the prevailing judicial guidance on the meaning of the duty to balance in the context of trustee investment (see *Nestlé v National Westminster Bank* [1993] 1 WLR 1260 (CA); [2000] WTLR 795 (Hoffmann J)). We therefore discuss whether it is necessary to dis-tinguish the duties relevant when investment policy is being formulated from those applicable when investment returns are being allocated to income or capital.

16.   We propose that an action for breach of trust should, in principle, lie against defaulting trustees in the event of a failure to discharge the duty to balance. The exercise or non-exercise of the statutory power of allocation should also be subject to review by the courts on the same basis as any other discretionary power conferred upon trustees. We consider, however, that the likelihood of a trustee being fixed with personal liability for breach of trust in this context is low. We anticipate that most disagreements would be resolved through further exercise of the power of allocation to restore a balance, without resort to formal methods of dispute resolution.

Rules of apportionment

17.   The existing equitable rules of apportionment are intended to give effect to the general equitable principle of impartiality. Although the rules largely achieve a defensible result in the limited circumstances where they do apply, they do not apply in every situation where appor-tionment would be necessary to balance the interests of income and capital beneficiaries. They are also unduly rigid and technical. We believe the potential availability of a statutory power of allocation for trust receipts and expenses informed by the duty to balance would render recourse to the equitable rules unnecessary. We therefore propose that all the existing equit-able rules of apportionment should be abrogated.

18.   The rule set out in section 2 of the Apportionment Act 1870 has long been criticised as being inconvenient and unfair in its application to trusts. Insofar as this statutory rule applies to trusts, we provisionally propose (unless a contrary intention is expressed in the terms of the trust) that it should be replaced by a statutory power to apportion to the extent that the trustees, in their absolute discretion, deem it just and expedient.

QUESTIONS

1. Consider the various contexts (in addition to those here discussed) in which it is necessary to make a distinction between income and capital. For example:
   (a) for the payment of income tax in respect of dividends earned partly before and partly after the death of the life tenant. Apportionment Act 1870,

section 2; Josling: *Apportionments for Executors and Trustees* (4th edn, 1976), pp. 4–10; H&M, pp. 566–567.

(b) for the treatment of distributions by companies as capital distributions or as dividends: *Bouch v Sproule* (1887) 12 App Cas 385; (1975) 39 Conv (NS) 355 (W.H. Goodhart); *Re Sechiari* [1950] 1 All ER 417; *Re Kleinwort's Settlements* [1951] Ch 860; *Re Rudd's Will Trusts* [1952] 1 All ER 254; (1953) 17 Conv (NS) 22 (A.J. Bland); *Re Malam* [1894] 3 Ch 578; *Re Lee* [1993] 3 All ER 926; [1993] All ER Rev 417 (C.H. Sherrin); (1995) 9 *Trust Law International* 55 (P. Duffield); H&M, pp. 568–569; P&S, pp. 392–393; Law Commission CP 175 (2004), paras. 5.6–5.12.

(c) for the allocation to income or capital dividends when sold and purchased by trustees cum dividend: *Scholefield v Redfern* (1863) 2 Drew & Sm 173; *Freman v Whitbread* (1865) LR 1 Eq 266; *Bulkeley v Stephens* [1896] 2 Ch 241; *Re Henderson* [1940] Ch 368; *Re Maclaren's Settlement Trusts* [1951] 2 All ER 414 at 420; *Re Ellerman's Settlement Trusts* [1984] LS Gaz R 430; (1986) 1 *Trust Law and Practice* 62 (I. Pittaway); Underhill and Hayton, pp. 510–511; H&M, p. 568; Law Commission CP 175 (2004), paras. 3.64–3.71.

(d) for the allocation of the proceeds of sale of mortgaged property where the monies are insufficient to repay in full: *Re Atkinson* [1904] 2 Ch 160, H&M, pp. 567–568.

(e) for the allocation of interest awarded for non-receipt from a trustee of money that ought to have been received: *Bartlett v Barclays Bank Trust Co Ltd (No 2)* [1980] Ch 515 [p. 968, below].

2. How important is the rule in *Howe v Lord Dartmouth* today after the enactment of Part II of the Trustee Act 2000? See p. 692, above.

VII DUTY IN RESPECT OF ACCOUNTS AND AUDIT[153]

A trustee must keep accounts of the trust and disclose them to the beneficiaries as requested.[154] Commonly, copies are given to the beneficiaries, but strictly a beneficiary is only entitled to a copy if he pays for it.

---

[153] H&M, pp. 569–570; Lewin, p. 1375; P&M, pp. 672–673; P&S, pp. 712–714; Pettit, p. 379–400; Snell, p. 651; T&H, pp. 354–358; U&H, pp. 818–827. For the duty of charitable trustees to account, see pp. 614, above.

[154] *Pearse v Green* (1819) 1 Jac & W 135 at 140, *per* Plumer MR.

TRUSTEE ACT 1925

22. Reversionary interests, valuations, and audit

(4) Trustees may, in their absolute discretion, from time to time, but not more than once in every three years unless the nature of the trust or any special dealings with the trust property make a more frequent exercise of the right reasonable, cause the accounts of the trust property to be examined or audited by an independent accountant, and shall, for that purpose, produce such vouchers and give such information to him as he may require; and the costs of such examination or audit, including the fee of the auditor, shall be paid out of the capital or income of the trust property, or partly in one way and partly in the other, as the trustees, in their absolute discretion, think fit, but, in default of any direction by the trustees to the contrary in any special case, costs attributable to capital shall be borne by capital and those attributable to income by income.

PUBLIC TRUSTEE ACT 1906

13. Investigation and audit of trust accounts[155]

(1) Subject to rules under this Act and unless the court otherwise orders, the condition and accounts of any trust shall, on an application being made and notice thereof given in the prescribed manner by any trustee or beneficiary, be investigated and audited by such solicitor or public accountant as may be agreed on by the applicant and the trustees or, in default of agreement, by the public trustee or some person appointed by him:

Provided that (except with the leave of the court) such an investigation or audit shall not be required within twelve months after any such previous investigation or audit, and that a trustee or beneficiary shall not be appointed under this section to make an investigation or audit.

(2) The person making the investigation or audit (hereinafter called the auditor) shall have a right of access to the books, accounts, and vouchers of the trustees, and to any securities and documents of title held by them on account of the trust, and may require from them such information and explanation as may be necessary for the performance of his duties, and upon the completion of the investigation and audit shall forward to the applicant and to every trustee a copy of the accounts, together with a report thereon, and a certificate signed by him to the effect that the accounts exhibit a true view of the state of the affairs of the trust and that he has had the securities of the trust fund investments produced to and verified by him or (as the case may be) that such accounts are deficient in such respects as may be specified in such certificate.

---

[155] See Public Trustee Rules 1912, rr. 31–37. Law Reform Committee 23rd Report (*The Powers and Duties of Trustees*) 1982 Cmnd 8733, para. 9.48 recommends the abolition of s. 13. It is only occasionally used and contains no powers to enforce the findings of the Public Trustee.

(3) Every beneficiary under the trust shall, subject to rules under this Act, be entitled at all reasonable times to inspect and take copies of the accounts, report, and certificate, and, at his own expense, to be furnished with copies thereto or extracts therefrom.

JUDICIAL TRUSTEES ACT 1896

1. Power of court on application to appoint judicial trustee.[156]

(6): see p. 646, above.

VIII DUTY TO PROVIDE INFORMATION. TRUST DOCUMENTS[157]

A trustee must provide information to the beneficiaries concerning the state of the trust.[158] For this purpose, it is convenient to keep a Minute Book and a Trust Diary, in which day-to-day events are recorded.

D. Hayton in *Trends in Contemporary Trust Law* (ed. A.J. Oakley) (1996), p. 52

The beneficiaries' rights to inspect trust documents are now seen as better based not on equitable proprietary rights but on the beneficiaries' rights to make the trustees account for their trusteeship.[159] Thus, beneficiaries under fixed or discretionary trusts have the right to see all documents relating to the management and administration of the trust by the trustees and to the distributive function of the trustees[160] except to the extent that such documents would reveal the reasons for the exercise of the trustees' sensitive discretions[161] or are confidential e.g. letters between trustees and a beneficiary relating to the beneficiary's personal needs or a letter of wishes from the settlor to his trustees if expressly or impliedly confidential.[162]

[156] See Judicial Trustee Rules 1983 (S.I. 1983 No. 370), rr. 9, 10, 12–14.

[157] H&M, pp. 570–573; Lewin, pp. 785–844; P&M, pp. 581–590; P&S, pp. 705–712; Pettit, pp. 396–399; Snell, pp. 650–651; T&H, pp. 415–434; U&H, pp. 827–844. See also D. Hayton in *Trends in Contemporary Trust Law* (ed. A. Oakley, 1996), pp. 49–52.

[158] But this does not put the trustees 'under any duty to proffer information to their beneficiary, or to see that he has proper advice merely because they are trustees for him and know that he is entering into a transaction with his beneficial interest with some person or body connected in some way with the trustees, such as a company in which the trustees own some shares beneficially': *Tito v Waddell (No 2)* [1977] Ch 106 at 243, *per* Megarry V-C; questioned at (1977) 41 Conv (NS) 438 (F.R. Crane).

[159] *Hartigan Nominees Pty Ltd v Rydge* (1992) 29 NSWLR 405; *A-G of Ontario v Stavro* (1994) 119 DLR (4th) 750 (beneficiaries of unadministered residuary estate legally and beneficially owned by executor subject to fiduciary duties); Ford and Lee, *Principles of the Law of Trusts* (1990), para 9290.

[160] See p. 717, n. 82, above. Exact rights will vary depending upon whether the beneficiary is interested in income or in capital.   [161] See p. 716, n. 83, above, and J.D. Davies (1995) 7 *Bond Law Review*, LR5.

[162] *Hartigan Nominees Pty Ltd v Rydge*, note 159 above; *Tierney v King* [1983] 2 Qd R 580, *Re Londonderry's Settlement* [1964] Ch 594.

Re Londonderry's Settlement[163]
[1965] Ch 918 (CA, **Harman, Danckwerts** and **Salmon LJJ**)

The trustees of a family settlement created by the Seventh Marquess of Londonderry decided, in accordance with the provisions of the settlement, to distribute the capital among the beneficiaries, and to bring the settlement to an end.

The defendant, a daughter of the settlor, was dissatisfied with the provision which the trustees decided to make for her and her children. She asked to see the minutes of the trustees' meetings, agenda and other documents prepared for their meetings, and the correspondence between the trustees, the settlor (then deceased), the trustees' solicitor, and other persons concerned with the administration of the trust. The trustees took the view that it was not in the interests of the family as a whole to disclose all these documents, and they supplied the complainant only with copies of the intended appointments of capital, and copies of the accounts of the trust. The question was whether she was entitled to inspect the other documents.

Held (reversing Plowman J). The trustees were not under a duty to supply the documents or to disclose the reasons for their decisions.

Harman LJ: I have found this a difficult case. It raises what in my judgment is a novel question on which there is no authority exactly in point although several cases have been cited to us somewhere near it. The court is really required here to resolve two principles that come into conflict, or at least apparent conflict. The first is that, as the defendant beneficiary admits, trustees exercising a discretionary power are not bound to disclose to their beneficiaries the reasons actuating them in coming to a decision. This is a long-standing principle and rests largely I think on the view that nobody could be called upon to accept a trusteeship involving the exercise of a discretion unless, in the absence of bad faith, he were not liable to have his motives or his reasons called in question either by the beneficiaries or by the court. To this there is added a rider, namely, that if trustees do give reasons, their soundness can be considered by the court. Compare the observations of James LJ in *Re Gresham Life Assurance Society, ex p Penney* (1872) 8 Ch App 446 at 449, 450 on the analogous position of directors.

It would seem on the face of it that there is no reason why this principle should be confined to decisions orally arrived at and should not extend to a case, like the present, where owing to the complexity of the trust and the large sums involved, the trustees, who act subject to the consent of another body called the appointors, have brought into existence various written documents, including, in particular, agenda for and minutes of their meetings from time to time held in order to consider distributions made of the fund and its income. It is here that the conflicting principle is said to emerge. All these documents, it is argued, came into existence for the purposes of the trust and are in the possession of the trustees as such and are, therefore, trust documents, the property of the beneficiaries, and as such open to them to inspect....

The defendant relied on certain observations in *O'Rourke v Darbishire* [1920] AC 581. The decision was that the plaintiff was not entitled to the production of what were called the 'trust documents', and I find Lord Parmoor making this observation at 619.

---

[163] (1965) 81 LQR 192 (R.E.M.). See *Chaine-Nickson v Bank of Ireland* [1976] IR 393.

'A *cestui que trust*, in an action against his trustees, is generally entitled to the production for inspection of all documents relating to the affairs of the trust. It is not material for the present purpose whether this right is to be regarded as a paramount proprietary right in the *cestui que trust*, or as a right to be enforced under the law of discovery.'

Lord Wrenbury says at 626.

'If the plaintiff is right in saying that he is a beneficiary, and if the documents are documents belonging to the executors as executors, he has a right to access to the documents which he desires to inspect upon what has been called in the judgments in this case a proprietary right. The beneficiary is entitled to see all the trust documents because they are trust documents and because he is a beneficiary. They are in a sense his own. Action or no action, he is entitled to access to them. This has nothing to do with discovery. The right to discovery is a right to see someone else's documents. A proprietary right is a right to access to documents which are your own. No question of professional privilege arises in such a case. Documents containing professional advice taken by the executors as trustees contain advice taken by trustees for their *cestuis que trust*, and the beneficiaries are entitled to see them because they are beneficiaries.'

General observations of this sort give very little guidance, for first they beg the question what are trust documents, and secondly their lordships were not considering the point here that papers are asked for which bear on the question of the exercise of the trustees' discretion. In my judgment category (a) mentioned in the notice of appeal, *viz.*, the minutes of the meetings of the trustees of the settlement; and part of (b), *viz.*, agenda prepared for trustees' meetings, are, in the absence of an action impugning the trustees' good faith, documents which a beneficiary cannot claim the right to inspect. If the defendant is allowed to examine these, she will know at once the very matters which the trustees are not bound to disclose to her, namely, their motives and reasons. Trustees who wish to preserve their rights in this respect must either commit nothing to paper or destroy everything from meeting to meeting. Indeed, if the defendant be right, I doubt if the last course is open, for she must succeed, if at all, on the ground that the papers belong to her, and if so, the trustees have no right to destroy them.

I would hold that even if documents of this type ought properly to be described as trust documents, they are protected for the special reason which protects the trustees' deliberations on a discretionary matter from disclosure. If necessary, I hold that this principle overrides the ordinary rule. This is, in my judgment, no less in the true interest of the beneficiary than of the trustees. Again, if one of the trustees commits to paper his suggestions and circulates them among his co-trustees; or if inquiries are made in writing as to the circumstances of a member of the class; I decline to hold that such documents are trust documents the property of the beneficiaries. In my opinion such documents are not trust documents in the proper sense at all. On the other hand, if the solicitor advising the trustees commits to paper an *aide-mémoire* summarising the state of the fund or of the family and reminding the trustees of past distributions and future possibilities I think that must be a document which any beneficiary must be at liberty to inspect. It seems to me, therefore, that category (b) in the notice of appeal embraces documents on both sides of the line.

As to (c), which is: 'correspondence relating to the administration of the trust property or otherwise to the execution of the trusts of the said settlement and passing between (i) the individuals for the time being holding office as trustees of or appointors under the said settlement; (ii) the said trustees and appointors or any of them on the one hand and the solicitors to the trustees on the other hand; (iii) the said trustees and appointors or any of them on the one hand and the beneficiaries under the said settlement on the other hand'; I cannot think that communications passing between individual trustees and appointors are documents in which beneficiaries have a proprietary right. On the other hand, as to category (ii), in general the letters of the trustees' solicitors to the trustees do seem to me to be trust documents in which the beneficiaries have a property. As to category (iii), I do not think letters to or from an individual beneficiary ought to be open to inspection by another beneficiary. Thus I think the judge's order went too far, but it is very difficult to frame a declaration which will not cut down the rights of the beneficiaries too much. I would propose that we should discuss this matter after my brethren have given their opinions on the matter.

Salmon LJ: There is another possible approach to the present case. The category of trust documents has never been comprehensively defined. Nor could it be—certainly not by me. Trust documents do, however, have these characteristics in common: (1) they are documents in the possession of the trustees as trustees; (2) they contain information about the trust which the beneficiaries are entitled to know; (3) the beneficiaries have a proprietary interest in the documents and, accordingly, are entitled to see them. If any parts of a document contain information which the beneficiaries are not entitled to know, I doubt whether such parts can truly be said to be integral parts of a trust document. Accordingly, any part of a document that lacked the second characteristic to which I have referred would automatically be excluded from the document in its character as a trust document.

I agree with my Lords that the appeal should be allowed.

(1965) 81 LQR 196–198 (R.E.M.)

It seems safe to say that the last of *Re Londonderry's Settlement* has not been heard. Perhaps the most obvious point which may arise is whether a beneficiary who is determined to discover all he can about the grounds upon which a discretion has been exercised may not achieve this by instituting litigation alleging that the trustees have exercised their discretion in some improper way, and then obtaining discovery of documents in those proceedings, as in *Talbot v Marshfield* (1865) 2 Drew & Sm 549. Will the courts permit the bonds of secrecy to be invaded by the simple process of commencing hostile litigation against the trustees? It is not easy to see how the courts can prevent this. True, questions of relevance may obviously arise; but on discovery the test of relevance is wide. The classical statement is that of Brett LJ: an applicant is entitled to discovery of any document 'which may fairly lead him to a train of inquiry' that may 'either directly or indirectly enable the party requiring the affidavit either to advance his own case or to damage the case of his adversary' (*Compagnie Financière et Commerciale du Pacifique v Peruvian Guano Co* (1882) 11 QBD 55 at 63). Indeed, the formal order of the court, . . . seems to recognise this possibility.

The other main point which plainly needs further exploration is the ambit of the term 'trust documents'. The negative proposition is now plain: not all documents held by trustees as such are 'trust documents'.[164] But even after a detailed examination of the judgments it is difficult to frame any positive proposition with any degree of confidence. Nor does the formal order of the court (see at 938) lessen the difficulty; indeed, it contributes its own quota of problems. The order states that without prejudice to any right of the defendant to discovery in any subsequent

---

[164] *Per* Danckwerts LJ at 935–936, at 861–862.

proceedings against the trustees, and subject to any order of the court in any particular circumstances, there are four categories of documents which the trustees are not bound to disclose to the defendant. The first of these categories is 'the agenda of the meetings of the trustees of the settlement'; the second and third categories consist of correspondence of the trustees *inter se* and with the beneficiaries; and the fourth category consists of minutes of the meetings of the trustees and other documents disclosing their deliberations as to the manner in which they should exercise their discretion or disclosing their reasons for any particular exercise of their discretion, or the materials thereof. It is thus only the minutes and the other documents in the fourth category which appear to be qualified by words relating to disclosure of the trustees' reasons for exercising their discretion in a particular way; the freedom from disclosure seems to apply to all agenda and correspondence, whether or not they would reveal any such reasons or the material on which they were based. Nor does the order make it plain how it applies to documents in the fourth category which not only disclose confidential matters but also deal with other points as well; the inclusion of any confidential matter seems to confer exemption upon the entire document, and not merely upon the confidential matter. The order did, however, declare that the trustees were bound to disclose to the defendant any written advice from their solicitors or counsel as to the manner in which the trustees were in law entitled to exercise their discretion.

Putting all the material together, it seems at present to be difficult to say more than that all documents held by trustees *qua* trustees are *prima facie* trust documents, but that there is a class of exceptions from this rule which is ill defined but includes confidential documents which the beneficiaries ought not to see. For greater precision than that we must await further decisions by the courts. The Court of Appeal has taken a firm step in the right direction; but that is all.[165]

Schmidt v Rosewood Trust Ltd
[2003] UKPC 26, [2003] 2 AC 709[166] **(Lords Nicholls of Birkenhead, Hope of Craighead, Hutton, Hobhouse of Woodborough and Walker of Gestingthorpe)**

The petitioner sought disclosure of documents relating to two settlements of which his father had been co-settlor. The petitioner claimed discretionary interests under the settlements and he was also the administrator of his father's estate. The trustees opposed disclosure because the petitioner was not a beneficiary under the settlement and his father was only an object of a power so he had no entitlement to trust documents. Disclosure was ordered by the High Court of the Isle of Man but was set aside on appeal to the Staff of Government Division. The petitioner appealed to the Privy Council.

---

[165] In *Wilson v Law Debenture Trust Corpn plc* [1995] 2 All ER 337 it was held that the *Re Londonderry* principle applied to pension fund trustees. Cf. (1992) 6 *Trust Law International* 119, 125 (Lord Browne-Wilkinson).

[166] (2004) LQR 1 (J. Davies); [2003] Conv 257 (I. Ferrier); [2003] All ER Rev 266 (P.J. Clarke). See also *Murphy v Murphy* [1999] 1 WLR 282; (1999) 115 LQR 206 (C. Mitchell); *Foreman v Kingstone and Cave* [2004] 1 NZLR 841; [2005] Conv 93 (G.L.H. Griffiths).

Held. The court could order the documents to be disclosed, but this did not depend on whether the beneficiary had a proprietary right to disclosure.

Lord Walker of Gestingthorpe:

43   Much of the debate before the Board addressed the question whether a beneficiary's right or claim to disclosure of trust documents should be regarded as a proprietary right. Mr. Brownbill [counsel for the trustees] argued that it should be classified in that way, and from that starting point he argued that no object of a mere power could have any right or claim to disclosure, because he had no proprietary interest in the trust property. Mr. Brownbill submitted that this point has been conclusively settled by the decision of the House of Lords in *O'Rourke v Darbishire* [1920] AC 581 [see p. 740, above].

[His Lordship considered the case and also *Clarke v Earl of Osmonde* (1821) Jac 108; *Re Cowin* (1886) 33 Ch D 179; *Re Londonderry's Settlement* [1965] Ch 918 [see p. 740, above]; and continued:]

50   Lord Wrenbury's observations in *O'Rourke v Darbishire* [1920] AC 581, 626–627, have also been cited in several Australian cases, and they were referred to by Lord Lowry in *AT & T Istel Ltd v Tully* [1993] AC 45, 65. The Board does not find it surprising that Lord Wrenbury's observations have been so often cited, since they are a vivid expression of the basic distinction between the right of a beneficiary arising under the law of trusts (which most would regard as part of the law of property) and the right of a litigant to disclosure of his opponent's documents (which is part of the law of procedure and evidence). But the Board cannot regard it as a reasoned or binding decision that a beneficiary's right or claim to disclosure of trust documents or information must always have the proprietary basis of a transmissible interest in trust property. That was not an issue in *O'Rourke v Darbishire*.

51   Their Lordships consider that the more principled and correct approach is to regard the right to seek disclosure of trust documents as one aspect of the court's inherent jurisdiction to supervise, and if necessary to intervene in, the administration of trusts. The right to seek the court's intervention does not depend on entitlement to a fixed and transmissible beneficial interest. The object of a discretion (including a mere power) may also be entitled to protection from a court of equity, although the circumstances in which he may seek protection, and the nature of the protection he may expect to obtain, will depend on the court's discretion: see Lord Wilberforce in *Gartside v Inland Revenue Commissioners* [1968] AC 553, 617–618 and in *Re Baden* [1971] AC 424, 456–457 [see p. 91, above], Templeman J in *Re Manisty's Settlement* [1974] Ch 17, 27–28 and Warner J in *Mettoy Pension Trustees Ltd v Evans* [1990] 1 WLR 1587, 1617–1618. Mr. Brownbill's submission to the contrary effect tends to prove too much, since he would regard the object of a discretionary trust as having a proprietary interest even though it is not transmissible (except in the special case of collective action taken unanimously by all the members of a closed class).

52   Their Lordships are therefore in general agreement with the approach adopted in the judgments of Kirby P and Sheller JA in the Court of Appeal of New South Wales in *Hartigan Nominees Pty Ltd v Rydge* [1992] 29 NSWLR 405. That was a case concerned with disclosure of a memorandum of wishes addressed to the trustees by Sir Norman Rydge (who was in substance, but not nominally, the settlor). Kirby P said, at pp 421–422:

'I do not consider that it is imperative to determine whether that document is a "trust document" (as I think it is) or whether the respondent, as a beneficiary, has a proprietary interest in it (as I am also inclined to think he does). Much of the law on the subject of access to documents has conventionally been expressed in terms of the "proprietary interest" in the document of the party seeking access to it. Thus, it has been held that a *cestui que trust* has a "proprietary right" to seek all documents relating to the trust: see *O'Rourke v Darbishire* [1920] AC 581, 601, 603. This approach is unsatisfactory. Access should not be limited to documents in which a proprietary right may be established. Such rights may be *sufficient;* but they are not *necessary* to a right of access which the courts will enforce to uphold the *cestui que trust*'s entitlement to a reasonable assurance of the manifest integrity of the administration of the trust by the trustees. I agree with Professor H.A.J. Ford's comment, in his book (with Mr W A Lee) *Principles of the Law of Trusts*, 2nd ed (1990) Sydney, Law Book Co, p 425, that the equation of rights of inspection of trust documents with the beneficiaries' equitable rights of property in the trust assets "gives rise to far more problems than it solves" (at p 425): "The legal title and rights to possession are in the trustees: all the beneficiary has are equitable rights against the trustees... The beneficiary's rights to inspect trust documents are founded therefore not upon any equitable proprietary right which he or she may have in respect of those documents but upon the trustee's fiduciary duty to keep the beneficiary informed and to render accounts. It is the extent of that duty that is in issue. The equation of the right to inspect trust documents with the beneficiary's equitable proprietary rights gives rise to unnecessary and undesirable consequences. It results in the drawing of virtually incomprehensible distinctions between documents which are trust documents and those which are not; it casts doubts upon the rights of beneficiaries who cannot claim to have an equitable proprietary interest in the trust assets, such as the beneficiaries of discretionary trusts; and it may give trustees too great a degree of protection in the case of documents, artificially classified as not being trust documents, and beneficiaries too great a right to inspect the activities of trustees in the case of documents which are, equally artificially, classified as trust documents."'

53   Mahoney JA, at p 435, favoured the proprietary basis but recognised that it extended to information of a non-documentary kind. Sheller JA, at p 444, considered that inquiry as to an applicant's proprietary interest was 'if not a false, an unhelpful trail'. All three members of the court expressed reservations about the reasoning and conclusions in *Re Londonderry's Settlement* [1965] Ch 918.

54   It will be observed that Kirby P said that for an applicant to have a proprietary right might be sufficient, but was not necessary. In the Board's view it is neither sufficient nor necessary. Since *Re Cowin* 33 Ch D 179 well over a century ago the court has made clear that there may be circumstances (especially of confidentiality) in which even a vested and transmissible beneficial interest is not a sufficient basis for requiring disclosure of trust documents; and *Re Londonderry's Settlement* and more recent cases have begun to work out in some detail the way in which the court should exercise its discretion in such cases. There are three such areas in which the court may have to form a discretionary judgment: whether a discretionary object (or some other beneficiary with only a remote or wholly defeasible interest) should be granted relief at all; what classes of documents should be disclosed, either completely or in a redacted form; and what safeguards should be imposed (whether by undertakings to the court, arrangements for professional inspection, or otherwise) to limit the use which may be made of documents or information disclosed under the order of the court....

66   Their Lordships have already indicated their view that a beneficiary's right to seek disclosure of trust documents, although sometimes not inappropriately described as a proprietary right, is best approached as one aspect of the court's inherent jurisdiction to supervise, and where appropriate intervene in, the administration of trusts. There is therefore in their Lordships' view no reason to draw any bright dividing line either between transmissible and

non-transmissible (that is, discretionary) interests, or between the rights of an object of a discretionary trust and those of the object of a mere power (of a fiduciary character). The differences in this context between trusts and powers are (as Lord Wilberforce demonstrated in *Re Baden* [1971] AC 424, 448–449) a good deal less significant than the similarities. The tide of Commonwealth authority, although not entirely uniform, appears to be flowing in that direction.

67 However, the recent cases also confirm (as had been stated as long ago as *Re Cowin* 33 Ch D 179 in 1886) that no beneficiary (and least of all a discretionary object) has any entitlement as of right to disclosure of anything which can plausibly be described as a trust document. Especially when there are issues as to personal or commercial confidentiality, the court may have to balance the competing interests of different beneficiaries, the trustees themselves, and third parties. Disclosure may have to be limited and safeguards may have to be put in place. Evaluation of the claims of a beneficiary (and especially of a discretionary object) may be an important part of the balancing exercise which the court has to perform on the materials placed before it. In many cases the court may have no difficulty in concluding that an applicant with no more than a theoretical possibility of benefit ought not to be granted any relief.

The Board remitted the matter to the High Court of the Isle of Man for reconsideration.

In Breakspear v Ackland [2008] EWML 220 (Ch) Briggs J held that trustees have a discretion as to whether a letter of wishes should be disclosed; beneficiaries have no proprietary right to require disclosure. On the facts disclosure was ordered.

QUESTIONS

1. If disclosure of documents to beneficiaries is not founded on a proprietary basis, on what basis is it founded?

2. Should a settlor's letter of wishes be disclosed to the objects of a trust power? See *Hartigan Nominees Pty Ltd v Rydge* 29 NSWLR 405; *Freeman v Kingstone and Cave* [2004] 1 NZLR 841; [2005] Conv 93 (G.L.H. Griffiths); U&H, pp. 837–839; *Breakspear v Ackland* [2008] EWML 220 (Ch).

15

POWERS OF TRUSTEES[1]

I GENERAL

Trustees have such powers as are given to them by statute or by the trust instrument. It is necessary therefore to read all the statutory provisions which give them their powers. Only the main provisions can be reproduced here.

TRUSTEE ACT 1925

69. Application of Act

(2) The powers conferred by this Act on trustees are in addition to the powers conferred by the instrument, if any, creating the trust, but those powers,[2] unless otherwise stated, apply if and so far only as a contrary intention is not expressed

---

[1] H&M, pp. 575–605; Lewin, pp. 1115–1182, 1335–1378; P&M, pp. 590–592, 611–616, 675–710; P&S, pp. 410–417, 592–604, 661–673; Pettit, pp. 453–483, 490–491; Snell, pp. 611–635; T&H, pp. 451–532; U&H, pp. 845–898. The Trust Law Committee published a Consultation Paper on the subject of introducing a Schedule A of Standard Powers of Trustees (October 1999): <http://www.kcl.ac.uk/deptsa/law/tlc/Consult.html>. The Committee acknowledged in its 2000 Annual Report that the Government is unlikely to create the legislative opportunity for such clauses in the foreseeable future.

[2] That is, the powers conferred by the Act.

in the instrument,[3] if any, creating the trust, and have effect subject to the terms of that instrument.

Ockleton: *Trusts for Accountants* (1987), p. 107

So if we want to know the powers of the trustees in relation to a particular trust, we should always look at the trust instrument first, for the powers conferred by the Act may be modified or excluded by it. It is for the settlor to decide what powers he gives to his trustee: the Act merely gives him a model, which he can accept (by saying nothing) or reject as he pleases. It is true, however, that s. 69 (2) does include the words 'unless otherwise stated'. The powers given to trustees despite anything in the trust instrument are those under s. 14 (power of trustees to give receipts),[4] s. 16 (power to raise money by sale, mortgage, etc)[5] and s. 27 (protection by means of advertisements).[6] In the case of all other powers of trustees, the settlor's wishes expressed in the trust instrument take precedence over the Act.

II   OVER PROPERTY[7]

TRUSTEE ACT 1925

12. Power of trustees for sale to sell by auction, &c

(1) Where a trustee has a duty or power to sell property,[8] he may sell or concur with any other person in selling all or any part of the property, either subject to prior charges or not, and either together or in lots, by public auction or by private contract, subject to any such conditions respecting title or evidence of title or other matter as the trustee thinks fit, with power to vary any contract for sale, and to buy in at any auction, or to rescind any contract for sale and to resell, without being answerable for any loss.

(2) A duty[9] or power to sell or dispose of land includes a duty[10] or power to sell or dispose of part thereof, whether the division is horizontal, vertical, or made in any other way.

(3) This section does not enable an express power to sell settled land to be exercised where the power is not vested in the tenant for life or statutory owner.

---

[3] *Re Delamere's Settlement Trust* [1984] 1 WLR 813 ('equal shares absolutely' in trustees' deed of appointment held to mean 'indefeasibly', thus giving rise to a contrary intention); [1985] Conv 153 (R. Griffith).
[4] See p. 750, below.   [5] See p. 749, below.   [6] See p. 717, above.
[7] H&M, pp. 578–579; Lewin, pp. 1397–1405; P&M, p. 591; P&S, p. 598; Pettit, pp. 464–467; Snell, pp. 612–616; T&H, pp. 479–484; U&H, pp. 870–872. For powers relating to trusts of land see Trusts of Land and Appointment of Trustees Act (TLATA) 1996, s. 6; Maudsley and Burn's *Land Law: Cases and Materials* (8th edn., 2004), pp. 271–275.   [8] As amended by the TLATA 1996, s. 25(1), Sch. 3, para. 3(1), (2A).
[9] Ibid.   [10] Ibid.

16. Power to raise money by sale, mortgage, &c

(1) Where trustees are authorised by the instrument, if any, creating the trust or by law to pay or apply capital money subject to the trust for any purpose or in any manner, they shall have and shall be deemed always to have had power to raise the money required by sale, conversion, calling in, or mortgage of all or any part of the trust property for the time being in possession.[11]

(2) This section applies notwithstanding anything to the contrary contained in the instrument, if any, creating the trust, but does not apply to trustees of property held for charitable purposes, or to trustees of a settlement for the purposes of the Settled Land Act, 1925, not being also the statutory owners.

57. Power of court to authorise dealings with trust property

(1) Where in the management or administration of any property vested in trustees, any sale, lease, mortgage, surrender, release, or other disposition, or any purchase, investment, acquisition, expenditure, or other transaction, is in the opinion of the court expedient, but the same cannot be effected by reason of the absence of any power for that purpose vested in the trustees by the trust instrument, if any, or by law, the court may by order confer upon the trustees, either generally or in any particular instance, the necessary power for the purpose, on such terms, and subject to such provisions and conditions, if any, as the court may think fit and may direct in what manner any money authorised to be expended, and the costs of any transaction, are to be paid or borne as between capital and income.

(2) The court may, from time to time, rescind or vary any order made under this section, or may make any new or further order.

(3) An application to the court under this section may be made by the trustees, or by any of them, or by any person beneficially interested under the trust.

(4) This section does not apply to trustees of a settlement for the purposes of the Settled Land Act, 1925.

In **Re Hope's Will Trust** [1929] 2 Ch 136, the Court approved under section 57(1) the sale of family portraits which were held upon trusts which should correspond, as nearly as the rules of law and equity would permit, with the limitations of real estate in tail. Eve J said at 140:

Having come to the clear conclusion that the sale is one which will be beneficial to all parties interested, and indeed is almost unavoidable, I find no difficulty in authorizing the trustees to carry it out under s. 57.

---

[11] But this does not authorise trustees to raise money by charging existing investments in order to purchase others: *Re Suenson-Taylor's Settlement Trusts* [1974] 1 WLR 1280.

III TO GIVE RECEIPTS[12]

TRUSTEE ACT 1925

14. Power of trustees to give receipts

(1) The receipt in writing of a trustee for any money, securities, investments[13] or other personal property or effects payable, transferable, or deliverable to him under any trust or power shall be a sufficient discharge to the person paying, transferring, or delivering the same and shall effectually exonerate him from seeing to the application or being answerable for any loss or misapplication thereof.

(2) This section does not, except where the trustee is a trust corporation, enable a sole trustee to give a valid receipt for—

   (a) proceeds of sale or other capital money arising under a…trust of land,[14]

   (b) capital money arising under the Settled Land Act, 1925.

(3) This section applies notwithstanding anything to the contrary in the instrument, if any, creating the trust.

IV TO COMPOUND LIABILITIES
AND TO SETTLE CLAIMS[15]

TRUSTEE ACT 1925

15. Power to compound liabilities

A personal representative, or two or more trustees acting together, or, subject to the restrictions imposed in regard to receipts by a sole trustee not being a trust corporation, a sole acting trustee where by the instrument, if any, creating the trust, or by statute, a sole trustee is authorised to execute the trusts and powers reposed in him, may if and as he or they think fit—

   (a) accept any property, real or personal, before the time at which it is made transferable or payable; or

   (b) sever and apportion any blended trust funds or property; or

   (c) pay or allow any debt or claim on any evidence that he or they think sufficient; or

---

[12] H&M, p. 579–580; Lewin, pp. 1376–1377; P&M, p. 547; P&S, pp. 598–599; Pettit, p. 467; Snell, p. 615; T & H, pp. 486–487; U&H, pp. 872–873.

[13] As inserted by Trustee Act (TA) 2000, s. 40(1), Sch. 2, Pt II, para. 19.

[14] As amended by TLATA 1996, s. 25(1), Sch. 3, para. 3(1), (3).

[15] H&M, pp. 581–582; Lewin, pp. 1367–1369; P&M, pp. 590; P&S, pp. 599–600; Pettit, pp. 470–471; Snell, pp. 622–624; T&H, pp. 487–489; U&H, pp. 875–876.

(d) accept any composition or any security, real or personal, for any debt or for any property, real or personal, claimed; or

(e) allow any time of payment of any debt; or

(f) compromise, compound, abandon, submit to arbitration, or otherwise settle any debt, account, claim, or thing whatever relating to the testator's or intestate's estate or to the trust;[16]

and for any of those purposes may enter into, give, execute, and do such agreements, instruments of composition or arrangement, releases, and other things as to him or them seem expedient, without being responsible for any loss occasioned by any act or thing so done by him or them if he has or they have discharged the duty of care set out in section 1(1) of the Trustee Act 2000.[17]

V TO INSURE[18]

TRUSTEE ACT 1925

19. Power to insure[19]

(1) A trustee may—

(a) insure any property which is subject to the trust against risks of loss or damage due to any event, and

(b) pay the premiums out of the trust funds.

(2) In the case of property held on a bare trust, the power to insure is subject to any direction given by the beneficiary or each of the beneficiaries—

(a) that any property specified in the direction is not to be insured

(b) that any property specified in the direction is not to be insured except on such conditions as may be so specified.

(3) Property is held on a bare trust if it is held on trust for—

(a) a beneficiary who is of full age and capacity and absolutely entitled to the property subject to the trust, or

---

[16] Re Earl of Strafford [1980] Ch 28 (surrender of beneficial interest as part of compromise of dispute as to ownership of chattels between trust and beneficiaries).

[17] As amended by TA 2000, s. 40 (1), Sch 2, Pt. II, para. 20. For the statutory duty of care see p. 687, above. See also Alsop Wilkinson v Neary [1996] 1 WLR 1220, (a trustee, against whom hostile litigation had been brought challenging the validity of a settlement, has no duty to defend the trust but must remain neutral leaving it to the rival claimants to the beneficial interest to fight their own battles).

[18] H&M, pp. 580–581; Lewin, pp. 1239–1246; P&M, p. 591; P&S, p. 599; Pettit, pp. 468–469; Snell, pp. 616–617; T&H, pp. 484–486; U&H, pp. 700–701. See also Whitehouse and Hassall, Trusts of Land, Trustee Delegation and the Trustee Act (2nd edn, 2001), pp. 285–288; Law Commission, Trustees' Powers and Duties (1999), (Law Com No. 260), pp. 68–71.   [19] As substituted by TA 2000, s. 34.

   (b) beneficiaries each of whom is of full age and capacity and who (taken together) are absolutely entitled to the property subject to the trust.

(4) If a direction under subsection (2) of this section is given, the power to insure, so far as it is subject to the direction, ceases to be a delegable function for the purposes of section 11 of the Trustee Act 2000 (power to employ agents).[20]

(5) In this section 'trust funds' means any income or capital funds of the trust.

20. Application of insurance money where policy kept up under any trust, power or obligation

(1) Money receivable by trustees or any beneficiary under a policy of insurance against the loss or damage of any property subject to a trust or to a settlement within the meaning of the Settled Land Act, 1925, shall, where the policy has been kept up under any trust in that behalf or under any power statutory or otherwise, or in performance of any covenant or of any obligation statutory or otherwise, or by a tenant for life impeachable for waste, be capital money for the purposes of the trust or settlement, as the case may be.[21]

(3) Any such money—

   (a) if it was receivable in respect of settled land within the meaning of the Settled Land Act, 1925, or any building or works thereon, shall be deemed to be capital money arising under that Act from the settled land, and shall be invested or applied by the trustees, or, if in court, under the direction of the court, accordingly;

   (b) if it was receivable in respect of personal chattels settled as heirlooms within the meaning of the Settled Land Act, 1925, shall be deemed to be capital money arising under that Act, and shall be applicable by the trustees, or, if in court, under the direction of the court, in like manner as provided by that Act with respect to money arising by a sale of chattels settled as heirlooms as aforesaid;

   (c) if it was receivable in respect of land subject to a trust of land or personal property held on trust for sale,[22] shall be held upon the trusts and subject to the powers and provisions applicable to money arising by a sale under such trust;

   (d) in any other case, shall be held upon trusts corresponding as nearly as may be with the trusts affecting the property in respect of which it was payable.

(4) Such money, or any part thereof, may also be applied by the trustees, or, if in court, under the direction of the court, in rebuilding, reinstating, replacing, or repairing the property lost or damaged, but any such application by the trustees shall be subject to the consent of any person whose consent is required by the instrument, if any, creating the trust to the investment of money subject to the

---

[20] See p. 695, above.   [21] As amended by TA 2000, ss. 34(2), (3), 40(3), Sch. 4, Pt. II.

[22] As amended by TLATA 1996, s. 25(1), Sch. 3, para. 3(1), (5).

trust, and, in the case of money which is deemed to be capital money arising under the Settled Land Act, 1925, be subject to the provisions of that Act with respect to the application of capital money by the trustees of the settlement.

VI IN CONNECTION WITH REVERSIONARY INTERESTS[23]

TRUSTEE ACT 1925

22. Reversionary interests, valuations and audit

(1) Where the trust property includes any share or interest in property not vested in the trustees, or the proceeds of the sale of any such property, or any other thing in action, the trustees on the same falling into possession, or becoming payable or transferable may—

    (a) agree or ascertain the amount or value thereof or any part thereof in such manner as they may think fit;

    (b) accept in or towards satisfaction thereof, at the market or current value, or upon any valuation or estimate of value which they may think fit, any authorised investments;

    (c) allow any deductions for duties, costs, charges and expenses which they may think proper or reasonable;

    (d) execute any release in respect of the premises so as effectually to discharge all accountable parties from all liability in respect of any matters coming within the scope of such release;

without being responsible in any such case for any loss occasioned by any act or thing so done by them if they have discharged the duty of care set out in section 1(1) of the Trustee Act 2000.[24]

(2) The trustees shall not be under any obligation and shall not be chargeable with any breach of trust by reason of any omission—

    (a) to place any *distringas* notice or apply for any stop or other like order upon any securities or other property out of or on which such share or interest or other thing in action as aforesaid is derived, payable or charged;[25] or

    (b) to take any proceedings on account of any act, default, or neglect on the part of the persons in whom such securities or other property or any of them or any part thereof are for the time being, or had at any time been, vested;

[23] H&M, p. 582; Lewin, pp. 1222–1223; P&S, p. 600; Pettit, pp. 471–472; Snell, pp. 623–624; T&H, pp. 322–323; U&H, pp. 875–876.

[24] As amended by TA 2000, s. 40(1), Sch. 2, Pt. II, para. 22(a). For the statutory duty of care see p. 000, above.   [25] See CPR, Pt. 50, r. 50.5, Sch. 1, RSC Ord. 50, rr. 10ff.

unless and until required in writing so to do by some person, or the guardian of some person, beneficially interested under the trust, and unless also due provision is made to their satisfaction for payment of the costs of any proceedings required to be taken:

Provided that nothing in this subsection shall relieve the trustees of the obligation to get in and obtain payment or transfer of such share or interest or other thing in action on the same falling into possession.

(3) Trustees may, for the purpose of giving effect to the trust, or any of the provisions of the instrument, if any, creating the trust or of any statute, from time to time (by duly qualified agents) ascertain and fix the value of any trust property in such manner as they think proper, and any valuation so made if the trustees have discharged the duty of care set out in section 1(1) of the Trustee Act 2000 shall be binding upon all persons interested under the trust.[26]

VII TO DELEGATE[27]

A GENERAL POWER TO DELEGATE

Originally, a trustee was expected, in theory, to perform all his duties personally: *delegatus non potest delegare*. Whether or not this was ever a practical proposition, it early became impracticable because of the increasing complications of business life. By 1925, it could be said that a trustee could delegate certain functions; but not discretionary powers. The trustee had to show that the appointment of some person to perform his functions was reasonably necessary in the circumstances, or was in accordance with ordinary business practice.[28] The trustee had to exercise proper care in the selection of the agent, had to employ him in his proper field, and had to exercise general supervision.[29] The power of a trustee to delegate functions was widened by the Trustee Act 1925, although the interpretation of the relevant provisions was a matter of controversy, especially as regards when a trustee would be liable for an agent's default.[30] These provisions have now been repealed by the Trustee Act 2000, which has created a new statutory regime for the delegation of trustees' powers.[31] It should be

---

[26] As amended by TA 2000, s. 40(1), Sch. 2, Pt. II, para. 22(b). For the statutory duty of care see p. 687, above.

[27] H&M, pp. 582–591; Lewin, pp. 1338–1361; P&M, pp. 611–616; P&S, pp. 661–673; Pettit, pp. 453–464; Snell, pp. 617–622; T&H, pp. 499–544; U&H, pp. 772–787.   [28] *Speight v Gaunt* (1883) 9 App Cas 1.

[29] *Speight v Gaunt,* ibid; *Learoyd v Whiteley* (1887) 12 App Cas 727; *Fry v Tapson* (1884) 28 Ch D 268.

[30] See *Re Vickery* [1931] 1 Ch 572 and *Re Lucking's Will Trusts* [1968] 1 WLR 866; (1959) 22 MLR 388 (G.H. Jones).

[31] Following recommendations of the Law Commission: *Trustees Powers and Duties*, 1999 (Law Com No. 260), pp. 44–67.

emphasised that these general powers of delegation are concerned with delegation by the trustee body collectively.

The provisions of the Trustee Act 2000 on delegation of powers are probably most important in respect of investment powers, so they have been identified in Chapter 14, but it is important to emphasise that these statutory powers of delegation are of general application. The key provisions are as follows:

TRUSTEE ACT 2000

11. **Power to employ agents,** p. 695, above.

12. **Persons who may act as agents,** p. 696, above.

13. **Linked functions etc.,** p. 696, above.

14. **Terms of agency,** p. 697, above.

16. **Power to appoint nominees,** p. 698, above.

17. **Power to appoint custodians,** p. 698, above.

19. **Persons who may be appointed as nominees or custodians,** p. 699, above.

20. **Terms of appointment of nominees and custodians etc.,** p. 700, above.

22. **Review of agents, nominees and custodians etc.,** p. 700, above.

23. **Liability for agents, nominees and custodians etc.,** p. 701, above.

24. **Effect of trustees exceeding their powers,** p. 701, above.

25. **Sole trustees,** p. 702, above.

26. **Restriction or exclusion of this Part etc.,** p. 702, above.

27. **Existing trusts,** p. 702, above.

Schedule 1, paragraph 3, p. 702, above.

B SPECIFIC POWERS OF DELEGATION

(i) Delegation by individual trustees for a limited period

TRUSTEE ACT 1925

25. Delegation of trustee's functions by power of attorney.[32]

(1) Notwithstanding any rule of law or equity to the contrary, a trustee may, by power of attorney, delegate the execution or exercise of all or any of the trusts, powers and discretions vested in him as trustee either alone or jointly with any other person or persons.

---

[32] As amended by Trustee Delegation Act 1999, s. 5.

(2) A delegation under this section—

    (a) commences as provided by the instrument creating the power or, if the instrument makes no provision as to the commencement of the delegation, with the date of the execution of the instrument by the donor; and

    (b) continues for a period of twelve months or any shorter period provided by the instrument creating the power.

(3) The persons who may be donees of a power of attorney under this section include a trust corporation.

(4) Before or within seven days after giving a power of attorney under this section the donor shall give written notice of it (specifying the date on which the power comes into operation and its duration, the donee of the power, the reason why the power is given and, where some only are delegated, the trusts, powers and discretions delegated) to—

    (a) each person (other than himself), if any, who under any instrument creating the trust has power (whether alone or jointly) to appoint a new trustee; and

    (b) each of the other trustees, if any;

but failure to comply with this subsection shall not, in favour of a person dealing with the donee of the power, invalidate any act done or instrument executed by the donee.[33]

(7) The donor of a power of attorney given under this section shall be liable for the acts or defaults of the donee in the same manner as if they were the acts or defaults of the donor.

(8) For the purpose of executing or exercising the trusts or powers delegated to him, the donee may exercise any of the powers conferred on the donor as trustee by statute or by the instrument creating the trust, including power, for the purpose of the transfer of any inscribed stock, himself to delegate to an attorney power to transfer, but not including the power of delegation conferred by this section.

(9) The fact that it appears from any power of attorney given under this section, or from any evidence required for the purposes of any such power of attorney or otherwise, that in dealing with any stock the donee of the power is acting in the execution of a trust shall not be deemed for any purpose to affect any person in whose books the stock is inscribed or registered with any notice of the trust.

(10) This section applies to a personal representative, tenant for life and statutory owner as it applies to a trustee except that subsection (4) shall apply as if it required the notice there mentioned to be given—

    (a) in the case of a personal representative, to each of the other personal representatives, if any, except any executor who has renounced probate;

---

[33] Subsections (5) and (6) identify a prescribed form which must be used where there is delegation by a single donor.

(b) in the case of a tenant for life, to the trustees of the settlement and to each person, if any, who together with the person giving the notice constitutes the tenant for life; and

(c) in the case of a statutory owner, to each of the persons, if any, who together with the person giving the notice constitute the statutory owner and, in the case of a statutory owner by virtue of section 23(1)(a) of the Settled Land Act 1925, to the trustees of the settlement.

(ii) Delegation to beneficiaries by trustees of land collectively[34]

TRUSTS OF LAND AND APPOINTMENT OF TRUSTEES ACT 1996[35]

9. Delegation by trustees

(1) The trustees of land may, by power of attorney, delegate to any beneficiary or beneficiaries of full age and beneficially entitled to an interest in possession in land subject to the trust any of their functions as trustees which relate to the land.

(2) Where trustees purport to delegate to a person by a power of attorney under subsection (1) functions relating to any land and another person in good faith deals with him in relation to the land, he shall be presumed in favour of that other person to have been a person to whom the functions could be delegated unless that other has knowledge at the time of the transaction that he was not such a person.

And it shall be conclusively presumed in favour of any purchaser whose interest depends on the validity of that transaction that that other person dealt in good faith and did not have such knowledge if that other person makes a statutory declaration to that effect before or within three months after the completion of the purchase.

(3) A power of attorney under subsection (1) shall be given by all the trustees jointly and (unless expressed to be irrevocable and to be given by way of security) may be revoked by any one or more of them; and such a power is revoked by the appointment as a trustee of a person other than those by whom it is given (though not by any of those persons dying or otherwise ceasing to be a trustee).

(4) Where a beneficiary to whom functions are delegated by a power of attorney under subsection (1) ceases to be a person beneficially entitled to an interest in possession in land subject to the trust—

(a) if the functions are delegated to him alone, the power is revoked,

(b) if the functions are delegated to him and to other beneficiaries to be exercised by them jointly (but not separately), the power is revoked if each

---

[34] For delegation by trustees of land who are also beneficiaries, see Trustee Delegation Act 1999, p. 759, below.

[35] See Whitehouse and Hassall, *Trusts of Land, Trustee Delegation and the Trustee Act* (2nd edn, 2001), pp. 46–58.

of the other beneficiaries ceases to be so entitled (but otherwise functions exercisable in accordance with the power are so exercisable by the remaining beneficiary or beneficiaries), and

(c) if the functions are delegated to him and to other beneficiaries to be exercised by them separately (or either separately or jointly), the power is revoked in so far as it relates to him.

(5) A delegation under subsection (1) may be for any period or indefinite.

(6) A power of attorney under subsection (1) cannot be an enduring power of attorney or lasting power of attorney within the meaning of the Mental Capacity Act 2005.[36]

(7) Beneficiaries to whom functions have been delegated under subsection (1) are, in relation to the exercise of the functions, in the same position as trustees (with the same duties and liabilities); but such beneficiaries shall not be regarded as trustees for any other purposes (including, in particular, the purposes of any enactment permitting the delegation of functions by trustees or imposing requirements relating to the payment of capital money).

9A. Duties of trustees in connection with delegation etc.[37]

(1) The duty of care under section 1 of the Trustee Act 2000[38] applies to trustees of land in deciding whether to delegate any of their functions under section 9.

(2) Subsection (3) applies if the trustees of land—

(a) delegate any of their functions under section 9, and

(b) the delegation is not irrevocable.

(3) While the delegation continues, the trustees—

(a) must keep the delegation under review,

(b) if circumstances make it appropriate to do so, must consider whether there is a need to exercise any power of intervention that they have, and

(c) if they consider that there is a need to exercise such a power, must do so.

(4) 'Power of intervention' includes—

(a) a power to give directions to the beneficiary;

(b) a power to revoke the delegation.

(5) The duty of care under section 1 of the 2000 Act applies to trustees in carrying out any duty under subsection (3).

(6) A trustee of land is not liable for any act or default of the beneficiary, or beneficiaries, unless the trustee fails to comply with the duty of care in deciding to

---

[36] As amended by the Mental Capacity Act 2005.
[37] As inserted by TA 2000, Sch. 2, Pt. II, para. 47.   [38] See p. 687, above.

delegate any of the trustees' functions under section 9 or in carrying out any duty under subsection (3).

(7) Neither this section nor the repeal of section 9(8) by the Trustee Act 2000 affects the operation after the commencement of this section of any delegation effected before that commencement.

(iii) Delegation by Trustees of Land who are Also Beneficiaries

TRUSTEE DELEGATION ACT 1999[39]

1. Exercise of trustee functions by attorney

(1) The donee of a power of attorney is not prevented from doing an act in relation to—

(a) land,

(b) capital proceeds of a conveyance of land, or

(c) income from land,

by reason only that the act involves the exercise of a trustee function of the donor if, at the time when the act is done, the donor has a beneficial interest in the land, proceeds or income.

(2) In this section—

(a) 'conveyance' has the same meaning as in the Law of Property Act 1925,[40] and

(b) references to a trustee function of the donor are to a function which the donor has as trustee (either alone or jointly with any other person or persons).

(3) Subsection (1) above—

(a) applies only if and so far as a contrary intention is not expressed in the instrument creating the power of attorney, and

(b) has effect subject to the terms of that instrument.

(4) The donor of the power of attorney—

(a) is liable for the acts or defaults of the donee in exercising any function by virtue of subsection (1) above in the same manner as if they were acts or defaults of the donor, but

(b) is not liable by reason only that a function is exercised by the donee by virtue of that subsection.

---

[39] See Whitehouse and Hassall, *Trusts of Land, Trustee Delegation and the Trustee Act* (2nd edn, 2001), pp. 157–189.

[40] This includes every assurance of property or of an interest in property by any instrument except a will: LPA 1925, s. 205(1)(ii).

(5) Subsections (1) and (4) above—

    (a) apply only if and so far as a contrary intention is not expressed in the instrument (if any) creating the trust, and

    (b) have effect subject to the terms of such an instrument.

(6) The fact that it appears that, in dealing with any shares or stock, the donee of the power of attorney is exercising a function by virtue of subsection (1) above does not affect with any notice of any trust a person in whose books the shares are, or stock is, registered or inscribed.

(8) The donee of a power of attorney is not to be regarded as exercising a trustee function by virtue of subsection (1) above if he is acting under a trustee delegation power; and for this purpose a trustee delegation power is a power of attorney given under—

    (a) a statutory provision, or

    (b) a provision of the instrument (if any) creating a trust,

under which the donor of the power is expressly authorised to delegate the exercise of all or any of his trustee functions by power of attorney.

(9) … this section applies only to powers of attorney created after the commencement of this Act.

2. Evidence of beneficial interest

(1) This section applies where the interest of a purchaser depends on the donee of a power of attorney having power to do an act in relation to any property by virtue of section 1(1) above.

    In this subsection 'purchaser' has the same meaning as in Part I of the Law of Property Act 1925.[41]

(2) Where this section applies an appropriate statement is, in favour of the purchaser, conclusive evidence of the donor of the power having a beneficial interest in the property at the time of the doing of the act.

(3) In this section 'an appropriate statement' means a signed statement made by the donee—

    (a) when doing the act in question, or

    (b) at any other time within the period of three months beginning with the day on which the act is done,

that the donor has a beneficial interest in the property at the time of the donee doing the act.

(4) If an appropriate statement is false, the donee is liable in the same way as he would be if the statement were contained in a statutory declaration.

---

[41] This is defined to include any person who acquires an interest in property for valuable consideration: LPA 1925, s. 205(1)(xxi).

(iv) Two-trustee rules

TRUSTEE DELEGATION ACT 1999

7. Two-trustee rules

(1) A requirement imposed by an enactment—

  (a) that capital money be paid to, or dealt with as directed by, at least two trustees or that a valid receipt for capital money be given otherwise than by a sole trustee, or

  (b) that, in order for an interest or power to be overreached, a conveyance or deed be executed by at least two trustees,

  is not satisfied by money being paid to or dealt with as directed by, or a receipt for money being given by, a relevant attorney or by a conveyance or deed being executed by such an attorney.

(2) In this section 'relevant attorney' means a person (other than a trust corporation within the meaning of the Trustee Act 1925)[42] who is acting either—

  (a) both as a trustee and as attorney for one or more other trustees, or

  (b) as attorney for two or more trustees,

  and who is not acting together with any other person or persons.

TRUSTEE ACT 1925

36. Appointment of trustees

(6A)[43] A person who is either—

  (a) both a trustee and attorney for the other trustee (if one other), or for both of the other trustees (if two others), under a registered power; or

  (b) attorney under a registered power for the trustee (if one) or for both or each of the trustees (if two or three),

  may, if subsection (6B) of this section is satisfied in relation to him, make an appointment under subsection (6)(b) of this section on behalf of the trustee or trustees.

(6B) This subsection is satisfied in relation to an attorney under a registered power for one or more trustees if (as attorney under the power)—

  (a) he intends to exercise any function of the trustee or trustees by virtue of section 1(1) of the Trustee Delegation Act 1999;[44] or

  (b) he intends to exercise any function of the trustee or trustees in relation to any land, capital proceeds of a conveyance of land or income from land by virtue of its delegation to him under section 25 of this Act or the instrument (if any) creating the trust.

---

[42] TA 1925, s. 68(1), para 18.
[43] As inserted by Trustee Delegation Act 1999, s. 8. For TA 1925, s. 36, see p. 624, above.
[44] See p. 759, above.

(6C) In subsections (6A) and (6B) of this section 'registered power' means an enduring power of attorney or a lasting power of attorney registered under the Mental Capacity Act 2005.[45]

(6D) Subsection (6A) of this section—

(a) applies only if and so far as a contrary intention is not expressed in the instrument creating the power of attorney (or, where more than one, any of them) or the instrument (if any) creating the trust; and

(b) has effect subject to the terms of those instruments.

> **QUESTION**
>
> In what circumstances might the general powers of delegation [p. 754, above] and the specific powers of delegation [pp. 755, above] be used? See H&M, pp. 583–591; Whitehouse and Hassall, *Trusts of Land, Trustee Delegation and the Trustee Act 2000* (2nd edn, 2001), pp. 46–55, 157–189, 239–270.

VIII OF MAINTENANCE[46]

The statutory power of maintenance gives to trustees a power to apply income for the benefit of beneficiaries who are minors, or who are not yet entitled to the income. Minors and persons contingently entitled would otherwise be unable to benefit from the income. The policy is to allow the gift to 'carry the intermediate income' unless the income is otherwise disposed-of, or there are good reasons to the contrary. Thus, the trustees may apply the income for the maintenance, education, and benefit of minor beneficiaries; and are required to pay the income to adult persons who are contingently entitled to the capital on the happening of some future event.

A THE STATUTORY POWER

TRUSTEE ACT 1925

31. Power to apply income for maintenance and to accumulate surplus income during a minority

(1) Where any property is held by trustees in trust for any person for any interest whatsoever, whether vested or contingent, then, subject to any prior interests or charges affecting that property—

---

[45] As amended by the Mental Capacity Act 2005, Sch. 6.

[46] H&M, pp. 591–598; Lewin, pp. 1145–1165; P&M, pp. 682–688; P&S, pp. 410–414; Pettit, pp. 472–478; Snell, pp. 627–632, 634–635; T&H, pp. 454–464; U&H, pp. 877–886. See generally (1953) 17 Conv (NS) 273 (B.S. Ker).

(i) during the infancy of any such person, if his interest so long continues, the trustees may, at their sole discretion, pay to his parent or guardian, if any, or otherwise apply for or towards his maintenance, education, or benefit, the whole or such part, if any, of the income of that property as may, in all the circumstances, be reasonable, whether or not there is—

   (a) any other fund applicable to the same purpose; or

   (b) any person bound by law to provide for his maintenance or education; and

(ii) if such person on attaining the age of eighteen[47] years has not a vested interest in such income, the trustees shall thenceforth pay the income of that property and of any accretion thereto under subsection (2) of this section to him, until he either attains a vested interest therein or dies, or until failure of his interest:

Provided that, in deciding whether the whole or any part of the income of the property is during a minority to be paid or applied for the purposes aforesaid, the trustees shall have regard to the age of the infant and his requirements and generally to the circumstances of the case, and in particular to what other income, if any, is applicable for the same purposes; and where trustees have notice that the income of more than one fund is applicable for those purposes, then, so far as practicable, unless the entire income of the funds is paid or applied as aforesaid or the court otherwise directs, a proportionate part only of the income of each fund shall be so paid or applied.

(2) During the infancy of any such person, if his interest so long continues, the trustees shall accumulate all the residue of that income by investing it, and any profits from so investing it[48] from time to time in authorised investments, and shall hold those accumulations as follows:—

(i) If any such person—

   (a) attains the age of eighteen[49] years, or marries under that age or forms a civil partnership under that age, and his interest in such income during his infancy or until his marriage or his formation of a civil partnership is a vested interest; or

   (b) on attaining the age of eighteen[50] years or on marriage or formation of a civil partnership under that age becomes entitled to the property from which such income arose in fee simple, absolute or determinable,[51] or absolutely, or for an entailed interest;

---

[47] Reduced from 21 by the Family Law Reform Act 1969 in the case of instruments made (not only those coming into effect) on or after 1 January, 1970. A will made before that date is not to be treated as made on or after that date by reason only that the will is confirmed by a codicil executed on or after that date; s.1, and Sch. 3, para. 5. But a deed of revocation and appointment made after that date is affected by a reduction in the age of majority: *Begg-McBrearty v Stilwell* [1996] 1 WLR 951.

[48] Substituted by TA 2000, s. 40(1), Sch. 2, para. 25.   [49] See, n. 47, above.   [50] Ibid.

[51] *Re Sharp's Settlement Trusts* [1973] Ch 331; (1974) 34 Conv (NS) 436 (D.J. Hayton).

the trustees shall hold the accumulations in trust for such person absolutely, but without prejudice to any provision with respect thereto contained in any settlement by him made under any statutory powers during his infancy, and so that the receipt of such person after marriage or the formation of a civil partnership, and though still an infant, shall be a good discharge; and

(ii) In any other case the trustees shall, notwithstanding that such person had a vested interest in such income, hold the accumulations as an accretion to the capital of the property from which such accumulations arose, and as one fund with such capital for all purposes, and so that, if such property is settled land, such accumulations shall be held upon the same trusts as if the same were capital money arising therefrom;

but the trustees may, at any time during the infancy of such person if his interest so long continues, apply those accumulations, or any part thereof, as if they were income arising in the then current year.

(3) This section applies in the case of a contingent interest only if the limitation or trust carries the intermediate income of the property, but it applies to a future or contingent legacy by the parent of, or a person standing *in loco parentis* to, the legatee, if and for such period as, under the general law, the legacy carries interest for the maintenance of the legatee, and in any such case as last aforesaid the rate of interest shall (if the income available is sufficient, and subject to any rules of court to the contrary) be five pounds per centum per annum.

(4) This section applies to a vested annuity in like manner as if the annuity were the income of property held by trustees in trust to pay the income thereof to the annuitant for the same period for which the annuity is payable, save that in any case accumulations made during the infancy of the annuitant shall be held in trust for the annuitant or his personal representatives absolutely.

(5) This section does not apply where the instrument, if any, under which the interest arises came into operation before the commencement of this Act.

B   CONTRARY INTENTION

TRUSTEE ACT 1925

69. Application of Act

(2), p. 747, above.

In **Re Turner's Will Trust** [1937] Ch 15, Robert Turner, the testator, gave a share of his residuary estate in trust for such of the children of his late son as should attain the age of 28. The will contained an express power of maintenance and a power to pay the income to such of them as should have attained the age of 21, and instructed the trustees to accumulate the surplus.

Two of the testator's grandchildren had attained 28 at the testator's death. The third grandchild, Geoffrey, was then aged 21, and died three years later. His share of the income had all been accumulated. The question was whether he had been entitled to such income under the Trustee Act 1925, section 31. If so, the fund would pass on his death for Estate Duty purposes.

The Court of Appeal, reversing Bennett J, held that Geoffrey had not been entitled to the income. The imperative terms of section 31 must be read subject to section 69(2), so that the contrary intention prevailed. ROMER LJ said at 27:

The fact that section 31 contains provisions that are directory is immaterial. Powers of maintenance, in the comprehensive meaning of that term, usually do. Nothing is more common, for instance, than a direction to trustees to accumulate during the minority income not applied in maintenance. Such a direction is merely ancillary to the power of maintenance strictly so called, and may well be regarded as a part of the power of maintenance in its comprehensive sense. Such a direction is indeed contained in sub-section 2 of section 31 of the Trustee Act, 1925, and is an essential part of the statutory power of maintenance conferred upon trustees by the section. In the same way the direction contained in cl. (ii) of subsection 1 can be regarded as being merely an essential part of the new statutory power. This statutory power of maintenance, that is to say, the totality of the provisions to be found in section 31 of the Act, is, in our opinion, one of the 'powers conferred by this Act' within the meaning of section 69, subsection 2, and therefore only applies if and so far as a contrary intention is not expressed in the instrument creating the trust and has effect subject to the terms of that instrument. For these reasons we are of opinion that the accumulations of the income of the presumptive share of Geoffrey Heap Turner made by the trustees did not form part of his estate, but accrued by way of addition to the shares of the defendants Robert Heap Turner and Doris Heap Lyons in the residuary estate of the testator.[52]

C INTERMEDIATE INCOME[53]

(1953) 17 Conv (NS) 275–276 (B.S. Ker)

The question now arises as to when a 'limitation or trust' carries the intermediate income of the property. The rules are as follows:

1. A contingent gift by will of *residuary* personalty carries with it all the income it earns from the testator's death, for the simple reason that there is no one besides the residuary legatee to whom it could go. North J said in *Re Adams* [1893] 1 Ch 329, at 334, 'Here no child has [a vested interest in the residue]. How does the matter stand as to the income? It is said that they take an interest in that also. I think it is fallacious to say that they take an interest in the income, *qua* income of the capital they take an interest in. *But it is undisposed-of income, and as such becomes part of the residue;* but, being part of the residue, the income belongs contingently to the children, in the same way as the capital belongs contingently to them.' If this income is accumulated until the contingency vesting the money in the beneficiaries happens the rules in sections 164–166 of the Law of Property Act, 1925, must be observed. (See *Bective v Hodgson* (1864) 10 HL Cas 656.)

---

[52] Followed in *Re Erskine's Settlement Trusts* [1971] 1 WLR 162.
[53] For a tabular presentation, see (1976) 95 Law Notes 110 (M.J. Wells).

2. The rule as to contingent *specific* gifts of personalty and contingent specific or residuary gifts of realty is contained in section 175 of the Law of Property Act, 1925: 'a contingent or future specific devise or bequest of property, whether real or personal, and a contingent residuary devise of freehold land, and a specific or residuary devise of freehold land to trustees upon trust for persons whose interests are contingent or executory shall, subject to the statutory provisions relating to accumulations, carry the intermediate income of that property from the death of the testator, except so far as such income, or any part thereof, may be otherwise expressly disposed of.' This section applies only to *wills* coming into operation after 1925, but it has been held in *Re Raine* [1929] 1 Ch 716, not to apply to a pecuniary legacy. Further, it draws a distinction between 'land' and 'freehold' land. This is because leaseholds rank as personal property and therefore the ordinary rules (*supra* and *infra*) as to the income of contingent gifts of personalty apply: see *Guthrie v Walrond* (1883) 22 Ch D 573, and *Re Woodin* [1895] 2 Ch 309, *per* Lindley LJ and Kay LJ.

Pecuniary Legacies

3. In view of the decision on *Re Raine* (*supra*) the rules of the general law as to when contingent pecuniary legacies bear interest require examination. The broad rule is that no interest is payable on a contingent pecuniary legacy from the testator's death while the gift is in suspense (see *per* Kay LJ, in *Re George* (1877) 5 Ch D 837). There are, however, the following exceptions in which the legacy, subject to any contrary intention in the will, carries interest from the testator's death...

Summarising, then: the three cases in which, apart from statute, contingent legacies carry interest from the date of death are—

    (a) where the testator was the father of, or *in loco parentis* to, the legatee,

    (b) where, without being either of the foregoing, the testator shows an intention to maintain (*Re Churchill* [1909] 2 Ch 431), or

    (c) where the testator has segregated the legacy for the legatee (*Re Medlock* (1886) 55 LJ Ch 738).

It will be noticed that section 31(3) of the Trustee Act, 1925, expressly mentions the rule in (a) only—the golden rule. Does it impliedly exclude the rules in (b) and (c), or does it merely single out that in (a) for the purpose of fixing interest at 5 per cent per annum? If it excludes (b) and (c) then section 31 will not apply at all to cases of the *Re Churchill* and *Re Medlock* kinds and this would need to be borne in mind when considering, in particular, subsection (1)(ii) and (2). The arguments both ways have already been set out... It is submitted that the correct view is that subsection (3) does embrace the *Re Churchill* and *Re Medlock* types of case and that the specific mention of the rule in (a) above is only for the purpose of establishing a suitable rate of interest. The learned author of *Williams on Wills* (p. 803) seems to take this view.

Before leaving subsection (3) it may be worth noticing that while the rule—(a) above—of the general law is that the donor of the legacy must be the *father* of the legatee, the statute, in adopting the rule has used the word 'parent' instead of father. At common law, of course, it is the father's duty to maintain his child—not the mother's unless she has deliberately taken upon herself a father's duty. Section 31(3) may thus have enlarged the law here to cover a legacy by a mother not *in loco parentis*. However, the term 'parent' would probably be held to mean 'parent responsible in law for the children's maintenance' and thus refer only to the legatee's father, unless the mother had assumed the duty of maintenance.

In **Re McGeorge** [1963] Ch 544,[54] the testator devised land to his daughter and provided that the devise 'shall not take effect until after the death of my … wife should she survive me'. If the daughter should die before the wife, leaving issue, the issue, on attaining the age of 21, were to take by substitution the devise to the daughter. Cross J held that the devise to the daughter carried the intermediate income; that the income must be accumulated, to be paid to whoever became entitled to it—that is, the daughter or her issue, depending on whether the daughter survived the widow. CROSS J said at 550:

The devise … is, it is said, a future specific devise within the meaning of the section [Law of Property Act 1925, section 175]; the testator has not made any express disposition of the income accruing from it between his death and the death of his widow, therefore that income is carried by the gift. At first sight it is hard to see how Parliament could have enacted a section which produces such a result. If a testator gives property to A after the death of B, then whether or not he disposes of the income accruing during B's life he is at all events showing clearly that A is not to have it. Yet if the future gift to A is absolute and the intermediate income is carried with it by force of this section, A can claim to have the property transferred to him at once, since no one else can be interested in it. The section, that is to say, will have converted a gift in remainder into a gift in possession in defiance of the testator's wishes. The explanation for the section taking the form it does is, I think, probably as follows. It has long been established that a gift of residuary personalty to a legatee in being on a contingency or to an unborn person at birth, carries the intermediate income so far as the law will allow it to be accumulated, but that rule had been held for reasons depending on the old land law not to apply to gifts of real property, and it was apparently never applied to specific dispositions of personalty. Section 175 of the Law of Property Act was plainly intended to extend the rule to residuary devises and to specific gifts whether of realty or of personalty. It is now, however, established at all events in courts of first instance that the old rule does not apply to residuary bequests whether vested or contingent which are expressly deferred to a future date which must come sooner or later. (See *Re Oliver* [1947] 2 All ER 162; *Re Gillett's Will Trusts* [1950] Ch 102, and *Re Geering* [1964] Ch 136). There is a good reason for this distinction. If a testator gives property to X contingently on his attaining the age of 30 it is reasonable to assume, in the absence of a direction to the contrary, that he would wish X if he attains 30 to have the income produced by the property between his death and the happening of the contingency. If, on the other hand, he gives property to X for any sort of interest after the death of A, it is reasonable to assume that he does not wish X to have the income accruing during A's lifetime unless he directs that he is to have it. But this distinction between an immediate gift on a contingency and a gift which is expressly deferred was not drawn until after the Law of Property Act, 1925, was passed. There were statements in textbooks and even in judgments to the effect that the rule applied to deferred as well as to contingent gifts of residuary personalty. (See *Jarman*, 7th edn (1930) p. 1006.)

The legislature, when it extended this rule to residuary devises and specific gifts, must, I think, have adopted this erroneous view of the law. I would have liked, if I could, to construe the reference to 'future specific devises' and 'executory interest' in the section in such a way as to make it consistent with the recent cases on the scope of the old rule applicable to residuary bequests. But to do that would be to rectify the Act, not to construe it, and I see no escape from the conclusion that whereas before 1926 a specific gift or a residuary devise which was not

[54] (1963) 79 LQR 184 (P.V.B.).

vested in possession did not *prima facie* carry intermediate income at all, now such a gift may carry intermediate income in circumstances in which a residuary bequest would not carry it.

It was argued in this case that the fact that the will contained a residuary gift constituted an express disposition of the income of the land in question which prevented the section from applying. I am afraid that I cannot accept this submission. I have little doubt that the testator expected the income of the land to form part of the income of residue during his widow's life-time, but he has made no express disposition of it. I agree with what was said in this connection by Eve J in *Re Raine* [1929] 1 Ch 716 at 719.

As the devise is not vested indefeasibly in the daughter but is subject to defeasance during the mother's lifetime the intermediate income which the gift carries by virtue of section 175 ought *prima facie* to be accumulated to see who eventually becomes entitled to it. It was, however, submitted by counsel for the daughter that she could claim payment of it under section 31(1) of the Trustee Act 1925. So far as material, that subsection provides that where any property is held by trustees in trust for any person for any interest whatsoever, whether vested or con-tingent, then, subject to any prior interests or charges affecting that property, if such person on attaining the age of 21 years has not a vested interest in such income, the trustees shall thenceforth pay the income of that property and of any accretion of such income made during his infancy to him until he either attains a vested interest therein or dies or until failure of his interest. There are, as I see it, two answers to the daughter's claim. The first—and narrower—answer is that her interest in the income of the devised land is in a vested interest. It is a future interest liable to be divested but it is not contingent. Therefore, section 31(1)(ii) does not apply to it. The second—and wider—answer is that the whole framework of section 31 shows that it is inapplicable to a future gift of this sort and that a will containing such a gift expresses a con-trary intention within section 69(2) which prevents the section from applying. By deferring the enjoyment of the devise until after the widow's death the testator has expressed the intention that the daughter shall not have the immediate income. It is true that as he has not expressly disposed of it in any other way, section 175 of the Law of Property Act, 1925, defeats that intention to the extent of making the future devise carry the income so that the daughter will get it eventually if she survives her mother or dies before her leaving no children to take by substitu-tion. But even if the words of section 31 fitted the case, there would be no warrant for defeating the testator's intention still further by reading it into the will and thus giving the daughter an interest in possession in the income during her mother's lifetime. In the result, in my judgment the income of the fund must be accumulated for 21 years if the widow so long lives.

IX OF ADVANCEMENT[55]

The statutory power of advancement relates to the payment of capital for special purposes. Those purposes related, and until recent times were limited, to specific occasions in the establishment in life of a beneficiary.[56] In modern cases however, a

[55] H&M, pp. 598–605; Lewin, pp. 1167–1182; P&M, pp. 694–707; P&S, pp. 414–417; Pettit, pp. 478–483; Snell, pp. 632–634; T&H, pp. 464–475; U&H, pp. 886–896; (1958) 22 Conv (NS) 413; (1959) 23 Conv (NS) 27, 423 (D.W.M. Waters).   [56] See *Pilkington v IRC* [1964] AC 612 [p. 770, below].

wide construction is given to the phrase 'advancement or benefit', and this was used to permit blocks of capital to be paid to contingent remaindermen in order to avoid Estate Duty liability in respect of that property on the death of a life tenant. The fiscal advantages can still be significant since, when the life tenant's interest determines in his lifetime and the remainderman becomes absolutely entitled, there is no charge to Inheritance Tax, unless the life tenant dies within seven years of the termination. Where, however, the property is held on trust for a minor contingently on obtaining a specified age not in excess of 25, and there is no prior interest in possession, there is no charge to tax upon the minor's attainment of that specified age, nor upon payments of capital being made to him.[57]

A   THE STATUTORY POWER

TRUSTEE ACT 1925

32. Power of advancement

(1) Trustees may at any time or times pay or apply any capital money subject to a trust, for the advancement or benefit, in such manner as they may, in their absolute discretion, think fit, of any person entitled to the capital of the trust property or of any share thereof, whether absolutely or contingently on his attaining any specified age or on the occurrence of any other event, or subject to a gift over on his death under any specified age or on the occurrence of any other event, and whether in possession or in remainder or reversion, and such payment or application may be made notwithstanding that the interest of such person is liable to be defeated by the exercise of a power of appointment or revocation, or to be diminished by the increase of the class to which he belongs:

Provided that—

(a) the money so paid or applied for the advancement or benefit of any person shall not exceed altogether in amount one-half of the presumptive or vested share or interest of that person in the trust property;[58] and

(b) if that person is or becomes absolutely and indefeasibly entitled to a share in the trust property the money so paid or applied shall be brought into account as part of such share; and

(c) no such payment or application shall be made so as to prejudice any person entitled to any prior life or other interest, whether vested or contingent, in

---

[57] Inheritance Tax Act (IHTA) 1984, s. 71.

[58] *Re Marquess of Abergavenny's Estate Act Trusts* [1981] 1 WLR 843 (where trustees had express power to raise and pay to the life tenant 'any part or parts not exceeding in all one-half in value of the settled fund', Goulding J held that an advance of one-half exhausted the exercise of the power, so that it could not be exercised in the future, even though the retained assets in the fund later increased in value). Cf. *Re Richardson* [1896] 1 Ch 512; *Re Gollin's Declaration of Trust* [1969] 1 WLR 1858. See [1982] Conv 158 (J.W. Price).

the money paid or applied unless such person is in existence and of full age and consents in writing to such payment or application.[59]

(2) This section does not apply to capital money arising under the Settled Land Act 1925.[60]

(3) This section does not apply to trusts constituted or created before the commencement of this Act.[61]

B ADVANCEMENT OR BENEFIT

Pilkington v Inland Revenue Commissioners[62]
[1964] AC 612 (HL, **Lord Reid, Viscount Radcliffe, Lords Jenkins, Hodson** and **Devlin**)

Mr. Pilkington, by his will dated 14 December, 1934, gave the income of his residuary estate upon trusts for his nephews and nieces (the beneficiaries) in equal shares. Each share was settled on protective trusts, and the will provided that the consent of a beneficiary to the exercise by the trustees of their statutory power of advancement should not cause a forfeiture. The capital was to be held upon trust for the children of each beneficiary in such shares as the beneficiary should appoint, and in default of appointment in equal shares.

Richard Pilkington was one of the beneficiaries. He was married and had three children, one of whom was Penelope, a child two years old and born after the death of the testator. The trustees decided, with Richard's consent, to advance one-half of Penelope's expectant share in the trust, and to pay it to the trustees of a new trust which was being set up for Penelope's benefit. The main object of the trustees was to save the Estate Duty which would be payable upon that part of the fund on Richard's death. The new trusts were that until Penelope attained the age of 21 the income should be applied for her maintenance, education, and benefit, and the surplus accumulated; that on her attaining the age of 21 the income should be paid to her; and that the capital should be paid to her on attaining the age of 30.

---

[59] *Henley v Wardell* (1988) The Times, 29 January (consent of prior beneficiary necessary, even though the statutory power was expressly enlarged so as to give to the trustees 'an absolute and uncontrolled discretion' to advance capital for the benefit of a beneficiary).

[60] As substituted by TLATA 1996, s. 25(1), Sch. 3, para. 3(8).

[61] The application of s. 32 is subject to the expression of a contrary intention: *Re Evans' Settlement* [1967] 1 WLR 1294. But 'very few settlements provide that the statutory power is not to apply—though some extend the power or contain express advancement provisions more extended than the statutory power': *Inglewood (Lord) v IRC* [1983] 1 WLR 366 at 373, *per* Fox LJ.

[62] (1963) 27 Conv (NS) 65 (F.R. Crane); *Re Wills' Will Trusts* [1959] Ch 1 (advancement upon new trusts); *Re Clore's Settlement Trusts* [1966] 1 WLR 955 (payment to charity held to be for the benefit of rich minor who felt himself under moral obligation to make the gift); *Re Pauling's Settlement Trusts* [1964] Ch 303 (advancement nominally to children was really made to benefit parents); p. 776, below; *Inglewood (Lord) v IRC*, ibid, at 372; *X v A* [2006] 1 WLR 741 (advancement to beneficiary for charitable causes did not improve her material situation and so was not allowed).

The question was whether the trustees could properly so exercise the power of advancement.

Held. (i) Such an exercise was within the statutory power as being for Penelope's benefit, although her interest under the trust would vest later than under the will; (ii) but the particular exercise was void for perpetuity.[63]

Viscount Radcliffe: The word 'advancement' itself meant in this context the establishment in life of the beneficiary who was the object of the power or at any rate some step that would contribute to the furtherance of his establishment. Thus it was found in such phrases as 'preferment or advancement' (*Lowther v Bentinck* (1874) LR 19 Eq 166), 'business, profession, or employment or . . . advancement or preferment in the world' (*Roper-Curzon v Roper-Curzon* (1871) LR 11 Eq 452) and 'placing out or advancement in life' (*Re Breeds' Will* (1875) 1 Ch D 226). Typical instances of expenditure for such purposes under the social conditions of the nineteenth century were an apprenticeship or the purchase of a commission in the army or of an interest in business. In the case of a girl there could be advancement on marriage (*Lloyd v Cocker* (1860) 27 Beav 645). Advancement had, however, to some extent a limited range of meaning, since it was thought to convey the idea of some step in life of permanent significance, and accordingly, to prevent uncertainties about the permitted range of objects for which moneys could be raised and made available, such words as 'or otherwise for his or her benefit' were often added to the word 'advancement'. It was always recognised that these added words were 'large words' (see Jessel MR in *Re Breeds' Will* (1875) 1 Ch D 226 at 228) and indeed in another case (*Lowther v Bentinck* (1874) LR 19 Eq 166 at 169) the same judge spoke of preferment and advancement as being 'both large words' but of 'benefit' as being the 'largest of all'. So, too, Kay J in *Re Brittlebank* (1881) 30 WR 99 at 100. Recent judges have spoken in the same terms—see Farwell J in *Re Halsted's Will Trusts* [1937] 2 All ER 570 at 571 and Danckwerts J in *Re Moxon's Will Trusts* [1958] 1 WLR 165 at 168. This wide construction of the range of the power, which evidently did not stand upon niceties of distinction provided that the proposed application could fairly be regarded as for the benefit of the beneficiary who was the object of the power, must have been carried into the statutory power created by section 32, since it adopts without qualification the accustomed wording 'for the advancement or benefit in such manner as they may in their absolute discretion think fit'.

So much for 'advancement', which I now use for brevity to cover the combined phrase 'advancement or benefit'. It means any use of the money which will improve the material situation of the beneficiary. It is important, however, not to confuse the idea of 'advancement' with the idea of advancing the money out of the beneficiary's expectant interest. The two things have only a casual connection with each other. The one refers to the operation of finding money by way of anticipation of an interest not yet absolutely vested in possession or, if so vested, belonging to an infant: the other refers to the status of the beneficiary and the improvement of his situation. The power to carry out the operation of anticipating an interest is not conferred by the word 'advancement' but by those other words of the section which expressly authorise the payment or application of capital money for the benefit of a person entitled 'whether absolutely or contingently on his attaining any specified age or on the occurrence of any other event, or

[63] *Re Abraham's Will Trusts* [1969] 1 Ch 463; *Re Hastings-Bass* [1975] Ch 25; *Mettoy Pension Trustees Ltd v Evans* [1990] 1 WLR 1587; *Stannard v Fisons Pension Trust Ltd* [1992] IRLR 27.

subject to a gift over on his death under any specified age or on the occurrence of any other event, and whether in possession or in remainder or reversion', etc.

I think, with all respect to the Commissioners, a good deal of their argument is infected with some of this confusion. To say, for instance, that there cannot be a valid exercise of a power of advancement that results in a deferment of the vesting of the beneficiary's absolute title (Miss Penelope, it will be remembered, is to take at 30 under the proposed settlement instead of at 21 under the will) is in my opinion to play upon words. The element of anticipation consists in the raising of money for her now before she has any right to receive anything under the existing trusts: the advancement consists in the application of that money to form a trust fund, the provisions of which are thought to be for her benefit. I have not forgotten, of course, the references to powers of advancement which are found in such cases as *Re Joicey* [1915] 2 Ch 115; *Re May's Settlement* [1926] Ch 136 and *Re Mewburn's Settlement* [1934] Ch 112, to which our attention was called, or the answer supplied by Cotton LJ in *Re Aldridge*[64] to his own question 'what is advancement?'; but I think that it will be apparent from what I have already said that the description that he gives (it cannot be a definition) is confined entirely to the aspect of anticipation or acceleration which renders the money available and not to any description or limitation of the purposes for which it can then be applied.

I have not been able to find in the words of section 32, to which I have now referred, anything which in terms or by implication restricts the width of the manner or purpose of advancement. It is true that, if this settlement is made, Miss Penelope's children, who are not objects of the power, are given a possible interest in the event of her dying under 30 leaving surviving issue. But if the disposition itself, by which I mean the whole provision made, is for her benefit, it is no objection to the exercise of the power that other persons benefit incidentally as a result of the exercise. Thus a man's creditors may in certain cases get the most immediate advantage from an advancement made for the purpose of paying them off, as in *Lowther v Bentinck* (1874) LR 19 Eq 166, and a power to raise money for the advancement of a wife may cover a payment made direct to her husband in order to set him up in business: *Re Kershaw's Trusts* (1868) LR 6 Eq 322. The exercise will not be bad therefore on this ground.

Nor in my opinion will it be bad merely because the moneys are to be tied up in the proposed settlement. If it could be said that the payment or application permitted by section 32 cannot take the form of a settlement in any form but must somehow pass direct into or through the hands of the object of the power, I could appreciate the principle upon which the Commissioners' objection was founded. But can that principle be asserted? Anyone can see, I think, that there can be circumstances in which, while it is very desirable that some money should be raised at once for the benefit of an owner of an expectant or contingent interest, it would be very undesirable that the money should not be secured to him under some arrangement that will prevent him having the absolute disposition of it. I find it very difficult to think that there is something at the back of section 32 which makes an advancement impossible. Certainly neither Danckwerts J nor the members of the Court of Appeal in this case took that view. Both Lord Evershed MR and Upjohn LJ [1961] Ch 466 at 481, 486 explicitly accept the possibility of a settlement being made in exercise of a power of advancement. Farwell J authorised one in *Re Halsted's Will Trusts* [1937] 2 All ER 570 at 572, a case in which the trustees had left their discretion to the court. The trustees should raise the money and 'have' it 'settled', he said. So too, Harman J

---

[64] (1886) 55 LT 554 at 556: 'it is a payment to persons who are presumably entitled to, or have a vested or contingent interest in, an estate or a legacy, before the time fixed by the will for their obtaining the absolute interest in a portion or the whole of that to which they would be entitled.'

in *Re Ropner's Settlement Trusts* [1956] 1 WLR 902 at 906, authorised the settlement of an advance provided for an infant, saying that the child could not 'consent or request the trustees to make the advance, but the transfer of a part of his contingent share to the trustees of the settlement for him must advance his interest and thus be for his benefit...' All this must be wrong in principle if a power of advancement cannot cover an application of the moneys by way of settlement.

The truth is, I think, that the propriety of requiring a settlement of moneys found for advancement was recognised as long ago as 1871 in *Roper-Curzon v Roper-Curzon* (1871) LR 11 Eq 452 and, so far as I know, it has not been impugned since. Lord Romilly MR's decision passed into the text-books and it must have formed the basis of a good deal of subsequent practice. True enough, as counsel for the Commissioners has reminded us, the beneficiary in that case was an adult who was offering to execute the post-nuptial settlement required: but I find it impossible to read Lord Romilly's words as amounting to anything less than a decision that he would permit an advancement under the power only on the terms that the money was to be secured by settlement. That was what the case was about. If, then, it is a proper exercise of a power of advancement for trustees to stipulate that the money shall be settled, I cannot see any difference between having it settled that way and having it settled by themselves paying it to trustees of a settlement which is in the desired form.[65]

It is not as if anyone were contending for a principle that a power of advancement cannot be exercised 'over the head' of a beneficiary, that is, unless he actually asks for the money to be raised and consents to its application. From some points of view that might be a satisfactory limitation, and no doubt it is the way in which an advancement takes place in the great majority of cases. But, if application and consent were necessary requisites of advancement, that would cut out the possibility of making any advancement for the benefit of a person under age, at any rate without the institution of court proceedings and formal representation of the infant: and it would mean, moreover, that the trustees of an adult could not in any circumstances insist on raising money to pay his debts, however much the operation might be to his benefit, unless he agreed to that course. Counsel for the Commissioners did not contend before us that the power of advancement was inherently limited in this way: and I do not think that such a limitation would accord with the general understanding. Indeed its 'paternal' nature is well shown by the fact that it is often treated as being peculiarly for the assistance of an infant.

The Commissioners' objections seem to be concentrated upon such propositions as that the proposed transaction is 'nothing less than a resettlement' and that a power of advancement cannot be used so as to alter or vary the trusts created by the settlement from which it is derived. Such a transaction, they say, amounts to using the power of advancement as a way of appointing or declaring new trusts different from those of the settlement. The reason why I do not find that these propositions have any compulsive effect upon my mind is that they seem to me merely vivid ways of describing the substantial effect of that which is proposed to be done and they do not in themselves amount to convincing arguments against doing it. Of course, whenever money is raised for advancement on terms that it is to be settled on the beneficiary, the money only passes from one settlement to be caught up in the other. It is therefore the same thing as a resettlement. But, unless one is to say that such moneys can never be applied by way of settlement, an argument which, as I have shown, has few supporters and is contrary to authority, it merely describes the inevitable effect of such an advancement to say that it is nothing less than

---

[65] Cf. *Hart v Briscoe* [1979] Ch 1; *Hoare Trustees v Gardner* [1979] Ch 10.

a resettlement. Similarly, if it is part of the trusts and powers created by one settlement that the trustees of it should have power to raise money and make it available for a beneficiary upon new trusts approved by them, then they are in substance given power to free the money from one trust and to subject it to another. So be it: but, unless they cannot require a settlement of it at all, the transaction they carry out is the same thing in effect as an appointment of new trusts.

In the same way I am unconvinced by the argument that the trustees would be improperly delegating their trust by allowing the money raised to pass over to new trustees under a settlement conferring new powers on the latter. In fact I think that the whole issue of delegation is here beside the mark. The law is not that trustees cannot delegate: it is that trustees cannot delegate unless they have authority to do so. If the power of advancement which they possess is so read as to allow them to raise money for the purpose of having it settled, then they do have the necessary authority to let the money pass out of the old settlement into the new trusts. No question of delegation of their powers or trusts arises. If, on the other hand, their power of advancement is read so as to exclude settled advances, *cadit quaestio*.[66]

I ought to note for the record (1) that the transaction envisaged does not actually involve the raising of money, since the trustees propose to appropriate a block of shares in the family's private limited company as the trust investment, and (2) there will not be any actual transfer, since the trustees of the proposed settlement and the will trustees are the same persons. As I have already said, I do not attach any importance to these factors nor, I think, do the Commissioners. To transfer or appropriate outright is only to do by short cut what could be done in a more roundabout way by selling the shares to a consenting party, paying the money over to the new settlement with appropriate instructions and arranging for it to be used in buying back the shares as the trust investment. It cannot make any difference to follow the course taken in *Re Collard's Will Trusts* [1961] Ch 293 and deal with the property direct. On the other point, so long as there are separate trusts, the property effectually passes out of the old settlement into the new one, and it is of no relevance that, at any rate for the time being, the persons administering the new trust are the same individuals.

I have not yet referred to the ground which was taken by the Court of Appeal as their reason for saying that the proposed settlement was not permissible. To put it shortly, they held that the statutory power of advancement could not be exercised unless the benefit to be conferred was 'personal to the person concerned, in the sense of being related to his or her own real or personal needs' [1961] Ch 466 at 481. Or, to use other words of the learned Master of the Rolls at 484, the exercise of the power 'must be an exercise done to meet the circumstances as they present themselves in regard to a person within the scope of the section, whose circumstances call for that to be done which the trustees think fit to do'. Upjohn LJ at 487 expressed himself in virtually the same terms.

My Lords, I differ with reluctance from the views of judges so learned and experienced in matters of this sort: but I do not find it possible to import such restrictions into the words of the statutory power which itself does not contain them. First, the suggested qualification, that the considerations or circumstances must be 'personal' to the beneficiary, seems to me uncontrollably vague as a guide to general administration. What distinguishes a personal need from any other need to which the trustees in their discretion think it right to attend in the beneficiary's interest? And, if the advantage of preserving the funds of a beneficiary from the incidence of death duty is not an advantage personal to that beneficiary, I do not see what is. Death duty is

---

[66] See *Re Hay's Settlement Trusts* [1982] 1 WLR 202 [p. 49, above].

a present risk that attaches to the settled property in which Miss Penelope has her expectant interest, and even accepting the validity of the supposed limitation, I would not have supposed that there was anything either impersonal or unduly remote in the advantage to be conferred upon her of some exemption from that risk. I do not think, therefore, that I can support the interpretation of the power of advancement that has commended itself to the Court of Appeal, and, with great respect, I think that the judgments really amount to little more than a decision that in the opinion of the members of that court this was not a case in which there was any occasion to exercise the power. That would be a proper answer from a court to which trustees had referred their discretion with a request for its directions; but it does not really solve any question where, as here, they retain their discretion and merely ask whether it is impossible for them to exercise it.

To conclude, therefore, on this issue, I am of opinion that there is no maintainable reason for introducing into the statutory power of advancement a qualification that would exclude the exercise in the case now before us. It would not be candid to omit to say that, though I think that that is what the law requires, I am uneasy at some of the possible applications of this liberty, when advancements are made for the purposes of settlement or on terms that there is to be a settlement. It is quite true, as the Commissioners have pointed out, that you might have really extravagant cases of resettlements being forced on beneficiaries in the name of advancement, even a few months before an absolute vesting in possession would have destroyed the power. I have tried to give due weight to such possibilities, but when all is said I do not think that they ought to compel us to introduce a limitation of which no one, with all respect, can produce a satisfactory definition. First, I do not believe that it is wise to try to cut down an admittedly wide and discretionary power, enacted for general use, through fear of its being abused in certain hypothetical instances. And moreover, as regards this fear, I think that it must be remembered that we are speaking of a power intended to be in the hands of trustees chosen by a settlor because of his confidence in their discretion and good sense and subject to the external check that no exercise can take place without the consent of a prior life tenant; and that there does remain at all times a residual power in the court to restrain or correct any purported exercise that can be shown to be merely wanton or capricious and not to be attributable to a genuine discretion. I think, therefore, that, although extravagant possibilities exist, they may be more menacing in argument than in real life.

The other issue on which this case depends, that relating to the application of the rule against perpetuities, does not seem to me to present much difficulty. It is not in dispute that, if the limitations of the proposed settlement are to be treated as if they had been made by the testator's will and as coming into operation at the date of his death, there are trusts in it which would be void ab initio as violating the perpetuity rule. They postpone final vesting by too long a date. It is also a familiar rule of law in this field that, whereas appointments made under a general power of appointment conferred by will or deed are held as taking effect from the date of the exercise of the power, trusts declared by a special power of appointment, the distinguishing feature of which is that it can allocate property among a limited class of persons only, are treated as coming into operation at the date of the instrument that creates the power. The question therefore resolves itself into asking whether the exercise of a power of advancement which takes the form of a settlement should be looked upon as more closely analogous to a general or to a special power of appointment.

On this issue I am in full agreement with the views of Upjohn LJ in the Court of Appeal [1961] Ch 466 at 488. Indeed, much of the reasoning that has led me to my conclusion on the first issue that I have been considering leads me to think that for this purpose there is an effective analogy between powers of advancement and special powers of appointment. When one asks what person can be regarded as the settlor of Miss Penelope's proposed settlement, I do not see how it is possible to say that she is herself or that the trustees are. She is the passive recipient of the benefit extracted for her from the original trusts; the trustees are merely exercising a fiduciary power in arranging for the desired limitations. It is not their property that constitutes the funds of Miss Penelope's settlement; it is the property subjected to trusts by the will of the testator and passed over into the new settlement through the instrumentality of a power which by statute is made appendant to those trusts. I do not think, therefore, that it is important to this issue that money raised under a power of advancement passes entirely out of the reach of the existing trusts and makes, as it were, a new start under fresh limitations, the kind of thing that happened under the old form of family resettlement when the tenant in tail in remainder barred the entail with the consent of the protector of the settlement. I think that the important point for the purpose of the rule against perpetuities is that the new settlement is only effected by the operation of a fiduciary power which itself 'belongs' to the old settlement.

In the conclusion, therefore, there are legal objections to the proposed settlement which the trustees have placed before the court. Again I agree with Upjohn LJ that these objections go to the root of what is proposed and I do not think that it would be satisfactory that the court should try to frame a qualified answer to the question that they have propounded, which would express the general view that the power to advance by way of a settlement of this sort does exist and the special view that the power to make this particular settlement does not. Nor, I think, is such a course desired either by the appellants or the trustees. They will, I hope, know where they stand for the future, and so will the Commissioners, and that is enough.

C APPLICATION OF THE MONEY

In **Re Pauling's Settlement Trusts** [1964] Ch 303,[67] one question was whether trustees, in making an advancement, were under an obligation to ensure that the money advanced was in fact applied for the purposes for which it was advanced. WILLMER LJ said at 334:

Furthermore, it is clear that the power under the first limb [of the express power of appointment, giving the trustees power to advance up to one-half of a child's expectant, presumptive, or vested share and to pay the same to him for his absolute use, or for his advancement, or otherwise for his benefit in such manner as the trustees should think fit] may be exercised, if the circumstances warrant it, either by making an out-and-out payment to the person to be advanced, or for a particular purpose specified by the trustees. Thus in argument an example was given that when George [one of the beneficiaries] was called to the Bar the trustees might have quite properly advanced to him a sum of capital quite generally for his living expenses to support him while starting to practice, provided they thought that this was a reasonable thing to do, and that he was a type of person who could reasonably be trusted to make proper use of the money. On the other hand, if the trustees make the advance for a particular purpose which they state, they can quite properly pay it over to the advancee if they reasonably think they can trust

---

[67] See p. 889, below.

him or her to carry out the prescribed purpose. What they cannot do is to prescribe a particular purpose, and then raise and pay the money over to the advancee leaving him or her entirely free, legally and morally, to apply it for that purpose or to spend it in any way he or she chooses, without any responsibility on the trustees even to inquire as to its application.

D   EFFECT OF INFLATION

Law Reform Committee 23rd Report (*The Powers and Duties of Trustees*) 1982 Cmnd 8733, paras. 4.43, 44, 47

4.43   One of our witnesses discussed at some length the effects of inflation on the cash sum (or its equivalent) received by way of advancement by a beneficiary entitled to an undivided share in a trust fund. The position is that the beneficiary retains his interest in the relevant share but has to bring into account the cash sum when the final division takes place. This means that the amount advanced is accounted for at its value at the time of the advancement and not at the value prevailing at the time of the division. In times of stable values this produces no injustice, but can lead to capricious results in times of inflation. In such times the value of the advanced property (if it has not been spent altogether) will have appreciated as well as the value of the remaining part of the trust fund. The result might well be that the beneficiary who has received part of his share by way of advancement will in fact, in the long run, receive a larger proportion of the whole fund than would be expected given the value of his initial, undivided, share.

4.44   In order to deal with this problem it is suggested that it would be fairer to treat advances and appropriations as fractional distributions of entitlement rather than as cash sums to be brought into hotchpot. Each advance would have to be assessed as a fraction of the relevant beneficiary's entitlement and this would involve a valuation not only of the property advanced but also of the remainder of the fund. Such a process would be unduly laborious where only a small advance is being made but in such circumstances the trustees should be allowed to use the cash method at their discretion, rather than the fractional method, which should be used in all other cases.

4.47   We have considerable reservations about the mixing of the fractional and the cash bases of accounting. If there are mixed cash and fractional sums to add back together it would be necessary to do so in reverse order so that the correct hotchpot is arrived at. This might involve complicated calculations. We are agreed, however, that some form of indexation is needed to arrive at a just result. We are of the opinion that trustees should no longer use the cash basis when bringing advances into account. Any such sums should in future be accounted for at the time of the final division at their value at the time of the advance multiplied by any increase in the Retail Price Index. At their discretion, the trustees should be able to use the exact fractional method which would be more appropriate in cases where, for example, the trust fund largely consisted of land. If both cash sums and fractions have to be brought into hotchpot in order to achieve proper equality, these sums should be added back in the reverse order to arrive at the correct figure.

16

FIDUCIARY DUTIES OF TRUSTEES[1]

I FIDUCIARY RELATIONSHIPS

The essential characteristics of a fiduciary relationship were identified by MILLETT LJ in **Bristol and West Building Society v Mothew** [1998] Ch 1 at 18:

A fiduciary is someone who has undertaken to act for or on behalf of another in a particular matter in circumstances which give rise to a relationship of trust and confidence. The distinguishing obligation of a fiduciary is the obligation of loyalty. The principal is entitled to the single-minded loyalty of his fiduciary. This core liability has several facets. A fiduciary must act in good faith; he must not make a profit out of his trust; he must not place himself in a position where his duty and his interest may conflict; he may not act for his own benefit or the benefit of a third person without the informed consent of his principal. This is not intended to be an exhaustive list, but it

[1] H&M, pp. 607–633; Lewin, pp. 575–672; P&M, pp. 330–370; P&S, pp. 773–819; Pettit, pp. 141–150, 442–452; Snell, pp. 145–182; T&H, pp. 757–764, 913–958; U&H, pp. 467–506, 804–818; Oakley, *Constructive Trusts* (3rd edn, 1997), chap. 3; Finn, *Fiduciary Obligations* (1977); Shepherd, *Law of Fiduciaries* (1981); (1989) 9 OJLS 285 (R. Flannigan); Bean, *Fiduciary Obligations and Joint Ventures* (1995); McKendrick, ed. *Commercial Aspects of Trusts and Fiduciary Obligations* (1992); Law Commission Report on Fiduciary Duties and Regulatory Rules 1995 (Law Com. No. 236); Birks, ed. *Privacy and Loyalty* (1997); R.P. Austin in *Trends in Contemporary Trust Law* (ed. A.J. Oakley, 1996), pp. 153–175.

is sufficient to indicate the nature of fiduciary obligations. They are the defining characteristics of the fiduciary. As Dr. Finn pointed out in his classic work *Fiduciary Obligations* (1977), p. 2, he is not subject to fiduciary obligations because he is a fiduciary; it is because he is subject to them that he is a fiduciary.

A TRUSTEES AS FIDUCIARIES

All trustees are in a fiduciary relationship with their beneficiaries. It follows that a trustee must not benefit from his position as trustee. He must not put himself in a position in which his duty to the trust may conflict with his personal interest. This, as will be seen, is manifested in various ways. A trustee must not trade in the trust estate, nor take profits or commissions. The rules have been laid down in the strongest terms; but the cases will show how difficult are the border-lines of its application. On the other hand, a trustee has always been entitled to reimbursement of out-of-pocket expenses properly incurred,[2] and there is no objection to a provision in the trust instrument that trustees shall be remunerated. Indeed the complications of the administration of trusts at the present day necessitate the appointment of professional trustees.

Virgo: *The Principles of the Law of Restitution* (2006, 2nd ed.), pp. 501

Whilst it is clear that an express trustee is a fiduciary, there is a great deal of uncertainty whether resulting and constructive trustees should be similarly characterized. As regards resulting trustees it seems that whether such a trustee is a fiduciary depends on the reason a resulting trust was recognized. So, for example, if the resulting trust arose from the failure of an express trust it is appropriate to treat the resulting trustee as a fiduciary.[3] Whether the constructive trustee should be regarded as a fiduciary is a controversial matter, but the preferable view is that the essence of the constructive trust is simply that there is a separation of legal and equitable title and that it does not automatically follow from this that the constructive trustee is subject to fiduciary duties because he or she has not knowingly subjected him or herself to fiduciary obligations.[4] But, it should be possible for a constructive trustee to be subject to such fiduciary obligations where he or she knew the facts by virtue of which the constructive trust was imposed.

---

[2] *Stott v Milne* (1884) 25 Ch D 710; *Re Chapman* (1894) 72 LT 66 (expenses unreasonable); *Turner v Hancock* (1882) 20 Ch D 303 at 305 *per* Jessel MR ('all their proper costs incident to the execution of the trusts'). Now see Trustee Act 2000, s. 31(1) [p. 669, above].

[3] See Chambers, *Resulting Trusts* (1997), pp. 196–200.

[4] See 'Restitution and Constructive Trusts' (1998) 114 LQR 399, 405 (Sir Peter Millett).

B OTHER FIDUCIARIES

Other relationships have been recognised as fiduciary, for example involving agents,[5] solicitors,[6] company directors,[7] company promoters,[8] partners,[9] confidential employees,[10] certain bailees[11] and certain public officials.[12] It is not always easy to determine when a fiduciary relationship exists, but the category is not closed.[13]

[5] *De Bussche v Alt* (1878) 8 Ch D 286; *New Zealand Netherlands Society 'Oranje' Inc v Kuys* [1973] 1 WLR 1126 at 1129, *per* Lord Wilberforce; *English v Dedham Vale Properties Ltd* [1978] 1 WLR 93 [p. 801, n. 75, below] ('self-appointed agent'); *Hooper v Gorvin* (2001) WTLR 575 (spokesperson for tenants); *Boardman v Phipps* [1967] 2 AC 46 [p. 801, below]; cf. *Royal Products Ltd v Midland Bank Ltd* [1981] 2 Lloyd's Rep 194; *Alimand Computers Systems v Radcliffes & Co* (1991) The Times, 6 November (solicitors are trustees of funds paid to them by clients, as stakeholders); *Kelly v Cooper* [1993] AC 205.

[6] *Brown v IRC* [1965] AC 244; (1964) 80 LQR 470; *Oswald Hickson, Collier & Co v Carter-Ruck* [1984] AC 720n; *Islamic Republic of Iran Shipping Lines v Denby* [1987] 1 Lloyd's Rep 367 (accountable for bribe); *Bristol and West Building Society v Mothew* [1998] Ch 1; *Bristol and West Building Society v May May & Merrimans* [1996] 2 All ER 801 (acting for more than one principal); *Longstaff v Birtles* [2002] EWCA Civ 1219, [2002] 1 WLR 470 (fiduciary duty may endure beyond the termination of a retainer); *Marks and Spencer plc v Freshfields Bruckhaus Deringer (a firm)* [2004] EWHC 1337 (Ch), [2004] 1 WLR 2331; *Hilton v Barker Booth and Eastwood (a firm)* [2005] UKHL 8, [2005] 1 WLR 567; (2005) 64 CLJ 291 (M. Conaglen); (2006) 122 LQR 1 (J. Getzler). See also *Hanson v Lorenz* [1987] 1 FTLR 23 (no liability to account to client for his profits from a joint venture where client had understood the agreement). As to whether a head of chambers is in a fiduciary position to the members, see *Appleby v Cowley* (1982) The Times, 14 April.

[7] *Regal (Hastings) Ltd v Gulliver* [1967] 2 AC 134n; *Plus Group Ltd v Pyke* [2002] EWCA Civ 370; (2003) CLJ 42 (P. Koh); *Primlake Ltd v Matthews Associates* [2006] EWHC 1227 (Ch), [2007] 1 BCLC 666 (*de facto* director); *Foster Bryant Surveying Ltd v Bryant* [2007] EWCA Civ 200, [2007] 2 BCLC 239. The duty is owed to the company and not to the shareholders: *Percival v Wright* [1902] 2 Ch 421. But note Peskin v Anderson [2001] 1 BCLC 372, 379 (Mummery LJ) (exceptionally a separate fiduciary duty might be owed to shareholders).

[8] *Erlanger v New Sombrero Phosphate Co* (1878) 3 App Cas 1218; *Gluckstein v Barnes* [1900] AC 240; *Jubilee Cotton Mills Ltd v Lewis* [1924] AC 958.

[9] *Featherstonhaugh v Fenwick* (1810) 17 Ves 298; *Clegg v Fishwick* (1849) 1 Mac & G 294.

[10] *Triplex Safety Glass Co v Scorah* [1938] Ch 211; *British Celanese Ltd v Moncrieff* [1948] Ch 564; *British Syphon Co v Homewood* [1956] 1 WLR 1190; *A-G v Guardian Newspapers Ltd (No 2)* [1990] 1 AC 109 (the 'Spycatcher' case). Cp. *A-G v Blake* [1998] Ch 439 (CA) (this aspect of liability was not considered by the House of Lords on appeal).

[11] *Aluminium Industrie Vaassen BV v Romalpa Aluminium Ltd* [1976] 1 WLR 676; *Re Andrabell Ltd* [1984] 3 All ER 407.

[12] *Reading v A-G* [1951] AC 507 (bribes received by sergeant while on duty in Cairo); *A-G v Goddard* (1929) 98 LJKB 743 (sergeant in the Metropolitan Police); *A-G for Hong Kong v Reid* [1994] 1 AC 324 [p. 815, below] (acting Director of Public Prosecutions).

[13] Finn, *Fiduciary Obligations* (1977); Finn, *Fiduciary Law and the Modern Commercial World* in McKendrick, *Commercial Aspects of Trusts and Fiduciary Obligations* (1992); Law Commission No. 236: *Fiduciary Duties and Regulatory Rules* (1995); *Privacy and Loyalty* (ed. P. Birks) (1997): L. Hoyano, chap. 8; L. Smith, chap. 9; J. Glover, chap. 10; D. Hayton, chap. 11. For the refusal of the court to impose fiduciary obligations where commercial relationships were entered into at arm's length and on an equal footing, see *Polly Peck International v Nadir (No 2)* [1992] 4 All ER 769; *Kelly v Cooper* [1993] AC 205; *Re Goldcorp Exchange Ltd* [1995] 1 AC 74 at 98, *per* Lord Mustill; *Sinclair Investment Holdings SA v Versailles Trade Finance* Ltd [2007] EWHC 915 (Ch);P&M, pp. 330–336; (1994) 110 LQR 238 (Sir Anthony Mason); (1998) 114 LQR 214 (Sir Peter Millett); Virgo, *The Principles of the Law of* Restitution (2nd ed., 2006) p. 502; (1997–8) 8 *King's College Law Journal* 1, 6–12 (Sir Anthony Mason); (1999) CLJ 500 (S. Worthington). Cp. (1997) 113 LQR 601, 619–626 (A.J. Duggan).

(1996) 26 *University of Western Australia Law Review* 1, 18 (P. Birks)

It is manifestly impossible to predict whether a relationship will or will not be accounted fiduciary when a case comes to court. In many of the leading cases distinguished judges have been almost equally divided as to whether or not a relationship was fiduciary.[14] The necessary elements can be spelled out: a fiduciary is one who has discretion, and therefore, power, in the management of another's affairs, in circumstances in which that one cannot reasonably be expected to monitor him or take other precautions to protect his own interests.[15] But it turns out that this has a very low predictive yield.

II NATURE OF FIDUCIARY DUTIES

Finn, *Fiduciary Law and the Modern Commercial World* (1992), pp. 8–10 in McKendrick, *Commercial Aspects of Trusts and Fiduciary Obligations*[16]

A Fiduciary—A Fiduciary Relationship?

The answer to this, the most fundamental question, continues to elude us.[17] The question itself presupposes that we have a developed conception of the purpose and burden of fiduciary law. Yet these are matters on which there is widespread disagreement throughout the common law world. The present Chief Justice of the High Court of Australia has justly observed that 'the fiduciary relationship is a concept in search of a principle'.[18] Confusion here has had a number of causes: the use of the 'fiduciary' to fill hiatuses in available doctrines—hence, for example, the modern propensity to manufacture a fiduciary relationship between the directors of a marginally solvent company and corporate creditors...; the dilution of fiduciary obligations to exact what is in essence a duty of good faith and fair dealing;[19] the colourable findings of fiduciary

---

[14] Contrast *Hospital Products Ltd v US Surgical Corpn* (1984) 156 CLR 41 (and the judicial disagreements within it) with *Warman International Ltd v Dwyer* (1995) 182 CLR 544. Also in Canada: *Lac Minerals Ltd v International Corona Resources Ltd* [1989] 2 SCR 574 and *Hodgkinson v Simms* [1994] 3 SCR 377; noted [1995] *Canadian Bar Review* 714 (L.D. Smith). See also the judgment of Meagher JA in *Breen v Williams* (1995) 35 NSWLR 522 at 570, where there is strong condemnation of the over-extension of 'fiduciary'.

[15] On the many attempts to combine these elements effectively: A. Scott, 'The Fiduciary Principle' (1949) 37 *California Law Review* 539; L.S. Sealy, 'Fiduciary Relationships' (1962) CLJ 69; E.J. Weinrib, 'The Fiduciary Obligation' (1975) 25 *University of Toronto Law Journal* 1; J.C. Shepherd, 'Towards a Unified Concept of Fiduciary Relationships' (1981) 97 LQR 51; I.R.M. Gautreau, 'Demystifying the Fiduciary Mystique' (1989) 68 *Canadian Bar Review* 1. Cf Wilson J's much cited analysis in *Frame v Smith* [1987] 2 SCR 99 at 136.

[16] See also *Bristol and West Building Society v Mothew* [1998] Ch 1 at 18 [p. 778, above].

[17] See generally P. Finn, 'The Fiduciary Principle', in *Equity, Fiduciaries and Trusts* (ed. Youdan) (1989); see also R. Flannigan, 'Fiduciary Obligation in the Supreme Court' (1990) 54 *Saskatchewan Law Review* 45.

[18] Sir Anthony Mason, 'Themes and Prospects', in *Essays in Equity* (ed. P.D. Finn) (1985), p. 246.

[19] A prevalent phenomenon in Canadian, New Zealand, and United States jurisprudence in particular: see Finn, 'The Fiduciary Principle', note 17 above; see also *Pacific Industrial Corpn SA v Bank of New Zealand* [1991] 1 NZLR 368; *Plaza Fibreglass Manufacturing Ltd v Cardinal Insurance Co* (1990) 68 DLR (4th) 586.

relationships to gain access to equitable, but particularly profit-based, remedies;[20] uncertainty as to what precisely are fiduciary duties and whether they encompass in some measure the law of undue influence,[21] breach of confidence,[22] and, in relation to professional advisers, a negligence-like duty of care,[23] etc. When this has been acknowledged, it should equally be said that, for somewhat different reasons, the laws of Britain and Australia hold most closely to the old orthodoxies.[24]

For reasons of space, but also because the matter has been dealt with elsewhere,[25] I will simply note without elaboration my own understanding of (i) when, in our respective systems, a person can properly be said to be a fiduciary; and (ii) what is the obligation imposed in consequence of a fiduciary finding.

At best, all one can give is a description of a fiduciary—and one which, if it expresses the fiduciary idea, is no more precise than a description of the tort of negligence. It is as follows:

> A person will be a fiduciary in his relationship with another when and in so far as[26] that other is entitled to expect[27] that he will act in that other's interests or (as in a partnership) in their joint interests, to the exclusion of his own several interest.

Put crudely, the central idea is service of another's interests. And the consequential obligation a fiduciary finding attracts is itself one designed essentially to procure loyalty in service. It can be cast compendiously in the following terms:

A fiduciary

(a) cannot misuse his position, or knowledge or opportunity resulting from it, to his own or to a third party's possible advantage; or

(b) cannot, in any matter falling within the scope of his service, have a personal interest or an inconsistent engagement with a third party—

unless this is freely and informedly consented to by the beneficiary or is authorised by law.[28]

Two themes, it should be noted, are embodied in this: one, concerned with misuse of position, aims to preclude the fiduciary from using his position to advantage interests other than his beneficiary's; the second, concerned with conflicts of interest or of duty, aims to preclude

---

[20] An excellent UK example is *English v Dedham Vale Properties Ltd* [1978] 1 WLR 93; cf. the judgment of Deane J in *Hospital Products Ltd v US Surgical Corpn* (1984) 55 ALR 417.

[21] See e.g. *National Westminster Bank plc v Morgan* [1985] AC 686; and cf. the treatment of *Tate v Williamson* (1866) 2 Ch App 55 in *Bank of Credit and Commerce International SA v Aboody* [1990] 1 QB 923.

[22] Cf *LAC Minerals Ltd v International Corona Resources Ltd* (1989) 61 DLR (4th) 14.

[23] The subject of some controversy in Canadian and New Zealand law in relation to the liability of particularly solicitors for non-disclosure: but for the Canadian reaction, see the comments of Southin J in *Girardet v Crease & Co* (1987) 11 BCLR 2d 361, at 362; and see Finn, 'The Fiduciary Principle', note 17 above, pp. 25–26, 28–30.

[24] In Australia, though the traditional line was held by the High Court in *Hospital Products Ltd v US Surgical Corpn* (1984) 55 ALR 417, the pressure for more 'creative' uses was blunted both by the evolution of unconscionability-based doctrines and by the scope for invention given Australian courts by the Trade Practices Act, 1974, s. 52.   [25] See Finn, 'The Fiduciary Principle', note 17 above.

[26] Relationships commonly are fiduciary in part, non-fiduciary in part.

[27] That entitlement may arise from what one party undertakes or appears to undertake—cf. *Croce v Kurnit* 565 F Supp 884 (1982)—for the other; from what actually is agreed between the parties; or, for reasons of public policy, from legal prescription.

[28] The above is an adaptation of the formulation of Deane J in *Chan v Zacharia* (1983) 53 ALR 417 at 435—the most comprehensive formulation to be found in modern Anglo-Australian law.

the fiduciary from being swayed in his service by considerations of personal or third-party interest.

The one general comment I would make both of the description given and of the rather severe obligation that fiduciary law imposes, is that our preparedness to discriminate amongst the host of 'service relationships' to be found in contemporary society and to designate some only as fiduciary (for example, solicitor or financial adviser and client) is informed in some measure by considerations of public policy aimed at preserving the integrity and utility of these relationships, given the expectation that the community is considered to have of behaviour in them, and given the purposes they serve in society. This, as will later be seen, is likely to have quite some bearing on how the courts are prepared to apply fiduciary duties to multi-function business enterprises and large professional partnerships.

Virgo: *The Principles of the Law of Restitution* (2006, 2nd ed.), pp. 503–504

The nature and ambit of fiduciary obligations[29]
A number of different principles can be identified relating to the nature and ambit of fiduciary obligations.

(1) In an important dictum from an American case Frankfurter J said:

'To say that a man is a fiduciary only begins the analysis: it gives direction to further inquiry. To whom is he a fiduciary? What obligation does he owe as a fiduciary? In what respects has he failed to discharge these obligations? And what are the consequences of his deviation from duty?'[30]

In other words, it is not enough to decide that the defendant is a fiduciary: this is simply the initial question. This has now been recognized explicitly in English law. In *Bristol and West Building Society v Mothew*[31] the Court of Appeal recognised that there is more than one category of fiduciary relationship and that different categories of relationship possess different characteristics and attract different kinds of fiduciary obligation. Crucially, it is dangerous to assume that all fiduciaries are subject to the same duties in all circumstances.[32]

(2) A particular relationship may fall within more than one category of fiduciary relationship. Also the different categories of relationship may last for varying periods and the duties owed by the fiduciary will differ depending on the category of relationship which is being considered.

(3) In *Bristol and West Building Society v Mothew*[33] Millett LJ recognised that not every breach of duty by a fiduciary is a breach of fiduciary duty. Rather, fiduciary duties are 'those duties which are peculiar to fiduciaries and the breach of which attracts legal consequences differing from those consequent upon the breach of other duties'.[34] So, for example, although all fiduciaries are under an obligation to use proper skill and care in the discharge of their duties, the breach of this obligation is not a breach of a fiduciary duty simply because the obligation

---

[29] For detailed examination of the nature and ambit of fiduciary duties see Finn, *Fiduciary Obligations* (1977).

[30] *Securities and Exchange Commission v Chenery Corpn* (1943) 318 US 80 at 85–86.

[31] [1998] Ch 1. For more general analysis of the nature of fiduciary obligations see Millett, 'Equity's Place in the Law of Commerce' (1998) 114 LQR 214, 218–223.

[32] *Henderson v Merrett Syndicates Ltd* [1995] 2 AC 145, 206 (Lord Browne-Wilkinson).

[33] [1998] Ch 1, 16. See also *Hilton v Barker, Booth and Eastwood* [2005] UKHL 8, [2005] 1 WLR 567, 575 (Lord Walker). [34] [1998] Ch 1, 16.

arises from the fact that the defendant has assumed responsibility to another person and not from the fact that the defendant is a fiduciary.

(4) All fiduciary duties are proscriptive in effect. This means that the duties do not identify what fiduciaries must do, but rather identify what they should not do.

(5) For a fiduciary to be liable for breach of fiduciary duty he or she must have breached the duty by an intentional act; unconscious omission is not sufficient.[35] But, crucially, a fiduciary will be held liable even if he or she did not act fraudulently or in bad faith and even if the fiduciary honestly thought that he or she was acting in good faith.[36]

(6) Generally a fiduciary obligation does not continue after the termination of the relationship which gave rise to the duty.[37]

Although fiduciary duties are traditionally characterised as proscriptive in effect, in **Item Software (UK) Ltd v Fassihi** [2004] EWCA (Civ) 1244, [2005] BCLC 91[38] it was held that a director was under a fiduciary duty to disclose his misconduct to his company and failure to do so would itself constitute a breach of fiduciary duty.

M. Conaglen, 'The Nature and Function of Fiduciary Loyalty' (2005) 121 LQR 452, 453[39]

...fiduciary duties serve a function which differs from that served by other legal duties. The concept of fiduciary 'loyalty' is an encapsulation of a subsidiary and prophylactic form of protection for non-fiduciary duties which enhances the chance that those non-fiduciary duties will be properly performed. The primary means by which this notion of loyalty is given effect is a range of fiduciary duties which seek to insulate fiduciaries from influences that are likely to distract from such proper performance. It is often observed that fiduciary doctrine is *applied* in a prophylactic manner, although frequently without much clarification of [what] that means...fiduciary doctrine's prophylactic aspect is more than merely the strictness of its application; the argument presented here is that fiduciary doctrine is prophylactic *in its very nature,* as it is designed to avert breaches of non-fiduciary duties by seeking to neutralise influences likely to sway the fiduciary away from properly performing those non-fiduciary duties. This understanding of fiduciary loyalty provides a theoretical underpinning for a number of tenets of fiduciary doctrine that are acknowledged in the case law but are otherwise unexplained.

Fiduciary doctrine is frequently conceptualised as exhorting more moral behaviour from fiduciaries. Properly understood, the doctrine is far more cynical, functional and instrumentalist in outlook, focusing on lessening the danger that a fiduciary's undertaking will not be properly performed.[40]

---

[35] *Bristol and West Building Society v Mothew* [1998] Ch 1, 19 (Millett LJ).

[36] *Murad v Al-Saraj* [2005] EWCA Civ 969, para 67 (Arden LJ).

[37] *A-G v Blake* [1998] Ch 439, 453 (CA).

[38] (2005) 64 CLJ 48 (J. Armour and M. Conaglen); (2005) 121 LQR 213 (A. Berg); (2007) 66 CLJ 348 (L. Ho and P. Lee). See also *Shepherds Investments Ltd v Andrew Walters* [2006] EWHC 836, (Ch).

[39] See also L. Smith, 'The Motive, Not the Deed' in *Rationalizing Property, Equity and Trusts* (ed. J. Getzler, 2003) pp. 53–81.   [40] Cf (2007) 27 OJLS 327 (R. Lee).

Where the fiduciary has profited from his breach of fiduciary duty the usual remedy is to make him liable to disgorge this gain to the principal.[41] But equity can also require the fiduciary to compensate the principal for loss suffered.[42]

III THE NO-CONFLICT PRINCIPLE[43]

During the administration of a trust a trustee may wish to purchase either the trust property itself or a beneficiary's interest under the trust. Equity has evolved two rules to resolve the conflict which may arise between the duty of the trustee to the beneficiaries and his personal interest.[44] The first rule, which is called the self-dealing rule, provides that a trustee may not sell to himself, and renders the transaction voidable at the option of the beneficiaries, regardless of how fair the transaction is. Under the second rule, the fair-dealing rule, if a trustee purchases a beneficiary's interest, the transaction is not voidable as of right by the beneficiary, but will not be set aside if the trustee has behaved fairly.

A SELF-DEALING AND FAIR-DEALING RULES[45]

In **Tito v Waddell (No 2)** [1977] Ch 106, MEGARRY V-C said at 240:

> (2) *Lease by a fiduciary to itself.* I turn to the other way that Mr. Mowbray put the point, based on the 1931 lease being a lease by a fiduciary to itself. The lease, of course, is in terms a lease by the resident Commissioner to the British Phosphate Commissioners, and as such is

---

[41] See p. 791, below.

[42] *Swindle v Harrison* [1997] 4 All ER 705; *JJ Harrison (Properties) Ltd v Harrison* [2001] WTLR 1327, 1339; (2003) 119 LQR 248 (M. Conaglen). In Australia it has been held that exemplary damages are not available for breach of fiduciary duty, at least where the breach of duty also constitutes a breach of contract: *Harris v Digital Pulse Pty Ltd* (2003) 56 NSWLR 298; (2006) OJLS 303 (A. Duggan). Cf. Canada (*Norbery v Wynrib* [1992] 2 SCR 226, 298–300 (McLachlin J)); New Zealand (*Aquaculture Corp. v New Zealand Green Mussels Ltd* [1990] 3 NZLR 299). The position in England is unclear. The Law Commission has, however, recommended that such damages should be awarded: Law Com. No. 247 (1997) paras. 5.54–5.56.

[43] H&M, pp. 612–614; Lewin, pp. 607–647; P&M, pp. 346–355; P&S, pp. 787–791; Pettit, pp. 448–452; Snell, pp. 154–174; T&H, pp. 941–945; U&H, pp. 806–818; (1936) 49 *Harvard Law Review* 521 (A.W. Scott); (1955) 8 CLP 91 (O.R. Marshall); Goff & Jones, *The Law of Restitution* (7th edn, 2007), pp. 728–737; (1968) 84 LQR 472 (G.H. Jones); Virgo, *Principles of the Law of* Restitution (2nd ed., 2006) pp. 505–507; R.C. Nolan, in *Restitution: Past, Present and Future* (eds. W. Cornish, R. Nolan, J. O'Sullivan, G. Virgo) (1998), pp. 87–125; D. Fox, ibid, pp. 127–131; E. Simpson, 'Conflicts' in *Breach of Trust* (eds. P. Birks and A. Pretto, 2002), pp. 75–94. See *Hilton v Barker Booth and Eastwood (a firm)* [2005] UKHL 8, [2005] 1 WLR 567 (solicitor's conflicting duties to two clients was a breach of duty); [2005] All ER Rev 273 (P.J. Clarke); (2006) LQR 1 (J. Getzler). (2005) 64 CLJ 291 (M. Conaglen); *Ultraframe (UK) Ltd v Fielding* [2005] EWHC 1638 (Ch), [2005] All ER (D), paras 1307–1317 (Lewison J).

[44] Cf. where it is the settlor who has placed the trustees in a position of conflict: *Sargeant v National Westminster Bank plc* (1990) 61 P & CR 518.

[45] (2006) 65 CLJ 366 (M. Conaglen): both the self-dealing and fair-dealing rules are applications of the no-conflict principle and liability depends on whether the fiduciary obtained the principal's fully informed consent.

literally far from being a lease by a person to himself. But of course equity looks beneath the surface, and applies its doctrines to cases where, although in form a trustee has not sold to himself, in substance he has. Again one must regard the realities. If the question is asked: 'will a sale of trust property by the trustee to his wife be set aside?', nobody can answer it without being told more; for the question is asked in a conceptual form, and manifestly there are wives and wives. In one case the trustee may have sold privately to his wife with whom he was living in perfect amity; in another the property may have been knocked down at auction to the trustee's wife from whom he has been living separate and in enmity for a dozen years....

(3)   *Self-dealing and fair-dealing.* Let me revert briefly to the subject of the rules about self-dealing and fair-dealing, though on the view I take I doubt if much turns on this. As I have indicated, Mr. Vinelott took what I may call the orthodox view, namely, that there were two separate rules. The self-dealing rule is (to put it very shortly) that if a trustee sells the trust property to himself, the sale is voidable by any beneficiary *ex debito justitiae*, however fair the transaction. The fair-dealing rule is (again putting it very shortly) that if a trustee purchases the beneficial interest of any of his beneficiaries, the transaction is not voidable *ex debito justitiae*, but can be set aside by the beneficiary unless the trustee can show that he has taken no advantage of his position and has made full disclosure to the beneficiary, and that the transaction is fair and honest.

On the other hand, Mr. Mowbray strenuously contended that there was only one rule, though with two limbs, and he formulated an elaborate statement to that effect which I do not think I need set out. I can well see that both rules, or both limbs, have a common origin in that equity is astute to prevent a trustee from abusing his position or profiting from his trust: the shepherd must not become a wolf. But subject to that, it seems to me that for all practical purposes there are two rules: the consequences are different, and the property and the transactions which invoke the rules are different. I see no merit in attempting a forced union which has to be expressed in terms of disunity. I shall accordingly treat the rules as being in essence two distinct though allied rules.

B   PURCHASE OF TRUST PROPERTY.
SELF-DEALING

Holder v Holder
[1968] Ch 353 (CA, **Harman, Danckwerts** and **Sachs LJJ**)

The testator was the owner of two farms in Gloucestershire. His third son Victor, the defendant, was tenant with one Denley of part of one farm; and, as his father became advanced in years, Victor undertook responsibility for the farming of the remainder of the land, making annual payments to his father.

The testator died in 1959, having appointed his widow, a daughter, and Victor his executors, and provided by his will that the estate should be divided equally between the widow and all the children. The executors took the preliminary steps towards the administration of the estate, which Victor later conceded were sufficient to prevent him from renouncing, as he attempted to do.

The farms were valued on the basis that Victor was tenant with Denley of part of the one farm and also tenant of the remainder of the land. The eldest son Frank, the plaintiff, disputed this.

Victor purported to renounce the executorship, and subsequently purchased the farms at a fair price at an auction. The plaintiff received a cheque in respect of his share of the proceeds of sale. He later changed his solicitors and the new solicitor took, for the first time, the point that Victor, having begun to administer the estate, could not renounce, and could not therefore be a purchaser.

Held (reversing Cross J). (i) In the special circumstances of the case, Victor, although an executor, was not precluded from purchasing; (ii) Frank, by receiving his share of the purchase money, had precluded himself from relief.

Harman LJ: The cross-appeal raises far more difficult questions and they are broadly three. First, whether the actions of Victor before probate made his renunciation ineffective. Secondly, whether on that footing he was disentitled from bidding at the sale. Thirdly, whether the plaintiff is disentitled from taking this point because of his acquiescence.

It was admitted at the bar in the court below that the acts of Victor were enough to constitute intermeddling with the estate and that his renunciation was ineffective. On this footing he remained a personal representative, even after probate had been granted to his co-executors, and could have been obliged by a creditor or a beneficiary to re-assume the duties of an executor. The judge decided in favour of the plaintiff on this point because Victor at the time of the sale was himself still in a fiduciary position and like any other trustee could not purchase the trust property. I feel the force of this argument, but doubt its validity in the very special circumstances of this case. The reason for the rule is that a man may not be both vendor and purchaser; but Victor was never in that position here. He took no part in instructing the valuer who fixed the reserves or in the preparations for the auction. Everyone in the family knew that he was not a seller but a buyer. In this case Victor never assumed the duties of an executor. It is true that he concurred in signing a few cheques for trivial sums and endorsing a few insurance policies, but he never, so far as appears, interfered in any way with the administration of the estate. It is true he managed the farms, but he did that as tenant and not as executor. He acquired no special knowledge as executor. What he knew he knew as tenant of the farms.

Another reason lying behind the rule is that there must never be a conflict of duty and interest, but in fact there was none here in the case of Victor, who made no secret throughout that he intended to buy. There is of course ample authority that a trustee cannot purchase. The leading cases are decisions of Lord Eldon—*Ex p Lacey* (1802) 6 Ves 625 and *Ex p James* (1803) 8 Ves 337 at 344. In the former case the Lord Chancellor expressed himself thus at 626:

> 'The rule I take to be this; not, that a trustee cannot buy from his *cestuy que trust*, but, that he shall not buy from himself. If a trustee will so deal with his *cestuy que trust*, that the amount of the transaction shakes off the obligation, that attaches upon him as trustee, then he may buy. If that case[46] is rightly understood, it cannot lead to much mistake. The true interpretation of what is there reported does not break in upon the law as to trustees. The rule is this. A trustee, who is entrusted to sell and manage for others, undertakes in the same moment, in which he becomes a trustee, not to manage for the benefit and advantage of himself.'

In *Ex p James* the same Lord Chancellor said at 344:

> 'This doctrine as to purchases by trustees, assignees, and persons having a confidential character, stands much more upon general principle than upon the circumstances of any individual case. It rests upon this; that the purchase is not permitted in any case, however honest the circumstances; the general interests of justice requiring it to be destroyed in every instance.'

---

[46] *Whichcote v Lawrence* (1798) 3 Ves 740 at 749.

These are no doubt strong words, but it is to be observed that Lord Eldon was dealing with cases where the purchaser was at the time of sale acting for the vendors. In this case Victor was not so acting: his interference with the administration of the estate was of a minimal character and the last cheque he signed was in August before he executed the deed of renunciation. He took no part in the instructions for probate, nor in the valuations or fixing of the reserves. Everyone concerned knew of the renunciation and of the reason for it, namely, that he wished to be a purchaser. Equally, everyone, including the three firms of solicitors engaged, assumed that the renunciation was effective and entitled Victor to bid. I feel great doubt whether the admission made at the bar was correct, as did the judge, but assuming it was right, the acts were only technically acts of intermeddling and I find no case where the circumstances are parallel. Of course, I feel the force of the judge's reasoning that if Victor remained an executor he is within the rule, but in a case where the reasons behind the rule do not exist I do not feel bound to apply it. My reasons are that the beneficiaries never looked to Victor to protect their interests. They all knew he was in the market as purchaser; that the price paid was a good one and probably higher than anyone not a sitting tenant would give. Further, the first two defendants alone acted as executors and sellers; they alone could convey: they were not influenced by Victor in connection with the sales.

I hold, therefore, that the rule does not apply in order to disentitle Victor to bid at the auction, as he did. If I be wrong on this point and the rule applies so as to disentitle Victor to purchase, there arises a further defence, namely, that of acquiescence...

On the whole I am of opinion that in the circumstances of this case it would not be right to allow the plaintiff to assert his right (assuming he has one) because with full knowledge of the facts he affirmed the sale. He has had £2,000 as a result. He has caused [Victor] to embark on liabilities which he cannot recoup. There can in fact be no *restitutio in integrum*, which is a necessary element in rescission...

Danckwerts LJ: ...The principle that a trustee cannot purchase part of the trust estate goes back to the statement of it by Lord Eldon in 1802 in *Ex p Lacey* (1802) 6 Ves 625...

It is said that it makes no difference, even though the sale may be fair and honest and may be made at a public auction: see *Snell's Equity*, 26th Edn, 1966 p. 260. But the court may sanction such a purchase, and if the court can do that (see *Snell's Equity*, p. 219), there can be no more than a practice that the court should not allow a trustee to bid. In my view it is a matter for the discretion of the judge.

In **Re Thompson's Settlement** [1986] Ch 99,[47] estates in Norfolk, Lincolnshire, and Perthshire were held under a settlement on trust for grandchildren and their issue. The estates were leased to companies of which the directors were the settlor and the trustees. The leases were later informally assigned, one to a new company and the other to a partnership. One of the trustees of the settlement was the managing director of the company, in which he and his family held a majority shareholding. The partnership was formed by another trustee of the settlement and his family. The trustees of the settlement sought a declaration whether the leases were voidable at the option of the beneficiaries.

---

[47] (1986) 1 *Trust Law & Practice* 66 (C.H. Sherrin); *Movitex Ltd v Bulfield* [1988] BCLC 104. A mortgagee cannot sell to himself when exercising his power of sale, but he can sell to a company in which he has an interest if he acts in good faith and obtains the best price reasonably obtainable: *Tse Kwong Lam v Wong Chit Sen* [1983] 1 WLR 1349; Maudsley and Burn's *Land Law: Cases and Materials* (8th edn, 2004), pp. 880–883.

In holding that the leases were voidable under the self-dealing rule, VINELOTT J said at 106:

The application raises a question of some general importance concerning the ambit of the rule (which has been called the self-dealing rule) that a dealing such as a sale between a trustee and himself can be set aside by a beneficiary *ex debito justitiae* and without proof that the transaction was in any way unfair...

Mr. Price's other and more radical submission founded upon *Holder v Holder* [1968] Ch 353 [p. 786, above], was that the self-dealing rule only applies to a sale by trustees to one of their number, alone or jointly with others, or to a purchase by trustees from one of their number, alone or jointly with others, and to analogous dealings with trust property or trust moneys such as the grant of a lease by or to trustees. He founded that submission upon the statement by Harman LJ, at p. 391, that 'the reason for the rule is that a man may not be both vendor and purchaser...' He submitted that in the instant case the only dealings analogous to the sale of property were the assignments or purported assignments of the leases which were never themselves trust property. He submitted that in such a case the fair-dealing rule applies (because it is founded on the principle that a man must not put himself in a position where his duty and interest conflict and because in relation to the trustees it was their duty to consider whether to consent to the assignments) but not the self-dealing rule which only applies if there is a sale or purchase by trustees or something analogous to it. I do not think that the self-dealing rule can be so confined. It is clear that the self-dealing rule is an application of the wider principle that a man must not put himself in a position where duty and interest conflict or where his duty to one conflicts with his duty to another: see in particular the opinion of Lord Dunedin in *Wright v Morgan* [1926] AC 788 which I have cited. The principle is applied stringently in cases where a trustee concurs in a transaction which cannot be carried into effect without his concurrence and who also has an interest in or owes a fiduciary duty to another in relation to the same transaction. The transaction cannot stand if challenged by a beneficiary because in the absence of an express provision in the trust instrument the beneficiaries are entitled to require that the trustees act unanimously and that each brings to bear a mind unclouded by any contrary interest or duty in deciding whether it is in the interest of the beneficiaries that the trustees concur in it.

The same principle also applies, but less stringently, in a case within the fair-dealing rule, such as the purchase by a trustee of a beneficiary's beneficial interest. There, there are genuinely two parties to the transaction and it will be allowed to stand if freely entered into and if the trustee took no advantage from his position or from any knowledge acquired from it.

In the instant case the concurrence of the trustees of the grandchildren's settlement was required if the leases were to be assigned to or new tenancies created in favour of the new company and the partnership. The beneficiaries were entitled to ask that the trustees should give unprejudiced consideration to the question whether they should refuse to concur in the assignments in the expectation that a surrender of the leases might be negotiated from the old company and the estates sold or let on the open market.

The decision of the Court of Appeal in *Holder v Holder* does not in my judgment assist Mr. Price. The reason why, in the words of Harman LJ, the rule did not apply was that Victor, though he might technically have been made an executor notwithstanding the purported renunciation, had never acted as executor in a way which could be taken to amount to acceptance of a duty to act in the interests of the beneficiaries under his father's will.

Mr. Parker submitted that whenever a trustee, alone or as a partner or as a director of a company takes an assignment of a lease of trust property he holds the lease as a constructive trustee. He submitted that in such a case it is the duty of the trustee as trustee to consider whether the trustees should negotiate a surrender of the lease by the tenant (who in such a case must be taken to wish to dispose of the lease) and that the trustees cannot be permitted to negotiate on his own behalf or on behalf of others for an assignment. He relied by analogy on the well-known case of *Keech v Sandford* (1726) Sel Cas Ch 61 [p. 791, below]. The principle established in *Keech v Sandford* has been held to apply to the purchase of a reversion by a trustee if the lease is renewable by contract or custom; but it has been held not to apply where there is no custom or right of renewal: see *Bevan v Webb* [1905] 1 Ch 620 and the cases there cited. Mr. Parker's submission seems to me to face considerable difficulty but I do not need to decide whether there are circumstances in which the principle in *Keech v Sandford* would apply by analogy to the purchase of a lease of trust property by a trustee of the reversion and I express no opinion on the question. It is sufficient for the purposes of the present case that the leases could not be vested in the new company or the partnership, whether by assignment or surrender and regrant, without the concurrence of the trustees of the grandchildren's trust, and that they were no more capable of binding the trust by so concurring than of binding the trust estates by a sale of the land to the new company or the partnership.

In **Kane v Radley-Kane** [1999] Ch 274,[48] Sir Richard Scott V-C held that the self-dealing rule applied to a personal representative who had appropriated property to satisfy a legacy to herself without the sanction of the court or the consent of the beneficiaries. It followed that the appropriation was voidable at the suit of a beneficiary.

C   PURCHASE FROM BENEFICIARY. FAIR-DEALING

In **Coles v Trecothick** (1804) 9 Ves 234, Lord Eldon LC said at 247:

Upon the question as to a purchase by a trustee from the *cestui que trust* I agree, the *cestui que trust* may deal with his trustee, so that the trustee may become the purchaser of the estate. But, though permitted, it is a transaction of great delicacy, and which the Court will watch with the utmost diligence: so much, that it is very hazardous for a trustee to engage in such a transaction....

As to the objection to a purchase by the trustee, the answer is, that a trustee may buy from the *cestui que trust*, provided there is a distinct and clear contract, ascertained to be such after a jealous and scrupulous examination of all the circumstances, proving, that the *cestui que trust* intended, the trustee should buy; and there is no fraud, no concealment, no advantage taken, by the trustee of information, acquired by him in the character of trustee. I admit, it is a difficult case to make out, wherever it is contended, that the exception prevails. The principle was clearly recognised in *Fox v Mackreth* (1788) 2 Bro CC 400; and was established long before.

In **Thomson v Eastwood** (1877) 2 App Cas 215, Lord Cairns LC said at 236:

They were cases of this kind—cases where a trustee has entered into dealings with his *cestui que trust*—dealings which may be legitimate, but which, on the other hand, are open to examination when they are complained of. A trustee, for example, buys from his *cestui que trust* the trust property; there is no rule of law which says that a trustee shall not buy trust property from a *cestui que trust*, but it is a well-known doctrine of Equity that if a transaction of that kind is

---

[48] [1998] All ER Rev 463 (C.H. Sherrin); (1998) 28 *Family Law* 526 (S. Cretney).

challenged in proper time, a Court of Equity will examine into it, will ascertain the value that was paid by the trustee, and will throw upon the trustee the onus of proving that he gave full value, and that all information was laid before the *cestui que trust* when it was sold.[49]

D LAW REFORM

Law Reform Committee 23rd Report: *The Powers and Duties of Trustees* 1982 Cmnd. 8733, para. 3.59

3.59 We appreciate that there are circumstances, such as in the case of family trusts, where transfers between trusts with common trustees are envisaged which are not possible as the law stands at present without the sanction of the court.[50] If a change is to be made, we think it is necessary for there to be some sort of safeguard on this kind of transaction. One possibility is to provide that such a transaction can be made without the sanction of the court provided that there are at least two independent trustees on each side and the common trustee or trustees take no part in the transaction. Alternatively, there could be a requirement of a supporting valuation by a genuinely independent valuer rather than a requirement that the common trustee plays no part in the transaction. Our conclusion is that, so long as the common trustees are not beneficiaries under either of the trusts concerned, the trustees should be able to do business with one another with the common trustees playing such part as it is thought fit, provided that the market value of any property dealt with has been certified by a truly independent valuer as being the proper market price for that property.

IV THE NO-PROFIT PRINCIPLE[51]

A THE RULE IN *KEECH V SANDFORD*

(i) *Renewal of a Lease*[52]

Keech v Sandford
(1726) Sel Cas Ch 61 (King LC)

The lessee of the profits of Romford market devised his estate to a trustee on trust for an infant. Prior to the expiration of the lease, the trustee applied to the lessor for a

---

[49] *Hill v Langley* (1988) The Times, 28 January.

[50] Settled Land Act 1925, s. 68 caters for the position where a tenant for life wants to deal with the settled land for his own benefit, even where he is one of the trustees.

[51] H&M, pp. 614–633; Lewin, pp. 576–607; P&M, pp. 355–370; P&S, pp. 791–817; Pettit, pp. 144–150; Snell, pp. 175–182; T&H, pp. 913–941, 949–952; U&H, pp. 473–501; (1968) 84 LQR 472 (G.H. Jones). See generally (1967) CLJ 83 (L.S. Sealy); (1981) 97 LQR 51 (J.C. Shepherd); (1983) 46 MLR 289 (W. Bishop and D.D. Prentice); Goff and Jones, *Law of Restitution* (7th edn, 2007), pp. 738–743; Virgo, *Principles of the Law of Restitution* (2nd edn, 2006) pp. 508–511; *Hospital Products Ltd v US Surgical Corpn* (1984) 156 CLR 41; (1986) OJLS 444 (R.P. Austin).

[52] White and Tudor's *Leading Cases in Equity* (9th edn, 1928), pp. 648ff; *Re Knowles' Will Trusts* [1948] 1 All ER 866; *Re Jarvis* [1958] 1 WLR 815; *Re Edwards' Will Trusts* [1982] Ch 30; *Chan v Zacharia* (1983) 154

renewal of the lease for the benefit of the infant. The lessor refused, on the ground that, because the lease was of the profits only and not of the land, his remedy for recovery of rent was not by distress, but upon the covenant only, by which an infant would not be bound. The trustee then took a lease for himself.

The infant sought to have the lease assigned to him.

Held. The lease should be assigned to the infant, with an account of the profits received by the trustee.

King LC: I must consider this as a trust for the infant; for I very well see, if a trustee, on the refusal to renew, might have a lease to himself, few trust estates would be renewed to *cestui que use;* though I do not say there is a fraud in this case, yet he should rather have let it run out, than to have had the lease to himself. This may seem hard, that the trustee is the only person of all mankind who might not have the lease; but it is very proper that rule should be strictly pursued, and not in the least relaxed; for it is very obvious what would be the consequences of letting trustees have the lease, on refusal to renew to *cestui que use.*

In **Re Biss** [1903] 2 Ch 40, Mr. Biss had carried on a profitable business as a common lodging-house keeper on premises leased to him under a seven-year lease. On its expiry he continued as a yearly tenant. He died, leaving a widow and three children, one of whom was an infant. The widow, who was his administratrix, and an adult son continued the business, and they applied for a renewal of the lease. This was refused, but a new three-year lease was then granted to the adult son. The question was whether he should be compelled, under the rule in *Keech v Sandford,* to hold the lease upon trust. The Court of Appeal decided that he could hold it beneficially. The son, in obtaining the lease, was not in breach of any fiduciary duty. COLLINS MR said at 57:

In the present case the appellant is simply one of the next-of-kin of the former tenant, and had, as such, a possible interest in the term. He was not, as such, a trustee for the others interested, nor was he in possession. The administratrix represented the estate and alone had the right to renew incident thereto, and she unquestionably could renew only for the benefit of the estate. But is the appellant in the same category? Or is he entitled to go into the facts to shew that he has not, in point of fact, abused his position, or in any sense intercepted an advantage coming by way of accretion to the estate? He did not take under a will or a settlement with interests coming after his own, but simply got a possible share upon an intestacy in case there was a surplus of assets over debts. It seems to me that his obligation cannot be put higher than that of any other tenant in common against whom it would have to be established, not as a presumption of law but as an inference of fact, that he had abused his position. If he is not under a personal incapacity to take a benefit, he is entitled to shew that the renewal was not in fact an accretion to the original term, and that it was not until there had been an absolute refusal on the part of the lessor, and after full opportunity to the administratrix to procure it for the estate if she could, that he accepted a proposal of renewal made to him by the lessor. These questions cannot be considered or discussed when the party is by his position debarred from keeping a personal advantage derived directly or indirectly out of his fiduciary or quasi-fiduciary position; but

CLR 178. See too (1969) 33 Conv (NS) 161 (S.M. Cretney) on the historical reasons for the rule; (1984) 58 *Australian Law Journal* 660 (J. Starke).

when he is not so debarred I think it becomes a question of fact whether that which he has received was in his hands an accretion to the interest of the deceased, or whether the connection between the estate and the renewal had not been wholly severed by the action of the lessor before the appellant accepted a new lease. This consideration seems to get rid of any difficulty that one of the next of kin was an infant. The right or hope of renewal incident to the estate was determined before the plaintiff intervened.[53]

(ii) Purchase of the Reversion

In **Thompson's Trustee in Bankruptcy v Heaton** [1974] 1 WLR 605,[54] PENNYCUICK V-C said at 606:

The action is concerned with a property known as Lissington Manor Farm in Lincolnshire, to which I shall refer as 'Lissington'. Summarily Mr. Thompson and Mr. Heaton acquired a leasehold interest in Lissington as partners in 1948. The partnership was dissolved in 1952 under some arrangement between them. Mr. Heaton and, subsequently, the company [William T. Heaton Ltd, a private company whose shares were owned by Mr. and Mrs. Heaton] remained in sole occupation of Lissington. Mr. Heaton died in 1966. Then in 1967 his executors acquired the freehold reversion in Lissington on behalf of the company. Since the commencement of the action the company has sold Lissington at a very substantial profit. [Mr. Thompson having become bankrupt] the plaintiff trustee in bankruptcy now contends that he is entitled in effect to half of that profit [on the ground that the farm was an undistributed asset of the partnership].

It remains to consider whether the defendants are accountable to the plaintiff in respect of the freehold reversion and the proceeds of sale of the freehold. It is well established that where someone holding a leasehold interest in a fiduciary capacity acquires a renewal of the leasehold interest he must hold the renewed interest as part of the trust estate. This principle is known as the rule in *Keech v Sandford* (1726) Sel Cas Ch 61: *Snell's Principles of Equity,* 27th edn (1973), p. 236. It is also, I think, well established that where someone holding a leasehold interest in a fiduciary capacity acquires the freehold reversion, he must hold that reversion as part of the trust estate: see *Protheroe v Protheroe* [1968] 1 WLR 519, where Lord Denning MR says at 521:

'The short answer to the husband's contention is this: although the house was in the husband's name, he was a trustee of it for both. It was a family asset which the husband and wife owned in equal shares. Being a trustee, he had an especial advantage in getting the freehold. There is a long established rule of equity from *Keech v Sandford* (1726) Sel Cas Ch 61 downwards that if a trustee, who owns the leasehold, gets in the freehold, that freehold belongs to the trust and he cannot take the property for himself.'

That decision is cited, with some implied criticism, in *Snell's Principles of Equity,* p. 238. It seems to me, however, that, apart from the fact that it binds me, this decision, like the rule in

---

[53] *Brenner v Rose* [1973] 1 WLR 443. See also *Harris v Black* (1983) 46 P & CR 366, where CA held that the court had jurisdiction at the suit of one trustee to compel his co-trustee to apply for the renewal of a lease under Part II Landlord and Tenant Act 1954. The matter was one for discretion and CA refused to exercise it.

[54] (1974) 38 Conv (NS) 288 (F.R. Crane); (1975) 38 MLR 226 (P. Jackson). See also *Chan v Zacharia* (1984) 154 CLR 178 (High Court of Australia); *Popat v Schonchhatra* [1997] 1 WLR 1367; *Don King Productions Inc v Warren* [2000] Ch 291.

Keech v Sandford is really in modern terms an application of the broad principle that a trustee must not make a profit out of the trust estate. This principle applies to all kinds of collateral advantages, for instance directors' remuneration received by a trustee acting as a director for a company controlled through the shares of the trust. In *Phillips v Phillips* (1885) 29 Ch D 673 the Court of Appeal applied the principle to the purchase of a reversion by a tenant for life. I ought to make one observation in this connection. Obviously the beneficiary under the trust in such circumstances cannot be compelled to accept and pay for the reversion. If he refuses to do so, either before or after the acquisition by the trustee, no doubt the latter is entitled to acquire and retain the reversion for his own use, but if the beneficiary does require that the reversion be brought into the trust estate, then the trustee must deal with it accordingly, subject of course to recoupment out of the trust estate.

There can, I think, be no doubt that so long as a partnership subsists each partner is under a corresponding obligation to his co-partners. See as to this point section 29 of the Partnership Act 1890 and *Lindley on Partnership* 13th edn (1971), p. 337....

The fiduciary relation here arises not from a trust of property but from the duty of good faith which each partner owes to the other. It is immaterial for this purpose in which partner the legal estate in the leasehold interest concerned is vested.

B   TRUSTEES AS COMPANY DIRECTORS[55]

Re Macadam[56]
[1946] Ch 73 (Ch D, **Cohen J**)

The articles of a company provided that the trustees of the testator's will may 'so long as they shall hold shares in the company as such trustees, appoint two persons...to be directors of the company'. The trustees appointed themselves.

The question was whether the trustees could retain, as their own, the directors' fees.

Held. They were accountable.

Cohen J: The question has been raised whether the plaintiffs are entitled to retain the directors' fees received by them from the company or whether they are accountable to the trust estate for the sums received by them as remuneration in respect of the office of director. I desire to say at once that nobody suggested any impropriety on their part in regard to this remuneration. The question was asked purely as one of law whether, having regard to all the provisions of the material documents, on general principles of law, they are accountable or not. My attention

---

[55] Companies Act 2006, ss. 170–181 provides a statutory statement of directors' duties which replaces many of the common law and equitable duties, such as the duty to avoid conflicts of interest, which is to be found in s. 175. This states that a director must avoid a situation where a direct or indirect interest (or duty) of his may conflict with that of the company, especially as regards the exploitation of property, information or opportunity. But this duty is not breached if the matter has been authorised by the directors.

[56] *Re Gee* [1948] Ch 284 (trustees appointed independently of the voters of the trust shares); *Re Francis* (1905) 74 LJ Ch 198; *Re Lewis* (1910) 103 LT 495 (independent appointment); *Re Llewellin's Will Trusts* [1949] Ch 225 (appointment authorised by trust instrument); *Re Keeler's Settlement Trusts* [1981] Ch 156 [p. 797, below] (appointment authorised by trust instrument); *Re Orwell's Will Trusts* [1982] 1 WLR 1337.

was called to a number of cases bearing on this matter, but I think that Mr. Gray and Mr. Timins were right in saying that they are all applications of the same general principle, though the consequence of applying that principle has resulted in some cases in the person concerned being allowed to retain the remuneration, and in others in his being held accountable. The principle, I think, is well stated in a passage from the speech of Lord Herschell in *Bray v Ford* [1896] AC 44 at 51 which was cited by Russell J in *Williams v Barton* [1927] 2 Ch 9 at 11. The citation is as follows: 'It is an inflexible rule of a court of equity that a person in a fiduciary position ... is not, unless otherwise expressly provided, entitled to make a profit; he is not allowed to put himself in a position where his interest and duty conflict.'

The first of the cases to which my attention was called was *Re Francis* (1905) 92 LT 77. [His Lordship referred also to *Re Dover Coalfield Extension Ltd* [1907] 2 Ch 76; affd [1908] 1 Ch 65, and to *Re Lewis* (1910) 103 LT 495, of which case he said:] It seems to me that the distinction between that case and this is that there he secured the appointment as salesman not by virtue of the exercise of any discretion in him as trustee, but by virtue of a bargain with his co-partners; whereas in the present case the plaintiffs got their appointment, by the exercise of a power which is vested in them—not, it is true, by the testator's will, but by the articles of the company approved by the court, but none the less vested in them as trustees.

The last, and perhaps the nearest, case to the present—although it is a much stronger case than the one I have to decide—is *Williams v Barton* [1927] 2 Ch 9 decided by Russell J from which I have already cited a short passage. In that case the headnote says:

'The defendant, one of two trustees of a will, was employed as a clerk by a firm of stockbrokers on the terms that his salary should consist of half the commission earned by the firm on business introduced by him. At the recommendation of the defendant, the firm was employed to value his testator's securities. The firm's charges were paid out of the testator's estate and, in accordance with their contract with the defendant, they paid to him half the fees so earned. The defendant took no part in making the valuations or in fixing the fees to be charged. In an action by his co-trustee claiming that the defendant was bound to treat the fees so paid to him as part of the testator's estate:— *Held*, that it was the defendant's duty as a trustee to give the estate the benefit of his unfettered advice in choosing stockbrokers to act for the estate, but, as the recipient of half the fees earned by the firm on business introduced by him, it was to his interest to choose his firm to act. The services rendered to the firm by the defendant remained unchanged but his remuneration for them was increased, and increased by virtue of his trusteeship. That increase was a profit which the defendant would not have made but for his position as trustee and he was therefore bound to treat it as part of the estate of his testator.'

After citing the passage which I have read from the speech of Lord Herschell in *Bray v Ford* [1896] AC 44, Russell J continued—and I think his remarks apply to this case too—

'The point is not an easy one and there is little, if any, authority to assist in its determination ... it seems to me evident that the case falls within the mischief which is sought to be prevented by the rule. The case is clearly one where his duty as trustee and his interest in an increased remuneration are in direct conflict. As a trustee it is his duty to give the estate the benefit of his unfettered advice in choosing the stockbrokers to act for the estate; as the recipient of half the fees to be earned by George Burnand & Co on work introduced by him his obvious interest is to choose or recommend them for the job.'

Pausing there, it seems to me that, with a certain substitution, that last sentence applies to this case. As trustees it is the duty of the plaintiffs to give the estate the benefit of their unfettered advice in choosing the persons to act as directors of the company, as, if appointed, they will receive such remuneration as may be voted to them; as recipients of the remuneration of direct-ors their obvious interest is to choose themselves for the job. Then the learned judge goes on:

'In the event that has happened they have been chosen, and chosen because the defendant was a trustee, with the result that half of what the estate pays must necessarily pass through them to the defendant as part of his remuneration for other services rendered, but as an addition to the remuneration which he would otherwise have received for those self-same services. The services rendered remain unchanged but the remuneration for them has been increased. He has increased his remuneration by virtue of his trusteeship. In my opinion this increase of remuneration is a profit made by the defendant out of and by reason of his trusteeship, which he would not have made but for his position as trustee.'

Then he goes on to deal with *Re Dover Coalfield Extension Ltd* [1907] 2 Ch 76; affd [1908] 1 Ch 65, 70, and says:

'But that case seems to me very different. At the request of the Dover company Mr. Cousins had entered into a contract with the Kent company to serve them as a director, the Kent company paying him remuneration for his services. The necessary qualification shares were provided by the Dover company and in respect of those shares he became a trustee for the Dover company. He had not, however, used his position as a trustee for the purpose of acquiring his directorship. He had, in fact, been appointed a director before he became a trustee of the shares. The profit which he gained was not procured by him by the use of his position as trustee but was a profit earned by reason of work which he did for the Kent company and which would not have been earned by him had he not been willing to do the work for which it was the remuneration. It was not (as in the present case) a profit acquired solely by reason of his use of his position as trustee and a profit in respect of which no extra services were rendered.'

That case is, as Mr. Christie rightly says, much stronger than the present case, because, first, the profit in a sense came directly out of the estate, and, secondly, because it was a profit earned in a sense without any work done by him. I think that the root of the matter really is: did he acquire the position in respect of which he drew the remuneration by virtue of his position as trustee? In the present case there can be no doubt that the only way in which the plaintiffs became directors was by exercise of the powers vested in the trustees of the will under art. 68 of the articles of association of the company. The principle is one which has always been regarded as of the greatest importance in these courts, and I do not think I ought to do anything to weaken it. As I have said, although the remuneration was remuneration for services as director of the company, the opportunity to receive that remuneration was gained as a result of the exercise of a discretion vested in the trustees, and they had put themselves in a position where their interest and duty conflicted. In those circumstances, I do not think this court can allow them to make a profit out of doing so, and I do not think the liability to account for a profit can be confined to cases where the profit is derived directly from the trust estate. I leave over the matter of the exact wording of the order, because I do not want to do anything to prejudice the question whether, in the circumstances, I ought not to allow the plaintiffs to retain the whole or a part of the remuneration. If I can be satisfied (and that is the point I have not considered) that they were the best persons to be directors, I do not think it would be right for me to expect them to do the extra work for nothing.

In **Re Keeler's Settlement Trusts** [1981] Ch 156, a settlement of shares in two companies authorised the trustees to be appointed directors of the companies. There was a professional charging clause, but no power authorising trustees to retain remuneration earned in their directorships. Trustee directors had been appointed. One question was whether they could retain past remuneration received as directors.[57] GOULDING J, in directing accounts and inquiries, said at 160:

In *Re Macadam* [1946] Ch 73 Cohen J held that certain trustees were in the circumstances of the case accountable for directors' fees received by them and, at 82 [quoted above], left over the question whether they might be allowed to retain them, in whole or in part, presumably under the inherent jurisdiction of the court...

In *Re Masters* [1953] 1 WLR 81 at 83 Danckwerts J commented on *Re Macadam* in which he had been junior counsel for the trustees, and said that to his knowledge the course suggested by Cohen J was adopted and the remuneration was in fact authorised. He said so in delivering a judgment which authorised a trust corporation to charge for acting as administrator and trustee of an intestate's estate.

I observe in passing that the reports of *Re Macadam* (1945) 62 TLR 48 at 52 and 115 LJ Ch 14 at 21 suggest that the question reserved by Cohen J was in fact ultimately disposed of by compromise.

In *Re Duke of Norfolk's Settlement Trusts* [1979] Ch 37, Walton J carefully reviewed the earlier authorities on the whole subject of the court's inherent jurisdiction to allow remuneration to trustees.... The test I have taken from the judgment of Walton J in the *Norfolk* case is whether any exceptional effort or skill was shown in acquiring the remuneration. That was his formulation at 54 of the report. He paraphrased it at 59:

'those cases where the trustees are held to be accountable for profits which they have made out of the trust, but are in general allowed to keep that proportion of the profits so made—doubtless, in many cases, the whole—which results from their own exertions above and beyond those expected of a trustee...'

I do not think that any and every effort or skill applied by a trustee in executing the office of a company director is to be regarded as exceptional or unexpected for this purpose, certainly not in the present case, where it is made perfectly clear by clause 4 of the settlement that a trustee may be proposed for appointment as a director of any company in which the trustees have an interest. The director trustee, in my judgment, may in a proper case be allowed to retain reasonable remuneration for effort and skill applied by him in performing the duties of the directorship over and above the effort and skill ordinarily required of a director appointed to represent the interests of a substantial shareholder. The latter is something that a prudent man of business would in general undertake in the management of his own investments, and so in my view is in general an exertion reasonably expected of a trustee. Compare the observation of Upjohn J in *Re Worthington* [1954] 1 WLR 526 at 529, cited in the *Norfolk* case [1979] Ch 37 at 55.

---

[57] A claim in respect of future remuneration was refused, following Walton J in *Re Duke of Norfolk's Settlement Trusts* [1979] Ch 37. This is no longer authoritative in view of the Court of Appeal's reversal of Walton J on this point [1982] Ch 61 [p. 675, above].

C   OTHER PROFITS OF FIDUCIARIES

The law on fiduciary duties has recognised many other situations where different fiduciaries, including trustees, are liable to account for incidental profits which they have made in breach of duty. 'Whenever it can be shewn that the trustee has so arranged matters as to obtain an advantage, whether in money or money's worth, to himself personally through the execution of his trust, he will not be permitted to retain it, but be compelled to make it over to his constituent.'[58]

In **Williams v Barton** [1927] 2 Ch 9, a trustee of a will was employed as a clerk by stockbrokers on the terms that his salary should be half the commission earned by the firm on business introduced by him. He persuaded his co-trustee to employ his firm to value the testator's securities. In holding that the trustee was accountable for the half-commission received by him, RUSSELL J said at 12:

The case is clearly one where his duty as trustee and his interest in an increased remuneration are in direct conflict. As a trustee it is his duty to give the estate the benefit of his unfettered advice in choosing the stockbrokers to act for the estate; as the recipient of half the fees to be earned by George Burnand & Co. on work introduced by him his obvious interest is to choose or recommend them for the job. . . . He has increased his remuneration by virtue of his trusteeship. In my opinion this increase of remuneration is a profit made by the defendant out of and by reason of his trusteeship, which he would not have made but for his position as trustee.

One of the most significant areas in which can arise the liability of fiduciaries to account for profits made in breach of fiduciary duty concerns company directors.

Hanbury & Martin: *Modern Equity* (17th edn, 2005), pp. 621–624

The leading case is the House of Lords decision in *Regal (Hastings) Ltd v Gulliver.*[59]

R. Ltd set up a subsidiary, A. Ltd, to acquire the leases of two cinemas. A. Ltd had a share capital of 5,000 £1 shares. The owner of the cinemas was only willing to lease them if the share capital of A. Ltd was completely subscribed for. However, R. Ltd had resources to subscribe for only 2,000 of the 5,000 shares and it was therefore agreed that the directors of R. Ltd should subscribe for the rest. When the business of R. Ltd was transferred to new controllers the directors made a profit from their holdings in A. Ltd. The new controllers of R. Ltd caused the company to sue the ex-directors of R. Ltd for an account of the profit. The directors were held liable. They had made

---

[58]   *Huntington Copper and Sulphur Co Ltd v Henderson* (1877) 4 R 294 at 308, *per* Lord Young; *Sugden v Crossland* (1856) 3 Sm & G 192 (payment of £75 to trustee in consideration of his retiring and appointing the payer as new trustee); *Re Smith* [1896] 1 Ch 71 (payment of £300 commission on investing trust funds in debentures of a particular company); *Brown v IRC* [1965] AC 244 (interest earned by Scottish solicitor on deposits of clients' moneys); (1964) 80 LQR 480; Solicitors Act 1974, s. 33, as amended by the Building Societies Act 1986, s. 120, Sch. 18, para. 11(1), (3). *Re Thomson* [1930] 1 Ch 203 (injunction granted to restrain executor from carrying on testator's business as yacht broker in competition with the trust); Partnership Act 1890, s. 30; *Moore v M'Glynn* [1894] 1 IR 74. See (2003) CLJ 403 (P. Koh).

[59]   [1967] 2 AC 134n.

the profit out of their position as directors and, in the absence of shareholder approval,[60] they were obliged to account.

There are a number of noteworthy features of *Regal*. First, the directors were found by the court to have acted bona fide, but the liability of a fiduciary to account for a profit made from his office 'in no way depends on fraud, or absence of bona fides'.[61] Secondly, the new controllers obtained a windfall.[62] Thirdly, it was arguable that the directors by purchasing the shares in A. Ltd had enabled R. Ltd to enter into a transaction which it was otherwise commercially impossible for the company to enter into. While there is some truth in this, the decision that R. Ltd did not have the necessary financial resources to enter into the transaction was made by the directors who were the very persons who benefited from this decision. Because of this a compelling argument can be made that a 'reasonable man looking at the relevant facts and circumstances of the particular case would think that there was a real sensible possibility of conflict'.[63]

A clear case of conflict of interest and duty arose in *Guinness plc v Saunders*,[64] where a director (Ward) agreed to provide his services in connection with a proposed take-over of another company (Distillers), on terms that he would be paid a fee the size of which depended on the amount of the take-over bid if successful. The bid was successful, and the fee paid to Ward was £5.2 million. The claim by Guinness for summary judgment for the repayment of this sum was upheld in the House of Lords. Ward's interest in obtaining a fee calculated on the above basis conflicted with his duty as director, which was to give impartial advice concerning the take-over. The agreement for the fee, made with two other directors, but not the board of directors, was void for want of authority. Ward had no arguable defence to Guinness's claim that he had received the money, paid under a void contract, as a constructive trustee.

The courts have imposed liability on directors to account where the directors have made the profit out of an economic opportunity, or information, even though they acquired it in a personal capacity, if it was information which could have been exploited by their company.[65]

In *Industrial Development Consultants Ltd v Cooley*,[66] the defendant was a director and general manager of the claimant company, which provided construction consultancy services. He attempted to interest a public Gas Board in a project, but was unsuccessful because the Gas Board's policy was not to employ development companies. The defendant was a distinguished architect who had worked in the gas industry for many years. For this reason the Gas Board decided to offer the contract to him personally, which he accepted, obtaining a release from the claimant by falsely representing that he was ill. He was held to be liable to account to the claimant for the profits of the contract.

[60] Lord Russell of Killowen considered that the shareholders could have ratified the directors' breach of duty: [1967] 2 AC 134n at 150. On this controversial aspect of the case, see (1958) 16 CLJ 93 at 102–106 (K. Wedderburn); *Prudential Assurance Co Ltd v Newman Industries Ltd (No 2)* [1981] Ch 257; (1981) 44 MLR 202.   [61] [1967] 2 AC 134n at 144.

[62] See (1979) 42 MLR 215 (D. Prentice).

[63] *Boardman v Phipps* [1967] 2 AC 46 at 124, *per* Lord Upjohn.

[64] [1990] 2 AC 663; (1990) 106 LQR 365 (J. Beatson and D. Prentice); (1990) 49 CLJ 220 (J. Hopkins); [1990] Conv 296 (S. Goulding).

[65] See *Canadian Aero Service Ltd v O'Malley* (1973) 40 DLR (3d) 371 (SCC).

[66] [1972] 1 WLR 443, [1972] 2 All ER 162 (the reports on the case are not identical); (1973) 89 LQR 187 (A. Yoran); (1972A) 30 CLJ 222 (J. Collier); (1972) 35 MLR 655 (H. Rajak); (1972) 50 CBR 623 (D. Prentice). See also *CMS Dolphin Ltd v Simonet* [2001] 2 BCLC 704; *Re Bhullar Bros Ltd* [2003] 2 BCLC 241; (2004) 120 LQR 198 (D. Prentice and J. Payne): (2004) 63 CLJ 33 (J. Armour).

The significance of the case is twofold. First, the court rejected Cooley's defence, that the information concerning the Gas Board's contract came to him in his private capacity, and not as director of the claimant company; this 'is the first case in which it was decided that the prohibition on exploiting a corporate opportunity applies also to an opportunity which was presented to the director personally and not in his capacity with the company'.[67] Secondly, the decision whether or not the contract went to the company lay not with the fiduciary, Cooley, but with a third party, the Gas Board.[68] In Cooley's case there were special circumstances; this was exactly the type of opportunity which the company relied on Cooley to obtain; furthermore, the absence of bona fides was clear. Also, the imposition of liability will provide directors with an incentive to channel opportunities to their companies and not exploit them for their personal advantage.

There are other decisions which suggest a more benign attitude towards directors.

> In Queensland Mines Ltd v Hudson[69] the claimant company had been interested in developing a mining operation and the defendant, the managing director, was successful in obtaining for the company the licences necessary to enable it to do so. However, because of financial problems it could not proceed. Hudson resigned as managing director and, with the knowledge of the company's board, successfully developed the mines. The Privy Council held that Hudson was not liable to account, for either of two reasons: (a) the rejection of the opportunity by the company because of cash difficulties took the venture outside the scope of Hudson's fiduciary duties or (b) because Hudson had acted with the full knowledge of the company's board, they should be taken to have consented to his activities.[70]

This decision causes difficulties.[71] First, to argue that a board's rejection of the opportunity immunises a director against liability is difficult to reconcile with Regal (Hastings) Ltd v Gulliver. Although in that case Lord Reid deliberately left open the question of the effect of board rejection,[72] it is difficult to see how there would still not be a serious conflict of interest if directors were permitted to acquire for themselves opportunities which they had rejected on behalf of the company. Secondly, only the shareholders could condone Hudson's breach, not the board.[73]

---

[67] (1973) 89 LQR 187, 189.

[68] Roskill J found that there was only a 10 per cent chance that the Gas Board would have awarded the contract to the company. Thus the company only benefited because Cooley had breached his duty.

[69] (1978) 18 ALR 1; [1980] Conv 200 (W. Braithwaite); applied in Jones v AMP Perpetual Trustee Company No 2 Ltd [1994] 1 NZLR 690. See also Island Export Finance Ltd v Umunna [1986] BCLC 460 (defendant not liable for developing a business opportunity after resigning as managing director because company was not actively pursuing the venture when he resigned, and his resignation was influenced, not by any wish to acquire the business opportunity, but by dissatisfaction with the company). See also Plus Group Ltd v Pyke [2002] 2 BCLC 201; (2003) 62 CLJ 42, 403 (P. Koh).

[70] (1978) 18 ALR 1 at 10. Lord Upjohn's reasoning in Boardman v Phipps [1967] 2 AC 46 was adopted on the basis that he had 'dissented on the facts, but not on the law' (at 3).

[71] (1979) 42 MLR 711 (G. Sullivan).

[72] [1967] 2 AC 134n at 152–153. In Peso-Silver Mines Ltd v Cropper (1966) 58 DLR (2d) 1 (SCC), it was held that board rejection did immunise a director against any action to account; criticised in (1967) 30 MLR 450 (D. Prentice); (1971) 49 Canadian Bar Review 80 (S.M. Beck).

[73] In Ultraframe (UK) Ltd v Fielding [2005] EWHC 1638 (Ch), [2005] All ER (D) 397 Lewison J held that a fiduciary who controls a company which has knowingly received money transferred in breach of duty is not liable to account for those funds simply by virtue of his interest in the company; (2006) 122 LQR 558 (D. Prentice and J. Payne).

D.D. Prentice and J. Payne, 'Director's Fiduciary Duties' (2006) 122 LQR 558–559

In a wide-ranging survey of director's duties, Lewison J [in *Ultraframe (UK) Ltd v Fielding* [2006] EWHC 1638, Ch) considered that the general duties on directors included 'two strands of fiduciary duties' which were the 'no conflict rule' (at [1307] *et seq.*) and the 'no profit rule' ([1318] *et seq.*). The first duty precludes a director from entering into a transaction where the director has an interest which conflicts with that of the company, and the second requires a director to account for any profit that he makes from his position unless there has been consent. Lewison J considered that such consent could be ad hoc, or as is common, 'consent to certain transactions is usually given by the articles of association of the company' (at [1318]). Perhaps a more felicitous way of formulating the no profit rule is that a director may not make 'unauthorised profits' (at [1322]). There are of course certain types of profit making to which consent cannot be given: these normally involve a misappropriation of a property that belongs to the company (*Cook v Deeks* [1916] 1 AC 554). As Lewison J points out, the no conflict rule ceases to operate as regards a director's future activities when he or she ceases to hold office (at [1309]). He also considered, citing amongst other cases, *Plus Group Ltd v Pyke* [2002] 2 BCLC 201, that the same rule applies where a director 'has no powers to exercise even during the currency of his directorship' (at [1310]), something which would occur where a director is effectively excluded from office. In such a situation the director 'might as well have resigned' (*Plus Group Ltd v Pyke* at 226). However, it should always be remembered that a director cannot abdicate his or her responsibilities or abandon his or her status without formally resigning. Accordingly, it must be only in the most exceptional circumstances that a director can avoid the no conflict rule by pleading impotence when it is his or her duty to act in the interests of the company and avoid conflict.

Although the no conflict rule 'ceases to apply to his future activities' (at [1309]) where a director resigns, this immunity does not extend to the no profit rule. As Lewison J points out:

> 'Resignation will not preclude a director from being in breach of the "no profit rule" if, after his resignation, he uses for his own benefit property of the company or information which he has acquired while a director' (at [1309]).

The liability of fiduciaries who profit from their position as fiduciaries is strict.[74]

Boardman v Phipps[75]
[1967] 2 AC 46 (HL, **Viscount Dilhorne, Lords Cohen, Hodson, Guest and Upjohn**)

Mr. Phipps left his residuary estate, which included 8,000 shares (approximately 27 per cent) in Lester and Harris Ltd, upon trust for his widow for life and after her

---

[74] (2005) 121 LQR 452 (M. Conaglen); (2006) 65 CLJ 278 (M. Conaglen).
[75] (1967) 31 Conv (NS) 63 (F.R. Crane); (1968) 84 LQR 472 (G.H.Jones) [p. 809, below]; [1978] Conv 114 (B.A.K. Rider); *New Zealand Netherlands Society 'Oranje' Inc v Kuys* [1973] 1 WLR 1126; (1973) 37 Conv (NS) 362 (F.R. Crane); (1975) 28 CLP 39 (J.D. Stephens); *English v Dedham Vale Properties Ltd* [1978] 1 WLR 93 (duty to account imposed upon 'self-appointed agent', where purchaser, without disclosure to vendor, applied for planning permission in vendor's name prior to contract and obtained it prior to completion); (1978) 94 LQR 347 (G. Samuel); 41 MLR 474 (A. Nicol); *United PAN-Europe Communications NV v Deutsche Bank AG* [2000] 2 BCLC 461; *Gwembe Valley Development Company Limited v Koshy (No 3)* [2003] EWCA

death for his four children. The trustees in 1955 were his widow (the life tenant), Mrs. Noble (his daughter), and Mr. Fox (a professional trustee and an accountant).

John Phipps, the plaintiff and respondent, was a son of the testator, and one of the beneficiaries. The defendants, now the appellants, were his brother Tom, also a beneficiary, and Mr. Boardman, who acted as solicitor to the trust and to the Phipps family.

In 1956, the appellants were dissatisfied with the way in which the business of Lester and Harris Ltd was conducted. They made enquiries and took various steps, recorded in more detail below, which culminated in the purchase by the appellants of all the shares in the company other than those owned by the trust. They then effected sales of the company's premises in Australia and in Coventry, and distributed the proceeds of sale as capital profits; and reorganised the part of the business which remained. The transactions were highly profitable both for the trust and for the appellants.

The steps by which this was effected were grouped by the court into three phases. In Phase I, lasting from December 1955 to April 1957, the appellants, acting on behalf of the trustees, obtained valuable information about the company. They made an unsuccessful bid in their own names for the remainder of the shares of the company at £3 per share. Fox and Mrs. Noble were informed, and approved. Mrs. Phipps, the testator's widow, aged and in failing health, was not consulted.

In Phase 2, April 1957 to August 1958, Boardman, again acting on behalf of the trustees, was attempting to reach a solution by effecting a sharing of the assets between the Harris family, and the directors and the Phipps family. The plan failed, but, again during this phase, Boardman obtained further information about the company and the potential value of its shares.

In Phase 3, from 1958 to 1961, an agreement was reached in March 1959 under which Boardman and Tom Phipps should buy the directors' holdings for £4 10s. per share and would make a bid for the remainder of the shares on the same terms. The life tenant had died in 1958. Boardman wrote to the remaindermen, including the respondent, asking their approval to his taking a personal interest in the negotiation. Throughout the negotiations, Boardman acted with unquestioned bona fides, and thought that he had the approval of the trustees while the trust lasted, and of the remaindermen after the life tenant's death. This was not so; he never obtained the approval of old Mrs. Phipps; and Wilberforce J found that the respondents had not been given complete information.

The agreements were carried out, and the profits distributed. The respondent then called upon the appellants to account for their profits on the ground that they held the shares as constructive trustees for the Phipps family.

Held. (Viscount Dilhorne and Lord Upjohn dissenting; and affirming WILBERFORCE J [1964] 1 WLR 993, and the Court of Appeal [1965] Ch 992). (i) The appellants, being persons who were enabled to make a profit by reason of a fiduciary relation, were liable

Civ 6048. Cf. *Swain v Law Society* [1983] 1 AC 598, [1982] 2 All ER 827 (Law Society held not accountable to premium-paying solicitors for commission received as a result of indemnity insurance scheme); [1982] Conv 447 (A.M. Kenny).

to account for it; but (ii) having acted bona fide throughout, were entitled to payment on a liberal scale for their work and skill.[76]

Lord Cohen: In the case before your Lordships it seems to me clear that the appellants throughout were obtaining information from the company for the purpose stated by Wilberforce J but it does not necessarily follow that the appellants were thereby debarred from acquiring shares in the company for themselves. They were bound to give the information to the trustees but they could not exclude it from their own minds. As Wilberforce J said [1964] 1 WLR 993 at 1011, the mere use of any knowledge or opportunity which comes to the trustee or agent in the course of his trusteeship or agency does not necessarily make him liable to account. In the present case had the company been a public company and had the appellants bought the shares on the market, they would not, I think, have been accountable. But the company is a private company and not only the information but the opportunity to purchase these shares came to them through the introduction which Mr. Fox gave them to the board of the company and in the second phase when the discussions related to the proposed split-up of the company's undertaking it was solely on behalf of the trustees that Mr. Boardman was purporting to negotiate with the board of the company. The question is this: when in the third phase the negotiations turned to the purchase of the shares at £4 10s. a share, were the appellants debarred by their fiduciary position from purchasing on their own behalf the 21,986 shares in the company without the informed consent of the trustees and the beneficiaries?

Wilberforce J and, in the Court of Appeal, both Lord Denning MR and Pearson LJ based their decision in favour of the respondent on the decision of your Lordships' House in *Regal (Hastings) Ltd v Gulliver* [1967] 2 AC 134n [p. 798, above]. I turn, therefore, to consider that case. Mr. Walton relied upon a number of passages in the judgments of the learned Lords who heard the appeal: in particular on (1) a passage in the speech of Lord Russell of Killowen where he says at 144G–145A:

'The rule of equity which insists on those, who by use of a fiduciary position make a profit, being liable to account for that profit, in no way depends on fraud, or absence of bona fides; or upon such questions or considerations as whether the profit would or should otherwise have gone to the plaintiff, or whether the profiteer was under a duty to obtain the source of the profit for the plaintiff, or whether he took a risk or acted as he did for the benefit of the plaintiff, or whether the plaintiff has in fact been damaged or benefited by his action. The liability arises from the mere fact of a profit having, in the stated circumstances, been made.'

(2) a passage in the speech of Lord Wright, where he says at 154B–C:

'That question can be briefly stated to be whether an agent, a director, a trustee or other person in an analogous fiduciary position, when a demand is made upon him by the person to whom he stands in the fiduciary relationship to account for profits acquired by him by reason of his fiduciary position, and by reason of the opportunity and the knowledge, or either, resulting from it, is entitled to defeat the claim upon any ground save that he made profits with the knowledge and assent of the other person. The most usual and typical case of this nature is that of principal and agent. The rule in such cases is compendiously expressed to be that an agent must account for net profits secretly (that is, without the knowledge of his principal) acquired by him in the course of his agency. The authorities show how manifold and various are the applications of the rule. It does not depend on fraud or corruption.'

[76] See p. 822, below.

These paragraphs undoubtedly help the respondent but they must be considered in relation to the facts of that case. In that case the profit arose through the application by four of the directors of Regal for shares in a subsidiary company which it had been the original intention of the board should be subscribed for by Regal. Regal had not the requisite money available but there was no question of it being ultra vires Regal to subscribe for the shares. In the circumstances Lord Russell of Killowen said at 146G–147A:

> 'I have no hesitation in coming to the conclusion, upon the facts of this case, that these shares, when acquired by the directors, were acquired by reason, and only by reason of the fact that they were directors of Regal, and in the course of their execution of that office.'

He goes on to consider whether the four directors were in a fiduciary relationship to Regal and concludes that they were. Accordingly, they were held accountable. Mr. Bagnall argued that the present case is distinguishable. He puts his argument thus. The question you ask is whether the information could have been used by the principal for the purpose for which it was used by his agents? If the answer to that question is no, the information was not used in the course of their duty as agents. In the present case the information could never have been used by the trustees for the purpose of purchasing shares in the company; therefore purchase of shares was outside the scope of the appellant's agency and they are not accountable.

This is an attractive argument, but it does not seem to me to give due weight to the fact that the appellants obtained both the information which satisfied them that the purchase of the shares would be a good investment and the opportunity of acquiring them as a result of acting for certain purposes on behalf of the trustees. Information is, of course, not property in the strict sense of that word and, as I have already stated, it does not necessarily follow that because an agent acquired information and opportunity while acting in a fiduciary capacity he is accountable to his principals for any profit that comes his way as the result of the use he makes of that information and opportunity. His liability to account must depend on the facts of the case. In the present case much of the information came the appellants' way when Mr. Boardman was acting on behalf of the trustees on the instructions of Mr. Fox and the opportunity of bidding for the shares came because he purported for all purposes except for making the bid to be acting on behalf of the owners of the 8,000 shares in the company. In these circumstances it seems to me that the principle of the *Regal* case [1967] 2 AC 134n applies and that the courts below came to the right conclusion.

That is enough to dispose of the case but I would add that an agent is, in my opinion, liable to account for profits he makes out of trust property if there is a possibility of conflict between his interest and his duty to his principal. Mr. Boardman and Tom Phipps were not general agents of the trustees but they were their agents for certain limited purposes. The information they had obtained and the opportunity to purchase the 21,986 shares afforded them by their relations with the directors of the company—an opportunity they got as the result of their introduction to the directors by Mr. Fox—were not property in the strict sense but that information and that opportunity they owed to their representing themselves as agents for the holders of the 8,000 shares held by the trustees. In these circumstances they could not, I think, use that information and that opportunity to purchase the shares for themselves if there was any possibility that the trustees might wish to acquire them for the trust. Mr. Boardman was the solicitor whom the trustees were in the habit of consulting if they wanted legal advice. Granted that he would not be bound to advise on any point unless he is consulted, he would still be the person they would consult if they wanted advice. He would clearly have advised them that they had no power to invest in shares of the company without the sanction of the court. In the first phase he would also have had to advise on the evidence then available that the court would be unlikely to give such sanction: but the appellants learnt much more during the second phase. It may well be that even in the third phase the answer of the court would have been the same but, in my opinion, Mr. Boardman would not have been able to give unprejudiced advice if he had been consulted by the trustees and was at the same time negotiating for the purchase of the shares on behalf of himself and Tom Phipps. In other words, there was, in my opinion, at the crucial date (March, 1959), a possibility of a conflict between his interest and his duty.

In making these observations I have referred to the fact that Mr. Boardman was the solicitor to the trust. Tom Phipps was only a beneficiary and was not as such debarred from bidding for the shares, but no attempt was made on the courts below to differentiate between them. Had such an attempt been made it would very likely have failed as Tom Phipps left the negotiations largely to Mr. Boardman and it might well be held that if Mr. Boardman was disqualified from bidding Tom Phipps could not be in a better position. Be that as it may, Mr. Bagnall rightly did not seek at this stage to distinguish between the two. He did, it is true, say that Tom Phipps as a beneficiary would be entitled to any information the trustees obtained. This may be so, but nonetheless I find myself unable to distinguish between the two appellants. They were, I think, in March, 1959, in a fiduciary position *vis-à-vis* the trust. That fiduciary position was of such a nature that (as the trust fund was distributable) the appellants could not purchase the shares on their own behalf without the informed consent of the beneficiaries; it is now admitted that they did not obtain that consent. They are therefore, in my opinion, accountable to the respondent for his share of the net profits they derived from the transaction.

I desire to repeat that the integrity of the appellants is not in doubt. They acted with complete honesty throughout and the respondent is a fortunate man in that the rigour of equity enables him to participate in the profits which have accrued as the result of the action taken by the appellants in March, 1959, in purchasing the shares at their own risk. As the last paragraph of his judgment clearly shows, the trial judge evidently shared this view. He directed an inquiry as to what sum is proper to be allowed to the appellants or either of them in respect of his work and skill in obtaining the said shares and the profits in respect thereof. The trial judge concluded by expressing the opinion that payment should be on a liberal scale. With that observation I respectfully agree.[77]

In the result I agree in substance with the judgments of Wilberforce J and of Lord Denning MR and Pearson LJ in the Court of Appeal, and I would dismiss the appeal.

Lord Upjohn (dissenting): It is of cardinal importance, and, in my view fundamental to the decision of this case, to appreciate that at this stage there was no question whatever of the trustees contemplating the possibility of a purchase of further shares in the company. Mr. Fox (whose evidence was accepted by the judge) made it abundantly plain that he would not consider any such proposition. The reasons for this attitude are worth setting out in full: (a) the acquisition of further shares in the company would have been a breach of trust, for they were not shares authorised by the investment clause in the will; (b) although not developed in evidence it must have been obvious to those concerned that no court would sanction the purchase of further shares in a small company which the trustees considered to be badly managed. It would have been throwing good money after bad. It would also have been necessary to bring in proposals for installing a new management. Mr. Fox was a busy practising chartered accountant who obviously would not have considered it; no one from start to finish ever suggested that Tom,

---

[77] See further p. 822, below for analysis of this equitable allowance.

who was running the family concern of Phipps & Son Ltd, would be willing to undertake this arduous task on behalf of the trustees; (c) the trustees had no money available for the purchase of further shares...

In these circumstances the respondent rather surprisingly seeks to hold the appellants accountable to him for his 5/18ths share of the 21,986 shares so purchased, on the footing that the appellants are constructive trustees of these shares for and on behalf of the trust. So I turn to the relevant law upon which this claim is based, but start by stating what is not in dispute, that the conduct of the appellants and each of them has never been anything except utterly honest and above board in every way. If they or either of them are accountable it is because of the operation of some harsh doctrine of equity upon consciences completely innocent in every way.

Rules of equity have to be applied to such a great diversity of circumstances that they can be stated only in the most general terms and applied with particular attention to the exact circumstances of each case. The relevant rule for the decision of this case is the fundamental rule of equity that a person in a fiduciary capacity must not make a profit out of his trust which is part of the wider rule that a trustee must not place himself in a position where his duty and his interest may conflict. I believe the rule is best stated in *Bray v Ford* [1896] AC 44 at 51 by Lord Herschell, who plainly recognised its limitations:

> 'It is an inflexible rule of a Court of Equity that a person in a fiduciary position, such as the respondent's, is not, unless otherwise expressly provided, entitled to make a profit; he is not allowed to put himself in a position where his interest and duty conflict. It does not appear to me that this rule is, as has been said, founded upon principles of morality. I regard it rather as based on the consideration that, human nature being what it is, there is danger, in such circumstances, of the person holding a fiduciary position being swayed by interest rather than by duty, and thus prejudicing those whom he was bound to protect. It has, therefore, been deemed expedient to lay down this positive rule. But I am satisfied that it might be departed from in many cases, without any breach of morality, without any wrong being inflicted, and without any consciousness of wrong-doing. Indeed, it is obvious that it might sometimes be to the advantage of the beneficiaries that their trustee should act for them professionally rather than a stranger, even though the trustee were paid for his services.'[78]

[His Lordship referred to *Aberdeen Rly Co v Blaikie Bros* (1854) 1 Macq 461; *Regal (Hastings) Ltd v Gulliver* [1967] 2 AC 134n; *Keech v Sandford* (1726) Sel Cas Ch 61, and continued:] Secondly, as to the position of Mr. Boardman himself. There is no doubt that from time to time he acted as solicitor to the trust and to the family and he was therefore throughout in a fiduciary capacity at least to the trustees. Whether he was ever in a fiduciary capacity to the respondent was not debated before your Lordships and I do not think it matters. I think, again, that some of the trouble that has arisen in this case, it being assumed rightly that throughout he was in such a capacity, is that it has been assumed that it has necessarily followed that any profit made by him renders him accountable to the trustees. This is not so. A solicitor who acts for a client from time to time is no doubt rightly described throughout as being in a fiduciary capacity to him but that means fundamentally no more than this, that if he has dealings with his clients, e.g., accepts a present from him or buys property from him, there is a presumption of undue influence and the onus is on the solicitor to justify the present or purchase (see, for example, *McMaster*

---

[78] See *Re Drexel Burnham Lambert UK Pension Plan* [1995] 1 WLR 32 (pension fund trustees also beneficiaries under scheme; court held to have jurisdiction to give directions as to exercise of trustees' discretion).

v Byrne [1952] 1 All ER 1362 at 1368). That principle has no relevance to the present case. There is no such thing as an office of being solicitor to a trust (*Saffron Walden Second Benefit Building Society v Rayner* (1880) 14 Ch D 406 at 409, *per* James LJ). Though these remarks of James LJ were admittedly obiter they represent the law. It is perfectly clear that a solicitor can if he so desires act against his clients in any matter in which he has not been retained by them provided, of course, that in acting for them generally he has not learnt information or placed himself in a position which would make it improper for him to act against them. This is an obvious application of the rule that he must not place himself in a position where his duty and his interest conflict. So in general a solicitor can deal in shares in a company in which the client is a shareholder, subject always to the general rule that the solicitor must never place himself in a position where his interest and his duty conflict; and in this connection it may be pointed out that the interest and duty may refer (and frequently do) to a conflict of interest and duty on behalf of different clients and have nothing to do with any conflict between the personal interest and duty of the solicitor, beyond his interest in earning his fees.

[His Lordship then referred to Wilberforce J and the Court of Appeal, and continued:] Before applying these principles to the facts, however, I shall refer to the judgment of Russell LJ, which proceeded on a rather different basis. He said [1965] Ch 992 at 1031:

'The substantial trust shareholding was an asset of which one aspect was its potential use as a means of acquiring knowledge of the company's affairs, or of negotiating allocations of the company's assets, or of inducing other shareholders to part with their shares. That aspect was part of the trust assets.'

My Lords, I regard that proposition as untenable.

In general, information is not property at all. It is normally open to all who have eyes to read and ears to hear. The true test is to determine in what circumstances the information has been acquired. If it has been acquired in such circumstances that it would be a breach of confidence to disclose it to another then courts of equity will restrain the recipient from communicating it to another. In such cases such confidential information is often and for many years has been described as the property of the donor, the books of authority are full of such references; knowledge of secret processes, 'know-how', confidential information as to the prospects of a company or of someone's intention or the expected results of some horse race based on stable or other confidential information. But in the end the real truth is that it is not property in any normal sense but equity will restrain its transmission to another if in breach of some confidential relationship.

With all respect to the views of Russell LJ, I protest at the idea that information acquired by trustees in the course of their duties as such is necessarily part of the assets of the trust which cannot be used by the trustees except for benefit of the trust. Russell LJ referred at 1031, at 864 to the fact that two out of three of the trustees could have no authority to turn over this aspect of trust property to the appellants except for the benefit of the trust; this I do not understand, for if such information is trust property not all the trustees acting together could do it for they cannot give away trust property.

We heard much argument upon the impact of the fact that the testator's widow was at all material times incapable of acting in the trust owing to disability. Of course trustees must act all of them and unanimously in matters affecting trust affairs, but in this case they never performed any relevant act on behalf of the trust at all; I quoted Mr. Fox's answer earlier for this reason. At no time after going to the meeting in December, 1956, did Mr. Boardman or Tom rely on any express or implied authority or consent of the trustees in relation to trust property. They understood rightly that there was no question of the trustees acquiring any further trust property by purchasing further shares in the company, and it was only in the purchase of other shares that they were interested.

There is, in my view, and I know of no authority to the contrary, no general rule that information learnt by a trustee during the course of his duties is property of the trust and cannot be used by him. If that were to be the rule it would put the Public Trustee and other corporate trustees out of business and make it difficult for private trustees to be trustees of more than one trust. This would be the greatest possible pity for corporate trustees and others may have much information which they may initially acquire in connection with some particular trust but without prejudice to that trust can make it readily available to other trusts to the great advantage of those other trusts.

The real rule is, in my view, that knowledge learnt by a trustee in the course of his duties as such is not in the least property of the trust and in general may be used by him for his own benefit or for the benefit of other trusts unless it is confidential information which is given to him (1) in circumstances which, regardless of his position as a trustee, would make it a breach of confidence for him to communicate to anyone for it has been given to him expressly or impliedly as confidential, or (2) in a fiduciary capacity, and its use would place him in a position where his duty and his interest might possibly conflict. Let me give one or two simple examples. A, as trustee of two settlements X and Y holding shares in the same small company, learns facts as trustee of X about the company which are encouraging. In the absence of special circumstances (such, for example, that X wants to buy more shares) I can see nothing whatever which would make it improper for him to tell his co-trustees of Y who feel inclined to sell that he has information that this would be a bad thing to do. Another example: A as trustee of X learns facts that make him and his co-trustees want to sell. Clearly he could not communicate this knowledge to his co-trustees of Y until at all events the holdings of X have been sold for there would be a plain conflict, reflected in the prices that might or might possibly be obtained...

As a result of the information they acquired, admittedly by reason of the trust holding, they found it worth while to offer a good deal more for the shares than in [the period January–April 1957]. I cannot see that in offering to purchase non-trust shares at a higher price they were in breach of any fiduciary relationship in using the information they had acquired for this purpose...

I have dealt with the problems that arise in this case at considerable length but it could, in my opinion, be dealt with quite shortly.

In *Barnes v Addy* (1874) 9 Ch App 244 at 251, Lord Selborne LC said:

'It is equally important to maintain the doctrine of trusts which is established in this court, and not to strain it by unreasonable construction beyond its due and proper limits. There would be no better mode of undermining the sound doctrines of equity than to make unreasonable and inequitable applications of them.'

That, in my judgment, is applicable to this case.

The trustees were not willing to buy more shares in the company. The active trustees were very willing that the appellants should do so themselves for the benefit of their large minority holding. The trustees, so to speak, lent their name to the appellants in the course of prolonged and difficult negotiations and, of course, the appellants thereby learnt much which would have otherwise been denied to them. The negotiations were in the end brilliantly successful.

And how successful Tom was in his reorganisation of the company is apparent to all. They ought to be very grateful.

In the long run the appellants have bought for themselves at entirely their own risk with their own money shares which the trustees never contemplated buying and they did so in circumstances fully known and approved of by the trustees.

To extend the doctrines of equity to make the appellants accountable in such circumstances is, in my judgment, to make unreasonable and unequitable applications of such doctrines.

I would allow the appeal and dismiss the action.

(1968) 84 LQR 472, 483–502 (G.H. Jones)[79]

Lord Hodson and Lord Guest were of the opinion that confidential information could properly be regarded as 'the property of the trust', and for this reason alone Phipps and Boardman must account for the fruit of that property.[80] Lord Hodson went on to say that because the appellants had acted as agents and had 'obtained knowledge by reason of their fiduciary position...they cannot escape liability by saying that they were acting for themselves and not as agents of the trustees'.[81] And Lord Guest based his final conclusion on the ground that 'Boardman and Tom Phipps...[had] placed themselves in a special position which was of a fiduciary character in relation to the negotiations with the directors....Out of such special position and in the course of such negotiations they obtained the opportunity to make a profit out of the shares and knowledge that the profit was there to be made.'[82]...

To say that the fiduciaries' profit was made solely through the use of property (the information) received qua fiduciaries, when the trust could not have utilised it and when the negotiations would have failed but for Boardman's business acumen and Boardman and Phipps' financial intervention, offends legal as well as common sense.[83]...

The main ground of the decision was that there was a conflict between Boardman and Phipps' self-interest and their fiduciary duty; they had made a profit out of their special position of trust. It is difficult to accept, however, that any reasonable person could conclude on these facts that there was any real (as distinct from a hypothetical) conflict of interest. In our view the reasoning of the dissenting law lords is convincing. Lord Upjohn's realistic, commonsense

---

[79] See also *Seager v Copydex Ltd* [1967] 1 WLR 923; (1970) 86 LQR 463 (G.H. Jones). See Virgo, *The Principles of the Law of Restitution* (2nd ed., 2006), pp. 528–529.

[80] In *Phipps v Boardman* the plaintiff in his writ had claimed that Boardman and Tom Phipps held 5/18ths of the shareholding as constructive trustees for the plaintiff (5/18ths being the extent of the plaintiff's beneficial interest in the trust fund), for an account of profits made by Boardman and Phipps from the holdings, and for an order to be made that they should transfer the shares held as constructive trustees to the plaintiff, and pay him 5/18ths of the profit: see [1965] Ch 992 at 1006. At first instance [1964] 1 WLR 993 at 1018, Wilberforce J had declared that the defendants were accountable and directed an account and an inquiry as to the allowances to which they were entitled. The order went on to say that 'further consideration [would be given] of order to transfer the shares held by the defendants and payment of any profit found on the taking of the account adjourned'. [81] [1967] 2 AC 46 at 111.

[82] At 118.

[83] In the Court of Appeal, Lord Denning MR suggested that the appellants should have told the trustees that the shares were a good buy, that they ought to purchase them, and that they should apply to the court for power to do so: see [1965] Ch 992 at 1020. No other judge in the Court of Appeal or House of Lords took up this point. Lord Upjohn considered that it was a 'difficult point', but was able to avoid it by saying that it was neither pleaded nor relied upon in argument: see [1967] 2 AC 46 at 131. In any event, is it realistic to assume that parties would contemplate an application to the court during the course of confidential and protracted negotiations?

approach is that of Justice Clark in the *Becker* case.[84] Both judges refused to apply blindly a rule of equity. In neither *Becker*'s case nor *Phipps v Boardman* had the profit been made at the expense of the fiduciary's principal. In both cases the fiduciary's actions had benefited the principal: the purchase of the debentures in the *Becker* case encouraged public confidence in a company which was in a parlous financial position; in *Phipps v Boardman* the long negotiations conducted with considerable skill by Boardman, and the purchase of the outstanding shares by Boardman and Tom Phipps, had resulted in great financial benefit to the trust....

Conclusion

'Rules of equity have to be applied to such a great diversity of circumstances that they can be stated only in the most general terms and applied with particular attention to the exact circumstances of each case.'[85]

The rule that a fiduciary must not profit from his trust is used to recover the fiduciary's unjust enrichment *and* to ensure that the conduct of all fiduciaries is maintained 'at a level higher than that trodden by the crowd'.[86]

In many cases these objects do not conflict. The dishonest fiduciary who is punished as a warning to others has been unjustly enriched. It is irrelevant that his gain has not been made at his principal's expense, in the sense that something has been taken 'from [the] plaintiff and added to the treasury of [the] defendant'. For he has abused his position of trust, and 'in equity and good conscience [he] should not be permitted to retain that by which [he] has been enriched'. In other cases, however, the fiduciary's enrichment has not been unjustly gained. There is then a variance between the two objects which underlie equity's inflexible rule. Some but not all courts and judges have been aware of this clash of principle. A conscious appreciation and consideration of the qualifications of the large generalisation of unjust enrichment[87]—the inherent fairness of the transaction, the fiduciary's honesty and concern to protect his principal's interests, and the fact that the principal has suffered no real loss (the 'complex equation' of loss and gain)—has helped them to decide that there was, on the particular facts, no real sensible possibility of conflict between duty and self-interest.

The boundaries between just and unjust enrichment do not inevitably compose the limits of equity's 'inflexible rule'. There may be cases where it is absolutely necessary to punish the fiduciary whose enrichment cannot be said to be unjustly gained. That wise public policy which desires to remove all temptation and to extinguish all possibility of profit may insist that a fiduciary whose integrity is beyond doubt and who has materially benefited his principal should be deprived of profit. But this decision should be taken only after due and careful regard has been paid to the relevant policy considerations, to the nature of the responsibilities which the particular fiduciary owes his principal and to the question whether it is necessary to make an example of the innocent and conscientious that others may learn from their fate.

Finally, there is the question of the extent and degree of the fiduciary's liability. In our view the principal should be allowed a proprietary claim only if the court considers it appropriate that he should be granted the additional benefits which naturally flow from such a grant. The

---

[84] *Manufacturers Trust Co v Becker* 338 US 304, 70 Sup Ct 127 (1949).

[85] *Boardman v Phipps* [1967] 2 AC 46 at 123, *per* Lord Upjohn.

[86] *Meinherd v Salmon* 249 NY 456 at 464, 164 NE 545 at 546 (1928), *per* Chief Judge Cardozo.

[87] *Fibrosa Spolka Akcyjna v Fairbairn Lawson Combe Barbour Ltd* [1943] AC 32 at 62–63, *per* Lord Wright.

honest fiduciary who is deemed to have breached his duty of loyalty but who has not been unjustly enriched and whose principal has suffered no loss should only be liable to account for his profits. On the other hand a fiduciary who is dishonest or who has otherwise manifestly disregarded his principal's interest should be held to be a constructive trustee of the benefits obtained at his principal's expense. If, as a matter of policy, the court imposes on him a further and penal liability for profits made by third parties, his liability should only be a personal one, to account to his principal for those profits.

That a claim for breach of fiduciary duty does not require proof of fault has been considered by the Court of Appeal.

Murad v Al-Saraj
[2005] EWCA Civ 959 (CA, **Lord Justices Clarke** and
Jonathan Parker and **Lady Justice Arden**)[88]

The Murads, two sisters, entered into a joint venture with Mr. Al-Saraj to buy a hotel for £4.1 million. It was agreed that £1 million would be provided by the Murads, £500,000 in cash by Al-Saraj, and the remainder from a bank loan. However, Al-Saraj's contribution in the end was made by offsetting certain unenforceable obligations owed to him by the vendor, including commission of £369,000 for Al-Saraj introducing the sisters to the vendor. The hotel was sold at a profit of £2 million. The trial judge found that the effect of the joint venture was that Al-Saraj was in a fiduciary relationship with the Murads, and that Al-Saraj had breached his fiduciary duty by not disclosing that he was making his contribution by set-off. He ordered that Al-Saraj should account for the entire profits he made from the acquisition of the hotel. Al-Saraj appealed on the primary ground that the account of profits should have been limited to the profits obtained by the breach of fiduciary duty, in the light of the judge's finding that, if the set-off had been disclosed to the Murads, they would have agreed to go ahead with the acquisition of the hotel but demanded a greater share of the profit. Rather, Al-Saraj should only be liable for the loss incurred by the Murads as a result of the non-disclosure of the set-off arrangement.

Held. Order for account of profits affirmed.

Lady Justice Arden:
17   Mr. Cogley [counsel for Al-Saraj] submits that both the nature of the fiduciary relationship and the consequences of the breach have an impact on the scope of any account of profits. Mr. Cogley submits that the account which was ordered went well beyond stripping Mr. Al-Saraj of the profit for breach of fiduciary duty. There has to be a link between the identified breach of duty and the profit.

18   Mr. Cogley submits that in all the earlier authorities there was a nexus between the profit and the breach of duty. In this he relies on *Boardman v Phipps* [1967] 2 AC 46 [p. 801, above], *Regal (Hastings) Limited v Gulliver* [1967] 2 AC 46 [p. 798, above]; *Gwembe Valley Development Company Limited v Koshy (No 3)* [2003] EWCA Civ 6048. Mr. Cogley submits

[88] [2005] All ER Rev 369 (J. Edelman and C. Mitchell); (2006) 122 LQR 11 (M. McInnes); (2006) 65 CLJ 278 (M. Conaglen).

that the effect of the judge's judgment at paragraph 287 is that some part of the profit must in fact have been authorised. He accepts that the common law principle that damages are to compensate a party for his loss, does not apply in this field. Nonetheless, he submits that there has to be some connection between the breach of duty and the remedy. In particular, he submits that there is a distinction to be drawn between the failure to make disclosure affecting the whole of a transaction and the failure to make disclosure affecting part only of the transaction. . . . .

30 Mr. Guy Newey QC, for the respondents, submits that a fiduciary who obtains a benefit as a result of a conflict between his interest and duty, is liable to account for that profit. It is not a question of there being a duty to inform; it is a principle of accountability.

31 Mr. Newey submits that there was a plain nexus in this case between the breach of duty and the account. In this regard, he relies on the judge's observation on the application for permission to appeal in this case that: 'the fiduciary has to take the position that he or she must disgorge all the profit made from the transaction.'. . . .

49 There has been some debate as to whether Mr. Al-Saraj was liable for breach of fiduciary duty because he was under a duty to disclose information which he failed to disclose, or whether he made a secret profit for which, in the absence of disclosure and the consent of the Murads, he is liable to account on the basis that such liability is an incident of the fiduciary relationship rather than a breach of duty. The judge's judgment suggests the former. The respondents rely on the latter because that leads them directly to the *Regal* case. For my own part, for the purposes simply of the question on this appeal, I do not think it matters which way the appellants' liability is analysed . . .

56 To test Mr. Cogley's argument on the extent of the liability to account, in my judgment it is necessary to go back to first principle. It has long been the law that equitable remedies for the wrongful conduct of a fiduciary differ from those available at common law. . . . Equity recognises that there are legal wrongs for which damages are not the appropriate remedy. In some situations therefore, as in this case, a court of equity instead awards an account of profits. As with an award of interest (as to which see *Wallersteiner v Moir (No 2)* [1975] QB 373 [see p. 967, below]), the purpose of the account is to strip a defaulting fiduciary of his profit. . . .

58 Furthermore, a loss to the person to whom a fiduciary duty is owed is not the other side of the coin from the profit which the person having the fiduciary duty has made: that person may have to account for a profit even if the beneficiary has suffered no loss.

59 I would highlight two well-established points about the reach of the equitable remedies:

(1) the liability of a fiduciary to account does not depend on whether the person to whom the fiduciary duty was owed could himself have made the profit.

(2) when awarding equitable compensation, the court does not apply the common law principles of causation. . . .

67 The fact that the fiduciary can show that that party would not have made a loss is, on the authority of the *Regal* case, an irrelevant consideration so far as an account of profits is concerned. Likewise, it follows in my judgment from the *Regal* case that it is no defence for a fiduciary to say that he would have made the profit even if there had been no breach of fiduciary duty.

68 In the present case, the conduct of Mr. Al-Saraj was held to be fraudulent. This was not the position of the directors in the *Regal* case. The principle, however, established by the *Regal* case applies even where the fiduciary acts in the mistaken belief that he is acting in accordance

with his fiduciary duty. As Lord Russell made clear in the passage cited above, liability does not depend on fraud or lack of good faith. The existence of a fraudulent intent will, however, be relevant to the question of the allowances to be made on the taking of the account (which subject I consider below)....

71   In my judgment it is not enough for the wrongdoer to show that, if he had not been fraudulent, he could have got the consent of the party to whom he owed the fiduciary duty to allow him to retain the profit. The point is that the profit here was in fact wholly unauthorised at the time it was made and has so remained. To obtain a valid consent, there would have to have been full and frank disclosure by Mr. Al-Saraj to the Murads of all relevant matters. It is only actual consent which obviates the liability to account.

72   Proposition (2) in paragraph 59 above is also established by many authorities. Most recently, in *Target Holdings Ltd v Redferns* [1996] AC 421, 436 [see p. 949, below], Lord Browne-Wilkinson held:

'[But] the basic equitable principle applicable to breach of trust is that the beneficiary is entitled to be compensated for any loss that he would not have suffered but for the breach.'

73   This principle is not applicable simply to fraudulent breaches of trust. As Lord Eldon LC said in *Caffrey v Darby* (1801) 6 Ves 488; 31ER 1159:

'It would be very dangerous, though no fraud could be imputed to the trustees, and no kind of interest or benefit to themselves was looked to, to lay down this principle; that trustees might without any responsibility act, as these did: in eight years, within which time the whole money ought to have been paid, receiving only £250; and taking no step as to the remainder. It would be an encouragement to bad motives; and it may be impossible to detect undue motives. If we get the length of neglect in not recovering this money by taking possession of the property, will they be relieved from that by the circumstance, that the loss has ultimately happened by something, that is not a direct and immediate consequence of their negligence: *viz.* the decision of a doubtful question of law? Even supposing they are right in saying, this was a very doubtful question, and they could not look to the possibility of its being so decided, yet, if they have been already guilty of negligence, they must be responsible for any loss in any way to that property: for whatever may be the immediate cause, the property would not have been in a situation to sustain that loss, if it had not been for their negligence. If they had taken possession of the property, it would not have been in his possession. If the loss had happened by fire, lightning, or any other accident, that would not be an excuse for them, if guilty of previous negligence. That was their fault.'

74   It may be asked why equity imposes stringent liability of this nature. The passage just cited from the judgment of Lord Eldon LC makes it clear that equity imposes stringent liability on a fiduciary as a deterrent—*pour encourager les autres*. Trust law recognises what in company law is now sometimes called the 'agency' problem. There is a separation of beneficial ownership and control and the shareholders (who may be numerous and only have small numbers of shares) or beneficial owners cannot easily monitor the actions of those who manage their business or property on a day-to-day basis. Therefore, in the interests of efficiency and to provide an incentive to fiduciaries to resist the temptation to misconduct themselves, the law imposes exacting standards on fiduciaries and an extensive liability to account. As Lord King said in the leading case of *Keech v Sandford* (1726) Sel Cas t King 61 [see p. 791, above]:

'I very well see, if a trustee, on the refusal to renew, might have a lease to himself, few trust-estates will be renewed to *cestuis que use*.'

75   I accept that any rule that makes a wrongdoer liable for all the consequences of his wrongful conduct or for actions which did not cause the injured party any loss needs to be justified by some special policy. But the authorities just cited show that in the field of fiduciaries there are policy reasons which have for a long time been accepted by the courts.

76   For policy reasons, the courts decline to investigate hypothetical situations as to what would have happened if the fiduciary had performed his duty. In the *Regal* case at page 154G, Lord Wright made the following point, to which I shall have to return below:

> 'Nor can the court adequately investigate the matter in most cases. The facts are generally difficult to ascertain or are solely in the knowledge of the person being charged. They are matters of surmise; they are hypothetical because the inquiry is as to what would have been the position if that party had not acted as he did, or what he might have done if there had not been the temptation to seek his own advantage, if, in short, interest had not conflicted with duty.'

77   Again, for the policy reasons, on the taking of an account, the court lays the burden on the defaulting fiduciary to show that the profit is not one for which he should account: see, for example, *Manley v Sartori* [1927] Ch 157. This shifting of the onus of proof is consistent with the deterrent nature of the fiduciary's liability. The liability of the fiduciary becomes the default rule....

82   I have already set out Lord Wright's observations in the *Regal* case about the difficulties of investigating the conduct of a defaulting trustee. Under the rule of equity applied in that case (and in part summarised in proposition (1) above), cases can be found where the fiduciary or trustee acted in all good faith believing that he was acting in the interests of his beneficiary but yet has been made to account for the profits obtained as a result of the breach of trust without limitation. Now, in a case like the *Regal* case, if the rule of equity under which the defendants were held liable to account for secret profits were not inflexible, the crucial issue of fact would be: what the company would have done if the opportunity to subscribe for shares in its subsidiary had been offered to it? In the passage just cited, as I have said, Lord Wright makes the point that it is very difficult to investigate that issue. However, while that may have been so in the past in the days of Lord Eldon and Lord King, that would not be the case today. The court has very extensive powers under the CPR for instance to require information to be given as to a party's case. If the witness cannot attend the hearing, it may be possible for his evidence to be given by way of a witness statement or it may be possible for him to give evidence by video-link. The reasons for the rule of equity are many and complex (for a recent discussion, see Conaglen, 'The Nature and Function of Fiduciary Loyalty' (2005) LQR 452). There have been calls for its re-examination (see, for example, the articles cited at (2005) LQR 452, 478 at footnote 151). It may be that the time has come when the court should revisit the operation of the inflexible rule of equity in harsh circumstances, as where the trustee has acted in perfect good faith and without any deception or concealment, and in the belief that he was acting in the best interests of the beneficiary. I need only say this: it would not be in the least impossible for a court in a future case, to determine as a question of fact whether the beneficiary would not have wanted to exploit the profit himself, or would have wanted the trustee to have acted other than in the way that the trustee in fact did act. Moreover, it would not be impossible for a modern court to conclude as a matter of policy that, without losing the deterrent effect of the rule, the harshness of it should be tempered in some circumstances. In addition, in such cases, the courts can provide a significant measure of protection for the beneficiaries by imposing on the defaulting trustee the affirmative burden of showing that those circumstances prevailed. Certainly the Canadian courts have modified the effect of equity's inflexible rule (see *Peso Silver Mines Ltd v Cropper* (1966) 58 DLR (2d) 1; see also the decision of the Privy Council on appeal from

Australia in *Queensland Mines v Hudson* (1978) 52 AJLR 399), though I express no view as to the circumstances in which there should be any relaxation of the rule in this jurisdiction. That sort of question must be left to another court.

83   In short, it may be appropriate for a higher court one day to revisit the rule on secret profits and to make it less inflexible in appropriate circumstances, where the unqualified operation of the rule operates particularly harshly and where the result is not compatible with the desire of modern courts to ensure that remedies are proportionate to the justice of the case where this does not conflict with some other overriding policy objective of the rule in question.

84   However that is not this case. Mr. Al-Saraj was found to have made a fraudulent misrepresentation to the Murads who had placed their trust in him. I do not consider that, even if we were free to revisit the *Regal* case, this would be an appropriate case in which to do so. The appropriate remedy is that he should disgorge all the profits, whether of a revenue or capital nature, that he made from inducing the Murads by his fraudulent representations from entering into the Parkside Hotel venture, subject to any allowances permitted by the court on the taking of the account....

Lord Justice Jonathan Parker concurred; Lord Justice Clarke dissented on the basis that the approach for assessing an account of profits should be more flexible.

D   BRIBES AND SECRET COMMISSIONS

Until the Privy Council decision in *A-G for Hong Kong v Reid* [1994] 1 AC 324, the liability of a fiduciary who received a secret profit depended on whether the profit was in the form of a bribe or of some other type. The first gave rise only to a personal relationship of debtor and creditor between the fiduciary and his principal,[89] the second to a proprietary relationship. In the case of the bribe the principal could sue the fiduciary or the briber[90] for the amount of the bribe; in the other case the fiduciary became a constructive trustee for the principal,[91] as a result of which he had a proprietary interest in the bribe so that he could trace into its product or substitute,[92] and, where the fiduciary was bankrupt, a claim ahead of his general creditors.

The Privy Council has now removed this inconsistency and held that in both cases a constructive trust arises in favour of the principal.

Attorney-General for Hong Kong v Reid
[1994] 1 AC 324 (PC, **Lords Templeman, Goff of Chieveley, Lowry, Lloyd of Berwick** and **Sir Thomas Eichelbaum**)[93]

Mr. Reid, a New Zealander, was Acting Director of Public Prosecutions in Hong Kong. In breach of his fiduciary duty to the Crown, he accepted bribes of NZ$2.5 million as

---

[89] *Lister & Co v Stubbs* (1890) 45 Ch D 1.

[90] *Mahesan v Malaysia Government Officers' Co-operative Housing Society Ltd* [1979] AC 374 at 383.

[91] *Boardman v Phipps* [1967] 2 AC 46 [p. 801, above].   [92] See p. 903, below.

[93] [1994] Conv 156 (A. Jones); (1994) CLJ 31 (A.J. Oakley); (1994) 110 LQR 178 (P. Watts); [1994] *Restitution Law Review* 57 (D. Crilley); [1994] All ER Rev 252 (P.J. Clarke); Goff and Jones, pp. 740–742; Virgo, *The*

an inducement to exploit his official position by obstructing the prosecution of certain criminals. He was convicted, sentenced to eight years' imprisonment and ordered to pay the Crown HK\$12.4 million, the equivalent of NZ\$2.5 million. Mr. Reid used the bribes to purchase three freehold properties in New Zealand, two for himself and his wife, and one for his solicitor. Neither his wife nor his solicitor could establish that they were bona fide purchasers for value without notice.

The Attorney-General for Hong Kong lodged a caveat against the titles to the properties, in order to prevent any dealing with them pending a full hearing. Mr. Reid argued that the Crown was entitled only to a personal claim for the value of the initial bribe and had no equitable interest in the properties. The Court of Appeal of New Zealand, following *Lister & Co v Stubbs* (1890) 45 Ch D 1, found for Mr. Reid.

Held (reversing the Court of Appeal) for the Crown. It had an equitable interest under a constructive trust.

Lord Templeman: A bribe is a gift accepted by a fiduciary as an inducement to him to betray his trust. A secret benefit, which may or may not constitute a bribe, is a benefit which the fiduciary derives from the trust property or obtains from knowledge which he acquires in the course of acting as a fiduciary. A fiduciary is not always accountable for a secret benefit but he is undoubtedly accountable for a secret benefit which consists of a bribe. In addition a person who provides the bribe and the fiduciary who accepts the bribe may each be guilty of a criminal offence. In the present case the first respondent was clearly guilty of a criminal offence.

Bribery is an evil practice which threatens the foundations of any civilised society. In particular bribery of policemen and prosecutors brings the administration of justice into disrepute. Where bribes are accepted by a trustee, servant, agent or other fiduciary, loss and damage are caused to the beneficiaries, master or principal whose interests have been betrayed. The amount of loss or damage resulting from the acceptance of a bribe may or may not be quantifiable. In the present case the amount of harm caused to the administration of justice in Hong Kong by the first respondent in return for bribes cannot be quantified.

When a bribe is offered and accepted in money or in kind, the money or property constituting the bribe belongs in law to the recipient. Money paid to the false fiduciary belongs to him. The legal estate in freehold property conveyed to the false fiduciary by way of bribe vests in him. Equity, however, which acts *in personam*, insists that it is unconscionable for a fiduciary to obtain and retain a benefit in breach of duty. The provider of a bribe cannot recover it because he committed a criminal offence when he paid the bribe. The false fiduciary who received the bribe in breach of duty must pay and account for the bribe to the person to whom that duty was owed. In the present case, as soon as the first respondent received a bribe in breach of the duties he owed to the Government of Hong Kong, he became a debtor in equity to the Crown for the amount of that bribe. So much is admitted. But if the bribe consists of property which increases in value or if a cash bribe is invested advantageously, the false fiduciary will receive a benefit from his breach of duty unless he is accountable not only for the original amount or value of the bribe but also for the increased value of the property representing the bribe. As soon as the bribe was received it should have been paid or transferred *instanter* to the person who suffered from the breach of duty. Equity considers as done that which ought to have been done.

Principles of the Law of Restitution (2nd ed., 2006) pp. 521–525; (1996) *Journal of Business Law* 22 (D.Cowan, R. Edmunds and J. Lowry); (1997) 1 *Corporate Finance & Insurance Law Review* 43 (C. Rotherham).

As soon as the bribe was received, whether in cash or in kind, the false fiduciary held the bribe on a constructive trust for the person injured. Two objections have been raised to this analysis. First it is said that if the fiduciary is in equity a debtor to the person injured, he cannot also be a trustee of the bribe. But there is no reason why equity should not provide two remedies, so long as they do not result in double recovery. If the property representing the bribe exceeds the original bribe in value, the fiduciary cannot retain the benefit of the increase in the value which he obtained solely as a result of his breach of duty. Secondly, it is said that if the false fiduciary holds property representing the bribe in trust for the person injured, and if the false fiduciary is or becomes insolvent, the unsecured creditors of the false fiduciary will be deprived of their right to share in the proceeds of that property. But the unsecured creditors cannot be in a better position than their debtor. The authorities show that property acquired by a trustee innocently but in breach of trust and the property from time to time representing the same belong in equity to the *cestui que trust* and not to the trustee personally whether he is solvent or insolvent. Property acquired by a trustee as a result of a criminal breach of trust and the property from time to time representing the same must also belong in equity to his *cestui que trust* and not to the trustee whether he is solvent or insolvent.

When a bribe is accepted by a fiduciary in breach of his duty then he holds that bribe in trust for the person to whom the duty was owed. If the property representing the bribe decreases in value the fiduciary must pay the difference between the value and the initial amount of the bribe because he should not have accepted the bribe or incurred the risk of loss. If the property increases in value, the fiduciary is not entitled to any surplus in excess of the initial value of the bribe because he is not allowed by any means to make a profit out of a breach of duty.

The courts of New Zealand were constrained by a number of precedents of the New Zealand, English and other common law courts which established a settled principle of law inconsistent with the foregoing analysis. That settled principle is open to review by the Board in the light of the foregoing analysis of the consequences in equity of the receipt of a bribe by a fiduciary. In *Keech v Sandford* (1726) Sel Cas Ch 61 a landlord refused to renew a lease to a trustee for the benefit of an infant. The trustee then took a new lease for his own benefit. The new lease had not formed part of the original trust property, the infant could not have acquired the new lease from the landlord and the trustee acted innocently, believing that he committed no breach of trust and that the new lease did not belong in equity to his *cestui que trust*. Lord King LC held nevertheless, at p. 62, that 'the trustee is the only person of all mankind who might not have the lease'; the trustee was obliged to assign the new lease to the infant and account for the profits he had received. The rule must be that property which a trustee obtains by use of knowledge acquired as trustee becomes trust property. The rule must, *a fortiori*, apply to a bribe accepted by a trustee for a guilty criminal purpose which injures the *cestui que trust*. The trustee is only one example of a fiduciary and the same rule applies to all other fiduciaries who accept bribes.

[His Lordship referred to *Fawcett v Whitehouse* (1829) 1 Russ & M 132 and *Sugden v Crossland* (1856) 3 Sm & G 192, and continued:] This case is of importance because it disposes succinctly of the argument which appears in later cases and which was put forward by counsel in the present case that there is a distinction between a profit which a trustee takes out of a trust and a profit such as a bribe which a trustee receives from a third party. If in law a trustee, who in breach of trust invests trust moneys in his own name, holds the investment as trust property, it is difficult to see why a trustee who in breach of trust receives and invests a bribe in his own name does not hold those investments also as trust property.

[His Lordship referred to *Tyrrell v Bank of London* (1862) 10 HL Cas 26; *Re Canadian Oil Works Corpn (Hay's Case)* (1875) 10 Ch App 593; *Re Morvah Consols Tin Mining Co, McKay's Case* (1875) 2 Ch D 1; *Re Caerphilly Colliery Co, Pearson's Case* (1877) 5 Ch D 336; *Metropolitan Bank v Heiron* (1880) 5 Ex D 319, and continued:] It has always been assumed and asserted that the law on the subject of bribes was definitively settled by the decision of the Court of Appeal in *Lister & Co v Stubbs* (1890) 45 Ch D 1.

In that case the plaintiffs, Lister & Co, employed the defendant, Stubbs, as their servant to purchase goods for the firm. Stubbs, on behalf of the firm, bought goods from Varley & Co and received from Varley & Co bribes amounting to £5,541. The bribes were invested by Stubbs in freehold properties and investments. His masters, the firm Lister & Co, sought and failed to obtain an interlocutory injunction restraining Stubbs from disposing of these assets pending the trial of the action in which they sought, *inter alia*, £5,541 and damages. In the Court of Appeal the first judgment was given by Cotton LJ who had been party to the decision in *Metropolitan Bank v Heiron* (1880) 5 Ex D 319. He was powerfully supported by the judgment of Lindley LJ and by the equally powerful concurrence of Bowen LJ. Cotton LJ said, at p. 12, that the bribe could not be said to be the money of the plaintiffs. He seemed to be reluctant to grant an interlocutory judgment which would provide security for a debt before that debt had been established. Lindley LJ said, at p. 15, that the relationship between the plaintiffs, Lister & Co, as masters and the defendant, Stubbs, as servant who had betrayed his trust and received a bribe:

> 'is that of debtor and creditor; it is not that of trustee and *cestui que trust*. We are asked to hold that it is—which would involve consequences which, I confess, startle me. One consequence, of course, would be that, if Stubbs were to become bankrupt, this property acquired by him with the money paid to him by Messrs. Varley would be withdrawn from the mass of his creditors and be handed over bodily to Lister & Co. Can that be right? Another consequence would be that, if the appellants are right, Lister & Co could compel Stubbs to account to them, not only for the money with interest, but for all the profits which he might have made by embarking in trade with it. Can that be right?'

For the reasons which have already been advanced their Lordships would respectfully answer both these questions in the affirmative. If a trustee mistakenly invests money which he ought to pay over to his *cestui que trust* and then becomes bankrupt, the moneys together with any profit which has accrued from the investment are withdrawn from the unsecured creditors as soon as the mistake is discovered. *A fortiori* if a trustee commits a crime by accepting a bribe which he ought to pay over to his *cestui que trust*, the bribe and any profit made therefrom should be withdrawn from the unsecured creditors as soon as the crime is discovered.

The decision in *Lister & Co v Stubbs* is not consistent with the principles that a fiduciary must not be allowed to benefit from his own breach of duty, that the fiduciary should account for the bribe as soon as he receives it and that equity regards as done that which ought to be done. From these principles it would appear to follow that the bribe and the property from time to time representing the bribe are held on a constructive trust for the person injured. A fiduciary remains personally liable for the amount of the bribe if, in the event, the value of the property then recovered by the injured person proved to be less than that amount.

His Lordship referred to *Powell and Thomas v Evans Jones & Co* [1905] 1 KB 11; *A-G v Goddard* (1929) 98 LJKB 743; *Regal (Hastings) Ltd v Gulliver* [1967] 2 AC 134n; *Reading v A-G* [1951] AC 507; and *Islamic Republic of Iran Shipping Lines v Denby* [1987] 1 Lloyd's Rep 367, and continued:

The authorities which followed *Lister & Co v Stubbs* do not cast any new light on that decision. Their Lordships are more impressed with the decision of Lai Kew Chai J in *Sumitomo Bank Ltd v Kartika Ratna Thahir* [1993] 1 SLR 735 ... After considering in detail all the relevant authorities Lai Kew Chai J determined robustly, at p. 810, that *Lister & Co v Stubbs* (1890) 45 Ch D 1, was wrong and that its 'undesirable and unjust consequences should not be imported and perpetuated as part of' the law of Singapore. Their Lordships are also much indebted for the fruits of research and the careful discussion of the present topic in the address entitled 'Bribes and Secret Commissions' [1993] *Restitution Law Review* 7 delivered by Sir Peter Millett to a meeting of the Society of Public Teachers of Law at Oxford in 1993. The following passage, at p. 20, elegantly sums up the views of Sir Peter Millett:

> '[The fiduciary] must not place himself in a position where his interest may conflict with his duty. If he has done so, equity insists on treating him as having acted in accordance with his duty; he will not be allowed to say that he preferred his own interest to that of his principal. He must not obtain a profit for himself out of his fiduciary position. If he has done so, equity insists on treating him as having obtained it for his principal; he will not be allowed to say that he obtained it for himself. He must not accept a bribe. If he has done so, equity insists on treating it as a legitimate payment intended for the benefit of the principal: he will not be allowed to say that it was a bribe.'

The conclusions reached by Lai Kew Chai J in *Sumitomo Bank Ltd v Kartika Ratna Thahir* and the views expressed by Sir Peter Millett were influenced by the decision of the House of Lords in *Boardman v Phipps* [1967] 2 AC 46 which demonstrates the strictness with which equity regards the conduct of a fiduciary and the extent to which equity is willing to impose a constructive trust on property obtained by a fiduciary by virtue of his office. In that case a solicitor acting for trustees rescued the interests of the trust in a private company by negotiating for a takeover bid in which he himself took an interest. He acted in good faith throughout and the information which the solicitor obtained about the company in the takeover bid could never have been used by the trustees. Nevertheless the solicitor was held to be a constructive trustee by a majority in the House of Lords because the solicitor obtained the information which satisfied him that the purchase of the shares in the takeover company would be a good investment and the opportunity of acquiring the shares as a result of acting for certain purposes on behalf of the trustees: see *per* Lord Cohen, at p. 103. If a fiduciary acting honestly and in good faith and making a profit which his principal could not make for himself becomes a constructive trustee of that profit then it seems to their Lordships that a fiduciary acting dishonestly and criminally who accepts a bribe and thereby causes loss and damage to his principal must also be a constructive trustee and must not be allowed by any means to make any profit from his wrongdoing. For the reasons indicated their Lordships consider that the three properties so far as they represent bribes accepted by the first respondent are held in trust for the Crown.

In **Daraydan Holdings Ltd v Solland International Ltd** [2004] EWHC 622 (Ch), [2005] Ch 119[94] the claimants claimed that commissions paid to the defendant, a former employee, in respect of contracts for the refurbishment of the claimants' properties

---

[94] [2005] All ER Rev 271 (P.J. Clarke); [2005] Conv 88 (M. Halliwell). See also *Sinclair Investment Holdings SA v Versailles* Trade Finance Ltd [2007] EWHC 915 (Ch); [2007] 2 All ER (Comm) 993, para. 105 (Rimer J).

were bribes and so the defendant was liable to account for them. Lawrence Collins J held that the claimant could recover the bribes because they derived directly from the claimants' property, since the contract price had been increased by the amount of the bribe, and the bribe money was paid from the money which had been paid by the claimants. In considering the defendants' liability the judge summarised the principles relating to liability for a fiduciary's receipt of bribes and the appropriate remedy, as follows:

52   An agent should not put himself in a position where his duty and interest may conflict, and if bribes are taken by an agent, the principal is deprived of the disinterested advice of the agent, to which the principal is entitled. Any surreptitious dealing between one principal to a transaction and the agent of the other is a fraud on the other principal. For this purpose sub-agents owe the same duty not to take bribes as agents, despite the absence of privity of contract between them and the principal: see *Bowstead & Reynolds on Agency*, 17th ed (2001), para 6–085 and *Powell & Thomas v Evan Jones and Co* [1905] 1 KB 11, 18.

53   In proceedings against the payer of the bribe there is no need for the principal to prove (a) that the payer of the bribe acted with a corrupt motive; (b) that the agent's mind was actually affected by the bribe; (c) that the payer knew or suspected that the agent would conceal the payment from the principal; (d) that the principal suffered any loss or that the transaction was in some way unfair: the law is intended to operate as a deterrent against the giving of bribes, and it will be assumed that the true price of any goods bought by the principal was increased by at least the amount of the bribe, but any loss beyond the amount of the bribe itself must be proved; (e) that the bribe was given specifically in connection with a particular contract, since a bribe may also be given to an agent to influence his mind in favour of the payer generally (e.g. in connection with the granting of future contracts).

54   The agent and the third party are jointly and severally liable to account for the bribe, and each may also be liable in damages to the principal for fraud or deceit or conspiracy to injury by unlawful means. Consequently, the agent and the maker of the payment are jointly and severally liable to the principal (1) to account for the amount of the bribe as money had and received and (2) for damages for any actual loss. But the principal must now elect between the two remedies prior to final judgment being entered: *Mahesan s/o Thambiah v Malaysia Officers' Co-operative Housing Society Ltd* [1979] AC 374, 383. The third party may also be liable on the basis of accessory liability in respect of breach of fiduciary duty:[95] *Bowstead & Reynolds on Agency*, para 8–221. The principal is also able to rescind the contract with the payer of the bribe....

78   Those who have supported *Lister & Co v Stubbs* (1890) 45 Ch D 1 rely on the policy that proprietary restitution is only justified where there has been a subtraction from the claimant's ownership or where the claimant has a proprietary basis for the claim. The general creditors have given value, and there is no reason why the agent's principal should have a preferred position. The policy against bribery is sufficiently vindicated through a personal remedy. Thus, according to Professor Roy Goode, proprietary remedies should only be available where the defendant receives gains which derive from the claimant's property, or where they stem from activity which the defendant was under an equitable obligation to undertake (if at all) for the plaintiff: the decision in *Lister & Co v Stubbs* was correct, because the bribe resulted from conduct in which the defendant should not have engaged at all: Goode, 'Property and Unjust Enrichment', in *Essays on the Law of Restitution*, ed Burrows (1991), pp 215, 230–231

[95] See p. 815, above.

and Goode, 'Proprietary Restitutionary Claims', in *Restitution: Past, Present and Future*, ed Cornish (1998), pp 63, 69. So also Professor Birks considers that proprietary restitution is only justified where the claimant has a proprietary base to his claim, i.e. where the defendant's breach of duty consists of misapplication of property belonging to the claimant; but in the case of bribery, the money paid to the agent comes from the third party, and not from the principal: Birks, *Introduction to the Law of Restitution*, 2nd ed (1989), p 386. See also Virgo, *The Principles of the Law of Restitution* (1999), p 543, Burrows, *The Law of Restitution*, 2nd ed (2002), p 500 and Tettenborn, *Law of Restitution in England and Ireland*, 2nd ed (1996), pp 231–233.

79   But the Privy Council preferred the views of Sir Peter Millett, in 'Bribes and Secret Commissions' [1993] *Restitution Law Review* 7, 20 [see p. 819, above]...

80   The decision of the Privy Council is regarded as black-letter law by *Bowstead & Reynolds on Agency*, para 6–082. It is also treated as representing the law by *Lewin on Trusts*, 17th ed (2000), para 20–34 and by *Snell's Equity*, 30th ed (2000), para 9–53. Goff & Jones, *The Law of Restitution*, 6th ed (2002), para 33–025, prefer *Attorney-General for Hong Kong v Reid* [1994] 1 AC 324 but consider that *Lister & Co v Stubbs* 45 Ch D 1 is a decision which is still technically binding.

81   *Attorney-General for Hong Kong v Reid* has been preferred at first instance to *Lister & Co v Stubbs* by Laddie J in *Ocular Sciences Ltd v Aspect Vision Care Ltd* [1997] RPC 289, 412–413 (a breach of confidence case) and by Toulson J (obiter) in *Fyffes Group Ltd v Templeman* [2000] 2 Lloyd's Rep 643. But Sir Richard Scott V-C in *Attorney-General v Blake* [1997] Ch 84, 96 and the Court of Appeal in *Halifax Building Society v Thomas* [1996] Ch 217, 229 treated *Lister & Co v Stubbs* as still binding, although neither of those cases was a case involving bribery of an agent.

[His Lordship considered whether a judge at first instance can follow a decision of the Privy Council which departs from an earlier decision of the Court of Appeal, and concluded that he could.]

85   The system of precedent would be shown in a most unfavourable light if a litigant in such a case were forced by the doctrine of binding precedent to go to the House of Lords....in order to have the decision of the Privy Council affirmed. That would be particularly so where the decision of the Privy Council is recent, where it was a decision on the English common law, where the Board consisted mainly of serving Law Lords, and where the decision had been made after full argument on the correctness of the earlier decision.

86   Accordingly, if this case were not distinguishable from *Lister & Co v Stubbs* 45 Ch D 1, I would have applied *Attorney-General for Hong Kong v Reid* [1994] 1 AC 324. There are powerful policy reasons for ensuring that a fiduciary does not retain gains acquired in violation of fiduciary duty, and I do not consider that it should make any difference whether the fiduciary is insolvent. There is no injustice to the creditors in their not sharing in an asset for which the fiduciary has not given value, and which the fiduciary should not have had.

87   But even if I were bound by *Lister & Co v Stubbs*, in my judgment there are two very significant differences between this case and that decision which in any event justify the restitutionary remedy. First, the facts of this case make it a case where there is a proprietary basis for the claim and where the bribe derives directly from the claimants' property. This is not a case where the price is presumed (for the purposes of the personal remedy) to have been increased by the amount of the bribe. Rather it is a case where the evidence is that the price was actually

increased by the amount of the bribe, and where the bribe was paid out of the money paid by the claimants for what they thought was the price. These factors make the claim one for the restitution of money extracted from the claimants.

　　88　　Secondly (and independently), the portion representing the bribe was paid as a result of a fraudulent misrepresentation of the Sollands, to which Mr. Khalid was a party, that the true price was the invoice price, when it fact the price had been inflated to pay the bribes...

In **Fyffes Group v Templeman** [2002] 2 Lloyds Law Rep 643[96] it was held that the person who had paid the bribe to the fiduciary was not liable to account because the principal of the bribed agent would have entered into the contract anyway.

E　THE EQUITABLE ALLOWANCE

The court may in appropriate cases authorise remuneration in favour of trustees or other persons acting in a fiduciary capacity even though they have breached their fiduciary duty.[97]

In **Brown v Litton** (1711) 1 P Wms 140, the plaintiff's testator was captain of a ship, and had $800 with him on a voyage. He died. The defendant, the mate, became captain, took the dollars, and traded successfully with them. On his return to England, the question was whether the defendant's obligation was to return the money with interest, or whether he was liable to account for the profits. LORD KEEPER HARCOURT held that he must account for the profits; but that he should be given a proper reward for his work.

In **Re Jarvis** [1958] 1 WLR 815, two sisters, Rosetta and Sheila, became entitled to half-shares in their deceased father's shop. The shop was largely destroyed by enemy bombing in 1940. Sheila had it repaired and built up the business. UPJOHN J held that Sheila was accountable as constructive trustee as to half for Rosetta 'subject to all just allowances for her time, energy and skill, for the assets she has contributed and the debts of the testator which she has paid'.

In **Boardman v Phipps** [1967] 2 AC 46 [p. 801, above], although the House of Lords held that the solicitor to the trust was accountable to the trust for the profits he had made, on the ground that the opportunity to make them arose from his fiduciary position, he was entitled to payment on a liberal scale in respect of his work and skill.[98]

In **O'Sullivan v Management Agency and Music Ltd** [1985] QB 428,[99] a contract between a manager and a young and unknown composer and performer of popular music, whose retail sale of records realised a gross figure of some £14.5 million between 1970 and 1978, was set aside for undue influence. The Court of Appeal held that the

---

[96] (2001) 117 LQR 207 (C. Mitchell).　　　[97] See p. 669, above.
[98] See also *Re Barbour's Settlement* [1974] 1 WLR 1198; cf. *Re Codd's Will Trusts* [1975] 1 WLR 1139.
[99] (1986) 49 MLR 118 (W. Bishop and D.D. Prentice).

defendants must account for the profits, but also should be entitled to a reasonable remuneration including a small profit element in respect of their skill and labour in promoting the plaintiff. Fox LJ said at 468:

Once it is accepted that the court can make an appropriate allowance to a fiduciary for his skill and labour I do not see why, in principle, it should not be able to give him some part of the profit of the venture if it was thought that justice as between the parties demanded that. To give the fiduciary any allowance for his skill and labour involves some reduction of the profits otherwise payable to the beneficiary. And the business reality may be that the profits could never have been earned at all, as between fully independent persons, except on a profit-sharing basis. But be that as it may, it would be one thing to permit a substantial sharing of profits in a case such as *Boardman v Phipps* where the conduct of the fiduciaries could not be criticised and quite another to permit it in a case such as the present where, though fraud was not alleged, there was an abuse of personal trust and confidence. I am not satisfied that it would be proper to exclude Mr. Mills and the M.A.M. companies from all reward for their efforts. I find it impossible to believe that they did not make a significant contribution to Mr. O'Sullivan's success. It would be unjust to deny them a recompense for that. I would, therefore, be prepared as was done in *Boardman v Phipps* to authorise the payment (over and above out of pocket expenses) of an allowance for the skill and labour of the first five defendants in promoting the compositions and performances and managing the business affairs of Mr. O'Sullivan, and that an inquiry (the terms of which would need to be considered with counsel) should be ordered for that purpose. Such an allowance could include a profit in the way that solicitors' costs do.

In **Guinness plc v Saunders** [1990] 2 AC 663,[100] [p. 799, above], the House of Lords refused remuneration to a company director, who was assumed to have acted bona fide but in circumstances which involved a clear conflict of interest and duty. LORD GOFF OF CHIEVELEY said at 701:

It will be observed that the decision [in *Boardman v Phipps* [1967] 2 AC 46 [p. 801, above] to make the allowance was founded upon the simple proposition that it would be inequitable now for the beneficiaries to step in and take the profit without paying for the skill and labour which has produced it. *Ex hypothesi*, such an allowance was not in the circumstances authorised by the terms of the trust deed; furthermore it was held that there had not been full and proper disclosure by the two defendants to the successful plaintiff beneficiary. The inequity was found in the simple proposition that the beneficiaries were taking the profit although, if Mr. Boardman (the solicitor) had not done the work, they would have had to employ an expert to do the work for them in order to earn that profit.

The decision has to be reconciled with the fundamental principle that a trustee is not entitled to remuneration for services rendered by him to the trust except as expressly provided in the trust deed. Strictly speaking, it is irreconcilable with the rule as so stated. It seems to me therefore that it can only be reconciled with it to the extent that the exercise of the equitable jurisdiction does not conflict with the policy underlying the rule. And, as I see it, such a conflict will only be avoided if the exercise of the jurisdiction is restricted to those cases where it cannot

---

[100] See Virgo, *The Principles of the Law of Restitution* (2nd ed., 2006), pp. 516–517. See also *Re Quarter Master UK Ltd* (Ch D, 15 July 2004); *Warman International Ltd v Dwyer* (1995) 128 ALR 201 at 212 (High Court of Australia); C. Harpum in *Privacy and Loyalty* (ed. P. Birks), pp. 154–160.

have the effect of encouraging trustees in any way to put themselves in a position where their interests conflict with their duties as trustees.

Not only was the equity underlying Mr. Boardman's claim in *Boardman v Phipps* clear and, indeed, overwhelming; but the exercise of the jurisdiction to award an allowance in the unusual circumstances of that case could not provide any encouragement to trustees to put themselves in a position where their duties as trustees conflicted with their interests. The present case is, however, very different. Whether any such an allowance might ever be granted by a court of equity in the case of a director of a company, as opposed to a trustee, is a point which has yet to be decided; and I must reserve the question whether the jurisdiction could be exercised in such a case, which may be said to involve interference by the court in the administration of a company's affairs when the company is not being wound up. In any event, however, like my noble and learned friend, Lord Templeman, I cannot see any possibility of such jurisdiction being exercised in the present case. I proceed, of course, on the basis that Mr. Ward acted throughout in complete good faith. But the simple fact remains that, by agreeing to provide his services in return for a substantial fee the size of which was dependent upon the amount of a successful bid by Guinness, Mr. Ward was most plainly putting himself in a position in which his interests were in stark conflict with his duty as a director. Furthermore, for such services as he rendered, it is still open to the board of Guinness (if it thinks fit, having had a full opportunity to investigate the circumstances of the case) to award Mr. Ward appropriate remuneration. In all the circumstances of the case, I cannot think that this is a case in which a court of equity (assuming that it has jurisdiction to do so in the case of a director of a company) would order the repayment of the £5.2 million by Mr. Ward to Guinness subject to a condition that an equitable allowance be made to Mr. Ward for his services.[101]

QUESTIONS

1. If trustees (and other fiduciaries) should not profit from their fiduciary position, what is the justification for remunerating them for services provided to their principal? See C. Harpum in *Privacy and Loyalty* (ed. P. Birks, 1997), pp. 154–160; Virgo, *The Principles of the Law of Restitution* (2006, 2nd ed.), pp. 517–519. See also p. 669, above.

2. In determining the borderline of a fiduciary liability, how relevant is it that:
   (a) the principal suffered no loss;
   (b) the principal benefited in addition to the fiduciary;
   (c) the fiduciary was bona fide;
   (d) the profit came through a decision of a third party (the Gas Board in *Industrial Development Consultants Ltd v Cooley* [1972] 1 WLR 443 [p. 799, above]);
   (e) the fiduciary is a trustee, solicitor, or director;
   (f) the defendant is a friend of the fiduciary?

---

[101] No reference was made to *O'Sullivan v Management Agency and Music Ltd* [1985] QB 428 [p. 822, above].

3. Do you think that fiduciary obligations should be imposed where there is also:

   (a) a breach of duty of care in tort: *Henderson v Merrett Syndicates Ltd* [1995] 2 AC 145 at 205, *per* Lord Browne-Wilkinson; (1995) 111 LQR 1 (J.D. Heydon); *Bristol and West Building Society v Mothew* [1998] Ch 1, 16 (Millet LJ).

   (b) a breach of contract: *Polly Peck International plc v Nadir (No 2)* [1992] 4 All ER 769; *Kelly v Cooper* [1993] AC 205; *Re Goldcorp Exchange Ltd* [1995] 1 AC 74; *United Dominions Corpn v Brian Pty Ltd* (1985) 157 CLR 1; (1994) 110 LQR 238 at pp. 245–248 (Sir Anthony Mason); (1998) 114 LQR 214, 217–218 (Sir Peter Millett).

4. The directors of a corporation purchased debentures at a discount, at prices varying from 3 per cent to 14 per cent of their face value. At the time of the purchase, the corporation was a going concern, but the market value of its property was insufficient to pay its outstanding debts. The purchase was made without failure to disclose any material facts to the sellers. On the liquidation of the corporation the directors stood to make a profit if their claims as debenture holders were allowed. The trustee for the debenture holders objected on the ground that the directors could not make a profit from the purchase of claims against an insolvent corporation.

   What result? *Manufacturers Trust Co v Becker* 338 US 304, 70 Sup Ct 127 (1949); (1968) 84 LQR at pp. 479ff (G.H. Jones). See also *Boardman v Phipps* [1967] 2 AC 46 at 90, where VISCOUNT DILHORNE quoted LINDLEY LJ in *Aas v Benham* [1891] 2 Ch 244 at 255–256: 'to hold that a partner can never derive any personal benefit from information which he obtains from a partner would be manifestly absurd'.

5. If you had been a Lord of Appeal in *Boardman v Phipps,* what would you have said?

6. Was *Boardman v Phipps* a case concerning constructive trusts, or personal accountability? H&M, p. 630; [1994] 2 *Restitution Law Review* 57, 61–62 (D. Crilley); (1968) 84 LQR at 502 (G.H. Jones); *A-G for Hong Kong v Reid* [1994] 1 AC 324 [p. 815, above].

7. Should the profits of a breach of fiduciary duty be held on constructive trust? Virgo, pp. 521–525; [1994] 2 *Restitution Law Review* 57 (D. Crilley); (1996) *Journal of Business Law* 22 (D. Cowan, R. Edmunds and J. Lowry).

8. Should liability for breach of fiduciary duty be strict? See M. Conaglen (2005) 121 LQR 452.

17

VARIATION OF TRUSTS[1]

I INTRODUCTION

A trustee must administer the trust in accordance with its terms; otherwise he commits a breach of trust. Sometimes, however, the observance of the terms is harmful to the beneficiaries. This appears in many contexts; and most especially in that of tax planning. In short, the old-fashioned settlement containing a succession of limited interests can be disadvantageous in terms of the liability to taxation on death. How can such a settlement, once established, be changed?

There is no difficulty if all the beneficiaries are of full age, under no disability, and all agree.[2] They can terminate the trust and share out; or agree to resettle upon other trusts. But it is usual in a family settlement that there are some beneficiaries of later generations who are minor or unborn, and who could not therefore join in a termination or reconstruction of the settlement. Could the court approve a reconstruction on behalf of minors or unborn beneficiaries when it was for their benefit? The House of Lords decided that it could not.[3] As LORD MORTON OF HENRYTON said in *Chapman v Chapman*:[4] 'if the court had power to approve, and did approve schemes such as the present scheme, the way would be open for a most undignified game of chess between the Chancery Division and the legislature'. If, however, there was a dispute between

---

[1] H&M, pp. 635–654; Lewin, pp. 1853–1903; P&M, pp. 741–760; P&S, pp. 462–478; Pettit, pp. 503–519; Snell, pp. 660–664; T&H, pp. 717–743; U&H, pp. 613–656; Harris, *Variation of Trusts* (1975).

[2] *Saunders v Vautier* (1841) 4 Beav 115 [p. 191, above]; affd (1841) Cr & Ph 240; *Re Chardon* [1928] Ch 464; *Re Smith* [1928] Ch 915 [p. 193, above]. See also Trusts of Land and Appointment of Trustees Act 1996, s. 6(2).   [3] *Chapman v Chapman* [1954] AC 429.

[4] Ibid. at 468.

the beneficiaries, which the beneficiaries were prepared to compromise, the Court could sanction the compromise.[5] It must be a real dispute; but it is hardly necessary to add that greater ingenuity was needed to find a dispute in some cases than was necessary to find a tax-saving compromise.

Various statutory provisions relate to variation of trusts, and these will be identified below.[6] The court also has inherent power to authorise certain acts by trustees which are beyond their powers. The inherent jurisdiction is narrow and is generally restricted to emergency and salvage operations.[7] Towering above these provisions and powers in significance is the Variation of Trusts Act 1958, under which most variations are now effected. It should be noted, however, that trustees may be given a power to amend the trust in the trust instrument itself.[8]

II TRUSTEE ACT 1925, SECTION 57

TRUSTEE ACT 1925

57. Power of court to authorise dealings with trust property: see p. 749, above.

Pettit: *Equity and the Law of Trusts* (10th edn, 2006), pp. 507–508

Of primary importance is the interpretation of the words 'management' and 'administration', which are largely, though very possibly not entirely, synonymous. The subject matter of both words in section 57 is trust property which is vested in trustees, and 'trust property' cannot by any legitimate stretch of the language include the equitable interests which a settlor has created in that property. The application of both words is confined to the managerial supervision and control of trust property on behalf of beneficiaries, and the section accordingly does not permit the remoulding of the beneficial interests. The object of section 57, it was said,[9] is

'to secure that trust property should be managed as advantageously as possible in the interests of the beneficiaries, and, with that object in view, to authorise specific dealings with the property which the court might have felt itself unable to sanction under the inherent jurisdiction, either because no actual "emergency" had arisen or because of inability to show that the position which called for intervention was one which the creator of the trust could not reasonably have

---

[5] See *Allen v Distillers Co (Biochemicals) Ltd* [1974] QB 384; *Re Barbour's Settlement* [1974] 1 WLR 1198; *Re Earl of Strafford* [1980] Ch 28 [p. 751, n. 16, above]; *Mason v Farbrother* [1983] 2 All ER 1078 [p. 828, below].

[6] See pp. 827–859, below; (1954) 17 MLR 420 (O.R. Marshall). See also Matrimonial Causes Act 1973, s. 24 (property adjustment orders in connection with divorce proceedings).

[7] *Re New* [1901] 2 Ch 534; *Re Tollemache* [1903] 1 Ch 955.

[8] See, for example, *Society of Lloyd's v Robinson* [1999] 1 WLR 756.

[9] Per Evershed MR and Romer LJ in *Re Downshire Settled Estates* [1953] Ch 218 at 248, 264, 268 ... And see *Municipal and General Securities Co Ltd v Lloyds Bank Ltd* [1950] Ch 212.

foreseen, but it was no part of the legislative aim to disturb the rule that the court will not rewrite a trust or to add to such exceptions to that rule as had already found their way into the inherent jurisdiction.'

Later in the judgment the majority adopted the statement of Farwell J in *Re Mair*,[10] that 'if and when the court sanctions an arrangement or transaction under section 57, it must be taken to have done it as though the power which is being put into operation had been inserted in the trust instrument as an overriding power'. Perhaps Farwell J put it even more clearly later in his judgment where he said[11] 'the effect of the court permitting the exercise by trustees of some power which is not in the trust document itself, and, therefore, something which the trustees could not do except by the direction of the court, is the same as though that power had been inserted as an overriding power in the trust document'.

Applications under section 57 are almost invariably heard and disposed of in private and accordingly not reported. There are, however, a few reported cases which show that in the exercise of its jurisdiction under this section the court has authorized the sale of settled chattels,[12] a partition of land[13] and a sale of land where the necessary consent could not be obtained.[14] It has authorized two residuary estates left on identical charitable trusts to be blended into one fund.[15] It has, apparently commonly, authorized capital money to be expended on paying off the tenant for life's debts, on having its replacement secured by a policy of insurance so that the beneficial interests remain unaltered,[16] but although it has in exceptional circumstances sanctioned a similar expenditure of capital to purchase the life tenant's interest, it is doubtful whether it would do so in an ordinary case, as it would come 'at least very near to altering the beneficial interests of the tenant for life'.[17] The court has also authorized the sale of a reversionary interest which under the trust instrument was not to be sold until it should fall into possession.[18] Finally . . . the section may be used to extend trustees' powers of investment.

In **Mason v Farbrother** [1983] 2 All ER 1078, the trustees of the Co-operative Wholesale Society's Pension and Death Fund Scheme sought a variation of the trust deed by the insertion of a wider investment clause. In sanctioning the variation under section 57, JUDGE BLACKETT-ORD V-C said at 1086:

That power was exercised by Danckwerts J in a charity case, *Re Shipwrecked Fishermen and Mariners' Royal Benevolent Society* [1959] Ch 220, so as to extend the investment powers of the trustees.

   Shortly afterwards, in *Re Coates' Will Trusts* [1959] 1 WLR 375, the view was put forward by Harman J that the proper way to proceed where trustees wished to obtain extended investment powers was by way of an application under the Variation of Trusts Act 1958,[19] and that

---

[10] [1935] Ch 562 at 565.   [11] Ibid at 566.   [12] *Re Hope's Will Trust* [1929] 2 Ch 136.

[13] *Re Thomas* [1930] 1 Ch 194.   [14] *Re Beale's Settlement Trusts* [1932] 2 Ch 15.

[15] *Re Harvey* [1941] 3 All ER 284. The contrary decision in *Re Royal Society's Charitable Trusts* [1956] Ch 87 . . ., where *Re Harvey* does not appear to have been cited, would seem to be wrong in the light of *Re Shipwrecked Fishermen and Mariners' Royal Benevolent Society* [1959] Ch 220 . . .

[16] *Re Salting* [1932] 2 Ch 57; *Re Mair* [1935] Ch 562. These cases must be read in the light of the observations of the majority of the Court of Appeal in *Re Downshire Settled Estates* [1953] Ch 218 at 249–251 . . . and see *Re Forster's Settlement* [1954] 3 All ER 714.   [17] *Re Forster's Settlement*, ibid, *per* Harman J at 720.

[18] *Re Cockerell's Settlement Trusts* [1956] Ch 372 . . .

[19] An application under Variation of Trusts Act 1958, s. 1 [p. 832, below], was not pursued. It was also held that the court could not vary the deed under its inherent jurisdiction to sanction a compromise. 'There

advice, in my experience, was acted on and many applications were made under that Act; but the law as laid down by Danckwerts J in *Re Shipwrecked Fishermen and Mariners' Royal Benevolent Society* has not been overruled, and I am satisfied that where in the management or administration of trust property it is in the opinion of the court expedient, I have the power to authorise the substitution for cll 5 and 6 of the 1929 deed of the sort of investment clause which is being put forward here.

The next question to be considered is whether there is any reason why this should not be done, based on the Trustee Investments Act 1961. I have indicated that after 1959 a great many applications were made by trustees of trusts under the Variation of Trusts Act 1958 to obtain wider investment powers, but Parliament then passed the 1961 Act extending investment powers of trustees and in two later cases, namely *Re Cooper's Settlement* [1962] Ch 826, and *Re Kolb's Will Trusts* [1962] Ch 531, Buckley J and Cross J respectively expressed the view that in the light of such a recent expression of the views of Parliament, it would not be right for the courts to continue to extend investment clauses with the enthusiasm with which they had done up to date; and for many years few applications, if any, were made.

But the rule was not an absolute one; it was said to apply in the absence of special circumstances, and the special circumstances in the present case are manifest: in a word, inflation since 1961. And also of course the fact that the trust is an unusual one in that it is not a private or family trust but a pension fund with perhaps something of a public element in it.

In my judgment, therefore, there is no reason why in a proper case an application such as the present one should not be acceded to under section 57 of the Trustee Act 1925. And it seems to me on the evidence that it is (in the words of the section) 'expedient' that the application should succeed. Therefore, the way that I think it is proper to deal with the application is by making an order under section 57 of the 1925 Act, and this I will do.[20]

In **Anker-Petersen v Anker-Petersen**, 6 December, 1990, reported (1998) 12 TLI 166, JUDGE PAUL BAKER QC held that both section 57 of the Trustee Act 1925 and the Variation of Trusts Act 1958 could be used to extend investment powers but, where there was no alteration of the beneficial interests, section 57 was preferable. His Honour said at 170:

The first point is whether applications which solely concern the powers of investment and other administrative powers of a settlement and do not affect the beneficial interests, should be brought under section 57 of the Trustee Act 1925 or under the Variation of Trusts Act 1958.

[His Honour read TA 1925, section 57 and the Variation of Trusts Act 1958, section 1 and considered various cases on whether section 57 can be used to extend investment powers and continued:] Where, however, no alteration of the beneficial interests [is] contemplated it appears to me more convenient to use section 57. In the first place the Trustees are the natural persons to make the applications and they are the normal applicants under section 57 (see sub-section (3)) but only exceptionally are they applicants under the Act of 1958: see *Re Druce's Settlement Trusts* [1962] 1 WLR 363.

is something to compromise, but the court cannot sweep the old away and substitute the new.' See *Re Powell-Cotton's Re-Settlement* [1956] 1 WLR 23 at 27, *per* Evershed MR.

[20] [1984] Conv 373 (H.E. Norman); [1984] All ER Rev 308 (P.J. Clarke). See *Trustees of the British Museum v A-G* [1984] 1 WLR 418, especially the comments by Megarry V-C on *Mason v Farbrother* at 425, 343 [p. 712, above].

Secondly, it is not essential to obtain the consent of every adult beneficiary under section 57 as it is under the Variation of Trusts Act 1958. Thirdly, the court is not required to give consent on behalf of every category of beneficiary separately but, more realistically, would consider their interests collectively in income on the one hand and in capital on the other.

These points lead to a less costly application without, in my judgment, imperilling the legitimate interests of the beneficiaries. It is also claimed that section 57 applications are cheaper and more convenient because they are taken in chambers whereas applications under the Act of 1958 are taken in open court. This is not something which is dictated by the statutory provisions, but rests in the practice of the court. It seems that immediately following the passing of the Variation of Trusts Act 1958 all applications for variation of investment clauses, whether under that Act or under section 57 of the Trustee Act, were heard in open court to ensure uniformity of practice: see the reporter's note to *Re Rouse's Will Trusts* [1959] 1 WLR 372 at 375. In more recent times the court has reverted to the practice obtaining before the Act of 1958 so that applications under section 57 are mostly heard in chambers: see *Re Downshire's Settled Estates* [1953] Ch 218 at 248 for the earlier practice, and *British Museum Trustees v A-G* [1984] 1 WLR 418 at 420B and 421B for the current practice.

This application being linked with an alternative application under the Variation of Trusts Act 1958 was heard in open court. I consider that I have jurisdiction under section 57 to enlarge the investment clause.

Following the enactment of Part II of the Trustee Act 2000[21] trustees' powers of investment have generally been widened, even as regards trusts which were created before the Act came into force.[22] It follows that there will be little need to vary investment powers in a trust deed, although such variation will still be necessary where the statutory powers of investment have been limited by the deed. Where the statutory powers have been qualified in this way it is unclear when, if ever, the courts would consider it to be expedient to vary the powers of investment.

III TRUSTEE ACT 1925, SECTION 53[23]

TRUSTEE ACT 1925

53. Vesting orders in relation to infants' beneficial interests

Where an infant is beneficially entitled to any property the court may, with a view to the application of the capital or income thereof for the maintenance, education, or benefit of the infant, make an order—

(a) appointing a person to convey such property; or

(b) in the case of stock, or a thing in action, vesting in any person the right to transfer or call for a transfer of such stock, or to receive the dividends or income thereof, or to sue for and recover such thing in action, upon such terms as the court may think fit.

---

21 See p. 692, above.   22 Trustee Act (TA) 2000, s. 7.
23 See (1957) 21 Conv (NS) 448 (O.R. Marshall).

Pettit: *Equity and the Law of Trusts* (10th edn, 2006), p. 506

Under this section it was held in *Re Gower's Settlement*[24] that where there was an infant tenant in tail in remainder of Blackacre with divers remainders over, the court could effectually authorize a mortgage of Blackacre (subject to the interests having priority over the infant's tenancy in tail) framed so as to vest in the mortgagee a security which would be as effective a bar against the infant's issue taking under the entail and the subsequent remaindermen as if the infant were of full age and had executed the conveyance in accordance with the Fines and Recoveries Act 1833.

It was expressly assumed in *Re Gower's Settlement*[25] that the requirement of the section that the mortgage should be made 'with a view to the application of the capital or income thereof for the maintenance, education or benefit of the infant' was satisfied. It was held that there was no such 'application' in *Re Heyworth's Settlements*[26] where it was proposed to put an end to the trusts created by the settlement by selling the infant's contingent reversionary interest to the life tenant for an outright cash payment. This decision was distinguished in *Re Meux's Will Trusts*[27] where the proceeds of sale were to be settled. It was held that the sale and settlement of the proceeds of sale were to be regarded as a single transaction, which did constitute an 'application' for the purposes of the section.[28] And in *Re Bristol's Settled Estates*[29] a person was appointed to execute a disentailing assurance to bar the infant's entail with a view to a settlement being made with the assistance of the court under the Variation of Trusts Act 1958.

IV MENTAL CAPACITY ACT 2005, SCHEDULE 2

The Mental Capacity Act 2005 gives the court power to appoint deputies where a person lacks capacity to make decisions. By section 18 the deputy has powers to control and manage the property of the person who lacks capacity, and to make settlement of that person's property. Schedule 2 makes provision for the variation of such settlements.[30]

MENTAL CAPACITY ACT 2005

Schedule 2, paragraph 6

Variation of Settlements

(1) If a settlement has been made by virtue of section 18, the court may by order vary or revoke the settlement if—

   (a) the settlement makes provision for its variation or revocation,

---

[24] [1934] Ch 365; *Re Lansdowne's Will Trusts* [1967] Ch 603...   [25] Ibid.
[26] [1956] Ch 364...   [27] [1958] Ch 154...; *Re Lansdowne's Will Trusts*, note 24 above.
[28] Cf. *Re Ropner's Settlement Trusts*.... [1956] 1 WLR 902—a decision on similar words in s 32 of the Trustee Act 1925.   [29] ...[1965] 1 WLR 469.
[30] A settlement made by a settlor before being found to lack capacity to do so may be varied under Variation of Trusts Act 1958: *Re CL* [1969] 1 Ch 587.

(b) the court is satisfied that a material fact was not disclosed when the settlement was made, or

(c) the court is satisfied that there has been a substantial change of circumstances.

(2) Any such order may give such consequential directions the court thinks fit.

V VARIATION OF TRUSTS ACT 1958[31]

A SECTION 1

VARIATION OF TRUSTS ACT 1958

1. Jurisdiction of courts to vary trusts

(1) Where property, whether real or personal, is held on trusts arising, whether before or after the passing of this Act, under any will, settlement or other disposition, the court may if it thinks fit by order approve on behalf of—

(a) any person having, directly or indirectly, an interest, whether vested or contingent, under the trusts who by reason of infancy or other incapacity is incapable of assenting, or

(b) any person (whether ascertained or not) who may become entitled, directly or indirectly, to an interest under the trusts as being at a future date or on the happening of a future event a person of any specified description or a member of any specified class of persons, so however that this paragraph shall not include any person who would be of that description, or a member of that class, as the case may be, if the said date had fallen or the said event had happened at the date of the application to the court, or

(c) any person unborn, or

(d) any person in respect of any discretionary interest of his under protective trusts, where the interest of the principal beneficiary has not failed or determined,[32]

any arrangement (by whomsoever proposed, and whether or not there is any other person beneficially interested who is capable of assenting thereto) varying or revoking all or any of the trusts, or enlarging the powers of the trustees of managing or administering any of the property subject to the trusts:

---

[31] H&M, pp. 643–654; Lewin, pp. 1867–1903; P&M, pp. 747–760; P&S, pp. 467–478; Pettit, pp. 511–519; Snell, pp. 660–664; T&H, pp. 723–732; U&H, pp. 622–646; Harris, *Variation of Trusts* (1975) chap. 3ff. The Act was based on the recommendation of Law Reform Committee Sixth Report (*Court's Power to Sanction Variation of Trusts*) (1957) Cmnd. 310. See generally (1958) 22 Conv (NS) 373 (M.J. Mowbray); (1963) 27 Conv (NS) 6 (D.M. Evans); (1965) 43 *Canadian Bar Review* 181 (A.J. Maclean); (1969) 33 Conv (NS) 113, 183 (J.W. Harris).   [32] *Gibbon v Mitchell* [1990] 1 WLR 1304. For protective trusts see p. 60, above.

Provided that except by virtue of paragraph (d) of this subsection the court shall not approve an arrangement on behalf of any person unless the carrying out thereof would be for the benefit of that person.

(2) In the foregoing subsection 'protective trusts' means the trusts specified in paragraphs (i) and (ii) of subsection (1) of section thirty-three of the Trustee Act, 1925, or any like trusts, 'the principal beneficiary' has the same meaning as in the said subsection (1) and 'discretionary interest' means an interest arising under the trust specified in paragraph (ii) of the said subsection (1) or any like trust.

(3) The jurisdiction conferred by subsection (1) of this section shall be exercisable by the High Court, except that the question whether the carrying out of any arrangement would be for the benefit of a person falling within paragraph (a) of the said subsection (1) who lacks capacity (within the meaning of the Mental Capacity Act 2005) to give his assent is to be determined by the Court of Protection.[33]

(6) Nothing in this section shall be taken to limit the powers conferred by section sixty-four of the Settled Land Act 1925, section fifty-seven of the Trustee Act 1925,[34] or the powers of the Court of Protection.[35]

B PERSONS ON WHOSE BEHALF APPROVAL MAY BE GIVEN

(i) Approval Given

In **Re Suffert's Settlement** [1961] Ch 1, the income of a family trust fund was held on protective trusts for Miss Suffert, a spinster aged 61, and after her death, upon trusts, as to capital and income, in favour of her issue; and in default of such issue, and subject to a general testamentary power of appointment, in trust for those persons who would be her statutory next-of-kin if she died a spinster.

Miss Suffert sought a variation of the settlement under which a fund of £500 would be held on trusts in favour of persons interested in the original trust, and the remainder of the fund, amounting to some £8,300, should be held on trust for herself absolutely.

At the date of the application to the court, her nearest relatives were three adult first cousins. One of them was made a party and consented to the variation. The other two were not made parties. The court was asked to approve on behalf of those two, and on behalf of unborn and unascertained persons who might become interested. BUCKLEY J held that he could approve the variation on behalf of the unborn and unascertained persons; but not on behalf of the two cousins. They were within the exception contained in paragraph (b) of section 1(1) of the Act. The two cousins should themselves decide whether to consent or refuse.

---

[33] As amended by Mental Capacity Act 2005.   [34] See p. 827, above.
[35] As amended by Mental Capacity Act 2005.

In **Re Moncrieff's Settlement Trusts** [1962] 1 WLR 1344, approval was requested on behalf of the statutory next-of-kin of Mrs. Parkin. Her next-of-kin at the date of the application was an infant adopted son, the first respondent. If she survived him, her next-of-kin would be the four infant grandchildren of her maternal aunt. They were made respondents to the summons, as were the trustees.

Buckley J approved the arrangement. He could do so on behalf of the first respondent under para (a) of section 1(1) on the grounds of infancy, and in respect of the four infant grandchildren under paragraph (b). It was not necessary therefore that the infant grandchildren should be made parties. BUCKLEY J said at 1346:

Section 1(1)(b) of the Variation of Trusts Act, 1958, enables me to approve the arrangement on behalf of 'any person (whether ascertained or not) who may become entitled, directly or indirectly, to an interest under the trusts as being at a future date or on the happening of a future event a person of any specified description or a member of any specified class of persons ... ' The first respondent would fall within that description, but the section goes on: 'so however that this paragraph shall not include any person who would be of that description, or a member of that class, as the case may be, if the said date had fallen or the said event had happened at the date of the application to the court ... ' The first respondent is excluded, therefore, from the persons on whose behalf I can sanction the arrangement under section 1(1)(b), but none of the other persons who might become entitled to participate in the estate of the settlor were she to survive the first respondent and then die intestate is excluded because none of them would be within the class of next-of-kin if she died today. Therefore, I am in a position to approve the arrangement on behalf of all persons whether ascertained or not who might become interested in the settlor's estate at a future date with the exception of the first respondent.

At the time the summons was drafted, the effect of that was not appreciated and certain persons were joined who would, in certain events, be the persons who would be the settlor's next-of-kin. In my view, it was unnecessary for those persons to be joined. Their interests can be looked after by the trustees, and they are persons who may never fall within the class of beneficiaries because they may predecease the settlor or the first respondent may survive the settlor. The summons could have been framed with the settlor as applicant and the first respondent and the trustees as respondents. I am not criticising counsel for the way in which the summons was framed because at the time it was settled it was not realised that it was not necessary to join all possible future next-of-kin.

His Lordship then considered the scheme and approved it on behalf of the infant respondents and all other persons who might thereafter become entitled to an interest in the trust fund.

(ii) *Approval Refused*

In **Knocker v Youle** [1986] 1 WLR 934,[36] income from a share of a trust fund was held on trust for the settlor's daughter for life, with remainder to appointees under her will. In default of appointment there was a gift over to the settlor's son or, if he were dead, to the settlor's four married sisters living at the son's death, or, if they were then dead,

---

[36] (1986) 136 NLJ 1057 (P. Luxton); [1987] Conv 144 (J.G. Riddall).

to their issue who should attain 21. In 1984, the settlor's wife and four sisters having died, the settlor's son and daughter sought a variation of the trusts of the settlement, but none of the very numerous issue of the four sisters was made a party since it was not practicable to obtain their consent. In holding that the court had no jurisdiction to approve the variation on their behalf, WARNER J said at 937:

There are two difficulties. First, it is not strictly accurate to describe the cousins as persons 'who may become entitled...to an interest under the trusts'. There is no doubt of course that they are members of a 'specified class'. Each of them is, however, entitled now to an interest under the trusts, albeit a contingent one (in the case of those who are under 21, a doubly contingent one) and albeit also that it is an interest that is defeasible on the exercise of the general testamentary powers of appointment vested in Mrs. Youle and Mr. Knocker. Nonetheless, it is properly described in legal language as an interest, and it seems to me plain that in this Act the word 'interest' is used in its technical, legal sense. Otherwise, the words 'whether vested or contingent' in section 1(1)(a) would be out of place.

What counsel invited me to do was in effect to interpret the word 'interest' in section 1(1) loosely, as a layman might, so as not to include an interest that was remote. I was referred to two authorities: Re Moncrieff's Settlement Trusts (Practice Note) [1962] 1 WLR 1344 [p. 834, above], and the earlier case, Re Suffert's Settlement [1961] Ch 1 [p. 833, above]. In both those cases, however, the class in question was a class of prospective next-of-kin, and of course it is trite law that the prospective or presumptive next-of-kin of a living person do not have an interest. They have only a spes successionis, a hope of succeeding, and quite certainly they are the typical category of persons who fall within section 1(1)(b). Another familiar example of a person falling within that provision is a potential future spouse. It seems to me, however, that a person who has an actual interest directly conferred upon him or her by a settlement, albeit a remote interest, cannot properly be described as one who 'may become' entitled to an interest.

The second difficulty (if one could think of a way of overcoming the first) is that there are, as I indicated earlier, 17 cousins who, if the failure or determination of the earlier trusts declared by the settlement had occurred at the date of the application to the court, would have been members of the specified class, in that they were then living and over 21. Therefore, they are prima facie excluded from section 1(1)(b) by what has been conveniently called the proviso to it, that is to say the part beginning 'so however that this paragraph shall not include...' They are in the same boat, if I may express it in that way, as the first cousins in Re Suffert's Settlement and the adopted son in Re Moncrieff's Settlement Trusts (Practice Note). The court cannot approve the arrangement on their behalf; only they themselves can do so.

Mr. Argles suggested that I could distinguish Re Suffert's Settlement and Re Moncrieff's Settlement Trusts (Practice Note) in that respect for two reasons. First, he suggested, that the proviso applied only if there was a single event on the happening of which one could ascertain the class. Here, he said, both Mr. Knocker and Mrs. Youle must die without exercising their general testamentary powers of appointment to the full before any of the cousins could take anything. But it seems to me that what the proviso is referring to is the event on which the class becomes ascertainable, and that that is a single event. It is, in this case, the death of the survivor of Mrs. Youle and Mr. Knocker, neither of them having exercised the power to the full; in the words of clause 7 of the settlement, it is 'the failure or determination of the trusts herein-before declared concerning the trust fund'.

The second reason suggested by Mr. Argles why I should distinguish the earlier authorities was that the event hypothesised in the proviso was the death of the survivor of Mr. Knocker and Mrs. Youle on the date when the originating summonses were issued, that is to say on 6 January, 1984. There is evidence that on that day there were in existence wills of both of them exercising their testamentary powers to the full. The difficulty about that is that the proviso does not say 'so however that this paragraph shall not include any person who would have become entitled if the said event had happened at the date of the application to the court'. It says 'so however that this paragraph shall not include any person who would be of that description, or a member of that class, as the case may be, if the said date had fallen or the said event had happened at the date of the application to the court'. So the proviso is designed to identify the presumptive members of the class at the date of the application to the court and does not advert to the question whether at that date they would or would not have become entitled.

I was reminded by counsel of the principle that one must construe Acts of Parliament having regard to their purpose, and it was suggested that the purpose here was to exclude the need to join as parties to applications under the Variation of Trusts Act 1958 people whose interests were remote. In my view, however, that principle does not enable me to take the sort of liberty with the language of this statute that I was invited to take. It is noteworthy that remoteness does not seem to be the test if one thinks in terms of presumptive statutory next-of-kin. The healthy issue of an elderly widow who is on her death bed, and who has not made a will, have an expectation of succeeding to her estate; that could hardly be described as remote. Yet they are a category of persons on whose behalf the court could, subject of course to the proviso, approve an arrangement under this Act. On the other hand, people in the position of the cousins in this case have an interest that is extremely remote. Nonetheless, it is an interest, and the distinction between an expectation and an interest is one which I do not think that I am entitled to blur. So, with regret, having regard to the particular circumstances of this case, I have to say that I do not think that I have jurisdiction to approve these arrangements on behalf of the cousins.

In **Re Christie-Miller's Settlement Trusts** [1961] 1 WLR 462, the question was whether persons who were possible objects of a power of appointment should be made parties to an application. The appointor was a party, and counsel agreed that the order should recite that he released the power. WILBERFORCE J held that it was not necessary to join as parties the possible objects of the power. Their possibility of ever becoming interested had been extinguished by the release.

C   HOW A VARIATION TAKES EFFECT

(i) *The Effect of Approval of the Court*

Re Holt's Settlement[37]
[1969] 1 Ch 100 (Ch D, **Megarry J**)

In 1959 the settlor settled £15,000 on trust for his daughter Mrs. Wilson for life, and after her death on trust for such of her children as should attain the age of 21.

---

[37] (1968) 84 LQR 162 (P.V.B.).

The fund was invested in a private company, and it increased in value to some £320,000. Mrs. Wilson wished to surrender her life interest in one-half of the fund in favour of her children, and to vary the trusts in such a way that the children would become entitled at the age of 30; and that one-half of the income of each child's share should be accumulated until the child attained the age of 25, or until the earlier expiry of 21 years from the date of the court's order.

In the application to Megarry J for approval, various questions arose: (i) whether, on a variation after 1964, the periods of perpetuity permitted by the Perpetuities and Accumulations Act 1964 could be utilised; (ii) whether the application was properly a variation of existing trusts or whether it was a revocation and resettlement; (iii) whether a variation under the Variation of Trusts Act 1958 took effect upon the court's order alone or upon some other basis.

Held. The application was approved. It took effect by virtue of the order of the court, and the new periods of perpetuity could be included.

Megarry J: Two main questions have been debated before me. I propose to consider these now, and to deal separately with certain details of the proposed arrangement. These questions are: first, does an order under the Act of 1958 ipso facto vary the terms of the trust without the execution of the arrangement or any other document by or on behalf of any beneficiary, apart from those on whose behalf section 1(1) of the Act empowers the court to approve the arrangement? Secondly, if after the commencement of the Perpetuities and Accumulations Act 1964, a variation is made in trusts constituted before the commencement of that Act, can that variation take advantage of the changes in the rules against perpetuities and accumulations which that Act has made?

Under the first head, the basic issue is whether an order under the Act of 1958 by itself varies the terms of the trust. Put rather differently, the question is whether the Act does no more than empower the court to supply on behalf of the infants, unborn persons and others mentioned in section 1(1) that binding approval which they cannot give, leaving the other beneficiaries to provide their own approvals in some other document which will bind them. In the present case the arrangement was drafted on the assumption that the order of the court will ipso facto vary the terms of the trusts; for the 'operative date' is defined as being the date of the order approving this arrangement, and the perpetuity period and the accumulation period (which are made use of in the terms of the trusts) each commences on the operative date.

The only authority directly on the point which has been cited to me is the decision in *Re Hambleden's Will Trusts* [1960] 1 WLR 82. I do not think I need read the provisions of the trusts in that case. It was a summons under the Act of 1958, and the judgment of Wynn-Parry J as reported is very short. The report does, however, include certain interlocutory observations. Wynn-Parry J made it clear that his view was that the order of the court ipso facto varied the trusts. He had had cited to him the decision of Vaisey J in *Re Joseph's Will Trusts* [1959] 1 WLR 1019 where that learned judge had inserted words in the order of the court which authorised and directed the trustees to carry the arrangement into effect. Wynn-Parry J said:

> 'I do not agree with that decision. I take the view that I have no jurisdiction to make an order including words directing the trustees to carry the arrangement into effect, and those words should be deleted from the draft minutes. Nothing is required except the approval of the court to the arrangement. If that approval is given the trusts are ipso facto altered, and the trustees are bound thereafter to give effect to the arrangement.'

Later in the course of the argument he said [1960] 1 WLR 82 at 85: 'If I approve an arrangement, I alter the trusts. *Res ipsa loquitur.*' Again, a little later, he said: 'if I approve an arrangement, I vary the trusts'. His judgment I will recite in its entirety:

> 'Very well. I hold that the effect of my approval is effective for all purposes to vary the trusts.
> Thereafter, the trusts are the trusts as varied. I approve the minutes of order, with the slight
> alterations which have been referred to, and the arrangement in the schedule.'

If that were a decision of the Court of Appeal I could venerate and obey, even without fully
comprehending. But the decision is at first instance, and so is of persuasive and not binding
authority. It is my misfortune not to be persuaded by such assertions, even though fourfold,
when made without explanation....

Where the arrangement is put into effect there is a disposition of an equitable interest, so that
unless there is some document signed by the adult beneficiaries, or by some agent authorised by
them in writing, the requirements of section 53(1)(c)[38] [of the Law of Property Act 1925] are
not satisfied. This contention is supported by a reference to the decision by the House of Lords in
Grey v IRC [1960] AC 1 [p. 113, above], that an oral direction by a beneficiary to his trustees to
hold property on certain trusts is a disposition, and that 'disposition' must be given its ordinary
wide meaning. It is further said that as there is here a transaction under which a moiety of a life
interest will pass from Mrs. Wilson to her children, this is *a fortiori* a 'disposition'. I may add
that there is the minor point that the common form of order under the Act does not normally
recite that all the adults have consented to the transaction, though where the insertion of such
a recital is required by the parties, the registrars insert it.

Let me say at once that there would seem to be no great difficulty in averting the consequences of this argument for the future. The adults could either execute the arrangement or,
perhaps more conveniently, give written authority to their solicitors or counsel to execute it on
their behalf. The latter course would usually be the more convenient, because not infrequently
changes (often minor) have to be made to the arrangement put before the court. It is, however,
a fact that many thousands of orders must have been made in the past on the footing of *Re
Hambleden's Will Trusts* [1960] 1 WLR 82. If the argument is right, there is the very real
difficulty that those orders will, perhaps in most cases, perhaps only in some, have effected no
variation of the trusts. This is a consideration which is particularly awkward in that a question
of jurisdiction is involved; for if the court has no jurisdiction to make an order which itself varies
the trusts, and orders have been made on the footing that the orders do ipso facto vary the
trusts, then it seems at least arguable that such orders were made without jurisdiction. It has
also been pointed out that the Inland Revenue has for some while acted upon the decision, and
that orders of the court have been stamped on the footing that they ipso facto vary the terms of
the trusts. Yet again, it is plain that present practice is convenient. It avoids the burden which
usually, perhaps, would not be very great, but in individual cases might be substantial, of getting
the necessary signatures of the adults either to the document itself or to written authorities.
I bear all those considerations in mind; nevertheless, it seems to me that there is very considerable force in the argument that has been advanced. The decision in *Re Hambleden's Will
Trusts* provides authority to the contrary but no explanation of the grounds for the decision.
Accordingly, a substantial part of the argument in this case has been directed to the discovery of
some basis upon which the convenient practice of *Re Hambleden's Will Trusts* can be rested.

---

[38] See p. 112, above.

In attempting to summarise Mr. Godfrey's argument for the settlor, I am sure I shall fail to do it justice. As I understood it, he submitted that the decision in *Re Hambleden's Will Trusts* was quite wrong but that in effect this did not matter. All that the court has to do, he said, is to approve the arrangement (i.e., the proposal made), and there was no question of the court approving anything which in law amounted to a disposition. The arrangement was not a disposition but merely a bargain or proposal, which was not within the ambit of section 53(1)(c) of the Law of Property Act, 1925. The court, he urged, was not concerned to see that the adults consented and certainly not that they executed any disposition. There might thus be no disposition at all; but the persons specified by section 1(1) of the Act of 1958 would be bound by the order of the court approving the arrangement, and the other beneficiaries could not in practice go back on what their counsel had assented to, at any rate so far as it had been acted upon. The result would be that, although there would be no new equitable interests actually created under the arrangement, all the beneficiaries would by a species of estoppel be treated as if they had those interests. I hope that Mr. Godfrey will forgive me if I say that I find this argument somewhat unattractive.[39] In particular, I find it very hard to believe that Parliament intended the court to approve on behalf of infants arrangements which depended for their efficacy upon the uncertainties of estoppel. I bear in mind, too, the wide meaning which *Grey v IRC* [1960] AC 1 gave to the word 'disposition' in section 53(1)(c).

Mr. Brookes, for the trustees, boldly asserted that, when correctly read, the Act of 1958 indirectly did what *Re Hambleden's Will Trusts* said it did. He went back to the words of section 1(1), and emphasised that the power of the court was a power exercisable 'by order' and that that power was a power to approve an arrangement 'varying or revoking' all or any of the trusts. In emphasising those phrases, he said that the right way to read the section was to say that the power of the court was merely a power to make an order approving an arrangement which in fact varied or revoked the trusts, and not an arrangement which failed to do any such thing. When the adults by their counsel assented to the arrangement, and the court on behalf of the infants by order approved the arrangement, then there was an arrangement which varied or revoked the trusts. So the order of the court both conferred jurisdiction and exercised it. His escape from section 53(1)(c) had a similar dexterity about it: by conferring an express power on the court to do something by order, Parliament in the Act of 1958 had provided by necessary implication an exception from section 53(1)(c). He buttressed his contention by a reference to *Re Joseph's Will Trusts* [1959] 1 WLR 1019. Vaisey J there accepted that the order which he made, directing the trustees to carry the order of the court into effect, was neither contemplated by the Act nor expressly authorised by it. Rather than read into the Act words that are not there, said Mr. Brookes, one should construe the Act as authorising an order which is efficacious to achieve its avowed object. He pointed to the long title of the Act which reads: 'An Act to extend the jurisdiction of courts of law to vary trusts in the interests of beneficiaries and sanction dealings with trust property'.

I hope that Mr. Brookes, too, will pardon me if I say that I did not find his argument compelling. Indeed, at times I think it tended to circularity. But I find it tempting; and I yield. It is not a construction which I think the most natural. But it is not an impossible construction; it accords with the long title; it accords with the practice which has been relied upon for many years in some thousands of cases; and it accords with considerations of convenience. The point

---

[39] See *Spens v IRC* [1970] 1 WLR 1173 at 1183–1185.

is technical, and I do not think that I am doing more than straining a little at the wording in the interests of legislative efficacy.

However that is not all. Mr. Millett, for Mrs. Wilson, the tenant for life, provided another means of escape from section 53(1)(c) in his helpful reply. Where, as here, the arrangement consists of an agreement made for valuable consideration, and that agreement is specifically enforceable, then the beneficial interests pass to the respective purchasers on the making of the agreement. Those interests pass by virtue of the species of constructive trust made familiar by contracts for the sale of land, whereunder the vendor becomes a constructive trustee for the purchaser as soon as the contract is made, albeit the constructive trust has special features about it.[40] Section 53(2), he continued, provides that 'this section does not affect the creation or operation of resulting, implied or constructive trusts'. Accordingly, because the trust was constructive, section 53(1)(c) was excluded. He supported this contention by the House of Lords decision in *Oughtred v IRC* [1960] AC 206 [see p. 118, above]. He relied in particular upon passages in the speeches (at 227, 231) of Lord Radcliffe and Lord Cohen, albeit that they were dissenting on the main point for decision. He pointed out that although Lord Jenkins (with whom Lord Keith concurred) had not decided the point, he had assumed for the purposes of his speech that it was correct (at 239), and that the rejection of the contention by Lord Denning (at 233) was in a very brief passage. Mr. Millett accepts that if there were to be some subsequent deed of family arrangement which would carry out the bargain, then this deed might well be caught by section 53(1)(c); but that, he said, cannot affect the 'arrangement', and the parties might well be willing to let matters rest on that. It seems to me that there is considerable force in this argument in cases where the agreement is specifically enforceable, and in its essentials I accept it. At all events it supports the conclusion that in such cases the practice established by *Re Hambleden's Will Trusts* [1960] 1 WLR 82 is right. For this and the other reasons that I have given, though with some hesitation, I accordingly hold this to be the case.

Finally, before turning to the second main point, I should mention that in this case the arrangement carries out its purpose by revoking all the existing trusts and establishing a new set of trusts. That being so, it is said that some difficulty arises on the wording of section 1(1) of the Act of 1958. This merely empowers the court to approve an arrangement 'varying or revoking all or any of the trusts', and so, it is said, the court cannot approve an arrangement which, instead of merely 'revoking' or merely 'varying', proceeds to revoke and then to set up new trusts, thereby producing an effect equivalent to the process of settlement and resettlement. The section, it is argued, says nothing of establishing new trusts for old. As a matter of principle, however, I do not really think that there is anything in this point, at all events in this case. Here the new trusts are in many respects similar to the old. In my judgment, the old trusts may fairly be said to have been varied by the arrangement whether the variation is effected directly, by leaving some of the old words standing and altering others, or indirectly, by revoking all the old words and then setting up new trusts partly, though not wholly, in the likeness of the old. One must not confuse machinery with substance; and it is the substance that matters. Comparing the position before and after the arrangement takes effect, I am satisfied that the result is a variation of the old trusts, even though effected by the machinery of revocation and resettlement.

[His Lordship considered *Re T's Settlement Trusts* [1964] Ch 158, and continued:] A line may, perhaps, one day emerge from a sufficiently ample series of reported decisions; but for the

---

[40] See p. 307, above.

present all that is necessary for me to say is whether the particular case before me is on the right side or the wrong side of any reasonable line that could be drawn. In this case I am satisfied that the arrangement proposed falls on the side of the line which bears the device 'variation'.[41]

I can now turn to the second main point, namely, that under the Perpetuities and Accumulations Act 1964. The settlement in this case was made prior to the commencement of that Act, and any variation will be made after that commencement. Section 15(5) provides that 'the foregoing sections of this Act shall apply...' (and there is then an exception with which I am not concerned) '...only in relation to instruments taking effect after the commencement of this Act....' There follows a reference to instruments made in the exercise of a special power of appointment. The Act received the Royal Assent on 16 July, 1964, so that this is the date of its commencement.

The kind of question that arises is this. Suppose an instrument taking effect in 1959, as the original trusts did in this case, and a variation made under the Act of 1958 which merely alters a few words: will such a variation allow the Act of 1964 to apply to the trusts in their revised form? Again, suppose that, as here, there is a revocation of the old trusts and a declaration of new trusts, so that in form there is a new start, although in substance merely a variation: does this alter the position? Could something be done by the second method which cannot be done by a method which in form as well as in substance is a mere variation? Is it possible to have a variation under the Act of 1958 once every generation, and then with each variation start afresh with a relaxed perpetuity rule and a new accumulation period bounteously provided by the Act of 1964?

Mr. Millett boldly answered 'Yes' to this last question, and harked back to those spacious days when strict settlements of land were common, and once a generation there was a process of settlement and resettlement, with all the old entails securely barred and new entails established. He pointed out that on each resettlement the settlors in effect changed, and that often there would be a similar result on a variation under the Act of 1958. When the settlement was first made the original settlor was the settlor; but when the first variation came to be made, then if there was any alteration in the beneficial interests (as distinct from the mere conferring of additional administrative powers *quoad* those beneficial interests) the beneficiaries concerned would be the settlors, transferring their interests to be held on new trusts. Thus in effect there would be a new start each time. Mr. Millett drew my attention to the decision of Plowman J in *Re Lloyd's Settlement* [1967] 2 WLR 1078, where, he said, this in effect was done. In that case a settlement *inter vivos* was made on 21 March, 1958 (21 March, 1959, in the headnote and 31 March, 1958, in the statement of facts seem to be erroneous). The settlement directed an accumulation, and in the result the only appropriate accumulation period was that of the settlor's life. The effect was to expose the trust property to Estate Duty risks in respect of an interest which would pass on the settlor's death, and accordingly in 1966 a variation of the trusts was sought under the Act of 1958. By then the Act of 1964 had come into effect. Under the trusts as varied by the arrangement, accumulation was directed for a period of 21 years from the date of the settlement; and this period is one which was made available for the first time by the Act of 1964. Accordingly, under the Act of 1958 a settlement made prior to the Act of 1964 was varied after that Act in a way which took advantage of the provisions of that Act. The case is shortly reported, setting out the facts at some length, the cases cited in the argument, and the order made; but unfortunately there is no statement of the reasons of the learned judge. Nevertheless it seems to me that the variation in fact there made supports Mr. Millett's contention.

---

[41] Megarry J considered the point more fully in *Re Ball's Settlement Trusts* [1968] 1 WLR 899 [p. 843, below].

Mr. Millett also referred me to *Lewin on Trusts,* 16th edn (1964), at p. 741, where an argument which is in accord with Mr. Millett's submission is advanced by the learned editor (the passage cannot have been the work of the late Mr. Lewin). I would only observe that there appears on page 742 to have been a slip in the statement of *Pilkington v IRC* [1964] AC 612, for the reference in the text should, it seems, be to a power of advancement rather than to a power of appointment, and the citation of the case is also erroneous. For myself, I find any analogy with powers of appointment and powers of advancement unsatisfactory. The mischief attacked by the rule against perpetuities in the case of powers of appointment, and now, since *Pilkington v IRC,* in the case of powers of advancement as well, is that the property is tied up *ab initio.* The power is conferred by the settlement, and that person exercising the power can do so only within pre-ordained limits. The power indeed 'belongs' to the old settlement, if I may respectfully adopt the language of Lord Radcliffe in the *Pilkington* case at 642. Under the Act of 1958, there are no such limits. The property, as it seems to me, is freely disposable. Under an arrangement approved by the court the trusts may be brought wholly to an end. On the other hand, they may be varied; and there is no limit, other than the discretion of the court and the agreement of the parties, to the variation which may be made. Any variation owes its authority not to anything in the initial settlement but to the statute and the consent of the adults coming, as it were, *ab extra.* This certainly seems to be so in any case not within the Act where a variation or resettlement is made under the doctrine of *Saunders v Vautier* (1841) 4 Beav 115 [p. 191, above], by all the adults joining together; and I cannot see any real difference in principle in a case where the court exercises its jurisdiction on behalf of the infants under the Act of 1958. It seems to me that the arrangement, coupled with the order of the court, constitute an 'instrument', or, since the singular includes the plural, 'instruments', which take effect after 15 July, 1964. Whether the documents are regarded as separate instruments or as together constituting one composite instrument, the effect is produced by the complex of documents; and what takes effect after 15 July, 1964, is the result of this complex of documents. In my judgment, therefore, it is permissible to insert provisions deriving their validity from the Act of 1964 into an arrangement approved under the Act of 1958.

That, I think, suffices to dispose of the two substantial points...

I can deal with the merits of this application quite shortly.

His Lordship approved the arrangement as being for the benefit of each of the beneficiaries categorised by section 1(1) of the Act.

In **Inland Revenue Commissioners v Holmden** [1968] AC 685, LORD REID said at 701:

Each beneficiary is bound because he has consented to the variation. If he was not of full age when the arrangement was made he is bound because the court was authorised by the Act to approve it on his behalf and did so by making an order... So the arrangement must be regarded as an arrangement made by the beneficiaries themselves. The court merely acted on behalf of or as representing those beneficiaries who were not in a position to give their own consent and approval.

And LORD HODSON at 705:

In my opinion, the effect of the arrangement varying the settlement was, as Harman LJ pointed out, to rewrite the settlement from the date of the order in the terms proposed and approved by the court.

(ii) Variation or Resettlement

In **Re Ball's Settlement Trusts**[42] [1968] 1 WLR 899, MEGARRY J, approving an arrangement 'revoking the trusts of the...settlement and resettling the subject matter of the...settlement', said at 903:

What section 1(1) of the Act authorises the court to approve is 'any arrangement...varying or revoking all or any of the trusts, or enlarging the powers of the trustees of managing or administering any of the property subject to the trusts'. The word 'resettling' or its equivalent nowhere appears. Accordingly, while there is plainly jurisdiction to approve the arrangement in so far as it revokes the trusts, in my view there is equally plainly no jurisdiction to approve the arrangement as regards 'resettling' the property, at any rate *eo nomine*. In this connection, I bear in mind the words of Wilberforce J in *Re T's Settlement Trusts* [1964] Ch 158. He there said at 162:

'I have no desire to cut down the very useful jurisdiction which this Act has conferred upon the court. But I am satisfied that the proposal as originally made to me falls outside it. Though presented as "a variation" it is in truth a complete new resettlement. The former trust funds were to be got in from the former trustees and held upon wholly new trusts such as might be made by an absolute owner of the funds. I do not think that the court can approve this.'

It seems to me that the originating summons correctly describes what is sought to be done in this case, and as so described there is clearly no jurisdiction for the court to approve the arrangement. But it does not follow that merely because an arrangement can correctly be described as effecting a revocation and resettlement, it cannot also be correctly described as effecting a variation of the trusts. The question then is whether the arrangement in this case can be so described. In the course of argument I indicated that it seemed desirable for the summons to be amended by substituting the words 'varying' for the word 'revoking' and deleting the reference to 'resettling', and that I would give leave for this amendment to be made. On the summons as so amended the question is thus whether the arrangement can fairly be said to be covered by the word 'varying' so that the court has power to approve it.

There was some discussion of the ambit of this word in *Re Holt's Settlement* [1969] 1 Ch 100 [p. 836, above]. It was there held that if in substance the new trusts were recognisable as the former trusts, though with variations, the change was comprehended within the word 'varying', even if it had been achieved by a process of revocation and new declaration. In that case, the new trusts were plainly recognisable as the old trusts with variations. In the present case, the new trusts are very different from the old. The settlor's life interest vanishes; so does the power of appointment, though that will now be released. In place of the provision in default of appointment for absolute interests for the two sons if they survive the settlor, and if not, for their issue stirpitally,[43] there is now a life interest for each son, and vested absolute interests for the children of the sons born before 1 October, 1977. There is a clean sweep of the somewhat exiguous administrative provisions and an equally exiguous new set in their place. The arrangement also makes altogether new provisions for insurance policies, both those which provide for death duties and are to be added to the trust fund and those which provide for the excluded persons and are to be held on separate trusts; but these portions of the arrangement, I should say, are not made part of the settlement as revised, but are to operate independently

---

[42] (1968) 84 LQR 459 (P.V.B.); *Allen v Distillers Co (Biochemical) Ltd* [1974] QB 384; [1974] *Annual Survey of Commonwealth Law* 524 (J. Hackney).   [43] Meaning a line of descendants from an ancestor.

and outside its terms. All that remains of the old trusts are what I may call the general drift or purport, namely, that a moiety of the trust fund is to be held on certain trusts for each son and certain of his issue. Is the word 'varying' wide enough to embrace so categorical a change?

[His Lordship referred to *Re Dyer* [1935] VLR 273, and continued:] If an arrangement changes the whole substratum of the trust, then it may well be that it cannot be regarded merely as varying that trust. But if an arrangement, while leaving the substratum, effectuates the purpose of the original trust by other means, it may still be possible to regard that arrangement as merely varying the original trusts, even though the means employed are wholly different and even though the form is completely changed.

I am, of course, well aware that this view carries me a good deal farther than I went in *Re Holt's Settlement* [1969] 1 Ch 100. I have felt some hesitation in the matter, but on the whole I consider that this is a proper step to take. The jurisdiction of the Act is beneficial and, in my judgment, the court should construe it widely and not be astute to confine its beneficent operation. I must remember that in essence the court is merely contributing on behalf of infants and unborn and unascertained persons the binding assents to the arrangement which they, unlike an adult beneficiary, cannot give. So far as is proper, the power of the court to give that assent should be assimilated to the wide powers which the ascertained adults have.

In this case, it seems to me that the substratum of the original trusts remains. True, the settlor's life interest disappears; but the remaining trusts are still in essence trusts of half of the fund for each of the two named sons and their families, with defined interests for the sons and their children in place of the former provisions for a power of appointment among the sons and their children and grandchildren and for the sons to take absolutely in default of appointment. In the events which are likely to occur, the differences between the old provision and the new may, I think, fairly be said to lie in detail rather than in substance. Accordingly, in my judgment, the arrangement here proposed, with the various revisions to it made in the course of argument, can properly be described as varying the trusts of the settlement. Subject to the summons being duly amended, I therefore approve the revised arrangement.

D   FRAUD ON A POWER

Parker and Mellows: *Modern Law of Trusts* (8th edn, 2003) pp. 754–755

Obviously a variation which is fraudulent or contrary to public policy will not be sanctioned.

Fraud has only arisen in connection with the doctrine of fraud on a power. In *Re Robertson's Will Trusts*,[44] the applicant had exercised a special power of appointment in favour of his children as a preliminary to the proposed arrangement. His purpose and intention in making the appointment was to benefit his children and not himself. Later he was advised that his financial position would in fact be improved if the appointment were made and the scheme approved. But Russell J held that to suppose his original purpose and intention had been changed or added to was unjustified. It followed that there was no fraud on the power, though, if there had been, the court would not have been able to approve the scheme.

However, subsequent case law appears to indicate a certain conflict as to the precise principles to be applied. In *Re Wallace's Settlement*[45] Megarry J said that the fact that protected life tenants had executed appointments in favour of their children in itself raised a case for

---

[44] [1960] 1 WLR 1050.   [45] [1968] 1 WLR 711.

inquiry because the life tenants benefited by the arrangement; however, on the evidence he was satisfied that there was no fraud on the power because the benefit to the life tenants was not substantial and they had intended to make the appointment before the arrangement was approved. On the other hand, in Re Brook's Settlement[46] Stamp J adopted a rather different approach. He held that the exercise of a special power of appointment amounted to a fraud on the power and he was unable to approve the variation. Here one of the purposes of the appointment (by a protected life tenant in favour of his children from which he would also benefit from a division of the capital) was to enable the life tenant to obtain what he could not otherwise get, namely capital rather than income. This was enough to invalidate the appointment. The important feature of Re Brook's Settlement is that the judge emphasised that the question is whether the purpose of the appointment amounted to a fraud, not, as was apparently suggested in Re Wallace's Settlement, the effect of the appointment on the financial position of the appointor. It is thought that Re Brook's Settlement applies the correct principle.

The difficulties that may thus arise as a result of a fraud on the power, however inadvertent, may in some circumstances be avoided by releasing the power. No question of a fraud on a power normally arises on a mere release. It has been held that, provided that the power in question can be released,[47] the court will approve an arrangement varying a settlement even though the objects of the power are ignored.[48] There appears to be some doubt as to whether the release should be effected by deed, or whether it can be inferred from the facts. The latter would seem to be sufficient.[49]

Even if the power cannot be released (if, for example, it was given to the donee as trustee) it still seems possible to apply to the court for an arrangement extinguishing the power because this amounts to varying or revoking a trust within section 1 of the Act. But because the power is not of itself capable of release the court is likely to impose conditions on the release. Thus in Re Drewe's Settlement,[50] Stamp J in approving an arrangement insisted that such a power could only be effected by deed and with the consent of the trustees.

E   PRINCIPLES APPLICABLE TO THE EXERCISE
OF THE DISCRETION

(i)   Observing the Settlor's Intention

Re Steed's Will Trusts[51]
[1960] Ch 407 (CA, Lord Evershed MR, Willmer and Upjohn LJJ)

The testator gave property which included Loft Farm to trustees 'upon protective trusts as defined by section 33 of the Trustee Act, 1925' for his housekeeper Miss Sandford for

---

46   [1968] 1 WLR 1661.

47   See Re Wills' Trust Deeds [1964] Ch 219; and see (1968) 84 LQR 64 (A.J. Hawkins).

48   Re Christie-Miller's Settlement [1961] 1 WLR 462; Re Courtauld's Settlement [1965] 1 WLR 1385; Re Ball's Settlement [1968] 1 WLR 899.

49   In Re Ball Megarry J insisted on a formal release, but in Re Christie-Miller and Re Courtauld an inferred release was regarded as sufficient.   50   [1966] 1 WLR 1518.

51   See also Re Michelham's Will Trusts [1964] Ch 550; Re Remnant's Settlement Trusts [1970] Ch 560 at 567 [p. 855, below].

her life, and after her death for such persons as she might by deed or will appoint; and in default of appointment upon trust for her next-of-kin.

The will declared (clause 9) that it was the testator's 'wish that she shall have the use and enjoyment of the capital value thereof if she needs it during her life. And . . . that if and when such property shall be sold my trustees may apply capital moneys from such sale to or for her benefit . . . provided that they shall consider the necessity for retaining sufficient capital to prevent her from being without adequate means at any time during her life . . .'

Miss Sandford exercised the power of appointment in her own favour.

The farm was let to her brother. There was some doubt whether he paid any rent, or was able to do so. The trustees decided that the farm should be sold, and they received a good offer. Miss Sandford asked the court to restrain the sale, and brought a summons under the Variation of Trusts Act 1958, asking the court to approve an arrangement under which the trustee should hold the property on trust for herself absolutely.

Held. The court refused its approval.

Lord Evershed MR: This is in more ways than one, including matters of procedure, a somewhat unusual case, as Mr. Newsom observed. It is also in many respects an unhappy case, and I cannot refrain from expressing my own sympathy for the plaintiff on the one side, and for the three defendant trustees on the other.

I propose in this judgment to forbear from entering, except where absolutely necessary, into matters of fact which might only serve to rub salt into existing wounds. Suffice it to say that the plaintiff was one who served loyally and most skilfully for a long period of time the testator and the testator's wife. In consideration for those services the testator included in his will provisions for her benefit . . .

It is, I think, quite plain on the evidence that the testator, while anxious to show his gratitude to the plaintiff, was no less anxious she should be well provided-for and not exposed to the temptation, which he thought was real, of being, to use a common phrase, sponged upon by one of her brothers. I fully realise that the plaintiff's natural affection for that brother is not a matter which one can in any sense condemn. Blood is, after all, thicker than water, and the happiness of the plaintiff, according to her own view at any rate, is very much linked up with the association with that brother and the brother's daughter and wife.

[His Lordship decided that the court ought not to interfere with the exercise by the trustees of their discretion; and continued]: I now come to what has caused me greater difficulty, namely, the effect of the Variation of Trusts Act 1958 . . .

In the present case, the proposed variation (that is, the 'arrangement') which the plaintiff puts forward may be most briefly and accurately stated as involving this: in clause 9 of the will the words: 'upon protective trusts as defined by section 33 of the Trustee Act 1925', should be omitted, and similarly in the next clause the words 'protective' should be omitted. If those words were omitted, the result would be that the plaintiff would become absolutely entitled to the property, because she would then be the life tenant, having appointed by irrevocable deed to herself the reversion; and that is what she seeks.

The trustees have taken the view that it is not an arrangement which, having regard to their conception of their duties and the wishes of their testator, they should approve. For my part, I do not think that approval on behalf of the trustees is the court's function in this case, though the court in exercising its general discretion will certainly pay regard to what the trustees say and the grounds for their saying it. Nor can I see, if this was the judge's view, that the court is called upon by the language of this section to approve the arrangement or proposal on behalf of the proposer; that is to say, whether they think she was wise or unwise to put her idea forward.

The duty of the court, as I read the section on the facts of this case, is that they must approve it on behalf of the only person or persons who might have an interest under the discretionary trusts and whose presence under the trusts now prevents the plaintiff saying that she can put an end to the settlement.

Having regard to the plaintiff's age, no doubt it is true to say that she will not and cannot now have children, but she might marry, and marry more than once. She says, with some reason, that having lived for 53 years unmarried she does not feel in the least likely to marry now. That may well be right, though many have said that before and subsequent events have proved them wrong. That, however, is neither here nor there. There does exist a discretionary trust, and a future husband of the plaintiff's is a person interested under those trusts, on whose behalf the court must now approve the proposal.

Having regard to what has happened between the plaintiff and her brother, it is possible that, strictly speaking, there has been a forfeiture, and if so, the future husband or husbands would be within paragraph (b) of the subsection, but if not, he would be within paragraph (d). Again, I think that does not, for present purposes, matter.

I repeat that the duty of the court is now to consider whether in the exercise of its discretion, which is framed in the widest possible language, it should approve the arrangement on behalf of what has been described in argument as the spectral spouse of the plaintiff. In doing that, what must the court consider? Not, I conceive, merely the material benefit or detriment of such spouse. Certainly not if he is to be regarded as being a person, under paragraph (d), though if he is to be regarded as falling under paragraph (b) it is expressly enjoined that the court shall not approve the arrangement unless it is for his benefit.

As I have said, I do not so read this Act as to mean that the court's duty in the exercise of this very wide and, indeed, revolutionary discretion is confined to saying: 'would it really much harm this spectral spouse if we approve the proposal?' Bearing in mind, of course, the admitted possibility that the spouse might cease to be spectral and become a reality, I think what the court is bound to do is to see whether, looked at on behalf of the person indicated, it approves the arrangement. It is the arrangement which has to be approved, not just the limited interest of the person on whose behalf the court's duty is to consider it.

If that is right, it then follows that the court must regard the proposal as a whole, and so regarding it, then ask itself whether in the exercise of its jurisdiction it should approve that proposal on behalf of the person who cannot give a consent, because he is not in a position to do so. If that is a right premise, then it follows that the court is bound to look at the scheme as a whole, and when it does so, to consider, as surely it must, what really was the intention of the benefactor. That such is a proper approach is at least supported by the provisions of RSC Ord. 55, r.14A (3A),[52] which provides that in the case of an application under this Act, where there is a living settlor the living settlor is to be a party before the court. That rule seems to me to reinforce what I conceive to underlie this provision, namely, that the court must, albeit that it is performing its duty on behalf of some person who cannot consent on his or her own part, regard the proposal in the light of the purpose of the trust as shown by the evidence of the will or settlement itself, and of any other relevant evidence available.

[52] Now Ord. 93, r. 6 (2) (CPR 1998, Sch. 1).

Having so formulated the duty, I have, for my part, come to the conclusion that it would not be right for the court in the exercise of its discretion to approve this variation or arrangement. I am not uninfluenced in coming to that conclusion by any means by the circumstance that the judge obviously did not think it was a proposal which should be approved, though it is quite true that for reasons which I have indicated it may be said he was looking at it and basing his jurisdiction upon an interpretation of the section which I have not been altogether able to share, namely, it was his duty to approve it on behalf of the proposer, the plaintiff, and also that the scheme must be regarded as intended to be in some sense *inter partes* and, therefore, that he had to approve it on behalf of the trustees.

Disagreeing, if that is a fair view of his judgment, with that premise, nevertheless it is quite clear, I think, that the judge was by no means unsympathetic to the feelings and views of the plaintiff, but, on the other hand, was no less clear in his mind that the arrangement was one which so cut at the root of the testator's wishes and intentions that it was not one which the court should approve.

After all, if the court is asked to approve this proposal on behalf of a spectral spouse (if I may revert to that phrase), it must ask, I take it, why is the spectral spouse there at all under the trust? If one asks that question, nearly everything else, as it seems to me, follows. There is no doubt why the spectral spouse is there. It was part of the testator's scheme, made as I think manifest by the language which I have read from the clauses in the will, that it was the intention and the desire of the testator that this trust should be available for the plaintiff so that she would have proper provision made for her throughout her life, and would not be exposed to the risk that she might, if she had been handed the money, part with it in favour of another individual about whom the testator felt apprehension, which apprehension is plainly shared by the trustees.

For those reasons, therefore, I also conclude adversely to the plaintiff that we should not exercise jurisdiction under the Act of 1958 to approve the arrangement which has been put forward, and which I have tried to define. That is the end of the case. I only repeat the sympathy I have felt in a distressing matter of this kind, both with the plaintiff and with the trustees, whose difficulties in discharging their duty are obvious. I should like to express the hope that perhaps time, the healer, will do much to put an end to these troubles.

Goulding v James
[1997] 2 All ER 239 (CA, **Butler-Sloss, Mummery LJJ** and **Sir Ralph Gibson**)[53]

Mrs. Froud made a will which provided for the creation of a trust under which her daughter, Mrs. Goulding, had a life interest subject to which her grandson, Marcus Goulding, would take absolutely if he attained the age of 40. There was evidence that the testatrix structured the settlement in this way because she did not want her daughter to have access to the capital since she did not trust her daughter's husband and she considered her grandson to be a 'free spirit'. The daughter and her son wished to vary the trust under the Variation of Trusts Act 1958, section 1(1)(c) so that each would have 45 per cent of the residuary estate absolutely, with the remaining 10 per cent of the estate being held on the trusts of a grandchildren's trust fund. The beneficiaries wished

---

[53]   (1997) 60 MLR 719 (P. Luxton).

the trust to be varied in this way since it would benefit the unborn great-grandchildren of the testatrix.

The trial judge refused to vary the trust since this would be contrary to the intention of the testatrix.

Held (reversing the trial judge). Trust varied.

Mummery LJ [after referring to passages from judgments of Megarry J in *Re Holt's Settlement* [1969] 1 Ch 100 at 120; *Re Ball's Settlement* [1968] 1 WLR 899–905 and *Spens v IRC* [1970] 1 WLR 1173 at 1184]: The effect of Megarry J's observations in those decisions is this. First, what varies the trust is not the court, but the agreement or consensus of the beneficiaries. Secondly, there is no real difference in principle in the rearrangement of the trusts between the case where the court is exercising its jurisdiction on behalf of the specified class under the 1958 Act and the case where the resettlement is made by virtue of the doctrine in *Saunders v Vautier* (1841) 4 Beav 115, and by all the adult beneficiaries joining together. Thirdly, the court is merely contributing on behalf of infants and unborn and unascertained persons the binding assents to the arrangement which they, unlike an adult beneficiary, cannot give. The 1958 Act has thus been viewed by the courts as a statutory extension of the consent principle embodied in the rule in *Saunders v Vautier.* The principle recognises the rights of beneficiaries, who are *sui juris* and together absolutely entitled to the trust property, to exercise their proprietary rights to overbear and defeat the intention of a testator or settlor to subject property to the continuing trusts, powers and limitations of a will or trust instrument.

The role of the court is not to stand in as, or for, a settlor in varying the trusts. As Mr. Green emphasised, the court acts 'on behalf of' the specified class and, in appropriate cases, supplies consent for persons incapable of consenting. The court does not, in Mr. Green's submission, simply approve an arrangement; it approves an arrangement 'on behalf of' a specified class. Mr. Green accepted that, in so acting, the court has a discretion. The court *may,* if it thinks fit, by order, approve on behalf of the specified beneficiaries. He pointed, however, to the proviso in section 1(1) of the 1958 Act, which highlights 'benefit' as a mandatory factor in the exercise of discretion. Except in para (d) cases, the court is directed not to approve an arrangement on behalf of any person, unless the carrying out thereof would be for the benefit of that person. Although Mr. Green accepted that in some cases, such as *Re Steed's Will Trusts,* the intentions, wishes and motives of the settlor or testator may be relevant and weighty, in this case he contended that they are not relevant, because they do not relate to the class of persons for whom the court approves the arrangement. Alternatively, if they are relevant, it is not a proper exercise of the discretion in this case to allow extrinsic evidence of Mrs. Froud's wishes to outweigh the undoubted benefit to be conferred on her great-grandchildren, on whose behalf the court is empowered to act.

[His Lordship then referred to the submissions of the trustees and continued:] In my judgment, the legal position is as follows.

(1) The court has a discretion whether or not to approve a proposed arrangement.

(2) That discretion is fettered by only one express restriction. The proviso to section 1 prohibits the court from approving an arrangement which is not for the benefit of the classes referred to in (a), (b) or (c). The approval of this arrangement is not prevented by that proviso, since it is plainly the case that it is greatly for the benefit of the class specified in section 1(1)(c).

(3) It does not follow from the fact of benefit to unborns that the arrangement must be approved. In *Re Van Gruisen's Will Trusts* [1964] 1 WLR 449 at 450, Ungoed-Thomas J said:

'It is shown that actuarially the provisions for the infants and unborn persons are more beneficial for them under the arrangement than under the present trusts of the will. That, however, does not conclude the case. The court is not merely concerned with this actuarial calculation, even assuming that it satisfies the statutory requirement that the arrangement must be for the benefit of the infants and unborn persons. The court is also concerned whether the arrangement as a whole, in all the circumstances, is such that it is proper to approve it. The court's concern involves, *inter alia*, a practical and business-like consideration of the arrangement, including the total amounts of the advantages which the various parties obtain, and their bargaining strength.'

(4) That overall discretion described by Ungoed-Thomas J is to be exercised with regard to all relevant factors properly considered in the statutory context. The context is that the court is empowered to approve an arrangement 'on behalf of' the members of a specified class. As Lord Denning MR said in *Re Weston's Settlements* [1969] 1 Ch 223 at 245, 'in exercising its discretion, the function of the court is to protect those who cannot protect themselves'. In relation to the members of the specified class who cannot act for themselves, the court is almost in the position of a 'statutory attorney', a striking expression used by Mr. E. I. Goulding QC in his illuminating submissions to the Court of Appeal in *Re Weston's Settlements* [1969] 1 Ch 223 at 236. The court is not in the position of a statutory attorney for the settlor or for the adult beneficiaries and the court is not, as was made clear in *Re Holmden's Settlement,* in the position of a statutory settlor.

(5) Viewed in that context, an important factor in this case is that Mrs. June Goulding and Mr. Marcus Goulding are *sui juris* and Mrs. Froud's intentions and wishes related to their beneficial interests under the testamentary trusts rather than to the contingent interests of her unborn great-grandchildren whom the court is concerned to protect. Mr. Halpern did not dispute that Mrs. June Goulding and Mr. Marcus Goulding are legally entitled to do what they want with their beneficial interests in the residuary estate. Mrs. June Goulding, for example, is entitled, contrary to the firmest of intentions expressed by her late mother, to assign her life interest to her husband or to dispose of it for a capital sum and give that capital sum to her husband. Mrs. Froud's contrary non-testamentary wishes could not inhibit Mrs. June Goulding's proprietary rights, as a person beneficially entitled to the life interest in residue.

(6) In these circumstances the critical question is what relevance, if any, can Mrs. Froud's intentions and wishes with regard to the interests in residue taken under the will by her daughter and grandson and with regard to the exclusion of her son-in-law from direct or indirect benefit, have to the exercise of the court's jurisdiction on behalf of unborn great-grandchildren of Mrs. Froud? On this crucial question the judge was impressed by Mr. Halpern's submission that Mrs. Froud's intentions and wishes are important and should be taken into account on the authority of the Court of Appeal decision in *Re Steed's Will Trusts*. I do not accept Mr. Halpern's submission that the Court of Appeal in that case laid down any rule, principle or guideline of general application on the importance of the intentions and wishes of a settlor or testator to applications to approve arrangements under the 1958 Act.

(7) A close examination of the facts and reasoning in *Re Steed's Will Trusts* reveals two significant special features of that case.

(a) The applicant in that case, unlike Mrs. June Goulding, had only a protected life interest held on the protective trusts in section 33 of the Trustee Act 1925. After exercising a power of appointment the protected life tenant applied to the court to lift the protective trusts, so that she would become absolutely entitled to a farm and legacy settled on those trusts. The applicant in that case did not have the same beneficial rights as Mrs. June Goulding has in relation to her life interest.

(b) Very different considerations affected the court's discretion in *Re Steed's Will Trusts*. The court was asked to approve the arrangement proposed by the protected life tenant on behalf of the person or persons specified in section 1(1)(d) of the 1958 Act, that is 'any person in respect of any discretionary interest of his under protective trusts where the interest of the principal beneficiary has not failed or determined'. The proviso as regards benefit does not apply to that paragraph, so that the court may approve an arrangement, the carrying-out of which would not be for the benefit of that person. The court may consider whether or not there is benefit as a discretionary factor, but lack of benefit for such a person is no barrier to the approval of the court. The relevant paragraph (d) person in *Re Steed's Will Trusts*, where the applicant was unmarried and past the age of child-bearing, was the applicant's 'spectral husband', as he was described. In deciding whether or not to approve on his behalf, the court was not in the position (which exists here) of having to balance mandatory benefit to a specified paragraph (c) class against other discretionary factors, such as the intentions and wishes of the testator.

The central fact in *Re Steed's Will Trusts* was that the testator had manifested in the terms of his will a particular purpose in creating a protective trust; that was to protect the life tenant from improvident dealings with property in favour of certain members of her family. The Court of Appeal was satisfied that the testator's purpose, evidenced in the will, was still justified at the time of the application to vary. That was a view also shared by the trustees, who opposed the application by the protected life tenant. In those circumstances there was an overwhelming reason for the continuation of the protective trusts and in the continuance of the interest of the paragraph (d) class of person. That explained and justified the court's refusal of approval. The court in that case was not engaged in the exercise demanded in this case of deciding whether a mandatory benefit, bargained on behalf of a specified class, is outweighed by some other countervailing discretionary factor, such as the purpose of the trust or the intention of the testatrix in making it. [His Lordship referred to a dictum of Lord Evershed MR in *Re Steed's Will Trusts* [1960] Ch 407, at 422 [p. 848, above], and continued:]

(8) The fact that the rules of court require a living settlor to be joined as a party to proceedings under the 1958 Act does not mean that the court attaches any overbearing or special significance to the wishes of a settlor. Mr. Halpern accepted that the nature of the jurisdiction under the 1958 Act is such that even the most carefully planned and meticulously drafted intentions of a settlor or testator are liable to be overridden by an arrangement agreed between *sui juris* beneficiaries and by the sanction of the court under the 1958 Act. Mr. Halpern also accepted that even the most determined settlor or testator cannot exclude the jurisdiction of the court under the 1958 Act. The court has a discretion to approve an arrangement under the Act, even though the settlement or will may make it crystal clear that the settlor or testator does not want any departure from any of the strict terms of the trust....

To sum up. The flaw in the judge's refusal to approve the arrangement is that, in reliance on the supposed scope of the decision in *Re Steed's Will Trusts*, he allowed extrinsic evidence of the subjective wishes of Mrs. Froud as regards her daughter, son-in-law and grandson to outweigh considerations of objective and substantial benefit to the class on whose behalf the court is empowered to act. If the judge had adopted the correct approach to the exercise of his discretion, he could only have come to the conclusion that the intentions and wishes of Mrs. Froud, expressed externally to her will in relation to the adult beneficiaries and an adult non-beneficiary, had little, if any, relevance or weight to the issue of approval on behalf of the future unborn great-grandchildren, whose interest in residue was multiplied five-fold under the proposed arrangement.

For all these reasons, I would allow this appeal. I would also approve the proposed arrangement set out in the draft minute of order.

(1997) 60 MLR 719, 725 (P. Luxton)

Although several earlier cases have, in discussing the Variation of Trusts Act 1958, drawn an analogy with the doctrine of *Saunders v Vautier,* they have all done so in the context of an analysis either of jurisdiction, or of the effect of a variation (so that an arrangement under the Act is treated as substituting new trusts for old). It does not follow from such cases that the analogy should be pressed into service to restrict the manner in which the court may exercise the discretion which the statute confers upon it. This is, however, precisely what the Court of Appeal has done in *Goulding v James.* It did not, however, draw such analogy to its logical conclusion, which would have resulted in the court, in the exercise of its overall discretion, having to exclude any consideration of the settlor's intentions, even if they related to the person on whose behalf the court was asked to give its consent. As it was bound by its earlier decision in *Re Steed,* the Court of Appeal chose to steer a middle course; but it has in so doing sought to lay down rules in an area which is essentially one of discretion. The essence of its reasoning can, perhaps, be expressed in the words of Laddie J[54] at first instance, summing up the applicants' argument that he went on to reject: namely, 'that the intentions of the settlor should always be taken into account and then always dismissed as being insufficiently weighty'. Earlier cases have indicated that the discretion is a wide one, and judges have previously avoided laying down rules of law respecting its exercise, no doubt because they felt that such rules would undesirably fetter the judicial discretion in ways not laid down in the Act itself. It is to be hoped that *Goulding v James* does not represent the beginning of a trend in the opposite direction.

(ii) *Benefit: Fiscal, Social and Moral*

Re Weston's Settlements[55]
[1969] 1 Ch 223 (CA, Lord Denning MR, Harman and Danckwerts LJJ)

In 1964 Mr. Weston made two settlements, one in consideration of the marriage of his elder son, who was born in 1942, and the other a voluntary settlement in favour of his younger son, born in 1949. Under each settlement, the son in question received a life interest with a general power of appointment over part of the fund and subject thereto

---

54 [1996] 4 All ER 865 at 869.

55 (1969) 85 LQR 15 (P.V.B.); (1968) 32 Conv (NS) 431 (F.R. Crane); (1976) 40 Conv (NS) 295 (T.G. Watkin). See also *D (a child) v O* [2004] EWHC (Ch) 1036, [2004] 3 All ER 780 (variation of bare trust of life policy to advance whole of capital for benefit of minor); [2004] All ER Rev 251 (P.J. Clarke).

on trust for such of his children as he shall appoint and in default of appointment on trust for his children absolutely. The investments of both settlements were in the Stanley Weston Group Ltd.

These settlements were subject to fiscal disadvantages, namely to Capital Gains Tax on disposal (introduced by the Finance Act 1965) and to Estate Duty upon the deaths of each of the sons. These problems were explained by Stamp J in the lower court [1969] 1 Ch 223 at 231–232.

The settlor and the two sons (and the family of the elder son) moved their homes to Jersey, and claimed to be resident and domiciled there. The settlor asked the court to appoint (under the Trustee Act 1925, section 41 [p. 634, above]) two persons of good repute, resident in Jersey, in the place of the existing English trustees; and asked the court to approve an arrangement under the Variation of Trusts Act 1958 which inserted in the trusts a power in the new trustees to discharge the property from the trusts of the English settlements and to subject it to identical trusts of a Jersey settlement.

Held (affirming Stamp J). The court refused.

Lord Denning MR: If the court gives its approval to the proposed scheme, the result will be that the new trustees will be able to sell the shares in the Stanley Weston Group and buy other shares, without being accountable for capital gains. There will be also considerable savings of Estate Duty on the deaths of the two sons Robert and Alan. In short, there will be a tremendous tax advantage to the sons and grandchildren of Mr. Stanley Weston. The question is whether the court ought to sanction the scheme.

There is one reported case in which a scheme on these lines was approved. It was *Re Seale's Marriage Settlement* [1961] Ch 574. In that case husband and wife married in 1931. They were both domiciled and resident in England: and a marriage settlement was made in an English trust in the ordinary form. They had three children who appear to have been born in England. But when the children were quite small the family emigrated to Canada. The children were brought up as Canadians and were likely to continue to live in Canada. The husband and wife intended to continue to live there. It was obviously advantageous for the settlement to be turned from an English settlement into a Canadian settlement—quite irrespective of tax advantages—and Buckley J made orders enabling Canadian trustees to be appointed and a Canadian settlement to be drawn up substantially in the same terms as the English settlement.

Those advising Mr. Weston ask the court to approve a similar scheme here. The judge refused. He said that this was a 'cheap exercise in tax avoidance' which he ought not to sanction: but he hoped that the case would be taken to the Court of Appeal so as to have the views of this court.

Before the Variation of Trusts Act 1958, there was much discussion as to the power of the court to sanction the variation of trusts. If the beneficiaries were all *sui juris*, they could agree between themselves to revoke or vary the trusts. If there were infant beneficiaries or unborn persons, it needed the consent of the court. But the jurisdiction of the court so to consent was very limited. The court could not sanction it except in case of a compromise of disputed rights: see *Chapman v Chapman* [1954] AC 429. By the Variation of Trusts Act 1958, this limitation was removed. The court has power to approve a variation or revocation of the trust, if it thinks fit, on behalf of infants or unborn persons. The statute gives no guide as to the way in which this discretion should be exercised. It says: 'the court may *if it thinks* fit by order approve...'. Likewise with the appointment of new trustees, the Trustee Act, 1925, gives no guide. It simply says the court may appoint new trustees 'whenever it is expedient'. There being no guidance in the statutes, it remains for the court to do the best it can.

Two propositions are clear: (i) in exercising its discretion, the function of the court is to protect those who cannot protect themselves. It must do what is truly for their benefit. (ii) It can give its consent to a scheme to avoid death duties or other taxes. Nearly every variation that has come before the court has tax avoidance for its principal object: and no one has ever suggested that this is undesirable or contrary to public policy.

But I think it necessary to add this third proposition: (iii) the court should not consider merely the financial benefit[56] to the infants or unborn children, but also their educational and social benefit. There are many things in life more worthwhile than money. One of these things is to be brought up in this our England, which is still 'the envy of less happier lands'. I do not believe it is for the benefit of children to be uprooted from England and transported to another country simply to avoid tax. It was very different with the children of the Seale family, which Buckley J considered. That family had emigrated to Canada many years before, with no thought of tax avoidance, and had brought up the children there as Canadians. It was very proper that the trust should be transferred to Canada. But here the family had only been in Jersey three months when they presented this scheme to the court. The inference is irresistible: the underlying purpose was to go there in order to avoid tax. I do not think that this will be all to the good for the children. I should imagine that, even if they had stayed in this country, they would have had a very considerable fortune at their disposal, even after paying tax. The only thing that Jersey can do for them is to give them an even greater fortune. Many a child has been ruined by being given too much.[57] The avoidance of tax may be lawful, but it is not yet a virtue. The Court of Chancery should not encourage or support it—it should not give its approval to it—if by so doing it would imperil the true welfare of the children, already born or yet to be born.

There is one thing more. I cannot help wondering how long these young people will stay in Jersey. It may be to their financial interest at present to make their home there permanently. But will they remain there once the capital gains are safely in hand, clear of tax? They may well change their minds and come back to enjoy their untaxed gains. Is such a prospect really for the benefit of the children? Are they to be wanderers over the face of the earth, moving from this country to that, according to where they can best avoid tax? I cannot believe that to be right. Children are like trees: they grow stronger with firm roots.

The long and short of it is, as the judge said, that the exodus of this family to Jersey is done to avoid British taxation. Having made great wealth here, they want to quit without paying the taxes and duties which are imposed on those who stay. So be it. If it really be for the benefit of the children, let it be done. Let them go, taking their money with them. But, if it be not truly for their benefit, the court should not countenance it. It should not give the scheme its blessing. The judge refused his approval. So would I. I would dismiss this appeal.[58]

---

[56] 'The word 'benefit' is, I think, plainly not confined to financial benefit, but may extend to moral or social benefit': *Re Holt's Settlement* [1969] 1 Ch 100 at 121, *per* Megarry J. See also *Re T's Settlement Trusts* [1964] Ch 158; *Re CL* [1969] 1 Ch 587; *Re Remnant's Settlement Trusts* [1970] Ch 560.

[57] Each settlement was worth some £400,000.

[58] Cf. *Re Windeatt's Will Trusts* [1969] 1 WLR 692, (variation approved by Pennycuick J where the 'family had been in Jersey for 19 years and had made a genuine and permanent home there. The children were born there'); *Re Whitehead's Will Trusts* [1971] 1 WLR 833 [p. 630, above] (where Pennycuick J approved appointment of trustees resident overseas where beneficiaries were resident and domiciled in Jersey). See also *Re Chamberlain* (unreported) discussed in (1976) 126 NLJ 1034 (J.B. Morcom) (transfer of funds from trust governed by English law to trust governed by law of Guernsey where primary beneficiaries were resident

Harman LJ: This is an essay in tax avoidance naked and unashamed, and none the worse for that, says the applicant. Indeed the judge agreed that this court is not the watch-dog of the Inland Revenue, and it is well known that much and perhaps the main use which has been made of the Act has been to produce schemes of variation of English trusts which will have the effect of reducing liabilities either on the capital of the trusts or the income of the beneficiaries....

Now, the linchpin of the scheme is not to be carried out under the Variation of Trusts Act at all. It is essential that the court should exercise its powers under the Trustee Act 1925, either by appointing new trustees out of the jurisdiction or giving leave to the existing trustees to make the appointment. It is not suggested that the present trustees are unsuitable or that any difficulty has arisen in the administration of the trusts. The scheme is entirely conditioned by the wish to avoid the incidence of Capital Gains Tax. For this purpose it is essential that the affairs of the trust should be administered from outside the United Kingdom and that this should be done by appointing two persons so resident as trustees. It is proposed that these trustees should then be empowered while still trustees of the English settlements to revoke the whole of the trusts of those instruments and to transfer the assets to themselves as trustees of the two settlements framed, it is said, so as to conform with the Jersey law.

Now, this law has never had any experience of trusts and so far as appears, the courts of Jersey have never made an order executing the trusts of a settlement. There is not, it appears, any Trustee Act in Jersey at all, and the effect of this last transaction must, so far as I can see, have nothing to recommend it from a trust point of view.[59]

In the circumstances the judge was entitled to consider whether the court 'should think fit' to accede to the scheme. The judge professed himself unsatisfied, and I think he was entitled to take that view. It is true that he expressed some dislike of tax avoidance of this sort, and in that he may have been mistaken, but he was in my opinion well justified in not being satisfied that a transfer of the whole trust to Jersey is expedient. The two young men who alone may be considered cannot be said to have proved that they truly intend to make Jersey their home. Indeed the younger of them has expressed no views on the subject at all. It seems to me most unlikely that two wealthy young men of this sort will be content at the threshold of their lives to settle down in the island and will not within a short time seek wider opportunities for their talents and wealth than that island affords. It follows, as it seems to me, that on the facts of this case no case has been made out for the removal of the trusts to Jersey rather than any other part of the world. These are English settlements and they should I think remain so unless some good reason connected with the trusts themselves can be put forward. I am of opinion, therefore, that the judge was entitled in the exercise of his discretion to say that to use the powers of the Trustee Act in this way was not justified and I would dismiss the appeal.

(iii) Family Harmony

In **Re Remnant's Settlement Trusts** [1970] Ch 560, a trust fund in favour of the children of two sisters, Mrs. Hooper and Mrs. Crosthwaite, was subject to forfeiture in

and domiciled in France and remaindermen in Indonesia); *Richard v The Hon AB Mackay* (14 March 1987), (1997) 11 TLI 23 [p. 630, above].

[59] See now Trusts (Jersey) Law 1984, as amended, and, generally, Matthews and Sowden, *Jersey Law of Trusts* (3rd edn, 1993).

respect of any of their children who practised Roman Catholicism or was married to a Roman Catholic, with an accruer provision in favour of the children of the other. The children of Mrs. Hooper were Protestant, those of Mrs. Crosthwaite were Roman Catholic. Pennycuick J was asked to approve an arrangement which deleted the forfeiture provision and accelerated the interest of the children of each sister in a sum of £10,000, part of the trust fund.

The deletion of the forfeiture clause was clearly not for the financial benefit of Mrs. Hooper's children; for they stood a very good chance of benefiting from it under the accruer provision. Nevertheless, PENNYCUICK J approved the arrangement. He said at 566:

The three considerations set out by Mrs. Crosthwaite, and elaborated by counsel, are these: first, that the forfeiture provisions represent a deterrent to each of the Hooper children from adopting the Roman Catholic faith should she be minded to do so; secondly, that they operate as a deterrent to each of the Hooper children in the selection of a husband when the time comes; and thirdly, that the forfeiture provisions represent a source of possible family dissension. I am not sure that there is very much weight in the first of those considerations because there is no reason to suppose that any of these children has any particular concern with the Roman Catholic faith. On the other hand, I do think there is very real weight in the second and in the third considerations. Obviously a forfeiture provision of this kind might well cause very serious dissension between the families of the two sisters. On the best consideration I can give it I think that the deletion of the forfeiture provisions on the terms contained in the arrangement, including the provision for acceleration in £10,000, should be regarded as for the benefit of the three Hooper children.

I have not found this an easy point, but I think I am entitled to take a broad view of what is meant by 'benefit', and so taking it, I think this arrangement can fairly be said to be for their benefit...

I conclude then that the carrying-out of this arrangement will be for the benefit of all the persons born and unborn on whose behalf I am concerned to approve the arrangement.

It remains to consider whether the arrangement is a fair and proper one. As far as I can see, there is no reason for saying otherwise, except that the arrangement defeats this testator's intention. That is a serious but by no means conclusive consideration. I have reached the clear conclusion that these forfeiture provisions are undesirable in themselves in the circumstances of this case and that an arrangement involving their deletion is a fair and proper one. I propose accordingly to approve the arrangement with one or two modifications which are not material to this judgment.

I would only like to add this word of caution. The effect of any particular forfeiture provision must depend on the nature of the provision itself and upon the circumstances in which it is likely to operate. A forfeiture provision is by no means always intrinsically undesirable. Again, you may have the position that a forfeiture provision benefits exclusively one or the other party concerned, and in that case it might be very difficult to say that the deletion of the provision was for the benefit of that party, unless there was the fullest financial compensation. However, I am not concerned to go further into those matters. It is sufficient for me to say that on the facts of this particular case the deletion of the forfeiture provisions, upon the terms of the arrangement, is for the benefit of everyone concerned and that the arrangement is a fair and proper one.

(1971) 34 MLR 98 (R.B.M. Cotterrell)

Even more difficult problems arise in cases such as *Re Remnant* and *Re Weston* where it becomes necessary to weigh the relative importance of countervailing financial and non-financial considerations. Thus the court may find itself forced to evaluate such considerations as the benefit to an English child in being brought up in England,[60] or the benefit to a mental patient in releasing a trust interest which she would probably have wished to release if sane.[61] In such circumstances it is hard to avoid the conclusion that benefit and the measure of it is simply what the court says it is.

Since each case in this area of the law must be largely a matter of decision on the facts, comparison of the reported cases is difficult. Nevertheless they offer some guidance in an area where there is little else to guide the court and it is unfortunate that no cases other than *Re Weston* were discussed in *Re Remnant*. In the case of *Re Tinker's Settlement*,[62] Russell J refused to approve a variation on behalf of unborn children under which they would lose a contingent interest under the trust on the ground that the variation would not be for their benefit even though it might prevent dissatisfaction and conflict in the family. While the remarks in *Re Tinker's Settlement*[63] which suggest that financial benefit must be present to satisfy the requirement of 'benefit' now seem unacceptable, the actual decision in the case has not been challenged and was approved by Cross J in *Re CL*.[64] The position in *Re Tinker* was strikingly similar to that in *Re Remnant* and, while grounds of distinction could have been found, it would have been more satisfactory to have some consideration of the relevant pre-*Weston* cases. In view of the awesome width of the court's present discretion, it will be regrettable if judges underestimate the importance of precedent, wisely used, as an aid to uniformity of treatment and coherence in trust variation law. Where such a heavy burden of decision is placed on the court these qualities seem particularly important and desirable.

(iv) Taking a Chance

The question arises whether the court should approve on behalf of a beneficiary who will in almost every conceivable set of circumstances be benefited, but might be prejudiced in one possible foreseeable situation. To what extent should the court take the chance of his receiving a benefit?

In **Re Holt's Settlement** [1969] 1 Ch 100,[65] MEGARRY J said at 121:

The point that at one stage troubled me concerns the unborn issue. Mr. Brookes, as in duty bound, put before me a contention that it was possible to conceive of an unborn infant who would be so circumstanced that a proposed rearrangement would be entirely to his disadvantage. He postulated the case of a child born to Mrs. Wilson next year, and of Mrs. Wilson dying in childbirth, or shortly after the child's birth. In such a case, he said, the benefit of the acceleration of interest resulting from Mrs. Wilson surrendering the moiety of her life interest

---

[60] *Re Weston's Settlements* [1969] 1 Ch 223 [p. 852, above].   [61] *Re CL* [1969] 1 Ch 587.

[62] [1960] 1 WLR 1011. The part of the proposed variation which conferred a purely financial benefit on the unborn children was approved.

[63] The case was not cited in *Re Weston's Settlements* or *Re Remnant's Settlement Trusts*, but see Cross J in *Re CL* [1969] 1 Ch 587 at 599.   [64] [1969] 1 Ch 587.

[65] For the facts see p. 836, above. See also *Re Robinson's Settlement Trusts* [1976] 1 WLR 806.

would be minimal, and there would be no saving of Estate Duty. All that would happen in regard to such an infant would be that the vesting of his interest would be postponed from age 21 to age 30; and the only possible advantage in that would be the non-financial moral or social advantage to which I have just referred. In support of this contention he referred me to the decision of Stamp J in *Re Cohen's Settlement Trusts* [1965] 1 WLR 1229. There, the scheme originally proposed was not approved by the court because there was a possibility of there being a beneficiary who would get no advantage whatsoever from the proposed arrangement; it would merely be to his detriment.

Mr. Millett, however, points out that there is an essential distinction between that case and this; for there, whatever the surrounding circumstances, the unborn person contemplated could not benefit from the arrangement. In the present case, he says, all that Mr. Brookes has done is to put forward the case of an infant who might be born next year; and it would be a result of the surrounding circumstances, and not of the time of birth or the characteristics of the infant, that that infant might derive no benefit from the arrangement proposed. Mr. Millet referred me to *Re Cohen's Will Trusts* [1959] 1 WLR 865,[66] where Danckwerts J held that in exercising the jurisdiction under the Act of 1958 the court must, on behalf of those persons for whom it was approving the arrangement, take the sort of risk which an adult would be prepared to take. Accordingly, says Mr. Millett, Mr. Brookes' special infant to be born next year was in the position that although there was the chance that its mother would die immediately afterwards, there was also the alternative chance that its mother would survive its birth for a substantial period of time. In the latter event, which was the more probable, the advantages of the arrangement would accrue to the infant. In short, he distinguishes the decision of Stamp J in *Re Cohen's Settlement Trusts* [1965] 1 WLR 1229 on the footing that that was the case of an unborn person whose prospects were hopeless, whatever the events, whereas in the present case the hypothetical unborn person has the normal prospects of events occurring which will either improve or not improve his position. Such an unborn person falls, he says, into the category of unborn persons on whose behalf the court should be prepared to take a risk if the arrangement appears on the whole to be for their benefit.

It seems to me that this is a proper distinction to make, and I accept it. Accordingly, I hold that the arrangement is for the benefit of the classes of persons specified in section 1(1) of the Act, and I approve it.

QUESTIONS

1. Which of the theories concerning the operation of the Variation of Trusts Act 1958 do you think is convincing? Should writing be required to effect a change in the beneficial interests of assenting adults? *Grey v IRC* [1960] AC 1 [p. 113, above]; *Oughtred v IRC* [1960] AC 206 [p. 118, above]; *Re Holt's Settlement* [1969] 1 Ch 100 [p. 836, above].

2. Do you think that the Variation of Trusts Act 1958 provides too generous fiscal advantages for those lucky enough to have interests under settlements? Do you think it right that minors should suffer from the disadvantage that they are unable to make fiscally advantageous changes in their interests under

---

[66] See (1960) 76 LQR 22 (R.E.M.).

settlements when adults in their situation could do so freely? L.R.C. Seventh Report, Cmnd. 310; (1965) 43 *Canadian Bar Review* 181 (A.J. Maclean).

3. Would a variation to avoid tax today be regarded as acceptable? Compare *Sieff v Fox* [2005] EWHC 1312 (Ch), [2005] 1 WLR 3811 [p. 658, above].

4. Why are different meanings given to the word 'benefit' in:

   (a) Variation of Trusts Act 1958; (1969) 33 Conv 122–131 (NS).

   (b) Trustee Act 1925, section 31(1) (power to apply income for maintenance education or benefit) [p. 762, above].

   (c) Trustee Act 1925, section 32(1) (power to apply capital of a settlement for the advancement or benefit of beneficiaries) [p. 769, above]?

PART VI

LIABILITY FOR BREACH
OF TRUST

18

BASIC PRINCIPLES[1]

I THE NATURE OF BREACH OF TRUST[2]

The nature of breach of trust was identified by MILLETT LJ in **Armitage v Nurse** [1998] Ch 241, who said at 251:

Breaches of trust are of many different kinds. A breach of trust may be deliberate or inadvertent; it may consist of an actual misappropriation or misapplication of the trust property or merely of an investment or other dealing which is outside the trustees' powers; it may consist of a failure to carry out a positive obligation of the trustees or merely of a want of skill and care on their part in the management of the trust property; it may be injurious to the interests of the beneficiaries or be actually to their benefit. By consciously acting beyond their powers (as, for example, by making an investment which they know to be unauthorised) the trustees may deliberately commit a breach of trust; but if they do so in good faith and in the honest belief that they are acting in the interest of the beneficiaries their conduct is not fraudulent. So a

---

[1] H&M, pp. 656–657, 666–682; Lewin, Part V; P&M, pp. 761–764, 776–794; P&S, pp. 736–744, 756–772; Pettit, pp. 520–522, 528–549; Snell, pp. 665–668, 672–683; T&H, pp. 1009–1029, 1054–1059, 1062—1070; U&H, pp. 1078–1081, 1117–1165; *Breach of Trust* (ed. P. Birks and A. Pretto) (2002). See the definitions of breach of trust discussed by Megarry J in *Tito v Waddell (No 2)* [1977] Ch 106 at 247–248. For criminal liability, see Debtors Act 1869, s. 4 and Theft Act 1968; *R v Barrick* (1985) 81 Cr App Rep 78; *R v Clark* [1998] 2 Cr App Rep 137; *R v Whitehouse and Morrison* [1999] 2 Cr App Rep (S) 259 (guidelines on sentencing); *A-G's Reference (No 1 of 1985)* [1986] QB 491 (making of secret profit for which a fiduciary was personally accountable held not to be theft within s. 5(1), (3)); (1975) 9 Conv (NS) 29 (R. Brazier); P&S, p. 719; Pettit, p. 549; U&H, pp. 1109–1115. As to whether this decision has been undermined by *A-G for Hong Kong v Reid* [1994] 1 AC 324, see Law Commission Report: *Conspiracy to Defraud* (1994) (Law Com No 228), paras. 4.20–4.24; (1994) 110 LQR 180 (J.C. Smith); Smith and Hogan (ed. D. Ormerod), *Criminal Law* (11th edn, 2005), pp. 684–685 and Simester and Sullivan, *Criminal Law: Theory and Doctrine* (3rd edn., 2007), pp. 461–462.

[2] H&M, pp. 656–657; P&M, pp. 761–763; P&S, pp. 736–738; Pettit, pp. 520–521; Snell, p. 665; T&H, pp. 1026–1029.

deliberate breach of trust is not necessarily fraudulent. Hence the remark famously attributed to Selwyn LJ by Sir Nathaniel Lindley MR in the course of argument in *Perrins v Bellamy* [1899] 1 Ch 797 at 798: 'My old master, the late Selwyn LJ, used to say "The main duty of a trustee is to commit *judicious* breaches of trust".'

II LIABILITY BETWEEN TRUSTEES[3]

A trustee is personally liable to compensate the beneficiaries for the loss which a breach of trust causes to the trust property, either directly or indirectly, and the burden of proof is on the claimant to prove a causal connection between the breach and the loss.[4]

The liability is joint and several. It is personal, not vicarious. A trustee is not vicariously liable for the acts of his co-trustees.[5] But, and this is of great significance, trustees are required to act jointly. One trustee cannot escape liability by leaving his co-trustees to do all the work.

A trustee's liability may be reduced by a provision in the trust instrument.[6] It is common also for professional trustees to protect themselves by insurance.[7]

A CONTRIBUTION

Where a trustee is liable for a breach of trust, it is possible for that trustee to apply to the court to require other trustees who were liable for the same breach to make a contribution towards the remedy.

Before 1979 the equitable rules of contribution provided that the liability was to be shared equally between co-trustees, even where one of them was more to blame than another.[8] These rules were superseded by:

CIVIL LIABILITY (CONTRIBUTION) ACT 1978[9]

1. Entitlement to contribution

(1) Subject to the following provisions of this section, any person liable in respect of any damage suffered by another person may recover contribution from any

---

[3] H&M, pp. 666–668; Lewin pp. 1588–1593; P&M, pp. 763–764, 776–779; P&S, pp. 742–743, 768–771; Pettit, pp. 528–532; Snell, pp. 674–676; T&H, pp. 1054–1059, 1063–1064; U&H, pp. 1078–1079, 1152–1165.

[4] See p. 948, below.

[5] *Townley v Sherborne* (1633) J Bridg 35 at 37–38; *Re Brier* (1884) 26 Ch D 238. See Whitehouse and Hassall, *Trusts of Land. Trustee Delegation and the Trustee Act 2000* (2nd edn, 2001), pp. 206–207. A trustee will, however, be liable for the acts of a co-trustee if the trustee was also at fault.

[6] See p. 867, below.

[7] See (1994) 2 Charity Commissioners' Report 24–27.

[8] See, for example, *Bahin v Hughes* (1886) 31 Ch D 390.

[9] The Act was based on the Law Commission Report on Contribution, 1977 (Law Com. No. 79). See para. 28. It came into force on 1 January 1979. For special time limits for claiming contribution, see Limitation Act 1980, s. 10.

other person liable in respect of the same damage[10] (whether jointly with him or otherwise).

2. Assessment of contribution

(1) Subject to subsection (3) below,[11] in any proceedings for contribution under section 1 above the amount of the contribution recoverable from any person shall be such as may be found by the court to be just and equitable having regard to the extent of that person's responsibility for the damage in question.

(2) Subject to subsection (3) below, the court shall have power in any such proceedings to exempt any person from liability to make contribution, or to direct that the contribution to be recovered from any person shall amount to a complete indemnity.

6. Interpretation

(1) A person is liable in respect of any damage for the purposes of this Act if the person who suffered it (or anyone representing his estate or dependants) is entitled to recover compensation from him in respect of that damage (whatever the legal basis of his liability, whether tort, breach of contract, breach of trust or otherwise).

In **Friends' Provident Life Office v Hillier Parker May and Rowden** [1997] QB 85, Hillier Parker had recommended Friends' Provident to make payments of interest to developers which were in fact overpayments. Friends' Provident sued Hillier Parker for negligence and breach of contract. Hillier Parker then claimed a contribution from the developers for breach of a constructive trust[12] in not making restitution of the money to Friends' Provident. In holding that a contribution was payable AULD LJ said at 108:

Here, Hillier Parker's case is that the developers were in breach of trust in dissipating the money, in failing to pay it back when asked to do so, and in denying Friends' Provident's entitlement to repayment. In my view, and in the light of my construction of sections 1(1) and 6(1) of the Act of 1978 under the heading of quasi-contract, whatever the precise form of remedy Friends' Provident might have in respect of that money, whether restitutionary or in damages, it is for compensation for damage it has suffered by its loss in the sense referred to by Viscount Haldane LC in *Nocton v Lord Ashburton* [1914] AC 932 and in the words of the Act.

---

[10] *Birse Construction Ltd v Haiste Ltd* [1996] 1 WLR 675 (two parties liable in respect of same damages suffered by a third party). The Act applies to restitutionary claims which can be characterised as involving the same damage as claims for compensation: *Friends' Provident Life Office v Hillier Parker May & Rowden* [1997] QB 85; *Niru Battery Manufacturing Co v Milestone Trading Ltd (No 2)* [2004] EWCA Civ 487, [2004] 2 All ER (Comm) 289; *Charter plc v City Index Ltd* [2007] EWCA Civ 1382 1 WLR 26 (application to claim for unconscionable receipt) [see p. 1008, below]. Cf. *Royal Brompton Hospital NHS Trust v Hammond* [2002] 1 WLR 1397.

[11] Subsection (3) limits liability to make a contribution where there has been prior agreement for an upper limit or statutory reduction of damages.

[12] As to when a constructive trust of mistaken payments might be recognised, see *Westdeutsche Landesbank Girozentrale v Islington London Borough Council* [1996] AC 669 [see p. 281, above].

Accordingly, assuming that the developers are trustees for Friends' Provident of all or some of the notional interest the subject of this action and are in breach of that trust by paying the money away for their own use, or in not repaying it on demand by Friends' Provident or in asserting that they, not Friends' Provident, were entitled to it, then, subject to any successful defence of estoppel, I would hold that section 1(1) of the Act of 1978 applies to a claim for restitutionary compensation based on such liability.

B INDEMNITY

Although the Civil Liability (Contribution) Act 1978 excluded the courts' inherent equitable jurisdiction to order a contribution, it does not exclude any right to an indemnity. One trustee will be required to indemnify fully another where the former bears the full liability for the breach of trust. The liability of one trustee to indemnify another is recognised only in very exceptional circumstances.

(i) Reliance on Solicitor-Trustee

In **Re Partington** (1887) 57 LT 654, the trustees of a fund were Mr. Allen, a solicitor, and Mrs. Partington, the widow of the testator. A breach of trust was committed. Mr. Allen had undertaken the whole administration of the trust. STIRLING J held that he had not communicated sufficiently to Mrs. Partington concerning the affairs of the trust to enable her to exercise a judgment upon the unauthorised investment. 'The trustee, Mrs. Partington, appears to me to have been misled by her co-trustee by reason of his not giving her full information as to the nature of the investments which he was asking her to advance the money upon, and I think he has been guilty of negligence also in his duty as a solicitor.' Mrs. Partington was entitled to an indemnity.

In **Head v Gould** [1898] 2 Ch 250, an attempt to obtain an indemnity against a solicitor trustee failed. KEKEWICH J said at 265:

True it is that the defendant Gould is a solicitor, and that he was appointed trustee for that very reason. True no doubt, also, that the legal business was managed by him, and I do not propose to absolve him from any responsibility attaching to him on that ground; but I do not myself think that Byrne J,[13] or any other judge ever intended to hold that a man is bound to indemnify his co-trustee against loss merely because he was a solicitor, when that co-trustee was an active participator in the breach of trust complained of, and is not proved to have participated merely in consequence of the advice and control of the solicitor . . .

(ii) Trustee as Beneficiary

In **Chillingworth v Chambers** [1896] 1 Ch 685, the plaintiff, Chillingworth, and defendant, Chambers, were trustees of a testamentary trust. The plaintiff was married to one of the beneficiaries, and, on her death, became himself a beneficiary.

---

[13] In *Re Turner* [1897] 1 Ch 536. See also *Lockhart v Reilly* (1856) 25 LJ Ch 697.

The trustees made an unauthorised investment in mortgages of leasehold property, some being made before Mrs. Chillingworth's death and some after. The mortgages proved insufficient. The deficiency of £1,580 was made good out of the plaintiff's interest.

He brought this action claiming contribution from Chambers, and failed. KAY LJ said at 707:

On the whole, I think that the weight of authority is in favour of holding that a trustee who, being also *cestui que trust*, has received, as between himself and his co-trustee, an exclusive benefit by the breach of trust, must indemnify his co-trustee to the extent of his interest in the trust fund, and not merely to the extent of the benefit which he has received. I think that the plaintiff must be treated as having received such an exclusive benefit.

III PROTECTION OF TRUSTEES

A TRUSTEE EXEMPTION CLAUSES[14]

The Trustee Act 2000 allows for the statutory duty of care to be excluded by the trust instrument.[15] As an alternative, the trust deed may include a clause which exempts a trustee from liability. Such a clause will not exclude the statutory duty of care, but it will operate to protect the trustee from personal liability for breach of duty. If a trustee can rely on such a clause it will mean that he is not liable to compensate the beneficiaries for loss suffered, but it will not prevent the trustee from being removed from the trust.[16] The effectiveness of trustee exemption clauses has been a matter of recent concern both for the judiciary and for the Law Commission.[17] The Law Commission has defined a trustee exemption clause as follows:

'...a clause in a trust instrument which excludes or restricts a trustee's liability for breach of trust, either by expressly excluding liability or by modifying the trustee's powers and duties. The term is used interchangeably with "trustee exoneration clauses" and "trustee exculpation clauses".'[18]

---

[14] H&M, pp. 507–509; Lewin, pp. 1603–1615; P&M, pp. 786–789; P&S, pp. 738–740; Pettit, pp. 532–534; Snell, p. 677; T&H, pp. 651–655; U&H, pp. 728–733; J. Penner, 'Exemptions' in *Breach of Trust* (eds. P. Birks and A. Pretto, 2002), pp. 241–267.

[15] Sch. 1, para. 7. See p. 689, above. The validity of a clause excluding duties, other than fiduciary duties, was accepted by the Privy Council in *Hayim v Citibank* [1987] AC 730. Specific statutory rules apply to exemption clauses relating to trustees of pension trusts (Pensions Act 1995, ss. 33, 34(6) [see p. 71, above]: no exclusion of liability for investment functions), unit trusts (Financial Services and Markets Act 2000, s. 253: exemption for negligence is not permitted) and debenture trusts (Companies Act 2006, s. 750: exemption for negligence is not permitted). [16] See Lewin, p. 1605.

[17] See p. 870, below.

[18] *Trustee Exemption Clauses*, Executive Summary, Law Com No. 301, 2006, p. 1.

In **Armitage v Nurse** [1998] Ch 241[19] clause 15 of a settlement stated that no trustee should be liable for any loss or damage suffered by the trust fund or income from the fund at any time or for any cause unless the loss or damage was caused by the trustee's 'own actual fraud'. The plaintiff, Paula, brought a claim for breach of trust. One of the questions for the Court to consider was the validity of the exemption clause. MILLETT LJ said at 250:

In my judgment, the meaning of the clause is plain and unambiguous. No trustee can be made liable for loss or damage to the capital or income of the trust property caused otherwise than by his own actual fraud. 'Actual fraud' means what it says. It does not mean 'constructive fraud' or 'equitable fraud'. The word 'actual' is deliberately chosen to exclude them....

The expression 'actual fraud' in clause 15 is not used to describe the common law tort of deceit. As the judge appreciated it simply means dishonesty. I accept the formulation put forward by Mr. Hill on behalf of the respondents which (as I have slightly modified it) is that it:

'connotes at the minimum an intention on the part of the trustee to pursue a particular course of action, either knowing that it is contrary to the interests of the beneficiaries or being recklessly indifferent whether it is contrary to their interests or not.'

It is the duty of a trustee to manage the trust property and deal with it in the interests of the beneficiaries. If he acts in a way which he does not honestly believe is in their interests then he is acting dishonestly. It does not matter whether he stands or thinks he stands to gain personally from his actions. A trustee who acts with the intention of benefiting persons who are not the objects of the trust is not the less dishonest because he does not intend to benefit himself.

In my judgment clause 15 exempts the trustee from liability for loss or damage to the trust property no matter how indolent, imprudent, lacking in diligence, negligent or wilful he may have been, so long as he has not acted dishonestly....

I accept the submission made on behalf of Paula that there is an irreducible core of obligations owed by the trustees to the beneficiaries and enforceable by them which is fundamental to the concept of a trust. If the beneficiaries have no rights enforceable against the trustees there are no trusts. But I do not accept the further submission that these core obligations include the duties of skill and care, prudence and diligence. The duty of the trustees to perform the trusts honestly and in good faith for the benefit of the beneficiaries is the minimum necessary to give substance to the trusts.[20]...

It is, of course, far too late to suggest that the exclusion in a contract of liability for ordinary negligence or want of care is contrary to public policy. What is true of a contract must be equally true of a settlement. It would be very surprising if our law drew the line between liability for ordinary negligence and liability for gross negligence. In this respect English law differs from civil law systems, for it has always drawn a sharp distinction between negligence, however gross, on the one hand and fraud, bad faith and wilful misconduct on the other. The doctrine of the common law is that: 'Gross negligence may be evidence of *mala fides*, but it is not the same thing': see *Goodman v Harvey* (1836) 4 Ad & El 870 at 876, *per* Lord Denman CJ. But while we regard the difference between fraud on the one hand and mere negligence, however gross, on the other as a difference in kind, we regard the difference between negligence and gross

---

[19] (1998) 57 CLJ 33 (N.J. McBride); [1998] Conv 100 (G. McCormack); [1997] All ER Rev 275 (P.J. Clarke).

[20] It follows logically from this that liability for breach of fiduciary duty cannot be excluded. For the nature of such duties, see Chapter 16.

negligence as merely one of degree. English lawyers have always had a healthy disrespect for the latter distinction. In *Hinton v Dibbin* (1842) 2 QB 646 Lord Denman CJ doubted whether any intelligible distinction exists; while in *Grill v General Iron Screw Collier Co* (1866) LR 1 CP 600 at 612 Willes J famously observed that gross negligence is ordinary negligence with a vituperative epithet....

It must be acknowledged that the view is widely held that these clauses have gone too far, and that trustees who charge for their services and who, as professional men, would not dream of excluding liability for ordinary professional negligence should not be able to rely on a trustee exemption clause excluding liability for gross negligence. Jersey introduced a law in 1989 which denies effect to a trustee exemption clause which purports to absolve a trustee from liability for his own 'fraud, wilful misconduct or gross negligence'.... If clauses such as clause 15 of the settlement are to be denied effect, then in my opinion this should be done by Parliament....[21]

In **Walker v Stones** [2001] QB 902[22] the trustees of a discretionary trust were also partners in a firm of solicitors.[23] Clause 15 of the so-called Bacchus trust deed exempted trustees from all liability other than 'wilful fraud or dishonesty'. The beneficiaries of the trust alleged that the trustees had acted in breach of trust by acting for the benefit of people who were not objects of the trust. SIR CHRISTOPHER SLADE considered there to be no material difference between the exemption clause in this case and that in *Armitage v Nurse* [1998] Ch 241 [p. 868, above]. His Lordship then said at 939:

At least in the case of a solicitor-trustee, a qualification must in my opinion be necessary to take account of the case where the trustee's so-called 'honest belief', though actually held, is so unreasonable that, by any objective standard, no reasonable solicitor-trustee could have thought that what he did or agreed to do was for the benefit of the beneficiaries. I limit this proposition to the case of a solicitor-trustee, first, because on the facts before us we are concerned only with solicitor-trustees and, secondly, because I accept that the test of honesty may vary from case to case, depending on, among other things, the role and calling of the trustee: compare *Twinsectra Ltd v Yardley* [1999] Lloyd's Rep Bank 438, at 464, *per* Potter LJ.[24] In that case, the court regarded the standard of honesty applicable in the case of the defendant solicitor, Mr. Leach, as being 'that to be expected of a reasonably prudent and honest solicitor': see at 465.

The word 'honest' at first sight points exclusively to a state of mind. But, as the *Twinsectra* case illustrates, its scope cannot be so limited. A person may in some cases act dishonestly, according to the ordinary use of language, even though he genuinely believes that his action is morally justified. The penniless thief, for example, who picks the pocket of the multi-millionaire is dishonest even though he genuinely considers the theft is morally justified as a fair redistribution of wealth and that he is not therefore being dishonest.

---

[21] See also *HIH Casualty v Chase Manhattan Bank* [2003] 1 All ER (Comm) 349; [2003] Conv 185 (A. Kennedy); *Barnes v Tomlinson* [2006] EWHC 3115 (Ch), [2007] WTLR 377 (dishonesty required consciousness of breach of duty or reckless carelessness as to the breach). Cf *Citibank NA v MBIA Assurance SA* [2007] EWCA Civ 11, [2007] 1 All ER (Comm) 475: guarantor's right to instruct trustee as regards exercise of trustee discretion and powers was valid without imposing liability on trustee. For criticism that this ignores the 'irreducible core of trust obligations' see (2007) 123 LQR 342 (A. Trukhtanov).

[22] [2000] All ER Rev 251 (P.J. Clarke).

[23] In *Bogg v Raper* (1998) The Times, 12 April the Court of Appeal recognised that a solicitor-trustee who had drafted an exemption clause in the trust under a will could rely on it, but only if he had drawn the testator's attention to the clause and its effect.

[24] Now see *Twinsectra Ltd v Yardley* [2002] 2 AC 164 [p. 990, below].

[His Lordship then considered Lord Nicholls of Birkenhead's analysis of dishonesty in *Royal Brunei Airlines Sdn Bhd v Tan* [1995] 2 AC 378 [p. 983, below], and continued:] There is an obvious difference of emphasis between the judgments in *Royal Brunei Airlines Sdn Bhd v Tan* and *Armitage v Nurse* [1998] Ch 241 so far as they relate to the concept of dishonesty and it has been suggested that they may be irreconcilable. I do not think they are. The decision in *Royal Brunei Airlines Sdn Bhd v Tan* was cited to the Court of Appeal in *Armitage v Nurse*. Millett LJ did not purport to distinguish *Royal Brunei Airlines Sdn Bhd v Tan*, either on the grounds that it related to the liability of accessories or on any other grounds. As already stated, I can see no grounds for applying a different test of honesty in the context of a trustee exemption clause, such as clause 15 of the Bacchus trust deed, from that applicable to the liability of an accessory in a breach of trust. It would be surprising if the court in *Armitage v Nurse* had regarded itself as differing from *Royal Brunei Airlines Sdn Bhd v Tan* without saying so or explaining why. I think that in the relevant passage from his judgment quoted above at 250–251 [see p. 868, above]—and in particular in saying that if trustees deliberately commit a breach of trust they are not dishonest provided that 'they may do so in good faith and in the honest belief that they are acting in the interests of the beneficiaries'—Millett LJ was directing his mind to the not uncommon case of what Selwyn LJ had once described as 'judicious breaches of trust'. I think it most unlikely that he would have intended this dictum to apply in a case where a solicitor-trustee's perception of the interests of the beneficiaries was so unreasonable that no reasonable solicitor-trustee could have held such belief. Indeed in my opinion such a construction of the clause could well render it inconsistent with the very existence of an effective trust.

Millett LJ analysed the permitted scope of trustee exemption clauses in *Armitage v Nurse* at 251–256. His analysis in my judgment clearly illustrates the need, as a matter of policy, for the courts to construe clauses of this nature no more widely than their language on a fair reading requires. I cannot believe it would be the intention of the draftsmen of clauses such as clause 15 of the Bacchus trust deed to exempt trustees from liability for a breach of trust in a case such as that postulated at the end of the immediately preceding paragraph.

For all these reasons Rattee J in my judgment erred in his approach to the construction of the effect of clause 15(1)(a)(iv) of the Bacchus trust deed. That clause in my judgment would not exempt the trustees from liability for breaches of trust, even if committed in the genuine belief that the course taken by them was in the interests of the beneficiaries, if such belief was so unreasonable that no reasonable solicitor-trustee could have held that belief.[25]

Law Commission: *Trustee Exemption Clauses* (2006) (No. 301), para. 7.1–7.4[26]

SUMMARY OF RECOMMENDATIONS

7.1   We recommend that a rule of practice should be recognised in the interests of securing settlor awareness of trustee exemption clauses.

7.2   We recommend that the main elements of the rule should be as follows:

> Any paid trustee who causes a settlor to include a clause in a trust instrument which has the effect of excluding or limiting liability for negligence must before the creation of the trust take such steps as are reasonable to ensure that the settlor is aware of the meaning and effect of the clause.

---

[25] In *Wight v Olswang* (1999) The Times, 18 May the Court of Appeal held that a clause which exempted liability for unpaid trustees should be construed narrowly.

[26] [2007] Conv 103 (A. Kenny).

7.3 We recommend that regulatory and professional bodies should make regulation to such effect in order to meet the particular circumstances of their membership and should enforce such regulation in accordance with their codes of conduct. Bodies whose membership includes the drafters of trusts should extend regulation to those who draft trust documentation containing trustee exemption provisions.

7.4 We recommend that Government should promote the application of this rule of practice as widely as possible across the trust industry.

In August 2006 The Society of Trust and Estate Practitioners issued a Practice Rule that its members should disclose clauses exempting trustees and executors from liability.

B RELIEF BY THE COURT[27]

TRUSTEE ACT 1925

61. Power to relieve trustee from personal liability

If it appears to the court that a trustee, whether appointed by the court or otherwise, is or may be personally liable for any breach of trust, whether the transaction alleged to be a breach of trust occurred before or after the commencement of this Act, but has acted honestly and reasonably, and ought fairly to be excused for the breach of trust and for omitting to obtain the directions of the court in the matter in which he committed such breach, then the court may relieve him either wholly or partly from personal liability for the same.

It is not possible to lay down with precision the occasions on which the section will be applied. The question has usually arisen in connection with the making of unauthorised investments,[28] and the payment of money to the wrong beneficiaries.

Where a trustee is in doubt, he should always take legal advice. Having done so, an amateur trustee will nearly always be covered; but relief is not automatic. A solicitor should likewise take counsel's opinion. Professional trustees, however, fall within the section, but the court is less willing to apply its provisions in their favour.[29]

The best general explanation of the section—or rather its predecessor, Judicial Trustees Act 1896, section 3—is found in *Perrins v Bellamy* [1898] 2 Ch 521, *per* Kekewich J and in *Re Stuart* [1897] 2 Ch 583, *per* Stirling J. In each case trustees were guilty of a breach of trust. In the former they were excused; but not in the latter.[30]

---

[27] H&M, pp. 674–676; Lewin, pp. 1615–1618; P&M, pp. 789–791; P&S, pp. 758–762; Pettit, pp. 546–548; Snell, pp. 682–683; T&H, pp. 1068–1069; U&H, pp. 1117–1125; J, Lowry and R. Edmunds, 'Excuses' in *Breach of Trust* (eds. P. Birks and A. Pretto, 2002), pp. 269–295. See generally (1955) 19 Conv (NS) 420 (L.A. Sheridan). See also Charities Act 1993, s. 73D (relief of liability of charity trustee by Charity Commission) [see p. 617, above].

[28] *Bartlett v Barclays Bank Trust Co Ltd* [1980] Ch 515 [p. 717, above] (trustees held not to have acted honestly).

[29] *National Trustees Co of Australasia Ltd v General Finance Co of Australasia Ltd* [1905] AC 373; *Re Pauling's Settlement Trusts* [1964] Ch 303 [p. 889, below]; *Re Rosenthal* [1972] 1 WLR 1273; Law Reform Committee 23rd Report (*The Powers and Duties of Trustees*) 1982 Cmnd. 8733, para. 2.16.

[30] For initial criticism of the relief, see *Maitland's Equity* (2nd edn, 1926), pp. 99–100; (1898) 14 LQR 159 (H.F. Maugham).

In **Perrins v Bellamy** [1898] 2 Ch 521, KEKEWICH J said at 527:

Broadly speaking, these trustees have committed a breach of trust, and they are responsible for it. But then the statute comes in, and the very foundation for the application of the statute is that the trustee whose conduct is in question 'is or may be personally liable for any breach of trust'. I am bound to look at the rest of the section by the light of those words, and with the view that, in cases falling within the section, the breach of trust is not of itself to render the trustee personally liable. Leaving out the intervening words, which merely make the section retrospective, I find when in general the trustee is to be relieved from personal liability. He is not to be held personally liable if he 'has acted honestly and reasonably, and ought fairly to be excused for the breach of trust'. In this case, as in the large majority of cases of breach of trust which come before the Court, the word 'honestly' may be left out of consideration. Cases do unfortunately occur from time to time in which trustees, and even solicitors in whom confidence has been reposed, run away with the money of their *cestuis que trust*, and where such flagrant dishonesty occurs breach of trust becomes a minor consideration. In the present case there is no imputation or ground for imputation of any dishonesty whatever. The Legislature has made the absence of all dishonesty a condition precedent to the relief of the trustee from liability. But that is not the grit of the section. The grit is in the words 'reasonably, and ought fairly to be excused for the breach of trust'. How much the latter words add to the force of the word 'reasonably' I am not at present prepared to say. I suppose, however, that in the view of the Legislature there might be cases in which a trustee, though he had acted reasonably, ought not fairly to be excused for the breach of trust. Indeed, I am not sure that some of the evidence adduced in this case was not addressed to a view of that kind, as, for instance, the evidence by which it was attempted to shew that these trustees, though they acted reasonably in selling the property, ought not fairly to be excused because the plaintiff Mrs. Perrins objected to their selling, and her objection was brought to their notice. In the section the copulative 'and' is used, and it may well be argued that in order to bring a case within the section it must be shewn not merely that the trustee has acted 'reasonably', but also that he ought 'fairly' to be excused for the breach of trust. I venture, however, to think that, in general and in the absence of special circumstances, a trustee who has acted 'reasonably' ought to be relieved, and that it is not incumbent on the Court to consider whether he ought 'fairly' to be excused, unless there is evidence of a special character shewing that the provisions of the section ought not to be applied in his favour. I need not pursue that subject further, because in the present case I find no ground whatever for saying that these trustees, if they acted reasonably, ought not to be excused. The question, and the only question, is whether they acted reasonably. In saying that, I am not unmindful of the words of the section which follow, and which require that it should be shewn that the trustee ought 'fairly' to be excused, not only 'for the breach of trust', but also 'for omitting to obtain the directions of the Court in the matter in which he committed such breach of trust'. I find it difficult to follow that. I do not see how the trustee can be excused for the breach of trust without being also excused for the omission referred to, or how he can be excused for the omission without also being excused for the breach of trust. If I am at liberty to guess, I should suppose that these words were added by way of amendment, and crept into the statute without due regard being had to the meaning of the context. The fact that a trustee has omitted to obtain the directions of the Court has never been held to be a ground for holding him personally liable, though it may be a reason guiding the Court in the matter of costs, or in deciding whether he has acted reasonably or otherwise, and especially so in these days when questions of difficulty, even as regards the legal estate, can be decided economically and expeditiously on originating summons. But if the Court comes to the conclusion that a trustee has acted reasonably, I cannot see how it can usefully proceed to consider, as an independent matter, the question whether he has or has not omitted to obtain the directions of the Court.

In **Re Stuart** [1897] 2 Ch 583, STIRLING J said at 590:

The effect of section 3 of the Judicial Trustees Act, 1896, appears to me to be this. The law as it stood at the passing of the Act is not altered, but a jurisdiction is given to the Court under special circumstances, the Court being satisfied as to the several matters mentioned in the section, to relieve the trustee of the consequences of a breach of trust as regards his personal liability. But the Court must first be satisfied that the trustee has acted honestly and reasonably. As to the honesty of the trustee in this case there is no question; but that is not the only condition to be satisfied, and the question arises whether the other conditions are satisfied. I quite agree that this section applies to a trustee making an improper investment of the trust funds as well as to any other breach of trust. This matter has been considered by Byrne J in *Re Turner* [1897] 1 Ch 536 at 542, where he says this:

> 'I think that the section relied on is meant to be acted upon freely and fairly in the exercise of judicial discretion, but I think that the Court ought to be satisfied, before exercising the very large powers conferred upon it, by sufficient evidence, that the trustee acted reasonably. I do not think that I have sufficient evidence in this case that he so acted; in fact, it does not appear from the letters that Mr. Turner acted in respect of this mortgage as he would probably have acted had it been a transaction of his own. I think that if he was—and he well may have been—a businesslike man, he would not, before lending his money, have been satisfied without some further inquiry as to the means of the mortgagor and as to the nature and value of the property upon which he was about to advance his money.'

That has since been approved by the Court of Appeal; and I willingly adopt what is there laid down as a guide to me in this matter. In my opinion the burden lies on the trustee who asks the Court to exercise the jurisdiction conferred by this section to shew that he has acted reasonably; and, certainly, it is fair in dealing with such a question to consider whether Mr. Box would have acted with reference to these investments as he did if he had been lending money of his own.

C IMPOUNDING A BENEFICIARY'S INTEREST[31]

TRUSTEE ACT 1925

62. Power to make beneficiary indemnify for breach of trust

(1) Where a trustee commits a breach of trust at the instigation or request or with the consent in writing of a beneficiary, the court may, if it thinks fit, make such order as to the court seems just, for impounding all or any part of the interest of the beneficiary in the trust estate by way of indemnity to the trustee or persons claiming through him.[32]

---

[31] H&M, pp. 673–674; Lewin, pp. 1623–1625; P&M, pp. 793–794; P&S, pp. 771–772; Pettit, pp. 537–538; Snell, pp. 680–681; T&H, p. 1065; U&H, pp. 1161–1163.

[32] As amended by the Married Women (Restraint upon Anticipation) Act 1949, s. 1(4) and Sch. 2.

(2) This section applies to breaches of trust committed as well before as after the commencement of this Act.

In **Re Somerset** [1894] 1 Ch 231, the trustees of a marriage settlement lent an excessive sum upon mortgage. They lent the money at the instigation, request, and consent in writing of the tenant for life, Mr. Somerset. When the security proved to be inadequate, Mr. Somerset and his infant children sued the trustees for breach of trust. Liability to the children was admitted, but the defendant trustees claimed, *inter alia*, that they were entitled to impound Somerset's life interest for the purposes of meeting the claim.

The Court of Appeal refused. Mr. Somerset, though approving the investment, had not intended to be a party to a breach of trust, and in effect left the trustees to determine whether the investment was a proper one for the sum advanced. LINDLEY MR said at 265:

Did the trustees commit the breach of trust for which they have been made liable at the instigation or request, or with the consent in writing of the Appellant? The section is intended to protect trustees, and ought to be construed so as to carry out that intention. But the section ought not, in my opinion, to be construed as if the word 'investment' had been inserted instead of 'breach of trust'. An enactment to that effect would produce great injustice in many cases. In order to bring a case within this section the *cestui que trust* must instigate, or request, or consent in writing to some act or omission which is itself a breach of trust, and not to some act or omission which only becomes a breach of trust by reason of want of care on the part of the trustees. If a *cestui que trust* instigates, requests, or consents in writing to an investment not in terms authorized by the power of investment, he clearly falls within the section; and in such a case his ignorance or forgetfulness of the terms of the power would not, I think, protect him—at all events, not unless he could give some good reason why it should, e.g., that it was caused by the trustee. But if all that a *cestui que trust* does is to instigate, request, or consent in writing to an investment which is authorized by the terms of the power, the case is, I think, very different. He has a right to expect that the trustees will act with proper care in making the investment, and if they do not they cannot throw the consequences on him unless they can shew that he instigated, requested, or consented in writing to their non-performance of their duty in this respect.

This is, in my opinion, the true construction of this section.

In **Re Pauling's Settlement Trusts (No 2)** [1963] Ch 576, Coutts and Co, the trustees of a family trust, were held liable for breach of trust in respect of a number of advances of capital to the children of the life tenant, Mrs. Younghusband. At first instance, Wilberforce J made his order without prejudice to any right which the defendant bank might have to impound the interests of any beneficiary during the lives of the wife and any surviving husband of hers. The bank claimed to be entitled to impound the life interest of Mrs. Younghusband. The plaintiffs sought the appointment of two new trustees in the place of the bank, who opposed this on the ground that such an appointment might negate their right to impound.

WILBERFORCE J appointed new trustees, holding that such an appointment would not imperil the defendants' right to impound. After dealing with a number of other matters, he said at 583:

Next I come to a separate series of objections which raise some difficult questions of law. The defendants, as I have already mentioned, have a claim to impound the life interest of Mrs. Younghusband now vested in the Guardian Assurance Co Ltd in order to recoup themselves against any money which they may be ordered to repay. What is said by the defendants is that that right to impound would be prejudiced if new trustees were appointed now and the trust fund handed over to them. That involves a consideration as to what is the nature of the right to impound which exists in favour of a trustee who has committed a breach of trust at the instigation of a beneficiary. I have to consider both the ordinary right which exists in equity apart from statute and also the further statutory right which has been conferred by section 62 of the Trustee Act, 1925, both of which are invoked by the defendants as plaintiffs in the Chancery action now pending. It seems to me that it is not possible to maintain, as is the defendants' contention here, that a trustee, having committed a breach of trust, is entitled to remain as a trustee until it has exercised its right to impound the income of the beneficiary in order to recoup itself. That seems to me an impossible proposition. It is quite true that, in the reported authorities, there is no case where the right to impound has been exercised by a former trustee as distinct from an existing trustee, but it seems to me in principle that it is impossible to contend that the right to impound is limited to the case where the trustee seeking the right is an actual trustee. The nature of the right to impound seems to me to turn on two things: first, that the money paid back to capital is in its origin the money of the trustee, and that when it comes to considering who should get the income of it, the trustee who has provided the money has a better right to it than the tenant for life who has instigated the breach of trust. The alternative way of putting the matter is that the trustee in breach of trust is in some way subrogated to the rights of the beneficiary. He stands in his position in order that he may be indemnified. That seems to me the way in which it was put by the Lords Justices in *Raby v Ridehalgh* (1855) 7 De GM & G 104. It does not seem to me that there is any support in authority or in principle for saying that the right depends upon the actual possession of the trust fund, and it appears to me that the analogy which has been sought to be drawn with the executor's right to retain is a false one and does not apply to this case. So much for the equitable right to impound as opposed to the statutory right.

As regards the statutory right, that depends on the language of section 62 of the Trustee Act, 1925, and at first sight it might look as if that right only exists in favour of a person who is actually a trustee. But, on consideration, that seems to me to be a misconstruction of the section. In the first place, the same objection against limiting the right in that way applies to the statutory jurisdiction. It seems to me an absurdity that it is required as a condition of exercising the right to obtain an impounding order, that the trustee who, *ex hypothesi*, is in breach of trust, must remain the trustee in order to acquire a right of indemnity. Further, it seems to me on the authorities, and, indeed, on the very terms of the section, that the section is giving an additional right, among other things, to deal with the case of a married woman beneficiary; that the statutory right is extending the equitable right and not limiting it, and that it is not right to read the section so as to apply only to a person who was formerly a trustee. The section begins with the words: 'where a trustee commits a breach of trust', thereby indicating that at the time the breach of trust is committed the person in question must be a trustee. Then further down in the section there is a reference to a trustee and that appears to me to be merely a reference back to the same person as the person who committed the breach of trust and not as an indication that the person in question must be a trustee at the date of the order. I would add to that, that here the writ which has been issued in the Chancery Division was issued at a time when the defendants were trustees, and, therefore, at the date of the writ the requirement of being a trustee was fulfilled. So that, although I entirely appreciate that the defendants may be anxious not to lose their right to impound the income of the tenant for life, that right could not, in my view, be prejudiced by appointing new trustees at this stage.

D   LIMITATION ACT AND LACHES[33]

(i) Time Limits

LIMITATION ACT 1980

2. Time limit for actions founded on tort

An action founded on tort shall not be brought after the expiration of six years from the date on which the cause of action accrued.

5. Time limit for actions founded on simple contract

An action founded on simple contract shall not be brought after the expiration of six years from the date on which the cause of action accrued.

21. Time limit for actions in respect of trust property

(1) No period of limitation prescribed by this Act shall apply to an action by a beneficiary under a trust, being an action—

    (a) in respect of any fraud or fraudulent breach of trust to which the trustee was a party or privy;[34] or

    (b) to recover from the trustee trust property or the proceeds of trust property in the possession of the trustee, or previously received by the trustee and converted to his use.[35]

---

[33] H&M, pp. 677–682; Lewin, pp. 1791–1850; P&M, pp. 778–785; P&S, pp. 762–768; Pettit, pp. 538–546; Snell, pp. 677–680; T&H, pp. 1069–1070; U&H, pp. 1125–1141; W. Swadling, 'Limitation' in *Breach of Trust* (eds. P. Birks and A. Pretto, 2002), pp. 319–351. See Cheshire and Burn, *Modern Law of Real Property* (17th edn, 2006), chap. 6; Preston and Newsom, *Limitation of Action* (4th edn, 1989), chap. 7; Franks, *Limitation of Actions* (1959), pp. 62–80; McGee, *Limitation Periods* (5th edn, 2006); Prime and Scanlan, *Modern Law of Limitation* (1993); (1989) CLJ 472 (H. McLean); *Tito v Waddell (No 2)* [1977] Ch 106 at 244–252; Law Reform Committee 21st Report (*Final Report on Limitation of Actions*) (1977) Cmnd 6923, pp. 53–54; Law Com. No. 270 (2001), paras. 2.39–2.45.

[34] *North American Land and Timber Co Ltd v Watkins* [1904] 1 Ch 242; *Thorne v Heard* [1894] 1 Ch 599; affd [1895] AC 495; *Armitage v Nurse* [1998] Ch 241 (deliberate but honest breach by trustees not fraud, fraud requires dishonesty). In *Cattley v Pollard* [2006] EWHC 3130 (Ch), [2007] Ch 353 it was held that this provision did not apply to claims for dishonest assistance in a breach of trust, where the normal six-year limitation period applied. See p. 982, below. But note *Statek Corp v Alford* [2008] EWHC 32 (Ch) where Evans–Lombe J held that the provision did apply to such accessorial liability.

[35] *Re Sharp* [1906] 1 Ch 793; *Re Howlett* [1949] Ch 767; *Wassell v Leggatt* [1896] 1 Ch 554; *Re Eyre-Williams* [1923] 2 Ch 533; *Re Clark* (1920) 150 LT Jo 94; *JJ Harrison (Properties) Ltd v Harrison* [2001] EWCA Civ 1467, [2002] 1 BCLC 162. See also *Re Landi* [1939] Ch 828; *Re Milking Pail Farm Trusts* [1940] Ch 996; (1941) 57 LQR 26 (R.E.M.); (1971) 35 Conv (NS) 6 (G. Battersby).

(2)[36] Where a trustee who is also a beneficiary under the trust receives or retains trust property or its proceeds as his share on a distribution of trust property under the trust, his liability in any action brought by virtue of subsection (1)(b) above to recover that property or its proceeds after the expiration of the period of limitation prescribed by this Act for bringing an action to recover trust property shall be limited to the excess over his proper share.

This subsection only applies if the trustee acted honestly and reasonably in making the distribution.

(3) Subject to the preceding provisions of this section, an action by a beneficiary to recover trust property or in respect of any breach of trust,[37] not being an action for which a period of limitation is prescribed by any other provision of this Act, shall not be brought after the expiration of six years from the date on which the right of action accrued.

For the purposes of this subsection, the right of action shall not be treated as having accrued to any beneficiary entitled to a future interest in the trust property until the interest fell into possession.[38]

(4) No beneficiary as against whom there would be a good defence under this Act shall derive any greater or other benefit from a judgment or order obtained by any other beneficiary than he could have obtained if he had brought the action and this Act had been pleaded in defence.

22. Time limit for actions claiming personal estate of a deceased person[39]

Subject to section 21 (1) and (2) of this Act—

(a) no action in respect of any claim to the personal estate of a deceased person or to any share or interest in any such estate (whether under a will or on intestacy) shall be brought after the expiration of twelve years from the date on which the right to receive the share or interest accrued; and

(b) no action to recover arrears of interest in respect of any legacy, or damages in respect of such arrears, shall be brought after the expiration of six years from the date on which the interest became due.

23. Time limit in respect of actions for an account

An action for an account shall not be brought after the expiration of any time limit under the Act which is applicable to the claim which is the basis of the duty to account.

---

[36] S. 21(2) was added by Limitation Amendment Act 1980, s. 5(1).

[37] In *Tito v Waddell (No 2)* [1977] Ch 106 at 249, Megarry J concluded that this provision did not apply to situations governed by the self-dealing and fair-dealing rules applicable to trustees. Those cases are covered by the doctrine of *laches*. See p. 886, below.

[38] *Re Somerset* [1894] 1 Ch 231; *Re Pauling's Settlement Trusts* [1964] Ch 303 [p. 889, below]; *A-G v Cocke* [1988] Ch 414 (s. 21(3) does not apply to an action by the A-G to enforce a charitable trust for the benefit of the public at large; nor where there is no claim for any recovery of trust property or allegation of breach of trust); [1988] Conv 292 (J. Warburton); [1988] All ER Rev 183 (P.J. Clarke); *Armitage v Nurse* [1998] Ch 241 (beneficiary under discretionary trust held not to have interest in possession for purposes of s. 21(3)).

[39] *Re Loftus* [2005] 2 All ER 700; [2006] Conv 245 (T. Prime).

36. Equitable jurisdiction and remedies

(1) The following time limits under this Act, that is to say—

   (a) the time limit under section 2 for actions founded on tort;

   (b) the time limit under section 5 for actions founded on simple contract;

shall not apply to any claim for specific performance of a contract or for an injunction or for any other equitable relief, except in so far as any such time limit may be applied by the court by analogy in like manner as the corresponding time limit under any enactment repealed by the Limitation Act 1939 was applied before 1st July 1940.

(2) Nothing in this Act shall affect any equitable jurisdiction to refuse relief on the ground of acquiescence or otherwise.

For the definition of a trustee, see the Limitation Act 1980, section 38(1); Trustee Act 1925, section 68(17). It includes personal representatives, certain fiduciary agents: *Burdick v Garrick* (1870) 5 Ch App 233, company directors: *Re Lands Allotment Co* [1894] 1 Ch 616; *Belmont Finance Corpn v Williams Furniture Ltd (No 2)* [1980] 1 All ER 393; a mortgagee in respect of the proceeds of sale: *Thorne v Heard* [1895] AC 495, but not a trustee in bankruptcy: *Re Cornish* [1896] 1 QB 99, nor the liquidator of a company in voluntary liquidation: *Re Windsor Steam Coal Co (1901) Ltd* [1928] Ch 609; affd [1929] 1 Ch 151. The definition also applies to implied and constructive trusts.[40]

(ii) Constructive Trusts and Breach of Fiduciary Duty

The application of the Limitation Act 1980 to constructive trusts and breach of fiduciary duty has recently been explored by the courts.

(a) Constructive Trusts

In **Paragon Finance v D B Thakerar and Co** [1999] 1 All ER 400, the defendant solicitor acted for both the plaintiff mortgage lender and the borrower. The defendant was required to inform the plaintiff of any sub-sale but failed to do so, even though the defendant was aware that the borrowers were sub-purchasers who were purporting to buy properties at prices which were much higher than that for which they had been sold to the original purchasers. The reason for this was that the borrowers were involved in a mortgage fraud. The plaintiffs sued the defendant *inter alia* for fraudulent breach of duty. One of the issues before the court concerned the appropriate limitation period for this type of claim. MILLETT LJ said at 408:

The plaintiffs submit that section 21(1)(a) of the 1980 Act taken with the extended definition of the words 'trust' and 'trustee' has the effect of excluding the application of any period of limitation to their claim for breach of this constructive trust. They say that it is irrelevant that

[40] In *James v Williams* [2000] Ch 1 [p. 287, above], an executor *de son tort* who held property on a constructive trust was held to be a trustee within s. 21(1)(b).

the trust in question had no independent existence apart from the fraud but is rather equity's response to the fraud. They submit that, if such a fact was ever relevant, it ceased to be so after the passing of the 1939 Act. This makes it necessary to consider the antecedent law and the effect of the 1939 Act.

Before 1890, when the Trustee Act 1888 came into operation, a claim against an express trustee was never barred by lapse of time. The Court of Chancery had developed the rule that, in the absence of laches or acquiescence, such a trustee was accountable without limit of time. The rule was confirmed by section 25(3) of the Supreme Court of Judicature Act 1873, which provided that no claim by a *cestui que trust* against his trustee for any property held on an express trust, or in respect of any breach of such trust, should be held to be barred by any statute of limitation.

The explanation for the rule was that the possession of an express trustee is never in virtue of any right of his own but is taken from the first for and on behalf of the beneficiaries. His possession was consequently treated as the possession of the beneficiaries, with the result that time did not run in his favour against them: see the classic judgment of Lord Redesdale in *Hovenden v Lord Annesley* (1806) 2 Sch & Lef 607 at 633–634.

The rule did not depend upon the nature of the trustee's appointment, and it was applied to trustees *de son tort* and to directors and other fiduciaries who though not strictly trustees, were in an analogous position and who abused the trust and confidence reposed in them to obtain their principal's property for themselves. Such persons are properly described as constructive trustees.

Regrettably, however, the expressions 'constructive trust' and 'constructive trustee' have been used by equity lawyers to describe two entirely different situations. The first covers those cases already mentioned, where the defendant, though not expressly appointed as trustee, has assumed the duties of a trustee by a lawful transaction which was independent of and preceded the breach of trust and is not impeached by the plaintiff. The second covers those cases where the trust obligation arises as a direct consequence of the unlawful transaction which is impeached by the plaintiff.[41] ...

The constructive trust on which the plaintiffs seek to rely is of the second kind. The defendants were fiduciaries, and held the plaintiffs' money on a resulting trust for them pending completion of the sub-purchase. But the plaintiffs cannot establish and do not rely upon a breach of this trust. They allege that the money which was obtained from them and which would otherwise have been subject to it was obtained by fraud and they seek to raise a constructive trust in their own favour in its place.

The importance of the distinction between the two categories of constructive trust lies in the application of the statutes of limitation. Before 1890 constructive trusts of the first kind were treated in the same way as express trusts and were often confusingly described as such; claims against the trustee were not barred by the passage of time. Constructive trusts of the second kind however were treated differently. They were not in reality trusts at all, but merely a remedial mechanism by which equity gave relief for fraud. The Court of Chancery, which applied the statutes of limitation by analogy, was not misled by its own terminology; it gave effect to the reality of the situation by applying the statute to the fraud which gave rise to the defendant's liability: see *Soar v Ashwell* [1893] 2 QB 390 at 393 *per* Lord Esher MR:

'If the breach of the legal relation relied on ... makes, in the view of a Court of Equity, the defendant a trustee for the plaintiff, the Court of Equity treats the defendant as a trustee ... by construction,

41 See p. 280, above.

and the trust is called a constructive trust; and against the breach which by construction creates the trust the Court of Equity allows Statutes of Limitation to be vouched.'

Lord Esher MR's reference to the breach of the legal relation shows that while the first kind of constructive trust was a creature of equity's exclusive jurisdiction the second arose in the exercise of its concurrent jurisdiction. That is why the statute was applied by analogy....

For a fuller discussion of the distinction between the two categories of constructive trust, see *Hovenden v Lord Annesley* (1806) 2 Sch & Lef 607 at 632–633, *Taylor v Davies* [1920] AC 636; *Clarkson v Davies* [1923] AC 100; *Selangor United Rubber Estates Ltd v Cradock (No 3)* [1968] 1 WLR 1555 and *Competitive Insurance Co Ltd v Davies Investments Ltd* [1975] 1 WLR 1240.

It was evidently considered unduly harsh that trustees should remain liable indefinitely for innocent breaches of trust when even common law actions for fraud were barred after six years, and section 8 of the 1888 Act introduced a period of limitation (effectively six years) for such claims. Its purpose was to provide protection for trustees who would otherwise be liable without limitation of time (laches and acquiescence apart) where the breach of trust was committed innocently: see *Re Richardson* [1920] 1 Ch 423 at 440. It excepted two cases from its provisions: (i) where the claim was founded upon any fraud or fraudulent breach of trust to which the trustee was part or privy, and (ii) where the proceeds were still retained by the trustee or had previously been received by the trustee and converted to his use. The same scheme was adopted by section 19 of the 1939 Act and section 21 of the 1980 Act....

Had the present case occurred before 1940, therefore, the defendants could have pleaded a limitation defence to the claim based on constructive trust. The question is whether the distinction between the two kinds of constructive trust survived the passing of the 1939 Act, section 19 of which was in virtually the same terms as section 21 of the 1980 Act, and both of which adopted the definition of 'trust' and 'trustee' in the 1925 Act....

I question whether so many different remedies should continue to be available for the same misapplication of property. They make proceedings of the present kind unnecessarily complex. But whatever the answer to this question, the present problem is a semantic one. The defendants cannot sensibly be described as constructive trustees at all. The expression is used in its remedial sense, though not in the sense in which it is used in the United States and Canada, where it is the basis of a discretionary proprietary remedy; in cases like the present a plaintiff is necessarily confined to a personal remedy. Before the Supreme Court of Judicature Act 1873 the expression was a catch-phrase which was employed by the Court of Chancery to justify the exercise of equity's concurrent jurisdiction in cases of fraud. 125 years later it is surely time to discard it. If we cannot bring ourselves to discard it, at least we can resolve not to take it literally.

In **Coulthard v Disco Mix Club Ltd** [2000] 1 WLR 707, the plaintiff, Coulthard, claimed that the defendant, DMC, had failed to account for moneys obtained through the exploitation of the plaintiff's 'mega-mixes' and these moneys were consequently held on constructive trust for the plaintiff. JUDGE JULES SHER QC said at 731:

There are however two distinct types of constructive trust. The first example is where the constructive trustee, although not expressly appointed as a trustee, has assumed the duties of a trustee before the events which are alleged to constitute the breach of trust. In that case he really is a trustee: he receives the trust property as the result of a transaction by which both parties intend to create a trust from the outset. The second type of constructive trust is merely the creation by the court by way of a suitable remedy to meet the wrongdoing alleged: there is no real trust and usually no chance of a proprietary remedy: the defendant is said to be liable to account as a constructive trustee. The trust is nothing more than a formula for equitable relief: *Selangor United Rubber Estates Ltd v Cradock (No 3)* [1968] 1 WLR 1555 at 1582.

The practical importance of the distinction lies in the application of the statutes of limitation. Before the Trustee Act 1888 a constructive trust of the second kind, which I shall refer to as the 'remedial constructive trust', was not treated like a real trust, where there was no question of limitation at all. The statute was applied to the wrongdoing which gave rise to the defendant's liability as constructive trustee: *Soar v Ashwell* [1893] 2 QB 390 at 393.

The present section 21 had its origin in section 8 of the 1888 Act and, despite the fact that section 1(3) of the 1888 Act defined a trustee as including a trustee whose trust arises by construction or implication of law, the constructive trustee under a remedial constructive trust was still held to be able to rely on the limitation defence: see *Taylor v Davies* [1920] AC 636 and *Clarkson v Davies* [1923] AC 100. There has been a great deal of academic controversy as to whether that position survived the passing of the 1939 Act. The view of Millett LJ in *Paragon Finance plc v D B Thakerar & Co* was that there are formidable arguments why it did survive. Those arguments, which are set out in his judgment in the *Paragon Finance* case, seem to me to be absolutely correct. In a nutshell and in Millett LJ's words ([1999] 1 All ER 400 at 414):

'There is a case for treating fraudulent breach of trust differently from other frauds, but only if what is involved really is a breach of trust. There is no case for distinguishing between an action for damages for fraud at common law and its counterpart in equity based on the same facts merely because equity employs the formula of constructive trust to justify the exercise of the equitable jurisdiction.'

... What *Paragon Finance plc v D B Thakerar & Co* makes clear is that the critical boundary in these cases lies between those cases where the defendant is a true trustee (be it of an express trust or a constructive trust) and those where he is not....

The touchstone of a true trusteeship is trust property. There is no allegation or evidence (save possibly in two minor respects) that DMC was required to keep moneys reaching it as a result of commercial exploitation of Mr. Coulthard's mixes separate from its own moneys. Everything in the pleading and evidence is consistent with the idea that DMC was free to mix such moneys with its own and then account at some later point in time to Mr. Coulthard, after deduction of the appropriate commission. In its essence the commercial relationship engendered personal claims between them rather than proprietary ones. At no stage in Mr. Coulthard's pleading or evidence is an asset or fund identified as an asset or fund which is or should have been held in a trustee capacity. That is why this dispute attracts the application of the six-year limit under section 5 of the 1980 Act, directly or by analogy. Had there been a true trust of property alleged, the relevant section would have been section 21; and to the extent to which there was fraud, or a receipt by the trustee and conversion to his use, there would not have been any limitation defence.[42]

(b) Breach of Fiduciary Duty

In **Coulthard v Disco Mix Club Ltd** [2000] 1 WLR 707, the plaintiff, Coulthard, also sued the defendant, DMC, for deliberate and dishonest breach of fiduciary duty. The

---

[42] See also *Cattley v Pollard* [2006] EWHC 3130 (Ch), [2007] Ch 353.

key question for the court was whether there was a limitation period for such claims and, if so, what it was. JUDGE JULES SHER QC said at 729:

> [The issue is] whether the time limits under the 1980 Act would be applied by analogy by virtue of section 36 of the 1980 Act to the claims in breach of fiduciary duty pleaded in this case. That section provides that the statutory time limits (for example, the six years for breach of contract) shall not apply to equitable relief except in so far as they may be applied by the court by analogy 'in like manner as the corresponding time limit under any enactment repealed by the Limitation Act 1939 was applied before 1st July 1940'.
>
> The best description of the circumstances in which the court of equity acted by analogy to the statute is, I think, contained in the speech of Lord Westbury in *Knox v Gye* (1872) LR 5 HL 656 at 674–675:
>
>> 'The general principle was laid down as early as the case of *Lockey v Lockey* (1719) Prec Ch 518), where it was held that where a Court of Equity assumes a concurrent jurisdiction with Courts of Law no account will be given after the legal limit of six years, if the statute be pleaded. If it could be doubted whether the executor of a deceased partner can, at Common Law, have an action of account against the surviving partner, the result will still be the same because a Court of Equity, in affording such a remedy and giving such an account, would act by analogy to the *Statute of Limitations.* For where the remedy in Equity is correspondent to the remedy at Law, and the latter is subject to a limit in point of time by the *Statute of Limitations,* a Court of Equity acts by analogy to the statute, and imposes on the remedy it affords the same limitation. This is the meaning of the common phrase, that a Court of Equity acts by analogy to the *Statute of Limitations,* the meaning being, that where the suit in Equity corresponds with an action at Law which is included in the words of the statute, a Court of Equity adopts the enactment of the statute as its own rule of procedure. But if any proceeding in Equity be included within the words of the statute, there a Court of Equity, like a Court of Law, acts in obedience to the statute ... Where a Court of Equity frames its remedy upon the basis of the Common Law, and supplements the Common Law by extending the remedy to parties who cannot have an action at Common Law, there the Court of Equity acts in analogy to the statute; that is, it adopts the statute as the rule of procedure regulating the remedy it affords.'
>
> Two things emerge from these passages. First, where the court of equity was simply exercising a concurrent jurisdiction giving the same relief as was available in a court of law the statute of limitation would be applied. But, secondly, even if the relief afforded by the court of equity was wider than that available at law the court of equity would apply the statute by analogy where there was 'correspondence' between the remedies available at law or in equity.
>
> Now, in my judgment, the true breaches of fiduciary duty, i.e. the allegations of deliberate and dishonest under-accounting, are based on the same factual allegations as the common law claims of fraud. The breaches of fiduciary duty are thus no more than the equitable counterparts of the claims at common law. The court of equity, in granting relief for such breaches would be exercising a concurrent jurisdiction with that of the common law. I have little doubt but that to such a claim the statute would have been applied.
>
> Mr. Bate argues that the court of equity will apply the statute by analogy only where the equitable remedy is being sought in support of a legal right or the court of equity is being asked to decide a purely legal right, and he cites passages from *Hicks v Sallit* (1854) 3 De GM & G 782 and *Hovenden v Lord Annesley* (1806) 2 Sch & Lef 607. I have no doubt that the principles of application by analogy to the statute (or, in obedience to the statute, as Lord Redesdale LC preferred to describe it in its application to the facts of *Hovenden's* case), are quite apposite in

the situations envisaged by Mr. Bate. But, in my judgment, they have a much wider scope than that: one could scarcely imagine a more correspondent set of remedies as damages for fraudulent breach of contract and equitable compensation for breach of fiduciary duty in relation to the same factual situation, namely, the deliberate withholding of money due by a manager to his artist. It would have been a blot on our jurisprudence if those selfsame facts gave rise to a time bar in the common law courts but none in the court of equity.

I have been greatly assisted in reaching the conclusion I have by the decision of the Court of Appeal in *Paragon Finance plc v D B Thakerar & Co* [1999] 1 All ER 400, sent to me by counsel after the hearing. Ebsworth J came to a different conclusion in *Kershaw v Whelan (No 2)* (1997) The Times, 10 February, but the judge based herself firmly on *Nelson v Rye* [1996] 1 WLR 1378 and did not have the benefit, as I have had, of the judgments of the Court of Appeal in the *Paragon Finance* case, which disapprove *Nelson v Rye*. I am happy to come to what seems to me to be the sensible conclusion that no distinction in point of limitation can be made between an action for damages for fraud at common law and its counterpart in equity based on the same facts. I should note in closing on this aspect that, of course, if there was any allegation of fraud or deliberate concealment which had not been discovered by Mr. Coulthard before the inception of the period of six years before action, the matter would be wholly different. There is no such allegation here. On his own evidence Mr. Coulthard had discovered, more than six years before action, the facts giving rise to the alleged dishonesty.

In **Cia de Seguros Imperio v Health (REBX) Ltd** [2001] 1 WLR 112, the claimant sued the defendant for breach of fiduciary duty and sought equitable compensation. CLARKE LJ said at 124:

I agree with Waller LJ that the outcome of the appeal turns on the correct application of section 36(1) of the Limitation Act 1980 to the facts of this case. The time limits in sections 2 and 5 of the Act do not apply directly. The claim with which the appeal is concerned is based on alleged breaches of fiduciary duty on the part of the defendant to act in what it honestly believed to be the best interests of the plaintiff. It was originally described in the prayer to the points of claim as a claim for damages. Detailed analysis of the position has revealed that the basis of the claim is equitable and that the claim is one for compensation. It was, however, no doubt described as a claim for damages because that is what, in truth, it is. As Waller LJ has put it, the reality of the claim is that it is a claim for damages which would be assessed in the same way as a claim for damages at common law. As I see it, it is a claim for equitable compensation, but not the kind of equitable compensation which may be awarded in lieu of rescission or specific restitution.

As a claim for equitable relief, it falls within the expression 'other equitable relief' in section 36(1) of the 1980 Act, which thus provides, so far as relevant, that the time limits in sections 2 and 5 shall not apply—

'except in so far as any such time limit may be applied by the court by analogy in like manner as the corresponding time limit under any enactment repealed by the Limitation Act 1939 was applied before 1 July 1940'.

It is not in dispute that the Limitation Act 1939 repealed statutes which contained similar provisions to sections 2 and 5 of the Act of 1980. It follows, as I see it, that those time limits may be applied by analogy 'in like manner' as those time limits were applied.

I agree with Waller LJ that that cannot mean that it is necessary to find an identical case decided before 1940 in which a court of equity in fact applied a previous statute by analogy. The section cannot, to my mind, have been intended to be read so narrowly. It must mean that the court is to have power to apply sections 2 and 5 by analogy in the kind of case in which equity would have done the same. In such a case the court will be applying the provision by analogy 'in like manner as the corresponding time limit...was applied before 1 July, 1940'. The correct approach is to identify if possible the principle which the courts of equity adopted and to apply a similar principle now.

I would certainly have expected a court of equity to apply the common law time limits by analogy on the facts of this case. As Waller LJ has pointed out, and as the judge demonstrated by a detailed analysis of the points of claim, the essential nature of the pleaded case is the same whether it is put as damages for breach of contract, damages for breach of duty or damages (or compensation) for breach of fiduciary duty. The only additional element is the defendant's alleged intention, which on the facts here adds nothing of substance to the claim for damages. Indeed it would be quite unnecessary to include this claim if it were not thought necessary to do so in order to advance the time-bar argument....

...there is a sufficient close similarity between the exclusive equitable right in question, namely the claim for compensation for breach of fiduciary duty, and the legal rights to which the statute applies—namely the claim for damages for breach of contract founded on simple contract and the claim in tort for damages for breach of duty—that a court of equity would (and will) ordinarily act on the statute of limitation by analogy. There is nothing in the particular circumstances of the case to make it unjust to do so. On the contrary, it is just to do so because there is no reason why, if the claims for damages for breach of contract and tort are time-barred, the claim for damages for breach of fiduciary duty should not be time-barred also.

(iii) Extension and Postponement of Time Limits

LIMITATION ACT 1980

28. Extension of limitation period in case of disability

   (1) Subject to the following provisions of this section, if on the date when any right of action accrued for which a period of limitation is prescribed by this Act, the person to whom it accrued was under a disability, the action may be brought at any time before the expiration of six years from the date when he ceased to be under a disability or died (whichever first occurred) notwithstanding that the period of limitation has expired.

   (2) This section shall not affect any case where the right of action first accrued to some person (not under a disability) through whom the person under a disability claims.

   (3) When a right of action which has accrued to a person under a disability accrues, on the death of that person while still under a disability, to another person under a disability, no further extension of time shall be allowed by reason of the disability of the second person.

   (4) No action to recover land or money charged on land shall be brought by virtue of this section by any person after the expiration of thirty years from the date on which the right of action accrued to that person or some person through whom he claims.

32. Postponement of limitation period in case of fraud, concealment or mistake[43]

(1) Subject to subsection (3) below, where in the case of any action for which a period of limitation is prescribed by this Act, either—

 (a) the action is based upon the fraud of the defendant;[44] or

 (b) any fact relevant to the plaintiff's right of action has been deliberately concealed from him by the defendant;[45] or

 (c) the action is for relief from the consequences of a mistake;

the period of limitation shall not begin to run until the plaintiff has discovered the fraud, concealment or mistake (as the case may be) or could with reasonable diligence have discovered it.[46]

References in this subsection to the defendant include references to the defendant's agent and to any person through whom the defendant claims and his agent.

(2) For the purposes of subsection (1) above, deliberate commission of a breach of duty in circumstances in which it is unlikely to be discovered for some time amounts to deliberate concealment of the facts involved in that breach of duty.

(3) Nothing in this section shall enable any action—

 (a) to recover, or recover the value of, any property, or

 (b) to enforce any charge against, or set aside any transaction affecting, any property;

to be brought against the purchaser of the property or any person claiming through him in any case where the property has been purchased for valuable consideration by an innocent third party since the fraud or concealment or (as the case may be) the transaction in which the mistake was made took place.

(4) A purchaser is an innocent third party for the purposes of this section—

 (a) in the case of fraud or concealment of any fact relevant to the plaintiff's right of action, if he was not a party to the fraud or (as the case may be) to the concealment of that fact and did not at the time of the purchase know or have reason to believe that the fraud or concealment had taken place; and

 (b) in the case of mistake, if he did not at the time of the purchase know or have reason to believe that the mistake had been made.

As regards the question of when the claimant could with reasonable diligence have discovered the fraud, MILLETT LJ said in **Paragon Finance v D B Thakerar & Co** [1999] 1 All ER 400 at 418:

The question is not whether the plaintiffs *should* have discovered the fraud sooner; but whether they *could* with reasonable diligence have done so. The burden of proof is on them. They

---

[43] See Cheshire and Burn, *Modern Law of Real Property* (17th edn, 2006), pp. 140–141.

[44] *Cattley v Pollard* [2006] EWHC 3130 (Ch), [2007] Ch 353.

[45] In *Bartlett v Barclays Bank Trust Co Ltd* [1980] Ch 515 at 537, the trustee unsuccessfully pleaded the forerunner of paragraph (b) (Limitation Act 1939, s. 26(b)). 'There was no cover-up by the bank. The bank had no inkling that it was acting in breach of trust', *per* Brightman J.

[46] See *Peco Arts Inc v Hazlitt Gallery Ltd* [1983] 1 WLR 1315.

must establish that they *could not* have discovered the fraud without exceptional measures which they could not reasonably have been expected to take. In this context the length of the applicable period of limitation is irrelevant. In the course of argument May LJ observed that reasonable diligence must be measured against some standard, but that the six-year limitation period did not provide the relevant standard. He suggested that the test was how a person carrying on a business of the relevant kind would act if he had adequate but not unlimited staff and resources and were motivated by a reasonable but not excessive sense of urgency. I respectfully agree.

An assignee, with notice, from a trustee is in the same position as the trustee was. In **Eddis v Chichester Constable** [1969] 2 Ch 345,[47] a tenant for life of a painting attributed to Caravaggio sold it in 1951, through the agency of one Mrs. Blois, to an art consortium who resold it in 1952 to the William Rockhill Nelson Gallery of Art, Kansas City, Missouri, USA. In 1963 the tenant for life died and the trustees for the first time became aware of the absence of the painting. In 1966 they sued the representative of the tenant for life for breach of trust and the art consortium for conversion. The Limitation Act 1939 was pleaded.

The main question was whether, assuming that the trustees' right of action was concealed by the fraud of the tenant for life, section 26[48] prevented time from running against the trustees in favour of the art consortium. The Court of Appeal, affirming GOFF J, held that time did not run against the trustees until the fraud was discovered.

(iv) Laches and Acquiescence[49]

LIMITATION ACT 1980

36. Acquiescence

(2) Nothing in this Act shall affect any equitable jurisdiction to refuse relief on the ground of acquiescence or otherwise.[50]

In **Nelson v Rye** [1996] 1 WLR 1378, LADDIE J said[51] at 1382:

It can be misleading to approach the equitable defences of laches and acquiescence as if they consisted of a series of precisely defined hurdles over each of which a litigant must struggle before the defence is made out.

---

[47] See also *Re Dixon* [1900] 2 Ch 561; *Re Eyre-Williams* [1923] 2 Ch 533; *GL Baker Ltd v Medway Building and Supplies Ltd* [1958] 1 WLR 1216.   [48] Now Limitation Act 1980, s. 32.

[49] G. Watt, '*Laches*, Estoppel and Election' in *Breach of Trust* (eds. P. Birks and A. Pretto, 2002), pp. 353–377.

[50] Thus preserving the doctrine of *laches*. See Cheshire and Burn, *Modern Law of Real Property* (17th edn, 2006), pp. 133–135; Brunyate, *Limitation of Actions in Equity*, (1932), chap. 7.

[51] The judge's decision that the Limitation Act 1980 did not apply to a claim founded on a breach of fiduciary duty was subsequently rejected in *Paragon Finance plc v D B Thakerar and Co* [1999] 1 All ER 400 [p. 883, above]. The dictum of Laddie J, although inapposite on the facts, remains a valid statement of the doctrine of *laches*.

[His Lordship cited *Lindsay Petroleum Co v Hurd* (1874) LR 5 PC 221 at 239, 240, and *Erlanger v New Sombrero Phosphate Co* (1878) 3 App Cas 1218 at 1279–1280, *per* Lord Blackburn, and continued:] So here, these defences are not technical or arbitrary. The courts have indicated over the years some of the factors which must be taken into consideration in deciding whether the defence runs. Those factors include the period of the delay, the extent to which the defendant's position has been prejudiced by the delay, and the extent to which that prejudice was caused by the actions of the plaintiff. I accept that mere delay alone will almost never suffice, but the court has to look at all the circumstances, including in particular those factors set out above, and then decide whether the balance of justice or injustice is in favour of granting the remedy or withholding it. If substantial prejudice will be suffered by the defendant, it is not necessary for the defendant to prove that it was caused by the delay. On the other hand, the plaintiff's knowledge that the delay will cause such prejudice is a factor to be taken into account. With these considerations in mind, I turn to the facts.

His Lordship held that the defences succeeded largely due to the plaintiff's wilful refusal to involve himself in his financial affairs.

In **Re Loftus** [2006] EWCA Civ 1124, [2007] 1 WLR 591, CHADWICK LJ said at para. 42:

The inquiry should require a broad approach, directed to ascertaining whether it would in all the circumstances be unconscionable for a party to be permitted to assert his beneficial right.[52]

(v) Law Reform

In **Cia de Seguros Imperio v Heath (REBX) Ltd** [2001] 1 WLR 112, SIR CHRISTOPHER STAUGHTON LJ said at 124:

It seems to me unfortunate that the claimant, an insurance company in Portugal, should have to endure a prolonged and expensive contest as to the rules of equity as they were 60 years ago and more. And all that for the purpose of determining whether claims that arose before September 1989 are time-barred.

It is not obvious to me why it is still necessary to have special rules for the limitation of claims for specific performance, or an injunction, or other equitable relief. And if it is still necessary to do so, I do not see any merit in continuing to define the circumstances where a particular claim will be time-barred by reference to what happened, or might have happened, more than 60 years ago. If a distinction still has to be drawn between common law and equitable claims for limitation purposes, I would hope that a revised statute will enact with some precision where that distinction should be drawn, rather than leave it to the product of researches into cases decided long ago.

The Law Commission (No. 270, 2001) has considered the form of the law on limitation periods in their application to claims for breach of trust and has made the following recommendations:

---

[52] *Cattley v Pollard* [2006] EWHC 3130 (Ch), [2007] Ch 353, paras. 151–157 (Richard Sheldon QC).

Law Commission No 270, 2001: *Limitation of Actions*, pp. 201–202, 204, 211–212

(1) The primary limitation period should start to run from the 'date of knowledge' rather than, for example, the date the cause of action accrues.

(2) The date of knowledge (which is when the primary limitation period should start to run) should be the date when the claimant has (actual or constructive) knowledge of the following facts:—

(a) the facts which give rise to the cause of action;

(b) the identity of the defendant; and

(c) where injury, loss or damage has occurred or a benefit has been received, that the injury, loss, damage or benefit are significant.

(3) For the purposes of the definition of the date of knowledge, a claimant will be deemed to know that the injury, loss, damage or benefit is significant if

(a) the claimant knows the full extent of the injury, loss, damage suffered by the claimant (or any other relevant person), or (in relation to a claim for restitution) of any benefit obtained by the defendant (or any other relevant person); or

(b) a reasonable person would think that, on the assumption that the defendant does not dispute liability and is able to satisfy a judgment, a civil claim was worth making in respect of the injury, loss, damage or benefit concerned.

(5) 'Actual knowledge' should not be defined in the proposed legislation and should be treated as a straightforward issue of fact which does not require elaboration.

(6) The claimant should be considered to have constructive knowledge of the relevant facts when the claimant in his or her circumstances and with his or her abilities ought reasonably to have known of the relevant facts.

(7) Unless the claimant has acted unreasonably in not seeking advice from an expert, the claimant should not be treated as having constructive knowledge of any fact which an expert might have acquired. Where an expert has been consulted, the claimant will not be deemed to have constructive knowledge of any information which the expert either acquired, but failed to communicate to the claimant, or failed to acquire.

(15) The primary limitation period applying under the core regime should be three years.

(16) A claim, other than in respect of a personal injury, should be subject to a long-stop limitation period of ten years.

(54) Subject to our recommendations in paragraph 56 below all claims for breach of trust should be subject to the core regime.

(55) Claims to recover trust property should be subject to the core regime; but in the case of a claim for the recovery of trust property held on a bare trust, the cause of action shall not accrue unless and until the trustee acts in breach of trust.

(56) Legislation should provide that where a claim by one beneficiary has become time-barred, that beneficiary should not be permitted to benefit from a successful claim by another beneficiary whose claim is not time-barred.

Pursuant to the application of the core regime, there is no need to provide a trustee with protection equivalent to that which is currently found in Limitation Act 1980, section 21(2).[53]

Neither the primary limitation period nor the long-stop limitation period should apply to claims for breach of trust or to recover trust property which are brought by either the Attorney-General or the Charity Commissioners.

(57) Neither the primary limitation period nor the long-stop limitation period in respect of a claim for breach of trust or to recover trust property by a beneficiary with a future or contingent interest will start until that interest has fallen into possession.

(58) The core regime should apply to claims in respect of the personal estate of a deceased person (including any claims in respect of a claim to arrears of interest on legacies).

E SUMMARY

The various forms of protection of trustees were before the Court of Appeal in **Re Pauling's Settlement Trusts** [1964] Ch 303.[54] Commander and Mrs. Younghusband were married in 1919; their marriage settlement contained in clause 11 a power of advancement for the trustees, Coutts & Co, to raise, with the written consent of Mrs. Younghusband, any part not exceeding one-half of the expectant or presumptive or vested share of any child of the wife, and to pay to him for his own absolute use, or advancement, or benefit, in such manner as the trustees should think fit. Between 1948 and 1954 the trustees made a number of advancements to the four children who, on some, though not every, occasion, received independent legal advice as to their rights under the settlement. The mother's consent was obtained in every case.

In 1954, as a result of a scheme of one son's for avoiding Estate Duty on his mother's death, the children first became aware that the advancements might have been in breach of trust. In 1958 they brought an action against the trustees claiming £29,160, on the ground that this sum had been improperly paid out by way of advancement to beneficiaries who were presumed to be subject to undue influence and who were not emancipated from parental control.

WILLMER LJ said at 338:

The bank also rely for relief from the consequences of any breach of trust upon section 61 of the Trustee Act, 1925. At this stage all we propose to say is that it would be a misconstruction of the section to say it does not apply to professional trustees, but, as was pointed out in the Judicial Committee of the Privy Council in *National Trustees Company of Australasia Ltd v General Finance Company of Australasia Ltd* [1905] AC 373 at 381 '... without saying that the remedial provisions of the section should never be applied to a trustee in the position of the appellants, their Lordships think it is a circumstance to be taken into account...' Where a banker undertakes to act as a paid trustee of a settlement created by a customer, and so

---

53 See p. 877, above.
54 See J. Payne, 'Consent' in *Breach of Trust* (eds. P. Birks and A. Pretto, 2002), pp. 298–318.

deliberately places itself in a position where its duty as trustee conflicts with its interest as a banker, we think that the court should be very slow to relieve such a trustee under the provisions of the section.

We propose to deal with the bank's plea of the Limitation Act 1939 and the pleas of laches, acquiescence and delay when we have considered the detailed transactions. It only remains to state that the question of law on which this case was reported in the court below, *Re Pauling's Settlement Trusts* [1962] 1 WLR 86, has not been argued before us, and many of the cases there cited have not been cited to us. Mr. Bagnall, however, accepts as accurate the proposition that

> 'The result of these authorities appears to me [Wilberforce J] to be that the court has to consider all the circumstances in which the concurrence of the *cestui que trust* was given with a view to seeing whether it is fair and equitable that, having given his concurrence, he should afterwards turn round and sue the trustees: that, subject to this, it is not necessary that he should know that what he is concurring in is a breach of trust, provided that he fully understands what he is concurring in, and that it is not necessary that he should himself have directly benefited by the breach of trust [1962] 1 WLR 86 at 108.'

We express no opinion on it.

[His Lordship then dealt with the impugned transactions *seriatim*. **Upjohn LJ** continued the reading of the judgment of the court, and, on the question of undue influence, said at 347:] At the time of this advance the son George was 23 years old. He had done his military service, and was up at Cambridge. The judge thought him an exceptionally able young man, well acquainted with his rights, and able to take care of himself. He had no separate advice about this £2,000 advance, but he had been advised about the Hodson loan transaction, and in the course of receiving the explanations then offered he must have realised what the power was which the trustees were purporting to exercise. Indeed, the fatal opinion of counsel advising on the possibility of using clause 11 to purchase a house in the Isle of Man was, on the evidence, familiar not only to George, but to Ann. The judge held that he was emancipated from parental control, and well enough acquainted with his position to make his consent to this advance binding upon him, and this court cannot reverse that finding, depending, as it does, so much upon the demeanour of the witness.

The case of the other son, Francis, is quite different. He was at this time 28 years old, and was apparently living for the most part with his grandmother, so that he was removed from immediate parental control. On the other hand, we now know that he was a schizophrenic. This diagnosis had been made in 1940 when he found one day of life in the Royal Air Force altogether too much for him, and was repeated by a doctor who saw him in 1951. He was not called by either side, it being agreed that his memory was not at all to be trusted. Consent to this, as to other transactions in which he was involved, was written out and sent to him by his father. There is no letter from him anywhere in the correspondence. No representative of the bank ever saw him. He was obviously left purposely in the background. On the other hand, he was capable of teaching in a boys school, which he did for two years towards the end of the war, and was accepted for entry to Edinburgh University after the war, where also he continued for two years as a student. Further, when he went with his brother to be advised over the Hodson loan, the partner in Farrer & Co who saw him thought him capable of understanding the transaction. Moreover, it has never been alleged that he was at any material time incapacitated from contracting or conducting business affairs by reason of his mental health, though we cannot think that if the bank had known of his history of ill-health they would have acted on the consents he returned signed to his father. But the bank did not know the facts. We have considered anxiously whether, before making an advance, they should have made some inquiry into his circumstances. It is alleged in the particulars of the statement of claim (paragraph 10) that the law presumes undue influence to exist between a person suffering from mental ill-health and the person with whom he resides; but in the end Mr. Bagnall rightly abandoned this plea, for there is no such presumption though actual undue influence may not be difficult to prove. The presumption exists only as to the medical adviser. On the whole, we do not feel able to say that the presumption of undue influence must be held to exist between Francis and his parents having regard to his age and his absence from home, and we conclude that the bank were not bound to make inquiries as to his state of mind or fitness as an object of the power they were affecting to exercise. Accordingly, though this was the plainest breach of trust, we agree with the judge that the bank have a good defence, for they obtained consents from the two children concerned, and they were emancipated . . .

The bank pleads the Limitation Act 1939, and as to this we wholly agree with what the judge said and need not repeat it. So, too, as to the defence of laches.[55] As to acquiescence, we think that this must be looked at rather broadly. We were, of course, pressed with the leading case of *Allcard v Skinner* (1887) 36 Ch D 145, but in that case the plaintiff had her rights fully explained to her by a brother, who was a barrister, and by her solicitor, and yet she took no steps until five or six years later. Even that gave rise to a difference of opinion in a very strong Court of Appeal. In this case it would be wrong, we feel, to place any disability upon the beneficiaries because it so happened that George was a member of the Bar, and had been in well-known chambers. He had not been in Chancery chambers where it may be said that these things are better understood; but the real truth of the matter is that a party cannot be held to have acquiesced unless he knew, or ought to have known, what his rights were. On the facts of this case we cannot criticise any of the plaintiffs for failing to appreciate their rights until another junior counsel, whom they consulted on a far-fetched and futile scheme of George's for avoiding Estate Duty on his mother's death, advised that the advances might be improper. That was in 1954, and thereupon the family, headed, of course, by George, took immediate steps to explore this matter. This is a most complicated action, and many matters had to be explored before an action for breach of trust could properly be mounted. The writ was issued in 1958, and we do not think it right to hold that the plaintiffs were debarred by acquiescence from bringing an action which otherwise, to the extent we have indicated, is justified.

We have already dealt with the impact of section 61 in general and in detail as we have gone through the various impugned transactions, and on that we need say nothing further.

---

[55] [1962] 1 WLR 86 at 115, *per* Wilberforce J:

'I must now deal with certain special defences. (1) *The Limitation Act 1939*. The relevant provision is section 19(2), and the whole question is whether the plaintiffs' rights are preserved by the proviso. In my judgment, they are. Undoubtedly they had 'a future interest' and, in my judgment, that interest did not fall into possession when the trustees by an (*ex hypothesi*) invalid advance raised a sum of money out of the capital. Mrs. Younghusband's consent to the advance was not, in my view, equivalent to a release of her life interest, and the only way (without a release) in which a capital sum could fall into possession would be by means of a valid advance. This defence, in my judgment fails. (2) *Laches*. There being an express statutory provision, providing a period of limitation for the plaintiffs' claims, there is no room for the equitable doctrine of *laches*.'

The Court of Appeal differed on the application of section 61 to one of the advances. WILBERFORCE J described it at 310:

On 13 September, 1948, the bank, as trustees, had also advanced to Francis and George a sum of £2,600 (Advance No. 5) which was applied in discharging a loan, which the bank, as trustee of a settlement of another customer of the bank, a Mrs. Hodson, had made to their mother and which had been charged as a mortgage on their mother's life interest under her uncle's will. This loan (known as the Hodson loan) was also secured by four life insurance policies on the mother's life of a total nominal value of £3,000, whose surrender value was then about £650. On this transaction the sons did have separate advice. Charles Russell & Co advised that it would be a proper exercise of the power of advancement provided that Francis and George received an adequate *quid pro quo* in the shape of the assignment to them of the four policies, coupled with covenants by the mother to maintain the premiums and to pay interest on the money advanced. However, the assignment of the life policies, as executed, contained no such covenants by the mother. Burrell of Farrer & Co approved the draft assignment on behalf of the sons without ever consulting them. The sons retained the life policies till 1953 when they gave them back to their mother, on joining with their mother in executing a mortgage dated 18 March, 1953, by the mother to the bank of her life interest under her uncle's will for the sum of £2,000. Apparently this was for the purpose of enabling the commander to raise further sums by charging them again.

The Court of Appeal held that the payment of the £2,000 was a clear breach of trust. UPJOHN LJ, with whom Harman LJ concurred, said at 358:

In my judgment, therefore, the only question that arises is whether the bank should be relieved from the consequences of their breach of trust under section 61 of the Trustee Act 1925, to any, and if so, what extent. This, I think, is a very difficult question. The judgment of the court has already pointed out that the bank were personally innocent, but they were ill-advised by their own solicitors; but the bank must accept responsibility for such negligence, and section 61 cannot possibly be invoked to relieve them from its consequences without more. The circumstance that seems to me to make the application of the section possible is that the bank received the letter quoted in the judgment of the court written by Burrell on behalf of Francis and George saying that the matter was in a satisfactory state. Thereafter it would have been quite unreasonable for the bank to take any further step to assure themselves that the transaction had been properly carried out, and they were lulled into a false sense of security. Section 61 is purely discretionary, and its application necessarily depends on the particular facts of each case. I think, in the circumstances of this case, that I am prepared to hold that the bank acted honestly (that is not in dispute) and reasonably and ought fairly to be excused to the extent of the surrender value of the policies transferred to the boys at the date of the transaction, about £650, but no doubt the exact figure can be ascertained. I do not see how the bank can properly be relieved to any greater extent. The fact that the mother paid the premiums for a few years, so enhancing the value of the policies, is (so far as the bank is concerned) as irrelevant as the fact that, as was to be expected, in due course the boys gave the policies back to their mother, and so, of course, to the commander, thereby losing all benefit from them.

QUESTIONS

1. Is the law on exemption of trustees' liability satisfactory? If not, should reform be left to Parliament, the judiciary, or to regulatory and professional bodies? See *Trustee Exemption Clauses,* Executive Summary, Law Com No. 301, 2006, pp. 1–4.

2. Would it be appropriate and workable to have a rule of law which states that trustees can exempt liability for negligence but not gross negligence? See *Armitage v Nurse* [1998] Ch 241 [p. 868, above].

3. Can a trustee make payments out of the trust fund to buy indemnity insurance to cover liability for breach of trust?

4. Are the existing rules on limitation periods for claims relating to breach of trust satisfactory?

19
PROPRIETARY CLAIMS AND REMEDIES[1]

I GENERAL PRINCIPLES

Where a trustee has misappropriated trust property in breach of trust the beneficiary may bring a claim to recover the property. Such claims will be founded on the beneficiary's equitable title to the property and so are properly characterised as proprietary claims. But, although the claim is founded on the beneficiary's proprietary rights, the remedy which is awarded is not necessarily a proprietary one.[2] There are two different types of remedy which are available in respect of equitable proprietary claims:

1. Personal remedies for the value of the property which has been received by the defendant but has not necessarily been retained.[3]

2. Proprietary remedies which enable the claimant to treat property in the hands of the defendant as belonging to the claimant. It does not necessarily follow that the claimant can recover the actual property which is in the defendant's hands. Rather, the claimant may simply be able to recover the value of the property, but the proprietary remedy creates a security interest in the property held by the

---

[1] H&M, pp. 682–716; Lewin, pp. 1655–1732; P&M, pp. 800–838; P&S, pp. 863–906; Pettit, pp. 550–564; Snell, pp. 683–690; T&H, pp. 1071–1132; U&H, pp. 1081–1104, 1208–1231; Goff and Jones, *Law of Restitution* (2007), (7th edn), chap. 2; Virgo, *The Principles of the Law of Restitution* (2nd edn, 2006), pp. 569–644.

[2] See *Boscawen v Bajwa* [1996] 1 WLR 328 at 334 (Millett LJ); *Trustee of the Property of FC Jones & Sons v Jones* [1997] Ch 159 at 168 (Millett LJ). See p. 968, below.

[3] See the action for unconscionable receipt of trust property, discussed at p. 971, below.

defendant so that the claimant can recover the value of the property in priority to the defendant's other creditors.[4]

In both situations, however, it is necessary for the claimant to establish that the defendant has received property in which the claimant has an equitable proprietary interest. This may require the claimant to rely on the tracing rules.

The essential features of proprietary claims and remedies were identified by MILLETT LJ in **Boscawen v Bajwa** [1996] 1 WLR 328. His Lordship said at 334:

Equity lawyers habitually use the expressions 'the tracing claim' and 'the tracing remedy' to describe the proprietary claim and the proprietary remedy which equity makes available to the beneficial owner who seeks to recover his property in specie from those into whose hands it has come. Tracing properly so-called, however, is neither a claim nor a remedy but a process. Moreover, it is not confined to the case where the plaintiff seeks a proprietary remedy; it is equally necessary where he seeks a personal remedy against the knowing recipient or knowing assistant. It is the process by which the plaintiff traces what has happened to his property, identifies the persons who have handled or received it, and justifies his claim that the money which they handled or received (and, if necessary, which they still retain) can properly be regarded as representing his property. He needs to do this because his claim is based on the retention by him of a beneficial interest in the property which the defendant handled or received. Unless he can prove this he cannot (in the traditional language of equity) raise an equity against the defendant or (in the modern language of restitution) show that the defendant's unjust enrichment was at his expense.

In such a case the defendant will either challenge the plaintiff's claim that the property in question represents his property (i.e., he will challenge the validity of the tracing exercise) or he will raise a priority dispute (e.g., by claiming to be a bona fide purchaser without notice).[5] If all else fails he will raise the defence of innocent change of position. This was not a defence which was recognised in England before 1991 but it was widely accepted throughout the common law world. In *Lipkin Gorman v Karpnale Ltd* [1991] 2 AC 548 the House of Lords acknowledged it to be part of English law also. The introduction of this defence not only provides the court with a means of doing justice in future, but allows a re-examination of many decisions of the past in which the absence of the defence may have led judges to distort basic principles in order to avoid injustice to the defendant.

If the plaintiff succeeds in tracing his property, whether in its original or in some changed form, into the hands of the defendant, and overcomes any defences which are put forward on the defendant's behalf, he is entitled to a remedy. The remedy will be fashioned to the circumstances. The plaintiff will generally be entitled to a personal remedy; if he seeks a proprietary remedy he must usually prove that the property to which he lays claim is still in the ownership of the defendant. If he succeeds in doing this the court will treat the defendant as holding the property on a constructive trust for the plaintiff and will order the defendant to transfer it in specie to the plaintiff.[6] But this is only one of the proprietary remedies which are available to a court of equity. If the plaintiff's money has been applied by the defendant, for example, not in the acquisition of a landed property but in its improvement, then the court may treat the land

---

[4] See p. 943, below for illustrations of the different types of proprietary remedy.
[5] See p. 937, below.   [6] See p. 944, below.

as charged with the payment to the plaintiff of a sum representing the amount by which the value of the defendant's land has been enhanced by the use of the plaintiff's money.[7] And if the plaintiff's money has been used to discharge a mortgage on the defendant's land, then the court may achieve a similar result by treating the land as subject to a charge by way of subrogation in favour of the plaintiff.[8]

There are several advantages which proprietary remedies have over personal remedies. For example, the claimant will rank above the general unsecured creditors of the defendant if the defendant becomes insolvent. Also, the claimant may benefit from any increase in the value of the property held by the defendant, although the claimant may also suffer if the property falls in value.

II IDENTIFYING THE CLAIMANT'S PROPERTY IN THE HANDS OF THE DEFENDANT[9]

Where the claimant wishes to bring a proprietary claim it is necessary first to establish that he had a proprietary interest, and then to establish that this interest subsists in the property which is held by the defendant. These questions are often considered together. Where property is held on trust for the claimant, it will be possible for him to establish an equitable proprietary interest. In order to show that this interest subsists in property held by the defendant the claimant will need to rely on the following and tracing rules.

A THE NATURE OF THE FOLLOWING AND TRACING RULES[10]

In **Foskett v McKeown** [2001] 1 AC 102,[11] LORD MILLETT said at 127:

The process of ascertaining what happened to the plaintiffs' money involves both tracing and following. These are both exercises in locating assets which are or may be taken to represent an asset belonging to the plaintiffs and to which they assert ownership. The processes of

---

⁷ See p. 945, below.   ⁸ See p. 945, below.

⁹ H&M, pp. 684–712; Lewin, pp. 1659–1708; P&M, pp. 800–838; P&S, pp. 863–869; Pettit, pp. 550–552; Snell, pp. 684–690; T&H, pp. 1072–1082; U&H, pp. 1081–1104; Smith, *The Law of Tracing* (1997); Virgo, *The Principles of the Law of Restitution* (2nd edn, 2006), pp. 619–635; (1959) 75 LQR 234 (R.H. Maudsley); (1971) 34 MLR 12 (F.O.B. Babafemi); (1975) 28 CLP 64 (A.J. Oakley); (1976) 40 Conv (NS) 277 (R.A. Pearce); (1976) 92 LQR 360, 367 (R.M. Goode); (1979) 95 LQR 78 (S. Khurshid and P.Matthews); (1981) 34 CLP 159 (P. Matthews); (1997) 11 *Trust Law International* 1 (P. Birks); (1999) 115 LQR 469 (S. Evans).

¹⁰ Smith, *The Law of Tracing* (1997), pp. 3–4; Virgo, *The Principles of the Law of Restitution* (2nd edn, 2006), pp. 619–624.   ¹¹ See further p. 915, below.

following and tracing are, however, distinct. Following is the process of following the same asset as it moves from hand to hand. Tracing is the process of identifying a new asset as the substitute for the old. Where one asset is exchanged for another, a claimant can elect whether to follow the original asset into the hands of the new owner or to trace its value into the new asset in the hands of the same owner. In practice his choice is often dictated by the circumstances...[12]

We speak of money at the bank, and of money passing into and out of a bank account. But of course the account holder has no money at the bank. Money paid into a bank account belongs legally and beneficially to the bank and not to the account holder. The bank gives value for it, and it is accordingly not usually possible to make the money itself the subject of an adverse claim. Instead a claimant normally sues the account holder rather than the bank and lays claim to the proceeds of the money in his hands. These consist of the debt or part of the debt due to him from the bank. We speak of tracing money into and out of the account, but there is no money in the account. There is merely a single debt of an amount equal to the final balance standing to the credit of the account holder. No money passes from paying bank to receiving bank or through the clearing system (where the money flows may be in the opposite direction). There is simply a series of debits and credits which are causally and transactionally linked. We also speak of tracing one asset into another, but this too is inaccurate. The original asset still exists in the hands of the new owner, or it may have become untraceable. The claimant claims the new asset because it was acquired in whole or in part with the original asset. What he traces, therefore, is not the physical asset itself but the value inherent in it.

Tracing is thus neither a claim nor a remedy. It is merely the process by which a claimant demonstrates what has happened to his property, identifies its proceeds and the persons who have handled or received them, and justifies his claim that the proceeds can properly be regarded as representing his property. Tracing is also distinct from claiming. It identifies the traceable proceeds of the claimant's property. It enables the claimant to substitute the traceable proceeds for the original asset as the subject matter of his claim. But it does not affect or establish his claim. That will depend on a number of factors including the nature of his interest in the original asset. He will normally be able to maintain the same claim to the substituted asset as he could have maintained to the original asset. If he held only a security interest in the original asset, he cannot claim more than a security interest in its proceeds. But his claim may also be exposed to potential defences as a result of intervening transactions. Even if the plaintiffs could demonstrate what the bank had done with their money, for example, and could thus identify its traceable proceeds in the hands of the bank, any claim by them to assert ownership of those proceeds would be defeated by the bona fide purchaser defence. The successful completion of a tracing exercise may be preliminary to a personal claim (as in *El Ajou v Dollar Land Holding plc* [1993] 3 All ER 717) or a proprietary one, to the enforcement of a legal right (as in *Trustees of the Property of FC Jones & Sons v Jones* [1997] Ch 159, see p. 898, below) or an equitable one.

In **Shalson v Russo** [2003] EWHC 1637 (Ch), [2005] Ch 281, at para 102, RIMER J described tracing 'as the process by which a claimant seeks to show that an interest he had in an asset has become represented by an interest in a different asset.'

---

[12] For further analysis of this doctrine of election, see *Boscawen v Bajwa* [1996] 1 WLR 328, at 341 (Millett LJ) and *Lipkin Gorman v Karpnale Ltd* [1991] 2 AC 548 at 573 (Lord Goff of Chieveley).

B   TRACING AT COMMON LAW[13]

Where the claimant has an existing legal interest in property, he will need to rely on the common law tracing rules to establish that the interest subsists in property held by the defendant. The common law tracing rules have traditionally been interpreted restrictively. In particular, it has generally been held that it is not possible to trace at law through a mixed fund,[14] although this view has been recently challenged on a number of occasions.

In **Trustee of the Property of FC Jones & Sons v Jones** [1997] Ch 159,[15] the defendant, the wife of a bankrupt, paid £11,700 into an account with a firm of commodity brokers. This money was drawn from a bank account with Midland Bank, which was jointly in her husband's name and in the name of another bankrupt. She used this money to deal in potato futures and paid £50,760 obtained from her deals into a bank deposit account with Raphaels. The trustee in bankruptcy claimed this money. The Court of Appeal held that the money in the husband's bank account belonged to the trustee in bankruptcy. The question for the court then was whether the trustee could trace this money into the bank account. MILLETT LJ said at 168:

In the present case equity has no role to play. The trustee must bring his claim at common law. It follows that, if he has to trace his money, he must rely on common law tracing rules, and that he has no proprietary remedy. But it does not follow that he has no proprietary claim. His claim is exclusively proprietary. He claims the money because it belongs to him at law or represents profits made by the use of money which belonged to him at law.

The trustee submits that he has no need to trace, since the facts are clear and undisputed. The defendant did not mix the money with her own. The trustee's money remained identifiable as such throughout. But, of course, he does have to trace it in order to establish that the money which he claims represents his money. Counsel for the defendant acknowledges that the trustee can successfully trace his money into her account at Raphaels, for his concession in respect of the £11,700 acknowledges this. I do not understand how his concession that the trustee is entitled to £11,700 of the money in court is reconcilable with his submission that the only cause of action available to the trustee is an action for money had and received. I say this for two reasons. In the first place, the trustee has never brought such an action, and any such action would now be long out of time. In the second place, in an action for money had and received it would be irrelevant what the defendant had done with the money after she received it. Her liability would be based on her receipt of the money, and she would be personally liable to a money judgment for

---

[13]   H&M, pp. 684–688; Lewin, pp. 1665–1666; P&M, pp. 800–806; P&S, pp. 869–880; Pettit, pp. 553–554; Snell, pp. 684–685; T&H, pp. 1082–1087, 1126–1127; U&H, pp. 1098–1101; Smith, *The Law of Tracing* (1997); Virgo, *The Principles of the Law of Restitution* (2nd edn, 2006), pp. 625–628; (1986) *University of Western Australia Law Review* 463 (M. Scott); P. Matthews, *Laundering and Tracing* (ed. P. Birks) (1995), p. 23.

[14]   *Taylor v Plumer* (1815) 3 M & S 562; *Banque Belge pour l'Etranger v Hambrouck* [1921] 1 KB 321; *Agip (Africa) Ltd v Jackson* [1990] Ch 265; affd [1991] Ch 547; *El Ajou v Dollar Land Holdings* [1993] 3 All ER 717; *Trustee of the Property of FC Jones & Sons v Jones* [1997] Ch 159, below.

[15]   (1997) 113 LQR 21 (N. Andrews and J. Beatson); (1997) 56 CLJ 30 (D. Fox); (1997) 11 *Trust Law International* 2 (P. Birks); [1996] All ER Rev 366 (P. Birks and W. Swadling); [1997] 5 *Restitution Law Review* 92 (R. Davern); (1997–98) 8 *King's College Law Journal* 123 (C. Mitchell).

£11,700. But, while the trustee would be entitled to a money judgment for that sum, he would not be entitled to any particular sum of £11,700 such as the money in court in specie.

But in my judgment the concession that the trustee can trace the money at common law is rightly made. There are no factual difficulties of the kind which proved fatal in this court to the common law claim in *Agip (Africa) Ltd v Jackson* [1991] Ch 547.[16] It is not necessary to trace the passage of the money through the clearing system or the London potato futures market. The money which the defendant paid into her account with the commodity brokers represented the proceeds of cheques which she received from her husband. Those cheques represented money in the bankrupts' joint account at Midland Bank which belonged to the trustee.

In *Lipkin Gorman v Karpnale Ltd* [1991] 2 AC 548 at 573 Lord Goff of Chieveley held that the plaintiffs could trace or follow their 'property into its product' for this 'involves a decision by the owner of the original property to assert his title to the product in place of his original property'. In that case the original property was the plaintiffs' chose in action, a debt owed by the bank to the plaintiffs. Lord Goff held, at 574, that the plaintiffs could 'trace their property at common law in that chose in action, or in any part of it, into its product, i.e. cash drawn by Cass from their client account at the bank'.

Accordingly, the trustee can follow the money in the joint account at Midland Bank, which had been vested by statute in him, into the proceeds of the three cheques which the defendant received from her husband. The trustee does not need to follow the money from one recipient to another or follow it through the clearing system; he can follow the cheques as they pass from hand to hand. It is sufficient for him to be able to trace the money into the cheques and the cheques into their proceeds.

In *Agip (Africa) Ltd v Jackson* [1990] Ch 265 at 285 I said that the ability of the common law to trace an asset into a changed form in the same hands was established in *Taylor v Plumer* (1815) 3 M & S 562. Lord Ellenborough CJ in that case had said, at 575:

'the product of or substitute for the original thing still follows the nature of the thing itself, as long as it can be ascertained to be such, and the right only ceases when the means of ascertainment fail, which is the case when the subject is turned into money, and mixed and confounded in a general mass of the same description.'

In this it appears that I fell into a common error, for it has since been convincingly demonstrated that, although *Taylor v Plumer* was decided by a common law court, the court was in fact applying the rules of equity: see Lionel Smith, 'Tracing in *Taylor v Plumer*: Equity in the Court of King's Bench' [1995] LMCLQ 240.

But this is no reason for concluding that the common law does not recognise claims to substitute assets or their products. Such claims were upheld by this court in *Banque Belge pour l'Etranger v Hambrouck* [1921] 1 KB 321 and by the House of Lords in *Lipkin Gorman v Karpnale Ltd* [1991] 2 AC 548. It has been suggested by commentators that these cases are undermined by their misunderstanding of *Taylor v Plumer* (1815) 3 M & S 562 but that is not how the English doctrine of *stare decisis* operates. It would be more consistent with that doctrine to say that, in recognising claims to substituted assets, equity must be taken to have followed the law, even though the law was not declared until later. Lord Ellenborough CJ gave no indication that, in following assets into their exchange products, equity had adopted a rule which was peculiar to itself or which went further than the common law.

---

[16] Tracing at law was not possible in that case because the money had been paid through the clearing system and so was no longer identifiable. See p. 901, below.

There is no merit in having distinct and differing tracing rules at law and in equity, given that tracing is neither a right nor a remedy but merely the process by which the plaintiff establishes what has happened to his property and makes good his claim that the assets which he claims can properly be regarded as representing his property. The fact that there are different tracing rules at law and in equity is unfortunate though probably inevitable, but unnecessary differences should not be created where they are not required by the different nature of legal and equitable doctrines and remedies. There is, in my view, even less merit in the present rule which precludes the invocation of the equitable tracing rules to support a common law claim; until that rule is swept away unnecessary obstacles to the development of a rational and coherent law of restitution will remain.

Given that the trustee can trace his money at Midland Bank into the money in the defendant's account with the commodity brokers, can he successfully assert a claim to that part of the money which represents the profit made by the use of his money? I have no doubt that, in the particular circumstances of this case, he can. There is no need to trace through the dealings on the London potato futures market. If the defendant, as the nominal account holder, had any entitlement to demand payment from the brokers, this was because of the terms of the contract which she made with them. Under the terms of that contract it is reasonable to infer that the brokers were authorised to deal in potato futures on her account, to debit her account with losses and to credit it with profits, and to pay her only the balance standing to her account. It is, in my opinion, impossible to separate the chose in action constituted by the deposit of the trustee's money on those terms from the terms upon which it was deposited. The chose in action, which was vested in the defendant's name but which in reality belonged to the trustee, was not a right to payment from the brokers of the original amount deposited but a right to claim the balance, whether greater or less than the amounted deposited; and it is to that chose in action that the trustee now lays claim.

Given, then, that the trustee has established his legal claim to the £11,700 and the profits earned by the use of his money, and has located the money, first, in the defendant's account with the commodity brokers and, later, in the defendant's account at Raphaels, I am satisfied that the common law has adequate remedies to enable him to recover his property. He did not need to sue the defendant; and he did not do so. He was entitled to bring an action for debt against Raphaels and obtain an order for payment. When he threatened to do so, Raphaels interpleaded, and the issue between the trustee and the defendant was which of them could give a good receipt to Raphaels. That depended upon which of them had the legal title to the chose in action. The money now being in court, the court can grant an appropriate declaration and make an order for payment.

In my judgment the trustee was entitled at law to the money in the joint account of the bankrupts at Midland Bank, which had vested in him by statute. He was similarly entitled to the balance of the money in the defendant's account with the commodity brokers, and the fact that it included profits made by the use of that money is immaterial. He was similarly entitled to the money in the defendant's account at Raphaels and able to give them a good receipt for the money. The defendant never had any interest, legal or equitable, in any of those moneys. The trustee is plainly entitled to the money in court and the judge was right to order that it be paid out to him.

Nourse LJ said at 172:

I recognise that our decision goes further than that of the House of Lords in *Lipkin Gorman v Karpnale Ltd* [1991] 2 AC 548 in that it holds that the action for money had and received entitles the legal owner to trace his property into its product, not only in the sense of property for which it is exchanged, but also in the sense of property representing the original and the profit made by the defendant's use of it.

Millett LJ has explained how that extension is justified on the particular facts of this case. But there is, I think, a broader justification to be found in the seminal judgment of Lord Mansfield CJ in *Clarke v Shee and Johnson* (1774) 1 Cowp 197, at 199–200 where he said of the action for money had and received:

> 'This is a liberal action in the nature of a bill in equity; and if, under the circumstances of the case, it appears that the defendant cannot in conscience retain what is the subject matter of it, the plaintiff may well support this action.'

In my view the defendant cannot in conscience retain the profit any more than the original £11,700. She had no title to the original. She could not have made the profit without her use of it. She cannot, by making a profit through the use of money to which she had no title, acquire some better title to the profit.

In **Agip (Africa) Ltd v Jackson** [1990] Ch 265,[17] the plaintiff had carried out oil explorations in Tunisia in the 1970s and early 1980s, and held an account with the Banque du Sud in Tunis to pay overseas suppliers. The plaintiff discovered that they had been defrauded of large sums of money by Z, its chief accountant. Z was not a director nor an authorised signatory of the company but it was his task to put the completed payment orders before the authorised signatory and obtain his signature. Afterwards Z was responsible for taking the payment orders to the bank for payment. Z affected the frauds by altering the names of the payees on the payment orders after obtaining the authorised signature. It was estimated that in a two-year period some $10.5 million had been diverted away from the proper payees of the plaintiff in this way. This action, though, was concerned with only one payment of $518,822 which was made to Baker Oil Services Ltd (Baker Oil), a company registered in the Isle of Man which held a dollar account at a branch of Lloyds Bank in London. This was a shell company which immediately before the transfer of the money to it had nothing standing to its credit in the account. Shortly after receiving the money the whole balance was transferred to the account of Jackson & Co, an accountancy firm the partners of which were the first and second defendants. They were also the directors and shareholders of Baker Oil. The third defendant was an employee of the partnership. The money was only held in the partnership account for the benefit of the partnership clients. From there it was then transferred to another company which held an account at the same branch of Lloyds Bank before being transferred overseas to the ultimate recipients and organisers of the frauds.

On discovering the frauds the plaintiff brought an unsuccessful action in Tunisia against the Banque du Sud for recovery of the money which had been debited to its account. It also obtained a judgment against Baker Oil, but this was unsatisfied and certain to remain so, as Baker Oil was now in liquidation.

---

[17] (1989) 105 LQR 528 (P. Birks); (1991) 107 LQR 71 (Sir Peter Millett); (1990) CLJ 217 (C. Harpum). On appeal (1991) 50 CLJ 409 (C. Harpum); [1992] Conv 367 (S. Goulding), from which the statement of the facts is taken.

The plaintiff brought a number of claims against the defendants. It failed in its attempt to trace at common law, but succeeded in claims to trace in equity [p. 909, below] and for assistance in breach of trust.[18] On the first point, MILLETT J (whose decision on all three claims was upheld by the Court of Appeal: [1991] Ch 547)[19] said at 285:

The common law has always been able to follow a physical asset from one recipient to another. Its ability to follow an asset in the same hands into a changed form was established in *Taylor v Plumer* (1815) 3 M & S 562. In following the plaintiff's money into an asset purchased exclusively with it, no distinction is drawn between a chose in action such as the debt of a bank to its customer and any other asset: *Re Diplock* [1948] Ch 465, at 519. But it can only follow a physical asset, such as a cheque or its proceeds, from one person to another. It can follow money but not a chose in action. Money can be followed at common law into and out of a bank account and into the hands of a subsequent transferee, provided that it does not cease to be identifiable by being mixed with other money in the bank account derived from some other source: *Banque Belge pour l'Etranger v Hambrouck* [1921] 1 KB 321. Applying these principles, the plaintiffs claim to follow their money through Baker Oil's account where it was not mixed with any other money and into Jackson & Co's account at Lloyds Bank.

The defendants deny this. They contend that tracing is not possible at common law because the money was mixed, first when it was handled in New York, and secondly in Jackson & Co's own account at Lloyds Bank.

The latter objection is easily disposed of. The cause of action for money had and received is complete when the plaintiff's money is received by the defendant. It does not depend on the continued retention of the money by the defendant. Save in strictly limited circumstances it is no defence that he has parted with it. *A fortiori* it can be no defence for him to show that he has so mixed it with his own money that he cannot tell whether he still has it or not. Mixing by the defendant himself must, therefore, be distinguished from mixing by a prior recipient. The former is irrelevant, but the latter will destroy the claim, for it will prevent proof that the money received by the defendant was the money paid by the plaintiff.

In my judgment, however, the former objection is insuperable. The money cannot be followed by treating it as the proceeds of a cheque presented by the collecting bank in exchange for payment by the paying bank. The money was transmitted by telegraphic transfer. There was no cheque or any equivalent. The payment order was not a cheque or its equivalent. It remained throughout in the possession of the Banque du Sud. No copy was sent to Lloyds Bank or Baker Oil or presented to the Banque du Sud in exchange for the money. It was normally the plaintiffs' practice to forward a copy of the payment order to the supplier when paying an invoice but this was for information only. It did not authorise or enable the supplier to obtain payment. There is no evidence that this practice was followed in the case of forged payment orders and it is exceedingly unlikely that it was.

Nothing passed between Tunisia and London but a stream of electrons. It is not possible to treat the money received by Lloyds Bank in London or its correspondent bank in New York as representing the proceeds of the payment order or of any other physical asset previously in its hands and delivered by it in exchange for the money. The Banque du Sud merely telexed a request to Lloyd's Bank to make a payment to Baker Oil against its own undertaking to reimburse Lloyds Bank in New York. Lloyds Bank complied with the request by paying Baker

---

[18] See p. 982, below for the action of dishonest assistance in a breach of trust.
[19] See Fox LJ at 563.

Oil with its own money. It thereby took a delivery risk. In due course it was no doubt reimbursed, but it is not possible to identify the source of the money with which it was reimbursed without attempting to follow the money through the New York clearing system. Unless Lloyds Bank's correspondent bank in New York was also Citibank, this involves tracing the money through the accounts of Citibank and Lloyds Bank's correspondent bank with the Federal Reserve Bank, where it must have been mixed with other money. The money with which Lloyds Bank was reimbursed cannot therefore, without recourse to equity, be identified as being that of the Banque du Sud. There is no evidence that Lloyds Bank's correspondent bank in New York was Citibank, and accordingly the plaintiff's attempt to trace the money at common law must fail.[20]

C   TRACING IN EQUITY[21]

The main difference between the equitable and common law tracing rules is that the equitable rules will not be defeated by the irretrievable mixing of property.[22] The equitable rules, however, do require it to be established that the property in which the claimant had an equitable proprietary interest passed to the defendant through the hands of a fiduciary in breach of duty.[23] This will be satisfied where, as is usually the case, the property had been held by a trustee or any other type of fiduciary. It must not be forgotten that the equitable tracing rules can only be relevant where the claimant has an equitable proprietary interest, sometimes described as an equitable proprietary base. This may arise by virtue of an express trust, a resulting trust,[24] or a constructive trust.[25]

(i) Fiduciary Relationship and Equitable Proprietary Interest

The fiduciary through whose hands the property must have passed in breach of duty may, but need not, be the defendant himself.

---

[20] See also *El Ajou v Dollar Land Holdings plc* [1993] 3 All ER 717; *Bank of America v Arnell* [1999] Lloyd's Rep Bank 399; (2000) 59 CLJ 28 (D. Fox).

[21] H&M, pp. 688–703; Lewin, pp. 1659–1708; P&M, pp. 807–832; P&S, pp. 880–900; Pettit, pp. 555–562; Snell, pp. 685–689; T&H, pp. 1087–1103, 1127–1132; U&H, pp. 1086–1104; Smith, *The Law of Tracing* (1997); Virgo, *The Principles of the Law of Restitution* (2nd edn, 2006), pp. 628–634; 'Equity's Identification Rules' (D. Hayton), chap. 1 in Birks, *Laundering and Tracing* (ed. P. Birks) (1995).

[22] *Re Hallett's Estate* (1880) 13 Ch D 696; *Sinclair v Brougham* [1914] AC 398; *Agip (Africa) Ltd v Jackson* [1991] Ch 547.

[23] *Re Hallett's Estate* (1880) 13 Ch D 696; *El Ajou v Dollar Land Holdings plc* [1993] 3 All ER 717 at 733 (Millett J); *Boscawen v Bajwa* [1996] 1 WLR 328 at 335 (Millett LJ). Although the need for such a relationship might be in doubt, after the decision of the House of Lords in *Foskett v McKeown* [2001] 1 AC 102 [p. 915, below] any comments about this were obiter so it is not yet possible to say for certain that the requirement has been removed and the rules for tracing at law and in equity are the same. See also (1997) *Trust Law International* 2 at 3 (P. Birks). The requirement has been rejected in New Zealand: *Elders Pastoral Ltd v Bank of New Zealand* [1989] 2 NZLR 180. For further criticism of a fiduciary relationship as the basis of equitable tracing; see (1990) 106 LQR 552 (P. Watts); (1987) 103 LQR 433 (R.M. Goode); *Re Goldcorp Exchange Ltd* [1995] 1 AC 74 at 98, per Lord Mustill; *El Ajou v Dollar Land Holdings* [1993] BCLC 735 at 753, *per* Millett J.

[24] See Chapter 6.   [25] See Chapter 7.

Re Diplock
[1948] Ch 465 (CA, **Lord Greene MR, Wrottesley** and **Evershed LJJ**)[26]

By his will, Mr. Diplock directed his executors to apply his residuary estate 'for such charitable institutions or other charitable or benevolent object or objects in England' as they should 'in their...absolute discretion select'. It was assumed that the will created a valid charitable trust; and the executors distributed some £203,000 among 139 different charities before its validity was challenged by the next-of-kin. The House of Lords held the bequest void in *Chichester Diocesan Fund and Board of Finance Inc v Simpson* [1944] AC 341 [p. 537, above]. The next-of-kin of the testator, having exhausted their remedy against the executors, made claims to recover the money from the charities. These claims against the different charities varied in details; but not on principle.

Held. The next-of-kin succeeded; both in respect of (i) a claim *in personam*. An unpaid or under-paid legatee was entitled to a personal claim in equity against an overpaid or wrongly paid legatee. This aspect of the case was later affirmed on appeal to the House of Lords in *Ministry of Health v Simpson* [1951] AC 251; and (ii) a claim *in rem*. The right to trace into a mixed fund was not restricted to cases where the defendant was the person who had mixed the moneys, or where the fiduciary relationship, necessary for a proprietary claim in equity, existed between the parties to the action.

Only the claim *in rem* is discussed in this extract.

Lord Greene MR: The first question which appears to us to fall for decision on this part of the present appeals may, we think, be thus formulated: did the power of equity to treat Diplock 'money' as recoverable from the charity, which undoubtedly existed down to the moment when the cheque was paid by the bank on which it was drawn, cease the moment that the 'money' by the process of 'mixture' came to be represented by an accretion to or an enlargement of the chose in action consisting of a debt already owing to the charity by its own bankers? Wynn-Parry J, in effect, decided that it did. His reason for taking this view, shortly stated, was as follows: the principle applicable was to be extracted from the decision in *Hallett's* case (1880) 13 Ch D 696, p. 911, below, and that principle was in no way extended by the decision in *Sinclair v Brougham* [1914] AC 398. The principle can operate only in cases where the mixing takes place in breach of a trust, actual or constructive, or in breach of some other fiduciary relationship and in proceedings against the trustee or fiduciary agent: here the mixing was not of this character, since it was effected by an innocent volunteer: there is no ground on which, according to principle, the conscience of such a volunteer can be held in equity to be precluded from setting up a title adverse to the claim: in every case, therefore, where a 'mixture' has been carried out by the charity, the claim whether it be against a mixed monetary fund or against investments made by means of such a mixed fund, must fail *in limine*.

Now we may say at once that this view of the inability of equity to deal with the case of the volunteer appears to us, with all respect to Wynn-Parry J, to be in conflict with the principles expounded, particularly by Lord Parker, in *Sinclair v Brougham*. If Lord Parker means what we think he meant, and if what he said is to be accepted as a correct statement of the law,

---

[26] Approved by the House of Lords in *Westdeutsche Landesbank Girozentrale v Islington London Borough Council* [1996] AC 669.

Mr. Pennycuick, who argued this part of the case on behalf of the charities, admittedly felt great difficulty in supporting this part of the reasoning of the learned judge. We shall deal further with Lord Parker's observations on this topic when we come to them in our examination of *Sinclair v Brougham*. But here we may conveniently summarise what we consider to be the effect of them as follows: where an innocent volunteer (as distinct from a purchaser for value without notice) mixes 'money' of his own with 'money' which in equity belongs to another person, or is found in possession of such a mixture, although that other person cannot claim a charge on the mass superior to the claim of the volunteer he is entitled, nevertheless, to a charge ranking *pari passu* with the claim of the volunteer. And Lord Parker's reasons for taking this view appear to have been on the following lines: equity regards the rights of the equitable owner as being 'in effect rights of property' though not recognised as such by the common law. Just as a volunteer is not allowed by equity in the case, e.g., of a conveyance of the legal estate in land, to set up his legal title adversely to the claim of a person having an equitable interest in the land, so in the case of a mixed fund of money the volunteer must give such recognition as equity considers him in conscience (as a volunteer) bound to give to the interest of the equitable owner of the money which has been mixed with the volunteer's own. But this burden on the conscience of the volunteer is not such as to compel him to treat the claim of the equitable owner as paramount. That would be to treat the volunteer as strictly as if he himself stood in a fiduciary relationship to the equitable owner which *ex hypothesi* he does not. The volunteer is under no greater duty of conscience to recognise the interest of the equitable owner than that which lies upon a person having an equitable interest in one of two trust funds of 'money' which have become mixed towards the equitable owner of the other. Such a person is not in conscience bound to give precedence to the equitable owner of the other of the two funds.

We may enlarge upon the implications which appear to us to be contained in Lord Parker's reasoning. First of all, it appears to us to be wrong to treat the principle which underlies *Hallett's* case as coming into operation only where the person who does the mixing is not only in a fiduciary position but is also a *party to the tracing action*. If he is a party to the action he is, of course, precluded from setting up a case inconsistent with the obligations of his fiduciary position. But supposing that he is not a party? The result cannot surely depend on what equity would or would not have allowed him to say if he had been a party. Suppose that the sole trustee of (say) five separate trusts draws 100l. out of each of the trust banking accounts, pays the resulting 500l. into an account which he opens in his own name, draws a cheque for 500l. on that account and gives it as a present to his son. A claim by the five sets of beneficiaries to follow the money of their respective trusts would be a claim against the son. He would stand in no fiduciary relationship to any of them. We recoil from the conclusion that all five beneficiaries would be dismissed empty-handed by a court of equity and the son left to enjoy what in equity was originally their money. Yet that is the conclusion to which the reasoning of the learned judge would lead us. Lord Parker's reasoning, on the other hand, seems to us to lead to the conclusion that each set of beneficiaries could set up its equitable interest which would prevail against the bare legal title of the son as a volunteer and that they would be entitled to share *pari passu* in so much of the fund or its proceeds as remained identifiable.

An even more striking example was admitted by Mr. Pennycuick to be the result of his argument, and he vigorously maintained that it followed inevitably from the principles of equity involved. If a fiduciary agent takes cash belonging to his principal and gives it to his son, who takes it innocently, then so long as the son keeps it unmixed with other cash in one trouser pocket, the principal can follow it and claim it back. Once, however, the son, being under no fiduciary duty to the principal, transfers it to his other trouser pocket in which there are repos-ing a coin or two of his own of the same denomination, the son, by a sort of process of accretion, acquires an indefeasible title to what the moment before the transfer he could not have claimed as his own. This result appears to us to stultify the beneficent powers of equity to protect and enforce what it recognises as equitable rights of property which subsist until they are destroyed by the operation of a purchase for value without notice.

The error into which, we respectfully suggest, the learned judge has fallen is in thinking that what, in *Hallett's* case was only the method (there appropriate) of bringing a much wider-based principle of equity into operation—*viz.*, the method by which a fiduciary agent, who has himself wrongfully mixed the funds, is prohibited from asserting a breach of his duty—is an element which must necessarily be present before equity can afford protection to the equitable rights which it has brought into existence. We are not prepared to see the arm of equity thus shortened.

It is now time to examine in some detail the case of *Sinclair v Brougham*. Before us it was argued, on behalf of the respondents, that the principle on which it was decided was not that applied in *Hallett's* case but a different one altogether, invented with a view to solving a par-ticular problem. We do not agree. The principle, in our view, was clearly the same; but in its application to new facts fresh light was thrown upon it, and it was shown to have a much wider scope than a narrow reading of *Hallett's* case itself would suggest...

The contest in *Sinclair v Brougham* was between shareholders and depositors in respect of a miscellaneous mass of assets distributable by the liquidator in the winding-up of a building society. The deposits had been made, and the assets were used, in connexion with a banking business carried on in the name of the society but beyond its powers. Each of the two classes claimed priority over the other. Until the case reached the House of Lords the possibility that they might rank *pari passu* does not appear to have been considered. The majority of the Court of Appeal, affirming Neville J, gave the shareholders priority over the depositors. Fletcher Moulton LJ would have given the depositors priority over the shareholders. The House of Lords held that both views were wrong and that on the principle on which *Hallett's* case was founded, the two classes shared rateably. In one respect, no doubt, this application of the principle is an extension of it since, although the right of individuals to trace their own money (if they could) was preserved in the order of the House, the order provided for tracing the aggregate contributions of the two classes as classes. *Hallett's* case was, of course, based on the right of an individual to follow what he could in equity identify as his own money. The extension of the principle in *Sinclair v Brougham* was the obvious and, indeed, on the facts, the only practical method of securing a just distribution of the assets. The importance of the point must not, however, be overlooked in considering the arguments and the speeches.....

[His Lordship considered the arguments of counsel and continued:] Now it is to be remem-bered that the arguments of counsel on either side were directed to claiming priority for their respective clients and much of the reasoning in the speeches is directed to negativing these claims to priority. The House held that although the equity underlying *Hallett's* case was appli-cable, the result of its proper application was that the conclusion sought by both arguments was wrong and that the fund was divisible rateably between the two classes of claimants. We may call attention in passing to the manner in which the House dealt with the argument of counsel for the shareholders that there could be no tracing save in favour of an individual who could follow and (in equity) identify his own property and that in consequence there could not be what would be in substance a tracing order in favour of a class. This argument does appear to raise a technical difficulty. But the House brushed it aside. Lord Sumner's speech contains the clearest exposition of the reasons for dealing with it in the manner approved by the House. He said [1914] AC 398 at 459:

> 'My Lords, I agree, without recapitulating reasons, that the principle on which *Hallett's* case is founded justifies an order allowing the appellants to follow the assets, not merely to the verge of actual identification, but even somewhat further in a case like the present, where after a process of exclusion only two classes or groups of persons, having equal claims, are left in and all superior claims have been eliminated. Tracing in a sense it is not, for we know that the money coming from A went into one security and that coming from B into another, and that the two securities did not probably depreciate exactly in the same percentage, and we know further that no one will ever know any more. Still I think this well within the "tracing" equity, and that among persons making up these two groups the principle of rateable division of the assets is sound.'

This does at least show that in applying the equitable principle equity is entitled to adopt that method of application which in the circumstances of the case will lead to an equitable result.

[His Lordship considered the facts of the case in more detail and continued:] The starting point of the claim of the depositors was the existence of a fiduciary relationship as between themselves and the directors: that relationship arose from the fact that the depositors had entrusted their money to the directors for the purpose of a business which could not lawfully be carried on, so that the directors must be treated as holding the money on behalf of the depositors. If the directors had paid the money of a depositor into their own banking account he would have had an action against them exactly similar to the action in *Hallett's* case and it would have been correctly said that the directors could not be heard to set up a title of their own to the money standing in the account adverse to the claim of the depositor. But nothing of the sort could be said if the directors paid the money into the account of the society at its bankers. Neither the conscience of the society nor of its liquidator (if it went into liquidation) could ever come into the picture on the basis of a fiduciary relationship since the only parties to that relationship were the directors and the depositors. The society could not have been a party to it, since it had no power to accept the depositor's money. If, therefore, in such a case, the depositor could claim a charge on the society's account with its bankers the claim must have been based on some wider principle.

What can that principle be? In our judgment it must be the principle clearly indicated by Lord Parker, that equity may operate on the conscience not merely of those who acquire a legal title in breach of some trust, express or constructive, or of some other fiduciary obligation, but of volunteers provided that as a result of what has gone before some equitable proprietary interest has been created and attached to the property in the hands of the volunteer.[27]

The decision of the House of Lords in *Sinclair v Brougham* [1914] AC 398 was overruled by the House of Lords in *Westdeutsche Landesbank Girozentrale v Islington London Borough Council* [1996] AC 669. This was not because of the analysis of tracing, but rather because of the conclusion that the plaintiffs in *Sinclair v Brougham* had had an equitable proprietary interest.

In **Westdeutsche Landesbank Girozentrale v Islington London Borough Council** [1996] AC 669, the plaintiff bank sought restitution of money it had paid to the defendant local authority pursuant to an interest-rate swap contract which was void

---

[27] See also *Re J Leslie Engineers Co Ltd* [1976] 1 WLR 292.

since the defendant lacked the capacity to enter into such a contract. The issue for the court was whether compound interest could be awarded and this depended on the plaintiff establishing a proprietary claim. The plaintiff argued that it had an equitable proprietary interest in the money by virtue of the principle recognised in *Sinclair v Brougham*.

In holding that the plaintiff had no proprietary interest in the money received by the defendant, LORD BROWNE-WILKINSON said at 709:[28]

[*Sinclair v Brougham*] concerned the distribution of the assets of the Birkbeck Permanent Benefit Building Society, an unincorporated body which was insolvent. The society had for many years been carrying on business as a bank which, it was held, was ultra vires its objects. The bank had accepted deposits in the course of its ultra vires banking business and it was held that the debts owed to such depositors were themselves void as being ultra vires. In addition to the banking depositors, there were ordinary trade creditors. The society had two classes of members, the A shareholders who were entitled to repayment of their investment on maturity and the B shareholders whose shares were permanent. By agreement, the claims of the ordinary trade creditors and of the A shareholders had been settled. Therefore the only claimants to the assets of the society before the court were the ultra vires depositors and the B shareholders, the latter of which could take no greater interest than the society itself.

The issues for decision arose on a summons taken out by the liquidator for directions as to how he should distribute the assets in the liquidation. In the judgments, it is not always clear whether this House was laying down general propositions of law or merely giving directions as to the proper mode in which the assets in that liquidation should be distributed. The depositors claimed, first, in quasi-contract for money had and received. They claimed secondly, as the result of an argument suggested for the first time in the course of argument in the House of Lords (at p. 404), to trace their deposits into the assets of the society.

His Lordship considered the personal claim for money had and received and concluded that the House of Lords was wrong to decide that no such claim was available, and continued:

The House of Lords held that, the ordinary trade creditors having been paid in full by agreement, the assets remaining were to be divided between the ultra vires depositors and the members of the society pro rata according to their respective payments to the society. The difficulty is to identify any single ratio decidendi for that decision. [His Lordship considered the judgments of Viscount Haldane LC and Lords Atkinson, Dunedin, Sumner and Parker and continued:] As has been pointed out frequently over the 80 years since it was decided, *Sinclair v Brougham* is a bewildering authority: no single ratio decidendi can be detected; all the reasoning is open to serious objection; it was only intended to deal with cases where there were no trade creditors in competition and the reasoning is incapable of application where there are such creditors. In my view the decision as to rights *in rem* in *Sinclair v Brougham* should also be overruled. Although the case is one where property rights are involved, such overruling should not in practice disturb long-settled titles. However, your Lordships should not be taken to be casting any doubt on the principles of tracing as established in *Re Diplock*.

---

[28] Lords Slynn of Hadley and Lloyd of Berwick concurred. Lords Goff of Chieveley and Woolf preferred to distinguish rather than to overrule *Sinclair v Brougham*.

If *Sinclair v Brougham,* in both its aspects, is overruled the law can be established in accordance with principle and commercial common sense: a claimant for restitution of moneys paid under an ultra vires, and therefore void, contract has a personal action at law to recover the moneys paid as on a total failure of consideration; he will not have an equitable proprietary claim which gives him either rights against third parties or priority in an insolvency; nor will he have a personal claim in equity, since the recipient is not a trustee.

In **Chase Manhattan Bank NA v Israel-British Bank (London) Ltd** [1981] Ch 105,[29] the plaintiff bank had paid $2 million to another bank in New York for the account of the defendant bank which carried on business in London. Later the same day the plaintiff bank made a book-keeping error and paid the same amount again. A month later the defendant bank became insolvent and then went into compulsory liquidation. The plaintiff bank sought restitution of the money it had paid by mistake. Since the defendant was insolvent the plaintiff brought a proprietary claim and the question arose whether the plaintiff bank was entitled in equity to trace the mistaken payment into the defendant bank's assets in priority to the general creditors.

Goulding J held that the mistaken payment gave rise to a constructive trust which entitled the plaintiff to trace the money.

The conclusion that money paid by mistake was held on constructive trust simply because of the operation of the mistake was doubted by Lord Browne-Wilkinson in **Westdeutsche Landesbank Girozentrale v Islington London Borough Council** [1996] AC 669 at 714 [p. 281, above]. However, his Lordship considered that money paid by mistake could be held on constructive trust once the recipient of the money was aware of the mistake, since his conscience would then be affected. It would follow that, once a constructive trust has been recognised, the equitable tracing rules would be available because the money would have passed through a fiduciary relationship.

In **Agip (Africa) Ltd v Jackson** [1990] Ch 265,[30] Millett J said at 289:[31]

There is no difficulty in tracing the plaintiffs' property in equity which can follow the money as it passed through the accounts of the correspondent banks in New York or, more realistically, follow the chose in action through its transmutation as a direct result of forged instructions from a debt owed by the Banque de Sud to the plaintiffs in Tunis into a debt owed by Lloyds Bank to Baker Oil in London.

The only restriction on the ability of equity to follow assets is the requirement that there must be some fiduciary relationship which permits the assistance of equity to be invoked. The requirement has been widely condemned and depends on authority rather than principle, but the law was settled by *Re Diplock* [1948] Ch 465 [p. 904, above]. It may need to be reconsidered but not, I venture to think, at first instance. The requirement may be circumvented since it is not necessary that the fund to be traced should have been the subject of fiduciary obligations before it got into the wrong hands; it is sufficient that the payment to the defendant itself gives rise to a fiduciary relationship: *Chase Manhattan Bank NA v Israel-British Bank (London) Ltd* [1981] Ch 105. In that case, however, equity's assistance was not needed in order to trace the

---

[29] (1980) CLJ 272 (A. Tettenborn), 275 (G. Jones); (1980) 43 MLR 489, 500 (W. Goodhart and G. Jones).
[30] The facts are described at p. 901, above.   [31] Affirmed [1991] Ch 547; see Fox LJ at 566.

plaintiff's money into the hands of the defendant; it was needed in order to ascertain whether it had any of the plaintiff's money left. The case cannot, therefore, be used to circumvent the requirement that there should be an initial fiduciary relationship in order to start the tracing process in equity.

The requirement is, however, readily satisfied in most cases of commercial fraud, since the embezzlement of a company's funds almost inevitably involves a breach of fiduciary duty on the part of one of the company's employees or agents. That was so in [the] present case. There was clearly a fiduciary relationship between Mr. Zdiri and the plaintiffs. Mr. Zdiri was not a director nor a signatory on the plaintiffs' bank account, but he was a senior and responsible officer. As such he was entrusted with possession of the signed payment orders to have them taken to the bank and implemented. He took advantage of his possession of them to divert the money and cause the separation between its legal ownership which passed to the payees and its beneficial ownership which remained in the plaintiffs. There is clear authority that there is a receipt of trust property when a company's funds are misapplied by a director and, in my judgment, this is equally the case when a company's funds are misapplied by any person whose fiduciary position gave him control of them or enabled him to misapply them.

The tracing claim in equity gives rise to a proprietary remedy which depends on the continued existence of the trust property in the hands of the defendant. Unless he is a bona fide purchaser for value without notice, he must restore the trust property to its rightful owner if he still has it. But even a volunteer who has received trust property cannot be made subject to a personal liability to account for it as a constructive trustee if he has parted with it without having previously acquired some knowledge of the existence of the trust: *Re Montagu's Settlement Trusts* [1987] Ch 264.

The plaintiffs are entitled to the money in court which rightfully belongs to them. To recover the money which the defendants have paid away the plaintiffs must subject them to a personal liability to account as constructive trustees and prove the requisite degree of knowledge to establish the liability.[32]

(ii) Unmixed Funds

Where property is taken by a person in a fiduciary relationship to the claimant, the claimant may claim that property from the fiduciary, or, if it has been sold, may claim the proceeds of sale, or may follow the property into the hands of a third party, but not if it comes into the hands of a bona fide purchaser for value without notice.[33]

(iii) Mixed Funds

In **Banque Belge Pour L'Etranger v Hambrouck** [1921] 1 KB 321, ATKIN LJ said at 335:

The question always was, had the means of ascertainment failed? But if in 1815 the common law halted outside the bankers' door, by 1879 equity had had the courage to lift the latch, walk in

---

[32] For the action of unconscionable receipt, see p. 971, below.
[33] *Thorndike v Hunt* (1859) 3 De G & J 563; *Taylor v Blakelock* (1886) 32 Ch D 560; *Thomson v Clydesdale Bank Ltd* [1893] AC 282; *Coleman v Bucks and Oxon Union Bank* [1897] 2 Ch 243.

and examine the books: *Re Hallett's Estate* (1880) 13 Ch D 696. I see no reason why the means of ascertainment should not now be available both for common law and equity proceedings.[34]

Re Hallett's Estate
(1880) 13 Ch D 696 (CA, **Sir George Jessel MR, Baggallay** and **Thesiger LJJ**)

Mr. Hallett was a solicitor. He was trustee of his own marriage settlement, and had paid some moneys from that trust into his own bank account. He was solicitor to Mrs. Cotterill, and had been entrusted by her with money for investment. Part of this money was improperly paid into Hallett's bank account. Hallett made various payments from, and into, the account, and also incurred further debts. At the date of his death, the account held sufficient funds to meet the claims of the trustees of the marriage settlement and of Mrs. Cotterill, but not the personal debts as well. In an action for the administration of Hallett's estate, the main question was whether the trust and Mrs. Cotterill could claim in priority to the creditors.

Held. (i) Both the trust and Mrs. Cotterill were entitled to a charge upon the moneys in the bank account in priority to the general creditors; (ii) (Thesiger LJ dissenting) the various payments by Hallett out of the account must be treated as payments of his own money and not that of the trust, nor of Mrs. Cotterill.

Jessel MR: There is no doubt, therefore, that Mr. *Hallett* stood in a fiduciary position towards Mrs. *Cotterill.* Mr. *Hallett,* before his death, I regret to say, improperly sold the bonds and put the money to his general account at his bankers. It is not disputed that the money remained at his bankers mixed with his own money at the time of his death; that is, he had not drawn out that money from his bankers. In that position of matters Mrs. *Cotterill* claimed to be entitled to receive the proceeds, or the amount of the proceeds, of the bonds out of money in the hands of Mr. *Hallett's* bankers at the time of his death, and that claim was allowed by the learned Judge of the Court below, and I think was properly so allowed. Indeed, as I understand the doctrines of Equity, it would have been too clear a case for argument, except for another decision of that learned Judge himself, *Ex p Dale & Co* (1879) 11 Ch D 772. The modern doctrine of Equity as regards property disposed of by persons in a fiduciary position is a very clear and well-established doctrine. You can, if the sale was rightful, take the proceeds of the sale, if you can identify them. If the sale was wrongful, you can still take the proceeds of the sale, in a sense adopting the sale for the purpose of taking the proceeds, if you can identify them. There is no distinction, therefore, between a rightful and a wrongful disposition of the property, so far as regards the right of the beneficial owner to follow the proceeds. But it very often happens that you cannot identify the proceeds. The proceeds may have been invested together with money belonging to the person in a fiduciary position, in a purchase. He may have bought land with it, for instance, or he may have bought chattels with it. Now, what is the position of the beneficial owner as regards such purchases? I will, first of all, take his position when the purchase is clearly made with what I will call, for shortness, the trust money, although it is not confined, as I will shew presently, to express trusts. In that case, according to the now well-established doctrine of Equity, the beneficial owner has a right to elect either to take the property purchased, or to hold

[34] *Chief Constable of Kent v V* [1983] QB 34 at 41, *per* Lord Denning MR.

it as a security for the amount of the trust money laid out in the purchase; or, as we generally express it, he is entitled at his election either to take the property, or to have a charge on the property for the amount of the trust money. But in the second case, where a trustee has mixed the money with his own, there is the distinction, that the *cestui que trust,* or beneficial owner, can no longer elect to take the property, because it is no longer bought with the trust-money simply and purely, but with a mixed fund. He is, however, still entitled to a charge on the property purchased, for the amount of the trust-money laid out in the purchase; and that charge is quite independent of the fact of the amount laid out by the trustee. The moment you get a substantial portion of it furnished by the trustee, using the word 'trustee' in the sense I have mentioned, as including all persons in a fiduciary relation, the right to the charge follows. That is the modern doctrine of Equity. Has it ever been suggested, until very recently, that there is any distinction between an express trustee, or an agent, or a bailee, or a collector of rents, or anybody else in a fiduciary position? I have never heard, until quite recently, such a distinction suggested. It *cannot,* as far as I am aware (and since this Court sat last to hear this case, I have taken the trouble to look for authority), be found in any reported case even suggested, except in the recent decision of Mr. Justice *Fry,* to which I shall draw attention presently. It can have no foundation in principle, because the beneficial ownership is the same, wherever the legal ownership may be. If you have goods bargained and sold to a man upon trust to sell and hand over the net proceeds to another, that other is the beneficial owner; but if instead of being bargained and sold, so as to vest the legal ownership in the trustee, they are deposited with him to sell as agent, so that the legal ownership remains in the beneficial owner, can it be supposed, in a Court of Equity, that the rights of the beneficial owner are different, he being entire beneficial owner in both cases? I say on principle it is impossible to imagine there can be any difference. In practice we know there is no difference, because the moment you get into a Court of Equity, where a principal can sue an agent as well as a *cestui que trust* can sue a trustee, no such distinction was ever suggested, as far as I am aware. Therefore, the moment you establish the fiduciary relation, the modern rules of Equity, as regards following trust money, apply. I intentionally say modern rules, because it must not be forgotten that the rules of Courts of Equity are not, like the rules of the Common Law, supposed to have been established from time immemorial. It is perfectly well known that they have been established from time to time—altered, improved, and refined from time to time. In many cases we know the names of the Chancellors who invented them. No doubt they were invented for the purpose of securing the better administration of justice, but still they were invented. Take such things as these: the separate use of a married woman, the restraint on alienation, the modern rule against perpetuities, and the rules of equitable waste. We can name the Chancellors who first invented them, and state the date when they were first introduced into Equity jurisprudence; and, therefore in cases of this kind, the older precedents in Equity are of very little value. The doctrines are progressive, refined, and improved; and if we want to know what the rules of Equity are, we must look, of course, rather to the more modern than the more ancient cases.

Now that being the established doctrine of Equity on this point, I will take the case of the pure bailee. If the bailee sells the goods bailed, the bailor can in Equity follow the proceeds, and can follow the proceeds wherever they can be distinguished, either being actually kept separate, or being mixed up with other moneys. I have only to advert to one other point, and that is this— supposing, instead of being invested in the purchase of land or goods, the moneys were simply mixed with other moneys of the trustee, using the term again in its full sense as including every person in a fiduciary relation, does it make any difference according to the modern doctrine of

Equity? I say none. It would be very remarkable if it were to do so. Supposing the trust money was 1,000 sovereigns, and the trustee put them into a bag, and by mistake, or accident, or otherwise, dropped a sovereign of his own into the bag. Could anybody suppose that a Judge in Equity would find any difficulty in saying that the *cestui que trust* had a right to take 1,000 sovereigns out of that bag? I do not like to call it a charge of 1,000 sovereigns on the 1,001 sovereigns, but that is the effect of it. I have no doubt of it. It would make no difference if, instead of one sovereign, it was another 1,000 sovereigns. . . .

[His Lordship referred to various authorities, including *Taylor v Plumer* (1815) 3 M & S 562, from which he quoted Lord Ellenborough:] 'and the right only ceases when the means of ascertainment fail'. That is correct. Now there comes a point which is not correct, but which I am afraid only ceases to be correct because Lord *Ellenborough's* knowledge of the rules of Equity was not quite commensurate with his knowledge of the rules of Common Law, 'which is the case when the subject is turned into money, and mixed and confounded in a general mass of the same description'. He was not aware of the rule of Equity which gave you a charge—that if you lent £1,000 of your own and £1,000 trust money on a bond for £2,000, or on a mortgage for £2,000, or on a promissory note for £2,000, Equity could follow it, and create a charge; but he gives that, not as law—the law is that it only fails when the means of ascertainment fail—he gives it as a case in which the means of ascertainment fail, not being aware of this refinement of Equity by which the means of ascertainment still remain. With the exception of that one fact, which is rather a fact than a statement of law, the rest of the judgment is in my opinion admirable. It goes on: 'the difficulty which arises in such a case is a difficulty of fact, and not of law, and the dictum that money has no ear-mark must be understood in the same way, i.e., as predicated only of an undivided and undistinguishable mass of current money.' There, again, as I say, he did not know that Equity would have followed the money, even if put into a bag or into an undistinguishable mass, by taking out the same quantity . . .

I think after those authorities it must now be considered settled that there is no distinction, and never was a distinction, between a person occupying one fiduciary position or another fiduciary position as to the right of the beneficial owner to follow the trust fund, and that those cases which have been cited at Law so far from establishing a distinction, establish the contrary; and that the mere error of supposing that Equity could not follow or distinguish money in the cases supposed, if error it was, and perhaps it was not so originally (I am not sure that the doctrine of equity had got so far at the first start, but it was certainly an error at a later period), is attributable really to the fact that the Judges who followed the earlier cases were not aware of what I may call the gradual refinement of the doctrine of equity. Therefore, looking at the authorities to find out the principle, you do not find out any such distinction established as that suggested by Mr. Justice *Fry,* or anything of the kind even mentioned in them; and I do not know of anything more mischievous than for a Judge to say, 'the cases before me establish no principle, but they quite establish something else which I will now enunciate, and therefore hold myself bound by those cases to establish another principle which was never suggested or thought of by the Judges who decided the original cases'. It is only out of my great respect and esteem for the learned Judge from whom this appeal comes that I have thought it right to go so fully into the cases to shew that there is no foundation whatever for the suggested distinction, and therefore his decision in this case rests on no trivial or slight distinction between this case and the case of *Ex p Dale* & *Co* (1879) 11 Ch D 772, but is grounded on the well-ascertained doctrines of equity.

[On the question whether the Rule in *Clayton*'s case (1816) 1 Mer 572 applied as between the claims of the beneficiaries and Hallett's estate,[35] his Lordship continued:] I will first of all consider the case on principle, and then I will consider how far we are bound by authority to come to a decision opposed to principle. It may well be, and sometimes does so happen, that we are bound to come to a decision opposed to principle. Now, first upon principle, nothing can be better settled, either in our own law, or, I suppose, the law of all civilised countries, than this, that where a man does an act which may be rightfully performed, he cannot say that that act was intentionally and in fact done wrongly. A man who has a right of entry cannot say he committed a trespass in entering. A man who sells the goods of another as agent for the owner cannot prevent the owner adopting the sale, and deny that he acted as agent for the owner. It runs throughout our law, and we are familiar with numerous instances in the law of real property. A man who grants a lease believing he has sufficient estate to grant it, although it turns out that he has not, but has a power which enables him to grant it, is not allowed to say he did not grant it under the power. Wherever it can be done rightfully, he is not allowed to say, against the person entitled to the property or the right, that he has done it wrongfully. That is the universal law.

When we come to apply that principle to the case of a trustee who has blended trust moneys with his own, it seems to me perfectly plain that he cannot be heard to say that he took away the trust money when he had a right to take away his own money. The simplest case put is the mingling of trust moneys in a bag with money of the trustee's own. Suppose he has a hundred sovereigns in a bag, and he adds to them another hundred sovereigns of his own, so that they are commingled in such a way that they cannot be distinguished, and the next day he draws out for his own purposes £100, is it tolerable for anybody to allege that what he drew out was the first £100, the trust money, and that he misappropriated it, and left his own £100 in the bag? It is obvious he must have taken away that which he had a right to take away, his own £100. What difference does it make if, instead of being in a bag, he deposits it with his banker, and then pays in other money of his own, and draws out some money for his own purpose? Could he say that he had actually drawn out anything but his own money? His money was there, and he had a right to draw it out, and why should the natural act of simply drawing out the money be attributed to anything except to his ownership of money which was at the bankers[?]

It is said, no doubt, that according to the modern theory of banking, the deposit banker is a debtor for the money. So he is, and not a trustee in the strict sense of the word. At the same time one must recollect that the position of a deposit banker is different from that of an ordinary debtor. Still he is for some purposes a debtor, and it is said if a debt of this kind is paid by a banker, although the total balance is the amount owing by the banker, yet considering the repayments and the sums paid in by the depositor, you attribute the first sum drawn out to the first sum paid in. That was rule first established by Sir *William Grant* in *Clayton's Case* (1816) 1 Mer 572,[36] a very convenient rule, and I have nothing to say against it unless there is evidence either of agreement to the contrary or of circumstances from which a contrary intention must be presumed, and then of course that which is a mere presumption of law gives way to those other considerations. Therefore, it does appear to me there is nothing in the world laid down by Sir *William Grant* in *Clayton's Case,* or in the numerous cases which follow it, which in the slightest degree affects the principle, which I consider to be clearly established.

---

[35] As there were sufficient moneys to satisfy both those prior claims, no question of competition between the marriage settlement trustees and Mrs. Cotterill arose. Fry J had held, below, that as between two *cestuis que trust* whose money had been paid by a trustee into his account, the rule in *Clayton's* case applied. See *Re Diplock* [1948] Ch 465 at 554. On the rule generally, see p. 935, below.   [36] See p. 935, below.

[His Lordship then held that he was not bound by *Pennell v Deffell* (1853) 4 De GM & G 372 and concluded:] Therefore in my opinion, the appeal must be allowed.[37]

Foskett v McKeown
[2001] 1 AC 102 (HL, **Lords Browne-Wilkinson, Steyn, Hoffmann, Hope** and **Millett**)[38]

In 1986 Mr. Murphy entered into a whole-life insurance policy. The sum assured was £1 million and the annual premium was £10,200. The policy stated that on Murphy's death a specified death benefit became payable, which would be the greater of (1) the sum assured and (2) the aggregate value of units notionally allocated to the policy under its terms at their bid price on the day of the receipt by the insurers of a written notice of death (the investment element). One of the functions of this investment element was to pay for the cost of life cover. This worked in the following way. On the receipt of a premium a notional allocation of units would take place and the insurers would cancel units to meet the cost of life cover for the next year. If premiums ceased to be paid, the policy would be converted into a paid-up policy and units would continue to be cancelled until there were no units left. Once there were no units left the policy would lapse so that death benefit or surrender value would no longer be available.

The policy and money paid under it were held on an express trust for Murphy's wife and children. Murphy paid five premiums. The first three were paid from his own money, but he then paid two other premiums from another trust, one in 1989 and the other in 1990. The money in this trust had been paid by purchasers to a Mr. Deasy in respect of the possible development of land in Portugal. Mr. Deasy held this money on trust for the purchasers. Murphy committed suicide and the insurers paid just over £1 million to two remaining trustees of the insurance policy. The purchasers claimed that, since at least two of the five premiums had been paid from money which had been held on trust for them, they should recover at least two-fifths of the £1 million with the remaining amount being paid to Murphy's children.

The Court of Appeal [1998] Ch 265 (Sir Richard Scott V-C and Hobhouse LJ, Morritt LJ dissenting)[39] held that the purchasers could recover the value of two of the premiums plus interest but could not receive any share of the proceeds of the policy. The purchasers appealed to the House of Lords.

Held (Lords Steyn and Hope dissenting). The purchasers were entitled to recover two-fifths of the £1 million which was held on trust for the children.

Lord Browne-Wilkinson: My Lords, there are many cases in which the court has to decide which of two innocent parties is to suffer from the activities of a fraudster. This case, unusually, raises the converse question: which of two innocent parties is to benefit from the activities of the

---

[37] See also *Re Oatway* [1903] 2 Ch 356, explained in *Re Tilley's Will Trusts* [1967] Ch 1179 [p. 930, below].
[38] (2001) 117 LQR 366 (A. Berg): (2000) 59 CLJ 440 (C. Rotherham); (2000) 63 MLR 905 (R. Grantham and C. Rickett); (2000) 14 *Trust Law International* 194 (P. Jaffey); [2000] *Restitution Law Review* 573 (Sir Robert Walker); [2001] Conv 94 (J. Stevens); [2001] LMCLQ 1 (D. Fox); (2001) 25 *Melbourne University Law Review* 295 (T.H. Wu).   [39] [1997] LMCLQ 465 (C. Mitchell); (1997) 56 CLJ 41 (R. Nolan).

fraudster[?] In my judgment, in the context of this case the two types of case fall to be decided on exactly the same principles, *viz.* by determining who enjoys the ownership of the property in which the loss or the unexpected benefit is reflected....

As to the appeal, at the conclusion of the hearing I considered that the majority of the Court of Appeal were correct and would have dismissed the appeal. However, having read the draft speech of Lord Millett I have changed my mind and for the reasons which he gives I would allow the appeal. But, as we are differing from the majority of the Court of Appeal I will say a word or two about the substance of the case and then deal with one minor matter on which I do not agree with my noble and learned friend, Lord Millett.

The crucial factor in this case is to appreciate that the purchasers are claiming a proprietary interest in the policy moneys and that such proprietary interest is not dependent on any discretion vested in the court. Nor is the purchasers' claim based on unjust enrichment. It is based on the assertion by the purchasers of their equitable proprietary interest in identified property.

The first step is to identify the interest of the purchasers: it is their absolute equitable interest in the moneys originally held by Mr. Deasy on the express trusts of the purchasers' trust deed. This case does not involve any question of resulting or constructive trusts. The only trusts at issue are the express trusts of the purchasers' trust deed. Under those express trusts the purchasers were entitled to equitable interests in the original moneys paid to Mr. Deasy by the purchasers. Like any other equitable proprietary interest, those equitable proprietary interests under the purchasers' trust deed which originally existed in the moneys paid to Mr. Deasy now exist in any other property which, in law, now represents the original trust assets. Those equitable interests under the purchasers' trust deed are also enforceable against whoever for the time being holds those assets other than someone who is a bona fide purchaser for value of the legal interest without notice or a person who claims through such a purchaser. No question of a bona fide purchaser arises in the present case: the children are mere volunteers under the policy trust. Therefore the critical question is whether the assets now subject to the express trusts of the purchasers' trust deed comprise any part of the policy moneys, a question which depends on the rules of tracing. If, as a result of tracing, it can be said that certain of the policy moneys are what now represent part of the assets subject to the trusts of the purchasers' trust deed, then as a matter of English property law the purchasers have an absolute interest in such moneys. There is no discretion vested in the court. There is no room for any consideration whether, in the circumstances of this particular case, it is in a moral sense 'equitable' for the purchasers to be so entitled. The rules establishing equitable proprietary interests and their enforceability against certain parties have been developed over the centuries and are an integral part of the property law of England. It is a fundamental error to think that, because certain property rights are equitable rather than legal, such rights are in some way discretionary. This case does not depend on whether it is fair, just and reasonable to give the purchasers an interest as a result of which the court in its discretion provides a remedy. It is a case of hard-nosed property rights.

Can then the sums improperly used from the purchasers' moneys be traced into the policy moneys? Tracing is a process whereby assets are identified. I do not now want to enter into the dispute whether the legal and equitable rules of tracing are the same or differ. The question does not arise in this case. The question of tracing which does arise is whether the rules of tracing are those regulating tracing through a mixed fund or those regulating the position when moneys of one person have been innocently expended on the property of another. In the former case (mixing of funds) it is established law that the mixed fund belongs proportionately to those whose moneys were mixed. In the latter case it is equally clear that money expended on maintaining or improving the property of another normally gives rise, at the most, to a proprietary lien to recover the moneys so expended. In certain cases the rules of tracing in such a case may give rise to no proprietary interest at all if to give such interest would be unfair: see *Re Diplock* [1948] Ch 465, at 548.

Both Sir Richard Scott V-C and Hobhouse LJ considered that the payment of a premium on someone else's policy was more akin to an improvement to land than to the mixing of separate trust moneys in one account. Hobhouse LJ was additionally influenced by the fact that the payment of the fourth and fifth premiums out of the purchasers' moneys conferred no benefit on the children: the policy was theirs and, since the first two premiums had already been paid, the policy would not have lapsed even if the fourth and fifth premiums had not been paid.

Cases where the money of one person has been expended on improving or maintaining the physical property of another raise special problems. The property left at the end of the day is incapable of being physically divided into its separate constituent assets, i.e. the land and the money spent on it. Nor can the rules for tracing moneys through a mixed fund apply: the essence of tracing through a mixed fund is the ability to re-divide the mixed fund into its constituent parts pro rata according to the value of the contributions made to it. The question which arises in this case is whether, for tracing purposes, the payments of the fourth and fifth premiums on a policy which, up to that date, had been the sole property of the children for tracing purposes fall to be treated as analogous to the expenditure of cash on the physical property of another or as analogous to the mixture of moneys in a bank account. If the former analogy is to be preferred, the maximum amount recoverable by the purchasers will be the amount of the fourth and fifth premiums plus interest: if the latter analogy is preferred the children and the other purchasers will share the policy moneys pro rata.

The speech of my noble and learned friend, Lord Millett, demonstrates why the analogy with moneys mixed in an account is the correct one. Where a trustee in breach of trust mixes money in his own bank account with trust moneys, the moneys in the account belong to the trustee personally and to the beneficiaries under the trust rateably according to the amounts respectively provided. On a proper analysis, there are 'no moneys in the account' in the sense of physical cash. Immediately before the improper mixture, the trustee had a chose in action being his right against the bank to demand a payment of the credit balance on his account. Immediately after the mixture, the trustee had the same chose in action (i.e. the right of action against the bank) but its value reflected in part the amount of the beneficiaries' moneys wrongly paid in. There is no doubt that in such a case of moneys mixed in a bank account the credit balance on the account belongs to the trustee and the beneficiaries rateably according to their respective contributions.

So in the present case. Immediately before the payment of the fourth premium, the trust property held in trust for the children was a chose in action, i.e. the bundle of rights enforceable under the policy against the insurers. The trustee, by paying the fourth premium out of the moneys subject to the purchasers' trust deed, wrongly mixed the value of the premium with the value of the policy. Thereafter, the trustee for the children held the same chose in action (i.e. the policy) but it reflected the value of both contributions. The case, therefore, is wholly analogous to that where moneys are mixed in a bank account. It follows that, in my judgment, both the policy and the policy moneys belong to the children and the trust fund subject to the purchasers' trust deed rateably according to their respective contributions to the premiums paid.

The contrary view appears to be based primarily on the ground that to give the purchasers a rateable share of the policy moneys is not to reverse an unjust enrichment but to give the purchasers a wholly unwarranted windfall. I do not myself quibble at the description of it being 'a windfall' on the facts of this case. But this windfall is enjoyed because of the rights which the purchasers enjoy under the law of property. A man under whose land oil is discovered enjoys a very valuable windfall but no one suggests that he, as owner of the property, is not entitled to the windfall which goes with his property right. We are not dealing with a claim in unjust enrichment.

Moreover the argument based on windfall can be, and is, much over-stated. It is said that the fourth and fifth premiums paid out of the purchasers' moneys did not increase the value of the policy in any way: the first and second premiums were, by themselves, sufficient under the unusual terms of the policy to pay all the premiums falling due without any assistance from the fourth and fifth premiums: even if the fourth and fifth premiums had not been paid the policy would have been in force at the time of Mr. Murphy's death. Therefore, it is asked, what value has been derived from the fourth and fifth premiums which can justify giving the purchasers a pro rata share. In my judgment this argument does not reflect the true position. It is true that, in the events which have happened, the fourth and fifth premiums were not required to keep the policy on foot until the death of Mr. Murphy. But at the times the fourth and fifth premiums were paid (which must be the dates at which the beneficial interests in the policy were established) it was wholly uncertain what the future would bring. What if Mr. Murphy had not died when he did? Say he had survived for another five years? The premiums paid in the fourth and fifth years would in those events have been directly responsible for keeping the policy in force until his death since the first and second premiums would long since have been exhausted in keeping the policy on foot. In those circumstances, would it be said that the purchasers were entitled to 100 per cent of the policy moneys? In my judgment, the beneficial ownership of the policy, and therefore the policy moneys, cannot depend upon how events turn out. The rights of the parties in the policy, one way or another, were fixed when the relevant premiums were paid when the future was unknown.

For these reasons and the much fuller reasons given by Lord Millett, I would allow the appeal and declare that the policy moneys were held in trust for the children and the purchasers in proportion to the contributions which they respectively made to the five premiums paid.

Lord Hoffmann: My Lords, I have had the advantage of reading in draft the speech of my noble and learned friend, Lord Millett. I agree with him that this is a straightforward case of mixed substitution (what the Roman lawyers, if they had had an economy which required tracing through bank accounts, would have called *confusio*).[40] I agree with his conclusion that Mr. Murphy's children, claiming through him, and the trust beneficiaries whose money he used, are entitled to share in the proceeds of the insurance policy in proportion to the value which they respectively contributed to the policy. This not based upon unjust enrichment except in the most trivial sense of that expression. It is, as my noble and learned friend says, a vindication of proprietary right. . . .

Lord Millett: My Lords, this is a textbook example of tracing through mixed substitutions. At the beginning of the story the plaintiffs were beneficially entitled under an express trust to a sum standing in the name of Mr. Murphy in a bank account. From there the money moved into and out of various bank accounts where in breach of trust it was inextricably mixed by Mr. Murphy with his own money. After each transaction was completed the plaintiffs' money

---

[40] Lord Hope of Craighead disagreed: [2001] 1 AC 102 at 120.

formed an indistinguishable part of the balance standing to Mr. Murphy's credit in his bank account. The amount of that balance represented a debt due from the bank to Mr. Murphy, that is to say a chose in action. At the penultimate stage the plaintiffs' money was represented by an indistinguishable part of a different chose in action, *viz.* the debt prospectively and contingently due from an insurance company to its policyholders, being the trustees of a settlement made by Mr. Murphy for the benefit of his children. At the present and final stage it forms an indistinguishable part of the balance standing to the credit of the respondent trustees in their bank account....

In the present case the plaintiffs do not seek to follow the money any further once it reached the bank or insurance company, since its identity was lost in the hands of the recipient (which in any case obtained an unassailable title as a bona fide purchaser for value without notice of the plaintiffs' beneficial interest). Instead the plaintiffs have chosen at each stage to trace the money into its proceeds, *viz.* the debt presently due from the bank to the account holder or the debt prospectively and contingently due from the insurance company to the policy holders.

Having completed this exercise, the plaintiffs claim a continuing beneficial interest in the insurance money. Since this represents the product of Mr. Murphy's own money as well as theirs, which Mr. Murphy mingled indistinguishably in a single chose in action, they claim a beneficial interest in a proportionate part of the money only. The transmission of a claimant's property rights from one asset to its traceable proceeds is part of our law of property, not of the law of unjust enrichment. There is no 'unjust factor' to justify restitution (unless 'want of title' be one, which makes the point). The claimant succeeds if at all by virtue of his own title, not to reverse unjust enrichment. Property rights are determined by fixed rules and settled principles. They are not discretionary. They do not depend upon ideas of what is 'fair, just and reasonable'. Such concepts, which in reality mask decisions of legal policy, have no place in the law of property.

A beneficiary of a trust is entitled to a continuing beneficial interest not merely in the trust property but in its traceable proceeds also, and his interest binds every one who takes the property or its traceable proceeds except a bona fide purchaser for value without notice. In the present case the plaintiffs' beneficial interest plainly bound Mr. Murphy, a trustee who wrongfully mixed the trust money with his own and whose every dealing with the money (including the payment of the premiums) was in breach of trust. It similarly binds his successors, the trustees of the children's settlement, who claim no beneficial interest of their own, and Mr. Murphy's children, who are volunteers. They gave no value for what they received and derive their interest from Mr. Murphy by way of gift....

[His Lordship considered the nature of tracing [see p. 896, above] and continued:] This is not, however, the occasion to explore these matters further, for the present is a straightforward case of a trustee who wrongfully misappropriated trust money, mixed it with his own, and used it to pay for an asset for the benefit of his children. Even on the traditional approach, the equitable tracing rules are available to the plaintiffs. There are only two complicating factors. The first is that the wrongdoer used their money to pay premiums on an equity-linked policy of life assurance on his own life. The nature of the policy should make no difference in principle, though it may complicate the accounting. The second is that he had previously settled the policy for the benefit of his children. This should also make no difference. The claimant's rights cannot depend on whether the wrongdoer gave the policy to his children during his lifetime or left the proceeds to them by his will; or if during his lifetime whether he did so before or after he had recourse to the claimant's money to pay the premiums. The order of events does not affect the fact that the children are not contributors but volunteers who have received the gift of an asset paid for in part with misappropriated trust moneys....

The tracing rules

The insurance policy in the present case is a very sophisticated financial instrument. Tracing into the rights conferred by such an instrument raises a number of important issues. It is therefore desirable to set out the basic principles before turning to deal with the particular problems to which policies of life assurance give rise.

The simplest case is where a trustee wrongfully misappropriates trust property and uses it exclusively to acquire other property for his own benefit. In such a case the beneficiary is entitled at his option either to assert his beneficial ownership of the proceeds or to bring a personal claim against the trustee for breach of trust and enforce an equitable lien or charge on the proceeds to secure restoration of the trust fund. He will normally exercise the option in the way most advantageous to himself. If the traceable proceeds have increased in value and are worth more than the original asset, he will assert his beneficial ownership and obtain the profit for himself. There is nothing unfair in this. The trustee cannot be permitted to keep any profit resulting from his misappropriation for himself, and his donees cannot obtain a better title than their donor. If the traceable proceeds are worth less than the original asset, it does not usually matter how the beneficiary exercises his option. He will take the whole of the proceeds on either basis. This is why it is not possible to identify the basis on which the claim succeeded in some of the cases.

Both remedies are proprietary and depend on successfully tracing the trust property into its proceeds. A beneficiary's claim against a trustee for breach of trust is a personal claim. It does not entitle him to priority over the trustee's general creditors unless he can trace the trust property into its product and establish a proprietary interest in the proceeds. If the beneficiary is unable to trace the trust property into its proceeds, he still has a personal claim against the trustee, but his claim will be unsecured. The beneficiary's proprietary claims to the trust property or its traceable proceeds can be maintained against the wrongdoer and anyone who derives title from him except a bona fide purchaser for value without notice of the breach of trust. The same rules apply even where there have been numerous successive transactions, so long as the tracing exercise is successful and no bona fide purchaser for value without notice has intervened.

A more complicated case is where there is a mixed substitution. This occurs where the trust money represents only part of the cost of acquiring the new asset. As James Barr Ames pointed out in 'Following Misappropriated Property into its Product' (1906) 19 *Harvard Law Review* 511, consistency requires that, if a trustee buys property partly with his own money and partly with trust money, the beneficiary should have the option of taking a proportionate part of the new property or a lien upon it, as may be most for his advantage. In principle it should not matter (and it has never previously been suggested that it does) whether the trustee mixes the trust money with his own and buys the new asset with the mixed fund or makes separate payments of the purchase price (whether simultaneously or sequentially) out of the different funds. In every case the value formerly inherent in the trust property has become located within the value inherent in the new asset.

The rule, and its rationale, were stated by Samuel Williston in 'The Right to Follow Trust Property when Confused with other Property' (1888) 2 *Harvard Law Review* 28, 29:

'If the trust fund is traceable as having furnished in part the money with which a certain investment was made, and the proportion it formed of the whole money so invested is known or ascertainable, the *cestui que trust* should be allowed to regard the acts of the trustee as done for his benefit, in the same way that he would be allowed to if all the money so invested had been his; that is, he should be entitled in equity to an undivided share of the property which the trust money contributed to purchase—such a proportion of the whole as the trust money bore to the whole money invested. The reason in the one case as in the other is that the trustee cannot be allowed to make a profit from the use of the trust money, and if the property which he wrongfully purchased were held subject only to a lien for the amount invested, any appreciation in value would go to the trustee.'

If this correctly states the underlying basis of the rule (as I believe it does), then it is impossible to distinguish between the case where mixing precedes the investment and the case where it arises on and in consequence of the investment. It is also impossible to distinguish between the case where the investment is retained by the trustee and the case where it is given away to a gratuitous donee. The donee cannot obtain a better title than his donor, and a donor who is a trustee cannot be allowed to profit from his trust.

In *Re Hallett's Estate* (1880) 13 Ch D 696, 709 [p. 911, above], Sir George Jessel MR acknowledged that where an asset was acquired exclusively with trust money, the beneficiary could either assert equitable ownership of the asset or enforce a lien or charge over it to recover the trust money. But he appeared to suggest that in the case of a mixed substitution the beneficiary is confined to a lien. Any authority that this dictum might otherwise have is weakened by the fact that Sir George Jessel MR gave no reason for the existence of any such rule, and none is readily apparent. The dictum was plainly obiter, for the fund was deficient and the plaintiff was only claiming a lien....

In my view the time has come to state unequivocally that English law has no such rule. It conflicts with the rule that a trustee must not benefit from his trust. I agree with Burrows [*The Law of Restitution* (1993), p. 368] that the beneficiary's right to elect to have a proportionate share of a mixed substitution necessarily follows once one accepts, as English law does, (i) that a claimant can trace in equity into a mixed fund and (ii) that he can trace unmixed money into its proceeds and assert ownership of the proceeds.

Accordingly, I would state the basic rule as follows. Where a trustee wrongfully uses trust money to provide part of the cost of acquiring an asset, the beneficiary is entitled at his option either to claim a proportionate share of the asset or to enforce a lien upon it to secure his personal claim against the trustee for the amount of the misapplied money. It does not matter whether the trustee mixed the trust money with his own in a single fund before using it to acquire the asset, or made separate payments (whether simultaneously or sequentially) out of the differently owned funds to acquire a single asset.

Two observations are necessary at this point. First, there is a mixed substitution (with the results already described) whenever the claimant's property has contributed in part only towards the acquisition of the new asset. It is not necessary for the claimant to show in addition that his property has contributed to any increase in the value of the new asset. This is because, as I have already pointed out, this branch of the law is concerned with vindicating rights of property and not with reversing unjust enrichment. Secondly, the beneficiary's right to claim a lien is available only against a wrongdoer and those deriving title under him otherwise than for value. It is not available against competing contributors who are innocent of any wrongdoing. The tracing rules are not the result of any presumption or principle peculiar to equity. They correspond to the common law rules for following into physical mixtures (though the consequences may not be identical). Common to both is the principle that the interests of the wrongdoer who was responsible for the mixing and those who derive title under him otherwise than for value are subordinated to those of innocent contributors. As against the wrongdoer and his successors, the beneficiary is entitled to locate his contribution in any part of the mixture and to subordinate their claims to share in the mixture until his own contribution has been satisfied. This has the effect of giving the beneficiary a lien for his contribution if the mixture is deficient.

Innocent contributors, however, must be treated equally *inter se*. Where the beneficiary's claim is in competition with the claims of other innocent contributors, there is no basis upon which any of the claims can be subordinated to any of the others. Where the fund is deficient, the beneficiary is not entitled to enforce a lien for his contributions; all must share rateably in the fund.

The primary rule in regard to a mixed fund, therefore, is that gains and losses are borne by the contributors rateably. The beneficiary's right to elect instead to enforce a lien to obtain repayment is an exception to the primary rule, exercisable where the fund is deficient and the claim is made against the wrongdoer and those claiming through him. It is not necessary to consider whether there are any circumstances in which the beneficiary is confined to a lien in cases where the fund is more than sufficient to repay the contributions of all parties. It is sufficient to say that he is not so confined in a case like the present. It is not enough that those defending the claim are innocent of any wrongdoing if they are not themselves contributors but, like the trustees and Mr. Murphy's children in the present case, are volunteers who derive title under the wrongdoer otherwise than for value. On ordinary principles such persons are in no better position than the wrongdoer, and are liable to suffer the same subordination of their interests to those of the claimant as the wrongdoer would have been. They certainly cannot do better than the claimant by confining him to a lien and keeping any profit for themselves.

Similar principles apply to following into physical mixtures: see *Lupton v White* (1808) 15 Ves 432; and *Sandeman & Sons v Tyzack and Branfoor Steamship Co Ltd* [1913] AC 680, at 695, where Lord Moulton said: 'if the mixing has arisen from the fault of "B", "A" can claim the goods'. There are relatively few cases which deal with the position of the innocent recipient from the wrongdoer, but *Jones v de Marchant* (1916) 28 DLR 561 may be cited as an example. A husband wrongfully used 18 beaver skins belonging to his wife and used them, together with 4 skins of his own, to have a fur coat made up which he then gave to his mistress. Unsurprisingly the wife was held entitled to recover the coat. The mistress knew nothing of the true ownership of the skins, but her innocence was held to be immaterial. She was a gratuitous donee and could stand in no better position than the husband. The coat was a new asset manufactured from the skins and not merely the product of intermingling them. The problem could not be solved by a sale of the coat in order to reduce the disputed property to a divisible fund, since (as we shall see) the realisation of an asset does not affect its ownership. It would hardly have been appropriate to require the two ladies to share the coat between them. Accordingly it was an all-or-nothing case in which the ownership of the coat must be assigned to one or other of the parties. The determinative factor was that the mixing was the act of the wrongdoer through whom the mistress acquired the coat otherwise than for value.

The rule in equity is to the same effect, as Sir William Page Wood V-C observed in *Frith v Cartland* (1865) 2 Hem & M 417, at 420: 'if a man mixes trust funds with his own, the whole will be treated as the trust property, except so far as he may be able to distinguish what is his own'. This does not, in my opinion, exclude a pro rata division where this is appropriate, as in the case of money and other fungibles like grain, oil or wine. But it is to be observed that a pro rata division is the best that the wrongdoer and his donees can hope for. If a pro rata division is excluded, the beneficiary takes the whole; there is no question of confining him to a lien. *Jones v de Marchant* (1916) 28 DLR 561 is a useful illustration of the principles shared by the common law and equity alike that an innocent recipient who receives misappropriated property by way of gift obtains no better title than his donor, and that if a proportionate sharing is inappropriate the wrongdoer and those who derive title under him take nothing.

Insurance policies

... In the present case the benefits specified in the policy are expressed to be payable 'in consideration of the payment of the first premium already made and of the further premiums payable'. The premiums are stated to be £10,220 payable at annual intervals from 6 November, 1985 throughout the lifetime of the life assured'. It is beyond argument that the death benefit of £1 million paid on Mr. Murphy's death was paid in consideration for all the premiums which had been paid before that date, including those paid with the plaintiffs' money, and not just some of them. Part of that sum, therefore, represented the traceable proceeds of the plaintiffs' money.

It is, however, of critical importance in the present case to appreciate that the plaintiffs do not trace the premiums directly into the insurance money. They trace them first into the policy and thence into the proceeds of the policy. It is essential not to elide the two steps. In this context, of course, the word 'policy' does not mean the contract of insurance. You do not trace the payment of a premium into the insurance contract any more than you trace a payment into a bank account into the banking contract. The word 'policy' is here used to describe the bundle of rights to which the policyholder is entitled in return for the premiums. These rights, which may be very complex, together constitute a chose in action, *viz.* the right to payment of a debt payable on a future event and contingent upon the continued payment of further premiums until the happening of the event. That chose in action represents the traceable proceeds of the premiums; its current value fluctuates from time to time. When the policy matures, the insurance money represents the traceable proceeds of the policy and hence indirectly of the premiums.

It follows that, if a claimant can show that premiums were paid with his money, he can claim a proportionate share of the policy. His interest arises by reason of and immediately upon the payment of the premiums, and the extent of his share is ascertainable at once. He does not have to wait until the policy matures in order to claim his property. His share in the policy and its proceeds may increase or decrease as further premiums are paid; but it is not affected by the realisation of the policy. His share remains the same whether the policy is sold or surrendered or held until maturity; these are merely different methods of realising the policy. They may affect the amount of the proceeds received on realisation but they cannot affect the extent of his share in the proceeds. In principle the plaintiffs are entitled to the insurance money which was paid on Mr. Murphy's death in the same shares and proportions as they were entitled in the policy immediately before his death.

Since the manner in which an asset is realised does not affect its ownership, and since it cannot matter whether the claimant discovers what has happened before or after it is realised, the question of ownership can be answered by ascertaining the shares in which it is owned immediately before it is realised. Where A misappropriates B's money and uses it to buy a winning ticket in the lottery, B is entitled to the winnings. Since A is a wrongdoer, it is irrelevant that he could have used his own money if in fact he used B's. This may seem to give B an undeserved windfall, but the result is not unjust. Had B discovered the fraud before the draw, he could have decided whether to keep the ticket or demand his money back. He alone has the right to decide whether to gamble with his own money. If A keeps him in ignorance until after the draw, he suffers the consequence. He cannot deprive B of his right to choose what to do with his own money; but he can give him an informed choice.

The application of these principles ought not to depend on the nature of the chose in action. They should apply to a policy of life assurance as they apply to a bank account or a lottery ticket. It has not been suggested in argument that they do not apply to a policy of life assurance. This question has not been discussed in the English authorities, but it has been considered in the United States. In a Note (1925) 35 *Yale Law Journal* 220–227 Professor Palmer doubted the claimant's right to share in the proceeds of a life policy, and suggested that he should be confined to a lien for his contributions. Professor Palmer accepted, as the majority of the Court of Appeal in the present case did not, that the claimant can trace from the premiums into the policy and that the proceeds of the policy are the product of all the premiums. His doubts were not based on any technical considerations but on questions of social policy. They have not been shared by the American courts. These have generally allowed the claimant a share in the proceeds proportionate to his contributions even though the share in the proceeds is greater than the amount of his money used in paying the premiums: see for example *Shaler v Trowbridge* (1877) 28 NJEq 595; *Holmes v Gilman* 138 NY 369 (1893); *Vorlander v Keyes* 1 F 2d 67 (1924); *Truelsch v Northwestern Mutual Life Insurance Co* 202 NW 352 (1925); *Baxter House v Rosen* 278 NY 2d 442 (1967); *Lohman v General American Life Insurance Co* 478 F 2d 719 (1973). This accords with Ames's and Williston's opinions in the articles to which I have referred.

The question is discussed at length in *Scott on Trusts* (4th edn), pp. 574–584, section 508.4. Professor Scott concludes that there is no substance in the doubts expressed by Palmer. He points out that the strongest argument in favour of limiting the beneficiary's claim to a lien is that otherwise he obtains a windfall. But in cases where the wrongdoer has misappropriated the claimant's money and used it to acquire other forms of property which have greatly increased in value the courts have consistently refused to limit the claimant to an equitable lien. In any case, the windfall argument is suspect. As Professor Scott points out, a life policy is an aleatory contract. Whether or not the sum assured exceeds the premiums is a matter of chance. Viewed from the perspective of the insurer, the contract is a commercial one; so the chances are weighted against the assured. But the outcome in any individual case is unpredictable at the time the premiums are paid. The unspoken assumption in the argument that a life policy should be treated differently from other choses in action seems to be that, by dying earlier than expected, the assured provides a contribution of indeterminate but presumably substantial value. But the assumption is false. A life policy is not an indemnity policy, in which the rights against the insurer are acquired by virtue of the payment of the premiums and the diminution of the value of an asset. In the case of a life policy the sum assured is paid in return for the premiums and nothing else. The death of the assured is merely the occasion on which the insurance money is payable. The ownership of the policy does not depend on whether this occurs sooner or later, or on whether the bargain proves to be a good one. It cannot be made to await the event.

The windfall argument has little to commend it in the present case. The plaintiffs were kept in ignorance of the fact that premiums had been paid with their money until after Mr. Murphy's death. Had they discovered what had happened before Mr. Murphy died, they would have intervened. They might or might not have elected to take an interest in the policy rather than enforce a lien for the return of the premiums paid with their money, but they would certainly have wanted immediate payment. This would have entailed the surrender of the policy. At the date of his death Mr. Murphy was only 45 and a non-smoker. He had a life expectancy of many years, and neither he nor the trustees had the means to keep up the premiums. The plaintiffs would hardly have been prepared to wait for years to recover their money, paying the premiums in the meantime. It is true that, under the terms of the policy, life cover could if necessary be maintained for a few years more at the expense of the investment element of the policy (which also provided its surrender value). But it is in the highest degree unlikely that the plaintiffs would have been willing to gamble on the remote possibility of Mr. Murphy's dying before the policy's surrender value was exhausted. If he did not they would recover nothing. They would obviously have chosen to enforce their lien to recover the premiums or have sought a declaration that the trustees held the policy for Mr. Murphy's children and themselves as tenants in common in the appropriate shares. In either case the trustees would have had no alternative but to surrender the policy. In practice the trustees were able to obtain the death benefit by maintaining the policy until Mr. Murphy's death only because the plaintiffs were kept in ignorance of the fact that premiums had been paid with their money and so were unable to intervene.

[His Lordship considered the reasoning of the Court of Appeal and continued:] Sir Richard Scott V-C considered that Mr. Murphy's children acquired vested interests in the policy at its inception. They had a vested interest (subject to defeasance) in the death benefit at the outset and before any of the plaintiffs' money was used to pay the premiums. The use of the plaintiffs' money gave the plaintiffs a lien on the proceeds of the policy for the return of the premiums paid with their money, but could not have the effect of divesting the children of their existing interest. The children owned the policy; the plaintiffs' money was merely used to maintain it. The position was analogous to that where trust money was used to maintain or improve property of a third party.

Sir Richard Scott V-C treated the policy as an ordinary policy of life assurance. It is not clear whether he thought that the children obtained a vested interest in the policy because Mr. Murphy took the policy out or because he paid the first premium, but I cannot accept either proposition. Mr. Murphy was the original contracting party, but he obtained nothing of value until he paid the first premium. The chose in action represented by the policy is the product of the premiums, not of the contract. The trustee took out the policy in all the recorded cases. In some of them he paid all the premiums with trust money. In such cases the beneficiary was held to be entitled to the whole of the proceeds of the policy. In other cases the trustee paid some of the premiums with his own money and some with trust money. In those cases the parties were held entitled to the proceeds of the policy rateably in proportion to their contributions. It has never been suggested that the beneficiary is confined to his lien for repayment of the premiums because the policy was taken out by the trustee. The ownership of the policy does not depend on the identity of the party who took out the policy. It depends on the identity of the party or parties whose money was used to pay the premiums.

So Sir Richard Scott V-C's analysis can only be maintained if it is based on the fact that Mr. Murphy paid the first few premiums out of his own money before he began to make use of the trust money. Professor Scott records only one case in which it has been held that in such a case the claimant is confined to a lien on the ground that the later premiums were not made in acquiring the interest under the policy but merely in preserving or improving it: see *Thum v Wolstenholme* (1900) 61 P 537. The case is expressly disapproved in *Scott on Trusts*, pp. 616–617, where it is said that the decision cannot be supported, and that the claimant should be entitled to a proportionate share of the proceeds, regardless of the question whether some of the premiums were paid wholly with the claimant's money and others wholly with the wrongdoer's money and regardless of the order of the payments, or whether the premiums were paid out of a mingled fund containing the money of both.

In my opinion there is no reason to differentiate between the first premium or premiums and later premiums. Such a distinction is not based on any principle. Why should the policy belong to the party who paid the first premium, without which there would have been no policy, rather than to the party who paid the last premium, without which it would normally have lapsed? Moreover, any such distinction would lead to the most capricious results. If only four annual premiums are paid, why should it matter whether A paid the first two premiums and B the second two, or B paid the first two and A the second two, or they each paid half of each of the four premiums? Why should the children obtain the whole of the sum assured if Mr. Murphy used his own money before he began to use the plaintiffs' money, and only a return of the premiums if Mr. Murphy happened to use the plaintiffs' money first? Why should the proceeds of the policy be attributed to the first premium when the policy itself is expressed to be in consideration of all the premiums? There is no analogy with the case where trust money is used to maintain or improve property of a third party. The nearest analogy is with an instalment purchase.

Hobhouse LJ adopted a different approach. He concentrated on the detailed terms of the policy, and in particular on the fact that in the event the payment of the fourth and fifth premiums with the plaintiffs' money made no difference to the amount of the death benefit. Once the third premium had been paid, there was sufficient surrender value in the policy, built up by the use of Mr. Murphy's own money, to keep the policy on foot for the next few years, and as it happened Mr. Murphy's death occurred during those few years. But this was adventitious and unpredictable at the time the premiums were paid. The argument is based on causation and as I have explained is a category mistake derived from the law of unjust enrichment. It is an example of the same fallacy that gives rise to the idea that the proceeds of an ordinary life policy belong to the party who paid the last premium without which the policy would have lapsed. But the question is one of attribution not causation. The question is not whether the same death benefit would have been payable if the last premium or last few premiums had not been paid. It is whether the death benefit is attributable to all the premiums or only to some of them. The answer is that death benefit is attributable to all of them because it represents the proceeds of realising the policy, and the policy in turn represents the product of all the premiums.

In any case, Hobhouse LJ's analysis of the terms of the policy does not go far enough. It is not correct that the last two premiums contributed nothing to the sum payable on Mr. Murphy's death but merely reduced the cost to the insurers of providing it. Life cover was provided in return for a series of internal premiums paid for by the cancellation of units previously allocated to the policy. Units were allocated to the policy in return for the annual premiums. Prior to their cancellation the cancelled units formed part of a mixed fund of units which was the product of all the premiums paid by Mr. Murphy, including those paid with the plaintiffs' money. On ordinary principles, the plaintiffs can trace the last two premiums into and out of the mixed fund and into the internal premiums used to provide the death benefit.

It is true that the last two premiums were not needed to provide the death benefit in the sense that in the events which happened the same amount would have been payable even if those premiums had not been paid. In other words, with the benefit of hindsight it can be seen that Mr. Murphy made a bad investment when he paid the last two premiums. It is, therefore, superficially attractive to say that the plaintiffs' money contributed nothing of value. But the argument proves too much, for if the plaintiffs cannot trace their money into the proceeds of the policy, they should have no proprietary remedy at all, not even a lien for the return of their money. But the fact is that Mr. Murphy, who could not foresee the future, did choose to pay the last two premiums, and to pay them with the plaintiffs' money; and they were applied by the insurer towards the payment of the internal premiums needed to fund the death benefit. It should not avail his donees that he need not have paid the premiums, and that if he had not then (in the events which happened) the insurers would have provided the same death benefit and funded it differently.

In the case of an ordinary life policy which lapses if the premiums are not paid, Sir Richard Scott V-C's approach gives the death benefit to the party whose money was used to pay the first premium, and Hobhouse LJ's approach gives it to the party whose money was used to pay the last premium. In the case of a policy like the present, Hobhouse LJ's approach also produces unacceptable and capricious results. The claimant must wait to see whether the life assured lives long enough to exhaust the amount of the policy's surrender value as at the date immediately before the claimant's money was first used. If the life assured dies the day before it would have been exhausted, the claimant is confined to his lien to recover the premiums; if he dies the day after, then the claimant's premiums were needed to maintain the life cover. In the latter case he takes at least a proportionate share of the proceeds or, if the argument is pressed to its logical conclusion, the whole of the proceeds subject to a lien in favour of the trustees of the children's settlement. This simply cannot be right.

Hobhouse LJ's approach is also open to objection on purely practical grounds. It must, I think, be unworkable if there is an eccentric pattern of payment; or if there is a fall in the value of the units at a critical moment. Like Sir Richard Scott V-C's approach, it prompts the question: why should the order of payments matter? It is true that the premiums paid with the plaintiff's money did not in the event increase the amount payable on Mr Murphy's death, but they increased the surrender value of the policy and postponed the date at which it would lapse if no further premiums were paid. Why should it be necessary to identify the premium the payment of which (in the events which happened) prevented the policy from lapsing? Above all, this approach makes it impossible for the ownership of the policy to be determined until the policy matures or is realised. This too cannot be right.

The trustees argued that such considerations are beside the point. It is not necessary, they submitted, to consider what the plaintiffs' rights would have been if the policy had been surrendered, or if Mr. Murphy had lived longer. It is sufficient to take account of what actually happened. I do not agree. A principled approach must yield a coherent solution in all eventualities. The ownership of the policy must be ascertainable at every moment from inception to maturity; it cannot be made to await events. In my view the only way to achieve this is to hold firm to the principle that the manner in which an asset is converted into money does not affect its ownership. The parties' respective rights to the proceeds of the policy depend on their rights to the policy immediately before it was realised on Mr. Murphy's death, and this depends on the shares in which they contributed to the premiums and nothing else. They do not depend on the date at which or the manner in which the chose in action was realised....

In the course of argument it was submitted that if the children, who were innocent of any wrongdoing themselves, had been aware that their father was using stolen funds to pay the premiums, they could have insisted that the premiums should not be paid, and in the events which happened would still have received the same death benefit. But the fact is that Mr. Murphy concealed his wrongdoing from both parties. The proper response is to treat them both alike, that is to say rateably. It is morally offensive as well as contrary to principle to subordinate the claims of the victims of a fraud to those of the objects of the fraudster's bounty on the ground that he concealed his wrongdoing from both of them....

It was Mr. Murphy's decision to use the plaintiffs' money to pay the later premiums. The children are merely passive recipients of an asset acquired in part by the use of misappropriated trust money. They are innocent of any personal wrongdoing, but they are not contributors. They are volunteers who derive their interest from the wrongdoer otherwise than for value and are in no better position than he would have been if he had retained the policy for the benefit of his estate. It is not, with respect to those who think otherwise, a case where there are competing claimants to a fund who are both innocent victims of a fraud and where the equities are equal. But if it were such a case, the parties would share rateably, which is all that the plaintiffs claim....

Accordingly, I agree with Morritt LJ in the Court of Appeal that, on well established principles, the parties are entitled to the proceeds of the policy in the proportions in which those proceeds represent their respective contributions. It should not, however, be too readily assumed that this means in the proportions in which the insurance premiums were paid with their money. These represent the cost of the contributions, not necessarily their value.

A mixed fund, like a physical mixture, is divisible between the parties who contributed to it rateably in proportion to the value of their respective contributions, and this must be ascertained at the time they are added to the mixture. Where the mixed fund consists of sterling or a sterling account or where both parties make their contributions to the mixture at the same time, there is no difference between the cost of the contributions and their sterling value. But where there is a physical mixture or the mixture consists of an account maintained in other units of account and the parties make their contributions at different times, it is essential to value the contributions of both parties at the same time. If this is not done, the resulting proportions will not reflect a comparison of like with like. The appropriate time for valuing the parties' respective contributions is when successive contributions are added to the mixture.

This is certainly what happens with physical mixtures. If 20 gallons of A's oil are mixed with 40 gallons of B's oil to produce a uniform mixture of 60 gallons, A and B are entitled to share in the mixture in the proportions of 1 to 2. It makes no difference if A's oil, being purchased later, cost £2 a gallon and B's oil cost only £1 a gallon, so that they each paid out £40. This is because the mixture is divisible between the parties rateably in proportion to the value of their respective contributions and not in proportion to their respective cost. B's contribution to the mixture was made when A's oil was added to his, and both parties' contributions should be valued at that date. Should a further 20 gallons of A's oil be added to the mixture to produce a uniform mixture of 80 gallons at a time when the oil was worth £3 a gallon—the oil would be divisible equally between them. (A's further 20 gallons are worth £3 a gallon—but so are the 60 gallons belonging to both of them to which they have been added.) It is not of course necessary to go through the laborious task of valuing every successive contribution separately in sterling. It is simpler to take the account by measuring the contributions in gallons rather than sterling. This is merely a short cut which produces the same result.

In my opinion the same principle operates whenever the mixture consists of fungibles, whether these be physical assets like oil, grain or wine or intangibles like money in an account. Take the case where a trustee misappropriates trust money in a sterling bank account and pays it into his personal dollar account which also contains funds of his own. The dollars are, of course, merely units of account; the account holder has no proprietary interest in them. But no one, I think, would doubt that the beneficiary could claim the dollar value of the contributions made with trust money. Most people would explain this by saying that it is because the account is kept in dollars. But the correct explanation is that it is because the contributions are made in dollars. In order to allocate the fund between the parties rateably in proportion to the value of their respective contributions, it is necessary to identify the point at which the trust money becomes mixed with the trustee's own money. This does not occur when the trustee pays in a sterling cheque drawn on the trust account. At that stage the trust money is still identifiable. It occurs when the bank credits the dollar equivalent of the sterling cheque to the trustee's personal account. Those dollars represent the contribution made by the trust. The sterling value of the trust's contribution must be valued at that time; and it follows that the trustee's contributions, which were also made in dollars, must be valued at the same time. Otherwise one or other party will suffer the injustice of having his contributions undervalued.

Lord Steyn (dissenting): There is in principle no difficulty about allowing a proprietary claim in respect of the proceeds of an insurance policy. If in the circumstances of the present case the stolen moneys had been wholly or partly causative of the production of the death benefit received by the children there would have been no obstacle to admitting such a proprietary claim. But those are not the material facts of the case. I am not influenced by hindsight. The fact is that the rights of the children had crystallised by 1989 before any money was stolen and used to pay the 1989 and 1990 premiums. Indeed Morritt LJ expressly accepts, at 302, at 426, that 'in the event, the policy moneys would have been the same if the later premiums had not been paid'. Counsel for the purchasers accepted that as a matter of primary fact this was a correct statement. But he argued that there was nevertheless a causal link between the premiums paid with stolen moneys and the death benefit. I cannot accept this argument. It would be artificial to say that all five premiums produced the policy moneys. The purchasers' money did not 'buy' any part of the death benefit. On the contrary, the stolen moneys were not causally relevant to any benefit received by the children. The 1989 and 1990 premiums did not contribute to a mixed fund in which the purchasers have an equitable interest entitling them to a rateable division. It would be an innovation to create a proprietary remedy in respect of an asset (the death benefit) which had already been acquired at the date of the use of the stolen moneys. Far from assisting the case of the purchasers the impact of wider considerations of policy in truth tend to undermine the case of the purchasers. One needs to consider the implication of a holding in favour of the purchasers in other cases. Suppose Mr. Murphy had surrendered the policy before going bankrupt. Assume Mr. Murphy had partly used his own money and partly used money stolen from the purchasers to pay premiums. The hypothesis is that the stolen money did not in any way increase the surrender value of the policy. Justice does not support the creation to the prejudice of trade creditors of a new proprietary right in the surrender value of the policy: compare Roy Goode, 'Proprietary Restitutionary Claims', essay in *Restitution: Past, Present and Future* (ed. Cornish), pp. 63 et seq. For these reasons I differ from the analysis of Morritt LJ and reject the argument of the purchasers.

There is one final matter of significance. In a critical final passage in his judgment Morritt LJ observed, at 303:

> 'In my view . . . common justice requires that the purchasers should have the right to participate in that which has followed from the use of their money together with the other moneys, taking their share out of that joint and common stock.'

The purchasers do not assert that they suffered any loss. They cannot assert that the children would be unjustly enriched if the purchasers' claim fails. In these circumstances my perception of the justice of the case is different from that of Morritt LJ. If justice demanded the recognition of such a proprietary right to the policy moneys, I would have been prepared to embark on such a development. Given that the moneys stolen from the purchasers did not contribute or add to what the children received, in accordance with their rights established before the theft by Mr. Murphy, the proprietary claim of the purchasers is not in my view underpinned by any considerations of fairness or justice. And, if this view is correct, there is no justification for creating by analogy with cases on equitable interests in mixed funds a new proprietary right to the policy moneys in the special circumstances of the present case.

(iv) Entitlement to Increase in Value

In **Re Tilley's Will Trusts** [1967] Ch 1179,[41] the testator, Mr. Tilley, appointed his widow as an executrix and gave her a life interest in his estate with remainder to his children, Charles and Mabel. Mrs. Tilley, with the help of a bank overdraft, embarked on a highly successful career as a dealer in property. By 1952, having dealt with some properties, she had accumulated £2,237 trust capital, and over the years had thoroughly confused this trust money with her own private funds. She had overdraft facilities for over £22,000 in 1939, and by 1945 the overdraft was £23,536. She died in 1959, leaving an estate valued at some £94,000. The plaintiff, as executor of Mabel's estate, brought an action for an account of what was due to Mabel's estate. The question was whether the property should be treated as Mrs. Tilley's, or whether all or part of it should be treated as belonging to the trusts of the testator's estate, and if so, in what proportions.

UNGOED-THOMAS J held that it was all her own free estate, on the ground that trust moneys had not been used for the property purchases. His Lordship said at 1193, that 'the trust moneys were not invested in properties at all but merely went in reduction of Mrs. Tilley's overdraft which was in reality the source of the purchase-moneys'. If, however, trust moneys had been applied in the purchase of the properties, these properties would have been owned partly by Mrs. Tilley and partly by the trust, in proportions in which moneys from those sources had been used to make the purchases.

UNGOED-THOMAS J said at 1182:

The plaintiff claims that Mabel's estate should, in virtue of Mabel's half-interest in the estate, subject to Mrs. Tilley's life interest, have half of the proportion of the profits of the purchases made by Mrs. Tilley to the extent to which the defendants, as her legal personal representatives, cannot show that those properties were purchased out of Mrs. Tilley's personal moneys. The defendants, on the other hand, say that the plaintiff is entitled only to a charge on the defendants' bank account for half the trust moneys paid into that bank account with interest, i.e., half the sum of £2,237, which is shown to have been paid into that bank account, and the interest on that amount.

I come first to the law. The plaintiff relied on the statement of the law in *Lewin on Trusts* (16th edn, 1964) at p. 223, and some of the cases cited in support of it. That statement reads:

'Wherever the trust property is placed, if a trustee amalgamates it with his own, his beneficiary will be entitled to every portion of the blended property which the trustee cannot prove to be his own....'

---

[41] (1968) CLJ 28 (G.H. Jones). See also *Scott v Scott* (1963) 109 CLR 649; Restatement of Restitution, § 142.

So the proposition in *Lewin on Trusts,* which I have read, is limited to cases where the amalgam of mixed assets is such that they cannot be sufficiently distinguished and treated separately; it is based on the lack of evidence to do so being attributable to the trustee's fault.

The defendants relied on *Re Hallett's Estate* (1880) 13 Ch D 696, with a view to establishing that the trustee must be presumed to have drawn out his own moneys from the bank account of mixed moneys in priority to trust moneys, with the result that property bought by such prior drawings must be the trustee's exclusive personal property. In that case the claim was against a bank balance of mixed fiduciary and personal funds, and it is in the context of such a claim that it was held that the person in a fiduciary character drawing out money from the bank account must be taken to have drawn out his own money in preference to the trust money, so that the claim of the beneficiaries prevailed against the balance of the account. *Re Oatway* [1903] 2 Ch 356 was the converse of the decision in *Re Hallett's Estate.* In that case the claim was not against the balance left in the bank of such mixed moneys, but against the proceeds of sale of shares which the trustee had purchased with moneys which, as in *Re Hallett's Estate,* he had drawn from the bank account. But, unlike the situation in *Re Hallett's Estate,* his later drawings had exhausted the account, so that it was useless to proceed against the account. It was held that the beneficiary was entitled to the proceeds of sale of the shares, which were more than their purchase price but less than the trust moneys paid into the account. The law is reviewed and the principles stated by Joyce J who said [1903] 2 Ch 356 at 359–361:

'Trust money may be followed into land or any other property in which it has been invested; and when a trustee has, in making any purchase or investment, applied trust money together with his own, the *cestuis que trust* are entitled to a charge on the property purchased for the amount of the trust money laid out in the purchase or investment. Similarly, if money held by any person in a fiduciary capacity be paid into his own banking account, it may be followed by the equitable owner, who, as against the trustee, will have a charge for what belongs to him upon the balance to the credit of the account. If, then, the trustee pays in further sums, and from time to time draws out money by cheques, but leaves a balance to the credit of the account, it is settled that he is not entitled to have the rule in *Clayton's* case (1816) 1 Mer 572 applied so as to maintain that the sums which have been drawn out and paid away so as to be incapable of being recovered represented *pro tanto* the trust money, and that the balance remaining is not trust money, but represents only his own moneys paid into the account. *Brown v Adams* (1869) 4 Ch App 764 to the contrary ought not to be followed since the decision in *Re Hallett's Estate.* It is, in my opinion, equally clear that when any of the money drawn out has been invested, and the investment remains in the name or under the control of the trustee, the rest of the balance having been afterwards dissipated by him, he cannot maintain that the investment which remains represents his own money alone, and that what has been spent and can no longer be traced and recovered was the money belonging to the trust. In other words, when the private money of the trustee and that which he held in a fiduciary capacity have been mixed in the same banking account, from which various payments have from time to time been made, then, in order to determine to whom any remaining balance or any investment that may have been paid for out of the account ought to be deemed to belong, the trustee must be debited with all the sums that have been withdrawn and applied to his own use so as to be no longer recoverable, and the trust money in like manner be debited with any sums taken out and duly invested in the names of the proper trustees. The order of priority in which the various withdrawals and investments may have been respectively made is wholly immaterial. I have been referring, of course, to cases where there is only one fiduciary owner or set of *cestuis que trust* claiming whatever may be left as against the trustee. In the present case there is no balance left. The only investment or property remaining which represents any part of the mixed moneys paid into the banking account is the Oceana shares purchased for £2,137. Upon these, therefore, the trust had a charge for the £3,000 trust money paid into the account. That is to say, those shares and the proceeds thereof belong to the trust. It was objected that the investment in the Oceana shares was made at a time when Oatway's own share of the balance to the credit of the account (if the whole had been then justly distributed) would have exceeded £2,137, the price of the shares; that he was therefore entitled to withdraw that sum, and might rightly apply it for his own purposes; and that consequently the shares should be held to belong to his estate. To this I answer that he never was entitled to withdraw the £2,137 from the account, or, at all events, that he could not be entitled to take the sum from the account and hold it or the investment made therewith, freed from the charge in favour of the trust, unless or until the trust money paid into the account had been first restored, and the trust fund reinstated by due investment of the money in the joint names of the proper trustees, which never was done. The investment by Oatway, in his own name, of the £2,137 in Oceana shares no more got rid of the claim or charge of the trust upon the money so invested, than would have been the case if he had drawn a cheque for £2,137 and simply placed and retained the amount in a drawer without further disposing of the money in any way. The proceeds of the Oceana shares must be held to belong to the trust funds under the will of which Oatway and Maxwell Skipper were the trustees.'

So, contrary to the defendants' contention, it is not a presumption that a trustee's drawings from the mixed fund must necessarily be treated as drawings of the trustee's own money where the beneficiary's claim is against the property bought by such drawings. Further, *Re Oatway* [1903] 2 Ch 356 did not raise the question whether a beneficiary is entitled to any profit made out of the purchase of property by a trustee out of a fund consisting of his personal moneys which he mixed with the trust moneys, and so the judgment was not directed to, and did not deal with, that question.

I return now to the judgments in *Re Hallett's Estate* (1880) 13 Ch D 696....

[His Lordship quoted extensively from the parts of the judgment which are extracted at p. 911, above, and continued:]

Sinclair v Brougham [1914] AC 398 considered *Re Hallett's Estate*. Lord Parker said at 442:

'The principle on which, and the extent to which, trust money can be followed in equity is discussed at length in *Re Hallett's Estate* by Sir George Jessel. He gives two instances. First, he supposes the case of property being purchased by means of the trust money alone. In such a case the beneficiary may either take the property itself or claim a lien on it for the amount of the money expended in the purchase. Secondly, he supposes the case of the purchase having been made partly with the trust money and partly with money of the trustee...'

The next sentence I shall come back to later.

'In such a case the beneficiary can only claim a charge on the property for the amount of the trust money expended in the purchase. The trustee is precluded by his own misconduct from asserting any interest in the property until such amount has been refunded. By the actual decision in the case, this principle was held applicable when the trust money had been paid into the trustee's banking account. I will add two further illustrations which have some bearing on the present case. Suppose the property is acquired by means of money, part of which belongs to one owner and part to another, the purchaser being in a fiduciary relationship to both. Clearly each owner has an equal equity. Each is entitled to a charge on the property for his own money, and neither can claim priority over the other. It follows that their charges must rank *pari passu* according to their respective amounts...'

—again, I emphasise this—

> 'Further, I think that as against the fiduciary agent they could by agreement claim to take the property itself, in which case they would become tenants in common in shares proportioned to amounts for which either could claim a charge.'

It seems to me that when Lord Parker says in the sentence, to which I first called particular attention [1914] AC 398 at 442, that 'in such a case the beneficiary can only claim a charge on the property for the amount of the trust money expended in the purchase' he is merely contrasting the charge with the right to take the whole property which is the matter he had just been dealing with; Lord Parker is not, as I see it, addressing his mind to the question of whether the beneficiary could claim a proportion of the property corresponding to his own contribution to its purchase. This interpretation of the passage seems to me to be the only interpretation which in principle is consistent with Lord Parker's view expressed at the end of the passage which I quoted, and to which I drew particular attention, where the purchase is made by the trustee wholly out of moneys of two different beneficiaries. In that case he says that they are not limited to charges for their respective amounts, but are together entitled to the whole property. But if each of two beneficiaries can, in co-operation with the other, take the whole property which has resulted in profit from the trustee's action in buying it with their money, why can they not do so if the trustee himself has also paid some part of the purchase price? And if the two beneficiaries can do so, why not one? Indeed, it was conceded in argument that the passage should be so interpreted as suggested.

In *Snell's Principles of Equity* (26th edn, 1966), the law is thus stated at p. 315:

> 'Where the trustee mixes trust money with his own, the equities are clearly unequal. Accordingly the beneficiaries are entitled to a first charge on the mixed fund, or on any land, securities or other assets purchased with it. Thus if the trustee purchases shares with part of the mixed fund, leaving enough of it to repay the trust moneys, and then dissipates the balance, the beneficiaries' charge binds the shares; for although under the rule in *Re Hallett's Estate* (1880) 13 Ch D 696 the trustee is presumed to have bought the shares out of his own money, the charge attached to the entire fund, and could be discharged only by restoring the trust moneys. Where the property purchased has increased in value, the charge will be not merely for the amount of the trust moneys but for a proportionate part of the increased value. Thus if the trustee purchases land with £500 of his own money and £1,000 of trust moneys, and the land doubles in value, he would be profiting from his breach of trust if he were entitled to all except £1,000; the beneficiaries are accordingly entitled to a charge on the land for £2,000.'

For the defendants it has been rightly admitted that if a trustee wrongly uses trust money to pay the whole of the purchase price in respect of the purchase of an asset a beneficiary can elect either to treat the purchased asset as trust property or to treat the purchased asset as security for the recouping of the trust money. It was further conceded that this right of election by a beneficiary also applies where the asset is purchased by a trustee in part of his own money and in part out of the trust moneys, so that he may, if he wishes, require the asset to be treated as trust property with regard to that proportion of it which the trust moneys contributed to its purchase.

Does this case fall within that principle? ...

It seems to me that if, having regard to all the circumstances of the case objectively considered, it appears that the trustee has in fact, whatever his intention, laid out trust moneys in or towards a purchase, then the beneficiaries are entitled to the property purchased and any profits which it produces to the extent to which it has been paid for out of the trust moneys.

But, even by this objective test, it appears to me that the trust moneys were not in this case so laid out. It seems to me, on a proper appraisal of all the facts of this particular case, that Mrs. Tilley's breach halted at the mixing of the funds in her bank account. Although properties bought out of those funds would, like the bank account itself, at any rate if the moneys in the bank account were inadequate, be charged with repayment of the trust moneys which then would stand in the same position as the bank account, yet the trust moneys were not invested in properties at all but merely went in reduction of Mrs. Tilley's overdraft which was in reality the source of the purchase-moneys.

The plaintiff's claim therefore fails and he is entitled to no more than repayment of the half of the £2,237...

(v) Lowest Intermediate Balance

In **Roscoe v Winder** [1915] 1 Ch 62, an agreement for the sale of the goodwill of a business provided that the purchaser, one Wigham, should collect certain of the book debts and pay that money over to the vendor. Wigham collected the debts and paid part of the money, £455 18s. 11d., into his private account. A few days later the balance in the account was reduced to £25 18s. At the date of Wigham's death, the balance had risen to £358 5s. 5d. The question was the extent to which the plaintiffs could claim a charge under the rules in *Hallett*'s case.

SARGANT J, in holding that Wigham had held the money as trustee, but that the charge was limited to £25 18s., the lowest intermediate balance subsequent to the appropriation, said at 67:

But there is a further circumstance in the present case which seems to me to be conclusive in favour of the defendant as regards the greater part of the balance of 358l. ss. 5d. It appears that after the payment in by the debtor of a portion of the book debts which he had received the balance at the bank on 19 May, 1913, was reduced by his drawings to a sum of 25l. 18s. only on 21 May. So that, although the ultimate balance at the debtor's death was about 358l., there had been an intermediate balance of only 25l. 18s. The result of that seems to me to be that the trust moneys cannot possibly be traced into this common fund, which was standing to the debtor's credit at his death, to an extent of more than 25l. 18s., because, although *prima facie* under the second rule in *Re Hallett's Estate* (1880) 13 Ch D 696 any drawings out by the debtor ought to be attributed to the private moneys which he had at the bank and not to the trust moneys, yet, when the drawings out had reached such an amount that the whole of his private money part had been exhausted, it necessarily followed that the rest of the drawings must have been against trust moneys. There being on 21 May, 1913, only 25l. 18s., in all, standing to the credit of the debtor's account, it is quite clear that on that day he must have denuded his account of all the trust moneys there—the whole 455l. 18s. 11d.—except to the extent of 25l. 18s.

Practically, what Mr. Martelli and Mr. Hansell have been asking me to do—although I think Mr. Hansell in particular rather disguised the claim by the phraseology he used—is to say that the debtor, by paying further moneys after 21 May into this common account, was impressing upon those further moneys so paid in the like trust or obligation, or charge of the nature of a trust, which had formerly been impressed upon the previous balances to the credit of that account. No doubt, Mr. Hansell did say 'No. I am only asking you to treat the account as a whole, and to consider the balance from time to time standing to the credit of that account as subject to one continual charge or trust.' But I think that really is using words which are not appropriate to the facts. You must, for the purpose of tracing, which was the process adopted in *Re Hallett's Estate,* put your finger on some definite fund which either remains in its original state or can be found in another shape. That is tracing, and tracing, by the very facts of this case, seems to be absolutely excluded except as to the 251. 18s.

Then, apart from tracing, it seems to me possible to establish this claim against the ultimate balance of 3581. 5s. 5d. only by saying that something was done, with regard to the additional moneys which are needed to make up that balance, by the person to whom those moneys belonged, the debtor, to substitute those moneys for the purpose of, or to impose upon those moneys a trust equivalent to, the trust which rested on the previous balance. Of course, if there was anything like a separate trust account, the payment of the further moneys into that account would, in itself, have been quite a sufficient indication of the intention of the debtor to substitute those additional moneys for the original trust moneys, and accordingly to impose, by way of substitution, the old trusts upon those additional moneys. But, in a case where the account into which the moneys are paid is the general trading account of the debtor on which he has been accustomed to draw both in the ordinary course and in breach of trust when there were trust funds standing to the credit of that account which were convenient for that purpose, I think it is impossible to attribute to him that by the mere payment into the account of further moneys, which to a large extent he subsequently used for purposes of his own, he intended to clothe those moneys with a trust in favour of the plaintiffs.

Certainly, after having heard *Re Hallett's Estate* (1880) 13 Ch D 696 stated over and over again, I should have thought that the general view of that decision was that it only applied to such an amount of the balance ultimately standing to the credit of the trustee as did not exceed the lowest balance of the account during the intervening period.[42]

(vi) The Rule in Clayton's Case

Goff and Jones: *The Law of Restitution* (7th edn, 2007), pp. 115–117

A trustee is a trustee of two different trusts. In breach of trust he mixes the trust funds of the two different trusts in one fund and then subsequently withdraws part of the fund. As Lord Millett said in *Foskett v McKeown,*[43] 'where the beneficiary's claim is in competition with the claims of other innocent contributors there is no basis upon which any of the claims can be subordinated to any of the others'. But this principle requires qualification.

If the mixed fund is in an active, unbroken banking account, such as a current (but not a deposit) account at a bank, then any withdrawals from the mixed fund will be borne between the two main trusts in accordance with the rule in *Clayton*'s case,[44] namely first in, first out.[45] For

---

[42] See also *Re Goldcorp Exchange Ltd* [1995] 1 AC 74; *Bishopsgate Management Investment Ltd v Homan* [1995] Ch 211 (held no tracing through overdrawn bank account whether overdrawn at time when money was paid in or subsequently); *Campden Hill Ltd v Chakrani* [2005] EWHC 911 (Ch); cf. *Space Investments Ltd v Canadian Imperial Bank of Commerce Trust Co (Bahamas) Ltd* [1986] 1 WLR 1072 [p. 939, below].

[43] [2000] 3 All ER 97, 124.   [44] (1816) 1 Mer 572.

[45] *Pennell v Deffell* (1853) 4 De GM & G 372; *Re Hallett's Estate* (1880) 13 Ch D 696, at 700, *per* Fry J (the point did not arise in the Court of Appeal); *Hancock v Smith* (1889) 41 Ch D 456, at 461, *per* Lord Halsbury LC; *Re Stenning* [1895] 2 Ch 433; *Mutton v Peat* [1899] 2 Ch 556; *Re Diplock* [1948] Ch 465.

example a trustee pays £500 from trust fund A into his bank account, which contains no other money, on 1 January; two days later he pays £500 from trust fund B into the same account. On 1 February, he withdraws £500. In accordance with the rule in *Clayton's* case the loss is wholly borne by trust fund A. The result is capricious and arbitrary. As Judge Learned Hand once said: 'when the law attempts a fiction, it is, or at least it should be, for some purpose of justice. To adopt [the fiction of first in, first out]... is to apportion a common misfortune through a test which has no relation whatever to the justice of the case.'[46]

If the mixed fund is not in an active, unbroken banking account, any loss is borne *pari passu* so that the parties recover proportionately in relation to their contributions. In the example just given, both trust funds would then bear the loss equally.

The scope of the rule in *Clayton's* case was considered by the Court of Appeal in *Barlow Clowes International Ltd v Vaughan*.[47] The authority of *Pennell v Duffell* and *Re Diplock* compelled the Court to conclude that the rule *prima facie* governed the competing claims of beneficiaries of different trusts and those of beneficiaries of a trust and innocent volunteers, whose moneys have been wrongfully mixed in a single current account. The Court also concluded that, on the particular facts, the 'North American' solution (namely, that 'credits to a bank account made at different times and from different sources [are treated] as a blend or cocktail with the result that when a withdrawal is made from the account it is treated as a withdrawal in the same proportions as the different interests in the account (here of the investors) bear to each other at the moment before the withdrawal is made'[48] was, on the particular facts, impracticable, although 'manifestly fairer'. However, the rule in *Clayton's* case should not be applied if it would be impracticable or result in injustice between the parties, such as investors whose moneys are to be paid into a common pool.[49] It is a 'mere rule of evidence, and not an invariable rule of law...'[50] If there was a 'shared misfortune, the investors will be presumed to have intended the rule not to apply.'[51] The fund should then be shared rateably in proportion to the amount due to the different parties who had contributed to the mixed fund. There is, however, one significant caveat to that rule. It is this: the investor's claim is to the lowest intermediate balance in the fund. Consequently, if it can be shown that his money was deposited in a fund which had been exhausted, he has no claim to sums subsequently deposited by other investors.

The decision in *Barlow Clowes* is a welcome relaxation of the rule in *Clayton's* case. Both Woolf and Leggatt LJJ regretted that *Clayton's* case was binding on the Court of Appeal. The 'fairness of rateable division is obvious.' Dillon LJ was less sure that it was unfair to adopt the 'first in, first out' rule; later investors might well be aggrieved if their claims were to rank *pari passu* with those of earlier investors.[52,53]

---

[46] *Re Walter J Schmidt & Co* 298 F 314, at 316 (1923). But precedent compelled the judge to apply the rule to the facts. See (1950) 36 *Cornell Law Quarterly* 170, 176 (Z. Chaffee). The fiction of *Clayton's* case was rejected by the New Zealand Court of Appeal in *Re Registered Securities Ltd* [1991] 1 NZLR 545. cf *Tracing in Bank Accounts: The Lowest Intermediate Balance Rule on Trial* (2000) 33 *Canadian Business Law Journal* 75.(The lowest intermediate balance rule is distinct from, and should not be confused with, *Clayton's* case).

[47] [1992] 4 All ER 22.   [48] At 35, *per* Woolf LJ.

[49] *Re Eastern Capital Futures Ltd* [1989] BCLC 371 (not possible to distinguish various customers of the company, now in liquidation); *Re Lewis's of Leicester Ltd* [1995] 1 BCLC 428 at 439.

[50] *Re British Red Cross Balkan Fund* [1914] 2 Ch 419 at 421, *per* Astbury J.

[51] At 42, *per* Woolf LJ.   [52] Cf Leggatt LJ (at 44) and Dillon LJ (at 32).

[53] See also (1999) 115 LQR 186 (K.R. Handley).

See also *Russell-Cooke Trust Co v Prentis* [2003] 2 All ER 478[54] which recognised that the rule in *Clayton's* case would be distinguished where a counter-intention could be presumed. Such a counter-intention would be readily presumed having regard to the investors' acts and omissions and the injustice of applying such an arbitrary rule. Indeed, LINDSAY J considered that *Clayton's* case is best described as the exception rather than the rule.

(vii) Loss of the Right to Trace[55]

Goff and Jones: *The Law of Restitution* (7th edn, 2007), pp. 118–122

As the law now stands, the claimant's equitable title is defeated and the right to trace is lost, either in whole or in part, in the following circumstances:

(a) if the property reaches the hands of a bona fide purchaser;[56]

(b) if it would be inequitable to allow the claimant to trace.

This limitation on the right to trace was recognised in *Re Diplock*. The Court of Appeal instanced two cases where it would be inequitable to allow the plaintiff to trace in equity.[57] In the third edition of this book we described them as an emasculated application of the defence of change of position.[58] Now that the House of Lords has recognised the defence as a general defence to all restitutionary claims,[59] the two examples, which we shall now discuss, should be seen as two possible illustrations of change of position.[60]

First, in the view of the Court of Appeal, the equitable proprietary claim will fail if an innocent volunteer improves his land; the land may not have necessarily increased in value, the property to which a lien could attach may be uncertain, and it would be inequitable to require the sale of the property subject to the charge.[61] These may have been persuasive reasons in *Re Diplock* for there were among the innocent volunteers, hospitals, one of which had used the Diplock money to build a new ward.[62] But on other facts it may not be inequitable to impose a lien. For example, the innocent volunteer may be a rich banker who has used the money wisely

---

[54] [2003] All ER Rev 269 (P.J. Clarke). See also *Commerzbank Aktiengesellschaft v IBM Morgan plc* [2004] EWHC 2771 (Ch), [2005] 1 Lloyd's Rep 298.

[55] H&M, pp. 707–712; Lewin, pp. 1714–1720; P&M, pp. 832–838; P&S, pp. 900–903; Pettit, pp. 562–564; Snell, pp. 689–690; T&H, pp. 1113–1126.

[56] See W. Swadling in *The Limits of Restitutionary Claims: A Comparative Analysis* (ed. W. Swadling) (1997), p. 79; [1994] LMCLQ 421 (P. Key); Virgo, *The Principles of the Law of Restitution*, (2nd edn, 2006) pp. 674–679. [57] [1948] Ch 465 at 546–547.

[58] Accord: *Boscawen v Bajwa* [1996] 1 WLR 328 at 340, *per* Millett LJ.

[59] *Lipkin Gorman v Karpnale Ltd* [1991] 2 AC 548.

[60] See generally Virgo, *The Principles of the Law of Restitution* (2nd edn, 2006) pp. 709–732. On the relationship between change of position and estoppel, see *Scottish Equitable plc v Derby* [2001] 3 All ER 818 and *National Westminster Bank plc v Somer International (UK) Ltd* [2002] 1 All ER 198; (2001) 60 CLJ 465 (P. Key).

[61] Contrast Proceeds of Crime Act 2002, s.306(2)(3): recoverable property is mixed with other property if it is used—'(c) for the restoration or improvement of land'.

[62] [1948] Ch 465, 547–550. The charities included Westminster and Guy's Hospitals, Queen Alexandra Cottage Homes, Heritage Crafts Schools, and Leaf Homeopathic Hospital.

to increase the value of his country house; and he has, furthermore, ample liquid assets to discharge any lien imposed over it.[63]

The second illustration given by the Court of Appeal was of the innocent volunteer who used the Diplock money to pay off his debts. The creditor who grants the discharge is, of course, a bona fide purchaser.[64] But if he was a secured creditor, should the next-of-kin be allowed to step into his shoes and enjoy the priority which he once enjoyed? The Court of Appeal held that the next-of-kin were not entitled to a comparable charge over the land of the charity, a hospital, which had received Diplock money for the specific purpose of paying off a secured bank loan. The facts were analogous to the cases where Diplock money was spent by charities on improvements to their land. It would be inequitable to compel the hospital to submit to a sale to discharge the charge.[65]

In *Boscawen v Bajwa*[66] Millett LJ found, not surprisingly, the reasoning of the Court of Appeal in *Re Diplock* puzzling. He would confine the observations of the *Diplock* Court to the particular facts before it. The hospital had changed its position to its detriment, for the next-of-kin were seeking immediately to enforce the charge whereas the original secured creditor was willing to wait. But the charge by subrogation should not have been enforceable until the hospital had had a reasonable opportunity to obtain a fresh advance from a willing lender, perhaps its original secured creditor.[67]

If this interpretation of the reasoning in *Re Diplock* is accepted, then it would appear that change of position may be a defence to an equitable proprietary claim.[68] Furthermore, as has been seen, *Lipkin Gorman v Karpnale Ltd*[69] may be interpreted as authority for the proposition that change of position is a defence to a legal proprietary claim.[70] It has been argued that it is 'alien to the security of property interests that the conduct of a person who receives the plaintiff's asset [generally money] should affect the plaintiff's right to enforce his property in it'.[71] This problem will normally arise if a good faith volunteer, having received money, changes his position to his detriment.[72] The holder of the equitable title prevails against the interests of the good faith volunteer, being earlier in time. But in our view, it is not inequitable to allow the good faith volunteer a defence of change of position. The burden of demonstrating change of position is a formidable one. The volunteer, acting in good faith, must demonstrate that, acting on the receipt of the benefit, he has so changed his position that it would be inequitable to compel restitution. For these reasons it is questionable whether the security of the claimant's title will be seriously undermined.

---

[63] Contrast the position of the fiduciary who uses trust property to improve property: see *Boscawen v Bajwa* [1996] 1 WLR 328 at 335 (Millett LJ).

[64] Unless he knew of the executor's mistake, an unlikely event.

[65] *Lipkin Gorman v Karpnale Ltd* [1991] 2 AC 548 at 549–550 (Lord Goff of Chieveley).

[66] [1996] 1 WLR 328 at 340–341.

[67] The Lord Justice did not think that the problems which would have arisen if fresh charges had been created in the meantime were insoluble: at 783. Contrast *Re Diplock*, above.

[68] In *Campden Hill Ltd v Chakrani* [2005] EWHC 911 (Ch) Hart J left open [the] question to what extent change of position affects the right to trace in equity...   [69] [1991] 2 AC 548.

[70] ...In *Foskett v McKeown*, Lord Millett was careful not to reject change of position as a defence to an equitable proprietary claim: [2000] 3 All ER 97, 122. ('...a claim in unjust enrichment is subject to a change of position defence , which usually operates by reducing or extinguishing the element of enrichment. An action like the present is subject to the bona fide purchase for value defence, which operates to clear the defendant's title.')   [71] [2000] *Restitution Law Review* 465, 488 (D. Fox).

[72] The bona fide purchaser has a complete defence.

(c) If the claimant's property disappears, as will be the case if the defendant buys wine with the trust money and drinks it.[73] The right to trace is also lost if the claimant's property is mixed by the defendant with his own property of a different kind, thereby forming a new product.[74]

Similarly, a proprietary claim will fail if trust money is paid into the trustee's personal account, which is overdrawn.

> 'The equitable remedies presuppose the continued existence of the money either as a separate fund or as part of a mixed fund or as latent in property acquired by means of such a fund. If, on the facts of any individual case, such continued existence is not established, equity is as helpless as the common law itself.'[75]

In *Bishopsgate Investment Management Ltd v Homan*[76] the Court of Appeal endorsed this principle and rejected the submission that the court should impose an equitable charge on all the assets of the company, now in liquidation, into whose overdrawn account trust moneys had been paid in fraudulent breach of trust. In doing so the Court distinguished dicta of Lord Templeman, giving the advice of the Privy Council in *Space Investments Ltd v Canadian Imperial Bank of Commerce*.[77] In *Space Investments* Lord Templeman concluded, *obiter,* that the beneficiaries of a trust instrument should be granted a lien over the general assets of a bank, which had agreed to hold moneys on trust in a separate fund but had failed to do so. This equitable charge should be 'in priority to any payments of customers' deposits and other unsecured debts'.[78] In his view:[79]

> 'This priority is conferred because the customers and other unsecured creditors voluntarily accept the risk that the trustee bank might become insolvent and unable to discharge its obligations in full. On the other hand, the settlor of the trust and the beneficiaries interested under the trust, never accept any risks involved in the possible insolvency of the trustee bank. On the contrary, the settlor could be certain that if the trusts were lawfully administered, the trustee bank could never make use of trust money for its own purposes and would always be obliged to segregate trust money and trust property in the manner authorised by law and by the trust instrument free from any risks involved in the possible insolvency of the trustee bank. It is therefore equitable that where the trustee bank has unlawfully misappropriated trust money by treating the trust money

---

[73] *Re Diplock* [1948] Ch 465 at 521.

[74] *Borden (UK) Ltd v Scottish Timber Products Ltd* [1981] Ch 25; but if the defendant has consciously mixed the claimant's property with his own, the principle in *Lupton v White* (1808) 15 Ves 432 suggests that the new product belongs in equity to the claimant, and the burden is on the defendant to demonstrate the extent of his contribution.

[75] *Re Diplock* [1948] Ch 465 at 521; see also *James Roscoe (Bolton) Ltd v Winder* [1915] 1 Ch 62 [p. 934, above]. Cf. *Shalson v Russo* [2005] Ch 281 at [138]–[140]. The rogue's current account into which the fraud moneys were paid was overdrawn but he had accounts in credit in other financial institutions. Rimer J refused to treat all these accounts as a single fund. It is only possible to trace assets and this requires their identification, following *Box v Barclays Bank* [1998] Lloyd's Rep Bank 185, 202.

[76] [1995] Ch 211, following *Re Goldcorp Exchange Ltd* [1995] 1 AC 74.   [77] [1986] 1 WLR 1072.

[78] At 1074, at 77. Cf. *Sinclair v Brougham* [1914] AC 398, where the depositors were given an equitable charge over the Society's general assets, and were not required to identify any specific asset acquired with their moneys, and *El Ajou v Dollar Land Holdings plc* [1993] 3 All ER 717 (money deposited in several bank accounts; equitable charge imposed over each account even though the plaintiff was unable to identify which sums went into each account). See Moriarty, chapter in *Laundering and Tracing* (ed. Birks, 1995), pp. 84–86.   [79] *Space Investments Ltd v Canadian Imperial Bank of Commerce* [1986] 1 WLR 1072.

as though it belonged to the bank beneficially, merely acknowledging and recording the amount in a trust deposit account with the bank, then the claims of the beneficiaries should be paid in full out of the assets of the trustee bank in priority to the claims of the customers and other unsecured creditors of the bank.... Where a bank trustee is insolvent, trust money wrongfully treated as being on deposit with the bank must be repaid in full so far as may be out of the assets of the bank in priority to any payment of customers' deposits and other unsecured debts.'

In *Bishopsgate Investment Management Ltd* the Court of Appeal held that Lord Templeman could not have intended these dicta to apply to the situation where trust moneys had been paid into an overdrawn account. This would effect a 'fundamental change in the well understood limitations to equitable tracing. Lord Templeman was only considering the position of an insolvent bank which had been taking deposits and lending money'.[80]

There is only one possible exception to the defence that money paid into an overdrawn account cannot be traced in equity, namely, the possibility of so-called 'backward tracing'. This might apply:

'where an asset was acquired by the [defendant company] with moneys borrowed from an overdrawn or loan account and there was an inference that when the borrowing was incurred it was the intention that it should be repaid by misappropriations of [the plaintiff's money]. Another possibility was that moneys misappropriated from [the plaintiffs] were paid into an overdrawn account of [the defendant company] in order to reduce the overdraft and so make finance available within the overdraft limits for [the defendant company] to purchase some particular asset.'[81]

It was Dillon LJ's view, as it was Vinelott J's in the court below, that 'it is at least arguable, depending on the facts, that there ought to be an equitable charge in favour of [the plaintiffs] on the asset in question of [the defendant company]'.[82] But Leggatt LJ emphatically rejected that possibility.[83]

In our view, it is desirable, in the new world of international fraud, to encourage the courts to create new rules and presumptions. For that reason, it is our view that it would be a mistake to reject the mere possibility of 'backward tracing':

'The availability of equitable remedies ought...to depend upon the substance of the transaction in question and not upon the strict order in which associated events happen.'[84]

(d) if, in claims arising from the administration of an estate, the claimants have already recovered in an action against the executors for *devastavit*. In *Re Diplock*[85] the Court of Appeal held that before the next-of-kin could bring a personal action against the charities they must first sue the executors, who had mistakenly paid the money; and any sums recovered from the executors should be credited rateably among the charities. The Court added that, '*prima facie* and subject to discussion',[86] the next-of-kin's proprietary claim should be similarly reduced.

---

[80] [1995] Ch 211 at 217, *per* Dillon LJ.

[81] At 216, *per* Dillon LJ, adopting the judgment of Vinelott J in the court below.

[82] At 217. In *Shalson v Russo* [2005] Ch 281 at [141] Rimer J preferred Dillon LJ's 'approach' in *Bishopsgate Investment Management Ltd*, as did Evans-Lombe J in the unreported case of *Jyske Bank (Gibraltar) Ltd v Spjeldnaes*, 23 July 1997, Transcript pp. 333–334, cited by Rimer J.

[83] At 221. See also *Foskett v McKeown* [1998] Ch 265.

[84] *Foskett v McKeown* [1998] 2 WLR 298, 315, where Sir Richard Scott VC accepted the possibility of backward tracing. Hobhouse LJ (at p. 321) and Morritt LJ (at p. 327) did not. [See also (1995) 54 CLJ 290 (L. Smith).]   [85] [1948] Ch 465.

[86] [1948] Ch 465 at 556. See also *John v Dodwell & Co* [1918] AC 563 at 575.

The limitation may be peculiar to claims arising from the administration of an estate, but it may also be applicable to claims arising under *inter vivos* trusts. If it is accepted, the amount which a wrongly paid volunteer must disgorge is directly dependent on how much money can be extracted from the executors. In our view the next-of-kin's proprietary claim against volunteers should not be reduced or destroyed by the sums recoverable from the executors. If they are able to identify their property in the hands of a volunteer they should be able to recover that property and it should be no defence to the volunteer that the next-of-kin have recovered *in personam* against the executors. The executors should then be allowed to claim, as is an insurer in comparable circumstances, to that part of the next-of-kin's fund which represents the difference between the total of the sums recovered from the executors and the volunteer and the loss suffered by the next-of-kin.[87] But the most practical and sensible rule, which has been adopted by statute in New Zealand and Western Australia,[88] is to require the claimant to sue the volunteer before suing the executors who should be liable only for any amount which the claimant has failed to recover from the volunteer. The volunteer would enjoy the usual defences.

In **Foskett v McKeown** [2001] 1 AC 102, 129 LORD MILLETT indicated that the defence of change of position would not be available to a claim founded on the vindication of the claimant's property rights. He expanded on this dictum extra-judicially in *Equity in Commercial Law* (eds. S. Degeling and J. Edelman) (2005) at pp. 315 and 325, where he said that a claim for a proprietary remedy is not subject to a change of position defence, although it might be available to a proprietary claim where the claimant seeks a personal remedy: see p. 968, below.

D THE FUTURE OF THE TRACING RULES

Although the orthodox approach to the analysis of tracing rules treats the rules at law and equity as distinct,[89] there are growing calls for the assimilation of these rules. Some commentators have asserted that the rules have already been assimilated[90] and there is some indication from recent case law that this view is shared by some members of the judiciary.

In **Foskett v McKeown** [2001] 1 AC 102, LORD STEYN said at 113:

In arguing the merits of the proprietary claim counsel for the purchasers from time to time invoked 'the rules of tracing'. By that expression he was placing reliance on a corpus of supposed rules of law, divided into common law and equitable rules. In truth tracing is a process of identifying assets: it belongs to the realm of evidence. It tells us nothing about legal or equitable rights to the assets traced. In a crystalline analysis Professor Birks ('The Necessity of a Unitary Law of Tracing', essay in *Making Commercial Law, Essays in Honour of Roy Goode* (1997), pp. 239–258) explained, at p. 257, that there is a unified regime for tracing and that 'it allows

---

[87] Cf. *Lord Napier and Ettrick v RF Kershaw Ltd* [1993] AC 713.

[88] New Zealand Administration Act 1952, s. 30B(5), added in 1960; Western Australia Trustee Act 1962, s. 65(7).   [89] See *Shalson v Russo* [2003] EWHC 1637 (ch), [2005] Ch 281, para. 104 (Rimer J).

[90] Smith, *The Law of Tracing*, (1997), p. 5; (1979) 95 LQR 78 (S. Khurshid and P. Matthews).

tracing to be cleanly separated from the business of asserting rights in or in relation to assets successfully traced'. Applying this reasoning Professor Birks concludes, at p. 258:

> 'that the modern law is equipped with various means of coping with the evidential difficulties which a tracing exercise is bound to encounter. The process of identification thus ceases to be either legal or equitable and becomes, as is fitting, genuinely neutral as to the rights exigible in respect of the assets into which the value in question is traced. The tracing exercise once success-fully completed, it can then be asked what rights, if any, the plaintiff can, on his particular facts, assert. It is at that point that it become relevant to recall that on some facts those rights will be personal, on others proprietary, on some legal, and on others equitable.'

I regard this explanation as correct. It is consistent with orthodox principle. It clarifies the correct approach to so called tracing claims. It explains what tracing is about without providing answers to controversies about legal or equitable rights to assets so traced.

LORD MILLETT said at 128:

Given its nature, there is nothing inherently legal or equitable about the tracing exercise. There is thus no sense in maintaining different rules for tracing at law and in equity. One set of tracing rules is enough. The existence of two has never formed part of the law in the United States: see *Scott on Trusts*, 4th ed (1989), section 515, at pp 605–609. There is certainly no logical justification for allowing any distinction between them to produce capricious results in cases of mixed substitutions by insisting on the existence of a fiduciary relationship as a precondition for applying equity's tracing rules. The existence of such a relationship may be relevant to the nature of the claim which the plaintiff can maintain, whether personal or proprietary, but that is a different matter. I agree with the passages which my noble and learned friend, Lord Steyn, has cited from Professor Birks's essay 'The Necessity of a Unitary Law of Tracing',[91] and with Dr Lionel Smith's exposition in his comprehensive monograph *The Law of Tracing* (1997): see particularly pp 120–130, 277–279 and 342–347.

III REMEDIES FOR PROPRIETARY CLAIMS[92]

A COMMON LAW PROPRIETARY REMEDIES

Where the claimant has brought a proprietary claim at common law usually the remedy will be a personal one for the value of the property. This is because the common law generally does not recognise proprietary remedies.[93] It will be sufficient, therefore, for the claimant to establish that the defendant has received property in which the

---

[91] In *Laundering and Tracing* (ed. P. Birks) (1995).

[92] H&M, pp. 694–705; Lewin, pp. 1735–1737; P&S, pp. 876–880, 903–906; T&H, pp. 1103–1112; U&H, pp. 1083–1088.

[93] Save for the action for ejectment to recover land and the discretionary remedy of delivery up of goods under s. 3(3) of the Torts (Interference with Goods) Act 1977.

claimant has a legal proprietary interest, without needing to show that the defendant has retained this property. This is a claim which is founded on the vindication of the claimant's proprietary rights, for which the remedy is personal and is called the action for money had and received. The defendant will have the defence of change of position to the extent that the defendant changed his position in good faith in reliance on the receipt of the property.[94]

In **Lipkin Gorman v Karpnale Ltd** [1991] 2 AC 548,[95] one of the partners of the appellant firm, a compulsive gambler named Cass, drew cheques on the firm's client account without authority and paid the proceeds to the Playboy Club, which was owned by the respondent. The Club being solvent, the appellant brought the common law personal action for money had and received against it. In order to succeed in that action the appellant had to establish, by the common law tracing rules, that the Club had received its property. LORD GOFF OF CHIEVELEY said at 572:

So, in the present case, the solicitors seek to show that the money in question was their property at common law. But their claim in the present case for money had and received is nevertheless a personal claim; it is not a proprietary claim, advanced on the basis that money remaining in the hands of the respondents is their property. Of course there is no doubt that, even if legal title to the money did vest in Cass immediately on receipt, nevertheless he would have held it on trust for his partners, who would accordingly have been entitled to trace it in equity into the hands of the respondents. However, your Lordships are not concerned with an equitable tracing claim in the present case, since no such case is advanced by the solicitors, who have been content to proceed at common law by a personal action, viz. an action for money had and received. I should add that in the present case, we are not concerned with the fact that money drawn by Cass from the solicitors' client account at the bank may have become mixed by Cass with his own money before he gambled it away at the club. For the respondents have conceded that, if the solicitors can establish legal title to the money in the hands of Cass, that title was not defeated by mixing of the money with other money of Cass while in his hands. On this aspect of the case, therefore, the only question is whether the solicitors can establish legal title to the money when received by Cass from the bank by drawing cheques on the client account without authority....

His Lordship held that they could.

B EQUITABLE PROPRIETARY REMEDIES

If the claimant can show that the defendant has received and retained property in which the claimant has an equitable interest, it is then necessary to consider what is the appropriate remedy to vindicate this equitable proprietary right. Unfortunately, in cases such as **Foskett v McKeown** [2001] 1 AC 102, although the distinction between

---

[94] See p. 937, above.
[95] (1991) 107 LQR 521 (P. Watts); (1992) 5 MLR 377 (E. McKendrick); [1992] Conv 124 (M. Halliwell); [1992] All ER Rev 262 (W. Swadling).

tracing and claiming was recognised,[96] the reasoning of the judges tended to confuse these two distinct issues. So, in *Foskett,* the majority of their Lordships considered together the distinct issues of whether it was possible for the plaintiffs to trace the proceeds of the insurance policy, and whether the appropriate remedy to vindicate the plaintiffs' property rights was a constructive trust or a charge. The distinction was, however, recognised by LORD HOPE OF CRAIGHEAD, albeit in a dissenting judgment, who said at 120:

But the result of the tracing exercise cannot solve the remaining question, which relates to the extent of the purchasers' entitlement. It is the fact that this is a case of mixed substitution which creates the difficulty. If the purchasers' money had been used to pay all the premiums there would have been no mixture of value with that contributed by others. Their claim would have been to the whole of the proceeds of the policy. As it is, there are competing claims on the same fund. In the absence of any other basis for division in principle or on authority—and no other basis has been suggested—it must be divided between the competitors in such proportions as can be shown to be equitable. In my opinion the answer to the question as to what is equitable does not depend solely on the terms of the policy. The equities affecting each party must be examined. They must be balanced against each other. The conduct of the parties so far as this may be relevant, and the consequences to them of allowing and rejecting the purchasers' claim, must be analysed and weighed up. It may be helpful to refer to what would be done in other situations by way of analogy. But it seems to me that in the end a judgment requires to be made as to what is fair, just and reasonable.[97]

There are three distinct proprietary remedies which can be employed to vindicate equitable proprietary rights.

Virgo, *The Principles of the Law of Restitution* (2nd edn, 2006), pp. 637–644

(i) Constructive Trust
The recognition that the defendant holds property on constructive trust for the claimant may have two different implications.

(1) Transfer of property
     Where the claimant can show that he or she has an equitable proprietary interest in property which is in the hands of the defendant the court may declare that the property is held on constructive trust for the claimant and it will order the defendant to transfer this property to the claimant.[98]

(2) Proportionate share
     A constructive trust may also be imposed where the claimant is considered to have a proportionate share in the property which is in the defendant's possession. This remedy is more attractive to the claimant than an equitable charge[99] where the property

---

[96] See p. 897, above.

[97] Cp. the views of the majority as to the relevance of considerations of fairness, justice and reasonableness [p. 916, above].   [98] *Boscawen v Bajwa* [1996] 1 WLR 328 at 334 (Millett LJ).

[99] See p. 945, below.

has increased in value. Where the claimant's money has been used by the defendant to purchase an asset with a contribution from the defendant's own money, the claimant can claim a share of this asset which is proportionate to the amount of money which he or she had contributed.[100] Similarly, this remedy is available where the defendant mixes money from two innocent parties and uses this mixture to buy an asset.[101] In such circumstances the claims of both parties are equal, so it is not appropriate for one to have priority over the other. Rather, they should share the asset proportionately, bearing pro rata an increase or decrease in its value.[102]....

(ii) Equitable charge or lien

An alternative remedy to the recovery of particular property or the award of a proportionate share is to impose a charge on the property to secure repayment of the amount which the defendant owed to the claimant. This enables the claimant to recover the value received and retained by the defendant plus interest, but does not enable the claimant to recover any more.

Where the claimant's money has been used by the defendant to improve or maintain the defendant's property it will not be appropriate for the court to require the defendant to hold the property on constructive trust for the claimant since the claimant cannot be considered to have a beneficial interest in it, as would be the case where the claimant's property is used to acquire an asset. Instead the court may treat the property as charged with a sum which represents the amount by which the value of the defendant's property has been increased by the use of the claimant's money.[103] Similarly, where the defendant has used the claimant's money to improve or maintain the property of a third party a charge over the property may be available, but only if it would not be unfair to the innocent third party.[104] Where the claimant's money has been used by the defendant to purchase an asset the claimant can claim a proportionate share in the property, but there is nothing to stop the claimant from claiming a charge over it if he wants.[105] A charge would be an appropriate remedy in such a case if the value of the asset has not increased....

(iii) Subrogation[106]

...Subrogation is a remedy which is designed to ensure a 'transfer of rights from one person to another...by operation of law'.[107] Essentially the function of the remedy is to enable the claimant to rely on the rights of a third party against a defendant, or the rights of a defendant against a third party. This is often described as the claimant being allowed to stand in the shoes of the third party. The typical case where subrogation will be an appropriate remedy in the context of a proprietary restitutionary claim is where the claimant's money is used by the defendant to discharge a debt which the defendant owed to a secured creditor. In such circumstances the claimant can be subrogated to the secured creditor's charge and gain the benefit of that security as against other creditors of the borrower. In effect the benefit of the charge

---

[100] *Re Tilley's Will Trusts* [1967] Ch 1179. See p. 930, above.

[101] *Edinburgh Corpn v Lord Advocate* (1879) 4 App Cas 823 at 841 (Lord Hatherley).

[102] *Re Diplock* [1948] Ch 465 at 532 (Lord Greene MR); *Foskett v McKeown* [2001] 1 AC 102 [p. 915, above].   [103] *Boscawen v Bajwa* [1996] 1 WLR 328 at 335 (Millett LJ).

[104] *Re Diplock* [1948] Ch 465 at 547 (Lord Greene MR); *Foskett v McKeown* [1998] Ch 265 at 278, (Sir Richard Scott V-C).   [105] *Re Hallett's Estate* (1880) 13 Ch D 696 at 711 (Jessel MR).

[106] For detailed analysis of the remedy of subrogation, see Mitchell and Waterson, *Subrogation: Law and Practice* (2007).   [107] *Orakpo v Manson Investments Ltd* [1978] AC 95 at 104 (Lord Diplock).

is treated as though it had been assigned to the claimant[108] so that he or she will obtain the benefit of that charge.[109]

In **Boscawen v Bajwa** [1996] 1 WLR 328,[110] MILLETT LJ said at 335:

Subrogation, therefore, is a remedy, not a cause of action; see Goff & Jones, *Law of Restitution*, 4th ed. (1993), pp. 589 et seq, *Orakpo v Manson Investments Ltd* [1978] AC 95, 104, *per* Lord Diplock and *Re TH Knitwear (Wholesale) Ltd* [1988] Ch 275, 284. It is available in a wide variety of different factual situations in which it is required in order to reverse the defendant's unjust enrichment. Equity lawyers speak of a right of subrogation, or of an equity of subrogation, but this merely reflects the fact that it is not a remedy which the court has a general discretion to impose whenever it thinks it just to do so. The equity arises from the conduct of the parties on well-settled principles and in defined circumstances which make it unconscionable for the defendant to deny the proprietary interest claimed by the plaintiff. A constructive trust arises in the same way. Once the equity is established the court satisfies it by declaring that the property in question is subject to a charge by the way of subrogation in the one case or a constructive trust in the other.

QUESTIONS

1. Was *Foskett v McKeown* [2001] 1 AC 102 [p. 915, above] correctly decided?

2. Is a fiduciary relationship necessary in order to trace? Ought it to be? H&M, pp. 688–690; Goff and Jones: *Law of Restitution* (7th edn) pp. 110–112; Virgo, *The Principles of the Law of Restitution* (2nd edn., 2006), p. 630; Smith, *The Law of Tracing* (1997), pp. 123–130; (1996) OJLS 61, 65 (R. Grantham); *Westdeutsche Landesbank Girozentrale v Islington LBC* [1994] 1 WLR 938, 947 (Dillon LJ), 953 (Leggatt LJ); *Campden Hill Ltd v Chakrani* [2005] EWHC 911 (Ch), para. 74, where HART J held that the fiduciary relationship can be established simply from the division of the legal and beneficial ownership of property.

3. What is the liability of an innocent volunteer, if he:
   (a) still has the property,
   (b) has mixed the property with his own,
   (c) no longer has the property?

   Re Diplock [1948] Ch 465 [p. 904, above]; *Foskett v McKeown* [2001] 1 AC 102 [p. 915, above]; [1983] Conv 135 (K. Hodkinson); Virgo, *The Principles of the Law of Restitution*, pp. 631–632.

---

[108] *Banque Financière de la Cité v Parc (Battersea) Ltd* [1999] 1 AC 221, 236 (Lord Hoffmann). See also *Boscawen v Bajwa* [1996] 1 WLR 328, 333 (Millett LJ).

[109] See also *Cheltenham and Gloucester plc v Appleyard* [2004] EWCA Civ 291; *Filby v Mortgage Express (No. 2) Ltd* [2004] EWCA Civ 759.

[110] (1995) 9 *Trust Law International* 124 (P. Birks); (1996) 55 CLJ 199 (N. Andrews); [1997] Conv 1 (A. Oakley).

4. Should it be possible to trace into a previously acquired asset? See: (1995) 54 CLJ 290 (L. Smith); *Bishopsgate Investment Management Ltd v Homan* [1995] Ch 211, 217 (Dillon LJ), 221 (Leggatt LJ); *Boscawen v Bajwa* [1996] 1 WLR 328, 341 (Millett LJ); *Foskett v McKeown* [1998] Ch 265, at 283; *Shalson v Russo* [2003] EWHC 1637 (Ch), [2005] Ch 281 at para. 141 (Rimer J); *Law Society v Haider* [2003] EWHC 2486 (Ch).

5. Should it be possible to trace the defendant's general assets even though no asset can be identified as representing the claimant's property? See *Space Investments Ltd v Canadian Imperial Bank of Commerce Trust Co (Bahamas) Ltd* [1986] 1 WLR 1072; *Re Goldcorp Exchange Ltd* [1995] 1 AC 74; *Bishopsgate Investment Management Ltd v Homan* [1995] Ch 211; H&M, pp. 696–698; Virgo, *The Principles of the Law of Restitution*, p. 634; [1995] LMCLQ 446 (L. Gullifer); (1999) 115 LQR 469 (S. Evans).

6. Can the tracing rules at law and in equity be treated as assimilated? If not, should they be so treated? *Nelson v Larholt* [1948] 1 KB 339 at 342–343 (Denning J); *Bristol and West Building Society v Mothew* [1998] Ch 1 at 23 (Millett LJ); (1997) 113 LQR 21 (N. Andrews and J. Beatson); Virgo, *The Principles of the Law of Restitution*, p. 635; Smith, *The Law of Tracing*, pp. 278–279; (1997) 11 *Trust Law International* 2 (P. Birks); (1998) 114 LQR 399, 409 and (1999) 14 *Amicus Curiae* 4 (Sir Peter Millett).

20

PERSONAL CLAIMS AND REMEDIES

I LIABILITY OF TRUSTEES

Where a trustee has breached a trust, the nature of the claim and the remedy will depend on the nature of the breach. Where the breach has involved the misappropriation of trust property, the beneficiaries may have a proprietary restitution claim, as was examined in Chapter 19. Where the trustee no longer has the misappropriated property, or where the breach did not involve the trustee taking anything for himself, the liability of the trustee will be personal. The nature of this liability and the remedies which are available will be examined in this chapter.

A GENERAL PRINCIPLES[1]

One of the most significant issues concerning personal liability for breach of trust relates to the appropriate tests of causation and remoteness.[2]

---

[1] H&M, pp. 656–666; Lewin, pp. 1557–1588; P&M, pp. 764–776; P&S, pp. 744–755; Pettit, pp. 520–528; Snell, pp. 666–673; T&H, pp. 1029–1054; U&H, pp. 1047–1078; R. Chambers, 'Liability' in *Breach of Trust* (eds. P. Birks and A. Pretto, 2002), pp. 1–40.

[2] A similar issue has arisen in the context of liability for breach of fiduciary duty. See p. 811, above.

Target Holdings Ltd v Redferns[3]
[1996] AC 421 (HL, **Lords Keith of Kinkel, Ackner, Jauncey of Tullichettle, Browne-Wilkinson** and **Lloyd of Berwick**)

Mirage Properties Ltd, who were the owners of commercial property in Birmingham, made a contract to sell it to Crowngate Developments Ltd for £775,000. Target Holdings Ltd agreed to lend Crowngate £1,525,000 on the security of the property. Redferns, who were acting as solicitors for both Crowngate and Target, held the mortgage advance on a bare trust for Target with authority to release the money to Crowngate only on receipt of the executed conveyances and mortgage of the property. However, they released the money before the documents were executed. It was admitted that this was a breach of trust. The property was in due course found to be worth only £500,000, through no fault on the part of Redferns.

Redferns argued that the breach of trust was technical and that Target had suffered no loss arising from the breach, because in due course it had received the documents and the same loss would have occurred even if there had been no breach. Target argued that the duty of a trustee who misapplied trust funds was to restore them, subject to giving credit for any money received on the sale of the mortgaged property.

Held (reversing the Court of Appeal [1994] 1 WLR 1089). For Redferns.

Lord Browne-Wilkinson: My Lords, this appeal raises a novel point on the liability of a trustee who commits a breach of trust to compensate beneficiaries for such breach. Is the trustee liable to compensate the beneficiary not only for losses caused by the breach but also for losses which the beneficiary would, in any event, have suffered even if there had been no such breach? ...

Before considering the technical issues of law which arise, it is appropriate to look at the case more generally. Target allege, and it is probably the case, that they were defrauded by third parties (Mr. Kohli and Mr. Musafir and possibly their associates) to advance money on the security of the property. If there had been no breach by Redferns of their instructions and the transaction had gone through, Target would have suffered a loss in round figures of £1.2 million (i.e. £1.7 million advanced less £500,000 recovered on the realisation of the security). Such loss would have been wholly caused by the fraud of the third parties. The breach of trust committed by Redferns left Target in exactly the same position as it would have been if there had been no such breach: Target advanced the same amount of money, obtained the same security and received the same amount on the realisation of that security. In any ordinary use of words, the breach of trust by Redferns cannot be said to have caused the actual loss ultimately suffered by Target unless it can be shown that, but for the breach of trust, the transaction would not have gone through, ... if the transaction had not gone through, Target would not have advanced the money at all and therefore Target would not have suffered any loss. But the Court of Appeal decided (see Ralph Gibson LJ at 1100; Peter Gibson LJ at 1104) and it is common ground before your Lordships that there is a triable issue as to whether, had it not been

[3] (1995) 139 SJ 894 (N.J. Patten QC counsel for the respondents); (1996) 112 LQR 27 (C.E.F. Rickett); [1995] All ER Rev 325 (P.J. Clarke); [1996] LMCLQ 161 (R. Nolan); (1995) 9 *Trust Law International* 86 (J.Ulph); [1997] Conv 14 (D. Capper). See also *Youyang Pty Ltd v Minter Ellison Morris Fletcher* (2003) 196 ALR 482; (2003) 119 LQR 545 (S. Elliott and J. Edelman) where *Target Holdings* was distinguished by the High Court of Australia.

for the breach of trust, the transaction would have gone through. Therefore the decision of the Court of Appeal in this case can only be maintained on the basis that, even if there is no causal link between the breach of trust and the actual loss eventually suffered by Target (i.e. the sum advanced less the sum recovered) the trustee in breach is liable to bear (at least in part) the loss suffered by Target.

The transaction in the present case is redolent of fraud and negligence. But, in considering the principles involved, suspicions of such wrongdoing must be put on one side. If the law as stated by the Court of Appeal is correct, it applies to cases where the breach of trust involves no suspicion of fraud or negligence. For example, say an advance is made by a lender to an honest borrower in reliance on an entirely honest and accurate valuation. The sum to be advanced is paid into the client account of the lender's solicitors. Due to an honest and non-negligent error (e.g. an unforeseeable failure in the solicitors' computer) the moneys in client account are transferred by the solicitors to the borrower one day before the mortgage is executed. That is a breach of trust. Then the property market collapses and when the lender realises his security by sale he recovers only half the sum advanced. As I understand the Court of Appeal decision, the solicitors would bear the loss flowing from the collapse in the market value: subject to the court's discretionary power to relieve a trustee from liability under section 61 of the Trustee Act 1925 [p. 871, above], the solicitors would be bound to repay the total amount wrongly paid out of the client account in breach of trust receiving credit only for the sum received on the sale of the security.

To my mind in the case of an unimpeachable transaction this would be an unjust and surprising conclusion. At common law there are two principles fundamental to the award of damages. First, that the defendant's wrongful act must cause the damage complained of. Second, that the plaintiff is to be put 'in the same position as he would have been in if he had not sustained the wrong for which he is now getting his compensation or reparation:' *Livingstone v Rawyards Coal Co* (1880) 5 App Cas 25 at 39, *per* Lord Blackburn. Although, as will appear, in many ways equity approaches liability for making good a breach of trust from a different starting point, in my judgment those two principles are applicable as much in equity as at common law. Under both systems liability is fault-based: the defendant is only liable for the consequences of the legal wrong he has done to the plaintiff and to make good the damage caused by such wrong. He is not responsible for damage not caused by his wrong or to pay by way of compensation more than the loss suffered from such wrong. The detailed rules of equity as to causation and the quantification of loss differ, at least ostensibly, from those applicable at common law. But the principles underlying both systems are the same. On the assumptions that had to be made in the present case until the factual issues are resolved (i.e. that the transaction would have gone through even if there had been no breach of trust), the result reached by the Court of Appeal does not accord with those principles. Redferns as trustees have been held liable to compensate Target for a loss caused otherwise than by the breach of trust. I approach the consideration of the relevant rules of equity with a strong predisposition against such a conclusion.

The considerations urged before your Lordships, although presented as a single argument leading to the conclusion that the views of the majority in the Court of Appeal are correct, on analysis comprise two separate lines of reasoning, *viz.*: (A) an argument developed by Mr. Patten (but not reflected in the reasons of the Court of Appeal) that Target is now (i.e. at the date of judgment) entitled to have the 'trust fund' restored by an order that Redferns reconstitute the trust fund by paying back into client account the moneys paid away in breach of trust. Once the trust fund is so reconstituted, Redferns as bare trustee for Target will have no answer to a claim by Target for the payment over of the moneys in the reconstituted 'trust fund'. Therefore, Mr. Patten says, it is proper now to order payment direct to Target of the whole sum improperly paid away, less the sum which Target has received on the sale of property; and (B) the argument accepted by the majority of the Court of Appeal that, because immediately after the moneys were paid away by Redferns in breach of trust there was an immediate right to have the 'trust fund' reconstituted, there was then an immediate loss to the trust fund for which loss Redferns are now liable to compensate Target direct.

The critical distinction between the two arguments is that argument (A) depends upon Target being entitled now to an order for restitution to the trust fund whereas argument (B) quantifies the compensation payable to Target as beneficiary by reference to a right to restitution to the trust fund at an earlier date and is not dependent upon Target having any right to have the client account reconstituted now.

Before dealing with these two lines of argument, it is desirable to say something about the approach to the principles under discussion. The argument both before the Court of Appeal and your Lordships concentrated on the equitable rules establishing the extent and quantification of the compensation payable by a trustee who is in breach of trust. In my judgment this approach is liable to lead to the wrong conclusions in the present case because it ignores an earlier and crucial question, *viz.*, is the trustee who has committed a breach under any liability at all to the beneficiary complaining of the breach? There can be cases where, although there is an undoubted breach of trust, the trustee is under no liability at all to a beneficiary. For example, if a trustee commits a breach of trust with the acquiescence of one beneficiary, that beneficiary has no right to complain and an action for breach of trust brought by him would fail completely. Again there may be cases where the breach gives rise to no right to compensation. Say, as often occurs, a trustee commits a judicious breach of trust by investing in an unauthorised investment which proves to be very profitable to the trust. A carping beneficiary could insist that the unauthorised investment be sold and the proceeds invested in authorised investments: but the trustee would be under no liability to pay compensation either to the trust fund or to the beneficiary because the breach has caused no loss to the trust fund. Therefore, in each case the first question is to ask what are the rights of the beneficiary: only if some relevant right has been infringed so as to give rise to a loss is it necessary to consider the extent of the trustee's liability to compensate for such loss.

The basic right of a beneficiary is to have the trust duly administered in accordance with the provisions of the trust instrument, if any, and the general law. Thus, in relation to a traditional trust where the fund is held in trust for a number of beneficiaries having different, usually successive, equitable interests, (e.g. A for life with remainder to B), the right of each beneficiary is to have the whole fund vested in the trustees so as to be available to satisfy his equitable interest when, and if, it falls into possession. Accordingly, in the case of a breach of such a trust involving the wrongful paying-away of trust assets, the liability of the trustee is to restore to the trust fund, often called 'the trust estate', what ought to have been there.

The equitable rules of compensation for breach of trust have been largely developed in relation to such traditional trusts, where the only way in which all the beneficiaries' rights can be protected is to restore to the trust fund what ought to be there. In such a case the basic rule is that a trustee in breach of trust must restore or pay to the trust estate either the assets which have been lost to the estate by reason of the breach or compensation for such loss. Courts of Equity did not award damages but, acting *in personam*, ordered the defaulting trustee to restore the trust estate: see *Nocton v Lord Ashburton* [1914] AC 932 at 952, 958, *per* Viscount

Haldane LC. If specific restitution of the trust property is not possible, then the liability of the trustee is to pay sufficient compensation to the trust estate to put it back to what it would have been had the breach not been committed: *Caffrey v Darby* (1801) 6 Ves 488; *Clough v Bond* (1838) 3 My & Cr 490. Even if the immediate cause of the loss is the dishonesty or failure of a third party, the trustee is liable to make good that loss to the trust estate if, but for the breach, such loss would not have occurred: see Underhill and Hayton, *Law of Trusts & Trustees,* 14th edn (1987), pp. 734–736; *Re Dawson* [1966] 2 NSWLR 211; *Bartlett v Barclays Bank Trust Co Ltd (Nos 1 and 2)* [1980] Ch 515. Thus the common law rules of remoteness of damage and causation do not apply. However there does have to be some causal connection between the breach of trust and the loss to the trust estate for which compensation is recoverable, *viz.* the fact that the loss would not have occurred but for the breach: see also *Re Miller's Deed Trusts* [1978] LS Gaz R 454; *Nestlé v National Westminster Bank Plc* [1993] 1 WLR 1260.

Hitherto I have been considering the rights of beneficiaries under traditional trusts where the trusts are still subsisting and therefore the right of each beneficiary, and his only right, is to have the trust fund reconstituted as it should be. But what if at the time of the action claiming compensation for breach of trust those trusts have come to an end? Take as an example again the trust for A for life with remainder to B. During A's lifetime B's only right is to have the trust duly administered and, in the event of a breach, to have the trust fund restored. After A's death, B becomes absolutely entitled. He of course has the right to have the trust assets retained by the trustees until they have fully accounted for them to him. But if the trustees commit a breach of trust, there is no reason for compensating the breach of trust by way of an order for restitution and compensation to the trust fund as opposed to the beneficiary himself. The beneficiary's right is no longer simply to have the trust duly administered: he is, in equity, the sole owner of the trust estate. Nor, for the same reason, is restitution to the trust fund necessary to protect other beneficiaries. Therefore, although I do not wholly rule out the possibility that even in those circumstances an order to reconstitute the fund may be appropriate, in the ordinary case where a beneficiary becomes absolutely entitled to the trust fund the court orders, not restitution to the trust estate, but the payment of compensation directly to the beneficiary. The measure of such compensation is the same, i.e. the difference between what the beneficiary has in fact received and the amount he would have received but for the breach of trust.

Thus in *Bartlett v Barclays Bank Trust Co Ltd (Nos 1 and 2)* [1980] Ch 515 by the date of judgment some of the shares settled by the trust deed had become absolutely vested in possession: see at 543. The compensation for breach of trust, though quantified by reference to what the fund would have been but for the breach of trust, was payable directly to the persons who were absolutely entitled to their shares of the trust fund: see at 544. Accordingly, in traditional trusts for persons by way of succession, in my judgment once those trusts have been exhausted and the fund has become absolutely vested in possession, the beneficiary is not normally entitled to have the exhausted trust reconstituted. His right is to be compensated for the loss he has suffered by reason of the breach.

I turn then to the two arguments urged before your Lordships.

Argument (A)
As I have said, the critical step in this argument is that Target is now entitled to an order for reconstitution of the trust fund by the repayment into client account of the moneys wrongly paid away, so that Target can now demand immediate repayment of the whole of such moneys without regard to the real loss it has suffered by reason of the breach.

Even if the equitable rules developed in relation to traditional trusts were directly applicable to such a case as this, as I have sought to show a beneficiary becoming absolutely entitled to a trust fund has no automatic right to have the fund reconstituted in all circumstances. Thus, even applying the strict rules so developed in relation to traditional trusts, it seems to me very doubtful whether Target is now entitled to have the trust fund reconstituted. But in my judgment it is in any event wrong to lift wholesale the detailed rules developed in the context of traditional trusts and then seek to apply them to trusts of quite a different kind. In the modern world the trust has become a valuable device in commercial and financial dealings. The fundamental principles of equity apply as much to such trusts as they do to the traditional trusts in relation to which those principles were originally formulated. But in my judgment it is important, if the trust is not to be rendered commercially useless, to distinguish between the basic principles of trust law and those specialist rules developed in relation to traditional trusts which are applicable only to such trusts and the rationale of which has no application to trusts of quite a different kind.

This case is concerned with a trust which has at all times been a bare trust. Bare trusts arise in a number of different contexts: e.g. by the ultimate vesting of the property under a traditional trust, nominee shareholdings and, as in the present case, as but one incident of a wider commercial transaction involving agency. In the case of moneys paid to a solicitor by a client as part of a conveyancing transaction, the purpose of that transaction is to achieve the commercial objective of the client, be it the acquisition of property or the lending of money on security. The depositing of money with the solicitor is but one aspect of the arrangements between the parties, such arrangements being for the most part contractual. Thus, the circumstances under which the solicitor can part with money from client account are regulated by the instructions given by the client: they are not part of the trusts on which the property is held. I do not intend to cast any doubt on the fact that moneys held by solicitors on client account are trust moneys or that the basic equitable principles apply to any breach of such trust by solicitors. But the basic equitable principle applicable to breach of trust is that the beneficiary is entitled to be compensated for any loss he would not have suffered but for the breach. I have no doubt that, until the underlying commercial transaction has been completed, the solicitor can be required to restore to client account moneys wrongly paid away. But to import into such trust an obligation to restore the trust fund once the transaction has been completed would be entirely artificial. The obligation to reconstitute the trust fund applicable in the case of traditional trusts reflects the fact that no one beneficiary is entitled to the trust property and the need to compensate all beneficiaries for the breach. That rationale has no application to a case such as the present. To impose such an obligation in order to enable the beneficiary solely entitled (i.e. the client) to recover from the solicitor more than the client has in fact lost flies in the face of common sense and is in direct conflict with the basic principles of equitable compensation. In my judgment, once a conveyancing transaction has been completed the client has no right to have the solicitor's client account reconstituted as a 'trust fund.'

Argument (B)
I have already summarised the reasons of the majority in the Court of Appeal for holding that Redferns were liable to pay to Target, by way of compensation, the whole sum paid away in breach of trust, less the sum recovered by Target. Mr. Patten supported this argument before your Lordships.

The key point in the reasoning of the Court of Appeal is that where moneys are paid away to a stranger in breach of trust, an immediate loss is suffered by the trust estate: as a result, subsequent events reducing that loss are irrelevant. They drew a distinction between the case in which the breach of trust consisted of some failure in the administration of the trust and the case where a trustee has actually paid away trust moneys to a stranger. There is no doubt that in the former case, one waits to see what loss is in fact suffered by reason of the breach, i.e. the restitution or compensation payable is assessed at the date of trial, not of breach. However, the Court of Appeal considered that where the breach consisted of paying away the trust moneys to a stranger it made no sense to wait: it seemed to Peter Gibson LJ [1994] 1 WLR 1089 at 1103 obvious that in such a case 'there is an immediate loss placing the trustee under an immediate duty to restore the moneys to the trust fund'. The majority of the Court of Appeal therefore considered that subsequent events which diminished the loss in fact suffered were irrelevant, save for imposing on the compensated beneficiary an obligation to give credit for any benefit he subsequently received. In effect, in the view of the Court of Appeal one 'stops the clock' at the date the moneys are paid away: events which occur between the date of breach and the date of trial are irrelevant in assessing the loss suffered by reason of the breach.

A trustee who wrongly pays away trust money, like a trustee who makes an unauthorised investment, commits a breach of trust and comes under an immediate duty to remedy such breach. If immediate proceedings are brought, the court will make an immediate order requiring restoration to the trust fund of the assets wrongly distributed or, in the case of an unauthorised investment, will order the sale of the unauthorised investment and the payment of compensation for any loss suffered. But the fact that there is an accrued cause of action as soon as the breach is committed does not in my judgment mean that the quantum of the compensation payable is ultimately fixed as at the date when the breach occurred. The quantum is fixed at the date of judgment at which date, according to the circumstances then pertaining, the compensation is assessed at the figure then necessary to put the trust estate or the beneficiary back into the position it would have been in had there been no breach. I can see no justification for 'stopping the clock' immediately in some cases but not in others: to do so may, as in this case, lead to compensating the trust estate or the beneficiary for a loss which, on the facts known at trial, it has never suffered.

[His Lordship referred to *Re Dawson* [1966] 2 NSWLR 211; *Canson Enterprises Ltd v Boughton & Co* (1991) 85 DLR (4th) 129; *Alliance & Leicester Building Society v Edgestop Ltd* (18 January 1991, unreported); *Bishopsgate Investment Management Ltd v Maxwell (No 2)* [1994] 1 All ER 261; *Nant-y-glo and Blaina Ironworks Co v Grave* (1878) 12 Ch D 738; *Jaffray v Marshall* [1993] 1 WLR 1285 and continued:]

For these reasons I reach the conclusion that, on the facts which must currently be assumed, Target has not demonstrated that it is entitled to any compensation for breach of trust. Assuming that moneys would have been forthcoming from some other source to complete the purchase from Mirage if the moneys had not been wrongly provided by Redferns in breach of trust, Target obtained exactly what it would have obtained had no breach occurred, i.e. a valid security for the sum advanced. Therefore, on the assumption made, Target has suffered no compensatable loss. Redferns are entitled to leave to defend the breach of trust claim.

However, I find it very difficult to make that assumption of fact. There must be a high probability that, at trial, it will emerge that the use of Target's money to pay for the purchase from Mirage and the other intermediate transactions was a vital feature of the transaction. The circumstances of the present case are clouded by suspicion, which suspicion is not dissipated by Mr. Bundy's untruthful letter dated 30 June informing Target that the purchase of the property and the charges to Target had been completed. If the moneys made available by Redferns' breach of trust were essential to enable the transaction to go through, but for Redferns' breach of trust Target would not have advanced any money. In that case the loss suffered by Target by reason of the breach of trust will be the total sum advanced to Crowngate less the proceeds of the security. It is not surprising that Mr. Sumption was rather muted in his submission that Redferns should have had unconditional leave to defend and that the order for payment into court of £1 million should be set aside. In my judgment such an order was fully justified.

I would therefore allow the appeal, set aside the order of the Court of Appeal and restore the order of Warner J.

The decision of the House of Lords in *Target Holdings Ltd v Redferns* is of importance for a number of reasons. First, the House of Lords has affirmed the importance of causation when determining liability for breach of trust. The trustee will only be liable to compensate the trust for loss suffered as a result of a breach of trust where that loss was caused by the breach. It remains unclear, however, to what extent common law rules of remoteness, foreseeability, and causation are relevant to claims for breach of trust.[4] Second, the House of Lords has recognised the importance of characterising the nature of the trust. A distinction is drawn between 'traditional' trusts and bare trusts. A 'traditional' trust is a continuing trust where the beneficiaries have a right to have the trust fund properly administered and the trustee is under a duty to restore the trust fund to what it would have been but for the breach of trust. Where, however, the trust is a bare trust, there is no obligation to reconstitute the trust once the commercial transaction has been completed. Rather, the trustee is simply required to compensate the beneficiary for loss suffered as a direct result of the breach of trust.

Lord Millett, *Equity's Place in the Law of Commerce* (1998) 114 LQR 214, 223–227

This brings us to the important but in some respects unsatisfactory case of *Target Holdings Ltd v. Redferns*.[5] The facts are familiar, and can be briefly summarised. They suggest a common kind of mortgage fraud. The borrower bought a property and interposed his own offshore companies between the vendor and himself, more than doubling the ostensible purchase price in the process. Armed with the contract between himself and one of his own companies, together with an inflated valuation, he obtained an excessive mortgage advance from the plaintiff. Even if there had been no downturn in the property market, the plaintiff would have suffered substantial loss; but the recession made it worse, and the plaintiff's advance proved largely irrecoverable. The plaintiff sued the borrower's solicitor, who had in the usual way acted for both mortgage lender and borrower. The plaintiff alleged fraud as well as negligence. There may have been some reason to suspect that the solicitor was implicated in the fraud, since he appears to have been aware of the whole transaction, including the arrangements for the uplift of the purchase price. If fraud was established the plaintiff would be able to recover the whole of its loss, including that part of the loss which was attributable to the fall in the property market.[6]

---

[4] See (2001) 60 CLJ 337 (G. Vos).   [5] [1996] AC 421.

[6] *Smith New Court Securities Ltd v Scrimgeour Vickers (Asset Management) Ltd* [1997] AC 254, disapproving dicta of Hobhouse LJ in *Downs v Chappell* [1997] 1 WLR 1271.

This part of the loss would not be recoverable in an action for negligence only.[7] In the course of the proceedings the plaintiff discovered that the solicitor had parted with the mortgage money without obtaining the executed mortgage and title deeds in exchange, and had lied to the plaintiff about what he had done. Fortunately he later obtained the documents, so no harm was done. These facts could perhaps have been relied upon as evidence that the solicitor was implicated in the fraud. But the plaintiff saw a way of recovering the full amount of its loss without having to prove fraud and without having to go to trial. It amended its pleadings to allege breach of trust and applied for summary judgment. The Court of Appeal gave summary judgment for the whole of the loss. The payment was a breach of trust; the solicitor was strictly liable in equity to restore the trust property; and he could not invoke common law rules about causation and remoteness of damage to limit his liability. The House of Lords reversed the decision. The plaintiff had obtained exactly what it would have obtained if no breach of trust had occurred, *viz.* a valid security for the sum advanced. In the absence of fraud, there was no warrant for awarding equitable compensation for the loss occasioned by the inadequacy of the security, let alone the fall in the property market, since neither loss was attributable to the relevant breach of duty.

This was eminently satisfactory. It put right the error which the Court of Appeal had made in failing to identify the relevant breach of trust, which was not in parting with the money but in failing to obtain the title deeds in return. This put the trust fund at risk—but the risk did not materialise. There are two disquieting features about the case nevertheless. First, Lord Browne-Wilkinson distinguished between traditional family trusts on the one hand and the bare trust which has become a valuable device in commercial and financial dealings. He accepted that the fundamental principles of equity apply as much to such trusts as they do to the traditional trust in relation to which those principles were originally formulated. But he suggested that it was important, if the trust concept was not to be rendered commercially useless, to distinguish between the basic principles of trust law and those specialist rules developed in relation to traditional trusts which are applicable only to such trusts and the rationale of which has no application to trusts of a quite different kind.

It is difficult to know what to make of this. It is impossible to dissent from the proposition that equity is flexible and that circumstances alter cases. It is also true that, as Lord Browne-Wilkinson pointed out, the circumstances in which the solicitor was entitled to part with his client's money were regulated by the client's instructions and were not part of the trusts on which the money was held. This is plainly correct. The only trust was a bare trust for the client; its instructions were superimposed on that trust. It was a form of *Quistclose* trust.[8] But nothing turns on this, except that it made the instructions revocable. Application of trust money in such circumstances otherwise than in accordance with the unrevoked instructions of the beneficial owner is still a breach of trust. Likewise trustee investment powers are not part of the trusts on which trust money is held, but an unauthorised investment of trust money is still a breach of trust.

But what is the specialist rule applicable only to family trusts which excludes the principle limiting the amount of recoverable compensation to the loss actually occasioned by the breach? If there is such a rule it must be of general application. Is it seriously to be supposed that the result in *Target Holdings Ltd v Redferns* would have been different if the trust in question had

---

[7] *Banque Bruxelles Lambert SA v Eagle Star Insurance Co. Ltd* [1997] AC 191.
[8] See (1985) 101 LQR 269. See p. 38, above.

been a traditional trust? Suppose trustees of a family settlement with power to invest on mort-gage decide to do so, but negligently part with the trust money without obtaining the executed mortgage and title deeds in exchange. Suppose, too, that a few days later they do obtain the necessary documents. And suppose that the property has been overvalued and the investment proves to be a bad one. Is it seriously suggested that the trustees are to be held liable for any-thing more than a few days' loss of interest?

Lord Browne-Wilkinson's speech is, with respect, disappointing in a second respect. He begins his analysis by referring to the basic right of a beneficiary to have the trust duly admin-istered in accordance with the provisions of the trust instrument, if any, and the general law, and of the trustee's liability to pay compensation for any loss to the trust estate which may be occasioned by his breach of trust. From there he proceeds to speak exclusively in terms of caus-ation, introducing the 'but for' test while at the same time rejecting other tests of causation and remoteness of damage which have been adopted by the common law. This fails to explain why the trustee's liability is strict, or why equity should not adopt the common law rules of causation and remoteness in toto.

It is misleading to speak of breach of trust as if it were the equitable counterpart of breach of contract at common law; or to speak of equitable compensation for breach of fiduciary duty as if it were common law damages masquerading under a fancy name. Forty years ago, the Chancery Judges bore down heavily on such solecisms. Woe betide a Chancery Junior who spoke of 'damages for breach of trust' or 'damages for breach of fiduciary duty'. The judges knew that misuse of language often conceals a confusion of thought. Nowadays these misleading expressions are in common use. It is time that the usage was stamped out.

Lord Diplock has said that a contracting party is under a primary obligation to perform his contract and a secondary obligation to pay damages if he does not.[9] It is tempting, but wrong, to assume that a trustee is likewise under a primary obligation to perform the trust and a secondary obligation to pay equitable compensation if he does not. The primary obligation of a trustee is to account for his stewardship. The primary remedy of the beneficiary—any benefi-ciary no matter how limited his interest—is to have the account taken, to surcharge and falsify the account, and to require the trustee to restore to the trust estate any deficiency which may appear when the account is taken. The liability is strict. The account must be taken down to the date on which it is rendered. That is why there is no question of 'stopping the clock'.

If the beneficiary is dissatisfied with the way in which the trustee has carried out his trust—if, for example, he considers that the trustee has negligently failed to obtain all that he should have done for the benefit of the trust estate, then he may surcharge the account. He does this by requiring the account to be taken on the footing of wilful default. In this context 'wilful default' bears a special and unusual meaning; it means merely lack of ordinary prudence or due diligence.[10] The trustee is made to account, not only for what he has in fact received, but also for what he might with due diligence have received. Since the trustee is, in effect, charged with negligence, and the amount by which the account is surcharged is measured by the loss occasioned by his want of skill and care, the analogy with common law damages for negligence is almost exact.[11] Although he is a fiduciary, his duty of care is not a fiduciary duty.[12] In this context it must be right to adopt the common law rules of causation and remoteness of damage

[9] *Moschi v Lep Air Services Ltd* [1973] AC 331.   [10] See, e.g. *Re Chapman* [1896] 2 Ch. 763.

[11] See *Henderson v Merrett Syndicates Ltd* [1995] 2 AC 145 at p. 205 *per* Lord Browne-Wilkinson.

[12] See *Permanent Building Society v Wheeler* (1994) 14 ACSR 109 at pp. 157–158 *per* Ipp J approved in *Bristol & West Building Society v Mothew* [1997] 2 WLR 436 at pp. 448–449.

to their fullest extent. The trustee's liability is enforced in the course of taking the trust account rather than by an action for damages, but the obligation of skill and care is identical to the common law duty of care.

Target Holdings Ltd v. Redferns was concerned with the other side of the account. Where the beneficiary complains that the trustee has misapplied trust money, he falsifies the account, that is to say, he asks for the disbursement to be disallowed. If, for example, the trustee lays out trust money in an unauthorised investment which falls in value, the beneficiary will falsify the account by asking the court to disallow both the disbursement and the corresponding asset on the other side of the account. The unauthorised investment will then be treated as having been bought with the trustee's own money and on his own behalf. He will be required to account to the trust estate for the full amount of the disbursement—*not* for the amount of the loss. That is what is meant by saying that the trustee is liable to restore the trust property; and why common law rules of causation and remoteness of damage are out of place.

If the unauthorised investment has appreciated in value, then the beneficiary will be content with it. He is not obliged to falsify the account which the trustee renders; he can always accept it. (It goes without saying that the trustee cannot simply 'borrow' the trust money to make a profitable investment for his own account and then rely on the fact that the investment was unauthorised to avoid bringing the transaction into the account. He must account for what he has done with the trust money, not merely for what he has properly done with it.) Where the beneficiary accepts the unauthorised investment, he is often said to affirm or adopt the transaction. That is not wholly accurate. The beneficiary has a right to elect, but it is merely a right to decide whether to complain or not.

Where the beneficiary accepts the unauthorised investment, the account must be taken as if the investment were fully authorised in every respect. The investment is shown as a trust asset and the cost of acquisition as an authorised disbursement. But the converse is equally true. Where the beneficiary elects to falsify the account, the unauthorised investment is not shown as an asset, the disbursement is disallowed, and the trustee is accountable in every respect as if he had not disbursed the money. He is liable to restore the money to the trust estate; as notionally restored it remains subject to all the trusts powers and provisions of the trust as if it had never been disbursed; and the account is taken accordingly.

All this is elementary, but it provides the solution to the problem in *Target Holdings Ltd v Redferns*. The solicitor held the plaintiff's money in trust for the plaintiff but with its authority to lay it out in exchange for an executed mortgage and the documents of title. He paid it away without obtaining these documents. This was an unauthorised application of trust money which entitled the plaintiff to falsify the account. The disbursement must be disallowed and the solicitor treated as accountable as if the money were still in his client account and available to be laid out in the manner directed. It was later so laid out. The plaintiff could not object to the acquisition of the mortgage or the disbursement by which it was obtained; it was an authorised application of what must be treated as trust money notionally restored to the trust estate on the taking of the account. To put the point another way; the trustee's obligation to restore the trust property is not an obligation to restore it in the very form in which he disbursed it, but an obligation to restore it in any form authorised by the trust.[13]

---

[13] See also Lord Millett in *Equity in Commercial Law* (eds. Degeling and Edelman)(2005), p. 310; (2004) 18 *Trust Law International* 116 (J. Edelman and S. Elliott); (2002) 65 MLR 588 (S. Elliott).

B PERSONAL REMEDIES FOR BREACH OF TRUST

Where a trustee is liable for a breach of trust there are two types of personal equitable remedy which may be awarded. The first is the equitable remedy of compensation.[14] Although the effect of this remedy is to restore the trust to the position which existed before the breach of trust had occurred, this is not a restitutionary remedy as such[15] because the function of the remedy is not to deprive the defendant trustee of gains made as a result of a breach of trust. The remedy is assessed by reference to what the trust lost rather than what the defendant gained. Second, the restitutionary remedy of an account of profits may be awarded. This is assessed by reference to gains made by the trustee as a result of the breach of trust. Where the defendant is liable to account for profits, these profits may be held on constructive trust.[16] It follows that this remedy will actually operate as a proprietary restitutionary remedy.[17] In *Harris v Digital Pulse Pty Ltd* (2003) 56 NSWLR 298 the New South Wales Court of Appeal held that exemplary damages were not available against a defendant who had breached a fiduciary or some other equitable duty.[18]

Both equitable compensation and an account of profits may be available in respect of the same breach of trust. But, where these remedies are inconsistent, the claimant will need to elect between them, usually before judgment is entered against the defendant, unless the claimant is not able to make an informed choice until later.[19] Once the election has been made the claimant cannot claim the other remedy.[20]

In **Personal Representatives of Tang Man Sit v Capacious Investments Ltd** [1996] AC 514 (PC), a landowner had agreed to assign houses to the plaintiff. No deed of assignment was executed and the landowner let the houses without the plaintiff's consent. The landowner died and the plaintiff sued his personal representatives for breach of trust. The trial judge declared that the plaintiff was the equitable owner of the houses from the date of the agreement. The defendant was ordered to assign the houses to the plaintiff, account for all profits from letting the houses, and to pay damages for breach of trust, to be assessed by reference to the loss of rental on the properties and their loss of value.

---

[14] See *Nocton v Lord Ashburton* [1914] AC 932 at 856–957 (Viscount Haldane LC); *Bishopsgate Investment Management Ltd v Maxwell (No 2)* [1994] 1 All ER 261; *Target Holdings Ltd v Redferns* [1996] AC 421; *Mahoney v Purnell* [1996] 3 All ER 61; *Bristol and West Building Society v Mothew* [1998] Ch 1 at 17 (Millett LJ); and *Swindle v Harrison* [1997] 4 All ER 705. See also the decision of the High Court of Australia in *Warman International Ltd v Dwyer* (1995) 128 ALR 201. For the assessment of equitable compensation where there has been a breach of fiduciary duty, see *Nationwide Building Society v Various Solicitors (No 3)* (1999) The Times, 1 March (compensation for actual loss); (2003) 119 LQR 246 (M. Conaglen). Cf. (2004) 18 *Trust Law International* 116 (J. Edelman and S. Elliott).

[15] Although Lord Browne-Wilkinson did suggest that it was in *Target Holdings Ltd v Redferns*, [1996] AC 421, 434, p. 951 above. See also *Swindle v Harrison* [1997] 4 All ER 705 at 714, where Evans LJ described the equitable remedy of compensation for breach of fiduciary duty as restitutionary.

[16] See *A-G for Hong Kong v Reid* [1994] 1 AC 324. See p. 815, above.   [17] See p. 944, above.

[18] (2006) 26 OJLS 303 (A. Duggan).

[19] Virgo, *The Principles of the Law of Restitution*, (2nd edn, 2006) pp. 442–445. See also Law Com. No. 247 (1997), pp. 47–49.

[20] *United Australia Ltd v Barclays Bank Ltd* [1941] AC 1; *Island Records Ltd v Tring International plc* [1996] 1 WLR 1256 at 1258 (Lightman J).

The plaintiff recovered part of the profits and proceeded with the assessment of the loss which he had suffered. In holding that the remedies of account of profits and damages for loss of use were inconsistent, LORD NICHOLLS OF BIRKENHEAD said at 520:

In agreement with the Court of Appeal their Lordships accept the defendant's submission that there is an inconsistency between an account of profits, whereby for better or worse a plaintiff takes the money the defendant received from the use he made of the property, and an award of damages, representing the financial return the plaintiff would have received for the same period had he been able to use the property. These remedies are alternative, not cumulative. A plaintiff may have one or other, but not both. (Strictly, the claim for damages might be more accurately formulated as a claim for compensation for loss sustained by a breach of trust. In the present case nothing turns on the historic distinction between damages, awarded by common law courts, and compensation, a monetary remedy awarded by the Court of Chancery for breach of equitable obligations. It will be convenient therefore to use the nomenclature of damages which has been adopted throughout this case.) ...

Two remedies
Their Lordships will consider first whether the plaintiff did choose to take the remedy of an account of profits, with the consequence that it could no longer pursue a claim for damages so far as this would be inconsistent with an account of profits. This issue lies at the heart of this case. This issue calls for consideration of the principles governing election between remedies.

The law frequently affords an injured person more than one remedy for the wrong he has suffered. Sometimes the two remedies are alternative and inconsistent. The classic example, indeed, is (1) an account of the profits made by a defendant in breach of his fiduciary obligations and (2) damages for the loss suffered by the plaintiff by reason of the same breach. The former is measured by the wrongdoer's gain, the latter by the injured party's loss.

Sometimes the two remedies are cumulative. Cumulative remedies may lie against one person. A person fraudulently induced to enter into a contract may have the contract set aside and also sue for damages. Or there may be cumulative remedies against more than one person. A plaintiff may have a cause of action in negligence against two persons in respect of the same loss.

Alternative remedies
Faced with alternative and inconsistent remedies a plaintiff must choose, or elect, between them. He cannot have both. The basic principle governing when a plaintiff must make his choice is simple and clear. He is required to choose when, but not before, judgment is given in his favour and the judge is asked to make orders against the defendant. A plaintiff is not required to make his choice when he launches his proceedings. He may claim one remedy initially, and then by amendment of his writ and his pleadings abandon that claim in favour of the other. He may claim both remedies, as alternatives. But he must make up his mind when judgment is being entered against the defendant. Court orders are intended to be obeyed. In the nature of things, therefore, the court should not make orders which would afford a plaintiff both of two alternative remedies.

In the ordinary course, by the time the trial is concluded a plaintiff will know which remedy is more advantageous to him. By then, if not before, he will know enough of the facts to assess where his best interests lie. There will be nothing unfair in requiring him to elect at that stage. Occasionally this may not be so. This is more likely to happen when the judgment is a default judgment or a summary judgment than at the conclusion of a trial. A plaintiff may not know how much money the defendant has made from the wrongful use of his property. It may be unreasonable to require the plaintiff to make his choice without further information. To meet this difficulty, the court may make discovery and other orders designed to give the plaintiff the information he needs, and which in fairness he ought to have, before deciding upon his remedy. A recent instance where this was done is the decision of Lightman J in *Island Records Ltd v Tring International plc* [1996] 1 WLR 1256. The court will take care to ensure that such an order is not oppressive to a defendant.

In the ordinary course the decision made when judgment is entered is made once and for all. That is the normal rule. The order is a final order, and the interests of the parties and the public interest alike dictate that there should be finality. The principle, however, is not rigid and unbending. Like all procedural principles, the established principles regarding election between alternative remedies are not fixed and unyielding rules. These principles are the means to an end, not the end in themselves. They are no more than practical applications of a general and overriding principle governing the conduct of legal proceedings, namely, that proceedings should be conducted in a manner which strikes a fair and reasonable balance between the interests of the parties, having proper regard also to the wider public interest in the conduct of court proceedings. Thus in *Johnson v Agnew* [1980] AC 367 the House of Lords held that when specific performance fails to be realised, an order for specific performance may subsequently be discharged and an inquiry as to damages ordered. Lord Wilberforce observed, at 398: 'election, though the subject of much learning and refinement, is in the end a doctrine based on simple considerations of common sense and equity.'

Cumulative remedies

The procedural principles applicable to cumulative remedies are necessarily different. Faced with alternative and inconsistent remedies a plaintiff must choose between them. Faced with cumulative remedies a plaintiff is not required to choose. He may have both remedies. He may pursue one remedy or the other remedy or both remedies, just as he wishes. It is a matter for him. He may obtain judgment for both remedies and enforce both judgments. When the remedies are against two different people, he may sue both persons. He may do so concurrently, and obtain judgment against both. Damages to the full value of goods which have been converted may be awarded against two persons for successive conversions of the same goods. Or the plaintiff may sue the two persons successively. He may obtain judgment against one, and take steps to enforce the judgment. This does not preclude him from then suing the other. There are limitations to this freedom. One limitation is the so-called rule in *Henderson v Henderson* (1843) 3 Hare 100. In the interests of fairness and finality a plaintiff is required to bring forward his whole case against a defendant in one action. Another limitation is that the court has power to ensure that, when fairness so requires, claims against more than one person shall all be tried and decided together. A third limitation is that a plaintiff cannot recover in the aggregate from one or more defendants an amount in excess of his loss. Part-satisfaction of a judgment against one person does not operate as a bar to the plaintiff thereafter bringing an action against another who is also liable, but it does operate to reduce the amount recoverable in the second action. However, once a plaintiff has fully recouped his loss, of necessity he cannot thereafter pursue any other remedy he might have and which he might have pursued earlier. Having recouped the whole of his loss, any further proceedings would lack a subject matter. This principle of full satisfaction prevents double recovery.

[His Lordship referred to *United Australia Ltd v Barclays Bank Ltd* [1941] AC 1 and *Mahesan s/o Thambiah v Malaysia Government Officers' Cooperative Housing Society Ltd* [1979] AC 374 and continued:]

The present case

Their Lordships turn to apply these principles in the present case. As already noted, to some extent at least the remedies claimed by the plaintiff included two alternative and inconsistent remedies. An account of the profits Mr. Tang had made from the lettings is an alternative remedy to damages for the loss of use of the houses. However, and this is the unusual feature of the present case, matters went awry at the time of summary judgment on 25 August, 1992. The plaintiff should have been required, so far as the two remedies were inconsistent, to choose which it would take. If it chose an account of profits, it could have damages only so far as, on the facts of this case, an award of damages was not inconsistent. In the event, the plaintiff was not required to elect. Instead the order gave the plaintiff both remedies. The judge ordered the defendant to account for the estate's profits and also to pay damages. The latter order was expressed in unqualified terms. The judge can hardly be blamed for this. The point was overlooked by everybody. No discussion seems to have taken place on the form of the order.

What happened thereafter was that the plaintiff proceeded to enforce both remedies ordered by the judge. The defendant produced an account showing receipts in excess of $1.8 million. The plaintiff proceeded to enforce payment by obtaining a charging order. The plaintiff also proceeded with the necessary preparatory steps for an assessment of damages. There is thus no question of the plaintiff having chosen to take an account of profits rather than payment of damages. Nor is there any question of the defendant having paid $1,807,774 in the mistaken belief that the plaintiff had done so.

Subsequently the plaintiff's choice was made abundantly clear. As appeared from the amended particulars of damage served in July 1993, the plaintiff was seeking damages and giving credit for the amounts received in respect of the secret profits. The company sought, and obtained, an assessment of damages on that footing.

In these unusual circumstances it would make no sense to treat receipt of the amount of $1,807,774 as an election by the plaintiff for an account of profits and against damages. To treat receipt of this payment as an election would lack a rational basis, given the terms of the judge's order, and given the continuing steps to proceed with the assessment of damages. It would also be extremely unfair to the plaintiff. It would mean that by accepting payment of one sum due under the court order of 25 August, 1992, the plaintiff had unknowingly and inadvertently disabled itself from enforcing payment of a much larger amount due under the same order. That would be unfair, because there is no reason to doubt that, in so far as the two remedies are inconsistent in the present case, the plaintiff, armed first with any further information it required, would have chosen damages had it been required to elect at the time judgment was entered.

The conclusion would be otherwise if in the light of all the circumstances it would be inequitable to permit the plaintiff, after receiving the secret profits payment, to proceed with the damages claim even though it gave credit for the amount received. There is no such inequity in this case. The defendant did not make the payment under any misapprehension about the plaintiff's intentions. The belatedness of the plaintiff's choice did not prejudice the defendant.

(i) Purchase of Unauthorised Investments

In **Knott v Cottee** (1852) 16 Beav 77, the testator, who died in 1844, bequeathed his personal estate to trustees upon trust to invest in 'the public or Government Stocks or Funds of Great Britain, or upon real security in England or Wales'.

The executor invested in foreign stocks and in Exchequer bills. In a suit by the beneficiaries, he was required to deposit the Exchequer bills in court, and on 18 November, 1846 they were sold, under an order of the court, at a loss. The court made a decree in 1848 declaring the investments to be unauthorised. By that time, the price of the bills had risen; if they had been sold then, there would have been a profit.

The question was whether the executor should be charged with the original sum due for investment plus 5 per cent., or with the sum which would have been produced if invested in Consols; and whether he should be credited with the proceeds of the Exchequer bills as sold in 1846, or with their (increased) value in 1848 when they were declared to be unauthorised. ROMILLY MR held that the executor should be charged with the amount improperly invested, and credited with the proceeds actually received on their sale. He said at 81:

As to the mode of charging the executor in respect of the Exchequer bills, I treat the laying out in Exchequer bills in this way: the persons interested were entitled to ear-mark them, as being bought with the testator's assets, in the same manner as if the executor had bought a house with the trust funds; and though they do not recognize the investment, they had a right to make it available for what was due; and though part of the property of the executor, it was specifically applicable to the payment. When the Exchequer bills were sold and produced £3,955, the Court must consider the produce as a sum of money refunded by the executor to the testator's estate on that day; and on taking the account, the Master must give credit for this amount as on the day on which the Exchequer bills were sold.

(ii) Improper retention of unauthorised investments[21]

In **Fry v Fry** (1859) 27 Beav 144, a testator, who died in 1834, provided by his will that the Langford Inn should be sold 'as soon as convenient after his decease...either by auction or private sale, and for the most money that could be reasonably obtained for the same'.

The trustees had difficulty in selling. In 1836 they advertised and offered to sell for £1,000. They refused an offer of £900. In 1843 the Bristol and Exeter Railway was opened, and deprived the Inn of most of its coaching traffic. It was again advertised in 1854, but no offer was received. It remained unsold.

ROMILLY MR held the trustees liable in consequence of their negligence for so many years in not selling the property. The estates of the trustees (who had died) would be liable for the difference between the amount eventually received and £900.

(iii) Improper sale of authorised investments

In **Re Massingberd's Settlement** (1890) 63 LT 296,[22] the trustees of a settlement had power to invest in Government or real securities. In 1875 they sold Consols and

---

[21] Trustee Act 2000, ss. 3 and 6(1)(b) [p. 692, above].
[22] *Phillipson v Gatty* (1848) 7 Hare 516.

reinvested in certain unauthorised mortgages. The mortgages were called in and the whole of the money invested was recovered.

Proceedings began in 1887, at which time Consols stood higher than they had done in 1875. The trustees argued that their obligation was only to produce the capital sum; but the Court of Appeal held that they must produce the stock sold or its present money equivalent.

The date of valuation is as at the date of judgment, or, exceptionally, at the date when the asset sold in breach of trust would have been properly sold at a later date (*Re Bell's Indenture* [1980] 1 WLR 1217 at 1233). It is not the date of the writ, as was assumed without argument in *Re Massingberd's Settlement,* where 'having regard to the stability of price of Consols over short periods in the 19th century the difference in price between the date of the writ and the date of the judgment of Kay J was insignificant' (*per* VINELOTT J in *Re Bell's Indenture* at 1233).

(iv) A profit in one transaction cannot be set off against a loss in another

Dimes v Scott
(1828) 4 Russ 195 (LC, **Lord Lyndhurst**)

By his will the testator, who died in 1802, left his estate upon trust for his widow for her life, and after her death upon trust for the plaintiff. The estate included an investment in an East India Company 10 per cent loan whose retention was not authorised by the will. Instead of selling this unauthorised investment within a year of the testator's death, the trustees retained it, and paid the whole income to the widow.

In 1813 the loan was repaid, and the proceeds were invested in 3 per cent Consols. The price of Consols was lower than it had been a year after the testator's death, and the trustees were able to purchase more Consols than they would have been able to purchase if they had made the switch a year from the testator's death.

The question was whether the trustees had committed a breach of trust by paying the whole income to the widow; and, if they had, whether they could set off, against that liability, the extra Consols which the delay had enabled them to purchase.

Held. The payments to the tenant for life were excessive; and the trustees could claim no credit in respect of the extra Consols.

Lord Lyndhurst: This testator left his property to trustees, who were directed to convert it into money, and to invest the proceeds in government or real securities; and he gave the interest of the money so to be invested to his widow for life, with remainder to the lady who is one of the present Plaintiffs. Part of his property consisted of a sum which he had subscribed to what is called the decennial loan. The trustees did not convert his share of this loan into money; but, suffering it to remain as they found it, paid the interest, which was £10 per cent, to the tenant for life. Was that a proper performance of their duty?

The directions of the will were most distinct; and, according to the case of *Howe v Lord Dartmouth* (1802) 7 Ves 137 [see p. 729, above] and the principles of this Court, it was the duty of the trustees to have sold the property within the usual period after the testator's death.

If they neglected to sell it, still, so far as regarded the tenant for life, the property was to be considered as if it had been duly converted. Had the conversion taken place, and the proceeds been invested in that which is considered in this Court as the fit and proper security, namely, £3 per cent stock, the tenant for life would not have been entitled to more than the interest which would have resulted from such stock. The executor is therefore chargeable with the difference between the interest which the fund, if so converted, would have yielded, and the £10 per cent which was actually produced by the fund, and was paid over by him to the tenant for life.

It is said, that, if the subscription to the decennial loan had been sold, and the produce invested in stock at the end of a year from the testator's death, the sale would have been much less advantageous to the estate than the course which has been actually followed; and that, if the executor is to be charged for not having made the conversion at the proper time, he ought on the other hand, to have the benefit of the advantage which has accrued from his course of conduct. The answer is this: with respect to the principal sum, at whatever period the subscription to the decennial loan was sold, the estate must have the whole amount of the stock that was bought; and if it was sold at a later period than the rules of the Court require, the executor is not entitled to any accidental advantage thence arising. As to the payments to the tenant for life, the executors are entitled to have credit only for sums I have adverted to, namely, the dividends on so much £3 per cent stock as would have been purchased with the proceeds of the subscription to the decennial loan, if the conversion had taken place at the proper time. On the other hand, he is chargeable with the whole of the difference between the amount of those dividends and the amount of the sums which have been received in respect of interest on the money which was continued in the decennial loan. I think, therefore, that the judgment of the *Master of the Rolls* [Lord Gifford] must be affirmed.

Hanbury & Martin: *Modern Equity* (17th edn, 2005), p. 665

The rule is harsh though logical. It has not been applied where the court finds that the gain and loss were part of the same transaction. There is often difficulty in determining whether the matter should or should not be regarded as a single transaction.

In *Fletcher v Green*[23] trust money was lent on mortgage to a firm of which one trustee was a partner. The trustees reclaimed the money; the security was sold at a loss and the proceeds paid into court and invested in Consols. The question was whether the trustees' accounts should credit them with the amount of the proceeds of sale or with the value of the Consols, which had risen in price. They were held entitled to take advantage of the rise. No reasons were given. The case is usually explained on the ground that the whole matter was treated as one transaction. If that is so, they should logically have been at risk in relation to a possible fall in the price of Consols; the trustees can hardly be allowed to take advantage of a rise but not the burden of a fall; but it would be hard on the trustees if they have to run the risk of loss on an investment made by the court.

In **Bartlett v Barclays Bank Trust Co Ltd** [1980] Ch 515, BRIGHTMAN J said at 538:

The general rule as stated in all the textbooks, with some reservations, is that where a trustee is liable in respect of distinct breaches of trust, one of which has resulted in a loss and the other in a gain, he is not entitled to set off the gain against the loss, unless they arise in the same transaction. The relevant cases are, however, not altogether easy to reconcile. All are centenarians

---

[23] (1864) 33 Beav 426.

and none is quite like the present. The Guildford development stemmed from exactly the same policy and (to a lesser degree because it proceeded less far) exemplified the same folly as the Old Bailey project. Part of the profit was in fact used to finance the Old Bailey disaster. By sheer luck the gamble paid off handsomely, on capital account. I think it would be unjust to deprive the bank of this element of salvage in the course of assessing the cost of the shipwreck. My order will therefore reflect the bank's right to an appropriate set-off.

(v) Beneficiary's loss reflective of company loss

In **Shaker v Al-Bedrawi** [2002] EWCA Civ 1452, [2003] Ch 350[24] it was recognised that a beneficiary of a trust of shares could not sue a trustee, who was also a director of the company and who had arranged for the wrongful payment of the company's money, where the beneficiary's loss reflected the loss of the company because the company had a cause of action to seek relief for this loss.

C   INTEREST

A trustee may be liable, not only to replace trust capital which has been misapplied, but also to pay interest on that sum from the date of misapplication. Judges have a discretion to award simple interest by virtue of the Supreme Court Act 1981, section 35A. But there is also an equitable jurisdiction to award compound interest. In **Westdeutsche Landesbank Girozentrale v Islington London Borough Council** [1996] AC 669, LORD GOFF OF CHIEVELEY at 692, summarised the situations when compound interest will traditionally be awarded and identified the rationale for the award of such interest:[25]

Now it is true that the reported cases on the exercise of the equitable jurisdiction, which are by no means numerous, are concerned with cases of breach of duty by trustees and other fiduciaries. In *A-G v Alford* (1855) 4 De GM & G 843, for example, which came before Lord Cranworth LC, the question arose whether an executor and trustee, who had for several years retained in his hands trust funds which he ought to have invested, should be chargeable with interest in excess of the ordinary rate of simple interest. It was held that he should not be chargeable at a higher rate. Lord Cranworth LC recognised that the court might in such a case impose interest at a higher rate, or even compound interest. But he observed that if so the court does not impose a penalty on the trustee. He said, at 851:

> 'What the court ought to do, I think, is to charge him only with the interest which he has received, or which it is justly entitled to say he ought to have received, or which it is so fairly to be presumed that he did receive that he is estopped from saying that he did not receive it.'

In cases of misconduct which benefits the executor, however, the court may fairly infer that he used the money in speculation, and may, on the principle *in odium spoliatoris omnia praesumuntur*,[26] assume that he made a higher rate, if that was a reasonable conclusion.

---

[24] See also *Barnes v Tomlinson* [2006] EWHC 3115 (Ch).

[25] See also *President of India v La Pintada Compania Navigacion SA* [1985] AC 104 at 115 (Lord Brandon of Oakbrook) and *Wallersteiner v Moir (No 2)* [1975] QB 373 at 397 (Buckley LJ).

[26] 'Everything can be presumed against a wrongdoer.'

Likewise in *Burdick v Garrick* (1870) 5 Ch App 233, where a fiduciary agent held money of his principal and simply paid it into his bank account, it was held that he should be charged with simple interest only. Lord Hatherley LC, at 241–242, applied the principle laid down in *A-G v Alford,* namely that:

'the court does not proceed against an accounting party by way of punishing him for making use of the plaintiff's money by directing rests, or payment of compound interest, but proceeds upon this principle, either that he has made, or has put himself in such a position that he is to be presumed to have made, 5 per cent, or compound interest, as the case may be. If the court finds . . . that the money received has been invested in an ordinary trade, the whole course of decision has tended to this, that the court presumes that the party against whom relief is sought has made that amount of profit which persons ordinarily do make in trade, and in those cases the court directs rests to be made.'

For a more recent case in which the equitable jurisdiction was invoked, see *Wallersteiner v Moir (No 2)* [1975] QB 373, below.

From these cases it can be seen that compound interest may be awarded in cases where the defendant has wrongfully profited, or may be presumed to have so profited, from having the use of another person's money. The power to award compound interest is therefore available to achieve justice in a limited area of what is now seen as the law of restitution, *viz.* where the defendant has acquired a benefit through his wrongful act.

In **Wallersteiner v Moir (No 2)** [1975] QB 373,[27] the defendant was a company director and international financier who was shown to have improperly used company funds for his own benefit in breach of fiduciary duty. He was held liable to pay compound interest at the rate of 1 per cent over the minimum lending rate.

SCARMAN LJ said at 406:

I agree that we have power under the equitable jurisdiction of the court to include interest in the judgment entered against Dr. Wallersteiner. This judgment we have already said is to be for £234,773 and interest, but at the time we had not heard argument as to the propriety of including interest. The principle on which equitable interest is awarded was stated by Lord Hatherley LC in *Burdick v Garrick* (1870) 5 Ch App 233 at 241, and has been frequently applied to situations in which there was a fiduciary relationship at the time when the money was appropriated. In *Atwool v Merryweather* (1867) LR 5 Eq 464n, interest was awarded to a company upon money recovered for it in a minority shareholder's action.

There is, therefore, ample authority to support the claim made by Mr. Moir on behalf of the companies to interest from the date on which the companies made their loan to I.F.T.—a loan which in default of defence this court has accepted was instigated by Dr. Wallersteiner in breach of his duty as a director.

The question whether the interest to be awarded should be simple or compound depends upon evidence as to what the accounting party has, or is to be presumed to have done with the money . . .

Dr. Wallersteiner was at all material times engaged in the business of finance. Through a complex structure of companies he conducted financial operations with a view to profit. The quarter-million pounds assistance which he obtained from the two companies in order to finance the acquisition of the shares meant that he was in a position to employ the money or its capital

[27] (1975) 39 Conv (NS) (J.T. Farrand); (1985) 101 LQR 30 (F.A. Mann).

equivalent in those operations. Though the truth is unlikely ever to be fully known, shrouded as it is by the elaborate corporate structure within which Dr. Wallersteiner chose to operate, one may safely presume that the use of the money (or the capital it enabled him to acquire) was worth to him the equivalent of compound interest at commercial rates with yearly rests, if not more. I, therefore, agree that he should be ordered to pay compound interest at the rates, and with the rests, proposed by Lord Denning MR and Buckley LJ. This being a case for equitable interest, no question arises as to interest under section 3 of the Law Reform (Miscellaneous Provisions) Act 1934;[28] I therefore express no opinion as to the true construction of subsection (1) of that section.

The House of Lords recognised in *Sempra Metals Ltd v IRC* [2007] UKHL 34, [2007] WLR 354[29] that compound interest is generally available in respect of claims regardless of whether they are founded in equity or at common law.

A further question relates to the rate at which compound interest should be awarded. Although this lies in the discretion of the court, guidance has been given in **Bartlett v Barclays Bank Trust Co Ltd (No 2)** [1980] Ch 515. BRIGHTMAN LJ said at 547:

In my judgment, a proper rate of interest to be awarded, in the absence of special circumstances, to compensate beneficiaries and trust funds for non-receipt from a trustee of money that ought to have been received is that allowed from time to time on the courts' short-term investment account, established under section 6(1) of the Administration of Justice Act 1965.[30] To some extent the high interest rates payable on money lent reflect and compensate for the continual erosion in the value of money by reason of galloping inflation. It seems to me arguable, therefore, that if a high rate of interest is payable in such circumstances, a proportion of that interest should be added to capital in order to help maintain the value of the corpus of the trust estate. It may be, therefore, that there will have to be some adjustment as between life tenant and remaindermen. I do not decide this point and I express no view upon it.

II LIABILITY OF THIRD PARTIES[31]

Where a third party has received trust property in breach of trust,[32] the beneficiaries of the trust have two types of remedy available to them. One is proprietary and this will be available where the third party has retained the trust property or its proceeds.[33] Typically, the third party will hold that property on constructive trust for

---

[28] See now Supreme Court Act 1981, s. 35A.   [29] (2007) CLJ 510 (G. Virgo).

[30] See also (1981) 78 LS Gaz 1029 for an opinion by L.H. Hoffmann QC, in favour of 'the prevailing London clearing banks' base rate'; [1982] Conv 93; *Guardian Ocean Cargoes Ltd v Banco do Brasil (No 3)* [1992] 2 Lloyd's Rep 193 (1 per cent above New York prime rate).

[31] H&M, pp. 309–324; Lewin, pp. 1623–1654, 1733–1782; P&M, pp. 370–407; P&S, pp. 820–862; Pettit, pp. 150–163; Snell, pp. 690–693; T&H, pp. 959–1006; U&H, pp. 1167–1204 ; Oakley, *Constructive Trusts* (3rd edn), pp. 181–242; Virgo, *The Principles of the Law of Restitution* (2nd edn, 2006), 533–537, 647–655. See generally (1986) 102 LQR 114, 267 (C. Harpum); (1996) 112 LQR 56 (S. Gardner); (2001) 21 OJLS 239 (S. Thomas).

[32] The same principles apply where property has been received in breach of fiduciary duty.

[33] See p. 943, above.

the beneficiary,[34] unless the third party is a bona fide purchaser of the legal estate for value without notice, actual, constructive, or imputed.[35] Where, however, the third party had received the property but it has since been dissipated, the beneficiary cannot claim a proprietary remedy. Instead, the beneficiary may seek to hold the third party personally liable for 'unconscionable receipt' of trust property. Similarly, where the third party has not received trust property but has assisted in the breach of trust,[36] the beneficiary may seek to hold the third party personally liable for dishonest assistance in a breach of trust. Traditionally, where a third party is held liable for 'unconscionable receipt' or 'dishonest assistance' he is held liable as though he is a constructive trustee or as having a constructive trust imposed on him.[37] This is, however, misleading, since his liability is not proprietary but is personal.[38] The third party does not have any property which belongs to the beneficiary as such and so no proprietary remedy can be awarded. Rather, where the third party is held liable for unconscionable receipt he is required to make restitution of the value of the trust property which has been received. Where the third party is liable for dishonest assistance he is typically required to compensate the trust for the loss suffered as a result of the assistance which had been provided.[39]

The essence of this liability was identified by MILLETT LJ in **Paragon Finance plc v DB Thakerar & Co** [1999] 1 All ER 400 at 408:

Regrettably, however, the expressions 'constructive trust' and 'constructive trustee' have been used by equity lawyers to describe two entirely different situations. The first covers those cases....where the defendant, though not expressly appointed as trustee, has assumed the duties of a trustee by a lawful transaction which was independent of and preceded the breach of trust and is not impeached by the plaintiff. The second covers those cases where the trust obligation arises as a direct consequence of the unlawful transaction which is impeached by the plaintiff....

The second class of case is different. It arises when the defendant is implicated in a fraud. Equity has always given relief against fraud by making any person sufficiently implicated in the fraud accountable in equity. In such a case he is traditionally, though I think unfortunately, described as a constructive trustee and said to be 'liable to account as constructive trustee'.

---

[34] Alternatively the beneficiary may only have a security interest in the property which was received by the third party. See p. 945, above.   [35] See p. 937, above.

[36] Or a breach of fiduciary duty.

[37] *Westdeutsche Landesbank Girozentrale v Islington London Borough Council* [1996] AC 669 at 705 (Lord Browne-Wilkinson).

[38] *Paragon Finance plc v DB Thakerar & Co* [1999] 1 All ER 400, 408 (Millett LJ) [below]; *Dubai Aluminium Co Ltd v Salaam* [2003] 2 AC 366, 404 (Lord Millett); *Restitution: Past, Present and Future* (eds. W. Cornish, R. Nolan, J. O'Sullivan and G. Virgo), p. 200 (P. Millett); (1999) CLJ 294, 301–302 (L. Smith); Oakley, *Constructive Trusts,* (3rd edn) pp. 186–190.

[39] See *Royal Brunei Airlines Sdn Bhd v Tan* [1995] 2 AC 378 [p. 983, below]; *Sinclair Investment Holdings SA v Versailles Trade Finance Ltd* [2007] EWHC 915 (Ch), (2004) 67 MLR 16 (S. Elliott and C. Mitchell). In *Ultraframe (UK) Ltd v Fielding* [2006] EWHC 1638 (Ch), [2005] All ER (D) 397 Lewison J held, at [1594] that the defendant who is liable for dishonest assistance may be required to disgorge profits made from the wrongdoing rather than being required to compensate the claimant for loss suffered; (2006) 122 LQR 558, 563 (D.D. Prentice and J. Payne).

Such a person is not in fact a trustee at all, even though he may be liable to account as if he were. He never assumes the position of a trustee, and if he receives the trust property at all it is adversely to the plaintiff by an unlawful transaction which is impugned by the plaintiff. In such a case the expressions 'constructive trust' and 'constructive trustee' are misleading, for there is no trust and usually no possibility of a proprietary remedy; they are 'nothing more than a formula for equitable relief': *Selangor United Rubber Estates Ltd v Cradock (No 3)* [1968] 1 WLR 1555 at 1582, *per* Ungoed-Thomas J.[40]

In **Dubai Aluminium Co Ltd v Salaam** [2002] UKHL 48, [2003] 2 AC 366, LORD MILLETT also said:

141 ... Equity gives relief against fraud by making any person sufficiently implicated in the fraud accountable in equity. In such a case he is traditionally (and I have suggested unfortunately) described as a 'constructive trustee' and is said to be 'liable to account as a constructive trustee'. But he is not in fact a trustee at all, even though he may be liable to account as if he were. He never claims to assume the position of trustee on behalf of others, and he may be liable without ever receiving or handling the trust property. If he receives the trust property at all he receives it adversely to the claimant and by an unlawful transaction which is impugned by the claimant. He is not a fiduciary or subject to fiduciary obligations; and he could plead the Limitation Acts as a defence to the claim.

142 In this second class of case the expressions 'constructive trust' and 'constructive trustee' create a trap. As the court recently observed in *Coulthard v Disco Mix Club Ltd* [2000] 1 WLR 707, 731 this 'type of constructive trust is merely the creation by the court ... to meet the wrongdoing alleged: there is no real trust and usually no chance of a proprietary remedy'. The expressions are 'nothing more than a formula for equitable relief': *Selangor United Rubber Estates Ltd v Cradock (No 3)* [1968] 1 WLR 1555, 1582, *per* Ungoed-Thomas J. I think that we should now discard the words 'accountable as constructive trustee' in this context and substitute the words 'accountable in equity'.

The most controversial and difficult issue relating to liability for both 'unconscionable receipt' and 'dishonest assistance' concerns the degree of fault which is required to establish such liability. Crucially, is liability to be assessed subjectively, with reference to the defendant's own thought process, or should it be assessed objectively, by reference to whether the reasonable person would have known that the third party was receiving trust property in breach of trust or was assisting a breach of trust? As regards liability for receipt, a further controversy relates to whether it is necessary to establish fault at all, on the ground that liability should instead be analysed as receipt-based rather than fault-based.[41]

In both cases of receipt of trust property and assisting in a breach of trust, the existence of the trust must be established.[42] Knowledge of a 'doubtful equity' does not suffice.[43]

---

[40] See also *Cattley v Pollard* [2006] EWHC 3130 (Ch), [2007] Ch 353.

[41] This distinction was recognised by the Privy Council in *Royal Brunei Airlines Sdn Bhd v Tan* [1995] 2 AC 378 [p. 983, below].   [42] *Box v Barclays Bank plc* [1998] Lloyd's Rep Bank 185.

[43] *Carl Zeiss Stiftung v Herbert Smith & Co (No 2)* [1969] 2 Ch 276; *Brinks Ltd v Abu-Saleh (No 3)* (1995) The Times, 23 October. A solicitor in doubt as to possible liability should apply to the court for directions: *Finers v Miro* [1991] 1 WLR 35.

A   UNCONSCIONABLE RECEIPT[44]

Where a person, not appointed as trustee, has received,[45] but no longer retains, property which is identifiable as trust property,[46] or the traceable product of such property, for his own benefit,[47] with knowledge that it is trust property transferred in breach of trust, or has acquired knowledge after such receipt and then dealt with the property inconsistently with the trust, he is liable to account for the value of the property received as though he was a constructive trustee. It is not necessary that the breach of trust is fraudulent. The receipt must, however, be a direct consequence of the alleged breach of trust or breach of fiduciary duty: *Brown v Bennett* [1999] 1 BCLC 649. This action will also be available where the defendant has received property which he knows to have been transferred in breach of fiduciary duty. The remedy is simply a personal liability to account for the value of the property received.[48]

(i) The fault requirement

It has been a matter of controversy for some time as to what degree of fault must be established before the defendant can be held liable for unconscionable receipt. Many cases have concluded that it is sufficient that the defendant had constructive notice of the breach of trust and that the property which had been received derived from this breach of trust.[49] Other cases have held that constructive knowledge is not

---

[44] P. Birks, 'Receipt' in *Breach of Trust* (eds. P. Birks and A. Pretto, 2002), pp. 212–240.

[45] In *Trustor v AB Smallbone (No 2)* [2001] 1 WLR 1177 it was held that property will have been received by the defendant if it can be identified in the defendant's hands in accordance with the normal rules of tracing in equity [see p. 903, above]. Property received by a subsidiary company will not have been received by the parent unless the subsidiary was acting as agent for the parent or the subsidiary's veil of incorporation can be pierced.

[46] In *Satnam Investments Ltd v Dunlop Heywood Ltd* [1999] 3 All ER 652 it was contemplated, but not decided, that this action might be available in respect of the receipt of confidential information which had been disclosed in breach of fiduciary duty: [1998] All ER Rev 233 (P.J. Clarke).

[47] Liability cannot arise in this category for receipt and dealing as agent for another: *Agip (Africa) Ltd v Jackson* [1991] Ch 547; *Polly Peck International plc v Nadir (No 2)* [1992] 4 All ER 769.

[48] *Crown Dilmun v Sutton* [2004] EWHC 52, para 204 (Peter Smith J). Cf. *Pulvers (a firm) v Chan* [2007] EWHC 2406 (Ch), para. 380 (Morgan J): equitable compensation available as a remedy for unconscionable receipt.

[49] See, for example, *Karak Rubber Co Ltd v Burden (No 2)* [1972] 1 WLR 602; *Rolled Steel Products (Holdings) Ltd v British Steel Corpn* [1986] Ch 246; *Belmont Finance Corpn Ltd v Williams Furniture Ltd (No 2)* [1980] 1 All ER 393; *International Sales and Agencies Ltd v Marcus* [1982] 3 All ER 551; *Agip (Africa) Ltd v Jackson* [1990] Ch 265 (not dealt with on appeal); *Polly Peck International plc v Nadir (No 2)* [1992] 4 All ER 769; (1990) 49 CLJ 217 (C. Harpum); (1993) 109 LQR 368 (M. Bryan); *El Ajou v Dollar Land Holdings plc* [1993] 3 All ER 717 (reversed on a different point at [1994] 2 All ER 685); *Houghton v Fayers* [2000] 1 BCLC 511. Similarly in New Zealand: *Westpac Banking Corpn v Savin* [1985] 2 NZLR 41; *Powell v Thompson* [1991] 1 NZLR 597; *Equiticorp Industries Group Ltd v Hawkins* [1991] 3 NZLR 700; *Lankshear v ANZ Banking Group (New Zealand) Ltd* [1993] 1 NZLR 481. A similar approach has also been adopted by the Supreme Court of Canada in *Citadel General Assurance Co v Lloyds Bank Canada* (1997) 152 DLR (4th) 411.

sufficient.[50] This controversy has, to some extent been resolved by the decision of the Court of Appeal in *Bank of Credit and Commerce International (Overseas) Ltd v Akindele* [2001] Ch 437, where the court held that the appropriate test of knowledge was one of unconscionability.

Bank of Credit and Commerce International (Overseas) Ltd v Akindele[51]
[2001] Ch 437 (CA, **Nourse, Ward** and **Sedley LJJ**)

Employees of a company, acting in fraudulent breach of their fiduciary duties, procured the company's entry into an artificial loan agreement with the defendant, pursuant to which the defendant paid US$10 million to the company in exchange for 250,000 shares in its holding company, on the basis that the company would arrange for the shares to be sold at a price which gave the defendant a 15 per cent annual return on his investment. The purpose of this scheme was to make it appear that the corporate group had more money than was in fact the case. In pursuance of this agreement, the defendant received US$16.679 million from the company. The claimants, who were liquidators of the company, claimed that the defendant was liable to account for this sum as a constructive trustee because he had received the money knowing of the breach of fiduciary duty.[52]

Held. To be liable for a receipt-based claim it was not necessary to show that the defendant had acted dishonestly.[53] It was sufficient that the defendant's knowledge of the provenance of the funds which he had received made it unconscionable for him to retain the benefit of the receipt. In this case there was insufficient evidence to conclude that the defendant's knowledge was such that it was unconscionable for him to retain the benefit of the money he had received and so the defendant was held not liable.

Nourse LJ: So far as the law is concerned, the comprehensive arguments of Mr. Sheldon and Mr. Moss have demonstrated that there are two questions which, though closely related, are distinct: first, what, in this context, is meant by knowledge; second, is it necessary for the recipient to act dishonestly? Because the answer to it is the simpler, the convenient course is to deal with the second of those questions first.

Knowing receipt—dishonesty
As appears from the penultimate sentence of his judgment, Carnwath J proceeded on an assumption that dishonesty in one form or another was the essential foundation of the claimants' case,

[50] *Re Montagu's Settlement Trusts* [1987] Ch 264; *Eagle Trust plc v SBC Securities Ltd* [1993] 1 WLR 484; *Cowan de Groot Property Ltd v Eagle Trust plc* [1992] 4 All ER 700; *Eagle Trust plc v SBC Securities Ltd (No 2)* [1996] 1 BCLC 121; *Hillsdown Holdings plc v Pensions Ombudsman* [1997] 1 All ER 862.
[51] (2000) 59 CLJ 447 (R. Nolan); (2000) 14 *Trust Law International* 229 (J. Penner); [2000] All ER Rev 319 (P. Birks and W. Swadling); [2000] All ER Rev 252 (P.J. Clarke); [2001] *Restitution Law Review* 99 (J. Stevens).
[52] The claimants also contended that the defendant was liable for dishonest assistance, but the Court of Appeal rejected this claim because the trial judge had correctly concluded that the defendant had acted honestly. See p. 982, below.
[53] Cp. *Bank of America v Arnell* [1999] Lloyd's Rep Bank 399; (2000) CLJ 28 (D. Fox).

whether in knowing assistance or knowing receipt. That was no doubt caused by the acceptance before him (though not at any higher level) by Mr. Sheldon...that the thrust of the recent authorities at first instance was that the recipient's state of knowledge must fall into one of the first three categories listed by Peter Gibson J in *Baden v Société Générale pour Favoriser le Développement du Commerce et de l'Industrie en France SA* [1993] 1 WLR 509 at 575–576, on which basis, said Carnwath J, it was doubtful whether the test differed materially in practice from that for knowing assistance. However, the assumption on which the judge proceeded, derived as I believe from an omission to distinguish between the questions of knowledge and dishonesty, was incorrect in law. While a knowing recipient will often be found to have acted dishonestly, it has never been a prerequisite of the liability that he should.

An authoritative decision on this question, the complexity of whose subject transactions has sometimes caused it to be overlooked in this particular context, is *Belmont Finance Corpn Ltd v Williams Furniture Ltd (No 2)* [1980] 1 All ER 393....

[His Lordship considered the facts of that case and the judgments of the court and continued:] [This case] is clear authority for the proposition that dishonesty is not a necessary ingredient of liability in knowing receipt. There have been other, more recent, judicial pronouncements to the same effect. Thus in *Polly Peck International plc v Nadir (No 2)* [1992] 4 All ER 769 at 777 Scott LJ said that liability in a knowing receipt case did not require that the misapplication of the trust funds should be fraudulent. While in theory it is possible for a misapplication not to be fraudulent and the recipient to be dishonest, in practice such a combination must be rare. Similarly, in *Agip (Africa) Ltd v Jackson* [1990] Ch 265 at 292 Millett J said that in knowing receipt it was immaterial whether the breach of trust was fraudulent or not. The point was made most clearly by Vinelott J in *Eagle Trust plc v SBC Securities Ltd* [1993] 1 WLR 484 at 497:

> 'What the decision in *Belmont (No 2)* [1980] 1 All ER 393 shows is that in a "knowing receipt" case it is only necessary to show that the defendant knew that the moneys paid to him were trust moneys and of circumstances which made the payment a misapplication of them. Unlike a "knowing assistance" case it is not necessary, and never has been necessary, to show that the defendant was in any sense a participator in a fraud.'

Knowing receipt—the authorities on knowledge
With the proliferation in the last twenty years or so of cases in which the misapplied assets of companies have come into the hands of third parties, there has been a sustained judicial and extrajudicial debate as to the knowledge on the part of the recipient which is required in order to found liability in knowing receipt. Expressed in its simplest terms, the question is whether the recipient must have actual knowledge (or the equivalent) that the assets received are traceable to a breach of trust or whether constructive knowledge is enough. The instinctive approach of most equity judges, especially in this court, has been to assume that constructive knowledge is enough. But there is now a series of decisions of eminent first instance judges who, after considering the question in greater depth, have come to the contrary conclusion, at all events when commercial transactions are in point. In the Commonwealth, on the other hand, the preponderance of authority has been in favour of the view that constructive knowledge is enough.

His Lordship considered *Karak Rubber Co Ltd v Burden (No 2)* [1972] 1 WLR 602 at 632 (Brightman J); *Belmont Finance Corpn Ltd v Williams Furniture Ltd (No 2)* [1980] 1 All ER 393 at 405 (Buckley LJ), at 412 (Goff LJ); *Rolled Steel Products (Holdings) Ltd v*

British Steel Corpn [1986] Ch 246 at 306–307 (Browne-Wilkinson LJ); *Agip (Africa) Ltd v Jackson* [1990] Ch 265 at 291 (Millett J); *Houghton v Fayers* [2000] 1 BCLC 511 at 516 (Nourse LJ) and continued:

Collectively, those observations might be thought to provide strong support for the view that constructive knowledge is enough. But it must at once be said that in each of the three cases in this court (including, despite some apparent uncertainty in the judgment of Goff LJ in *Belmont Finance Corpn Ltd v Williams Furniture Ltd (No 2)* [1980] 1 All ER 393 at 412) actual knowledge was found and, further, that the decisions in *Karak Rubber Co Ltd v Burden (No 2)* [1972] 1 WLR 602 and *Agip (Africa) Ltd v Jackson* [1990] Ch 265 were based on knowing assistance, not knowing receipt. Thus in none of the five cases was it necessary for the question to be examined in any depth and there appears to be no case in which such an examination has been conducted in this court. The groundwork has been done in other cases at first instance. I will refer to those of them in which the question has been considered in depth.

The seminal judgment, characteristically penetrative in its treatment of authority and, in the best sense, argumentative, is that of Sir Robert Megarry V-C in *Re Montagu's Settlement Trusts* [1987] Ch 264. It was he who first plumbed the distinction between notice and knowledge. It was he who, building on a passage in the judgment of this court in *Re Diplock* [1948] Ch 465 at 478–479 first emphasised the fundamental difference between the questions which arise in respect of the doctrine of purchaser without notice on the one hand and the doctrine of constructive trusts on the other. Reading from his earlier judgment in the same case, he said [1987] Ch 264 at 278:

> 'The former is concerned with the question whether a person takes property subject to or free from some equity. The latter is concerned with whether or not a person is to have imposed upon him the personal burdens and obligations of trusteeship. I do not see why one of the touchstones for determining the burdens on property should be the same as that for deciding whether to impose a personal obligation on a [person]. The cold calculus of constructive and imputed notice does not seem to me to be an appropriate instrument for deciding whether a [person's] conscience is sufficiently affected for it to be right to bind him by the obligations of a constructive trustee.'

He added that there is more to being made a trustee than merely taking property subject to an equity.

The practical importance of that distinction had been explained by Sir Robert Megarry V-C in his earlier judgment. The question in that case was whether the widow and executrix of the will of the 10th Duke of Manchester was liable to account to the 11th Duke in respect of certain settled chattels or the proceeds of sale thereof. Having found that the 10th Duke had had no knowledge that the chattels received by him were still subject to any trust and that he believed that they had been lawfully and properly released to him by the trustees, Sir Robert Megarry V-C continued, at 272:

> 'If liability as a constructive trustee depended on his knowledge, then he was not liable as a constructive trustee, and his estate is not liable for any chattels that have been disposed of, as distinct from any traceable proceeds of them. Even if he was not a constructive trustee and was a mere volunteer, his estate is liable to yield up any chattels that remain, or the traceable proceeds of any that have gone ... But unless he was a constructive trustee, there appears to be no liability if the chattels have gone and there are no traceable proceeds.'

Sir Robert Megarry V-C summarised his conclusions in eight subparagraphs, at 285. I read the first three:

'(1) The equitable doctrine of tracing and the imposition of a constructive trust by reason of the knowing receipt of trust property are governed by different rules and must be kept distinct. Tracing is primarily a means of determining the rights of property, whereas the imposition of a constructive trust creates personal obligations that go beyond mere property rights.

(2) In considering whether a constructive trust has arisen in a case of the knowing receipt of trust property, the basic question is whether the conscience of the recipient is sufficiently affected to justify the imposition of such a trust.

(3) Whether a constructive trust arises in such a case primarily depends on the knowledge of the recipient, and not on notice to him; and for clarity it is desirable to use the word "knowledge" and avoid the word "notice" in such cases.'

The effect of Sir Robert Megarry V-C's decision, broadly stated, was that, in order to establish liability in knowing receipt, the recipient must have actual knowledge (or the equivalent) that the assets received are traceable to a breach of trust and that constructive knowledge is not enough.

In *Eagle Trust plc v SBC Securities Ltd* [1993] 1 WLR 484 at 503 Vinelott J did not think it would be right to found a decision that the statement of claim in that case disclosed no cause of action solely on the authority of *Re Montagu's Settlement Trusts* [1987] Ch 264. However, on the ground that he (unlike Sir Robert Megarry V-C) was dealing with a commercial transaction, he arrived at the same conclusion and held that in such a transaction constructive knowledge is not enough. He cited, at 504, a well-known passage in the judgment of Lindley LJ in *Manchester Trust v Furness* [1895] 2 QB 539 at 545, the latter part of which reads thus:

'In dealing with estates in land title is everything, and it can be leisurely investigated; in commercial transactions possession is everything, and there is no time to investigate title; and if we were to extend the doctrine of constructive notice to commercial transactions we should be doing infinite mischief and paralysing the trade of the country.'

The decision of Vinelott J was followed by Knox J in *Cowan de Groot Properties Ltd v Eagle Trust plc* [1992] 4 All ER 700 (another case of a commercial transaction) and the decisions of both of them by Arden J at the trial of the action in *Eagle Trust* case: see *Eagle Trust plc v SBC Securities Ltd (No 2)* [1996] 1 BCLC 121.

We were also referred to three decisions in New Zealand and one in Canada. In each of *Westpac Banking Corpn v Savin* [1985] 2 NZLR 41; *Equiticorp Industries Group Ltd v Hawkins* [1991] 3 NZLR 700; and *Lankshear v ANZ Banking Group (New Zealand) Ltd* [1993] 1 NZLR 481, the preferred view was that constructive knowledge was enough, although in the last-named case the point went by concession. All of them were cases of commercial transactions. In *Westpac Banking Corpn v Savin* [1985] 2 NZLR 41, a decision of the Court of Appeal, Richardson J, having expressed a provisional preference for the view that constructive knowledge was enough, said, at 53:

'Clearly courts would not readily import a duty to inquire in the case of commercial transactions where they must be conscious of the seriously inhibiting effects of a wide application of the doctrine. Nevertheless there must be cases where there is no justification on the known facts for allowing a commercial man who has received funds paid to him in breach of trust to plead the shelter of the exigencies of commercial life.'

CHAPTER 20: PERSONAL CLAIMS & REMEDIES

In *Citadel General Assurance Co v Lloyds Bank Canada* (1997) 152 DLR (4th) 411, another case of a commercial transaction, the Supreme Court of Canada held, as a matter of decision, that constructive knowledge was enough.

The Baden *case*
It will have been observed that up to this stage I have made no more than a passing reference to the fivefold categorisation of knowledge accepted by Peter Gibson J in *Baden v Société Générale pour Favoriser le Développement du Commerce et de l'Industrie en France SA* [1993] 1 WLR 509 at 575–576:

(i)   actual knowledge;
(ii) wilfully shutting one's eyes to the obvious;
(iii) wilfully and recklessly failing to make such inquiries as an honest and reasonable man would make;
(iv) knowledge of circumstances which would indicate the facts to an honest and reasonable man;
(v)   knowledge of circumstances which will put an honest and reasonable man on inquiry.

Reference to the categorisation has been made in most of the knowing receipt cases to which I have referred from *Re Montagu's Settlement Trusts* [1987] Ch 264 onwards. In many of them it has been influential in the decision. In general, the first three categories have been taken to constitute actual knowledge (or its equivalent) and the last two constructive knowledge.

Two important points must be made about the *Baden* categorisation. First, it appears to have been propounded by counsel for the plaintiffs, accepted by counsel for the defendant and then put to the judge on an agreed basis. Secondly, though both counsel accepted that all five categories of knowledge were relevant and neither sought to submit that there was any distinction for that purpose between knowing receipt and knowing assistance (a view with which the judge expressed his agreement: see [1993] 1 WLR 509 at 582), the claim in constructive trust was based squarely on knowing assistance and not on knowing receipt: see at 572. In the circumstances, whatever may have been agreed between counsel, it is natural to assume that the categorisation was not formulated with knowing receipt primarily in mind. This, I think, may be confirmed by the references to 'an honest and reasonable man' in categories (iv) and (v). Moreover, in *Agip (Africa) Ltd v Jackson* [1990] Ch 265 at 293, Millett J warned against over-refinement or a too ready assumption that categories (iv) and (v) are necessarily cases of constructive knowledge only, reservations which were shared by Knox J in *Cowan de Groot Properties Ltd v Eagle Trust plc* [1992] 4 All ER 700 at 761.

Knowing receipt—the recipient's state of knowledge
In *Royal Brunei Airlines Sdn Bhd v Tan* [1995] 2 AC 378 [p. 983, below], which is now the leading authority on knowing assistance, Lord Nicholls of Birkenhead, in delivering the judgment of the Privy Council, said, at 392, that 'knowingly' was better avoided as a defining ingredient of the liability, and that in that context the *Baden* categorisation was best forgotten. Although my own view is that the categorisation is often helpful in identifying different states of knowledge which may or may not result in a finding of dishonesty for the purposes of knowing assistance, I have grave doubts about its utility in cases of knowing receipt. Quite apart from

its origins in a context of knowing assistance and the reservations of Knox and Millett JJ, any categorisation is of little value unless the purpose it is to serve is adequately defined, whether it be fivefold, as in the *Baden* case [1993] 1 WLR 509, or twofold, as in the classical division between actual and constructive knowledge, a division which has itself become blurred in recent authorities.

What then, in the context of knowing receipt, is the purpose to be served by a categorisation of knowledge? It can only be to enable the court to determine whether, in the words of Buckley LJ in *Belmont Finance Corpn Ltd v Williams Furniture Ltd (No 2)* [1980] 1 All ER 393 at 405, the recipient can 'conscientiously retain [the] funds against the company' or, in the words of Sir Robert Megarry V-C in *Re Montagu's Settlement Trusts* [1987] Ch 264 at 273, '[the recipient's] conscience is sufficiently affected for it to be right to bind him by the obligations of a constructive trustee'. But, if that is the purpose, there is no need for categorisation. All that is necessary is that the recipient's state of knowledge should be such as to make it unconscionable for him to retain the benefit of the receipt.

For these reasons I have come to the view that, just as there is now a single test of dishonesty for knowing assistance, so ought there to be a single test of knowledge for knowing receipt. The recipient's state of knowledge must be such as to make it unconscionable for him to retain the benefit of the receipt. A test in that form, though it cannot, any more than any other, avoid difficulties of application, ought to avoid those of definition and allocation to which the previous categorisations have led. Moreover, it should better enable the courts to give common-sense decisions in the commercial context in which claims in knowing receipt are now frequently made, paying equal regard to the wisdom of Lindley LJ on the one hand and of Richardson J on the other.

His Lordship then considered the evidence and concluded that the defendant's knowledge did not make it unconscionable for him to retain the benefit of the receipt since he was unaware of any facts which questioned the propriety of the transaction into which he had entered. His Lordship also concluded that, even if the appropriate test was whether the defendant had actual or constructive knowledge that the money he had received was traceable to a breach of fiduciary duty, this test also was not satisfied.

In **Criterion Properties plc v Stratford UK Properties LLC** [2004] UKHL 28, [2004] 1 WLR 1856 the claimant, Criterion Properties plc, and defendant, Oaktree, formed a limited partnership. Fearing that the claimant might be taken over by another company the managing director and another director of the claimant signed a so-called 'poison pill' agreement with the defendant. This gave the defendant the right to have its interest in the partnership bought out on favourable terms if another company gained control of the claimant or if the chairman or managing director ceased to be involved in its management. The managing director was dismissed and the defendant sought to exercise its option to be bought out. The issue was whether the 'poison pill' agreement was valid. The Court of Appeal, [2003] EWCA Civ 1783, [2003] 1 WLR 2108, considered that this turned on whether it was unconscionable for the defendant to hold the claimant to the agreement. The House of Lords considered that this was not the relevant issue. Rather, it was whether the claimant's directors had authority to sign the agreement. In the course of his judgment LORD NICOLLS OF BIRKENHEAD considered *BCCI v Akindele:*

2   As explained by Lord Scott, the issues arising on this application for summary judgment were clouded in the courts below by a faulty elision of two different issues to which different principles apply. The only relevant issue on this application is whether the second supplementary agreement was a valid and binding agreement. It is accepted by Criterion, for the purposes of this application, that Oaktree's directors acted honestly. Thus this issue of validity turns solely on whether the directors who signed the agreement on behalf of Criterion did so within the actual or apparent scope of their authority. This issue, in turn, depends upon an application of ordinary agency principles, having due regard to the rule in *Royal British Bank v Turquand* (1856) 6 E & B 327 and sections 35A and 35B of the Companies Act 1985 (as substituted by section 108(1) of the Companies Act 1989).

3   Unfortunately, in the courts below this 'want of authority' issue was approached on the basis that the outcome turned on whether Oaktree's conduct was unconscionable. This seems to have been the test applied by the Court of Appeal in *Bank of Credit and Commerce International (Overseas) Ltd v Akindele* [2001] Ch 437 both to questions of 'want of authority' and to liability for what traditionally has been labelled 'knowing receipt'.

4   I respectfully consider the Court of Appeal in *Akindele*'s case fell into error on this point. If a company (A) enters into an agreement with B under which B acquires benefits from A, A's ability to recover these benefits from B depends essentially on whether the agreement is binding on A. If the directors of A were acting for an improper purpose when they entered into the agreement, A's ability to have the agreement set aside depends upon the application of familiar principles of agency and company law. If, applying these principles, the agreement is found to be valid and is therefore *not* set aside, questions of 'knowing receipt' by B do not arise. So far as B is concerned there can be no question of A's assets having been misapplied. B acquired the assets from A, the legal and beneficial owner of the assets, under a valid agreement made between him and A....

The meaning of unconscionability for the purposes of the action for unconscionable receipt has been clarified to some extent by resorting to cases on the defence of change of position, which is a defence to claims in unjust enrichment.[54] That defence is not available if the defendant has acted in bad faith and the defendant will be considered to have acted in bad faith where he was acting unconscionably. This includes dishonesty and a failure to act in a commercially acceptable way,[55] but not negligence.[56] The meaning of unconscionability was also considered by the Court of Appeal in *Criterion Properties plc v Stratford UK Properties LLC,*[57] when determining whether the defendant could hold the claimant to an unauthorised agreement. Whether enforcement of the agreement was unconscionable depended on factors such as the fault of both parties and the actions and knowledge of the defendant in the context of the commercial relationship as a whole.

----

[54] See p. 937, above. See also (2001) 21 OJLS 239 (S.B. Thomas), who suggests economic analysis can provide a framework for the determination of unconscionability. See also (1998) 57 CLJ 291 (D. Fox).

[55] *Niru Battery Manufacturing Co v Milestone Trading Ltd* [2002] EWHC 1425, Comm, [2002] 2 All ER (Comm) 705, 741; endorsed by CA [2003] EWCA Civ 1446 (Civ); *Abou-Rahmah v Abacha* [2006] EWCA Civ 1492, [2007] 1 All ER (Comm) 827.

[56] *Maersk Air Ltd v Expeditors International (UK) Ltd* [2003] 1 Lloyd's Rep 491, 499.

[57] [2002] EWCA Civ 1783, [2003] 1 WLR 2108.

(ii) Should Liability for Receipt of Property in Breach of Trust be Strict?

At common law, where the defendant has received property belonging to the claimant but the defendant no longer retains that property or its traceable proceeds, the claimant can bring a personal restitutionary claim for money had and received. To establish such a claim the claimant must show that he retained legal title to the property at the point when the defendant received it or its traceable proceeds.[58] The defendant's liability is strict. Consequently, the fact that the defendant was unaware of the claimant's proprietary rights is irrelevant, save where the defendant provided consideration for the property and so can claim a defence of bona fide purchase. The defendant may also have a defence of change of position. This defence is available where the defendant's position has changed in reliance on the receipt of the benefit such that it is inequitable to require him or her to make restitution to the claimant.[59]

If the common law claim for restitution of the value of the claimant's property which the defendant has received is a strict liability claim, why does the similar equitable claim of unconscionable receipt require proof of fault? Both claims are grounded on the fact that the defendant has received property belonging to the claimant, either at law, for the action for money had and received, or in equity, for the action of unconscionable receipt. In fact, equity does recognise one type of strict liability restitutionary claim. This is where the defendant mistakenly received property belonging to another in the administration of an estate, as in *Ministry of Health v Simpson* [1951] AC 251 (the *Diplock* litigation).[60] Why should such a strict liability claim not be available generally in equity to mirror precisely the equivalent common law claim? The harshness of such a strict liability claim could be mitigated by the defence of change of position, recognised by the House of Lords in *Lipkin Gorman v Karpnale Ltd* [1991] 2 AC 548.

[58] *Lipkin Gorman v Karpnale Ltd* [1991] 2 AC 548, p. 943; (1991) 107 LQR 527 (P. Watts); (1991) CLJ 407 (W.R. Cornish); [1992] Conv 124 (M. Halliwell); (1992) 55 MLR 377 (E. McKendrick); [1992] All ER Rev 202 (P.J. Clarke); 255 (W.J. Swadling); (1994) 57 MLR 38 (S. Fennell). It is a matter of some controversy whether such a restitutionary claim should be characterised as being grounded on the reversal of the defendant's unjust enrichment or the vindication of property rights. For the former view, see [1997] *New Zealand Law Review* 623 (P. Birks); (2001) 117 LQR 412 (A. Burrows). For the latter view see Virgo, *The Principles of the Law of Restitution* (2nd edn, 2006), pp. 11–14; [1997] *New Zealand Law Review* 668 (R. Grantham and C. Rickett).

[59] *Lipkin Gorman v Karpnale Ltd* ibid; Virgo, ibid, pp. 689–714. See also *South Tyneside Metropolitan Borough Council v Svenska International plc* [1995] 1 All ER 545; (1994) 58 MLR 505 (P. Key); *Phillip Collins Ltd v Davis* [2000] 3 All ER 808; *Scottish Equitable plc v Derby* [2001] 3 All ER 818; *National Westminster Bank plc v Somer International* [2002] 1 All ER 198; *National Bank of Egypt International Ltd v Oman Housing Bank SAOC* [2002] EWHC 1760 (Comm), [2003] 1 All ER (Comm) 246; *Dextra Bank & Trust Co Ltd v Bank of Jamaica* [2002] 1 All ER (Comm) 193 (PC); *Papamichael v National Westminster Bank plc* [2003] 1 Lloyd's Rep 341; *Maersk Air Ltd v Expeditors International (UK) Ltd* [2003] 1 Lloyd's Rep 491; *Rose v AIB Group (UK) plc* [2003] EWHC 1737 (Ch), [2003] 1 WLR 2791; *Commerzbank AG v Gareth Price-Jones* [2003] EWCA Civ 1663, [2005] 1 Lloyd's Rep 298; *Credit Suisse (Monaco) SA v Attar* [2004] EWHC 374 (Comm); *Barros Mattos Junior v Macdaniels* [2004] EWHC 1188 (Ch), [2005] 1 WLR 247. Cp *Foskett v McKeown* [2001] 1 AC 102 at 129 (Lord Millett): change of position defence not available for claims involving the vindication of property rights. See p. 941, above.

[60] See also *Nelson v Larholt* [1948] 1 KB 339; *Baker (GL) Ltd v Medway Building and Supplies Ltd* [1958] 1 WLR 1216.

However, the authorities do not yet establish strict liability for innocent volunteers in equity other than in the context of administration of estates.[61]

Nevertheless, there have been persuasive calls for the recognition of such a claim, most notably by Lord Nicholls of Birkenhead writing extra-judicially.[62] This was considered by NOURSE LJ in **Bank of Credit and Commerce International (Overseas) Ltd v Akindele** [2001] Ch 437 at 455:[63]

We were referred in argument to 'Knowing Receipt: The Need for a New Landmark', an essay by Lord Nicholls of Birkenhead in *Restitution Past, Present and Future* (1998), p. 231, a work of insight and scholarship taking forward the writings of academic authors, in particular those of Professor Birks, Professor Burrows and Professor Gareth Jones. It is impossible to do justice to such a work within the compass of a judgment such as this. Most pertinent for present purposes is the suggestion made by Lord Nicholls, at p 238, in reference to the decision of the House of Lords in *Lipkin Gorman v Karpnale Ltd* [1991] 2 AC 548:

> 'In this respect equity should now follow the law. Restitutionary liability, applicable regardless of fault but subject to a defence of change of position, would be a better-tailored response to the underlying mischief of misapplied property than personal liability which is exclusively fault-based. Personal liability would flow from having received the property of another, from having been unjustly enriched at the expense of another. It would be triggered by the mere fact of receipt, thus recognising the endurance of property rights. But fairness would be ensured by the need to identify a gain, and by making change of position available as a defence in suitable cases when, for instance, the recipient had changed his position in reliance on the receipt.'

Lord Nicholls goes on to examine the *Re Diplock* [1948] Ch 465 principle, suggesting, at p. 241, that it could be reshaped by being extended to all trusts but in a form modified to take proper account of the decision in *Lipkin Gorman v Karpnale Ltd* [1991] 2 AC 548.

No argument before us was based on the suggestions made in Lord Nicholls's essay. Indeed, at this level of decision, it would have been a fruitless exercise. We must continue to do our best with the accepted formulation of the liability in knowing receipt, seeking to simplify and improve it where we may. While in general it may be possible to sympathise with a tendency to subsume a further part of our law of restitution under the principles of unjust enrichment, I beg leave to doubt whether strict liability coupled with a change of position defence would be preferable to fault-based liability in many commercial transactions, for example where, as here, the receipt is of a company's funds which have been misapplied by its directors. Without having heard argument it is unwise to be dogmatic, but in such a case it would appear to be commercially unworkable and contrary to the spirit of the rule in *Royal British Bank v Turquand* (1856) 6 E & B 327 that, simply on proof of an internal misapplication of the company's funds, the burden should shift to the recipient to defend the receipt either by a change of position or perhaps in some other way. Moreover, if the circumstances of the receipt are such as to make it

---

[61] Although *Baker (GL) Ltd v Medway Building and Supplies Ltd* [1958] 1 WLR 1216 recognised a strict liability equitable claim where assets were distributed from an *inter vivos* trust.

[62] In *Restitution: Past, Present and Future* (eds. W.R. Cornish, R. Nolan, J. O'Sullivan and G. Virgo, 1998) pp. 231–245. See also Lord Millett, *Equity in Commercial Law* (eds. Degeling and Edelman, 2005), pp. 311–312; Lord Walker, (2005) 27 *Sydney Law Review* 187; 'Receipt' in *Breach of Trust* (eds. Birks and Pretto, 2002) (P. Birks).

[63] See also *Grupo Torras SA v Al-Sabah (No 5)* [2001] Lloyd's Rep Bank 36, 62.

unconscionable for the recipient to retain the benefit of it, there is an obvious difficulty in saying that it is equitable for a change of position to afford him a defence.[64]

In **Twinsectra Ltd v Yardley** [2002] 2 AC 164, LORD MILLETT said at para. 105:

Liability for 'knowing receipt' is receipt-based. It does not depend on fault. The cause of action is restitutionary and is available only where the defendant received or applied the money in breach of trust for his own use and benefit: see *Agip (Africa) Ltd v Jackson* [1990] Ch 265 at 291–292; *Royal Brunei Airlines Sdn Bhd v Tan* [1995] 2 AC 378 at 386. There is no basis for requiring actual knowledge of the breach of trust, let alone dishonesty, as a condition of liability. Constructive notice is sufficient, and may not even be necessary. There is powerful academic support for the proposition that the liability of the recipient is the same as in other cases of restitution, that is to say strict but subject to a change of position defence.[65]

In **Criterion Properties plc v Stratford UK Properties LLC** [2004] UKHL 28, [2004] 1 WLR 1856 [see p. 977, above] LORD NICHOLLS OF BIRKENHEAD continued immediately after the previous extract, as follows:

If, however, the agreement *is* set aside, B will be accountable for any benefits he may have received from A under the agreement. A will have a proprietary claim, if B still has the assets. Additionally, and irrespective of whether B still has the assets in question, A will have a personal claim against B for unjust enrichment, subject always to a defence of change of position. B's personal accountability will not be dependent upon proof of fault or 'unconscionable' conduct on his part. B's accountability, in this regard, will be 'strict'.

Virgo, *The Principles of the Law of Restitution* (2nd edn, 2006), pp. 653–654

This is a very important dictum which raises a number of significant points. First, the dictum is clearly obiter because it had not been determined whether the agreement in the case was valid.[66] It follows that the fault-based cause of action of unconscionable receipt continues to exist, although what constitutes unconscionability for these purposes remains unclear.

Secondly, to establish any proprietary claim it is necessary first to show that the defendant has received property in which the claimant has a proprietary interest, either at law or in equity. Where property has been transferred pursuant to an invalid transaction, such as the putative unauthorised agreement in *Criterion Properties*, legal title will pass, but it is possible to establish that an equitable proprietary interest has been created if, for example, the defendant is aware that the transaction is invalid. It might be possible to establish this in a case like *Criterion Properties* itself. In fact, the creation of an equitable proprietary interest could have been established more simply, by virtue of the fact that the defendants in that case were directors who, had they entered into an unauthorised transaction, would have profited from a breach of fiduciary duty and so would hold the profits on constructive trust for the claimant.[67] If the profits had been dissipated then a claim for the value of the profits would be appropriate.

---

[64] See also (2000) 116 LQR 412 (L. Smith); (2001) 3 *Trust Law International* 151 (P. Jaffey) (the action for knowing receipt should be characterised as tortious).

[65] See also *Dubai Aluminium Co Ltd v Salaam* [2002] UKHL 448, [2003] 2 AC 366, 391 (Lord Millett).

[66] See p. 977, above. [67] See p. 815, above.

Thirdly, the recognition of unjust enrichment as the principle which underpins the personal claim is significant but unfortunate. It is significant because it follows that Lord Nicholls has expressly recognised a strict liability claim. But if the emphasis is on unjust enrichment then the elements of that cause of action need to be identified. Where the defendant has received a valuable benefit from the claimant under a contract which is subsequently found to be invalid for lack of authority, it is obvious that the defendant will have been enriched[68] at the claimant's expense. But what is the ground of restitution? Is it mistake as to the validity of the agreement, or total failure of consideration or even absence of consideration on the basis that no benefit could be properly received if the agreement is invalid? ... But this speculation is unnecessary, because reliance on the unjust enrichment principle is irrelevant in this context. Where the defendant has received, but not retained, property in which the claimant has a proprietary interest, it should be sufficient to found the claim on the vindication of the claimant's property rights, in the same way as the common law claim in *Lipkin Gorman* is properly analysed as a proprietary claim for which personal remedies are available. But, despite this, the real significance of Lord Nicholls' approach is that, as he explicitly states, liability is strict.

Finally, if this strict-liability receipt-based claim in equity is recognised, does it follow that there is no longer any need to recognise the fault-based claim? Certainly there would be much less need to rely on the fault-based claims, because of the difficulties of establishing fault. However, the key significance is that the defence of change of position would not be available to the fault-based claim, whereas it would be available to the receipt-based claim. But this raises a nice irony. If a claimant relies on the receipt-based claim there is no need to prove fault, but the defendant can defeat that claim by relying on the defence of change of position. That defence is itself defeated if the defendant had acted in bad faith and, as has already been seen,[69] recent cases on the defence of change of position have relied on the notion of unconscionability to determine whether or not the defendant can be considered to have acted in bad faith. It follows that, even though Lord Nicholls had rejected the need for a fault-based claim, fault is inevitably introduced through the back door when considering whether or not the defence of change of position might be available to the defendant.

In *Farah Constructions Pty Ltd v Say-Dee Pty Ltd* [2007] HCA 2[70] the High Court of Australia confirmed the importance of fault to the equitable action of 'knowing receipt'.

B DISHONESTLY ASSISTING A BREACH OF TRUST[71]

Where a third party assists the trustees in a breach of trust, or a fiduciary in breach of fiduciary duty,[72] the third party will be personally liable to the trust, or the fiduciary's

---

[68] In *Criterion* it was not possible to establish that the defendant had been enriched because no assets had been received by the defendant. As Lord Scott recognised at para. 27 ([2004] 1 WLR 1846, 1855), the creation of contractual rights through an executory contract does not constitute the receipt of an asset. Cp. *BBCI v Akindele* [2001] Ch. 437 where the defendant had received $17m. under the impugned agreement.

[69] See p. 978 above.

[70] (2007) *Trust Law International* 55 (D. Hayton); (2007) 66 CLJ 515 (M. Conaglen and R. Nolan); (2008) 124 LQR 26 (P. Ridge and J. Dietrich).

[71] 'Assistance' in *Breach of Trust* (eds. Birks and Pretto, 2002), pp. 139–212 (C. Mitchell).

[72] This was said to be 'arguable' in respect of breach of fiduciary duty by directors: *Brown v Bennett* [1999] 1 BCLC 649. But now see *Barlow Clowes International Ltd v Eurotrust International Ltd* [2005] UKPC 37, [2006] 1 WLR 1476, para. 28 [p. 997, below].

principal, as appropriate.[73] This has been described as an 'equitable tort'.[74] Opinions have varied as to the degree of knowledge of the breach of trust, or breach of fiduciary liability, which is required to found liability. An innocent third party with no reason to suspect the breach will not be liable. The question is whether dishonesty is required or whether negligence suffices. Some cases have recognised that constructive notice of the breach of trust is enough.[75] Other cases considered that want of probity must be established,[76] and others that dishonesty was required.[77] The requirement of dishonesty has now been confirmed by the Privy Council in *Royal Brunei Airlines Sdn Bhd v Tan* [1995] 2 AC 378, below, although the appropriate test of dishonesty has proved to be a controversial matter, with different interpretations adopted by the House of Lords[78] and the Privy Council.[79]

It was also recognised in **Royal Brunei Airlines Sdn Bhd v Tan** [1995] 2 AC 378 that the breach of trust in which the third party assisted need not itself have been fraudulent. This overturns the previous rule, deriving from *Barnes v Addy* (1874) 9 Ch App 244, that there must have been a dishonest and fraudulent design on the part of the trustees. LORD NICHOLLS OF BIRKENHEAD, delivering the judgment of the Board, also considered that the term 'knowing assistance', used throughout the case law, should be avoided, as the word 'knowing' was an inapt criterion. Dishonesty was the touchstone of liability. His Lordship further suggested that in this context the five categories of knowledge laid down by PETER GIBSON J in *Baden v Société Générale pour Favoriser le Développement du Commerce et de l'Industrie en France SA* [1993] 1 WLR 509n,[80] were 'best forgotten'.

Royal Brunei Airlines Sdn Bhd v Tan[81]
[1995] 2 AC 378 (PC, **Lords Goff of Chieveley, Ackner, Nicholls of Birkenhead** and **Steyn** and **Sir John May**)

The plaintiff airline appointed Borneo Leisure Travel Sdn Bhd ('BLT') to act as its general travel agent. BLT was required to account to the plaintiff for the proceeds of

[73] For analysis of the appropriate remedies see (2004) 67 MLR 16 (S. Elliott and C. Mitchell) *Sinclair Investment Holdings SA v Versailles Trade Finance Ltd* [2007] EWHC 915 (Ch). A six-year limitation period might apply: *Cattley v Pollard* [2006] EWHC 3130 (Ch), [2007] Ch 353. Cf. *Statek Corp v Alford* [2008] EWHC 32 (Ch).

[74] *Abou-Rahmah v Abacha* [2006] EWCA Civ 1492, [2007] 1 All ER (Comm) 827, para. 2, Rix LJ.

[75] *Selangor United Rubber Estates Ltd v Cradock (No 3)* [1968] 1 WLR 1555 (Ungoed-Thomas J); *Karak Rubber Co Ltd v Burden (No 2)* [1972] 1 WLR 602; *Baden v Société Générale pour Favoriser le Développement du Commerce et de l'Industrie en France SA* [1993] 1 WLR 509n.

[76] *Carl Zeiss Stiftung v Herbert Smith & Co (No 2)* [1969] 2 Ch 276; *Belmont Finance Corpn Ltd v Williams Furniture Ltd* [1979] Ch 250; *Lipkin Gorman v Karpnale Ltd* [1989] 1 WLR 1340 and *Polly Peck International plc v Nadir (No 2)* [1992] 4 All ER 769.

[77] *Agip Africa Ltd v Jackson* [1990] Ch 265, affirmed [1991] Ch 547.

[78] *Twinsectra Ltd v Yardley* [2002] UKHL 12, [2002] 2 AC 164 [p. 990. below].

[79] *Barlow Clowes International Ltd v Eurotrust International Ltd* [2005] UKPC 37, [2006] 1 WLR 1476 [p. 997, below].

[80] Set out in *Bank of Credit and Commerce International (Overseas) Ltd v Akindele* [2001] Ch 437 at 454 [p. 976, above].

[81] (1995) 111 LQR 545 (C. Harpum); [1995] Conv 339 (M. Halliwell); (1995) CLJ 505 (R. Nolan); [1995] 3 *Restitution Law Review* 105 (J. Stevens); (1995) 145 NLJ 1379 (C. Passmore and N. Sieve); (1995) 9 *Trust Law*

ticket sales, after deducting commission. The terms of the agreement constituted BLT a trustee of the money for the plaintiff. The money was not paid into a separate bank account but was used in the business of BLT, which was conceded to be a breach of trust. BLT fell into arrears in accounting to the plaintiff and the agreement was terminated. As BLT was insolvent, the plaintiff sought a remedy against Mr. Tan, who was the principal shareholder and director of BLT. It was conceded that Tan had assisted in the breach of trust with actual knowledge. The Court of Appeal of Brunei Darussalam held him not liable on the ground that the breach of trust in which he had assisted had not been shown to be a dishonest and fraudulent design on the part of BLT, which was considered essential to accessory liability in cases of long standing and high authority. In fact BLT's breach was dishonest, because Tan's state of mind was to be imputed to the company.[82] The issue on appeal to the Privy Council was whether the breach of trust which is a prerequisite to accessory liability must itself be a dishonest and fraudulent breach by the trustee, a view deriving from a dictum of Lord Selborne LC in *Barnes v Addy* (1874) 9 Ch App 244 at 251–252. The resolution of this issue also required consideration of the question whether the person assisting in the breach of trust must have acted dishonestly (as opposed to negligently) in order to incur liability, and a consideration of the meaning of 'dishonesty'.

Held. Tan was personally liable for dishonestly assisting in BLT's breach of trust. There was no further requirement of dishonesty on the part of BLT.

Lord Nicholls of Birkenhead:

The honest trustee and the dishonest third party
It must be noted at once that there is a difficulty with the approach adopted on this point in the *Belmont*[83] case. Take the simple example of an honest trustee and a dishonest third party. Take a case where a dishonest solicitor persuades a trustee to apply trust property in a way the trustee honestly believes is permissible but which the solicitor knows full well is a clear breach of trust. The solicitor deliberately conceals this from the trustee. In consequence, the beneficiaries suffer a substantial loss. It cannot be right that in such a case the accessory liability principle would be inapplicable because of the innocence of the trustee. In ordinary parlance, the beneficiaries have been defrauded by the solicitor. If there is to be an accessory liability principle at all, whereby in appropriate circumstances beneficiaries may have direct recourse against a third party, the principle must surely be applicable in such a case, just as much as in a case where both the trustee and the third party have been dishonest. Indeed, if anything, the case for liability of the dishonest third party seems stronger where the trustee is innocent, because in such a case the third party alone was dishonest and that was the cause of the subsequent misapplication of the trust property.

The position would be the same if, instead of *procuring* the breach, the third party dishonestly *assisted* in the breach. Change the facts slightly. A trustee is proposing to make a payment out of

---

International 102 (G. McCormack); (1996) 112 LQR 56 (S. Gardner); (1996) 59 MLR 443 (A. Berg); [1996] LMCLQ 1 (P. Birks).

[82] This was accepted by the Privy Council. See *El Ajou v Dollar Land Holdings plc* [1994] 2 All ER 685.
[83] *Belmont Finance Corpn Ltd v Williams Furniture Ltd* [1979] Ch 250, upholding Lord Selborne's principle.

the trust fund to a particular person. He honestly believes he is authorised to do so by the terms of the trust deed. He asks a solicitor to carry through the transaction. The solicitor well knows that the proposed payment would be a plain breach of trust. He also well knows that the trustee mistakenly believes otherwise. Dishonestly he leaves the trustee under his misapprehension and prepares the necessary documentation. Again, if the accessory principle is not to be artificially constricted, it ought to be applicable in such a case.

These examples suggest that what matters is the state of mind of the third party sought to be made liable, not the state of mind of the trustee. The trustee will be liable in any event for the breach of trust, even if he acted innocently, unless excused by an exemption clause in the trust instrument[84] or relieved by the court.[85] But *his* state of mind is essentially irrelevant to the question whether the *third party* should be made liable to the beneficiaries for the breach of trust. If the liability of the third party is fault-based, what matters is the nature of his fault, not that of the trustee. In this regard dishonesty on the part of the third party would seem to be a sufficient basis for his liability, irrespective of the state of mind of the trustee who is in breach of trust. It is difficult to see why, if the third party dishonestly assisted in a breach, there should be a further prerequisite to his liability, namely, that the trustee also must have been acting dishonestly. The alternative view would mean that a dishonest third party is liable if the trustee is dishonest, but if the trustee did not act dishonestly that of itself would excuse a dishonest third party from liability. That would make no sense.

Earlier authority
The view that the accessory liability principle cannot be restricted to fraudulent breaches of trust is not to be approached with suspicion as a latter-day novelty. Before the accessory principle donned its *Barnes v Addy* straitjacket, judges seem not to have regarded the principle as confined in this way.

[His Lordship considered *Fyler v Fyler* (1841) 3 Beav 550; *A-G v Leicester Corpn* (1844) 7 Beav 176; and *Eaves v Hickson* (1861) 30 Beav 136, and continued:] What has gone wrong? Their Lordships venture to think that the reason is that ever since the *Selangor*[86] case highlighted the potential uses of equitable remedies in connection with misapplied company funds, there has been a tendency to cite and interpret and apply Lord Selborne's formulation in *Barnes v Addy* (1874) 9 Ch App 244, 251–252 as though it were a statute. This has particularly been so with the accessory limb of Lord Selborne LC's apophthegm. This approach has been inimical to analysis of the underlying concept. Working within this constraint, the courts have found themselves wrestling with the interpretation of the individual ingredients, especially 'knowingly' but also 'dishonest and fraudulent design on the part of the trustees', without examining the underlying reason why a third party who has received no trust property is being made liable at all. One notable exception is the judgment of Thomas J in *Powell v Thompson* [1991] 1 NZLR 597, 610–615. On this point he observed at 613:

'Once a breach of trust has been committed, the commission of which has involved a third party, the question which arises is one as between the beneficiary and that third party. If the third party's conduct has been unconscionable, then irrespective of the degree of impropriety in the trustee's conduct, the third party is liable to be held accountable to the beneficiary as if he or she were a trustee.'

84 See p. 867, above.   85 TA 1925, s. 61. See p. 871, above.
86 *Selangor United Rubber Estates Ltd v Cradock (No 3)* [1968] 1 WLR 1555.

To resolve this issue it is necessary to take an overall look at the accessory liability principle. A conclusion cannot be reached on the nature of the breach of trust which may trigger accessory liability without at the same time considering the other ingredients including, in particular, the state of mind of the third party. It is not necessary, however, to look even more widely and consider the essential ingredients of recipient liability. The issue on this appeal concerns only the accessory liability principle. Different considerations apply to the two heads of liability. Recipient liability is restitution-based, accessory liability is not.

No liability

The starting point for any analysis must be to consider the extreme possibility: that a third party who does not receive trust property ought never to be liable directly to the beneficiaries merely because he assisted the trustee to commit a breach of trust or procured him to do so. This possibility can be dismissed summarily. On this the position which the law has long adopted is clear and makes good sense. Stated in the simplest terms, a trust is a relationship which exists when one person holds property on behalf of another. If, for his own purposes, a third party deliberately interferes in that relationship by assisting the trustee in depriving the beneficiary of the property held for him by the trustee, the beneficiary should be able to look for recompense to the third party as well as the trustee. Affording the beneficiary a remedy against the third party serves the dual purpose of making good the beneficiary's loss should the trustee lack financial means and imposing a liability which will discourage others from behaving in a similar fashion.

The rationale is not far to seek. Beneficiaries are entitled to expect that those who become trustees will fulfil their obligations. They are also entitled to expect, and this is only a short step further, that those who become trustees will be permitted to fulfil their obligations without deliberate intervention from third parties. They are entitled to expect that third parties will refrain from intentionally intruding in the trustee–beneficiary relationship and thereby hindering a beneficiary from receiving his entitlement in accordance with the terms of the trust instrument. There is here a close analogy with breach of contract. A person who knowingly procures a breach of contract, or knowingly interferes with the due performance of a contract, is liable to the innocent party. The underlying rationale is the same.

Strict liability

The other extreme possibility can also be rejected out of hand. This is the case where a third party deals with a trustee without knowing, or having any reason to suspect, that he is a trustee. Or the case where a third party is aware he is dealing with a trustee but has no reason to know or suspect that their transaction is inconsistent with the terms of the trust. The law has never gone so far as to give a beneficiary a remedy against a non-recipient third party in such circumstances. Within defined limits, proprietary rights, whether legal or equitable, endure against third parties who were unaware of their existence. But accessory liability is concerned with the liability of a person who has not received any property. His liability is not property-based. His only sin is that he interfered with the due performance by the trustee of the fiduciary obligations undertaken by the trustee. These are personal obligations. They are, in this respect, analogous to the personal obligations undertaken by the parties to a contract. But ordinary, every day business would become impossible if third parties were to be held liable for *unknowingly* interfering in the due performance of such personal obligations. Beneficiaries could not reasonably expect that third parties should deal with trustees at their peril, to the extent that they should become liable to the beneficiaries even when they received no trust property and even when they were unaware and had no reason to suppose that they were dealing with trustees.

Fault-based liability

Given, then, that in some circumstances a third party may be liable directly to a beneficiary, but given also that the liability is not so strict that there would be liability even when the third party was wholly unaware of the existence of the trust, the next step is to seek to identify the touchstone of liability. By common accord dishonesty fulfils this role. Whether, in addition, negligence will suffice is an issue on which there has been a well-known difference of judicial opinion. The *Selangor* decision [1968] 1 WLR 1555 in 1968 was the first modern decision on this point. Ungoed-Thomas J at 1590, held that the touchstone was whether the third party had knowledge of circumstances which would indicate to 'an honest, reasonable man' that the breach in question was being committed or would put him on inquiry. Brightman J reached the same conclusion in *Karak Rubber Co Ltd v Burden (No 2)* [1972] 1 WLR 602. So did Peter Gibson J in 1983 in the *Baden* case [1993] 1 WLR 509n. In that case the judge accepted a five-point scale of knowledge which had been formulated by counsel.

Meanwhile doubts had been expressed about this test by Buckley LJ and Goff LJ in the *Belmont* case [1979] Ch 250 at 267, 275. Similar doubts were expressed in Australia by Jacobs P in *DPC Estates Pty Ltd v Grey* [1974] 1 NSWLR 443 at 459. When that decision reached the High Court of Australia, the doubts were echoed by Barwick CJ, Gibbs J and Stephen J: see *Consul Development Pty Ltd v DPC Estates Pty Ltd* (1975) 132 CLR 373 at 376, 398, and 412.

Since then the tide in England has flowed strongly in favour of the test being one of dishonesty: see, for instance, Sir Robert Megarry V-C in *Re Montagu's Settlement Trusts* [1987] Ch 264 at 285, and Millett J in *Agip (Africa) Ltd v Jackson* [1990] Ch 265 at 293. In *Eagle Trust plc v SBC Securities Ltd* [1993] 1 WLR 484 at 495, Vinelott J stated that it could be taken as settled law that want of probity was a prerequisite to liability. This received the imprimatur of the Court of Appeal in *Polly Peck International plc v Nadir (No 2)* [1992] 4 All ER 769 at 777, *per* Scott LJ. [His Lordship then considered the divergent judicial views in New Zealand and continued:]

Dishonesty

Before considering this issue further it will be helpful to define the terms being used by looking more closely at what dishonesty means in this context. Whatever may be the position in some criminal or other contexts (see, for instance, *R v Ghosh* [1982] QB 1053), in the context of the accessory liability principle acting dishonestly, or with a lack of probity, which is synonymous, means simply not acting as an honest person would in the circumstances. This is an objective standard. At first sight this may seem surprising. Honesty has a connotation of subjectivity, as distinct from the objectivity of negligence. Honesty, indeed, does have a strong subjective element in that it is a description of a type of conduct assessed in the light of what a person actually knew at the time, as distinct from what a reasonable person would have known or appreciated. Further, honesty and its counterpart dishonesty are mostly concerned with advertent conduct, not inadvertent conduct. Carelessness is not dishonesty. Thus for the most part dishonesty is to be equated with conscious impropriety.

However, these subjective characteristics of honesty do not mean that individuals are free to set their own standards of honesty in particular circumstances. The standard of what constitutes honest conduct is not subjective. Honesty is not an optional scale, with higher or lower values according to the moral standards of each individual. If a person knowingly appropriates another's property, he will not escape a finding of dishonesty simply because he sees nothing wrong in such behaviour....

Negligence

It is against this background that the question of negligence is to be addressed. This question, it should be remembered, is directed at whether an honest third party who receives no trust property should be liable if he procures or assists in a breach of trust of which he would have become aware had he exercised reasonable diligence. Should he be liable to the beneficiaries for the loss they suffer from the breach of trust?

The majority of persons falling into this category will be the hosts of people who act for trustees in various ways: as advisers, consultants, bankers, and agents of many kinds. This category also includes officers and employees of companies, in respect of the application of company funds. All these people will be accountable to the trustees for their conduct. For the most part they will owe to the trustees a duty to exercise reasonable skill and care. When that is so, the rights flowing from that duty form part of the trust property. As such they can be enforced by the beneficiaries in a suitable case if the trustees are unable or unwilling to do so. That being so, it is difficult to identify a compelling reason why, in addition to the duty of skill and care *vis-à-vis* the trustees which the third parties have accepted, or which the law has imposed upon them, third parties should also owe a duty of care directly to the beneficiaries. They have undertaken work for the trustees. They must carry out that work properly. If they fail to do so, they will be liable to make good the loss suffered by the trustees in consequence. This will include, where appropriate, the loss suffered by the trustees being exposed to claims for breach of trust.

Outside this category of persons who owe duties of skill and care to the trustees, there are others who will deal with trustees. If they have not accepted, and the law has not imposed upon them, any such duties in favour of the trustees, it is difficult to discern a good reason why they should nevertheless owe such duties to the beneficiaries.

There remains to be considered the position where third parties are acting for, or dealing with, dishonest trustees. In such cases the trustees would have no claims against the third party. The trustees would suffer no loss by reason of the third party's failure to discover what was going on. The question is whether in this type of situation the third party owes a duty of care to the beneficiaries to, in effect, check that a trustee is not misbehaving. The third party must act honestly. The question is whether that is enough.

In agreement with the preponderant view, their Lordships consider that dishonesty is an essential ingredient here. There may be cases where, in the light of the particular facts, a third party will owe a duty of care to the beneficiaries. As a general proposition, however, beneficiaries cannot reasonably expect that all the world dealing with their trustees should owe them a duty to take care lest the trustees are behaving dishonestly.

Unconscionable conduct

Mention, finally, must be made of the suggestion that the test for liability is that of unconscionable conduct. Unconscionable is a word of immediate appeal to an equity lawyer. Equity is rooted historically in the concept of the Lord Chancellor, as the keeper of the Royal Conscience, concerning himself with conduct which was contrary to good conscience. It must be recognised, however, that unconscionable is not a word in everyday use by non-lawyers. If it is to be used in this context, and if it is to be the touchstone for liability as an accessory, it is essential to be clear on what, *in this context*, unconscionable *means*. If unconscionable means no more than dishonesty, then dishonesty is the preferable label. If unconscionable means something different, it must be said that it is not clear what that something different is. Either way, therefore, the term is better avoided in this context.

The accessory liability principle

Drawing the threads together, their Lordships' overall conclusion is that dishonesty is a necessary ingredient of accessory liability. It is also a sufficient ingredient. A liability in equity to make good resulting loss attaches to a person who dishonestly procures or assists in a breach of trust or fiduciary obligation. It is not necessary that, in addition, the trustee or fiduciary was acting dishonestly, although this will usually be so where the third party who is assisting him is acting dishonestly. 'Knowingly' is better avoided as a defining ingredient of the principle, and in the context of this principle the *Baden* scale of knowledge is best forgotten.

In **Agip (Africa) Ltd v Jackson**,[87] payment orders from Agip to third parties were fraudulently altered by Agip's accountant, who changed the names of the payees to those of companies formed by the defendants, who were two accountants in partnership and their employee. The money was transferred to the accounts of the companies and ultimately paid to third parties abroad, from whom it was irrecoverable. Agip sought to recover from the defendants, who had throughout followed the instructions of their client, a French lawyer acting for unknown principals. At first instance [1990] Ch 265, MILLETT J held that dishonesty was the test for accessory liability and that the defendants, who had acted with at least reckless indifference, were accordingly liable for assisting in the fraudulent breach of fiduciary duty by Agip's accountant.[88] This was upheld by the Court of Appeal [1991] Ch 547, although uncritical reference was made to the *Selangor* line of cases.

MILLETT J said at 294:

Mr. Jackson and Mr. Griffin are professional men. They obviously knew that they were laundering money. They were consciously helping their clients to make arrangements designed for the purpose of concealment from, *inter alios*, the plaintiff. It must have been obvious to them that their clients could not afford their activities to see the light of day. Secrecy is the badge of fraud. They must have realised at least that their clients *might* be involved in a fraud on the plaintiffs.

Can Mr. Jackson and Mr. Griffin possibly have believed that their arrangements had an honest purpose? They pleaded no such belief. They have given no evidence. On their behalf it was submitted that they were entitled to be reassured by the fact that they were taking over arrangements which had been established for some years, that they were introduced to them by a partner in a well-known and reputable firm of chartered accountants and that, if there was any wrongdoing, it would surely have come to light long before. Had Mr. Jackson and Mr. Griffin given evidence to this effect, I might or might not have believed it. But I will not assume it when they do not tell me so. . . .

I am led to the conclusion that Mr. Jackson and Mr. Griffin were at best indifferent to the possibility of fraud. They made no inquiries of the plaintiffs because they thought that it was none of their business. That is not honest behaviour. The sooner that those who provide the services of nominee companies for the purpose of enabling their clients to keep their activities

---

[87] (1991) 50 CLJ 409 (C. Harpum); [1992] Conv 367 (S. Goulding); (1992) 12 LS 332 (H. Norman); (1993–94) 4 *King's College Law Journal* 82 (P. Oliver).

[88] Two were personally liable and the third was vicariously liable.

secret realise it, the better. In my judgment, it is quite enough to make them liable to account as constructive trustees.

In the Court of Appeal Fox LJ said at 567:

The judge held, and it is not challenged, that Mr. Bowers did not participate in the furtherance of the fraud at all; although he was a partner in Jackson & Co he played no part in the movement of the money and gave no instructions about it. Mr. Jackson and Mr. Griffin are in quite a different position. Mr Jackson set up the company structures. Mr. Jackson and Mr. Griffin controlled the movement of the money from the time it reached Baker Oil to the time it was paid out of the account of Jackson & Co in the Isle of Man bank. On the evidence, and in the absence of evidence from Mr. Jackson and Mr. Griffin themselves, I agree with the judge that both of them must be regarded as having assisted in the fraud. That, however, by no means concludes the matter. There remains the question of their state of mind. Did they have the necessary degree of knowledge?

[His Lordship reviewed the evidence and concluded:] In the circumstances I think that the judge rightly came to the conclusion that they must have known they were laundering money, and were consequently helping their clients to make arrangements to conceal some dispositions of money which had such a degree of impropriety that neither they nor their clients could afford to have them disclosed....

In the end, it seems to me that the most striking feature in the case is that in August 1984 Mr. Jackson and Mr. Griffin were being given advice on the possibility that a payment or payments might involve a fraud on Agip. Having got to that point it seems to me that persons acting honestly would have pursued the matter with a view to satisfying themselves that there was no fraud. But there is nothing to show that they did that. They made no inquiries of Agip at all. They let matters continue. In the circumstances, I conclude that Mr. Jackson and Mr. Griffin are liable as constructive trustees. Mr. Bowers is liable for the acts of Mr. Jackson, who was his partner, and of Mr. Griffin, who was employed by the partnership.

Accordingly, I think that the judge came to the right conclusion and I would dismiss the appeal.

Twinsectra Ltd v Yardley
[2002] UKHL 12, [2002] 2 AC 164 (HL, **Lords Slynn of Hadley, Steyn, Hoffmann, Hutton** and **Millett**)[89]

Mr. Yardley borrowed money from the claimant to purchase property. It had been agreed that the money would be held by a solicitor, Mr. Sims, who undertook that it would only be used for the purchase of property. Yardley borrowed the same amount of money from Barclays Bank without telling the claimant. Yardley's solicitor, Mr. Leach, was aware of the arrangement. In breach of the undertaking, Sims paid most of the loan to Yardley in discharge of debts he owed to Yardley. The claimant brought a number of claims to recover its money, one of which was a claim for dishonest assistance against Leach, who had been paid the money by Sims and who paid it out upon Yardley's instructions. A substantial sum of this money was used for purposes other than the

---

[89] (2003) LQR 8 (T. M. Yeo and H. Tjio); (2002) CLJ 52 (R. Thornton); [2002] Conv 386 (J. Ross); [2002] All ER Rev 231 (P.J. Clarke).

acquisition of property. The trial judge held that, although the defendant had shut his eyes to the details of the transaction, he had not acted dishonestly because he believed that the money was at the disposal of Yardley. The Court of Appeal substituted a finding of dishonesty.

Held (Lord Millett dissenting). Leach had not acted dishonestly.[90]

Lord Hutton:

27.   Whilst in discussing the term 'dishonesty' the courts often draw a distinction between subjective dishonesty and objective dishonesty, there are three possible standards which can be applied to determine whether a person has acted dishonestly. There is a purely subjective standard, whereby a person is only regarded as dishonest if he transgresses his own standard of honesty, even if that standard is contrary to that of reasonable and honest people. This has been termed the 'Robin Hood test' and has been rejected by the courts. As Sir Christopher Slade stated in *Walker v Stones* [2000] Lloyds Rep PN 864 at 877, para. 164:

> 'A person may in some cases act dishonestly, according to the ordinary use of language, even though he genuinely believes that his action is morally justified. The penniless thief, for example, who picks the pocket of the multi-millionaire is dishonest even though he genuinely considers that theft is morally justified as a fair redistribution of wealth and that he is not therefore being dishonest.'

Secondly, there is a purely objective standard whereby a person acts dishonestly if his conduct is dishonest by the ordinary standards of reasonable and honest people, even if he does not realise this. Thirdly, there is a standard which combines an objective test and a subjective test, and which requires that before there can be a finding of dishonesty it must be established that the defendant's conduct was dishonest by the ordinary standards of reasonable and honest people and that he himself realised that by those standards his conduct was dishonest. I will term this 'the combined test'.

28.   There is a passage in the earlier part of the judgment in *Royal Brunei* which suggests that Lord Nicholls considered that dishonesty has a subjective element.

Thus in discussing the honest trustee and the dishonest third party at [1995] 2 AC 378 at 385 he stated:

> 'These examples suggest that what matters is the state of mind of the third party.... But [the trustee's] state of mind is essentially irrelevant to the question whether the third party should be made liable to the beneficiaries for breach of trust.'

29.   However, after stating, at 387, that the touchstone of liability is dishonesty, Lord Nicholls went on at 389 to discuss the meaning of dishonesty:

> 'Before considering this issue further it will be helpful to define the terms being used by looking more closely at what dishonesty means in this context. Whatever may be the position in some criminal or other contexts (see, for instance, *R v Ghosh* [1982] QB 1053), in the context of the accessory liability principle acting dishonestly, or with a lack of probity, which is synonymous, means simply not acting as an honest person would in the circumstances. This is an objective standard.'

---

[90] It was held unanimously that the money in Sims' keeping was held on trust for the claimant. See p. 242, above.

30.   My noble and learned friend Lord Millett has subjected this passage and subsequent passages in the judgment to detailed analysis and is of the opinion that Lord Nicholls used the term 'dishonesty' in a purely objective sense so that in this area of the law a person can be held to be dishonest even though he does not realise that what he is doing is dishonest by the ordinary standards of honest people. This leads Lord Millett on to the conclusion that in determining the liability of an accessory dishonesty is not necessary and that liability depends on knowledge.

31.   In *R v Ghosh* [1982] QB 1053 Lord Lane CJ held that in the law of theft dishonesty required that the defendant himself must have realised that what he was doing was dishonest by the ordinary standards of reasonable and honest people. The three sentences in Lord Nicholls' judgment, at 389 [p. 987, above], which appear to draw a distinction between the position in criminal law and the position in equity, do give support to Lord Millett's view. But considering those sentences in the context of the remainder of the paragraph and taking account of other passages in the judgment, I think that in referring to an objective standard Lord Nicholls was contrasting it with the purely subjective standard whereby a man sets his own standard of honesty and does not regard as dishonest what upright and responsible people would regard as dishonest. Thus after stating that dishonesty is assessed on an objective standard he continued, at 389:

'At first sight this may seem surprising. Honesty has a connotation of subjectivity, as distinct from the objectivity of negligence. Honesty, indeed, does have a strong subjective element in that it is a description of a type of conduct assessed in the light of what a person actually knew at the time, as distinct from what a reasonable person would have known or appreciated. Further, honesty and its counterpart dishonesty are mostly concerned with advertent conduct, not inadvertent conduct. Carelessness is not dishonesty. Thus for the most part dishonesty is to be equated with conscious impropriety. However, these subjective characteristics of honesty do not mean that individuals are free to set their own standards of honesty in particular circumstances. The standard of what constitutes honest conduct is not subjective. Honesty is not an optional scale, with higher or lower values according to the moral standards of each individual. If a person knowingly appropriates another's property, he will not escape a finding of dishonesty simply because he sees nothing wrong in such behaviour.'

Further, at 391, **Lord Nicholls** said:

'Ultimately, in most cases, an honest person should have little difficulty in knowing whether a proposed transaction, or his participation in it, would offend the normally accepted standards of honest conduct. Likewise, when called upon to decide whether a person was acting honestly, a court will look at all the circumstances known to the third party at the time. The court will also have regard to personal attributes of the third party, such as his experience and intelligence, and the reason why he acted as he did.'

32.   The use of the word 'knowing' in the first sentence would be superfluous if the defendant did not have to be aware that what he was doing would offend the normally accepted standards of honest conduct, and the need to look at the experience and intelligence of the defendant would also appear superfluous if all that was required was a purely objective standard of dishonesty. Therefore I do not think that Lord Nicholls was stating that in this sphere of equity a man can be dishonest even if he does not know that what he is doing would be regarded as dishonest by honest people.

33.   Then, at 392, Lord Nicholls stated the general principle that dishonesty is a necessary ingredient of accessory liability and that knowledge is not an appropriate test:

[His Lordship read from Lord Nicholls' judgment following the heading 'The accessory liability principle' [see p. 989, above] and continued:] I consider that this was a statement of general principle and was not confined to the doubtful case when the propriety of the transaction in question was uncertain.

34. At 387 Lord Nicholls stated that there is a close analogy between 'knowingly' interfering with the due performance of a contract and interfering with the relationship between a trustee and a beneficiary. But this observation was made in considering and rejecting the possibility that a third party who did not receive trust property should never be liable for assisting in a breach of trust. I do not think that in referring to 'knowingly' procuring a breach of contract Lord Nicholls was suggesting that knowingly assisting in a breach of trust was sufficient to give rise to liability. Such a view would be contrary to the later passage, at 392, dealing directly with this point.

35. There is, in my opinion, a further consideration which supports the view that for liability as an accessory to arise the defendant must himself appreciate that what he was doing was dishonest by the standards of honest and reasonable men. A finding by a judge that a defendant has been dishonest is a grave finding, and it is particularly grave against a professional man, such as a solicitor. Notwithstanding that the issue arises in equity law and not in a criminal context, I think that it would be less than just for the law to permit a finding that a defendant had been 'dishonest' in assisting in a breach of trust where he knew of the facts which created the trust and its breach but had not been aware that what he was doing would be regarded by honest men as being dishonest.

36. It would be open to your Lordships to depart from the principle stated by Lord Nicholls that dishonesty is a necessary ingredient of accessory liability and to hold that knowledge is a sufficient ingredient. But the statement of that principle by Lord Nicholls has been widely regarded as clarifying this area of the law and, as he observed, the tide of authority in England has flowed strongly in favour of the test of dishonesty. Therefore I consider that the courts should continue to apply that test and that your Lordships should state that dishonesty requires knowledge by the defendant that what he was doing would be regarded as dishonest by honest people, although he should not escape a finding of dishonesty because he sets his own standards of honesty and does not regard as dishonest what he knows would offend the normally accepted standards of honest conduct.

[His Lordship considered the facts and concluded:]

43. It is only in exceptional circumstances that an appellate court should reverse a finding by a trial judge on a question of fact (and particularly on the state of mind of a party) when the judge has had the advantage of seeing the party giving evidence in the witness box. Therefore I do not think that it would have been right for the Court of Appeal in this case to have come to a different conclusion from the judge and to have held that Mr. Leach was dishonest in that when he transferred the monies to Mr. Yardley he knew that his conduct was dishonest by the standards of responsible and honest solicitors.

Lord Millett (dissenting):

107. The accessory's liability for having assisted in a breach of trust... is fault-based, not receipt-based. The defendant is not charged with having received trust moneys for his own benefit, but with having acted as an accessory to a breach of trust. The action is not restitutionary; the claimant seeks compensation for wrongdoing. The cause of action is concerned with attributing liability for misdirected funds. Liability is not restricted to the person whose breach of trust or fiduciary duty caused their original diversion. His liability is strict. Nor is it

limited to those who assist him in the original breach. It extends to everyone who consciously assists in the continuing diversion of the money. Most of the cases have been concerned, not with assisting in the original breach, but in covering it up afterwards by helping to launder the money. Mr. Leach's wrongdoing is not confined to the assistance he gave Mr. Sims to commit a breach of trust by receiving the money from him knowing that Mr. Sims should not have paid it to him (though this is sufficient to render him liable for any resulting loss); it extends to the assistance he gave in the subsequent misdirection of the money by paying it out to Mr. Yardley's order without seeing to its proper application.

114.   In taking dishonesty to be the condition of liability, however, Lord Nicholls used the word in an objective sense. He did not employ the concept of dishonesty as it is understood in criminal cases. He explained the sense in which he was using the word at [1995] 2 AC 378 at 389 as follows:

[His Lordship read the dictum of Lord Nicholls [at p. 987, above] and continued:]

Dishonesty as a state of mind or as a course of conduct?

115.   In *R v Ghosh* [1982] QB 1053 Lord Lane CJ drew a distinction between dishonesty as a state of mind and dishonesty as a course of conduct, and held that dishonesty in section 1 of the Theft Act 1968 referred to dishonesty as a state of mind. The question was not whether the accused had in fact acted dishonestly but whether he was aware that he was acting dishonestly. The jury must first of all decide whether the conduct of the accused was dishonest according to the ordinary standards of reasonable and honest people. That was an objective test. If he was not dishonest by those standards, that was an end of the matter and the prosecution failed. If it was dishonest by those standards, the jury had secondly to consider whether the accused was aware that what he was doing was dishonest by those standards. That was a subjective test. Given his actual (subjective) knowledge the accused must have fallen below ordinary (objective) standards of honesty and (subjectively) have been aware that he was doing so.

116.   The same test of dishonesty is applicable in civil cases where, for example, liability depends upon intent to defraud, for this connotes a dishonest state of mind. *Aktieselskabet Dansk Skibsfinansiering v Bothers* [2001] 2 BCLC 324 was a case of this kind (trading with intent to defraud creditors). But it is not generally an appropriate condition of civil liability, which does not ordinarily require a guilty mind. Civil liability is usually predicated on the defendant's conduct rather than his state of mind; it results from his negligent or unreasonable behaviour or, where this is not sufficient, from intentional wrongdoing.

117.   A dishonest state of mind might logically have been required when it was thought that the accessory was liable only if the principal was guilty of a fraudulent breach of trust, for then the claim could have been regarded as the equitable counterpart of the common law conspiracy to defraud. But this requirement was discarded in *Royal Brunei Airlines Sdn Bhd v Tan* [1995] 2 AC 378.

118.   It is, therefore, not surprising that Lord Nicholls rejected a dishonest state of mind as an appropriate condition of liability.

[His Lordship referred to various dicta of Lord Nicholls and continued:] In my opinion, in rejecting the test of dishonesty adopted in *R v Ghosh* [1982] QB 1053, Lord Nicholls was using the word to characterise the defendant's conduct, not his state of mind.

119.   Lord Nicholls had earlier drawn an analogy with the tort of procuring a breach of contract. He observed, at 387, that a person who knowingly procures a breach of contract, or who knowingly interferes with the due performance of a contract, is liable in damages to the innocent party. The rationale underlying the accessory's liability for a breach of trust, he said,

was the same. It is scarcely necessary to observe that dishonesty is not a condition of liability for the common law cause of action. This is a point to which I must revert later; for the moment, it is sufficient to say that procuring a breach of contract is an intentional tort, but it does not depend on dishonesty. Lord Nicholls was not of course confusing knowledge with dishonesty. But his approach to dishonesty is premised on the belief that it is dishonest for a man consciously to participate in the misapplication of money.

120. This is evident by the way in which Lord Nicholls dealt with the difficult case where the propriety of the transaction is doubtful. An honest man, he considered, would make appropriate enquiries before going ahead. This assumes that an honest man is one who would not knowingly participate in a transaction which caused the misapplication of funds....

121. In my opinion Lord Nicholls was adopting an objective standard of dishonesty by which the defendant is expected to attain the standard which would be observed by an honest person placed in similar circumstances. Account must be taken of subjective considerations such as the defendant's experience and intelligence and his actual state of knowledge at the relevant time. But it is not necessary that he should actually have appreciated that he was acting dishonestly; it is sufficient that he was....

125. The modern tendency is to deprecate the use of words like 'fraud' and 'dishonesty' as synonyms for moral turpitude or conduct which is morally reprehensible. There is much to be said for semantic reform, that is to say for changing the language while retaining the incidents of equitable liability; but there is nothing to be said for retaining the language and giving it the meaning it has in criminal cases so as to alter the incidents of equitable liability.

Should subjective dishonesty be required?

126. The question for your Lordships is not whether Lord Nicholls was using the word dishonesty in a subjective or objective sense in *Royal Brunei Airlines Sdn Bhd v Tan* [1995] 2 AC 378. The question is whether a plaintiff should be required to establish that an accessory to a breach of trust had a dishonest state of mind (so that he was subjectively dishonest in the *R v Ghosh* sense); or whether it should be sufficient to establish that he acted with the requisite knowledge (so that his conduct was objectively dishonest). This question is at large for us, and we are free to resolve it either way.

127. I would resolve it by adopting the objective approach. I would do so because:

(1) consciousness of wrongdoing is an aspect of *mens rea* and an appropriate condition of criminal liability: it is not an appropriate condition of civil liability. This generally results from negligent or intentional conduct. For the purpose of civil liability, it should not be necessary that the defendant realised that his conduct was dishonest; it should be sufficient that it constituted intentional wrongdoing.

(2) the objective test is in accordance with Lord Selborne's statement in *Barnes v Addy* (1874) LR 9 Ch App 244 and traditional doctrine. This taught that a person who knowingly participates in the misdirection of money is liable to compensate the injured party. While negligence is not a sufficient condition of liability, intentional wrongdoing is. Such conduct is culpable and falls below the objective standards of honesty adopted by ordinary people.

(3) the claim for 'knowing assistance' is the equitable counterpart of the economic torts. These are intentional torts; negligence is not sufficient and dishonesty is not necessary. Liability depends on knowledge. A requirement of subjective dishonesty introduces an unnecessary and unjustified distinction between the elements of the equitable claim and those of the tort of wrongful interference with the performance of a contract.

132.   It would be most undesirable if we were to introduce a distinction between the equitable claim and the tort, thereby inducing the claimant to attempt to spell a contractual obligation out of a fiduciary relationship in order to avoid the need to establish that the defendant
had a dishonest state of mind. It would, moreover, be strange if equity made liability depend
on subjective dishonesty when in a comparable situation the common law did not. This would
be a reversal of the general rule that equity demands higher standards of behaviour than the
common law.

133.   If we were to reject subjective dishonesty as a requirement of civil liability in this
branch of the law, the remaining question is merely a semantic one. Should we return to the
traditional description of the claim as 'knowing assistance', reminding ourselves that nothing
less than actual knowledge is sufficient; or should we adopt Lord Nicholls' description of the
claim as 'dishonest assistance', reminding ourselves that the test is an objective one?

134.   For my own part, I have no difficulty in equating the knowing mishandling of money
with dishonest conduct. But the introduction of dishonesty is an unnecessary distraction, and
conducive to error. Many judges would be reluctant to brand a professional man as dishonest
where he was unaware that honest people would consider his conduct to be so. If the condition
of liability is intentional wrongdoing and not conscious dishonesty as understood in the criminal
courts, I think that we should return to the traditional description of this head of equitable
liability as arising from 'knowing assistance'.

Knowledge

135.   The question here is whether it is sufficient that the accessory should have actual
knowledge of the facts which created the trust, or must he also have appreciated that they did
so? It is obviously not necessary that he should know the details of the trust or the identity of
the beneficiary. It is sufficient that he knows that the money is not at the free disposal of the
principal. In some circumstances it may not even be necessary that his knowledge should extend
this far. It may be sufficient that he knows that he is assisting in a dishonest scheme.

136.   That is not this case, for in the absence of knowledge that his client is not entitled to
receive it there is nothing intrinsically dishonest in a solicitor paying money to him. But I am
satisfied that knowledge of the arrangements which constitute the trust is sufficient; it is not
necessary that the defendant should appreciate that they do so. Of course, if they do not create
a trust, then he will not be liable for having assisted in a breach of trust. But he takes the risk
that they do.

137.   The gravamen of the charge against the principal is not that he has broken his word,
but that having been entrusted with the control of a fund with limited powers of disposal he has
betrayed the confidence placed in him by disposing of the money in an unauthorised manner.
The gravamen of the charge against the accessory is not that he is handling stolen property,
but that he is assisting a person who has been entrusted with the control of a fund to dispose
of the fund in an unauthorised manner. He should be liable if he knows of the arrangements by
which that person obtained control of the money and that his authority to deal with the money
was limited, and participates in a dealing with the money in a manner which he knows is
unauthorised. I do not believe that the man in the street would have any doubt that such conduct
was culpable.

His Lordship then considered the facts of the case and concluded that, because Leach
knew of the terms of the undertaking, he should be held liable for assisting a breach
of trust.

Barlow Clowes International Ltd v Eurotrust International Ltd
[2005] UKPC 37, [2006] 1 WLR 1476 (PC, **Lords Nicholls of Birkenhead, Steyn, Hoffmann, Walker of Gestingthorpe and Carswell**)[91]

The appellant had been used to operate a fraudulent offshore investment scheme. Clowes, the perpetrator of the scheme, was convicted of fraud. Some of the investors' money had been paid through bank accounts maintained by the defendant company, which was administered from the Isle of Man. The appellant claimed that the defendant and its directors, including Mr. Henwood, had dishonestly assisted Clowes to misappropriate the money. The defendants were held liable. On appeal Mr. Henwood was held not liable because the evidence did not support a finding of dishonesty. The appellant appealed to the Privy Council.

Held, allowing the appeal. The test of dishonesty was whether, in the light of the defendant's knowledge, his assistance was contrary to ordinary standards of honest behaviour. The evidenced supported a finding that Mr. Henwood had acted dishonestly.

Lord Hoffmann:

10 The judge stated the law in terms largely derived from the advice of the Board given by Lord Nicholls of Birkenhead in *Royal Brunei Airlines Sdn Bhd v Tan* [1995] 2 AC 378. In summary, she said that liability for dishonest assistance requires a dishonest state of mind on the part of the person who assists in a breach of trust. Such a state of mind may consist in knowledge that the transaction is one in which he cannot honestly participate (for example, a misappropriation of other people's money), or it may consist in suspicion combined with a conscious decision not to make inquiries which might result in knowledge: see *Manifest Shipping Co Ltd v Uni-Polaris Insurance Co Ltd* [2003] 1 AC 469. Although a dishonest state of mind is a subjective mental state, the standard by which the law determines whether it is dishonest is objective. If by ordinary standards a defendant's mental state would be characterised as dishonest, it is irrelevant that the defendant judges by different standards. The Court of Appeal held this to be a correct state of the law and their Lordships agree.

11 The judge found that during and after June 1987 Mr. Henwood strongly suspected that the funds passing through his hands were moneys which Barlow Clowes had received from members of the public who thought that they were subscribing to a scheme of investment in gilt-edged securities. If those suspicions were correct, no honest person could have assisted Mr. Clowes and Mr. Cramer to dispose of the funds for their personal use. But Mr. Henwood consciously decided not to make inquiries because he preferred in his own interest not to run the risk of discovering the truth.

12 Their Lordships consider that by ordinary standards such a state of mind is dishonest. The judge found that Mr. Henwood may well have lived by different standards and seen nothing wrong in what he was doing. He had an

'exaggerated notion of dutiful service to clients, which produced a warped moral approach that it was not improper to treat carrying out clients' instructions as being all-important. Mr. Henwood may well have thought this to be an honest attitude, but, if so, he was wrong.'

[91] (2006) 65 CLJ 18 (M. Conaglen and A. Goymour); (2006) 122 LQR 171 (T.M.Yeo); [2006] All ER Rev 255 (P.J. Clarke); [2006] *Restitution Law Review* 175 (G. Mcmeel); [2005] *New Zealand Law Journal* 410 (J. Palmer); (2006) *Trust Law International* 122 (J.E. Penner); [2006] Conv 188 (D. Ryan); (2006) 57 *Northern Ireland Law Quarterly* 494 (A. Woodcock); (2006) 17 *King's College Law Journal* 105 (M. Bryan); (2008) LS 1 (J. Lee); *Statek Corp v Alford* [2008] EWHC 32 (Ch), para. 98, Evans–Lombe J.

13   Lord Neill of Bladen, who appeared for Mr. Henwood, submitted to their Lordships that such a state of mind was not dishonest unless Mr. Henwood was aware that it would by ordinary standards be regarded as dishonest. Only in such a case could he be said to be *consciously* dishonest. But the judge made no finding about Mr. Henwood's opinions about normal standards of honesty. The only finding was that by normal standards he had been dishonest but that his own standard was different.

14   In submitting that an inquiry into the defendant's views about standards of honesty is required, Lord Neill relied upon a statement by Lord Hutton in *Twinsectra Ltd v Yardley* [2002] AC 164, 174, with which the majority of their Lordships agreed. [Their Lordships read the dictum of Lord Hutton at paras. 35 and 36 [see p. 993, above] and continued:]

15   Their Lordships accept that there is an element of ambiguity in these remarks which may have encouraged a belief, expressed in some academic writing, that the *Twinsectra* case had departed from the law as previously understood and invited inquiry not merely into the defendant's mental state about the nature of the transaction in which he was participating but also into his views about generally acceptable standards of honesty. But they do not consider that this is what Lord Hutton meant. The reference to 'what he knows would offend normally accepted standards of honest conduct' meant only that his knowledge of the transaction had to be such as to render his participation contrary to normally acceptable standards of honest conduct. It did not require that he should have had reflections about what those normally acceptable standards were.

16   Similarly in the speech of Lord Hoffmann, the statement (in para 20) that a dishonest state of mind meant ' consciousness that one is transgressing ordinary standards of honest behaviour' was in their Lordships' view intended to require consciousness of those elements of the transaction which make participation transgress ordinary standards of honest behaviour. It did not also require him to have thought about what those standards were.

17   On the facts of the *Twinsectra* case, neither the judge who acquitted Mr. Leach of dishonesty nor the House undertook any inquiry into the views of the defendant solicitor, Mr. Leach, about ordinary standards of honest behaviour. He had received on behalf of his client a payment from another solicitor whom he knew had given an undertaking to pay it to Mr. Leach's client only for a particular use. But the other solicitor had paid the money to Mr. Leach without requiring any undertaking. The judge found that he was not dishonest because he honestly believed that the undertaking did not, so to speak, run with the money and that, as between him and his client, he held it for his client unconditionally. He was therefore bound to pay it upon his client's instructions without restriction on its use. The majority in the House of Lords considered that a solicitor who held this view of the law, even though he knew all the facts, was not by normal standards dishonest.

18   Their Lordships therefore reject Lord Neill's submission that the judge failed to apply the principles of liability for dishonest assistance which had been laid down in the *Twinsectra* case. In their opinion they were no different from the principles stated in *Royal Brunei Airlines Sdn Bhd v Tan* [1995] 2 AC 378 which were correctly summarised by the judge.

19   Their Lordships now address the grounds upon which the Staff of Government Division allowed Mr. Henwood's appeal. Having set out the Acting Deemster's findings at some length, they said that she could not have held Mr. Henwood liable unless she could find that he had 'solid grounds for suspicion, which he consciously ignored, that the disposals in which Mr. Henwood participated involved dealings with misappropriated trust funds'.

20   Their Lordships think that, on the facts of this case, this was a substantially accurate way of putting the matter, although they will return to the question of whether Mr. Henwood

needed to have had any knowledge or suspicions about the precise terms on which the misappropriated moneys were held. The question for the Staff of Government Division was therefore whether there was evidence upon which the Acting Deemster could make her finding that he had the necessary state of mind.

[Their Lordships considered that there was such evidence, and continued:]

27   The appellate court then went on to say that because Mr. Henwood knew the general nature of the businesses of the members of the Barlow Clowes group, it was not a necessary inference that he would have concluded that the disposals were of moneys held in trust. That was because there was no evidence that Mr. Henwood 'knew anything about, for example, the actual conduct of the businesses of members of the Barlow Clowes group, the contractual arrangements made with investors, the mechanisms for management of funds under the group's control, the investment and distribution policies and the precise involvement of Mr. Cramer in the group's affairs'.

28   Their Lordships consider that this passage displays two errors of law. First, it was not necessary...that Mr. Henwood should have concluded that the disposals were of moneys held in trust. It was sufficient that he should have entertained a clear suspicion that this was the case. Secondly, it is quite unreal to suppose that Mr. Henwood needed to know all the details to which the court referred before he had grounds to suspect that Mr. Clowes and Mr. Cramer were misappropriating their investors' money. The money in Barlow Clowes was either held on trust for the investors or else belonged to the company and was subject to fiduciary duties on the part of the directors. In either case, Mr. Clowes and Mr. Cramer could not have been entitled to make free with it as they pleased. In *Brinks Ltd v Abu-Saleh* [1996] CLC 133, 155 Rimer J expressed the opinion that a person cannot be liable for dishonest assistance in a breach of trust unless he knows of the existence of the trust or at least the facts giving rise to the trust. But their Lordships do not agree. Someone can know, and can certainly suspect, that he is assisting in a misappropriation of money without knowing that the money is held on trust or what a trust means: see the *Twinsectra* case [2002] 2 AC 164, para 19 (Lord Hoffmann) and para 135 (Lord Millett). And it was not necessary to know the 'precise involvement' of Mr. Cramer in the group's affairs in order to suspect that neither he nor anyone else had the right to use Barlow Clowes money for speculative investments of their own.

29   Their Lordships accordingly consider that there was abundant evidence on which the judge was entitled to make the findings of fact which she did about the disposal of £577,429 of the transaction 11 money on 8 June 1987...

In **Abou-Rahmah v Abacha** [2006] EWCA Civ 1492, [2007] 1 All ER (Comm) 827,[92] the Court of Appeal considered the test of dishonesty for the action for dishonest assistance. ARDEN LJ said:

64   This is the first opportunity since the decision in the *Barlow Clowes* case that this court has had to consider the element of dishonesty required for liability as an accessory in a breach of trust. As the facts of this case show, a claim based on liability for assistance in a breach of trust can arise in the context of ordinary commercial transactions, and there is thus a need for the law to be clear. The decision of the Privy Council in *Royal Brunei Airlines Sdn Bhd v Tan* [1995] 2 AC 378, on appeal from the Court of Appeal of Brunei Darussalem, had been taken to establish for the purposes of English law that dishonesty was required before liability for

---

[92] (2007) 66 CLJ 22 (G. Virgo); [2007] Conv 168 (D. Ryan); [2007] *Restitution Law Review* 135 (J. Lee).

assisting in a breach of trust could be imposed (see, for example, *Lewin on Trusts,* 17th ed 40–22 to 40–25; 'Knowing receipt: the need for a new landmark', by Lord Nicholls, Chapter 17, *Restitution, Past Present and Future,* ed Cornish, Nolan, O'Sullivan and Virgo (Hart, 1998)). Indeed, in the *Twinsectra* case, Lord Hutton accepted that the House should follow the holding in the *Royal Brunei* case that dishonesty was a necessary ingredient of liability for assistance in a breach of trust precisely because 'the statement of that principle by Lord Nicholls had been widely regarded as clarifying this area of the law' (para.[36]). The decision in the *Royal Brunei* case was based on English authorities and drew no distinction between the law of Brunei and that of England and Wales. Lord Nicholls, giving the advice of the Privy Council, held that 'the standard of what constitutes honest conduct is not subjective' (page 389) and gave other indications that consciousness of wrongdoing was not required for accessory liability for breach of trust.

65   The subsequent decision of the House of Lords in *Twinsectra Ltd v Yardley* [2002] 2 AC 164 was widely interpreted as requiring both an objective and subjective test to be applied to the question of standard. In the case of the subjective test, that would mean that the defendant would not be guilty of dishonesty unless he was conscious that the transaction fell below normally acceptable standards of conduct. The Privy Council in the *Barlow Clowes* case has now clarified that this is a wrong interpretation of the *Twinsectra* decision. It is not a requirement of the standard of dishonesty that the defendant should be conscious of his wrongdoing. *Snell's Equity* now refers to this as the 'better view' (31st ed, para.28–46 as updated).

66   On the basis of this interpretation, the test of dishonesty is predominantly objective: did the conduct of the defendant fall below the normally acceptable standard? But there are also subjective aspects of dishonesty. As Lord Nicholls said in the *Royal Brunei* case, honesty has 'a strong subjective element in that it is a description of a type of conduct assessed in the light of what a person actually knew at the time, as distinct from what a reasonable person would have known or appreciated' (page 389 and see generally pp 389 to 391). In this case, the judge applied the *Barlow Clowes* decision without asking himself, on the basis that *Twinsectra* was binding on him under the doctrine of precedent and the *Barlow Clowes* case, as a decision of the Privy Council, was only persuasive authority, whether the interpretation in that case was one he would himself have come to . . . Adherence to the doctrine of precedent is important as it helps to create and maintain legal certainty. On the other hand special factors can arise with respect to decisions of the Privy Council, as opposed to the other courts for jurisdictions outside England and Wales, as the decisions of that body have frequently paved the way for changes in the law of England and Wales and are from time to time taken to decide authoritatively questions of English law. The members of the Privy Council are also usually members of the Appellate Committee of the House of Lords. These factors led Baroness Hale in the recent case of *Re Spectrum Plus Ltd* [2005] 2 AC 680 at [163] to call for reconsideration of the rule of precedent that the Court of Appeal or the High Court is bound by decisions of the Court of Appeal in a case where the earlier decision of the Court of Appeal has been expressly disapproved by the Privy Council on appeal from a country where the law on the subject is the same as that of England and Wales. [Her Ladyship cited certain criminal law cases where the Court of Appeal followed a decision of the Privy Council rather than a decision of the House of Lords, and continued:]

68   Accordingly, in my judgment, before this court or the High Court decides to follow a decision of the Privy Council in place of a decision of the House of Lords the circumstances

must be quite exceptional and the court must be satisfied that in practice the result would be a foregone conclusion. In my judgment, the circumstances of this case are also exceptional and justify the course which the judge took for the following reasons:

i. The decision in *Twinsectra* is of course binding on this court and the judge. But the *Barlow Clowes* decision does not involve a departure from, or refusal to follow, the *Twinsectra* case. Rather, the *Barlow Clowes* case gives guidance as to the proper interpretation to be placed on it as a matter of English law. It shows how the *Royal Brunei* case and the *Twinsectra* case can be read together to form a consistent corpus of law.

ii. The meaning of dishonesty in the *Twinsectra* case appeared to involve an additional subjective element, namely an awareness on the part of the accessory that his conduct was dishonest. The decision under appeal in the *Barlow Clowes* case was an appeal from the Isle of Man but no distinction was drawn between the law of [the] Isle of Man and the law of England and Wales. It would appear therefore that the Privy Council was also intending to clarify English law since that is the only logical implication from the methodology of interpretation of an English authority. That interpretation could hardly have been an interpretation which only applied in the Isle of Man but not in England and Wales. The approach of the Privy Council was both striking and bold: one writer has referred to it as taking judicial re-interpretation 'to new heights' (Virgo, *Mapping the Law, Essays in memory of Peter Birks,* ed Burrows and Rodger (2006)(Oxford) chapter 5, page 86). The decision in the *Barlow Clowes* case could probably have been reached without consideration of the *Twinsectra* decision for the purpose of English law, and it is significant that the Privy Council took another course.

iii. Furthermore, the members of the Privy Council in the *Barlow Clowes* case are (or were at the date of the hearing of the appeal) all members of the Appellate Committee of the House of Lords. Their number was five, and that does not represent a majority of the Appellate Committee as in *Holley* [one of the criminal law cases previously cited by her Ladyship]. But the approach in *Barlow Clowes* was to clarify the meaning of the speeches of Lord Hutton and Lord Hoffmann in the *Twinsectra* case. The view expressed by Lord Hutton represented the view of the majority. Two members of the constitution of the Appellate Committee which sat in *Twinsectra* (Lord Steyn and Lord Hoffmann) were parties to the decision in *Barlow Clowes*. It is difficult to see that another constitution of the Appellate Committee would itself come to a different view as to what the majority in *Twinsectra* had meant. Put another way, I do not see how in these particular circumstances this court could be criticised for adopting the interpretation of the *Twinsectra* decision unanimously adopted by the Privy Council, consisting of members of the Appellate Committee at least two of whom were parties to the *Twinsectra* decision, in preference to its own.

iv. There is no overriding reason why in respect of dishonesty in the context of civil liability (as opposed to criminal responsibility) the law should take account of the defendant's views as to the morality of his actions.

69   For all the above reasons, I consider that the judge was right to proceed on the basis that the law as laid down in the *Twinsectra* case, as interpreted in the Privy Council in *Barlow Clowes*, represented the law of England and Wales.

Her Ladyship concluded, however, that, one the facts of the case, the defendant bank's general suspicions, did not constitute dishonesty. Rix and Pill LJJ considered that it was not necessary to examine the conflict between *Twinsectra* and *Barlow Clowes* because the defendant's conduct was not even objectively dishonest; however RIX LJ did say:

> 16   Without intending or attempting myself to restate the authorities, I would merely haz-ard this analysis. It would seem that a claimant in this area needs to show three things: first, that a defendant has the requisite knowledge; secondly, that, given that knowledge, the defendant acts in a way which is contrary to normally acceptable standards of honest conduct (the object-ive test of honesty or dishonesty); and thirdly, possibly, that the defendant must in some sense be dishonest himself (a subjective test of dishonesty which might, on analysis, add little or nothing to knowledge of the facts which, objectively, would make his conduct dishonest).
>
> 17   It is the third element which raises a problem of definition in the light of *Twinsectra* and *Barlow Clowes*....
>
> 23   I do not need to enter into that controversy for the purposes of this appeal. It is sufficient to concentrate on what was said in *Barlow Clowes* about the element of knowledge required to set up an investigation of the subsequent element of dishonesty. For in this respect, the Privy Council underlined that there may be sufficient knowledge (a) in suspicion and (b) despite ignorance that money is held on trust at all....
>
> 37   ... It is one thing to be negligent in failing to spot a possible money launderer, providing the negligence does not extend to shutting one's eyes to the truth. It is another thing, however, to have good grounds for suspecting money laundering and then to proceed as though one did not. Money laundering is a serious crime, for the very reason that *ex hypothesi* its subject mat-ter is the proceeds of crime. It is true that such proceeds are not necessarily those of a breach of trust—they could be the proceeds of drug dealing. But I am doubtful that that possibility provides any protection where there is a breach of trust. It is also true that the growing concern now experienced about money laundering and the international precautions now taken against it must be viewed in the context of public policy rather than on the level of an equitable tort designed to provide remedies in the civil law against knowing assistance in breach of trust. Nevertheless, I do not see why a bank which has, through its managers, a clear suspicion that a prospective client indulges in money laundering, can be said to lack that knowledge which is the first element in the tort.

C   AGENT ASSUMING TRUSTEE'S DUTIES

An agent of the trustees, such as a solicitor or banker, will not incur liability merely by reason of being in possession of trust property knowing it to be such. His receipt is merely ministerial and the transfer is not normally a breach of trust. He may be liable, however, if he has received for his own benefit property transferred to him in breach of trust or if he assists the trustees in a breach of trust. The cases suggest that he will not be liable if he acts honestly and in accordance with the instructions of his principal,[93] *a fortiori* where the existence of the trust is not established.[94]

---

[93] *Morgan v Stephens* (1861) 3 Giff 226; *Barnes v Addy* (1874) 9 Ch App 244; *Mara v Browne* [1896] 1 Ch 199; *Competitive Insurance Co Ltd v Davies Investments Ltd* [1975] 1 WLR 1240 (a liquidator unaware of the trust). See generally (1986) 102 LQR 111, 130ff (C. Harpum).

[94] *Carl Zeiss Stiftung v Herbert Smith & Co (No 2)* [1969] 2 Ch 276.

In **Williams-Ashman v Price and Williams** [1942] Ch 219, solicitors had received trust money into the firm's account and, on the trustee's instructions, in some cases those of a sole trustee, had made unauthorised investments. BENNETT J said at 228:

Mara v Browne [1896] 1 Ch 199 seems to me to be a decision that an agent in possession of money which he knows to be trust money, so long as he acts honestly, is not accountable to the beneficiaries interested in the trust money unless he intermeddles in the trust by doing acts characteristic of a trustee and outside the duties of an agent. After all, the beneficiaries have their remedy against the persons who are the real trustees. I have stated that, in my opinion, Mr. Alfred Williams acted throughout the transactions honestly. Indeed, the contrary is not suggested. He acted throughout on the instructions of his principals. He never intermeddled in the trust. He has, I think, acted incautiously. Many people might take the view that he ought to have ascertained by reference to the declaration of trust what the trusts were before he did what he was asked to do first by Dr. MacGowan and Mr. Streather [the trustees] and afterwards, when Mr. Streather had died, by Dr. MacGowan alone. But considerations of this kind do not assist the plaintiff unless he can establish that when the money came into the possession of the firm, Mr. Alfred Williams or the firm came under a duty to him as a beneficiary interested in the trust fund. It is only if the plaintiff can establish the existence of such a duty that he can establish a liability on the firm arising out of the breaches of trust committed by the express trustees.

The plaintiff is, I think, trying to use the passage from Stirling J's judgment and the statement from Underhill's *Law of Trusts and Trustees* to support a proposition which neither Stirling J nor the late Sir Arthur Underhill could have had in mind when they used the words relied on.[95]

Blyth v Fladgate [1891] 1 Ch 337 was plainly a case where the defendants, a firm of solicitors, were saddled with the liability of trustees because they had dealt with trust moneys in breach of trust and without instructions from their principals. The facts were that at a time when there was but one trustee of a marriage settlement, trust moneys had been invested in Exchequer bills which had been deposited with the bankers of the solicitors and were so deposited when the sole trustee died. Afterwards, while there was no trustee, the bills were sold and the proceeds of sale were placed to the credit of the solicitors with their bankers and afterwards paid by the solicitors to a mortgagor who, as security for their repayment, executed a mortgage in favour of three persons who were subsequently appointed to be trustees of the settlement. The advance on this mortgage was held improper and a breach of trust, and for this breach the solicitors were held to be responsible as constructive trustees because, having in their possession money which they knew was trust money, they had made an improper investment of it without instructions from or the authority of any principal. Stirling J's observations must be read in relation to the facts with which he was dealing. In *Mara v Browne* [1896] 1 Ch 199 the Court of Appeal laid down clearly the principles which govern the rights of the plaintiff and defendant firm in respect of the two sums of 200l. and 700l. received by the firm from Miss Pullen. On the facts, as I find them to be, the firm is not responsible to the plaintiff for the breaches of trust committed by the express trustees of the declaration of trust in respect of these two sums. The result is that the action fails and must be dismissed with costs.

---

[95] 'Where the trust funds come into the custody and under the control of a solicitor, or indeed of any one else, with notice of the trusts, he can only discharge himself of liability by showing that the property was duly applied in accordance with the trusts': Underhill (9th edn), p. 548, and relied on by Stirling J in *Blyth v Fladgate* [1891] 1 Ch 337.

D LIABILITY OF PARTNER

Another question which arises concerns the vicarious liability of partners in a partnership for one of their number who is held liable to account as a constructive trustee.

PARTNERSHIP ACT 1890

Liability of the firm for wrongs

10. Where, by any wrongful act or omission of any partner acting in the ordinary course of the business of the firm, or with the authority of his co-partners, loss or injury is caused to any person not being a partner in the firm, or any penalty is incurred, the firm is liable therefor to the same extent as the partner so acting or omitting to act.

The application of the provision where a partner is liable to account as a constructive trustee was considered by the House of Lords in **Dubai Aluminium Co Ltd v Salaam** [2002] UKHL 48, [2003] 2 AC 366[96] where a partner in a firm of solicitors was held liable for dishonestly assisting a fraudulent scheme. In holding that the firm was liable for the acts of the solicitor even though these were unauthorised, because the fraudulent scheme was closely connected with the acts which the dishonest solicitor was authorised to do, LORD NICHOLLS OF BIRKENHEAD considered the interpretation of section 10 of the Partnership Act:

10 ... There is nothing in the language of section 10 to suggest that the phrase 'any wrongful act or omission' is intended to be confined to common law torts. On the contrary, the reference to incurring a penalty points away from such a narrow interpretation of the phrase. The liability of co-partners for penalties incurred, for instance, for breach of revenue laws was well established when the 1890 Act was passed: see *Lindley on Partnership*, 6th ed (1893), p 160, and *Attorney-General v Stannyforth* (1721) Bunb 97.

11 In addition to the language the statutory context points in the same direction. Section 10 applies only to the conduct of a partner acting in the ordinary course of the firm's business or with the authority of his co-partners. It would be remarkable if a firm were liable for fraudulent misrepresentations made by a partner so acting, but not liable for dishonest participation by a partner in conduct directed at the misappropriation of another's property. In both cases the liability of the wrongdoing partner arises from dishonesty. In terms of the firm's liability there can be no rational basis for distinguishing one case from the other. Both fall naturally within the description of a 'wrongful act'.

12 In 1874 Lord Selborne LC's famous statement in *Barnes v Addy* (1874) LR 9 Ch App 244, 251–252, made plain that a stranger to a trust could be liable in equity for assisting in a breach of trust, even though he received no trust property. On the interpretation of section 10 advanced for Mr. Al Tajir and Mr. Salaam, a firm could never be vicariously liable for such conduct by one of their partners. I can see nothing to commend this interpretation of the statute...

---

[96] (2003) 119 LQR 364 (C. Mitchell). See also *Balfron Trustees Ltd v Peterson* [2002] WTLR 157 (vicarious liability of employer for employee).

17   I do not think the issue of vicarious liability is quite so straightforward when, as here, the act in question was not authorised. In order to identify the crucial issue it is necessary first to be clear on what is meant in this context by 'acting in the ordinary course of business'.

18   Partnership is the relationship which subsists between persons carrying on a business in common with a view of profit: section 1 of the Partnership Act 1890. Partnership is rooted in agreement, express or tacit, between the partners. So is the conduct of the partnership business. Clearly, the nature and scope of a business carried on by partners are questions of fact. Similarly, what the ordinary course of the business comprises, in the sense of what is the normal manner in which the business is carried on, is also a question of fact. So also is the scope of a partner's authority.

19   Vicarious liability is concerned with the responsibility of the firm to other persons for wrongful acts done by a partner while acting in the ordinary course of the partnership business or with the authority of his co-partners. At first sight this might seem something of a contradiction in terms. Partners do not usually agree with each other to commit wrongful acts. Partners are not normally authorised to engage in wrongful conduct. Indeed, if vicarious liability of a firm for acts done by a partner acting in the ordinary course of the business of the firm were confined to acts authorised in every particular, the reach of vicarious liability would be short indeed. Especially would this be so with dishonesty and other intentional wrongdoing, as distinct from negligence. Similarly restricted would be the vicarious responsibility of employers for wrongful acts done by employees in the course of their employment. Like considerations apply to vicarious liability for employees.

20   Take the present case. The essence of the claim advanced by Dubai Aluminium against Mr. Amhurst is that he and Mr. Salaam engaged in a criminal conspiracy to defraud Dubai Aluminium. Mr. Amhurst drafted the consultancy agreement and other agreements in furtherance of this conspiracy. Needless to say, Mr. Amhurst had no authority from his partners to conduct himself in this manner. Nor is there any question of conduct of this nature being part of the ordinary course of the business of the Amhurst firm. Mr. Amhurst had authority to draft commercial agreements. He had no authority to draft a commercial agreement for the dishonest purpose of furthering a criminal conspiracy.

21   However, this latter fact does not of itself mean that the firm is exempt from liability for his wrongful conduct. Whether an act or omission was done in the ordinary course of a firm's business cannot be decided simply by considering whether the partner was authorised by his co-partners to do the very act he did. The reason for this lies in the legal policy underlying vicarious liability. The underlying legal policy is based on the recognition that carrying on a business enterprise necessarily involves risks to others. It involves the risk that others will be harmed by wrongful acts committed by the agents through whom the business is carried on. When those risks ripen into loss, it is just that the business should be responsible for compensating the person who has been wronged.

22   This policy reason dictates that liability for agents should not be strictly confined to acts done with the employer's authority. Negligence can be expected to occur from time to time. Everyone makes mistakes at times. Additionally, it is a fact of life, and therefore to be expected by those who carry on businesses, that sometimes their agents may exceed the bounds of their authority or even defy express instructions. It is fair to allocate risk of losses thus arising to the businesses rather than leave those wronged with the sole remedy, of doubtful value, against the individual employee who committed the wrong. To this end, the law has given the concept of 'ordinary course of employment' an extended scope.

23 If, then, authority is not the touchstone, what is? Lord Denning MR once said that on this question the cases are baffling: see *Morris v C W Martin & Sons Ltd* [1966] 1 QB 716, 724. Perhaps the best general answer is that the wrongful conduct must be so closely connected with acts the partner or employee was authorised to do that, for the purpose of the liability of the firm or the employer to third parties, the wrongful conduct *may fairly and properly be regarded* as done by the partner while acting in the ordinary course of the firm's business or the employee's employment. Lord Millett said as much in *Lister v Hesley Hall Ltd* [2002] 1 AC 215, 245. So did Lord Steyn, at pp 223–224 and 230. McLachlin J said, in *Bazley v Curry* (1999) 174 DLR (4th) 45, 62: 'the policy purposes underlying the imposition of vicarious liability on employers are served only where the wrong is so connected with the employment that it *can be said* that the employer has introduced the risk of the wrong (and is thereby fairly and usefully charged with its management and minimisation)' (emphasis added.) To the same effect is Professor Atiyah's monograph *Vicarious Liability* (1967), p 171: 'the master ought to be liable for all those torts which *can fairly be regarded* as reasonably incidental risks to the type of business he carried on' (emphasis added).

24 In these formulations the phrases 'may fairly and properly be regarded', 'can be said' and 'can fairly be regarded' betoken a value judgment by the court. The conclusion is a conclusion of law, based on primary facts, rather than a simple question of fact.

25 This 'close connection' test focuses attention in the right direction. But it affords no guidance on the type or degree of connection which will normally be regarded as sufficiently close to prompt the legal conclusion that the risk of the wrongful act occurring, and any loss flowing from the wrongful act, should fall on the firm or employer rather than the third party who was wronged. It provides no clear assistance on when, to use Professor Fleming's phraseology, an incident is to be regarded as sufficiently work-related, as distinct from personal: see Fleming, *The Law of Torts*, 9th ed (1998), p 427....

26 This lack of precision is inevitable, given the infinite range of circumstances where the issue arises. The crucial feature or features, either producing or negativing vicarious liability, vary widely from one case or type of case to the next. Essentially the court makes an evaluative judgment in each case, having regard to all the circumstances and, importantly, having regard also to the assistance provided by previous court decisions. In this field the latter form of assistance is particularly valuable....

His Lordship noted that it was correct to assume that Mr. Amhurst had been drafting the relevant agreements in his capacity as partner, and continued:

35 This is a factually meagre basis on which to decide a question of vicarious responsibility for assumed dishonest conduct. But there is no other factual material available. Perforce the House must do its best with this material. Proceeding on this footing, in this context 'acting in his capacity as a partner' can only mean that Mr. Amhurst was acting for and on behalf of the firm, as distinct from acting solely in his own interests or the interests of others. He was seeking to promote the business of the firm.

36 On this assumed factual basis, I consider the firm is liable for Mr. Amhurst's dishonest assistance in the fraudulent scheme, the assistance taking the form of drafting the necessary agreements. Drafting agreements of this nature for a proper purpose would be within the ordinary course of the firm's business. Drafting these particular agreements is to be regarded as an act done within the ordinary course of the firm's business even though they were drafted for a dishonest purpose. These acts were so closely connected with the acts Mr. Amhurst was

authorised to do that for the purpose of the liability of the Amhurst firm they may fairly and properly be regarded as done by him while acting in the ordinary course of the firm's business.

Lord Millett:

110   Section 9 is not concerned with the liability of the firm at all but with the liability of the individual partners. It provides that every partner in a firm is liable jointly with the other partners for all debts and obligations of the firm incurred while he was a partner. Section 12 makes every partner jointly and severally liable for loss for which the firm was liable under sections 10 and 11 while he was a partner in the firm. Where section 10 makes the firm vicariously liable for loss caused by a partner's wrongdoing, therefore, section 12 makes the liability the joint and several liability of the individual partners. Sections 11 and 13 are not concerned with wrongdoing or with vicarious liability but with the original liability of the firm to account for receipts. I explained the difference between the two sections in *Bass Brewers Ltd v Appleby* [1997] 2 BCLC 700, 711. Section 11 deals with money which is properly received by the firm in the ordinary course of its business and is afterwards misappropriated by one of the partners. The firm is not vicariously liable for the misappropriation; it is liable to account for the money it received, and cannot plead the partner's wrongdoing as an excuse for its failure to do so. Section 13 deals with money which is misappropriated by a trustee who happens to be a partner and who in breach of trust or fiduciary duty afterwards pays it to his firm or otherwise improperly employs it in the partnership business. The innocent partners are not vicariously liable for the misappropriation, which will have occurred outside the ordinary course of the firm's business. But they are liable to restore the money if the requirements of the general law of knowing receipt are satisfied.

111   ... The critical distinction between section 10 on the one hand and sections 11 and 13 on the other is not between liability at common law and liability in equity, but between vicarious liability for wrongdoing and original liability for receipts. The firm (section 10) and its innocent partners (section 112) are vicariously liable for a partner's conduct provided that three conditions are satisfied: (i) his conduct must be wrongful, that is to say it must give rise to fault-based liability and not, for example, merely receipt-based liability in unjust enrichment; (ii) it must cause damage to the claimant; and (iii) it must be carried out in the ordinary course of the firm's business.

A firm of solicitors will not be vicariously liable for a solicitor who has committed a wrong as an express trustee.[97]

E   CONTRIBUTION

It was seen in Chapter 18 that where two or more people are liable in respect of the same damage, the court has a discretion as to the extent of the liability of each defendant by virtue of the Civil Liability (Contribution) Act 1978.[98] The application of this Act, where one party is liable to account as a constructive trustee for unconscionable

---

[97]   *Walker v Stones* [2001] QB 902; [2001] 15 *Trust Law International* 18, 25 (M. Doherty and R. Fletcher). Similarly if a solicitor is a 'trustee *de son tort*' or a constructive trustee *stricto sensu*: *Dubai Aluminium Co Ltd v Salaam* [2002] UKHL 48, [2003] 2 AC 366, para. 143 (Lord Millett).

[98]   See p. 864, above.

receipt of property in breach of trust, was considered in **City Index Ltd v David Gawler** [2007] EWCA Civ 1382. In that case the Court of Appeal held that even though the remedy for unconscionable receipt was restitutionary, it could also be characterised as compensatory, since the defendant was liable to make good the loss suffered by the trust or principal to the extent of the value which the defendant had received. It followed that a defendant who was liable for unconscionable receipt could be considered to be liable for the same damage as a defendant who was liable for negligence and so a claim for contribution might lie.

QUESTIONS

1. 'The obligation of a defaulting trustee is essentially that of effecting restitution to the trust estate.':

   Target Holdings Ltd v Redferns [1996] AC 421 [p. 949, above]; *Bartlett v Barclays Bank Trust Co Ltd (No 2)* [1980] Ch 515 at 543, *per* Brightman LJ; *Re Dawson* [1966] 2 NSWLR 211, *per* Street J (quoted Underhill and Hayton, p. 829); *Re Bell's Indenture* [1980] 1 WLR 1217 at 1236–1237; (1982) 126 SJ 631 (A.M. Kenny).

   In what ways is the obligation of a defaulting trustee different from that of a contractual or tortious wrongdoer?

2. Is the test of unconscionability as propounded by the Court of Appeal in *Bank of Credit and Commerce International (Overseas) Ltd v Akindele* [2001] Ch 437 [see p. 972, above] workable? See (2001) 21 OJLS 239 (S.B. Thomas); (2000) CLJ 446 (R. Nolan).

3. How is dishonesty defined for the action of dishonestly assisting a breach of trust? Do you prefer the analysis of ARDEN LJ or RIX LJ in *Abou-Rahmah v Abacha* [2006] EWCA Civ 1492, [2007] 1 All ER (Comm) 827 [p. 999, above]? See Virgo (2007) 66 CLJ 22.

4. What is the difference between the test of unconscionability for unconscionable receipt and the test of dishonesty for dishonest assistance? What is the reason for the different tests?

5. Should the tests of 'unconscionability' and 'dishonesty' be defined differently for disputes arising in a commercial context and disputes arising in a traditional private trust context?

6. Should liability for receipt of trust property be strict?

7. Is the distinction between personal accountability and constructive trusteeship important?

8. Is the defence of change of position available to defendants who are sued for unconscionable receipt or dishonest assistance?

PART VII

EQUITABLE ORDERS

21

EQUITABLE ORDERS

I GENERAL PRINCIPLES

It was seen in Chapter 1 that equity has a creative function to provide remedies to moderate the rigours of the common law. The creative function is illustrated most effectively by the law relating to trusts and trustees, as has been seen through all the preceding chapters. But this creativity is also exemplified by a number of equitable orders, the significance of which is not limited to the law of trusts and trustees. Some of these orders, such as rescission[1] of contracts in equity or rectification of documents,[2] are of real commercial significance. This chapter, however, will illustrate the creativity of equity by reference to the remedy of specific performance and the variety of injunctions and orders. The latter are of particular commercial importance both domestically and through international commercial litigation in England.

When considering the equitable jurisdiction to make an order, whether it be an injunction or specific performance, a number of key principles need to be borne in mind:

(i)   the equitable jurisdiction can be used to enforce legal and equitable rights;

(ii) the orders are discretionary but their availability is dependent on recognised principles. Nevertheless, they are flexible and can be adapted to deal with new situations;

(iii) they are only available where common law remedies are inadequate;

---

[1] H&M, pp. 851–870; P&S, pp. 71–80; Pettit, pp. 706–717; Snell, pp. 317–329.
[2] H&M, pp. 870–877; P&S, pp. 80–82; Pettit, pp. 717–727; Snell, pp. 331–343.

   (iv) breach of these orders constitutes the crime of contempt of court for which the punishment is imprisonment or a fine. A third party may be liable as an accessory;

   (v) there are a variety of defences available to the defendant, including that the claimant did not come to equity with clean hands, laches,[3] estoppel, acquiescence and hardship to the defendant; and

   (vi) in some situations, rather than make the relevant order, the court can order that damages be paid in lieu of the order. See p. 1037, below.

II INJUNCTIONS[4]

A GENERAL PRINCIPLES

SUPREME COURT ACT 1981

37. Powers of High Court with respect to injunctions and receivers

   (1) The High Court may by order (whether interlocutory or final) grant an injunction....in all cases in which it appears to the court to be just and convenient to do so.

   (2) Any such order may be made either unconditionally or on such terms and conditions as the court thinks just.

The equitable jurisdiction to grant injunctions is wide-ranging. The injunction can prohibit the defendant from acting or make the defendant act in a particular way. It can be awarded in interlocutory proceedings[5] before the trial, usually to maintain the status quo. *Quia timet* injunctions can be granted where interference with the claimant's rights is threatened or feared but has not yet occurred.

B MANDATORY INJUNCTIONS[6]

In **Redland Bricks Ltd v Morris** [1970] AC 652 the appellant's excavation of clay had left a pit into which the respondent's land was slipping. The respondent obtained an injunction which required the appellant to restore support to the respondent's land within six months. The appellant appealed to the House of Lords on the grounds that

---

   [3] See p. 886, above.
   [4] H&M, pp. 765–849; P&S, pp. 44–68; Pettit, pp. 567–662; Snell, pp.379–425.
   [5] See CPR r. 25.1(1)(a).   [6] H&M, pp. 779–782; P&S, pp. 56–57; Pettit, pp. 610–617.

damages were an adequate remedy. In allowing the appeal the House of Lords considered the nature of the jurisdiction to grant a mandatory injunction.

LORD UPJOHN said:

My Lords, this appeal raises some interesting and important questions as to the principles upon which the court will grant *quia timet* injunctions, particularly when mandatory.

[His Lordship considered the facts and continued:] It is, of course, quite clear and was settled in your Lordships' House nearly a hundred years ago in *Darley Main Colliery Co. v Mitchell* (1886) 11 App Cas 127, that if a person withdraws support from his neighbour's land that gives no right of action at law to that neighbour until damage to his land has thereby been suffered; damage is the gist of the action. When such damage occurs the neighbour is entitled to sue for the damage suffered to his land and equity comes to the aid of the common law by granting an injunction to restrain the continuance or recurrence of any acts which may lead to a further withdrawal of support in the future.

The neighbour may not be entitled as of right to such an injunction, for the granting of an injunction is in its nature a discretionary remedy, but he is entitled to it 'as of course' which comes to much the same thing and at this stage an argument on behalf of the tortfeasor, who has been withdrawing support that this will be very costly to him, perhaps by rendering him liable for heavy damages for breach of contract for failing to supply e.g., clay or gravel, receives scant, if any, respect. A similar case arises when injunctions are granted in the negative form where local authorities or statutory undertakers are enjoined from polluting rivers; in practice the most they can hope for is a suspension of the injunction while they have to take, perhaps, the most expensive steps to prevent further pollution.

But the granting of an injunction to prevent further tortious acts and the award of compensation for damage to the land already suffered exhausts the remedies [to] which at law and (under this heading) in equity the owner of the land is entitled. He is not prejudiced at law for if, as a result of the previous withdrawal of support, some further slip of his land occurs he can bring a fresh action for this new damage and ask for damages and injunctions.

But to prevent the jurisdiction of the courts being stultified equity has invented the *quia timet* action, that is an action for an injunction to prevent an apprehended legal wrong, though none has occurred at present, and the suppliant for such an injunction is without any remedy at law.

[His Lordship considered the decision of the Court of Appeal [1967] 1 WLR 967 and continued:] My Lords, *quia timet* actions are broadly applicable to two types of cases: first, where the defendant has as yet done no hurt to the plaintiff but is threatening and intending (so the plaintiff alleges) to do works which will render irreparable harm to him or his property if carried to completion. Your Lordships are not concerned with that and those cases are normally, though not exclusively, concerned with negative injunctions. Secondly, the type of case where the plaintiff has been fully recompensed both at law and in equity for the damage he has suffered but where he alleges that the earlier actions of the defendant may lead to future causes of action. In practice this means the case of which that which is before your Lordships' House is typical, where the defendant has withdrawn support from his neighbour's land or where he has so acted in depositing his soil from his mining operations as to constitute a menace to the plaintiff's land. It is in this field that the undoubted jurisdiction of equity to grant a mandatory injunction, that is an injunction ordering the defendant to carry out positive works, finds its main expression, though of course it is equally applicable to many other cases. Thus, to take the simplest example, if the defendant, the owner of land, including a metalled road over which the plaintiff has a right of way, ploughs up that land so that it is no longer usable, no doubt a mandatory injunction will go to restore it; damages are not a sufficient remedy, for the plaintiff has no right to go upon the defendant's land to remake his right of way.

The cases of *Isenberg v East India House Estate Co. Ltd.* (1863) 3 De GJ & S 263 and *Durell v Pritchard* (1865) 1 Ch App 244 have laid down some basic principles, and your Lordships have been referred to some other cases which have been helpful. The grant of a mandatory injunction is, of course, entirely discretionary and unlike a negative injunction can never be 'as of course'. Every case must depend essentially upon its own particular circumstances. Any general principles for its application can only be laid down in the most general terms:

1. A mandatory injunction can only be granted where the plaintiff shows a very strong probability upon the facts that grave damage will accrue to him in the future.... It is a jurisdiction to be exercised sparingly and with caution but in the proper case unhesitatingly.

2. Damages will not be a sufficient or adequate remedy if such damage does happen. This is only the application of a general principle of equity ...

3. Unlike the case where a negative injunction is granted to prevent the continuance or recurrence of a wrongful act the question of the cost to the defendant to do works to prevent or lessen the likelihood of a future apprehended wrong must be an element to be taken into account:

   (a) where the defendant has acted without regard to his neighbour's rights, or has tried to steal a march on him or has tried to evade the jurisdiction of the court or, to sum it up, has acted wantonly and quite unreasonably in relation to his neighbour he may be ordered to repair his wanton and unreasonable acts by doing positive work to restore the status quo even if the expense to him is out of all proportion to the advantage thereby accruing to the plaintiff. As illustrative of this see *Woodhouse v Newry Navigation Co.* [1898] 1 IR 161;

   (b) but where the defendant has acted reasonably, though in the event wrongly, the cost of remedying by positive action his earlier activities is most important for two reasons. First, because no legal wrong has yet occurred (for which he has not been recompensed at law and in equity) and, in spite of gloomy expert opinion, may never occur or possibly only upon a much smaller scale than anticipated. Secondly, because if ultimately heavy damage does occur the plaintiff is in no way prejudiced for he has his action at law and all his consequential remedies in equity.

So the amount to be expended under a mandatory order by the defendant must be balanced with these considerations in mind against the anticipated possible damage to the plaintiff and if, on such balance, it seems unreasonable to inflict such expenditure upon one who for this purpose is no more than a potential wrongdoer then the court must exercise its jurisdiction accordingly. Of course, the court does not have to order such works as upon the evidence before it will remedy the wrong but may think it proper to impose upon the defendant the obligation of doing certain works which may upon expert opinion merely lessen the likelihood of any further injury to the plaintiff's land. Sargant J pointed this out in effect in the celebrated 'Moving Mountain' case, *Kennard v Cory Bros. and Co. Ltd.* [1922] 1 Ch 265 at the foot of p. 274 (his judgment was affirmed in the Court of Appeal [1922] Ch 1).

4. If in the exercise of its discretion the court decides that it is a proper case to grant a mandatory injunction, then the court must be careful to see that the defendant knows exactly in fact what he has to do and this means not as a matter of law but as a matter of fact, so that in carrying out an order he can give his contractors the proper instructions.

C INTERLOCUTORY INJUNCTIONS[7]

In **American Cyanamid Co v Ethicon Ltd** [1975] AC 396 the defendants were about to launch on the British market a surgicial suture which the plaintiff alleged infringed its patent. The plaintiff sought an interlocutory injunction to restrain the product launch. This was granted by the trial judge but reversed by the Court of Appeal on the ground that no *prima facie* case of infringement of the patent had been established. In granting the injunction the House of Lords considered when an interlocutory injunction should be granted. LORD DIPLOCK said, at p. 405:

The grant of an interlocutory injunction is a remedy that is both temporary and discretionary. It would be most exceptional for your Lordships to give leave to appeal to this House in a case which turned upon where the balance of convenience lay. In the instant appeal, however, the question of the balance of convenience, although it had been considered by Graham J and decided in Cyanamid's favour, was never reached by the Court of Appeal. They considered that there was a rule of practice so well established as to constitute a rule of law that precluded them from granting any interim injunction unless upon the evidence adduced by both the parties on the hearing of the application the applicant had satisfied the court that on the balance of probabilities the acts of the other party sought to be enjoined would, if committed, violate the applicant's legal rights. In the view of the Court of Appeal the case which the applicant had to prove before any question of balance of convenience arose was '*prima facie*' only in the sense that the conclusion of law reached by the court upon that evidence might need to be modified at some later date in the light of further evidence either detracting from the probative value of the evidence on which the court had acted or proving additional facts. It was in order to enable the existence of any such rule of law to be considered by your Lordships' House that leave to appeal was granted.....

My Lords, when an application for an interlocutory injunction to restrain a defendant from doing acts alleged to be in violation of the plaintiff's legal right is made upon contested facts, the decision whether or not to grant an interlocutory injunction has to be taken at a time when *ex hypothesi* the existence of the right or the violation of it, or both, is uncertain and will remain uncertain until final judgment is given in the action. It was to mitigate the risk of injustice to the plaintiff during the period before that uncertainty could be resolved that the practice arose of granting him relief by way of interlocutory injunction; but since the middle of the 19th century this has been made subject to his undertaking to pay damages to the defendant for any loss sustained by reason of the injunction if it should be held at the trial that the plaintiff had not been entitled to restrain the defendant from doing what he was threatening to do. The object of the interlocutory injunction is to protect the plaintiff against injury by violation of his right for which he could not be adequately compensated in damages recoverable in the action if the uncertainty were resolved in his favour at the trial; but the plaintiff's need for such protection must be weighed against the corresponding need of the defendant to be protected against injury resulting from his having been prevented from exercising his own legal rights for which he could not be adequately compensated under the plaintiff's undertaking in damages if the uncertainty were resolved in the defendant's favour at the trial. The court must weigh one need against another and determine where 'the balance of convenience' lies.

[7] H&M, pp. 782–801; P&S, pp. 51–55; Pettit, pp. 594–610.

In those cases where the legal rights of the parties depend upon facts that are in dispute between them, the evidence available to the court at the hearing of the application for an interlocutory injunction is incomplete. It is given on affidavit and has not been tested by oral cross-examination. The purpose sought to be achieved by giving to the court discretion to grant such injunctions would be stultified if the discretion were clogged by a technical rule forbidding its exercise if upon that incomplete untested evidence the court evaluated the chances of the plaintiff's ultimate success in the action at 50 per cent or less, but permitting its exercise if the court evaluated his chances at more than 50 per cent....

The use of such expressions as 'a probability', 'a *prima facie* case', or 'a strong *prima facie* case' in the context of the exercise of a discretionary power to grant an interlocutory injunction leads to confusion as to the object sought to be achieved by this form of temporary relief. The court no doubt must be satisfied that the claim is not frivolous or vexatious, in other words, that there is a serious question to be tried.

It is no part of the court's function at this stage of the litigation to try to resolve conflicts of evidence on affidavit as to facts on which the claims of either party may ultimately depend nor to decide difficult questions of law which call for detailed argument and mature considerations. These are matters to be dealt with at the trial. One of the reasons for the introduction of the practice of requiring an undertaking as to damages upon the grant of an interlocutory injunction was that 'it aided the court in doing that which was its great object, *viz.* abstaining from expressing any opinion upon the merits of the case until the hearing': *Wakefield v Duke of Buccleugh* (1865) 12 LT 628, 629. So unless the material available to the court at the hearing of the application for an interlocutory injunction fails to disclose that the plaintiff has any real prospect of succeeding in his claim for a permanent injunction at the trial, the court should go on to consider whether the balance of convenience lies in favour of granting or refusing the interlocutory relief that is sought.

As to that, the governing principle is that the court should first consider whether, if the plaintiff were to succeed at the trial in establishing his right to a permanent injunction, he would be adequately compensated by an award of damages for the loss he would have sustained as a result of the defendant's continuing to do what was sought to be enjoined between the time of the application and the time of the trial. If damages in the measure recoverable at common law would be adequate remedy and the defendant would be in a financial position to pay them, no interlocutory injunction should normally be granted, however strong the plaintiff's claim appeared to be at that stage. If, on the other hand, damages would not provide an adequate remedy for the plaintiff in the event of his succeeding at the trial, the court should then consider whether, on the contrary hypothesis that the defendant were to succeed at the trial in establishing his right to do that which was sought to be enjoined, he would be adequately compensated under the plaintiff's undertaking as to damages for the loss he would have sustained by being prevented from doing so between the time of the application and the time of the trial. If damages in the measure recoverable under such an undertaking would be an adequate remedy and the plaintiff would be in a financial position to pay them, there would be no reason upon this ground to refuse an interlocutory injunction.

It is where there is doubt as to the adequacy of the respective remedies in damages available to either party or to both, that the question of balance of convenience arises. It would be unwise to attempt even to list all the various matters which may need to be taken into consideration in deciding where the balance lies, let alone to suggest the relative weight to be attached to them. These will vary from case to case.

Where other factors appear to be evenly balanced it is a counsel of prudence to take such measures as are calculated to preserve the status quo. If the defendant is enjoined temporarily from doing something that he has not done before, the only effect of the interlocutory injunction in the event of his succeeding at the trial is to postpone the date at which he is able to embark upon a course of action which he has not previously found it necessary to undertake; whereas to interrupt him in the conduct of an established enterprise would cause much greater inconvenience to him since he would have to start again to establish it in the event of his succeeding at the trial.

Save in the simplest cases, the decision to grant or to refuse an interlocutory injunction will cause to whichever party is unsuccessful on the application some disadvantages which his ultimate success at the trial may show he ought to have been spared and the disadvantages may be such that the recovery of damages to which he would then be entitled either in the action or under the plaintiff's undertaking would not be sufficient to compensate him fully for all of them. The extent to which the disadvantages to each party would be incapable of being compensated in damages in the event of his succeeding at the trial is always a significant factor in assessing where the balance of convenience lies, and if the extent of the uncompensatable disadvantage to each party would not differ widely, it may not be improper to take into account in tipping the balance the relative strength of each party's case as revealed by the affidavit evidence adduced on the hearing of the application. This, however, should be done only where it is apparent upon the facts disclosed by evidence as to which there is no credible dispute that the strength of one party's case is disproportionate to that of the other party. The court is not justified in embarking upon anything resembling a trial of the action upon conflicting affidavits in order to evaluate the strength of either party's case.

A relevant factor in support of the grant of the injunction in this case was that the defendant's product was not yet on the market whereas the plaintiff had an established market.

D FREEZING INJUNCTIONS[8]

The creative function of equity is particularly well illustrated by an important remedy developed in the 1970s to deal with the problem of a defendant who seeks to hide his assets or take them out of the jurisdiction to prevent the claimant from enforcing a judgment for damages against him. To avoid this problem equity was relied on to create a new form of interim injunction, known then as a *Mareva* injunction (after one[9] of the early cases which first recognised it, involving a ship of that name—see p. 1018, below) and now known as a freezing injunction. This is an injunction which can be used by judges to freeze some or all of the defendant's assets to prevent the defendant from removing them from the jurisdiction, or dissipating them, and so ensure that any judgment can be enforced against the defendant. For example, the order might mean that the defendant would not be able to gain access to money which has been credited to his bank account. Such orders can be granted either before or after[10] judgment has

---

[8] H&M, pp. 842–849; P&S, pp. 61–68; Pettit, pp. 640–653.

[9] The first case to recognise this injunction was *Nippon Yusen Kaisha* v *Karageorgis* [1975] 1 WLR 1093.

[10] *Babanaft International Co SA v Bassatne* [1990] Ch 13.

been obtained. This is an injunction which has proved to be a significant feature of the English law of civil procedure.

Lord Denning, *The Due Process of Law* (1980), p. 134

The greatest piece of judicial law reform in my time.

(i) *The Jurisdiction to grant a Freezing Injunction*

Mareva Compania Naviera SA v International Bulkcarriers SA
[1975] 2 Lloyd's Rep 509 (CA, **Lord Denning MR**, **Roskill** and **Ormrod LJJ**)

Shipowners sued the charterers of the *Mareva* for recovery of hire payments and sought an injunction to restrain them from taking any of the money they had received under the charter from a London bank and out of the jurisdiction. The trial judge granted the injunction until the matter was heard by the Court of Appeal. The shipowner appealed on the basis that the injunction should continue until judgment was obtained.

Held. Appeal allowed.

Lord Denning MR: [The shipowners] have applied for an injunction to restrain the disposal of those moneys which are now in the bank. They rely on the recent case of *Nippon Yusen Kaisha v Karageorgis* [1975] 1 WLR 1093. Mr. Justice Donaldson [the trial judge] felt some doubt about that decision because we were not referred to *Lister v Stubbs* [1890] 45 Ch D 1 [p. 815, above]. There are observations in that case to the effect that the Court has no jurisdiction to protect a creditor before he gets judgment. Lord Justice Cotton said:

> 'I know of no case where, because it was highly probable that if the action were brought to a hearing the plaintiff could establish that a debt was due to him from the defendant, the defendant has been ordered to give security until that has been established by the judgment or decree.'

and Lord Justice Lindley said:

> '...we should be doing what I conceive to be very great mischief if we were to stretch a sound principle to the extent to which the appellants ask us to stretch it...'

Mr. Justice Donaldson felt that he was bound by *Lister v Stubbs* and that he had no power to grant an injunction. But, in deference to the recent case, he did grant an injunction, but only until 17:00 today (23 June, 1975), on the understanding that by that time this Court would be able to reconsider the position.

Now Mr. Rix has been very helpful. He has drawn our attention not only to *Lister v Stubbs* but also to section 45 of the Judicature Act, 1925, which repeats section 25(8) of the Judicature Act, 1875. It says:

> 'A *mandamus* or an injunction may be granted or a receiver appointed by an interlocutory order of the court in all cases in which it shall appear to the court to be just or convenient.'

In *Beddow v Beddow* (1878) 9 Ch D 89, Sir George Jessel, the then Master of the Rolls, gave a very wide interpretation to that section. He said:

> 'I have unlimited power to grant an injunction in any case where it would be right or just to do so.'

There is only one qualification to be made. The Court will not grant an injunction to protect a person who has no legal or equitable right whatever. That appears from *North London Railway Co v Great Northern Railway Co* (1883) 11 QBD 30. But, subject to that qualification, the statute gives a wide general power to the Courts. It is well summarized in Halsbury's *Laws of England*, vol. 21, 3rd ed., p. 348, para. 729:

> '...now, therefore, whenever a right, which can be asserted either at law or in equity, does exist, then, whatever the previous practice may have been, the Court is enabled by virtue of this provision, in a proper case, to grant an injunction to protect that right.'

In my opinion that principle applies to a creditor who has a right to be paid the debt owing to him, even before he has established his right by getting judgment for it. If it appears that the debt is due and owing—and there is a danger that the debtor may dispose of his assets so as to defeat it before judgment—the Court has jurisdiction in a proper case to grant an interlocutory judgment so as to prevent him disposing of those assets. It seems to me that this is a proper case for the exercise of this jurisdiction. There is money in a bank in London which stands in the name of these time charterers. The time charterers have control of it. They may at any time dispose of it or remove it out of this country. If they do so, the shipowners may never get their charter hire. The ship is now on the high seas. It has passed Cape Town on its way to India. It will complete the voyage and the cargo discharged and the shipowners may not get their charter hire at all. In face of this danger, I think this Court ought to grant an injunction to restrain the defendants from disposing of these moneys now in the bank in London until the trial or judgment in this action. If the defendants have any grievance about it when they hear of it, they can apply to discharge it. But meanwhile the plaintiffs should be protected. It is only just and right that this Court should grant an injunction. I would therefore continue the injunction.

The legitimacy of granting freezing orders was confirmed by the House of Lords[11] and has now been recognised by statute:

SUPREME COURT ACT 1981

Powers of High Court with respect to injunctions and receivers

37(3) The power of the High Court under subsection (1) to grant an interlocutory injunction restraining a party to any proceedings from removing from the jurisdiction of the High Court, or otherwise dealing with, assets located within that jurisdiction shall be exercisable in cases where that party is, as well as in cases where he is not, domiciled, resident or present within that jurisdiction.

The freezing injunction is now governed by Civil Procedure Rule r 25,1(1)(f): it is an order:

(i)   restraining a party from removing from the jurisdiction assets located there; or

(ii) restraining a party from dealing with any assets whether located within the jurisdiction or not.[12]

---

[11] *Siskina v Distos Compania Naviera* [1979] AC 210.
[12] See also CPR Practice Direction 25, para. 6.

(ii) Factors relevant to the grant of a freezing injunction

A freezing injunction can only be granted if the claimant has satisfied the usual requirements for an interlocutory injunction as recognised in *American Cyanamid Co v Ethicon Ltd.* [1975] AC 396 [p. 1015, above], namely that there is a serious issue to be tried and the balance of convenience favours the grant of the injunction.

In **Third Chandris Shipping Corporation v Unimarine SA** [1979] QB 645 LORD DENNING MR identified the following factors as relevant to the decision to grant a freezing order:[13]

It is just four years ago now since we introduced here the procedure known as *Mareva* injunctions. All the other legal systems of the world have a similar procedure. It is called in the civil law *saisie conservatoire*. It has been welcomed in the City of London and has proved extremely beneficial. It enables a creditor in a proper case to stop his debtor from parting with his assets pending trial . . . In *Siskina v Distos Compania Naviera* [1979] AC 210 the House of Lords placed this restriction upon the procedure. It applies only in the case of an 'interlocutory order'. In order to obtain a *Mareva* injunction there has to be in existence a substantive cause of action on which the plaintiff is suing or about to sue in the High Court in England or is enforcing or about to enforce by arbitration in England. . . .

Much as I am in favour of the *Mareva* injunction, it must not be stretched too far lest it be endangered. In endeavouring to set out some guidelines, I have had recourse to the practice of many other countries which ha[s] been put before us. They have been most helpful. These are the points which those who apply for it should bear in mind:

(i)   The plaintiff should make full and frank disclosure of all matters in his knowledge which are material for the judge to know . . .

(ii)   The plaintiff should give particulars of his claim against the defendant, stating the ground of his claim and the amount thereof, and fairly stating the points made against it by the defendant.

(iii)   The plaintiff should give some grounds for believing that the defendant has assets here . . . The existence of a bank account in England is enough, whether it is in overdraft or not.

(iv)   The plaintiff should give some grounds for believing that there is a risk of the assets being removed before the judgment or award is satisfied. The mere fact that the defendant is abroad is not by itself sufficient . . .

(v)   The plaintiff must, of course, give an undertaking in damages—in case he fails in his claim or the injunction turns out to be unjustified. In a suitable case this should be supported by a bond or security: and the injunction only granted on it being given, or undertaken to be given.

In setting out those guidelines, I hope we shall do nothing to reduce the efficacy of the present practice. In it speed is of the essence. *Ex parte* is of the essence. If there is delay, or if advance warning is given, the assets may well be removed before the injunction can bite.

---

[13] See also *Z Ltd v A* [1982] 1 All ER 556; *Ninemia Maritime Corp v Trave Schiffahrtgesellschaft (The Niedersachsen)* [1984] 1 All ER 398; *Ketchum International plc v Group Public Relations Holdings Ltd* [1997] 1 WLR 4; *Fourie v Le Roux* [2007] UKHL 1, [2007] 1 WLR 320.

In **Camdex International Ltd v Bank of Zambia (No. 2)** [1997] 1 WLR 632 the claimant had obtained a freezing order against the Zambian central bank. The bank had printed high-denomination Zambian banknotes in England which were caught by the injunction but which were important to the Zambian economy. The Court of Appeal held that the banknotes should be released from the order. Sir Thomas Bingham MR provided further clarification of the function of the freezing order. He said, at p. 636:

It seems to me that in a situation such as this, it is important to go back to first principles. A *Mareva* injunction is granted to prevent the dissipation of assets by a prospective judgment debtor, or a judgment debtor, with the object or effect of denying a claimant or judgment creditor satisfaction of his claim or judgment debt. Here, it is plain that the defendant wants to transfer these banknotes to Zambia. In doing so it would not, as it seems to me, dissipate any asset available to satisfy the judgment debt because the asset has, in the open market, no value. It is not an asset of value to the plaintiff or other creditors of the defendant if it were put up on the market and sold. It is true that the denial of this asset to the defendant would put the defendant in a position of such extreme difficulty that the defendant would seek to pay a price beyond the market value of the asset in order to recover it, but that is, as it would seem to me, what would in ordinary parlance be described as holding someone to ransom. I do not for my part consider that this is an empty application. The relaxation of the injunction to permit removal of the bank notes would, in my judgment, improve the position of the defendant... I feel driven to conclude that the judge did give inadequate weight to the quite extraordinary circumstances affecting the exercise of the equitable jurisdiction in this case. In his judgment he said that he did have misgivings about a private institution acquiring a central bank's rights and advancing those interests in preference to those of other international governmental or quasi-governmental organisations. However, he went on to say that he was faced with a judgment debtor who had decided to make enforcement as difficult as possible, and who was seeking to remove from the jurisdiction an asset which was of considerable value to itself and which it might be willing to purchase from the judgment creditor once execution had been levied upon it.

Of course one agrees with the judge, without qualification, that a judgment debt should, in the ordinary way and in any ordinary situation, be paid. It is, however, relevant that the defendant is a body to whom the ordinary procedures of bankruptcy and winding up are not available. The situation is one in which, on the evidence, severe national hardship to the people of Zambia would follow if the state defaulted in its international obligations.

Aldous LJ, at p. 638 said:

The purpose of *Mareva* relief is, and always has been, to prevent a defendant from removing from the jurisdiction his assets or dissipating them. It is not, and never has been, an aid to obtaining preference for repayment from an insolvent party.

(iii) World-wide Freezing Injunctions

It has been recognised that freezing orders can be granted to restrain the dissipation of assets abroad.[14]

---

[14] See now CPR r 25(1)(f), p. 1019, above. See also see also *Derby & Co Ltd v Weldon (Nos 3 and 4)* [1990] Ch 65 and *Derby & Co Ltd v Weldon (No 6)* [1990] 3 All ER 263.

In **Derby & Co Ltd v Weldon** [1990] Ch 48 the Court of Appeal recognised that the court had jurisdiction to freeze assets abroad. It also granted an order to require the defendant to disclose the location of its assets abroad.

MAY LJ said at p. 55:

In *Babanaft International Co SA v Bassatne* [1990] Ch 13 this court was prepared to make a post-judgment worldwide *Mareva* order subject to a proviso preserving the personal effect of such an order on and to the particular defendants against whom it was directed. The court in *Babanaft* indicated that in its view a pre-judgment worldwide *Mareva* was legitimate, but of course that comment was then obiter. However, in *Republic of Haiti v Duvalier* [1990] 1 QB 202, decided during the hearing of the instant appeal, another division of this court made a pre-judgment worldwide *Mareva,* again subject to the personal proviso to which I have already referred. The court recognised that such an injunction was a most unusual measure, such as should very rarely be granted. Nevertheless the court quoted the dictum of Kerr LJ in *Babanaft* [1990] Ch 13, 33D: 'some situations... cry out—as a matter of justice to plaintiffs—for disclosure orders and *Mareva*-type injunctions covering foreign assets of defendants even before judgment'.

PARKER LJ said at p. 56:

The mere fact that the plaintiff shows a good arguable case and a real risk of disposal or hiding of English assets—the requisites for an internal *Mareva*—clearly cannot by itself be sufficient to justify an extraterritorial *Mareva* either worldwide or at all. Such a *Mareva* would clearly be unjustified if, for example, there were sufficient English assets to cover the appropriate sum, or if the court were not satisfied that there were foreign assets or that there was a real risk of disposal of the same, or if it would in all the circumstances be oppressive to make the order.... There are in essence only three issues; (i) has the plaintiff a good arguable case; (ii) has the plaintiff satisfied the court that there are assets within and, where an extraterritorial order is sought, without the jurisdiction; and (iii) is there a real risk of dissipation or secretion of assets so as to render any judgment which the plaintiff may obtain nugatory[?] Such matters should be decided on comparatively brief evidence.

[His Lordship quoted from the judgment of Lord Diplock in *American Cyanamid Co v Ethjicon Ltd* [1975] AC 396 [p. 1015, above], rejecting the need to resolve conflicts of evidence in interlocutory proceedings, and continued:] In my view the difference between an application for an ordinary injunction and a *Mareva* lies only in this, that in the former case the plaintiff need only establish that there is a serious question to be tried, whereas in the latter the test is said to be whether the plaintiff shows a good arguable case. This difference, which is incapable of definition, does not however affect the applicability of Lord Diplock's observations to *Mareva* cases.

NICHOLLS LJ said, at p. 62:

In my view each case must depend on its own facts. An order restraining a defendant from dealing with any of his assets overseas, and requiring him to disclose details of all his assets wherever located, is a draconian order. The risk of prejudice to which, in the absence of such an order, the plaintiff will be subject is that of the dissipation or secretion of assets *abroad*. This risk must, on the facts, be appropriately grave before it will be just and convenient for such a draconian order to be made.

(iv) Effect on third parties

A matter of particular significance concerns the effect of freezing orders on third parties. This was considered by the House of Lords in **Customs and Excise Commissioners v Barclays Bank plc** [2006] UKHL 28, [2007] 1 AC 181[15] where the Customs and Excise Commissioners were trying to recover outstanding payments of VAT from two companies and obtained a freezing order in respect of funds held by the companies in the defendant bank. The bank was informed of the orders but failed to prevent payment out of the accounts. The claimant sued the bank for negligence. In holding that the bank did not owe a duty of care to the claimant, the House of Lords considered the nature of the court's jurisdiction to grant injunctions. LORD BINGHAM OF CORNHILL said at para. 9:

The prescribed standard form contains a penal notice:

'If you [] disobey this order you may be held to be in contempt of court and may be imprisoned, fined or have your assets seized.

Any other person who knows of this order and does anything which helps or permits the respondent to breach the terms of this order may also be held to be in contempt of court and may be imprisoned, fined or have their assets seized.'

The first of these warnings is addressed to the subject of the order, the second to any party (such as a bank) who knows of it. The form provides that anyone served with or notified of the order may apply to the court to vary or discharge it on notice to the applicant's solicitor. The effect of the order as it affects parties other than the applicant and the subject of the order is again stated:

'It is a contempt of court for any person notified of this order knowingly to assist in or permit a breach of this order. Any person doing so may be imprisoned, fined or have their assets seized.'

The form records an undertaking by the applicant to pay the reasonable costs of any person other than the subject of the order:

'which have been incurred as a result of this order including the costs of finding out whether that person holds any of the respondent's assets and if the court finds that this order has caused such person loss, and decides that such person should be compensated for that loss, the applicant will comply with any order the court may make.' ...

10   It is very well established that the purpose of a freezing injunction is to restrain a defendant or prospective defendant from disposing of or dealing with assets so as to defeat, wholly or in part, a likely judgment against it. The purpose is not to give a claimant security for his claim or give him any proprietary interest in the assets restrained: *Gangway Ltd v Caledonian Park Investments (Jersey) Ltd* [2001] 2 Lloyd's Rep 715, para 14, *per* Colman J. The ownership of the assets does not change. All that changes is the right to deal with them.

11   The court will punish a party who breaches one of its orders if the breach is sufficiently serious and the required standard of knowledge and intention is sufficiently proved. This rule applies to freezing injunctions, as the prescribed form and the notices given to the bank in this case make clear. The leading authority on *Mareva* injunctions leaves no room for doubt. In *Z*

[15] (2006) 122 LQR 535 (S. Gee).

Ltd v A–Z and AA–LL [1982] QB 558, 572, Lord Denning MR said: 'Every person who has knowledge of [the order] must do what he reasonably can to preserve the asset. He must not assist in any way in the disposal of it. Otherwise he is guilty of a contempt of court.' He repeated this point at pp 573–574 and 575. Eveleigh LJ devoted his judgment in the case wholly to the requirements of contempt in this context. That the power to punish for contempt is not a mere paper tiger is well illustrated by the judgment of Colman J in *Z Bank v D1* [1994] 1 Lloyd's Rep 656....

13   In 1981 Robert Goff J observed that 'the banks in this country have received numerous notices of [*Mareva*] injunctions which have been granted' (*Searose Ltd v Seatrain UK Ltd* [1981] 1 WLR 894, 895), and there is no reason to think that the pace has slackened since. Thus receiving notice of such injunctions is, literally, an everyday event. And the Commissioners are right that they were not claiming substantive relief against the bank as a claimant seeks it against a defendant. But I think the bank is right to say that that is not the whole story, for three main reasons. First, the effect of notification of the order is to override the ordinary contractual duties which govern the relationship of banker and customer. This is not something of which a bank can complain or of which the bank does complain. A bank's relationship with its customers is subject to the law of the land, which provides for the grant of freezing injunctions. But the effect is none the less to oblige the bank to act in a way which but for the order would be a gross breach of contract. Such a situation must necessarily be very unwelcome to any bank which values its relationship with its customer. Secondly, the order exposes the bank to the risk that its employees may be imprisoned, the bank fined and its assets sequestrated. Of course, this is only a risk if the bank breaches the order in a sufficiently culpable way. But it is not a risk which exists independently of the order, and not a risk to which anyone would wish to be exposed....

The *Mareva* jurisdiction has developed as one exercised by court order enforceable only by the court's power to punish those who break its orders. The documentation issued by the court does not hint at the existence of any other remedy. This regime makes perfect sense on the assumption that the only duty owed by a notified party is to the court.

LORD HOFFMANN said at para. 29:

A freezing order is an injunction made against the putative debtor to which the bank is not a party. But the existence of the injunction may have an effect upon third parties in two ways. First, it is a contempt of court to aid and abet a breach of an injunction by the party against whom the order was made. Secondly, it is an independent contempt of court to do an act which deliberately interferes with the course of justice by frustrating the purpose for which the order was made: see *Attorney-General v Times Newspapers Ltd* [1992] 1 AC 191 and *Attorney-General v Punch Ltd* [2003] 1 AC 1046 for the general principle and *Z Ltd v A–Z and AA–LL* [1982] QB 558, 578 for an explanation by Eveleigh LJ of its application to *Mareva* injunctions. The purpose of serving the bank with the order is therefore to give the bank notice that payment out of the account will frustrate its purpose and, if done deliberately, will be a contempt of court. However, as Lord Hope of Craighead said in *Attorney-General v Punch Ltd* [2003] 1 AC 1046, 1066, for the third party to be liable for contempt:

'it has...to be shown there was an intention on his part to interfere with or impede the admin-istration of justice. This is an essential ingredient, and it has to be established to the criminal standard of proof.'

III SEARCH ORDERS[16]

A THE NATURE OF THE ORDER

Another significant application of the equitable jurisdiction to supplement domestic and international litigation is the search order, sometimes known as the *Anton Piller* order after one of the first cases[17] to recognise the legitimacy of the order.

Anton Piller KG v Manufacturing Process Ltd
[1976] Ch 55 (CA, Lord Denning MR, Ormrod and Shaw LJJ)

The plaintiff claimed the defendant company had given confidential information to manufacturers which was damaging to the plaintiff's business. The plaintiff applied for an order for permission to enter the defendant's premises and to remove documents into the custody of the plaintiff's solicitor.

Held. Order granted.

Lord Denning MR: During the last 18 months the judges of the Chancery Division have been making orders of a kind not known before. They have some resemblance to search warrants. Under these orders, the plaintiff and his solicitors are authorised to enter the defendant's premises so as to inspect papers, provided the defendant gives permission.

Now this is the important point: the court orders the defendant to give them permission. The judges have been making these orders on *ex parte* applications without prior notice to the defendant... it is obvious that such an order can only be justified in the most exceptional circumstances...

Let me say at once that no court in this land has any power to issue a search warrant to enter a man's house so as to see if there are papers or documents there which are of an incriminating nature, whether libels or infringements of copyright or anything else of the kind. No constable or bailiff can knock at the door and demand entry so as to inspect papers or documents. The householder can shut the door in his face and say 'Get out'. That was established in the leading case of *Entick v Carrington* (1765) 2 Wils KB 275. None of us would wish to whittle down that principle in the slightest. But the order sought in this case is not a search warrant. It does not authorise the plaintiffs' solicitors or anyone else to enter the defendants' premises against their will. It does not authorise the breaking down of any doors, nor the slipping-in by a back door, nor getting in by an open door or window. It only authorises entry and inspection by the permission of the defendants. The plaintiffs must get the defendants' permission. But it does do this: it brings pressure on the defendants to give permission. It does more. It actually orders them to give permission—with, I suppose, the result that if they do not give permission, they are guilty of contempt of court.

This may seem to be a search warrant in disguise. But it was fully considered in the House of Lords 150 years ago and held to be legitimate. The case is *United Company of Merchants of*

---

[16] H&M, pp. 839—841; P&S, pp. 68—71; Pettit, pp. 653–660.
[17] The first reported case to make such an order was *EMI Ltd v Pandit* [1975] 1 WLR 302 (Templeman J).

England, Trading to the East Indies v Kynaston (1821) 3 Bli (OS) 153. Lord Redesdale said, at pp. 163–164:

> 'The arguments urged for the appellants at the Bar are founded upon the supposition, that the court has directed a forcible inspection. This is an erroneous view of the case. The order is to permit; and if the East India Company should refuse to permit inspection, they will be guilty of a contempt of the court.... It is an order operating on the person requiring the defendants to permit inspection, not giving authority of force, or to break open the doors of their warehouse.'

That case was not, however, concerned with papers or things. It was only as to the value of a warehouse; and that could not be obtained without an inspection. But the distinction drawn by Lord Redesdale affords ground for thinking that there is jurisdiction to make an order that the defendant 'do permit' when it is necessary in the interests of justice...

It seems to me that such an order can be made by a judge *ex parte*, but it should only be made where it is essential that the plaintiff should have inspection so that justice can be done between the parties: and when, if the defendant were forewarned, there is a grave danger that vital evidence will be destroyed, that papers will be burnt or lost or hidden, or taken beyond the jurisdiction, and so the ends of justice be defeated: and when the inspection would do no real harm to the defendant or his case.

Nevertheless, in the enforcement of this order, the plaintiffs must act with due circumspection. On the service of it, the plaintiffs should be attended by their solicitor, who is an officer of the court. They should give the defendants an opportunity of considering it and of consulting their own solicitor. If the defendants wish to apply to discharge the order as having been improperly obtained, they must be allow[ed] to do so. If the defendants refuse permission to enter or to inspect, the plaintiffs must not force their way in. They must accept the refusal, and bring it to the notice of the court afterwards, if need be on an application to commit.

You might think that with all these safeguards against abuse, it would be of little use to make such an order. But it can be effective in this way: it serves to tell the defendants that, on the evidence put before it, the court is of opinion that they ought to permit inspection—nay, it orders them to permit—and that they refuse at their peril. It puts them in peril not only of proceedings for contempt, but also of adverse inferences being drawn against them; so much so that their own solicitor may often advise them to comply. We are told that in two at least of the cases such an order has been effective. We are prepared, therefore, to sanction its continuance, but only in an extreme case where there is grave danger of property being smuggled away or of vital evidence being destroyed.

Ormrod LJ: I agree with all that Lord Denning MR has said. The proposed order is at the extremity of this court's powers. Such orders, therefore, will rarely be made, and only when there is no alternative way of ensuring that justice is done to the applicant.

There are three essential pre-conditions for the making of such an order, in my judgment. First, there must be an extremely strong *prima facie* case. Secondly, the damage, potential or actual, must be very serious for the applicant. Thirdly, there must be clear evidence that the defendants have in their possession incriminating documents or things, and that there is a real possibility that they may destroy such material before any application *inter partes* can be made.

The form of the order makes it plain that the court is not ordering or granting anything equivalent to a search warrant. The order is an order on the defendant *in personam* to permit inspection. It is therefore open to him to refuse to comply with such an order, but at his peril either of further proceedings for contempt of court—in which case, of course, the court will have the widest discretion as to how to deal with it, and if it turns out that the order was made improperly in the first place, the contempt will be dealt with accordingly—but more important, of course, the refusal to comply may be the most damning evidence against the defendant at the subsequent trial. Great responsibility clearly rests on the solicitors for the applicant to ensure that the carrying-out of such an order is meticulously carefully done with the fullest respect for the defendant's rights, as Lord Denning MR has said, of applying to the court, should he feel it necessary to do so, before permitting the inspection.[18]

The jurisdiction to make such an order has now been recognised by statute.

CIVIL PROCEDURE ACT 1997

7. Power of courts to make orders for preserving evidence, etc.

(1) The court may make an order under this section for the purpose of securing, in the case of any existing or proposed proceedings in the court—

(a) the preservation of evidence which is or may be relevant, or

(b) the preservation of property which is or may be the subject-matter of the proceedings or as to which any question arises or may arise in the proceedings.

(2) A person who is, or appears to the court likely to be, a party to proceedings in the court may make an application for such an order.

(3) Such an order may direct any person to permit any person described in the order, or secure that any person so described is permitted—

(a) to enter premises in England and Wales, and

(b) while on the premises, to take in accordance with the terms of the order any of the following steps.

(4) Those steps are—

(a) to carry out a search for or inspection of anything described in the order, and

(b) to make or obtain a copy, photograph, sample or other record of anything so described.

(5) The order may also direct the person concerned—

(a) to provide any person described in the order, or secure that any person so described is provided, with any information or article described in the order, and

(b) to allow any person described in the order, or secure that any person so described is allowed, to retain for safe keeping anything described in the order, and

---

[18] The validity of the *Anton Piller* order was recognised by the House of Lords in *Rank Film Distributors Ltd v Video Information Centre* [1982] AC 380. See also *Ex p Island Records* [1978] Ch 122; *Yousif v Salama* [1980] 1 WLR 1540; *Emanuel v Emanuel* [1982] 2 All ER 342; *Coca Cola v Gilbey* [1995] 4 All ER 711; *Tate Access Floors Inc v Boswell* [1991] Ch 512; *AT & T Istel Ltd v Tully* [1993] AC 45.

(6) An order under this section is to have effect subject to such conditions as are specified in the order.

(7) This section does not affect any right of a person to refuse to do anything on the ground that to do so might tend to expose him or his spouse or civil partner to proceedings for an offence or for the recovery of a penalty.

(8) In this section—

'court' means the High Court, and ' premises' includes any vehicle;

and an order under this section may describe anything generally, whether by reference to a class or otherwise.

The procedure for granting search orders and other related orders is governed by the Civil Procedure Rules.[19]

Civil Procedure Rule r 25.1

(1) The court may grant the following interim remedies: ...

   (c) an order—

     (i)   for the detention, custody or preservation of relevant property;

     (ii) for the inspection of relevant property;

     (iii) for the taking of a sample of relevant property;

     (iv) for the carrying out of an experiment on or with relevant property;

     (v) for the sale of relevant property which is of a perishable nature or which for any other good reason it is desirable to sell quickly; and

     (vi) for the payment of income from relevant property until a claim is decided;

   (d) an order authorising a person to enter any land or building in the possession of a party to the proceedings for the purposes of carrying out an order under sub-paragraph (c);

   (g) an order directing a party to provide information about the location of relevant property or assets or to provide information about relevant property or assets which are or may be the subject of an application for a freezing injunction;

   (h) an order (referred to as a 'search order') under section 7 of the Civil Procedure Act 1997 (order requiring a party to admit another party to premises for the purpose of preserving evidence etc);

   (i) an order under section 33 of the Supreme Court Act 1981 or section 52 of the County Courts Act 1984 (order for disclosure of documents or inspection of property before a claim has been made).

---

[19] See also CPR Practice Direction 25, paras. 7 and 8.

B PROCEDURAL SAFEGUARDS[20]

In **Columbia Picture Industries Inc v Robinson** [1987] Ch 38[21] the plaintiffs wished to sue the defendant for breach of copyright involving the sale of pirate videos from a particular shop. The plaintiffs were granted search and freezing orders. Items were seized from the defendant's premises including items which were not relevant to the breach of copyright claim. The defendant ceased trading. The defendant applied for the search order to be set aside and for damages. Scott J held that the plaintiffs had failed to make full and frank disclosure of all relevant matters and had acted oppressively in executing the order. Although it was too late to set the order aside, the plaintiffs were liable to compensate the defendant for the loss of his business. SCOTT J said at p. 70:

There is, accordingly, no doubt at all but that *Anton Piller* orders have become established as part of the tools of the administration of justice in civil cases. It may be thought, as, I think, Lord Denning MR thought, that they play a part not unlike that played by search warrants in the area of crime and suspected crime. But the legitimate purposes of *Anton Piller* orders are clearly identified by the leading cases which have established the legitimacy of their use. One, and perhaps the most usual purpose, is to preserve evidence necessary for the plaintiff's case. *Anton Piller* orders are used to prevent a defendant, when warned of impending litigation, from destroying all documentary evidence in his possession which might, were it available, support the plaintiff's cause of action. Secondly, *Anton Piller* orders are often used in order to track to its source and obtain the possession of the master tape or master plate or blueprint by means of which reproductions in breach of copyright are being made. This purpose is, perhaps, no more than a sub-division of the first.

It is implicit in the nature of *Anton Piller* orders that they should be applied for *ex parte* and dealt with by the courts in secrecy...

Anton Piller orders and procedure have, therefore, these characteristics: no notice to the defendant of what is afoot, and secrecy. A third and, perhaps, the most significant feature of *Anton Piller* orders is that they are mandatory in form and are designed for immediate execution. The respondent to the order is required by the order to permit his premises to be entered and searched and, under most if not all orders, to permit the plaintiff's solicitors to remove into the solicitors' custody articles covered by the order.

Further, *Anton Piller* orders are almost invariably accompanied by *Mareva* injunctions freezing the bank accounts of the respondent and restraining him from making any disposition of his assets. *Anton Piller* orders and *Mareva* injunctions granted *ex parte* always reserve liberty for the respondent to apply on short notice for them to be discharged. This provides a reasonable safeguard in the case of *Mareva* injunctions. They can be lifted on very short notice. Harm may already have been done but can be expected to be of a limited nature. But in relation to any *Anton Piller* order, the liberty to apply to have it discharged is of little, if any, value to the respondent. He does not know the order has been made until it has been served upon him. At the same time as the order is served, the respondent comes under an immediate obligation to consent to the entry onto and search of his premises and the removal of material from his premises

---

[20] See also *Hytrac Convevors Ltd v Conveyors International Ltd* [1983] 1 WLR 44; *Universal Thermosensors Ltd v Hibben* [1992] 3 All ER 257; Practice Direction [1994] 4 All ER 52, [1996] 1 WLR 1552.

[21] (1987) 4 CLJ 50 (N. Andrews); [1986] All ER Rev 225 (A. Zuckerman).

specified by the order. If he does not consent, he is at risk of committal to prison for contempt of court. This is so even if the reason for his refusal to consent is his intention to apply to have the order discharged...

A decision whether or not an *Anton Piller* order should be granted requires a balance to be struck between the plaintiff's need that the remedies allowed by the civil law for the breach of his rights should be attainable and the requirement of justice that a defendant should not be deprived of his property without being heard. What I have heard in the present case has disposed me to think that the practice of the court has allowed the balance to swing much too far in favour of plaintiffs and that *Anton Piller* orders have been too readily granted and with insufficient safeguards for respondents.

The draconian and essentially unfair nature of *Anton Piller* orders from the point of view of respondents against whom they are made requires, in my view, that they be so drawn as to extend no further than the minimum extent necessary to achieve the purpose for which they are granted, namely, the preservation of documents or articles which might otherwise be destroyed or concealed. Anything beyond that is, in my judgment, impossible to justify. For example, I do not understand how an order can be justified that allows the plaintiffs' solicitors to take and retain all relevant documentary material and correspondence. Once the plaintiffs' solicitors have satisfied themselves what material exists and have had an opportunity to take copies thereof, the material ought, in my opinion, to be returned to its owner. The material need be retained no more than a relatively short period of time for that purpose.

Secondly, I would think it essential that a detailed record of the material taken should always be required to be made by the solicitors who execute the order before the material is removed from the respondent's premises. So far as possible, disputes as to what material was taken, the resolution of which depends on the oral testimony and credibility of the solicitors on the one hand and the respondent on the other hand, ought to be avoided. In the absence of any corroboration of a respondent's allegation that particular material, for instance, divorce papers, was taken, a solicitor's sworn and apparently credible denial is likely always to be preferred. This state of affairs is unfair to respondents. It ought to be avoided so far as it can be.

Thirdly, no material should, in my judgment, be taken from the respondent's premises by the executing solicitors unless it is clearly covered by the terms of the order. In particular, I find it wholly unacceptable that a practice should have grown up whereby the respondent to the order is procured by the executing solicitors to give consent to additional material being removed. In view of the circumstances in which *Anton Piller* orders are customarily executed (the execution is often aptly called 'a raid'), I would not, for my part, be prepared to accept that an apparent consent by a respondent had been freely and effectively given unless the respondent's solicitor had been present to confirm and ensure that the consent was a free and informed one.

Fourthly, I find it inappropriate that seized material the ownership of which is in dispute, such as allegedly pirate tapes, should be retained by the plaintiffs' solicitors pending the trial. Although officers of the court, the main role of solicitors for plaintiffs is to act for the plaintiffs. If the proper administration of justice requires that material taken under an *Anton Piller* order from defendants should, pending trial, be kept from the defendants, then those responsible for the administration of justice might reasonably be expected to provide a neutral officer of the court charged with the custody of the material. In lieu of any such officer, and there is none at present, the plaintiffs' solicitors ought, in my view, as soon as solicitors for the defendants are on the record, to be required to deliver the material to the defendants' solicitors on their undertaking for its safe custody and production, if required, in court. Finally, the nature of

Anton Piller orders requires that the affidavits in support of applications for them ought to err on the side of excessive disclosure. In the case of material falling into the grey area of possible relevance, the judge, not the plaintiffs' solicitors, should be the judge of relevance.

In **Chappell v United Kingdom** (1990) 12 EHHR 1, the European Court of Justice held that the execution of a search order did not violate Article 8 of the European Convention on Human Rights. The defendant had been allowed to claim the privilege against self-incrimination[22] as a legitimate reason for refusing to comply with a search order.[23] Although this privilege is no longer available in the context of intellectual property disputes,[24] it may still be pleaded in respect of other disputes where the execution of the search order may assist with a criminal prosecution. However, in *C plc v P* [2007] EWCA Civ 493, [2007] 3 WLR 437[25] it was held that the privilege did not extend to documents or things which have 'an existence independent of the will' of the person who sought to plead it. It followed in that case that the privilege was not available to a defendant who had been required to hand over a computer to an independent expert pursuant to a search order, on the hard drive of which computer indecent images of children were found.

IV SPECIFIC PERFORMANCE[26]

A THE FUNCTION OF SPECIFIC PERFORMANCE

A different type of equitable remedy is that of specific performance: to require a party to perform a contractual obligation, but only where damages for breach of contract are inadequate.

Co-operative Insurance Society v Argyll Stores (Holdings) Ltd
[1998] AC 1 (HL) (**Lords Browne-Wilkinson, Slynn of Hadley, Hoffmann, Hope** and **Clyde)**[27]

The plaintiff granted the defendant a lease of a unit in a shopping centre in Sheffield. The defendant covenanted to keep the premises open for retail trade during usual business hours. After a business review the defendant announced that it would close the shop. The plaintiff sought specific performance of the covenant. The trial judge

---

[22] Civil Evidence Act 1968, s. 14.
[23] *Rank Film Distributors Ltd v Video Information Centre* [1982] AC 380.
[24] Supreme Court Act 1981, s. 72.   [25] (2007) 66 CLJ 528 (R. Moules).
[26] H&M, pp. 723–763; P&S, pp. 32–43; Pettit, pp. 661–691; Snell, pp. 345–377; Jones and Goodhart, *Specific Performance* (2nd edn, 1996); White and Tudor *Leading Cases in Equity* (9th edn, 1928), vol. ii, pp. 372 et seq.; Burrows, *Remedies for Torts and Breach of Contract* (3rd edn, 2004), Ch. 20.
[27] (1997) 56 CLJ 488 (G. Jones); (1998) 61 MLR 421 (A. Phang); [1998] Conv 396 (P. Luxton).

granted an order for damages but not specific performance. This was reversed by the Court of Appeal. The defendant appealed to the House of Lords.

Held. The court would not grant a mandatory injunction to require the business to be carried on.

Lord Hoffmann: A decree of specific performance is of course a discretionary remedy and the question for your Lordships is whether the Court of Appeal was entitled to set aside the exercise of the judge's discretion. There are well-established principles which govern the exercise of the discretion but these, like all equitable principles, are flexible and adaptable to achieve the ends of equity, which is, as Lord Selborne LC once remarked, to 'do more perfect and complete justice' than would be the result of leaving the parties to their remedies at common law: *Wilson v Northampton and Banbury Junction Railway Co.* (1874) LR 9 Ch App 279, 284. Much therefore depends upon the facts of the particular case and I shall begin by describing these in more detail.

[His Lordship described the facts and continued:] Specific performance is traditionally regarded in English law as an exceptional remedy, as opposed to the common law damages to which a successful plaintiff is entitled as of right. There may have been some element of later rationalisation of an untidier history, but by the 19th century it was orthodox doctrine that the power to decree specific performance was part of the discretionary jurisdiction of the Court of Chancery to do justice in cases in which the remedies available at common law were inadequate. This is the basis of the general principle that specific performance will not be ordered when damages are an adequate remedy. By contrast, in countries with legal systems based on civil law, such as France, Germany and Scotland, the plaintiff is *prima facie* entitled to specific performance. The cases in which he is confined to a claim for damages are regarded as the exceptions. In practice, however, there is less difference between common law and civilian systems than these general statements might lead one to suppose. The principles upon which English judges exercise the discretion to grant specific performance are reasonably well settled and depend upon a number of considerations, mostly of a practical nature, which are of very general application. I have made no investigation of civilian systems, but *a priori* I would expect that judges take much the same matters into account in deciding whether specific performance would be inappropriate in a particular case.

The practice of not ordering a defendant to carry on a business is not entirely dependent upon damages being an adequate remedy. In *Dowty Boulton Paul Ltd v Wolverhampton Corporation* [1971] 1 WLR 204 Sir John Pennycuick V-C refused to order the corporation to maintain an airfield as a going concern because: 'it is very well established that the court will not order specific performance of an obligation to carry on a business': see p. 211. He added: 'it is unnecessary in the circumstances to discuss whether damages would be an adequate remedy to the company': see p. 212. Thus the reasons which underlie the established practice may justify a refusal of specific performance even when damages are not an adequate remedy.

The most frequent reason given in the cases for declining to order someone to carry on a business is that it would require constant supervision by the court. In *JC Williamson Ltd v Lukey and Mulholland* (1931) 45 CLR 282, 297–298, Dixon J said flatly: 'specific performance is inapplicable when the continued supervision of the court is necessary in order to ensure the fulfilment of the contract'.

There has, I think, been some misunderstanding about what is meant by continued superintendence. It may at first sight suggest that the judge (or some other officer of the court) would literally have to supervise the execution of the order. In *CH Giles and Co Ltd v Morris* [1972] 1

WLR 307, 318 Megarry J said that 'difficulties of constant superintendence' were a 'narrow consideration' because: 'there is normally no question of the court having to send its officers to supervise the performance of the order... Performance... is normally secured by the realisation of the person enjoined that he is liable to be punished for contempt if evidence of his disobedience to the order is put before the court;...'

This is, of course, true but does not really meet the point. The judges who have said that the need for constant supervision was an objection to such orders were no doubt well aware that supervision would in practice take the form of rulings by the court, on applications made by the parties, as to whether there had been a breach of the order. It is the possibility of the court having to give an indefinite series of such rulings in order to ensure the execution of the order which has been regarded as undesirable.

Why should this be so? A principal reason is that, as Megarry J pointed out in the passage to which I have referred, the only means available to the court to enforce its order is the quasi-criminal procedure of punishment for contempt. This is a powerful weapon; so powerful, in fact, as often to be unsuitable as an instrument for adjudicating upon the disputes which may arise over whether a business is being run in accordance with the terms of the court's order. The heavy-handed nature of the enforcement mechanism is a consideration which may go to the exercise of the court's discretion in other cases as well, but its use to compel the running of a business is perhaps the paradigm case of its disadvantages and it is in this context that I shall discuss them.

The prospect of committal or even a fine, with the damage to commercial reputation which will be caused by a finding of contempt of court, is likely to have at least two undesirable consequences. First, the defendant, who *ex hypothesi* did not think that it was in his economic interest to run the business at all, now has to make decisions under a sword of Damocles which may descend if the way the business is run does not conform to the terms of the order. This is, as one might say, no way to run a business. In this case the Court of Appeal made light of the point because it assumed that, once the defendant had been ordered to run the business, self-interest and compliance with the order would thereafter go hand in hand. But, as I shall explain, this is not necessarily true.

Secondly, the seriousness of a finding of contempt for the defendant means that any application to enforce the order is likely to be a heavy and expensive piece of litigation. The possibility of repeated applications over a period of time means that, in comparison with a once-and-for-all inquiry as to damages, the enforcement of the remedy is likely to be expensive in terms of cost to the parties and the resources of the judicial system.

This is a convenient point at which to distinguish between orders which require a defendant to carry on an activity, such as running a business over a more or less extended period of time, and orders which require him to achieve a result. The possibility of repeated applications for rulings on compliance with the order which arises in the former case does not exist to anything like the same extent in the latter. Even if the achievement of the result is a complicated matter which will take some time, the court, if called upon to rule, only has to examine the finished work and say whether it complies with the order...

This distinction between orders to carry on activities and orders to achieve results explains why the courts have in appropriate circumstances ordered specific performance of building contracts and repairing covenants: see *Wolverhampton Corporation v Emmons* [1901] 1 KB 515 (building contract) and *Jeune v Queens Cross Properties Ltd* [1974] Ch 97 (repairing covenant). It by no means follows, however, that even obligations to achieve a result will always be enforced by specific performance. There may be other objections, to some of which I now turn.

One such objection, which applies to orders to achieve a result and *a fortiori* to orders to carry on an activity, is imprecision in the terms of the order. If the terms of the court's order, reflecting the terms of the obligation, cannot be precisely drawn, the possibility of wasteful litigation over compliance is increased. So is the oppression caused by the defendant having to do things under threat of proceedings for contempt. The less precise the order, the fewer the signposts to the forensic minefield which he has to traverse. . . .

Precision is of course a question of degree and the courts have shown themselves willing to cope with a certain degree of imprecision in cases of orders requiring the achievement of a result in which the plaintiffs' merits appeared strong; like all the reasons which I have been discussing, it is, taken alone, merely a discretionary matter to be taken into account: see Spry, *Equitable Remedies,* 4th ed. (1990), p. 112. It is, however, a very important one . . .

There is a further objection to an order requiring the defendant to carry on a business, which was emphasised by Millett LJ in the Court of Appeal. This is that it may cause injustice by allowing the plaintiff to enrich himself at the defendant's expense. The loss which the defendant may suffer through having to comply with the order (for example, by running a business at a loss for an indefinite period) may be far greater than the plaintiff would suffer from the contract being broken. As Professor R.J. Sharpe explains in 'Specific Relief for Contract Breach', ch. 5 of *Studies in Contract Law* (1980), edited by Reiter and Swan, p. 129:

> 'In such circumstances, a specific decree in favour of the plaintiff will put him in a bargaining position *vis-à-vis* the defendant whereby the measure of what he will receive will be the value to the defendant of being released from performance. If the plaintiff bargains effectively, the amount he will set will exceed the value to him of performance and will approach the cost to the defendant to complete.'

This was the reason given by Lord Westbury LC in *Isenberg v East India House Estate Co. Ltd.* (1863) 3 De GJ & S 263, 273 for refusing a mandatory injunction to compel the defendant to pull down part of a new building which interfered with the plaintiff's light and exercising instead the Court of Chancery's recently-acquired jurisdiction under Lord Cairns's Act 1858 [Chancery Amendment Act 1858—p. 1037, below], to order payment of damages:

> '. . . I hold it . . . to be the duty of the court in such a case as the present not, by granting a mandatory injunction, to deliver over the defendants to the plaintiff bound hand and foot, in order to be made subject to any extortionate demand that he may by possibility make, but to substitute for such mandatory injunction an inquiry before itself, in order to ascertain the measure of damage that has been actually sustained.'

It is true that the defendant has, by his own breach of contract, put himself in such an unfortunate position. But the purpose of the law of contract is not to punish wrongdoing but to satisfy the expectations of the party entitled to performance. A remedy which enables him to secure, in money terms, more than the performance due to him is unjust. From a wider perspective, it cannot be in the public interest for the courts to require someone to carry on business at a loss if there is any plausible alternative by which the other party can be given compensation. It is not only a waste of resources but yokes the parties together in a continuing hostile relationship. The order for specific performance prolongs the battle. If the defendant is ordered to run a business, its conduct becomes the subject of a flow of complaints, solicitors' letters and affidavits. This is wasteful for both parties and the legal system. An award of damages, on the other hand, brings the litigation to an end. The defendant pays damages, the forensic link between them is severed, they go their separate ways and the wounds of conflict can heal.

B RESTRICTIONS ON SPECIFIC PERFORMANCE

In **Hill v C.A. Parsons & Co Ltd** [1972] Ch 305 LORD DENNING MR said at p. 314:

Suppose, however, that the master insists on the employment terminating on the named day? What is the consequence in law? In the ordinary course of things, the relationship of master and servant thereupon comes to an end: for it is inconsistent with the confidential nature of the relationship that it should continue contrary to the will of one of the parties thereto. As Viscount Kilmuir LC said in *Vine v National Dock Labour Board* [1957] AC 488, referring at p. 500 to the *ordinary* master and servant case: 'if the master wrongfully dismisses the servant, either summarily or by giving insufficient notice, the employment is effectively terminated, albeit in breach of contract'. Accordingly, the servant cannot claim specific performance of the contract of employment. Nor can he claim wages as such after the relationship has been determined. He is left to his remedy in damages against the master for breach of the contract to continue the relationship for the contractual period. He gets damages for the time he would have served if he had been given proper notice, less, of course, anything he has, or ought to have earned, in alternative employment... I would emphasise, however, that that is the consequence in the *ordinary* course of things. The rule is not inflexible. It permits of exceptions. The court can in a proper case grant a declaration that the relationship still subsists and an injunction to stop the master treating it as at an end.... Let me give an example taken from the decided cases. Suppose that a senior servant has a service agreement with a company under which he is employed for five years certain—and, in return, so long as he is in the service, he is entitled to a free house and coal—and at the end to a pension from a pension fund to which he and his employers have contributed. Now, suppose that, when there is only six months to go, the company, without any justification or excuse, gives him notice to terminate his service at the end of three months. I think it plain that the court would grant an injunction restraining the company from treating the notice as terminating his service. If the company did not want him to come to work, the court would not order the company to give him work. But, so long as he was ready and willing to serve the company, whenever they required his services, the court would order the company to do their part of the agreement, that is, allow him his free house and coal, and enable him to qualify for the pension fund.... It may be said that, by granting an injunction in such a case, the court is indirectly enforcing specifically a contract for personal services. So be it. Lord St. Leonards did something like it in *Lumley v Wagner* (1852) 1 De GM & G 604 and I see no reason why we should not do it here.

In **Beswick v Beswick** [1968] AC 58 the House of Lords considered whether it was possible specifically to perform a contract to pay money. In that case the defendant had agreed with his uncle that, in exchange for receiving his uncle's coal business, he would pay his uncle a weekly sum and, on his uncle's death, he would pay an annuity to his uncle's widow. On his uncle's death the defendant failed to pay his aunt. She sued the defendant in her personal capacity and as administratrix of her husband's estate. In holding that the contractual obligation could be enforced, LORD UPJOHN said:

But surely on a number of grounds this is a case for specific performance.

First, here is the sale of a business for full consideration wholly executed on A's part who has put C into possession of all the assets. C is repudiating the obligations to be performed by him. To such a case the words of Kay J in *Hart v Hart* [1881] 18 Ch D 670, 685 are particularly appropriate:

> '...when an agreement for valuable consideration between two parties has been partially performed, the court ought to do its utmost to carry out that agreement by a decree for specific performance.'

The fact that A by the agreement was to render such services as consultant as he might find convenient or at his own absolute discretion should decide may be ignored as *de minimis* and the contrary was not argued. In any event the fact that there is a small element of personal service in a contract of this nature does not destroy that quality of mutuality (otherwise plainly present) want of which may in general terms properly be a ground for refusing a decree of specific performance. See, for example, *Fortescue v Lostwithiel and Fowey Railway Co* [1894] 3 Ch 621.

In the courts below, though not before your Lordships, it was argued that the remedy of specific performance was not available when all that remained was the obligation to make a money payment. Danckwerts LJ rightly demolished this contention as untenable for the reasons he gives: [1967] Ch 538, 560–561.

But when the money payment is not made once and for all but in the nature of an annuity there is an even greater need for equity to come to the assistance of the common law. Equity is to do true justice to enforce the true contract that the parties have made and to prevent the trouble and expense of a multiplicity of actions. This has been well settled for over a century: *Swift v Swift* (1841) 3 Ir Eq R 267. In that case an annuity of £40 p.a. was payable to a lady quarterly and Lord Plunket LC enforced specific performance of it. He said, ibid 275–276:

> 'It is said she has a complete remedy at law for the breach of this contract, and that, therefore, this court should not interfere. Now, the remedy at law could only be obtained in one of two ways, either by at once recovering damages for all the breaches that might occur during the joint lives of herself and the defendant, or by bringing four actions in each year, and recovering in each the amount of a quarterly payment of the annuity. Those are the two modes of redress open to the plaintiff at law and I am called on to refuse relief here on the ground that such remedies are equally beneficial and effectual for the plaintiff as that which this court could afford. To refuse relief on such a ground would not, in my opinion, be a rational administration of justice. I do not see that there is any authority for refusing relief, and certainly there is no foundation in reason for doing so.'

Then, after referring to the case of *Adderley v Dixon* (1824) 1 Sim & St 607 he continued, at 276–277:

> 'Applying this to the present case, leaving the plaintiff to proceed at law and to get damages at once for all the breaches that might occur during the joint lives of her and the defendant, would, in effect, be altering the entire nature of the contract that she entered into: it would be compelling her to accept a certain sum, a sum to be ascertained by the conjecture of a jury as to what was the value of the annuity. This would be most unreasonable and unjust: her contract was for the periodical payment of certain sums during an uncertain period; she was entitled to a certain sum of money, and she agreed to give up that for an annuity for her own and the defendant's lives, and to insist on her now accepting a certain sum of money in the shape of damages for it, would be in effect to make her convert into money, what she, having in money, exchanged for an annuity. As to her resorting four times every year to a Court of Law for each quarterly payment of this annuity, it is a manifest absurdity to call that a beneficial or effectual remedy for the plaintiff; and resting the case on that ground alone, I think I am warranted by the highest authority in granting the relief sought.'

It is in such common-sense and practical ways that equity comes to the aid of the common law and it is sufficiently flexible to meet and satisfy the justice of the case in the many different circumstances that arise from time to time.

To sum up this matter: had C repudiated the contract in the lifetime of A the latter would have had a cast-iron case for specific performance. Can it make any difference that by the terms of the agreement C is obliged to pay the annuity after A's death to B? Of course not. On the principle I have just stated it is clear that there can be nothing to prevent equity in A's specific-performance action making an appropriate decree for specific performance directing payment of the annuity to A but during his life and thereafter to B for her life.[28]

V DAMAGES IN LIEU OF
EQUITABLE ORDERS[29]

The jurisdiction to grant damages in lieu of ordering injunctions or specific perform-ance was available under section 2 of the **Chancery Amendment Act 1858**:

In all cases in which the Court of Chancery has jurisdiction to entertain an application for an injunction against a breach of any covenant, contract, or agreement, or against the commission or continuance of any wrongful act, or for the specific performance of any covenant, contract, or agreement, it shall be lawful for the same court, if it shall think fit, to award damages to the party injured, either in addition to or in substitution for such injunction or specific performance, and such damages may be assessed in such manner as the court shall direct.

This jurisdiction has now been replaced by section 50 of the **Supreme Court Act 1981**.

In **Jaggard v Sawyer** [1995] 1 WLR 269[30] the defendant built a house in a private cul-de-sac, the access to which involved breach of a covenant. The plaintiff, one of nine residents who had entered into the covenant with the defendant, sought an injunction to restrain the defendant's continuing breach of covenant and trespass. The trial judge considered that it would be oppressive to grant the order, but damages were awarded in lieu of the injunction. These were assessed as one-ninth of what the defendant might reasonably have been required to pay the residents for release of the covenant. The plaintiff's appeal against this award was dismissed. MILLETT LJ said at p. 283:

This appeal raises yet again the questions: what approach should the court adopt when invited to exercise its statutory jurisdiction to award damages instead of granting an injunction to restrain a threatened or continuing trespass or breach of a restrictive covenant? And if the court accedes to the invitation on what basis should damages be assessed?

Before considering these questions, it is desirable to state some general propositions which are established by the authorities and which are, or at least ought to be, uncontroversial.

---

[28] Now see Contracts (Rights of Third) Parties Act 1999, p. 169, above.

[29] H&M, pp. 755–758, 808–816; P&S, pp. 43–44, 48–51; Pettit, 580–587; (1975) CLJ 224 (J. A. Jolowicz); [1981] Conv 286 (T. Ingman and J. Wakefield).   [30] See also *Bracewell v Appleby* [1975] Ch 408.

(1) The jurisdiction was originally conferred by section 2 of the Chancery Amendment Act 1858, commonly known as Lord Cairns's Act. It is now to be found in section 50 of the Supreme Court Act 1981. It is a jurisdiction to award damages 'in addition to or in substitution for such injunction or specific performance'.

(2) The principal object of Lord Cairns's Act is well known. It was described by Turner LJ in *Ferguson v Wilson* (1866) LR 2 Ch App 77, 88. It was to enable the Court of Chancery, when declining to grant equitable relief and leaving the plaintiff to his remedy at law, to award the plaintiff damages itself instead of sending him to the common law courts to obtain them. From the very first, however, it was recognised that the Act did more than this. The jurisdiction of the Court of Chancery was wider than that of the common law courts, for it could give relief where there was no cause of action at law. As early as 1863, Turner LJ himself had recognised the potential effect of Lord Cairns's Act. In *Eastwood v Lever* (1863) 4 De GJ & S 114, 128, he pointed out that the Act had empowered the courts of equity to award damages in cases where the common law courts could not. The Act, he said, was not 'confined to cases in which the plaintiffs could recover damages at law'. Damages at common law are recoverable only in respect of causes of action which are complete at the date of the writ; damages for future or repeated wrongs must be made the subject of fresh proceedings. Damages in substitution for an injunction, however, relate to the future, not the past. They inevitably extend beyond the damages to which the plaintiff may be entitled at law. In *Leeds Industrial Co-operative Society Ltd v Slack* [1924] AC 851 the House of Lords confirmed the jurisdiction of the courts to award damages under the Act in respect of an injury which was threatened but had not yet occurred. No such damages could have been awarded at common law.

(3) The nature of the cause of action is immaterial; it may be in contract or tort. Lord Cairns's Act referred in terms to 'a breach of any covenant, contract, or agreement, or against the commission or continuance of any wrongful act'. The jurisdiction to award damages in substitution for an injunction has most commonly been exercised in cases where the defendant's building has infringed the plaintiff's right to light or where it has been erected in breach of a restrictive covenant. Despite dicta to the contrary in *Woollerton and Wilson Ltd v Richard Costain Ltd* [1970] 1 WLR 411 there is in my opinion no justification for excluding cases of threatened or continuing trespass on the ground that trespass is actionable at law without proof of actual damage. Equitable relief, whether by way of injunction or damages under Lord Cairns's Act, is available because the common law remedy is inadequate; but the common law remedy of damages in cases of continuing trespass is inadequate not because the damages are likely to be small or nominal but because they cover the past only and not the future.

(4) The power to award damages under Lord Cairns's Act arises whenever the court 'has jurisdiction to entertain an application' for an injunction or specific performance. This question must be determined as at the date of the writ. If the court would then have had jurisdiction to grant an injunction, it has jurisdiction to award damages instead. When the court comes to consider whether to grant an injunction or award damages instead, of course, it must do so by reference to the circumstances as they exist at the date of the hearing.

(5) The former question is effectively one of jurisdiction. The question is whether, at the date of the writ, the court *could* have granted an injunction, not whether it *would* have done: *City of London Brewery Co v Tennant* (1873) LR 9 Ch App 212. Russell LJ put it neatly in *Hooper v Rogers* [1975] Ch 43, 48 when he said that the question was 'whether...the judge could have (however unwisely...) made a mandatory order'. There have been numerous cases where

damages under Lord Cairns's Act were refused because at the date of the writ it was impossible to grant an injunction or specific performance: for one well known example, see *Lavery v Pursell* (1888) 39 Ch D 508. The recent case of *Surrey County Council v Bredero Homes Ltd* [1993] 1 WLR 1361 appears to have been a case of this character.

(6) It is not necessary for the plaintiff to include a claim for damages in his writ. As long ago as 1868 Lord Chelmsford LC held that damages may be awarded under Lord Cairns's Act 'though not specifically prayed for by the bill, the statute having vested a discretion in the judge, which he may exercise when he thinks the case fitting without the prayer of the party': see *Betts v Neilson* (1868) LR 3 Ch App 429, 441.

It would be absurd as well as misleading to insist on the plaintiff including a claim for damages in his writ when he is insisting on his right to an injunction and opposing the defendant's claim that he should be content to receive damages instead. By a parity of reasoning it is not in my opinion necessary for a plaintiff to include a claim for an injunction in order to found a claim for damages under the Act. It would be absurd to require him to include a claim for an injunction if he is sufficiently realistic to recognise that in the circumstances he is unlikely to obtain one and intends from the first to ask the court for damages instead. But he ought to make it clear whether he is claiming damages for past injury at common law or under the Act in substitution for an injunction.

(7) In *Anchor Brewhouse Developments Ltd. v Berkley House (Docklands Developments) Ltd* (1987) 38 BLR 87 Scott J granted an injunction to restrain a continuing trespass. In the course of his judgment, however, he cast doubt on the power of the court to award damages for future trespasses by means of what he described as a 'once-and-for-all payment'. This was because, as he put it, the court could not by an award of damages put the defendant in the position of a person entitled to an easement; whether or not an injunction were granted, the defendant's conduct would still constitute a trespass; and a succession of further actions for damages could accordingly still be brought. This reasoning strikes at the very heart of the statutory jurisdiction; it is in marked contrast to the attitude of the many judges who from the very first have recognised that, while the Act does not enable the court to license future wrongs, this may be the practical result of withholding injunctive relief; and it is inconsistent with the existence of the jurisdiction, confirmed in *Leeds Industrial Co-operative Society Ltd v Slack* [1924] AC 851, to award damages under the Act in a *quia timet* action. It is in my view fallacious because it is not the award of damages which has the practical effect of licensing the defendant to commit the wrong, but the refusal of injunctive relief. Thereafter the defendant may have no right to act in the manner complained of, but he cannot be prevented from doing so. The court can in my judgment properly award damages 'once and for all' in respect of future wrongs because it awards them in substitution for an injunction and to compensate for those future wrongs which an injunction would have prevented. The doctrine of *res judicata* operates to prevent the plaintiff and his successors in title from bringing proceedings thereafter to recover even nominal damages in respect of further wrongs for which the plaintiff has been fully compensated.

It has always been recognised that the practical consequence of withholding injunctive relief is to authorise the continuance of an unlawful state of affairs. If, for example, the defendant threatens to build in such a way that the plaintiff's light will be obstructed and he is not restrained, then the plaintiff will inevitably be deprived of his legal right. This was the very basis upon which before 1858 the Court of Chancery had made the remedy of injunction available in such cases. After the passing of Lord Cairns's Act many of the judges warned that the jurisdiction to award damages instead of an injunction should not be exercised as a matter of course so as to legalise the commission of a tort by any defendant who was willing and able to pay compensation. In *Shelfer v City of London Electric Lighting Co* [1895] 1 Ch 287, 315–316 Lindley LJ said:

> 'But in exercising the jurisdiction thus given attention ought to be paid to well-settled principles; and ever since Lord Cairns's Act was passed the Court of Chancery has repudiated the notion that the legislature intended to turn that court into a tribunal for legalizing wrongful acts; or in other words, the court has always protested against the notion that it ought to allow a wrong to continue simply because the wrongdoer is able and willing to pay for the injury he may inflict.'

and Buckley J said in *Cowper v Laidler* [1903] 2 Ch 337, 341:

> 'The court has affirmed over and over again that the jurisdiction to give damages where it exists is not so to be used as in fact to enable the defendant to purchase from the plaintiff against his will his legal right to the easement.'

The plaintiff is, therefore, in good company when she says in her skeleton argument (prepared when she was acting in person):

> 'What Judge Jack has in effect done in his judgment is to grant Mr. and Mrs. Sawyer a right of way in perpetuity over my land for a once-and-for-all payment. I do not understand how the court can have power to produce such a result as it effectively expropriates my property...Ashleigh Avenue is a private roadway and Judge Jack has turned it into a public highway. Surely he does not have the jurisdiction to do this?'

It will be of small comfort to her to be told that the jurisdiction is undoubted, though it is to be exercised with caution. What does need to be stressed, however, is that the consequences to which the plaintiff refers do not result from the judge's exercise of the statutory jurisdiction to award damages instead of an injunction, but from his refusal to grant an injunction. Lord Cairns's Act did not worsen the plaintiff's position but improved it. Thenceforth, if injunctive relief was withheld, the plaintiff was not compelled to wait until further wrongs were committed and then bring successive actions for damages; he could be compensated by a once-and-for-all payment to cover future as well as past wrongs. Of course, the ability to do 'complete justice' in this way made it easier for the courts to withhold the remedy of an injunction, and it was therefore necessary for the judges to remind themselves from time to time that the discretion to withhold it, which had existed as well before 1858 as after it, was to be exercised in accordance with settled principles; that a plaintiff who had established both a legal right and a threat to infringe it was *prima facie* entitled to an injunction to protect it; and that special circumstances were needed to justify withholding the injunction.

Nevertheless references to the 'expropriation' of the plaintiff's property are somewhat overdone, not because that is not the practical effect of withholding an injunction, but because the grant of an injunction, like all equitable remedies, is discretionary. Many proprietary rights cannot be protected at all by the common law. The owner must submit to unlawful interference with his rights and be content with damages. If he wants to be protected he must seek equitable relief, and he has no absolute right to that. In many cases, it is true, an injunction will be granted almost as of course; but this is not always the case, and it will never be granted if this would cause injustice to the defendant. Citation of passages in the cases warning of the danger of 'expropriating' the plaintiff needs to be balanced by reference to statements like that of Lord

Westbury LC in *Isenberg v East India House Estate Co Ltd* (1863) 3 De GJ & S 263, 273 where he held that it was the duty of the court not

> 'by granting a mandatory injunction, to deliver over the defendants to the plaintiff bound hand and foot, in order to be made subject to any extortionate demand that he may by possibility make, but to substitute for such mandatory injunction an inquiry before itself, in order to ascertain the measure of damage that has been actually sustained.'

When the plaintiff claims an injunction and the defendant asks the court to award damages instead, the proper approach for the court to adopt cannot be in doubt. Clearly the plaintiff must first establish a case for equitable relief, not only by proving his legal right and an actual or threatened infringement by the defendant, but also by overcoming all equitable defences such as laches, acquiescence or estoppel. If he succeeds in doing this, he is *prima facie* entitled to an injunction. The court may nevertheless in its discretion withhold injunctive relief and award damages instead. How is this discretion to be exercised? In a well known passage in *Shelfer v City of London Electic Lighting Co* [1895] 1 Ch 287, 322–323, AL Smith LJ set out what he described as 'a good working rule' that

> '(1) If the injury to the plaintiff's legal right is small,
> (2) and is one which is capable of being estimated in money,
> (3) and is one which can be adequately compensated by a small money payment,
> (4) and the case is one in which it would be oppressive to the defendant to grant an injunction:—
>   then damages in substitution for an injunction may be given.'

Laid down just 100 years ago, AL Smith LJ's check-list has stood the test of time; but it needs to be remembered that it is only a working rule and does not purport to be an exhaustive statement of the circumstances in which damages may be awarded instead of an injunction.

Reported cases are merely illustrations of circumstances in which particular judges have exercised their discretion, in some cases by granting an injunction, and in others by awarding damages instead. Since they are all cases on the exercise of a discretion, none of them is a binding authority on how the discretion should be exercised. The most that any of them can demonstrate is that in similar circumstances it would not be wrong to exercise the discretion in the same way. But it does not follow that it would be wrong to exercise it differently.

The outcome of any particular case usually turns on the question: would it in all the circumstances be oppressive to the defendant to grant the injunction to which the plaintiff is *prima facie* entitled? Most of the cases in which the injunction has been refused are cases where the plaintiff has sought a mandatory injunction to pull down a building which infringes his right to light or which has been built in breach of a restrictive covenant. In such cases the court is faced with a *fait accompli*. The jurisdiction to grant a mandatory injunction in those circumstances cannot be doubted, but to grant it would subject the defendant to a loss out of all proportion to that which would be suffered by the plaintiff if it were refused, and would indeed deliver him to the plaintiff bound hand and foot to be subjected to any extortionate demands the plaintiff might make. In the present case, as in the closely similar case of *Bracewell v Appleby* [1975] Ch 408, the plaintiff sought a prohibitory injunction to restrain the use of a road giving access to the defendants' house. The result of granting the injunction would be much the same; the house would not have to be pulled down, but it would be rendered landlocked and incapable of beneficial enjoyment.

In the cases of oversailing cranes and other trespasses to the plaintiff's airspace, on the other hand, the court has not been faced with a similar *fait accompli*. The grant of an injunction would merely restore the parties to the same position, with each of them enjoying the same bargaining strength, that they had enjoyed before the trespass began.

[His Lordship considered *Goodson v Richardson* (1974) LR 9 Ch App 221, and continued:] In considering whether the grant of an injunction would be oppressive to the defendant, all the circumstances of the case have to be considered. At one extreme, the defendant may have acted openly and in good faith and in ignorance of the plaintiff's rights, and thereby inadvertently placed himself in a position where the grant of an injunction would either force him to yield to the plaintiff's extortionate demands or expose him to substantial loss. At the other extreme, the defendant may have acted with his eyes open and in full knowledge that he was invading the plaintiff's rights, and hurried on his work in the hope that by presenting the court with a *fait accompli* he could compel the plaintiff to accept monetary compensation. Most cases, like the present, fall somewhere in between.

In the present case, the defendants acted openly and in good faith and in the not unreasonable belief that they were entitled to make use of Ashleigh Avenue for access to the house that they were building. At the same time, they had been warned by the plaintiff and her solicitors that Ashleigh Avenue was a private road, that they were not entitled to use it for access to the new house, and that it would be a breach of covenant for them to use the garden of No. 5 to gain access to No. 5A. They went ahead, not with their eyes open, but at their own risk. On the other hand, the plaintiff did not seek interlocutory relief at a time when she would almost certainly have obtained it. She should not be criticised for that, but it follows that she also took a risk, namely, that by the time her case came on for trial the court would be presented with a *fait accompli*. The case was a difficult one, but in an exemplary judgment the judge took into account all the relevant considerations, both those which told in favour of granting an injunction and those which told against, and in the exercise of his discretion he decided to refuse it. In my judgment his conclusion cannot be faulted.

Having decided to refuse an injunction and to award the plaintiff damages instead, the judge had to consider the measure of damages. He based them on her share of the amount which, in his opinion, the plaintiff and the other residents of Ashleigh Avenue could reasonably have demanded as the price of waiving their rights. In this he applied the measure of damages which had been adopted by Brightman J in *Wrotham Park Estate Co Ltd v Parkside Homes Ltd* [1974] 1 WLR 798, a case which has frequently been followed. It would not be necessary to consider this matter further but for the fact that in the recent case in this court of *Surrey County Council v Bredero Homes Ltd.* [1993] 1 WLR 1361 doubts were expressed as to the basis on which this measure of damages could be justified and whether it was consistent with the reasoning of Lord Wilberforce in *Johnson v Agnew* [1980] AC 367. It is, therefore, necessary to examine those cases further.

In *Surrey County Council v Bredero Homes Ltd* [1993] 1 WLR 1361 the plaintiffs claimed damages from the original covenantor, a developer, for breach of a restrictive covenant against building more than 72 houses, and sought to measure the damages by reference to the additional profit which the defendant had made by building the extra houses. Their claim to substantial damages failed. The case is not authority on the proper measure of damages under Lord Cairns's Act, since (as Dillon LJ made clear, at p. 1367C) the plaintiffs' claim was for damages at common law and not under the Act. Unfortunately, he did not make it clear why this was so. He said, at p. 1364:

'The plaintiffs therefore seek damages. They have never sought an interim injunction to restrain the defendant from developing the land otherwise than in accordance with the first planning permission. They never sought an injunction at the trial requiring the defendant to pull down the completed houses. They recognised that there was never any practical possibility of such an injunction being granted.'

If this is to be understood as meaning that the plaintiffs were confined to their remedy at law because they had not included a claim to an injunction in the writ, or because there never was any practical possibility, whether at the date of the writ or at the date of the trial, of obtaining an injunction, then I cannot agree with it. But examination of the facts stated in the headnote reveals that the defendant had disposed of all the houses on the estate before the plaintiffs commenced proceedings, and that the purchasers were not joined as parties. Any claim to damages under Lord Cairns's Act must have failed; at the date of the writ the court could not have ordered the defendant to pull down the houses, since this was no longer something which was within its power to do.

Unfortunately, however, Dillon LJ cast doubt on the correctness of the measure of damages which had been adopted by Brightman J in *Wrotham Park Estate Co Ltd v Parkside Homes Ltd* [1974] 1 WLR 798, a case which was decided under Lord Cairns's Act. He said [1993] 1 WLR 1361, 1366:

'The difficulty about the decision in the *Wrotham Park* case is that in *Johnson v Agnew* [1980] AC 367, 400G, Lord Wilberforce, after citing certain decisions on the scope and basis of Lord Cairns's Act which were not cited to Brightman J, stated in the clearest terms that on the balance of those authorities and on principle he found in the Act no warrant for the court awarding damages differently from common law damages.'

Johnson v Agnew concerned a contract for the sale of land. The vendor obtained a decree of specific performance with which the purchaser failed to comply. The vendor's mortgagees then sold the land. The vendor was compelled to return to the court and ask it to dissolve the decree and award her damages instead. At first instance she was refused damages, but in this court she was awarded damages under Lord Cairns's Act by reference to the value of the land at the date when specific performance became impossible. An appeal by the purchaser to the House of Lords failed. Before the House of Lords neither party argued that the measure of damages under Lord Cairns's Act differed from the measure of damages at common law: see [1980] AC 367, 379B–C, 387A, F. The vendor placed no reliance on the wording of section 2 of the Act which provided that damages might be assessed 'in such manner as the court shall direct' which, as Lord Wilberforce explained, referred only to procedure. Where the parties differed was whether the damages, whether at common law or under the Act, had invariably to be measured by reference to the value of the land ascertained at the date of the breach of contract.

In the course of his speech Lord Wilberforce referred, at p. 400E–F, to the view expressed by Megarry J in *Wroth v Tyler* [1974] Ch 30 that the words 'in substitution for specific performance' allowed the court to assess damages under the Act as on the date when specific performance could have been ordered, that is to say as at the date of the judgment of the court, and said that if that was intended to establish a different basis from that applicable at common law then he could not agree with it.

This statement must not be taken out of context. Earlier in his speech Lord Wilberforce had clearly recognised that damages could be awarded under Lord Cairns's Act where there was no cause of action at law, and he cannot have been insensible to the fact that, when the court awards damages in substitution for an injunction, it seeks to compensate the plaintiff for loss arising from future wrongs, that is to say, loss for which the common law does not provide a remedy. Neither *Wroth v Tyler* nor *Johnson v Agnew* [1980] AC 367 was a case of this kind. In each of those cases the plaintiff claimed damages for loss occasioned by a single, once-and-for-all, past breach of contract on the part of the defendant. In neither case was the breach a continuing one capable of generating further losses. In my view Lord Wilberforce's statement that the measure of damages is the same whether damages are recoverable at common law or under the Act must be taken to be limited to the case where they are recoverable in respect of the same cause of action. It cannot sensibly have any application where the claim at common law is in respect of a past trespass or breach of covenant and that under the Act is in respect of future trespasses or continuing breaches of covenant.

> 'In my view *Wrotham Park Estate Co Ltd v Parkside Homes Ltd* [1974] 1 WLR 798 is only defensible on the basis of the third or restitutionary principle... The plaintiffs' argument that the *Wrotham Park* case can be justified on the basis of a loss of bargaining opportunity is a fiction.'[31]

I find these remarks puzzling. It is plain from his judgment in the *Wrotham Park* case that Brightman J's approach was compensatory, not restitutionary. He sought to measure the damages by reference to what the plaintiff had lost, not by reference to what the defendant had gained. He did not award the plaintiff the profit which the defendant had made by the breach, but the amount which he judged the plaintiff might have obtained as the price of giving its consent. The amount of the profit which the defendant expected to make was a relevant factor in that assessment, but that was all.

Both the *Wrotham Park* and *Bredero Homes* cases (unlike the present) were concerned with a single past breach of covenant, so that the measure of damages at common law and under the Act was the same. *Prima facie* the measure of damages in either case for breach of a covenant not to build a house on neighbouring land is the diminution in the value of the plaintiff's land occasioned by the breach. One element in the value of the plaintiff's land immediately before the breach is attributable to his ability to obtain an injunction to prevent the building. Clearly a defendant who wished to build would pay for the release of the covenant, but only so long as the court could still protect it by the grant of an injunction. The proviso is important. It is the ability to claim an injunction which gives the benefit of the covenant much of its value. If the plaintiff delays proceedings until it is no longer possible for him to obtain an injunction, he destroys his own bargaining position and devalues his right. The unavailability of the remedy of injunction at one and the same time deprives the court of jurisdiction to award damages under the Act and removes the basis for awarding substantial damages at common law. For this reason, I take the view that damages can be awarded at common law in accordance with the approach adopted in the *Wrotham Park* case, but in practice only in the circumstances in which they could also be awarded under the Act.

This may be what Steyn LJ had in mind when he said that the loss of bargaining opportunity was a fiction. If he meant it generally or in relation to the facts which obtained in the *Wrotham*

---

[31] *Surrey County Council v Bredero Homes Ltd.* [1993] 1 WLR 1361, 000 (Steyn LJ).

Park case, then I respectfully disagree. But it was true in the circumstances of the case before him, and not merely for the reason given by Rose LJ (that the plaintiffs did not object to the extra houses and would have waived the breach for a nominal sum). The plaintiffs did not bring the proceedings until after the defendant had sold the houses and was no longer susceptible to an injunction. The plaintiffs had thereby deprived themselves of any bargaining position. Unable to obtain an injunction, they were equally unable to invoke the jurisdiction to award damages under Lord Cairns's Act. No longer exposed to the risk of an injunction, and having successfully disposed of the houses, the defendant had no reason to pay anything for the release of the covenant. Unless they were able to recover damages in accordance with restitutionary principles, neither at common law nor in equity could the plaintiffs recover more than nominal damages.

In the present case the plaintiff brought proceedings at a time when her rights were still capable of being protected by injunction. She has accordingly been able to invoke the court's jurisdiction to award in substitution for an injunction damages which take account of the future as well as the past. In my view there is no reason why compensatory damages for future trespasses and continuing breaches of covenant should not reflect the value of the rights which she has lost, or why such damages should not be measured by the amount which she could reasonably have expected to receive for their release.

In my judgment the judge's approach to the assessment of damages was correct on the facts and in accordance with principle. I would dismiss the appeal.[32]

In **Johnson v Agnew** [1980] AC 367[33] the House of Lords recognised that if specific performance of a contract for the sale of land was ordered the contract remained effective, so that if the order was not complied with the plaintiff could apply to the court for the contract to be terminated and damages be awarded for breach of contract. In determining the assessment of these damages LORD WILBERFORCE said at p. 399:

It is now necessary to deal with questions relating to the measure of damages. The Court of Appeal, while denying the vendors' right to damages at common law, granted damages under Lord Cairns' Act. Since, on the view which I take, damages can be recovered at common law, two relevant questions now arise.

(1) Whether Lord Cairns' Act provides a different measure of damages from the common law: if so, the respondents would be in a position to claim the more favourable basis to them.

(2) If the measure of damages is the same, on what basis they should be calculated.

Since the decision of this House, by majority, in *Leeds Industrial Co-operative Society Ltd v Slack* [1924] AC 851 it is clear that the jurisdiction to award damages in accordance with section 2 of Lord Cairns' Act (accepted by the House as surviving the repeal of the Act) may arise in some cases in which damages could not be recovered at common law: examples of this would be damages in lieu of a *quia timet* injunction and damages for breach of a restrictive covenant

[32] See also *Gafford v Graham* [1999] 7 P and CR 73; *Amec Developments Ltd v Jury's Hotel Management* [2001] EGLR 81; *Experience Hendrix LLC v PPX Enterprises Inc* [2003] EWCA Civ 323, [2003] 1 All ER (Comm) 830; *O'Brien Homes Ltd v Lane* [2004] EWHC 303 (QB); *WWF–World Wide Fund for Nature v World Wrestling Federation Entertainment* [2007] EWCA Civ 286, [2008] 1 WLR 445. See also *A-G v Blake* [2001] 1 AC 268.

[33] (1979) 95 LQR 321 (P. Baker); (1980) 39 CLJ 58 (A. Oakley); [1979] Conv 293 (F. Crane).

to which the plaintiff was not a party. To this extent the Act created a power to award damages which did not exist before at common law. But apart from these, and similar cases where damages could not be claimed at all at common law, there is sound authority for the proposition that the Act does not provide for the assessment of damages on any new basis. The wording of section 2 'may be assessed in such manner as the court shall direct' does not so suggest, but clearly refers only to procedure.

In *Ferguson v Wilson* (1866) LR 2 Ch 77, 88, Turner LJ sitting in a court which included Sir Hugh Cairns himself expressed the clear opinion that the purpose of the Act was to enable a court of equity to grant those damages which another court might give; a similar opinion was strongly expressed by Kay J in *Rock Portland Cement Co Ltd v Wilson* (1882) 52 LJ Ch 214, and *Fry on Specific Performance,* 6th ed. p. 602 is of the same opinion. In *Wroth v Tyler* [1974] Ch 30 [p. 1043, above] however, Megarry J, relying on the words 'in lieu of specific performance' reached the view that damages under the Act should be assessed as on the date when specific performance could have been ordered, in that case as at the date of the judgment of the court. This case was followed in *Grant v Dawkins* [1973] 1 WLR 1406. If this establishes a different basis from that applicable at common law, I could not agree with it, but in *Horsler v Zorro* [1975] Ch 302, 316 Megarry J went so far as to indicate his view that there is no inflexible rule that common law damages must be assessed as at the date of the breach. Furthermore, in *Malhotra v Choudhury* [1980] Ch 52 the Court of Appeal expressly decided that, in a case where damages are given in substitution for an order for specific performance, both equity and the common law would award damages on the same basis—in that case as on the date of judgment. On the balance of these authorities and also on principle, I find in the Act no warrant for the court awarding damages differently from common law damages, but the question is left open on what date such damages, however awarded, ought to be assessed.

(2) The general principle for the assessment of damages is compensatory, i.e., that the innocent party is to be placed, so far as money can do so, in the same position as if the contract had been performed. Where the contract is one of sale, this principle normally leads to assessment of damages as at the date of the breach—a principle recognised and embodied in section 51 of the Sale of Goods Act 1893. But this is not an absolute rule: if to follow it would give rise to injustice, the court has power to fix such other date as may be appropriate in the circumstances.

In cases where a breach of a contract for sale has occurred, and the innocent party reasonably continues to try to have the contract completed, it would to me appear more logical and just rather than tie him to the date of the original breach, to assess damages as at the date when (otherwise than by his default) the contract is lost. Support for this approach is to be found in the cases. In *Ogle v Earl Vane* (1867) LR 2 QB 275; LR 3 QB 272 the date was fixed by reference to the time when the innocent party, acting reasonably, went into the market; in *Hickman v Haynes* (1875) LR 10 CP 598 at a reasonable time after the last request of the defendants (buyers) to withhold delivery. In *Radford v de Froberville* [1977] 1 WLR 1262, where the defendant had covenanted to build a wall, damages were held measurable as at the date of the hearing rather than at the date of the defendant's breach, unless the plaintiff ought reasonably to have mitigated the breach at an earlier date.

In the present case if it is accepted, as I would accept, that the vendors acted reasonably in pursuing the remedy of specific performance, the date on which that remedy became aborted (not by the vendors' fault) should logically be fixed as the date on which damages should be assessed. Choice of this date would be in accordance both with common law principle, as indicated in the authorities I have mentioned, and with the wording of the Act 'in substitution for ... specific performance'.

QUESTIONS

1. Why is it important to emphasise that the freezing injunction is made through the exercise of an equitable jurisdiction?

2. What can a court do to reverse the effects of breaching a freezing injunction either by the defendant or a third party? See (2006) 122 LQR 535 (S. Gee).

3. Does the search order provide sufficient protection for the rights of the defendant?

4. When should damages be awarded in lieu of an injunction and in lieu of specific performance?

INDEX

Please note that references to footnotes contain the letter 'n' following the page number